WORD MEANINGS
in the
New Testament

WORD
MEANINGS
in the
New Testament

One-volume Edition

Ralph Earle, Th.D.

BAKER BOOK HOUSE
Grand Rapids, Michigan 49506

The Amplified New Testament, © The Lockman
Foundation, 1954, 1958.

The Bible: An American Translation (Goodspeed), by
J. M. Powis Smith and Edgar J. Goodspeed.
Copyright 1923, 1927, 1948 by the University of
Chicago Press.

The Bible: A New Translation, by James Moffatt.
Copyright 1954 by James Moffatt. By permission of
Harper and Row, Publishers, Inc.

The Holy Bible, New International Version (NIV),
copyright © 1973, 1978, by the International Bible
Society.

The Jerusalem Bible (JB), copyright © 1966 by
Darton, Longman, and Todd, Ltd., and Doubleday
and Co., Inc.

*The Modern Language Bible—the New Berkeley
Version in Modern English*, copyright © 1945, 1959,
1969 by Zondervan Publishing House.

The *New American Standard Bible* (NASB), copyright
© The Lockman Foundation, 1960, 1962, 1963, 1968,
1971, 1972, 1973, 1975, 1977.

The *New English Bible* (NEB), © The Delegates of the
Oxford University Press and The Syndics of the
Cambridge University Press, 1961, 1970.

New International Version of the New Testament
(NIV), copyright © 1973 by New York Bible Society
International.

The New Testament in the Language of the People
(Williams), by Charles B. Williams. Copyright 1937
by Bruce Humphries, Inc.; assigned 1949 to the
Moody Bible Institute, Chicago.

The New Testament in Modern English (Phillips),
revised edition © J. B. Phillips, 1958, 1960, 1972.
Used by permission of the Macmillan Publishing Co.,
Inc.

The *Revised Standard Version of the Bible* (RSV),
copyright 1946, 1952, 1971, 1973 by the Division of
Christian Education of the National Council of the
Churches of Christ in the United States of America.

Weymouth's New Testament in Modern English
(Weymouth), by Richard Francis Weymouth. By
special arrangements with James Clarke and Co.,
Ltd., and permission of Harper and Row Publishers,
Inc.

Contents

Preface

In his book *More New Testament Words* (Harper, 1958), William Barclay quotes Gregory Thaumaturgus as saying that "if one aims at readiness of speech and beauty of discourse, he will get at them by no other discipline than the study of words, and their constant practice." Who should be more concerned than a preacher about the use of words? But no less interested should be any serious student of the Bible.

Barclay also expresses his own feelings in the matter. He writes: "The more I study words, the more I am convinced of their basic and fundamental importance. On the meaning of words everything depends" (p. 9).

That is what this volume is all about. It deals with the meaning of interesting and significant words in the New Testament. Its purpose is twofold: (1) to help the preacher understand the Scriptures more clearly and expound their message more accurately and effectively; and (2) to help all students of the Word to discover the rich mine of truth to be found in a study of the original languages of the biblical text. All Greek words are transliterated, and the discussion is on a practical rather than technical level.

Two generations ago Marvin Vincent's *Word Studies in the New Testament* (4 vols.) appeared, and it proved to be a gold mine of preaching material. A generation ago A. T. Robertson's *Word Pictures in the New Testament* (6 vols.) added a new dimension of resources. It seems that the time has now come for a new attempt to be made in this field. It is hoped that *Word Meanings in the New Testament* will prove to be of some value in further sharpening the preacher's tools for the exposition of the Word of God, which was written in ancient language.

The format is a bit different from the works just cited. The material is handled under convenient headings. Usually the first quoted word or phrase of the heading is from the King James Version.

Several good English versions of the New Testament have appeared in recent years. But no translation can possibly bring out the varied nuances of the Greek. That is why word studies are important for anyone who would adequately understand and expound the Word of God.

Across more than a dozen years this volume has engaged my attention, interspersed with a heavy schedule of preaching, teaching, translating (the New International Version), and the writing of a dozen other books (the annual *Peloubet's Notes*). I thank God for health and strength to complete this task. Almost fifty years of teaching the Greek New Testament have given me a passion for communicating more accurately the inspired words of Scripture. I pray that this volume will contribute to that end.

Abbreviations and Sources

References for quoted material, or other citations, will often direct the reader to an author who may have written more than one work, and to a specific page or pages. The particular volume from which a quotation has been taken may not be parenthetically cited, but the reader is hereby advised that the quotation will be found in the author's commentary or work that includes in its title the name of the book of the Bible under consideration. For example, if an entry concerned with a word from a verse in the Book of Acts includes a quotation of F. F. Bruce, with a page reference, the quotation can be found in his *Acts of the Apostles*, one of two works by Bruce in the list of sources that follows.

For convenience, translations of the Bible or the New Testament by one or two persons are listed under the name(s) of the translator(s), rather than by title, as are composite translations.

Abbott	T. K. Abbott, *A Critical and Exegetical Commentary on the Epistles to the Ephesians and to the Colossians*. International Critical Commentary. Edinburgh: T. & T. Clark, 1897.
A-S	G. Abbott-Smith, *A Manual Greek Lexicon of the New Testament*. Second edition. Edinburgh: T. & T. Clark, 1923.
Alford	Henry Alford, *The Greek Testament*. 4 vols. Chicago: Moody Press, 1958 (reprint).
ASV	*American Standard Version*. Camden: Thomas Nelson & Sons, 1901.
ANT	*The Amplified New Testament*. Grand Rapids: Zondervan, 1965.
Anchor	*The Anchor Bible*. Garden City, N.Y.: Doubleday, 1964.
AG	W. F. Arndt and F. W. Gingrich, *A Greek-English Lexicon of the New Testament*. Second edition. Chicago: University of Chicago Press, 1979.
Ballantine	William G. Ballantine, *The Riverside New Testament*. Boston: Houghton Mifflin, 1923.
NTW	William Barclay, *A New Testament Wordbook*. London: SCM Press, 1955.
BBC	*Beacon Bible Commentary*. 10 vols. Kansas City: Beacon Hill, 1964–1968.
Beare	F. W. Beare, "The Epistle to the Ephesians" (Exegesis), *The Interpreter's Bible*, vol. 10. New York: Abingdon-Cokesbury Press, 1953.
Beet	J. Agar Beet, *A Commentary on St. Paul's Epistle to the Romans*. Ninth edition. London: Hodder & Stoughton, 1900.
Beginnings	*The Beginnings of Christianity*. 5 vols. Edited by F. J. Foakes Jackson and Kirsopp Lake. London: Macmillan, 1920.

Bengel	John Albert Bengel, *Gnomon of the New Testament*. 5 vols. Edinburgh: T. & T. Clark, 1860.
Bernard	J. H. Bernard, *A Critical and Exegetical Commentary on the Gospel According to St. John*. 2 vols. International Critical Commentary. Edinburgh: T. & T. Clark, 1928.
	_____, *The Pastoral Epistles*. Cambridge Greek Testament. Cambridge: University Press, 1899.
Blass and Debrunner	F. Blass and A. Debrunner, *Grammar of New Testament Greek*. Translated and revised by Robert W. Funk. Chicago: University of Chicago Press, 1961.
Bloomfield	S. T. Bloomfield, *The Greek Testament with English Notes*. 2 vols. Fifth edition. Philadelphia: H. C. Peck & Theo. Bliss, 1836.
Bruce	F. F. Bruce, *The Acts of the Apostles*. Grand Rapids: Wm. B. Eerdmans, 1951.
	_____, *Epistle to the Hebrews*. New International Commentary on the New Testament. Grand Rapids: Wm. B. Eerdmans, 1964.
Burton	E. D. Burton, *A Critical and Exegetical Commentary on the Epistle to the Galatians*. International Critical Commentary. Edinburgh: T. & T. Clark, 1921.
	_____, *Syntax of the Moods and Tenses in New Testament Greek*. Second edition. Chicago: University of Chicago Press, 1893.
Calvin	John Calvin, *The Epistles of Paul the Apostle to the Romans and to the Thessalonians*. Edited by David Torrance and T. F. Torrance. Translated by Ross Mackenzie. Grand Rapids: Wm. B. Eerdmans, 1961.
CGT	*Cambridge Greek Testament*. Cambridge: University Press, 1886.
CGTC	*Cambridge Greek Testament Commentary*.
Clarke	Ada Clarke, *The New Testament of Our Lord and Saviour Jesus Christ*. 2 vols. New York: Methodist Book Concern, n.d.
Cranfield	C. E. B. Cranfield, *First Epistle of Peter*. London: SCM Press, 1950.
Creed	John M. Creed, *The Gospel According to St. Luke*. London: Macmillan, 1930.
Cremer	Hermann Cremer, *Biblio-Theological Lexicon of New Testament Greek*. Edinburgh: T. & T. Clark, 1878.
BS	Adolph Deissmann, *Bible Studies*. Edinburgh: T. & T. Clark, 1901.
LAE	_____, *Light from the Ancient East*. New York: George H. Doran, 1927.
HDCG	*Dictionary of Christ and the Gospels*. 2 vols. Edited by James Hastings. New York: Charles Scribner's Sons, 1906 (vol. I) and 1908 (vol. II).
HDAC	*Dictionary of the Apostolic Church*. 2 vols. Edited by James Hastings. New York: Charles Scribner's Sons, 1915 (vol. I) and 1918 (vol. II).
HDB	*Dictionary of the Bible*. Edited by James Hastings. 5 vols. New York: Charles Scribner's Sons, 1852–1922.
Dodd	Charles H. Dodd, *The Apostolic Preaching and Its Developments*. London: Hodder & Stoughton, 1970 (reprint).
Eadie	John Eadie, *Commentary on the Epistle to the Colossians*. Grand Rapids: Zondervan, 1957 (reprint).
	_____, *Commentary on the Epistle to the Ephesians*. Grand Rapids: Zondervan, n.d.
Easton	B. S. Easton, *The Pastoral Epistles*. New York: Charles Scribner's Sons, 1947.

Edersheim	Alfred Edersheim, *The Life and Times of Jesus the Messiah*. 2 vols. Eighth edition. New York: Longmans, Green & Co., 1903.
Ellicott	Charles J. Ellicott, *Commentary on St. Paul's Epistle to the Ephesians*. London: Longmans, Green, Reader, and Dyer, 1868.
	_____, *Commentary on St. Paul's Epistles to the Philippians, Colossians, and to Philemon*. Andover, Mass.: Warren F. Draper, 1890.
	_____, *A Critical and Gramatical Commentary on St. Paul's Epistle to the Ephesians*. Boston: W. H. Holliday, 1885.
ERV	*English Revised Version* (1881–1885).
EGT	*Expositor's Greek Testament*. 5 vols. Grand Rapids: Wm. B. Eerdmans, n.d.
Frame	James E. Frame, *A Critical and Exegetical Commentary on the Epistles of St. Paul to the Thessalonians*. International Critical Commentary. Edinburgh: T. & T. Clark, 1912.
Geldenhuys	Norval Geldenhuys, *Commentary on the Gospel of Luke*. New International Commentary on the New Testament. Grand Rapids: Wm. B. Eerdmans, 1951.
Godet	Frederick L. Godet, *Commentary on St. Paul's Epistle to the Romans*. Grand Rapids: Zondervan, n.d.
	_____, *Commentary on the First Epistle to the Corinthians*. Grand Rapids: Zondervan, 1956 (reprint).
	_____, *Commentary on the Gospel of John*. 2 vols. Grand Rapids: Zondervan, n.d.
	_____, *Commentary on the Gospel of St. Luke*. 2 vols. New York: Funk & Wagnalls, n.d.
Goodspeed	*See* J. M. P. Smith.
Grosheide	F. W. Grosheide, *The First Epistle to the Corinthians*. New International Commentary on the New Testament. Grand Rapids: Wm. B. Eerdmans, 1953.
NTC	William Hendriksen, *New Testament Commentary: Exposition of the Gospel According to John*. 2 vols. Grand Rapids: Baker Book House, 1953.
	_____, *New Testament Commentary: Exposition of the Gospel According to Luke*. Grand Rapids: Baker Book House, 1978.
	_____, *New Testament Commentary: Exposition of the Gospel According to Matthew*. Grand Rapids: Baker Book House, 1973.
Hobart	William K. Hobart, *Medical Language of St. Luke*. Grand Rapids: Baker Book House, 1954 (reprint).
Hodge	Charles Hodge, *Commentary on the Epistle to the Romans*. Grand Rapids: Wm. B. Eerdmans, 1950 (reprint).
NIV	*The Holy Bible, New International Version*. Grand Rapids: Zondervan, 1978.
ICC	*International Critical Commentary*.
ISBE	*International Standard Bible Encyclopedia*. 5 vols. Edited by James Orr. Grand Rapids: Wm. B. Eerdmans, 1939.
IB	*Interpreter's Bible*. 12 vols. Edited by G. A. Buttrick, et al. Nashville: Abingdon, 1953–1956.
JB	*Jerusalem Bible*. New York: Doubleday, 1966.
KJV	*King James Version* (1611).

Knox   Ronald Knox, *The Holy Bible: A Translation from the Latin Vulgate in the Light of the Hebrew and Greek Originals*. New York: Sheed and Ward, 1954.

Ladd   George E. Ladd, *Commentary on the Revelation of John*. Grand Rapids: Wm. B. Eerdmans, 1972.

Lange   John Peter Lange, *Commentary on the Holy Scriptures*. Grand Rapids: Zondervan, n.d.

Lenski   R. C. H. Lenski, *The Interpretation of the Acts of the Apostles*. Columbus, Ohio: Wartburg Press, 1944.

————, *The Interpretation of St. Luke's Gospel*. Columbus, Ohio: Wartburg Press, 1934.

Lias   J. J. Lias, *The First Epistle of Paul to the Corinthians*. Cambridge Greek Testament. Cambridge: University Press, 1886.

————, *The Second Epistle of Paul to the Corinthians*. Cambridge Greek Testament. Cambridge: University Press, 1892.

LS-J   H. G. Liddell and Robert Scott, *A Greek-English Lexicon*. Revised and enlarged by H. S. Jones. Oxford: Clarendon Press, 1940.

Lightfoot   J. B. Lightfoot, *Notes on the Epistles of St. Paul*. Grand Rapids: Zondervan, 1957 (reprint, notes on Rom. 1–7, I Cor. 1–7, Eph. 1:1–14, and I and II Thess.).

————, *Saint Paul's Epistle to the Colossians and to Philemon*. Grand Rapids: Zondervan, n.d.

————, *Saint Paul's Epistle to the Philippians*. Grand Rapids: Zondervan, 1953.

Lock   Walter Lock, *A Critical and Exegetical Commentary on the Pastoral Epistles*. International Critical Commentary. Edinburgh: T. & T. Clark, 1924.

Lumby   J. Rawson Lumby, *The Acts of the Apostles*. Cambridge Greek Testament. Cambridge: University Press, 1912.

Marshall   I. Howard Marshall, *The Gospel of Luke*. New International Greek Testament Commentary. Grand Rapids: Wm. B. Eerdmans, 1978.

Mayor   J. B. Mayor, *The Epistle of James*. Grand Rapids: Zondervan, 1954 (reprint).

McDowell   Edward McDowell, *The Meaning and Message of the Book of Revelation*. Nashville: Broadman Press, 1951.

Metzger   Bruce Metzger, *A Textual Commentary on the Greek New Testament*. New York: United Bible Society, 1978.

Meyer   H. A. W. Meyer, *A Critical and Exegetical Handbook to the Acts of the Apostles*. New York: Funk & Wagnalls, 1883.

————, *A Critical and Exegetical Handbook to the Epistles to the Corinthians*. Edinburgh: T. & T. Clark, 1877.

————, *A Critical and Exegetical Handbook to the Epistles to the Galatians and the Ephesians*. New York: Funk & Wagnalls, 1884.

————, *A Critical and Exegetical Handbook to the Epistles to the Philippians and Colossians, and to Philemon*. New York: Funk & Wagnalls, 1885.

————, *A Critical and Exegetical Handbook to the Epistle to the Romans*. New York: Funk & Wagnalls, 1884.

Milligan   George Milligan, *St. Paul's Epistles to the Thessalonians*. Grand Rapids: Wm. B. Eerdmans, 1952 (reprint).

Berkeley	*The Modern Language Bible—The New Berkeley Version in Modern English*. Grand Rapids: Zondervan, 1969.
Moffatt	James Moffatt, *The Bible: A New Translation*. New York: Harper and Row, 1954.
Montgomery	Helen (Barrett) Montgomery, *The New Testament in Modern English*. Philadelphia: Judson Press, 1944.
Moule	H. C. G. Moule, *Ephesian Studies*. London: Pickering and Inglis, n.d.
	_____, *The Epistle of St. Paul to the Romans*. Expositor's Bible. New York: A. C. Armstrong & Sons, 1906.
Grammar	James H. Moulton, *The Grammar of New Testament Greek*. 2 vols. Vol. 1, 1906. Third edition, 1908. Vol 2. Edited by W. F. Howard, 1919, 1928. Darby, Penn.: Darby Books, 1980 (reprint).
VGT	James H. Moulton and George Milligan, *The Vocabulary of the Greek Testament*. Grand Rapids: Wm. B. Eerdmans, 1949.
Moulton and Geden	W. F. Moulton and A. S. Geden, *Concordance to the Greek Testament*. Revised by H. K. Moulton. Edinburgh: T. & T. Clark, 1963.
Mounce	Robert H. Mounce, *The Book of Revelation*. New International Commentary on the New Testament. Grand Rapids: Wm. B. Eerdmans, 1977.
NAB	*New American Bible*. New York: P. J. Kenedy and Sons, 1970.
NASB	*New American Standard Bible*. Camden: Thomas Nelson & Sons, 1973.
Confraternity	*New Catholic Edition of the Holy Bible*. New York: Catholic Book, 1957.
NEB	*New English Bible*. Cambridge: University Press, 1961, 1970.
DNTT	*New International Dictionary of New Testament Theology*. 3 vols. Edited by Colin Brown. Grand Rapids: Zondervan, 1978.
NIGTC	*New International Greek Testament Commentary*.
Olshausen	Hermann Olshausen, *Biblical Commentary on the New Testament*. 6 vols. American edition. New York: Sheldon, 1863.
OED	*Oxford English Dictionary*. 13 vols.
Page	T. E. Page, *Acts of the Apostles*. London: Macmillan, 1886.
Phillips	J. B. Phillips, *The New Testament in Modern English*. New York: Macmillan, 1960.
Plummer	Alfred Plummer, *A Critical and Exegetical Commentary on the Gospel According to St. Luke*. International Critical Commentary. Fifth edition. Edinburgh: T. & T. Clark, 1922.
	_____, *A Critical and Exegetical Commentary on the Second Epistle of St. Paul to the Corinthians*. International Critical Commentary. Edinburgh: T. & T. Clark, 1915.
	_____, *The Gospel According to St. John*. Cambridge Greek Testament. Cambridge: University Press, 1882.
Plummer and Robertson	Alfred Plummer and A. T. Robertson, *A Critical and Exegetical Commentary on the First Epistle of St. Paul to the Corinthians*. International Critical Commentary. Edinburgh: T. & T. Clark, 1911.
Ramsay	William M. Ramsay, *A Historical Commentary on St. Paul's Epistle to the Galatians*. New York: Putnam, 1900.
RSV	*Revised Standard Version*. Camden: Thomas Nelson & Sons, 1952.
Ridderbos	H. N. Ridderbos, *The Epistle of Paul to the Churches of Galatia*. New International Commentary on the New Testament. Grand Rapids: Wm. B. Eerdmans, 1953.

Rob. Gram.	A. T. Robertson, *A Grammar of the Greek New Testament in the Light of Historical Research*. Fifth edition. New York: Harper & Brothers, 1931.
WP	_____, *Word Pictures in the New Testament*. 6 vols. New York: Richard R. Smith, 1930–1933.
Robinson	Joseph A. Robinson, *St. Paul's Epistle to the Ephesians*. London: James Clarke, 1903.
SH	William Sanday and A. C. Headlam, *A Critical and Exegetical Commentary on the Epistle to the Romans*. International Critical Commentary. Edinburgh: T. & T. Clark, 1895.
LXX	Septuagint.
Simpson	E. K. Simpson, *The Pastoral Epistles*. Grand Rapids: Wm. B. Eerdmans, 1954.
Smith	J. M. P. Smith and Edgar J. Goodspeed, *The Bible: An American Translation*. Chicago: University of Chicago Press, 1923, 1927, 1948.
Spencer	Francis A. Spencer, *The New Testament of Our Lord and Saviour Jesus Christ*. New York: MacMillan, 1937.
Swete	H. B. Swete, *The Gospel According to St. Mark*. London: Macmillan, 1898.
	_____, *The Apocalypse of St. John*. Grand Rapids: Wm. B. Eerdmans, 1951 (reprint).
Taylor	Vincent Taylor, *The Gospel According to St. Mark*. London: Macmillan, 1963.
Thayer	J. H. Thayer, *A Greek-English Lexicon of the New Testament*. New York: American Book Co., 1886.
TDNT	*Theological Dictionary of the New Testament*. 10 vols. Edited by G. Kittel and G. Friedrich. Translated by G. W. Bromiley. Grand Rapids: Wm. B. Eerdmans, 1964–1976.
TWBB	*A Theological Word Book of the Bible*. Edited by Alan Richardson. London: SCM Press, 1950.
Trench	R. C. Trench, *Synonyms of the New Testament*. Ninth edition, 1880. Grand Rapids: Wm. B. Eerdmans, 1947 (reprint).
TCNT	*Twentieth Century New Testament* (1904, revised edition).
Vincent	Marvin Vincent, *A Critical and Exegetical Commentary on the Epistles to the Philippians and to Philemon*. International Critical Commentary. Edinburgh: T. & T. Clark, 1897.
	_____, *Word Studies in the New Testament*. 4 vols. Grand Rapids: Wm. B. Eerdmans, 1946 (reprint).
Vine	W. E. Vine, *An Expository Dictionary of New Testament*. 4 vols. Westwood, N.J.: Fleming H. Revell Co., 1940.
Wand	John W. C. Wand, *The General Epistles of St. Peter and St. Jude*. London: Methuen, 1934.
WNID	*Webster's New International Dictionary*. Second edition.
Westcott	B. F. Westcott, *Gospel According to St. John*. Grand Rapids: Wm. B. Eerdmans, 1950 (reprint).
	_____, *St. Paul's Epistle to the Ephesians*. Grand Rapids: Wm. B. Eerdmans, 1950 (reprint).
	_____, *Epistle to the Hebrews*. London: Macmillan, 1892.
Weymouth	R. F. Weymouth, *Weymouth's New Testament in Modern English*. New York: Harper and Row.

Williams	Charles B. Williams, *The New Testament in the Language of the People*. Chicago: Moody Press, 1954.
NTPE	Charles K. Williams, *The New Testament: A New Translation in Plain English*. Grand Rapids: Wm. B. Eerdmans, 1963.
Winer	George B. Winer, *A Grammar of the Idioms of the Greek Language of the New Testament*. New York: Robert Carter and Bros., 1850.
Wuest	Kenneth S. Wuest, *Expanded Translation of the Greek New Testament*. Grand Rapids: Wm. B. Eerdmans, 1956–1959.
	_____, *Romans in the Greek Testament*. Grand Rapids: Wm. B. Eerdmans, 1955.
Young	Robert Young, *Young's Literal Translation of the Holy Bible*. Grand Rapids: Baker Book House, n.d. (reprint).

Pronunciation Guide
for Transliterated
Greek Words

a = *ah*

ai = *ai* (as in *aisle*)

au = *ow* (as in *cow*)

c = *k*

e = *eh* (short *e*)

ē = *ay* (representing Greek *eta*)

ei = *ay* (as in *eight*)

eu = *you* (as in *eulogy*)

i = short *i* or *ee*

ō = *oh* (representing Greek *omega*)

oi = *oi* (as in *boil*)

ou = *oo* (as in *food*)

y = short *i* or *ee* (as in *daily*)

(British usage differs somewhat from American usage.)

Matthew

1:1 ***Generation*** The Greek word is *genesis*, which we have taken over into English with the meaning "origin." The opening expression of Matthew, *Biblos geneseōs*, is found in Gen. 2:4 (LXX), where it means "history of the origin," and Gen. 5:1, where it means "a record of the genealogy." The latter fits here (cf. NIV) as a heading for verses 2–17.

2 ***Begat*** The verb is *gennaō*. Arndt and Gingrich give the meaning "beget," but immediately add: "Literally *become the father of*" (p. 155). Since "begat" (KJV) is obsolete now, "was the father of" is better.

17 ***Generations*** Here we have the noun *genea*, which is translated (KJV) "generation" 37 of the 42 times it occurs in the NT. Hermann Buechsel thinks that here it has the sense of "age" or "period" (TDNT, 1:663). But "generations," used loosely, fits best.

18 ***Espoused*** The verb *mnēsteuo* means "woo and win, betroth," and in the passive "be betrothed, become engaged" (AG, p. 525). Since "espoused" is used mainly today for championing a cause, some would suggest "engaged" as best here. But a Jewish betrothal was more binding than a modern engagement (see note at v. 19). So "pledged to be married" is more accurate.

19 ***Make Her a Public Example*** The verb *deigmatizō* (only here and Col. 2:15) means "expose to public disgrace" (cf. NIV). This was the Jewish custom with an adulteress.

Put Away *Apolyō* meant to "loose" or "let go." But it was the regular term used for a man divorcing his wife. As suggested above, a Jewish betrothal was legally binding. It could be broken only by a legal divorce, with papers passed. So "to divorce quietly" (RSV, NIV) expresses the true idea.

25 ***Knew*** The verb is *ginōskō*, which does mean "know." But this is a euphemism for "have sexual relations with." A chaste translation that conveys the meaning is: "But he had no union with her until she gave birth to a son" (NIV). Incidentally, this implies that he did after Jesus was born—contrary to the Catholic dogma of the perpetual virginity of Mary.

2:1 ***Wise Men*** The Greek word here translated "wise men" (and in vv. 7, 16) is *magoi*. Elsewhere it is used for Bar-Jesus, who is called a "sorcerer" and a "false prophet" (Acts 13:6, 8). The cognate verb, *mageuo*, "practice magic," is used to describe Simon Magus (Acts 8:9). So the best translation in Matthew is "Magi."

Who were these Magi? They were astrologers from Persia, Babylonia, or possibly Arabia. It is not stated how many there were. The idea that there were three evidently comes from the mention of three kinds of gifts (v. 11).

4 ***Christ*** The Greek word *Christos* has the definite article. It literally means "the anointed one." Our word "Messiah" comes from the Hebrew, and also means "anointed one." What Herod asked the Jewish religious leaders was where "the Messiah," prophesied in the OT, was to be born. But since Herod was speaking Greek, he used *Christos*.

6 ***Rule*** The verb is *poimainō*, from *poimēn*, "shepherd." So it literally means "tend a flock." The term came to be used for shepherding people. This is brought out by "will shepherd" (NASB) or "will be the shepherd of" (NIV).

7 Privily   The Greek adverb *lathra* means "secretly." It comes from the verb *lanthano*, which means "be hidden."

12 Departed   The verb *anachoreo* occurs four times in this chapter (vv. 12, 13, 14, 22). In KJV it is translated "departed" the first three times and "turned aside" in verse 22 ("departed" all four places in NASB).

Arndt and Gingrich indicate that the basic meaning is "go away" and that this fits verse 13 ("gone," NEB, NIV). But it also has the special meaning of "return" in verse 12 and "withdraw, retire, take refuge" (p. 63) in verses 14 and 22 (cf. "withdrew," NIV). This is a good example of the distinctions that can often be found in one Greek word.

16 Mocked   The verb *empaizo* means "ridicule" or "mock." But in this passage it has the special meaning of "deceive" or "trick" (cf. NASB, RSV, NEB)—so, "outwitted" (NIV).

Exceeding Wroth   *Thymoo* occurs only here in the NT. In the passive, as here, it means "become angry." Modified by *lian*, it means "was very angry."

Coasts   The Greek word is *horia* (always plural in NT). It literally means "boundaries," but is used in the sense of "region" or "district." In connection with a town (as here) it signifies "environs" (NASB) or "vicinity" (NIV). Occurring 11 times, it is rendered "coasts" all but once in the KJV, but obviously it has no relation to a shoreline.

23 Nazarene   The quotation here is said to come from "the prophets"—not one particular prophet. Hans Schaeder is right when he says, "It is hard to find an OT prophecy directly corresponding to Mt. 2:23" (TDNT, 4:875).

The Greek *Nazarenos* is always used by Mark (4 times), and in two passages in Luke (4:34; 24:19) that are rather clearly dependent on Mark. In Matthew (twice), Luke (once), John (3 times), and Acts (7 times) we find the form here, *Nazoraios*. But Matthew indicates here that the term is equivalent in meaning to *Nazarenos*—that is, an inhabitant of Nazareth.

A. T. Robertson writes: "It may be that this term of contempt (John 2:46; 7:52) is what is meant, and that several prophecies are to be combined like Pss. 22:6, 8; 79:11, 19; Isa. 53:2, 3, 4. The name Nazareth means a shoot or

branch, but it is by no means certain that Matthew has this in mind. It is best to confess that we do not know" (WP, 1:21). It is only fair to state that the connection of *Nazareth* with *neser*, "branch," is disputed.

3:1 Repent   The verb *metanoeo* literally means "change one's mind," then "feel remorse, repent, be converted" (AG, pp. 511–12). We should always remember that repentance is more than an emotional response (feeling sorry); it also involves the intellect and will.

2 The Kingdom of Heaven   Literally it is "the kingdom of the heavens," but the singular and plural of "heaven" are used interchangeably (plural about one-third of the time). The expression is found only in Matthew (33 times). The other Gospels have "the kingdom of God." Matthew was writing to Jews who preferred to use a euphemistic substitute for God, such as "heaven."

3 Wilderness   Today the term "wilderness" suggests a heavily wooded area. But the "Desert of Judea" (v. 1, NIV) was, and is, almost devoid of vegetation. We call that a "desert." See also discussion at Mark 1:3.

4 Girdle   See discussion at Mark 1:6.

Meat   See discussion at Acts 27:33.

6 Confessing   *Homologeo* is used in 1 John 1:9: "If we confess our sins." But the verb here is the compound *exomologeo*. *Ex* means "out." So we almost get here the idea of "confessing out" one's sins.

The Greek verb *baptizo* here is in the imperfect tense, and "confessing" is the present participle in Greek. Both tenses indicate action going on. So this sentence literally says: "They were being baptized by him in the Jordan River as they were confessing their sins."

12 Fan   Arndt and Gingrich define *ptyon* as follows: "*winnowing shovel*, a fork-like shovel, with which the threshed grain was thrown into the wind; thus the chaff was separated from the grain" (p. 727). One can still see this being done at harvesttime in the Middle East on many a threshing floor.

14 Forbad   The imperfect tense of *diakolyo* literally means "tried to deter" (NIV) or "tried to prevent" (NASB).

4:4 *It Is Written* The Greek has *gegraptai,* the perfect passive of *graphō,* "write." The perfect tense expresses completed action and a permanent state resulting from it. So the word could justifiably be translated: "It has been written and still stands written." It is a strong affirmation of the unchanging character of the Scriptures.

It should be noted that Jesus met every temptation of Satan by answering with Scripture. He used only one weapon, the same as we have: "the sword of the Spirit, which is the word of God" (Eph. 6:17).

14 *Esaias* This is the Greek form. But whenever familiar OT names appear in the NT, it is more logical to give the Hebrew, not Greek, form, so that their identity can be readily recognized. So here it should be "Isaiah."

18 *Net* A rare compound, *amphiblēstron* (only here in NT), is used for "net." This noun comes from the verb *amphiballō,* which, in turn, occurs only in the parallel passage in Mark (1:16) for "casting." The verb means "cast" (perhaps "around," *amphi*). The noun indicates a circular "casting net" used in fishing.

21 *Mending* The verb is *katartizō.* It means "put in order, restore to its former condition." Arndt and Gingrich say that with nets it means "by cleaning, mending, folding together" (p. 417). They were "preparing their nets" (NIV) for the next day.

24 *Fame* The Greek word *akoē* comes from the verb *akouō,* "hear." So the noun means "that which is heard." Today we call this "news" (NASB, NIV).

Syria The term here comprises not only Syria proper, but also Phoenicia (modern Lebanon) and Palestine.

Possessed with Devils "Those which were possessed with devils" is all one word in Greek, *daimonizomenous,* which in English simply means "demon-possessed" (NIV), or "demoniac" (NASB).

Lunatic Again "those which were lunatic" is all one word in Greek, *selēniazomenous*—literally, "moonstruck." The people of that time thought that epileptic seizures were caused by overexposure to the moon. The correct translation is "epileptics" (NASB, NIV).

Those That Had the Palsy Once more we have just one word in Greek, *paralytikous,* from which we get "paralytics," which term is the proper translation (NASB, NIV).

5:3 *Blessed* Some, including John Wesley (1755), use the translation "happy." But the Greek word *makarios* was used by Aristotle and others to describe the blessedness that the gods enjoy and also "of men to denote the state of godlike blessedness hereafter in the isles of the blessed" (TDNT, 4:362). Friedrich Hauck goes on to say that it "refers overwhelmingly to the distinctive religious joy which accrues to man from his share in the salvation of the kingdom of God" (p. 367). He also notes: "The NT, like the LXX in many cases, prefers a predicative *makarios* first, then the person with article (cf. Mt. 5:3ff; Rev. 1:3; 14:13, etc.), and finally the reason for the blessedness, or a description of it in a subsidiary clause" (ibid.).

9 *The Children* The Greek does not have *ta tekna,* "the children," but simply *whioi,* "sons." When the article is omitted in Greek, the emphasis is on kind or quality. So the meaning here is that peacemakers will be called "sons of God" (NASB, NIV) because they exhibit the character of their heavenly Father.

15 *Candle* The Greek word *lychnos* means an oil-burning lamp. These lamps were made of clay and were small enough to be hidden in the palm of one's hand.

"Candlestick," as everywhere else in the Bible, should be translated "lampstand" (NASB) or simply "stand" (NIV). We are specifically told that the seven-branched golden "candlestick" (KJV) of the OT was fed by olive oil (Zech. 4:2–3, 12).

Bushel The Greek word is *modion,* found also in Mark 4:21 and in Luke 11:33. It literally means a "peck-measure" (NASB), one-fourth of a bushel. It was probably the "meal-tub" (NEB) found in each home.

18 *Jot* The word is *iōta,* which is the name of the smallest letter of the Greek alphabet. It is like our small *i,* but with no dot over it. We have taken this word over into English to represent a very small thing, as when we say, "It doesn't make one iota of difference." So a good translation here is "the smallest letter" (NASB, NIV).

Incidentally, the smallest letter of the Hebrew alphabet is called *yodh,* which is like our small apostrophe. The Greek iota is pronounced "yota."

Tittle   This word has disappeared from our modern vocabularies. The Greek is *keraia* (here and in Luke 16:17). It literally means "horn," that is, the tiny projection on one Hebrew letter that distinguishes it from another letter of the alphabet. So the most helpful translation is "the least stroke of a pen" (NIV). Jesus used very strong language here to assert the authority of God's Word.

20 *Scribes*   The word *grammateus* occurs 67 times in the Greek New Testament. In the KJV it is translated "scribe" in every place but one, Acts 19:35, where it is rendered "townclerk." It also has a Greek (non-Jewish) setting in 1 Cor. 1:20, where the NIV reads "scholar."

The dominant use of the term is in the Synoptic Gospels, where it is found 24 times in Matthew, 22 times in Mark, and 15 times in Luke. The only place where it occurs in John is in 8:3—a part of the story of the woman taken in adultery. But John 7:53–8:11 is not in the earliest Greek manuscripts (Papyrus 66 and 75 of the early third century, plus Vaticanus and Sinaiticus, the only two manuscripts we have from the fourth century). So, many say that apparently John did not use the term. Luke wrote Acts, where he uses it 3 times in its Jewish connotation (4:5; 6:12; 23:9).

The word comes from *gramma*, which was used for a letter of the alphabet, as in Gal. 6:11. So it was originally used for a public scribe, secretary, or recorder, and was a regular title at Athens and elsewhere. That is the way it is used in Acts 19:35 for the "city clerk" at Ephesus.

But the usual NT usage relates to the Jewish scribe. To most people today, "scribe" means one who writes for others (from the Latin *scribo*, "I write"). But the Jewish scribe of Jesus' day was something far beyond this.

Joseph H. Thayer defines the biblical usage thus: "a man learned in the Mosaic law and in the sacred writings, an interpreter, teacher." He goes on to say: "The *grammateis* (pl.) explained the meaning of the sacred oracles . . . examined into the more difficult and subtle questions of the law . . . added to the Mosaic law decisions of various kinds thought to elucidate its meaning and scope." He concludes: "Since the advice of men skilled in the law was needed in the examination of causes and the solution of difficult questions, they were enrolled in the Sanhedrin; and accordingly in the New Testament they are often mentioned in connection with the priests and elders of the people"

(p. 121). The more adequate translation is therefore "teacher of the law."

22 *But I Say unto You*   This expression occurs 6 times in this chapter (vv. 22, 28, 32, 34, 39, 44). In the Greek it reads: *egō de legō hymin*.

Legō means "I say." When the pronoun *egō* is expressed separately, it denotes special emphasis. Also, the place of greatest emphasis in a Greek sentence is the beginning. So in translating *egō de legō hymin*, the "I" (*ego*) should be underscored: "But *I* say to you."

Either Jesus was the greatest egotist who ever lived, or He was what He claimed to be— the Son of God. Nineteen centuries of Christian history have proved that the latter is the case.

Raca   This seems to be an Aramaic word (only here in NT) that perhaps meant "empty." J. Jeremias suggests "blockhead!" (TDNT, 6:975).

Fool   The Greek word is *mōre*, vocative of the adjective *mōros*, "foolish." The accusative form *mōron* we have taken over into English. A. B. Bruce writes: "*Raca* expresses contempt for a man's head—you stupid! *Mōre* expresses contempt for his heart and character—you scoundrel" (EGT, 1:107). Both utterances are sins against humanity.

26 *Farthing*   The Greek word is *kodrantēs*, a Roman copper coin worth a quarter of a cent. It is found (in NT) only here and in Mark 12:42.

29–30 *Offend*   The Greek verb is *scandalizō*, from which we get "scandalize." It comes from the noun *scandalon*, which first meant the bait-stick in a snare or the trigger on a trap. Then it came to be used for the trap or snare itself. So the verb literally means to "ensnare" or "trap."

Abbott-Smith agrees with ASV (1901) in translating *scandalizō* as "cause to stumble" (p. 407). But Arndt and Gingrich prefer "cause to sin" (p. 752). Gustav Staehlin says that in this passage Jesus evidently meant "entice to sin" (TDNT, 7:352).

The NASB is a revision of the ASV, and so has "makes you stumble." But the NIV is a fresh translation of the Greek text and reads, "causes you to sin." Modern commentators are generally agreed on this meaning.

32 *Fornication*   The Greek word is *porneia*, which occurs 26 times in the NT and is always (in KJV) translated "fornication." It sometimes has this meaning in distinction from *moicheia*, which regularly means "adultery" but occurs only twice in the NT (Matt. 15:19; Mark 7:21).

On the other hand, Abbott-Smith notes that here and in 19:9 it equals *moicheia* (p. 373). Arndt and Gingrich give this definition of *porneia: "prostitution, unchastity, fornication,* of every kind of unlawful sexual intercourse" (p. 699).

Today "fornication" means "sexual intercourse between a man and woman not married to each other" (*American Heritage Dictionary*, p. 517). According to this, it is not an accurate translation here; the meaning is more accurately "marital unfaithfulness" as in the NIV.

33 *Forswear Thyself* The verb is *epiorkeō* (only here in NT). Arndt and Gingrich give two meanings: (1) "swear falsely, perjure oneself"; (2) "break one's oath"; and then add that here "both meanings are possible" (p. 296). J. Schneider uses only "false swearing" as the meaning here (TDNT, 5:467). Actually, the two meanings are very closely related.

39 *Evil* "Resist not evil" (KJV) is an obvious contradiction of the general teaching of the Bible. We *are* to resist evil. But the Greek here is not *ponēria*, "evil," but *tō ponērō*, "the evil one." Commentators are usually agreed, however, that this does not mean the devil. Henry Alford suggests: "the evil man; 'him who injures thee'" (1:52), although he allows the possibility of taking the adjective *ponērō* as neuter rather than masculine, which would mean "the evil thing." But the context favors the reference to a person.

40 *Coat ... Cloak* Today "coat" means an outer garment, but the Greek word here, *chitōn,* means "the garment worn next the skin ... *a tunic*" (A-S, p. 481). "Cloak" is *himation,* used for the outer garment. The two Greek words may be translated "shirt ... coat" (NASB) or "tunic ... cloak" (NIV).

41 *Compel* The verb *angareuō* occurs (in NT) only here and in connection with Simon being compelled to carry Jesus' cross (27:32; Mark 15:21). The word is of Persian origin, or even Babylonian (AG, p. 6). It meant "impress into service."

Jesus said: "If someone forces you to go one mile, go with him two miles" (NIV). From this we get the popular expression "go the second mile."

46 *Publicans* The Greek word *telōnēs* occurs 22 times in the NT (9 in Matthew, 3 in

Mark, 10 in Luke). It is always translated "publican" in the KJV.

This is derived from the Latin *publicanus.* But the *publicani* were wealthy Romans who contracted with the government to collect the taxes from certain designated areas. The so-called "publicans" of the Gospels were local tax collectors who did the actual collecting from the people, turning over the taxes to the *publicani.*

6:1 *Alms* The earliest Greek manuscripts do not have *eleēmosynēn* (alms) but *dikaiosynēn* (righteousness). That is, the first verse of this chapter is not a part of the discussion of almsgiving. Rather, it is an introduction to the next three paragraphs: (1) Giving, vv. 2–4; (2) Praying, vv. 5–15; (3) Fasting, vv. 16–18.

To Be Seen The two most common verbs for "see" in the NT are *blepō* (135 times) and *horaō* (59 times). But here it is *theaomai* (24 times), which means "look upon, view attentively, contemplate" (Thayer, p. 284). From this verb comes the noun *theatron,* "theater." What Jesus is saying is: "Don't make a theatrical show of your religious activity." To put it more briefly, we might say, "Don't parade your piety."

Jesus did not say, "Don't let anyone see your righteous acts." That would contradict what He says in 5:16. What He is dealing with here, as in the whole of the Sermon on the Mount, is the matter of our motives. We are not to practice our righteousness "to be seen" by people. That is a wrong motive.

2 *Alms* In this verse the Greek does have *eleēmosynēn.* It comes from the noun *eleos* (mercy, pity, compassion) and the verb *eleeō,* "to have pity or mercy on, to show mercy" (A-S, p. 145). So our word here means "almsgiving" or "charitable giving." We are to give for God's glory and the blessing of others, not for our own honor.

2, 5, 16 *Hypocrites* Our plural "hypocrites" is an exact transliteration of the Greek singular *hypocritēs.* This word meant "an actor on the stage." Arndt and Gingrich write of its occurrences here: "In these three passages the meaning 'play-actor' is strongly felt" (p. 845). The word is also found in 7:5; 15:7; 22:18; 23:13–15; 24:51; Mark 7:6; Luke 6:42; 12:56; 13:15.

In those days actors wore masks on their faces, with hidden megaphones in them so that they could be heard. So a hypocrite is one who wears a false face.

Have Their Reward The Greek verb here for "have" is not the simple *echō*, "have," which occurs over 700 times in the NT. Rather, it is the compound *apechō*, which is found only 11 times.

The full meaning of this word was not known until the discovery, less than 100 years ago, of papyri in the dry sands of southern Egypt. Many of the multiplied thousands of papyri from the NT period consist of receipts. These regularly have this verb *apechō*. On the basis of this, Deissmann says that the true meaning here is: "They have received their reward in full" (cf. NIV). He goes on to say: "it is as though they had already given a receipt, and they have absolutely no further claim to reward" (LAE, p. 111). The contrast is between the cheap rewards that men can give and the eternal rewards that only God can give.

4, 6, 18 *Openly* The oldest Greek manuscripts do not have this. It was added by later copyists.

6 *Closet* The Greek word is *tameion*. It was used by Xenophon for an "inner room" (NASB). It has the same meaning in 24:26 and Luke 12:3. We are not to make a public display of our praying, as the hypocrites did (v. 5), but to go inside the house and seek the privacy of our bedroom or study—but not necessarily a clothes "closet"!

7 *Use . . . Vain Repetitions* This is all one word in Greek, *battalogēsēte* and is used only here in the NT. It means "*babble*, speak without thinking" (AG, p. 137). That is what too many people do when praying in public. Our praying should be thoughtful as well as fervent. We are not heard for our "much speaking."

In the so-called Lord's Prayer in this same chapter (vv. 9–13) Jesus gives us the pattern—brief, right to the point, every word counting. We should avoid repeating "Lord," "God," or any other words too often in our praying, especially in public.

9 *Hallowed Be* The Greek is *hagiasthētō*, the aorist passive imperative of *hagiazō*, the verb meaning "sanctify." So this prayer literally reads: "Let Your name be sanctified."

It is significant that this is the first petition in the Lord's Prayer. It is primary. We should first pray that God's holy name will be sanctified everywhere.

But we also need to make it personal and relevant: "Let Your name be sanctified in *my* life *today*." We sanctify His holy name by holy living. If our lives are not holy, we desecrate that sacred Name by secular living.

There are 6 petitions in the Lord's Prayer. The first 3 are for God's glory and the extension of His kingdom, not ours. Only then do we pray for ourselves—the last 3 petitions.

Again, we should make these petitions personal: "Let Your kingdom come fully in my heart, as I acknowledge You as King of my life"; "Let Your will be done in my heart as in heaven."

11 *Daily* The Greek word is *epiousios*. There is no clear occurrence of this term anywhere in Greek literature outside of this verse and Luke 11:3. In the third century Origen suggested it was coined by Matthew and Luke. Some scholars claim to have found the word in a papyrus, but Bruce Metzger challenges this.

Unfortunately, there is much dispute as to the exact derivation and meaning of this rare word. Cremer devotes about four pages to a discussion of it. Arndt and Gingrich list no less than four distinct meanings championed by different scholars: "(1) necessary for existence; (2) for today; (3) for the following day; (4) for the future" (p. 297). But they do not express a preference.

TDNT devotes nearly 10 pages to the discussion of *epiousios* (2:590–99), and more than half the space is given to footnotes citing scholars by the dozens! Werner Foerster ends his lengthy treatment by favoring "the bread which we need, give us today" (p. 599). But most modern versions have stayed with the traditional "daily bread"—and probably rightly so.

12 *Debts* The Greek word *opheilēma* is found (in NT) only here and in Rom. 4:4, where it may be translated "what is due" (NASB) or "an obligation" (NIV). But here it clearly has a moral connotation, meaning "sin."

This is shown by the fact that Luke, in his form of the Lord's Prayer, has *hamartias*, "sins." Jesus was probably speaking in Aramaic, as most NT scholars agree. And in Aramaic the one word *hobha* means "debt" or "sin." As Matthew Black observes, " 'Sin' was conceived of in terms of a debt" (*An Aramaic Approach to the Gospels and Acts*, p. 102). For his Greek readers, Luke translated the Aramaic word by *hamartias*, "sins." So we should obviously understand it in that sense.

Why do some congregations, when reciting the Lord's Prayer, say, "Forgive us our trespasses, as we forgive those who trespass against us"? The answer is that this is taken from the Anglican Book of Common Prayer. But it is not a correct rendition.

13 *For Thine Is the Kingdom . . .* The last half of verse 13, a closing doxology, is not found in the earliest manuscripts, nor in the church fathers. It is evidently a liturgical addition adopted to give a smoother ending to the prayer. However, it is doubtless wise to include it when reciting the Lord's Prayer in public today.

14–15 *Trespasses* The Greek noun *paraptōma* comes from the verb *parapiptō*. This is compounded of *para*, "beside," and *piptō*, "fall." So it literally means "fall beside"—that is, off the road. It indicates a "false step," which is sin.

Paul uses this word frequently; but aside from his Epistles it is found only here and in Mark 11:25. Matthew alone uses it for faults against our fellowmen. Wilhelm Michaelis notes that "the severity of offences against men is emphasized by the use of *paraptōmata* for them too." He adds: "There are no *paraptōmata* against one's neighbour which do not affect one's relation to God, and *vice versa*" (TDNT, 6:171).

16 *Of a Sad Countenance* This is all one word in Greek, the adjective *skythrōpos* (only here and Luke 24:17). It means "with a sad, gloomy, or sullen look" (AG, p. 758). With the verb *ginomai*, "become," it may be translated: "Do not put on a gloomy face" (NASB).

19–20 *Rust* The Greek word *brōsis* is used elsewhere in the NT for eating food, either physical or spiritual food. But here alone it means rust or corrosion which eats metal.

22 *Single* *Haplous* occurs only here and in the parallel passage in Luke (11:34). Literally it means "simple, single, sincere." When used of the eye—in contrast to *ponēros*, "bad" (v. 23, NASB, NIV)—it means "clear, sound, healthy" (AG, p. 86).

24 *Serve* The verb is *douleuō*, which literally means "be a slave to." A man today may work two jobs. But no one can be a slave to two "masters"—Greek *kyriois*, "lords" or "owners."

Mammon The Greek word *mamōnas* is found only here and in Luke 16:9, 11, 13. It comes from an Aramaic root. Friedrich Hauck notes that the derivation is uncertain but thinks it most likely comes from a word meaning "that in which one trusts" (TDNT, 4:388). He goes on to say: "In the NT *mamōnas* occurs only on the lips of Jesus. In the first instance it means 'property,' 'earthly goods,' but always with a derogatory sense of the materialistic, anti-godly and sinful. In the earthly property which man gathers (Mt. 6:19ff.), in which he erroneously seeks security (Lk. 2:15ff.), to which he gives his heart (Mt. 6:21), and because of which he ceases to love, Jesus finds the very opposite of God (Mt. 6:24 par.). Because of the demonic power immanent in possessions, surrender to them brings practical enslavement (Mt. 6:19ff.). The righteous must resolutely break free from this entanglement and stand in exclusive religious dependence on God, Mt. 6:24 par." (p. 389).

25, 31, 34 *Take No Thought* This unfortunate translation in the KJV has led some conscientious people into strange folly. For example, to "take no thought" for our life (v. 25), as to what we eat (v. 31), or for tomorrow (v. 34) has been interpreted to forbid buying life insurance. As a result many young widows and children have been left in helpless circumstances.

The Greek verb is *merimnaō* (from *merimna*), which means "be anxious." The true admonition is "Do not be anxious" (NASB) or "Do not worry" (NIV).

27 *Stature* See discussion at Luke 12:25.

7:3–5 *Mote* The Greek word *karphos* (only here and Luke 6:41–42) indicates "a small piece of straw, chaff, wood, etc., to denote something quite insignificant" (AG, p. 405). It is best rendered "speck" (NASB) or "speck of sawdust" (NIV).

Beam The Greek *dokos* is also found only here and in Luke 6:41–42. It may equally well be translated as "beam" (KJV), "log" (RSV, NASB), or "plank" (NIV).

6 *Pearls* The Greek word for "pearl" is *margaritēs*, from which we get Marguerite and Margaret—a beautiful connotation for those names.

13–14 *Strait* The adjective *stenos* (only here and Luke 13:24) simply means "narrow." Everyone who enters the kingdom of God comes through the narrow door of self-denial, of repentance toward God and faith in Jesus.

13 *Broad* The Greek word is *eurychōros* (only here in NT). It is compounded of *eurys*, "broad," and *chōra*, "country." So it suggests the fact that the broad way is wide-open country, with no fences or boundaries—a correct description of the "broad way." There are no rules or regulations to hinder one from doing just what he pleases. On the broad road one may go anywhere he wants to and live as undisciplined a life as he chooses. He need not worry about getting off the road. He can't! But—it leads to destruction. Any other way but the narrow road of doing God's will is the wide-open road to final doom.

14 Narrow This is not the same adjective noted above, describing the gate. Rather, we are told here that the "way," or "road" is *tethlimmenē*. This is the perfect passive participle of *thlibō*, which means "press" or "compress." So the participle can be translated "restricted" or "confined." Only those who are willing to live godly lives in an ungodly world, to be holy in heart and life, can find their way home to heaven. It is only for those who do the will of God (v. 21).

20 Know The verb is *ginōskō*, which does mean "know." Some people have found difficulty in harmonizing Jesus' statement here with His admonition in verse 1. But there is no contradiction. We are not to judge people, but we cannot help but "recognize" (NIV) the obvious in their lives.

28 Were Astonished The verb is *ekplēssō*. It is compounded of *ek*, "out of," and *plēssō*, "strike." The people were "struck out of their minds" with amazement at Jesus' teaching.

8:2 Worshiped See discussion at Mark 5:6.

5 Centurion The Greek is *hekatontarchos*. It is compounded of *hekaton*, "a hundred," and *archōn*, "ruler." So it literally means "ruler of a hundred (men)." Our word "centurion" comes from the Latin. It means an officer commanding "a century" (100 men) in the Roman army.

6 Sick of the Palsy All one word in the Greek, *paralyticos*, the adjective "paralyzed" (NIV).

Grievously Tormented The Greek is *deinōs basanizomenos*. The adverb *deinōs* (only here and Luke 11:53) means "terribly." The verb *basanizō* means "torture, torment" (cf. v. 29). The combination may be translated "suffering great pain" (NASB) or "in terrible suffering" (NIV).

10 Verily This is *amēn* in the Greek, which occurs about 150 times in the NT. In the KJV it is transliterated as "Amen" nearly 50 times in the Epistles and Revelation. But in the Gospels it is translated "verily" ("Verily I say unto you") 100 times (30 in Matthew, 14 in Mark, 6 in Luke, and 50 times in John). One reason for the large number in John is that it is regularly the double "*amēn amēn*" in that Gospel.

The whole phrase (in the Synoptic Gospels) may be translated "Truly I say to you" (NASB) or "I tell you the truth" (NIV). Jesus spoke with divine authority.

11 Sit Down The Greek verb *anaklinō* comes from *klinē*, "couch." So it means in the passive, as here, "*lie down, recline* at a meal" (AG, p. 56). It is correctly translated "recline *at table*" (NASB), or more broadly, "take their places at the feast" (NIV).

15 Ministered See discussion at Mark 1:31.

20 Nests The Greek noun *kataskēnōsis* (only here and Luke 9:58) is compounded of *kata*, "down," and *skēnē*, "tent." The birds "tent down" in the trees in their nests.

24 Tempest The word *seismos* literally means "a shaking." Elsewhere in the NT (13 times) it is translated "earthquake." And so in English we have the "seismograph" for measuring the intensity of earthquakes.

But here the *seismos* is on the water, brought on by violent winds. In the parallel passages in Mark (4:37) and Luke (8:23) we find a different word, *lailaps*, "whirlwind." This gives the source of the shaking: It was due to the downrush of violent gusts of wind, which churned the water into an angry monster reaching out wet hands to seize its helpless victims and drag them down to a watery grave.

The explanation of these sudden, violent storms is to be found in the topography of the Lake of Galilee. The surface of the lake is nearly 700 feet below sea level. Bordering the lake are hills and mountains. The cold winds rush down from these hills sometimes with tremendous force.

28 Gadarenes See discussion at Mark 5:1.

Fierce The adjective *chalepos* means "terrible" in 2 Tim. 3:1 and "fierce" or "violent" (NIV) here, the only two places where it occurs in the NT.

32 *Ran Violently* This is a bit of over-translation. The single Greek word, *hōrmēsen*, simply means "rushed." See discussion at Mark 5:13.

A Steep Place The noun *krēmnos* means "a steep bank." It is used (in NT) only here and in the parallel passages in Mark (5:13) and Luke (8:33).

9:1 ***His Own City*** One might assume that this meant Nazareth, Jesus' hometown. But here it means Capernaum, the place He had chosen as the headquarters of His great Galilean ministry (see 4:13).

2 *Sick of the Palsy* The adjective *paralyticos* occurs five times each in Matthew and Mark. Luke the physician uses another expression in his Gospel.

We have already noted that in 8:6 it should be translated as an adjective—"paralyzed" (NASB, NIV). But here it is used as a substantive and is properly translated "a paralytic."

Be of Good Cheer The Greek is *tharsei*, the imperative (always in NT) of the verb *pharseō*. The verb occurs (sing. or pl.) 7 times in the NT.

In the KJV *tharsei* is translated "be of good comfort" in verse 22, as well as in Mark 10:49. The rest of the time it is "be of good cheer." It may be rendered "Take courage" (NASB) or "Take heart" (NIV).

Be Forgiven The earliest Greek manuscripts have here and in Mark 2:5 *aphientai* (pres. indic.), "are forgiven" (NASB, NIV), and *apheontai* (perf. indic.), "have been forgiven," in Luke 5:20. To translate these, "Thy sins be forgiven thee" makes them sound like a wish or command, whereas Jesus was simply making a statement of fact.

9 *Receipt of Custom* This is one Greek word, *telōnion*, found only here and in the parallel passages (Mark 2:14; Luke 5:27). It means "tax office" (AG, NASB). But since this might suggest some sort of office building, the NIV has "tax collector's booth." Anyone who has walked the streets of the old city of Jerusalem will appreciate this reference to a small booth on a narrow street.

It was in the busy city of Capernaum that Jesus called a businessman to leave the employ of the Roman Empire and accept service in the kingdom of heaven. No wonder that Matthew's favorite word is "kingdom" and that "the kingdom of heaven" is a phrase found only in his Gospel (over 30 times). He was kingdom-conscious, and he knew full well that his call by the Master of men was not a demotion but a promotion. Appropriately, his first act after forsaking his business to follow Jesus was to give a large feast in honor of his new Employer (9:10; cf. Luke 5:29).

10–11 *Sinners* These men were *called* "sinners" by the Pharisees because they did not keep all the minute regulations of the "tradition of the elders." They were not necessarily wicked men. Thus the NIV puts these words in quotation marks.

13 *To Repentance* This phrase is not found in the earliest Greek manuscripts. A. B. Bruce says: "It is a clear case of harmonising assimilation" (EGT, 1:151)—that is, with Luke 5:32, where it is genuine.

15 *Children of the Bridechamber* See discussion at Mark 2:19.

16–17 *Piece . . . New . . . Bottles* See discussion at Mark 2:21–22.

23 *Minstrels* The Greek word *aulētas* occurs (in NT) only here and in Rev. 18:22. It means "flute-players" (NASB, NIV). They were used for both festive occasions and for mourning (AG, p. 121).

36 *Fainted . Scattered Abroad* The Greek says that they were *eskylmenoi* and *errimmenoi* (both perfect passive participles). The first is the verb *skyllō*, which originally meant "flay" or "skin," and then "harass" (AG, p. 758). The second is the verb *hriptō*, which means "throw," and so here "cast down, prostrate" (A-S, p. 398). The combination may be translated "distressed and downcast" (NASB) or "harassed and helpless" (NIV).

10:1–2 ***Disciples . . . Apostles*** In verse one Jesus prepares "his twelve disciples" to go out on their first mission. But in verse two they are called "the twelve apostles" (cf. Mark 3:14). What is the difference?

"Disciple" is the broader term; it takes in every true follower of the Master. The Greek word is *mathētēs*, from the verb *manthanō*, "learn." So a disciple is primarily a "learner."

As followers of Jesus we are to be, first of all, learners. We are to learn from Him by listening to Him, learn the truth that will set us free (John 8:32) and keep us from error. But we are also to learn from Him by looking at Him—

learn how to live a life of holiness and happiness, a life of beauty and blessing.

The word "apostle" has a very different connotation. The Greek is *apostolos*, "one sent on a mission"—from the verb *apostellō*, "send with a commission." Thayer defines the verb as meaning: "to order (one) to go to a place appointed" (p. 67).

So the apostle is primarily a "missionary"— a word that comes from the Latin. In a very true sense every Christian is to be a missionary. All are sent by the Master to share His good news of salvation.

This is the first occurrence of *apostolos* in the NT. It occurs once also in Mark and John. But it is found 6 times in Luke, 30 times in Acts, and over 40 times in Paul's Epistles.

4 Canaanite　See discussion at Mark 3:18.

7 Is at Hand　This is the third time we have had the statement "The kingdom of heaven is at hand." The first time it was on the lips of John the Baptist (3:2). Then Jesus used it as His opening proclamation (4:17). Now He tells His 12 apostles to proclaim it.

"Is at hand" is one word, *ēngiken*, the perfect tense of *engizō*. The verb comes from the adjective *engys*, which means "near," in relation to either place or time.

Actually, both of these concepts fit here. Jesus declared: "The kingdom of heaven is near" (NIV). In His person it was near the disciples right then. It was also coming soon in a special way at Pentecost and in the missionary work that followed. And it will come in its final fulfillment at the return of Christ.

9 Brass　This should be "copper" (*chalcon*). In those days they had gold, silver, and copper coins, just as we have today (cf. Mark 6:8).

10 Scrip . . . Coats　See discussion at Mark 6:8–9.

10 Meat　The Greek *trophē* occurs 16 times in the NT and is translated "meat" 13 times in the KJV. Twice it is correctly rendered "food" (Acts 14:17; Jas. 2:15).

The word comes from the verb *trephō*, which means "nourish" or "feed." So the noun means "nourishment" or "food." Here the context suggests "support" (NASB) or "keep" (NIV).

16 Harmless　*Akeraios* is defined by Thayer as literally meaning "unmixed, pure," and so, when used of a person, "without admixture of evil, free from guile, innocent, simple" (p. 22).

It occurs only here and in Rom. 16:19 and Phil. 2:15 (see discussion at the latter). We are to be "as shrewd as snakes and as innocent as doves" (NIV). This suggests that we are to be tough-minded but tender-hearted.

17 Councils　See discussion at Mark 13:9.

19 Take No Thought　The first part of this verse is better rendered: "But when they arrest you, do not worry about what to say or how to say it" (NIV). (See discussion at Mark 13:11.)

24 Master . . . Lord　The first word is *didaskalos*. It comes from *didaskō*, "teach," and so means "teacher." Yet in the KJV it is translated "master" 46 times in the Gospels. In the Epistles (except in Jas. 3:1) it is correctly translated in the KJV "teacher" (10 times). In our present passage "teacher" is doubly meaningful, since it is paired off with "disciple," which means "learner."

"Lord" translates *kyrios*, which is correctly rendered "lord" (or "Lord") many times in the NT. But here and in numerous other passages it refers to a "master" of slaves. What Jesus said in this verse was: "A student is not above his teacher, nor a servant above his master" (NIV).

41–42 In the Name of　A. B. Bruce says that *eis onoma* means "having regard to the fact that he is a prophet or righteous man" (EGT, 1:168)—hence "because he is" (NIV).

42 Cold Water　As the italics in the KJV indicate, the word "water" is not in the Greek, which simply has the adjective *psychros*, "cold" (only here and Rev. 3:15–16). Cold water was a great luxury in Palestine, much of which is hot desert.

11:8 Soft Clothing

The Greek has only *ta malaka*, "the soft (things)," which is represented literally by "soft *clothing*" (KJV, NASB)—the italics indicating that only the adjective "soft" (neut. pl.) occurs here. In those days only wealthy people could afford to wear "soft" clothes. So the idea is that of "fine clothes" (NIV).

12 Suffereth Violence . . . Violent　The Greek simply has *biazetai . . . biastai*. The first word is the verb *biazō*, which occurs (in NT) only here and in Luke 16:16. There the KJV has: " . . . the kingdom of God is preached, and every man presseth into it." Similarly the NASB has in Matt. 12:12, " . . . the kingdom of heaven suffers violence, and violent men take it by force"; and in Luke 16:16, " . . . the gospel of the kingdom of God is preached, and every one is forcing his way into it."

The second word is the noun *biastēs* (only here in NT), which means: "1. strong, forceful. 2. violent" (A-S, p. 81)—used as a substantive. Both noun and verb come from *bia*, "strength, force, violence" (only in Acts, four times).

The disconcerting fact—a real problem in exegesis—is that the form *biazetai* may be either passive or middle. The KJV and NASB obviously take it as the former, and not in the best sense.

Thayer takes it (in Matthew) as passive, but in a good sense. He would translate: *"The kingdom of heaven is taken by violence, carried by storm,* i.e. a share in the heavenly kingdom is sought for with the most ardent zeal and the intensest exertion." He goes on to say: "The other explanation: *the kingdom of heaven suffereth violence* sc. from its enemies, agrees neither with the time when Christ spoke the words, nor with the context" (p. 101). We might note that Thayer takes the verb as middle in Luke 16:16, with the sense "to force one's way into," and so "to get a share in the kingdom of God by the utmost earnestness and effort."

We would agree with this general interpretation. But we would also take it as middle in Matthew: ". . . the kingdom of heaven has been forcefully advancing, and forceful men lay hold of it" (NIV).

16 *Markets* The Greek noun is *agora*. It means the marketplace or the plaza in each city where people did their buying and visited with each other.

17 *Piped . . . Mourned* The Greek has *ēulēsannen . . . ethrēnēsamen.* The verb *auleō* means "play on a flute," and the verb *thrēneō* means "lament" or "wail." So the correct translation is (NIV; cf. NASB):

> We played the flute for you, and you did not dance;
> we sang a dirge, and you did not mourn.

The picture here is that of children in the marketplace playing the games of wedding and funeral. First, someone tries playing wedding and pipes a merry tune. But the others look glumly on with "I won't play" written on their faces. So the player tries to catch the spirit of the occasion and begins to wail a funeral dirge, but with the same result.

23 *Hell* The Greek word is *hadēs*. It is best simply transliterated as "HADES" (NASB) or translated as "the depths" (NIV). Incidentally, the first clause of this verse should be taken as a question: "And you, Capernaum, will you be lifted up to the skies?" (NIV). By the use of *mē* the Greek indicates that a negative answer is expected (cf. NASB). Capernaum had been chosen by Jesus as the main headquarters of His Galilean ministry, but the religious leaders there rejected Him.

28 *Give You Rest* "Give rest" is one word in Greek, *anapausō*—literally, "I will rest (you)." It is His presence that brings rest. We do not receive "rest" as a gift to be kept in cold storage. His warm presence rests our hearts.

Heavy Laden This is the perfect passive participle of *phortizō* (only here and Luke 11:46). It means to be "loaded down" or "burdened" (NIV). The latter has the advantage of tying in to the noun "burden" in verse 30, which is *phortion*, "load, burden."

30 *Easy* The adjective *chrēstos* commonly means "pleasant." Wearing Christ's easy yoke is actually pleasant!

12:1 *Corn*
The same Greek word as here is translated "corn fields" in Luke 6:1 and Mark 2:23 (see the discussion there)—the only places it occurs in the NT. In all three places it is in the plural.

The noun is *sporimos*. It comes from *speirō*, the verb meaning to "sow." So literally it indicates land that has been sown with seed. The correct translation (for America) is "grainfields." In the British Isles wheat is still called "corn" (see NEB).

4 *Showbread* See discussion at Mark 2:26.

14 *Held a Council* The Greek is *symboulion elabon.* This combination of the noun with the verb *lambanō* is found only in Matthew (see 22:15; 27:1, 7; 28:12). In his parallel passage Mark (3:6) has the verb *didōmi*, "give."

Symboulion literally means "counsel," and the verb *lambanō* means "take"—so, "take counsel." The idea here is "counseled together" (NASB), or, better (see AG, p. 778), "plotted" (NIV).

20 *Smoking Flax* "Flax" is *linon*. In the only other place where it occurs in the NT (Rev. 15:6) it is correctly translated "linen."

"Smoking" is the present passive participle

of the verb *typhō*, "smoke" or "smolder" (only here in NT). Since *linon* was used for a wick, a good translation here is: "a smoldering wick he will not snuff out" (NIV).

The interpretation of this passage accepted by most commentators appears to be that the Messiah would not use harsh, severe methods in dealing with those whose lamps of spiritual life were burning feebly. He would not snuff out their flickering flame. Rather, He would try to revive it with the fresh oil of His grace. This offers a suggestion to pastors in dealing with spiritually weak persons in their congregations.

22–28 Devils There is only one "devil" (*diabolos*). But the Greek word here is *daimonion*, from which we get "demon." It should always be translated "demon" in the NT. It occurs 60 times in the Greek NT and in the KJV is translated "devil" all but one time (Acts 17:18, "gods").

36 Idle The adjective is *argos*, which is compounded of the alpha-privative *a-* and *ergon*, "work." So it literally means "inactive, idle." Abbott-Smith says that it is used here metaphorically in the sense of "inactive, ineffective, worthless" (p. 57). Arndt and Gingrich suggest that it means "a *careless word* which, because of its worthlessness, had better been left unspoken" (p. 104).

40 Whale The Greek word is *kētos* (only here in NT). In Greek literature it is used for "sea monster" (NASB).

The problem with "whale" is that a whale, which is a mammal, does not have a large enough throat to swallow a man. But a shark, which is a fish, does. So "huge fish" (NIV) is more accurate.

44 Empty This is the present participle *scholazonta*. It means "unoccupied" (NASB, NIV).

Garnished This is the perfect passive participle of *cosmeō*, from which we get "cosmetics." It means "put in order" (NASB, NIV), or perhaps "decorate" (AG, p. 444).

13:3 Parables This is the first of 50 occurrences in the NT of the word *parabolē*, which we have taken over into English as "parable." It occurs 17 times in Matthew, 13 times in Mark, and 18 times in Luke—plus twice in Hebrews (9:9; 11:19), where it is translated "figure" (KJV).

The Greek word comes from *paraballō*, which means "lay beside" or "compare." So a parable is "*a comparison, illustration, analogy, figure . . .* specifically of the pictures and narratives drawn from nature and human life which are characteristic of the synoptic teaching of our Lord, *a parable*" (A-S, p. 338). It is generally agreed that John has no parables.

Matthew, who is very systematic and also fond of significant numbers, gives us in chapter 13 seven parables of the Kingdom—"the kingdom of heaven is like" (vv. 24, 31, 33, 44, 45, 47, NIV). The parable of the sower (vv. 3–9) is not so identified.

See also discussion at Mark 3:23.

5 Stony See discussion at Mark 4:5.

Sprung Up The verb *exanatellō* is found only here and in Mark 4:5. *Ana* means "up" and *ex* means "out of." (We always work backward in handling Greek compounds.) So the meaning here is that the seed grew up through the ground and out into the air. It "sprang up quickly."

7 Sprung Up This is a different verb from that found in verse 5. Here it is *anabainō*, which is less forceful. It means "came up" (NASB) or "grew up" (NIV).

8 Fruit See discussion at Mark 4:7.

11 Mystery Our English word comes directly from the Greek *mysterion*, which comes from *mystēs*, "one who has been initiated." Jesus indicated that the disciples had been initiated into the secrets of the Kingdom.

15 Is Waxed Gross This is one word in Greek—*epachynthē*. The verb *pachynō* comes from *pachys*, "thick," and so in the passive literally means "grow fat." But here it is used metaphorically in the sense of "has become dull" (NASB) or "has become calloused" (NIV). That is what happens to the hearts of people who refuse to obey God's Word.

21 Offended See discussion at Mark 4:17.

25 Tares The word *zizania* (pl.) occurs only in this parable (eight times, in vv. 25, 26, 27, 29, 30, 36, 38, 40). It refers to a bearded "darnel" (NEB), a "weed" (NIV) that looks very much like wheat until it is ripe. But the use of it could cause dizziness or nausea.

Would anyone do such a dirty trick? Henry Alford tells how in a field belonging to him someone maliciously sowed charlock over the wheat (1:143).

30, 39 Reapers The Greek word (only here in NT) is *theristēs*. It is from the same stem as the noun *therismos*, which is translated "harvest" earlier in both verses. This connection is brought out in English by using "harvesters" (NIV).

31 Grain of Mustard Seed See discussion at Mark 4:31.

32 Herbs See discussion at Mark 4:32.

36 Declare The verb is *diasapheō*. It comes from *saphēs*, "clear," and so means "make clear," or "explain" (NASB, NIV).

41 Things That Offend The KJV margin says "Or, scandals." The Greek here says *scandala*, the plural of *scandalon* from which we get "scandal." But the Greek *scandalon* was a trap or snare. So a better translation here for the whole phrase is "everything that causes sin" (NIV).

45 Merchant Man The Greek word is *emporos* (only here and in Rev. 18:3, 11, 15, 23). It comes from *en*, "on," and *poros*, "a journey." It means a man carrying on trade. We would call him simply a "merchant."

46 Of Great Price The Greek adjective *polytimos* is compounded of *polys*, "much," and the noun *timē*, which means "value." So "of great value" (NASB, NIV) is perhaps preferable.

47 Net The Greek word *sagēnē* (only here in NT) means "a drag-net, seine" (A-S, p. 400). Even today one can see fishermen pulling in these nets full of fish on the shores of the Lake of Galilee or on the beaches of the Mediterranean.

48 Vessels The usual word translated "vessel" in KJV (19 times) is *skeuos*. But here we find a rare term, *angos* (only here in NT). It means "a container" (cf. NASB). But these containers for fish were "baskets" (NIV).

52 Instructed The Greek has *mathēteutheis*, the aorist passive participle of *mathēteuō*. In the passive this means "become a disciple," as in Matt. 27:57 (cf. NIV). That seems to be the best translation here (NASB).

57 Own Country See discussion at Mark 6:1.

14:1 Tetrarch The Greek word *tetrarchēs* is a compound of *tetra*, "four," and *archōn*, "ruler." Strabo, a Greek geographer at the time of Christ's birth, uses the term for a ruler of the fourth part of a region. "Later, when the original sense was wholly lost," it came to be used as the "title of a petty dependent prince, whose rank and authority were lower than those of a king" (AG, p. 814).

"Herod the tetrarch" was Herod Antipas, a son of Herod the Great. He ruled over Galilee and Perea (Transjordan) from 4 B.C. to A.D. 39. Luke also refers to him as "the tetrarch" (Luke 3:19; 9:7; Acts 13:1).

Fame "Heard" is the verb *akouō* and "fame" is the noun *akoē*, derived from it. So the Greek literally says: "heard the hearing."

The verb occurs some 437 times in the NT. The noun occurs 24 times. It has several distinct meanings. It may mean the act of hearing, the organ of hearing (the ears), or that which is heard. The last is what we have here. The word may be translated "news" (NASB) or "reports" (NIV).

2 Mighty Works This is one word in Greek, the plural of *dynamis*. In the KJV it is translated "power" 77 out of the 120 times it occurs in the NT. In the Synoptic Gospels it is the most common term used to designate the miracles of Jesus. Probably the best translation here is "miraculous powers" (NASB, NIV). Apparently Antipas thought that if John the Baptist had risen from the dead, he could work miracles.

4 Said The Greek verb is in the imperfect tense (*elegen*) of continuous or repeated action. This is brought out in English by "had been saying."

6 Birthday The Greek word is *genesia* (only here and Mark 6:21), the neuter, plural of the adjective *genesios*, "relating to birth," which is derived from *genesis*, "birth" (see Matt. 1:18). In late Greek *genesia* came to mean a "birthday feast." Perhaps it is plural to indicate the celebrations that took place.

8 Being Before Instructed On the surface this seems to be a contradiction of Mark 6:24, which says that the girl went out and asked her mother what to say. But a correct translation of the Greek takes care of this problem. The right wording here in Matthew is: "having been prompted by her mother" (NASB)—aorist passive participle—or, more simply, "prompted by her mother" (NIV). That is, she went out and got her mother's prompting as to what she should say.

11 Charger See discussion at Mark 6:25.

13, 15 Desert The Greek adjective *erēmos* means "solitary, lonely, desolate, deserted" (A-S, p. 179).

16 Give Ye In the Greek the "ye" (*hymeis*) is emphatic: "You give them something to eat" (NASB, NIV), with emphasis on "you." The interesting point is that they did exactly this (v. 19) when Jesus multiplied the loaves and fish. When our Lord commands us to do something, He provides the enablement for doing it. Our only responsibility is to obey Him.

20 Filled See discussion at Mark 6:42.

Baskets See discussion at Mark 6:43.

22 Constrained See discussion at Mark 6:45.

24 In the Midst of the Sea We have here a problem in textual criticism. The wording above is based on the bulk of the Greek manuscripts and is parallel to the undisputed Greek reading in Mark 6:47. In John 6:19 we read that the disciples had rowed 25 or 30 *stadia*—3 or 3½ miles—which would be to about the middle of the lake. Our best single manuscript (Vaticanus, 4th cent.) and some others have here in Matthew: "many stadia away from the land" (NASB). This reading is represented in the NIV: "a considerable distance from the land." For further discussion of *stadion* see comments at Luke 24:13.

Tossed The Greek verb is *basanizō*, which literally means "torture" or "torment." The latter is the KJV translation 8 out of the 12 times it occurs in the NT. But here we find "tossed (with waves)" and in the parallel passage in Mark 6:48 "toiling (in rowing)." For the Matthew passage the NASB has "battered" and the NIV "buffeted."

26 Troubled See discussion at Mark 6:50.

31 Doubt This is one of four Greek verbs translated "doubt" in the NT. It is *distazō* (only

here and 28:17), which comes from *dis*, "twice." So it suggests hesitating between two opinions.

35 Diseased The Greek here (*kakos echontas*) literally means "having badly." Since there are definite Greek words in the NT for "disease," a better translation here is "who were ill" (NASB) or "their sick" (NIV).

36 Edge The Greek word is *kraspedon* (Matt. 9:20; 14:36; 23:5; Mark 6:56; Luke 8:44). In 23:5 it clearly means "tassel," as in the Septuagint. Here it probably refers to "the edge of his cloak" (NIV) or "the fringe of his cloak" (NASB).

15:2–3 Transgress The verb (only here and Acts 1:25) is *parabainō*. *Bainō* means "go" and *para* "beside." Homer, our earliest Greek author, uses it in the literal sense of "go beside." In later writers, such as Herodotus, it means "go past" or "overstep." Thucydides speaks of sinning against one of the gods by transgressing the law. In the papyri this verb is used for breaking legal provisions.

Its use in the Septuagint is especially significant. J. Schneider writes: "The usage found in the papyri and inscriptions is plainly to be seen in the LXX, except that here there is little or no trace of the sphere of private law. Man becomes guilty in respect of God's commandments and ordinances" (TDNT, 5:737). However, we should note that the Pharisees did use the verb for breaking their man-made laws. Schneider goes on to say of this passage: "Transgression is sin only where there is disregard for the *entolē* [command] of God. Human tradition, though it purports to be plain exposition of the commandments of God, is in truth a sin against these commandments if the human ordinance obscures the pure and original will of God, and turns it into its opposite" (p. 739). This warning against treating human ordinances as having divine authority still needs to be sounded.

The current idiom for "transgress the commandment" is "break the command" (NIV). Jesus accused the Pharisees of doing this by their tradition (vv. 3–6).

6 Have Ye Made . . . of None Effect This is all one word in Greek, *ēkyrōsate*. The verb *akyroō* is compounded of the alpha privative *a* and *kyros*, "authority." So it means to "invalidate" (NASB) or "nullify" (NIV). In the NT the word occurs only here and in Mark 7:13; Gal. 3:17.

14 *Ditch* This is the way *bothynos* is translated (KJV) in the parallel passage (Luke 6:39). But KJV translates it "a pit" in Matt. 12:11, the only other place in the NT where it occurs. There is no article in the Greek in all three passages. So the correct translation everywhere is "a pit" (RSV, NASB, NIV; A-S, p. 83; AG, p. 144). In those days sometimes a man would dig a pit and carelessly leave it unguarded, to the peril of the blind.

15 *Declare* In the best Greek text *phrazō* is found only here in the NT. It means "interpret" or "explain" (NASB, NIV).

19 *Blasphemies* The Greek word is *blasphēmiai*, from which we get "blasphemies." But today "blasphemy" is used only for an irreverent utterance against God. In the KJV the term *blasphēmia* is translated "blasphemy" 16 out of the 19 times it occurs in the NT. But scholars are agreed that in about half these instances, involving only human beings, the correct rendering is "slander(s)" (RSV, NASB, NIV).

21 *Coasts* Four different Greek words in the NT are translated "coast" in the KJV, and not one of them means "coast" in the sense of shoreline as used today. Here (and in 16:13; Acts 19:1) the word is *meros*, which literally means "part," and is so translated in the KJV in 24 out of its 43 occurrences in the NT. The correct translation here is "district" (RSV, NASB) or "region" (NIV).

22 *Coasts* This is another Greek word, *horion*, which literally means "boundary," but is always plural in the NT. In the KJV it is translated "coasts" 10 out of the 11 times it occurs. (The exception is Matt. 4:13.) That is because in the time of the KJV "coast" meant "the border, bound, or limit, of a country," or "a district" (*Oxford English Dictionary*, 2:555). But that meaning is obsolete today.

26–27 *Dogs* On the surface it seems out of character for Jesus to refer to this Gentile woman as a dog. But He did not use the common word for "dog," *kyon* (5 times in NT), which was indeed a term of reproach (cf. Phil. 3:2; Rev. 22:15). Instead, He used the diminutive word, *kynarion*, "little dog" (only here and the parallel passage, Mark 7:27–28), which referred to the pet dogs of the family. This can be brought out in verse 26 by saying "their dogs" (NIV). In verse 27 the woman picked up this same Greek term and applied it beautifully.

28, 30 *Made Whole ... Healed* The first (one word) is the verb *iaomai*. It occurs 28 times in the NT and is translated in the KJV as "heal" 26 times and "make whole" twice (here and Acts 9:34).

In verse 30 the verb is *therapeuō*, which gives us "therapy," "therapeutic," etc. It occurs 44 times and is translated (KJV) "heal" 38 times, "cure" 5 times, and "worship" once (Acts 17:25).

Therapeuō first meant "*serve* a deity" and is so used in Acts 17:25. Then it came to be used as a medical term, with the meaning "treat" and finally "heal."

It is probably best to translate both verbs here as "healed" (NASB, NIV). That is what we would say today.

31 *Whole* This is another word, the adjective *hygiēs*, which means "healthy, sound" (cf. "hygienic"). It may also be translated "well" (NIV).

32 *Faint* See discussion at Mark 8:3.

37 *Baskets* This is not the same word (*kophinos*) that is used in connection with the feeding of the 5,000 (Matt. 14:20; 16:9; Mark 6:43; 8:19; Luke 9:17; John 16:13). Instead it is *spyris*, used in connection with the feeding of the 4,000 (Matt. 15:37; 16:10; Mark 8:8, 20), plus Acts 9:25. The latter passage tells how Saul was let down in a *spyris* from the wall at Damascus. This shows that it must have been a large basket. It was a "hamper" in size (AG, p. 764). So the 7 baskets here may well have held as much as the 12 baskets of the earlier feeding.

Some negative critics have said that we have two different traditions of *one* feeding. But the completely consistent use of these two distinct words for basket is a strong argument against this.

39 *Magdala* The very oldest manuscripts have *Magadan*, and this fourth-century reading is attested by the three great fourth-century church fathers—Eusebius, Jerome, and Augustine. It is adopted in RSV, NASB, NIV, and other modern versions. It appears to have been another name for Magdala, or a part of that hometown of Mary Magdalene.

16:1 *Tempting* The verb *peirazō* occurs 39 times in the NT and is translated (in KJV) "tempt" 31 times. But its primary meaning in the Septuagint and NT is "to test, try, prove," often in a good sense, but sometimes "in a bad sense ... of the attempts made to ensnare Jesus

in his speech" (A-S, 351)—as we have it here. Admittedly it is used in Matt. 4:3 and elsewhere of temptations by Satan. But most scholars feel that the correct translation here is "test" (RSV, NASB, NIV).

Sign   See discussion at Mark 8:11.

3 *Lowering*   See comments at Mark 10:22, the only other place (in NT) where the verb *stygnazō* occurs. There it is used of a gloomy human face, here of the "overcast" (NIV) face of the sky.

7 *Reason*   See discussion at Mark 8:16–17.

12 *Doctrine*   See discussion at Mark 1:27. We might note that Matthew alone gives the explanation found in this verse—a characteristic of his Gospel (cf. 17:13).

13 "*I . . . Am*"   The Greek does not say this. Rather, it reads: "Who do people say the Son of Man is?" (NIV; cf. NASB).

15 *You*   Literally the Greek reads "But you"—*hymeis* (you) placed first in the sentence for strong emphasis—"who do you say me to be?" This should be indicated in English as follows: " 'But what about you?' he asked. 'Who do you say I am?' " (NIV). It was interesting to know the opinions of others. But the all-important question was what *they* thought about Him. And the deity of Jesus is still the foundation doctrine of Christianity.

16 *You*   Again the "you" (sing. here) is emphatic: *su*, "thou" (KJV). One of the problems of our English language today is that "you" is used for both the singular and the plural. This creates a real problem in translating the Bible.

The Christ   The Greek is *ho Christos*, "the anointed One"—that is, "the Messiah" (Heb.). Jesus was the long-expected Messiah of the Jews.

Matthew alone adds: "The Son of the living God." He was the *divine* Messiah. Peter received this vital knowledge by direct revelation from God (v. 17).

18 *Peter . . . Rock*   For discussion of this crucial matter, see my treatment in *Beacon Bible Commentary*, 6:155.

Church   In the four Gospels the Greek word *ecclēsia* occurs only here and in 18:17 (twice). But it is found 24 times in Acts and over 60 times in Paul's Epistles. It is used for both the whole Body of Believers (the Church of Jesus Christ) and for local congregations—but never for a building, as today.

Ecclēsia comes from the verb *kaleō*, "call," and *ek*, "out." So it literally means "called out."

The word has two significant backgrounds for its NT use for "church." The first is the Greek secular use for the "assembly" of free (called out) citizens in a Greek city. We find this usage three times in the NT (Acts 19:32, 39, 41), for the city "assembly" at Ephesus.

The second, more significant, use is found in the Septuagint. There it refers to the "congregation" of Israel. This usage is reflected in two passages in the NT (Acts 7:38; Heb. 2:12). The latter is a quotation from the Septuagint.

Ecclēsia occurs 115 times in the NT. In the remaining 110 times it refers to the church, either local (87 times) or general (23 times). It is interesting to note that all 9 times in Ephesians it means the Church of Jesus Christ (His Bride; cf. Eph. 5:25–27).

Hell   This is not *Gehenna*, which means "hell," but "Hades" (NASB, NIV), the place of departed spirits.

Prevail   The verb is *katischyō* (only here and Luke 21:36; 23:23). Literally it means "be strong." Here it means "win a victory over" (AG, p. 424), and so "overpower" (NASB) or "overcome" (NIV).

21 *From That Time . . . Began*   Peter's confession at Caesarea Philippi marks the main turning point in Jesus' ministry. Hitherto He had spoken in parables to great crowds of people. Now He concentrates on preparing His disciples for His death, resurrection, and ascension.

22 *Be It Far from Thee*   The Greek has only two words: *hileōs soi. Hileōs* means "gracious" or "merciful" (cf. Heb. 8:12, the only other place in NT where this word occurs.). *Soi* literally means "to you" (sing.). So the whole phrase may mean, "*May God be gracious to you, Lord,* i.e., may God in his mercy spare you this, *God forbid!*" (AG, p. 376). James Holt Moulton remarks: "With the development of a deprecatory force in such phrases we may compare that in our vernacular expression, 'Mercy on us!' " (*Rob. Gram.*, 1:240).

It will readily be seen that this unusual expression can be translated in various ways. It rather obviously is an exclamation. So we find:

"God forbid, Lord!" (RSV; cf. NASB) and "Never, Lord!" (NIV).

23 *Satan* See discussion at Mark 8:33.

Offense The Greek word is *scandalon*, which originally meant the bait-stick of a snare or the trigger of a trap, and then the trap itself. Probably the best translation here is "stumbling block" (NASB, NIV).

24 *Deny . . . Take Up . . . Follow* The first two verbs are in the aorist tense of momentary action; but the third is in the present tense of continuous action. Christ calls His disciples to: (1) a crucial conversion; (2) a complete commitment; (3) a continuous consecration (or course of following Him fully).

25–26 *Life . . . Soul* The same Greek word *psychē* is translated "life" twice in verse 25 and "soul" twice in verse 26. Is this consistent? The ASV (1901) has "life" in all four places, and so does the RSV (1952). But the NASB and NIV both have "life" in verse 25 and "soul" in verse 26, in line with the KJV. Why?

There is general agreement that "life" fits best in verse 25. Schweizer says that the saving (finding) of the life in the last part of the verse shows that it is "true and full life as God the Creator made and fashioned it. . . . Jesus is thus telling man that he will achieve full life only when he no longer clings to it but finds it in loss or sacrifice" (TDNT, 9:642).

But what about verse 26? The translators of the NIV, and others, have felt that *psychē* in this verse refers to the immortal "soul," which is of eternal worth.

17:4 *Tabernacles* The Greek word is *skēnē*, which means "tent" or "booth." It is used for the Tabernacle built at Mount Sinai (Heb. 8:5; 9:2–3, 6, 8, 21). But that was a large structure, as tabernacles usually are today. What Peter had in mind was making small "booths" (RSV) of branches. These would be "shelters" (NIV).

15 *Lunatic* See discussion at Matt. 4:24, the only other place where the verb *selēniazō* occurs in the NT.

17 *Faithless* *Apistos* is compounded of the alpha-privative *a-* and *pistos*, "believing" (A-S, p. 362). Today "faithless" is used interchangeably with "unfaithful"—that is, with respect to one's obligations. So a more accurate translation here is "unbelieving."

24 *Tribute Money* All the Greek has is *ta didrachma*, "the two-drachma." This was the Temple tax which every adult male Jew was required to pay each year (Hastings, DB, 3:428). The word *didrachma* occurs only here (twice) in the NT.

25 *Custom* The Greek says "*telē ē cēnson.*" *Telē* is the plural of *telos*, which literally means "end." See the discussion at Rom. 13:7. For *cēnsos* ("poll tax") see the discussion at Mark 12:14.

27 *A Piece of Money* This is all one word in Greek, *statēr* ("stater," NASB). This was "a four-drachma coin" (NIV), which would pay the tax for both Peter and Jesus. *Statēr* is found only here in the NT.

18:6–9 *Offend* The verb *scandalizō* (see discussion at 5:29–30) means far more than is indicated by the word "offend." It means "causes . . . to stumble" (NASB) or "causes . . . to sin" (NIV).

6 *Millstone* See discussion at Mark 9:42, the only other place (in NT) where *onikos* occurs.

Drowned The verb is *katapontizō*, found in the NT only here and in 14:30, where Peter began to "sink" in the water.

22 *Seventy Times Seven* The Greek here is *hebdomēkontakis hepta*. The second word unquestionably means "seven," but the problem is with the first, longer word, which occurs only here in the NT.

In the Septuagint we find this expression at Gen. 4:24. There the Hebrew clearly indicates that the meaning is "seventy-seven times" (H. A. W. Meyer, *A Critical and Exegetical Handbook to the Gospel of Matthew*, p. 332). J. H. Moulton feels that the Genesis passage is decisive for the meaning here. He comments: "A definite *allusion* to the Genesis story is highly probable: Jesus pointedly sets against the natural man's craving for seventy-sevenfold revenge the spiritual man's ambition to exercise the privilege of seventy-sevenfold forgiveness" (Rob. Gram., 1:98).

28 *Pence* The Greek is *denaria*. A *denarius* (Latin) was a Roman silver coin worth about 18 or 20 cents. So the 100 *denaria* would be about $20.00. The 10,000 talents would equal about $10 million.

31 *Told* We have already noted the verb *diasapheō* in 13:36, the only other place in the NT where it is found. There it clearly means "explain." But for the present passage Arndt and Gingrich suggest "tell plainly, in detail, report" (p. 188). It is translated "told" in KJV and NIV, more adequately as "reported" in RSV and NASB, but most adequately as "reported in detail" (William Hendriksen, NTC, p. 708).

34 *Tormentors* The noun *basanistēs* occurs only here in the NT. It comes from the verb *basanizō*, "examine by torture," and more generally, "torture" (A-S, p. 76). Johannes Schneider says that here in the NT *basanistēs* means "tormentor" (TDNT, 1:563). Arndt and Gingrich give "torturer, jailer" (p. 134), since it was the jailer who did the torturing. So we have the translation "jailers" (RSV, NIV).

19:3 *For Every Cause* This phrase is not found in the parallel passage in Mark (10:2–12), for Gentile readers would not be aware, as would Matthew's readers, of the Jewish connotation. It highlights the controversy in the first century B.C. between the schools of Hillel and Shammai.

The conflict arose over the interpretation of Deut. 24:1—"When a man hath taken a wife, and married her, and it come to pass that she find no favor in his eyes, because he hath found some uncleanness in her: then let him write her a bill of divorcement . . ." Shammai held that "uncleanness" meant fornication: "A man shall not divorce his wife unless he has found in her a matter of shame." His colleague, Hillel (*ca.* 60 B.C.—A.D. 20), who was much more liberal, emphasized the previous clause, "she find no favor in his eyes." He would allow a man to divorce his wife if she did anything that he disliked, even if she burned his food in cooking it.

5 *Cleave* The verb is *kollaō*, from *kolla*, "glue." So it literally means (in the passive) "be glued to." What is needed in modern marriage, in these days of rampaging divorce, is more of the glue of unselfish love!

6 *Joined Together* The Greek says "yoked together" (*synzeugnymi*). (See Mark 10:9, the only other place in the NT where this verb occurs.) When two people are married, they are supposed to put their necks into the same yoke and stay together the rest of their lives.

9 *Except for Fornication* This exception is found only in Matthew. *Porneia* does not here mean "fornication" (KJV) but "immorality" (NASB) or "marital unfaithfulness" (NIV). (See discussion at Matt. 5:32.)

20:2 *Agreed* The Greek verb is *symphoneō*, compounded of *syn*, "together," and *phonē*, "sound." So it literally means to "sound together," or "agree in sound" (cf. our "symphony"). Then it came to have the general meaning of "agree." The word is used in 18:19 of agreeing together in prayer.

Penny The Greek word is *denarion* (Latin, *denarius*). It was a Roman silver coin worth about 18 or 20 cents.

8 *Steward* The word is *epitropos* (see discussion at Gal. 4:2). The only other place it occurs in the NT is Luke 8:3. The usage is slightly different in the three places. Here a good translation is "foreman" (NASB, NIV).

15 *Good* Here is the common Greek adjective for "good" in the ethical sense—*agathos*. But the context suggests "generous" (NASB, NIV)—which could be thought of as our treating others as God treats us (TDNT, 1:15–16).

22–23 *And Be Baptized . . .* These two rather lengthy clauses are not in the oldest and best Greek manuscripts and so are omitted in most modern versions. They were evidently imported by a later copyist from Mark 10:38–39. Probably no competent scholar would argue in favor of their genuineness here.

25 *Exercise Dominion* The same verb, *katakyrieuō* is translated "exercise lordship" (KJV) in the parallel passage (Mark 10:42). "Lord it over" (NASB, NIV) exactly catches the thought of the Greek. "Exercise authority" (KJV, NASB, NIV) is the verb *katexousiazō* (only in these two passages). The first verb occurs also in Acts 19:16; 1 Pet. 5:3.

26–27 *Minister . . . Servant* See discussion at Mark 10:44.

28 *Minister . . . Ransom* The verb is *diaconeō*, the first meaning of which was: "wait on someone at table," and then more generally, "serve" (AG, p. 184). So a better translation is: "Just as the Son of Man did not come to be served, but to serve, and to give his life a ransom for many" (NASB, NIV). We find the same Greek wording in Mark 10:45, the outstanding theological passage in that Gospel. *Lytron*, "ransom," was the price paid for freeing a slave.

For   See discussion at Mark 10:45.

21:12 *Tables*   These "tables of the money-changers" were the forerunners of the banks of our time. The Greek word for "table" is *trapeza*, and one sees this word over every bank in Athens today.

Moneychangers   The Greek word *kollybistēs* is found (in NT) only here and in the parallel passages (Mark 11:15; John 2:15).

13 *Thieves*   The Greek word *lēstēs* does not mean "thief" but "robber." The money changers forced the Jews to exchange their Greek money for the Phoenician half-shekel in paying their annual Temple tax, and charged them a heavy commission for making the exchange. They were thus acting as robbers.

15 *They Were Sore Displeased*   This is one word in the Greek, the verb *aganakteō*. It simply means "they were indignant" (NIV).

19–20 *Withered Away*   This is too strong a translation. Mark indicates that Jesus cursed the fig tree on Monday morning (11:12–14). The next morning the disciples saw it "withered" (v. 20) and called Jesus' attention to it (v. 21). In both these verses in Mark the perfect tense is used, indicating that it was *withered away*.
But in Matthew we are told that as soon as Jesus cursed the fig tree, "Immediately the tree withered" (NIV, cf. NASB). Here the verb is in the aorist tense. Probably it should be treated as an ingressive aorist: "began to wither." This would help to take care of what on the surface seems like a conflict between these two accounts. We should note that one of the characteristics of Matthew is that he "telescopes" two successive events into one continuous narrative. In verse 20 "withered away" is exactly the same form (aorist) as in verse 19 and should be treated the same.

27 *We Cannot Tell*   The Greek says, "We don't know"—*ouk oidamen*. This was probably a deliberate lie, as indicated by their discussion (vv. 25–26). They were concerned about themselves, not the truth.

33 *Tower*   See discussion at Mark 12:1.

41 *Miserably Destroy*   The Greek here is very strong: *kakous kakōs apolesei autous*—literally, "bad (men), he will destroy them badly." A

good translation is: "He will bring those wretches to a wretched end" (NASB, NIV).

22:2, 4, 9 *Marriage*   The Greek has the plural of *gamos*. Josephus distinguished between the singular of this word as meaning a wedding and the plural as meaning the wedding celebration—which usually lasted from one to three weeks. So the correct translation here is "wedding feast" (NASB) or "wedding banquet" (NIV).

5 *Made Light Of*   This is the verb *ameleō*—the alpha privative *a-* plus *melei*, "it is a care" (or concern). So it means to have no concern. Arndt and Gingrich suggest "paid no attention."

Merchandise   *Emporia* is found only here in the NT. Today we would say "business" (NASB, NIV).

6 *Entreated Them Spitefully*   This is all one word in the Greek, *hybrisan*. The verb *hybrizō* means "to outrage, insult, treat insolently" (A-S, p. 453). The simplest translation is "mistreated them" (NASB, NIV). The KJV uses "entreat," which now means "ask" or "beg" and is obviously not the sense here.

9–10 *Highways*   In verse 9, "highways" is a translation of three Greek words: *diexodous tōn hodōn*. The term *diexodos* (only here in NT) is a combination of three words: *hodos*, "way"; *ex*, "out"; *dia*, "through." So it literally means "a way out through." Arndt and Gingrich say that the whole expression here "is sometimes taken to mean *street-crossing*, but is probably the place where a street cuts *through* the city boundary and goes *out* into the open country" (p. 194). Henry Alford says that the *diexodoi* "are the places of resort at the meetings of streets, the squares, or confluences of ways" (1:219–20). A. B. Bruce comments: "In the open spaces of the city, strangers from the country as well as the lower population of the town could be met with; the foreign element = Gentiles, mainly in view" (EGT, 1:271).
This serves as a good example of two things: (1) the difficulty of making an exact translation of the Greek; (2) the fact that the general meaning is fairly clear.
In verse 10 "highways" is simply *hodous*, "ways." It is probably best translated "streets" (NASB, NIV).

10 *Wedding*   Our two oldest Greek manuscripts, Vaticanus and Sinaiticus of the fourth century, plus Regins (L), have *nymphon*. It means "wedding hall" (NASB, NIV).

10–11 *Guests* The Greek in both places has the present participle of *anakeimai*, "recline at table." That is why the NASB has "dinner-guests." The setting is the wedding feast or banquet.

11 *Had Not on a Wedding Garment* The Greek says: *ouk endedymenon endyma gamou*—literally, "not clothed with wedding clothes." So it may be translated "not dressed in wedding clothes" (NASB) or "not wearing wedding clothes" (NIV). Similarly, "not having a wedding garment" (v. 12, KJV) would simply be "without wedding clothes."

15 *Took Counsel* See discussion at Matt. 12:14.

Entangle The Greek verb is *pagideuō* (only here in NT). It comes from the noun *pagis*, "a trap or snare." So the whole clause means "how they might trap Him in what He said" (NASB).

17 *Tribute* See discussion at the parallel passage, Mark 12:14.

21 *Render* See discussion at Mark 12:17.

35 *Lawyer* See discussion at Luke 10:25.

36 *Which* See discussion at Mark 12:28.

37 *Heart ... Soul ... Mind* See discussion at Mark 12:30.

23:2 *Seat* The Greek word is *cathedra* (only here, 21:12, and Mark 11:15). The statement of Jesus here is related to our use of the expression *ex cathedra* (literally, "from a seat") as meaning "with authority" or "from the seat of authority."

5 *Phylacteries* This comes directly from the Greek, *phylactēria* (only here in the NT). The phylacteries were "small boxes containing scripture verses bound on forehead and arm during prayer, in accordance with Deut. 8:6." They "could be regarded as protections against demonic influences, like amulets" (AG, p. 868).

Borders The Greek word is *kraspedon* (see discussion at 14:36). J. Schneider writes: "In the Bible it denotes the 'hem of a garment' or especially the 'tassel' which the Jews bore on each of the four corners of their outer garment

as a constant reminder of all the commandments (Nu. 15:38f.; Dt. 22:12). ... In Mt. 23:5 Jesus lashes the Pharisees for their purely outward display of piety. Using wool of the prominent hyacinth blue and white, they made their tassels as long as possible in order to gain a reputation for zealous prayer and strict observance of the commandments" (TDNT, 3:904). A good translation here is "the tassels of their prayer shawls" (NIV).

6 *Uppermost Rooms ... Chief Seats* See discussion at Mark 12:39.

7 *Rabbi* The word comes directly from the Hebrew into Greek and English. The Hebrew term *rab* meant "great" and was used for someone who occupied a high and respected position. *Rabbi* means "my great one."

Edward Lohse writes: "The one called *rabbi* is recognized thereby to be higher in rank than the speaker" (TDNT, 6:961). It was especially the custom among the Jews for a pupil to address his teacher with this term. Lohse comments: "The pupil followed his teacher with obedience and respect and expressed this by addressing him as *rabbi*, 'my master' but also 'my teacher' " (p. 962).

In the NT we find *rabbi* used only in Matthew (5 times), Mark (4 times), and John (8 times). Luke never uses *rabbi*, because his Greek readers would not be familiar with the term.

The KJV translates *rabbi* as "Master" 9 out of the 17 times it occurs in the NT. But it is better to transliterate it—"rabbi."

8, 10 *Master ... Master* In verse 8 the word is *didaskalos*, the common Greek term for "teacher" (from the verb *didaskō*, "teach"). This term is applied to Christ many times in the Gospels.

In verse 10 we have a rare term twice, *kathēgētēs* (only here in NT). It comes from the verb *kathēgeomai*, "to go before, guide." So it properly means "a·guide." But it was commonly used in classical Greek, as well as the papyri, in the sense of "teacher," and in modern Greek it means "professor." The only definition given by Arndt and Gingrich is "teacher." Jesus was telling His disciples that He was their only real "Teacher," with divine authority. They were not to take His place. But Jesus was clearly more concerned about attitudes than technical titles, as shown by verse 12.

12 *Abased ... Humble* It is the same Greek verb (*tapeinoō*) in both cases. It is better to translate it: "humbled . . . humbles" (NASB, NIV).

15 *Proselyte* Our word comes right from the Greek *prosēlytos*. The word was used for a "convert" (NIV) to Judaism. It occurs (in NT) only here and in Acts 2:10; 6:5; 13:43, where the NIV spells it out as "convert(s) to Judaism."

16, 18 *He Is a Debtor . . . He Is Guilty* The Greek is exactly the same in both places: the one word *opheilei*. It means "*he is obligated, bound* (by his oath)" (AG, p. 599).

17, 19 *Sanctifieth* The verb is *hagiazō*. When applied to persons, it means "make holy." But when applied to things, as here, it means "make sacred" (cf. NIV).

23 *Anise* The Greek word *anēthon* means "dill" (NASB, NIV). It was a plant used for seasoning.

Judgment. . . Faith The two Greek words—*crisis . . . pistis*—basically mean "judgment . . . faith." But in the context here they clearly have their other authentic meanings: "justice . . . faithfulness" (NASB, NIV).

24 *Strain At* The one who reads the KJV gets the mental picture of a person straining in the air to catch a little gnat and swallowing a camel betimes. But this is not the correct sense.

The Greek verb *diulizō* (only here in NT) does not mean "strain at," but "strain out." The true picture is that of a pious Pharisee straining his drinking water through a piece of thin cloth so that he won't accidentally eat an unclean animal (the tiny gnat), while at the same time he swallows—literally, "drinks down"—one of the biggest ceremonially "unclean" animals, the camel. What a picture of the folly of picayunish legalism!

25 *Platter* *Paropsis* first meant "a side-dish of dainties," but later was used for "the *dish* itself on which the dainties are served" (A-S, p. 347). So the correct translation is "dish" (NASB, NIV).

Extortion . . . Excess The first word is *harpagē* (only here; Luke 11:39; Heb. 10:34). It comes from the verb *harpazō*, which means "seize by force." So the noun first indicates "robbery," a meaning that fits the passage in Hebrews. Then it means "what has been stolen, plunder"—preferred by Arndt and Gingrich for this passage. The cup and dish are full of stolen

things. A third meaning, "greed," fits the parallel passage in Luke (11:39), where Jesus says, "You are full"—meaning the Pharisees. The NIV uses "greed" here, taking cup and dish to represent the Pharisees.

The second word, "excess," translates *akrasia* (only here and 1 Cor. 7:5). It means "lack of self-control," and so "self-indulgence" (NASB, NIV).

27 *Whited* The Greek has the perfect passive participle of the verb *koniaō* (only here and Acts 23:3). It comes from *konia*, "dust" or "lime," and so means to "whitewash."

29 *Garnish* The verb *cosmeō* means "put in order," and then "adorn" (NASB) or "decorate" (NIV). Our word "cosmetics" comes from this root.

24:1 *Temple* This would be a good place to discuss the two words for "temple" in the NT. In the chapter in which we have just been working the word *naos* occurs 5 times (23:16 [twice], 17, 21, 35). On the other hand, in chapter 21 *hieron* occurs 5 times (vv. 12 [twice], 14, 15, 23). Here in chapter 24 it is the latter term (twice in verse 1). What is the difference?

Naos comes from the verb *naiō*, "dwell." It was used in classical Greek for the dwelling place of the gods. Otto Michel cites many instances of this (TDNT, 4:880–81). The word was also used in the Septuagint for the Temple of God at Jerusalem.

With respect to the NT use of the term, J. H. Thayer writes that *naos* is "used of the temple at Jerusalem, but only of the sacred edifice (or sanctuary) itself, consisting of the Holy place and the Holy of holies" (p. 422).

The other word is *hieron*. It is the substantive neuter of the adjective *hieros*, "sacred." So it means sacred place. It is used of the temple of Artemis at Ephesus (Acts 19:27). In the Septuagint it is used twice for the Temple at Jerusalem (Ezek. 45:19; 1 Chron. 29:4). In the NT it occurs 71 times—45 of these in the Gospels, 25 in Acts, and only once elsewhere (1 Cor. 9:13). On the other hand, *naos* occurs only 19 times in the Gospels, 3 times in Acts, 8 times in Paul's Epistles, and 16 times in Revelation—for a total of 46.

The reason for the greater frequency of *hieron* in the Gospels and Acts is that it refers to the whole Temple area, where the people gathered in the Temple courts and Jesus often taught. Only the priests could go into the *naos*, the sanctuary itself. Because of this distinction the NIV sometimes translates *hieron* as "temple area" (e.g., Matt. 21:12, 15) or "temple courts" (e.g., Matt. 21:23; 26:55).

Michel claims that in the NT *hieron* and *naos* are used "with no real distinction between the terms in either meaning or range" (TDNT, 4:882). This is perhaps an overstatement, for he does modify this somewhat in a footnote on page 885: "Though it seems that we might often make a distinction between *naos* and *hieron*, this is not always possible."

He cites Matt. 27:5 as an instance of the use of *naos* for the whole Temple area (p. 884). But we tend to agree with Thayer when he says that Judas Iscariot in his desperation might even have pushed on into the holy place (p. 422).

3 World   The normal Greek term for "world" in the NT is *cosmos,* which we have taken over into English in a broad sense. It occurs 187 times and is translated (KJV) as "world" except in 1 Pet. 3:3 ("adorning").

But here the Greek word is *aiōn,* from which we get "aeon." It is translated "world" 38 times in the KJV, and "age" only twice (Eph. 2:7; Col. 1:26). Most often (71 times) it is rendered "ever," in such combinations as "forever" or "evermore." This would seem to show that the dominant emphasis of *aiōn* is that of time rather than space. Abbott-Smith says that in the NT it is used "of an indefinitely long period, *an age, eternity*" (p. 15).

Most recent versions have "age" in our passage and similar ones. That seems best.

8 Sorrows   See discussion at Mark 13:8.

15 The Abomination of Desolation   This expression comes from the Book of Daniel (9:27; 11:31; 12:11). The Greek word for "abomination" is *bdelygma.* It means "detestable thing" (A-S, p. 78). "Desolation" is *erēmōsis,* which means "making desolate, laying waste." The first reference in Daniel was to the desecration of the Temple by erecting an altar to a pagan god. Jesus was probably referring to the image of the future Antichrist. The expression occurs here and in Mark 13:14.

26 Secret Chambers   The Greek word *tameion* originally meant "storeroom" and is used in that sense in Luke 12:24. But in the other three places where it occurs in the NT (Matt. 6:6; 24:26; Luke 12:3) it refers to "inner rooms" (NASB, NIV). The shift in meaning is easily understood, since storerooms were always inner rooms for the sake of security.

33 It   In Greek, no pronoun is expressed—as in Latin, it is included in the verb—so *estin* can be translated either "it is" (KJV, NIV) or "He is" (NASB). But since the parallel passage in Luke (21:31) says "the kingdom of God is near," it would seem best to use "it" rather than "He."

36 Nor the Son   The oldest Greek manuscripts add this after "angels of heaven," so Matthew agrees with Mark (13:32) in reporting Jesus as saying that He did not know the time of His second coming. This is part of His *kenosis*—His self-emptying (see Phil. 2:7, NASB)—connected with His incarnation.

41 Grinding at the Mill   The Greek word is *mylos.* Today the word "mill" conjures up the picture of a large building, or group of buildings, used for processing grain or textiles. But the reference here is clearly to the little hand mill in each Palestinian home, used each morning to grind wheat or barley into meal for baking bread. These "mills" are about as big around as a dinner plate. To help the reader, NIV has "grinding with a hand mill."

42 Watch   The verb is *grēgoreō,* the first meaning of which is "be awake." It is used in this literal sense in verse 43: If the owner had known what time the thief was coming, he would have kept awake.

Furthermore, the verb is here in the present tense of continuous action: "keep watch" (NIV) or "be on the alert" (NASB). It is like our expression "Keep your eyes open!" (See also Matt. 24:43 and 25:13.)

43 Goodman of the House   This is one word in the Greek, *oikodespotēs,* compounded of *oikos,* "house," and *despotēs,* "lord." Occurring 12 times in the NT, it is translated 4 ways in the KJV—"householder," "goodman of the house," "master of the house," "goodman." Today we would say "head of the house" (NASB) or "owner of the house" (NIV).

Watch   This is the literal meaning of the noun *phylakē.* It comes from the verb *phylassō,* which means to "guard." Used first for "a guarding," it came to mean "sentinel," then "prison," and finally "the time during which guard was kept by night" (A-S, p. 475). It has this last meaning here: "at what time of night" (NIV; cf. NASB).

45, 47 Make Him Ruler   This is one word in Greek, the verb *kathistēmi.* It comes from *kata,* "down," and *histēmi*—literally, "make to stand." So the compound means "set" or "appoint." A good translation here is "put in charge."

51 Cut Him Asunder Literally, "he will dichotomize" him—*dichotomēsei*. That is, "he will cut him to pieces" (NIV; cf. NASB).

25:2 Foolish It is the adjective *mōron* (in the neuter), which we have taken over into English for a mentally retarded person who has a mental age between 8 and 12 years. In the Greek it was first used of the nerves, "dull, sluggish," and then of the mind, "dull, stupid, foolish" (A-S, p. 299).

Wise The Greek adjective is *phronimos*. It comes from the verb *phroneō*, "to have in mind, be mindful of, think of" (A-S, p. 474). The wise virgins used their heads! They were thoughtful, foresighted, providing for emergencies—which often happen. Incidentally, "foolish" comes before "wise" here in the Greek.

4 Vessels The word *angeion* occurs only here in the NT. It is used in a second-century papyrus for a jar of oil, as here (VGT, p. 3). Since today we use "vessel" mostly for a ship, the better translation here is "flasks" (NASB) or "jars" (NIV).

5 Slumbered and Slept The first verb *nystazō* (only here and 2 Pet. 2:3) means to "nod" and is in the (ingressive) aorist. The second verb, *katheudō*, "sleep," is in the imperfect tense of action going on in the past. So a literal translation here would be: "They all began to nod"—"became drowsy" (NIV)—"and were sleeping."

6 Cometh This word is not in the Greek, which simply says: "Look! The bridegroom!" It could be rendered, "Here's the bridegroom!" (NIV).

8 Are Gone Out This translation would require the aorist tense of completed action in the past. But the Greek has the present tense of continuing action—*sbennyntai*. The correct translation is: "Our lamps are going out" (RSV, NASB, NIV).

This has homiletical significance. We should warn people not only against losing their spiritual light but also against letting it burn low. The foolish virgins, whose lamps were "going out," lost out entirely in getting into the wedding feast, a type of the marriage supper of the Lamb (Rev. 19:9).

14 Travelling into a Far Country This is all one word in the Greek, the present participle of the verb *apodēmeō*, which means "go on a journey." It is correctly translated this way in verse 15. But in verse 14 and elsewhere in the NT (Matt. 21:33; Mark 12:33; Luke 20:9) the KJV wrongly adds "into a far country." The one exception is Luke 15:13, where "into a far country" is in the Greek text.

15–28 Talents Our word comes right from the Greek *talanton*. This was originally a certain weight. Then it came to be used for "a sum of money, whether gold or silver, equivalent to a talent in weight" (A-S, p. 439). Aside from this parable the word is found (in NT) only in 18:24.

Our modern use of "talents" for abilities is drawn from this parable, according to the *Oxford English Dictionary* (11:54), which cites these interesting words from a book published in 1671: "Our Lord having herein given him an extraordinary talent." It seems altogether proper for us to use this parable in emphasizing the fact that we are stewards of our God-given talents. If we use them, they will increase. If we do not use them, we are "wicked" and "lazy" (v. 26, NIV), and our fate will be "outer darkness" (v. 30).

There is a practical point here, also. People with limited talents are most apt to do nothing. As Christian workers we need to watch for these and encourage them to use what they have.

19 Reckoneth The Greek is *synairei logon*. The verb *synairō*, "take up together," occurs only here and in 18:23–24. There the whole expression is translated "take account" (v. 23) and the verb alone "to reckon" (v. 24). The simplest translation is "settle(d) accounts" (NASB, NIV).

21, 23 Well Done The commendation is exactly the same in both places. (The KJV "thou" in italics is an obtrusion in verse 21.) We will not be rewarded by the Lord on the basis of how *much* we have done, but on how *well* we have used the talents He has given us. Only two things are required of us: that we be "good" and "faithful." And the reward for good work is more work!

24, 26 Strawed The verb is *diaskorpizō*, which means "scatter." If it is to be taken as parallel to the previous clause—"reaping where you did not sow" (NASB)—then it would mean "scattered seed" (NIV, cf. NASB). But Abbott-Smith says that here it is used "of winnowing

23

grain" (p. 111), and the RSV has "winnow(ed)." Arndt and Gingrich write: "Of seed *scatter*, unless it could be taken to mean *winnow*" (p. 188). A. B. Bruce has for verse 24: "You did not scatter with the fan" (EGT, 1:303). This would be winnowing, which would be an added statement, rather than a parallel. Either idea fits well. (This is another example of the difficulty of making an *exact* translation of the Greek New Testament.)

27 *Exchangers* Here we find the plural of *trapezitēs* (only here in NT), which means "money changer" or "banker" (NIV). The word obviously comes from *trapeza*, "table." See discussion at 21:12, where we have *kollybistēs* for "money-changers" (KJV).

Usury The noun *tokos* comes from *tiktō*, "give birth to a child." So it properly means "offspring." It is here used metaphorically for "the produce of money lent out" (A-S, p. 447). The same usage is found in Luke 19:23, the only other place where this noun occurs in the NT. Since "usury" today means an *exorbitant* rate of interest, the better translation in both places is "interest" (RSV, NASB, NIV).

31 *Holy* This is not in any of the oldest Greek manuscripts, so must it have been an addition made by a later copyist.

26:3 *And the Scribes* These words are
not in any of the oldest Greek manuscripts.

4 *Consulted* The verb *symbouleuō* is compounded of *bouleuō*, "take counsel," and *syn*, "together." So it means to "take counsel together," or "plot" (AG, cf. NASB, NIV).

5 *Uproar* *Thorybos* means "noise" or "clamor," then "turmoil," and finally a "disturbance" or "riot" (NASB, NIV). The chief priests knew that they would be in trouble with the Roman government if a riot occurred. With hundreds of thousands of Jews in Jerusalem for the Passover, religious feelings ran high.

7 *Alabaster Box* See discussion at Mark 14:3.

Very Precious Ointment "Very precious" (KJV) translates the adjective *barytimos*, which is compounded of *barys*, "heavy," and *timē*, "value" or "price." The word for "ointment" is *myron*, which may be translated "ointment" or "perfume." The preferable translation is either

"very costly perfume" (NASB) or "very expensive perfume" (NIV).

10 *Wrought a Good Work* The Greek could be rendered, "She has worked a good work on me." How much more beautiful, however, is the translation, "She has done a beautiful thing to me" (RSV, NIV)! Some would question whether the Greek adjective here, *kalos*, really means "beautiful," but it is actually the first meaning given in lexicons. Cremer says that it means "beautiful, pleasing" (p. 339). It is used this way in the aesthetic sense.

15 *Covenanted with Him For* This is not an incorrect translation of the Greek here, but it is the least likely of the options. The verb *histēmi* means "put, place, set." One way of taking it here is "set" or "fix." Arndt and Gingrich write: "This meaning is perhaps correct for Mt. 26:15 ... *they set out* (= *offered, allowed*) (*for*) *him 30 silver coins*." But they go on to say that some scholars, "probably rightly," prefer the meaning *weigh out* on the scales" (p. 382).

The RSV has simply: "They paid him thirty pieces of silver." The NASB reads: "They weighed out to him thirty pieces of silver." The NIV says: "They counted out for him thirty silver coins." All of these probably represent correctly what happened.

18 *Such a Man* The Greek has one word—*deina* (only here in NT). It means "*a certain one*, whom one cannot or will not name" (A-S, p. 100). It could be translated "so-and-so" (AG, p. 173). Probably "a certain man" (NASB, NIV) is best. Jesus did not wish Judas Iscariot to know where this home was, for He wanted a quiet evening with His disciples just before His crucifixion.

20 *Sat* See discussion at Mark 14:18.

22 *Is It I?* See discussion at Mark 14:19.

23 *Dish* See discussion at Mark 14:20.

27 *Drink Ye All of It* This particular wording seems to imply that the disciples were to drain the cup to the last drop. But the Greek does not say this. "All of it" in this sense would be *panta* (neut. pl. acc.; direct object). Instead, the Greek has *pantes* (masc. pl. nom.; subject). So the correct translation is, "Drink from it, all of you" (NASB, NIV). What is called for is the participation of all in the Communion service.

28 Testament We should note first that the word for "new" (*kainē*) is not found here in the two third-century papyri or our two fourth-century manuscripts (similarly in Mark 14:24). It was evidently copied into Matthew and Mark from Luke 22:20, where it is genuine.

The Greek word is *diathēkē*, which (in KJV) is translated "covenant" 20 times and "testament" 13 times. There is general agreement, however, that it should be "covenant" except in Heb. 9:16–17. The idea of a "blood covenant" (signed in blood) was common in that day and culture.

More than half (17) of the occurrences of *diathēkē* are in Hebrews.

28 Remission This is a correct translation of *aphesis*, the basic meaning of which is "release." But Arndt and Gingrich suggest for this passage: *forgiveness of sins* i.e. cancellation·of the guilt of sin" (p. 125). "Forgiveness" (NASB, NIV) is probably better understood today than "remission."

31 Be Offended Once more we have the verb *scandalizō* (see discussion at 5:29–30). The best translation here (and in v. 33) is "fall away" (NASB, NIV).

34–35 Deny The verb *aparneomai* is correctly translated "deny" in 16:24; Mark 8:34; and Luke 12:9. However, "disown" is better in connection with Peter's so-called denials. We commonly speak of "denying ourselves" of our own sovereignty and selfish desires. We may also deny a statement that is made. We may deny other people of some things they need. But none of these ideas will apply to Peter. He *disowned* Jesus.

36 Gethsemane This Greek name (only here and Mark 14:32) is from the Hebrew, meaning "oil-press." The Mount of Olives was an appropriate place for pressing out of ripe olives the oil which was used for lamps, food, and a healing ointment.

37 Very Heavy The verb *adēmoneō* (here; Mark 14:33; and Phil. 2:26) means (A-S, p. 9) to "be troubled" (NIV) or "distressed" (NASB). Jesus was facing Calvary.

38 Watch See discussion at Mark 14:34.

45 Sleep On Now, and Take Your Rest In the Greek language the second person plural of the present tense uses the same form for both the indicative and the impera-

tive. So the above translation (KJV) is allowable.

But this seems to conflict with verse 46. Fortunately, this seeming conflict can easily be eliminated by taking this as interrogative; the Greek uses exactly the same words in the same order for a question as for a statement. The context indicates that the words here should be taken as a question: "Are you still sleeping and taking your rest?" (RSV, NASB; cf. NIV). Jesus was gently chiding His disciples for sleeping while He was praying, especially after He had told them, "Stay here and keep watch with me" (v. 38, NIV).

47 Staves The Greek *xylon* means "wood," and so anything made of wood. Here it obviously means "clubs" (RSV, NASB, NIV).

48–49 Kiss See discussion at Mark 14:44.

50 Wherefore Art Thou Come? Here we might reverse the procedure of verse 45. The Greek words could well be translated: "Do what you came for" (NIV; cf. NASB).

51 Ear See discussion at Mark 14:47.

55 Thief See discussion at Mark 14:48.

58 Palace In Homer the Greek word here, *aulē*, meant an open courtyard in front of a house. In the time of Christ it usually indicated a "courtyard" (NASB, NIV) around which the home was built. Probably *aulē* means "palace" only in Matt. 26:3 and Mark 15:16 (AG, p. 121).

63 Held His Peace This is a rather odd idiom, though it is still commonly used as an imperative: "Hold your peace!" The Greek simply says that Jesus "remained silent" (NIV)—the imperfect of *siōpaō*, "be silent."

Adjure This English word is a rather technical legal term today. The Greek has *exorkizō* (only here in NT). The clearest translation is: "I charge you under oath." When thus charged by the high priest, Jesus was obligated to answer, and He did so.

64 Thou Hast Said This is a literal translation of the Greek *su eipas*. Exactly the same expression is found in verse 25. Rather clearly it is an affirmative answer there; Judas *was* guilty. A. Carr comments: "This is a formula of assent both in Hebrew and Greek, and is still used in Palestine in that sense" (*Gospel According to St. Matthew*, CGT, p. 290).

Power　The Jews sometimes used "power" as a substitute for "God," just as we have already noted that they preferred "the kingdom of heaven" to "the kingdom of God." So "the Mighty One" represents the sense.

67 Buffeted　The verb *kolaphizō* literally means to "strike with the fist." It is used that way here and in Mark 14:65. So we prefer "struck him with their fists" (NIV; cf. NASB), which makes a clear picture.

69 Palace　Since Peter was sitting "outside" (NASB, NIV; "without," KJV), he was clearly in the "courtyard." (See discussion on verse 58.)

71 Porch　The Greek word here, different from that in Mark 14:68, is *pylon*. It comes from *pyle*, "gate," and so means "gateway" (NASB, NIV).

73 Bewrayeth　This is an obsolete form for "betrays." The best translation is, "for your accent gives you away" (NIV). The people in Jerusalem knew from Peter's accent that he was from Galilee, just as in the United States Midwesterners can recognize the accent of Southerners or New Englanders.

74 To Curse and to Swear　See discussion at Mark 14:71. There is one slight difference here. For "curse," Matthew has the verb *katathematizō* (only here in NT), "curse vehemently." But the two have much the same meaning: "he began to call down curses on himself" (NIV). And then he placed himself under oath that he was telling the truth. It was a serious sin that he committed under the pressure of the circumstances.

27:1 Took Counsel　See discussion at Matt. 12:14.

3 Repented　There are two Greek verbs that are always translated "repent" in the KJV: *metamelomai* (5 times) and *metanoeō* (34 times). It is *metamelomai* here (and in 21:29, 32; 2 Cor. 7:8; Heb. 7:21).

Metanoeō basically means to "change one's mind." So it is properly translated "repent" in most instances. It involves the intellect and will. *Metamelomai* has to do more with the emotions, and so does not indicate true biblical repentance. If Judas Iscariot had really "repented," he would not have committed suicide (v. 5).

The difference between these two verbs is very well described by Michel. He writes:

"*Metanoein* and *metamelesthai* are distinct in classical Greek. *Metanoein* means a change of heart either generally or in respect of a specific sin, whereas *metamelesthai* means 'to experience remorse.' *Metanoein* implies that one has later arrived at a different view of something (*nous*), *metamelesthai* that one has a different feeling about it (*melei*)" (TDNT, 4:626). He also quotes Josephus as saying: "Alongside *metanoia*, the change of will, is *metamelos*, remorse, through which man suffers the pain of self-accusation" (p. 628).

It seems clear that the correct translation of *metameletheis* here (aor. pass. part.) is not "repented" (KJV) but "felt remorse" (NASB) or "was seized with remorse" (NIV). See further discussion at 2 Cor. 7:8.

5 Temple　The word here is not *hieron*, the Temple courts, but *naos*, the "sanctuary" (NASB). See discussion at Matt. 24:1.

11 Thou Sayest　See discussion at Matt. 26:64. There the verb *legō* is in the aorist tense (*eipas*). Here it is the present tense (*su legeis*). See also discussion at Luke 23:3.

15 Was Wont　This expression, found four times in the KJV, is now obsolete. Twice it translates the verb *ethō* (here and Mark 10:1). *Ethō* is also found in Luke 4:16, where it is correctly translated "(as his) custom was," and in Acts 17:2—"(as his) manner was." The related noun *ethos*, "custom," has been taken over into English.

16 Notable　The adjective *episēmos* (from *sēma*, "a mark," and *epi*, "upon") literally means "bearing a mark." It occurs only twice in the NT. In Rom. 16:7 it is used in a good sense—"notable" or "outstanding" (NASB, NIV). But here it is used in a bad sense—"notorious" (NASB, NIV).

19 Judgment Seat　This is one word in the Greek—*bēma*. It is used in the parallel passage in John (19:13). Roman custom demanded that a governor must be seated on the *bēma* when he gave an official sentence. See further discussion at Rom. 14:10.

27 Common Hall　The Greek word is *praitōrion*, the Greek form of the Latin "Praetorium" (NASB, NIV). See discussion at Mark 15:16.

28 Scarlet Robe　In Mark 15:17 and John 19:2 it says that the soldiers "clothed him with purple." Here it says that they "put on him a scarlet robe." How are we to reconcile the two statements?

The Greek word for "robe" is a rare one in the NT—*chlamys* (only here and v. 31), the specific name of the short cloak that was worn over the tunic. The color of this was "scarlet"—*kokkinos* (only here; Heb. 9:19; and four times in Revelation). R. C. Trench states that the *chlamys* was "a garment of dignity and office." He goes on to say that "the employment of *chlamys* in the record of the Passion leaves little doubt that these profane mockers obtained, as it would have been so easy for them in the praetorium to obtain, the cast-off cloke of some high Roman officers, and with this arrayed the sacred person of the Lord" (p. 186).

But what about the "purple"? If this was a cast-off *chlamys*, as Trench suggests, the bright scarlet could easily have faded into purple. Furthermore, the Greek word for "purple" in John 19:2, 5 is *porphyreos*. *The Oxford English Dictionary* gives the following as the first definition of the adjective "purple": "Of the distinguishing colour of the dress of emperors, kings, etc.; . . . Gr. *porphyreos*, in early use meaning crimson; hence, imperial, royal" (8:1625).

29 Platted The verb *plekō* is used (in NT) only here and in the parallel passages (Mark 15:17; John 19:2). It means to "twist" or "weave."

32 Compelled See discussion at Matt. 5:41.

34 Vinegar The earliest and best Greek manuscripts have *oinos* here, the same as in the parallel passage in Mark (15:23). This word simply means "wine" (NASB, NIV).

Gall The Greek word *cholē* means "gall." But Abbott-Smith thinks that here it "probably" signifies "myrrh" (cf. Mark 15:23). H. B. Swete says that "wine drugged with myrrh was usually offered to condemned malefactors . . . through the charity (it is said) of the women of Jerusalem . . . the intention being to deaden the sense of pain." But Jesus declined to drink it. "He had need of the full use of His human faculties, and the pain which was before Him belonged to the cup which the Father's will had appointed" (p. 358).

38, 44 Thieves See discussion at Mark 14:48. Jesus was not crucified between two thieves, but between two "robbers" (NASB, NIV). Actually they were militant revolutionar-

ies against the Roman government (cf. Mark 15:7).

42 If He Be the King of Israel The oldest Greek manuscripts do not have the "if" (*ei*). They simply say, "He's the king of Israel!" (NIV; cf. NASB). This was sarcasm at its cruel worst!

48 Sponge . . . Vinegar See discussion at Mark 15:36.

51 Veil There were two curtains in the ancient Tabernacle and in the Temple. One was at the outer entrance to the holy place. But the Greek word here is *katapetasma*, which in the NT always represents the inner curtain, between the Holy Place and the Holy of Holies. The word is also found in the parallel passages (Mark 15:38; Luke 23:45), as well as in Heb. 6:19; 9:3; 10:20. Through Christ's death (Heb. 10:20) the way is opened to us right into the presence of God.

55 Ministering See discussion at Mark 15:41.

62 Preparation See discussion at Mark 15:42.

63–64 Deceiver . . . Error The first word is *planos*, "deceiver." The second is *planē*, "deception." Since these are the same root in Greek, this should be brought out in English: "deceiver . . . deception" (NASB, NIV).

65–66 Watch The Greek word (only here and Matthew 28:11, the only places in NT) is *coustōdia*, from the Latin *custodia* (cf. Eng. custodian). It means a "guard" (NASB, NIV).

In verse 65 the Greek *"Echete coustōdian"* may be translated "You have a guard" (NASB) or "Take a guard" (NIV). As we have noted before, in the second person plural of the present tense the same form may be indicative or imperative. Both make sense, but William Hendriksen says that 28:14 indicates clearly that Pilate is speaking about a guard under his control—that is, a Roman guard. He also asserts that the Temple guard (controlled by the high priests) would have no authority outside the Temple (NTC, p. 982). So "Take a guard" would seem to be better.

28:1 In the End The Greek has one word, *opse*. It is an adverb of time. First it meant "long after, late," then "late in the day, at evening." That is its meaning in the only

other places it occurs in the NT (Mark 11:19; 13:35). But finally it came to mean "after" (Moulton, *Grammar*, p. 72), the only meaning that fits here. For the Sabbath ended at sunset Saturday, and this seems clearly to be Sunday morning.

Began to Dawn   We have here the present participle—literally, "at the dawning"—of *epiphōskō* (only here and Luke 23:54). The verb is compounded of *phōs*, "light," and *epi*, "upon."

The First Day of the Week   This is literally "first of sabbaths" (*mian sabbatōn*). We find basically the same expression in Mark 16:2 and Luke 24:1. Since the word *sabbaton*, "sabbath," also means "week," the above translation is correct. In the NT the singular and plural of *sabbaton* are used interchangeably.

3 *Countenance*   The Greek word *eidea* (only here in NT) comes from *eidon*, "I saw." It means "appearance" (NASB, NIV). Of "countenance" (KJV) R. C. Trench says: "It is not a happy translation; 'appearance' would be better" (*Synonyms*, p. 266).

4 *Did Shake*   The Greek word is *eseisthēsan* (aor. pass.), "were shaken." This has the same root as the noun *seismos*, "earthquake" (v. 2). The guards at the tomb were "all shook up" inside by the violent earthquake. Being superstitious, they thought that the gods of the skies were after them, especially when an angel immediately appeared.

9 *All Hail*   The Greek is *chairete*, which literally means "rejoice." It was a common form of Greek greeting, taken over by the Jews. Arndt and Gingrich suggest that here it would be equivalent to our "Good morning" (p. 874). The NASB margin even has "hello." Probably the simplest translation is "Greetings" (NIV).

11 *Watch*   See discussion at Matthew 27:65–66.

14 *Secure You*   The Greek says: "We will make you *amerimnous*." This adjective (only here and 1 Cor. 7:22) is compounded of *alpha*-negative and *merimna*, "care, anxiety." So it means "free from anxiety or care." The idea can be expressed this way: "Keep you out of trouble" (NASB, NIV).

15 *Is Commonly Reported*   This is all one word: *diephēmisthē*. The verb *diaphamizō* is found only here, 9:31, and Mark 1:45 (see discussion there). It may be translated "widely spread" (NASB) or "widely circulated" (NIV).

18 *Power*   The Greek does not have *dynamis*, "power," but *exousia*, "authority" (NASB, NIV).

19 *Teach*   The verb is not *didaskō*, "teach," but *mathēteuō*, "make disciples" (only here; 13:52; 27:57; and Acts 14:21). The verb comes from the noun *mathētēs*, "disciple." The correct translation is therefore "make disciples" (NASB, NIV). In verse 20 we do find the verb *didaskō*—"teaching."

20 *Alway*   The Greek literally says "all the days" (*pasas tas hēmeras*). A. B. Bruce comments: ". . . of which, it is implied there may be many; the vista of the future is lengthening" (EGT, 1:340). Henry Alford similarly says: "all the (*appointed*) days—for they are numbered by the Father, though by none but Him" (1:308).

Probably "always" gives the sense correctly, if we recognize that this means Christ's "continual presence" with us (Bengel). We like Hendriksen's suggestion that it means "day in day out," no matter what troubles or difficulties may come (*NT Commentary: Matthew*, p. 1003).

End of the World   This should be "end of the age" (*aiōnos*). No matter how long Christ's coming tarries, He will be with us here through the presence of the Holy Spirit.

Mark

1:1 Gospel The Greek word, as is commonly known, is *euangelion*, which literally means "good news." It comes from the verb *euangelizō*, "announce glad tidings." In the New Testament "the gospel" is the good news of salvation through Jesus Christ.

What did Mark mean when he wrote, "The beginning of the gospel of Jesus Christ"? Today we use the term *Gospel* (capitalized) for one of the four accounts of Christ's life and ministry. So some have taken this as meaning the beginning of this particular Gospel. But the word *euangelion* was not then used for a book (one of our four Gospels). As Gerhard Friedrich points out, *euangelion* was not used for a book of the New Testament until the second century (TDNT, 2:735–36). So Mark is not referring to the "beginning" of his Gospel.

What does he mean, then? Rather obviously, the reference is to the ministry of John the Baptist, which immediately follows (vv. 2–8). That was the beginning of the good news about Jesus Christ (vv. 7–8).

Of "Jesus Christ" is in the genitive case in the Greek text. Unfortunately, this case has several varying usages. "The gospel of Jesus Christ" might be taken as meaning the gospel belonging to Him (possessive genitive). But the more obvious meaning is the good news *about* Christ (objective genitive). So the best translation is "the gospel about Jesus Christ." This is the "gospel" we preach today.

The Son of God The words *whiou theou* are found in our oldest extant manuscript of the Greek New Testament (Vaticanus of the fourth century), as well as in two fifth-century manuscripts. They are missing in the original text of Sinaiticus, the only other fourth-century manuscript. Unfortunately, we have no third-century papyrus of Mark's Gospel. It is interesting to note that F. C. Grant, in his "Exegesis of the Gospel of Mark" in *The Interpreter's Bible*, says that the two words "were probably in the original" (7:648). Most scholars agree that the theological purpose of Mark in his Gospel was to stress the deity of Jesus.

2 As It Is Written The Greek verb is in the perfect tense (*gegraptai*), which stresses both completed action and a continuing state. The full force of the Greek is: "Even as it has been written and still stands written"—a mighty affirmation of the divine inspiration and authority of the Old Testament Scriptures. This should be remembered when we read the simple English translation "As it is written." Emphasizing the "is" will help to bring this out.

The Prophets or Isaiah the Prophet? The evidence of the Greek manuscripts (Vaticanus, Sinaiticus, Bezae, Theta—representing the Alexandrian, Western, and Caesarean families of texts) clearly indicates that "Isaiah the prophet" (NASB, NIV) is the correct reading. If so, why, one may ask, do so many of the later manuscripts have "the prophets"?

The answer seems obvious. Mark quotes first (v. 2) from Mal. 3:1. But then (v. 3) he quotes from Isaiah (40:3). Some later scribe, bothered by this seeming inconsistency, sought to straighten out the matter by changing the text.

It would seem that Mark had mainly in mind the quotation from Isaiah—which is found in all the other three Gospels—and inserted, somewhat parenthetically, the shorter quotation from Malachi.

3 *Wilderness* Today the term "wilderness" conjures up a mental picture of a wooded area, often with heavy underbrush. But the so-called Wilderness of Judea, which stretches from Jerusalem and Bethlehem eastward some 20 miles down to the Jordan River and the Dead Sea, is a barren region of rugged hills and valleys. So it would seem that "desert" communicates the true picture more accurately.

4 *Baptism of Repentance* John preached a repentance-baptism. He baptized people only "as they were confessing out their sins" (v. 5, literal Greek). He required genuine repentance as a condition for being baptized.

What is repentance? The Greek noun *metanoia* literally means "a change of mind." It is more than emotional sorrow, which too often does not produce any change of life. Rather, it is a change of mind, or attitude, toward God, sin, and ourselves. Deep repentance involves a real turnabout in life and prepares us to believe savingly in Jesus Christ.

Remission "Remission" is a correct translation but the term is rarely heard today. The Greek word *aphesis* was used for a "release" from captivity (Luke 4:18; 14:9) and also for a "pardon" from punishment or a "cancellation" of guilt. Arndt and Gingrich suggest "forgiveness" for the rest of the passages in the NT where it occurs.

Of One of the most common archaic forms in the King James Version is the use of the preposition "of" for "by." The Greek here clearly says, "were being baptized by [*hypo*] him in the Jordan River."

6 *Girdle* A more contemporary translation here for "a girdle of a skin about his loins" (KJV) is "a leather belt around his waist" (as in NIV). Incidentally, "camel's" hair in this verse comes right out of the Greek, which has *camelou*, "of a camel."

7 *Shoes* The only meaning that Arndt and Gingrich's *Lexicon* gives for *hypodēma* is "sandal." In those days people wore sandals, not the enclosed shoes of today. "Thongs of whose sandals" is therefore a better translation.

10 *Opened* We are told that as Jesus was coming up out of the water, He saw the heavens "opened" (KJV). Matthew (3:16) and Luke (3:21) both have the verb *anoigō*, which means simply "open." But Mark has a much stronger word, *schizō*. It means "split, divide, separate,

tear apart, tear off" (AG, p. 797), from which comes "schizophrenic," split personality.

Incidentally, this highlights Mark's frequent use of stronger or more dramatic terms than we find in the parallel passages in Matthew and Luke. The early church was unanimous in saying that Mark's Gospel gives us the preaching of Peter. It seems clear that these strong expressions were used by Peter in his preaching, reflecting his vigorous personality. Mark, his "son" in the ministry (1 Pet. 5:13), caught this and incorporated it in his Gospel.

12 *Immediately* In contrast to Matthew (4:1–11) and Luke (4:1–13), Mark gives us only a brief reference to the temptation of Jesus (vv. 12–13). But some of the distinctive characteristics of his Gospel show up even in this brief compass.

The first is "immediately." This translates the adverb *euthys*, which Mark uses often (42 out of the 54 times it occurs in the New Testament). See W. F. Moulton and A. S. Geden, *A Concordance to the Greek Testament*, p. 400.

This reflects the main characteristic of Mark's Gospel—rapid action. Whereas John gives us in his Gospel a studied *portrait* of Jesus, the lines of which were drawn with loving care after a long lifetime of meditating on his Lord, and Matthew and Luke give us a series of colored *slides*, Mark presents a *moving picture* of Jesus' life. Most verses of the first chapter begin with "and," plus the fact that *euthys* occurs no less than 11 times here. We see Jesus moving rapidly from one scene of action to another.

The KJV translates this key word several different ways: "straightway" (v. 10), "immediately" (v. 12), "forthwith" (v. 29), which are proper enough. However "anon" (v. 30) is both inaccurate and archaic. In other chapters we find "as soon as" (5:36; 11:2), which is good, but twice the KJV uses "by and by" (Matt. 13:21; Luke 17:7), which, like "anon," conveys a quite different idea than what *euthys* really means.

For those Greek students who might check the *Englishman's Greek Concordance* and find *eutheōs* occurring far more frequently than *euthys*, a word of explanation is in order. This valuable reference work uses the *Textus Receptus*, which is based on the late Greek manuscripts. For an accurate tally on the frequency of Greek words in the NT, one needs to check Moulton and Geden's *Concordance*. (See also for these particular words the discussion in VGT, pp. 261–62.)

16 *Sea* The Greek word is *thalassa*. It occurs 92 times in the NT and is always translated "sea" in the KJV. This is correct in many places. But most of the 17 times it occurs in Matthew and the 19 times it occurs in Mark the reference is to the Sea of Galilee. This is hardly a "sea" in modern terminology, for it is only about 13 miles long and 7 miles wide. Also, since it has an inlet and an outlet it is more properly a lake. Thus the translation here and in most places in Matthew and Mark should be "lake." Luke, who was used to traveling the Mediterranean Sea, uses for the smaller body of water *limnē*, which specifically means "lake." In Revelation *thalassa* is used for the oceans in general, and so is correctly translated "sea" (26 times).

The use of *thalassa* for "lake" is labeled by Arndt and Gingrich a "Semitic usage" (p. 350). Without question "lake" communicates a more accurate picture to the reader today but the expression "Sea of Galilee" is retained by the NIV as being the traditional name. See also discussion at Luke 5:1.

24 What Have We to Do with Thee ... The demon said to Jesus, "What have we to do with thee?" (KJV; cf. NASB). It may also be translated, "What do you want with us?" (NIV; cf. RSV). The Greek says *ti hēmin kai soi*—literally, "What to us and to you?"

In his commentary on the Greek text of Mark, Vincent Taylor notes that in classical Greek the question would mean, "What have we in common?" But he thinks that here it probably means, "Why do you meddle with us?" (*The Gospel According to St. Mark*, p. 174). Ezra Gould combines these in his commentary in the ICC series: "What have we in common which gives you the right to interfere with us?" (p. 23).

25 Hold Thy Peace The Greek literally says, "Be muzzled!" (*phimōthēti*)—the same word found in Luke's parallel passage (4:35). It means "Be quiet!" (NIV; cf. RSV, NASB).

26 Torn The Greek verb is *sparassō*, which means to "pull to and fro" or "convulse." Luke (4:35) has the verb *hriptō*, "throw down." The idea seems to be "throwing him into convulsions" (NASB), or "shook the man violently" (NIV).

27 Doctrine The KJV usually translates *didachē* as "doctrine" (29 times; "has been taught" once). But the noun comes from the verb *didaskō*, "teach." Today "doctrine" has a formal, theological sense that *didachē* does not

have. A more accurate translation is "teaching."

28 Fame The Greek noun is *akoē*, which comes from the verb *akouō*, "hear." So it means "something that is heard"—a report or "news about him" (NIV; cf. NASB).

30–31 Fever "Sick of a fever" (KJV) is all one word in the Greek, the participle *pyressousa*. The verb *pyressō* (only here and Matt. 8:14) comes from the noun *pyr*, which means "fire." A fever burns like a fire in our bodies.

The noun *pyretos* ("fever," v. 31) is found also in Matt. 8:15; Luke 4:38–39; John 4:52; Acts 28:8. It suggests a state of fiery burning.

31 Ministered unto When the mother-in-law of Simon was healed of her fever, she "ministered unto" Jesus and His disciples. The verb is *diaconeō*, the earliest meaning of which was "wait on someone at table" (AG, p. 184). The verb here is in the imperfect (probably inchoative). So the best translation would be "began to wait on them."

They had just come home from the synagogue service (v. 29). Instead of dinner being ready, Peter's mother-in-law was sick. When healed, she proceeded to help serve the meal.

32, 34 Devils In verse 32 we find *daimonizomenous*, which means "demon-possessed." In verse 34 the word *daimonia* occurs twice. It does not mean "devils" (KJV) but "demons" (RSV, NASB, NIV). There is only one "devil" (Greek *diabolos*), but there are many demons. We should always be careful to make the distinction.

36 Followed The verb *katadiōkō* (only here in NT) is an intensive compound of *diōkō*, which means "run after, pursue." It carries the idea of "*search for* eagerly, *hunt for*" (AG, p. 410). Probably the best translation here is "hunted for Him" (NASB). They had to search for some time before they found Jesus.

38 Towns *Kōmopoleis* is compounded of *kōmē*, "village," and *polis*, "city." So it literally means "village-cities." Swete calls them "country towns" and adds: "There were many such in Galilee" (p. 26).

41 Moved with Compassion The Greek has the aorist passive participle here, *splangchnistheis*. To bring out the force of the aorist we should translate it "gripped with compassion." This was Jesus' instant reaction to human need. He was deeply moved in His heart at the sight of suffering.

43 Straitly Charged The Greek participle *embrimēsamenos* expresses very strong feeling. In classical Greek it suggested snorting in anger. But most authorities agree that the idea here is that of "sternly warned" (NASB). "Jesus sent him away at once with a strong warning" (NIV) probably captures the correct picture.

But why did Jesus do this? Verses 44–45 furnish the answer. The Master did not want His miraculous healing ministry spectacularly publicized, because it hindered Him from His far more important preaching and teaching ministry. Then, as now, people were more concerned for their bodies than for their souls.

45 Publish The Greek word is *kēryssō*, which means to "herald" or "proclaim." The man doubtless thought he was doing a great thing, but he was disobeying Jesus.

Blaze Abroad This is a one-word compound in Greek, the verb *diaphēmizō*. It means "*make known* by word of mouth, *spread the news about*"—here, "spread widely, disseminate" (AG, p. 190). The cleansed leper was a powerful publicity agent, but it was not the kind of publicity that Jesus wanted.

2:1 In the House The Greek literally says: "It was heard, 'He is in a house.' " But this is the Greek way of saying, "The people heard that he had come home" (NIV). Jesus had slipped out of town very early on the morning after the sunset healing service (1:32–35). Doubtless many who missed that opportunity hoped to get healed the next day, but Jesus was gone (v. 39). Now the word got around that He was back home, and the crowd gathered again (2:2).

4 Uncovered the Roof *Apestegasan tēn stegēn*—literally, "unroofed the roof." This is typical of the vivid, vigorous language of Peter, reflected in Mark's Gospel. Mark alone also adds: "and after digging through it." Luke says that they went up on the roof and lowered the paralytic "through the tile." The typical home in Palestine had a flat roof, with outside steps leading to it. On top of the crossbeams were laid branches of trees, or tiles as here, covered with dirt. The four friends dug down through the dirt, broke through the tiles, and lowered the man down in front of Jesus. Matthew gives none of these details.

Bed The three Synoptic Gospels use three different Greek words for the "bed" on which the paralytic was lying. Matthew has *klinē*, the common word for bed, which occurs 9 times in the NT. Luke has the diminutive form, *klinidion*—only found in this incident (Luke 5:19, 24). But Mark, typically, uses an entirely different word: *krabattos*, a "pallet." Marvin Vincent describes it as: "A rude pallet, merely a thickly padded quilt or mat, held at the corners, and requiring no cords to let it down" (WS, 1:170). Swete says that it was "the poor man's bed . . . small and flexible, and therefore better adapted for the purpose of the bearers than the *klinē* which Mt. and Lc. (5:18) substitute. Lc., who seems to feel the difficulty as to *klinē*, uses *klinidion* as the story advances (v. 19)" (p. 32). *Krabattos* occurs mostly in Mark (2:4, 9, 11–12; 6:55), but also in John (5:8–12) and Acts (5:15; 9:33).

5 Be Forgiven Thee The Greek very clearly says "are forgiven" (NASB, NIV)—*aphientai*, present indicative. Luke puts it even more strongly: *apheōntai*, perfect passive, "Your sins have been forgiven you." It was not a wish but a declaration.

7 Speak Blasphemies The Greek is stronger than the KJV implies. It says: "Why does this fellow talk like that? He's blaspheming!" (NIV). *Blasphēmei* is a complete sentence (present indicative of the verb).

9 Easier *Eukopōteron* is the comparative form of the adjective *eukopos*. *Eu* means "good" and *kopos*, "labor." So the idea here is: "Which is easier to do?" Actually, it would be easier *to say*, "Your sins are forgiven," than *to say*, "Get up, take your mat and walk," because the results of the latter could be checked by the observer, but not the results of the former. Jesus' question must be read carefully to get the right answer.

10 Power Again the Greek word is *exousia*, "authority," not *dynamis*, "power" (KJV).

11 House The correct contemporary translation is: "I tell you, get up, take your mat, and go home."

15 Sinners The "sinners" referred to here were not men who led wicked lives, but simply those who did not keep all the minute rules and regulations of the "tradition of the elders." So the Pharisees dubbed them "sinners." That is why the word is put in quotation marks in the NIV. See discussion at Matt. 9:10–11.

17 *To Repentance* This phrase is not found in the oldest Greek manuscripts and so is left out in most modern versions.

18 *Used to Fast* The Greek clearly says "were fasting" (*ēsan . . . nēsteuontes*). It was a regular Jewish fast day, which the Pharisees and the disciples of John the Baptist were observing. But Jesus' disciples were eating. This is what caused the controversy (v. 18).

19 *Children of the Bridechamber* The Greek has "sons of the bridal chamber" (*nymphōn*). Arndt and Gingrich say that the whole expression means "*the bridegroom's attendants*, that group of the wedding guests who stood closest to the groom and played an essential part in the wedding ceremony" (p. 545).

21 *Piece* The Greek word is *epiblēma*. It comes from the verb *epiballō*, which means "lay on" or "put on." So the noun, used in this parabolic saying in all three Synoptics (see Matt. 9:16; Luke 5:36), clearly means a "patch" (RSV, NASB, NIV).

New The Greek word is *agnaphos*, which means "unbleached" or "unshrunk." Both it and the word for "cloth" (*hrakos*) are found (in NT) only here and in the parallel passage in Matt. 9:16. "Unshrunk cloth" is the correct translation (RSV, NASB, NIV).

22 *Bottles* Today "bottles" refers to glass or plastic containers, which the common people did not use in the time of Christ. The Greek word here is *askos*, which means "*a leather bag, especially wine-skin*" (AG, p. 116).

New In this verse two different Greek words are used for "new." The first word, used with "wine," is *neos*, from which we get our word "new." The second, used at the end with "wineskins," is *kainos*.

R. C. Trench distinguishes between these two words as follows: "Contemplate the new under aspects of *time*, as that which has recently come into existence, and this is *neos*. . . . But contemplate the new, not now under aspects of time, but of *quality*, the new, as set over against that which has seen service, the outworn, the effete or marred through age, and this is *kainos*" (pp. 219–20).

When grape juice ("new wine") is placed in a wineskin, it soon begins to ferment. But the new leather wineskin will stretch as the volume of the fermenting wine increases. If, on the other hand, fresh grape juice is put into a used wineskin which has already stretched, the fermentation will cause the skin to burst, and both wine and wineskin will be lost. The best translation at the end of the verse is "fresh wineskins" (NASB).

23 *Corn Fields* In the British Isles wheat is still called "corn." But in the United States "corn" means maize, which of course was not grown in Palestine in Jesus' day. The two common grains grown there were wheat and barley. So a better translation is "grainfields" (NASB, NIV, RSV).

It is also clear that "ears of corn" as used here conveys a confusing picture to the North American reader. What is meant is "heads of grain" (NASB, NIV). The RSV corrected only half the problem when it used "ears of grain."

26 *Showbread* The Greek literally says "the loaves of the presentation" (or "placing before")—*tous artous tēs protheseōs*. They were the biscuitlike loaves presented to the Lord and placed before the altar.

A beautiful translation is "the bread of the Presence" (RSV)—that is, the bread which symbolized God's presence in the midst of His people (in the sanctuary). But there is a dispute as to whether "presentation" definitely implies that idea.

3:1 *Withered* In keeping with his love of strong language (reflecting Peter), Mark has here the perfect passive of the verb *xērainō*, "dry out." The full force would be "all dried up." Matthew and Luke use the adjective *xēros*, which Mark also has here in verse 3. Evidently Peter was impressed with the extreme immobility of the hand.

2 *Watched* Mark and Luke (6:7) both have the verb *paratēreō*. Marvin Vincent writes: "The compound verb, with *para, by the side of*, means to *watch carefully* or *closely*, as one who dogs another's steps" (WS, 1:174). Wycliffe, in the first English translation of the Bible (1382), had "They aspieden him"—that is, "they spied on him." That is exactly what these observers were doing. Moulton and Milligan note that this verb was used for keeping a careful eye on criminals (VGT, p. 490). Luke indicates that it was the Pharisees and the teachers of the law who were doing this (Luke 6:7). "Watched him closely" is a good translation here.

3 Stand Forth The Greek literally says, "Get up [or, stand up] into the midst." The meaning evidently is: "Stand up in front of everyone" (NIV). Arndt and Gingrich (p. 214) note that the imperative form of the verb here—*egeire*—means "Get up."

5 Being Grieved The simple verb *lypeō* in the passive means "become sad, sorrowful, distressed" (AG, p. 482). But here it is the compound, *syllypeō*. The prepositional prefix, *syn* (assimilated as *syl* with the following *lypeō*) has what is called the "intensive force," strengthening the main verb. Arndt and Gingrich would translate the whole phrase here: "deeply grieved at the hardening of their heart" (p. 784). A bit more contemporary rendering is "deeply distressed at their stubborn hearts" (NIV).

"When he had looked round upon" is the aorist participle, *periblepsamenos*. It indicates a momentary flash of anger at the stubborn, unreasonable attitude of these religious leaders, who didn't want Him to heal a needy man on the Sabbath. But "being grieved" is the present participle, *syllypoumenos*, indicating a continuing deep distress at their selfishness. We should react, as Jesus did, with anger at the sight of cruelty to human beings. At the same time we should feel a continuing compassion for the sinner.

9 Ship There were no "ships" on the Lake of Galilee. Actually the Greek here is *ploiarion*, "small boat"—probably a rowboat.

10 Pressed Upon The verb is *epipiptō*, which literally means "fall upon." The picture is that of the many people that were "pushing forward" (NIV) to touch Jesus for healing. There was danger that He would be pushed into the lake. He had to get into the small boat for safety.

14 Ordain The Greek verb is simply *poieō*, which means "do" or "make." Vincent Taylor writes: "In *kai epoiēsen dōdeka* the verb means 'to appoint,' a meaning which is not classical, but which is used in the LXX . . . of *appointing* priests." He goes on to say: "This use of *poieō* should be classified as an example of 'translation Greek,' influenced by the LXX" (*Mark*, p. 230). Probably "ordained" (KJV) is too strong; "appointed" (NASB, NIV) is better.

18 Canaanite The word should be "cananaean" (NASB) but this is not used elsewhere and needs explanation. In his parallel passage, Luke (6:15) has *zēlōtēs*, "zealot." Swete and several other good commentators prefer to take this as meaning that Simon was a zealous person. But probably it indicates that he was "an adherent of the party later known as 'the zealots.' " Vincent Taylor goes on to say: "Although the Zealots belonged to a later time, being especially active in leading the people to armed revolt against the Romans (cf. Josephus, BJ, iv. 3.9), they were preceded, from the time of Judas of Galilee onwards, by many, including Pharisees of the left wing, with strong nationalistic tendencies; and to such Simon may have belonged" (*Mark*, p. 234).

19 Betrayed The verb is *paradidōmi*, which means "hand over." But it is regularly used of Judas betraying Jesus. In effect he was "handing over" Jesus to His enemies.

21 Friends The Greek is *hoi par'autou*—literally, "those from the side of Him." This could mean "friends." But verse 31 rather clearly indicates that they were "Jesus' mother and brothers," who set out when they "heard" (v. 21) and finally "arrived" (v. 31). So "family" is better.

Lay Hold On It is true that the verb *krateō* does sometimes mean "take hold of, grasp, seize." But the first definition given by Arndt and Gingrich is "*take into one's possession or custody*" (p. 448). There was certainly no hostile intent here. So "take custody of" (NASB) or "take charge of" (NIV) is better.

He Is Beside Himself This is all one word in the Greek: *exestē*. In the second aorist, as here, the verb means "lose one's mind, be out of one's senses." What His family said was, "He is out of his mind" (NIV). Paul was charged with the same thing (Acts 26:24; 2 Cor. 5:13).

A. T. Robertson gives a good explanation of the situation. He writes: "Mary probably felt that Jesus was overwrought and wished to take him out of the excitement and strain that he might get rest and proper food" (WP, 1:281).

23 Parables The Greek word *parabolē* literally means "a placing beside," and so "a comparison," and its 50 uses in the NT are almost all in the Synoptics. See discussion at Matt. 13:3.

Characteristically the word refers to an illustrative story. But here it is used for short sayings. It is interesting to note that while Matthew and Luke give these sayings of Jesus, they do not call them "parables."

How many parables did Jesus speak? If we

think strictly of illustrative stories, we would probably have only 30, which is what R. C. Trench has in his very helpful *Notes on the Parables*. If we include such short sayings as here, the list could run to 70 or more.

29 *In Danger of* The Greek word *enochos* was a legal term, meaning "guilty" (AG, p. 268). It is more than "in danger of." The one who "blasphemes against the Holy Spirit"—that is, attributes to Satan the gracious work of the Holy Spirit (see vv. 22, 30)—is already "caught" (the force of the adjective) and found guilty.

Damnation "Damnation" is the KJV translation of *crisis*, which simply means "judgment."

But the oldest and best Greek manuscripts have *hamartēma* or *hamartia*—"sin." It is "an eternal sin" (NASB, NIV), from which a person can never be set free.

34 *About* "He looked round about" (KJV) translates the participle *periblepsamenos*, which we have already met in verse 5—"looked round about." But here we are concerned with the second occurrence of "about"—"sat about him." Here "about" translates *cyclō*, in a circle (cf. English "cycle"). "Those seated in a circle around him" is what the Greek says.

4:1 *Great* The Greek *pleistos* is the superlative of *polys*, "much." The simplest and clearest translation (with *ochlos*, "crowd") is "a very large crowd." In the New Testament the superlative form of an adjective usually has the elative force, "very." It is common in the New Testament to use the positive form for the comparative sense and the comparative form for the superlative sense, leaving the superlative for the elative sense ("very").

5 *Stony* "Stony ground" suggests soil covered with many small stones. But that is not the true picture, as the rest of the description shows.

The Greek is *petrōdes*, from *petra*, "rock." It clearly refers to thin soil on top of solid rock, allowing no chance for deep roots that would enable the plants to survive. The correct translation is "rocky ground" (NASB) or "rocky places" (NIV). The same expression is found in the plural in verse 16.

7 *Fruit* Today we do not speak of wheat plants bearing "fruit." So the correct translation of *karpos* here is "grain" or "crop." The same is true in verses 8 and 29.

17 *Are Offended* The Greek verb is *scandalizō*, from which we get "scandalize." It comes from the noun *scandalon*, which meant the bait stick in a trap or snare, and then the trap or snare itself. So the verb means "to trap." Jesus is talking about superficial converts whose faith is so feeble that they are quickly trapped by the hard realities of life and "fall away" (NASB, NIV) from the faith. "Offended" is too weak a translation. See discussion at Matt. 5:29–30.

19 *Lusts* The noun *epithymia* means "desire, longing, craving" (AG, p. 293). It is even used in a good sense sometimes in the New Testament (Luke 22:15; Phil. 1:23; 1 Thess. 2:17). Today "lust" has negative connotations and is usually related to sex. Here the meaning is "desires for other things" not in God's will.

21 *Candle . . . Bushel* See the discussion of these terms at Matt. 5:15.

22 *Hid . . . Secret* The first adjective is *cryptos* (cf. "cryptic"). It comes from the verb *cryptō*, which means "hide" or "conceal." Rather than "hid," today we would say "hidden" (NASB, NIV).

The second adjective is *apocryphos*, which comes from *apocryptō*, "conceal" or "keep secret." The so-called Apocryphal Books were considered to be "secret" writings, and so they were excluded from the Hebrew canon, though they were included in the Greek Septuagint, the Latin Vulgate, and the early editions of the King James Version. Protestants agree with the Jews in rejecting them.

Be Manifested . . . Come Abroad The first expression translates the verb *phaneroō*, in the passive, which means *"become visible or known, be revealed"* (AG, p. 852). The second is the verb for "come" (*erchomai*) with *eis phaneron*, "come into the open." What Jesus is saying is that things are hidden or kept secret so that at the proper time and place they may be "brought out into the open" (NIV).

Swete gives an excellent explanation of what Jesus meant: "If the Gospel was for the moment treated as a secret, it was so only because this temporary secrecy was essential to its successful proclamation after the Ascension" (p. 78).

24 *Measure . . . Mete . . . Measure* The Greek has *metrō . . . metreite . . . metrēthēsetai:* "With the measure (by which) you measure, it will be measured to you." This is a proverbial saying and expresses a significant law of life. Arndt and Gingrich give the sense well: "The measure you give will be the measure you get" (p. 514). And Swete offers a helpful application. He writes: "Here the sense is: 'your attention to the teaching will be the measure of the profit you will receive from it' " (p. 79).

In the last clause of this verse the modification "that hear" is not found in the earliest and best manuscripts. The Greek simply says, "and it will be added to you."

27 *Grow Up* The verb *mēkynō* occurs only here in the NT. In the middle voice, as here, it literally means "become long" or "grow" (RSV, NASB, NIV).

28 *Of Herself* This is one word in the Greek, *automatē*, from which we get the adverb "automatically." *Autos* is the Greek word for "self." Incidentally, an "automobile" is a vehicle that moves by itself.

The Greek word is found (in NT) only here and in Acts 12:10, where the prison gate opened automatically for Peter to escape. Today we would say "by itself" (NASB) or "all by itself" (NIV). Incidentally, the Greek word occurs in the emphatic position at the very beginning of the sentence, which supports the NIV.

Blade . . . Ear . . . Full Corn The first word is *chortos*, which literally means "grass." Here it is used for "stalks of grain in their early, grass-like stages" (AG, p. 884). The second word is *stachys*, which means a "head" of grain. The third word ("córn") is *sitos*, which first meant "wheat" and then "grain" in general. The best translation is: "First the stalk, then the head, then the full kernel in the head" (NIV).

It should be noted that this parable of the growing seed (vv. 26–29) is found only in Mark's Gospel. It is obviously related to the parable of the sower (vv. 2–8, 13–20), which is recorded also in Matthew (13:1–9, 18–23) and Luke 8:4–8, 11–15). Besides these, Mark has only two other parables of Jesus—the mustard seed (vv. 30–32) and the wicked tenants (12:1–11).

30 *Liken . . . Comparison* Here we first have the aorist subjunctive of the verb *homoioō*, which comes from the adjective *homoios*, "like, resembling." For "comparison" the Greek has *parabolē*. The literal rendering of the question is: "How shall we liken the kingdom of God, or in what parable shall we place it?" Probably the clearest translation is: "What

shall we say the kingdom of God is like, or what parable shall we use to describe it?" (NIV).

31 *Grain of Mustard Seed* The Greek has "grain [*kokkos*] of mustard [*sinapi*]." Obviously the whole expression simply means "mustard seed."

Less than All The Greek has the comparative of the adjective *micros*, "small, little." We have taken it over into English for a prefix, as in "microscopic." So the Greek literally says that the mustard seed is "smaller than all the seeds that are upon the ground" (NASB).

The problem is that the mustard seed is not the smallest seed known to botanists today, though it apparently was to the ancients. In any case, it was used proverbially for "the smallest thing." So the NIV has: "which is the smallest seed you plant in the ground." It should be noted that the Greek word *gē* may be translated "earth" (KJV) or "ground" (NASB, NIV).

32 *Herbs* Technically either "herbs" or "garden plants" is correct. But since "herb" is used with special culinary and medicinal senses, "plant" is better (see note under "plant" in the *American Heritage Dictionary*, pp. 1002–3). The Greek word here, *lachanos*, comes from the verb *lachainō* ("dig") and so means any plant that is put in the garden.

34 *Expound* The Greek word is *epilyō*. *Lyō* means "loose" and *epi* means "upon." So this verb (only here and Acts 19:39) literally means "set free" or "release." But here it is used figuratively in the sense of "explain, interpret" (AG, p. 295).

36 *Sent Away* Here we have the aorist participle (*aphentas*) of the verb *aphiēmi*. Arndt and Gingrich give as the first meaning "let go, send away," and they list this passage under that definition. But they say that here the meaning "leave" is "also possible." Since it was the disciples, not Jesus, who acted—the participle is in the plural—it seems more likely that "leaving" (NASB, NIV) is better than "sent away." Jesus might dismiss the crowd, but would the disciples do so?

Took The verb *lambanō* would mean "took." But here we have the compound *paralambanō*, which means "take along."

37 *Great Storm* The Greek says that there was a great *lailaps* of wind. This word is defined by Arndt and Gingrich as "whirlwind, hurricane" (p. 462). It is obviously a very strong word. The whole expression can be translated "a fierce gale of wind" (NASB) or "a furious squall" (NIV).

Now Full The Greek does not have the aorist tense, suggesting completed action (see the Blass-Debrunner *Grammar*), but the present infinitive of continuing action. So a better translation is "already filling up" (NASB) or "nearly swamped" (NIV). If the boat had been "now full" (KJV), it would have been at the bottom of the lake!

38 Pillow The Greek word *proskephalaion* (only here in NT) is compounded of *kephalē*, "head," and *pros*, "toward"—so, the place where one lays his head. In the stern of the boat this would be an oarsman's cushion on which Jesus rested.

39 Ceased The verb *kopazō* literally means "grow weary." This is brought out well by the rendering "died down" (NASB, NIV). The wind gave up its furious blowing when its Master spoke.

5:1 Gadarenes The KJV has "Gergesenes" in Matthew and "Gadarenes" in Mark and Luke. But the earliest and best Greek manuscripts have "Gadarenes" in Matthew, and "Gerasenes" in Mark and Luke (see NASB, NIV). All three readings are found in each account in the different manuscripts, showing that there was a great deal of uncertainty in the early church as to which was the correct reading in each Gospel.

But this is not a crucial matter, for all three names apply basically to the same general region. Gergasa may represent the village of Khersa, the ruins of which have been found near the only hill close to the eastern shore of the Lake of Galilee. Gadara was the nearest large city, about 6 miles away. Gerasa (modern Jerash), the most prominent city in that whole region, was about 30 miles southeast of the lake.

3 No Man ... No ... Not We have noted before that Mark likes strong language (Peter's language). Here is a good example. The Greek has *oude ... ouketi ... oudeis*—"neither ... no longer ... no one." While Matthew's account, as usual, is much shorter (8:28–34), Luke's account is almost as graphic (8:26–39). But Mark alone adds: "No one was strong enough to subdue him" (v. 4); and "Night and day among the

tombs and in the hills he would cry out and cut himself with stones" (v. 5, both NIV).

6 Worshiped It is true that *proskyneō* (from *kyneō*, "kiss") means "to make obeisance, do reverence to, worship" (A-S, p. 386). Arndt and Gingrich note that the verb was "used to designate the custom of prostrating oneself before a person and kissing his feet, the hem of his garment, the ground, etc.; the Persians did this in the presence of their deified king, and the Greeks before a divinity or something holy" (p. 716). But it was also used for a slave prostrating himself before his master (Matt. 18:26).

The pertinent question remains: Would the demon-possessed man be worshiping Jesus, even though he called Him "Son of the Most High God" (NASB, NIV, RSV)? Probably "fell on his knees in front of him" (NIV) is a safer translation.

7 Torment The verb *basanizō* comes from the noun *basanos*, which first meant a "touchstone" (a dark stone used in testing metals), then "examination by torture," and finally "torment, torture." The noun occurs (in NT) only in Matt. 4:24 and Luke 16:23, 28.

Thayer says that the verb properly meant to test metals by the touchstone, secondly "to question by applying torture," and thirdly "to torture" (p. 96). So while "torment" (KJV, NASB) may be all right, it would seem that the demons were afraid that Jesus would immediately "torture" (NIV) them in Gehenna.

13 Ran Violently The verb *hormaō* occurs (in NT) only in the three Synoptic accounts of this incident (cf. Matt. 8:32; Luke 8:33), plus Acts 7:57; 19:29. Our medical term "hormone"—a substance that moves from one bodily organ to another, to stimulate the second one—comes from this. The verb means to "rush" headlong or impulsively.

17 Pray Today we use "pray" mostly for addressing God. So "plead" is more appropriate.

19 Friends The Greek *tous sous* literally means "those who are yours." This could be translated "your people" (NASB) or more helpfully "your family" (NIV).

20 Decapolis This is simply a transliteration of the Greek word for "Ten City(ies)." The name occurs (in NT) only here, in 7:31, and in Matt. 4:25. The name was given to a league of 10 cities, 9 of which were on the east side of the Jordan.

22 *Rulers of the Synagogue* This is one word in Greek, *archisynagōgōn*. It comes from *archōn*, "ruler," and *synagōgē* (literally, "a gathering together"). Swete comments: "In a small synagogue there might be but one such officer (Lc. xiii. 14), in larger synagogues there were sometimes several (Acts xiii. 15). The *archisynagōgos* was the supervisor of the worship of the synagogue" (p. 96).

23 *Little Daughter* This is one word in Greek, *thygatrion*, the diminutive of *thygatēr*, "daughter." It is used only by Mark (here and 7:25). Vincent refers to it as "this little endearing touch" (WS, 1:188).

Lieth at the Point of Death The Greek is *eschatōs echei*—literally, "has last." A. T. Robertson suggests: "Has it in the last stages" (WP, 1:298)—that is, "is dying" (NIV). *Eschatōs* is found only here in the NT.

26 *Suffered* The verb is *paschō*, which in the NT practically always has the unfavorable sense of "suffer, endure" (AG, pp. 633–34). Vincent comments: "To be taken here, as everywhere in the New Testament, in the sense of *suffering pain*, not merely *subjected to treatment*" (WS, 1:189). He goes on to give adequate illustration of this suffering in a lengthy prescription for medical treatment of a persistent hemorrhage, as found in the Talmud. It is difficult to believe that the rabbis would recommend such ridiculous measures for this ailment—a treatment that only witch doctors would give today.

As a layman, Mark—perhaps from Peter—reports bluntly but truthfully: "and had spent all she had, yet instead of getting better she grew worse" (NIV). The "beloved physician," Luke (see Col. 4:14), protects his profession by observing that "no one could heal her" (Luke 8:43); her illness was incurable.

30 *Virtue* Today "virtue" means "goodness." But the Greek word here is *dynamis*, "power." It was supernatural, healing power that went out from Jesus. He had to give of himself in order to heal her, and this is true of our spiritual healing ministry to others.

36 *Heard* The verb is not *akouō*, "hear"—though Luke (8:50) has that—but *parakouō*. Literally this verb means "hear beside," or "overhear" (cf. NASB). But later it came to mean "hear without heeding, take no heed" (A-S, p. 341). In the only other place in the NT where it occurs (Matt. 18:17, twice), it clearly means

this—"neglect to hear" (KJV), or "refuses to listen" (NASB, NIV). So it probably here means "ignoring." Swete notes: "In the Septuagint *parakouein* is uniformly to neglect or refuse to hear, or to act as if one did not hear. . . . The Lord heard the words said . . . but spoke as if He had not heard, passed them by in silence and followed His own course" (p. 101). Moulton and Milligan (VGT, p. 486) confirm this meaning from the papyri.

38 *Tumult* Arndt and Gingrich give for *thorybos* here the meaning "turmoil, excitement, uproar" and say that it is used "of the milling about of a throng in a house of mourning" (p. 363). We would call this a "commotion" (NASB, NIV).

41 *Damsel* The Greek *korasion* is the diminutive of *korē*, "girl." So it correctly means "little girl" (NASB, NIV). It was a tender, endearing term for a girl 12 years old. Probably *Talitha koum* (Aramaic) were the very words the mother used each morning to waken the girl.

6:1 *Own Country* The Greek word *patris* comes from *patēr*, "father," and so literally means "belonging to one's fathers." It was sometimes used for "fatherland" or "homeland" and may carry that connotation in John 4:44 ("his own country," NIV). But in its other occurrences in the NT it clearly means "home town" (Matt. 13:54, 57; Mark 6:1, 4; Luke 4:23–24). That this is the correct meaning is demonstrated conclusively by Luke 4:23, where the people of Nazareth say to Jesus, "Do here in your home town what we have heard that you did in Capernaum" (NIV). Capernaum was just as much "thy country" (KJV) or "your own country" (RSV) as was Nazareth.

It might be noted that *patris* is used for "home town" frequently in the papyri and inscriptions of that period—so much so that Moulton and Milligan say of *patris:* " 'native place,' 'native town,' rather than 'native land' " (VGT, p. 499).

Scrip The Greek word is *pēra*, which Arndt and Gingrich define as "*knapsack, traveler's bag* which Jesus' disciples were directed not to take with them when they were sent out, since it was not absolutely necessary." They go on to say: "But perhaps this passage has in mind the more specialized meaning *beggar's bag*. . . . Such a bag was part of a Cynic itinerant preacher's equipment" (p. 656). Adolf Deissmann cites an inscription from the Roman period in which *pēra* is clearly used for a "beggar's collecting-bag," and he thinks that this special meaning "makes excellent sense in our text" (LAE, p. 109).

In the Greek text "bread" comes before "bag." So this command seems to mean: "You are not to take any food, any bag for begging food, or any money for buying food." Incidentally, *zōnē* does not mean "purse" (KJV) but "belt(s)" (RSV, NASB, NIV).

9 Coats The Greek word *chitōn* does not mean the outer garment (coat) but the inner garment, or "tunic."

19 Quarrel The Greek says that Herodias "had it in for him" (cf. AG, p. 265). The imperfect tense of *enechō* suggests a "grudge" (RSV, NASB, NIV) held continuously. Herodias resented John's righteous proclamation.

20 Observed The verb is *syntēreō*. The only definition that Abbott-Smith gives is "to preserve, keep safe, keep close" (p. 433). The first meaning given by Arndt and Gingrich is "*protect, defend* against harm or ruin" (p. 792). This is the connotation of the verb in the Septuagint and the papyri. There is general agreement among scholars that this is the meaning here.

Herodias wanted to assassinate John. But Herod Antipas "feared" John, knowing he was a holy man. So he kept John safely in prison to protect him from assassination.

Did Many Things Variant readings occur at this point in the Greek manuscripts. Our two earliest manuscripts (fourth cent.), with some others, have *ēporei*, "was perplexed," which Vincent Taylor says "should probably be preferred" (*Mark*, p. 313). The bulk of the later manuscripts have *epoiei*, which simply means "did." *Polla* literally means "many things." But Mark commonly uses it in the adverbial sense of "greatly."

21 Convenient Herodias had been watching for an opportunity to kill John the Baptist. Now her "opportune time came" (NIV). It was "a strategic day" (NASB) to carry out her purpose of getting revenge.

Supper The noun *deipnon* was used for the main meal of the day, toward evening (cf. the Lord's Supper, 1 Cor. 11:20). But it also means "a formal dinner, banquet." That seems clearly to be its meaning here.

Lords, High Captains, Chief Estates The first Greek term, *megistasin*, literally means "greatest ones." The second noun, *chiliarchos*, designates "the leader of a thousand soldiers," and so, in general, a high-ranking military officer. The third category here is literally "first ones [*prōtois*] of Galilee." The use of "estates" (KJV) is misleading. Probably the best translation is: "Gave a banquet for his high officials and military commanders and the leading men of Galilee" (NIV).

25 Charger The Greek *pinax* indicates a shallow wooden dish, or "platter" (RSV, NASB, NIV).

31 Rest The verb *anapauō* is an intensive form of *pauō*, which in the middle voice means "cease, leave off." The compound (in mid.) means "take rest." The disciples were so busy they needed to cease their activity for a while.

39 Companies The Greek reads: *symposia symposia* (pl.). The noun *symposion* (only here in NT) literally means "a drinking together" and was used for a drinking party. Then it came to be used finally for "*a party* or *group* of people eating together" (AG, p. 780).

40 Ranks The Greek here is *prasiai prasiai* (pl.). The noun *prasia* literally means "garden bed." Mark alone mentions the "green grass" (v. 39). As Peter looked at the groups of people in their bright, oriental garments reclining on the green grass of the hillside, he may well have exclaimed, "Flower beds!" He probably repeated this reaction in his preaching, and Mark preserves it for us.

41 Blessed The verb *eulogeō* may be translated "bless" or "give thanks." For this passage Arndt and Gingrich prefer "gave thanks" (p. 322). In connection with the feeding of the 4,000 (8:1–10) we find the verb *eucharisteō* used for giving thanks for the bread (v. 7) and *eulogeō* used for blessing the fish (v. 8). Hermann Beyer writes: "If *eucharistein* is sometimes used for *eulogein* (and the two together at Mk. 8:6, 7), this does not denote any distinction of sense" (TDNT, 2:762). We "offer thanks" or "say the blessing" over our food.

42 Filled The Greek verb is *chortazō*. It comes from *chortos*, "grass," which occurs at the end of verse 39. To "be grassed" obviously means first to be filled with grass, and then simply to be filled. In the passive, as here, it signifies "eat one's fill, be satisfied" (AG, p. 883). In modern Greek it carries this connotation (VGT, p. 690). The translation "satisfied" (RSV, NASB, NIV) is stronger than "filled" (KJV).

43 Baskets The Greek word is *kophinos*, which Abbott-Smith defines as "*a basket*, probably of wicker-work, such as were carried by Jews for food" (p. 255). Since there were 12 of these, it seems likely that they were the empty lunch baskets of the 12 apostles.

45 Constrained The verb is *anangkazō*, which basically means "compel," or "force." Jesus "made" (NASB, NIV) the disciples get into the boat. It may be that John 6:15 suggests the reason for this urgency. Jesus knew that the people intended to make Him king by force, and He did not want His disciples involved in this false political move.

50 Troubled Here we have the passive of the verb *tarassō*. Arndt and Gingrich say that it means "be troubled, frightened, terrified" (p. 805). It would seem that under the circumstances "terrified" fits best.

53 Drew to the Shore It is the aorist passive of the verb *prosormizō*, which is found only here in the NT. In the passive it means "come into (the) harbor, come to anchor." They were in a large fishing boat (probably Peter's) and would need to anchor a bit offshore.

7:2 Unclean The Greek adjective *koinos* means "common." But in this verse, says Friedrich Hauck, "a more precise translation" would be "unclean" (TDNT, 3:797). The next two verses indicate that this is what is meant here. C. E. B. Cranfield notes that in 1 Maccabees 1:47, 62 the adjective means "ritually unclean" (*Mark*, CGTC, p. 232).

Unwashed The adjective *aniptos* (only here and Matt. 15:20) comes from the verb *niptō* (wash a part of the body) and *alpha*-negative. So it means "unwashed." But the context indicates very clearly that it means more precisely "ceremonially unwashed" (NIV).

3 Oft The Greek literally says, "unless they wash their hands with (the) fist" (*pygmē*, only here in NT). Swete thinks this could mean "with the hand held out with clenched fingers while the attendant pours water over it" (*Mark*, p. 136). H. A. W. Meyer prefers: "They place the closed fist in the hollow of the hand, rub and roll the former in the latter" (*Mark and Luke*, p. 88). K. L. Schmidt suggests: "One clenched fist

(*pygmē*) rubbing in the hollow hand, or up to the elbow or joint of the hand" (TDNT, 6:916). In any case, it is a prescribed ceremonial washing that is referred to.

The content of verses 3 and 4 occurs only in this Gospel. That is because Mark was writing for the Romans, who would not be acquainted with these Jewish customs.

11 Corban This term (only here in NT) is a Hebrew word for "a gift devoted to God," as Mark is careful to explain to his Gentile readers. Matthew, in his parallel passage, simply has the common Greek word for gift (*dōron*), which Mark uses in his explanation.

19 Purging All Meats After the saying that physical food does not go into the heart, but rather into the stomach, from which the process of elimination takes place (cf. NASB, NIV), the KJV adds: "purging all meats" (by this process). Why then do we find such very different translations as "Thus he declared all foods clean" (RSV; cf. NASB) or "In saying this, Jesus declared all foods 'clean' " (NIV)?

The simple answer is that the participle "cleansing" is in the masculine (*catharizōn*), not the neuter, in all the earliest Greek manuscripts. So it cannot modify *aphedrōna*—"draught" (KJV) or "latrine" (NASB, margin)—but refers to Christ.

22 Lasciviousness The Greek word *aselgeia* means "licentiousness, debauchery, sensuality" (AG, p. 114). It is a strong term for unbridled living.

Pride The word *hyperēphania* is found only here in the NT. It comes from the adjective *hyperēphanos* (several times in NT), which is compounded of *hyper*, "above," and *phainomai*, "appear"—and so, "appearing above others." The noun means "haughtiness, arrogance, disdain" (A-S, p. 458).

In Paul's Epistles we have several lists of vices, but this is the longest list found in the teachings of Jesus as recorded in the Gospels.

27–28 Dogs See comments at Matt. 15:26–27.

34 Ephphatha This Aramaic word means "Be opened" or "Be released." C. E. B. Cranfield comments: "The idea is not of the particular part of the person being opened, but of the whole person being opened or released. . . . One whom Satan has kept shut up and bound is being released" (*Mark*, CGTC, p. 252). (See next note.)

35 String The Greek noun *desmos* means "bond" or "fetter," from the verb *deō*, "bind." Not only were his ears opened, but the fetter that bound his tongue was broken, and he was released. Then "he began to speak plainly" (NIV), his speech impediment gone.

8:3 Faint The verb *eklyō* (always passive in NT) means "*become weary* or *slack, give out*" (AG, p. 243). Jesus did not want His listeners to give out on the long journey home—walking all day without food.

8 Baskets See comments at Matt. 15:37.

11 Sign The word *sēmeion* is used in John's Gospel for the miracles of Jesus, but not in the Synoptics. That may be partly because of the use of the word here and in parallel passages. Cranfield observes: "The Synoptists use *sēmeion* to denote an outward compelling proof of divine authority—something which unbelief demands but Jesus resolutely refuses to give" (*Mark*, CGTC, p. 257).

15 Take Heed, Beware The Greek is: "*Horate, blepete*." The two verbs, *horaō* and *blepō*, both mean "see." But they also both carry in some passages the added force of "Look out!" or "Beware!" or "Watch out!" It is rare to find them together.

16–17 Reason The KJV has "reason" in both verses; the NASB, "discuss" (cf. NIV). Both are correct, but the second fits better.

The verb is *dialogizomai*, from which we get our word "dialogue"—"a conversation between two or more people" (*American Heritage Dictionary*, p. 364). Arndt and Gingrich give two sets of meanings for the Greek verb: (1) "consider, ponder, reason"; (2) "consider and discuss, argue" (p. 186). "Discuss" seems to fit best here.

17 Perceive . . . Understand The Greek has two similar verbs—*noeō* and *syniēmi*. The first means "perceive, apprehend, understand, gain an insight into" (AG, p. 540). The second means "understand, comprehend, gain (an) insight into" (AG, p. 790). Swete gives the force of Jesus' question to His disciples: "Have ye not yet learnt the habit of attending to and reflecting upon the facts that pass under your observation from day to day?" (*Mark*, p. 161).

29 You See discussion at Matt. 16:15.

31 Rejected The Greek verb *apodokimazō* literally means "reject after testing" (or scrutinizing). The religious leaders looked Jesus over—checked Him out, as it were—and then deliberately rejected Him.

32 Openly The noun here is *parrēsia*, which Arndt and Gingrich define as "*outspokenness, frankness, plainness* of speech, that conceals nothing and passes over nothing" (p. 630). In the dative case, as here, it is used adverbially.

The translation "openly" fits some other places in the New Testament very well. But since Jesus was sharing only with His 12 apostles the truth of His coming death and resurrection, "plainly" (NIV) is more accurate here.

33 Satan This is a Hebrew word taken over into Greek as well as English. It means "adversary" and could possibly be translated that way here.

9:3 Fuller The Greek word *gnapheus* (only here in NT) means "*bleacher, fuller*, one who cleans woolen cloth" (AG, p. 162). So the clearest translation here is "whiter than anyone in the world could bleach them" (NIV).

5 Tabernacles The Greek word is *skēnas*, "tents." It seems clearly here to refer to booths made of boughs from trees. "Shelters" (NIV) is probably simplest.

15 Were Greatly Amazed Mark's fondness for strong words shows up again here. It is interesting that both *thambeō* "be amazed," and the compound *ekthambeō* (here), "be greatly amazed," are found only in Mark's Gospel. The latter may be translated "were overwhelmed with wonder" (NIV). What amazed the people was probably the afterglow of His transfiguration, still showing on His face.

18 Teareth Him The verb *hrēssō* (only here and Luke 9:42) means "throw down, dash to the ground" (AG, p. 735). The demon, as was often the case, was cruel and vicious.

Foameth *Aphrizō*, "foam at the mouth" is found only here and at the end of verse 20. Again we see Mark's fondness for retaining vivid words.

Pineth Away The verb *xērainō* in the passive, as here, literally means "dry up" or "wither." But for this passage Arndt and Gingrich give: "he becomes stiff" (cf. "becomes rigid," NIV).

20 *Tare* The verb *sysparassō* is found only here and in Luke 9:42. It is a strong verb, meaning "threw [the boy] into a convulsion."

Wallowed *Kyliō* is found only here in the New Testament. It means "rolled around."

23 *If You Can* In verse 22 the distraught father said: "But if you can do anything, take pity on us and help us." In verse 23 Jesus picked up his words in a question: " 'If you can'?" The Greek literally says: "The 'If you can' "—which could be translated: "As to the 'If you can.' " "Believe" is not in the oldest manuscripts.

29 *And Fasting?* Our two oldest Greek manuscripts of the New Testament, Vaticanus and Sinaiticus (fourth cent.), simply say "by prayer," not "by prayer and fasting" (KJV). In the fifth century there was a great deal of emphasis on asceticism, leading to monasticism and clerical celibacy. So "fasting" was added here.

We have heard it publicly stated: "If you pray and God doesn't answer your prayer, then fast and He will *have* to do it." But this is pagan magic (manipulating Deity), not true Christianity. A. T. Robertson says of these disciples: "They were powerless because they were prayerless" (WP, 1:343).

36 *When He Had Taken in His Arms* This is all one word in Greek, the aorist participle of *enangkalizomai*—a verb used only by Mark (see 10:16). It is a typical Marcan touch, adding vivid detail to the narrative.

42 *Millstone* The Greek literally says "a mill-stone pertaining to a donkey" (*mylos onikos*)—that is, "a mill-stone worked by donkey-power" (AG, p. 570). This would be a "large mill-stone" (NIV), in contrast to the small stones used by women for grinding grain each morning in their homes.

43 *Asbestos* This is the Greek word (with the definite article) which is translated "that never shall be quenched" (KJV) or "never goes out" (NIV), or, more simply, "the unquenchable" (RSV, NASB). It literally means "inextinguishable." The adjective occurs only two other places in the NT (Matt. 3:12; Luke 3:17). "Into the fire that never shall be quenched" at the end of verse 45 (KJV) is not in the oldest manuscripts.

The reported discovery of asbestos is an interesting story. It is told that a man who was burning some wood in his fireplace noticed

that a bird's nest in one of the small branches did not ignite with the wood. Investigation in the forest produced more of the material. Some scientist who knew the Greek gave to the substance the name "asbestos."

47 *With One Eye* The compound Greek word *monophthalmos* literally means "one-eyed." It occurs (in NT) only here and in Matt. 18:9.

10:5 *Hardness of Your Heart* This is one word in Greek, *sclērocardia*, found only here and in the parallel passage (Matt. 19:8). According to Arndt and Gingrich (p. 756) it is a biblical and ecclesiastical term, not found in secular Greek. Its spiritual significance is obvious.

14 *Much Displeased* The verb *aganakteō* means "be aroused, indignant, angry" (AG, p. 4). So the stronger term "indignant" (NASB, NIV) is better.

16 *Blessed* *Eulogeō*—literally, "speak well of," but usually translated "bless"—is found over 40 times in the NT. But Mark typically uses a strong compound, *kateulogeō* (only here in NT). Swete says of Jesus: "He blessed them fervently, in no perfunctory way, but with emphasis" (p. 208).

22 *Sad* The verb *stygnazō* is found (in NT) only here and in Matt. 16:3. There it is used of the gloomy appearance of the sky. Vincent says that it means "to have a gloomy, lowering look" (WS, *Mark*, p. 436). So, "face fell" (NASB, NIV) describes the situation well.

32 *Leading the Way* The Greek participle is *proagōn*. It is composed of *agō*, "lead," and *pro*, "before." The compound verb means "go before" or "lead the way." The thing that astonished the disciples and made them afraid was the boldness, courage, and determination with which Jesus headed for Jerusalem, after He had told them what would happen to Him there (8:31; 9:31). Swete puts it well: "The Lord walked in advance of the Twelve with a solemnity and determination which foreboded danger" (p. 219).

37 *At Your Right* The Greek word for "right" is here in the neuter plural. But it simply means "right side" (AG, p. 175). This was the place of highest honor.

37, 40 Left ... Left While the word for "right" is the same in both verses, two different words are used for "left"—both of them again in the plural. In verse 37 it is *aristerōn*, in verse 40 *euōnymōn*. They seem to be used with no distinction in meaning.

42 Exercise Lordship This is one word in Greek, the verb *katakyrieuō*, from *kyrios*, "lord." The best English translation is "lord it over them" (RSV, NASB, NIV).

44 Minister The Greek word is *diaconos*, from which we get "deacon." But at that time it simply meant "servant," basically one who waited on tables. Today the term "minister" usually suggests pastor or preacher, which obviously is not the meaning here.

Servant *Doulos* comes from *deō*, "bind," and so means a bondservant or slave. The one who wants to be first must be willing to be "slave of all" (NASB, NIV).

45 For The Greek preposition is *anti*. Moulton and Milligan make the assertion: "By far the commonest meaning of *anti* is the simple 'instead of' " (VGT, p. 46). Arndt and Gingrich write: "Gen. 44:33 shows how the meaning *in place of* can develop into *in behalf of, for* someone, so that *anti* becomes *hyper*" (p. 73). But Hermann Buechsel says that in this passage *anti* has the first of these two meanings. He goes on to say of Jesus: "What He does on their behalf is simply to take their place" (TDNT, 1:373).

11:3 Quotation Marks There are no quotation marks in the Greek text. This very helpful device was introduced at a later time. So one of the real problems confronting translators and expositors of the Bible is when and where to insert quotation marks in the translation. This verse furnishes a good example.

The problem here concerns the last words of the verse: "And straightway he will send him [the colt] hither" (KJV). The reader would naturally assume that Jesus is saying that the one in charge of the colt will promptly send the animal to Jesus. The NASB interprets it that way. But the JB, RSV, NEB, NAB, and NIV, by the appropriate use of quotation marks, all take these words as a part of what the two disciples were to say to the man with the colt. We would agree with this handling of the matter: "If anyone asks you, 'Why are you doing this?' tell him, 'The Lord needs it and will send it back here shortly' " (NIV).

4 A Place Where Two Ways Met This is all one word in the Greek, the noun *amphodon*, which is found only here in the NT. It is compounded of *amphi*, which means "on both sides," and *hodos*, "way, road." So literally it signifies "a road around anything" (Thayer). Arndt and Gingrich give this definition: "*a city quarter*, surrounded and crossed by streets, then *street*." Alfred Plummer writes: "It originally meant a road around some building and then it seems to have been used for any public road or street" (CGT, *Mark*, p. 257). The best translation of the whole expression here is: "outside in the street" (NASB, NIV).

8 Branches This is the word *stibas* (only here in NT). It comes from *steibō*, which means "tread on." Its original meaning was "a spread or layer of leaves, reeds, rushes, soft leafy twigs, straw, etc., serving for a bed," and so "a branch full of leaves, soft foliage" (Thayer). The NAB has "reeds" and the NEB "brushwood." But since the parallel passage in Matthew (21:8) clearly says "branches of trees," probably the best translation is "leafy branches" (RSV, NASB) or simply "branches" (KJV, NIV). After noting the earlier meaning of *stibas*, Arndt and Gingrich say that in the NT it obviously means "leaves, leafy branches."

19 When The Greek *hotan* is a temporal particle meaning "when" (*hote*) or "whenever." Arndt and Gingrich suggest the latter for this passage (cf. NASB). The statement may be intended to indicate that each evening during Passion Week Jesus went out to Bethany to stay at the home of Martha, Mary, and Lazarus.

12:1 By The Greek preposition is *en*, the basic meaning of which is "in." That fits much better here (RSV, NASB, NIV).

Place The word *hypolēnion* (only here in NT) means a "*vat* or *trough* placed beneath the wine-press to hold the wine" (AG). So "vat" (NASB) or "pit" (NIV) is correct.

Tower *Pyrgos* does mean "tower." But there were various kinds of towers for different uses. Here it was clearly a watchtower, which was always built in a vineyard to prevent the stealing of ripe grapes. Moulton and Milligan (VGT) give examples from the inscriptions and papyri of that period for the use of *pyrgos* for "watchtower" (NIV).

Went into a Far Country This is all one word in Greek: *apedēmēsen*. The verb is *apodēmeō*, which simply means "go on a journey." So "went on a journey" (NASB) or "went away on a journey" (NIV) is correct.

4 *And at Him They Cast Stones* This is not found in any good Greek manuscript and so is omitted in modern versions.

Wounded in the Head This is all one word in the Greek, the verb *kephalioō*, from *kephalē*, "head." It means "strike on the head" (AG, cf. NIV).

14 *Tribute* Today "tribute" means a sum of money paid by one nation (or its ruler) to another nation for protection. So this term does not fit here. The Greek word used is *cēnsos*, borrowed from the Latin *census*. This suggests a poll-tax. Rather obviously "give tribute" (KJV) should be either "pay a poll-tax" (NASB) or, more generally, "pay taxes" (RSV, NIV). Moulton and Milligan cite the use for a head tax in an inscription of that time (VGT, p. 343).

15 *Knowing Their Hypocrisy* This verse and its two parallels (Matt. 22:18; Luke 20:23) furnish an interesting example of how the three Synoptic accounts supplement each other. Three different verbs and three different nouns are used.

Let us look first at the nouns. Matthew has *ponēria*, Luke has *panourgia*, while Mark has *hypocrisis*. In his excellent commentary on the Greek text of Mark, Swete writes: "Malice (*ponēria*) lay at the root of their conduct, unscrupulous cunning (*panourgia*) supplied them with the means of seeking their end, whilst they sought to screen themselves under the pretence (*hypocrisis*) of a desire for guidance and an admiration of fearless truthfulness" (p. 259).

Now to the verbs. Mark uses *eidōs*, a form of the verb *oida* (know intuitively). Matthew has *gnous*, the aorist of *ginōskō* (know by experience or experimentation). Luke has *katanoēsas*. The verb is *katanoeō*, which means "notice" or "observe" (AG). Swete comments: "The Lord detected their true character intuitively (*eidōs*), He knew it by experience (*gnous*), and He perceived it by tokens which did not escape His observation (*katanoēsas*)." He adds: "Thus each Evangelist contributes to the completeness of the picture."

17 *Render* All three Synoptic Gospels (cf. Matt. 22:21; Luke 20:35) have *apodote*, the aorist imperative of *apodidōmi*. One meaning of this verb is "give back, return." We are to

give back to the government in taxes for the services we have received, and we are to give back to God what belongs to Him—the human soul.

28 *Which* The Greek has *poia* (fem. of *poios*), which literally means "of what kind." But Arndt and Gingrich say that here and in Matt. 22:36 it equals *tis*, "which?" This seems to be the judgment of the best scholars (see VGT, Vincent Taylor, and grammars by Blass and Moulton).

29 *One Lord* The Greek literally says: "Hear, O Israel, [the] Lord our God, [the] Lord is one" (cf. NIV). These were the opening words of the *Shema* (Deut. 6:4–5), which every devout Jew is supposed to recite daily. Mark is the only one of the Synoptists that gives them here. Vincent Taylor comments: "The connexion of these words with those that follow is vital; for the command to love God is not simply a duty; it is an obligation arising out of the fact that He is One, in comparison with whom the gods of the heathen are idols, and that He has chosen Israel in covenant-love" (*Luke*, p. 486).

30 *Heart . . . Soul . . . Mind . . . Strength* It is difficult to draw a sharp distinction between these terms, especially the first three. The meaning of the commandment is that we are to love the Lord with all our being. Vincent Taylor puts it well: "The intention is not to distinguish faculties and powers, but to insist on a complete response" (*Luke*, p. 486).

34 *Discreetly* The adverb *nounechōs* (only here in NT) is compounded of *nous*, "mind," and *echō*, "have." So it means having one's mind on what he is doing. Lexicons give "sensibly, discreetly" (A-S) or "wisely, thoughtfully" (AG).

38 *Love* The verb is *thelō*, which means "wish." For this passage Arndt and Gingrich give "take pleasure in, like." This is the idea here (cf. RSV, NASB, NIV).

Long Clothing The Greek word is *stolē*, which we have taken over into English for a broad scarf worn over the shoulders by women. But in ancient Rome it was a long robe worn by matrons.

Ulrich Wilckens gives a good survey of the history of this word. In classical Greek it was used for "the 'upper garment,' especially that which is long and flowing" (TDNT, 7:687). In the LXX it is used 98 times, over 40 times for the sacred vestments of the priests. As to the

NT, Wilckens writes: "In Mk. 12:38 (Lk. 20:46) Jesus warns against the scribes who go about in the long and flowing robes" because they think they "should be given appropriate honour by the people" (pp. 690–91).

39 *Chief Seats . . . Uppermost Rooms* The Greek has two compound words— *prōtokathedria* and *prōtoklisia*. The prefix *prōto* means "first" or "chief." *Kathedra*, from which we get "cathedral," means "seat." A cathedral is properly only a church building which is the seat of a bishop. *Klisia* means "a place for reclining," especially at the table while eating, according to the Roman custom of that day (adopted by many Jews). Vincent Taylor says that *prōtokathedria* "is the bench before the ark containing the sacred scrolls of the Law and the Prophets, a place of honour in the synagogue . . . facing the people" (p. 494). A good translation of this verse is: "and chief seats in the synagogues, and places of honor at banquets" (NASB; cf. NIV).

41 *Treasury* The Greek word is *gazophylakion*. It is compounded of *gaza*—a Persian word taken over into Greek and meaning "treasure"—and *phylakē*, from the verb *phylassō*, "guard." So it was a place of guarded treasure.

Money The Greek has *chalkon*, "copper." So the people were throwing copper coins into the receptacles in the treasury, which was located in the Court of the Women. (Only men could go beyond this into the more secluded, sacred Court of Israel.)

42 *Mites* The Greek word is *lepta*. A *lepton*, the smallest coin in circulation, was a small copper coin, worth about one-eighth of a cent. So a good translation is "two very small copper coins" (NIV).

Farthing This is *kodrantēs* (Latin *quadrans*), worth about a fourth of a cent. For his Roman readers Mark computes the value of two *lepta* as equaling one *quadrans*.

13:8 *And Troubles* These words (KJV) are not in the oldest and best Greek manuscripts.

Sorrows The Greek word *ōdin* (also in the parallel passage, Matt. 24:8) is used literally in 1 Thess. 5:3, where we find "travail upon a woman with child" (KJV). It comes from the verb *ōdinō*, "suffer birth pains" (Gal. 4:19, 27; Rev. 12:2). So the correct translation here is "birth pangs" (NASB) or "birth pains" (NIV). Later Jewish rabbis spoke of "the birth pangs of the Messiah." Billerbeck thinks this was a technical expression already in the time of Christ (H. L. Strack and P. Billerbeck, *Kommentar zum Neuen Testament*, 1:950). George Bertram indicates that the Jews spoke of "the birth-pangs of the Messianic age" (TDNT, 9:672).

9 *Councils* The Greek is *synedria*, plural of *synedrion*. Ezra Gould comments: "The word is used of the local tribunals to be found in Jewish towns, modelled somewhat after the Sanhedrim[n], the great council in Jerusalem." He goes on to say: "The synagogues were the ecclesiastical tribunal of the town, as the *synedria* were the municipal courts" (*Mark*, ICC, pp. 244–45). The "rulers and kings" would be Gentiles.

11 *Take (No) Thought Beforehand* This is one word in Greek, *promerimnate* (only here in NT). *Pro*, of course, means "before" or "beforehand." The verb *merimnaō* means "have anxiety, be anxious, be (unduly) concerned" (AG). Jesus was not telling them, "take no thought" (KJV), but "do not be anxious beforehand" (NASB) or "do not worry beforehand" (NIV). This verse has often been misunderstood and misapplied.

Neither Do Ye Premeditate These words are not found in the earliest Greek manuscripts.

18 *Your Flight* These words also are not in the oldest manuscripts, which simply have, "Pray that this will not take place in winter" (NIV). A. B. Bruce remarks about the addition: "More impressive without. What [is] meant [is] obvious" (EGT, 1:430).

22 *Seduce* It is the strong compound *apoplanaō* (only here and 1 Tim. 6:10 in NT). It means "lead astray" (NASB, RSV) or "deceive" (NIV).

34 *Taking a Far Journey* This is all one word in the Greek, the adjective *apodēmos* (only here in NT). It means "away on a journey" (AG).

14:3 *Box* For "alabaster box" (KJV) the Greek has simply *alabastron*. Arndt and Gingrich give this definition: "*alabaster*, then an *alabaster flask* for ointment, a vessel with a rather long neck which was broken off when

the contents were used" (p. 34). It is obvious that the word "box" conveys the wrong picture to readers today. A better translation is "alabaster jar" (RSV, NIV).

Spikenard   The adjective *pistikos* is found only here and in John 12:3. (This anointing by Mary of Bethany is recorded by Matthew, Mark, and John; Luke 7:36–50 describes a different anointing.)

The word evidently comes from *pistis*, "faith," and so in later writers was used in the sense of "faithful" or "trustworthy." Arndt and Gingrich say: "From this as a basis the word has been interpreted to mean *genuine, unadulterated*" (p. 662). With *nardos* it means "pure nard" (RSV, NASB, NIV).

5 Murmured   The verb is *embrimaomai*. It was used with the meaning "to snort," then "to be very angry." For this passage Arndt and Gingrich suggest "scold, censure." So it may be translated, "And they rebuked her harshly" (NIV).

13 Pitcher   The Greek word (only here and Luke 22:10) is *ceramion*, from which we get "ceramics." So it indicates an earthenware "jar" (RSV, NIV), such as was always used by women (not men) for carrying water.

14 Goodman   The whole expression "goodman of the house" is one word in Greek, *oikodespotēs*. It is compounded of *oikos*, "house," and *despotēs*, "master" or "lord." It is perhaps best rendered "owner of the house" (NASB, NIV).

The Guestchamber   *Katalyma* is also found in the parallel passage in Luke (22:11). Aside from that it occurs in the NT only in Luke 2:7 ("the inn"). The Greek here in Mark has "my guest room" (RSV, NIV; cf. NASB).

15 Furnished   The Greek has the perfect passive participle of the verb *strōnnyō*, "spread," which we found in 11:8 in connection with the Triumphal Entry. But here and in Luke 22:12 it evidently means that the room was furnished with carpets and couches for people to recline on while eating.

18 Sat   We are accustomed to medieval pictures—such as Leonardo da Vinci's *Last Supper*—that portray Jesus sitting at the table with His disciples. But the Greek verb *anakeimai* means "recline," not "sit." Jews had adopted the Roman custom of reclining on couches while eating.

19 Is It I?   The Greek has *mēti egō*. Since *mē* indicates that a negative answer is expected, this is best represented in English by "Surely not I?" (NASB, NIV).

20 Dish   The noun *tryblion* is found (in NT) only here and in the parallel passage (Matt. 26:23). It may be translated either way. But perhaps "bowl" fits a bit better for the large container of sauce into which they dipped the bread.

31 The More Vehemently   This is one word in Greek, the adverb *ekperissos*, found only here in the NT. It means "more exceedingly" (A-S, p. 140), and so "emphatically."

33 To Be Sore Amazed   This is another example of Mark's fondness for strong terms. Matthew says that Jesus began "to be sorrowful" (the verb *lypeō*). But Mark has the verb *ekthambeō*. He is the only one of the NT writers to use it (four times: 9:15; 14:33; 16:5–6). It is always in the passive and means "to be amazed, terrified" (A-S, p. 138). It may be translated "to be deeply distressed." Facing the dense outer darkness of the Cross, when He would take on himself the condemnation for all our sins, was a terrifying experience. No wonder He prayed (v. 34): "My soul is overwhelmed with sorrow to the point of death" (NIV). Swete comments: "The Lord was overwhelmed with sorrow, but His first feeling was one of terrified surprise. Long as He had foreseen the Passion, when it came clearly into view its terrors exceeded His anticipations" (p. 322).

34 Watch   Both Matthew (26:38) and Mark have the present imperative of continuous action. So "keep watch" (NASB, NIV) is a more adequate translation.

35 Fell   Matthew (26:39) says that Jesus "fell" (aorist tense) on His face, praying. But Mark uses the imperfect tense for both verbs. Literally he says: "And having gone a little farther, He was falling on the ground and was praying." We get a picture of Jesus *staggering*, stumbling under the weight of the world's sins, and finally falling *prostrate* on the ground—all the while *praying* in agony of soul. We cannot overestimate the spiritual crisis through which Jesus passed in Gethsemane on that awful night before His crucifixion. No wonder He "prayed that, if it were possible, the hour might pass from him."

36 Abba Matthew and Luke have Jesus saying *patēr*, "father." But Mark uses the Aramaic term *Abba*. Kittel says that it was "used in the everyday life of the family" (TDNT, 1:6). The Jews, out of reverence, avoided using this familiar word in addressing God. But Jesus was able to do it, and so are we. (See Rom. 8:15 and Gal. 4:6, the only two other places in the NT where this Aramaic word occurs.)

40 Heavy Again Mark uses a strong term, the verb *katabarynō* (only here in NT). In the present passive participle here it means "weighed down"—from *baros*, "weight." The compound verb here may well be translated "very heavy" (RSV, NASB).

41 It Is Enough The Greek is *apechei*, the impersonal third singular of *apechō*. "It is enough" (KJV, RSV, NASB) comes from the Vulgate *sufficit*, but "is perhaps to be preferred" (AG, p. 85) to other meanings.

44 Token The Greek word is *syssēmon* (only here in NT). It means a "*signal* previously agreed upon" (AG, p. 794). So a good translation is "had arranged a signal with them" (NIV). Rengstorf comments: "What Mt. 26:48 simply calls a *sēmeion* [sign] is thus interpreted as something which Judas had very carefully arranged beforehand" (TDNT, 7:269).

Kiss The verb is *phileō*. In all three Synoptic Gospels it is used in connection with Judas' betrayal of Jesus (cf. Matt. 26:48; Luke 22:47). Elsewhere in the NT (22 times) it is always translated "love." Its use for "kiss" shows that it expresses the love of affection, not of unselfish devotion. In verse 45 and Matt. 26:49 "kissed" is the compound verb *kataphileō*, which means "to kiss fervently, kiss affectionately" (A-S, p. 240). This makes Judas' deed all the more dastardly.

45 Master The Greek word is *rabbi*. (It is not found twice here in the best Greek text.) It is a Hebrew term taken over into Greek. In Jewish circles it was applied to outstanding teachers of the law. In John 1:38 it is interpreted as *didascalos*, the Greek word for "teacher." It is best simply to transliterate it as "Rabbi" (NASB, NIV).

47 Ear The common word for "ear" in the Greek NT is *ous* (37 times). But here and in John 18:10 it is *ōtarion*. We also find the synonym *ōtion* (Matt. 26:51; Luke 22:51; John 18:26). Because these are both diminutives, it has sometimes been suggested that it was only the lobe of the ear that was cut off. But Moulton and Milligan present clear evidence that these two words were used in Koine Greek (300 B.C.–A.D. 300) as equivalent to *ous*, and so simply mean the outer ear (VGT, p. 704).

48 Thief The KJV translates *lēstēs* as "thief" 11 times and as "robber" 4 times. But the Greek word for thief is *kleptēs* (cf. "kleptomaniac"). *Lēstēs* means "robber," which is far more serious. But Josephus uses *lēstēs* for the Jews who were revolutionaries against the Roman government. So Jesus could well be saying, "Am I leading a rebellion?" (NIV).

51 A Linen Cloth *Sindōn* means "linen." It is used for the linen cloth in which the body of Jesus was wrapped for burial (Matt. 27:59; Mark 15:46; Luke 23:53). The only other place where the word occurs in the NT is here in verses 51–52. Concerning its meaning here, Arndt and Gingrich comment that it is "the *tunic* or *shirt* (cf. Hdt. 2, 95) which was the only garment worn by the youth who tried to follow Jesus after Jesus' arrest, unless it was simply a sheet that he wrapped about his body" (p. 751).

This brief incident is found only in this Gospel. It might be Mark's way of saying, "I was there." If the Last Supper took place in the home of John Mark's mother (cf. Acts 12:12), Judas Iscariot may have returned there first to betray Jesus. We can then understand how John Mark would be roused, perhaps grab a sheet to cover his body, and rush to the garden to warn Jesus.

54 Warmed Himself One of the outstanding features of Mark's Gospel is the addition of little details, like this one. The Greek literally says: "warming himself (*thermainomenos*) at the light (*phōs*)." The fire would serve for both heating and lighting. Incidentally, our word "thermometer" is a combination of two Greek words: *thermē*, "heat," and the verb *metreō*, "measure."

65 Strike . . . with the Palms of . . . Hands The Greek literally says that the servants "took (or, "received") him with blows." The last word is *hrapismasin*. The noun *hrapisma* literally means "a blow with a club, rod, or whip." Arndt and Gingrich go on to say, however, of this passage: "But even here it may have the meaning that is certain for the other passages in our literature, *a slap in the face*" (p. 734). It may have been either one.

68 Porch *Proaulion* (only here in NT) literally means "forecourt." This would be the "entryway" by the outside door.

71 To Curse and to Swear If we should hear today that someone, when cornered, "began to curse and to swear," we would assume that this meant he used profanity. This is not the meaning here, however. "To curse" is *anathematizein* ("anathematize"). It means to "bind oneself with an oath or under a curse." "To swear" is *omnynai*, "to take an oath," as one does in court. What Peter was saying was: "I swear that I am telling you the truth; may God curse me if I am not."

15:1 Held a Consultation This is the wording in KJV, RSV, NASB. It is based on the Greek reading *symboulion poiēsantes*. "Reached a decision" (NIV) translates *symboulion hetoimasantes*.

Actually, it is very difficult to make a decision between these two. The first reading has the support of Vaticanus (fourth cent.) and two fifth-century manuscripts (AW). The second reading is found in Sinaiticus (fourth cent.) and one fifth-century manuscript (C). Both are found in later manuscripts. Swete and Vincent Taylor both think that *poiēsantes* was the original reading, as do C. E. B. Cranfield (CGTC) and William Hendriksen (who translates it "passed a resolution"). But Arndt and Gingrich prefer *hetoimasantes* (p. 778). So one can take his choice between NASB and NIV.

2 Thou Sayest It See discussion at Luke 23:3.

3 But He Answered Nothing This clause (KJV) is not found in the earliest and best manuscripts.

3, 4 Accused . . . Witness Against In the Greek the same verb is found in both places (cf. NIV). *Katēgoreō* was a technical legal term for bringing charges against a person in court (cf. NASB, v. 4).

4 Answerest Thou Nothing? The form of the Greek (introduced by *ouk*) indicates that a positive answer is expected: "Aren't you going to answer?" (NIV).

6 Released The Greek has the imperfect tense of *apolyō*. This tense suggests continuous, repeated, or customary action in the past. The third category fits perfectly here: ". . . he used to release" (RSV, NASB) or "Now it was the custom at the Feast to release a prisoner whom the people requested" (NIV). Incidentally, the last verb here (*paraiteomai*) does not mean "desire" but "request" (AG, p. 616).

16 Hall *Aulē* is frequently used for a courtyard (cf. 14:54, 66). But here it means "palace" (RSV, NASB, NIV). This usage is well supported in the literature of that period.

Praetorium This was a Latin word, which the Greeks took over as *praitōrion*. It originally indicated the tent of a Roman praetor (a high administrator). Finally it was used to designate the governor's official residence. That is its meaning in the Gospels. In the KJV, the parallel passage in Matthew (27:27) *praitōrion* is rendered "common hall."

23 Myrrh See discussion of "Gall" at Matt. 27:34.

36 Sponge Our word "sponge" comes from the Greek *spongos*. It is found only here and in the parallel passages in Matthew (27:48) and John (19:29).

Vinegar The word *oxos* is found only here and in the parallel passages in the other three Gospels (Matt. 27:48; Luke 23:36; John 19:29–30). Arndt and Gingrich write of it: "*sour wine, wine vinegar;* it relieved thirst more effectively than water and, because it was cheaper than regular wine, it was a favorite beverage of the lower ranks of society and of those in moderate circumstances . . ., especially of soldiers" (p. 574).

37 Gave Up the Ghost This is all one word in Greek, *exepneusen* (only here and Luke 23:46). It literally means "breathed out," and so "breathed his last" (RSV, NASB, NIV).

38 Veil See discussion at Matt. 27:51.

41 Ministered The verb *diaconeō* at first meant to "wait on someone at table" (AG, p. 184). Then it came to have the general meaning of "serve." Here the idea clearly is that these devoted women followed Jesus and "cared for his needs" (NIV)—perhaps especially the matters of food and clothing. It was a service of love to their Master.

42 *Preparation* The Greek is *paraskeuē*. It is identified here as "the day before the sabbath." This is all one word in Greek, *prosabbaton* (only here in NT). Since the Jewish Sabbath was from sunset Friday to sunset Saturday, this was definitely Friday afternoon. It is of interest to note that in modern Greek the sixth day of the week is still called *Paraskeue*. All of this seems clearly to indicate a Friday crucifixion.

43 *Honorable Counsellor* The Greek adjective *euschēmōn* means "prominent, of high standing." The noun *bouleutēs* (only here and Luke 23:50) means "member of a council" (AG). Joseph was therefore "a prominent member of the Council"—that is, of the Great Sanhedrin at Jerusalem.

45 *Centurion* See discussion at Luke 23:47.

16:8 *Trembled and Were Amazed* The Greek literally says, "For trembling and amazement held them." The first noun is *tromos*. It comes from the verb *tremō*, which means "tremble," usually with fear (see 5:33; Luke 8:47; 2 Pet. 2:10). So *tromos* means "*trembling, quaking*, especially from fear" (A-S, p. 450). In the other passages in the NT where it occurs (1 Cor. 2:3; 2 Cor. 7:15; Eph. 6:5; Phil. 2:12) it has the noun *phobos* (fear) associated with it.

The second noun is *ecstasis*, which we have taken over into English as "ecstasy." It has already occurred in 5:42, where it is translated "astonishment" (KJV).

The noun comes from the verb *existēmi* which literally means "put out of its place," and so metaphorically "to drive one out of his senses" (A-S, p. 160). Arndt and Gingrich say that the noun literally means "being beside oneself" (p. 245). The women were overcome with amazement at what happened at the tomb.

Luke

1:1 Forasmuch As The word is *epeidēper* (only here in NT). It is a classical term meaning "'inasmuch as' with reference to a fact already well known" (Blass-Debrunner, *Grammar*, p. 456). Abbott-Smith says that it is "a stately compound, frequent in classics and suitable for the formal introduction of Luke" (p. 165).

The fact is that the preface to Luke's Gospel (vv. 1–4) is written in the purest classical Greek of any part of the NT. Luke was probably the only non-Jewish NT writer. He wrote as a Greek for Greeks. His preface is in the conventional style of the introductory sentences of the books of the great Greek historians such as Herodotus and Thucydides.

Have Taken in Hand The verb is *epicheireō* (only here and Acts 9:29; 19:13)—one of the many Lukan terms found only in his Gospel and Acts. It is composed of *cheir*, "hand," and *epi*, "upon." So it literally means to "put one's hand to." It may be translated "have undertaken" (NASB, NIV).

Set Forth *Anatassomai* (only here in NT) literally means to "arrange in proper order." It can be translated "draw up" (NIV) or "compile" (NASB).

Declaration This is not the best translation of *diēgēsis* (only here in NT), which comes from the verb *diēgeomai*, "set out in detail." The noun means "a narrative" or, still better, "an account" (NASB, NIV).

Those Things The Greek has simply "the things"—*tōn pragmatōn*, from which we get "pragmatic." The noun comes from the verb *prassō*, which means "do." So it literally means "that which has been done." It could be trans-

lated "events" (AG, p. 697). Norval Geldenhuys comments: "Luke here uses *pragma* instead of *hrēma*, and in this way makes it clear that it is here not a question of mere narratives, but of actual historical facts, i.e., of things that have really taken place" (*Commentary on the Gospel of Luke*, p. 56). In this preface, Luke is strongly asserting the historical basis and accuracy of his Gospel.

Most Surely Believed This is one long word in Greek—*peplērophorēmenōn*, the perfect passive participle of *plērophoreō*, which literally means "bring in full measure" or "fill completely." It may be translated "that have been accomplished" (AG, p. 670; cf. NASB) or "that have been fulfilled" (NIV). Alfred Plummer gives the force of it: "Of the things which have been carried through to the end, of the matters which have been accomplished, fully established" (*Luke*, p. 3).

2 Delivered We have here the second aorist (classical form) of *paradidōmi*. In the first volume to appear of *The New International Greek Testament Commentary*, I. Howard Marshall writes: "The verb is a technical term for the handing down of material, whether orally or in writing, as authoritative teaching" (*The Gospel of Luke*, pp. 41–42). An accurate translation here is "handed down" (NASB, NIV).

Eyewitnesses *Autoptēs* (only here in NT) is composed of *autos*, "oneself," and the perfect tense of *horaō*, "see." So it signifies "one who has seen for himself." That is what an eyewitness is. Luke had probably never seen Jesus, but he had consulted with many eyewitnesses in Palestine.

Ministers The noun here is *hypēretēs*. Occurring 20 times in the NT, it is translated (KJV) "officer" 11 times, "minister" 5 times, and "servant" 4 times.

Hypēretēs comes from *hypo*, "under," and *eretēs*, "rower." So it literally means "an underrower." It emphasizes the subordinate position such a person holds. For instance, Luke calls John Mark the *hypēretēs* of Paul and Barnabas (Acts 13:5)—certainly not "minister" (KJV), but "servant."

3 Having Had . . . Understanding This is one word in the Greek—*parēkolouthēkoti*. It is compounded of *akoloutheō*, "follow," and *para*, "beside." So it literally means "follow closely." In the classics, it has the sense of "trace, investigate," and Luke uses it that way here.

"Perfect" (KJV) apparently translates *akribōs*, an adverb meaning "with exactness, carefully." The combination is well represented by "having investigated everything carefully" (NASB; cf. NIV). Luke was not claiming to have "perfect understanding." Rather, as a reliable historian, he claims to have made a thorough investigation of the events he is recording.

In Order This is the adverb *kathexēs*, which means "successively in order" (A-S, p. 223). The word is used (in NT) only by Luke (five times). It means here "in orderly sequence" (AG, p. 388). Geldenhuys says that it "does not necessarily point only to chronological order, but to context, linking up and systematic co-ordination. He aimed, therefore, not merely at chronological order, but also at logical and artistic arrangement" (p. 57).

Most Excellent *Kratiste* (vocative case). In the NT it occurs only here and in Acts 23:26; 24:3; 26:25—another Lukan term. Since in the three places in Acts it is used in addressing the Roman governors Felix and Festus, it is generally assumed that Theophilus was a Roman official of high rank.

4 Know This is not the simple verb *ginōskō*, but the compound *epiginōskō*. Geldenhuys says that *epignōs* "expresses the definiteness and sureness of the knowledge, with special reference to the trustworthiness of the information imparted" (p. 57).

Certainty *Asphaleia* comes from roots meaning "not tripped up." As Plummer says, "Theophilus shall know that the faith which he has embraced has an impregnable historical foundation" (p. 5).

Instructed The verb *katecheō* (only Luke and Paul) "originally means 'to sound in the ears', and then 'to teach by word of mouth' or merely 'to instruct' " (Geldenhuys, p. 57). We get from it our words "catechize" and "catechism." Possibly Theophilus was still a catechumen.

5 Judea The Greek *Ioudaia* is the feminine form of the adjective meaning "Jewish." So here it means the Jewish country, Palestine, all of which was ruled by Herod the Great. On the other hand *Iouda* in verse 39 refers to Judah, the southern part of Palestine.

Zacharias This priest had the Hebrew name Zechariah (very common in OT). Since he did, it is better to use the Hebrew form "Zechariah" (NIV) rather than the Greek form. The same goes for "Abia," which should be the familiar "Abijah" (NASB, NIV).

7, 18 Well Stricken in Years The Greek literally says "having gone ahead"—perfect passive participle of *probainō*, "in their days." The simplest translation is "advanced in years" (NASB) or "well along in years" (NIV).

9 His Lot Was The single Greek word is *elache*, the second aorist of *langchanō*, "be chosen by lot." So the clear translation is: "He was chosen by lot." There were thousands of priests, so one man was chosen by lot for each day. "No priest was permitted to offer incense more than once in his lifetime" (Marshall, p. 54).

22 Beckoned The verb *dianeuō* means "nod, beckon." The Greek emphasizes repeated action (pres. part.)—"kept nodding" (AG) or "kept making signs" (NASB, NIV).

Speechless Marshall writes: "*Kōphos* can mean 'dumb' (11:14) or 'deaf' (7:22) or both (Philo, Spec. 4:197f.). The third meaning is supported by the fact that Zechariah is regarded as deaf, as well as dumb, in 1:62" (*Luke*, NIGTC, p. 61).

Today we speak of a person as "standing there speechless, not knowing what to say." But the idea here is that Zechariah was "mute" (NASB) or "unable to speak" (NIV).

23 Ministration The word *leitourgia* was used in classical Greek for service that wealthy citizens performed for the state. In the

51

Septuagint it designated priestly service rendered to God, and that is exactly what we have here. So it may be rendered "priestly service" (NASB) or simply "service" (NIV). (For further discussion see the comments at Phil. 2:17.)

25 *Reproach* The noun *oneidos* (only here in NT) comes from the verb *oneidizō*, which means to "reproach." It means a matter of reproach, or "disgrace" (NASB, NIV). In those days it was considered a disgrace for a woman not to have children.

26 *City* The word is *polis*, the common Greek term for a city. But Nazareth was a small, insignificant village. So it is more accurate to use "town" (NIV). Marshall comments: "Modern versions rightly translate *polis* as 'town,' rather than 'city'; Luke uses it frequently, and even of villages" (p. 64).

Luke identifies Nazareth as "a town in Galilee" because he was writing to Greeks outside of Palestine, who would not know where it was located.

27 *Espoused* See discussion at Matt. 1:18.

28 *Thou That Art Highly Favored* This is all one word in Greek: *kecharitōmenē*, the perfect passive participle of the verb *charitoō* (only here and Eph. 1:6, where it is translated "make us accepted").

The base stem of this verb is the noun *charis*, which is translated "grace" (KJV) 130 out of the 156 times it occurs in the NT. But it also means "favor."

Abbott-Smith defines *charitoō* as follows: "to endow with *charis*, i.e. 1. (a.) to make graceful; (b.) to endue with grace (i.e. divine favor)" (p. 480). The last definition is applied to the NT passages. So "favored one" (NASB) or "you who are highly favored" (NIV) will fit. "Blessed art thou among women" (KJV) is not in the early Greek manuscripts.

32 *The Highest* *Hypsistos* is the superlative of the adjective for "high." It is best translated "the Most High." It is used in the Septuagint as a title for God, stressing His transcendence. In the NT it is used that way mostly by Luke, 7 out of 9 times (TDNT, 8:619).

34 *I Know Not a Man* The verb *ginōskō*, "know," is used here (also in Matt. 1:25) as a euphemism for having sexual relations. We find the same usage in the OT (Gen. 4:1, etc.).

35 *That Holy Thing* This seems like a strange designation for the Child Jesus. It is true that the Greek has the neuter: *to gennōmenon hagion*. But it may be neuter by analogy with *teknon*, "child."

Three viable suggestions have been made for alleviating the difficulty of syntax: (1) "The child to be born will be called holy, the Son of God" (RSV); (2) "The holy offspring shall be called the Son of God" (NASB); (3) "The holy one to be born will be called the Son of God" (NIV).

36 *Cousin* *Syngenis* (only here in NT) is broader in meaning than "cousin." It means a female "relative" (NASB, NIV).

38 *Handmaid* The Greek is *doulē*, feminine of *doulos*, "servant." Since *doulos* comes from the verb *deō*, "bind," and so means "bond servant," NASB has here "bondslave." That is, Mary placed herself completely at God's disposal, even though she knew the outcome would bring shame and disgrace on her in the eyes of her neighbors.

41 *Filled with the Holy Spirit* This expression, which becomes the key phrase of the Book of Acts, has already appeared in verse 15 and occurs again in verse 67. Luke gives more attention to the Holy Spirit than do Matthew and Mark.

43 *Lord* In verse 15 "Lord" (*kyrios*) is used for God, as it is very frequently in the Septuagint (to translate *Yahweh*, "Lord"). But here it refers to Jesus. In Luke's Gospel "Lord" is used for Jesus over 20 times. This is a tremendous affirmation of His deity. Marshall comments: "The use of *kyrios* in narrative to refer to Jesus is distinctive of Luke" (p. 81). It is Luke's favorite way of emphasizing the deity of Jesus.

45 *For* The Greek conjunction *hoti* has two very different functions (in our thinking). It may be taken as causal and translated "because" or "for," as here in the KJV. But it also very frequently simply means "that." It is interpreted this way here in the NASB and NIV.

Marshall has a good treatment of this problem. He writes: "The *hoti* clause may express the reason why Mary is blessed—because what she believed will certainly come true ...; or it may give the content of what she believed. The analogy of Acts 27:25 favours the second interpretation (so most translations ...), which surely includes the former: 'Blessed is she who believed that God will fulfil his word (because he *will* fulfil it)' " (p. 82). This both/and interpretation is excellent.

46 *Magnify* Mary's song (vv. 46–55) is called the Magnificat because the first word of it in Latin is *magnificat*, "magnifies" (the verb is usually first in a Latin sentence). In the Greek also the verb comes first here: *megalynei*, "makes great." It means "exalts" (NASB) or "praises" (NIV; see AG, p. 497).

47 *Rejoices* The verb is *agalliaō*, "to rejoice greatly" (A-S, p. 3). In these two lines (vv. 46b–47) we have a good example of poetic parallelism, the main feature of Hebrew poetry in the OT. Both lines say essentially the same thing, Luke majors on joy and praise throughout his Gospel. (Incidentally, it is obvious that these two lines should have been put in the same verse!)

God My Savior This phrase is a familiar one in the Septuagint, where it represents the Hebrew expression "God of my salvation" (Marshall, p. 82). In the NT it is primarily Christ who is Savior.

48 *Regarded* The word is *epiblepō*, "look upon" (see its use in 9:38). It occurs also in Jas. 2:3.

Low Estate This is a single word, *tapeinōsis*. It means "humble state" (NASB, NIV).

52 *Mighty . . . Seats* The first word is *dynastēs*, from which we get "dynasty." It means "prince" or "ruler" here and in 1 Tim. 6:15. In its only other occurrence in the NT (Acts 8:27) it means a high official.

"Seats" is *thronōn*, "thrones." So the correct translation here is: "He has brought down rulers from their thrones" (NASB, NIV).

Them of Low Degree This is one word, the adjective *tapeinos*. It simply means "the humble" (NIV).

56 *Returned* *Hypostrephō* is a favorite verb with Luke—21 times in his Gospel, 11 times in Acts, plus Gal. 1:17; Heb. 7:1.

58 *Neighbors* This is the adjective *perioikos* (only here in NT). It is compounded of *oikos*, "house," and *peri*, "around"—literally, "dwelling around." Used as a substantive, it means "neighbor."

Cousins This is the plural of the adjective *syngenēs*, "related," and so means "relatives." In verse 36 we saw the feminine form.

59 *Circumcise* Our English word comes from the Latin, meaning "cut around." This is also the exact meaning of the Greek verb, *peritemnō* (18 times in NT).

60 *Not So* *Ouchi* is an emphatic "No!" (NIV) or "No indeed" (NASB).

61 *Kindred* *Syngeneia* (only here and Acts 7:3, 14) is obviously related to the two words for "relative" that we found in verses 36 and 58. It, too, should be translated "relatives" (NASB, NIV).

63 *Writing Table* This is one word, *pinakidion* (only here in NT). It was a wax-coated, small, wooden "writing tablet" (NIV)—something quite different from a "writing table" (KJV).

64 *Immediately* The Greek word here, *parachrēma*, is found only in Luke's writings (10 times in the Gospel, 6 times in Acts), except for Matt. 21:19–20.

65 *Dwelling Round* This is the participle of the verb *perioikeō*, "dwell around" (only here in NT). It is obviously related to the adjective *perioikos*, found only in verse 58 (see discussion there).

Were Noised Abroad The Greek has the imperfect tense of *dialaleō* (only here and 6:11), which in the passive, as here, means "talk over" or "talk about" (cf. NASB, NIV).

68 *Visited* The verb is *episkeptomai*, which Marshall says "is used of God 'visiting' men in the sense that he comes to bless and save them" (p. 90). It occurs again in verse 78 and 7:16 in the same sense. Divine visitation is an important emphasis in the Scriptures.

Redeemed The Greek literally says "made redemption." The noun is *lytrōsis* (only here; 2:38; Heb. 9:12). This was a technical legal term in the Greek papyri of the NT period. It meant a "ransoming," the releasing of a person through the payment of a ransom price. God was providing a redemption for humanity through the ransom price of His Son's own blood.

69 Horn The Greek word *keras* literally means "a horn." It is used in the Bible as a symbol of strength—from the horn of a fighting animal. "Horn of salvation" means "a mighty Savior" (Marshall, p. 91).

75 Holiness . . . Righteousness The first word is *hosiotēs* (only here and Eph. 4:24; see discussion there). The second word is *dikaiosynē*. Marshall comments: "The two words may express duty to God and man respectively" (p. 92). We would suggest that "holiness" may relate more to the inner life and "righteousness" to our outward walk.

2:1 Decree The Greek word is *dogma*. It was first used for imperial decrees and later for ecclesiastical "dogmas."

All the World The Greek for "world" here is not *cosmos*, which occurs 187 times in the NT and is translated "world" all but once (1 Pet. 3:3, "adorning"). Rather, it is *oikoumenē* (15 times; translated "world" except in Luke 21:26, "earth").

This noun comes from the verb *oikeō*, which means "inhabit." So it properly means "the inhabited earth" (cf. NASB). In classical writers it designated "the countries occupied by Greeks, as distinguished from barbarian lands" (A-S, p. 313). But later writers used it in the sense of the Roman Empire. They considered this to be "all the world." That is why the NIV has "the entire Roman world."

Taxed The verb is *apographō*. It occurs three times here (vv. 1, 3, 5) and in Heb. 12:23 (names enrolled in heaven). Here in Luke (in the middle voice) it means "register (oneself)"—"official registration in the tax lists" (AG, p. 89). The decree was that all should "enroll" (RSV) or "register" (NASB, NIV) for a later taxation—that is, "that a census should be taken."

2 Taxing This is the noun *apographē* (only here and Acts 5:37). Deissmann quotes an interesting edict of a Roman governor of Egypt in A.D. 104: "The enrolment by household being at hand, it is necessary to notify all who for any cause soever are outside their nomes [local areas] to return to their domestic hearths, that they may also accomplish the customary dispensation of enrolment" (LAE, p. 271). The correct translation of *apographē*, which comes from *apographō*, is "census" (NASB, NIV).

Incidentally, the above quotation from Egypt sheds important light on verse 3: "And everyone went to his own town to register"

(NIV). It also helps to explain verse 4. Joseph had to go to his old family town, Bethlehem, to register.

5 Espoused See discussion at Matt. 1:18.

Great with Child This is one word in Greek, the adjective *engkyos* (only here in NT). It comes from the verb *kyō*, "conceive," and so means "pregnant" or "expecting a child" (NIV).

7 Wrapped . . . in Swaddling Clothes This is the verb *sparganoō* (only here and v. 12). It means to wrap in clothes. Howard Marshall says that "these were strips of cloth like bandages, wrapped around young infants to keep their limbs straight" (p. 106).

Manger The word is *phatnē* (only here, vv. 12 and 16, and 13:15). In the latter place it evidently means "stall," but not here. J. M. Creed writes: "The manger or feeding-trough would probably be a movable receptacle placed on the ground" (*Luke*, p. 34). The sheep were out in the fields (v. 8).

Inn There has been much discussion about the meaning of the Greek word *katalyma*. In the only other places where it occurs in the NT—Mark 14:14 and Luke 22:11, where it refers to the upper room of the Last Supper—it clearly means "guest room" (NASB, NIV). Furthermore, in Luke 10:34 we find for "inn" the word *pandocheian* (only there in NT). So Creed favors "guest chamber" here. He comments: "Here too it probably denotes a single reception room in which the travellers would sleep" (p. 34). Marshall says that "the reference may be to a room rather than to an inn . . . and to a room in a private house rather than to a room in an inn" (p. 107).

8 Abiding in the Field This is one word in the Greek, the present participle of the verb *angrauleō* (only here in NT). It means "living out in the fields" (NIV).

9 Shone Round About The compound verb *perilampō*—"around" and "lamp"—occurs (in NT) only here and Acts 26:13. The simple verb *lampō*, "shine," occurs half a dozen times.

14 Peace The Greek word is *eirēnē*, from which we get the name "Irene" (a peaceful person). The term first indicated an interlude of peace between wars, as we use it today. Then it came to suggest a peaceful state of mind.

But in the Septuagint *eirēnē* was regularly

used to translate the Hebrew *shalom*, which carries the thought of well-being or salvation. The result is that in the NT "the principal meaning is salvation in a deeper sense" (TDNT, 2:411). Foerster goes on to say that *eirēnē* can mean "peace as a feeling of peace and rest" or "peace as a state of reconciliation with God" or "peace as the salvation of the whole man in an ultimate eschatological sense." He feels that "the last is basic" (p. 412).

Marshall declares that *eirēnē* here "is used to indicate the full sum of the blessings associated with the coming of the Messiah (Is. 9:5f.; Mi. 5:4)." He concludes that "*eirēnē* is thus tantamount to *sotēria*," or salvation (p. 112).

Good Will Toward Men

This familiar phrase, heard so often at Christmastime, is based on the reading *eudokia* (nominative case), found in the late manuscripts (ninth cent. and following). Our earliest Greek manuscripts (fourth and fifth cents.) have the genitive form *eudokias*, "of good will."

But *eudokia* means more than "good will." Arndt and Gingrich note that the expression here has often been interpreted: "among men characterized by good will." But they go on to say that evidence from Qumran (Dead Sea Scrolls) and recent literary analysis of Luke point toward "favor," and "thus would refer to the persons upon whom divine favor rests" (p. 319).

G. Schrenk observes that "*eudokia* is not a classical word. It is almost completely restricted to Jewish and Christian literature, and occurs for the first time in the Greek Bible" (TDNT, 2:742). God's favor rests on those who accept His salvation. This is indicated by John 3:16.

22 Her

The KJV has "her purification." But the United Bible Societies' Greek textual apparatus lists only one manuscript with *autēs*, "her"—ms. 76 (from the 12th cent.). It appears that all our known Greek manuscripts from the 4th through the 11th centuries all have *autōn*, "their." So, correctly, recent versions have "their purification."

We are thus left with the problem of interpreting "their purification." The OT law required that the mother of a male child must offer a sacrifice 40 days after the birth of her son (Lev. 12:1–8). This is probably why "their" was finally changed to "her."

But to what does "their" refer? Some scholars suggest Joseph and Mary. More reasonable is the idea that "their" refers to the Jews—so, "Jewish." Marshall makes another suggestion:

"It is most likely that Luke has run together the cleansing of the mother and the offering of the child" (p. 116).

25 Just

The Greek adjective *dikaios* is translated (in KJV) "righteous" 41 times, "just" 33 times, "right" 5 times, and "meet" twice. The best translation here is "righteous" (NASB). In Jewish eyes that meant "conforming to the Law."

Devout

Eulabēs (here and Acts 2:5; 8:2; 22:12) means "devout, God-fearing, reverent." In a sense "righteous" described more Simeon's outward life and "devout" his inner life.

The Consolation of Israel

Verse 26 indicates that this phrase equals "the coming of the Messiah" (Christ). Luke's frequent mention of the Holy Spirit should be noted here (vv. 25–27).

27 Temple

The Greek word here is *hieron*, which means "temple courts" (NIV)—the whole Temple area, which covered about 25 acres.

After the Custom

The Greek says "according to the *eithismenon*." The last word is the perfect passive participle of the verb *ethizō* (only here in NT) and so may be translated "the established custom" (A-S, p. 129).

29 Lord

This is not the usual word for Lord, *kyrios* (749 times in NT), which is also used for the "master" of slaves (Eph. 6:5, 9; Col. 4:1). It is *despotēs* (only 10 times in NT), from which we get "despot."

Thayer says that *despotēs* "denoted absolute ownership and uncontrolled power" (p. 130). This is brought out by the NIV: "Sovereign Lord."

32 To Lighten

The noun "light" is the common Greek word *phōs*. But this is followed immediately by *eis apocalypsin*, "for revelation" (NIV). "To lighten" or "enlighten" would be the infinitive of the verb *photizō*. But that is not used here.

33 Joseph

The word "Joseph" is not found in any Greek manuscript earlier than the 9th century. All the earlier manuscripts have "His father" (NASB; cf. NIV). It is obvious that late scribes, anxious to protect the doctrine of the virgin birth of Christ, changed "His father" to Joseph. But Joseph was the legal, foster father of Jesus.

34 Fall The noun *ptōsis* (from the verb *piptō*, "fall") occurs elsewhere in the NT only in Matt. 7:27. There it refers to the great "fall" of the house built on the sand rather than on the rock. This suggests that those Israelites who did not build on the solid Rock, Christ Jesus, would fall.

Rising Again This is one word in the Greek, *anastasis*, which in the NT is translated (in KJV) "resurrection" 39 out of the 42 times it occurs. The Jews who accepted Christ would experience a spiritual resurrection.

That Will Be Spoken Against This is all one word in Greek, the present passive participle of *antilegō*. It literally means "speak against," and so "contradict" or "oppose" (cf. NASB)—or even "refuse" (AG, p. 74).

36 *Prophetess* The Greek *prophētis* is the feminine of *prophētēs*, "prophet." It is found (in NT) only here and in Rev. 2:20.

37 *Widow of . . .* The Greek says, "a widow until 84 years." It is not quite clear whether this means that she was a widow for 84 years or that she had reached the age of 84. Probably the latter is better (cf. NASB, NIV).

38 *Gave Thanks* The verb *anthomologeomai* (only here in NT) is a combination of *anti*, "over against," and *homologeomai*, "confess, acknowledge." Michel writes: "The praise of Anna is an answer to the act of God (*anti-*) which she has experienced in her old age. It implies 'acknowledgment,' 'obedience,' 'proclamation'" (TDNT, 5:213).

Looked for This is the same verb, *prosdechomai*, that was translated "waiting for" in verse 25. It has a future outlook and so may be translated "looking forward to" (NIV).

Redemption See discussion at 1:68. Here "the redemption of Jerusalem" (best Greek text) means the coming of the Messiah to deliver His people.

40 *Child* This is not *pais*, but the diminutive form *paidion*, "young child."

In Spirit This expression is not in the oldest Greek manuscripts and so is omitted in recent versions. It was obviously an addition (from 1:80) made by a later scribe.

Grew . . . Waxed Strong Both verbs *auxanō* and (*krataioō*) are in the imperfect tense—"was growing and becoming stronger." Jesus had a normal physical growth: He was a healthy, vigorous child.

Filled with Wisdom This is the present participle of *plēroō*—"being filled" day by day "with wisdom." His mind, as well as His body, was growing.

Grace Here we find Paul's favorite term, *charis* (over 100 times in his Epistles). Matthew and Mark do not have it at all; John has it 4 times. But Luke uses it 8 times in his Gospel and 16 times in Acts.

Alfred Plummer comments on this verse: "The intellectual, moral, and spiritual growth of the child, like the physical, was *real*. His was a perfect humanity developing perfectly, unimpeded by hereditary or acquired defects. It was the first instance of such a growth in history. For the first time a human infant was realizing the ideal of humanity" (p. 74).

43 *Child* This is *pais*. Since Jesus was now 12 years old, it is better translated "boy" (NASB, NIV).

Joseph and His Mother The oldest Greek manuscripts have "his parents" (NASB). This is another example of later Catholic scribes changing the text to protect the Virgin Birth.

44 *Company* The Greek word is *synodia* (only here in NT). It is compounded of *hodos*, "way," and *syn*, "together." So it means a company of travelers, what was called a "caravan" (NASB).

46 *Doctors* The Greek says *didaskalōn*, "teachers"—that is, teachers of the Law. They were the religious instructors of the people. A look at the *Oxford English Dictionary* (3:570–71) will show that at first "doctor" was used only for a teacher. Finally, in modern times, it came to be applied to physicians and surgeons, its popular use today. The correct translation here is "teachers" (all recent versions).

48 *Sorrowing* This is the present passive participle of *odynaō*—"suffer pain or distress." Marshall well observes that this "may perhaps indicate the first fulfilment of Simeon's prophecy"—v. 35—"a sword will pierce your own soul" (p. 128).

49 My Father's Business The Greek literally says, "in the things of my Father." Most modern translations prefer "in my Father's house." Marshall observes that the latter rendering is "required by the context, since the point at issue is *where* Jesus is to be found" (p. 129).

51 Kept The Greek verb is not *tēreō*, "keep," but *diatēreō*, "keep carefully" (only here and Acts 15:29). It means "treasured" (Marshall, NASB, NIV).

52 Stature The Greek word *hēlikia* has two distinct meanings. In John 9:21, 23, it clearly means "age." Just as clearly it means "stature" (physical height) in Luke 19:3. Concerning its use in this verse Marshall comments: "Here the thought is of the maturity associated with increasing age" (p. 130).

After noting that in classical Greek *hēlikia* is used primarily for "age" but also for "physical size," J. Schneider goes on to say: "The sense of 'size' or 'growth' or 'stature' is not found in the papyri" (TDNT, 2:941). He also declares: "The meaning 'age' is also predominant in the Septuagint" (p. 942).

We are loathe to give up the idea that Luke is here speaking of Jesus' normal development mentally, physically, socially, and spiritually. But we must leave the matter open.

3:1 Reign . . . Governor . . . Tetrarch

There are three interesting words here. The first is the noun *hēgemonia* (only here in NT). It comes from *hēgemōn* (22 times in NT), which almost always denotes a Roman governor. Why, then, did Luke use this noun for the reign of the emperor, instead of using *monarchia*?

The answer may perhaps be found as a part of the solution of a chronological problem here. If we take "the fifteenth year of the reign of Tiberius Caesar" as counted from the time of his full accession to the throne, Jesus would have been 32, not 30 (cf. v. 23), when He began His ministry. But if we begin two years earlier, when Tiberius became coregent with his father, it comes out just right. So the weaker term *hēgemonia* may purposely have been used for his period of rule. F. L. Godet writes: "It has long been maintained that this last mode of reckoning, as it is foreign to the Roman writers, could only be attributed to Luke to meet the requirements of harmonists. Wieseler, however, has just proved, by inscriptions and medals, that it prevailed in the East, and particularly at Antioch whence Luke appears originally to have come, and where he certainly resided for some time" (1:166–67).

The second expression, "being governor," is the verb *hēgemoneuō* (only here and 2:2). It is related to the verb *hēgeomai*, "lead," and so first meant to "be a leader." Here it indicates being a governor.

The third expression, "being tetrarch," is the present participle of *tetrarcheō* (only here, three times). It obviously comes from the noun *tetrarchēs* (Matt. 14:1; Luke 3:19; 9:7; Acts 13:1), which originally meant a ruler of the fourth part of a region but later was used for any dependent prince.

2 Being the High Priests The Greek is *epi archiereōs*. Marshall says that *epi* with the genitive (as here) means "in the time of." He also comments: "*Archiereus* is correctly used in the singular, despite the fact that two names follow, since there was only one high priest at the time" (p. 134). Caiaphas was actually high priest (A.D. 18–37). But his father-in-law, Annas, who had been high priest A.D. 6–15, still held the reins of power while five of his sons and his son-in-law were in office.

3 Repentance See discussion at Mark 1:4.

5 Filled . . . Low . . . Straight . . . Smooth The word for "valley," *pharanx* (only here in NT), primarily means a "chasm" or "ravine." Such places must be filled in.

"Mountain" is the usual word, *horos* (65 times in NT). "Hill" is *bounos* (only here and 23:30). "Shall be brought low" is the verb *tapeinoō*, translated "humble" (KJV) 8 out of the 14 times it occurs in the NT.

"Crooked" (*skolois*) is a strong adjective. Here it means "curved, bent, winding." The other 3 times it occurs in the NT (Acts 2:40; Phil. 2:15; 1 Pet. 2:18) it is used metaphorically in the sense of "crooked, perverse, unjust" (A-S, p. 409). *Eutheias* (fem. pl. of *euthys*), "straight" is preceded by *eis*, "into." The crooked will be made into straight ways.

"Rough ways" is the plural of the adjective *trachys* (only here and Acts 27:29). "Smooth" is the adjective *leios* (only here in NT).

11 Coats The Greek word *chitōn* does not mean a coat—the outer garment—which in Greek is *himation*. Rather, it is the "tunic" (NASB, NIV), worn under the outer cloak.

Meat The Greek word is *brōma*, which means any kind of "food."

14 Do Violence The verb is *diaseiō* (only here in NT). It literally means "shake violently." In those days it was a technical, legal term, meaning "extort money by violence" much like our current slang expression "shake down" (AG, p. 188).

Accuse Falsely This is a single word, the verb *sykophanteō* (only here and 19:8). Sir William Ramsay says that the passage means: "If I have accused any defaulter before the government and had him condemned to pay up arrears" (HDB 5:396, n.).

The Liddell-Scott-Jones *Greek-English Lexicon* defines the verb as: "prosecute vexatiously, blackmail"—frequently of blackmail by officials—and so "extort by false charges or threats" (p. 1671).

4:1 Full of the Holy Spirit This key phrase (*plērēs pneumatos hagiou*) is found (in NT) only here and three times in Acts (6:3; 7:55; 11:24). It is the key phrase of that book, along with "filled with the Holy Spirit."

2 Devil The word *diabolos* occurs 38 times in the NT. In 3 instances it is plural and refers to human beings, and so may be translated literally as "slanderers" (1 Tim. 3:11; 2 Tim. 3:3; Titus 2:3). The other 35 times it is singular and is a title for Satan. Matthew and Luke each use it 6 times ("devil"), but Mark not at all. He prefers *satanas*, "Satan" (6 times). Matthew also uses *satanas* 4 times and Luke has it 6 times (out of a total of 36 times in NT).

4 But by Every Word of God These words are not in the very earliest Greek manuscripts and so should be omitted here (cf. NASB, NIV).

5 Into an High Mountain These words, found in Matthew (4:8), are not found in the oldest manuscripts of Luke.

Moment The word is *stigmē* (only here in NT). It comes from the verb *stizō*, "prick," and means a "prick" or "point," and so "a moment."

14 Fame *Phēmē* (only here and Matt. 9:26) comes from the verb *phēmi*, "say," and so denotes a "saying" or "report." It simply means "news" (NASB, NIV).

17 Book The Greek *biblion* means a "scroll." All the sacred Scriptures of the Jews (our OT) were written on scrolls, not in bound books.

Opened The verb is *anaptyssō* (only here in NT). It means to "unroll," which is what has to be done with a scroll. Verse 20 reads: "Then he rolled up the scroll" (NIV).

18 To Preach the Gospel This is one word, *euangelisasthai*. It means to "preach good news" (NIV).

He Hath Sent . . . Brokenhearted This clause is not in the earliest Greek manuscripts.

Recovering of Sight This is one word, the noun *anablepsis* (only here in NT). It comes from the verb *anablepo*, "see again."

Them That Are Bruised This is one word, the perfect passive participle of *thrauō* (only here in NT), "break in pieces." So it probably means "the oppressed" (NIV).

20 Minister See discussion at 1:2. This man was the "attendant" (NASB, NIV) who brought the scroll to Jesus and then returned it to its place.

23–24 Country See discussion at Mark 6:1.

29 Cast Down Headlong This is one word in the Greek, the verb *katakrēmnizō* (only here in NT). It means "throw over a precipice," and so "throw him down the cliff" (NASB, NIV).

34 Let Us Alone In Greek this is the single word *ea*. Thayer says that this was "an interjection expressive of indignation, or of wonder mixed with fear" (p. 162). The KJV rendering (above) is based on the assumption that it is derived from the present imperative of the verb *eaō*, "let alone." But most scholars today take it as a natural, instinctive sound, "Ha!" (NASB, NIV).

What Have We to Do with Thee? The Greek is *ti hēmin kai soi*—literally, "What to us and to you [sing.]?" That would mean, "What have we in common?" But Marshall notes that in the Septuagint it translates a phrase that means, "Why are you interfering with me?" He says that it is a rhetorical question, implying, "Do not meddle with me" (p. 193).

35 Hold Thy Peace This is the verb *phimoō* (only here in Luke). It is used literally in 1 Cor. 9:9; 1 Tim. 5:18. See discussion at Mark 1:25.

36 They Were All Amazed The NASB gives a literal translation of the Greek: "Amazement came upon them all." The word for "amazement" is *thambos* (only here; 5:9; and Acts 3:10). Marshall says it is "wonder, perhaps mingled with fear."

38 A Great Fever The Greek expression here was used by Galen, a prominent physician. It may reflect Luke's familiarity with medical language, which appears in his Gospel and Acts.

39 Ministered See discussion at Mark 1:31.

41 Christ The name Christ does not precede "the Son of God" in the earliest Greek manuscripts.

42 Stayed Him We have here the imperfect of *katechō*, which means "to hold back, detain, restrain" (A-S, p. 241). Luke uses it in his Gospel and Acts, but it is not found in Mark or Matthew. The Greek says here that the people "tried to keep Him from going away from them" (NASB).

5:1 Pressed Upon This is a strong verb, *epikeimai*, which literally means "lie upon." It would seem that Jesus was almost in danger of being pushed into the lake by the people, all of whom were trying to get close to Him to hear the Word of God. So He got into a boat, so that all could see and hear Him.

Lake This is the first occurrence of *limnē*, which (in NT) is used only in Luke's Gospel (5 times) and in Revelation (5 times, always for the lake of fire). Matthew and Mark call the Lake of Galilee (Gennesaret) "the sea"—the popular designation of it by those who lived on its shores and fished its waters. But Luke had traveled on the Mediterranean Sea, and so he correctly recognized "the Sea of Galilee" (about 13 miles long and 7 miles wide) as a lake. See also discussion at Mark 1:16.

2-3 Ships These were obviously two small "boats," not "ships" as we use that term today.

4, 9 Draught The noun *agra* (only here) was used for what was taken in hunting or fishing, and so means a "catch" (NASB, NIV).

5 Master *Epistatēs* is found only in Luke (5:5; 8:24, 45; 9:33, 49; 17:13). A. Oepke observes: "Except in the last instance, it is used only by the disciples. The transcription *rabbi* used by the other Evangelists is avoided by the Hellenist Luke" (TDNT, 2:623).

The noun comes from the verb *ephistēmi*, "set over." So it means "any sort of a superintendent or overseer." Thayer goes on to say that it was used by the disciples "when addressing Jesus, who called him thus 'not from the fact that he was a teacher, but because of his authority' (Bretschneider)" (p. 243).

6 Brake The verb *diarressō* is in the (inchoative) imperfect—"began to break" (NASB, NIV).

7 Beckoned The verb *kataneuō* (only here) means to make a sign by nodding the head. The simplest translation is "signaled" (NASB, NIV).

Partners The adjective *metochos* (only here and Heb. 1:9; 3:1, 14; 6:4; 12:8) comes from the verb *metechō*, "share." So it properly means "sharing." But here and in Heb. 1:9 it is used as a substantive with the meaning "partner."

10 Partners This is a different word, *koinōnoi*—the plural of the adjective *koinōnos*, which means "common" (*koinos*). Here it is used as a substantive meaning "partners" (cf. 2 Cor. 8:23; Philem. 17). *Koinōnia* means not only a "fellowship" in worship but a "partnership" in service.

Catch The Greek word is *zōgreō* (only here and 2 Tim. 2:26). It means "to take alive," and "was used in the LXX for saving persons alive from danger" (Marshall, p. 205). Peter would rescue sinners from eternal loss.

12 Full of Leprosy Matthew (8:2) and Mark (1:40) simply say that "a leper" (Greek, *lepros*) came to Jesus. Luke says, *anēr plērēs lepras*—"a man full of leprosy." This is another of many evidences of the medical interest of Luke the physician.

16 Withdrew . . . Prayed "He withdrew himself into the wilderness and prayed" (KJV). This suggests one trip and one prayer. The Greek, however, paints a different picture. Literally it says: "But He himself"—*autos*—"was"—*ēn*, imperfect of customary or repeated action—"withdrawing"—present participle of the verb *hypochōreō* (only here and 9:10), "used with *ēn* in the sense 'retire to a place and spend some time there'" (AG, p. 848)—"in solitary places"—*en tais erēmois*—"and praying"—*kai proseuchomenos*, present participle of continuing action. The full force of the Greek gives us this: "But Jesus often withdrew to lonely places and prayed" (NIV). Luke, with his special emphasis on the prayer life of Jesus, is the only one who records this item.

17 Doctors of the Law This is one word in the Greek, *nomodidaskaloi* (three times in NT). It is compounded of *didaskalos,* "teacher," and *nomos,* "law." So the plural means "teachers of the law," and it is correctly translated that way in 1 Tim. 1:7 (KJV). In Acts 5:34 it is singular, used of Gamaliel. These were the men who taught the law of Moses to the people in the synagogues each Sabbath. K. H. Rengstorf writes of *nomodidaskalos:* "This word is not found in secular Greek, nor in the LXX, Josephus or Philo. . . . It is rather a Christian construction designed to mark off Jewish from Christian teachers at the decisive point, namely the absolutising of the *nomos*" (TDNT, 2:159).

18 Taken with a Palsy This is one word in Greek, *paralelymenos*—the perfect passive participle of *paralyō* (only here; v. 24; Acts 8:7; 9:33; Heb. 12:12). In the parallel passages in Matthew (9:2) and Mark (2:3) the Greek has the adjective *paralyticos,* used as a substantive—"a paralytic." A. B. Bruce says that Luke's participial form of the verb was "more in use among physicians, and the more classical" (EGT, 1:497). The best translation here is "a man who was paralyzed" (NASB).

19 Tiling The Greek word is *ceramos* (only here in NT), from which we get "ceramic." It was used first for potter's clay, then for a pottery dish, and finally, as here, for "tile." Luke alone notes that this house had a tile roof.

27 Receipt of Custom See discussion at Matt. 9:9.

29 Feast We do not find here the usual Greek word for "feast" in the NT. Rather it is *dochē* (only here and 14:13)—another Lukan term. It comes from *dechomai,* "receive" or "welcome." So a good translation is "reception" (NASB).

36–38 Piece . . . New . . . Bottles See discussion at Mark 2:21–22.

6:1 Second Sabbath After the First "Second . . . after the first" is one word in Greek, *deuteroprōtō. Deutero* means "second," *prōtō,* "first"—literally, "second-first." Of this strange compound Plummer says: "In the whole of Greek literature, classical, Jewish, or Christian, no such word is found independently of

this text" (p. 166). Arndt and Gingrich observe: "Even many ancient interpreters, understandably, could make nothing of it . . . and it may owe its origin solely to a scribal error" (p. 177). It seems best to follow the reading of the oldest manuscripts, which have simply "Sabbath."

Corn See discussion at Mark 2:23.

Plucked The verb *tillō* occurs (in NT) only here and in the parallel passages (Matt. 12:1; Mark 2:23). Probably today we would use "pick" (NASB, NIV).

Rubbing The verb is *psōchō* (only here in NT). Plummer comments: "According to Rabbinical notions, it was reaping, thrashing, winnowing, and preparing food all at once"—all of which were forbidden on the Sabbath. He then adds: "Lk. alone mentions the rubbing, and the word *psōchein* seems to occur elsewhere only in the medical writer Nicander" (p. 167).

4 Showbread See discussion at Mark 2:26.

6 Right Hand Matthew and Mark have simply "hand." As a physician, Luke notes more precisely that it was the man's "right hand."

7 Watched See discussion at Mark 3:2.

11 Madness The Greek word *anoia* (only here and 2 Tim. 3:9) is compounded of *alpha*-negative and *nous,* "mind." So it means "folly," but here "fury" or "rage."

Communed *Dialaleō* (only here and 1:65) literally means "talk" (*laleō*) "through" or "with" (*dia*). The whole expression here simply means "discussed together" (NASB). The imperfect tense suggests that this discussion "began" (NIV) at this point and continued.

12 Continued All Night The Greek has *ēn,* "was," and *dianyktereuōn,* the present participle of *dianyktereuō* (only here in NT), which means "pass the night" (*nyks*). This is one of 6 times when Luke mentions Jesus praying, when the other Gospels do not. Before selecting His 12 apostles, the nucleus of His Church, He spent the night in prayer, seeking His Father's guidance.

15 Zelotes See discussion at Mark 3:18.

16 Traitor The noun *prodotēs* comes from the verb *prodidōmi,* which means "betray." The noun is found only here and Acts 7:52; 2 Tim. 3:4.

17 *Plain* *Pedinos* (only here in NT) means a level place. The message that follows (vv. 20–49) is often labeled "The Sermon on the Plain" (so Marshall, p. 243). Others refer to it as "Luke's version of the Sermon on the Mount."

19 *Virtue* The Greek word is *dynamis*, "power."

20 *Blessed* See discussion at Matt. 5:3.

22 *Separate . . . from Their Company* This is all one word in Greek, *aphorisōsin*. The verb *aphorizō* literally means "mark off by boundaries," and so "separate from." Abbott-Smith thinks that here it refers to excommunication (p. 72). But probably it has a broader application to social ostracism.

30 *Ask Them Not Again* This is the verb *apaiteō* (only here in NT), with *mē*, "not." The expression means: "Do not demand it back" (NASB, NIV).

36 *Merciful* This verse is Luke's parallel to Matt. 5:48. Probably on one occasion Jesus said "perfect" and on another occasion "merciful," *oiktirmōn* (only here and Jas. 5:11)—showing kindness to all as God does (v. 35). This expresses perfect love.

38 *Running Over* The verb *hyperekchynaō* is found only here in the NT. It expresses the superabundance of God's giving back to us when we give generously.

41–42 *Mote . . . Beam* See discussion at Matt. 7:3–5.

7:2 *Dear* The Greek adjective *entimos* is compounded of *en*, "in," and *timē*, "honor" or "value." So it means "honored, respected"— that is, "valued highly" (NIV).

4 *Instantly* Today this adverb means "at that moment." But the Greek *spoudaios* means "earnestly."

11 *The Day After* The adverb *exēs* means "next" (in a series). Here the *Textus Receptus* has *en tēs hexēs*, suggesting that the feminine noun *hēmera*, "day," should be supplied—"on the next day." But the best Greek text has *en tō hexēs*, suggesting that *chronō* (masc.), "time,"

be supplied. This would mean "soon afterward" (NIV; cf. NASB).

14 *Bier* The Greek *soros* (only here in NT) means "coffin." However, it was not an expensive, covered coffin, for the young man sat up.

16 *Visited* See discussion at Luke 1:68.

17 *Rumor* This is somewhat of a pejorative term. The Greek simply has *logos*, "word." It means "report" (NASB) or "news" (NIV).

25 *Delicately* This is the dative case of the noun *tryphē* (only here and 2 Pet. 2:13). It means "in luxury."

30 *Lawyers* See discussion at Luke 10:25.

32 *Piped . . . Mourned* See discussion at Matt. 11:17.

34 *Gluttonous Man . . . Winebibber* The first expression is *phagos*, from the second aorist of *esthiō*, "eat." The second is a compound word *oinopotēs* (*oinos*, wine, and *potēs*, "drinker). Both words are found (in NT) only here and in the parallel passage (Matt. 11:19).

36 *Sat Down to Meat* This is one word in Greek, the verb *kataklinō*. It is used only by Luke (9:14–15; 14:8; 24:10). Compounded of *kata*, "down," and *klinē*, "couch," it means "reclined at the table" on couches.

37 *Alabaster Box of Ointment* The Greek is *alabastron myrou*. It should be translated "alabaster jar of perfume" (NIV). See discussion at Mark 14:3.

38, 44 *Wash* The Greek verb *brechō* means to "wet," not "wash." In its other occurrences in the NT it is translated "rain" (Matt. 5:45; Luke 17:29; Jas. 5:17; Rev. 11:6)—a meaning it has in the later Greek writers of that period.

38 *Did Wipe . . . Kissed . . . Anointed* The three Greek verbs are in the imperfect tense— "kept wiping them with the hair of her head, and kissing His feet, and anointing them with perfume" (NASB).

41 *Creditor* The Greek word *daneistēs* (only here in NT) means "moneylender" (NIV). We might note that the word for "debtors," *chreopheiletēs*, occurs only here and in 16:5.

8:1 *He Went* The verb *diodeuō* is compounded of *hodos*, "way," and *dia*, "through." It is a Lukan term (only here and Acts 17:1). It means "traveled about" (NIV).

Showing the Glad Tidings This is one word in the Greek, the present participle *euangelizomenos*. It is preceded by *keryssōn*, "heralding" or "proclaiming." These are the two main verbs used for "preach" in the NT. The NASB gives a good literal translation: "proclaiming and preaching the kingdom of God." Since *euangelizō* means "announce good news," the NIV has "proclaiming the good news of the kingdom of God" (cf. Marshall, p. 316).

3 *Ministered* See discussion at Mark 15:41.

Him The Greek manuscripts—even the fourth- and fifth-century ones—are rather evenly divided between *autois*, "them," and *auto*, "him." It is impossible to be certain now as to which was the original meaning. But that makes little difference in the sense. "Them" would mean Jesus and the Twelve (cf. v. 1).

6 *Moisture* The word *ikmas* occurs only here in the NT. Arndt and Gingrich indicate that it was used by Greek writers "of the moisture in the soil, without which plants cannot live." They also note that it had a medical usage.

7 *Sprang Up with It* This is one word, the verb *synphyō* (only here in NT). It means "grew up with it." In verses 6 and 8 Luke uses the simple verb *phyō* (only there and Heb. 12:15).

14 *Bring . . . Fruit to Perfection* This is one word in Greek, *telesphorousin*. The verb *telesphoreō* (only here in NT) is compounded of *telos*, "end," and *pherō*, "bear." It means "bring (no) fruit to maturity" (NASB).

15 *Patience* The noun *hypomonē* is translated "patience" in the KJV 29 of the 32 times it occurs in the NT. But it does not mean that. Rather it means "perseverance" (NASB; cf. NIV).

19 *Come At Him* Today this expression suggests hostile intention. The verb *syntynchanō* (only here in NT) means "come together with." So the idea here is "get to Him" (NASB) or "get near him" (NIV).

22 *Launched Forth* Only the widely traveled Luke (of all NT writers) uses the verb *anagō* (in the middle or passive) as a technical nautical term for "put out to sea" in a boat. He does this a dozen times in Acts.

23 *Sailed* The verb *pleō*, "sail," is used only by Luke (here and four times in Acts), except for Rev. 18:17.

Fell Asleep The verb *aphypnoō* is found only here in the NT.

Storm See discussion at Mark 4:37.

Filled with Water The Greek has *syneplē-rounto* (imperfect), "they were being filled"—"being swamped" (NIV).

Master, Master See discussion at Luke 5:5.

26 *Arrived* The verb *katapleō* (only here in NT) literally means "sail down"—that is, to the land.

Gadarenes See discussion at Mark 5:1.

Over Against This is the adverb (used as a preposition) *antipera* (only here in NT). It means "opposite" (NASB), or here "across the lake from" (NIV).

31 *Deep* The Greek word is *abysson*—"Abyss" (NIV; cf. NASB). It was used for the "underworld" or "abode of the dead." In the KJV it is translated "deep" here and in Rom. 10:7, but "bottomless pit" 7 times in Revelation.

43–44 *Issue* The noun *hrysis* (only here and Mark 5:25) comes from the verb *hreō*, "flow." So it means a "flowing." Used here with "blood" (*haima*) it means "bleeding" (NIV) or "hemorrhage" (NASB).

44 *Stanched* This is the second aorist of *histēmi*. It means "stopped." The flowing of blood came to an end.

45 *Throng . . . Press* The first verb is *synechō*, which literally means "hold together," but here and 19:43 "hem in, press on every side" (A-S, p. 428). The second verb is *apothlibō* (only here in NT), which is compounded of *apo* (intensive) and *thlibō*, "press," and so means "press hard."

46 *Virtue* See discussion at Mark 5:30.

52 Wept . . . Bewailed The first verb is *klaiō*, which indicates "any loud expression of pain or sorrow, especially for the dead" (A-S, p. 247). The second verb is *koptō*. It properly means to "strike" and in the middle, as here, "*to beat one's breast* with grief, *to mourn*" (A-S, p. 254). Both verbs are in the imperfect tense of continuous action. So the best translation is: "were wailing and mourning" (NIV).

Weep Not This is the verb *klaiō* again, in the present imperative. It means "stop wailing."

53 Laughed . . . to Scorn This is the imperfect tense of the verb *katagelaō*, which (in NT) occurs only here and in the parallel passages (Matt. 9:24; Mark 5:40). It means "laugh at, ridicule" (TDNT, 1:659). Of the usage here the author writes: "This obviously denotes scornful laughter on the basis of supposedly better information and therefore of a superiority which is not slow to make itself felt" (p. 660).

54 Put Them All Out These words are not in the earliest Greek manuscripts. They were brought over by a later scribe from Mark 5:40 and so do not belong here in an accurate version of the Bible.

9:1 Called . . . Together The verb *synkaleō* (*kaleō*, "call"; *syn*, "together") is used (in NT) only by Luke (7 times) plus Mark 15:16. The disciples had been separated (8:51).

His Twelve Disciples The best Greek text simply has "the Twelve."

3 Scrip See discussion at Mark 6:8.

5 Shake Off Luke alone uses the verb *apotinassō* (here and Acts 28:5). Marshall comments: "The action of shaking off the dust of a gentile city from one's feet was practised by Jews; they removed what was ceremonially unclean before returning to their own land, lest they should defile it" (p. 354). In this case it was a "testimony" that the town which rejected the gospel was unclean; its people were not a part of the true Israel.

7 Perplexed *Diaporeō* is another Lukan term (only here and Acts 2:12; 5:24; 10:17). The prefix *dia* could suggest "greatly perplexed" (NASB). Abbott-Smith says that the verb means "to be quite at a loss, be in great perplexity" (p. 110).

9 Beheaded The verb *apokephalizō* occurs (in NT) only here and in the parallel passages (Matt. 14:10; Mark 6:16, 28). It comes from *kephalē*, "head," and *apo*, "away from."

10 Went Aside The verb *hypochōreō* is another Lukan term (only here and 5:16; see discussion there).

12 Victuals *Episitismos* (only here in NT) comes from *sitos*, "wheat," then "grain" in general. So it means "provision."

14 Company *Klisia* (only here in NT) is in the plural (*klisias*). So it should be translated "groups." This noun comes from the verb *klinō*, "recline." Here the reference is to people reclining to eat.

20 But Whom . . . ? See discussion at Matt. 16:15.

29 Glistering This is the present participle of the verb *exastraptō* (only here in NT). It means "to flash out like lightning, to shine, be radiant" (Thayer, p. 222).

31 Decease Today this term means "death." But the Greek word here is *exodos*—literally, the "way out," and so "departure." It is this word, in its Latin form "exodus," which is used for the Israelites leaving Egypt.

The primary reference is probably to Jesus' death, which soon occurred at Jerusalem. But we should include His resurrection and ascension as His "departure" to heaven. In the light of the Exodus under Moses, the thought of salvation should also be included.

32 When They Were Awake This is all one word in Greek, the aorist participle of *diagrēgoreō* (only here in NT). The simple verb *grēgoreō* means "be awake." So the compound would mean "be fully awake."

There is a great deal of debate as to what is signified here. Several commentators argue that the disciples "remained awake," in spite of their drowsiness. Alford translates it "having kept awake" (*Greek Testament*, 1:530). The NASB goes the other way: "Now Peter and his companions had been overcome with sleep; but when they were fully awake. . . ." The NIV tries to leave the door a bit open by saying: "Peter and his companions were very sleepy, but when they became fully awake. . . ." That is probably the best we can do with this passage.

33 Departed Verses 31 and 32, plus the first clause of 33, are found only in Luke. (The Transfiguration is also recorded in Matt. 17:1–8 and Mark 9:2–8.) The verb for "departed" is *diachōrizomai* (only here in NT). The infinitive phrase means "while they were beginning to go away."

Tabernacles See discussion at Mark 9:5.

35 My Beloved Son Instead of *agapētos* (used here by Matthew and Mark), Luke has *eklelegmenos*, the perfect passive participle of *eklegō*, "choose." This is found in Papyri 45 and 75 of the third century and in both fourth-century manuscripts—our oldest witnesses. So the correct translation is "This is My Son, My Chosen One" (NASB) or "This is my Son whom I have chosen" (NIV).

36 Kept It Close The Greek is *esigēsan*, the aorist of *sigaō*, which simply means to "be silent." So "kept silent" (NASB) catches it.

39 Teareth The verb is *sparassō* (only here and Mark 1:26; 9:26). It means "convulse," and so here "throws him into convulsions."

42 Tare See discussion at Mark 9:20.

43 Mighty Power The single Greek word is *megaleiotēs* (only here and Acts 19:27; 2 Pet. 1:16). It means "grandeur, sublimity, majesty." The simplest meaning is "greatness." In 2 Pet. 1:16 the reference is to the Transfiguration, which Peter witnessed.

45 Hid This is the perfect passive participle of *parakalyptō* (only here in NT). This is an intensive compound of *kalyptō*, "cover." So it means "completely covered over." Today we would say "hidden" (NIV) or "concealed" (NASB).

46 Reasoning The word is *dialogismos*. Here it clearly means "argument."

49 Forbad This is the imperfect of *kōlyō*, "hinder, restrain." It means "tried to stop him" (NIV).

51 Received Up In the Greek there is a noun, *analēmpsis* (only here in NT), which means "a taking up," and so "His ascension" (NASB).

10:1 Appointed Luke alone uses the verb *anadeiknymi* (here and Acts 1:24). It was used by classical Greek writers in the sense of "appoint" or "commission."

Seventy The manuscript evidence for either "seventy" or "seventy-two" is very divided. Our third-century papyrus (75) and fourth-century Vaticanus have 72. But the other fourth-century manuscript, Sinaiticus, has 70. One fifth-century manuscript (D) has 72, while the other three (A, C, W) have 70. We would agree with Geldenhuys that "it seems impossible to decide" which is the original reading.

3 Lambs The word *arēn* (pl. *arnas*) occurs only here in the NT. It emphasizes how helpless the disciples were in themselves as they faced the "wolves" of opposition.

4 Purse Luke alone uses *ballantion* (here; 12:33; 22:35–36). It was an old Greek term for a money bag.

Scrip See discussion at Mark 6:8.

Shoes See discussion at Mark 1:7.

Salute The verb *aspazomai*, "greet," is common in the NT. But the command here to "greet no one on the way" seems strange. The reason for it is that oriental greetings were "long and time-consuming" (Marshall, p. 418). The disciples were on a brief, urgent mission. They must not palaver on the road.

5 Peace The common Hebrew greeting is still "Shalom." The Greek word is *eirēnē*. In the NT this "peace" is associated with salvation. W. Foerster writes: "The greeting which they give on entering a house is not a wish. It is a gift which is either received or rejected as such" (TDNT, 2:413).

6 Son of Peace This is a common expression in both Hebrew and Greek. Primarily it means "a peaceable person." Here it probably suggests a person worthy of peace, or willing to accept God's peace.

11 Cleaveth The verb is *kollaō*, to "glue." Today we would say "sticks to our feet" (NIV).

Wipe Off Luke likes compound words, as does Paul. The verb is *apomassō* (only here in NT), "wipe off" or "wipe clean."

15 Which Art Exalted to Heaven This should be translated as a question, and the Greek *mē* indicates that a negative answer is expected: "And you, Capernaum, will not be exalted to heaven, will you?" (NASB). Marshall comments: "The force of the question, 'Do you really expect to be raised to heaven because I visited you?' " (p. 425).

Hell See discussion at Matt. 11:23.

16 Heareth The very common verb *akouō* "is used here in the sense of hearing and accepting" (Marshall, p. 426). This is brought out in modern English by "listens to" (NASB, NIV), which means "obeys."

Despiseth The verb *atheteō* basically means to "set aside" or "do away with." So here it means "rejects." The one who rejects the messenger rejects the message, and so the ultimate Messenger, Christ Himself.

20 Written We do not have here the simple verb *graphō*, "write," but *engraphō*, "engrave." G. Schrenk notes that this compound verb was used of solemn "entry in a document" and "always with a sense of something firmly laid down in a written compact." It was used frequently by Philo in connection with a list of citizens. In Luke 10:20, "The well-known image from civic life is combined with the biblical conception of inscription in a book—the book of life" (TDNT, 1:769).

21 Rejoiced See discussion at Luke 1:47.

In Spirit Most scholars are agreed that the best Greek text reads: "in the Holy Spirit." This is in line with Luke's strong emphasis on the Holy Spirit. "In spirit" would mean in His own spirit—that is, inwardly.

Thank In the KJV the verb *exomologeō* is correctly translated "confess"—its basic meaning in the middle, as here—in 8 out of its 11 occurrences. It is also correctly rendered "promise" in Luke 22:6, where it is active. But "thank" (here and Matt. 11:25) is not found in the lexicons. The right word is "praise."

22 Will Reveal This sounds like a simple future tense. But the Greek has *bouletai . . . apocalypsai*—"wills to reveal" (NASB) or "chooses to reveal" (NIV).

25 Lawyer *Nomikos* (from *nomos*, "law") occurs once in Matthew (22:35) and 6 times in Luke's Gospel, plus twice in Titus (3:9, 13). Since "lawyer" today means an attorney, the NIV has translated *nomikos* all 7 times in the

Gospels as "an expert in the law"—that is, the Mosaic law.

Tempted The Greek has *ekpeirazōn*, "testing Him out." He wanted to see how Jesus would answer a theological question.

30 Went Down The KJV implies that the robbery took place after the man arrived at his destination. But the Greek clearly says that he "was going down" the Jericho Road when it happened (imperfect tense).

Thieves The Greek does not have *kleptais*, "thieves," but *lēstais*, "robbers" (NASB, NIV). There is a difference.

Half Dead The adjective *hēmithanēs* (only here in NT) is compounded of *hēmi*, "half," and the stem *than*, meaning "dead."

31 Chance *Synkyria* (only here in NT) means "chance" or "coincidence."

31–32 He Passed By on the Other Side This is all one word in the Greek, the second aorist of the verb *antiparerchomai* (only here in NT). *Erchomai* means "go," *para* "beside," and *anti* "opposite to."

33 As He Journeyed This is the present participle of *hodeuō* (only here in NT), which comes from the noun *hodos*, "way" or "road." So it means "as he traveled."

34 Bound Up This is the verb *katadeō* (only here in NT). It is an intensive compound of *deō*, "bind," and so means "bind up." It was a medical term. The Samaritan did a thorough job.

Wounds The noun *trauma* is found only here in the NT. We have taken the word over into English, but we use it for emotional, rather than physical, wounds.

Pouring In *Epicheō* (only here in NT) is from *cheō*, "pour," and *epi*, "upon." The Samaritan poured "oil" as a salve and "wine" for an antiseptic (alcohol) *on* the man's wounds.

Beast *Ktēnos* means a domestic animal, not a wild animal. This animal was a "donkey," a small animal which was the common beast of burden then—as in the Holy Land even today.

Inn The word here is *pandocheion* (only here in NT). This was an actual inn, where a traveler might find lodging. For another kind of "inn" (KJV), see discussion at 2:7.

35 Host This is *pandocheus* (only here in NT). It is compounded of *pas*, "all," and *dechomai* "welcome"—one who welcomed all travelers. It should be translated "innkeeper" (NASB, NIV).

Thou Spendest More This is the verb *prosdapanaō* (only here in NT). It comes from *dapanaō*, "spend," and *pros*, "in addition to" (AG, p. 709).

40 Was Cumbered The verb *perispaō* (only here in NT) means "*be pulled* or *dragged away*," and so "*become* or *be distracted, quite busy, overburdened*" (AG, p. 650).

Help A short word in English, but a long word in Greek—*synantilabētai*. It is compounded of *lambanō*, "take," *anti*, "over against," and *syn*, "with." So it means "to take hold with at the side." It is used (in NT) only here and in Rom. 8:26.

41 Thou Art Careful The Greek word *merimnas* really means "you are worried" (NASB, NIV).

Troubled The verb *thorybazō* indicates that Martha was "bothered" (NASB) or "upset" (NIV).

11:2 Hallowed Be See discussion at Matt. 6:9.

4 Sins See discussion of "debts" at Matt. 6:12.

7 Shut This is the perfect tense of *kleiō*, which means "shut, lock, bar" (AG, p. 434). The context indicates that the best translation is "locked"—that is, with a bar inside that fastened the door securely against intruders. When the man said, "I can't" (NIV), he meant "I won't."

Bed Several different words are used for "bed" in the Gospels, but *koitē* occurs only here. Elsewhere in the NT it is found only in Heb. 13:4 ("marriage bed," NIV), in Rom. 9:10 (of conception), and in Rom. 13:13 ("sexual immorality," NIV). Luke alone uses the term here in its primary and general meaning of "bed."

8 Importunity The Greek word is *anaideia* (only here in NT). In its original, literal sense it

meant "shamelessness." Marshall comments: "This can mean the attitude of the man at the door, his 'sheer impudence' in coming at such an hour with his request, or less probably his 'unblushing persistence' in continuing to demand an answer" (p. 465). It does seem, however, that "persistence" is the best rendering here.

17 Thoughts Six different Greek words are translated as "thought" (noun) in the KJV. This one is *dianoēma* (only here in NT), which comes from *dia*, "through," and a derivation of *nous*, "mind." It seems to say that Jesus "knew what was going through their minds."

17–18 Divided The common verb for "divide" is *merizō*, used throughout the NT. But here we have the compound *diamerizō*. It occurs twice in Matthew, once in Mark, and once in John; but 6 times in Luke, and twice in Acts. This reflects Luke's fondness for compound words.

20 Finger of God *Daktylos*, "finger," occurs 8 times in the NT. Elsewhere it is used literally. But here it means the power of God. In his parallel passage, Matthew (12:28) has "Spirit of God."

21 Armed This is the perfect passive participle of *kathoplizō* (only here in NT), which means to "arm fully." So the correct translation is "fully armed" (NASB, NIV). The verb is compounded of *kata* (intensive) and *hopla*, "arms, weapons."

Keepeth The verb is *phylassē*. It means "guards."

Palace Why is this KJV rendering changed to "homestead" in the NASB and "house" in the NIV? Arndt and Gingrich give these definitions for the Greek word here (*aulē*): (1) "courtyard"; (2) "farm, house"; (3) "(outer) court;" of the temple; (4) "the (court) of a prince," and so "palace." They prefer 2 here, but would allow 4.

22 Armor The Greek word is *panoplia*, compounded of *pan*, "all," and *hopla*, "arms." Elsewhere in the NT it occurs only in Eph. 6:11, 13, where it is translated "whole armor" (of God). See discussion there.

25 Garnished The verb *cosmeō* comes from the noun *cosmos*, the earliest meaning of which was "order." So the verb meant "to order, arrange, prepare." But just as the noun came to mean "ornament, adornment," so the verb finally meant "to adorn, furnish" (A-S, pp. 254–55). Here the idea is, "put in order."

29 Were Gathered Thick Together   This is the present participle of *epathroizō* (only here in NT), which means "assemble beside." "The people" (KJV) is in Greek "the crowds." The idea, then, is "as the crowds increased" (NIV; cf. NASB).

37–38 Dine . . . Dinner   The first word is the verb *aristaō*, the second is the noun *ariston*. The latter is found also in 14:12 and Matt. 22:4 ("dinner," KJV). The former occurs again in John 21:12, 15. The *ariston* was the morning meal among the Jews, so "dinner" in the modern context is incorrect. The more general term "meal" is a better rendering.

38 Washed   The Greek verb is *baptizō*, "ceremonially washed" (NASB). This custom before meals, prescribed by the Pharisees, was not required by the original Mosaic law.

40 Ye Fools   This is one word in the Greek, *aphrones*. The adjective *aphrōn* comes from *alpha*-negative and *phrēn*, "mind." So it means "without reason, senseless, foolish" (A-S, p. 72). A better translation, then, is "You foolish ones" (NASB) or "You foolish people!" (NIV).

41 Such Things as Ye Have   The Greek is *ta enonta*—literally, "the things being inside" (present participle of *eneimi*); that is, "what is inside." The Pharisees were full of greed inside (v. 39). They needed to "give alms from the heart" (*Grammar*, 3:247).

42 Rue   The Greek word *pēganon* is found only here in the NT. It was "a plant about 3 feet high with grey-green foliage and yellow flowers" (Marshall, p. 497).

43 Uppermost Seats   *Prōtokathedria* is translated "chief seats" in Matt. 23:6; Mark 12:39; and "highest seats" in Luke 20:46 (the only other NT occurrences of the term). It means "the front seats" (NASB).

44 Which Appear Not   This is the adjective *adēlos*, "unseen, unobserved" (only here and 1 Cor. 14:8). Here it probably refers to "unmarked graves" (NIV).

46 Grievous to Be Borne   This is the adjective *dysbastaktos* (only here in NT). It means "hard to bear" (NASB).

53 To Urge   This is the present infinitive of *apostomatizō*, which meant "to question" (NASB) or "besiege him with questions" (NIV).

54 Catch   *Thēreuō* (only here in NT) was a term used in hunting, for catching one's prey. It can mean "ensnare." The Pharisees were trying to catch Jesus in a trap by getting Him to say something unwise.

12:1 An Innumerable Multitude of People

The Greek literally says "the myriads (*myriadōn*) of the crowd" (*ochlou*). The Greek word *myrias* (genitive, *myriados*) means "ten thousand." Here it is used "hyperbolically, of vast numbers" (A-S, p. 298). The whole expression may be translated "a crowd of many thousands."

14 Divider   This rendering of the noun *meristēs* (only here in NT) has the advantage of showing the connection with the verb *merizō* ("divide") in verse 13. But today we would say "arbiter."

16 Brought Forth Plentifully   This is a good translation of the single word *euphorēsen*, from which we get "euphoric." The verb *euphoreō* (only here in NT) literally means "bear well."

17–18 Bestow   The Greek verb is *synagō*, which means "gather together." A better translation is "store." "Fruits" in verse 18 is *siton*, literally "wheat," and then "grain" (NASB, NIV).

20 Fool   See discussion at Luke 11:40.

22 Take No Thought   See discussion at Matt. 6:25.

24 Ravens   Luke has the term *korax* (only here in NT). Matthew (6:26) has "birds."

25 Stature   The Greek word is *hēlikia*, which Abbott-Smith says indicated "a stage of growth whether measured by age or stature" (p. 199). The only place in the NT where it is unmistakably used for "stature" is Luke 19:3. J. Schneider says that in Matt. 6:27 and Luke 12:25 "the context demands that *hēlikia* should mean 'span of life' and that *pēchus* ['cubit'] should be a measure of time. Jesus is saying that anxious care is futile. No one can thereby add even a fraction to his life" (TDNT, 2:942). See further discussion at Luke 2:52. A good translation here is: "Who of you by worrying can add a single hour to his life?" (NIV). The irony is that worry will actually shorten our lives!

29 Neither Be Ye of Doubtful Mind This is the negative *mē* with the verb *meteōrizō* (only here in NT), which literally means to "be in midair"—perhaps like our being "all up in the air" about something. The verb comes from the adjective *meteōros*, which Arndt and Gingrich say suggests "hovering between hope and fear, restless, anxious" (p. 514).

K. Deissner notes that in the Septuagint the verb has the bad sense of lifting oneself up, being arrogant. But in one papyrus it clearly means "Do not be upset" (TDNT, 4:630). Martin Luther had, "Do not fly high."

After noting the preceding and following verses here, Deissner concludes: "In this context, the only admonition which makes sense is that we be not anxious, unsettled or insecure, since God guarantees all gifts" (p. 631). So perhaps the best rendering is "Do not keep worrying" (NASB) or "Do not worry about it" (NIV).

35 Loins . . . Girded About This is clearly the literal meaning of the Greek, but hardly contemporary language. In those days men wore loose garments without a belt while resting in the house. But they put a belt around their waist before going out or beginning to work. So the idea here is: "Be dressed ready for service"—as suggested by verse 37 where the same verb occurs.

39 Goodman of the House See discussion at Matt. 24:43.

42 Portion of Meat This is one word in Greek, *sitometrion* (only here in NT). *Sitos* literally means "wheat" and *metrion* "measure." So the compound indicates "a measured allowance of food," or simply "food allowance."

49 What Will I . . . Kindled? The KJV renders the Greek quite literally. But Marshall indicates that Semitic usage supports this translation: "How I wish that it was already kindled" (p. 546). Incidentally the verb for "kindled," *anaptō*, occurs (in NT) only here and in Jas. 3:5.

50 Am I Straitened This is the verb *synechomai*, which literally means "I am held together." For this passage Arndt and Gingrich suggest: "How great is my distress" (p. 789). But H. Koester prefers: "How I am totally governed by this" (TDNT, 7:884). Jesus was looking earnestly forward to completing His task.

51 Division The noun *diamerismos* is found only here in the NT. It is a strong term, meaning "dissension, disunity" (AG, p. 186).

54 Shower The Greek *ombros* (only here in NT) is a strong word, meaning "rain-storm, thunderstorm" (AG, p. 565).

58 Hale The verb *katasyrō* (only here in NT) means "drag away" or "drag off."

Officer The Greek word *praktōr* (only here in NT) indicates "one who executes sentence on debtors who are unwilling or unable to pay" (K. H. Rengstorf, TDNT, 7:539).

13:2, 4 Sinners The Greek has two different words for "sinners" in these two verses. In verse 2 it is *hamartōlos*, the most common word for "sinner" (47 times in NT). In verse 4 it is *opheiletēs*, which properly means "debtor" and is so translated (KJV) 5 of the 7 times it occurs in the NT. Only here is it rendered "sinner." It is translated "culprits" in the NASB and "guilty" in the NIV, to differentiate it from the word in verse 2. It must be admitted, however, that in the Aramaic the same word was used for "debts" and "sins" (cf. Matt. 6:12; Luke 11:4).

7 Dresser of His Vineyard This is one word in the Greek, *ampelourgon* (only here in NT). It is compounded of *ampelōn*, "vineyard," and *ergon*, "work." So it means "worker in a vineyard."

Cumbereth The verb is *katargeō*, which literally means to "make idle or inactive." In the NT it is used in its literal sense only here—"use up." Marshall comments: "The tree not only takes up space, but in fact exhausts the ground by taking nourishment from it" (p. 555).

8 Dung It The Greek has *balō kopria* (neut. pl.)—literally, "put manure" (on it). (The word *koprion* occurs only here in the NT.) A good translation is "put in fertilizer" (NASB) or "fertilize it" (NIV).

11 Bowed Together This is the present participle of the verb *synkyptō* (only here in NT), which means "bent over."

Lift Up Herself The verb *anakyptō* means "straighten oneself." Probably the whole expression here is best translated "could not straighten up at all" (NASB, NIV). According to

Hobart (*Medical Language of St. Luke*, pp. 20–22) the verb here was a technical medical term.

22 *Journeying* The Greek has the present participle of *poieō*—"making"—and *poreia*, "way" or "journey." This is well represented by "as he made his way."

24 *Strive* The Greek verb is *agōnizō*, from which we get "agonize." It was originally used mainly for striving to win in an athletic competition, particularly in the marathon race. On Jesus' saying here Ethelbert Stauffer writes: "The struggle for the kingdom of heaven allows of no indolence, indecision or relaxation. Only those who press into it can attain entrance" (TDNT, 1:137). The NIV has here: "Make every effort."

Strait The adjective *stenos* (only here and Matt. 7:13–14) means "narrow."

29 *Sit Down* The verb *anaklinō* means to "recline at table" (NASB). So it could be translated "take their places at the feast" (NIV). This reminds us of the marriage supper of the Lamb.

32 *I Shall Be Perfected* This is one word in Greek, *teleioumai*. The verb *teleioō* comes from *telos*, "end." So it means "reach the end" or "complete." Probably Jesus was not talking about perfection of character. Rather, what He meant was, "I will reach my goal" (NIV; cf. NASB).

14:1 *Watched* See discussion at Mark 3:2.

2 *Had the Dropsy* The Greek says that the man was *hydrōpikos*. This adjective (only here in NT) means "suffering from dropsy"—a disease that causes the body to swell up because of fluid forming in the cavities and tissues.

3 *Lawyers* See discussion at Luke 10:25.

5 *Pit* The word is *phrear*, which is translated "well" in John 4:11–12 (KJV)—the standard definition in lexicons. It is perhaps best here.

Donkey The Greek text underlying the KJV has *onos*, "donkey." But our three oldest manuscripts of Luke (Papyri 45 and 75 of the 3rd century and Vaticanus of the 4th century) have *whios*, "son" (see NASB, NIV). "A donkey or an ox" might seem to be a more logical combination. But Plummer suggests that the meaning is: "when your son, or even your ox, falls into a well" (p. 355).

7 *Chief Rooms* This is one word in the Greek, *prōtoklisias*. *Prōtos* means "first" or "chief"; *klisia* means a place of reclining at the table (on couches), as the wealthy people did in that day. So this compound word means "places of honor at the table."

8 *Sit . . . Highest Room* The Greek has: *mē kataklithēs eis tēn prōtoklisian*: "Do not recline in the place of honor."

9–10 *The Lowest Room* *Ton eschaton topon* is literally "the last place" (NASB).

10 *Go Up* This is a double compound in Greek, the verb *prosanabainō* (only here in NT). *Bainō* means "go," *ana* "up," and *pros* "to."

12 *Dinner* The Greek is *ariston ē deipnon*—the earlier and later of the usual two meals a day eaten at that time in the late morning and late afternoon. In the culture of our day this would be "a luncheon or dinner."

13 *Feast* See discussion at Luke 5:29.

13, 21 *Maimed* The Greek adjective *anapeiros* (only here in NT) means "crippled."

28 *Count . . . Cost* The verb *psēphizō* (only here and Rev. 13:18) comes from *psēphos*, "a pebble." So it literally means to "count" or "calculate" (NASB) with pebbles. The NIV uses "estimate."

The noun is *dapanē* (only here in NT). It means "cost" or "expense."

To Finish The Greek literally says "for completion"—*apartismos* (only here in NT). In verses 29 and 30 "to finish" is the verb *ekteleō* (only here in NT).

32 *Ambassage* The noun *presbeia* (only here and 19:14) comes from the verb *presbeuō*, "be an ambassador." It literally means "an embassy," but here is used in the concrete sense of "ambassadors" (AG, p. 699). It may be translated "a delegation."

35 *Dunghill* The word *kopria* is found only here and in 13:8 (which see). Today we would say "the manure pile."

15:2 *Murmured* The compound *diagongyzō* (only here and 19:7) means "grumble" (NASB)—perhaps "aloud" (AG, p. 182). It is stronger than the simple *gongyzō*, which occurs eight times in the NT.

Receiveth *Lambanō* means "receive." *Dechomai* is stronger, meaning "welcome." But the verb here is *prosdechomai,* "welcome to" (Himself). The separatistic Pharisees were shocked that Jesus would socialize with "sinners"— those who did not observe meticulously the ceremonial rites. The Pharisees would never eat with such people lest they be defiled.

6 Friends . . . Neighbors These words are both masculine in the Greek. "Friends" is *philous. Geitonas,* "neighbors," can be either, but the definite article with it is masculine. The man would naturally call together only his male friends and neighbors, especially in that culture.

8 Pieces of Silver The Greek word is *drachmas* (only here and v. 9, where it is sing.). This was the basic Greek silver coin, worth about the same as the Roman *denarius* (about 20¢). It is often suggested that the 10 drachmas may have been the woman's dowry. So they had a special sentimental value.

Diligently The adverb is *epimelōs* (only here in NT). Since the stem *mel* means "care," the translation "carefully" is accurate.

9 Friends . . . Neighbors Very appropriately the Greek words here are feminine— *philas* and *geitonas* with the feminine definite article. The woman would share her joys only with other women. See discussion at Luke 15:6.

12 The Portion of Goods That Falleth to Me "Portion" is the common *meros,* which means "part" or "share." The Greek for "goods" is *ousia* (only here and v. 13 in NT). It means "property" or "possession." The expression "portion that falleth to me" is *to epiballon meros.* Adolf Deissmann notes that this is "a technical formula, also used in the Papyri," and especially "of the paternal inheritance" (BS, p. 230). The whole expression above can be translated "my share of the estate." Since he was the younger son, this would be only one-third of the family estate (Deut. 21:17).

13 Gathered . . . Together The verb *synagō* probably means "turn into cash" (Marshall, p. 607; cf. AG, p. 782). The father's property would need to be converted into usable currency before the son went on his journey.

Wasted The verb *diaskorpizō* means to "scatter abroad," and so here "squandered" (NASB, NIV).

Riotous The adverb *asōtōs* (only here in NT) means "dissolutely, loosely," used "of debauched, profligate living" (AG, p. 119). It describes a "dissipated life" (Foerster, TDNT, 1:507).

16 Husks The Greek word *keration* literally means "little horn." It was used in the plural (as here) for pods of the carob tree, which still grows in that part of the world. There is an interesting rabbinical statement that fits this parable: "When the Israelites are reduced to carob pods, then they repent" (quoted by Marshall, p. 609).

25 Music . . . Dancing The first word is *symphonia,* from which we get "symphony." It literally means "a sounding together." The second word is *choros,* from which we get "chorus." Both words are found only here in the NT.

29 Serve The verb *douleuō* literally means "be a slave to." This is caught in the NIV: "All these years I've been slaving for you."

16:1 Accused
The verb is *diaballō* (only here in NT). In the Greek of that period we find it used with the meaning: "*bring charges with hostile intent,* either falsely and slanderously . . . or justly" (AG, p. 181).

Measures The *batos* (only here in NT) was a Hebrew liquid measure called a "bath" in the OT. According to Josephus (*Ant.* 8:57), it held about eight gallons.

7 Bill The Greek word is *grammata* (pl.). In the singular (*gramma;* cf. "grammar") it originally meant a letter of the alphabet (see discussion at Gal. 6:11). Then, mostly in the plural, it came to mean "a document" or "piece of writing." Arndt and Gingrich suggest for here: "a promissory note" (p. 165).

Measures The *koros* (only here in NT) was a Hebrew dry measure called "*cor*" in the OT. According to Josephus (*Ant.* 15:314) it held about 10 bushels.

8 Wisely *Phronimōs* (only here in NT) comes from *phrēn* (*phrenos,* gen.), "mind." So it means that the manager used his head in this situation. "Wisely" (KJV) is not the best translation because wisdom in the Bible always carries a moral connotation; the "wise man" is the one who does right. So "shrewdly" (NASB, NIV) is the better rendering. Similarly "wiser" should be "more shrewd."

9 Ye Fail The Greek says "it fails" (NASB)—*eklipē* (third sing.)—that is, when money is gone.

13 Serve See discussion at Matt. 6:24.

14 Who Were Covetous This is one word in Greek, the adjective *philargyros* (only here and 2 Tim. 3:2). It means "loving money"—so, "who loved money."

Derided This is a very strong verb in Greek, *ekmyktērizō* (only here and 23:35). It literally means "turn up the nose"—and so, "were sneering at Jesus" (NIV).

16 Presseth The verb is *biazō*, which occurs (in NT) only here and in Matt. 11:12 (see discussion there).

17 Tittle See discussion at Matt. 5:18, the only other place where *keraia* occurs in the NT.

19 Fared Sumptuously The verb is *euphrainō*, which is used four times in chapter 15 (vv. 23–24, 29, 32) in the sense of making merry. The adverb is *lamprōs* (only here in NT), which means "splendidly." The combination may be translated "gaily living in splendor" (NASB) or "lived in luxury" (NIV).

20 Full of Sores This is one word, the perfect (hence, "full of") passive participle of *helkoō* (only here in NT), a common Greek medical term. Today we would say, "covered with sores."

21 Licked The verb *epileichō* occurs only here in the NT. Was Luke the physician, who alone records this story, thinking of a possible healing effect? We would agree with what R. C. H. Lenski (contrary to many commentators) says here: "These dogs licked the beggar's sores as they would have licked their own to clean and to ease them with their soft tongues. Dogs did that, no one else would" (p. 848).

23 Hell This is the Greek word *hadēs*, which (in KJV) is translated "hell" 10 of the 11 times it occurs in the Textus Receptus. (In 1 Cor. 15:55 it is "grave.") It means "the underworld as the place of the dead" (AG, p. 16). In Rev. 21:14 we are told that "death and Hades were thrown into the lake of fire" which "is the second death" (hell) (NIV). The word is transliterated properly in the NIV as "Hades" everywhere but here. It would be preferred here as well, as in NASB.

26 Gulf The Greek word is *chasma* (only here in NT), from which we get "chasm." That is the best translation.

17:1 Offences This is the basic translation (KJV) of the Greek *scandala* (plural) 10 out of the 15 times in the NT. It is the word from which we get "scandal." A more adequate translation is "stumbling-blocks" (NASB), or, better still, "things that cause people to sin" (NIV; see AG, p. 753). Gustav Staehlin writes: "The *scandalon* is an obstacle in coming to faith and a cause of going astray in it" (TDNT, 7:345). See also discussion at Matt. 5:29–30.

2 Offend See discussion at Matt. 5:29–30.

3 Trespass Against Thee All the Greek has is *hamartē* (2 aorist subj. of *hamartanō*, to "sin"). So the correct translation is "If your brother sins" (NASB, NIV)—not just "against thee." However, "against you" is genuine in verse 4.

6 Sycamine This is practically a transliteration of the Greek *sycaminos* (only here in NT). In 19:4 we have *sycomorea* (only there in NT). Hunzinger writes: "The fact that Lk. seems to make a distinction between the two favours the view that he follows more precise usage and is referring to the mulberry [in 17:6]. But in the light of LXX usage and contemporary examples he might just as well be speaking of the sycamore fig, which was especially firm and deeply rooted" (TDNT, 7:758). He agrees that in 19:4 *sycomorea* "can denote only the sycamore fig" (p. 758).

Considering all the evidence, it seems best to use "sycamore" in 19:4 and "mulberry" in 17:6. *Sycē* means "a fig tree." So both these were a species of fig tree.

7 Feeding Cattle This is one Greek word, the present participle of the verb *poimainō*. It comes from *poimēn*—masculine, "a shepherd"; feminine, "a flock of sheep." So the verb means "tending sheep" (NASB) or "looking after the sheep" (NIV).

By and By The Greek word here, *eutheōs*, always means "immediately" (NASB), never "by and by." See also discussion at Mark 1:12.

20 With Observation The Greek uses *meta* ("with") and *paratērēsis* (only here in NT). The noun comes from the verb *paratēreō*, "watch closely." Arndt and Gingrich translate the passage here: "*The Kingdom of God is not coming* *with observation* i.e., in such a way that its rise can be observed" (p. 622). The Pharisees were looking for spectacular signs to hail the coming of the Kingdom. But Jesus replied, "The kingdom of God does not come visibly" (NIV).

21 Within You Jesus went on to explain why the Kingdom would not come visibly: "The kingdom of God is within you" (KJV, NIV). Some commentators and translators prefer "in your midst" (NASB). But the Greek preposition here is not *en*, "in"; it is *entos* (only here and Matt. 23:26), which means "within." Alfred Plummer discusses both translations. His conclusion is that if "within you" is adopted, the meaning will be, "Instead of being something externally visible, the Kingdom is essentially spiritual; it is in your hearts, if you possess it at all" (p. 406). It would seem that this is what Jesus meant.

37 Eagles It is generally agreed by commentators that here and in Matt. 24:28 *aetoi* means "vultures." This is shown by the fact that in Matthew the word for body (*ptōma*) means "dead body."

18:1 Faint Abbott-Smith (p. 154) says that the verb *engkakeō* comes from *kakos*, "cowardly," and so means "lose heart" (cf. NASB). Arndt and Gingrich prefer for this passage "become weary, tired" (p. 215). Grundmann agrees: "not grow weary" (TDNT, 3:486). When the answer is delayed, we should "not give up" (NIV).

2, 4 Regard The verb *entrepō* in the middle (as here) means "have regard for, respect." This judge neither reverenced God nor respected man—two wonderful qualifications for a judge!

3 Came The verb *erchomai* is here in the imperfect tense: "kept coming."

Avenge The verb *ekdikeō* does sometimes mean "avenge." But here the verb is followed in the Greek by *apo*, "from." So the idea is, "Give me legal protection from my opponent" (NASB) or "Grant me justice against my adversary" (NIV; cf. AG, p. 238; TDNT, 2:444). Plummer says that the meaning is "preserve me against his attacks" (p. 412).

5 Troubleth The Greek literally says, "keeps causing me trouble," and so, "keeps bothering me."

Weary Me This is a weak translation for the verb *hypōpiazō*, which literally means "to strike under the eye, give a black eye" (A-S, p. 463). It seems unlikely that the woman would dare to strike the judge in the face. But he may have feared that the woman would "give him a black eye" in the community. The least translation we can use is "wear me out" (RSV, NASB, NIV).

7–8 Avenge Here we have the verb *poieō*, "do" or "make," and the noun *ekdikēsis*, "vindication." Arndt and Gingrich translate this: "see to it that justice is done" (p. 238). The simplest translation is "bring about justice."

12 I Possess The verb here, *ktaomai*, means "get, gain, acquire" (A-S, p. 259), not "possess." We do not pay tithes on our possessions, but on our income. So the correct rendering is "all I get."

25 Needle In their parallel passages Matthew (19:24) and Mark (10:25) have *hraphis*, which means a sewing needle. But Luke the physician has *belonē* (only here in NT). W. K. Hobart (*Medical Language of St. Luke*, p. 60) says this was a surgical needle (cf. also William Hendriksen, p. 847).

42 Saved The verb *sōzō* occurs 111 times in the NT. It is translated (KJV) "save" 94 times, "make whole" or "be whole" 11 times, "heal" 3 times, plus 3 other ways. In the Gospels and the first part of Acts it is used frequently for physical healing. In the latter part of Acts and in the Epistles it almost always refers to spiritual salvation. (Exceptions are 1 Tim. 2:15; Jas. 5:15; Jude 5.) Since the reference here in Luke is to physical condition, the correct translation is "made you well" (NASB) or "healed you" (NIV).

19:4 Sycamore See discussion at Luke 17:6.

8 Taken . . . by False Accusation See discussion at Luke 3:14.

Fourfold Here we have the adjective *tetraplous* (only here in NT) used as an adverb. It means "four times as much."

11 He Added and Spake The first verb is *prostithēmi*, which does mean "add." But we have here a special combination that means "he proceeded to tell" (AG, p. 919).

12 A Certain Nobleman The Greek says "a certain man *eugenēs*"—literally "well-born," and so the translation, "a man of noble birth."

13 Pounds The Greek word is *mnas*, which occurs (in NT) only here and in verses 16, 18, 20, 24–25. It is easier for us to use the Latin form "minas." The Greek *mina* was worth 100 drachmas, or about $20.00.

Occupy The verb *pragmateuomai* (only here in NT) means "do business" or "trade." The idea is caught well in the NIV: "Put this money to work."

14 Message This is *presbeia*, which was translated "ambassage" in 14:32—the only other place in the NT where it occurs (see discussion there). A good translation is "a delegation."

We Will Not Have The Greek is *ou thelomen:* "We don't want" (NIV; cf. NASB). The verb *thelō* means "wish" or "desire."

15 Every Man Had Gained by Trading This is all one word in Greek, the aorist middle participle of the verb *diapragmateuomai* (only here in NT). The prefix *dia* means "through"—so "gained through trading" (cf. "occupy," v. 13).

16 Gained This is a different verb, *prosergazomai* (only here in NT), which means "to gain besides, by working or trading" (A-S, p. 384) or "make more, earn in addition" (AG, p. 713). This servant had gained 1,000 percent profit!

17 Well This is the adverb *euge* (only here in NT). It means "Well done," which communicates the idea better than just "well."

20 Napkin The *soudarion* was "a scarf or neckcloth used to protect the back of the head from the sun" (Marshall, p. 706).

21–22 Austere This English word comes directly from the Greek adjective *austēros* (only here in NT). It means "severe, strict," or "exacting" (NASB).

23 Bank The Greek word is *trapeza*, which (except for "meat" in Acts 16:34) is translated (in KJV) "table" all the other 13 times it occurs in the NT. The reference here is to the money changers' tables (see Matt. 21:12; Mark 11:15; cf. John 2:15). Goppelt writes: "The most famil-

iar table of the artisan or trader is that of the moneychangers. . . . While other salesmen often displayed their wares on the ground, these put their coins on the table. . . . On this basis *trapeza* comes to have the transfer sense of 'bank' . . . to put (interest-bearing) money in the 'bank,' Lk. 19:23" (TDNT, 8:211).

Usury See discussion at Matt. 25:27.

27 Slay The strong compound, *katasphazō*, is found only here in the NT. It means "to slaughter, strike down." Again we note that Luke was fond of compounds, as was Paul. These were 2 vigorous, well-educated thinkers.

36 Spread Matthew (21:8) and Mark (11:8) both have the simple verb, *strōnnyō*. But again Luke uses a compound, *hypostrōnnyō* (only here in NT). It means "to spread out underneath." The people took off their outer cloaks and spread them out under Jesus on the road.

37 Descent Another compound, *katabasis* (only here in NT). It comes from the verb *katabainō*, "go down." Instead of going around the base of the Mount of Olives from Bethany (on the east side), Jesus and His company climbed the gentle slope to the summit overlooking the city to the west, and then began the descent toward Jerusalem.

43 Cast In this verse there are three *hapax legomena* (words found only once in NT). The first is the compound verb *paremballō*, "to throw up against"—a military term. The second is the noun *charax* ("trench"). It means a "palisade" or "rampart," built against the walls of a city so the attackers could surmount those walls and capture the city. The third word is the compound verb *periikyloō*, "to surround, encircle." Josephus uses the same word for the Roman armies surrounding Jerusalem in A.D. 70.

44 Lay . . . Even with the Ground This is one word, the verb *edaphizō* (only here in NT). It means "dash [you] to the ground." It can also mean "level [you] to the ground" (NASB). This all happened literally to Jerusalem in A.D. 70.

46 Thieves Again we note that the Greek word *lēstōn* means "robbers," not "thieves."

48 Were Very Attentive to Hear Him "Were very attentive" is the imperfect of the verb *ekkremannymi* (only here in NT), which means "hang on." So the whole expression means "were hanging upon His words" (NASB) or "hung on his words" (NIV).

20:5 Reasoned The verb is *syllogizomai* (only here in NT), which means to "reason, discuss, debate." Mark has the more common *dialogizomai* here, but Luke is fond of compounds with *syn*, as is also Paul.

6 Stone Again we have a compound verb, *katalithazō* (only here in NT). The prefix *kata* has the intensive force: "stone to death." *Lithos* is the common Greek noun for "a stone."

9 Let It Forth The verb *ekdidōmi* is found (in NT) only here and in the parallel passages (Matt. 21:33, 41; Mark 12:1). It means "let out for hire," and so "rented it out" (NASB).

9–10, 14, 16 Husbandmen The noun *geōrgos* comes from *gē*, "earth," and *ergon*, "work"; so it means "a tiller of the soil" or "farmer."

12 Wounded We have already noted the noun *trauma* in 10:34. Here we have the verb *traumatizō* (only here and Acts 19:16). Luke the physician is the only NT writer who uses these terms.

13 Beloved The adjective *agapētos* literally means "beloved," but it also sometimes carries the sense of "only." The tenants knew (or assumed) that this "son" was the only "heir" (v. 14).

It May Be This is one word, the adverb *isōs* (only here in NT), which means "perhaps."

16 God Forbid The Greek says, *Mē genoito*—literally, "May it never be!" (NASB; cf. NIV). Aside from this passage, the expression is used only by Paul (14 times: 10 in Romans, 3 in Galatians, and once in 1 Corinthians). This reflects the close relationship between Paul and Luke, a fact which is emphasized in the NT and the Early Church fathers.

18 Broken . . . Grind to Powder The two verbs, *synthlaō* and *likmaō*, are found (in NT) only here and in Matthew's parallel passage (21:44). The first means "crush together" or "dash to pieces." The second in classical Greek meant "winnow" and in the Septuagint "scatter" (as chaff or dust). But Deissmann gives an example in a papyrus of the meaning "crush" or "destroy" (BS, p. 226). Marshall comments: "The imagery may be that of a pot falling on a stone and being dashed in pieces (*synthlaō*); alternatively the stone may fall on the pot and destroy it (*likmaō*)" (p. 732). The "stone" is Christ (v. 17). The picture here is of inevitable judgment on those who reject Jesus Christ as Savior and Lord.

20 Spies The adjective *engkathetos* (only here in NT) means "hired to lie in wait." Here it is used (in the pl.) as a substantive, "spies."

Feign The verb *hypocrinomai* (only here in NT) means "pretend, make believe." These men were acting as "hypocrites" (same root).

22 Tribute See discussion at Rom. 13:6.

23 Why Tempt Ye Me? This is not in the best Greek manuscripts. It is clearly a copyist's later addition, not a part of the original text (see any up-to-date version of the NT).

24 Penny See discussion at Matt. 20:2.

36 Equal unto the Angels This is one word in Greek, *isangeloi* (only here in NT). It is compounded of *isos*, "equal," and *angelos*, "angel." The redeemed saints will be sexless and immortal.

47 Damnation This is an overtranslation. The Greek word here, *crima*, simply means "judgment"—or at most, "condemnation" (NASB).

21:2 Poor In his parallel passage Mark (12:42) uses the common adjective for "poor," *ptōchos*. But Luke, typically, has a stronger term, *penichros*, "needy, very poor" (only here in NT). It would be appropriate to translate it "penniless."

Mites See discussion at Mark 12:42.

5 Goodly Stones The Greek language has two words meaning "good"; *agathos*, which primarily suggests ethical goodness; and *kalos*, which means aesthetically good, or "beautiful." The latter is used here, and so an accurate translation is "beautiful stones."

Gifts This is not the common word for gifts, *dōra*. Rather, it is *anathēma* (only here in NT), which means "something dedicated or consecrated to the deity" and is used particularly "of the consecrated offerings laid up in the temple" (Behm, TDNT, 1:354). So a more adequate translation is "votive gifts" (NASB) or "gifts dedicated to God" (NIV).

9 Commotions This is the strong word *akatastasia*, which in the context means "insurrections" or "revolutions."

By and By Again (see 17:7) we have this misleading translation for *eutheōs*, which means "immediately" (NASB) or "right away" (NIV). Wars and revolutions took place throughout the next 40 years, but they finally culminated in the Jewish revolution against Rome and the ensuing war (A.D. 66–70), which ended with the destruction of Jerusalem and its Temple in fulfillment of verse 6.

11 Famines and Pestilences Interestingly, the Greek is *limoi kai loimoi*. *Limos*, "famine," occurs a dozen times in the NT. But the noun *loimos*, "pestilence," is found only here (in the best Greek text). Famines are often accompanied by pestilences.

Fearful Sights This is one word, *phobētra* (only here in NT). It comes from *phobos*, "fear" or "terror."

14 Meditate Before The verb is *promeletaō* (only here in NT). It means "prepare beforehand" (NASB). Arndt and Gingrich note that it was a "technical term for practicing a speech" (p. 708).

What Ye Shall Answer This is all one word in Greek, the aorist passive infinitive of *apologeomai*, which means "speak in one's own defense, defend oneself" (AG, p. 95). Today "apologize" means saying; "I'm sorry; I was wrong." But the original meaning was defending oneself as being in the right (see discussion at 1 Cor. 9:3). So the meaning here is "to defend yourselves."

15 Gainsay nor Resist The first verb is *anthistēmi*, "stand against," and the second is *antilegō*, "speak against." We can translate "resist or refute" (NASB); "resist or contradict" (NIV).

19 Patience The word is *hypomonē*. It does not mean "patience," but "perseverance" (see discussion at 8:15).

This verse in Luke is his parallel to Matt. 24:13; Mark 13:13. Both of those say: "But he that shall endure [*hypomeinas*] unto the end, the same shall be saved" (KJV). The verb is the same root as Luke's noun here.

It is obvious that the verse in Luke should be saying essentially the same thing as Matthew and Mark. And this is what we find: "By your

perseverance you will win your souls" (NASB); "By standing firm you will save yourselves" (NIV).

Possess The verb *ktaomai* does not mean "possess," but "acquire, gain." The evidence of the earliest Greek manuscripts is split rather evenly between *ktēsasthe* (aor. imperative, represented in the KJV) and *ktēsesthe* (fut. indic., adopted by RSV, NASB, NIV).

20 Armies The word *stratopedon* (only here in NT) first meant "a military camp," and then "army."

21 Countries It is true that *chōra*, "country," is plural here. But the meaning very clearly is that those who are "in the country"—that is, the surrounding countryside—are not to enter the city of Jerusalem.

Incidentally, "depart out" is the verb *ekchoreō* (only here in NT), which is compounded of *ek*, "out," and *chora*, which first meant "place." The meaning of the last part of this verse clearly is: "Let those in the city get out, and let those in the country not enter the city" (NIV). The siege of Jerusalem (v. 20) ended with the Roman army capturing the city and putting to death a large part of its population (v. 24). This was the "desolation" (v. 20).

25 Distress The noun is *synochē* (only here and 2 Cor. 2:4), which comes from the verb *synechō*—"hold together" or "press together," and so "oppress."

Koester gives examples from the papyri of "dismay" or even "anguish" on the part of people because of astrological signs. He goes on to say: "*Synochē* thus comes to mean 'anxiety,' 'despair,' quite clearly . . . on the basis of astrological pronouncements" (TDNT, 7:886). This shows the connection with the first part of this verse.

Perplexity The word *aporia* (only here in NT) means "perplexity" or "anxiety." It comes from the verb *aporeō*, "to be at a loss."

26 Hearts Failing This is the present participle of the verb *apopsychō* (only here in NT). It literally means "to stop breathing," and so the more simple translation, "faint."

Looking After This is the noun *prosdokia* (only here and Acts 21:11). It means "expectation."

28 Look Up The verb is *anakyptō*. It is used of the physical straightening up of the body (13:11). But here it seems to be used for the lifting of one's spirits—"to be elated" (A-S, p. 31). That fits in with the next expression, "lift up your heads" (literal Greek).

30 Shoot Forth The verb *proballō* (only here and Acts 19:33) means "put forward." Here it clearly means "sprout leaves."

34 Overcharged The verb *bareō* means (in the passive, as here) "be weighed down."

Surfeiting The noun *kraipalē* (only here in NT) means "carousing, intoxication." It fits well with "drunkenness."

36 Be Accounted Worthy The verb is *katischyō*, which means "be strong." Here it carries the idea of "be able."

37 Abode The verb *aulizomai* (only here and Matt. 21:17) means "spend the night." Jesus spent His nights on the Mount of Olives during Passion Week.

22:4 Communed The verb *synlaleō* is compounded of *laleō*, "talk," and *syn*, "with, together." Today we would say "discussed."

4, 52 Captains The Greek word *stratēgos* is used only by Luke (these 2 times in the Gospel, and 8 times in Acts). In the plural (as here) it indicates the "officers of the temple guard" of which there were to be no less than 7 (Joachim Jeremias, *Jerusalem in the Time of Jesus*, p. 166).

5 Covenanted *Syntithēmi* (only here; John 9:22; Acts 23:20) means "agreed." Arndt and Gingrich suggest: "they came to an agreement with him, to pay him money" (p. 792).

6 In the Absence of This is all in the little Lukan word *ater* (only here and v. 35). It means "apart from."

Multitude *Ochlos* occurs 175 times in the NT. In the KJV it is translated "people" 82 times, "multitude" 79 times, "press" 5 times, "company" 7 times, and "number" twice. Most modern versions use the more contemporary word "crowd" in place of "multitude." It could possibly mean "disturbance" (AG, p. 600).

10 Pitcher See discussion at Mark 14:13.

11 Goodman See discussion at Mark 14:14.

Guestchamber See discussion at Mark 14:14.

12 Upper Room *Anagaion* (only here and Mark 14:15) means "an extra room built onto the roof of a typical Palestinian home" (Marshall, p. 792).

Furnished See discussion at Mark 14:15.

20 Testament See discussion at Matt. 26:28.

24 Strife *Philoneikia* (only here in NT) literally means "love of strife," and also the "strife" itself. It may be translated "a dispute."

25 Exercise Lordship Over This is the verb *kyrieuō* (only here in the Gospels; 6 times in Paul's Epistles). A more forceful translation is: "lord it over," which is the characteristic attitude of unchristian rulers.

Benefactors *Euergetēs* occurs only here in NT. But Deissmann says of the use of this title: "It would not be difficult to collect from inscriptions . . . over a hundred instances, so widespread was the custom" (LAE, p. 253).

26 He That Is Chief In the Greek this is the definite article, *ho*, plus the present participle of the verb *hēgeomai*, "lead." In Heb. 13:7 this verb is used to indicate leaders in the church. So here Jesus is saying that church leaders should be servants.

27 Sitteth at Meat *Anakeima*, translated five times in the KJV as "sit at meat," actually means "recline at table" on couches around the table.

28 Temptations The noun *peirasmos* in the plural means "trials." "Temptations" connotes something else. Seesemann says that "it is more natural to take the plural *peirasmoi* in the sense of 'dangers,' 'afflictions,' 'troubles' " (TDNT, 6:35).

29 Appoint The verb *diatithēmi* (only in the middle voice in NT) means "assign" or "confer." Behm says of this passage: "As the eschatological *basileia* (kingdom) is ordained for Jesus by the sovereign declaration of the will of God, so it is decided by the sovereign resolve of Jesus that the disciples should reign with Him" (TDNT, 2:105–6).

31 Hath Desired to Have The verb *exaiteomai* (only here in NT) means "ask for, demand." It is stronger than "desired."

31–32 You "You" is plural in verse 31 but singular in verse 32. This is indicated in the KJV by "You . . . thee," and in the NIV by footnote with verse 31 and "you, Simon" in verse 32 (cf. also RSV). Unfortunately, this is not brought out in the NASB.

31 Sift The verb *siniazō* is found only here in the NT. Verses 31 and 32 are a revealing picture of what is going on in the spirit world. The Book of Job is the crowning example of a man whom Satan sifted.

32 Converted Today we use this term for what happens when one is born again and becomes a Christian. But the verb *epistrephō* means "turn back" (cf. NIV) or "turn again" (cf. NASB). Bertram writes: "The verb is not used here as a technical term for Peter's conversion. It is used . . . for the change which is prepared by this saying of Jesus and brought about by the revelation of the Risen Lord" (TDNT, 7:727).

35–36 Scrip See discussion at Mark 6:8.

37 Have an End This is a literal translation of *telos echei*. Concerning its meaning, Marshall (p. 826) prefers the translation: "My life's work is at an end." But "accomplished" (KJV)—or better "fulfilled" (NASB, NIV)—is the verb *teleō*, which comes from *telos*, "end." So it would seem that the real meaning is: "the references to me [in the Scriptures] are being fulfilled."

39 As He Was Wont The Greek says *kata to ethos*—a Lukan phrase (see 1:9; 2:42)—"according to the [His] custom."

41 Cast The noun *bolē* (only here in NT) is from the verb *ballō*, "to throw." So the contemporary translation is "throw."

44 Agony . . . More Earnestly . . . Sweat . . . Drops Verses 43 and 44 are omitted in some of the earliest manuscripts. But many leading NT scholars accept them as genuine. So they are included, with appropriate footnotes, in such versions as the NASB and NIV.

Verse 44 is almost unique in having four *hapax legomena* ("said once," hence words found only once in the NT): *agōnia*, "agony"; *ektenesteron*, "more earnestly"; *hidrōs*, "sweat";

thrombos, "drop." The picture of Jesus' anguish of soul is painted in vivid colors here.

49 What Would Follow In the Greek this is the neuter definite article, *to*, with *esomenon* (the future participle of *eimi*, the verb "to be"). So it literally means "that which will be," or "what was going to happen."

51 Suffer Ye Thus Far The Greek has: *Eate hepōs toutou*. The last two words mean "up to this (point)." The verb *eaō* means "let go, leave alone." Arndt and Gingrich suggest for the whole expression: "Stop! No more of this!"

52 Thief See discussion at Mark 14:48.

55 Hall The noun *aulē* occurs 12 times in the NT. Only here and in Mark 15:16 is it translated "hall," which is clearly a mistake. The primary meaning is "courtyard," and that fits here.

59 Confidently Affirmed The verb *diischyrizomai* (only here and Acts 12:15) means "insist, maintain firmly" (AG, p. 195).

70 Ye Say that I Am This is a literal translation of the Greek. But *hoti*, "that," also means "because." So the sentence could be translated "You say (it), because I am." This leads to: "Yes, I am" (NASB); "You are right in saying I am" (NIV).

23:1 Multitude
The KJV translators were very fond of the word "multitude." They used it 79 times to render the Greek word *ochlos*, which means "people" or "crowd." They also used it 30 times to translate *plēthos*, the Greek word here.

But *plēthos* has a special meaning in this passage. As in Acts 23:7, it designates "the 'totality' of all the members of the council present" (G. D. Delling, TDNT, 6:279)—that is, the Sanhedrin. So it may be translated "assembly."

In verse 27 the same word (*plēthos*) refers to a large number of people. It is translated "company" (KJV), "multitude" (NASB), "number" (NIV). Incidentally, *plēthos* is used by Luke 25 times (8 in his Gospel, 17 in Acts) out of the 32 times it occurs in the NT.

2 Perverting The verb *diastrephō* (here in the present participle) does mean "perverting" (KJV) or "misleading" (NASB). Today we would probably say "subverting" (NIV).

Luke alone records this political charge which the Sanhedrin brought against Jesus in

Pilate's court. As in Acts, we find Luke, the Greek, very conscious of Roman government orientation. Of course, the accusation that Jesus was "forbidding to pay taxes to Caesar" was a flat lie (cf. 20:20–25).

3 *Thou Sayest* This is the literal translation of the Greek *Su legeis*, which is found at this point in all three Synoptic Gospels (cf. Matt. 27:11; Mark 15:2) and also in John 18:37 with a clause following it. But there is a problem concerning its meaning.

It could, and probably should, be taken as an affirmation: "You said it!" That is the way A. T. Robertson treats it: "By his answer (*thou sayest*) Jesus confesses that he is" (WP, 1:225). A. B. Bruce puts it very briefly: "*Su legeis* = yes" (EGT, 1:324). Alford comments: "*Su legeis* is not to be rendered as a *doubtful answer*—much less with Theophylact, as meaning, '*Thou sayest it, not I*'; but as a *strong affirmative*" (1:287–88).

In spite of the fact that some recent commentators take Jesus' answer as a denial or, at best, an evasion, we prefer the interpretation that it was affirmative. We would adopt either "*It is as* you say" (NASB) or "Yes, it is as you say" (NIV). See further the discussion at Matt. 26:64.

4, 14 *Fault* The Greek has *aition*, the neuter of the adjective *aitios*, meaning "responsible, guilty"—here used as a substantive. We find the same word in verse 22, where it is translated "cause" (with the additional phrase, "of death"). Arndt and Gingrich helpfully translate the whole expression in verse 22: "reason for capital punishment" (p. 26).

Pilate, as governor conducting a Roman trial, was not saying that he found no "fault" in Jesus' character. He was affirming that he found no crime worthy of punishment.

5 *Were the More Fierce* This is all one word in Greek, *epischyon* (only here in NT). It is the imperfect of the verb *epischyō*—literally, "grow stronger," but here used metaphorically as "be more urgent" (A-S, p. 175). The best translation is "kept on insisting" (NASB).

14 *Perverteth* In verse 2 we found the verb *diastrephō* (see discussion there). Here we have another compound of *strephō* ("turn"), *apostrephō*, which means "turn [someone] away from." Arndt and Gingrich say that here it means "cause them to revolt" (p. 100). A good rendering is: "inciting the people to rebellion."

16, 22 *Chastise* The verb *paideuō* (from *pais*, "child") is used for chastising children. But in this context it obviously means "punish."

18 *All at Once* This is one word in Greek, *pamplēthei* (only here in NT). It is compounded of *pan*, "all," and *plēthos* (see discussion at verse 1). So it means "all together."

19, 25 *Sedition* The noun *stasis* means "uprising, riot, revolt, rebellion" (AG, p. 764). A good translation here is "insurrection."

23 *Were Instant* The verb here, *epekeinto*, means "they were insistent."

27 *Bewailed . . . Lamented* The first verb is *koptō*, which in the middle voice (as here) means "*to beat one's breast* with grief, *to mourn*, bewail" (A-S, p. 254). The second is *thrēneō*, which also means to "mourn" or "wail for." These two verbs are traditionally found together in the culture of that time, especially in describing women weeping. They wailed loudly and almost uncontrollably.

31 *Green* The adjective *hygros* (only here in NT) literally means "wet, moist." J. Schneider comments: "Jesus compares Himself with green (damp and sappy) wood, the Jewish people, with dry. Sappy wood is not so easily burned as dry. Yet God has not spared Jesus; He goes on His way to the cross and death. How much more will Judaism, if impenitent, learn the seriousness of divine judgment" (TDNT, 5:38).

32–33, 39 *Malefactors* Aside from these three occurrences, the word *kakourgos*—from *kakos*, "evil," and *ergon*, "work" ("evilworker")—is found only in 2 Tim. 2:9. "Malefactors," from the Latin, is a literal translation but not contemporary English. A good rendering today is "criminals."

33 *Calvary* This is the only place where this word occurs in the KJV. In the parallel passages in the other three Gospels (Matt. 27:33; Mark 15:22; John 19:17) the same Greek word *kranion*—which we have taken over as "cranium"—is correctly and literally translated (in KJV) as "skull."

Why, then, did the translators use "Calvary" here? The answer is that they got it from the Latin Vulgate, which has *calvaria* here as the translation of the Greek *kranion*. The facts of the case are that the KJV (1611) was a revision of the Bishops' Bible (1568), which had in it many Latinisms. That is why, for example, we have "charity" for "love" (*agapē*) in 1 Corinthians 13.

35 Derided   See discussion at Luke 16:14.

41 Amiss   The word is *atopos*. It is compounded of *alpha*-negative and *topos*, "place." So it literally means "out of place." Here it means "wrong."

43 Paradise   See discussion at 2 Corinthians 12:4.

44 Earth   The Greek word *gē* is often used for the earth. But sometimes it means "the ground." Rather obviously it here means "land"—that is, the land of Palestine, or perhaps more specifically the land of Judea. It is correctly translated as "land" in the parallel passages (Matt. 27:45; Mark 15:33).

45 Veil   See discussion at Matt. 27:51.

46 Gave Up the Ghost   See discussion at Mark 15:37.

47 Centurion   The Greek word is *hekatontarchēs* (or *hekatontarchos* in some manuscripts) which occurs 4 times in Matthew, 3 times in Luke (cf. 7:2, 6) and 14 times in Acts. It is composed of *hekaton*, "one hundred," and *archōn*, "ruler." It meant the officer over 100 men.

Mark was writing his Gospel for the Romans. So he used the Latinism *centuriōn* (15:39, 44–45), which we have taken over into English.

48 Came Together   The verb is *symparaginomai* (only here in NT). It is composed of *ginomai*, "become," *para*, "beside," *syn*, "together."

Sight, Beholding   The noun is *theoria* (only here in NT); the verb is *theōreō*, "look at, observe." Obviously both came from the same root of "seeing."

50 Counsellor   See discussion at Mark 15:43.

51 Consented   The verb is *synkatatithēmi* (only here in NT). In the middle (as here) it means "*to deposit* one's vote *with*, hence, *to agree with, assent to*" (A-S, p. 430).

53 Hewn in Stone   This is one word in Greek, the adjective *laxeutos* (only here in NT).

54 Drew On   The verb is *epiphōskō* (only here and Matt. 28:1). It literally means "shine forth" or "dawn." But the context indicates that this was late Friday afternoon ("Preparation Day," NIV), with the Sabbath about to begin at sunset. E. Lohse suggests: "The reference is obviously to the shining of the first star as the Sabbath comes" (TDNT, 7:20, n. 159). In Matt. 28:1, however, it means "at dawn on the first day of the week."

55 Followed After   The verb *katakoloutheō* (only here and Acts 16:7) is another of Luke's compounds. The simple verb, very common, is *akoloutheō*, "follow."

24:4 Shining   This is the participle of the verb *astraptō* (only here and 17:24), which comes from the noun *astrapē*, "lightning." So the meaning here is "clothes that gleamed like lightning."

11 Idle Tales   This is one word (sing.), *lēros* (only here in NT). It means "silly talk" or "nonsense."

13 Threescore Furlongs   The Greek word for "furlong" is *stadion* (pl., *stadia*). The *stadion* was a measure of length, 600 Greek feet (about 607 Eng. ft.). The term was also used for what we call a "stadium" (Latin ending), a place where races were run. In this passage 60 *stadi* equals "about seven miles." See further discussion at 1 Cor. 9:24.

14–15 Talked Together . . . Communed Together   The verb *homileō*, from which we get "homiletics," is found only here and in Acts 20:11; 24:26. It comes from *homilos*, "crowd." So it first meant "be in company with" and then "converse with."

17 Communications   The Greek literally says, "What are these words that [you] *antiballete* with one another?" The verb *antiballō* (only here in NT) literally means "put or place against." Arndt and Gingrich suggest for this passage: "What are the words you are exchanging with each other?" (p. 74; cf. NASB). They say it means: "What is the subject of your discussion?"

As Ye Walk, and Are Sad   The best Greek text has: "And they stood still, *skythrōpoi*." The adjective *skythrōpos* (only here and Matt. 6:16) means "looking sad" (NASB) or with "faces downcast" (NIV).

18 Art Thou Only a Stranger? The Greek has *monos paroikeis*. The verb *paroikeō* (only here and Heb. 11:9) literally means "dwell beside," but in later writers took on the meaning "dwell as a stranger." Marshall says that the force of the question is, "Are you alone so much of a stranger in Jerusalem that you do not know what everybody there is talking about?" (p. 894).

21 Redeem The verb *lytroō* (only here; Titus 2:14; and 1 Pet. 1:18) literally means "to free by paying a ransom" (*lytron*). F. Buechsel thinks that in those other two passages it carries this full force, but that on the lips of these Jews it here has the weaker meaning of "set free" (TDNT, 4:349–51).

22 Early The adjective *orthrinos* (only here in NT) means "early in the morning."

25 Fools See discussion at Gal. 3:1. The correct translation is "foolish," not "fools."

Slow The adjective *bradys* (only here and Jas. 1:19) is here used "figuratively of mental and spiritual slowness" (AG, p. 147).

26 Ought Not? The Greek has *ouchi*, "was it not?" and the impersonal *edei*, "it was necessary." So the literal translation is: "Was it not necessary . . .?" (NASB). "Christ" is literally "the Christ," that is, "the Messiah."

28 Made as Though The verb *prospoieō* (only here in NT) in the middle means "to make as if" (A-S, p. 387). Some have translated it "pretended." We agree with Marshall when he writes: "But this is too strong here, since, although on one level of understanding he intends to stay with them, he is merely giving them the opportunity to invite him in, and will not force his presence on them" (p. 897). Incidentally, *porrōteron*, "farther"—the correct form found in modern versions—occurs only here in the NT.

29 Constrained The verb *parabiazomai* (only here and Acts 16:15) means "use force," and so "urge strongly."

Evening *Espera* is another Lukan term (only here and Acts 4:3; 28:23).

31 Vanished Out of Their Sight The Greek literally says that He "became invisible"—*aphantos* (only here in NT)—"from them."

37 Terrified . . . Affrighted The first term translates the aorist passive participle of *ptoeō* (only here and 21:9), "terrify." The second Greek word is *emphobos*, which literally means "in fear." A good translation is "startled and frightened."

39 Handle The verb is *psylaphaō* (only here; Acts 17:27; Heb. 12:18; 1 John 1:1). It means "touch."

41 Meat The Greek word is *brōsimos* (only here in NT). It is an adjective meaning "eatable," and so "anything . . . to eat."

42 And of an Honeycomb This is not in the oldest Greek manuscripts and so is correctly not included in modern versions.

44 Prophets This is properly capitalized in modern versions, since it was the title of a section of the Hebrew Scriptures.

45 Understanding The Greek word is *nous*, which simply means "mind." The verb "understand" (KJV) is *syniēmi*, which is properly translated thus.

46 Behoved There is nothing in the Greek to represent this unknown word.

49 Endued Probably this English term was derived from the Greek form here, *endysēthe*. But the verb *endyō* simply means "be clothed with." This is the only place (out of 28 times) in the NT (KJV) that it is translated "be endued with."

51 Parted The verb *diistēmi* is another Lukan term. It occurs (in NT) only here, in 22:59, and in Acts 27:28.

John

1:1 *Word* The Greek term is *logos*. This word is found about 330 times in the New Testament and is translated 25 different ways in the King James Version, including 218 times as "word" (small *w*) and 50 times as "saying." Just what does it mean?

In the city of Ephesus, 6 centuries before John wrote his Gospel there, Heraclitus used the term *logos* for the rational principle, power, or being which *speaks* to men both from without and from within. Plato used it for the divine force creating the world. With Aristotle it was "insight." In general, the Greeks thought of *logos* as "reason" or "thought," whereas the Jewish emphasis was on *logos* as "word."

Philo, a Jew who lived in Alexandria in the time of Christ, sought to combine these 2 ideas—thought and speech. He used the term *logos* over 1,300 times. It has been said that with Philo the Logos is often personified but never truly personalized.

The apostle John, under divine inspiration, goes beyond all this. He presents Jesus Christ as the eternal Logos, the true concept of God and also the Word (v. 1) expressing that concept fully in His incarnation (v. 14).

Aside from three times in the first verse here and once in verse 14, "Logos" is used for Christ in only two other places in the NT (1 John 1:1; Rev. 19:13). This fact tends to tie together these three books as written by John.

Was Three times in verse 1 and once in verse 2 we find *ēn*, the imperfect of the verb "to be" (*eimi*). The imperfect tense emphasizes continuous existence—in this case eternal existence ("in the beginning").

With There are several prepositions in the NT that mean "with." But this is an especially strong one—*pros*, which suggests "close proximity" (A-S, p. 383), or "in company with" (AG, p. 711). It also means "toward." All this adds up to the concept that the Logos was eternally in face-to-face fellowship with God.

Was God The Greek has *theos ēn ho logos*. *Theos* is placed first for emphasis. Also it is without the definite article, so it emphasizes quality rather than individuality. The Logos is not equivalent to "God"; there is also God the Father and God the Holy Spirit. But He is fully *divine*. We could translate this clause either literally—"*God* was the Word"—or as, "The Word was *deity*." It is an emphatic declaration of the deity of the Logos, who in verse 14 is identified with Jesus.

2 *Was* See comment at John 1:1.

3 *Were Made* Here we have a complete change of verb—from *ēn*, the imperfect of *eimi*, to *egeneto*, the aorist of *ginomai*, "become." In the Greek this verb literally says: "All things came into being through Him, and apart from Him not even one thing came into being which has come into being." The eternal Logos *was* divine, and He *became* the Creator of all things. In contradistinction to the erroneous teaching of Jehovah's Witnesses, these three verses teach that Jesus Christ (cf. v. 14) was eternally God and is the Creator of the universe.

5 *Comprehended It Not* One of the constant problems of translating the NT is that a given Greek word can mean two or more very different things in our way of thinking. The verb here is *katalambanō*. Basically it means "take hold of." This can mean either "comprehend" mentally, or "seize hold of" with hostile intent. It is used both ways in different passages in the NT. We would prefer "overpowered" in the text here and "understood" in the margin (for the NIV). Examples of single words that can go both ways are "master" and "apprehend"—which may mean either "arrest" or "understand."

6 Was In the Greek an interesting contrast takes place at this point again. We have already seen that the verb *ēn*—"was continuously"—is used three times in verse 1 and once in verse 2: the *Logos* existed eternally. But in verse 3 we find three times the verb *ginomai*, "come into being"—used of creation.

This same verb is used in verse 6 for John the Baptist. The Logos always "was." John the Baptist came into being. So we translate: "There came a man" (NASB, NIV).

11 His Own ... His Own These two expressions are not the same in Greek, and they should not be the same in English (as they are in KJV). The first is neuter and so means "His own things." The second is masculine, "His own people." This distinction should be brought out in any accurate translation. The first clause may be translated, "He came to his own home" (RSV)—the Promised Land, Jerusalem, the Temple. Arndt and Gingrich translate the second clause: "His own people did not accept him" (p. 619). The Greek verb here is not the simple *lambanō*, "receive," but the compound *paralambanō*, "take to oneself," and so "accept." What the Gospels show repeatedly is that Jesus' own people did not accept Him; instead they rejected Him as their Messiah.

12 Power The word here is not *dynamis*, which rightly means "power," but *exousia*, which means "authority"—that is, "the right" (NASB, NIV).

The Sons of God That would be *hoi whioi theou*. But the text has *tekna theou*, "children of God" (NASB, NIV).

13 The Will of Man The Greek word for "man" here is not the generic *anthrōpos*, "human being," but *anēr* (genitive *andros*), which means a male individual. In the KJV it is translated "man" 156 times, but "husband" 50 times. It would seem that this is one place where it should be rendered that way: "a husband's will" (NIV)—there is no definite article in the Greek.

14 Was Made Again we have the Greek *egeneto*, "became" (RSV, NASB, NIV). The Logos always "was" (v. 1). But He "became flesh" (v. 14) in His incarnation.

Dwelt The Greek has the verb *skēnoō*, from *skēnē*, "tent." So it literally means "tented" among us. The force of this is brought out well in the NIV: "lived for a while among us"—only 33 years.

15 Is Preferred Before Me The Greek literally says "has become before me." B. F. Westcott writes: " 'After' and 'before' are both used in a metaphorical sense from the image of progression in a line. He who comes later in time comes 'after;' and he who advances in front shews by that his superior power" (p. 13). So we can say: "is preferred before me" (KJV), "ranks before me" (RSV), "has a higher rank than I" (NASB), or "has surpassed me" (NIV).

He Was Before Me The Greek has *prōtos mou ēn*. *Prōtos* means "first"—literally, "He was first of me." What does this mean? Westcott says: "It expresses not only relative, but (so to speak) absolute priority. He was first altogether in regard to me, and not merely former as compared with me" (ibid.).

16 For The Greek preposition is *anti*. In the light of its use in the papyri, James H. Moulton and George Milligan affirm: "By far the commonest meaning of *anti* is the simple 'instead of' " (VGT, p. 46). So the idea here is "one grace in place of another." The NIV has sought to bring this out by saying: "We have all received one blessing after another."

17 Truth The basic meaning of *alētheia* is "truth." But this word also means "reality" (AG, p. 36). Bultmann says that in Greek usage "*alētheia* takes more and more the sense of 'true and genuine reality' " (TDNT, 1:239). He also declares: "In John *alētheia* denotes 'divine reality' " (1:245).

18 The Only Begotten Son The oldest Greek manuscripts (third and fourth centuries) all have *monogenēs theos*—"only begotten God." This, then, becomes the strongest possible statement of the full deity of Jesus. He is "the only begotten God" (NASB). The deity of Jesus is the recurring theme of John's Gospel, and to induce belief in this foundation doctrine of the Christian faith was the purpose for which it was written (20:31).

Declared The Greek verb is *exegeomai*, from which we get *exegete*—the Son has exegeted the Father. Literally the verb means "lead out." In a sense Christ has led the Father out for all of us to see.

But the verb came to mean: "explain, interpret, tell, report, describe" (AG, p. 275). Marvin Vincent writes: "John's meaning is that the Word *revealed* or *manifested* and *interpreted* the Father to men" (WS, 2:61). Hermann Buechsel says that the correct meaning of the verb here is "to reveal" (TDNT, 2:908).

In the Greek the verb is preceded by the pronoun *ekeinos*, "that one." J. H. Bernard says that here it is very emphatic: "It is *He* who interpreted (the Father)" (1:33).

28 Bethabara Recent versions have *Bethany*. Why? The simple reason is that all the oldest Greek manuscripts (third, fourth, and fifth centuries) have *Bēthania*. How did it come to be changed to *Bēthabara*?

Fortunately, in this case we know the answer. Origen (third century) tells us that he could not find any Bethany near the Jordan River, although he admits that *Bēthania* is the reading of "nearly all the manuscripts." So he deliberately changed *Bēthania* to *Bēthabara*, and the latter became the dominant reading in the late manuscripts. There is no question but that "Bethany" is correct.

42 A Stone Which is it, "a stone," or "Peter"? The simple answer is, "Both." Cephas is the Aramaic word for "a rock." John translates this for his readers as *petros*, the Greek word for "rock" or "stone." But since the Greek *petros* is rendered as "Peter" everywhere else in the KJV NT (161 times), probably it is better here also (NASB, NIV).

51 Verily, Verily See discussion at Matt. 8:10. The double *Amēn, amēn* is found only in John's Gospel.

2:3 Wanted Today "want" means "wish for." But the verb here, *hystereō*, means "fail, give out, lack" (AG, p. 849). So the correct sense is: "when the wine gave out" (NASB), or "When the wine was gone" (NIV).

4 What Have I to Do with Thee? The Greek literally says, "What to me and to thee?"—*Ti emoi kai soi*. Bernard says that this is "a phrase, translated from the Hebrew, occurring several times in the Greek Bible [Septuagint], and always suggestive of diversity of opinion or interest." He goes on to say:

"The phrase does not always imply reproach, but it suggests it. Here it seems to be a gentle suggestion of misunderstanding: 'I shall see to that; it will be better that you should leave it to me'" (1:75).

8 Draw Out This is the literal meaning of *antleō*. It is generally assumed that the command was to draw some water out of the stone water jars. But B. F. Westcott notes:

> The original word is applied most naturally to drawing water from the well (iv. 7, 15), and not from a vessel like the waterpot. Moreover the emphatic addition of *now* seems to mark the continuance of the same action of drawing as before, but with a different end. Hitherto they had drawn to fill the vessels of purification: they were charged *now* to "draw and bear to the governor of the feast." It seems most unlikely that water taken from vessels of purification could have been employed for the purpose of the miracle (p. 38).

We believe that the filling up of the water jars showed the completion of Judaism with its ceremonial cleansings. The unlimited supply of water from the well, turned into wine, symbolized the beginning of Christianity with its endless, joyful supply of God's grace.

8, 9 Governor of the Feast This is one word in the Greek, *architriklinos* (found only here in the NT). The prefix *archi* comes from *archōn*, "ruler" or "chief." Abbott-Smith says that *archi* is a prefix "denoting high office and dignity" (p. 62). He also notes that *triklinos* means "a room with three couches," on which the guests reclined as they ate. So the *architriklinos* was "*the superintendent of a banquet*, whose duty it was to arrange the tables and food." The word may be translated "headwaiter" (NASB) or, perhaps better, "master of the banquet" (NIV).

11 Miracles The Greek word is *sēmeion*. In the KJV it is translated "sign" 52 times, "miracle" 22 times, "wonder" 3 times, and "token" once—for a total of 78 times. In John's Gospel it is translated "miracle" 13 times and "sign" 4 times.

Unfortunately, this obscures the true meaning of *sēmeion*, which is "sign." The three Synoptic Gospels describe Jesus' miracles mostly as *dynameis*—literally "powers," but usually and properly translated (in KJV) as "mighty works." John, on the other hand, is concerned to show that Jesus' miracles—of which he only relates 7—had spiritual significance. For instance, feeding the 5,000 illustrated the fact that He was the Bread of Life (6:35); and raising Lazarus underscored the truth that He was the Resurrection and the Life (11:25). So John regularly refers to Jesus' miracles as "signs." Here he says that the turning of the water into wine was "the first of his miraculous signs" (NIV). It caused His disciples to believe in Him.

3:3 *Again*   The Greek word is *anōthen*, the first and basic meaning of which is "from above." Josephus (first cent.) clearly uses it in the sense of "again" or "anew." Which does it mean here?

J. H. Bernard writes: "*Anōthen*, in the Synoptists (generally) and always in the other passages where it occurs in John, means 'from above' . . . ; so also in James 1:17; 3:15, 17. This is its meaning here, the point being not that spiritual birth is a *repetition*, but that it is being born into a higher life" (1:102).

B. F. Westcott has a rather long "additional note" in which he traces the rendering of *anōthen* in the church fathers and ancient versions (as well as more recent ones). He concludes: "There seems then to be no reason to doubt that the sense given by the Vulgate and A. V. is right, though the notion is not that of mere repetition (*again*), but of analogous process (*anew*)" (p. 63).

Among recent commentators, William Hendriksen favors "from above" (1:132), as does Buechsel (TDNT, 1:378).

We have always been impressed with the fact that Nicodemus clearly understood Jesus to mean "again" (see v. 4) and that Jesus did not respond: "That isn't what I meant." But we would agree heartily with the conclusion given in Arndt and Gingrich's *Lexicon* that the whole expression "is purposely ambiguous and means both *born from above* and *born again*" (p. 77). There are many cases where we must take an either/or position; but in very many instances the both/and approach is richer and more rewarding. The new birth is a birth from above, by the Holy Spirit.

8 *Wind and Spirit*   Both these English words in this verse translate the same Greek word: *pneuma*. It has 3 meanings: breath (cf. *pneumonia*), wind (cf. *pneumatic*), and spirit—for both the human spirit and the Holy Spirit. The verb "blows" (*pnei*) is from the same root. So in the Greek the connection between "wind" and "Spirit" is closer than appears in English. It is very natural to speak, as is often done today, of "the winds of the Spirit" blowing in our midst.

10 *A Master*   The Greek clearly says "the teacher" (NASB), and so "Israel's teacher" (NIV). Nicodemus ranked as "the teacher of Israel." And yet he was ignorant of spiritual birth.

13 *Which Is in Heaven*   This clause in the KJV is not found in any Greek manuscript earlier than the ninth century. We now have two papyrus manuscripts of John's Gospel from close to A.D. 200—only about 100 years after that Gospel was written (probably about A.D. 95). Also, both our great Greek manuscripts from the fourth century do not have it. It seems obvious that no reasonable-minded person would argue that this clause was in John's Gospel as originally written, when it is not in the third- and fourth-century manuscripts that we have.

15 *Should Not Perish*   This clause in the KJV is genuine in verse 16. But it was imported into verse 15 from verse 16 by late copyists. None of the oldest manuscripts have it in verse 15, where it obviously was not a part of the original text.

16 *Everlasting Life*   In the Greek the last two words of verses 15 and 16 are exactly the same—*zōēn aiōnion*. The KJV translates them "eternal life" in 15 and "everlasting life" in 16.

The adjective *aiōnios* comes from the noun *aiōn*, which was first used for "lifetime" or "age." But Plato used it in the sense of "eternity." Sasse writes: "Plato distinguishes between *aiōn* as timeless, ideal eternity, in which there are no days or months or years, and *chronos* as the time which is created with the world as a moving image of eternity" (TDNT, 1:198).

When it comes to the adjective *aiōnios*, the first meaning given is "eternal" (TDNT, 1:208). Evidently the KJV translators used "everlasting" in verse 16 to avoid repetition. But one of the key expressions in John's Gospel is "eternal life," which has qualitative force, not just quantitative meaning. It is the life of eternity which God plants in our hearts when Christ, the Eternal One, comes in to abide. So it is better to use "eternal" also in verses 16 and 36 (RSV, NASB, NIV).

Incidentally, *aiōnios* occurs 17 times in John's Gospel and not more than 6 times in any other NT book. In the KJV it is translated "eternal" in 42 of the 71 times it occurs.

20 *Reproved*   Arndt and Gingrich give as the first meaning of the verb *elengchō:* "bring to light, expose, set forth" (p. 249). It seems that the best translation here is "exposed" (RSV, NASB, NIV). Buechsel writes: "This meaning is suitable in Jn. 3:20" (TDNT, 2:474).

4:14 Well The Greek word for "well" in verses 11 and 12 is *phrear*, which means "*a well purposely dug,*" and also a "pit" or "shaft" (AG, p. 865). But Jesus used a different word in verse 14—*pēgē*, which means a "spring" or "fountain" (AG, p. 655). The woman was talking about a hole in the ground. Jesus was promising her a bubbling "spring of water welling up to eternal life" (RSV, NIV).

24 A Spirit The Greek language has no indefinite article. So *pneuma ho theos* might possibly be translated "God is a spirit" (KJV). But since *pneuma* is first, it has almost an adjectival force: "Spirit"—not material body—"is God." This is brought out best by the translation, "God is spirit" (RSV, NASB, NIV).

27 The Woman There is no article in the Greek. So the correct translation is "a woman" (RSV, NASB, NIV). The Jewish rule was that no man should ever talk with *any* woman in public—not even his own wife, sister, or mother.

29 Is Not This the Christ? In English this question suggests that a positive answer ("Yes") is expected. But in the Greek *mēti* indicates that a negative answer—"this is not the Christ, is it?" (NASB)—is anticipated. B. F. Westcott writes: "The words suggest the great conclusion as something beyond hope. The form of the sentence grammatically suggests a negative answer, but hope bursts through it" (1:163). Perhaps this is best brought out by "Can this be the Christ?" (RSV) or "Could this be the Christ?" (NIV).

31 Master The Greek word is *Rabbi*. It is used for Christ 14 times in the NT—translated (in KJV) "Master" 9 times and "Rabbi" 5 times. Three times it is used for a Jewish rabbi (Matt. 23:7, 8). The best way is to transliterate it here as "Rabbi" (RSV, NASB, NIV), since the KJV translates 6 other Greek words as "master."

46, 49 Nobleman The Greek word is *basilikos*, which is properly an adjective (from *basileus*, "king") and is properly translated "royal" in the KJV in the other three places where it occurs in the NT (Acts 2:20, 21; Jas. 2:8). The best translation here, where it is used as a substantive, is "royal official."

5:2 Sheep Market The Greek simply has the adjective *probatikos*, "pertaining to sheep"; so the KJV translators supplied *market* (in italics). But all authorities agree that the correct reference is to the "Sheep Gate" (NIV) in the wall of Jerusalem, through which sheep were brought to the Temple.

Hebrew The Greek word is *Hebraisti*, which originally meant "Hebrew." But there is general agreement that here (as well as in 19:13, 17, 20) it means "Aramaic" (NIV). Gutbrod gives that meaning for *Hebraisti* in John's Gospel (TDNT, 3:389).

Porches The Greek word here is *stoa*, which students of Greek history and philosophy will connect with Athens, where the philosophers taught. Besides this verse, the word occurs (in NT) only in 10:23 and Acts 3:11; 5:12. In those three places it is "Solomon's porch" (KJV). We know that this was a covered colonnade inside the east wall of the Temple area. Since we think of "porches" as on the outside of buildings, that term hardly fits in these passages. A better translation is "covered colonnades" (NIV).

Incidentally, Bible students used to wonder why there were "five" colonnades. When the Pool of Bethesda in Jerusalem, north of the Temple area, was excavated, it was found to consist of two rectangular adjacent pools, with colonnades running the full length on both sides and at both ends, with one between the pools—making five in all.

3 Waiting for the Moving of the Water This last part of verse 3 and all of verse 4 are not found in the two third-century papyrus manuscripts of John's Gospel (66 and 75)—made only about 100 years after John was written—in our only two fourth-century manuscripts, or in two of the four manuscripts from the fifth century. It is completely clear to any honest observer that this legend, about an angel who came down and "troubled the water," was not a part of the original Gospel of John. It was added centuries later to explain the man's reference in verse 7.

6, 9, 11, 14, 15 Whole The adjective *hygiēs*, from which we get *hygiene*, is translated (in KJV) "whole" 11 out of the 12 times it occurs in the NT. The exception is Titus 2:8 ("sound speech"). As might be expected, the word means "healthy, well." It occurs twice each in Matthew (12:13; 15:31) and Mark (3:5; 5:34), and once in Luke (6:10), but 6 times in John (see 7:23), and once each in Acts (4:10) and Titus (2:8). The best contemporary translation of Jesus' question here is: "Do you want to get well?" (NIV; cf. NASB).

8, 9, 10, 11 Bed See discussion at Mark 2:4.

13 Conveyed Himself Away This is the verb *ekneuō* (only here in NT). It means "turn aside, withdraw" (cf. RSV). The simplest translation is "slipped away" (NASB, NIV).

20 Loveth There is a beautiful touch here in the Greek that cannot very well be brought out in English translation. When we are told that God "loved" the world (John 3:16), the verb is *agapaō*. This is also the verb that is used when we are told to love God (Matt. 22:37), our neighbor (Matt. 5:43), and our fellow Christians (John 13:34). It means to have a love that seeks the best good of its object, a love of full loyalty. The verb *agapaō* occurs 142 times in the NT and is always translated "love" (or "beloved," 7 times).

But the verb here is *phileō*, which signifies affectionate love. It is translated "kiss" 3 out of the 22 times it occurs (in NT)—of Judas kissing Jesus (Matt. 26:48; Mark 14:44; Luke 22:47).

Only here is it used to express the relationship within the Trinity. How beautiful to read that the Father has affectionate love for His Son! B. F. Westcott comments: "And so it is through the Son that the personal love of God is extended to believers" (1:190). The basis of this statement is John 16:27, where we read that "the Father himself loves"—*philei*, same as in 5:20—"you because you have loved [*phileō*] me." The last clause suggests that we are to have affectionate love, as well as loyalty love, toward God. Emotions do have a part in true religion.

21 Quickeneth The verb is *zōopoieō*, which means "make [*poieō*] alive" (*zōos*). Here the best translation is "gives them life" (RSV, NASB, NIV). The verb here signifies "communicating spiritual life" (Alfred Plummer, p. 137)—that is, to the spiritually dead. In verses 28–29 it is the physically dead who will be resurrected. But in verses 21–26 it is a spiritual resurrection.

24 Everlasting See discussion at 3:16.

35 Light . . . Light John the Baptist is called a burning and shining "light" (KJV), in whose "light" the people rejoiced for a while. But the first word is *lychnos*, which literally

meant an oil-burning "lamp" (usually of clay in NT times), and so should be translated "lamp" (RSV, NASB, NIV).

The second word is *phōs*, which is correctly translated "light." We get our word *photograph* from *phōtō* (dative case) and *graphō*, "write"—writing by light.

37 Shape The Greek word is *eidos*—"that which is seen, appearance, external form" (A-S, p. 131). It comes from the verb *eidon*, "I saw." So it refers to a visible "form" (RSV, NASB, NIV). God cannot be seen with physical eyes.

39 Search The verb is *eraunaō*, which means "search, examine" (A-S, p. 178). But our problem here is that in the present tense the same second person plural form (*eraunate*) may be either indicative or imperative. We cannot be sure which is intended here.

The KJV takes it as imperative, "Search." But scholars are pretty well agreed that the indicative fits better. Plummer writes: "The context seems to be strongly in favour of the indicative" (p. 142). J. H. Bernard declares: "Jesus is not exhorting the Jews here; He is arguing with them, and rebuking them for their stubborn rejection of Him" (1:253).

As early as the English Revised Version (NT, 1881), the change was made to the indicative. That wise move has been followed by most versions since. B. F. Westcott comments: "The word *eraunan* describes that minute, intense investigation of the Scripture which issued in the allegorical interpretations of the *Midrash*" (p. 201). He was on the revision committee that adopted "Ye search the Scriptures" (ERV, 1881). Today we would say, "You diligently study the Scriptures" (NIV).

40 Will Not Come This sounds like a simple future tense of the verb "come." But the Greek uses two verbs, with "come" as an infinitive: "You are unwilling to come to Me" (NASB). In many places the KJV fails to bring this out. The force of what Jesus says is this: "You refuse to come to me" (RSV, NIV).

41, 44 Honor The Greek word here has no relation to the verb translated "honor" four times in verse 23. There it is *timaō*, from the noun *timē* that means "esteem, honor." But here it is the noun *doxa*, which means "glory" (RSV, NASB) or "praise" (NIV).

45 Trust The Greek verb is *elpizō*, which is incorrectly translated "trust" (KJV) in 18 of its 31 occurrences in the NT. *Elpizō* comes from the noun *elpis*, which means "expectation" or "hope." Even the KJV translates the noun as "hope" 53 out of the 54 times it occurs in the NT. (The exception is Heb. 10:23, "faith," which is obviously an error.) Why did they not translate the verb correspondingly? We don't know. The correct translation here is "set your hope" (RSV, NASB; cf. NIV).

6:5-13 *Bread . . . Loaves* In the Greek the same word, *artoi* (pl.), is used for "bread" in verses 5 and 7 and for "loaves" in verses 9, 11, and 13. These loaves were about the size of a small, thin pancake.

6 *Prove* The verb *peirazō* has three successive meanings: (1) "test"; (2) "prove" by testing; (3) "approve" as the result of testing. It is obvious that the first meaning is intended here. So the correct translation is "test" (RSV, NASB, NIV).

7 *Two Hundred Pennyworth of Bread* The Greek literally says, "bread of two hundred denarii"—that is, "Two hundred denarii worth of bread" (NASB). The denarius was a Roman silver coin worth about 20 cents. But it also represented a day's wages (Matt. 20:2). To help the modern reader to see what a large sum of money for that day Philip had in mind, the NIV has: "Eight months' wages" (taking out Sabbaths and feast days). See also discussion at John 12:5.

10 *Men . . . Men* The Greek uses two different words here. The first is *anthrōpous*, which means human beings of both sexes. The second is *andres*, which means male individuals. So Jesus gave orders to have the "people" sit down, and then 5,000 "men" sat down (RSV, NASB, NIV). Matthew, writing to Jews, notes that there were "about five thousand men"—*andres*—"beside women and children" (Matt. 14:21). According to Jewish custom the women and children could not eat with men in public.

12 *Filled* The verb is *empiplēmi*, which means "to fill full, fill up, satisfy" (A-S, p. 149)—and so, "when they had eaten their fill" (RSV).

16, 17 *Sea . . . Ship* The Lake of Galilee was only 13 miles long and 6 or 7 miles wide—hardly a "sea" (KJV) in modern parlance. Furthermore, the "ship" (KJV) was only a fishing boat, perhaps only a dozen or 20 feet long. So the correct translation is "lake" and "boat"

(NIV). See also discussions at Mark 1:16 and Luke 5:1.

19 *Five and Twenty or Thirty Furlongs* The Greek says more clearly and simply: "Twenty-five or thirty" *stadia*. For discussion of *stadia* see note at Luke 24:13. The distance here was "three or three and a half miles" (NIV)—that is, halfway across the lake.

24 *Took Shipping* The Greek very clearly says: "got into the boats" (RSV, NIV).

41, 43, 61 *Murmur* See discussion at 1 Cor. 10:10.

69 *Christ, the Son of the Living God* This reading (KJV) has only very late and poor support in the Greek manuscripts (9th cent. and following). All but one of the manuscripts from the 3rd, 4th, 5th, 6th, and 8th centuries have "the Holy One of God" (RSV, NASB, NIV).

7:1 *Jewry* The Greek word *Ioudaia* occurs 44 times in the NT. In 42 cases it is correctly rendered in the KJV as "Judaea" (spelled "Judea" today). Twice (Luke 23:5 and here), for some unknown reason, it is rendered "Jewry."

16, 17 *Doctrine* Today "doctrine" has a technical connotation. In religious circles it refers to theological dogmas. The Greek word here, *didachē*, simply means "teaching" (in all up-to-date versions).

17 *Will Do* See discussion at John 5:40.

20 *Devil* The Greek word is *daimonion*, "demon," not *diabolos*, "devil."

23 *Every Whit Whole* The Greek literally says, "made a whole man well" (*hygiē*). This may be translated: "made an entire man well" (NASB), or "for healing the whole man" (NIV).

31 *People* The Greek word is *ochlos*, "crowd" (NIV). Rudolf Meyer writes:

> The term *ochlos* acquires a special sense in John's Gospel. . . . The word *ochlos* is especially common in Jn. 7 and 12. In 7:11 Jesus is sought by the Jews at the Feast of Tabernacles; the Jews are the *ochloi* in v. 12. What is meant in v. 11f. is the Jewish public. There is a further reference to the Jews in vv. 15–19, when they debate with Jesus, and in v. 20 *ochlos* is used again for the Jewish crowd. In 7:31f., however, the Pharisees are contrasted with the multitude. Many of the crowd believe in Jesus,

so that the high-priest and scribes are forced to take action against Him. Reference is again made to this crowd in vv. 40–49 in connection with the speech which Jesus made on the last day of the Feast of Tabernacles. Some regard Jesus as a prophet, some as the Messiah, whereas others doubt His Messiahship (v. 43). . . . Jn. 7:45f. takes up again the reason for arresting Jesus given in v. 31f.

After discussing the Greek of verses 48-49, Meyer observes:

> John thus differentiates the *archontes* (rulers) and *Pharisaioi*, who radically reject Jesus, from the wretched mob which does not know the Law. . . . Nevertheless, for all the obscurities of usage, one may suspect that the author had a specific purpose in the striking employment of *ochlos* in Jn. 7 and 12. In the first instance the term refers to the pilgrims at the feast. It is also natural to suppose that the *ochlos* is made up of Galileans, very probably those who wanted to make Him king, cf. 6:14f. But *ochlos* can also denote the common people of Jerusalem. Perhaps more emphatically than in the Synoptists, this is for the most part opposed to the ruling classes (TDNT, 5:588–89).

38 *Belly* It is true that *koilia* does literally mean "belly." But this is not all it means. Arndt and Gingrich give three uses of the word. The first is "an organ of nourishment: the digestive apparatus in its fullest extent." So it can very properly be translated "stomach," as in 1 Cor. 6:13 and Phil. 3:19 (NIV). The second use is "as an organ of reproduction"—the "womb" (Luke 1:41, NIV). In the third place, "*koilia* denotes the hidden, innermost recesses of the human body"; so "innermost being" (NASB) fits very well. Arndt and Gingrich suggest for John 7:38: "rivers of the living water shall flow from his heart" (p. 437; cf. RSV).

J. H. Bernard writes: " 'Out of his belly' is only an emphatic way of saying 'From him shall flow' " (1:283). So a good rendering here is simply this: "Streams of living water shall flow from within him" (NIV). We are told in verse 39 that this prediction refers to the Holy Spirit, who wants to fill our hearts and flow out through our lives.

7:53—8:11 The notes on this passage in NASB and NIV are accurate. The story of the woman taken in adultery is not found in the oldest and best Greek manuscripts. No Greek church father before Euthymius (12th cent.) comments on the passage, and he declared that the accurate copies of the Gospel did not contain it.

While the evidence is overwhelming that John 7:53–8:11 was not a part of the Gospel of John as originally written, yet New Testament scholars agree that it is probably a correct oral tradition of an actual incident in Jesus' life. So it may be used for purposes of illustration.

13 *Bearest Record . . . Record* The Greek has the verb *martyreō*, "testify," and the noun *martyria*, "testimony." So the literal translation is: "You are testifying about yourself; your testimony is not true." The same combination, basically, is found in verse 14 (cf. NIV).

54 *Honor* The verb twice is *doxazō;* the noun is *doxa*. The regular meaning of the verb is "glorify" and of the noun "glory" (NASB, NIV).

9:6 *Clay* The noun *pēlos* occurs twice in verse 6, and once each in verses 11, 14, and 15. Elsewhere it is found (in NT) only in Rom. 9:21, where the reference to the "potter" definitely favors the translation "clay." But its first meaning in classical Greek was "mud" (TDNT, 6:118; cf. NIV).

8 *Blind* "That he was blind" (KJV) is not found in any early Greek manuscripts. They all have: "that he was a beggar" (cf. NASB, NIV).

35 *Son of God* Both of our third-century papyrus Greek manuscripts of John's Gospel, as well as our two fourth-century manuscripts and two of the fifth century, have "Son of Man" (NASB, NIV), which is undoubtedly the correct reading. It is the title that Jesus regularly used for Himself (over 80 times), and it identified Him as the Messiah. Jesus was asking the healed man if he believed in Him as the promised Messiah of Israel.

10:4 *His Own Sheep* The best Greek text has *ta idia panta*—"all his own" (NASB, NIV).

6 *Parable* Our word "parable" comes from the Greek word *parabolē*, which literally means a "placing beside," and so, a comparison. The word occurs 50 times in the NT—all but two of those in the Synoptic Gospels (the others in Hebrews).

But that word does not occur in John's Gospel, and so "parable" should not be in the English. The Greek word here is *paroimia*. In 2 Pet. 2:22 it means "proverb," which was its common connotation in ancient Greek literature. Aside from that passage it occurs (in NT) only in John's Gospel (10:6; 16:25, 29). Here it "means 'hidden, obscure speech,' which stands in need of interpretation" (TDNT, 5:856). What we have in John 10:1–5 is not a "parable" (KJV), but an allegory. The word *paroimia* is correctly translated "figure of speech" (NASB, NIV). It is generally agreed that there are no parables in John's Gospel.

16 Fold In the KJV the word "fold" occurs twice in this verse. But there are two different Greek words here. The first is *aulē*, which is correctly translated "fold," or "sheep pen" (NIV). But the second is *poimnē*, which means "flock."

Is this distinction important? It is! The Roman Catholic church has insisted that *it* is the only true "fold," into which everyone must come in order to be saved. But what Jesus said was that there would be one "flock," His own sheep, though they belong to many denominational folds.

18 Power Again the KJV translates *exousia* as "power." But the correct translation is "authority" (NASB, NIV). This fits in also with the last sentence of the verse: "This command I received from my Father" (NIV). His Father had authorized Him to do it.

20 Is Mad The Greek verb is *mainomai*. Arndt and Gingrich say that it means "be mad, be out of one's mind" (p. 486). Herbert Preisker writes: "In the NT *mainomai* is used only to characterize the messengers of God with their unheard of proclamation. Thus we read in Jn. 10:19ff. that a division arose among the Jews because of the message of Jesus. Those who did not understand His claim or preaching, who had no ear for the uniqueness of His Word, rejected Him, and their reason was that He had an evil spirit and was out of His mind. The unheard of seems to be madness to unbelief" (TDNT, 4:361).

11:1, 30 Town The word *kōmē* occurs 28 times (in NT) and is translated (in KJV) "village" 17 times and "town" 11 times. The correct meaning always is "village" (NASB, NIV).

3, 5 Love In verse 3 we read that the two sisters of Lazarus sent word to Jesus, "Lord, the one you love is sick." Verse 5 reads: "Jesus loved Martha and her sister and Lazarus." But in verse 6 we read that when Jesus heard that Lazarus was sick, "he stayed where he was two more days" (all NIV). How can we harmonize verses 5 and 6?

The answer lies in the fact that two different Greek verbs for "love" are used in verses 3 and

5. In the former it is *phileō*, which means to have affectionate love. (It is also translated "kiss" in the NT.) But in verse 5 it is *agapaō*. This posits a higher kind of love (*agapē*) that seeks the best good of its object. Jesus delayed two days because He wanted to raise the faith of the two sisters to a higher level by raising Lazarus after he had been dead four days. The highest motivation for love is not our feelings or affections, but rather an honest, intelligent facing of the question: "What is best for the one I love?" That is how God acts. See also discussion in 5:20.

8, 28 Master In verse 8 the Greek word is *Rabbi*; in verse 28 it is *didaskalos*, "teacher." It is best to use the transliteration "Rabbi" in verse 8 and the literal translation "Teacher" in verse 28 (NASB, NIV).

17, 31, 38 Grave The noun *mnēmeion* is related to the verb *mnēmoneuō*, "remember." So its original meaning was "a memorial or monument" (TDNT, 4:680). In the New Testament it means "a sepulchre, tomb" (J. H. Thayer, p. 416). It is translated (in KJV) "sepulchre" 29 times, "grave" 8 times, and "tomb" 5 times. Probably the best rendering is "tomb" every time. Verse 38 demands it here.

12:2 Supper The Greek word is *deipnon*. Arndt and Gingrich define it as: "*dinner, supper*, the main *meal* (toward) evening" (p. 173). For many passages, including this one, they give the meaning: "(*formal*) dinner, banquet." Since today "supper" is used mostly for a light meal late in the evening, the best translation here is "dinner" (NIV).

That Sat at the Table All this translates one word in Greek, *anakeimenōn*, which is a participle of *anakeimai*. Arndt and Gingrich say that this verb is used "always of reclining at table" (p. 55)—that is, on couches around the table, according to the Roman custom of that time.

3 Pound Our metric term "liter," which represents about a quart, comes from the Greek word here, *litra*, which was used for the Roman "pound" (12 ounces). It would be roughly a "pint" (NIV) of liquid.

Odor of the Ointment The first noun is *osmē*, which means "fragrance." The second noun is *myron*, which means "perfume." So the best translation here is: "And the house was filled with the fragrance of the perfume" (NIV). How much more beautiful that is than saying, "and the house was filled with the odor of the ointment" (KJV)! Today we use *odor* almost exclusively for bad smells. For "pure nard" (NIV) see discussion at Mark 14:3.

5 *Three Hundred Pence* This expression certainly does not communicate to the modern reader the value of the perfume that Mary poured on Jesus' feet. The Greek says "300 denarii." The Roman silver denarius was a day's wage (Matt. 20:2). So—allowing for 52 Sabbaths and a dozen or more religious feast days—the 300 denarii would represent "a year's wages" (NIV). That was a lot of money to pour out on Jesus, as Judas Iscariot felt. See also discussion at John 6:7.

6 *Bare* This (KJV) is old-fashioned spelling for the verb "bear." But even this translation does not adequately represent what the Greek says. The verb is *bastazō*. Arndt and Gingrich say that it means here: "take surreptitiously, pilfer, steal" (p. 137). "He used to help himself to what was put into it" (NIV; cf. NASB). Incidentally, the word for "bag" (KJV) is really "money box" (NASB; see AG, p. 162), or "money bag" (NIV). Judas Iscariot acted as treasurer for the 12 apostles.

13 *Hosanna* This word had a strong Hebrew background in the Messianic psalms. In the NT it is found only in connection with Jesus' triumphal entry into Jerusalem (see Matt. 21:9, 15; Mark 11:9, 10). Luke omits it in his account, because the Hebrew word would not be understood by his Greek readers. Writing of Mark's Gospel, Lohse says: "By adopting the *Hosanna* which was familiar to every Jew the Evangelist wants to emphasize that every Messianic expectation has now been realized" (TDNT, 9:683). This strong Messianic connotation is further strengthened by the two lines that follow:

> "Blessed is he who comes in the name of the Lord!"
> "Blessed is the King of Israel!" (NIV)

The meaning of "Hosanna" from the Hebrew is usually given as "Save, I pray." On the lips of the people it would correspond to the cry in England: "God save the King!" (or, Queen).

32 *Lifted Up* We often hear this verse quoted and applied to lifting up Jesus in our lives, so that many will be drawn to Him. But the next verse clearly states that the reference was to His being lifted up on the Cross. And it is clear that the Jews understood it this way (see v. 34).

38 *Report* This is the word used in KJV, RSV, NASB. The NIV has "message." The Greek word is *akoē*, which comes from the verb *akouō*, "hear." So it was first used for "the sense or organ of hearing," and is translated "ear" four times in the NT (e.g., Mark 7:35). Then it came to be used for what was heard—a "rumour" (Matt. 24:6) or "report." Kittel goes on to say: "In this sense *akoē* approximates closely to *angelia* [announcement] and *kerygma*, and can be a technical term for 'proclamation' or 'preaching.' . . . The emphasis always falls, of course, on the one who hears the proclamation. . . . With this signification there is a return to the prophetic usage (R. 10:16; Jn. 12:38–Is. 53:1)" (TDNT, 1:221).

47 *Believe* The old Greek manuscripts and the versions of the early church have the verb *phylassō*, "guard" or "keep" (RSV, NASB, NIV), not *pisteuō*, "believe" (KJV). This is a helpful stress on obedience.

13:1 *Unto the End* The Greek has *eis telos*. The word *telos* means "end." So the translation is literally correct. But what is the meaning? To the end of His life? To the end of time? Eternally?

In 1 Thess. 2:16 *eis telos* is correctly translated "to the uttermost" (KJV). Frederick Godet writes: "In our passage, this meaning seems to be the only possible one. . . . This phrase signifies therefore the manifestation of His love even to its complete outpouring" (2:244). Godet paraphrases the last clause: "He perfectly testified to them all his love" (p. 242). Westcott favors the meaning "utterly, completely," and adds: "If . . . we take the words as expressing *loved them with a perfect love*, the thought comes out clearly" (2:146).

The ERV (NT, 1881) adopted "to the uttermost." A good rendering is, "He now showed them the full extent of his love" (NIV).

2, 4 *Supper* See discussion at John 12:2.

3 *Went* The Greek is present tense (*hypagei*). "Went" (KJV) is the wrong tense, for Jesus had not yet returned to the Father. The correct idea is: "was going back" (NASB), or "was returning" (NIV). He would be doing this in a few days.

4 *Garments* The word *himatia* is often used for "garments" in general. But in a considerable number of passages in the NT it clearly refers to the outer garments, in contrast to the *chitōn*, the inner garment. Jesus did not take off all His clothes but simply laid aside His "outer clothing" (NIV) to work.

4, 5 *Girded* "Gird" is not a verb in common usage today. "Took a towel, and girded himself" is better rendered: "wrapped a towel around his waist" (NIV). Similarly, "the towel wherewith he was girded" would be "the towel that was wrapped around him" (NIV). Aside from these two verses, the verb *diazonnymi* is found only in 21:7 ("girt," KJV).

5 *Basin* Today we use the term *basin* in many different ways. But the Greek word here is *niptēr* (only here in NT), which comes from the verb *niptō*, "wash." So it definitely means a washbasin used only for that purpose.

10 *Washed . . . Wash* These are two different verbs in the Greek. The first is *louō*, which means to bathe the whole body. The second is *niptō* (used in vv. 5–6, 8, 12), which means to wash a part of the body (see R. C. Trench, *Synonyms of the New Testament*, p. 161). So the correct translation is: "A person who has had a bath needs only to wash his feet" (NIV).

The picture is that of a person who has bathed, but then walks the dusty streets to the market in open sandals and no socks, as was the custom in those days. When he returns home, his feet will be dirty. He does not need to take another bath, but simply to wash his feet.

This has a very important spiritual application. A person who has experienced "the bath of regeneration" (Titus 3:5, Weymouth) and then feels somewhat contaminated in mind and spirit by contact with the world does not need to be "saved" (regenerated) all over again. He only needs to claim the cleansing of the blood for the partial, temporary soiling of his soul. Young Christians, especially, need to learn this truth. They can immediately ask for and receive the needed washing of the stain.

12 *Was Set Down* Today this is a colloquial expression that describes something entirely different from what took place here. So it communicates the wrong idea to the modern reader.

The expression is one word in Greek, *anepesen*. The verb *anapiptō* is compounded of *piptō*, "fall," and *ana*, "up." In classical Greek it meant to "fall back," but in later writers (time of NT) to "recline" for eating a meal.

Goppelt calls attention to the fact that in OT times people sat for meals (and even later at Qumran). He goes on to say: "In view of this practice it is surprising that in the NT, apart from OT quotation (1C. 10:7 = Ex. 32:6), the reference is always to reclining at table and never to sitting for meals" (TDNT, 8:210). Goppelt later expresses the opinion that "one may assume that the words were used in a weak sense for 'to sit down for a meal' " (p. 211). But most NT scholars take this verb (and similar ones in NT) to mean "reclined *at table*" (NASB). It must be admitted that "resumed his place" (RSV) and "returned to his place" (NIV) leave the matter somewhat open.

13–14 *Master* The Greek word *didaskalos* means "Teacher" (from the verb *didaskō*, "teach") and should be so translated (see NASB, NIV).

16 *Servant . . . Lord* The word translated "servant" (KJV) is *doulos*, which comes from the verb *deō*, "bind," and so means a "bond servant"—what we call a "slave" (NASB). The word translated "lord" (KJV) is *kyrios*, the same as in verses 13 and 14. However, today we do not speak of the "lord" of a slave, but the "master" (NASB, NIV). The Greek used the same word for lord and slave-master. But we do not.

He That Is Sent This is all one word in Greek, *apostolos*, which occurs 81 times in the NT. Only here is it translated "he that is sent." Twice it is rendered "messenger" (2 Cor. 8:23; Phil. 2:25), where Paul uses it for human messengers. The rest of the time it is "apostle."

Since the reference here is to a human "messenger," that is perhaps the best translation here (NIV). It so happens that "sent" at the end of verse 16 is not the verb *apostellō* from which *apostolos* comes, but *pempō*. So in the Greek there is no etymological connection between "he that is sent" and "he that sent him"—though, of course, there is a logical connection.

18 *Eateth* The common verb for "eat" in the Greek NT is *esthiō* (65 times). But here we find *trōgō*. Except for Matt. 24:38 it is found only in John's Gospel (6:54, 56, 57, 58; 13:18).

Goppelt writes: "*Trōgō* means, literally 'to gnaw,' 'to bite,' '(audibly) to chew,' and then it takes on the weaker sense 'to eat,' first of herbivorous animals, Hom. Od. 6, 90, then men, Hdt. I, 71. . . . In the later Hellenistic period, under Ionic influence, the word was often used popularly instead of *esthiō* as the present of aorist *ephagon*" (TDNT, 8:236). Since John was probably the latest writer in the NT (ca. A.D. 95), that may be the reason he uses *trōgō*. It is interesting to note that the Septuagint has *esthiō* in Ps. 41:10(9), quoted here.

23 Leaning The verb is *anakeimai*, which KJV generally takes as meaning "sit" (see discussion at Luke 22:27). But this passage shows clearly that it means "reclining" (NASB, NIV), for John was not sitting on Jesus' breast! It is used again in verse 28 ("at the table," KJV).

24 Beckoned The verb is *neuō*, which Arndt and Gingrich say means "*nod to someone* as a signal" (p. 536). That fits well in Acts 24:10 (NASB), the only other place in the NT where this verb occurs. It seems to us that "nod" fits well in both passages, though NASB has "gestured" here, and NIV has "motioned" in both places. "Nodded," of course, would be with the head, while "gestured" and "motioned" would be with the hand. It is interesting to note that the German has *winkte*—that is, "winked."

Incidentally "and said" (instead of "that he should," KJV) is found in B (fourth century) and C (fifth century). It is adopted in NASB and NIV, making it direct discourse.

25 Lying The best Greek text has *anapiptō* (see discussion at v. 12), which may be translated here "leaning back" (NASB, NIV). The *Textus Receptus* has *epipiptō* (followed by KJV), which is almost always rendered "fall upon" (or, "on").

26, 27, 30 Sop Only here (in NT), including twice in verse 26, is the Greek word *psōmion* found. It means "a piece of bread" (NIV) or "morsel" (NASB). In modern Greek the word *psōmi* is used for "bread."

38 Deny For "disown" (NIV) see discussion at Matt. 26:34. The best Greek text here has the simple verb *arneomai*, but it is used interchangeably with the compound *aparneomai*.

14:1 *Ye Believe*

Again we have the problem as to whether this is to be taken as indicative (KJV) or imperative (NASB, NIV). Exactly the same form, *pisteuete*, is used in both clauses of the second half of this verse. As we have noted before, in the second person plural of the present tense the indicative and imperative forms are the same. Only the context can suggest which meaning is intended.

Which is better here? Westcott writes: "The double imperative suits the context best. The changed order of the object (Believe in God and

in me believe) marks the development of the idea. 'Believe in God, and yet more than this, let your faith find in *Me* one on whom it can rest.' In Christ belief in God gained a present reality. . . . The belief is 'in Christ,' and not in any propositions about Christ" (2:167). That is why the NIV uses "trust" instead of "believe."

2 Mansions The Greek word is *monē*, which comes from the verb *menō*, "remain" or "dwell." The noun occurs (in NT) only here and in verse 23, where it is translated "abode" (KJV, NASB) or "home" (NIV).

The rendering "mansions" in verse 2 comes from the Latin Vulgate *mansiones*. The correct rendering of *monai* is "dwelling places" (NASB) or "rooms" (NIV). In today's language a "house" cannot have many "mansions"; it has many rooms. The mistranslation here has led many people to get excited about having a mansion in heaven—for which there is no biblical basis.

15 Keep The *Textus Receptus* (on which KJV is based) has the aorist imperative, *tērēsate*. But the fourth-century Vaticanus manuscript has the future *tērēsete*. Also the third-century Papyrus 66 and the fourth-century Sinaiticus have the aorist subjunctive, which would be translated the same as the future indicative. So the best translation here is: "If you love Me, you will keep My commandments" (NASB; cf. NIV).

Actually this makes the passage stronger. It clearly makes obedience the real test of true love.

16 The Paraclete The Greek word *paraclētos* occurs five times in the NT. It is used only by John—four times in the Gospel (14:16, 26; 15:26; 16:7) and once in the First Epistle (2:1).

There is little doubt about the meaning of *paraclētos* in 1 John 2:1. The use of the Greek word for an "Advocate" (NASB) or lawyer in court is well established. Adolf Deissmann quotes a second-century papyrus: "Father Ion, I need thee not, neither as judge (nor) as paraclete"—misspelled "paracrete" (LAE, p. 336, n. 5). Behm writes: "The use as noun, attested in secular Gk. from the 4th cent. B.C. in the sense of a 'person called in to help, summoned to give assistance,' gives us the meaning of 'helper in court' " (TDNT, 5:801). While the word *paraclētos* does not occur in the Septuagint or in Josephus, it is used in Philo (first cent.) for "advocate." Behm adds: "Thus the history of the term in the whole sphere of known Greek and Hellenistic usage outside the NT yields the clear picture of a legal advisor or helper or advocate in the relevant court" (TDNT, 5:803).

But what about the meaning of *paraclētos* in John's Gospel? Interestingly, Westcott favors using "advocate" here also. He writes: "In the Gospel again the sense of advocate, counsel, one who pleads, convinces, convicts, in a great controversy, who strengthens on the one hand and defends on the other, meeting formidable attacks, is alone adequate." He goes on to say: "Christ as the Advocate pleads the believer's cause with the Father against the accuser Satan (I John ii. 1 . . .). The Holy Spirit as the advocate pleads the believer's cause against the world (John xvi. 8ff. . . .), and also Christ's cause with the believer, John xiv. 26, xv. 26, xvi. 14" (pp. 212–13).

Most scholars, however, feel that "Advocate" does not fit best in the Gospel. As is well known, *paraclētos* comes from the verb *parakaleō*—"call to one's side to help." In what ways? Behm comments: "The only thing one can say for certain is that the sense of 'comforter' favored by, e.g., Wycliffe, Luther and the A.V. in John's Gospel, does not fit any of the NT passages. Neither Jesus nor the Spirit is described as a 'comforter' " (TDNT, 5:804).

If not "comforter," what then? We have always felt that the only word that takes in all the work of the Holy Spirit for us as the Paraclete is "Helper." He helps us in whatever way we need help. If it is comfort we need, He gives that. And the context here—Jesus' announcement that He was going away (13:33–14:7)—left the disciples in need of a Comforter. And if we take "Comforter" in the literal Latin sense of "Strengthener," we find the Holy Spirit filling that role. But we also need guidance (16:13). And He will be our constant Companion (14:16). He also acts as Teacher (14:26). So, personally, we were happy when the NASB came out with "Helper." This is all-inclusive.

Why, then, does the NIV (as well as RSV) have "Counselor"? The reason is that that seems to convey the main meaning of the term. A lawyer is referred to now as a legal "counsel." When we need advice, we seek counsel from some capable person. So, whatever our need, the Holy Spirit is ready to be our Counselor at all times. For further discussion see the note in Leon Morris, *The Gospel According to John* ("The New International Commentary on the New Testament"), pages 662–66.

18 Comfortless The Greek says *orphanous*, plural of the adjective *orphanos*, which means "orphaned"—literally, "deprived of one's parents." Here it is used figuratively of Jesus' disciples, who had depended on Him. The best translation is "as orphans" (NASB, NIV). The added clause, "I will come to you," refers to His coming to them in the person of the Holy Spirit on the Day of Pentecost.

15:1 Husbandman The Greek word is *geōrgos*, which is a compound of *gē*, "earth" or "soil," and *ergon*, "work." So it refers to one who works the soil. The literal meaning, then, is "farmer" or "gardener" (NIV). The context indicates that here it refers to a "vinedresser" (RSV, NASB). And *ampelos*, "vine," definitely means a grapevine.

2 Purgeth It is true that the Greek verb here, *kathairō*, does mean "make clean." But when speaking of a grapevine, we would say, "prunes" (RSV, NASB), or "trims clean" (NIV). The purpose of pruning is that the vine may bear "more fruit." So we should take God's pruning process gratefully.

22 Cloak The Greek word is *prophasis*, which Arndt and Gingrich define as: "valid excuse." So the best translation here is "excuse" (RSV, NASB, NIV).

16:1 Be Offended See discussion at Matt. 5:29. The best translation here for the verb *scandalizō* is "go astray" (NIV).

8 Reprove The Greek word is *elengchō*. Buechsel says that it means (in NT): "to show someone his sin and to summon him to repentance." He goes on to say: "The word does not mean only 'to blame' or 'to reprove,' nor 'to convince' in the sense of proof, nor 'to reveal' or 'expose,' but 'to set right,' namely, 'to point away from sin to repentance.' " And he adds: "The noteworthy and impressive battle against sin which is part of NT Christianity is reflected in the rich use of *elengchō* and related words" (TDNT, 2:474). The correct translation is "convict" (NIV).

16 Because I Go to the Father This clause (KJV) is not found in the oldest and best Greek manuscripts. It was evidently added by a later scribe from verse 10 or verse 17.

21 In Travail "She is in travail" is all one word in Greek, *tiktē*. The verb *tiktō* means "give birth to." So the proper contemporary translation of the whole clause is: "giving birth to a child" (NIV).

23 Ask . . . Ask Two different Greek words are used for "ask" in this verse. The first is *erōtaō*, which means "ask a question" (cf. NASB, which brings this out clearly). The second is *aiteō*, which means to "ask for" (something). Again the NASB makes it clear: "If you shall ask the Father for anything."

In verse 24 "asked" is the verb *aiteō*. The NIV does bring this out by translating it "asked for" (also NASB).

25, 29 Proverb The Greek word is *paroimia*. See discussion at 10:6 ("Parable"). The best translation here is "figurative language" (NASB; cf. NIV).

27 Loveth . . . Loved The Greek verb in both cases is *phileō*, which expresses affectionate love. This is a beautiful touch!

30 Ask The verb is *erōtaō* (see discussion at v. 23). Here the NIV translates it adequately: "ask you questions."

17:2 Power The Greek word is *exousia*, which means "authority" (NASB, NIV), not "power" (KJV), which would be *dynamis*.

15 Evil This should be "the evil one" (NASB, NIV). See discussion at Matt. 6:13.

19 Through the Truth The Greek says *en alētheia*, "in truth" (NASB). This means "truly" (NIV).

23–26 Love Throughout these verses the verb is *agapaō* and the noun is *agapē*. These express the highest kind of love—unselfish, loyal, devoted.

18:1 Brook The Greek word is *cheimarros* (only here in NT). Arndt and Gingrich define it as "winter torrent, ravine, wadi" (p. 879).

Cedron This word is also found only here in the NT. The OT form is *kidron*. It means: "*The Kidron valley*, a wadi or watercourse (dry except in the rainy season), adjoining Jerusalem on the east and emptying into the Dead Sea" (AG, p. 426). We have crossed this on a bridge many times—always bone dry in summer, but almost a torrent in winter.

1, 26 Garden The Greek word *kēpos* occurs twice in 19:41, and also in Luke 13:19. In all those places it is translated "garden" in the NIV. But here the NIV has "olive grove," which is what it actually was in this instance.

3, 12 Band The Greek *speira* (also in Matt. 27:27; Mark 15:16; Acts 10:1; 21:31; 27:1) represents the Roman "cohort." This was 1/10 of a legion (6,000 men), and so properly consisted of 600 soldiers. But there may well have been only about a third of these on duty. In any case, however, it was a sizable group that came to arrest Jesus!

3 Lanterns and Torches The first word is the Greek *phanos* (only here in NT), which comes from the verb *phainō*, "shine, give light." It means "torch," and then "lantern."

The second Greek word is *lampas*, from which we get our word "lamp." It can be translated "torch" or "lantern." So the KJV and NASB (rendering as shown) and NIV (with opposite order of words here) are correct.

12 Captain The Greek word is *chiliarchos*. It comes from *chilioi*, "a thousand," and *archōn*, "ruler." So it refers to an officer in charge of 1,000 troops. In today's armies he would not be called a "captain" (KJV). So "commander" (NASB, NIV) is more correct.

17 Art Not Thou This form in English suggests that a positive answer ("Yes") is expected. But the Greek, by the use of *mē*, indicates that a negative answer is expected. This is properly represented by "You are not also one of this man's disciples, are you?" (NASB), or "Surely you are not another of this man's disciples?" (NIV). The KJV makes this mistake a number of times, as in verse 25.

19 Doctrine See discussion at Mark 1:27.

22 Struck . . . with the Palm of His Hand The Greek literally says that the officer "gave a *rhapisma* to Jesus." The earliest meaning of this noun was "a blow with a club (or rod)." But here it means "a slap in the face" (cf. NIV).

24 Had Sent This tense in KJV is wrong. The Greek has the aorist tense—"sent" (NASB, NIV). It was at this time that Annas sent Jesus to Caiaphas, not previously.

28 Hall of Judgment The Greek word *praitōrion* occurs twice in this verse. For its meaning see the discussion at Mark 15:16. It is correctly translated here as "palace of the Roman governor" (NIV), or transliterated as "Praetorium" (NASB).

30 Malefactor "Malefactor" is, of course, the Latin for "evildoer" (NASB), which is exactly what the Greek here, *kakon poiōn* (or *kakopoiōn*) means. Probably what the Jews meant by this was "a criminal" (NIV).

37 Thou Sayest that I Am In commentaries and Greek grammars one will find a wide divergence of opinion as to how this should be treated. Blass-Debrunner (leading German grammar) prefers "because I am." Westcott, in the best of the older commentaries on John, says that this "seems to be both unnatural as a rendering of the original phrase, and alien from the context" (p. 285). But both the NASB and NIV follow this idea. For a good discussion see Leon Morris, *The Gospel According to John*, p. 770. The KJV is largely neutral (and literal).

38 Fault *Aitia* basically means "cause" or "reason." Here it is used as a technical legal term (AG, p. 26), meaning "guilt" (NASB) or "basis for a charge" (NIV). A character "fault" would have no place for handling in a Roman court!

40 Robber The Greek word *lēstēs* does mean "robber" or "bandit." But Josephus uses it in the sense of "revolutionary, insurrectionist" (AG, p. 473). Hence: "had taken part in a rebellion" (NIV).

19:3 And Came to Him This clause (not in KJV) is found in the earliest Greek manuscripts. The Greek *ērchonto pros auton* can be taken as inchoative imperfect: "they began to come up to Him" (NASB). But it is better to take it as the more common repetitive imperfect: "went up to him again and again" (NIV). The best commentators (Westcott, Morris, Brown, etc.) favor the second one.

4, 6 Fault See discussion at John 18:38.

10 Crucify . . . Release The oldest and best Greek manuscripts have these in reverse order (see RSV, NASB, NIV).

19, 20 Title The Greek word *titlos* (only here in NT) means "inscription" (NASB), "notice" or "sign" (NIV).

13, 17, 20 Hebrew See discussion at John 5:2.

23 Coat The Greek has *chitōn*, which means the "undergarment" (NIV) or "tunic" (NASB).

30 Ghost The Greek reads more easily, "gave up his spirit" (NIV)—*pneuma*. Today "ghost" is used for the spirit of a person already dead.

31 Preparation See discussion at Mark 15:42.

39 Hundred Pound The Greek says: "100 *litras*" (see discussion at 12:3). Since the *litra* was only 12 ounces (see NASB margin), 100 *litras* would be "seventy-five pounds" (NIV).

20:7 Napkin See discussion of *soudarion* at Luke 19:20. Arndt and Gingrich suggest that it may have been a "face-cloth" (NASB)—"for wiping perspiration, corresponding somewhat to our handkerchief" (p. 759). But perhaps here "burial cloth" fits best (NIV).

17 Touch Me Not The verb *haptō*, in the middle voice, means "touch, take hold of, hold someone or something" (AG, p. 102). Jesus was telling Mary not to hold on to Him in the flesh—as she clung to Him—but to let Him go so that He could come in the person of the Holy Spirit on the Day of Pentecost. Then He could be with all believers everywhere all the time. The correct translation here is, "Stop clinging to Me" (NASB) or "Do not hold on to me" (NIV).

19, 26 Shut The verb *kleiō* means "shut, lock, bar" (AG, p. 434), and it is in the perfect passive participle here—"locked tight." The context, "for fear of the Jews," shows that here it means "locked" (NIV)—that is, with a bar drawn across the inside.

21:5 Meat The Greek word here is *prosphagion* (only here in the NT)—literally, "something eaten with" (bread). But it was often used simply for "fish" (AG, p. 719). That fits best here (RSV, NASB, NIV).

7 Girt . . . Naked The KJV reads: "He girt his fisher's coat unto him, (for he was naked)." Obviously "girt" is not a contemporary English word (see discussion at 13:4, 5). And "fisher's coat" is *ependytēs* (only here in NT) which simply means an "outer garment" or "coat."

What about "naked"? The Greek word is *gymnos*, from which we get *gymnasium*. It did sometimes mean "naked, stripped, bare." But Arndt and Gingrich note that often it was used by Greek writers in the sense: "*without an outer garment*, without which a decent person did not appear in public" (p. 167). So the best translation here is: "he put his outer garment on (for

95

he was stripped for work)" (NASB) or "he wrapped his outer garment around him (for he had taken it off)" (NIV).

8 Two Hundred Cubits A cubit (*pēchys*) was about 18 inches in length. So the distance here was "about a hundred yards" (NIV).

12 Dine The verb *aristaō* properly means "eat breakfast" (AG, p. 106). "Come and dine" (KJV) is hardly what one would say at about six o'clock in the morning! Rather Jesus was inviting the disciples to "come and have breakfast" (NASB, NIV).

15–17 Love Putting it into contemporary English, we have Jesus asking Peter three times, "Do you love Me?" and Peter answering each time, "You know that I love You" (NASB). But two different Greek verbs are used (see NASB margin). Twice Jesus asked, "*Agapas me?*" and Peter answered, "*Philō se.*" But the third time Jesus dropped down to Peter's lower word and inquired, "*Phileis me?*" Again Peter answered, "*Philō se.*"

What is the difference? Many commentators find no difference—just a slight literary variation. But we tend to agree with Westcott when

he writes that Peter "lays claim only to the feeling of natural love (*philō se, amo te*, v.), of which he could be sure. He does not venture to say that he has attained to that higher love (*agapan*) which was to be the spring of the Christian life" (p. 367). He goes on to say: "When the Lord puts the question 'the third time,' He adopts the word which St. Peter had used. Just as the idea of comparison was given up before ("more than these," v. 15), so now the idea of the loftiest love is given up. It is as if the Lord would test the truth of the feeling which St. Peter claimed" (p. 368). William Hendriksen also makes this distinction in his excellent commentary on John.

This difference is brought out in the NIV by using "truly love" for *agapaō* and just "love" for *phileō*. The point, then, is that Peter was hurt because the third time Jesus even questioned the apostle's affection and friendship. See also discussions at 5:20 and 11:3, 5.

Feed In verses 15 and 17 the Greek verb is *boskō*, which properly means "feed." But in verse 16 it is *poimainō*, which comes from *poimēn*, "shepherd." So the correct translation is "Shepherd My sheep" (NASB) or "Take care of my sheep" (NIV).

Acts

1:1 *Treatise*   The Greek term is *logos*, which occurs 330 times in the NT and is translated more than 20 different ways in the KJV. Basically it means "word" (218 times), but also "saying" (50 times), "account" or "speech" (8 each), or even "thing" (5 times). Here alone it is rendered "treatise."

The closest parallel is found in Xenophon's *Anabasis* (which we had the good fortune to read in Greek in college). In Book 2 he refers to one "book" (*logos*) of his history (2:1). That is exactly what we have here. The "former book" (NIV) is Luke's Gospel. Both "books" (Luke and Acts) are addressed to Theophilus ("God-lover").

3 *Infallible Proofs*   This is one word in Greek, *tekmēriois*—a strong term (only here in NT). J. R. Lumby says, "A *tekmērion* is such an evidence as to remove all doubt" (*The Acts of the Apostles*, CGT, p. 81). Jesus presented Himself alive by many "convincing proofs" (NASB, NIV).

4 *Being Assembled Together with Them*   This is all one word in Greek, the participle *synalizomenos*. There has been a great deal of discussion as to whether this means "gathering them together" (NASB; but the participle is passive!); "staying with" (RSV), or "eating with" (NIV). Arndt and Gingrich have a good brief discussion of this problem (pp. 783-84). They leave the matter open.

7 *Times . . . Seasons*   The first word (in the sing.) is *chronos*, which simply means the passing of time. But the second word is *kairos*, meaning a fixed, appointed time. F. F. Bruce says here that "*chronous* refers to the time that must elapse before the final establishment of the Kingdom; *kairous* to the critical events accompanying its establishment" (p. 70).

Power   The Greek word is *exousia*, which should be translated "authority"—as is done correctly in versions today.

8 *Power*   Here the word is *dynamis*, from which we get *dynamite*, *dynamic*, and *dynamo*. These English words suggest: (1) adequate power; (2) personal power; (3) perpetual power.

13 *Zelotes*   See discussion at Mark 3:18 ("Canaanite"). Luke also used "the Zealot" (NASB, NIV) in his Gospel (6:15).

14 *With One Accord*   This is one word in Greek, *homothymadon* (10 times in Acts, but nowhere else in NT except Rom. 15:6). It is composed of *homos*, "same," and *thymos*, "mind" or "spirit," and so means "with one mind" (NASB).

15 *Disciples*   Instead of *mathētōn* ("disciples," KJV), the early Greek manuscripts have *adelphōn*, "brothers" (cf. NASB). Since there were women in the group (v. 14), the NIV has "believers."

Names   In the papyri of that period, as well as in the Septuagint, *onoma* ("name") is used for "person" (cf. NASB).

16 *Men and Brethren*   As indicated by italics in the KJV, the Greek has only "Men brethren" (*Andres adelphoi*). This is good Greek, but impossible English. We would simply say "Brothers" (NIV).

17 Numbered We have here the perfect passive participle of the compound verb *katarithmeō* (only here in NT). The simple verb *arithmeō* gives us our word *arithmetic*. The compound in the perfect tense emphasizes the fact that Judas Iscariot was really counted as one of the 12 apostles.

Part The Greek word *klēros* literally means a "lot" that is cast to decide a choice, as in verse 26. Here it means a "portion" (NASB) received by divine appointment. It was originally the lot that was cast, and then what was received as a result. That is why the word *lot* is used today for a field, because the land was originally assigned on the basis of casting lots (see Josh. 18:10, 11; 19:1, 10, etc; Judg. 1:3).

20 Bishopric The Greek word is *episcopē*, from which we get our word *episcopal*. An *episcopos* was an overseer, but that word is translated "bishop" (KJV) in four out of five times it occurs in the NT. Here *episcopē* means "office" (NASB) or "place of leadership" (NIV).

23 Appointed The Greek has the aorist of *histēmi*, which means "put, place, set." For this passage Arndt and Gingrich suggest "put forward" (NASB) or "proposed" (NIV).

24 Which Knowest the Hearts This is all one word in Greek, the noun *cardiognōstēs* ("heart-knower"), which occurs (in NT) only here and 15:8.

25 By Transgression Fell This is the single word *parebē*. The verb *parabainō* literally means "go beside." Then it took on the sense of "overstep" or "transgress." On its use here J. Schneider writes: "Literally, of course, it simply states the fact that Judas has withdrawn from his apostolic office. . . . But the choice of the word *parebē* carries an unmistakable reference to the guilt of Judas" (TDNT, 5:738–39).

2:1 Pentecost *Pentēcostē* is a feminine substantive from the adjective *pentēcostos*, "fiftieth" (AG, p. 643)—found three times in the NT (see 20:16; 1 Cor. 16:8). The feast was so called because it occurred on the 50th day after Passover. In the OT it is called the Feast of Weeks (Deut. 16:9–10).

Was Fully Come The Greek literally says, "was being fulfilled" (present infinitive of *synplēroō*). This may refer to the completion of the seven weeks preceding Pentecost (so *Begin-*

nings of Christianity, 4:16; F. F. Bruce, *Acts*, p. 81).

Of One Accord This translates the word *homothymadon*, which is found in 1:14 (see discussion there) and here in the *Textus Receptus*. But the early Greek manuscripts have *homou*, which simply means "together" (NASB, NIV).

2 A Rushing Mighty Wind The Greek literally says "a violent wind being borne along" (*pheromenēs pnoēs biaias*). It was a reverberating roar that made the 120 fully alert for what was to follow.

3 Cloven Tongues The Greek reads: *diamerizomenai glōssai*. The verb *diamerizō* means "divide, separate, distribute." The present participle here may be either passive ("being distributed") or middle ("distributing themselves"). A. T. Robertson (WP, 3:21) prefers the latter. The tongues "as of fire" separated, and one tongue of fire rested on each person.

5 Devout Men The Greek adjective *eulabeis* ("devout, God-fearing") is used only by Luke. In its other three occurrences (Luke 2:25; Acts 8:2; 22:12) it clearly refers to Jews, not Gentiles. So here we should probably put together "Jews" and "devout men"—"God-fearing Jews" (NIV).

6 Was Noised Abroad This expression suggests wide advertising. The Greek simply says, "When this sound (*phōnē*) happened." There is no way of being certain whether this is the "sound" (*ēchos*) of verse 2 or the inspired preaching of verse 4.

Multitude The Greek word *plēthos* means "a great number." The term is used mainly by Luke—25 times in his Gospel and in Acts—and only 7 times elsewhere in the NT. "Crowd" (NIV) is more contemporary than "multitude" (KJV, NASB).

8 Tongue The Greek word here is the same as what is found in verse 6—*dialectos*, the common Greek word for "language." So it definitely should be translated "language" here. In the Greek we have *glōssais*, "tongues," in verses 4 and 11, and *dialectō*, "language," in verses 6 and 8. This proves conclusively that the speaking in tongues (v. 4) was not ecstatic utterance but speaking in known, intelligent languages of that day (see v. 11).

10 Proselytes "Jews and proselytes" is in verse 11 in our printed Greek Testament and so is placed there in the NIV.

Our word "proselyte" is taken over directly from the Greek *prosēlytos*, which literally means "one who has come over," and so a "convert." In the NT it means (pl.) Gentile "converts to Judaism" (NIV).

12 Were . . . Amazed As in verse 7, the verb is *existēmi*, which means "put out of its place," and so "drive one out of his senses" (A-S, p. 160). It indicates an overwhelming feeling of amazement.

Were in Doubt The verb *diaporeō*—here in the imperfect tense of continuousness (cf. NASB)—means "be quite at a loss, be in great perplexity" (A-S, p. 110). It is used only by Luke (Luke 9:7; Acts 2:12; 5:24; 10:17).

14 Said This is not the common verb *legō*, "say," but a strong compound *apophthengomai* (only here, v. 4, and 26:25). It means "speak out, declare boldly or loudly" (AG, p. 102).

The three verbs in this verse suggest that Peter did three things that every preacher in the pulpit should do today: (1) Stood up; (2) Spoke up; (3) Spoke out.

22 Approved This is the perfect passive participle of *apodeiknymi*. It means "attested" (NASB) or "accredited" (NIV). Moulton and Milligan also note that it was used in the papyri of that period in the sense of proclaiming an appointment to public office (VGT, p. 60). Jesus' miracles were His divine credentials, proclaiming God's appointment of Him as the Messiah.

Miracles . . . Wonders . . . Signs These are the three words used to describe the miracles of Jesus. The first is *dynamesi*, "powers." The miracles demonstrated divine power. The second is *terasi*. Jesus' miracles struck the viewers with amazement and wonder. The third word, *sēmeiois*, indicates the significance of the miracles. They were "signs" of divine power, and also they symbolized some spiritual truth. That is why John in his Gospel always refers to Jesus' miracles as "signs." (For further discussions see my treatment in *Beacon Bible Commentary*, 7:285–86.)

23 Delivered This is the adjective *ekdotos* (only here in NT). It comes from the verb *ekdidōmi*, "give over." So it means "delivered up" (NASB) or "handed over" (NIV).

Determinate Counsel The first word is in Greek the perfect passive participle of *horizō*. This comes from the noun *horos*, "boundary." So it means literally to "mark off by boundaries," and then "to determine, appoint, designate" (A-S, p. 323). The second word is *boulē*, which means "counsel" or "purpose." So the expression may be translated "predetermined plan" (NASB) or "set purpose" (NIV).

Foreknowledge The Greek word is *prognōsis*—only here and 1 Pet. 1:2. This is one of the many parallels between Peter's First Epistle and his speeches in Acts.

Wicked The Greek has the adjective *anomos*, which is composed of alpha-privative *a-* and *nomos*, "law." So it literally means "lawless" or "without law" (as in 1 Cor. 9:21)—that is, Gentiles. In Jewish literature this adjective is often used to indicate the Romans (*Beginnings*, 4:23). This fits perfectly here, for it was actually the Romans who crucified Jesus.

Incidentally, in verse 23 we have a striking combination of divine sovereignty and human freedom. These both have to be held in balance.

24 Pains See discussion of "Sorrows" at Mark 13:8.

25 Moved The verb *saleuō* means "shake," as with the wind (cf. Matt. 11:7). Here it is used metaphorically in the sense of "*cast down* from a sense of security and happiness" (A-S, p. 400). So the best translation is "shaken" (NASB, NIV).

27, 31 Hell The Greek is *hadēs*, "Hades" (NASB). *Hadēs* meant the place of departed spirits, or "the grave" (NIV).

28 Countenance The word *prosōpon* literally means "face" or "countenance." But it also came to mean "presence," which fits best here (NASB, NIV).

30 Christ "He would raise up Christ" (KJV) is not in the oldest Greek manuscripts, and so will not be found in scholarly versions today.

33 Shed Forth The verb *ekcheō* means "pour out." It is so translated (KJV) 11 out of the 18 times it occurs in the NT ("shed" 4 times and "shed forth" only here). The proper rendering is "poured out" (NIV). The KJV correctly has "pour out" in verses 17 and 18—used of the Holy Spirit, as here.

37 Pricked The strong verb *katanyssō* (only here in NT) means "to pierce, to sting sharply, to stun, to smite" (WP, 3:34). It describes vividly the Holy Spirit's work of conviction.

43 Fear The Greek word is *phobos*, which basically means "fear." But it often, as here, means reverential fear, and so "awe" (NASB, NIV).

45 Sold . . . Parted The impression given here is that all the believers immediately sold their possessions and distributed the proceeds among the needy. But that would require both these verbs to be in the aorist tense of punctiliar action.

Instead they are in the imperfect tense of continuous or repetitive action (*epipraskon kai diemerizon*). As needs arose, properties were sold and money made available. This thought is further developed in the discussion of Acts 4:34–35.

46 From House to House The Greek says *kat' oikon*. This could be translated "at home" (ASV). But Arndt and Gingrich (p. 406) suggest "in the various houses" and cite papyrus support for this usage. "In their homes" (NIV) could be taken either way.

Meat The word is *trophē*, which means "nourishment" or "food," not "meat" as that word is taken today.

47 Such as Should Be Saved This translation is unjustified. The Greek simply says: "And the Lord was adding together those who were being saved" (*tous sōzomenous*). Incidentally, "the church" (KJV) is not in the early manuscripts.

3:7 Feet . . . Ancle Bones This should be simply "feet and ankles" (NIV). Both nouns, *basis* and *sphydron* (sing.), are found only here in the NT. And the verb *stereoō* ("make firm or solid," and so "strengthen") occurs elsewhere (in NT) only in verse 16 and 16:5.

All three of these words are found frequently in medical writers. This reflects the medical interest of "Luke, the doctor" (Col. 4:14, NIV), who wrote Acts.

8 Leaping Up The compound verb *exallomai* occurs only here in the NT, one of the many *hapax legomena* in Luke's writings. "Leaping" in the last part of the verse is the simple verb *allomai*.

10 Amazement See discussion at Mark 16:8.

11 Porch See discussion at John 5:2.

12 Holiness This is a rather strong translation for *eusebeia*, which simply means "piety" (NASB) or "godliness" (NIV).

13 Son The Greek does not have "Son" (KJV), which would be *whios*. Rather it is *pais*, which means "child," but also "servant, slave, attendant." In fact, in the KJV it is translated "servant" 10 times and "son" only 3 times (3:13, 26; John 4:51). Regarding the use of *pais* here, Arndt and Gingrich say: "In this connection it has the meaning *servant*, because of the identification of the 'servant of God' of certain OT passages with the Messiah" (p. 609). The so-called Servant Songs of Isaiah reflect this usage (cf. Isa. 42:1; 50:10; 52:13). That is why this translation is used in NASB and NIV.

13, 14 Denied *Arneomai* does commonly mean "deny." But we deny statements, not persons. So the better translation is "disowned" (NASB, NIV).

15 Prince The Greek word is *archēgos*, an adjective meaning "beginning, originating" but used mostly as a substantive with the sense of "founder, author" or "prince, leader" (A-S, p. 62). Both meanings are possible here: "Prince" (NASB); "author" (NIV).

16 Perfect Soundness This is one word in Greek, *holoklēria* (only here in NT). It means "completeness, soundness" (A-S, p. 315).

19 Be Converted The verb *epistrephō* is used in the Septuagint most often in the sense of "return." That is the best translation here (NASB).

Refreshing The noun *anapsyxis* (only here in NT) comes from the verb *anapsychō* (also only once in NT, at 2 Tim. 1:16). The verb is used frequently in the sense of "revive, refresh oneself" (A-S, p. 35). So the expression here could be translated "times of revival." These are "times of refreshing."

Blotted Out The verb *exaleiphō* is better translated "wiped away" (NASB; cf. NIV).

20 Preached The best Greek text does not have *prokekērygmenon*, "preached before" but *prokecheirismenon*, "appointed for" (ASV, RSV,

NASB, NIV). F. F. Bruce translates this passage: "And that He may send Jesus, who has been appointed Messiah for you" (*Acts*, p. 112).

21 Restitution The noun *apokatastasis* (only here in NT) means "restoration" (NASB; cf. NIV). It was used in the second century B.C. for the renewal of the sanctuary of a goddess and for the repair of a public road (VGT, p. 63). Josephus speaks of the "restoration" of the Jews from exile (*Ant.* 11. 3. 8).

Universalists have seized on "the times of restitution of all things" to bolster their claim that all people will ultimately be saved. But it is the "restoration of all things about which God spoke by the mouth of His holy prophets from ancient time" (NASB). The OT indicates clearly that there are two classes of people: those who accept God's offer of redemptive salvation and those who reject it. The latter are lost.

26 Son Jesus "Jesus" is not in the early Greek manuscripts. For a discussion of "Son" (KJV) versus "Servant" (NASB, NIV), see the treatment at Acts 3:13 ("Son").

4:1 Captain For the meaning of *stratēgos* see the discussion at Luke 22:4. This man was "captain of the temple guard" (NASB, NIV).

2 Being Grieved The Greek verb *diaponeō* (only here and 16:18) means to be "greatly disturbed" (NASB, NIV). The religious leaders were not "grieved"; they were angry and upset.

Through The Greek has *en*, "in" (NASB, NIV). That is, the apostles were preaching that "in the case of Jesus" a real resurrection had unquestionably taken place. The "priests" and "captain of the Temple guard" were all "Sadducees," and the Sadducees did not believe in any resurrection (23:8). They were greatly disturbed to have their doctrinal position challenged.

3 Hold The noun *tērēsis* comes from the verb *tēreō*, which means "watch over, guard, keep, preserve" (A-S, p. 445). So it is used in 1 Cor. 7:19 for a "keeping" of the commandments. But here and in 5:18 (the only two other places it occurs in NT), it means "jail" (NASB, NIV). Deissmann gives an example of this use in an early papyrus (BS, p. 267).

4 Was On the basis of this statement many people have declared: "The Book of Acts says that 3,000 were saved on the Day of Pentecost (chapter 2), and then in the fourth chapter that 5,000 more believed." But the Greek verb here is not *ēn*, "was," but *egenēthē*, "became," or "came to be" (NASB). The NIV spells it out carefully: "the number of men grew to about five thousand." This figure includes the 3,000 saved on the Day of Pentecost.

13 Unlearned . . . Ignorant In the Greek the first word is the adjective *agrammatos* (only here in NT), which literally means "unlettered." In the papyri of that period it is used very frequently in the sense of "illiterate" (VGT, p. 6). But Thayer thinks that here it means "unversed in the learning of the Jewish schools" (p. 8). The leaders knew that these disciples of Jesus had not received rabbinical training. (See further my discussion in BBC, 7:302.)

The second word is the noun *idiōtēs*, from which we get *idiot*. But the word comes from the adjective *idios*, "one's own." So the basic meaning is "a *private person*, as opposed to the State or an official." Then it came to mean: "one without professional knowledge, unskilled, uneducated, unlearned" (A-S, p. 213). "Unschooled, ordinary men" (NIV), or "uneducated and unschooled men" (NASB), puts it well.

24 Lord The usual Greek word for "Lord" in the NT is *kyrios*. But here we have *despota* (vocative form of *despotēs*) from which we get *despot*. Rengstorf notes that the earliest use of *despotēs* was for "the master of the house who normally rules unconditionally his family and household" (TDNT, 2:44). It was also used for "the absolute ruler in the sense of an unlimited possibility of the exercise of power unchecked by any law, as exemplified in the Persian monarch" (pp. 44–45). In the Septuagint "it serves especially to emphasize the power of God" (p. 45) or "to denote the omnipotence of God" (p. 46). Rengstorf also says: "In Josephus *despota* is the most common form of address in prayer" (p. 45, n. 13). That is what we have here.

Incidentally, "art God" (KJV) is not in the two fourth-century manuscripts, one of the fifth-century manuscripts, nor Papyrus 74 (seventh cent.). So it is omitted in recent scholarly versions.

Probably the best translation of *despota* when addressed to God is "Sovereign Lord" (RSV, NIV). This emphasizes His supreme power as Ruler.

26 Christ The Greek word *christos* means "Anointed One" (NIV).

27, 30 Child See discussion of "Son" at Acts 3:13.

27 Of a Truth The oldest Greek manuscripts add: "in this city" (see NASB, NIV).

34 Sold See the discussion at Acts 2:45. In the present passage (4:34–35) it is even more clear that there was not the practice of selling all private property and turning the proceeds into a common treasury. By the use of five imperfects, plus a present participle, this mistaken interpretation is clearly proved wrong. The force of the Greek is well brought out in the NIV of verses 34–35: "For from time to time those who owned lands or houses sold them, brought the money from the sales and put it at the apostles' feet, and it was distributed to anyone as he had need." For further discussion, see BBC, 7:306–7.

36 Consolation The Greek word is *paraklēsis*. It comes from the verb *parakaleō*, which has three distinct meanings: (1) "beseech"; (2) "exhort"; (3) "comfort." Some scholars prefer "exhortation," feeling that Barnabas was an exhorter, while Paul was a teacher. But the ideas of "exhortation" and "consolation" can be combined in the one word "encouragement" (RSV, NASB, NIV). So this is doubtless best.

5:1 Sapphira This name (only here in NT) comes from *sapphiros* (only in Rev. 21:19), meaning "sapphire." This woman didn't adorn her name by what she did here!

2 Kept Back The verb *nosphizō* (only here; v. 3; Titus 2:10) in the middle voice (as always in NT) means "set apart for oneself." That is why NASB and NIV have "kept back . . . for himself." Ananias cared more for himself than he did for God or the needy ones around him.

Being Privy to It This is one word in Greek, *syneiduiēs*, the perfect participle (with present meaning) of *synoida*, "know together." What it means is: "with his wife's full knowledge" (NASB, NIV). They acted in collusion.

5, 10 Gave Up the Ghost The Greek says *exepyxen*. The verb *ekpsychō* (only here; v. 10; 12:23) means "to expire, breathe one's last" (A-S, p. 143). W. K. Hobart writes: "The very rare word *ekpsychein* seems to be almost altogether confined to the medical writers and very seldom used by them" (*The Medical Language of St. Luke*, p. 37). This is one of the many evidences that the Third Gospel and Acts were written by Luke, the beloved physician.

11 Church Here the Greek word *ecclēsia* occurs for the first of 23 times in Acts. (For a discussion of its meaning, see Matt. 16:18.) Aside from Acts it is used most frequently in 1 Corinthians (22 times), Revelation (20), and Ephesians and 2 Corinthians (9 times each).

16 Vexed The verb *ochleō* (only here in NT) comes from *ochlos*, "crowd." It means to be "disturbed" or "troubled" (crowded?), and here "tormented" (NIV).

17 Indignation The noun *zēlos* has eight times in the NT the good meaning "zeal"— which is what we have taken over into English. But the same number of times it has the bad sense of "jealousy," as here (NASB, NIV).

18 Common The adjective *dēmosia* comes from *dēmos*, "the people" (from which we get *democracy*). Probably the last two words of the verse are best translated "the public jail" (NASB, NIV).

18, 19, 21, 22, 23, 25 Prison The word "prison" occurs 6 times in these 6 verses. In the NIV it is "jail" all 6 times. The Greek has *tērēsis* in verse 18; *phylakē* in verses 19, 22, and 25; and *desmōtērion* in verses 21 and 23. This distinction in the Greek is brought out in the NASB by "jail" (v. 18), "prison" (19, 22, 25), and "prison house" (21, 23).

We have already discussed *tērēsis* at Acts 4:3, where it is translated "hold" (KJV). *Phylakē* comes from *phylassō*, "guard." So it means a place where prisoners are guarded. *Desmōtērion* (found also in 16:26; Matt. 11:2) comes from the adjective *desmios*, "bound." So it signifies a place where prisoners are bound. See discussion of "hold" at Acts 4:3.

21 Senate The word *gerousia* comes from *gerōn* (only found in John 3:4), which means "an old man." So it means "a council of elders." Lexicographers agree with other scholars in holding that in the NT *gerousia* means the Sanhedrin. So probably we should treat the *kai* ("and") as "even"—one of its meanings. The reference is not to two councils, but one. This is well brought out in the NIV: "they called together the Sanhedrin—the full assembly of the elders of Israel—and sent to the jail for the apostles."

6:1 Disciples This is the first of 28 times in Acts that we find this term. It is applied to Christians in general. For the meaning of "disciple" see the discussion at Matt. 10:1.

Grecians The Greek is *Hellēnistōn*, "Hellenists." These were Greek-speaking Jewish Christians.

Hebrews *Hebraious* evidently means Aramaic-speaking Jewish Christians. There were cultural and linguistic differences between these two groups.

Neglected The verb *paratheōreō* (only here in NT) literally means "look beside." So the best translation here is "overlooked" (NASB, NIV).

Ministration The Greek noun is *diaconia*, which means "service." The related verb *diaconeō* is translated "serve" in verse 2. One of its earliest uses in Greek was for serving food at tables. The noun apparently means "serving of food" (NASB) or "distribution of food" (NIV). (See further discussion in BBC, 7:323–24.)

3 Business The Greek word is *chreia*. F. F. Bruce writes: "The NT force of *chreia* is usually 'need,' but in Hellenistic Greek it generally means 'office,' as here" (*Acts* p. 152).

4 Prayer It is widely agreed that *proseuchē* here means public prayer, which would be associated with the "ministry" (*diaconia*) "of the word."

8 Faith The best Greek text has *charitos*, "grace" (RSV, NASB, NIV).

9 Libertines Today this term has a bad connotation. But the Greek *Libertinōn* simply means "Freedmen" (NASB, NIV)—that is, captives or slaves who had been set free (see BBC, 7:328). They evidently met in one synagogue.

11 Suborned The verb *hypoballō* (only here in NT) literally means "throw under." It then meant "instigate (secretly)" (AG, p. 843). Here it may be translated "secretly induced" (NASB) or "secretly persuaded" (NIV).

7:6 Strange The Greek adjective *allotrios* comes from *allos*, "another." So it means "belonging to another, not one's own" (AG, p. 40). Today we would not speak of France, for instance, as a "strange" country, but as a "foreign" country. So the best contemporary translation here is "foreign" (NASB) or "not their

own" (NIV). The reason the NIV finally adopted the latter (in 1978) is that the Septuagint specifically says "not its own" (singular with *sperma*, "seed").

11 Sustenance The Greek word *chortasma* (only here in NT) comes from *chortos*, "grass." It is always used in the papyri and Septuagint of "fodder for domesticated animals." But Arndt and Gingrich think that here it means "food for men" (p. 884). Why not both? It is doubtless best to translate it "food" (NASB, NIV). Both men and flocks would suffer in the famine.

12 Corn *Sitia* is plural for *sition* (only here in NT), a diminutive of *sitos*, "wheat" (called "corn" in British circles). But *sitos* came to be used for "grain" in general. Abbott-Smith says that the plural *sitia* means "bread, food, provisions" (p. 407). This would basically be wheat or "grain" (NASB, NIV).

14 Sent . . . and Called The Greek literally says "having sent" (*aposteilas*) . . . "he called" (*metekalesato*). Interestingly, the verb *metakaleō* occurs only in Acts (7:14; 10:32; 20:17; 24:25). It means "to call from one place to another." Abbott-Smith says that in the middle (always in NT) it means "to send for" (p. 287). The NIV combines the two verbs in the simple translation "sent for." Both the Hebrew and Greek have very fulsome language that often has to be simplified somewhat to make good English.

19 Dealt Subtlely The verb *katasophizomai* (only here in NT) would naturally suggest "deal wisely with" (cf. Exod. 1:10), from *sophia*, "wisdom." But it actually conveys the sense "to deal craftily with, outwit" (A-S, p. 238). So it may be translated "took shrewd advantage of" (NASB) or "dealt treacherously with" (NIV).

Cast Out The Greek literally is "make" (*poiein*) the children "cast out"—the adjective *ekthetos* (only here in NT). Obviously the verb and adjective together mean "throw out" (NIV) or "expose" (NASB).

Young Children The noun *brephos* first meant "an unborn child," as in Luke 1:41, 44. Then it came to be used for "a newborn child, a babe" (Luke 2:12, 16; 18:15; Acts 7:19; 1 Pet. 2:2). So here we may use "infants" (NASB) or "newborn babies" (NIV).

20 Exceeding Fair The Greek says that he was *asteios* "to God." The adjective (only here and Heb. 11:23 in NT) means: "1. beautiful, well-formed." Arndt and Gingrich go on to say: "However, this adjective applied to Moses in Scripture seems also to have been understood (as the addition of *t. theō* shows) in the sense 2. acceptable, well-pleasing" (p. 117). It may be that "to God" or "before God" gives a strong superlative force to the adjective (*Beginnings*, 4:75). That is the way it is taken in the KJV. In modern Greek *theo* is used as a prefix to adjectives with the force of "very" (Bruce, *Acts*, p. 167).

20, 21 Nourished The verb *anatrephō* may be used in two ways: "1. of physical nurture *bring up*, care for . . . of the infant Moses Ac 7:20. . . . 2. of mental and spiritual nurture *bring up*, rear, train . . . Ac 7:21" (AG, p. 62). This plausible distinction is brought out in the NIV by the use of "cared for" (v. 20) and "raised" (v. 21).

22 Was Learned The verb *paideuō* (aorist passive, *epaideuthē*) comes from *pais*, "child," and meant first of all "train children." Then it came to be used more generally for "instruct." The best translation here is: "was educated" (NASB, NIV).

24 Defended The Greek has a very rare verb, *amynomai*, which means "retaliate," or "help, come to the aid of" (AG, p. 47).

Oppressed The verb is *kataponeō* (only here and 2 Pet. 2:7). It means "subdue, torment, wear out, oppress" (AG, p. 416).

26 Would Have Set Them at One The verb *synallassō* (only here in NT) is in the imperfect tense of attempted but unsuccessful action. So the best translation is "tried to reconcile them" (NASB, NIV).

33 Shoes *Hypodēma* literally means "something bound under" (the foot). In those days they did not wear shoes, but "sandals" (NASB, NIV).

38 Church The Greek word is *ecclēsia*. But this is used in the Septuagint many times for the "congregation" or "assembly" (of Israel), and that is the way it should be rendered here (cf. NASB, NIV). The translation "church" should be reserved for the Christian group.

45 Jesus The Greek does have the familiar word *Iēsous*. But this is the Greek equivalent of the Hebrew "Joshua" (or, *Yehoshua*). The reference here (and in Heb. 4:8) is very clearly to Joshua, Moses' successor. It is misleading to the unsuspecting reader to have "Jesus" here (KJV), when elsewhere that word refers to Jesus Christ.

48 Temples Made with Hands Should it be "temples" (KJV) or "houses" (NASB, NIV)? Neither word occurs in the Greek, which simply has the adjective *cheiropoiētois*, "handmade." So either noun may be put with it. But since "house" (*oikon*) occurs in verse 49, that fits best here.

53 Disposition The noun *diatagē* means "ordinance, direction," and here "*by directions of angels* (i.e., by God's directing angels [to transmit it])" (AG, p. 189).

8:1 Consenting We have here the present participle of *syneudokeō*. In analyzing a compound Greek word, we begin in the latter part, the basic root, and work backward through the prefixes. So this verb means "think well together with" that is, "give approval to." The principle here may be translated "in hearty agreement with" (NASB) or "giving approval to" (NIV).

Death The noun *anairesis* comes from the verb *anaireō*, which basically means "take up" (as in 7:21). But the verb came to have the stronger meaning of "take away, make an end of, destroy," and finally "kill" (A-S, p. 30). So the noun (only here in NT) means "a slaying, murder," or "death."

At That Time The Greek literally says "on that day" (NASB, NIV). The great persecution broke out immediately.

2 Carried . . . to His Burial The verb is *synkomizō* (only here in NT), which literally means "*to bring together, collect*" (in Herodotus and Xenophon) and then "*to take up* a body for burial (Sophocles)" (A-S, p. 431). So the simple translation here is "buried" (NASB, NIV).

Lamentation *Kopetos* (only here in NT) meant "a beating of the head and breast." This was the typical Oriental way of showing deep mourning.

3 Made Havoc The verb *lymainō* probably comes from the noun *lymē*, "outrage." It was used by Greek writers for "the mangling by wild beasts, e.g. lions . . . boars . . . leopards . . . wolves" (*Beginnings*, 4:88). The imperfect tense may suggest that Saul "was trying to destroy the church" (AG, p. 481). But it could be taken as the inchoative imperfect: "began ravaging the church" (NASB). We would somewhat prefer the continuous imperfect: "was ravaging the church," like a wild boar rooting up the vines in a vineyard (Ps. 80:13, where the Septuagint used this word).

Every House The Greek has *kata tous oikous*. R. J. Knowling comments: "The expression may denote 'entering into every house,' . . . or perhaps, more specifically, the houses known as places of Christian assembly." He adds: "In any case the words, as also those which follow, show the thoroughness and relentlessness of Saul's persecuting zeal" (EGT, 2:210).

Haling This is "an old English form of *hauling*, i.e. violently pulling" (Meyer, p. 318). The Greek verb is *syrō*, which means "drag someone away (by force)" (AG, p. 794). It is used of dragging in a net (John 21:8).

4 Scattered Abroad *Diasparentes* (second aorist passive participle of *diaspeirō*) gives us our word Diaspora, meaning "dispersion." The verb meant "to sow in separate or scattered places" (WP, 3:102). That is what happened to the gospel as a result of this dispersion.

4, 5 Preaching . . . Preached The verb in verse 4 is *euangelizomai*, "announce good news," while in verse 5 it is *kēryssō*, "herald" or "proclaim" (from the noun *kēryx*, "a herald" who makes an official proclamation). So it is best to use "preaching" (NASB) in verse 4, and "proclaimed" (NIV) in verse 5. "Began proclaiming" (NASB) takes the imperfect here as inchoative; it may also be continuous. A. T. Robertson makes it both: "began to preach and kept on at it." He adds: "Note *euaggelizomenoi* in verse 4 of missionaries of good news . . . while *ekērussen* here presents the preacher as a herald" (WP, 3:102).

6 Gave Heed We have here the imperfect of the verb *prosechō*. *Echō* means "hold," and *pros* means "to." Originally it was followed by *ton noun*, "the mind"—"hold the mind to something." Then the *ton noun* was frequently omitted, but understood. So the word *proseichon* means "were giving attention to" (NASB) or "paid close attention to" (NIV).

9 Used Sorcery The Greek has *prouparchen . . . mageuōn*. A. T. Robertson writes: "An ancient idiom (periphrastic), the present active participle *mageuōn* with the imperfect active verb from *prouparchō*, the idiom only here and Luke 23:12 in the N.T. Literally 'Simon was existing previously practising magic.' This old verb *mageuō* is from *magos* (a *magus*, seer, prophet, false prophet, sorcerer) and occurs here alone in the N.T." (WP, 3:104).

9, 11 Bewitched The Greek has *existanōn*: "Present active participle of the verb *existanō*, later form of *existēmi*, to throw out of position, displace, upset, astonish, chiefly in the Gospels in the N.T." (WP, 3:104). The verb is correctly translated (in KJV) "amazed" or "astonished" 12 out of the 17 times it occurs, and it should be one of those here.

10 The Great Power of God The Greek literally says: "This one is the power of God that is called Great" (cf. NASB, NIV).

11 Had Regard This is the same verb, *proseichon*, that is translated "gave heed" in verses 6 and 10. The NASB deserves credit for translating it the same way in all three places.

Sorceries The Greek word is *mageia* (only here in NT). The simplest translation is "magic" (NIV). But since it is plural here, "magic arts" (NASB) may be better.

20 Thy Money Perish with Thee The Greek literally says, "May your money [silver] be with you for [unto] perishing." The "may" is expressed by the optative form, *eiē*. F. F. Bruce writes: "In *eiē* we have a real optative, expressing a wish (cf. Lk. i. 38; Mk. xi. 14, etc.). There are 38 such proper optatives in the NT, fifteen of them being accounted for by the phrase *mē genoito*. Of the remaining twenty-three, Paul is responsible for fifteen. The optative was dying out in Hellenistic Gk., and has disappeared in Mod. Gk., except for *mē genoito*, which is of literary origin" (*Acts*, pp. 187–88). We might add that aside from Luke 20:16 (see discussion there on "God forbid"), *mē genoito* occurs only in Paul's Epistles. So he is responsible for 29 of the 38 optatives in the NT.

21 Right *Eutheia* is the feminine form of the adjective *euthys*, "straight." Morally, as here, it means "straightforward, right" (A-S, p. 186).

22 Thought *Epinoia* (only here in NT) means "thought" or "conception," here "intent"

(AG, p. 296). F. F. Bruce says it indicates "an evil thought or intent" (*Acts*, p. 188).

25 Preached . . . Preached The first word "preached" translates the verb *laleō*, "speak" (aorist participle), whereas the second "preached" is the verb *euangelizomai* (in the imperfect indicative). This distinction is brought out well in the NASB: "had . . . spoken . . . were preaching."

27, 34, 36, 38, 39 Eunuch The word *eunouchos* occurs (in NT) only in these five verses and three times in Matt. 19:12. In the latter passage it is used in the first place for men who "are by nature incapable of marrying and begetting children," and in the third place "of those who abstain from marriage, without being impotent." But in the second time in Matt. 19:12 and in all five occurrences here it is used "of physically castrated men. . . . They served, especially in the orient, as keepers of the harem (Esth. 2:14) and not infrequently rose to high positions in the state" (AG, p. 323).

37 This verse is not found in the oldest Greek manuscripts (third, fourth, and fifth centuries). So it is omitted in all scholarly versions today. It is easy to see why a later scribe would add it.

9:1 Breathing Out The verb *empneō* (only here in NT) first meant "breathe on" (*en*), and then simply "breathe." Knowling says of Paul that "threatening and murdering were as it were the atmosphere which he breathed, and in and by which he lived" (EGT, 2:229).

2 Of This Way The Greek simply says "being of the way" (*tēs hodou ontas*). This expression, "the Way" (capitalized in recent versions), is found six times in Acts (9:2; 19:9, 23; 22:4; 24:14, 22). "This appears to be one of the earliest names for the Church in Greek" (*Beginnings*, 4:100). The best translation here is "who belonged to the Way" (NIV; cf. NASB).

5–6 It Is Hard . . . Said unto Him The last part of verse 5 and the first part of verse 6 are omitted in practically all the Greek manuscripts. In fact, the first part of verse 6 is only found in the Latin, not at all in the Greek. It is obvious that "it is hard for thee to kick against the pricks" was imported here from 26:14, where it is the genuine Greek text.

20 Christ The early Greek manuscripts all have "Jesus" (cf. RSV, NASB, NIV).

25 By the Wall The Greek says "through [*dia*] the wall." This was obviously "through an opening in the wall" (NASB, NIV).

31 The Churches The plural is not found in any Greek manuscript earlier than the ninth century. All the old manuscripts have the singular *ecclēsia*, "the church" (NASB, NIV).

Edified The Greek has the present participle of *oikodomeō*, which literally meant "build a house" (*oikos*), and then simply "build." It is better to say here, "being built up" (NASB).

39 Coats See discussion at Matt. 5:40.

10:1 Centurion The Greek word *hekatontarchēs* is found—along with the variant form *hekatontarchos*—only in Matthew (4 times), Luke (3 times), and Acts (14 times). It is an interesting fact that every centurion mentioned in the NT is spoken of in a favorable light. For the meaning of the term see the discussion at Matt. 8:5.

Band See discussion at John 18:3, 12.

7 Household Servants This is a single word in Greek, *oiketēs*. In the other three NT places where it occurs (Luke 16:13; Rom. 14:4; 1 Pet. 2:18) it is translated (in KJV) simply as "servant." But it does mean a household servant, since it is derived from *oikos*, "house." The Greek language had several different words for servant.

9 Housetop The Greek word, only in the Synoptic Gospels (6 times) and here in Acts, is *dōma*, from which we get *dome* (by way of the Latin *domus*). It is a bit ironical that all the roofs of the houses in that day were flat, not dome-shaped as we use the term today.

10 Very Hungry Most modern versions have simply "hungry" (RSV, NASB, NIV). The Greek adjective is *prospeinos* (only here in NT). Since it is compounded of *pros*, "to," and *peina*, "hunger," the King James translators added the "very." But the meaning evidently is that Peter arrived ("to") at the state of being hungry.

Trance The Greek word is *ecstasis*, from which we get *ecstasy* (see discussion at Mark 16:8). There and in Luke 5:26 it is translated (in KJV) as "amazed" (cf. Acts 3:10, "amazement"). In Mark 5:42 it is rendered "astonishment." But here and in Acts 11:5 and 22:17 it is "trance."

The word is a combination of *stasis*, "standing," and *ec*, "out." So it suggests the idea of standing out of oneself, which is what a trance is.

11 Sheet The Greek word *othonē* is found (in NT) only here and in 11:5, where Peter recounts this vision. It basically means "linen." The diminutive *othonion* is used for the linen cloths that were wrapped around Jesus' dead body (Luke 24:12; John 19:40; 20:5, 6, 7). Here *othonē* is used for a large sheet let down from heaven by its four corners. J. R. Lumby observes: "The significance of the outstretched sheet, as a figure of the wide world, and the four corners as the directions into which the Gospel was now to be borne forth into all the world has often been dwelt upon" (*Mark*, CGT, p. 211).

14, 15 Common The Greek adjective is *koinos*, the literal meaning of which is "common." But the Pharisees used the word in the sense of "ceremonially unclean." In Mark 7:2 it is translated (in KJV) as "defiled." (See discussion there.) In Rom. 14:14, where it occurs three times, it is rendered "unclean." (See discussion there.) In Heb. 10:29 the KJV has "unholy," which is used in verses 14 and 15 here by the NASB. The NIV has "impure." All of these are correct.

17 Doubted The Greek verb is *diaporeō*. Only Luke uses this term—in Luke 9:7 (see discussion there), and in Acts 2:12 (see discussion there), 5:24, and here. In the Gospel it is correctly translated (in KJV) as "was (were) perplexed." That is the correct idea here.

Had Made Inquiry for The verb is *dierōtaō* (only here in NT). It is compounded of *erōtaō*, "ask," and *dia*, "through." So it suggests a bit of searching. Abbott-Smith defines it as "to find by inquiry" (p. 115).

20 Doubting Nothing The verb *diakrinō* literally means "judge between." In Hellenistic Greek it came to have in the middle voice (as here) the meaning: "to be divided in one's mind, to hesitate, doubt" (A-S, p. 108). The correct idea is probably "without hesitation" (cf. NIV).

28 Common See discussion at Acts 10:14, 15.

29 Without Gainsaying This is one word in Greek, *anantirrētōs* (only here in NT). Arndt

and Gingrich define it as "without raising any objection" (p. 58; cf. NASB, NIV).

34 Respecter of Persons The noun *prosōpolēmptēs* (only here in NT) comes from *prosōpon*, "face," and *lambanō*, "receive." So it literally means "receiver of face." The meaning here is clearly, "God is not one to show partiality" (NASB) or, "God does not show favoritism" (NIV).

38 Doing Good The verb *euergeteō* (only here in NT) is compounded of *eu*, "well," and *ergon*, "work." The cognate noun *euergetēs* is likewise found only once in the NT (Luke 22:25; see discussion there). In the light of Luke 22:25-26 Bertram makes this observation: "Only Christ can really be called *euergetēs*. . . . All human benefits may be traced back to Him, or to God" (TDNT, 2:655).

11:8 Not So This is one word in Greek, the adverb *mēdamōs*, found (in NT) only here and in the parallel verse (10:14). It is an emphatic negative: "By no means" (NASB) or "Surely not" (NIV).

20 Grecians The Greek word thus translated is *Hellēnistas*, which in 6:1 rather obviously means "Greek-speaking Jews." But here it almost as clearly means Gentiles. So some ancient Greek manuscripts have *Hellēnas*, "Greeks." Commentators are agreed that it is very difficult to decide between these two readings. The first edition of the United Bible Societies' *Greek New Testament* has *Hellēnas*, while the third edition has *Hellēnistas*.

Bruce Metzger suggests that probably the chief objection of modern scholars to *Hellēnistas* is the belief that it always means "Greek-speaking *Jews*." He then adds: "But since *Hellēnistas* is derived from *hellēnizein*, it means strictly 'one who uses Greek . . .'; whether the person be a Jew or a Roman or any other non-Greek must be gathered from the context." After noting that in 6:1 the contrast is clearly "between Greek-speaking Jewish Christians and Semitic-speaking Jewish Christians," and in 9:29—the only other place where the word occurs (in NT)—the meaning is not clear, he goes on to say: "In the present passage, where the preponderant weight of the external evidence combines with the strong transcriptional probability in support of *Hellēnistas*, the word is to be understood in the broad sense of 'Greek-speaking persons,' meaning thereby the mixed population of Antioch in contrast to the *Ioudaioi* of verse 19" (*A Textual Commentary on* the Greek New Testament, pp. 388–89). This is basically the conclusion of J. H. Ropes (*Beginnings* 3:106), Kirsopp Lake and Henry J. Cadbury (*Beginnings*, 4:128), and F. F. Bruce (pp. 235–36).

26 Christians The Greek word *Christianos* (sing.) occurs only three times in the NT (see 26:28; 1 Pet. 4:16). Up to this time the followers of Jesus are generally called "disciples." Grundmann says of *Christianoi*: "It denotes Christ's adherents, those who belong to Him. It seems most likely that the term was first used by non-Christians, though this does not have to imply that it was meant derisively." He further observes: "A reason for coining the term *Christianoi* is that the Christians in Antioch were now viewed as a separate society rather than as a section of the Jewish synagogue" (TDNT, 9:537).

12:1 Vex The verb *kakoō* is from the adjective *kakos*—"bad, evil, mean, injurious." So it meant to "harm" or "mistreat" (NASB).

5 Without Ceasing This is one word in Greek, the adverb *ektenōs*. It means "fervently, earnestly" (A-S, p. 142) or "eagerly, fervently, constantly" (AG, p. 245). The church prayed earnestly and continuously.

6 Keepers The Greek word is *phylax* (only here, v. 19, and 5:23). It comes from the verb *phylassō*, to "guard." So the correct translation is "guards" (NASB) or "sentries" (RSV, NIV). The word for "prison" is *phylakē* (see discussion at 5:23).

8 Gird Thyself The verb is *zōnnymi* (found in NT only here and John 21:18). Today we would say, "Dress yourself" (RSV), or "Put on your clothes" (NIV).

10 Ward The Greek word is *phylakē*, which is translated "prison" (in KJV) 36 out of the 47 times it occurs in the NT (cf. v. 6). Only here is it rendered "ward." It first meant the act of "watching," and then the person of the watcher, the "guard" (Bertram, TDNT, 9:241–42). It would seem that the best translation here is "guard" (RSV, NASB) or "guards" (NIV).

Of His Own Accord This is all one word in Greek, *automatē*, which occurs (in NT) only here and in Mark 4:28 (see discussion there).

13 Rhoda This is the Greek word for "Rose," which is still used for a girl's name.

15 Thou Art Mad See discussion at Acts 26:24-25.

20 Highly Displeased This is one word in Greek, the present participle of the verb *thymomacheō* (only here in NT). It is compounded of *thymos*, "hot anger," and *machomai*, to "fight." So it means "have a hot quarrel" (A-S, p. 210) or "be very angry with" (cf. NASB).

Chamberlain The noun is *koitōn* (only here in NT), which comes from *koitē*, "bed"—especially the marriage bed. So it signifies "a trusted personal servant" (NIV).

21 Made an Oration This is the imperfect tense of the verb *dēmēgoreō* (only here in NT). It is compounded of *dēmos*, "people," and *agoreuō*, "speak in the assembly." So it means "delivered a public address to the people" (NIV).

23 Eaten of Worms This is the verb *skōlēkobrōtos* (only here in NT). It is compounded of *skōlex*, "worm," and *bibrōskō*, "eat." It was a terrible way to die.

Gave Up the Ghost The Greek word is found (in NT) only here and in 5:5, 10 (see discussion there).

13:5 Minister When people today hear the word "minister," they automatically think of a pastor or preacher. John Mark was neither one.

The Greek word is *hypēretēs*, which literally means "under rower" on a boat. The general idea was "servant, helper, assistant" (AG, p. 842), with the prominent idea of subordination. In classical Greek the word was used for the aide of a military commander. Regarding our passage here, Rengstorf observes: "According to the usage of the time *hypēretēs* here can only mean that John Mark was at the disposal of Barnabas and Paul to meet their needs and carry out their wishes. They were the ones, then, who on the basis of their own work decided what he should do as their assistant" (TDNT, 8:541). The proper translation is "helper" (NASB, NIV). See also discussion at Luke 1:2.

7 Deputy The Greek word is *anthypatos*, which in the NT occurs only in Acts (13:7, 8, 12; 18:12; 19:38). It indicates a "proconsul" (RSV, NASB, NIV), who was the administrator of a senatorial province. The imperial provinces were governed by propraetors (see BBC, 7:404).

Prudent The adjective *synetos* means "intelligent" (NIV; cf. RSV, NASB). It comes from the verb *syniemi*, "bring together," and so "understand."

10 Subtlety Today the adjective *subtle* means "keen" or "clever," usually in a good sense. But the Greek noun here is *dolos*, which first meant a "bait" (Homer) or "snare," and finally "deceit" (RSV, NASB, NIV).

Mischief The Greek word is *rhadiourgia* (only here in NT). Xenophon uses it for "laziness" but also for "lewdness," while Plutarch uses it for a "fraud" (cf. NASB). In the papyri of the NT period it is used for a "theft" (A-S, p. 396). It may be translated "villainy" (RSV) or "trickery" (NIV). Bauernfeind writes: "The 'wickedness' of Elymas implies a loosening of all ethical restraints as a result of connection with the *diabolos* [devil], magic, and pseudo-prophecy" (TDNT, 6:973).

12 Doctrine The Greek word *didachē* occurs 30 times in the NT. In the KJV it is translated "doctrine" in all but one place (Titus 1:9). But it does not mean "doctrine" in the sense in which we use that term today. It comes from the verb *didaskō* "teach," and so simply means "teaching" (all recent versions).

18 Suffered He Their Manners KJV reference Bibles give a helpful marginal note at this point, as do the RSV, NASB, and NIV. The very earliest Greek manuscripts have *etropophorēsen*, "bore with" (RSV), whereas some early ones and many late ones have *etrophophorēsen*, "cared for." It is easy to see how copyists could have confused the two. Actually, of course, God both "cared for them" and at the same time "endured their conduct" (NIV), or "put up with them" (NASB).

20 About 450 Years This expression belongs at the end of verse 19 (RSV, NASB) or as a summary statement before the main declaration of verse 20 (NIV). The United Bible Societies' Greek text ties it in with the statement in verse 19. The KJV, by inserting it in the middle of verse 20, creates a chronological problem. It is impossible to find 450 years of rule by judges (between Joshua and King Saul). The time is considerably shorter, whatever date one adopts for the exodus from Egypt.

41 Despisers The Greek noun is *kataphronētēs* (only here in NT), which comes from the verb *kataphroneō*—"look down on, despise, scorn, treat with contempt." So the noun means "despiser, scoffer" (AG, p. 420). The more contemporary noun is "scoffers" (RSV, NASB, NIV).

42 Jews ... Gentiles There is no mention of "Jews" or "Gentiles" in any Greek manuscript before the ninth century. The words were added by later copyists and so got into the KJV, which is based on later manuscripts. Commentators agree that it was Paul and Barnabas who were leaving the synagogue and "the people" who invited them to speak again (cf. NASB, NIV).

45 Envy The Greek word is *zēlos*, from which we get *zeal*. It did have that meaning at first and is translated that way 6 times in the KJV. Six times it is rendered "envying" or "envy" and once "jealousy."

In the Septuagint *zēlos* is normally used in a good sense and applied to God (TDNT, 2:879). But it would seem that in our passage here it probably has the strong sense of "jealousy" (RSV, NASB, NIV).

48 Ordained This is the perfect passive participle of the verb *tassō*, which was used primarily in a military sense: "draw up in order, arrange in place, assign, appoint order" (A-S, p. 440). The participle may be taken in the middle sense: "as many as had set themselves unto eternal life." R. J. Knowling comments: "There is no countenance here for the *absolutum decretum* of the Calvinists, since verse 46 had already shown that the Jews had acted through their own choice." He goes on to say: "The Jews as a nation had been ordained to eternal life—they had rejected this election—but those who believed amongst the Gentiles were equally ordained by God to eternal life, and it was in accordance with His divine appointment that the Apostles had turned to them" (EGT, 2:300).

50 Coasts See discussion at Matt. 15:22.

14:5 Assault
The noun *hormē* (only here and in Jas. 3:4) comes from the verb *hormaō*, which means "rush" (see discussion at Mark 5:13). Of the noun Bertram says: "The word develops many meanings which mostly denote the beginning of a swift and even hostile movement" (TDNT, 5:467). He also suggests that it denotes "violent movement uncontrolled by human reason" (p. 470). Abbott-Smith thinks that

here it means "a hostile movement, onset, assault" (p. 323).

Use Them Despitefully   The verb is *hybrizō*, discussed at Matt. 22:6.

9 Healed   The verb is *sōzō*, which is usually translated "save." But it is used here and in a few other passages for physical healing. In most of the NT it is used "especially of salvation from spiritual disease and death" (A-S, p. 436).

12 Jupiter . . . Mercurius   These are the Roman names for those gods. The Greek names were "Zeus" and "Hermes" (see RSV, NASB, NIV).

13 Gates   The Greek word is *pylōn*, which we have taken over into English for a large, ornamental entrance. Here it means "the *gate-way* or *gate-tower* of a walled town" (A-S, p. 394).

15 Of Like Passions   The adjective *homoiopathēs* (only here and Jas. 5:17) is compounded of *homoios*, "like," and *paschō*, "suffer." So it means "of like nature or feelings."

16 Suffered   The verb *eaō* means "let" (NIV). The past, as here, may be translated "allowed" (RSV) or "permitted" (NASB). Today we do not use "suffer" in this sense.

21 Taught Many   The verb here is not *didaskō*, "teach." Rather it is *mathēteuō*, "make disciples" (from *mathētēs*, the regular word for "disciple" in the NT).

23 Ordained   The verb is *cheirotoneō* (only here and 2 Cor. 8:19). It comes from *cheir*, "hand" and *teinō*, "stretch out." So it regularly means "to vote by stretching out the hand." It is so used in 2 Corinthians. But here it was evidently a direct appointment by Paul and Barnabas. The better translation is "appointed" (RSV, NASB, NIV).

26 Recommended   The verb *paradidōmi* literally means "hand over." So the better translation here is "commended" (RSV, NASB) or "committed" (NIV).

27 Rehearsed   The verb is *anangellō* (also in 15:4, where it is translated "declared" in KJV). The word properly means "to bring back word, report" (A-S, p. 28). So the best translation is "reported" (NIV). It was a case of the returned missionaries reporting to their home base.

15:2 Dissension   The noun here is *stasis*, which comes from the verb *histēmi*, "stand" or "set." The noun has three distinct meanings in Greek literature and in the NT: "1. *a standing place, status* . . . Heb. 9⁸. 2. *insurrection, sedition:* Mk. 15⁷, Lk. 23¹⁹,²⁵, Ac. 19⁴⁰, 24⁵. 3. In poets and late prose, *strife, dissension* . . . Ac. 15², 23⁷, ¹⁰" (A-S, p. 415). This is a good example of the difficulty of translating the Greek NT. Perhaps the best rendering here is "dispute" (NIV).

Disputation   The noun *zētēsis* comes from the verb *zēteō*—"seek," and then metaphorically "search after, inquire into." So the noun means "a questioning, inquiry, debate" (A-S, p. 196). The last term probably fits best here (RSV, NASB, NIV). The same word is translated "disputing" in verse 7.

3 Conversion   In evangelical circles today this term is used a great deal, but in our English Bibles it occurs only here. That is true of the Greek noun *epistrophē*. Literally it means "a turning about." And that is what a true conversion is. In the case of these Gentiles it was a turning from false gods to the true God.

8 Which Knoweth the Hearts   See discussion at Acts 1:24.

12 Gave Audience   The same translation occurs in 22:22. In both places the Greek is simply *ēkouon*, the imperfect (3rd pl.) of *akouō* ("hear" or "listen"). So the correct translation is "they were listening" (NASB) or simply "they listened" (NIV). In 13:16 the aorist imperative of the same verb is translated "give audience" (KJV). The proper translation, of course, is "listen" (NASB) or "listen to me!" (NIV).

14 Simeon   This is the Hebrew form of "Simon." The reference is to Peter (v. 7). It is natural that James, head of the Jewish Christian church in Jerusalem, should use this Hebrew form.

19 My Sentence Is   The Greek has *egō krinō*, "I judge." So the idea is: "It is my judgment" (NASB, NIV). James was speaking as moderator of the Jerusalem Council.

Trouble   The verb is *parenochleō* (only here in NT). Arndt and Gingrich define it as "cause difficulty (for), trouble, annoy" (p. 625).

23 Apostles and Elders and Brethren   This sounds like three groups. But the Greek says: *Hoi apostoloi kai hoi presbyteroi* *adelphoi*—"The apostles and the elders, brothers" (cf. RSV, NASB, NIV).

Send Greeting This is one word in Greek, *chairein*, and it occurs at the very end of the verse (cf. RSV, NASB, NIV). In the thousands of papyrus letters that we now have from this period, this very word occurs regularly right after the addressor(s) and addressee(s)—just as we find it here (cf. NIV). But in the NT we find this usual word for "greeting" at the beginning of a letter in only two other places (23:26; Jas. 1:1). In place of this Paul always has a twofold greeting—*charis kai eirēnē*, "grace and peace"—which has greater spiritual significance. Incidentally, *chairein* is the present infinitive of the verb *chairō*, "rejoice" or "be glad."

29 Fare Ye Well This is better written as one word, "Farewell" (RSV, NASB, NIV). The Greek is *Errōsthe*, the perfect passive imperative of the verb *rhōnnymi*, "be strong." In the papyrus letters of that period it was used for "Farewell" or "Good-bye." In the NT it occurs only here and in 23:30 (in some manuscripts).

39 Contention The Greek literally says, "There came a *paroxysmos*," from which we get *paroxysm*. The term is found (in NT) only here and in Heb. 10:24, where it means "provocation." Obviously it is a strong word. (For a solution to this problem see BBC, 7:450.)

16:1 *To Derbe and Lystra* There has been a lot of discussion as to whether Timothy lived in Derbe or Lystra, because of the wording of the KJV. But the Greek is clear: The *eis* is repeated, "He came to Derbe and to Lystra." To avoid the perennial confusion, the NIV spells it out even more specifically: "He came to Derbe and then to Lystra." It was at Lystra that Timothy lived.

7 The Spirit All the best Greek manuscripts have "the Spirit of Jesus" (RSV, NASB, NIV). This striking expression is found only here in the NT.

9 Prayed It is particularly appropriate that the verb used here, *parakaleō*, literally means "call alongside (to help)." That fits in perfectly with the man's plea for help. The Greek has the participial form: "beseeching" (RSV) or "begging" (NIV).

10 We The use of the first person plural of the verb—*exētēsamen*, "we sought" (RSV, NASB)—shows that Luke, the author of Acts, joined the missionary party at this time. These so-called we passages occur periodically from now on in this book.

Preach the Gospel This is one word in the Greek, the verb *euangelizō*, "proclaim glad tidings." From it we get our word *evangelize*. Paul heard the call to begin the evangelization of Europe, and we are glad he obeyed the call!

11 Loosing The verb *anagō* in the middle or passive voice (as here) is a nautical term meaning "put out to sea" (NIV; cf. NASB). In this sense it is used only by Luke (Luke 8:22 and 13 times in Acts).

We Came with a Straight Course This is all one word in Greek, the verb *euthydromeō* (only here and 21:1). It means "ran a straight course" (NASB). (See further comment in BBC, 7:445.)

12 Colony We take this word directly from the Greek *kolōnia* (only here in NT) and Latin *colonia*. This was clearly "a Roman colony" (RSV, NASB, NIV). (For further comments, see BBC, 7:446.)

13 Out of the City The Greek literally says "outside the gate" (RSV, NASB). The noun is *pylē*, "a gate." This was obviously "the city gate" (NIV).

Prayer Was Wont to Be Made This translation is based on the *Textus Receptus*, which reads: *enomizeto proseuchē einai*. The verb *nomizō* comes from the noun *nomos*, the regular word for "law" in the NT. But the earliest meaning of *nomos* was "usage" or "custom." So *nomizō* first meant "hold by custom" (A-S, p. 304). The meaning here would be "where prayer was customarily made."

But throughout the rest of the NT *nomizō* means "consider, suppose." And the United Bible Societies' Greek text, based on some early manuscripts, has *enomizomen proseuchēn*. Since *proseuchē* means not only "prayer" but "a place of prayer," this gives us the translation "where we supposed there was a place of prayer" (RSV; cf. NASB, NIV).

There is no way of being certain as to the exact original text. Bruce Metzger comments: "In view of the wide range of variables in lexicography, syntax, palaeography, and textual attestation, the difficulties presented by this verse are well-nigh baffling" (*Textual Commentary*, p. 447). Fortunately, no essential meaning is jeopardized by these variants.

14 Seller of Purple This is all one word in the Greek, *porphyropōlis* (only here in NT). The adjective *porphyreos* is found four times (John 19:2, 5; Rev. 17:4; 18:6). The noun *porphyra* also occurs four times (Mark 15:17, 20; Luke 16:19; Rev. 18:12) with the meaning "purple robe."

Actually, the last of these three words had three distinct meanings: (1) a purple shellfish; (2) a purple dye extracted from this shellfish; (3) cloth dyed with this purple. Obviously such cloth would be expensive, since the dye would be very limited in amount. So Lydia was evidently a person of considerable means.

The correct translation of *porphyropōlis* is "a seller of purple fabrics" (NASB, A-S, p. 374) or "a dealer in purple cloth" (NIV). Lydia was well able to have the whole missionary party stay at her large home (v. 15).

15 Constrained See discussion at Luke 24:29.

16 Prayer *Proseuchē* here clearly means "the place of prayer" (RSV, NASB, NIV). In the Greek it is preceded by the definite article. This meaning is ignored in the KJV.

Of Divination The Greek simply has the noun *pythōn* (only here in NT), which we have taken over as the name of a large snake. Arndt and Gingrich define the Greek word as follows: "the serpent or dragon that guarded the Delphic oracle; it lived at the foot of Mt. Parnassus, and was slain by Apollo. Later the word came to designate a *spirit of divination*, then also a ventriloquist, who was believed to have such a spirit dwelling in his (or her) belly" (p. 728).

By Soothsaying This is the present participle of the verb *manteuomai* (only here in NT). It comes from the noun *mantis*, "diviner." Today we would say "by fortune-telling" (NASB, NIV).

18 Grieved A better translation for the verb *diaponeō* is "annoyed" (RSV), or even "greatly annoyed" (NASB). See further discussion at Acts 4:2. Today we connect "grieved" with sorrow.

19 Drew The verb *helkō* is stronger than this. In the aorist, as here, it means "dragged" (RSV, NASB, NIV).

Marketplace See discussion of *agora* at Matt. 11:16.

20 Magistrates The noun *stratēgos* (sing.) first meant a military commander, or general. But since military leaders were often put in charge of civil affairs, the term came to be used in a wider sense. Bauernfeind says that "*stratēgos* became one of the main terms for leading provincial or municipal officials" (TDNT, 7:704). It is interesting to note that only Luke the historian (the only Greek writer of Holy Scripture) uses this term in the NT—twice in his Gospel and eight times in Acts. He was well acquainted with the Greek world.

Do Exceedingly Trouble The verb *ektarassō* (only here in NT) is a strong word meaning "to throw into great trouble, agitate" (A-S, p. 142). Here it suggests, "are throwing our city into confusion" (NASB) or "into an uproar" (NIV). It was a serious accusation to bring, since the main thing the Roman rulers insisted on was peace and order. This civic charge is spelled out even more seriously in verse 21, where it has political and racial overtones.

22 Beat The verb *rhabdizō* (only here and 2 Cor. 11:25) comes from the noun *rhabdos*, "rod." So it means "to be beaten with rods" (NASB). This was a very cruel form of punishment, leaving the back lacerated and bleeding.

24 Stocks The word *xylon* has quite a history of usage. It first meant "wood" (1 Cor. 3:12; Rev. 18:12). Then it meant a piece of wood, and so anything made of wood. It was used for a staff or club (Matt. 26:47, 55; Mark 14:43, 48; Luke 22:52). Only here (in NT) is it used for wooden "stocks," into which prisoners' feet were fastened. It is used a number of times in the NT for the cross on which Jesus was hanged. Finally, in late writers, it came to be used for a "tree," as we find in Luke 23:31. In Revelation (2:7; 22:2, 14, 19) it is used for the "tree" of life.

25 Sang Praises This is one word in Greek, the verb *hymneō*, from which we get *hymn*. So, "were . . . singing hymns" (NIV) fits well. Hymns are usually addressed to God.

26 Bands The Greek word is *desma* (neut. pl. of *desmos*). It comes from *deō*, "bind." Here it would be "chains" (NASB, NIV), with which the prisoners were bound.

27 Keeper of the Prison The Greek noun *desmophylax* (only here and vv. 23, 36 in NT) is compounded of *desmos* (see previous note) and *phylax*, "guard." In the KJV it is translated "jailor" (v. 23). The correct rendering is "jailer" in all three places (RSV, NASB, NIV).

Prisoners   The Greek word is *desmios* (in the sing.). It means "bound one" and occurs a number of times in Acts. See discussion of "prison" at 5:18ff.

31 House   The word is *oikos*, "house." But here, as in many other places, it clearly means "household" (RSV, NASB, NIV).

35 Sergeants   The Greek word *rhabdouchos* (only here and v. 38) literally means "one who carries a rod or staff (of office)." The technical Roman name was "lictor." They could be called "officers" (NIV) or "police" (RSV).

17:3 *Opening and Alleging*   The first verb is *dianoigō*. It is composed of the verb *anoigō*, "open," and *dia*, "through," and so it means "open up completely." In Luke 24:32 it is used the same way as here: Jesus "opened the Scriptures" (NIV) to the two disciples on the road to Emmaus. Obviously it means "explain" or "interpret."

The second verb is *paratithēmi*, which literally means "place beside." In the middle voice, as here, it means "to bring forward, quote as evidence" (A-S, p. 343). So NASB has here: "explaining and giving evidence." A simpler translation is "explaining and proving" (RSV, NIV). Paul was bringing forward passages from "the Scriptures" (our OT) to prove his point that the Messiah had to suffer and be resurrected. Only then could he declare effectively that Jesus was really the Messiah.

4 Believed   The Greek has *epeisthēsan*, which can only mean "were persuaded" (RSV, NASB, NIV).

Consorted with   The verb is *prosklēroō* (only here in NT). It literally means "assign by lot," from *klēros*, a "lot" that is cast or drawn. In the passive, as here, the verb means "be attached to, join" (AG, p. 716). Foerster favors: "They attached themselves to" (TDNT, 3:766). The simplest translation is "joined" (RSV, NASB, NIV).

5 Lewd Fellows of the Baser Sort   The Greek word for "lewd" is the adjective *ponēros* that in the ethical sense means "wicked, evil, bad, base, worthless, vicious, degenerate" (AG, p. 690). "Fellows" is simply "men" (*andras*). "Of the baser sort" translates the adjective *agoraios*—"frequenting the *agora*," or "a lounger in the *agora*." So it seems that the best

translation is "wicked men from the market place" (NASB) or "bad characters from the marketplace" (NIV).

Gathered a Company   This is one word in the Greek, the aorist participle of the verb *ochlopoieō*, which has not been found elsewhere. It is composed of *poieō*, "make," and *ochlos*, "crowd." The logical translation is "formed a mob" (AG, p. 600).

6 Drew   See discussion of "haling" at Acts 8:3. The same verb *syrō* is translated "drew" at 14:19. It really means "dragged" in all three places.

6, 8 Rulers of the City   This is one word in Greek, *politarchēs* (only here in NT). It is composed of *polis*, "city," and *archōn*, "ruler." So it clearly means "city-ruler."

Until recently this term had not been found anywhere else in Greek literature. "So earlier critics accused Luke of having invented this word. But once more Luke has been completely exonerated by archaeology as being an accurate historian. No less than nineteen inscriptions have been discovered, ranging from the second century B.C. to the third century A.D., which contain this word. Fourteen of these inscriptions belong to Macedonia, and five of them refer to Thessalonica itself" (BBC, 7:455).

6 Turned . . . Upside Down   This is the Greek verb *anastatoō* (only here, 21:38; Gal. 5:12). Deissmann says that it means "incite to tumult, stir up sedition, unsettle" (LAE, p. 84). In Roman eyes this was the worst crime a person could commit. (See also v. 7.)

World   This is not the common term for "world," *cosmos*, but *oikoumenē*, "inhabited earth"—that is, the Roman world.

11 More Noble   This is the comparative form of *eugenēs*, which occurs in 1 Cor. 1:26 and Luke 19:12 (see discussion there). It literally means "well-born." But here *eugenesteroi* signifies "of more noble character" (NIV) or "more noble-minded" (NASB).

Readiness of Mind   See discussion at 2 Cor. 8:11, 12, 19.

12 Honorable   See discussion at Mark 15:43.

13 Stirred Up   The *Textus Receptus* (on which the KJV is based) has only one participle here, *saleuontes*. The verb *saleuō* basically means "agitate" or "shake," as by stormy wind or waves. Here it is used of "agitating" the crowds (NASB, NIV).

The oldest and best Greek manuscripts include a second participle, *tarassontes*, which means "inciting" (RSV) or "stirring up" (NASB, NIV). The Jews from Thessalonica were creating a major disturbance in Berea.

16 Stirred　　The Greek verb is *paroxynō* (only here and 1 Cor. 13:5). It means "provoked" (RSV, NASB) or "greatly distressed" (NIV). Arndt and Gingrich say on this passage: "*his spirit was aroused within him* (by anger, grief, or a desire to convert them)" (p. 629).

Wholly Given to Idolatry　　This is the Greek adjective *kateidōlos* (only here in NT). It means "full of idols" (lexicons, RSV, NASB, NIV).

17 Disputed　　The verb *dialegomai* is translated "reasoned" (KJV) in verse 2 and should be the same here (NASB, NIV). The basic idea is "discuss" (A-S, AG).

Devout Persons　　The Greek has the present participle of *sebō*, "worship." It refers to Gentiles who were worshiping the true God in the Jewish synagogues. Hence it means "God-fearing Greeks" (NIV; cf. NASB).

18 Babbler　　*Spermologos* (only here in NT) literally means "seedpicker." Abbott-Smith says that it was used properly of birds but "in Attic slang, of an idler who lives on scraps picked up in the agora" (p. 413). Kirsopp Lake and Henry Cadbury translate it "cocksparrow." They say that the word "was used first of birds that pick up grain, then of men who picked up odds and ends in the market; it was then transferred to men who were zealous seekers of the second-rate at second hand, and finally to generally worthless persons" (*Beginnings*, 4:211).

Setter Forth　　The noun *katangeleus* (only here in NT) comes from the verb *katangellō*, "proclaim." So it means "proclaimer" (NASB).

Strange　　*Xenos* means "strange" or "foreign." The second term probably fits better here (RSV, NIV). It does not mean "odd."

Gods　　In the NT the word *daimonion* is regularly used in the sense of "demon." But here alone it is used as in classical Greek (Herodotus, Plato) for "the Divine power, Deity" or "an

inferior divinity" (A-S, p. 97). Lake and Cadbury comment: "It is noteworthy that *daimonia* in the bad sense is not found in Acts, and that in the rest of the NT it is not found in the Greek sense" (*Beginnings*, 4:212). So "foreign gods" is the correct translation.

22 Mars' Hill　　The Greek expression is the same here as in verse 19, where it is properly translated "Areopagus." It is *Areios Pagos* (only these two places in NT). Ares was the Greek name for Mars, the god of war—hence, "Mars' hill" (KJV). The supreme council of Athens met on this hill for some time, and so was given the name "Areopagus." But in the first century its meeting place was in front of the Stoa Basileios in the Agora. Lake and Cadbury say that "the Areopagus here is much more likely to mean the council than the place" (*Beginnings*, 4:212). That is why the NIV has in both verses "meeting of the Areopagus." In any case the same Greek expression should be translated the same way in verses 19 and 22.

Too Superstitious　　For Paul to have said, "I perceive that in all things you are too superstitious" (KJV) would have been very unwise, especially in addressing the intelligentsia of Athens. The Greek has the superlative form of the adjective *deisidaimon* (only here in NT) which means "reverent to the deity, religious" (A-S, p. 100). Deissmann says: "The A.V. 'too superstitious' is an incorrect translation" (LAE, p. 285, n. 3). He translates the expression here: "extremely religious" (p. 285). Most new versions have "very religious" (RSV, NASB, NIV).

23 TO THE UNKNOWN GOD　　There is no definite article in the Greek (*AGNŌSTŌ THEŌ*). So the correct translation is "TO AN UNKNOWN GOD" (NASB, NIV).

26 Of One Blood　　The oldest Greek manuscripts (third and fourth centuries) have only *ex henos*, "from one" (RSV, NASB). The word "blood" was added by later copyists. The meaning clearly is "from one man" (NIV)—that is, Adam.

29 Godhead　　This English term might be thought of as referring to the Father, as the Head of the Trinity. But *theios* is an adjective meaning "divine." So the correct translation is "the Deity" (RSV), "the Divine Nature" (NASB), or "the divine being" (NIV).

30 Winked at　　The Greek verb is *hypereidon* (only here in NT). It comes from *eidon* (aorist tense), "looked," and *hyper*, "over." So it means "overlooked" (RSV, NASB, NIV).

31 Appointed The Greek word is *estēsen*, the aorist of *histēmi*, "set." So it simply means "set" (NIV) or "fixed" (RSV, NASB).

18:3 Same Craft . . . Occupation
The first expression is one word in Greek, *homotechnos* (only here in NT). It is composed of *homos*, "same," and *technē*, "trade." So it means "of the same trade" (RSV, NASB). The second word is *technē*, which should also obviously be translated "trade" (RSV, NASB).

4 Persuaded The Greek has the imperfect tense of continuous (not completed) action. This is brought out accurately by "trying to persuade" (NASB, NIV). As we know from many other passages in Acts, Paul did not succeed in persuading everybody.

5 Pressed in the Spirit No Greek manuscript earlier than the ninth century has "spirit" (*pneuma*). Instead, all the early manuscripts have "word" (*logos*). The verb, *synechō*, literally means "hold together." The whole phrase could be translated "constrained by the Word" (dative case, no preposition in the Greek). The idea is properly expressed by "devoted himself exclusively to preaching" (NIV, cf. NASB). It seems altogether likely that Silas and Timothy had brought Paul generous love offerings from the churches in Philippi and Thessalonica (cf. Phil. 4:16). As a result Paul was able to lay aside his tentmaking and give his whole time to preaching the Word.

6 Blasphemed The Greek verb *blasphēmeō* means "blaspheme" when directed toward God, but "revile" or "rail at" when directed toward human beings. Unfortunately, we cannot be certain as to which was the case here. The statement that Paul testified to the Jews that Jesus was the Messiah (v. 5) may suggest that the Jews reacted by cursing Jesus (v. 6), and so "blasphemed" (KJV, NASB) would be correct. But it may be that they "reviled" Paul (RSV) or "became abusive" toward him (NIV). In any case, the Greek does not say "opposed themselves" (KJV). They "opposed Paul" (NIV) or his message.

8, 17 Chief Ruler of the Synagogue The word is *archisynagōgos*—from *archōn*, "ruler" or "chief," and *synagōgē*, "synagogue." In the seven previous places where this word occurs in the NT (four times in Mark, twice in Luke,

and Acts 13:15), it is (in KJV) correctly translated "ruler of the synagogue." Why this incorrect double ("chief ruler") was adopted here is a conundrum.

9 Be Not Afraid . . . Speak . . . Hold Not Thy Peace The first two verbs are imperfect; the third is aorist. So the literal translation is: "Stop being afraid, but go on speaking, and do not become silent." It would seem that Paul had become fearful for his life. He needed the divine assurance (v. 10).

12 Deputy See discussion at Acts 13:7.

14 Wrong . . . Lewdness The first word is *adikēma* (only here; 24:20; Rev. 18:5). It means a "wrong" or "misdeed." The second is *rhadiourgēma* (only here in NT), which means a "crime." The first would suggest a misdemeanor, subject to civil law, the second a criminal offense. These are the two types of cases tried in Roman courts, as in our courts today.

17 The Greeks These two words (*hoi Hellēnes*) are not found in the earliest Greek manuscripts (third and fourth cents.). See further discussion in BBC, 7:469. The NIV correctly communicates what probably happened.

20 Consented Not The verb *epineuō* (only here in NT) is compounded of *neuō* (only in John 13:24), "nod," and *epi*, "upon" or "at." It means to nod one's head in agreement. Paul did not do this; he "declined" (RSV, NIV).

21 Bade Them Farewell This is all one word in Greek, *apotaxamenos*, which in verse 18 is translated "took his leave." The simplest rendering is "left" (both places in NIV) or "took leave" . . . "taking leave" (RSV, NASB).

I Must by All Means Keep This Feast That Cometh in Jerusalem These words are not found in the earliest Greek manuscripts (third and fourth cents.) and so are rightly omitted in most of the new versions of the Bible.

24 Eloquent The Greek word is *logios* (only here in NT). Kittel writes of it: "This word is found from the time of Pindar . . . in the two-fold sense of a. 'eloquent,' 'skilled in speech' . . . and b. 'skilled in knowledge,' 'educated,' 'cultured.' " He goes on to say: "Sense a. does not seem to occur in Josephus, but sense b. is common." He concludes: "It is not possible to decide with certainty between the two senses . . . the sense of 'learned' is at least very probable.

If most expositors prefer 'eloquent' this is due to v. 25 . . . and the picture of Apollos derived from 1 Cor. 1:12; 3:5f." (TDNT, 4:136–37). Lake and Cadbury settle for "eloquent" in their translation of Acts, but acknowledge, after considerable discussion: "We are still left, therefore, without any decisive evidence of its meaning here" (*Beginnings*, 4:233). So we may take our choice between "eloquent" (KJV, RSV, NASB) and "learned" (NIV). It appears altogether likely that Apollos was both!

25 Fervent in the Spirit   See discussion at Rom. 12:11.

27 Receive   *Apodechomai* is a strong compound. It means "accept gladly" or "welcome" (NASB, NIV).

28 Mightily   The adverb *eutonōs* (only here and Luke 23:10) means "vigorously" (NIV).

Convinced   The verb *diakatelenchomai* (only here in NT) means "refute completely" (AG, p. 184).

Publicly   The adjective *dēmosios* comes from the noun *dēmos*, "the common people" (cf. *democratic*). In the dative feminine it is used adverbially in the sense of "publicly." The word occurs only in Acts (5:18; 16:37; 18:28; 20:20).

19:1 Upper Coasts

The adjective "upper" is *anōterikos* (only here in NT). The noun is *merē* (pl.), "part." As we use the term today, "coasts" is misleading. In fact, it is just the opposite of what the Greek says. The correct picture is "the upper country" (RSV, NASB), or simply "the interior" (NIV). From Galatia and Phrygia (18:23) Paul traveled through the interior of the province of Asia to its seaport capital, Ephesus.

Disciples   The identity of these disciples is one of the most puzzling questions faced by commentators in the Book of Acts. A view that prevailed in earlier times, beginning with Chrysostom (fourth century), maintained these were disciples of John the Baptist. This idea is also set forth by Adam Clarke: "It is likely that these were Asiatic Jews, who, having been at Jerusalem about twenty-six years before this, had heard the preaching of John, and received his baptism, believing in the *coming* Christ, whom John had proclaimed; but it appears that till this time they had got no farther [*sic.*] instruction in the Christian religion" (p. 841).

Alexander differed from Clarke: "*Certain* (i.e.

some, a few) *disciples*, not of Apollos, or of John the Baptist, but of Christ, as the word always means when absolutely used . . . and as appears from the way in which Paul treated them" (p. 648). Similarly, Lake and Cadbury say: "This must mean Christians, both from the use of *mathetas* in Acts and from the context" (*Beginnings*, IV, 237). Bruce echoes this and adds a point, when he comments: "Presumably disciples of Christ, in accordance with the meaning elsewhere of *mathetes* thus used absolutely; had they been disciples of John, we should have expected this to be explicitly stated" (*Acts*, p. 253).

2 Since   The Greek literally says, "Did you receive the Holy Spirit, having believed [aorist participle, *pisteusantes*]?" Obviously this could be interpreted: "as a result of believing." So it is hardly honest exegesis to put undue emphasis on the word "since" (KJV). However, we do not agree with the translation "when you believed" (RSV, NASB, NIV). We would prefer to stick close to the Greek. "Having believed" could then be interpreted in either of two ways: "as a result of believing," or "subsequent to believing."

Whether There Be Any   This is a correct translation of the Greek. Yet in John 7:39 the same construction in the Greek is translated, "The Holy Ghost was not yet given." Perhaps that is the best translation here (cf. ASV— "Nay, we did not so much as hear whether Holy Spirit was *given*"). As has often been pointed out, John the Baptist talked about the Holy Spirit (Matt. 3:11 and parallels). But it is evident that these men clearly did not know that the Spirit had been poured out at Pentecost. It seems that these "disciples" had not been in contact with the Christian church. Perhaps they had left Palestine before Pentecost and had been isolated from the followers of Jesus ever since.

There is still something to be said for the literal translation here (KJV, RSV, NEB, Phillips). Page insists that "the only possible rendering of the Greek" is: "We did not even hear of the existence of a Holy Spirit" (p. 203). Bruce suggests a solution which is true to the Greek and yet makes place for the above interpretation, when he writes: "Possibly *pneuma hagion* is to be understood here in a special sense, of the Holy Spirit as sent at Pentecost with outward manifestation" (*Acts*, p. 354).

9 Divers   The current meaning of this word hardly fits this passage!

The correct translation of the Greek *tines* is "some" (RSV, NASB, NIV).

School The Greek word is *scholē* (only here in NT). Abbott-Smith defines it thus: "1. *leisure*. 2. Later (from Plato on) (a) that for which leisure is employed, a *disputation, lecture;* (b) the place where lectures are delivered, *a school*" (p. 436). Probably "lecture hall" (NIV) gives a more accurate picture.

10 *Asia* Again we would call attention to the fact that "Asia" (13 times in Acts and 6 times in the Epistles and Revelation) never means the continent of Asia (as today) but always the Roman province of Asia (helpfully indicated thus in NIV).

12 *Handkerchiefs* The Greek word here, *soudarion*, is in Luke 19:20 translated "napkin" (KJV, RSV), "piece of cloth" (NIV), but (consistently) "handkerchief" (NASB). It occurs elsewhere in the NT only in John 11:44—"napkin" (KJV), "cloth" (RSV, NASB, NIV)—and John 20:7—"napkin" (KJV, RSV), "face-cloth" (NASB), "burial cloth" (NIV). All have "handkerchiefs" here in Acts.

Aprons The word *simikinthion* (only here in NT) was used for a workman's apron.

13 *Vagabond* The Greek has *perierchomenōn*, present participle of the verb *perierchomai*. *Erchomai* means "go" and *peri* "around." So the idea is "itinerant" (RSV), "who went from place to place" (NASB), or "who went around" (NIV).

Exorcists A sensational film, *The Exorcist*, made this word familiar to the American public. It comes from the Greek noun used here, *exorkistes* (only here in NT). It literally means "one who administers an oath" (*orkos*). "I adjure," later in this verse (RSV, NASB), is *orkizō*, "put on oath." See also discussion at Matt. 26:63.

19 *Curious Arts* The Greek has one word, the adjective *periergos* (only here and 1 Tim. 5:13). It is composed of *ergon*, "work," and *peri*, "around," and so means "busy about trifles and neglectful of important matters" (Thayer, p. 502). Deissmann notes that the neuter plural here (*ta perierga*) was a technical term for "magic" (BS, p. 323, n. 5). So, instead of "used curious arts" it would be better to say "practiced magic arts" (RSV), or, more simply, "practiced magic" (NASB).

Books The noun here, *biblos* (from which we get *Bible*), was a variant form of *byblos*, the Greek name for the Egyptian papyrus plant, from which the "paper" then in use was made. Since formal writing in that period was on rolls or scrolls, not bound books as we know them, the better translation is "scrolls" (NIV). Lake and Cadbury comment: "The *bibloi* of the magicians were doubtless parchments or papyri of relatively small size with magical charms written on them" (*Beginnings*, 4:243). The value of these scrolls was about $10,000; but this represented 50,000 days' wages—a lot to burn!

21 *In the Spirit* There is some question whether "in the spirit" means Paul's human spirit (KJV, ASV; cf. NEB, "made up his mind") or the Holy Spirit (RSV, "in the Spirit"). As is frequently the case, the best answer is, "Both." Alexander expresses the combination thus: "*In the spirit*, i.e., under the divine direction, or in his own mind as determined by the Holy Ghost" (p. 663).

24 *Diana* This was the Latin name for the goddess. The Greek name, given here, was *Artemis*. It occurs again in verses 27, 28, 34, and 35 (and nowhere else in NT).

Gain The noun *ergasia* comes from *ergon*, "work." So it basically means "work" or "business" (RSV, NASB, NIV). See also Acts 19:25.

Craftsmen The Greek noun is *technites*, from which we get *technicians*. It is found again only in verse 38; Heb. 11:10; and Rev. 18:22.

25 *Sirs* The Greek has *andres*, "Men" (RSV, NASB, NIV).

Craft The Greek text has *ergasia*, translated "gain" (KJV) in verse 24. It should be translated "business" in both places.

27 *Craft* The Greek has an entirely different word from that which is translated "craft" (KJV) in verse 25. Here it is *meros*, "part" or "portion."

Set at Nought The Greek says, "in danger of coming into *apelegmos*." This word, which is not found anywhere else except in later Christian writings, means "refutation, exposure, discredit." Arndt and Gingrich suggest for this passage: "come into disrepute."

29, 31 Theater Our word *theater* (Am. spelling) comes from the Greek word *theatron* (only here and 1 Cor. 4:9). The noun is derived from the verb *theaomai:* "look upon, contemplate, view." So it was a place where people viewed plays, etc., in a leisurely way.

31 Chief of Asia This is one word in Greek, *Asiarchēs,* "an Asiarch" (from *Asia* and *archōn,* "chief"). It is found only here in the NT. Abbott-Smith defines it as "one of ten officers elected by the various cities in the province of Asia whose duty it was to celebrate at their own charges the public games and festivals" (p. 64). The proper translation is "Asiarchs" (RSV, NASB), or "officials of the province" (NIV).

Adventure Himself The Greek literally says "give himself" (*dounai heauton*). Today we would simply say "venture" (RSV, NASB, NIV).

32, 39, 41 Assembly This is the only place in the NT where we find *ecclēsia* used in its regular secular sense in that day for an "assembly" of free, voting citizens in a Greek city. Elsewhere in the NT it is used for the "congregation" of Israel (Acts 7:38; Heb. 2:12), or for a (the) Christian church (about 110 times). See also discussion at Matt. 16:18.

35 Townclerk It is interesting to discover that the Greek word here is *grammateus.* Elsewhere in the NT (65 times) it is translated "scribe" (KJV). In the NIV it is usually rendered as "teacher of the law" (see further discussion at Matt. 5:20). But here it means the "city clerk" (NIV).

38 The Law Is Open The Greek has *agoraioi agontai.* The meaning of the verb *agō* in this passage is "*to spend* or *keep* a day" (A-S, p. 8). The adjective *agoraios* occurs (in NT) only here and 17:5 (see discussion there). Abbott-Smith translates the whole expression: "courtdays are kept" (p. 6). It may be rendered "the courts are open" (RSV, NIV) or "the courts are in session" (NASB).

Deputies See discussion at Acts 13:7.

Implead Except for Rom. 8:33 the verb *engkaleō* is found only in Acts (six times). Here only (v. 38) is it translated "implead" (KJV). The correct meaning is "bring charges against" (RSV, NASB) or "press charges" (NIV). See also verse 40.

40 To Be Called in Question Here *engkaleō* is in the passive. Instead of "in danger to be called in question . . . uproar" (KJV), it is better to read: "in danger of being charged with rioting" (RSV, NIV, cf. NASB). See also verse 38.

Concourse *Systrophē* (only here and 23:12) means "a riotous gathering" (A-S, p. 435). It may be translated "commotion" (RSV, NIV) or "disorderly gathering" (NASB, AG, p. 795).

20:1 Called unto Him The recent versions have "sent for." Why the difference from the KJV?

The answer is that the *Textus Receptus* (sixteenth century) has *proskalesamenos,* which would be "called to himself." But the earliest Greek manuscripts have *metapempsamenos,* which means "sent for." The basic meaning is much the same.

Embraced The verb is *aspazomai,* "salute." It is translated that way 42 times in KJV, "greet" 15 times, "embrace" twice, and "take leave" once (Acts 21:6). The last of these is adopted here in RSV and NASB. The NIV has "said good-by."

Why, then, "embraced"? A comment in Thayer's *Lexicon* may give the answer. It says that "a salutation was made not merely by a slight gesture and a few words, but generally by embracing and kissing" (p. 81).

Just before *aspasamenos,* some ancient Greek manuscripts have *parakalesas.* Since this verb can mean either "comforted" or "exhorted" (RSV, NASB), the NIV has "encouraging," which combines these two ideas. Paul was always trying to encourage his new converts. The same word occurs again in verse 2.

3 Laid Wait The Greek has *genomenēs epiboulēs autō*—"when a plot was made against him" (RSV; cf. NASB, NIV). The noun *epiboulē,* "plot," is found only in Acts (9:24; 20:3, 19; 23:30 [q.v.])—always of plots made against Paul.

8 Lights The Greek word is *lampas* (sing.) from which we get our word *lamp.* That is the way it is translated (in the plural, as here) in the parable of the 10 virgins (Matt. 25:1, 3, 4), and that is the way it should be translated here (NASB, NIV). "Lights" suggests to us electric lights. But these were little clay lamps filled with olive oil. The fumes from these clay lamps would tend to make folk get drowsy (v. 9).

9 Third Loft This is one word in Greek, *tristegos* (only here in NT). It means "third story" (RSV, NIV) or "third floor" (NASB).

10 Embracing Him This is the aorist participle *symperilabōn*. The verb *symperilambanō* (only here in NT) is a double compound: *lambanō*, "lay hold of"; *peri*, "around"; *sym* (*syn*), "together." So it means "throw one's arms around" (AG, p. 779; cf. NIV).

13 Go Afoot This is the present infinitive of *pezeuō* (only here in NT). It comes from the adjective *pezos*, "on foot," and so means "*to travel on foot* or *by land*" (A-S, p. 350). After preaching all night, Paul wanted a quiet day by himself. So he walked the 20 miles to Assos.

24 None of These Things Move Me This clause is not found in the very earliest Greek manuscripts and so is rightly omitted in recent versions.

Course The noun *dromos* (only here; 13:25; 2 Tim. 4:7) comes from *dramōn*, the second aorist participle of *trechō*, "run." So it means a racecourse—a fitting figure for one's life or ministry. The NIV has "race" here.

27 Shunned This is the same verb and exactly the same form (aorist middle) that is translated "kept back" (KJV) in verse 20. Recent versions consistently have the same rendering in both verses: "I did not shrink" (RSV, NASB); "I have not hesitated" (NIV).

28 Overseers This is the plural of the word *episcopos*, from which we get our word *episcopal* (see discussion at Phil. 1:1). In the other four places where this term occurs (Phil. 1:1; 1 Tim. 3:2; Titus 1:7; 1 Pet. 2:25), it is translated in KJV as "bishops." Since today the term "bishop" regularly indicates the administrator of a diocese, the NIV uses "overseer." For it is very clear both here in Acts and in the Pastoral Epistles that at that time each church had several *episcopoi*.

Another important point needs to be made here. In verse 17 these men are called the "elders" (*presbyteroi*) of the church at Ephesus. Yet here Paul addresses them as "overseers" (*episcopoi*). This shows unquestionably that the "bishops" (overseers) and the "elders" (presbyters) were the same persons in the first-generation Christian church. (See further the discussion at Titus 1:5–7.)

Feed The Greek verb is *poimainō*. It comes from *poimēn*, and so literally means to "act as a shepherd." It is more than feeding; it is tending the flock in every way. So the correct translation here is "shepherd the church" (NASB) or "Be shepherds of the church" (NIV). Our word "pastor" comes from the Latin word for a shepherd. So a pastor should not only feed his flock each Sunday on the Word of God but tend his flock during the week. As we indicated earlier, it is a great responsibility!

29 Grievous It should be obvious to even the casual reader that this adjective does not fit at all with "wolves." The Greek word is *barys*. It is true that the basic meaning of this term is "heavy." Then it came to mean "burdensome" or "severe" (2 Cor. 10:10). But it was also used by Homer, Xenophon, Philo, and Josephus in the sense of "fierce, cruel, savage" (AG, p. 134). Schrenk says in Acts 20:29 it "refers to dangerous, rending wolves." He adds: "Here *barys* denotes the violent man" (TDNT, 1:558).

34 Ministered We do not find here the Greek verb *diaconeō*, which is translated "minister" 22 of the 37 times it occurs in the NT. Rather, it is *hypēreteō*—properly, "serve as a rower on a ship." But in classical Greek it is always used metaphorically in the sense of "minister" or "serve." In the NT it occurs only in Acts (13:36; 20:34; 24:23).

35 Laboring We find here a strong word in the Greek, the verb *kopiaō*. It comes from the noun *kopos*, which means "a striking, beating," and then "laborious toil, trouble" (A-S, p. 254). So the verb means "work hard." And the Christian ministry is "hard work" (NIV), but very rewarding.

21:3 Discovered
The verb *anaphainomai* (only here and Luke 19:11) means (in the aor. part.) "when we had come in sight of" (RSV, NASB) or "after sighting" (NIV).

4 Finding The verb *aneuriskō* (only here and Luke 2:16) implies finding after some searching.

5 Shore *Aigialos* (see also 27:39, 40) is here best translated "beach" (RSV, NASB, NIV).

6 Took Ship The Greek says "we went up into the ship" (*enebēmen eis to ploion*). The verb *embainō* means "go in." So the whole expression here would be: "we went on board the ship" (RSV, NASB) or "we went aboard the ship" (NIV).

7 Finished The verb *dianyō* (only here in NT) means "finish" or "complete." In later writers it also means "continue" (cf. NIV).

Course The noun *ploos* (only here and 27:9, 10) means "voyage." Again we note the use of nautical terms by Luke.

8 That Were of Paul's Company This added expression (cf. RSV, NASB, NIV) is not found in any Greek manuscript earlier than the ninth century. It is clearly an addition by a late copyist—not genuine.

Evangelist See discussion at Eph. 4:11.

15 Took Up Our Carriages In modern times (our own boyhood days) we did not take up carriages; the "carriages"—pulled by horses—took us!

Actually, this whole expression is only one word in Greek, the aorist middle participle of *episkeuazō* (only here in NT). This verb means "make preparations." So the correct translation is "got ready" (NASB, NIV).

17 Gladly The adverb is *asmenōs* (only here in NT). It comes from the verb meaning "be glad."

19 Particularly The Greek literally says "according to each [or, every] one"—*kata hen hekaston*. This suggests giving all the particulars. But today the adverb "particularly" is not ordinarily used in this sense. Rather, it means "1. To a great degree; especially. 2. With particular reference or emphasis" (*Am. Herit. Dict.*, p. 956). The proper contemporary translation here would be: "related one by one" (RSV) or "reported in detail" (NIV).

24 Be at Charges with Them The verb *dapanaō* comes from the noun *dapanē*, "expense" (see discussion at Luke 14:28). So the meaning here is: "Pay their expenses" (RSV, NASB, NIV).

Walkest Orderly This is one word in Greek, *stoicheis*. The verb *stoicheō* means "walk in line," and then metaphorically, "walk by rule" (A-S, p. 418). (See further discussion at Gal. 5:25.)

25 Fornication See discussion at Matt. 5:32.

26 Accomplishment The noun is *ekplērōsis* (only here in NT). It comes from the verb *ekplēroō* (only in 13:33), "fill full" or "fulfill." So it can be translated "completion" (NASB) or "fulfilled" (RSV).

Offering ... Offered The first is the noun *prosphora*. It is related to the second, the verb *prospherō*, "offer"—literally "bring to" (from *pherō*, "carry," and *pros*, "to"). The noun is used in the NT for sacrificial offerings offered in the Temple. The noun occurs 9 times in the NT, the verb 48 times.

29 Temple The Greek word here is *hieron*, the neuter of the adjective *hieros*, "sacred." It occurs 71 times in the NT—45 times in the Gospels, 25 times in Acts, and once in the Epistles (1 Cor. 9:13). In the KJV it is always translated "temple." But it refers to the whole Temple area, covering some 25 acres and composed mostly of open courts. Since most people think of a "temple" as a building, it is better to translate *hieron* as "temple area" (NIV). The Greek word for the Temple building itself—composed of the Holy Place and the Holy of Holies—is *naos*, which occurs 46 times in the NT and is translated "temple" all but one time (Acts 19:24, "shrine"). See also discussion at Matt. 24:1 and Acts 24:18.

30 Was Moved It is true the verb *kineō* basically means "move." But here "aroused" (RSV, NASB, NIV) fits better.

Drew See discussion at Acts 16:19.

31, 33 Chief Captain The Greek word is *chiliarchos* (first of 18 times in Acts). It is composed of *chilioi*, "a thousand," and *archōn*, "ruler." So it refers to an officer in charge of a thousand men—a military "tribune" (RSV) or "commander" (NIV). See also discussion at John 18:12.

31 Band See discussion at John 18:3.

34 Castle The word is *parembolē*. In Acts (21:34, 37; 22:24; 23:10, 16, 32) it is always translated "castle" (KJV). But it means the "barracks" (RSV, NASB, NIV) where the Roman troops in Jerusalem were quartered, just north of the Temple area.

35, 40 Stairs The word *anabathmos* (only here in NT) comes from the verb *anabainō*, "go up." So it literally means "a going up." In the plural, as here, it indicates a flight of stairs.

38 *Madest an Uproar* This is the aorist participle of the verb *anastatoō* (see discussion at 17:6). The best translation here is "stirred up a revolt" (RSV, NASB; cf. NIV).

Murderers The noun *sicarios* (only here in NT) comes from *sica*, "a dagger." Those who wore a dagger under their clothing were called *Sicarii*. That is what the plural here precisely means. We would call them "assassins" (RSV, NIV).

40 *When He Had Given . . . License* This is one word in Greek, the aorist middle participle of *epitrepō*, "give permission."

40 *Hebrew* The Greek adjective here is *Hebraios*. But it is generally agreed that the language spoken in Palestine in the time of Christ was not Hebrew but "Aramaic" (NIV), a sister Semitic *dialectos*, "dialect" (NASB), "language" (RSV).

22:1 *Men, Brethren, and Fathers* These are not three different groups of people. The "men" (*andres*) is a Greek style that is redundant in English. The correct translation is simply "Brethren and fathers" (RSV, NASB) or, as we would say today, "Brothers and fathers" (NIV).

2 *Hebrew* See Acts 21:40.

5 *Estate of the Elders* This is all one word in Greek, *presbyterion*, "presbytery" (only here; Luke 22:66; 1 Tim. 4:14). It is generally agreed that this is simply another way of referring to the Great Sanhedrin at Jerusalem. So most versions translate it "council" (NIV) or "Council of the elders" (NASB).

6 *Shone* The verb is *periastraptō*, "flash around." It is found (in NT) only here and in the historical account of Saul's conversion (9:3).

9 *Heard Not the Voice* On the surface this seems to be a flat contradiction of Acts 9:7—"hearing a voice." But there is no contradiction in the Greek. In both cases the verb is *akouō*, "hear," and the noun is *phōnē*, "voice." But in 9:7 *phōnē* is in the genitive case. This emphasizes the idea of hearing some kind of a sound. In 22:9, however, *phōnē* is in the accusative case, indicating a message heard. This is brought out helpfully in the NIV by "they heard the sound" (9:7) and "they did not understand the voice" (22:9). They heard the sound but did not catch the words. They were like the bystanders who, when the Father's voice came from heaven with words of assurance for His Son, "said it had thundered" (John 12:28–29, NIV).

17 *Trance* See discussion at Acts 10:10.

24, 29 *Examined* The verb *anetazō* (only here in NT) means "to examine judicially" (A-S, p. 36). It was a technical judicial term at that time.

28 *Sum* Here we have a good example of how words change their meaning. The Greek word here is the adjective *kephalaios*, which comes from *kephalē*, "head." So it literally means "of the head." It was used metaphorically for "principal, chief." In the only other place where it appears in the NT (Heb. 8:1) it means "the chief point." But here it means "the sum total, amount" (A-S, p. 245). So we find: "I had to pay a big price" (NIV).

Freedom The Greek word is *politeia* (only here and Eph. 2:12), which clearly means "citizenship" (RSV, NASB, NIV). For this reason it seems wise to translate *Romaios* (vv. 26, 27, 29), as "Roman citizen" (RSV, NIV). Also, "But I was *free* born" should be "But I was born a citizen" (RSV, NASB, NIV).

23:1 *Earnestly Beholding* This is one word in Greek, *atenisas*, the aorist participle of *atenizō*. This verb occurs 14 times in the NT and is translated 11 different ways in the KJV! It is found twice each in Luke and 2 Corinthians, and 10 times in Acts. Coming from the adjective *atenes*—"strained, intent, stretched"—it means "look intently at."

Council The Greek word is *synedrion*, "Sanhedrin" (NIV). It is compounded of *hedra*, "a seat," and *syn*, "together." So it literally means "a sitting together." The Sanhedrin at Jerusalem was the supreme court of the Jews. The word occurs three times each in Matthew and Mark, once each in Luke and John, and 14 times in Acts.

Conscience Our word "conscience" comes from the Latin *conscientia*, which is compounded of *scio*, "know," and *con*, "together." So it means a "knowing together." The Greek word here, *syneidēsis*, has exactly the same meaning. It was used first in the sense of "consciousness" (Heb. 10:2, NASB; cf. 1 Pet. 2:19). Then under Hebrew influence, it took on the ethical significance of our term "conscience"—

a moral monitor in man. The word occurs about 30 times in the NT (19 times in Paul's Epistles, 5 times in Hebrews, 3 times in Peter's Epistles, and twice in Acts; cf. 24:16).

8 Both The adjective *amphotera* first meant "both" of two. But it came later to be used when more than two things were involved. Arndt and Gingrich (p. 47) suggest "all" here (RSV, NASB, NIV).

9 Strove The verb *diamachomai* (only here in NT) is an intensive compound of *machomai*, "fight." So here it means "contend sharply" (AG, p. 186). Some Pharisees "*began* to argue heatedly" (NASB), or "argued vigorously" (NIV). There was a fight going on in the Sanhedrin.

Let Us Not Fight Against God The late Greek manuscripts have this: *mē theomachōmen*. It is clearly an addition made by a copyist and is not genuine.

11 Be of Good Cheer See discussion at Matt. 9:2.

12 Banded Together The Greek reads: *poiēsantes systrophēn*. The noun *systrophē* is found only here and in 19:40. There it means a disorderly gathering. Here it may mean a "plot" or "conspiracy" (AG, p. 795). The verb is the aorist participle of *poieō*, "make." These men "made a plot" (RSV) or "formed a conspiracy" (NASB, NIV). It is stronger than just "banded together."

12, 14, 21 Bound . . . Under a Curse This is all one word in Greek, *anethematisan*. The verb *anathematizō* (only here and Mark 14:71) means "bind with an oath" (cf. RSV, NASB, NIV).

13 Conspiracy The Greek word is *synōmosia* (only here in NT). It comes from the verb *synomnymi*, "conspire."

16 Lying in Wait All this is the noun *enedra* (only here and 25:3). It means an "ambush" (RSV, NASB).

21 Lie in Wait This is the associated verb *enedreuō* (only here and Luke 11:54).

23, 32 Horsemen This is the plural of *hippeus*, which comes from *hippos*, "horse." Interestingly, this is the only use of "horsemen"

in the NT (except for a related Greek word in Rev. 9:16).

24 Beasts Today "beast" means a wild animal. But the Greek word here, *ktēnos*, means "animal, i.e. domesticated animal . . . pack-animal, animal used for riding" (AG, p. 455). It is obviously the last meaning that fits here. So the best translation is "mounts" (RSV, NASB, NIV).

26 Sendeth Greeting See discussion at Acts 15:23.

27 Having Understood The Greek verb is *manthanō*, "learn." So the correct translation is "having learned" (RSV, NASB; cf. NIV). This, of course, was a lie; he learned this later.

29 Accused . . . Laid to His Charge In the Greek these two expressions are closely related. The first is the present passive participle of the verb *engkaleō*, which literally means "call in," and so "accuse." The second is a noun derived from this—*engklēma* (only here and 25:16), "accusation." So the best translation is "accused . . . accusation" (NASB).

30 When It Was Told *Menyō* does mean "disclose." But it is used here in the forensic sense "inform" (A-S, p. 291; AG, p. 519).

Laid Wait The Greek noun *epiboulē* (only here and 9:24; 20:3 [q.v.], 19) means "a plan against," and so "a plot." Probably the best translation here is: "When I was informed of a plot to be carried out against the man" (NIV).

35 Judgment Hall See discussion at Mark 15:16. We would favor the "Praetorium" (NASB; cf. RSV).

24:1 Orator The Greek word *rhētōr* (only here in NT) gives us our word *rhetorician*. It first meant "public speaker, orator." But then it came to be used specifically for "a speaker in court . . . attorney" (AG, p. 735). The correct translation is "attorney" (NASB) or "lawyer" (NIV). (See further discussion in BBC, 7:531.)

Informed The verb *emphanizō* literally means "make visible, reveal." But here it apparently means "bring formal charges against" (AG, p. 257; cf. NASB, NIV). It had this technical meaning in that period.

3 Most Noble The Greek word is *kratiste*, vocative case of the adjective *kratistos*. It first meant (in Homer) "strongest." But it then became a honorary form of address to superiors: "most noble, most excellent." Also see discussion at Luke 1:3.

4 *Clemency* *Epieikeia* meant "clemency" or "gentleness"—so translated (KJV) in 2 Cor. 10:1, the only other place where it occurs in the NT. Arndt and Gingrich suggest for our passage here: "with your (customary) graciousness" (p. 292).

A Few Words One word in Greek, the adverb *syntomōs*. It means "briefly" (RSV, NIV).

5 *A Pestilent Fellow* This is one word in Greek, *loimos*. In the only other place where it occurs in the NT, it is used in its literal sense of "pestilence" (Luke 21:11). Here it is used metaphorically for "a pest" (NASB) or "troublemaker" (NIV).

Ringleader *Prōtostatēs* (only here in NT) literally means "one who stands in first place." It is used in Thucydides and Xenophon for a soldier in the front rank. Then it came to be used more generally for "a leader." The dictionary defines "ringleader" as "a person who leads others, especially in unlawful or improper activities" *American Heritage Dictionary*, p. 1119). That meaning is especially appropriate here.

Sect The Greek noun is *hairesis*, from which we get our word *heresy*. It has an interesting history.

Hairesis comes from the verb *haireō*, "take." So it first meant a taking or capture. In the middle this verb means "take for oneself, choose." So the noun came to mean "a choice." Third, it meant "that which is chosen," and so "an opinion," and especially "a peculiar opinion, heresy." That is the way it is used in 2 Pet. 2:1, and perhaps in 1 Cor. 11:19; Gal. 5:20. Fourth, in late writers it came to mean a "sect" or "party." In the KJV it is translated "heresy" in the last three references just noted. In Acts it is translated "sect" in five places (5:17; 15:5; 24:5; 26:5; 28:22). In 5:17 it is the sect of the Sadducees. In 15:5 and 26:5 it is the sect of the Pharisees. In 24:5 and 28:22 the Christians are called a "sect."

That leaves one more passage, 24:14. The KJV has "heresy," which may be right. But probably it is better to use "sect" (RSV, NASB, NIV), as a parallel to "the Way." Schlier says, "The usage in Acts corresponds exactly to that of Josephus and the earlier rabbis" (TDNT, 1:182). This is "sect."

Profane The verb *bebēloō* occurs only twice in the NT. In Matt. 12:5 it refers to desecrating the Sabbath by manual labor. Here it refers to desecrating the Temple. While "profane" is correct, today we say "desecrate" (NASB, NIV).

Temple This is *hieron*, the Temple area, not *naos*, the sanctuary. For the basis of this false charge see 21:28–29.

6b–8a These words are definitely not in the earliest Greek manuscripts, and so they should be omitted (see notes in RSV, NASB, NIV).

9 *Saying* The Greek verb *phaskō* is stronger than this. It means "affirming" (RSV) or "asserting" (NIV). In the NT it occurs only here, 25:19, and Rom. 1:22 (NIV, "claimed").

12 *Raising Up the People* The Greek literally says: "making an *epistasis* of a crowd." The noun means "attack, onset" (AG, p. 300). Thayer says that it is used here for "a tumultuous gathering" (p. 243). The whole expression means at least "stirring up a crowd" (RSV, NIV) and perhaps "causing a riot" (NASB).

14 *The Way* This expression (the definite article with *hodos*, "way") is used five times in Acts (19:9, 23; 22:4; 24:14, 22) for Christianity as "the Way." Contrary to the KJV, it should be capitalized (RSV, NASB, NIV).

Law . . . Prophets The Law and the Prophets were the two main divisions of the OT, and so these two words should be capitalized (NASB, NIV).

16 *Exercise* The verb is *askeō* (only here in NT). Windisch says that it has the sense of "I exercise or exert myself," and he adds: "In taking pains to have a conscience void of offence towards God and man, Paul is careful to listen constantly to the admonishing and warning voice of conscience in order not to offend God or man and not to neglect any obligations towards them" (TDNT, 1:494). Such strong language as "take pains" (RSV), "do my best" (NASB), or "strive" (NIV) fits well here.

Conscience See discussion at Acts 23:1.

Void of Offense This is one word in Greek, the adjective *aproskopos*. It literally means "not causing to stumble" (active) or "not stumbling" (passive). It is the latter here. So it means "blameless" (NASB) or "clear" (RSV,

NIV). Paul sought to live all the time with a clear conscience.

18 Purified   This is the perfect passive participle of *hagnizō*. The verb comes from the adjective *hagnos*, "pure," which is related to *hagios*, "holy" (TDNT, 1:122). In the Septuagint *hagnizō* is always used for ceremonial purification. And that is its meaning in Acts. This is obvious in the other two places where the verb occurs in this book (21:24, 26). According to the very strict Jewish requirement, Paul had to be ceremonially purified before he could enter the Temple area (*hieron*). The perfect tense (here) in Greek emphasizes completed action ("having been purified," NASB). Even more it emphasizes the continuing state: "I was ceremonially clean when they found me in the temple courts" (NIV). Incidentally, the NIV sometimes uses "temple courts" for *hieron* to make its meaning clear.

22 Deferred   The verb *anaballō* (only here in NT) means "defer" or "put off" (RSV, NASB). But Arndt and Gingrich point out that this was also a technical legal term for adjourning a trial (p. 50). So, "adjourned the proceedings" (NIV) gives the correct sense.

23 Liberty   The noun is *anesis*, in the accusative case *anesin* (see discussion at 2 Cor. 2:13 and 2 Thess. 1:7). Paul uses it in the sense of relaxation from pressure (*thlipsis*). Here it would be relief from the pressures of imprisonment.

25 Temperance   The popular idea of "temperance" today is avoidance of alcoholic beverages. But the Greek word here, *engkrateias* (only here; Gal. 5:23; 2 Pet. 1:6), means "self-control" (RSV, NASB, NIV).

27 Came into . . . Room   The Greek literally says "received a successor" (*diadochos*). This noun (only here in NT) is from the verb *diadechomai* (also only once in NT, at Acts 7:45). The verb means "receive in turn." Today we would translate the expression here: "was succeeded by" (RSV, NASB, NIV).

25:2 The High Priest   Instead of *ho archiereus* (sing.), "the high priest," the earliest Greek manuscripts have *hoi archiereis* (pl.), "the chief priests." Abbott-Smith says that these would have included "ex-high-priests and members of high-priestly families" (p. 62)—that is, male members.

3 Laying Wait   The Greek literally says "making an ambush"—*enedra*. See discussion at Acts 23:16.

5 Able   This is the adjective *dynatos* (in the pl.). It is related to *dynamis*, "power," and so means "powerful." Lenski says that it means "those empowered among you"—that is, "the duly empowered representatives of the Sanhedrin" (*Acts*, p. 990). It was not those who were "able" to make the trip, but "the influential men" (NASB) or "leaders" (NIV).

6 More than Ten Days   The earliest Greek manuscripts say "not more than eight or ten days."

7 Complaints   The Greek word (only here in NT) is *aitiōma*, which means "a charge" or "accusation." This was not a matter of complaining but of bringing legal charges against Paul in court. Festus was "sitting on the judgment seat" (v. 6), the only place from which he could issue a verdict.

8 Answered for Himself   This is one word in Greek, the present participle of *apologeomai*—"speak in one's own defense, defend oneself" (AG, p. 95). It is true that our word *apologize* comes from this verb. But whereas *apologize* now means saying, "I'm sorry; I was wrong," *apologeomai* meant just the opposite: "I was right, and I'll prove it." The original meaning of our word *apology* was "a defense," as one can see in English literature. So here the text means "Paul said in his own defense" (NASB; cf. RSV) or "Paul made his defense" (NIV).

9 Pleasure   The Greek word is *charis*, which occurs 156 times in the NT and 130 times is translated "grace" (in KJV). It is rendered "pleasure" only here and in 24:27. A better translation would be "favor" (RSV, NASB, NIV).

11 Appeal   The verb is *epikaleō*. In the middle, as here, it means "to appeal to someone." It "is a common legal term in the NT" (TDNT, 3:497). This use occurs again in verses 12, 21, and 25, as well as in 26:32 and 28:19. As a Roman citizen, Paul had the choice privilege of appealing his case directly to the emperor at Rome. When he did so, no other official could put him on trial.

13 Salute   The common meaning of the verb *aspazomai* is "greet." But Arndt and Gingrich note that in the case of an official visit, as here, it would mean "pay one's respects to" (p. 117, cf. NASB, NIV).

14 Paul's Cause The Greek literally says "the things concerning Paul." Today we would say "Paul's case" (RSV, NASB, NIV).

In Bonds *Desmios* is clearly here, as elsewhere in the NT, used as a substantive, meaning "prisoner" (RSV, NASB, NIV). In fact, it is translated that way (in KJV) 14 out of its 16 occurrences in the NT.

15 Informed See discussion at Acts 24:1.

Judgment We do not have here one of the common Greek words for "judgment" in the NT—*crima* or *crisis* (both from the verb *crinō*, "judge")—but a strong compound, *katadikē* (only here in NT). It means "sentence" (RSV) or even "sentence of condemnation" (NASB; cf. NIV). They not only wanted Paul to be tried by the governor; they wanted him to be condemned.

16 To Die These words (*eis apōleian*) are not found in the earliest Greek manuscripts. It is easy to see why a later copyist added them. The verb for "deliver" (KJV) is *charizomai* (from *charis*, "grace"). It usually has a good meaning: "give freely or graciously," as God gives to us His favor. But here it is a matter of giving a prisoner over to his enemies. So a scribe tried to help out with "to die." The best translation is simply "hand over" (NASB, NIV).

19 Superstition The Greek word is the noun *deisidaimonia* (only here in NT). It is related to the adjective *deisidaimon*, found only in Acts 17:22 (see discussion there). Perhaps the best translation here is "religion" (NIV).

23 Pomp The Greek word is *phantasia* (only here in NT). Originally meaning "imagination" (cf. our word *fantasy*, which comes from it), the term finally came to mean "show" or "display," as here.

Place of Hearing The Greek word *akroatērion* (only here in NT) comes from the verb *akroaomai*, "listen." So this is a good literal translation. The modern equivalent would be "audience room" (NIV) or "auditorium" (NASB).

Chief Captains See discussion at Acts 21:31, 33.

25 Augustus This was the Latin equivalent of the Greek *Sebastos* (only here, v. 21, and 27:1). Both words mean "revered," or "worthy of reverence." This is what the Roman emperors claimed to be.

26:3 Questions The noun *zētēma* occurs
only in Acts (15:2; 18:15; 23:29; 25:19; 26:3). Arndt and Gingrich say that it is used in Acts "with the meaning it still has in Modern Greek (*controversial*) *question, issue*" (p. 339). So it may be translated "controversies" (RSV, NIV).

Patiently The noun *makrothymia* (14 times in NT) is translated (in KJV) "longsuffering" 12 times and "patience" twice. But here we have the adverb *makrothymōs* (only here in NT), which means "patiently."

4 Manner of Life This is one word in Greek, *biōsis* (only here in NT). It comes from *bios*, "life" (cf. *biology*), emphasizing the course of life. Our *biography* comes from *bios* and *graphō*, "write." A biography is a written record of the course of someone's life.

5 Most Straitest This, of course, is not good English. The Greek has a single word, the adjective *akribēs* (only here in NT) in the superlative *akribestatēn*. The adjective means "exact, strict." So the superlative form means "strictest" (RSV, NASB, NIV).

Religion *Thrēskeia* (only here in NT) primarily refers to "*religion* in its external aspect" (A-S, p. 208). K. L. Schmidt points out that *thrēskeia* is used commonly by Philo and Josephus, and that Josephus uses it mostly "for Jewish worship of God" (TDNT, 3:156–57).

7 Twelve Tribes Interestingly, this is one word in Greek, the adjective *dōdekaphylos* (only here in NT) in the singular, used as a substantive. It is composed of *dōdeka*, "12," and *phylē*, "tribe." Possibly the singular emphasizes the unity of the 12 tribes as the people of God.

Instantly The Greek has *en ekteneia*. The noun *ekteneia* (only here in NT) means "zeal, intentness, earnestness" (A-S, p. 142). *En* is used here in its instrumental sense of "by" or "with." So the correct translation is "earnestly" (RSV, NASB, NIV). Deissmann suggests that *ekteneia* has here "the ethical sense of *endurance*" (BS, p. 262).

10 Voice The word *psēphos* (only here and Rev. 2:17) literally meant "a small smooth stone" or "pebble." Since pebbles were used in voting at that time, the word came to mean "vote" (RSV, NASB, NIV). A black stone was cast for conviction, a white one for acquittal (AG, p. 892). On the surface this suggests that Paul had been a member of the Sanhedrin (but see discussion in BBC, 7:552–53).

11 Compelled Them to Blaspheme This is probably not a true statement. The verb for "compelled," *anangkazō*, is in the imperfect tense, which indicates that Paul did not succeed in making them do it. The correct translation is "tried to force them to blaspheme" (NASB, NIV).

Being Exceedingly Mad This is one word in Greek, the present participle of the verb *emmainomai* (only here in NT), which means "rage against" (A-S, p. 148). Arndt and Gingrich translate it here "being furiously enraged at" (p. 255).

14 Pricks The word is *kentron*. Aside from this passage, it is used (in NT) only in 1 Cor. 15:55, 56, and in Rev. 9:10, in which places it means "sting." But here (in the plural) it means "goads" (RSV, NASB, NIV), with which the oxen were guided (and "goaded" to move). God was trying to guide Paul, but, like a stubborn ox, he was kicking against the goads.

24 Thou Art Beside Thyself This is all one word in Greek, *mainē*, which in 12:15 is translated "Thou art mad." The verb *mainomai* means "be mad, be out of one's mind" (AG, p. 486). The latter fits best here (cf. NASB, NIV).

Mad This is the Greek noun *mania* (only here in NT), which we have taken over into English in the sense of "craze." Since "doth make thee mad" (KJV) could today mean "makes you very angry," a better translation would be: "is driving you insane" (NIV). This would be followed (v. 25) by: "I am not insane" (NIV). "I am not mad" could now be construed as, "I'm not angry."

28 Almost Thou Persuadest Me These words are the basis of the very moving invitation song "Almost Persuaded." But is this what King Agrippa meant?

Literally the Greek says: "In a little [*en oligō*] you are persuading me [*me peitheis*] to make a Christian [*Christianon poiēsai*]."

The majority of commentators today feel that this does not indicate that Agrippa was almost persuaded to be a Christian. It seems most likely that Agrippa was rejecting Paul's appeal. Whether he was actually sarcastic or not, we cannot be sure. (See further discussion of this point in BBC, 7:560–61.)

27:1 Band See discussion at John 18:3.

2 Launched See discussion at Luke 8:22. The verb *anagō*, a technical nautical term for "put out to sea" (NASB, NIV), is found in this sense in Acts 13:13; 16:11; 18:21; 20:3, 13; 21:1, 2; 27:2, 4, 12, 21; 28:10, 11.

3 Touched The verb *katagō* literally means "bring down." Here and in 28:12 it applies to bringing a boat down from the high seas to a harbor. So the correct translation is "put in" (RSV, NASB); or, more simply, "landed" (NIV).

Entreated "Entreated" is obviously an obsolete form for "treated." Today it means "asked"—a wrong meaning here. The Greek verb is *chraomai*. Literally it means "make use of." Here alone in the NT it has the sense of "treat."

Courteously The Greek adverb (only here in NT) is *philanthrōpōs*. It is compounded of *philos*, "loving," and *anthrōpos*, "a human being." So it means "kindly" (RSV).

To Refresh Himself The Greek literally says "to obtain care." The verb is *tynchanō* (in aor. infin.) and the noun *epimeleia* (only here in NT).

4 Sailed Under The verb *hypopleō* (only here and v. 7) is composed of *pleō*, "sail," and *hypo*, "under." But obviously they didn't sail *under* the island of Cyprus. They "sailed under the lee of Cyprus" (RSV), to get protection from the heavy winds.

5 Sea *Pelagos* (only here and Matt. 18:6) basically means "the depths" (Matt.), and so here "the open sea" (NIV).

8 Hardly The adverb *molis* comes from *molos*, "toil." So it means "with difficulty" (RSV, NASB, NIV). This adverb occurs also in verses 7 and 16. Paul was having a difficult voyage!

10, 21 Hurt First meaning "insolence" and then "insult" (2 Cor. 12:10, the only other place it occurs in NT), *hybris* here means "damage" (NASB) or "disaster" (cf. NIV). Incidentally, *hybris* is translated "harm" in verse 21 (KJV), even though the reference is exactly the same as here.

Damage *Zēmia* (only here and Phil. 3:7, 8) is best translated "loss" (RSV, NASB, NIV), as indeed it is rendered in verse 21 (KJV). In Philippians it is opposed to "gain."

10 Lading *Phortion* means "burden" or "load." Here it obviously means "cargo" (RSV, NASB, NIV).

11 Master *Kybernētēs* (only here and Rev. 18:17) comes from the verb *kybernaō*, "to guide." So it means a "steersman" or "pilot" (NASB, NIV).

Owner of the Ship This is one word in Greek, *nauklēros* (only here in NT). "Shipowner" was the regular meaning of the word, as Arndt and Gingrich note. Then they add: "But it can also mean *captain*, since the sailing-master of a ship engaged in state service was called a *nauklēros*" (p. 534). See further discussion in BBC, 7:571.

12 Haven The word *limēn* (only here and v. 8) means "harbor" (RSV, NASB, NIV).

13 Blew Softly The verb *hypopneō* (only here in NT) literally means "blow underneath." So it came to mean "blow gently" (cf. RSV, NIV).

Loosing Thence The verb *airō* (literally, "take up") occurs over 100 times in the NT. Only here is it translated as "loose." Arndt and Gingrich suggest for this passage (alone) the technical nautical term "weighed anchor" (RSV, NASB, NIV).

Close By The adverb *asson* (only here in NT) means "nearer." This is well expressed by "close inshore" (RSV).

14 Euroclydon The earliest Greek manuscripts have "Euraquilo" (NASB). It is what we would call the "Northeaster" (NIV; cf. RSV).

15 Caught This is a strong compound in Greek, *synarpazō*. It means "seize and carry away." This is what the wind did to the ship.

Bear Up into The verb *antophthalmeō* (only here in NT) is compounded of *anti*, "over against," and *ophthalmos*, "eye." In classical Greek it was used in the sense of "face" (cf. RSV, NASB) or "withstand." Abbott-Smith suggests that here it is used as a nautical term, "beat up against the wind" (p. 42).

16 Running Under This is the aorist participle of *hypotrechō* (only here in NT). *Trechō* is the common verb for "run" in the NT. Here the compound is a nautical term: "running under the lee of" (RSV), and so "running under the shelter of" (NASB).

To Come By The Greek says "to become *perikrateis*." This adjective (only here in NT) means "having full command of." This is reflected well in NASB: "to get the ship's boat under control."

Boat This is not the ordinary word for "boat" in the NT. Rather, it is *skaphē* (only here and verses 30, 32). It means "light boat" or "skiff." The correct idea is caught in the NIV: "We were hardly able to make the lifeboat secure."

17 Undergirding The Greek verb is *hypozōnnymi* (only here in NT). This was a technical nautical term, such as Luke alone uses in the NT. The meaning of the first part of verse 17 is spelled out very well in the NIV: "When the men had hoisted it aboard, they passed ropes under the ship itself to hold it together." (See further discussion of this "undergirding" in BBC, 7:574–75—a very full treatment.)

Quicksands The Greek has *syrtis* (only here in NT). This was the name of two large shoals or sandbars on the Libyan coast of Africa. They were the graveyard of the Mediterranean for hapless sailors.

Strake This is the same verb, *chalaō*, that is correctly translated "let down" in verse 30 and in 9:25. That (NASB) or "lowered" (RSV, NIV) is what is clearly meant here.

Sail Only here in the NT is the noun *skeuos* translated "sail" (KJV). Once it is rendered "stuff" (Luke 17:31) and twice "goods" (Matt. 12:29; Mark 3:27). The other 19 times (in KJV) it is "vessel."

What does it mean here? In the Septuagint *skeuos* is once used (in the plural) for the ship's gear (TDNT, 7:359). Maurer says that the meaning in our passage is uncertain. But he adds: "Probably the reference is not so much to taking down the sails as to throwing the drag anchor overboard to lessen the speed of the ship" (TDNT, 7:362). That is why we find: "let down the sea anchor" (NASB) and "lowered the sea anchor" (NIV).

18 Lightened the Ship The Greek says: *ekbolēn epoiounto.* The noun *ekbolē* (only here in NT), comes from the verb *ekballō,* "throw out." So it means "a throwing out" (A-S, p. 136). The verb *poieō* means "do" or "make." The correct translation, then, is "began to throw the cargo overboard" (RSV, NIV; cf. NASB).

21 Abstinence This definitely means abstinence from eating food (cf. RSV, NASB, NIV). The Greek word here is *asitia* (only here in NT). It is composed of *alpha*-negative and *sition,* "wheat" (in the plural, "food"). So it means going without food.

27 Shipmen The noun *nautēs* (sing.) occurs (in NT) only here, verse 30, and Rev. 18:17. It comes from *naus,* "ship" (only in 27:41 in NT). Today we would call them "sailors" (RSV, NASB, NIV).

28 Fathoms The Greek word *orguia* (only here in NT) represented the length of an outstretched arm. For modern equivalents see the NIV.

29, 30, 40 Anchors The Greek word *angkyra* is found (in NT) only here and in Heb. 6:19 (where it is used figuratively).

33, 34, 36 Meat The word *trophē* literally means "nourishment," and so "food" (RSV, NASB, NIV). It definitely does not mean "meat" as we use that term today. Verse 35 indicates that the "meat" here was bread.

38 Lightened This time the Greek verb is *kouphizō* (only here in NT). It comes from *kouphos,* "light."

39 Creek The Greek word is *kolpos.* Properly, it meant "the bosom" (John 13:23, etc.). Here it means "a bosom-like hollow, as a bay" (A-S, p. 253).

Shore The Greek word *aigialos* means "beach." So the whole expression here should be: "bay with a beach" (RSV, NASB, cf. NIV).

40 Taken Up The verb is *periaireō,* which in verse 20 means "abandoned" (RSV, NASB). R. J. Knowling says that "the meaning cannot be as A.V., following Vulgate, 'having taken up'; in fact it is the very reverse. The sailors loosed the cables of the anchors which were fastened within the ship, that they might fall off into the sea" (EGT, 2:534).

Committed Themselves On the basis of what we have just noted, this is obviously wrong. The sailors committed the anchors to the sea, not "themselves." In the Greek there is no object expressed. But if we have to supply one, it would be "them"—that is, the anchors.

28:1, 4 Escaped The verb *diasōzō* is composed of *sōzō,* the common verb for "save" in the NT, and *dia,* "through." So it means "bring safely through." The same verb is translated "escaped" (KJV) in 27:44. But in 27:43 it is rendered simply as "save." The RSV does the same. The NASB has "bring . . . safely through" (27:43) and "brought safely through" (28:1), but "brought safely" (27:44) and "saved" (28:4). It must be acknowledged that the context sometimes requires modifications such as this.

2 Barbarous People See discussion at Col. 3:11.

4, 5 Beast *Thērion* does basically mean "wild animal" or "beast." But in some secular Greek literature it is clearly used, as here, in the sense of "snake" (NIV).

7 Courteously The Greek adverb is *philophronōs* (only here in NT). It is compounded of *philos,* "friendly," and *phrēn,* "mind" or "heart." So it means "in a friendly manner," or "hospitably" (RSV, NIV).

8 A Bloody Flux The Greek word is *dysenterion* (only here in NT). It comes from *enteron,* "intestine," and so means "dysentery" (RSV, NASB, NIV). Incidentally, the Greek physicians were the only scientific doctors of ancient times. That is why most medical terms, like this one, come from the Greek. And Luke, "the beloved physician" (Col. 4:14), naturally uses more of these than does any other NT writer.

8, 9 Healed These are two different verbs in the Greek. In verse 8 it is *iaomai,* used most frequently by Luke (17 out of the 28 times in NT). In verse 9 it is *therapeuō,* from which we get *therapy* and *therapeutics.* It first meant to "do service." Then it became a medical term, meaning "treat, cure, heal." Luke uses this 19 out of the 44 times it occurs in the NT. Surprisingly, Matthew uses it 16 times, emphasizing the healing ministry of Jesus.

Because two different Greek verbs are used in these two verses, the RSV, NASB, and NIV wisely use "healed" in verse 8 and "cured" in verse 9. The English translation should convey the distinctions of the Greek text when possible.

11 Sign *Parasēmos* (only here in NT) is an adjective that in the Septuagint carries the sense of "marked with a sign." Then it was used as a substantive, meaning "figurehead" (RSV, NASB, NIV).

Castor and Pollux The Greek has just one word, *Dioskourois* (only here in NT). The Dioscuri signified Castor and Pollux, the twin sons of Zeus. That was the insignia on this ship.

13 *Fetched a Compass* The bulk of the Greek manuscripts have *perielthontes*, the second aorist participle of *perierchomai*, "go around," and so "made a circuit" (RSV). The two fourth-century manuscripts (Vaticanus and Sinaiticus) have *perielontes*, the second aorist participle of *periaireō*, "cast off." Scholars agree that we cannot be certain as to the original text here.

16 *The Centurion . . . Guard* These words are not found in any Greek manuscript earlier than the ninth century, and so they are necessarily omitted in any scholarly translation.

23 *Expounded* The verb *ektithēmi* literally means to "set out." Metaphorically it signifies "set forth" or "expound." The verb occurs (in NT) only in Acts (7:21; 11:4; 18:26; 28:23).

27 *Is Waxed Gross* The verb *pachynō* (only here and Matt. 13:15, where we have the same quotation from the Septuagint) comes from the adjective *pachys*, "thick." So in the passive, as here, it meant "grow fat." Here it is used metaphorically of the spiritual heart, and so means "has become calloused" (NIV) or "dull" (NASB).

30 *Hired House* This is one word in Greek, *misthōma* (only here in NT). It originally meant "price" or "hire," or even "rent" (AG, p. 523). Instead of "in his own hired house," the RSV has "at his own expense"—which Arndt and Gingrich say "is possible." But they prefer "in his own rented lodgings" (p. 523). We would favor that or "in his own rented quarters" (NASB). We are not convinced that he would have rented an entire "house" (NIV).

Romans

1:1 *Servant, Apostle* In all but four of Paul's Epistles he begins by calling himself an apostle. The four exceptions are the two Thessalonian letters, Philemon, and Philippians. In these he did not feel the need of calling attention to his apostolic authority, for the readers were thoroughly loyal to him.

But in the case of the Epistle to the Romans we have Paul's fullest and most systematic presentation of the great doctrines of "the redemption that is in Christ Jesus" (3:24). It was important that he support this with an assertion of his apostleship.

However, he begins by calling himself first *a servant*, and then *an apostle*. The only other place where he does this is in his Epistle to Titus. Why does he do it here?

Paul was writing to the Christians in the capital of the Roman Empire. He had never seen them. This was his first approach to them. The great Apostle of the Gentiles did not address them with a haughty bearing. Very humbly he said, "I am a slave of Jesus Christ." It was typical of Paul's true nobility of spirit. And it doubtless helped to open the hearts of the many who heard his Epistle read in the church.

The word *servant* is a translation of *doulos,* which means "slave." It is from *deō,* "bind," and so is literally "bond servant."

Cremer points out the implications of this for those who call themselves servants of Christ. He says, "The normal moral relation of man to God is that of a *doulos tou theou* (slave of God) whose own will, though perfectly free, is bound to God" (p. 216). He then goes on to point out that this expression, "slave of God," has a twofold meaning. It denotes first "that relation of subservience and subjection of will which beseems all who confess God and Christ, and are devoted to Him." Secondly, it indicates "a peculiar relation of devotedness, in which a man is at God's disposal and is employed by Him."

There is an interesting paradox in this word. The Christian becomes a slave of Christ by free choice, and yet he is owned by Christ because the latter purchased him with the price of His own blood.

This twofold idea is expressed in the case of the "love slave" of the OT times, described in Deut. 15:12–17. If an Israelite bought a Hebrew slave, he must let him go free in the sabbatical year. But if the slave loved his master and chose, of his own free will, to remain with him, then a hole was bored through the lobe of the slave's ear. He then became a bond servant for life.

This paradox is well expressed by Vincent. He writes: "The word involves the ideas of belonging to a master, and of service as a slave. The former is emphasized in Paul's use of the term, since Christian service, in his view, has no element of servility, but is the expression of love and free choice. . . . On the other hand, believers belong to Christ by purchase, and own Him as absolute Master" (3:2). Rengstorf notes that the word indicates "unconditional commitment" to God (TDNT, 2:275).

The phrase "servant of God" (or "servant of the Lord") has a strong background in the OT. Many times the prophets are called servants of the Lord—with *doulos* used in the Septuagint. It is found thus in Amos 3:7 and frequently in Jeremiah (e.g., 7:25), as also in Dan. 9:6 and Ezra 9:11. The first time that it is found in the NT is in Rom. 1:1.

This suggests that Paul's use of the term was not only an evidence of humility, but also a declaration of the fact that he belonged in the noble succession of prophets of the Lord. Sanday and Headlam have described this well in their comment: "But it is noticeable how quietly St. Paul steps into the place of the prophets and leaders of the Old Covenant, and how quietly he substitutes the name of His own Master in a connexion hitherto reserved for that of Jehovah" (p. 3).

The idea of being a slave of Christ takes on added significance when we think of the fact that He became a slave for our sakes. That is beautifully stated in Phil. 2:7, where we read that Christ "emptied himself" and "took upon him the form of a servant" (*doulos*). This was necessary for our salvation. And only as we become His slaves can we hope to be used in saving others.

The phrase "slave of the Lord" would carry more significance for the readers of Paul's Epistles because of the current phrase "slave of the emperor." Deissmann points out the frequent occurrence of this phrase in the inscriptions of that period. For instance, a Greek inscription found in Phrygia (in Asia Minor) contains this wording: "Agathopus, slave of the lord Emperor" (LAE, p. 376).

All over the Roman Empire there were those who were known as slaves of the emperor. How happy Paul was to write to Rome, "I am a slave of Jesus Christ, the King of Kings and Lord of Lords!" Thank God for the privilege of being freed from slavery to sin and Satan, that we might be Christ's slaves, and His alone. For His slavery spells true freedom.

But while Paul is a slave he is also an "apostle." We get our English word directly from the Greek *apostolos*. As is commonly known, this comes from the verb *apostellō*, which means "send on a mission, or with a commission." Hence an apostle is a "sent one." But, more than that, he is one sent with a message. The word suggests a messenger-missionary. It is used by the famous Greek historian Herodotus in the sense of "messenger," or "envoy" (VGT, p. 70).

Separated unto the Gospel The idea of Paul's special commission as an apostle is further enhanced by the phrase "separated unto the gospel of God." The verb here, *aphorizō*, means "mark off by boundaries," and so "set apart, devote to a special purpose." Paul was conscious that he was set apart, separated from all other pursuits in life, that he might devote himself wholly to the special purpose of preaching the gospel.

Such a consciousness must grip every preacher if he is to be true to his vocation. Until we are really separated we cannot hope to make a success in the ministry. It has been often and well said that if a person can feel content to do anything else in life rather than preach and teach the Word he does not belong in the ministry. A preacher must have an inescapable conviction that he is called and separated by God to this special purpose.

2 *In the Holy Scriptures* The Greek is *en graphais hagiais*—perhaps the earliest occurrence of this phrase anywhere. It is noticeable that the definite article is missing in the Greek. This grammatical construction emphasizes kind or quality. Sanday and Headlam have indicated well the significance of this feature in the passage before us. They write: "In *graphais hagiais* the absence of the article throws the stress on *hagiais;* the books are 'holy' as containing the promises of God Himself, written down by inspired men" (p. 6).

In the same vein Vincent says that they are "books which are *holy* as conveying God's revelations" (3:3). They are holy because they contain holy truth.

The word *graphai* is from *graphō*, "write," and simply means "writings." But in all the 50 or more occurrences of it (singular or plural) in the NT, it refers to the Sacred Scriptures, either the OT or some particular passage in it. Only here do we find the adjective "holy" with it.

The force of this compound expression is clearly indicated by Denney. He writes, "It emphasizes the Divine character of these as opposed to other writings. That is *hagion* which belongs to God, or is connected with the OT as God's book" (EGT, 2:585).

3–4 *The Seed of David . . . the Son of God* Ask a conservative, "Was Jesus human or divine?" and he will answer emphatically, "Divine!" Ask a liberal the same question and he may reply, "Human." Both are right and both are wrong. For the correct answer is "Both." Jesus was both human *and* divine.

This dual truth is expressed forcibly in the third and fourth verses. The third states that He became, or "was made," from the seed of David—that is, from Davidic ancestry—"according to the flesh" (*kata sarka*). The fourth affirms that He was "declared to be the Son of God with power, according to the spirit of holiness [*kata pneuma hagiōsynēs*], by the resurrection from the dead."

The Greek for "which was made" is *genomenou.* It is the aorist participle of *ginomai*, the simplest meaning of which is "become." The verb indicates "transition from one state or mode of subsistence to another." By His physical birth Jesus became a human being, descended from David, and so Heir to the throne of Israel.

But He was also "declared" the Son of God. The Greek word is *horisthentos*, which comes from *horos*, "boundary." So it means "marked off by boundaries." In the metaphorical sense, as here, it means "designated."

Jesus did not become the Son of God by His resurrection. He was God's Son from all eternity. But His resurrection designated Him as such to mankind. James Denney has well expressed it in these words: "The resurrection only declared Him to be what He truly was" (EGT, 2:586).

What is meant by the phrase "spirit of holiness"? Some modern commentators agree with the early church fathers in taking it as a reference to the Holy Spirit. Others refer it to the divine nature in Jesus, implying that *sarx* means the human nature. But it seems best to take it as referring to Jesus' human spirit, which was completely holy. Sanday and Headlam express the consensus of the best commentators when they write: "The *pneuma hagiōsynēs*, though not the Divine nature, is that in which the Divinity or Divine Personality resided" (p. 9).

These two verses sum up the twin truths that He who was from all eternity Son of God became Son of Man by a human birth and that He was then designated as God's Son by His resurrection from the dead. The purpose of the latter was that mankind might know beyond dispute that He was divine.

The word *anastasis* ("resurrection") means "a rising up." It is used in a Greek inscription for the erection of a monument. The resurrection of Jesus Christ was God's monument to the deity of His Son, erected to confirm the faith of all generations to come.

Before we leave these two verses there is one other word that deserves attention. Paul uses the very full expression "his Son Jesus Christ our Lord" (v. 3).

The word for *Lord* is *kyrios*. In the Septuagint (Greek) version (LXX) of the OT, made before the time of Christ, *kyrios* is used regularly to translate the Hebrew name Jehovah (or Yahweh). But Jehovah is the God of the Israelites, the only true God, the "high and lofty One that inhabiteth eternity, whose name is Holy" (Isa. 57:15).

When the early Christians applied to Jesus the term *kyrios*, they thereby expressed their faith that He was really God. Though men may use *lord* in a lesser sense, with Paul and the other writers of the NT the word as applied to

Jesus involved a declaration of His deity. James Denney says: " 'Our Lord' is the most compendious expression of the Christian consciousness" (EGT, 2:586). By the use of this term the believers declared that Jesus was all that the term *Jehovah* implied in the OT.

5 Grace Here we meet the term *grace* for the first time in this Epistle. Though a small word both in English and in Greek (*charis*), its meanings are many and varied.

The oldest sense in which *charis* was used, going clear back to Homer, was that of "sweetness" or "attractiveness." Then it came to mean "favor," "goodwill," "loving kindness," especially when shown to an inferior, as by a master to his servant or by a king to his subjects. So in the OT (LXX) it is used of God's favor to man.

A new element is then introduced, that of *unearned* favor. Thayer says that the writers of the NT use *charis* "pre-eminently of that kindness by which God bestows favors even upon the ill-deserving, and grants to sinners the pardon of their offences, and bids them accept of eternal salvation through Christ" (p. 666).

The word *charis* occurs about 160 times in the NT. It is translated a number of ways in KJV: favor, thank, pleasure, liberality, benefit, thanks, joy, thankworthy, acceptable. But by far the most common rendering is "grace" (130 times).

When Paul says here, "We have received grace," he apparently refers to God's wonderful favor, shown in his salvation. The great apostle never got over marveling that God should have saved him, the chief of sinners. He expresses more fully his feelings when writing to Timothy: "Howbeit for this cause I obtained mercy, that in me first Jesus Christ might shew forth all longsuffering" (1 Tim. 1:15–16).

Cremer sums up the NT meaning of *charis* in these words: "*Charis* has been distinctively appropriated in the NT to designate the relation and conduct of God towards sinful man as revealed in and through Christ, especially as an act of *spontaneous favor*, of favor wherein no mention can be made of obligation" (p. 574).

7 Saints The word translated "saints" in the NT is *hagioi*. It is the plural of the adjective *hagios*, "holy," which occurs over 200 times in the NT. About 60 of these times it is used as a substantive and is rendered "saints."

So the literal meaning of *saints* is "holy ones." That is the way Father Spencer renders it in his translation of the NT from the original Greek. The reason for Father Spencer's choice is obvious. Among Catholics the term *saint* has a technical connotation. It refers only to one who has been officially canonized by the church. But it is obvious that Paul uses the term as a general designation for all Christians. In what sense, however, can they be called holy?

If we restrict the word *holy* to the character or state resulting from entire sanctification, there is no answer. Obviously the term *holy* has a wider usage.

The primary idea of the word *holy*, as used in the OT, is that of *separation*. It describes both persons and things as set apart to God and to His service. But since what was consecrated to God must be unblemished, the word came to mean "free from blemish, spot, or stain."

In the NT the ethical or moral, rather than the formal and ceremonial, use came to the front. Since God is holy in character, that which is set apart to Him and for His use must be holy in character. Thus we have the essential idea of holiness as Godlikeness.

In referring to Christians as "saints," Paul is emphasizing the fact that they are set apart to God. He is also implying that, as such, they should become more and more holy in character, more like the God they serve.

Grace, Peace This is Paul's typical greeting, found at the beginning of all his Epistles. The typical Greek salutation was *chairein*, derived from *charis*. The universal Hebrew greeting, then as now, was *Shalom*, "Peace." Paul combines the two in his letters to these churches composed of both Jews and Gentiles.

The first seven verses of this Epistle constitute the salutation. It is remarkable how much theology Paul packs into his greeting to the church at Rome. He declares the deity and humanity of Jesus, the position of Christians as "saints," and the relationship of Father and Son. Paul is so eager for the Roman church to be thoroughly and correctly indoctrinated that even in his opening salutation he lays a basic foundation of Christian teaching.

8 ***Through Jesus Christ*** Paul declares that he is constantly (present tense) thanking God "through Jesus Christ." Everything we receive from God is through Christ Jesus (cf. Eph. 1:3) and so our praise to God should be rendered through Christ. Vincent writes: "In penitence and in thanksgiving alike, Jesus Christ is the one mediator through whom we have access to God" (3:6). Sanday and Headlam bring out the idea in their paraphrase of this passage:

"Through Him Who as High Priest presents all our prayers and praises" (p. 18).

Your Faith This expression has been interpreted two ways. It could be taken as referring to the strength or superiority of their faith in Christ. That is treating "faith" as a subjective attitude of the believer. But it seems best to take it objectively. Thus Sanday and Headlam say: "Here it is practically equivalent to 'your Christianity' " (p. 19). Wuest writes: "The faith of the saints here refers to the fact that they are Christians and to the lives they lived" (p. 19).

Spoken of The Greek word here is *katangellō*. The simple verb *angellō* means "announce." The compound suggests spreading tidings throughout, down among (*kata*), "with the included idea of *celebrating* or *commending*" (Vincent, 3:7). Probably the best translation would be: "is being proclaimed."

The Whole World The term for *world* here is *cosmos*, which we have taken over in English. It means "the ordered universe," being the opposite of "chaos." (Cosmetics, derived from this Greek word, are supposed to put a person's face in order!)

What does the apostle mean by "the whole world"? Commentators generally classify the expression as "hyperbolical." But this is not necessary. In the NT the phrase regularly refers to the Roman Empire as such. It of course could not include the western hemisphere, still undiscovered. Nor would it take in the Far East. Europe and the Middle East would be all that was intended. Since Rome was the capital city, it does not seem unreasonable to suggest that the faith of the Roman church was being proclaimed throughout the empire.

9 ***My Witness*** The word for *witness* is *martys;* from the genitive form, *martyros*, we get our English word *martyr*. This is due to the fact that in later times those who witnessed for Christ had to pay for it with their lives.

But here we have the term in its earlier, nontechnical meaning of one who bears testimony to what he knows—what he has seen or heard or otherwise experienced. Paul had to appeal to God as his Witness in this case, because no one else would have heard his daily private prayers for the Roman Christians. By this appeal the apostle solemnly asserts his faithfulness in prayer for them.

Sacred Service The word *latreuo* (*serve*) is used in the Septuagint for service to God and occasionally of serving heathen gods. But it is always of service to a higher power, whether supposed or actual. Says Vincent: "The word was used in a special sense to denote the service rendered to Jehovah by the Israelites as His peculiar people" (*ibid.*). In the NT it is used of the Christian's service to God.

Praying Without Ceasing The expression "without ceasing" is one word in the Greek, the adverb *adialeiptōs*. It means "without letting up or leaving off." Paul was incessant in his praying.

The term is found elsewhere in the NT only in 1 Thessalonians, where it occurs three times. In 1 Thess. 1:3, Paul says that he remembers unceasingly the faithfulness of the Christians at Thessalonica. But it immediately follows a statement that he is praying for them. In 2:13 he says he thanks God unceasingly for them. Finally, in 5:17 occurs that great command: "Pray without ceasing." The great apostle practiced what he preached; he himself set the example of unceasing prayer. Robertson says of Paul: "He seems to have had prayer lists" (4:325). And these included the people of the many churches he had founded on his missionary journeys.

10 Fourfold Fervor Paul's eagerness to see the Romans is expressed by 3 particles packed in close succession—*ei pōs ēdēpote*. They might be translated "if somehow now at last."

The common word for *now* in the Greek NT is *nyn*, which simply indicates present time. But the particle used here, *ēdē*, has "a certain suggestion of surprise or relief" that the goal has been reached as soon as it has, and is translated by Sanday and Headlam, "now, after all this waiting" (p. 20). Paul had an earnest desire to see the Romans. He looked forward eagerly to having this desire fulfilled soon.

A Prosperous Journey The KJV brings out the etymological force of the word *euodoō* in its translation "have a prosperous journey." It comes from *eu*, "well," "good," and *hodos*, "way." However, as Sanday and Headlam note, "The word has usually dropped the idea of *hodos* and means 'to be prospered' in any way" (*ibid.*). An example is 1 Cor. 16:2, where the same word is used for prospering financially. But it seems that the context here in Romans would favor giving the term its original meaning as translated in the KJV.

By Where did Paul hope to find this "good way," this "prosperous journey"? The KJV says

"by the will of God." But the Greek has *en*, which is usually translated "in." The best, safest, and most prosperous way of life lies "in the will of God." That is the road Paul was following. It is our privilege to take it, too.

11 Some Spiritual Gift The Greek expression is *ti charisma pneumatikon*. Sanday and Headlam say concerning it: "St. Paul has in mind the kind of gifts—partly what we should call natural and partly transcending the ordinary workings of nature—described in I Cor. XII–XIV" (p. 21). Adam Clarke agrees with this. He writes (2:39):

> This probably means some of the *extraordinary gifts* of the Holy Spirit, which, being given to them, might tend greatly to establish their faith in the Gospel of Christ; and it is very likely that such gifts were only conferred by means of *apostles;* and as the *apostle* had not yet been at Rome, consequently the Roman Christians had not yet received any of these miraculous gifts, and thus they differed widely from all the other Churches which had been raised by the apostle's ministry.

With all due respect to the very high scholarship of Adam Clarke and of Sanday and Headlam, we must confess some hesitation at accepting this interpretation. We find it difficult to believe that such a purpose would have engaged Paul's earnest attention.

It seems to us far more likely that the apostle would be concerned to share with them some spiritual grace that would help to establish these Roman believers in their Christian experience. We cannot see how a miraculous gift would do this, except the gift of the Holy Spirit himself. To us it seems most reasonable to hold that Paul was talking about a further gift of God's grace, "to the end ye may be established." This fits in with the basic meaning of the term. Vincent says: "*Charisma* is a gift of grace (*charis*), a *favor* received without merit on the recipient's part" (3:7).

12 Comfort The KJV reads: "that I may be comforted together with you." That is a common meaning of *symparakaleō*. The verb, however, may be translated a number of different ways. Probably the best rendering here is "strengthened together." He hopes that he and the Roman Christians may be mutually strengthened by their spiritual fellowship when he is able to come to them.

The language of verse 12 reveals the beautiful humility of Paul's character. Though he has much to impart to the believers at Rome, yet he graciously expresses himself as expecting to receive help and blessing from contact with the humblest of God's children. The writer remembers receiving a wonderful interpretation of a certain scriptural passage from the lips of a Pullman car porter. The basic prerequisite of all true learning is an attitude of humility. If we have this, we can learn much from the persons and events of our daily living. And he who has nothing to learn from others will not be able to teach others in any helpful way.

13 *Personal Purpose* Paul tells the Roman Christians that he had often purposed to come to them. The word is *protithēmi*, which means "set or place before." Here the word is in the second aorist middle. So it would mean: "I set before myself, proposed to myself, purposed, determined." But Paul was unable to carry out this intended plan.

Let The KJV has Paul saying, "But I was let hitherto." Here is a typical illustration of changed English word meanings since this translation was made. The Greek verb is *kōlyo*, which means "cut off," and so "hinder, prevent." Three hundred fifty years ago, *let* was used in the sense of "hinder." But that is definitely not true today. "Hindered" is found in most modern versions.

As Among Other Gentiles The question has often been raised—and, in fact, debated in scholarly circles—as to whether the Christian church at Rome was composed mostly of Jews or Gentiles. The last part of verse 13 would seem to indicate that the majority were Gentiles. For Paul expresses the wish that he may "get" (second aorist of *echō*) "some fruit among you also, even as among other Gentiles." James Denney writes: "Nothing could indicate more clearly that the Church at Rome, as a whole, was Gentile" (EGT, 2:588).

However, we shall find in the second chapter (v. 17) that Paul also addresses the Jews in the Roman church. Obviously the congregation there was composed of both Jews and Gentiles, unless we are to assume that they met in separate groups and that this Epistle was directed to both groups. That does not seem likely.

Fruit The term *karpos*, "fruit," is used in various ways in the NT, where it occurs some 70 times. In the majority of instances it is employed in a metaphorical or spiritual sense.

We find it seven times in the seventh chapter of Matthew, where we are twice told, "By their fruits ye shall know them" (vv. 16, 20).

That is simply a statement of the obvious fact that one's inward character can be recognized fairly accurately by one's outward conduct, for the latter is the fruit of the former.

The chapter where the term occurs most often, however, is the fifteenth of John's Gospel, where we find it eight times. Here the emphasis is on "bearing" or "bringing forth" fruit. It would appear that the term can be taken as referring either to the result of Christian service or to an inward growth in grace.

The latter idea is underscored by the great passage in Gal. 5:22–23 on "the fruit of the Spirit." There it refers to the inward graces of Christlike character which are produced in the heart of the sanctified believer by the indwelling Holy Spirit.

Which is the primary reference in this passage in Romans? That would be hard to say. We would agree with Denney in allowing both emphases. He writes: "*Karpos* denotes the result of labor: it might either mean new converts or the furtherance of the Christians in their new life" (EGT, 2:588).

14 *Debtor* To all missionary-minded persons—and that should mean all Christians—the term *debtor* is full of significance. For every child of God is deeply in debt.

The world *opheiletēs* means "one held by some obligation, bound to some duty" (Thayer). Wuest says: "The word refers to a personal, moral obligation as contrasted to a necessity in the nature of the case, which latter idea is expressed by *dei*" (p. 23).

What made Paul say, "I am debtor"? It was his realization of what a vast amount of unnumbered blessings he had received from God. All this put him under obligation.

How was he to discharge this debt? Paul's whole Christian career furnishes the answer. The only way he could repay his debt was in loving service to others. Thus he would express his loyalty and gratitude to God. So, while his primary debt was to God, he could say: "I am debtor both to the Greeks, and to the Barbarians."

Barbarians Our word is simply a transliteration of the Greek *barbaros*. The term was applied by the Greeks to any foreigner who did not speak the Greek language. With typical sophisticated prejudice they said of such a foreigner: "All he says is 'bar-bar-bar.'" So they called him a *barbaros*.

Thayer defines the word as indicating "one whose speech is rude, rough, harsh"; hence, "one who speaks a foreign or strange language which is not understood by another." He goes on to say: "The Greeks used *barbaros* of any foreigner ignorant of the Greek language and the Greek culture, whether mental or moral, with the added notion, after the Persian war, of rudeness and brutality" (p. 95). But he adds that Paul did not intend any reproach to foreigners here, but used the phrase "Greeks and Barbarians" as the equivalent of "all peoples." While Paul was well acquainted with the language and culture of Greece, he would not refer to non-Greeks in any disparaging way.

Wise, Unwise We are so accustomed to thinking of these terms in a mental frame of reference that it is difficult for us to get the biblical point of view. In the Scriptures, both Old Testament and New, the primary emphasis of wisdom is moral rather than mental.

The Greek adjective *sophos* ("wise") is used here in the dative plural. Of the cognate noun *sophia* ("wisdom") Trench has this to say: "We may affirm with confidence that *sophia* is never in Scripture ascribed to other than God or good men, except in an ironical sense . . . nor are any of the children of this world called *sophoi* except with this tacit or expressed irony . . . there can be no wisdom disjoined from goodness" (p. 283).

Of those described by the adjective *anoetos* ("unwise") Trench declares: "In the *anoetos* there is always a moral fault lying behind the intellectual" (*ibid.*). Again we would say that in the Bible "wisdom" is more of a moral matter than a mental one. The best of the Greek philosophers recognized this distinction, as Trench points out. It is the dominant idea connected with wisdom in the sacred Scriptures.

16 Power Here Paul makes one of the great assertions of this Epistle: "For I am not ashamed of the gospel of Christ: for it is the power of God unto salvation to every one that believeth." The initial *for* is related to the previous verse and tells us why he is "ready to preach the gospel to you that are at Rome also." The apostle knew that he had a great gospel worthy of being preached in the capital city of the greatest empire the world had ever seen.

Rome boasted of her power which consisted of military might. But Paul declares that his gospel is the "power of God." It is more than human might.

The Greek word translated "power" is *dynamis*, from which we get *dynamite, dynamic, dynamo*. It means: "strength, ability, power . . . inherent power, power residing in a thing by virtue of its nature, or which a person

or thing exerts or puts forth" (Thayer). The gospel, then, is the inherent power of an infinite God exerted in the salvation of mankind. What a glorious conception of truth! "The Gospel has all God's omnipotence behind it" (SH, p. 23). And Grundmann asserts: "The power to save and deliver is grounded only in the omnipotence of God and must proceed from it" (TDNT, 2:309).

Salvation The Greek word is *soteria*, from *soter*, "savior." Sanday and Headlam state: "The fundamental idea contained in *soteria* is the removal of dangers menacing to life and the consequent placing of life in conditions favorable to free and healthy expansion" (*ibid.*). They further point out that in the earlier books of the OT the term is used for "deliverance from physical peril." Later it is applied more to "the great deliverances of the nation." Finally it is associated with "Messianic deliverance," both "in the lower forms of the Jewish Messianic expectation" and "in the higher form of the Christian hope" (*ibid.*).

The basic idea of salvation is *deliverance*. It is a divine deliverance both *from* sin and *to* holiness.

17 Righteousness The term *righteousness* is, of course, one of the key words of this Epistle. In fact, the whole thesis of Romans is summed up in verses 16 and 17. The *gospel* is God's *power* unto *salvation*, which consists of God's *righteousness*, which comes by *faith*. That is the message of the NT in a nutshell.

The Greek word *dikaiosyne* comes from *dikaios*, "righteous." Cremer defines this as "what is right, conformable to right" (p. 183). With regard to *dikaiosyne* he says: "In its scriptural sense, both in the OT and NT, righteousness is the state commanded by God and standing the test of His judgment, the character and acts of man approved of Him, in virtue of which the man corresponds with Him and His will as his ideal and standard" (pp. 190–91). In the Pauline thought it is "the righteousness which God not only demands, but gives to man" (*ibid.*, p. 192).

Vincent gives an extended treatment of the two terms we are considering. He begins by saying that "*dikaiosyne* is *rightness* as characterizing the entire being of man" (3:10). He ends his discussion with the statement: "Righteousness thus expresses the relation of being right into which God puts the man who believes" (3:14).

In common with many other commentators Vincent declares that "righteousness of God" here does not mean an attribute of God but that righteousness which He bestows on the believer. Some support is found for this in the fact that the definite article does not occur here. It is either "a righteousness of God" or "God's righteousness."

But Sanday and Headlam protest, perhaps wisely, against this one-sided view. After giving carefully the arguments for both views they call for acceptance of both. They write: "The righteousness of which the apostle is speaking not only proceeds from God but *is* the righteousness of God Himself" (p. 25). This seems to be the most reasonable interpretation.

From Faith to Faith This phrase rather obviously means from a lesser faith to a greater faith. But what is the application? It is generally taken as indicating the change from a lower to a higher faith in the individual. But again Sanday and Headlam call for a dual interpretation: "The phrase means 'starting from a smaller quantity of faith to produce a larger quantity,' at once intensively and extensively, in the individual and in society" (p. 28).

18 *Irreverence* Paul states that God's wrath (*orgē theou*) is revealed from heaven against all "ungodliness and unrighteousness." The latter term (*adikia*) has reference to the lack of a right attitude inwardly and right conduct outwardly. It is used 26 times in the NT.

But the former term, *asebeia*, occurs only 6 times—twice here in Romans, twice in the Pastorals, and twice in the brief Epistle of Jude. In every case it is translated in the KJV "ungodliness" or "ungodly."

Today if a person is described as "ungodly," immediately we think of immorality and licentious living. But that is not at all the connotation of *asebeia*, nor indeed the original meaning of the English word. For *ungodly* literally means "ungodlike" (compare the German suffix—*lich*, which is the equivalent of the English—*ly*). An "ungodly" person is one who is "ungodlike" in heart and life, even though he may be respected as a model citizen in his community.

Actually, the essential idea of *asebeia* is "irreverence." Thayer defines it as "want of reverence towards God, impiety, ungodliness" (p. 79). E. R. Bernard writes: "As *anomia* is disregard and defiance of God's law, so *asebeia* is the same attitude towards God's Person. It expresses the insult and blasphemy involved in sin" (HDB, 4:532).

Every alert preacher will quickly sense the homiletical significance of this word. There are multiplied thousands who live lives that are circumspect and socially acceptable, but are nevertheless "ungodly" or "godless" because they pay no attention to God. A lack of reverence for God and sacred things—for instance, the time and place of worship—is what constitutes real ungodliness. A generation that desecrates the Lord's Day and lives without any reference to God is guilty of the sin of *asebeia*. Against such an attitude of indifference to the divine, God's wrath is revealed.

God's Wrath Some have contended that the idea of a God of wrath is entirely incompatible with that of a God of righteousness, to say nothing of a God who is love. But there can be no righteousness without wrath. And a love which is not righteous is not divine. True love can never condone sin.

Sanday and Headlam have expressed well the real meaning of God's wrath. They write: "Wrath is only the reaction of the Divine righteousness when it comes into collision with sin" (p. 35).

Hence it is entirely consistent that the two ideas should be linked so closely together here in verses 17 and 18. There can be no revelation of divine righteousness without an accompanying revelation of divine wrath. Trench says that God "would not love good, unless He hated evil, the two being so inseparable, that either He must do both or neither" (p. 134).

Hold It is here declared that some men "hold the truth in unrighteousness." The impression given by this translation is that men continue to hold the truth in their minds while they live unrighteous lives. In other words, their conduct contradicts their creed.

This may be the meaning here. For the first definition given for *katechō* in Abbott-Smith's *Lexicon* is "possess, hold fast," a sense which it obviously has in Luke 8:15 ("keep"), 1 Cor. 11:2 ("keep"), 15:2 ("keep in memory"), and Heb. 3:6; 10:23 ("hold fast"). This treats *katechō* as an intensive form of *echō*, "have or hold."

But the prefix *kata* literally signifies "down," and so we get the meaning "hold down." The second definition for *katechō* in Abbott-Smith (listed first in Thayer's *Lexicon*) is "to hold back, detain, restrain." That is clearly its meaning in 2 Thess. 2:7, where the old English "letteth" is used. The correct translation in that passage is "restrains" or "hinders."

But what is the preferable rendering here? Abbott-Smith supports KJV. But the majority of scholars agree with the more recent translations. The RV (1881) has "hold down." The AVS (1901) reads "hinder." The RSV (1946) renders

137

the word "suppress." And since the Greek preposition *en* may mean "by" as well as "in," the helpful interpretation is given: "who by their wickedness suppress the truth." One may give lip service to orthodoxy and yet hinder or hold down the truth by unrighteous living.

Incidentally, it is interesting to note that in John Wesley's translation of NT (final edition, 1790) the word is rendered "detain." Most scholars would agree with Sanday and Headlam's interpretation: "It is the truth which is 'held down,' hindered, thwarted, checked in its free and expansive operation" (p. 42).

20 *Eternal Power and Godhead* That which is known of God (v. 19) is the revelation of Him in nature. His invisible attributes are manifested in His visible creation. The universe is a projection of His personality. For those who have eyes to see, God may be observed every day and every night in the world around us (cf. Ps. 19:1–3).

What is it that may thus be understood? Paul answers, "his eternal power and Godhead."

The last word is a translation of *theiotēs*, found only here in the NT. It is similar to *theotēs*, which also occurs only once in the NT, in Col. 2:9. Both are translated "Godhead" in the KJV.

Is there any real difference in meaning between the two words? Many deny it. The RSV translates both "deity," thus agreeing with the KJV. TDNT makes no distinction.

But the ASV has "divinity" in Rom. 1:20 and "Godhead" in Col. 2:9. This distinction is supported by Vincent. He writes on the passage here in Romans: "Better, *divinity*. *Godhead* expresses *deity* (*theotēs*). *Theiotēs* is *godhood*, not *godhead*. It signifies the sum-total of the divine attributes" (3:16).

A high authority in the field is Archbishop Trench, who wrote the definitive work *Synonyms of the New Testament*. He insists on a distinction between the two terms under discussion. Speaking of *theiotēs* in Rom. 1:20 he says:

> Yet it is not the personal God whom any man may learn to know by these aids: He can be known only by the revelation of Himself in his Son; but only his divine attributes, his majesty and glory. . . . It is not to be doubted that St. Paul uses this vaguer, more abstract, and less personal word, just because he would affirm that men may know God's power and majesty . . . from his works; but would *not* imply that they may know Himself from these, or from anything short of the revelation of his Eternal Word" (p. 8).

Cremer supports this distinction. He writes: "*Theiotēs* is to be distinguished from *theotēs* thus, *theotēs* = *that which God is*, *theiotēs* = *that which is of God*" (p. 281).

For purposes of exact theological accuracy it would appear that these two terms should be kept distinct. Men see the attributes of God in His creation. But they can see His person only in His Son, Jesus Christ our Lord.

Sanday and Headlam are in general agreement with this. They write: "*Theotēs* = Divine Personality, *theiotēs* = Divine nature and properties" (p. 43).

Defenseless The expression "without excuse" (v. 20) is one word in Greek, *anapologētous*. It is composed of this alpha-privative *a-*, which negates the meaning of the word to which it is attached, and the term from which we get our English word *apology*, which now means "excuse."

But the original meaning of *apology* was "defense," which can still be found in the old English classics. Hence our word here literally means "defenseless." The first definition given in Thayer's *Lexicon* is "without defence." Those who close their eyes to the revelation of God in nature will have no defense in the day of judgment. How much more those who refuse to read or follow God's written Revelation, the Bible!

23–26 *Exchanged for* In verse 23 we read: "They changed the glory of the uncorruptible God into an image made like to corruptible man"—which is what the humanists are still doing. Verse 25 says that they "changed the truth of God into a lie." Verse 26 reads: "Even their women did change the natural use into that which is against nature."

The ASV has "changed . . . for" in verse 23, "exchanged . . . for" in verse 25, and "changed . . . into" in verse 26. Perhaps the RSV is more consistent in using "exchanged . . . for" in all three places.

The Greek text has "*allassō . . . en*" in verse 23, *metallassō . . . en*" in verse 25, and *metallassō . . . eis*" in verse 26. Both verbs may mean "change" or "exchange." Since *eis* and *en* mean practically the same thing—the latter has disappeared in modern Greek—it would seem best to translate all three passages the same way.

24 *Lusts* God gave men up "to uncleanness through the lusts of their own hearts." The word *lusts* is *epithumia*, which occurs some 37 times in the NT. Its primary meaning is "desire." It is translated this way in three places in the KJV (Luke 22:15; Phil. 1:23; 1 Thess. 2:17), where it obviously refers to good desire. Three times (Rom. 7:8; Col. 3:5; 1 Thess. 4:5) it is rendered "concupiscence," an old Latin term which has come to us from the Vulgate. In the remaining instances in the NT it signifies bad desire and is translated "*lusts*" in the KJV. That is the rendering here in the RSV.

24–28 *Gave Them Up* Three times in this passage we read: "God gave them up" (vv. 24, 26, 28). The KJV changes to "God gave them over" in verse 28, but the Greek is exactly the same in all three places.

The verb is *paradidōmi*, which means "give or hand over," "give or deliver up," as to prison or judgment. Here it clearly refers to a judicial punishment for men's willful, deliberate rejection of God. To have God let one go is the worst fate that can overtake any human being. Yet that is the inevitable result of stubborn refusal to let God have His way. A. T. Robertson writes: "The words sound to us like clods on the coffin as God leaves men to work their own wicked will" (4:330).

25 *More Than* In the KJV we read that apostate men "worshipped and served the creature more than the Creator." But the revised versions rightly have "rather than." It is not a matter of worshiping other things more than God, but of substituting them for God. Sanday and Headlam comment: "Not merely '*more than* the Creator' (a force which the preposition might bear), but *passing by* the Creator altogether,' 'to the neglect of the Creator' " (p. 46). The Greek preposition is *para*.

26 *Affections* The word *affections* is at once more narrow and intense than *desire*. The Greek *pathos* is something quite different from what we have made it in English. Used only three times in the NT, it is translated in KJV three different ways: "affections" here, "inordinate affection" in Col. 3:5, and "lust" in 1 Thess. 4:5. It always carries a bad connotation.

Vincent notes that *pathos* refers to "the diseased condition out of which lusts spring." He defines *epithymiai* as "evil longings" and *pathē* (pl.) as "ungovernable affections." He then comments: "Thus it appears that the divine punishment was the more severe, in that they were given over to a condition, and not merely to an evil desire" (3:19). The best translation is *passions*.

27 *Burned Out* We read here that men "burned in their lust one toward another." Sexual perversion, one of the pressing problems of our own day, seems to be referred to here.

The Greek verb *ekkaiō* ("burn") is found only here in the New Testament. The simple verb *kaiō* ("kindle, light") occurs a dozen times. But the compound is stronger. Vincent says: "The preposition indicates the rage of the lust" (3:20).

The passive form here literally means "burned out." The RSV has rendered the passage very well: "were consumed with passion for one another."

28 *Like, Reprobate* Often in the NT there is a significant connection between Greek words which does not show up at all in the English translations. Verse 28 has a striking example of this.

The KJV reads: "And even as they did not like to retain God in their knowledge, God gave them over to a reprobate mind." No one would ever guess that *like* and *reprobate* are from the same Greek root. Yet such is the case. The former is the verb *edokimasan*. The latter is the adjective *adokimon*.

The verb *dokimazō* occurs 23 times in the NT. In the KJV it is translated 10 times "prove," 4 times "try," 3 times "approve," twice each "discern" and "allow," and once each "examine" and "like." It will be obvious that the last rendering, which occurs only in Rom. 1:28, is the farthest removed from the dominant meaning of the word.

Actually, the verb *dokimazō* has two main meanings: (1) "test" or "prove"; (2) "approve" as the result of testing. It was used of testing metals or coins, to see if they were genuine.

This gives a startling connotation to the passage under consideration. Humanity had tested Deity and disapproved of Him. Consequently man had rejected God.

But now comes the other side of the picture: "God gave them over to a reprobate mind." The word "reprobate" (*adokimon*) means "rejected after testing." Since they rejected God, He rejected them.

The word for "knowledge," *epignōsis*, literally means "full knowledge." Charles B. Williams brings out the connection of the Greek words in his NT translation as follows: "And so, as they did not approve of fully recognizing God any longer, God gave them up to minds that He did not approve."

Inconvenient The KJV translates the last clause: "to do those things which are not convenient." C. B. Williams renders it: "to practices that were improper." Verkuyl (Berkeley Version) translates it: "to practice what is not decent." Goodspeed similarly says, "indecent conduct." All of these are stronger than the KJV.

The expression is a participle of the word *kathēkō*, which occurs elsewhere in the NT only in Acts 22:22. There it is rendered "fit"—"It is not fit that he should live"—and means "proper." The translation "convenient" would hardly "fit" that passage!

Actually, the expression was a technical term with the Stoics, meaning "what is morally fitting" (SH, p. 47). So Paul was talking about what was improper rather than inconvenient.

29–31 Filled with. . . . Verse 29 begins a long list of vices which were current in the Roman world of Paul's day. Twenty-three are enumerated here.

The list is introduced by *peplerōmenous*, the perfect passive participle of *pleroō*, which means "fill to the full." After 4 general terms for wickedness—5 in the KJV, but "fornication" is not in the oldest MSS—there is the adjective *mestos*. The cognate verb *mestoō* is found only in Acts 2:13, where the crowd accused the disciples on the Day of Pentecost of being "tanked up" with wine. Both of these words suggest being filled to the brim.

It will be impossible to comment on each of these 23 vices. But a few observations might be made.

Sanday and Headlam suggest that the first term *adikia*, is "a comprehensive term, including all that follows" (p. 47). All sins may be summed up in the word *unrighteousness*. The next three terms are best translated "evil, covetousness, malice." The first of these, *ponēria*, suggests "active mischief." The last has more the idea of "inward viciousness of disposition" (*ibid.*).

The first two terms after *full* indicate a play on words: *phthonon, phonon*. The third, *debate*, has caused some people to condemn all debating as sinful! But *eridos* really means "strife." The fifth, *malignity*, signifies "the tendency to put the worst construction upon everything" (*ibid.*).

The next two words, translated *whisperers, backbiters*, are found only here in the NT. The former has the idea of secrecy, but not the latter. The RSV translates them, "gossips, slanderers."

The term *despiteful* is perhaps better rendered "insolent." It comes from a verb meaning "to insult." The word *proud* is better "haughty."

It means literally "appearing above," and so "stuck up." The term *boasters* comes from a word meaning "wandering." So it suggests "empty pretenders, swaggerers, braggarts" (Rob., 4:332).

The first two terms in verse 31 also contain a play on words—*asynetous, asynthetous*. Sanday and Headlam define the second as meaning "false to their engagements" (p. 48). All four words in this verse begin with *a* (alpha privative), equivalent to our prefix *non* or suffix *less*. The RSV reflects this in its striking translation (which also carries over the alliterative feature of the first two words): "foolish, faithless, heartless, ruthless." That makes the original Greek live for the English reader.

32 Have Pleasure The King James translation in the last clause, "have pleasure," goes beyond the original. The Greek word means literally "think well with." It carries the idea of "hearty approval." The RSV correctly reads: "approve those who practice them."

2:1 Inexcusable In 1:20, Paul declared that the Gentiles who refused to recognize God's revelation of Himself in nature were "without excuse." Here he declares that the Jews, who possessed God's revelation in the Law, were likewise "inexcusable."

These are the only two occurrences in the NT of the double compound, *anapologētos*. This word, as noted already, is composed of *a*-privative (negative) and a derivative from the verb *apologeomai*. The latter, in turn, may be divided into *apo*, "from, away from," and *logeomai* from *legō*, "speak." Hence the literal meaning of the verb is "speak oneself off" (Vine, 2:58). Liddell and Scott, in their classical *Greek-English Lexicon*, give as the first definition "to talk oneself out of a difficulty." Hence it came to have the common usage, "to speak in defense, defend oneself." So the compound adjective means "defenseless."

In some ways this is a stronger expression than "without excuse" or "inexcusable." We may say that a certain person's fumbling action or serious mistake was "inexcusable." But the term "defenseless" suggests a court scene, where the defendant stands before the judge condemned because he has not been able to defend his action. It is exactly this legal or forensic use which is found in early Greek writers, such as Polybius (second century B.C.). So the implication here is that the self-righteous Jew was defenseless before God and would be so at the final judgment.

As Paul addressed himself to the Gentile

world in chapter 1, so here he speaks to the Jews. "O man, whosoever thou art that judgest" is to be interpreted by "thou art called a Jew" (v. 17).

1–3 Do The verb *prassō* occurs once in each of the first three verses of this chapter. In the KJV it is translated "doest" (v. 1), "commit" (v. 2), and "do" (v. 3). It occurs 38 times in the NT and is translated by 7 different English words in the KJV.

The more common Greek word for *do* (*poieō*) occurs a total of 576 times in the NT and is translated by more than 50 different words in the KJV. Its most common renderings are *do* (357 times) and *make* (114 times).

Paul declares: "You, the one judging, are practicing [*prasseis*] the same things." Some scholars hold that *poieō* and *prassō* are used indiscriminately and so mean the same thing. But others find a difference of suggestion in the two terms. One of the latter group is A. T. Robertson, who comments here: "The critic practises (*prasseis*, not single acts *poieō*, but the habit *prassō*) the same things that he condemns" (4:334). Apparently Paul is not talking about an occasional lapse but the habitual practice of wrong.

Some might question the assertion that the self-righteous Jews were practicing "the same things" as the Gentiles. But if this is interpreted in terms of rejecting light it will be seen that the charge is justified.

3 Thou Ordinarily in Greek the pronoun is included in the verb and indicated by the ending. When it is expressed separately it carries emphasis.

So here the *su* ("thou shalt escape") underscores the point the apostle is making. Sanday and Headlam paraphrase this emphatic meaning: "thou, of all men." They state further: "There is abundant illustration of the view current among the Jews that the Israelite was secure simply as such by virtue of his descent from Abraham and of his possession of the Law" (p. 55).

A. T. Robertson's comment is particularly pertinent. He writes: "The Jew posed as immune to the ordinary laws of ethics because a Jew. Alas, some Christians affect the same immunity" (4:334).

4 Despisest Paul accuses his supposed reader of despising the goodness of God. The Greek verb is *kataphroneō*, which literally means "think down on." A. T. Robertson's comment is incisive: "This upstart Jew actually thinks down on God" (4:335).

Of course, it should not be inferred that this accusation fitted all Jews. Paul has in mind the self-righteous Jew, who is in the same category as the self-righteous Gentile. Paul himself was a Jew, not a Jew-hater, and all anti-Semitism today is utterly unchristian.

Goodness The Greek word *chrēstotēs* is defined by Abbott-Smith as "goodness of heart, kindness." Sanday and Headlam render it "kindly disposition."

The term occurs 10 times in the NT. In the KJV it is rendered "goodness" 4 times, "kindness" 4 times, and once each "good" and "gentleness." It speaks of God's gracious kindness toward us.

Forbearance The noun *anochē* occurs only here and in 3:25 (v. 26 in the Greek). It comes from *anechō*, which means "hold back." So here it suggests "a delay of punishment." It was used in classical Greek for a truce of arms.

Trench points out very well the significance of this word here. He writes: "It is that forbearance or suspense of wrath, that truce with the sinner, which by no means implies that the wrath will not be executed at the last; nay, involves that it certainly will, unless he be found under new conditions of repentance and obedience" (p. 200).

Long-suffering The Greek word is *makrothymia*. It means "patience." The cognate verb *makrothymeō* means to be long-tempered rather than short-tempered. The noun occurs 14 times in the NT. In the KJV it is translated "patience" twice and "longsuffering" the other times.

Hogg and Vine express beautifully the meaning of this word, as follows: "Longsuffering is that quality of self-restraint in the face of provocation which does not hastily retaliate or promptly punish; it is the opposite of anger, and is associated with mercy, and is used of God" (Vine, 3:12).

Repentance The idea of repentance is rather prominent in the NT. The verb *metanoeō* occurs 34 times and is always translated "repent" in the KJV. The noun *metanoia* is found 24 times and is always rendered "repentance."

It may seem strange that the noun is found only once in the Epistle to the Romans, here in 2:4, while the verb is not found at all. Furthermore, the other verb translated "repent"— *metamellomai*, which occurs 6 times in the

NT—is likewise not in Romans. Elsewhere in his Epistles, however, Paul uses all three terms.

As is well known, the basic meaning of *metanoia* is "a change of mind." Thayer adds:

> . . . as it appears in one who repents of a purpose he has formed or of something he has done . . . esp. the change of mind of those who have begun to abhor their errors and misdeeds, and have determined to enter upon a better course of life, so that it embraces both a recognition of sin and sorrow for it and hearty amendment, the tokens and effects of which are good deeds (pp. 405–6).

Too often sorrow is confused with repentance. But though the two may be closely related in experience, they are far apart in essential meaning. Vincent has well written (on Matt. 3:2): "*Sorrow* is not, as popularly conceived, the primary nor the prominent notion of the word" (1:23).

The relation of sorrow and repentance is clearly indicated in 2 Cor. 7:10, where Paul declares: "For godly sorrow worketh repentance to salvation not to be repented of: but the sorrow of the world worketh death." The latter may only signify remorse or regret over the consequences of misdoing. The former is a Spirit-inspired sorrow for *sin*, which leads one to repent of his sins and turn away from them. It involves an abhorrence of sin because it is sin, not just a shrinking from the results of sin.

Cremer, followed by Vincent, holds that the full meaning of *metanoeō* is "to think differently after," giving the prepositional prefix both its meanings of time and change. Regarding its relation to sorrow, Cremer comments: "The feeling of sorrow, pain, mourning, is thus included in the word" (p. 441).

Chamberlain, in *The Meaning of Repentance*, protests against the misunderstandings and mistranslations of both Catholics and Protestants. The Reformers rightly rejected the Catholic translation, "Do penance"; but though Calvin correctly defined the meaning of repentance, the Protestant church as a whole has failed to follow through in its preaching on the subject.

Chamberlain calls repentance "a mental transfiguration" (p. 47). He gives this admirable definition: "Repentance is the reorientation of a personality with reference to God and his purpose" (p. 22).

5 Hardness One of the most dreaded afflictions of old age today is arteriosclerosis, or hardening of the walls of the arteries. Like most medical terms, this one is derived from the Greek.

The word translated "hardness" is *sclērotēs*. Abbott-Smith says that it is used metaphorically for stubbornness. It occurs only here in the NT.

Not much is known yet about the cause and cure of physical sclerosis. But the Bible sheds some light on the cause and cure of spiritual sclerosis. It is primarily the result of rejection of light. To obey God fully is to keep one's heart tender and one's spiritual being alive. But disobedience is always followed by a hardening of the spiritual arteries. The consequences of this are just as pathetic as, and far more tragic than, arteriosclerosis.

Impenitent Heart Robertson's paraphrase for "impenitent heart" is "an unreconstructed heart." It is the heart that has refused to repent.

The Greek adjective *ametanoētos* occurs only here in the NT. It literally means "unrepentant."

Treasurest Up The English word *thesaurus* comes directly from the Greek word *thēsauros*. Its primary meaning is "a place of safekeeping," and so a "treasury" or "storehouse" (A-S). It then came to mean the "treasure" which was stored. This noun occurs 18 times in the NT and is always translated "treasure" in the KJV. It was a favorite word with Jesus, being used by Him 15 of the 18 times it occurs in the Synoptic Gospels.

But the word here is the verb *thēsaurizō*. This is found only 8 times in the NT but is translated 6 different ways in the KJV! Three times it is rendered "lay up" and once each "in store," "lay up treasure," "treasure up," "heap treasure together," and "keep in store." It is clear that the basic meaning is that of storing.

But what is the apostle talking here about storing up? God's wrath! The one who continues unrepentant is steadily storing up wrath for himself against the day of judgment.

Jesus exhorted those who would follow Him to lay up treasure in heaven (e.g., Matt. 6:19–20), riches that can be enjoyed throughout eternity. What a tragedy for one instead to treasure up wrath!

The word *wrath* refers to an inward attitude of abhorrence of wrong. God's holy character demands that He treat unrepented, and so unforgiven, sin with such an attitude. "Wrath and love are mutually inclusive, not exclusive, in God" (TDNT, 5:425).

The expression "the day of wrath" obviously is the same as "the day of the Lord" which occurs frequently in the Minor Prophets. It is the day of God's judgment of sin and sinners.

7 *Patience* One of the more interesting words in the Greek NT is *hypomonē*. It occurs 32 times. Twenty-nine times it is translated in the KJV as "patience." In 2 Cor. 1:6 it is rendered "enduring." In 2 Thess. 1:4 it reads "patient waiting." Here it is translated "patient continuance."

There is, surprisingly, a wider spread in the RSV, where *hypomonē* is translated seven different ways. A check of all the passages shows that the word is rendered "steadfastness" 12 times, "endurance" 8 times, "patience" and "patient endurance" 4 times each, and once each "patiently endure," "enduring patiently," and "perseverance." In Romans it is translated twice each by "patience," "endurance," and "steadfastness."

In looking for some pattern of translation it was discovered that "steadfastness" was used always in the Thessalonian letters, the Pastoral Epistles, and the General Epistles. The rendering "patient endurance" occurs only in Revelation (4 out of 7 times). This would seem to reflect the preferences of individual translators—a factor that is almost unavoidable in a work translated by a committee, as was the case with KJV, ASV, and RSV.

It will be seen that the dominant meaning given to this word is "patience" in the KJV and "steadfastness" or "endurance" in the RSV. Which is closer to the basic connotation of the term?

The word *hypomonē* is a compound of *hypo*, meaning "under," and *menō*, the verb "remain." Literally, then, it means, "remain under." This suggests that the primary idea is that of endurance—"the steadfast and patient endurance of suffering" (TDNT, 4:587).

Thayer's *Lexicon* gives as the first meaning "steadfastness, constancy, endurance . . . in the NT the characteristic of a man who is unswerved from his deliberate purpose and his loyalty to faith and piety by even the greatest trials and sufferings" (p. 644). In line with this is the statement: "Patience is the quality that does not surrender to circumstances or succumb under trial" (Vine, 2:116).

Cremer supports fully the idea that the dominant meaning of *hypomonē* is endurance. He says: "The word occurs only in the later Greek, and answers to the usual *karteria*, *karterēsis*, holding out, enduring" (p. 420).

The interesting fact is pointed out by Cremer that in the Septuagint this word is used to translate some Hebrew terms indicating

hope, "hope being the basis of *hypomonē*." The close connection between hope and endurance is obvious in the passage in Romans now being studied. It is the hope of future glory that enables one to endure patiently the hardships of this life.

In seeking the exact shade of meaning of *hypomonē* it is necessary to note its synonym, *makrothymia*. The latter occurs 14 times in the NT. Twelve times it is rendered "long-suffering." Twice (Heb. 6:12; Jas. 5:10) it is translated "patience."

The classic distinction between *hypomonē* and *makrothymia* is that given by Trench. He says that "*makrothumia* will be found to express patience in respect of persons, *hypomonē* in respect of things" (p. 189). The latter describes the man "who, under a great siege of trials, bears up, and does not lose heart or courage" (*ibid.*). This distinction may not always hold good (cf. Heb. 6:15; Jas. 5:7–8), but in general it is valid.

In this connection it is interesting to note that *hypomonē* is never used of God, while *makrothymia* is. God continually has to exercise forbearance or long-suffering toward sinful men. But He does not have to endure circumstances relating to things, for they are under His control. It is only the free will of intelligent beings which causes God difficulty.

One more word needs to be said. It is clear that in this passage *hypomonē* means more than passive endurance. It obviously has the sense of active perseverance or steadfastness. For the Greek literally reads "steadfastness of [or *in*] good work." The Christian is not only to endure the difficult circumstances of life. Positively and actively he is to persevere in good work.

Immortality The word rendered "immortality" in the KJV is *aphtharsia*. Most scholars are agreed that the King James translation here is not the best; the word does not primarily mean immortality. That idea is conveyed in the word *athanasia*, literally "deathlessness."

In the KJV, *aphtharsia* is rendered "incorruption" four times, "immortality" and "sincerity" twice each. It comes from the verb *phtheirō*, which means "destroy, corrupt, spoil." So its basic meaning is "incorruption." It is used in 1 Cor. 15:42 of the resurrection body, which will be exempt from corruption.

8 *Factiousness* Words often have a long and varied history. Their travels sometimes take them far afield from their intellectual birthplace. Etymology does not always give the correct meaning of a term as it is used at a later time.

The word translated "contentious" in the KJV is a noun, *erithia* (or, *eritheia*). It occurs 7 times in the NT. Five times it is rendered "strife" and once each "contention" and "contentious."

The word is derived from *erithos*, "a hired laborer." The verb *eritheuō* meant to "act as a hireling." The middle *eritheuomai* signified "to hire paid canvassers and promote a party spirit." So the noun *erithia* means "the spirit of faction" (SH, 57). Ellicott gives its three meanings as "labor for hire," "scheming or intriguing for office," "party-spirit" (p. 133). The latter is the prevailing meaning in the NT. However, Ellicott thinks that the context here in Romans may suggest more the idea of contentiousness. But Sanday and Headlam define the ones described here as "those whose motive is factiousness" (p. 57).

Indignation and Wrath　　The last two nouns of verse 8 in the best Greek text are *orgē* and *thymos*. The difference between these two terms is expressed clearly by Trench, who writes: "In *thymos* . . . is more of the turbulent commotion, the boiling agitation of the feelings," while in *orgē* "is more of an abiding and settled habit of mind" (p. 731). He speaks of *thymos* as being "more passionate, and at the same time more temporary" (*ibid.*). It corresponds to the Latin *fumus*, from which has come the English word *fuming*.

Cremer's distinction is somewhat different. He says that "*thymos* denotes the inward excitement, and *orgē* the outward manifestation of it" (p. 287). But all agree that *thymos* expresses stronger, more stirred emotions. Abbott-Smith defines it as "passion, hot anger." He says that in the plural it means "impulses or outbursts of anger" (p. 210).

Due to a change of order in the Greek text the ASV reverses the King James translation, reading "wrath and indignation." The RSV has "wrath and fury." It is generally agreed that *orgē* denotes God's fixed attitude of abhorrence of sin, while *thymos* indicates the outflow of that attitude in judgment on the stubborn, rebellious sinner. James Denney puts it in succinct fashion: "*Orgē* is wrath within; *thymos* wrath as it overflows" (EGT, 2:596).

Before leaving these words it might be of interest to note the frequency with which they occur in the NT. *Orgē* is found 36 times. Thirty-one of these times it is translated "wrath" in the KJV, 3 times "anger," and once each "vengeance" and "indignation." *Thymos* occurs 18

times. It is translated "wrath" 15 times, "fierceness" twice, and "indignation" once.

9 Tribulation　　The Greek word is *thlipsis*. It is found 45 times in the NT; 21 times it is translated "tribulation," 17 times "affliction."

The word comes from the verb *thlibō*, which means "press," a term used for pressing out grapes in a winepress. A winepress can be seen today near the Garden Tomb. It is cut in the rock. The ripe grapes would be put in the rock basin and then women and children would squeeze out the juice by walking around on the grapes with their bare feet.

The figure suggests the heavy pressures of life that sometimes become almost unbearable. One feels as if he is being trodden down until he cannot take it any longer.

In this passage it is the tribulation of the wicked that is mentioned. A striking parallel may be found in Isa. 63:1–3, where the Lord says that He has "trodden the winepress alone" and adds: "for I will tread them in mine anger, and trample them in my fury." The reference is to God destroying the enemies of Israel. Here it is the wicked who will experience God's wrath and fury for their willful disobedience.

There is another figure which is suggested by the English word *tribulation*. This term comes from the Latin *tribulum*, which means a threshing instrument.

In NT times there were two ways of threshing grain. If the amount was very small, one might use a flail. Usually, however, the grain was piled about a foot and a half deep on the smooth, hard threshing floor. These threshing floors can still be seen outside the villages of Lebanon, Syria, and Jordan, with oxen pulling a threshing sled around on the grain. This sled is about four feet long and two and a half feet wide. Attached to the bottom are sharp stones or pieces of metal. These tear the grain loose from the stalks, and the oxen's feet help in the process. One may still see two yoke of oxen, each pulling a threshing sled ridden by women or children, just as it was done back in the days of David, a thousand years before the birth of Christ.

Anguish　　The Greek word *stenochōria* is compounded of *stenos*, "narrow," and *chōra*, "space." Abbott-Smith defines it as "narrowness of space, want of room." So, metaphorically it means "distress." Sanday and Headlam give its meaning as "torturing confinement," although they add: "But the etymological sense is probably lost in usage" (p. 57).

After commenting on the literal and figurative senses of the word, Trench makes this appropriate observation: "The fitness of this image is attested by the frequency with which on the other hand a state of joy is expressed in the Psalms and elsewhere as a bringing into a large room" (p. 203). Trench also notes that in ancient England there was a custom of placing heavy weights on the chests of condemned persons until they were literally crushed to death.

The word *stenochōria* is used in the NT only by Paul, twice in Romans and twice in 2 Corinthians. Although translated "anguish" here, in the KJV it is rendered "distress" in the other three passages. In three out of the four occurrences it is associated with *thlipsis*. They both include the idea of "pressed" or "compressed."

11 *No Partiality* The phrase "respect of persons" is all one word in the Greek, *prosōpolēmpsia*. It comes from *prosōpon*, "face," and a form of the verb *lambanō*, "receive." So it means literally "receiving of face." That is a typical Oriental expression for what we call partiality. The RSV translates this verse: "For God shows no partiality."

The word is used only four times in the NT (Rom. 2:11; Eph. 6:9; Col. 3:25; Jas. 2:1). In all four places it is translated "respect of persons" in the KJV.

This word and a cognate noun and verb are not found in the Septuagint nor in other pre-Christian writings. Moulton and Milligan state that they "may be reckoned amongst the earliest definitely Christian words" (VGT, p. 553). Mayor says: "In its strict sense the Greek would mean to accept the outside surface for the inner reality, the mask for the person" (p. 78).

12 *Without Law* The expression "without law" is one word in the Greek, the adverb *anomōs*. We have no equivalent adverb in English. So we have to translate it by a phrase.

The adverb is used twice in the twelfth verse but nowhere else in the NT. It is not listed in Moulton and Milligan's *Vocabulary of the Greek Testament Illustrated from the Papyri and Other Non-literary Sources*.

The word is composed of alpha-privative *a*- and the adverbial form of *nomos*, "law." Literally it would mean "unlawfully"—a sense found in classical Greek—or "lawlessly." The latter is the common usage in Greek writers and is illustrated in 2 Maccabees 8:17. There we read that Judas Maccabeus instructed his small army not to fear the vast forces of the enemy but to fight nobly, keeping before their eyes the fact that the Syrians had desecrated "lawlessly" the holy place.

But all lexicographers and commentators are agreed that here it means "without law." The only question would be as to what is meant by "law." Many hold that the Mosaic law is intended; others, law in general. Probably the comment of Vincent is wise: "Both law in the abstract and the Mosaic law. The principle laid down is general, though apparently viewed with special reference to the law of Moses" (3:27).

12–15 *Law, the Law* One of the outstanding problems in the exegesis of Romans is the interpretation of the terms *law* and *the law*. It has sometimes been suggested that the former refers to law in general, as a universal principle, while the latter refers to the law of Moses. This distinction is based on the fact that in Greek the anarthrous use (without the article) emphasizes *kind* or *quality*, whereas the articular construction (with the article) emphasizes individual identity. Similarly in English if we say "man" we are thinking of a human being as such, but if we say "the man" we are indicating some definite individual.

However, anyone who has read Romans in the Greek knows that the problem is not that simple. Many times the law of Moses seems rather clearly indicated by the context when there is no article in the Greek. (Greek has no indefinite article.)

One of the best discussions on this point will be found in Sanday and Headlam's outstanding commentary on Romans. They write:

> There are really three main uses: (1) *ho nomos* = the law of Moses; the article denotes something with which the readers are familiar. . . . (2) *nomos* = law in general (e.g., 2:12, 14; 3:2–5; 4:15; 5:13). (3) But there is yet a third usage where *nomos* without the article really means the Law of Moses, but the absence of the article calls attention to it not as proceeding from Moses; but in its quality *as law* (p. 58).

It might be noted that the word *law* (*nomos*) occurs eight times in verses 12–15 (not counting the adverb *anomōs*, noted above). In only two of these cases does the article occur. In verse 14 the Greek reads literally: "For whenever Gentiles who do not have law do by nature the things of the law, these not having [a] law are [a] law to themselves." Verse 15 adds: "Which shew the work of the law written in their hearts."

15 *Conscience* The English word *conscience* comes from the Latin *scio*, "know," and *con,* "together"—a knowing with or together. The Greek term here translated "conscience" has exactly the same meaning. It is *syneidēsis,* from the participle of *oida,* "know," and *syn,* "with." Sometimes the English has synonyms derived from both languages, as *compassion* (Latin) and *sympathy* (Greek). Both mean "a suffering with."

What is the meaning of *conscience?* It is a favorite word with Paul. He uses it 21 out of the 32 times it occurs in the NT. In fact, if we add Acts 23:1 and 24:16—which are parts of Paul's speeches before the Sanhedrin and Felix—we could say that it is used by Paul 23 times. Sanday and Headlam note that it is one of the few technical terms of Paul that are more Greek than Jewish (p. 61).

But what is the significance of the idea of "co-knowledge"? It is "the knowledge or reflective judgment which a man has *by the side of* or *in conjunction with* the original consciousness of the act" (*ibid.,* p. 60).

While the term is not found in Aristotle, it rose "into philosophical importance in the more introspective moral teaching of the Stoics" (*ibid.*). Apparently Paul was acquainted with the writings of the Stoics, for he quoted one of their poets in his speech before the Areopagus (Acts 17:28).

Sanday and Headlam summarize the Pauline usage of the term thus:

> The "Conscience" of St. Paul is a natural faculty which belongs to all men alike (Rom. 2:15), and pronounces upon the character of actions, both their own (2 Cor. 1:12) and those of others (2 Cor. 4:2; 5:11). It can be over-scrupulous (1 Cor. 10:25), but is blunted or "seared" by neglect of its warnings (1 Tim. 4:2) (p. 61).

Accusing, Excusing   The literal Greek here reads: "accusing or *even* excusing." The idea is definitely suggested that most of the time conscience condemns. Only occasionally does it commend. This would be true of the average person apart from salvation.

One Another   In the KJV verse 15 ends with the words "one another." This phrase is often taken externally—one person in relation to another accusing or excusing.

But probably Vincent's argument is well taken. He says: "As the other parts of the description refer to the individual soul in itself and not to relations with others, the explanation expressed in Rev. [ERV]—the mutual relations and interchanges of the individual thoughts—seems preferable" (3:28).

Sanday and Headlam show the possible relation between the two ideas. They write: "In the present passage St. Paul is describing an internal process, though one which is destined to find external expression; it is the process by which are formed the moral judgments of men upon their fellows" (p. 62).

This paragraph shows clearly that the basis of God's judgment of men will be their reaction to the light God has given them, whether through universal conscience or through the specific revelation in the Bible. That puts those of us who have had abundance of light under tremendous responsibility—including the obligation to obey Christ's great commission (Matt. 28:18–20).

17 *Jew*   The Greek word for *Jew* is *Ioudaios.* Strictly speaking, then, a Jew is a Judean; that is, from the tribe of Judah. That is the earliest use of the term, as found in 2 Kings 16:6 and in Jeremiah (32:12; 34:9; 38:19). Josephus apparently uses it for the first time as applied to Daniel and his companions (*Ant.* xi.5.7). The term came into common use during and after the Babylonian captivity.

It is an anachronism to call Abraham or Moses a Jew. The first is properly referred to as a "Hebrew." The other, with the masses under his leadership, was an "Israelite." But since most of those who returned from the Exile were from the former Kingdom of Judah, the usual designation for them thereafter was "Jews." This is what we find in the intertestamental period and mainly in the NT.

When Paul wrote to the Romans, the term *Hebrews* designated primarily a language group—the Aramaic-speaking as distinguished from the Greek-speaking Jews (cf. Acts 6:1, where "Hellenists" and "Hebrews" are both Jews). The word *Jew* referred mostly to nationality. The term *Israelite* suggested a covenant relation to God. Trench says: "This name was for the Jew his special badge and title of honor" (p. 142).

Why, then, does Paul use *Jew?* Sanday and Headlam suggest that the term "here approaches in meaning (as in the mouth of a Jew it would have a tendency to do) to *Israelites,* a member of the Chosen People, opposed to the heathen" (p. 64).

Probably the term *Jew* in Jesus' day carried a sense of pride of both race and religion. The Jews considered themselves superior to the Gentiles because they were God's favored people, children of Abraham as to race, and descendants of those who received the law at Sinai.

Leaning on the Law This verse mentions three sources of Jewish pride. The people were proud to be named Jews; they rested on the law; they boasted of a special relationship to God.

The word translated "restest in" is literally "rests upon." It is a compound formed with *epi*, which means "upon." The RSV renders it "rely upon." The word occurs only here and in Luke 10:6.

The trouble was that the Jews were depending for their salvation on something outward rather than inward. It was possession of the Mosaic law rather than possession of God's Spirit. It was an outward symbol rather than an inward reality. Robertson comments: "It is a picture of blind and mechanical reliance on the Mosaic Law" (4:338).

18 *Prove* In this verse is found an expression that may be translated more than one way. The Greek reads: *dokimazeis ta diapheronta.*

We have already found *dokimazō* in Rom. 1:28. There we noted that it had two distinct meanings: (1) test; (2) approve as the result of testing. Similarly, *ta diapheronta* may mean "the things that differ" or "the things that excel."

This gives two possible translations: "distinguish the things that differ," or "approve the things that excel." The former idea is adopted by a number of private translators. Weymouth has, "appreciate distinctions." Moffatt has a very free paraphrase: "with a sense of what is vital in religion." Goodspeed reads, "can tell what is right." Phillips paraphrases it: "truly to appreciate moral values."

But the KJV, ERV, ASV, and RSV all agree in adopting the second idea. It should simply be noted that "more" before "excellent" in the KJV is not justified.

Which of the two translations is preferable? Sanday and Headlam agree with the standard English versions. Robertson writes: "As in Phil. 1:10 it is difficult to tell which stage of the process (prove or approve) Paul has in mind" (4:338). Moulton and Milligan note both meanings in the papyri, with the second prominent. James Denney concludes: "There are no grounds on which we can decide positively for either" (EGT, 2:599).

Instructed The word *instructed* is *katechoumenos*, from which we get the term *catechumen* for one who is being instructed in the Christian religion. The verb (participial form above) means properly "to give oral instruction."

Since the most usual form of early Christian instruction, as in later times, was apparently by an oral question-and-answer method, the word *catechism* came to be applied to a book used for such instruction.

20 *Instructor* It should be noted that the word for *instructor* here has no relation to the word *instructed* in verse 18. In verse 20 it is *paideutēn*, found elsewhere only in Heb. 12:9. There it is accurately translated "corrected" in KJV. The RSV and the NASB have "corrector" here (v. 20), rather than "instructor," thus indicating that there are two different words in the Greek. This term comes from the verb *paideuō*, which literally means "train children" and is rendered "chastise" frequently in the KJV of the twelfth chapter of Hebrews.

22 *Sacrilege* The KJV has "commit sacrilege." But since that is a somewhat ambiguous term for the modern mind, it might easily be equated with *profane*. The RSV and NASB give the true and exact meaning, "rob temples."

The Greek word is *hierosyleis*, found only here in the NT. It comes from *hieron*, "temple," and *sylaō*, "plunder" (found only in 2 Cor. 11:8). In Acts 19:37 the town clerk at Ephesus declared that Paul and his companions were not temple-robbers (*hierosyloi*, only there in the NT). This seems to show "that the robbery of temples was a charge to which the Jews were open in spite of their professed horror of idol-worship" (SH, p. 66). Josephus (*Ant.* IV.8.10) has this pertinent passage: "Let no one blaspheme those gods which other cities esteem such; nor may any one steal what belongs to strange temples, nor take away the gifts that are dedicated to any god." Evidently some Jews were guilty of doing this very thing. One wonders whether deliberate desecration of what others consider sacred is the best way to win them to the true faith!

23 A Question? Verse 23 is put in the form of a question in the KJV as well as in the revised versions. But the opinion of Sanday and Headlam is worth considering. They say: "It is probably best not to treat this verse as a question. The questions which go before are collected by a summary accusation" (*ibid.*). It seems to us that this (cf. Phillips, NEB) accords somewhat better with verse 24 and alleviates the rather awkward connection of the two verses as they read in our standard versions. It should be remembered that in the early Greek manuscripts there is no way of distinguishing between a question and an assertion.

24 *Is Blasphemed* Paul writes to the insincere, inconsistent Jews that through them the name of God is "blasphemed" among the Gentiles. The English word comes directly from the Greek *blasphēmeō*. But does it mean the same as our English word *blaspheme?* Abbott-Smith's Lexicon gives these meanings: "1. to speak lightly or profanely of sacred things, esp. to speak impiously of God, to blaspheme. . . . 2. to revile, rail at, slander."

It is interesting to note that in the other two occurrences of this word in Romans it is rendered "be slanderously reported" (3:8) and "be evil spoken of" (14:16). In both of these instances God is not involved and so *blaspheme* would hardly be the appropriate term.

A check of the NT shows that the word is used almost equally in reference to God and in reference to man. The term occurs 35 times. In 19 instances God (or the Word of God) is the object and so *blaspheme* is used in the KJV. In one instance (Acts 19:37) we find "blasphemers of your goddess." In Matt. 27:39 those that passed by the cross "reviled" Christ; in Mark 15:29 they "railed" on Him; and in Luke 23:39 those hanged with Him "railed" on Him. But in the other 12 instances the object is man. Ten of these times the word is translated "speak evil of." That is its proper meaning in relation to man. But to speak evil of God is to blaspheme Him. Moulton and Milligan note that the etymological meaning of the cognate adjective *blasphēmos* is "injurious speaking" (VGT, p. 112). Only when related to God did the word take on the technical meaning which it has in English.

25–29 *Circumcision* In this closing paragraph of the second chapter of Romans the word *circumcision* occurs 6 times and *uncircumcision* 4 times. Still more interesting is the fact that of the 36 occurrences of *peritomē* (*circumcision*) in the NT, 15 are in Romans and 7 in Galatians. It is in these two books that Paul gives greatest attention to the problem of the Jew and the Gentile in relation to salvation. Furthermore, aside from twice in John's Gospel (7:22, 23) and 3 times in Acts (7:8; 10:45; 11:12) the word is found only in Paul's Epistles. The great apostle was vitally concerned with this question.

The word *akrobystia*, "uncircumcision," is found 20 times in the NT. Again we find it most frequently in Romans (11 times) and Galatians (3 times). With the exception of one time in Acts (11:3), it occurs only in Paul's Epistles.

In Greek the terms for *circumcision* and *uncircumcision* have no apparent relationship.

Peritomē comes from the verb *peritemnō*, "cut around," which is the literal meaning of "circumcise." The English term is derived from the Latin. *Akrobystia* meant first the physical part removed in circumcision and then abstractly "uncircumcision."

In this passage Paul is arguing for the truth that the formal rite of circumcision meant nothing unless it was accompanied by a faithful adherence to the Law. He went a step further and insisted that true circumcision was not "outward in the flesh," but "of the heart, in the spirit." He is simply emphasizing the universal teaching of the NT that true religion is in the spiritual realm, not the material.

The rite of circumcision is an ancient one. It was practiced among the Arabians, Moabites, Ammonites, Edomites, and Egyptians (ISBE, 1:656). It is first mentioned in the Bible in the seventeenth chapter of Genesis. It was required of Abraham and his descendants as a sign of the covenant between God and His people. Since the Moabites, Ammonites, and Edomites were descended from Abraham, this fact would sufficiently explain their observance of this custom. The Egyptians may have adopted the rite from the Israelites while the latter were living in that country. Josh. 5:5 states that the Israelites that came out of Egypt were circumcised, but that those born in the wilderness were not. This situation was remedied at Gilgal, which received its name thereby (Josh. 5:9). Since the first clear evidence of circumcision in Egypt comes from the 14th century before Christ (HDB, 1:442)—approximately the time of Moses—there does not seem to be any reason for denying the possibility that the Egyptians borrowed the rite from the Israelites. Of course, many scholars would prefer to assume that the Israelites borrowed from the Egyptians.

Ishmael was circumcised at the age of 13 (Gen. 17:25), and among Moslems circumcision is usually performed between the ages of 6 and 16, although it is not enjoined in the Koran (HDB, 1:443).

But Isaac was circumcised when 8 days old (Gen. 21:4), in accordance with God's instructions to Abraham (Gen. 17:12), and that custom obtains among orthodox Jews to the present time. It is then that the child is named (cf. Luke 2:21). It is a very solemn, elaborate religious ceremony, attended by relatives and friends.

On the significance of this ceremony for the Jews, Macalister makes this comment:

> Among the Jewish teachers circumcision was regarded as an operation of purification,

and the word foreskin has come to be synonymous with obstinacy and imperfection. The rite was regarded as a token in the flesh of the effect of Divine grace in the heart (*ibid.*).

Jeremiah accuses the Israelites of his day of being "uncircumcised in the heart" (9:26). This language is based on Deut. 30:6—"And the Lord thy God will circumcise thine heart, and the heart of thy seed, to love the Lord thy God with all thine heart, and with all thy soul, that thou mayest live."

Paul makes the spiritual application of this for Christians in Col. 2:11—"In whom also ye are circumcised with the circumcision made without hands, in putting off the body of the sins of the flesh by the circumcision of Christ." The language of Deut. 30:6 suggests that this spiritual circumcision of the heart is necessary if one would love the Lord with all his being. The application of this to the NT experience of heart cleansing is too obvious to be missed.

3:2 Oracles The Greek term *logia* is used four times in the NT and regularly translated "oracles." In Acts 7:38 it refers to the contents of the Mosaic law. Here in Rom. 3:2 it indicates God's "commands in the Mosaic law and his Messianic promises" (Thayer). In Heb. 5:12 the reference is to "the substance of the Christian religion," and in 1 Pet. 4:11 to "the utterances of God through Christian teachers" (*ibid.*). In every case it means the words or utterances of God.

Logion literally means "a little word" or "a brief utterance." By Greek writers it was used of divine oracles, since they were usually brief. In the Septuagint it was used for the breastplate of the high priest, which he must wear when seeking to find out God's will. It is always related to the idea of God speaking.

In Philo the word *logia* refers to the OT prophecies and the Ten Commandments. In the Septuagint it occurs 5 times in Isaiah and frequently in the Psalms—17 times in Psalm 119—for "the word of the Lord" (SH, p. 70). It came to be used in the early church for the sayings of Jesus. But in this passage it means the sacred writings of the OT. Denney says that the expression *ta logia tou theou* "must be regarded as the contents of revelation, having God as their author, and at the time when Paul wrote, identical with the OT scriptures" (EGT, 2:603).

3 Unbelief In this verse the KJV uses "did not believe" and "unbelief." The ASV reads "were without faith" and "want of faith." But RSV and NEB have "were unfaithful" and

"faithlessness," and Williams reads "proved unfaithful" and "unfaithfulness." Moffatt says "proved untrustworthy" and "faithlessness." The Greek words are *apisteō* and *apistia.*

It will be seen that a number of recent translations prefer the idea of unfaithfulness to that of unbelief. The same division of opinion may be found among the commentators. Sanday and Headlam prefer "unbelief." So does Denney. He interprets Paul as arguing that, though many Jews did not believe God's promises in the OT, that would not in any way affect God's faithfulness in keeping His promises. The truth of God's Word is not dependent on man's acceptance of it.

The main argument in favor of the rendering "unfaithfulness" is the expressed contrast between it and the "faithfulness" of God. While the Greek word *pistis* most commonly means "faith," it is obvious that when applied to God it rather means "faithfulness." Probably all scholars today would agree that the KJV erred in translating it "faith" in this passage. *Pistis* occurs 244 times in the NT and in the KJV is translated "faith" 239 times. The verb *pisteuō* occurs 248 times and is translated "believe" 239 times.

But while all agree on "faithfulness" for *pistis* in reference to God, there is still a dispute about *apisteō* and *apistia*. The truth of the matter is that while "disbelieve" and "unbelief" are the most common meanings of these terms, "there is no real objection to taking *ēpistēsan, apistian, pistin,* all to refer to faithfulness rather than just faith" (4:342).

Make Without Effect The verb is *katargeō*. It means "to make idle or inactive . . . to render inoperative or invalid, to abrogate, abolish" (A-S, 238). It is used 25 times by Paul and only twice elsewhere in the NT (Luke 13:7; Heb. 2:14). Vincent writes of this word: "Dr. Morison acutely observes that it negatives the idea of *agency* or *operation*, rather than of *result* or *effect*. It *is* rather *to make inefficient* than *to make without effect*" (3:32). The RSV renders it "nullify."

4 God Forbid This expression occurs 15 times in the KJV of the NT. Fourteen times it is used by Paul—10 of those times in Romans—and once by Luke (20:16).

This forceful phrase is the translation of *mē genoito*, which literally means, "Let it not be" or "May it not come to pass." Wuest renders it: "May such a thing never occur" (p. 53). Moffatt translates it, "Never!" The RSV follows Goodspeed in rendering it, "By no means!" The KJV is probably stronger than the Greek will support. But the words express more than a weak wish. They should be given some force, which can be represented in English by the exclamation point.

Burton has an apt comment on these words. He writes:

> The phrase *mē genoito* is an Optative of Wishing which strongly deprecates something suggested by a previous question or assertion. Fourteen of the fifteen NT instances are in Paul's writings, and in twelve of these it expresses the apostle's abhorrence of an inference which he fears may be (falsely) drawn from his argument (p. 79).

Sanday and Headlam comment: "It is characteristic of the vehement impulsive style of this group of Epp. that the phrase is confined to them (ten times in Rom., once in I Cor., twice in Gal.)" (p. 71).

Let God Be True It is obvious that these words carry something more than their literal sense in English, for God is always and inevitably true. Probably the best meaning is that found in ASV, "Let God be found true." The verb is *ginomai*, which means "become." Sanday and Headlam write: "The transition which the verb denotes is often from a latent condition to an apparent condition, and so here, 'prove to be,' 'be seen to be' " (p. 71). Vincent says: "The phrase is used with reference to men's apprehension" (3:33).

It Is Written The Greek form *gegraptai* occurs some 66 times in the NT. It is the regular formula for introducing quotations from the OT. This is its third occurrence in Romans (cf. 1:17; 2:24), and it is found 12 times more. It is the perfect passive of the verb *graphō*, "write." The perfect tense indicates completed action and also a continuing state resulting from that completed action. So the full force of this single word would be: "It has been written and still stands written." The common English rendering, "It is written," conveys this idea best of any brief translation, unless one were to prefer, "It stands written."

5 Commend This verse speaks of our unrighteousness commending the righteousness of God. Just what does this mean?

The word *commend* is *sunistēmi*. The verb literally means "place together." It has two distinct uses in the NT: (1) commend; (2) show, prove, establish. It seems rather obvious that

the second meaning is the one that fits this passage, although Robertson writes: "Either makes good sense here" (4:342). Denney has "demonstrates" (EGT, 2:604).

Vengeance The phrase "who taketh vengeance" is literally "the one inflicting the anger" (*ho epipherōn tēn orgēn*). The verb is found only here and in Jude 9, where it is rendered "bring against." The RSV translates the phrase here "inflict wrath." When does God inflict anger? "The reference is to the Last Judgment" (SH, p. 73).

8 Damnation The first of these two words occurs 11 times in the KJV. It may be justified in 2 Pet. 2:1, where the Greek word (*apoleia*) means "destruction." But in the other 10 passages it is stronger than the Greek original. Here and in 6 other places it translates *krima*, while in the remaining three passages it is the rendering of *krisis*. Both these Greek words mean "judgment." They come from *krinō*, "judge." *Krima* can be translated "condemnation," but not "damnation."

9 Better or Worse? The first verb in verse 9 has caused considerable trouble to translators and commentators. This is shown readily by the fact that the KJV renders it, "Are we better than they?"; RV (1881) has, "Are we in worse case than they?" (with the marginal reading: "Do we excuse ourselves?"); the ASV (1901) goes back to the King James rendering; and RSV adopts this meaning when it translates it, "Are we Jews any better off?" (but margin: "at any disadvantage?").

The word is *proechometha*, which is the first person plural of the present middle or passive indicative—the same form is used for both—of *proechō*. This verb, found only here in NT, literally means "hold before." From its use in running a race it came to mean "excel." Hence the passive would mean "Are we excelled?" The question then would signify: "Are we Jews worse off than the Gentiles?"—the meaning adopted in RV. But the context does not seem to support this. In the middle it could mean: "Do we excuse ourselves?" (RV margin). Meyer similarly would translate it: "Do we put forward (anything) in our defense?" (p. 120).

Perhaps the best solution is to adopt the sense expressed in KJV, ASV, and RSV: "Are we [Jews] any better off?" That seems to fit the context best, repeating the question of verse 1. This passage may serve as an example of the great difficulty that often attaches to the translation of even one word in the Greek. It should also be a warning against hasty condemnation of those who offer a new and different version. For in this case equally good scholars—intellectually and spiritually—come to opposite conclusions and offer exactly opposite translations. The work of translating the Scriptures demands the very highest qualities of learning and devotion.

Not at All A somewhat similar situation appears in the very next words in the Greek, *ou pantōs*. Sanday and Headlam state the case clearly: "Strictly speaking *ou* should qualify *pantōs*, 'not altogether,' 'not entirely,' as in 1 Cor. v. 10 ... but in some cases, as here, *pantōs* qualifies *ou*, 'altogether not,' 'entirely not,' i.e., 'not at all' " (p. 77). Intelligent translation involves far more than just looking up words in a lexicon!

Proved The ninth verse also includes a word that so far has not been found anywhere else (VGT), inside or outside the NT—*proaitiaomai*. The KJV translates it: "We have before proved." But there is general agreement among scholars that the correct meaning is rather this: "We before laid to the charge of" (ASV). Vincent writes: "The reference is not to logical proof, but to forensic accusation" (3:35). What Paul is saying is that he has already brought against both Jews and Gentiles the formal charge that they are under sin; that is, in its grip.

12 *Together* The word translated *together* in the second clause is *hama*. In its full force it means "one and all." It emphasizes the fact that not only *all* collectively but *everyone* individually has turned aside from God. Not only has the human race as a whole fallen from God's favor, but each and every member of it has sinned.

Unprofitable The verb in this same clause is *ēchreiōthēsan*. In the KJV and the ASV it is translated, "They are become unprofitable." The RSV has, "They have gone wrong."

These are translations of the Greek text quoted from the Septuagint. But the original Hebrew word used in the OT (Ps. 14:3) and rendered, "They are become filthy" (KJV and ASV; "corrupt," RSV), literally means "go bad, become sour." The picture is that of milk turning sour until it is not only useless but repulsive.

19 *Guilty Before God* The universality of sin, and so of judgment, is expressed here in unequivocal terms. Summarizing what has been emphasized in the first three chapters up to this point, this verse declares that "all the world may become guilty before God." In the English and American Revised versions this is changed to "all the world may be brought under the judgment of God." The RSV reads: "the whole world may be held accountable to God."

The variations are all translations of one word, *hypodikos*, found only here in the NT. This adjective comes from *hypo*, "under," and *dikē*, which means "a judicial hearing; hence its result, the execution of a sentence, punishment" (A-S). Thayer says that *dikē* means "a sentence of condemnation." So *hypodikos* properly suggests "under sentence of condemnation." Cremer writes: "It denotes one who is bound to do or suffer what is imposed for the sake of justice, because he has neglected to do what is right" (p. 204). Abbott-Smith gives this definition: "brought to trial." Vincent prefers "liable to pay penalty."

So what Paul is saying in this passage is that all the world is brought to trial before God, is under the judgment of God, is guilty before God, is under a sentence of condemnation before God. It is a sweeping statement that takes in all humanity outside of Jesus Christ.

20 *Justified* The verb *dikaioō* ("justify") occurs in verse 20 for the third time in this Epistle (cf. 2:13; 4:3). It is found 39 times in the NT, 27 in Paul's Epistles, 6 in Luke's two writings, 3 in James, 2 in Matthew, once in Revelation. The soteriological emphasis of Romans is shown by the fact that the word occurs 15 times in this Epistle alone.

Because *dikaioō* is central to the message of Romans, a more extended treatment of it is in order. The verb comes from the adjective *dikaios*. In early Greek writers this was used "of persons, observant of *dikē*, custom, rule, right, *righteous* in performing duties to gods and men" (A-S, 115–16). Thayer says the adjective means: "righteous, observing divine and human laws; one who is such as he ought to be"; and so, "approved of God, acceptable to God" (pp. 148–49). Cremer observes: "Righteousness in the biblical sense is a condition of rightness the standard of which is God, which is estimated according to the divine standard, which shows itself in behaviour comformable to God, and has to do above all things with its relation to God, and with the walk before Him" (p. 184). In other words, according to the Bible one is "right" only when he is right with God. That is a strong preaching point.

The verb *dikaioō* is defined by Abbott-Smith in its NT and LXX usage as: "to show to be right-

151

eous, to declare, pronounce righteous" (p. 116). Thayer notes that the proper meaning, "according to the analogy of other verbs ending in oō," is "to make *dikaios;* to render righteous or such as he ought to be." But he thinks "this meaning is extremely rare, if not altogether doubtful." He holds that the normal usage is "to show, exhibit, evince one to be righteous, such as he is and wishes himself to be considered." His conclusion is that *dikaioō* means "to declare, pronounce, one to be just, righteous, or such as he ought to be"; negatively, "to declare guiltless," positively, "to judge, declare, pronounce, righteous and therefore acceptable" (p. 150).

Cremer says that *dikaioō* denotes "the activity which is directed to the restoration or production of a *dikaion*" (p. 193). In the NT it means "to recognize, to set forth, as righteous, to justify" (p. 195). As used by Paul it "denotes nothing else than the *judicial act* of God, whereby man is pronounced free from guilt and punishment" (p. 197).

An observation might be in order at this point. It is sometimes assumed that lexicographers and grammarians write with complete scientific objectivity. But such is definitely not the case, nor is it possible. Every man works with certain presuppositions in the background of his thinking. It is impossible to escape this. So when Thayer (editing Grimm) states that the proper meaning of *dikaioō* is "make righteous," but then asserts that this meaning is rare and that the verb usually means "pronounce righteous" he is—in a measure, at least—giving a subjective opinion.

Sanday and Headlam in their monumental commentary on Romans have a careful discussion of *dikaioō*. They hold that its proper meaning is "pronounce righteous," and add: "It cannot mean 'to make righteous' " (p. 30).

Burton, in one of the most thorough commentaries on Galatians, traces extensively the usage of *dikaioō* in classical Greek, LXX, the Apocrypha and Pseudepigrapha, and finally in the NT. His conclusion is that in the NT it has the forensic meaning, "to recognize as acceptable [to God]" (p. 473).

Schrenk, in Kittel's massive *Theological Dictionary of the New Testament*, begins his discussion by saying, "*Dikaioō* derives from *dikaios,* and means 'to make righteous' " (2:211). In LXX it is a forensic term, and this aspect, he holds, is dominant in the NT, especially in Paul's Epistles. He says that the judicial acquittal "is neither exclusively objective in the cross nor exclusively subjective in experience" (2:216). In Gal. 2:16 the verb means "to become a righteous man in the eyes of God" (*ibid.*). He

also notes that whenever this word is used, faith (*pistis*) "is always included." Paul links the two together in 9 passages. In other words, justification by God never takes place apart from faith on the part of man.

All of this highlights the perennial debate on imputation versus impartation. Some teach that in justification Christ's righteousness is *imputed* to the sinner. Others hold that in the one act of justification God *makes* us righteous and then *pronounces* us righteous. To say that God declares righteous what is actually unrighteous is to make God a liar. God, by His very nature, is true and cannot assert what is not so.

Vincent has stated this truth very effectively. He discusses the classical usage of *dikaioō*, noting that the primitive meaning is "to make right." Then it came to mean "to judge a thing to be right" (3:38). In the NT it indicates "the act or process by which a man is brought into a right state as related to God" (*ibid.*, p. 39). He further says: "Justification aims directly at *character.* It contemplates making *the man himself* right" (*ibid.*).

Coming to grips then with the issue noted above, Vincent makes this fine statement of the case: "Justification which does not actually remove the wrong condition in man which is at the root of his enmity to God, is no justification. In the absence of this, a legal *declaration* that the man is right is a fiction" (p. 40).

It is interesting to note that the *Oxford English Dictionary* (5:643) straddles the issue, making place for both conceptions. For the theological definition of *justification* it says: "The action whereby man is justified, or freed from the penalty of sin, and accounted or made righteous by God." We would change that last *or* to *and.* For the theological meaning of *justify* it gives: "To declare free from the penalty of sin on the ground of Christ's righteousness, or to make inherently righteous by the infusion of grace." Again we would substitute *and* in place of *or.*

God has provided more than a legal pardon. He imparts Christ's righteousness to the one who believes. Then, and then only, can He recognize us as righteous.

21 *The Righteousness of God* The early part of verse 21 speaks of "the righteousness of God" (KJV), "a righteousness of God" (ASV), "the righteousness of God" (RSV). What are we to choose?

As might be expected, ASV gives the most literal translation. The Greek does not have the definite article here. However, the phrase could very accurately be rendered "God's righteousness." A. T. Robertson defines it as a "God kind of righteousness" (3:346).

Basically, the problem is the same as in 1:17. There it was noted that Sanday and Headlam suggest a twofold interpretation. The same holds good here. "The righteousness which he has in view is essentially the right-eousness of God; though the aspect from which it is regarded is as a condition bestowed upon man, that condition is the direct outcome of the Divine attribute of righteousness, working its way to larger realization amongst men" (p. 82).

This righteousness is not a law-righteous-ness (v. 21) but a faith-righteousness (v. 22). It comes by faith in Jesus Christ and is bestowed on all who believe. The ASV appears inconsis-tent in adding the definite article before right-eousness in verse 22. In the Greek the expres-sion is exactly the same as in verse 21.

22 Difference The KJV reads, "for there is no difference." The revised versions have "dis-tinction." To some the change of words may seem to be "a distinction without a difference"!

But there is a difference between the terms, as suggested by the phrase just quoted. Two things may be essentially different and yet no distinction be made between them in practice. The precise point being made by Paul here is that God makes no distinction between Jews and Gentiles; He treats both the same way. So probably "distinction" is preferable here. The Greek word *diastolē* is used in the NT only by Paul—here, in 10:12, and in 1 Cor. 14:7. In the last Scripture it is used of "a distinction" in mu-sical sounds. The usage in 10:12 is the same as here. It would seem best to translate it "distinc-tion" in all three places.

23 All Have Sinned . . . This is the most definite statement on the subject in the entire Bible. The language of the KJV is familiar to all: "For all have sinned, and come short of the glory of God." The ASV reads: "For all have sinned, and fall short of the glory of God." This may seem more awkward, but it is more accu-rate. For the King James rendering could be taken as meaning: "All have sinned, and [have] come short of the glory of God." It thereby fails to bring out the distinction between the tenses in the Greek. Actually, the first verb is in the aorist tense, "sinned," and the second is in the present tense, "are falling short." Not only is it true that all have sinned in the past; it is also true that all (apart from the grace of God) fall short, here and now, of God's glory as He

wishes it to be manifested *to* them and *through* them.

The Glory of God The word *doxa* was used in classical Greek for "opinion" or "reputation." In the NT it means "recognition, honor," and then "brightness, splendor, glory." In the OT the glory of God "is used of the aggregate of the divine attributes and coincides with His self-revelation." Vincent goes on to say that the phrase here means "the honor or approbation which God bestows" (3:42).

24 Redemption The phrase "the redemp-tion that is in Christ Jesus" could well be taken as the theme of the Epistle to the Romans. It is through this redemption that we are "justified freely by his grace." This is the message of Ro-mans in a nutshell.

The word *redemption* is *apolytrōsis*, which oc-curs only 10 times in the NT (Luke, Pauline Epistles, and Hebrews). In Romans it is used again only in 8:23.

Abbott-Smith defines the meaning as "re-lease effected by payment of ransom" (p. 53). This is because it incorporates the word *lytron*, which means "ransom." The latter is used fre-quently in the papyri for the price paid to free slaves. Deissmann writes: "*Lytron* for a slave's redemption-money is found . . . several times . . . in inscriptions from Thessaly" (LAE, p. 328). He also says: "When anybody heard the Greek word *lytron*, 'ransom,' in the first century, it was natural for him to think of the purchase-money for manumitting slaves" (p. 327).

Some have tried to eliminate the idea of "ransom" from *apolytrōsis* and make it mean simply "deliverance." But Sanday and Headlam's words are well supported when they say: "We can hardly resist the conclusion that the idea of the *lytron* retains its full force . . . describing the Death of Christ. The emphasis is on the *cost* of man's redemption" (p. 86). They add a salutary word of warning: "We need not press the metaphor yet a step fur-ther by asking (as the ancients did) to whom the ransom or price was paid."

Trench agrees with this emphasis. He writes: "For *apolytrōsis* is not recall from captiv-ity merely . . . but recall of captives from captiv-ity through the payment of a ransom for them" (p. 290).

25 Propitiation It is stated that God set forth Christ to be a "propitiation." The Greek word is *hilastērion*. It occurs elsewhere in the NT only in Heb. 9:5, where it is translated "mercy seat." An adjective, it is used in both places with the article as a substantive.

The adjective comes from the verb *hilaskomai*. This was used in the middle voice in classical Greek in the sense of appeasing or conciliating the gods. In the LXX it is used passively with the meaning "become propitious, be appeased" (Thayer, p. 301). The verb occurs only twice in the NT, in Luke 18:13—of the penitent publican in the parable of the Pharisee and the publican ("God *be merciful* to me a sinner")—and in Heb. 2:17 ("to *make reconciliation* for the sins of the people").

Then there is the noun *hilasmos*. As in the case of the adjective and verb, it occurs twice in the NT—1 John 2:2 and 4:10. It is translated "propitiation" in KJV. Cremer prefers "expiation"; that is, a covering of sin.

As a neuter substantive *hilastērion* has the sense "a means of appeasing, or expiating, a propitiation." Thayer goes on to distinguish two meanings in the two passages in the NT. He suggests that in Heb. 9:5 as "the lid of expiation" it refers to "the well-known cover of the ark of the covenant in the Holy of holies, which was sprinkled with the blood of the expiatory victim on the annual day of atonement (this rite signifying that the life of the people, the loss of which they had merited by their sins, was offered to God in the blood as the life of the victim, and that God by this ceremony was appeased and their sins expiated)" (p. 301). But Thayer holds that in Rom. 3:25 *hilastērion* means "an expiatory sacrifice."

Deissmann insists that the idea of mercy seat should not be attached to the word in Rom. 3:25. He says that here it signifies "means of propitiation," or "propitiatory gift" (BS, p. 130). He further writes: "The crucified Christ is the votive-gift of the Divine Love for the salvation of men" (p. 133).

James Denney suggests this rendering: "Whom God set forth in propitiatory power"— taking *hilastērion* as an adjective. He then makes this observation: "It is in His blood that Christ is endued with propitiatory power; and there is no propitiatory power of blood known to Scripture unless the blood be that of sacrifice" (EGT, 2:611).

In his commentary on *The Epistles of St. John* (Greek text), Bishop Westcott has an additional note on the use of *hilasmos*. After pointing out the classical idea of propitiating the gods—from Homer on—he contrasts the usage of the biblical writers as follows:

> They show that the scriptural conception of *hilaskesthai* is not that of appeasing one who is

angry, with a personal feeling, against the offender; but of altering the character of that which from without occasions a necessary alienation, and interposes an inevitable obstacle to fellowship. Such phrases as "propitiating God" and God "being reconciled" are foreign to the language of the NT. Man is reconciled (p. 87).

W. E. Vine, in *An Expository Dictionary of New Testament Words*, develops this truth a little further. He indicates with regard to the Greek gods that "their good will was not conceived as their natural attitude, but something to be earned first" (3:223). But this idea is entirely foreign to the biblical point of view. God's nature guarantees that His attitude is always based on holy love. Man does not need to change that attitude. "It is God who is propitiated by the vindication of His holy and righteous character, whereby, through the provision He has made in the vicarious and expiatory sacrifice of Christ, He has so dealt with sin that He can shew mercy to the believing sinner in the removal of his guilt and the remission of his sins" (*ibid.*). In agreement with Westcott, Vine says: "Never is God said to be reconciled, a fact itself indicative that the enmity exists on man's part alone, and that it is man who needs to be reconciled to God, and not God to man" (*ibid.*).

In discussing the meaning of *hilastērion* in Rom. 3:25, William Owen Carver has this to say: "Greek fathers generally and prominent modern scholars understand Paul here to say that God appointed Christ Jesus to be the 'mercy-seat' for sinners" (ISBE, 4:2467). Dr. Carver prefers this interpretation as the most natural.

Samuel R. Driver has a long discussion of the Hebrew terms used for the idea of propitiation. His final conclusion is this: " 'Propitiation' is in the OT attached especially to the sin-offering, and to the sacrifice of the blood (or life); and Christ, by the giving up of His sinless life, annuls the power of sin to separate between God and the believer, by a sacrifice analogous to those offered by the Jewish priests, but infinitely more efficacious" (HDB, 4:132).

Sanday and Headlam interpret the term here as meaning propitiatory sacrifice. They give a quotation from the Jewish Mishna which is worth reproducing:

> When a man thinks, I will just go on sinning and repent later, no help is given him from above to make him repent. He who thinks, I will but just sin and the Day of Atonement will bring me forgiveness, such an one

gets no forgiveness through the Day of Atonement (p. 88).

It seems best to relate the term *hilastērion* to the mercy seat in the ancient Tabernacle, since all agree that it clearly has that meaning in the LXX and in the only other place where it occurs in the NT, Heb. 9:5. Just as the high priest once a year, on the Day of Atonement, took the blood of the sin offering and sprinkled it on the mercy seat in the Holy of Holies, so Christ as our great High Priest took the blood of His own sacrifice and offered it as the propitiation for our sins. The Epistle to the Hebrews seems clearly to indicate that Christ is Himself the Priest, the Altar, and the Sacrifice. He is the Fulfillment of all the typology of the Tabernacle.

To Declare His Righteousness

God set forth Christ as a propitiating Sacrifice literally "for a showing [or proof] of His righteousness." Sanday and Headlam comment: "In what sense can the Death of Christ be said to demonstrate the righteousness of God? It demonstrates it by showing the impossibility of simply passing over sin" (p. 89).

In a similar vein Denney writes: "God's righteousness, therefore, is demonstrated at the Cross, because there, in Christ's death, it is made once for all apparent that He does not palter with sin" (EGT, 2:613).

Remission

The KJV says that this was "for the remission of sins that are past." The ASV more correctly reads, "because of the passing over of the sins done aforetime."

The Greek word elsewhere translated "remission" is *aphesis*, which occurs 17 times in the NT. It properly means "dismissal, release, pardon, remission of penalty" (A-S).

But the term used here is *paresis*, which occurs only this one time in the NT. Abbott-Smith defines its meaning as "a letting go, dismissal, passing by."

Trench criticizes the translators of the RV (1881) for retaining "remission" here. He wisely observes that there must have been some reason for Paul's changing from *aphesis* to *paresis*, and that such a change should be indicated in the English translation. He would define *paresis* as "the present passing by of sin, the suspension of its punishment" (p. 119).

For the meaning of this passage Trench offers the following explanation: "There needed a signal manifestation of the righteousness of God, on account of the long praetermission or passing over of sins, in his infinite forbearance, with no adequate expression of his wrath

against them, during all those long years which preceded the coming of Christ; which manifestation of God's righteousness found place, when He set forth no other and no less than his own Son to be the propitiatory sacrifice for sin" (p. 117).

Thayer sums up well the significance of *paresis* thus: ". . . because God had patiently let pass the sins committed previously (to the expiatory death of Christ), i.e., had tolerated, had not punished (and so man's conception of his holiness was in danger of becoming dim, if not extinct)."

This does not mean that there was no punishment for sin during the OT period. It simply means that God did not deal fully and adequately with sin until Calvary.

28 Faith

The central theme of Romans is usually held to be "Justification by Faith." The classic statement of that is, "Therefore we conclude that a man is justified by faith without the deeds of the law."

Since justification is by faith alone, it is obviously important that we understand the nature of faith. For true faith brings forgiveness of sins and a new life in Christ.

Cremer traces the origin of the Greek word *pistis*. He writes: "In classical Greek, *pistis* . . . signifies, primarily, the *trust* which I entertain, which one puts in any person or thing" (p. 478). Closely related is the idea of *fidelity*.

As for the meaning of *pistis* in the NT, Cremer holds that there are three distinguishable ideas. These are: "a conviction, which is not, like the profane *pistis*, merely an opinion held in good faith without reference to its proof, but a full and convinced *acknowledgment* of God's saving revelation or truth; a *cleaving* thus demanded of the person who acknowledges to the object acknowledged, therefore *personal fellowship* with the God and Lord of salvation (so especially in John), *and surrender to Him*; and lastly, a *behavior* of unconditional and yet perfectly intelligent and assured confidence" (p. 479).

Faith is a rather rare term in the OT. There one finds such expressions as "doing His will," "walking in the way of His commandments," "remembering the Lord," "waiting upon the Lord." Cremer says: "In the NT, on the other hand, *pistis* appears as the generic name for this whole bearing" (p. 480).

The fundamental conception of NT faith, says Cremer, is "a firmly relying trust" (p. 482). With that goes "*acknowledgment* and *conviction* with reference to the truths of the gospel." He adds: "We may describe *pistis* generally to be *trust or confidence cherished by firm conviction"* (p. 482).

Cremer also says: "In general *pistis* . . . is a bearing towards God and His revelation which recognizes and confides in Him and in it, which not only acknowledges and holds to His word as true, but practically applies and appropriates it" (p. 482). Faith is . . . "confident and selfsurrendering acknowledgment and acceptance of Christ's gracious revelation" (p. 483).

Faith is far more than intellectual assent. It is moral commitment. It is the personal surrender of one's will to God's will. Without the element of submission there is no real faith. There is no such thing as trust without obedience. Whitehouse says: "Obedience . . . is the inevitable concomitant of believing" (TWBB, p. 76).

Faith is actually the reaction of one's whole being—intellectual, emotional, moral, spiritual—to God and His Word. It is belief of the mind, submission of the heart, obedience of the will. Faith is best thought of as the total response of the human personality to the divine command.

The noun *pistis* is allied with the verb *peithō*, which means "persuade." Thayer says that in the NT *pistis* means "a conviction or belief respecting man's relationship to God and divine things, generally with the included idea of trust and holy fervor born of faith and conjoined with it" (p. 512).

Thayer goes on to say that in relation to God, *pistis* is "the conviction that God exists and is the creator and ruler of all things, the provider and bestower of eternal salvation through Christ," while in reference to Christ it denotes "a strong and welcome conviction or belief that Jesus is the Messiah, through whom we obtain eternal salvation in the kingdom of God" (p. 513).

Faith is more than intellectual belief. It is a conviction. One may believe that a thing is so because of adequate evidence. But real faith is a divinely wrought conviction of the truth of God's Word, involving an acceptance of it as binding the believer to action.

Vine emphasizes these two aspects. He writes: "The main elements in faith in its relation to the invisible God, as distinct from faith in man . . . are (1) a firm conviction, producing a full acknowledgment of God's revelation or truth . . . (2) a personal surrender to Him" (2:71).

Whitehouse declares that the NT usage of *pistis* "owes little or nothing to Plato" (TWBB, p. 75). He affirms that its main background is Hebrew. The latter he defines thus: "The core of this Hebrew concept is firmness, reliability,

or steadfastness. To believe is to hold on to something firmly, with conviction and confidence" (*ibid.*).

What Paul says is that a man is not justified by any doing of good deeds, by keeping the law. Rather, he is justified wholly and only because of a right attitude toward God: an attitude of trust and obedience, of belief and commitment, of conviction and confidence.

4:1 *What Shall We Say Then . . .* The three standard Bible versions in use in America today differ strikingly in their translation of the first verse of this chapter. The KJV reads: "What shall we say then that Abraham our father, as pertaining to the flesh, hath found?" The ASV has: "What then shall we say that Abraham, our forefather, hath found according to the flesh?" The RSV says: "What then shall we say about Abraham, our forefather according to the flesh?" (The NASB is similar to KJV.) The second translation differs from the first in attaching "according to the flesh" (*kata sarka*) to "found," rather than to "forefather." The meaning would then be: "What did Abraham gain by his own works [or, racial origin], apart from the grace of God?" The third differs from the other two in leaving out the word *found*. Why these differences?

The answer is that the three translations represent three variant readings in the Greek manuscripts. "Found" (*heurēkenai*) occurs after "say" (*eroumen*) in the fourth-century manuscript Sinaiticus, and in three fifth-century manuscripts (Alexandrinus, Ephraemi, Bezae), as well as in several later ones. Nestle adopts this reading, which is followed in KJV. It attaches "according to the flesh" to "forefather."

The reading found in ASV is based on the text of a few rather late manuscripts (K, L, P, etc.), which place "found" just before "according to the flesh." Since this version does not ordinarily follow the late manuscripts, it may be that its translators simply felt that "according to the flesh" should go with "found," regardless of the order of the Greek.

The RSV bases its reading on the text of the oldest manuscript, Vaticanus, of the early fourth century, and a very few others. These omit *heurēkenai* ("found") altogether. This reading was adopted by Westcott and Hort and is defended by Sanday and Headlam.

Three observations might be made. The first is that most of the thousands of variant readings in the Greek manuscripts have little or no effect on the meaning of the passage. The second is that some do affect the exact meaning and so require careful study before any conclusion is drawn. The third is that no fundamental doctrine of the Christian faith is in any way threatened by these variant readings. The foundations of our faith are secure.

3–10 Counted, Reckoned In colloquial American English *reckon* is equivalent to *guess*, or at most *think*. That is what a person means when he says, "I reckon so."

Very different is the correct meaning of the word. Literally it signifies to "count" or "compute." It is a mathematical term, with all the exactness that mathematics demands.

"Counted" (vv. 3, 5) and "reckoned" (vv. 4, 9, 10) are the same verb in the Greek, *logizomai*. In its 41 occurrences in the NT it is translated a dozen different ways in the KJV. The dominant renderings are *think, impute, reckon, count, account*.

Abbott-Smith says that the verb is used "properly of numerical calculation, *to count, reckon*." Secondly, it is used "metaphorically, without reference to numbers, by a reckoning of characteristics or reasons." Hence it means "to reckon, take into account . . . consider, calculate." That is its usage here. It is a bookkeeping term. Abraham's faith was credited to him as righteousness.

6–24 Imputed The same Greek word (*logizomai*) is translated "impute" 6 times in this chapter (vv. 6, 8, 11, 22, 23, 24). Altogether, *logizomai* occurs 11 times in this one chapter alone. In fact, almost half (19 out of 41) of its occurrences in the NT are in the Book of Romans. This accords with the central theme of Romans, justification by faith. The Greek word is used only 6 times in the NT outside of Paul's Epistles. He is the theologian who is particularly concerned with the forensic aspect of redemption.

The term *imputation* is not one to fear or avoid. It simply indicates the fact that, when a sinner believes in Jesus Christ as his Savior, God imputes—reckons, counts, credits—the righteousness of Christ to him. It in no way obviates the accompanying "impartation" of righteousness in the regenerating of the sinner. God at the same moment makes us righteous, by imparting to us and implanting in us the nature of Christ, and declares us righteous (imputation). See discussion of *dikaoō* (3:20).

7–8 Blessed . . . The same word (*makarios*, "blessed") is used in these verses as in the Beatitudes of Jesus (Matt. 5:3–12). It was used in Homer and Hesiod, the earliest Greek writers, chiefly of the gods and the departed. An ancient model letter reads thus: "The death of——, now blessed [*makariou*], hath grieved us exceedingly."

The adjective is found 50 times in the NT. Only twice (1 Tim. 1:11; 6:15) is it used of God. It occurs most frequently in the Gospels of Matthew (13 times) and Luke (15 times), always in the sayings of Jesus. It is found 7 times in the Book of Revelation.

Closely related is the noun *makarismos*, "blessedness" (vv. 6, 9), found elsewhere in the NT only in Gal. 4:15. It has two meanings: a state of blessedness and a declaration of blessedness. Vine argues for the latter sense in the NT. Abbott-Smith agrees with this.

Aristotle distinguished between divine blessedness (*makarios*) and human blessedness (*eudaimonia*). The latter word is not found at all in the Scriptures, because of its pagan associations. But the former occurs in the LXX to describe those who have found God's favor. This was often conceived by the Hebrews as manifested in material prosperity. But Jesus gave it a higher meaning. Blessedness is more than a superficial feeling of happiness, based on pleasant circumstances. It is God's favor experienced in the hearts and lives of those who believe and obey Jesus Christ, His Son.

9–12 Circumcision The words *peritomē* (circumcision) and *akrobystia* (uncircumcision) each occur 6 times in these 4 verses. The former also is found 6 times in 2:25–29 (see discussion there). The latter occurs 4 times in that place. These are the two prominent passages on circumcision in the NT. (The Greek nouns are sometimes translated as adjectives in the KJV.)

The important point that Paul makes here is that Abraham was justified by faith before he was circumcised. It is obvious, therefore, that circumcision is not essential to salvation. It was Abraham's righteousness which was counted to him for righteousness, not works such as circumcision.

This raises the question as to the basis of man's acceptance with God in OT times. As already noted, Paul teaches that there has always been one basis of acceptance with God—namely, faith. But there is no true faith without obedience. Faith is an attitude of obedience to the will of God. Faith and obedience may be distinguished in academic discussion but they can never be divorced in practical experience.

16 Seed Abraham had two seeds: one "of the law," and the other "of the faith." The promise to Abraham is valid for both. That is the main argument of verses 13–25.

There are 3 words translated "seed" in the NT. The first two, *spora* (once) and *sporos* (5 times), come from *speirō* (sow). Hence they clearly mean seed sown.

The third—used here in verses 13, 16, 18—is *sperma* (likewise derived from *speirō*), which has been taken over into English ("sperm"). It occurs 44 times in the NT. In only 8 cases does it refer to seed sown in the ground. The rest of the time it means "descendants." That is the translation of *sperma* in RSV of verses 13, 16, and 18. The word *descendants* does not occur at all in the KJV.

Sure   It is stated that God's promise was "of faith . . . by grace," in order that it "might be sure to all the seed." The adjective *bebaios* means "firm, secure" (A-S). It can be defined as "valid and therefore inviolable" (Thayer). Deissmann has a lengthy discussion of *bebaios* and *bebaiōsis* and shows that in the Greek usage of that day they clearly carried the sense of "legally guaranteed security" (BS, p. 109). Hence RSV reads here, "guaranteed to all his descendants."

17 Calleth Those Things . . .   In the latter part of the 17th verse God is described as the One who "calleth those things which be not as though they were." But faith is not fiction. The RSV has: "Calls into existence the things that do not exist." In spite of the opposition of Sanday and Headlam to this translation of the somewhat ambiguous Greek—literally, "calling the things not being as being"—it seems best to adopt this interpretation. It has the support of such eminent scholars as Lipsius, Lietzmann, Weiss, Zahn, and W. H. P. Hatch. Sanday and Headlam admit that it is the view of "most commentators."

As argument for it one might note that not only does it make the verse more meaningful but also it accords better with the preceding parallel clause, "who quickeneth the dead." Not only does God revive the dead; He actually creates new existences. That appears to be the meaning of the passage.

19 Not   The KJV says that Abraham "considered not his own body now dead," in spite of the fact that he was about a hundred years old. That is, he refused to accept the natural implications of his age.

But the oldest and best manuscripts—Vaticanus and Sinaiticus of the fourth century, Alexandrinus and Ephraemi of the 5th century—omit the word "not" (*ou*). This makes the passage even more striking. Abraham consid-

ered his body dead, as it actually was for the purpose of reproduction. Yet in spite of that he believed that God could give him a son.

20 Staggered Not   This verse says that Abraham "staggered not at the promise of God through unbelief." The verb "stagger" is *diakrinomai*, which means "to be divided in one's mind, to hesitate, doubt" (A-S). It is translated "waver" twice in Jas. 1:6. There was no unbelief in Abraham's heart to cause him to waver in his faith or hesitate to believe God's promise. Unwavering faith makes sturdy, steady, stable Christians.

Strong faith glorifies God. That is the lesson of verse 20. Abraham might well have "staggered" at the seeming impossibility of God's promise. Instead he rose nobly to the occasion with a strong faith that dared to believe God regardless of natural circumstances. That is real faith.

5:1 Peace with God   The KJV reads: "Therefore being justified by faith, we have peace with God through our Lord Jesus Christ." The three American revisions agree. But the English RV says, "Let us have peace." Why the change?

Again the answer is found in the fact of variant readings. The very earliest manuscripts have *echōmen* (with omega in the middle). This is the hortatory subjunctive, "let us have." But a later scribe changed the reading to *echomen* (with omicron in the middle), the simple indicative, "we have."

There are two main types of unintentional errors in the Greek manuscripts. (It must be remembered that all copies of the NT from the 1st to the 15th centuries were laboriously written by hand.) The first can be labeled "errors of the eye." These would occur when a scribe was making a single copy from a manuscript which lay before him. If two lines began or ended with the same Greek letters he would be apt to leave out a line. Probably most manuscripts have examples of this. Other errors of the eye would consist of omitting a phrase beginning with the same letters as a preceding phrase or repeating a phrase instead of writing it only once. Also two words that look much alike might be confused. Since the early Greek manuscripts have no division into words, sometimes the letters would be separated at the wrong place, giving an entirely different sense. The miracle is that mistakes were not made much more often!

The other class of unintentional confusion could be called "errors of the ear." These would occur when one scribe was reading from a master manuscript, while as many as 40 scribes sat before him, each making a copy of that manuscript from dictation. This "assembly line" procedure was the ancient publishing house. Today a million copies of a book can be run off the press, all of them exactly the same. Before the 15th century it was practically impossible to make even *two* copies of any sizable book exactly alike. There is no extant manuscript of the Greek NT without some mistakes in it. But by a careful comparison of many manuscripts most of these errors can be eliminated.

It is obvious that errors of the ear would occur easily when the writing scribe heard a word that sounded like another. Very probably in the early centuries of the Christian era *echomen* (ind.) and *echōmen* (subj.) were pronounced exactly alike. So some scribes wrote one and some the other.

One factor that guarded against a hopeless confusion in situations like this was that individual scribes could make a check against written manuscripts. Then, too, the scribes would gain a familiarity with the text of the NT. Tradition would be handed down from generation to generation as to the exact wording of a given text.

It is difficult to decide between the two readings in Rom. 5:1. Westcott and Hort have the subjunctive form. Nestle followed this in his sixteenth edition (1936) but has the indicative in his twenty-first edition (1952), as does the Bible Society's text (1966). Weymouth, Moffatt, Goodspeed, Ballantine (Riverside), Montgomery, Twentieth Century, Verkuyl (Berkeley), Knox, Wand, and Williams all have the subjunctive, "let us." Phillips has a very good paraphrase: "Let us grasp the fact that we *have* peace."

What conclusion should we reach? With regard to the manuscript evidence Sanday and Headlam say: "Clearly overwhelming evidence for *echōmen*" (p. 210). James Denney agrees that the manuscript evidence is overwhelmingly in favor of the subjunctive. However, this is his conclusion of the matter: "But the uninterrupted series of indicatives afterwards, the inappropriateness of the verb *echein* to express 'let us realize, let us make our own,' the strong tendency to give a paraenetic turn to a passage often read in church, the natural emphasis on *eirēnēn* (peace), and the logic of the situation, are all in favour of *echomen* [ind.], which is accordingly adopted by Meyer, Weiss, Lipsius, Godet and others, in spite of the manuscripts" (EGT, 2:623).

But Sanday and Headlam defend the sub-

junctive. They note that Paul is apt to change from argument to exhortation and that the subjunctive might be translated, "We should have"—something of a combination of inference and exhortation.

The verb is in the present tense. So it does not mean, "Let us get or obtain peace," but, "Let us keep on having or enjoying peace." (Cf. NEB: "Let us continue at peace.") It is therefore an exhortation to enjoy the peace that God has given us in the forgiveness of our sins. We should refuse to let doubts or fears rob us of the precious heritage that is rightfully ours.

2 Access Through our Lord Jesus Christ "we have access by faith into this grace wherein we stand." The word *access* is *prosagōgē*. Literally, it means "a bringing to." Besides this passage the term occurs in the NT only in Eph. 2:18; 3:12. Ellicott favors translating it "introduction" in Ephesians. The question is whether it should be rendered that way in Romans.

James Denney says that the word "has a certain touch of formality. Christ has 'introduced' us to our standing as Christians" (EGT, 2:623). Christ is not only the Door but also the One who stands there to welcome us in.

Cremer argues for *access* rather than *introduction*. But Sanday and Headlam take the opposite position. They write: "The idea is that of introduction to the presence-chamber of a monarch. The rendering 'access' is inadequate, as it leaves out of sight the fact that we do not come in our own strength but need an 'introducer'—Christ" (p. 121).

The Glory of God The word for *glory*, *doxa*, has had a long and interesting history. Its original meaning was "opinion, estimation," and then it came to mean "reputation." In the LXX it took on a meaning not found in classical Greek—"brightness, splendor." In this passage it seems to have special reference to the future glory awaiting the Christian in the next life. Sanday and Headlam comment: "It is the Glory of the Divine Presence (Shekinah) communicated to man (partially here, but) in full measure when he enters into that Presence; man's whole being will be transfigured by it" (p. 121).

3 Patience Paul says that we "glory in tribulations"—*he* certainly did!—because we know that "tribulation worketh patience." One can actually rejoice in hardship when he knows that great benefit will result from it.

"Patience" is the translation of *hypomonē*. This comes from *hypo*, "under," and *menō*, "remain." So it literally means "a remaining under."

The word *patience* is really too weak a translation. Denney says that the Greek word "has more of the sense of bravery and effort than the English 'patience': it is not so passive" (EGT, 2:624).

The real meaning is "patient enduring, endurance" (A-S). Thayer gives "steadfastness, constancy, endurance." He defines the word as follows: "In the NT the characteristic of a man who is unswerved from his deliberate purpose and his loyalty to faith and piety by even the greatest trials and sufferings" (p. 644). The best translation is "endurance" or "steadfastness."

4 *Experience* The Greek word is *dokimē*. It comes from the adjective *dokimos*, which means "tested, accepted, approved." It is connected with the verb *dokimazō*—"test, try, prove," and then "approve" as the result of testing. The noun used here has this twofold usage. It means first "the process of trial, *proving, test*" and secondly "the result of trial, *approved, approvedness*" (A-S).

The word occurs only in Paul's Epistles, where it is found with both senses a total of 7 times. In the KJV it is translated four different ways: "proof," "experience," "trial," "experiment."

Sanday and Headlam give a good definition for the word, as used in this passage: "The character which results from the process of trial, the temper of the veteran as opposed to that of the raw recruit" (p. 125). Denney defines it as "a spiritual state which has shown itself proof under trial" (EGT, 2:624). He also says: "Perhaps the best English equivalent of *dokimē* would be *character*."

It should be obvious that "experience" is hardly an adequate—if indeed an accurate—translation. The ASV more correctly uses "steadfastness" instead of "patience," and "approvedness" in place of "experience." Perhaps the RSV is still better—it is certainly more simple and clear—when it reads: "Endurance produces character." That says exactly what Paul meant.

5 *Not Ashamed* Paul goes on to say: "And hope maketh not ashamed." The RSV reads: "And hope does not disappoint us."

The Greek verb is *kataischynō*, which means "disgrace, dishonour, put to shame" (A-S). But Sanday and Headlam would translate it here: "does not disappoint," "does not prove illusory" (p. 125).

Shed The reason that hope does not disappoint us is that "the love of God is shed abroad in our hearts by the Holy Ghost which is given unto us." God's love, in the indwelling presence of the Holy Spirit, holds our hope steady.

The verb "shed abroad" is *ekchunnō*, a late form of *ekcheō*. The dominant meaning of the latter, even in KJV, is "pour out" (11 out of 18 times). That is the way the former should be translated here. The RSV correctly reads: "God's love has been poured into our hearts through the Holy Spirit." Only by the baptism with the Holy Spirit can our hearts be filled with divine love.

6, 8, 10 *Weak, Sinners, Enemies* In these verses, Christ is declared to have died for us, first, "while we were yet weak" (v. 6); secondly, "while we were yet sinners" (v. 8); thirdly, "while we were enemies" (v. 10). Weak, sinners, enemies—these describe in ascending scale the condition of the natural man before God. At best he is weak, too weak to live a fully righteous life. Worse still, he is a sinner, disobeying God's law. But worst of all, he is actually an enemy of the Almighty, defying his Maker by rebelling against His will. This is Paul's picture of every man without God.

6 *Weak* *Asthenos*, "weak," is translated "without strength" in the KJV and "helpless" in the RSV. It comes from the alpha-privative *a*- and *stenos*, "strength." So it literally means "without strength." Abbott-Smith defines it as "weak, feeble." Thayer adds "infirm" and suggests that here the meaning is "sluggish in doing right." In the Gospels and Acts it is used in a physical sense as "sickly." It almost always has this connotation in classical Greek. But Moulton and Milligan cite one example of the moral sense in Epictetus (*Dissertation* I.8.8), where it is coupled with *apaideutois* (undisciplined). Arndt and Gingrich give its primary meaning as "weak, powerless." It is used for the "impotent" man (Acts 4:9), who had no power to lift himself.

Hence it aptly describes the unregenerate man, who is "weak" and "helpless," unable to help himself but completely dependent on a Higher Power. Until the unsaved person is willing to recognize and confess his utter helplessness and hopelessness he cannot be a recipient of God's redeeming grace in Christ Jesus.

8 *Sinners* The second word, *sinners*, is *hamartolos*, which comes from the verb *hamartanō*. This in turn is from alpha-privative and *meiromai*. So it means "not to become a participator in, not to attain, not to arrive at the goal" (Cremer, p. 98). It is used by Homer of missing the mark in shooting. From Homer on it carried the moral sense, "to miss the right, to go wrong, to sin" (*ibid.*). In the Septuagint it means "missing the divinely appointed goal, deviation from what is pleasing to God" (*ibid.*, p. 99).

A "sinner," then, is not necessarily one who has gone far astray in wicked living. Rather, every man without Christ is a sinner because he has missed the goal of God's purpose for us as human beings; namely, that we should live holy lives in fellowship with a holy God. Apart from Christ no man is complete (Col. 2:10).

10 Enemies As though it were not enough to be weak and helpless, and further to miss the mark of God's goal for human living, man has gone so far as to rebel against his Creator and thus to become actually an enemy of God.

In Homer *echthros* meant "hated" or "hateful." In the NT it is used actively with the connotation "hating, hostile." Arndt and Gingrich give its primary meaning as "hostile." In the KJV it is used as a substantive and is translated "enemy" (30 times) or "foe" (twice).

This term shows the seriousness of sin. Reduced to the final analysis, sin is rebellion against God. It is not only a failure, but a refusal, to do God's will. Only when understood thus can the serious consequences of sin be properly appreciated.

11 Atonement One of the many criticisms made of RSV is that it has robbed us of the great word *atonement*. Several facts should be noted in relation to that objection.

The first is that in the OT the term *atonement* occurs 87 times in the RSV as against 74 times in the KJV. There it is the translation of the Hebrew noun meaning a "covering" or of the verb meaning "to cover." It is a ceremonial, sacrificial term.

The second fact is that *atonement* occurs only once in the NT in the KJV. It is definitely an OT concept.

Third, the Greek word *katallagē*, here translated "atonement" in the RSV, is rendered "reconciling" in 11:5 and "reconciliation" in 2 Cor. 5:18, 19. These are the only other occurrences of the word in the NT. It is clear that the RSV translators felt that the best meaning of the Greek word was "reconciliation."

Fourth, the verb *katallassō*, from which comes the noun *katallagē*, occurs 6 times in the NT and is always translated "reconcile" in the RSV. These occurrences are all in Paul's doctrinal Epistles (Rom. 5:10 [twice]; 1 Cor. 7:11; 2 Cor. 5:18, 19, 20). The passage in 1 Corinthians uses it of a wife being reconciled to her husband. It should be obvious that reconciliation is the correct meaning of these terms.

The lexicons all agree with this. Thayer notes that the earliest use of *katallagē* was for "the business of moneychangers, exchanging equivalent values." Then it came to mean "adjustment of a difference, reconciliation, restoration to favor," and "in the NT, of the restoration of the favor to sinners that repent and put their trust in the expiatory death of Christ" (p. 333).

Cremer writes of Rom. 5:11 that the language here "is decidedly opposed to the supposition that either a change of feeling on the part of man, brought about by the divine redemption, is referred to, or an alteration in his relation to God to be accomplished by man himself." Rather, "it is God who forms the relation between Himself and humanity anew" (pp. 91–92).

Arndt and Gingrich note that this reconciliation, "according to Paul, is brought about by God alone; he 'reconciles men to himself' " (p. 415). Vine declares that the word signifies not "atonement" but "reconciliation" (1:86).

Sanday and Headlam deal at length with the question as to whether "reconciliation" signifies a change in the attitude of man to God or in that of God to man. They object to the view that would make it only the former. They emphasize the fact that the expression "we have now received the reconciliation" implies "that the reconciliation comes to man from the side of God and is not directly due to any act of his own." They conclude: "We infer that the natural explanation of the passages which speak of enmity and reconciliation between God and man is that they are not on one side only, but are mutual" (p. 130).

F. J. Taylor agrees with this emphasis on reconciliation as a divine work. He says: "To reconcile is the distinctive activity of God himself and the world of men is the object of reconciliation" (TWBB, p. 185). In connection with the passage in Romans he comments: "The paradox which Paul is proclaiming is that, although God looks upon men as enemies, yet he reconciles them to himself and has done this by the one decisive act of the cross of Christ" (*ibid.*).

The paradox is due to the fact that, while man is provisionally and potentially reconciled to God, he remains an enemy of God until he accepts the reconciliation which is offered. The act of reconciliation is divine, but the acceptance is human. We have not actually "received the reconciliation" until we take God's offer of pardon. All men have received the offer; only a few have appropriated it by faith.

This truth is well stated by James Denney. He writes: "*Katallagē* is not a change in our disposition toward God, but a change in His attitude toward us. We do not give it . . . we receive it, by believing in Christ Jesus" (EGT, 2:626).

Because acceptance of the divinely provided reconciliation is necessary for its actual reception, there is involved a change on man's part. Barmby emphasizes the truth, but notes that here the main emphasis is on "an accomplished reconciliation available for all mankind" (pp. 124–25).

The KJV translation, "atonement," is due to the fact that at that time the term was equivalent to "reconciliation." The *Oxford English Dictionary* says that *atone* originally was "short for the phrase 'set or make at one' " and that the noun was formed by a combination of the phrase "at onement," the latter being a common word in the 16th century. Numerous examples are given of the use of *atone* and *atonement* in the sense of "reconcile" and "reconciliation" (1:539).

In Lange's *Commentary* the American editor, Philip Schaff, has a good note on the meaning of *katallagē*. He writes: "The translation atonement, at the close of Romans v. 11, is etymologically correct (at-one-ment = reconciliation), but theologically wrong in the present use of the term = *propitiation*, expiation." He then goes on to say: "The *katallagē*, in the Christian sense, signifies the great change in the relation between God and man, brought about by the voluntary atoning sacrifice of Christ, whereby God's wrath has been removed, His justice satisfied, and man reunited to Him as his loving and reconciled Father" (Lange, p. 166).

12–21 *Sin, Death* The words *sin* (*hamartia*) and *death* (*thanatos*) occur frequently in this passage. The former carries the definite article four times—twice in verse 12 and once each in verses 20 and 21. The latter has the article 5 times—twice in verse 12 and once each in verses 14, 17, and 21. While it is true that in Greek the definite article is often used with abstract nouns—where the English idiom calls for no article—yet the striking use of the article here and in chapter 6 suggests that sin and death are personified. In that case they should be capitalized—Sin and Death. They are pictured in verse 12 as two monsters entering the world, first Sin and then Death following.

12 *Entered into, Passed upon* In this verse there are two verbs compounded on the same root. *Eisēlthen* is translated "entered"; *diēlthen,* "passed." Literally the latter means "came through" (*dia*). The first part of the verse refers to the initial entrance of sin into the world, because of Adam's disobedience. The second part asserts the consequence: "Death came through into all men." That is, it "made its way to each individual member of the race" (SH, p. 133). The universality of death rests upon the universality of sin—"for that [better, 'because'] all have sinned." The RSV expresses the thought very accurately: "And so death spread to all men because all men sinned" (aorist tense).

13 *Imputed* This verse states that "sin is not imputed when there is no law." The Greek verb is *ellogeō.* The only other place where it occurs in the NT is Philemon 18. There Paul says: "If he hath wronged thee, or oweth thee ought, put that on mine account"; that is, "charge it to me." The word is a bookkeeping term. It suggests making an entry in a ledger to one's account. Moulton and Milligan cite examples of this usage in the papyri. "Counted" (RSV) is perhaps the best translation here.

14 *Adam's Transgression* "Transgression" is *parabasis.* It comes from *parabainō,* which literally means "go beside." That is its meaning in Homer, but later writers used it in the sense of "go past." It then came to have the metaphorical meaning "overstep" or "violate."

The noun had a similar history. In Aristotle it means "a going aside." Later writers used it in the sense of "an overstepping," and so metaphorically "transgression." It means the overpassing of a line. Adam was guilty of stepping over the line when he ate of the forbidden fruit. The ones who lived between him and the giving of the law through Moses "had not sinned" in the same way, since they had no direct divine command to disobey.

The noun *parabasis* occurs here for the third and last time in Romans (cf. 2:23; 4:15). In 2:23 it is translated "breaking" in the KJV and the RSV, but elsewhere "transgression." The ASV uniformly renders it "transgression" (7 times).

Figure The word *figure* is *typos* (type). It comes from *typtō,* which means "strike" or "smite." So it literally means "the mark of a blow." It was used for an impress or impression made by a die. Hence it came to signify "figure" or "image," as in Acts 7:43. But in the doctrinal sense, as here, it means "type." Arndt and

Gingrich say it is used of "the *types* given by God as an indication of the future, in the form of persons or things" (p. 838). Sanday and Headlam define it thus: "An event or person in history corresponding in certain characteristic features to another event or person" (p. 136). That is what is meant when one speaks of "types" in the OT.

Here it is stated that Adam was a "type" of Christ—"him that was to come." Obviously Adam was not in his transgression a type of Christ. It is rather that his disobedience affected the whole human race, and that Christ's obedience did likewise (cf. v. 19). They each functioned as a federal head of humanity.

15 Offence The Greek word is *paraptōma*. Previous to this in Romans it occurs only in 4:25. There and 6 times here in 6 verses (5:15–20) it is translated "offence" in the KJV. But though the word occurs in 16 other places in the NT, a different translation is used in all of them. In Matthew (4 times) and Mark (twice) it is rendered "trespass," as also 3 times in Paul's Epistles. In Rom. 11:11, 12 it is translated "fall"; in Jas. 5:16 and Gal. 6:1, "fault"; and the other 3 times, "sins." The inconsistency of the translators is shown by the fact that in Eph. 2:1 in the phrase "dead in trespasses and sins" the word is rendered "trespasses," but in the 5th verse "sins" in the expression "dead in sins." The RSV translates it "trespass" in every instance in the NT.

The noun is from the verb *parapiptō*, which means "fall beside." Hence it suggests "a false step." It came to have the ethical connotation of "a lapse or deviation from truth and uprightness; a sin, misdeed" (Thayer). Arndt and Gingrich prefer "transgression" and note that it is used as a rule "of sins against God" (p. 627). Moulton and Milligan note that in the papyri it seems to mean a "slip" or "lapse" (VGT, p. 489).

Cremer states the word occurs "only in later Greek, and but seldom there," and that it normally means "fault" or "mistake." He holds, as Moulton and Milligan also imply, that this "lax sense" is not the one which the word carries in the NT. He continues: "*Paraptōma* does not in Scripture, as in profane Greek, imply palliation or excuse; it denotes sin as a missing and violation of right" (p. 498).

Paraptōma is one of nine Greek nouns for sin listed by Trench in his *Synonyms of the New Testament*. He calls them "a mournfully numerous group of words" (p. 239). He notes that in Polybius the term is used for "an error, a mistake in judgment, a blunder," and thinks this is its meaning in Gal. 6:1 (p. 246). But he agrees with

the other authorities cited that in other passages it carries a much stronger meaning.

It seems clear that *offense* in its present sense does not accurately express the correct idea. The Greek word means a "falling beside" or deviation from the path, whether due to carelessness or willfulness. *Trespass* appears to be the nearest equivalent in modern English.

15–16 Free Gift, Gift Here the RSV is apparently in error. Three different Greek words in verses 15 and 16 are indiscriminately rendered "free gift." The KJV and the ASV—rather more wisely, it seems—translate one (both times) as "free gift" and the other two as "gift."

The first word is *charisma*, found near the beginning of verse 15 and the end of verse 16. Only here is it translated "free gift" in the KJV. In its 15 other occurrences it is rendered simply "gift." It comes from *charizomai*, which means "give freely." Abbott-Smith defines it thus: "*A gift of grace, a free gift*, especially of extraordinary operations of the Spirit in the Apostolic Church [e.g., 1 Cor. 12:4, 9, 28, 30, 31], but including all spiritual graces and endowments" (pp. 479–80). Thayer says it means "a favor which one receives without any merit of his own" and that in this passage it suggests "the economy of divine grace, by which the pardon of sin and eternal salvation is appointed to sinners in consideration of the merits of Christ laid hold of by faith" (p. 667). Arndt and Gingrich define it as "a gift freely and graciously given." Cremer gives its meaning here as "the effect of God's gracious dealing, the positive blessing bestowed upon sinners through grace" (p. 577).

The significant thing for its use in the NT is that *charisma* includes the word *charis*. The latter occurs some 156 times in the NT and is rendered "grace" 130 of these times. Hence *charisma* suggests a gift of God's free, unmerited favor.

The second word, used in verse 15, is *dōrea*. Aside from its adverbial use in the accusative (9 times) it occurs 11 times and is always rendered "gift" in the KJV. It is from the verb *didōmi*, which means "give." It must be admitted that Vine says *dōrea* "denotes a free gift, stressing its gratuitous character" (1:146–47). But it does seem best to make a distinction in translation between this and *charisma*. It would appear that Paul intended some difference when he chose to use differing terms.

The third word, *dōrēma*, is found only here and in Jas. 1:17. It is from *dorein*, "to present, bestow," and so means a "gift" or "boon." Sanday and Headlam, however, suggest the latter rendering for *dōrea*, which "is reserved for the highest and best gifts" (p. 140).

Probably the best treatment of these three words in this passage is that found in the KJV and the ASV, translating *charisma* as "free gift" and the other two as "gift." This at least suggests that there is a distinctive feature in the first not found in the others, which in fact is the case.

19 Made The verb *kathistēmi* occurs twice here, once in the aorist passive and then in the future passive. It is rendered "made" in the standard English versions. It means literally "to set down," and so "to set in order, appoint, make, constitute" (A-S). Vincent says that "appoint to office or position" is "its most frequent use in the NT" (3:64). Thayer thinks that here it means "constitute" in the sense of "declare, show to be" (p. 314). But Arndt and Gingrich would give it the full force of "make, cause (someone to become something)."

Sanday and Headlam translate the verb "were constituted . . . shall be constituted," but add: "The Greek word has the same ambiguity as the English." They hold that men were constituted sinners "prior to and independently of their own deliberate act of sin" (p. 142). But Denney says, more correctly, that this did not take place "immediately and unconditionally," but "mediately through their own sin" (EGT, 2:630). Yet there is truth in Meyer's statement: "*Thus through the disobedience of the one man,* because all had part in it, *has the position of all become that of sinners*" (p. 217). Because Adam was the federal head of the human race, there is a sense in which all mankind was involved in his disobedience and fall.

Although *constitute* more specifically expresses the meaning of *kathistēmi*, probably *made* conveys correctly the meaning here. It means "put in the category of."

20 Abound The last part of this verse reads: "But where sin abounded, grace did much more abound." However, two very different words are rendered "abound." The first, *pleonazō*, is defined by Abbott-Smith as "to abound, superabound." The second, *hyperperisseuō* (elsewhere in the NT only in 2 Cor. 7:4) he translates "to abound more exceedingly."

But in this passage Thayer suggests, for the former word, "to increase." Arndt and Gingrich agree. The RSV has: "But where sin increased, grace abounded all the more." That would seem to be the best translation, so as to avoid

the impression that the two words *abound* are the same in the Greek.

6:1 Continue It is apparent that in this section Paul is answering the supposed arguments of opponents. In 5:20 he had declared: "Where sin increased, grace abounded all the more" (RSV). It seemed logical then to assume that the more one sinned, the more opportunity there was given for the display of God's grace. But Paul's emphatic reaction was *mē genoito:* "Not at all!" (Williams); "By no means" (RSV). He repudiated utterly any such suggestion.

"Shall we continue?" is *epimenōmen*. It is the deliberative subjunctive, and so may well be rendered, "Are we to continue?" (Williams, Spencer, Goodspeed, RSV).

The verb *epimenō* literally means "remain on" (Moffatt). Metaphorically it means "persevere" or "persist." Vincent prefers the latter here.

2 Dead The Greek is *hoitines apethanomen*, which means "we who died" (RSV). It is the aorist tense, which emphasizes the crisis experience rather than the resultant state. Monsignor Knox gives a striking translation of this sentence: "We have died, once for all, to sin; can we breathe its air again?" James Denney says: "To have died to sin is to be utterly and for ever out of any relation to it" (EGT, 2:632).

3 Into What does it mean to be baptized "into Jesus Christ"? The preposition *eis* usually means "into." But this rendering does not fit some passages, as for instance Luke 8:48, "go in [*eis*] peace." Dana and Mantey say of *eis*: "It was derived from *en* (in) and gradually took over its functions, so much so that in Modern Greek *en* does not occur" (p. 103).

A. T. Robertson writes: "The translation 'into' makes Paul say that the union with Christ was brought to pass by means of baptism, which is not his idea, for Paul was not a sacramentarian" (4:361). It must be admitted, however, that most commentators give the sacramentarian interpretation to this passage. Many state flatly the doctrine of baptismal regeneration. But it does not take any extended observation to discover that many baptized individuals give no evidence whatever of being united with Christ. To say that the rite of water baptism actually gives spiritual life is to affirm a belief in magic, not religion. We cannot agree with the statement of Sanday and Headlam, "It is Baptism which makes a man a Christian" (p. 156). Francis Xavier baptized thousands of pagans, crying: "I make Christians." But the task is not as simple as that.

4 Newness of Life Christ's resurrection should be paralleled in the fact that we "walk in newness of life." The Christian life is the resurrected life. The verb *peripateō* literally means "go about, walk around." But in a number of Greek authors, such as Epictetus, it came to be used in the figurative sense of the walk of life. Arndt and Gingrich add: "In the NT this use of the word is decidedly Pauline" (p. 655). They further indicate that it means "live, conduct oneself." Vincent says it implies "habitual conduct" (3:67).

The noun *kainotēs*, "newness," is found only here and in Rom. 7:6. On the phrase here Vincent comments: "A stronger expression than *new life*. It gives more prominence to the main idea, *newness*, than would be given by the adjective" (2:67). The use of a noun for an adjective is a Hebraistic construction. Meyer also agrees that the phrase is "a stronger way of bringing out the idea of *kainotēs*" (p. 232). Denney adds his support when he says: "The construction makes the new quality of the life prominent" (EGT, 2:633).

Lightfoot gives a different slant. He would make "of life" a genitive of apposition and translate the phrase "in a new state, which is life" (p. 296). But probably Godet is more nearly correct when he writes of Paul's words: "By this turn of expression he gives less prominence to the idea of life (in contrast to that of *death*) than to the new nature of the second life in contrast to the nature of that which it excludes" (p. 241).

Many translators have tried to bring out the full force of this strong expression. Moffatt renders it: "live and move in the new sphere of Life." Monsignor Knox has a close echo: "live and move in a new kind of existence." Phillips reads: "rise to life on a new plane altogether." Williams also ties together the two clauses by translating the latter: "we shall share a resurrection life like His." Goodspeed renders the last phrase simply, "live a new life." The Berkeley Version has: "conduct ourselves in a new way of living." Weymouth expresses it well: "live an entirely new life."

Lightfoot calls attention to the basic meaning of "newness." He says: "The idea uppermost in *kainotēs* is 'strangeness,' and therefore a change" (p. 296). Trench points out the fact that *kainos* means new in *quality*, in distinction from *neos*, which means new in *time*. So the phrase here suggests a new quality of life rather than just a newly begun life.

5 Planted If we have been "planted together" in the likeness of Christ's death, we shall also be in the likeness of His resurrection. Death is not the end. It is only the prelude to a new life.

The Greek for "planted together" is the adjective *symphytos*, found only here in the NT. It comes from *symphyō*, which signifies "to make to grow together." So it means "grown along with, united with" (A-S). This definition is supported by Moulton and Milligan. Sanday and Headlam say of this adjective: "The word exactly expresses the process by which a graft becomes united with the life of a tree. So the Christian becomes 'grafted into' Christ" (p. 157). Meyer observes: "This figurative expression represents the most intimate union of being" (p. 233). He interprets the first clause of this verse as referring to "that moral death to sin . . . in which the spiritual communion in death with Christ consists" (*ibid.*). Godet would translate *symphytoi* as "one and the same plant with Him" (p. 243).

It should be obvious that the Christian life is entirely dependent on union with Christ. When by faith we become united with Him in His death, we become dead to sin. This is to be followed by the living of the resurrected life—a new life in Christ Jesus. That is the heart of the Christian message. There is no Christianity without Christ, in doctrine or experience.

6 Old Man The Greek reads literally as follows: "Knowing this, that our old man was crucified with Him, in order that the body of sin might be destroyed, with the result that no longer we should be serving Sin [the sin]."

The first problem that confronts us is the meaning of "our old man." The word *man* is *anthrōpos*, which means a human being. It is the generic term referring to a person without distinction between male and female. The Greek has another word for "man," *anēr*, which means "man" as distinct from "woman." It may also be translated "husband," a combination usage which is common to many languages, though not proper in English.

The word for "old" is *palaios*. Again, there are two terms in Greek for "old." The other, *archaios*, has been taken over in the English word *archaic*. Etymologically the latter signifies that which has been from the beginning (*archē*), while the former suggests what has existed for a long time. In usage they are somewhat synonymous. But Trench notes that *archaios* "will often designate the ancient as also the venerable, as that to which the honour due to antiquity belongs" (p. 251).

On the other hand, *palaios* suggests "old in the sense of more or less worn out" (*ibid.*, p. 252). It means "old because it has been superseded by that which is new" (Vine, 3:135). Cremer writes: "*Palaios* is that which already has long been *aged, old, ancient,* whether it still is or is no more" (p. 117). In the papyri it is used for "old coinage," now superseded, or, in one instance, "where dates which had been gathered for some time are contrasted with new, freshly gathered ones" (VGT, p. 475). Arndt and Gingrich observe that *palaios* means "old = in existence for a long time, often with the connotation of being antiquated or outworn" (p. 610). That states the case very accurately.

The NT usage supports this definition. In the Synoptic Gospels it is used for "old garment" (Matt. 9:16; Mark 2:21; Luke 5:36) and "old wineskins" (Matt. 9:17; Mark 2:22; Luke 5:37). It designates "old wine" (Luke 5:39) and "old leaven" (1 Cor. 5:7–8). Once it is used significantly for "the old testament" (2 Cor. 3:14); or better, "the old covenant."

In two passages in the NT it is clearly used in a sense which is not at all derogatory. Reference is made to "treasures new and old" (Matt. 13:52) and to the "old commandment" of love (1 John 2:7).

Completing the use of *palaios* in the NT, it may be noted that the phrase "old man" occurs in three places (Rom. 6:6; Eph. 4:22; Col. 3:9). It is distinctly a Pauline expression.

Cremer says this phrase means "human nature as it is in contrast with this renewal, as the individual is naturally" (p. 105). Arndt and Gingrich say it is the "earlier, unregenerate man." Westcott defines it as "the whole character representing the former self" and adds this pertinent observation: "There is much in the general temper of the world—self-assertion, self-seeking—which answers to 'the old man' " (*Ephesians*, p. 68). Vincent labels it "the old, unrenewed self." Sanday and Headlam say simply, "our old self." Denney agrees. It is the old, self-assertive self, which wants to have its own way rather than letting God have His way. Meyer calls it "our old ego." Lange says: "The old man is the whole sinfulness of man." It is what is commonly referred to as carnality or the carnal nature.

Perhaps the best definition of "the old man" is that given by Godet. He writes: "The expression: *our old man,* denotes human nature such as it has been made by the sin of him in whom it was wholly concentrated, fallen Adam reappearing in every human *ego* that comes into the world under the sway of the preponderance of self-love, which was determined by the primitive transgression. This corrupted nature bears the name of *old* only from the viewpoint of the believer who already possesses a renewed nature" (p. 244).

Paul asserts that this old man "was crucified with" (*synestaurōthe*). Apparently "Him" or "Christ" must be added to complete the sense.

Some have claimed this simply means that all the elect were crucified with Christ at Calvary. But the idea that we were crucified with Christ 1,900 years ago does not help us unless there is an actual death of the selfish ego here and now. Calvary's provisions must be realized in personal Christian experience. What was potential and provisional at Calvary needs to be actualized in each believer's heart through faith in Jesus Christ. When one surrenders himself fully to be united with his Lord in obedience to His will, he is crucified with Christ.

Most commentators say Paul taught that this crucifixion of the old man takes place at one's baptism. But A. T. Robertson affirms: "This took place not at baptism, but only pictured there. It took place when 'we died to sin' (verse 1)" (4:362).

The Body of Sin
Vincent echoes a very widely held view when he writes: "The phrase *body of sin* denotes the body belonging to, or ruled by the power of sin" (3:69). Wuest says: "The reference is therefore to the believer's physical body before salvation, possessed by or dominated and controlled by the sinful nature" (p. 101). Denney declares: "*To sōma tēs hamartias* is the body in which we live" (EGT, 2:633).

But Meyer recognizes the incompatibility of this interpretation with the statement that the body of sin is "destroyed." He says: "Consequently not the body *in itself,* but *in so far* as it is the sin-body" (p. 235). Sanday and Headlam write in a similar vein: "It is not the body, *simply as such,* which is to be killed, but the body *as the seat of sin*" (p. 158). But what does that mean? The language is rather nebulous.

Lange takes cognizance of the same problem. With the help of his American editor, Philip Schaff (in brackets), he comments: "It is self-evident, from Paul and the whole Bible, that there is not the slightest reference here to a [literal] destruction of the body [i.e., of his physical organism which is only dissolved in physical death, and which, instead of being annihilated, is to be sanctified. . . . —P. S.]" (p. 203).

How much simpler—and, it seems to us, more sensible—it is to take "the body of sin" as meaning the sinful nature, or carnality! The real difficulty is that most theologians will not allow that this is destroyed. For instance, Wuest says of the believer: "He has been *permanently* delivered from its power, when at the same time that nature is left in him *permanently*" (p. 99).

Destroyed Commentators are quick to point out that *katargeō* means "render idle, inactive, inoperative, to cause to cease." Sanday and Headlam define it as "paralyzed, reduced to a condition of absolute impotence and inaction, as if it were dead" (p. 158).

The word (cf. 3:3) occurs 27 times in the NT and is translated some 18 different ways in KJV. But the most common rendering (5 times) is "destroy." Here Arndt and Gingrich would translate it "done away with."

The KJV has "destroyed." The ASV (1901) changed it to "done away." But the RSV returned to "destroyed." Godet says, "The translation *destroyed* probably renders the thought best."

7 Freed This verse reads literally: "For the one who died has been justified from Sin [the sin]." The meaning commonly given to *dikaioō* is "declare righteous" or "make righteous" (cf. 3:20). But does that fit here?

The verb occurs 40 times in the NT. In the KJV it is rendered "to justify" 37 times, and once each "to free," "to be righteous," "justifier." Here it has "is freed." The ASV has "is justified," with "released" in the margin. The RSV returned to the KJV "is freed."

Here is an instance where it appears that the revisers of 1881 and 1901 were lacking in sanctified imagination. One of the main criticisms of the English and American revised versions is that too often they give a wooden, literal translation instead of representing the thought of the original language in free, idiomatic English. It was said of them when they first came out that they were "strong in Greek, but weak in English." That is a correct characterization. Hence they were good versions for the study, but poor ones for the pulpit.

But to get back to *dikaioō*. Arndt and Gingrich trace the history of this word. At first, as in Polybius, it meant "show justice, do justice." In the LXX it signifies "justify, vindicate, treat as just." But "Paul, who has influenced later writers, uses the word almost exclusively of God's judgment." In his Epistles it means "be acquitted, be pronounced and treated as righteous . . . be justified" (p. 196).

But Arndt and Gingrich go on to point out a very significant further use of the word. In the

LXX of Psalm 72 (Eng., 73):13 it means "make free or pure," and twice in noncanonical books it is used in the passive with the sense "be set free, made pure." It seems to have this same connotation in Acts 13:39—"from which you could not be justified [freed] by the law of Moses." That is evidently its meaning here in this passage.

There is still another use which suggests that in 1 Cor. 6:11 it should be rendered "you have become pure." For, "In the language of the mystery religions . . . *dikaiousthai* refers to a radical inner change which the initiate experiences" (*ibid.*, p. 197).

Wuest notes that the verb is used here in a different sense from that found in 3:21—5:11, because in the earlier passage Paul is dealing with the doctrine of justification, while in chapter 6 he is treating the doctrine of sanctification. Wuest then continues with this comment: "The one, Paul says, who died off once for all from the sinful nature, has been set free completely from it, with the present result that he is in a state of permanent freedom from it . . . *and it is his responsibility to maintain that freedom from it moment by moment*" (p. 103).

In explanation of the thought of this verse Sanday and Headlam write: "The idea is that of a master claiming legal possession of a slave: proof being put in that the slave is dead, the verdict must needs be that the claims of law are satisfied and that he is no longer answerable; Sin loses its suit" (p. 159).

What is the dying mentioned in Rom. 6:7? Meyer insists that the reference is to physical death. He claims that the thought of ethical death—though held by Erasmus, Bengel, and others—is foreign to this passage; it does not appear until the eighth verse. Denney, however, points out the unreasonableness of this view in the light of the context. He says: "But it [dying with Christ] is no new idea; it is the idea of the whole passage; and unless we bring it in here, the quittance *from sin* . . . remains inexplicable" (EGT, 2:633).

Typical of the emphasis on physical death is this comment from Weiss: "Only when the soul is in death separated from the body in which sin has attained the dominion, has it been, as it were, given to itself again, and has it returned to its normal state released from sin" (3:51). It is easy to see how this idea that sin is resident in the physical body could lead to the extremes of ascetic practice which appeared in the ancient and medieval church. The whole notion is pagan, not Christian. It is the basis of the fanatical asceticism common in Oriental countries to this day. The teaching that one cannot be freed

from sin until he is released from this physical
body is surely a hopeless theology! Those who
hold such wrong ideas about the human body
should read Paul's words to the Corinthian
Christians, "Know ye not that your body is the
temple of the Holy Ghost?" (1 Cor. 6:19). That
is the Christian conception.

11 Reckon The eleventh verse is the sequel
to the sixth. Our death to sin which was provisional and potential at Calvary we are to make
experiential and actual now. Only as by faith
we "reckon" ourselves to be dead to sin can we
realize in our hearts that which Christ's death
has made possible.

The word *logizomai* occurs 11 times in chapter 4. There it is translated 3 different ways:
"count" twice, "reckon" 3 times, and "impute" 6
times. Its most frequent rendering in the KJV
is "think" (9 out of a total of 41 times). Twice it
is translated "suppose." Does this passage
mean that we are to "think" or "suppose" ourselves dead to sin?

As already noted (on 4:3) the modern American colloquialism "I reckon" means "I guess" or
"I suppose." But Paul believed in a "know so"
Christian experience, not in a "guess so" or
"hope so" one. With him, "reckon" meant something far different.

Arndt and Gingrich note that the original
meaning of *logizomai* was "reckon, calculate."
They divide this into two categories. The first is
"count, take into account." In this connection
logizomai is sometimes a technical commercial
term, meaning "credit." The second idea is that
as a result of calculation it may signify "evalu-
ate, estimate, look upon as, consider." This last
word is the rendering they prefer for Rom.
6:11. It is also the one adopted in the RSV and
Berkeley (as also by Moffatt and Williams).

But we feel that it is not strong enough. By
faith we are to "account" ourselves as being actually dead to sin. We must believe that it is so
and then live day by day in the light of that
truth.

Through The KJV ends this verse with the
phrase "through Jesus Christ our Lord." But
the Greek reads *en Christō Iesou*." This is rendered correctly "in Christ Jesus" in all translations today. It is only as we are "in Christ Jesus" that we can be alive to God. It is not simply "through" His death on the Cross. Far more
significantly it is by actually being "in Christ,"
united to Him by faith, that we become and
continue "alive unto God."

Sanday and Headlam note the significance
of the phrase "in Christ." They write: "This

phrase is the summary expression of the doctrine which underlies the whole of this section
and forms ... one of the main pillars of St.
Paul's theology" (p. 160).

One more observation might well be made.
It is only as we keep "alive unto God" that we
can and will remain "dead indeed unto sin."
Life can never be a vacuum. If it is not filled
with God and good, it will inevitably be in-
vaded by sin.

16–17 Servants Three times in verses 16
and 17 the word *doulos* occurs. Found 125
times in the NT, it is rendered "servant" 118
times in the KJV. Six times it is translated
"bond" and once "bondman."

Only once in the NT of this version do we
find the term *slave*. There (Rev. 18:13) it is the
rendering of *sōma*, which means "body." In all
the other 145 instances *sōma* is translated
"body" in the KJV. The ASV does the same
thing. In the RSV the term "slave" occurs 32
times. Why the difference?

Most lexicons agree in giving "slave" as the
first meaning of *doulos*. Properly an adjective
meaning "enslaved," it is used mostly as a substantive in the NT. Abbott-Smith treats it under the adjective. But Moulton and Geden's concordance lists it separately, as does also the
lexicon by Arndt and Gingrich.

The proper goal of all Bible translations
should be to present the Word of God in terms
that convey correctly to the reader the true
meaning of the original. These terms should be
used in the sense with which the reader is familiar.

Judged by this standard it seems that *slave*
is the more accurate rendering for *doulos*. Today *servant* normally signifies one who works
for wages. But in NT times slavery was exceedingly common; it is said that one-half of the
population of the Roman Empire consisted of
slaves. The *doulos* of the NT, in most instances
at least, was what we would now call a "slave,"
not a "servant."

Arndt and Gingrich make this interesting observation: " 'Servant' for 'slave' is largely confined to Biblical translations and early American times ... in normal usage at the present
time the two words are carefully distinguished" (p. 204).

The first part of this statement is supported
by *The Oxford English Dictionary*. Under "servant" it says: "In all the Bible translations from
Wyclif to the Revised Version of 1880–4, the
word very often represents the Hebrew *ebed* or
the Greek *doulos*, which correspond to *slave*";
and declares: "In the North American colonies

in the 17–18th centuries, and subsequently in the United States, *servant* was the usual designation for a slave" (9:508).

Adolph Deissmann bemoans the fact that "the word *slave* with its satellites has been translated *servant*, to the total effacement of its ancient significance, in our Bibles" (LAE, p. 319). The very prevalent custom of slavery forms an essential background for understanding Paul's language at many places in his Epistles. He is not talking about hired servants who are free to come and go as they wish, but of *slaves*, who are subject to the will of their masters.

Only thus can we understand the phrase "servants of sin" (v. 17). The Greek clearly means "slaves of sin." And that is what men are until freed by Christ.

Trench points out the basic connotation of *doulos* when he writes: "The *doulos* . . . is properly the 'bondman,' from *deō* . . . one that is in a permanent relation of servitude to another, his will altogether swallowed up in the will of the other" (p. 30).

There are half a dozen different words for *servant* in the Greek NT. *Doulos* should here be translated *slave*. That is done by Goodspeed, Knox, Spencer, Williams, and the RSV.

18–22 *Free, Servants* The idea of slavery carries over clearly into the succeeding verses of this section. In verse 20 the expression "slaves of sin" occurs again. "Sin" carries the definite article, which, as noted above, suggests that it is personified as a monster who is master over his slaves.

Verses 18 and 22 speak of "being made free from sin." Deissmann calls attention to the fact that the exact verb and preposition here are used as technical expressions in the legal documents for freeing slaves in the time of Christ (LAE, p. 326, n. 1). So this language was entirely familiar to Paul's Roman readers and much more meaningful than it is to us today. They knew—some of them doubtless by personal experience—exactly what it meant to be freed from actual slavery.

But the apostle presents here an astounding thought. We are freed from the slavery of sin that we may enter a new slavery! We become "slaves to righteousness" (v. 18) or "slaves to God" (v. 22)—evidently parallel ideas. "Righteousness" and "God" are both in the dative case and should be translated with the same preposition.

In these two verses the expression "become servants" is the verb *douloō*. In the active voice it means "enslave." But in the passive, as here,

it means "become a slave to someone" (AG, p. 205). Paul calls upon his readers to be freed from the slavery of sin that they might find the glorious freedom of a higher slavery. They are to be slaves to God.

19–22 *Holiness* Some are jarred by the fact that the revised versions have changed "holiness" in these verses to "sanctification." It might come as a surprise to these to know that the Greek word here, *hagiasmos*, occurs 10 times in the NT, and in the KJV is translated "holiness" 5 times and "sanctification" 5 times. It is the term which is used in the familiar passage, "This is the will of God, even your sanctification" (1 Thess. 4:3).

There are other terms—*hagiotēs*, *hagiōsynē*—which clearly mean "holiness." It would seem wiser to follow the revised versions in translating *hagiasmos* as "sanctification." As a verbal noun it properly describes the work of sanctification, rather than the resultant state.

However, it must be noted that Meyer goes to the opposite extreme. He writes: "The word *hagiasmos* is found only in the Septuagint, Apocrypha and in the NT (in the latter it is always holiness, not sanctification . . .), but not Greek writers" (p. 249). On the other hand, many competent scholars take issue with Meyer.

23 *Wages, Gift* The closing verse of this chapter states graphically the contrasting rewards for serving sin and serving God. Though all men are slaves to sin, until freed by Christ, yet they do receive wages—but what wages! All that sin can offer is eternal death.

In contrast is "the free gift of God," eternal life. And this is only "in Christ Jesus our Lord." Here is the heart of Paul's theology.

The word *opsōnion* originally meant the provisions or pay for soldiers. But in the papyri and inscriptions it is used in the general sense of "wages."

"Gift" in the KJV is changed to "free gift" in the revised versions. In the NT there are several derivatives of the verb *didōmi*, "give," such as *dōma*, *dōrēma*, *dōron*, and *dōrean*. But the word here is *charisma*, from *charis*, "grace." So it means something graciously given.

7:2 *Which Hath a Husband* In this verse the expression "which hath an husband" is all one word in the Greek, *hypandros*, found only here in the NT. Literally it means "under a man." That is the Oriental conception of a married woman.

Be Dead   The KJV says, "if the husband be dead." But the Greek clearly says, "if her husband dies" (RSV). It is the event of death and not the resultant state of being dead that is indicated by *apothanē*.

Loosed   When the woman's husband dies she is "loosed." The revised versions all have "discharged."

The Greek verb is *katargeō*, which is translated "destroyed" in 6:6. In 3:3 it is rendered "make without effect"; in 3:31, "make void"; in 4:14, "made of none effect"; and in verse 6 of this chapter, "delivered." In other words, it is translated 6 different ways in its 6 occurrences in Romans.

For the two places where it is found in this chapter Abbott-Smith suggests "separated, discharged or loosed from." Thayer says: "severed from, separated from, discharged from, loosed from." Arndt and Gingrich prefer "released."

It is a favorite word with Paul. He uses it 25 out of the 27 times it occurs in the NT. The great apostle shows a marked affinity for strong terms, in keeping with his forceful personality.

Any of the translations suggested—separated, discharged, loosed, released—will fit well in this passage, as in verse 6. In both cases the idea is that all authority and power is terminated by a complete severance of the previously existing relationship.

3 Married   In this verse the case is raised of a woman with a living husband being "married" (KJV) to, or "joined" (ASV) to, or "lives with" (RSV), another man.

The lack of uniformity in translation is due to the fact that the Greek literally reads: "if she becomes to another man." This would normally be translated in English as "if she becomes another man's" (Moffatt).

Obviously, the question is whether this definitely indicates marriage, or whether it could also describe an illicit relationship. The latter idea can be included in "joined" or "lives with." Knox translates it, "if she gives herself to another man." Spencer gives a very weak rendering, "goes with." Weymouth has "unites herself to." It should perhaps be noted that both Weymouth and the RSV have "marries" at the end of the verse, though the same expression is used in the original.

While the Greek does not unequivocally indicate marriage, it seems that the context suggests it. Goodspeed, Verkuyl, and Williams

translate it so. In verse 4 it clearly carries this sense.

Called   The word *called* presents an interesting study. *Chrēmatizō* originally meant "to transact business," and so "to consult, deliberate." In the papyri it sometimes means "to make answer." In Josephus, the LXX, and the NT its common meaning is "to instruct, admonish."

But it also sometimes meant "to assume a name, be called." That sense is found in the NT only here and in Acts 11:26. However, it is clearly present in Polybius, Strabo, Plutarch, Philo, Josephus, and the papyri. In fact, the verb is used that way in an Oxyrhynchus papyrus of A.D. 58, which is within two years, probably, of the time when Paul wrote Romans.

5 In the Flesh   The word *sarx* occurs 150 times in the NT. With 3 exceptions ("carnal" in Rom. 8:6, 7; Heb. 9:10) it is translated "flesh" in the KJV. And in the first 2 of these 3 places it is more consistently rendered "flesh" in the revised versions. So far so good. But even when we have rendered it uniformly as "flesh"—which probably should be done—we are still faced with the fact that Paul uses the term in two distinct ways. So it will be necessary to look at the history of the word.

Vincent notes that in classical Greek *sarx* occurs only in the physical sense. He adds: "Paul's use of this and other psychological terms must be determined largely by the OT usage as it appears in the Septuagint" (3:74).

Paul uses *flesh* to indicate what we commonly call "blood relationship" (e.g., Rom. 1:3; 9:3–8). He also employs it for the physical body (e.g., Rom. 2:28). It is not entirely synonymous with *sōma*, "body." The latter is used for the church (e.g., Eph. 1:23), but not *sarx*—for obvious reasons. In a comprehensive sense *flesh* means "humanity" (e.g., Rom. 3:20; literally, "all flesh").

But there is still another very significant use. In some passages, says Vincent, "*the flesh* would seem to be interchangeable with *the old man*" (3:76).

Rom. 5:7 is apparently the earliest occurrence in the NT of this use of *flesh* for the old self or the carnal mind. It is obvious that Paul does not mean the physical body; for while still in that body he writes, "when we were in the flesh." Clearly he refers to the time when he was under the control of the carnal nature. This implies that he was no longer in such a state.

Just how many times the term *sarx* is used

in a spiritual, rather than a physical, sense it is difficult to determine. A check of the 150 passages would seem to indicate that it is used of the carnal nature perhaps some 27 times. Most of these are in Paul's Epistles, though this usage is clear in 1 Peter (e.g., 4:2) and probably occurs in 2 Peter and 1 John.

Eight of the occurrences of *sarx* in a spiritual sense are found in the eighth chapter of Romans. So further discussion will be postponed until then.

Motions This verse speaks of the "motions" of sin. The Greek word is *pathēmata*. It is used of Christ's sufferings (1 Pet. 1:11). But it also occurs here and in Gal. 5:24 in the sense of "passions." That is correctly the translation in the revised versions, as well as in Goodspeed, Berkeley, Weymouth, and Williams—to name only a few.

The odd rendering "motions" in the KJV is doubtless due to the fact that in earlier English *motion* was sometimes used in the sense of "emotion." But that meaning is now obsolete.

6 Delivered "Delivered" is the same word (*katargeō*) as "loosed" in verse 2. The revised versions render it "discharged" in both places. "Delivered" is the translation here in Tyndale, Cranmer, and the Geneva Bible. Either word conveys the meaning well.

Letter The term *letter* is *gramma* (cf. grammar). By it Paul probably means, not a literal interpretation of the Scriptures, as is often held, but rather the law of Moses. He is contrasting the new dispensation of the Spirit with the old dispensation of the Law. That is the main key to the understanding of chapters 7 and 8.

7–25 I, Me, My In this unique section Paul changes from the second and third persons to the first. He does not even use the editorial "we." Very directly he uses "I," "me," and "my." He is describing his own spiritual experience at some stage of his life. Five times in this brief section the emphatic pronoun "I" (*ego*) occurs. Eleven times we find "me" (*me, moi, emoi*). Four times he says "my" (*mou*). In these verses Paul is reliving vividly a crucial period in his life.

7 Lust The apostle says that through the law he became aware of the presence of "lust," or "coveting" (ASV). The word *epithymia* is translated "lust" in the KJV in 31 of its 38 occurrences. Of itself the term simply means "desire,

longing." In secular Greek it was predominantly a neutral term, "desire." It is used in a good sense in Josephus and in a few passages in NT (e.g., Luke 22:15; Phil. 1:23; 1 Thess. 2:17—the only places where it is translated "desire" in the KJV). It is interesting to note that the corresponding verb *epithymeō* is rendered "desire" 8 of its 16 times. The other renderings are "lust" (4 times), "covet" (3 times), and "fain" (once).

But in the NT the bad sense of *epithymia*, "lust," is dominant. This usage goes back as far as Plato. It is found commonly in the Apocrypha and Philo. The latter includes it in a list of vices, as is done in 1 Pet. 4:3.

The word was used frequently by the Stoics, and regularly in a derogatory sense. But it must be remembered that these philosophers condemned all emotional display, such as desire, pleasure, grief, or fear. So it is not evident that for them it meant immoral lust. They leaned toward the ideal of strict Buddhism that human salvation lies only through the negation of all desire. The perfect man is the one who desires nothing. But that is very far removed from the Christian ideal. A burning desire for God and for holiness is the basis of the highest character.

Burton Scott Easton has a significant comment that throws light on the use of the term here. He says: "A special abbreviation peculiar to Jewish Greek was created by the use of *epithymeō* in Exod. 20:17 to render 'covet' in the Tenth Commandment; this desire for one's neighbor's possession being of course sinful (Rom. 7:7, 8; 13:9; Acts 20:33)" (p. 187). He notes that both the verb and the noun are of themselves morally neutral, and that in the NT the evil character of desire is usually indicated by a modifying word or phrase.

As Scott has pointed out, the use of *epithymeō* in the tenth commandment for "covet" is due to the LXX. But Sanday and Headlam feel the verb carries the idea of "lust." They write: "The Greek word has a wider sense than our 'covet'; it includes every kind of illicit desire" (p. 179).

Denney thinks that Paul quoted the tenth commandment here because "its generality made it the most appropriate to quote" (EGT, 2:639). It may be that it was intended as a sort of summary conclusion of all the commandments. Wrong desire is the root of all sin.

Paul introduces this section with the question, "Is the law sin?" His answer is: "No, the law is not sin; it is that which makes me conscious of sin." The danger of drawing a wrong deduction—which the apostle is warning against in this verse—is well pointed out in this observation by A. T. Robertson: "Some people today oppose all inhibitions and prohibitions because they stimulate violations. That is half-baked thinking" (4:367). One is reminded of the common accusation that prohibition was responsible for the rise of racketeering. But nothing is said of the daily crop of crimes and deaths due to drinking.

The word *epithymia* is translated "concupiscence" in verse 8. This is a typical example of a Latinism due to the influence of the Vulgate. The term was familiar to medieval theologians, who used Latin almost entirely, but it is not meaningful to the modern English reader. The translators of KJV apparently yielded to ecclesiastical pressure and adopted the Latinisms of the Bishops' Bible—of which the KJV was a revision—instead of following the strong Protestant terminology of the Geneva Bible. The ASV uses "coveting" here, as in verse 7, thus preserving the etymological connection with the verb "covet." The RSV does much the same.

8 Occasion   Paul states that the commandment became the occasion—but not cause—of sin. The word *aphormē* first meant the starting point or base of operations for an expedition, especially a military campaign. That led to the more general meaning of resources necessary to carry through an undertaking. Moulton and Milligan write: "This Pauline word is well established in the vernacular with meanings varying from 'incitement' or 'prompting' to the more ordinary 'occasion' or 'opportunity'" (VGT, pp. 98–99). Arndt and Gingrich note that the term is used commonly in Koine Greek for "occasion, pretext, opportunity," and that that is its regular sense in the New Testament and early Christian literature. Possibly "occasion" is the more exact meaning here, as it is in modern Greek, although "opportunity" fits well. The term occurs only in Paul's Epistles (7 times).

9 Revived   Paul writes that "when the commandment came, sin ['the sin'] revived." It has been suggested that this may well be rendered, "Sin sprang into life." It had been lying down, like a sleeping lion. But the command, "Thou shalt not covet," had roused the monster Sin into action. What the apostle means, of course, is that sin is basically disobedience, and there must be a law to disobey before one is conscious of sin. He does not mean that there was no nature of sin within his heart, but rather that the sinful nature had been relatively dormant.

11 Deceived   The apostle declares that Sin took advantage of his consciousness of law to deceive and kill him. The word *deceive* is *exapataō*, which literally means "completely make one lose one's way." The language suggests the picture of Sin luring one off the main highway onto a dark side road and then quickly murdering its victim. That is what sin does with innocent youth.

12–13 Holy, Just, Good   In the seventh verse Paul had asked the question posed by the opposition: "Is the law sin?" Here he gives the answer. He asserts that the law is holy, just, and good. Vincent points out the significance of these three terms as follows: "Holy as God's revelation of Himself; *just* (Rev., *righteous*) in its requirements, which correspond to God's holiness; *good*, salutary, because of its end" (3:79).

So the law was not the cause of spiritual death; it was sin (v. 13). The monster Sin is shown to be "exceeding" (*hyperbolē*) sinful by the very fact that it takes advantage of something good as the occasion for doing its dastardly work.

14–25 Regenerate or Unregenerate?   Dispute as to where the autobiographical section of Romans (7:7–25) fits into Paul's life has been widespread. It is rather generally agreed that the apostle is describing his own experience. But was it his preconversion or postconversion state that is related so vividly? Is this a picture of an unregenerate or a regenerate man?

David Brown feels that the best solution is to divide the passage into two parts, taking verses 7–13 as describing the unregenerate man and verses 14–25 the regenerate man. He writes:

> From v. 7 to the end of v. 13 the apostle speaks entirely in the *past tense;* whereas from v. 14 to the end of the chapter he speaks exclusively in the *present tense.* And as the words of v. 9, "I was alive without the law *at one time*" (*pote*), clearly refer to his unconverted state, so . . . all from v. 14 to the end of the chapter is a description of his converted state (JFB, 4:231).

This view is also defended by Hodge. He too notes the change from the past tense to the present tense. Of course both he and Brown insist that the conflict between the old carnal nature and the new Christ nature continues in the believer throughout life. Hodge holds that the language of verses 15, 16, 19, and 22 cannot be attributed to an unregenerated individual.

In contrast, Adam Clarke maintains that this piece of autobiography cannot be applied to a Christian. He says:

> It is difficult to conceive how the opinion could have crept into the Church, or prevailed there, that "the apostle speaks here of his *regenerate state;* and that what was, in such a state, true of himself, must be true of all others in the same state." This opinion has, most pitifully and most shamefully, not only lowered the standard of Christianity but destroyed its influence and disgraced its character. It requires but little knowledge of the spirit of the Gospel, and of the scope of this epistle, to see that the apostle is, here, either personating a Jew under the law and without the Gospel, or showing what his own state was when he was deeply convinced that by the deeds of the law no man could be justified (2:86).

With Clarke's reasons for taking this position one can well sympathize. But part of the force of his argument is vitiated by this statement which he makes:

> From all this it follows that the epithet *carnal*, which is the characteristic designation of an unregenerate man, cannot be applied to St. Paul *after his conversion;* nor, indeed, to any Christian in that state (*ibid.*).

When he wrote that, he must have forgotten 1 Cor. 3:3—"And I, brethren, could not speak unto you as unto spiritual, but as unto carnal, even as unto babes in Christ." It is evident that, in Paul's thinking, new converts may be carnal.

Most of the Greek fathers, together with Erasmus and other modern scholars, held that the reference here is to the legal Jew, one who tries to fulfill the law but finds no real salvation in it. Augustine at first held this view, but changed it after his dispute with Pelagius. From that time he interpreted the passage as a description of the Christian and his struggles with his sinful nature. This view was adopted by Jerome and also by the Reformers.

H. C. G. Moule held that through verse 11 the passages describe the unregenerate state. But the tone changes after that. The man now "wills not," even "hates," what he practices. He "delights, rejoices, with the law of God." Says Moule: "He who can truly speak thus of an inmost sympathy, a sympathy of delight, with the most holy Law of God, is no half-Christian" (p. 192). But the thing that is missing here is any reference to the Holy Spirit. That comes in chapter 8.

The final word on the interpretation of Rom. 7:7–25 will perhaps never be said. But as far as the *application* of it in preaching is concerned, we feel that Riddle has the best point of view. He writes: "To refer it to a movement possible both before and after conversion, a state with reference to the law, *encourages* unbelievers to go to Christ, and *rouses* believers to go to him" (Lange, p. 246).

14 *Spiritual, Carnal* Paul declares that the law is *pneumatikos*, but he is *sarkinos*. The first adjective comes from *pneuma*, which means "spirit." It is used both of the human spirit and the Holy Spirit. In some passages it is very difficult to decide which of the two is intended, as will be discovered by comparing the English versions.

Brown feels that the law is "spiritual" because it comes from God, who is Spirit and so breathes spirituality in its nature and intent. Perhaps the simplest way is to take "spiritual" here as meaning "divine." The law was God-initiated and God-inspired. It reflects His holy character and reveals it to man.

The second adjective, "carnal," poses somewhat more of a problem. The reading of the late manuscripts, translated in the KJV, is *sarkikos*, which means "fleshly" in contrast to spiritual. It signifies a state of being dominated, or at least strongly influenced, by the flesh (*sarx*). Paul uses *sarx* in two ways: for the physical body, and for the carnal nature; in the previous sentence we mean *flesh* in the second sense.

But the earliest manuscripts have *sarkinos* in Rom. 7:14. Trench notes that adjectives ending in -*inos* generally indicate the stuff of which a thing is made. So *sarkinos* would properly be "fleshy"; that is, made of flesh (p. 272). That creates a problem of interpretation.

In spite of the fact that apparently *sarkinos* must be adopted as the correct reading, it would seem that the meaning here is "carnal" in contrast to "spiritual," referring to character rather than to substance. Brown interprets it as indicating "the sinful principle in the renewed man" (JFB, 4:233).

Meyer emphasizes *sarkinos* as meaning "made of flesh" and uses this as further support of his position that it is Paul under the law, before his conversion, who is here described. He feels that this term is "far stronger" than *sarkikos* (p. 275). Lange favors making *sarkinos* equal *sarkikos*. This would allow it to refer to the believer. It seems difficult to maintain the usual distinction between the two Greek terms, as far as this passage is concerned. In any case, it is clear that *carnal* means under the domination of the flesh, in contrast to *spiritual*, which means under the domination of the Spirit.

The question has often been raised as to why Paul closes this chapter on the melancholy tone of verse 25*b*. But it should be noted that 25*a* is an index finger pointing the way to chapter 8, where the life of glorious victory through the indwelling Holy Spirit is described.

But why then is 25*b* added? Godet gives a helpful explanation when he suggests that 25*b* is a summary of what Paul has been saying in the previous verses. Writes Godet: "He simply sums up in order to conclude" (p. 291). This makes all the more striking the contrast in chapter 8.

8:1 *Therefore*   The most significant single chapter in the NT on the Holy Spirit is the eighth chapter of Romans. While the Holy Spirit is mentioned only once before in the Epistle, He is referred to 19 times in this chapter. Here is portrayed clearly the fact that victorious Christian living comes only from the indwelling power and presence of the Spirit of God.

The Spirit-filled life is possible only "through Jesus Christ our Lord" (7:25). That is the force of the "therefore" in verse 1. The Greek word is not the more usual *oun*, found some 500 times in the NT, and translated in the KJV "therefore" 263 times and "then" 197 times. Rather it is *ara*, found only about 5 times. While *oun* is frequently merely a resumptive connective ("then"), *ara* has a more dominant inferential emphasis; that is, it underscores the conclusion drawn from a previous statement. Paul sometimes uses the two particles together, and when he does *ara* "expresses the inference and *oun* the transition" (AG, p. 103). So *ara* here emphasizes the connection of this verse with 7:25*a*.

Now   There are about a dozen different Greek words which are translated "now" in our English New Testaments. Some of them are merely resumptive, between what precedes and what follows. For instance, *de* is rendered "and" or "but" hundreds of times. But it is also translated "now" some 166 times in the KJV. This is obviously the weakest meaning of *now*, simply introducing or resuming the narrative.

In this passage the word is *nun*. Abbott-Smith says that it is used "properly of time, *now*, i.e. at the present time: as opposed to past . . . [or] future" (p. 306). Occurring some 139 times, it is translated "now" 121 times in the KJV.

Its use here emphasizes the fact that one does not have to wait until he gets to heaven to know that he is saved. Freedom from condemnation is an experience that can be enjoyed in this life. It is the happy lot of all who are "in Christ Jesus."

No Condemnation   The Greek word translated "no" is a strong term, *ouden*. Denney writes: "The *ouden* is emphatic; condemnation is in every sense out of the question" (2:644). Wuest translates it: "There is not even one bit of condemnation" (p. 127).

The word for "condemnation" is also a strong term, *katakrima*. The simple noun *krima* means "judgment," but in the KJV it is translated that way only 13 times, while 7 times it is rendered "damnation" and 5 times "condemnation." The latter 2 might be classified as overtranslations. The noun comes from the verb *krinō*, "judge."

But *katakrinō* means "condemn" and is so rendered in the KJV in 17 out of its 19 occurrences. "Damn," in the other 2 (Mark 16:16; Rom. 14:13), is probably not best, in view of the vulgar use of that word today.

So *katakrima* clearly means "condemnation." It is translated this way in all three places in the NT.

2 *Law of the Spirit, Law of Sin and Death*   The secret of victory for the Christian is stated here: "For the law of the Spirit of life in Christ Jesus hath made me free from the law of sin and death." Vincent defines "law" (*nomos*) as "regulative principle" (3:85). Abbott-Smith suggests "a force or influence impelling to action" (p. 304). Thayer calls it "the impulse to action" (p. 427).

Every unsanctified person is conscious of an inner influence or impulse moving him to do wrong. This is "the law of sin" which produces death, since death is always the consequence of sin (Rom. 6:23). But in the believer this is to be replaced by a new, vitalizing force, "the law of the Spirit," which gives life. In other words, the indwelling Holy Spirit moves us constantly to do the right. More than that, the Spirit actually provides life, the power and strength to do what we should. He is not only an Influence; He is a positive Force, enabling us to live righteously. What a wonderful exchange: to lose an inner influence toward sin and receive a living Person who will guide and empower!

3 *Weak Through the Flesh*   The exact interpretation of this verse is a bit difficult. The first clause has no grammatical relationship to the rest of the sentence. It is probably a nominative absolute, although, being neuter, it could be accusative. If the former, it would be translated "the inability of the law"; if the latter, "that which is impossible for the law." Alford favors the second. Denney thinks there is no way of deciding between the two. Sanday and Headlam conclude: "On the whole the passive sense appears to us to be more in accordance with the Biblical use of *adynaton* and also to give a somewhat easier construction" (p. 192). They would thus agree with Alford in adopting the accusative.

But Vincent disagrees. He labels it: "An absolute nominative in apposition with the divine act—*condemned sin*" (3:85). In other words, "God condemned sin, which condemnation was *an impossible thing* on the part of the law" (*ibid.*). The RSV reflects this meaning in its rendering: "For God has done what the law, weakened by the flesh, could not do." As Paul avers in the previous chapter, the law itself was holy (7:12). But its fatal weakness was that it furnished no power for carrying out its commands.

For Sin God sent His Son "for sin" (*peri hamartias*). The Greek phrase is used more than 50 times in the Book of Leviticus, besides elsewhere in the OT (LXX), for the "sin offering." So this could be translated "as a sin offering." The ERV (1881) reads: "as an offering for sin." Both the ASV and the RSV reverted to the King James rendering, "for sin." Williams has "as a sacrifice for sin." But the majority of the best commentators feel that the context favors the wider, more general sense of "for sin," or "concerning sin." That is, Christ came to deal with the entire problem of sin.

4 Righteousness of the Law The word *dikaiōma* is here given its most usual meaning, "righteousness" (so 4 times in the KJV, which translates it 4 different ways—righteousness, ordinance, judgment, justification—in its 10 occurrences in the NT). But that meaning does not seem to fit very well here. Arndt and Gingrich note that in the LXX it generally means "regulation, requirement, commandment" and suggest "the requirements of the law" as the best translation here. Tyndale caught the correct sense when he rendered it "the righteousness required of [by] the law." Vincent translates *dikaiōma* as "righteous requirement." The RV has "ordinance" (so ASV). But the RSV has "the just requirement." We would recommend Vincent's rendering as best.

The last half of verse 4 shows how one may fulfill "the righteous requirement of the law." It is by continually walking (present tense) "not after the flesh, but after the Spirit." The Spirit-filled, Spirit-directed life alone can fulfill God's law, which is summed up in the word *love* (Gal. 5:14).

5 The Spirit The Greek word for *spirit* is *pneuma*. It comes from the verb *pneō*, which means "blow" or "breathe." Hence the noun signifies first of all a blowing or breathing, and so "wind" or "breath." The noun and verb occur together in John 3:8—"The wind bloweth where it listeth" (*to pneuma . . . pnei*). This is the only place in the NT where *pneuma* is translated "wind," although that sense is common in classical Greek.

The second meaning, "breath," is found twice in the NT. In 2 Thess. 2:8 the KJV reads: ". . . whom the Lord shall consume with the spirit of his mouth." But *pneuma* here rather clearly means "breath." That is the way it is translated in the ERV (1885), the ASV (1901), the RSV, and most scholarly translations of this century.

The other passage is Rev. 13:15: "And he had power to give life unto the image of the beast." But John Wesley (1755) correctly translates *pneuma* here as "breath," as do the revised versions and private translations. Clearly this is the meaning.

In the second stage of development *pneuma* was used for the "spirit" of man. When a man dies he stops breathing. Since it was held that the spirit left the body at death, *pneuma*, "breath," was also used for *spirit*. This usage occurs several times in the NT. Vincent defines it as "the inward, self-conscious principle which feels and thinks and wills" (3:86). Arndt and Gingrich similarly call it "the source and seat of insight, feeling, and will, generally as the representative part of the inner life of man" (p. 681). It is differentiated from the *sōma* (body), the material part of man. Its distinction from "soul" (cf. 1 Thess. 5:23) is a psychological problem which is outside the province of this particular volume.

But our main interest in *pneuma* is in its use for the Holy Spirit, the Spirit of God, the Spirit of Christ. That is the most common usage in the Epistles of Paul. He employs the word in that sense literally scores of times. That is its significance in the eighth chapter of Romans.

Mind This verse is in the form of antithetic parallelism, so common in the wisdom literature of the OT (cf. Prov. 10:15). Paul writes: "For they that are after the flesh do mind the things of the flesh; but they that are after the

Spirit the things of the Spirit." Wuest renders the first part: "For those who are habitually dominated by the flesh, put their minds on the things of the flesh" (p. 131).

Godet notes that it is difficult to render the verb *phronein* ("mind") into French (and English), "because it includes at once *thinking* and *willing*" (p. 302). Vincent comments: "The verb primarily means *to have understanding;* then *to feel* or *think . . . to direct the mind to something,* and so *to seek* or *strive for . . .* so here. The object of their thinking and striving is fleshly" (3:90). Denney says of the ones described in the first clause: "Their 'mind,' i.e., their moral interest, their thought and study, is upon *ta tēs sarkos*" (EGT, 3:646).

6–7 The Carnal Mind In verse 6 we find the expression "to be carnally minded," and in verse 7 "the carnal mind." In the Greek the two phrases are exactly the same: *to phronēma tēs sarkos*, literally, "the mind of the flesh."

The meaning of the passage turns on two words: *phronēma* and *sarx*. We shall note both of these.

The first comes from the verb *phroneō*, which in turn is derived from *phrēn*. The last term is found in the earliest Greek literature (Homer, etc.) in a physical sense, as referring to the parts about the heart, the "midriff." Then it came to be used of the heart itself, as the seat of the passions, such as fear, joy, and grief. Thirdly, it took on the meaning "mind," as the seat of the mental faculties, perception, and thought. This noun, *phrēn*, is found only one place in the NT (1 Cor. 14:20). There it is used in the plural and means "thinking, understanding."

The verb *phroneō* is found in Homer in the sense of "have understanding." First meaning "think," it came to have the idea of "set one's mind on, be intent on." Kennedy says that "*phroneō* seems always to keep in view the *direction* which thought (of a practical kind) takes" (EGT, 3:420). Sanday and Headlam write (on verse 5): "*Phronein* denotes the whole action of the *phrēn*, i.e. of the affections and will as well as of the reason" (p. 195).

This background will help us to understand the meaning of the word in this passage. The noun *phronēma* is found only in the eighth chapter of Romans (vv. 6, 7, 27). It means "that which is in the mind . . . the thought." Sanday and Headlam define it as follows: "The content of *phronein*, the general bent of thought and motive" (p. 195). Alford says that the noun means "thoughts, cares, and aims" (2:388).

The carnal mind, then, is the mind domi-

nated by the flesh. The carnally minded individual is the one who sets his mind on fleshly things, gives his attention to them, makes them his concern and goal.

But what does "flesh" mean? The Greek word *sarx* has been the subject of endless dispute. We cannot hope to settle the argument in this brief study, but simply to point out some implications.

The noun *sarx* occurs 151 times in the NT. It is translated "carnal" (carnally) 3 times (Rom. 8:6, 7; Heb. 9:10) and "fleshly" once (Col. 2:18). The other 147 times it is rendered "flesh."

In the Greek classics *sarx* is used for "the soft substance of the animal body," then for the "body" as a whole, and finally of "the physical nature as subject to sensation and desire"; in Paul's Epistles it usually means "the flesh as the seat and vehicle of sinful desires" (A-S, 402–3). Arndt and Gingrich write: "In Paul's thought especially, the *flesh* is the willing instrument of sin, and is subject to sin to such a degree that wherever flesh is, all forms of sin are likewise present, and no good thing can live in the *sarx*" (p. 175). This statement places sin in the body, apparently, and thus means that one cannot be free from sin until the spirit is released from the body in death. This common theological emphasis leaves no hope for full deliverance from sin in this life.

More accurate is the definition by Thayer: "*Sarx*, when either expressly or tacitly opposed to *pneuma* (*tou theou*), has an ethical sense and denotes mere human nature, the earthly nature of man apart from divine influence, and therefore prone to sin and opposed to God; accordingly it includes whatever in the soul is weak, low, debased, tending to ungodliness and vice" (p. 571). In a somewhat similar vein Cremer writes: "Thus *sarx* comes at length, in distinct and presupposed antithesis to *pneuma*, to signify *the sinful condition in and according to its bodily manifestations*" (p. 520). Again he says that "*sarx* denotes *sinfully-conditioned human nature*" (*ibid.*).

But does the sinful human nature manifest itself only in the physical body? How about wicked thoughts? A man may outwardly manifest nothing improper and be thinking very evil thoughts. One of the greatest theological fallacies is the locating of sin in the body of man. Actually sin is a wrong condition of the heart, a wrong attitude of the mind, a wrong bent of the will.

6 Death Sanday and Headlam have an excellent comment on *thanatos* (death). They say: "Not merely is the *phronēma tēs sarkos* death in *effect*, inasmuch as it has death for its goal, but it is also a present death, inasmuch as its present condition contains the seeds which by their own inherent force will develop into the death both of body and soul" (p. 195).

9 If   Paul says that his readers are in the Spirit "if so be that the Spirit of God dwell in you." The phrase "if so be" translates the Greek word *eiper*. Denney comments that the term here has its proper force: "if, as is the fact" (EGT, 2:646). Beet renders it "if, as I assume" (p. 217). Godet translates it "if really" (2:72). This is reflected in the RSV: "if the Spirit of God really dwells in you."

The Spirit of Christ   The last part of the verse asserts: "Now if any man have not the Spirit of Christ, he is none of his." It is interesting to note that "Spirit of Christ" and "Spirit of God" are used interchangeably here. The Holy Spirit can be described in both ways. He proceeds from both the Father and the Son.

"He is none of his" is literally "this one is not of him." The RSV renders it: "does not belong to him." It is doubtless best to take *autou*, "of him," as a genitive of possession. It means "he is no true Christian" (SH, p. 197). The force of this statement is correctly interpreted by Beet, who writes: "It also implies that the Holy Spirit is the only medium of union with Christ" (p. 218). It is the Holy Spirit who regenerates the sinner that believes in Jesus Christ as Savior.

Taking the term *spirit* in its modern sense, we speak of one person as showing a good spirit, and another a bad spirit. As Christians, it is our obligation to manifest the spirit of Christ—the temper and disposition of mind which He displayed, the same reactions to life that marked His relations to men.

10 The Body   Paul affirms: "And if Christ be in you, the body is dead because of sin." Obviously this is a difficult statement to understand.

It should first be noted that *sōma* (body) should be taken literally. That it refers to the physical body is almost certain. But what does Paul mean by saying that if you are a Christian your body is dead?

The best explanation is that offered by Godet. He writes: "The term *dead* here signifies: irrevocably smitten with death. The human body . . . begins to die the instant it begins to live" (2:74). Denney comments: "The experience we call death is inevitable for it [the body]" (EGT, 2:646). Hodge renders the clause

thus: "although the body must die on account of sin" (p. 496).

The Spirit   The last clause reads: "but the Spirit is life because of righteousness." However, both ASV and RSV have "spirit." Which is correct?

Almost all modern commentators are agreed that "spirit" here should not be spelled with a capital letter. Denney says: ". . . the spirit (i.e., the human spirit, as is shown by contrast with *sōma*)" (EGT, 2:646). Godet writes: "The contrast between *spirit* and *body* leads us rather to apply the former term to the spiritual element in the believer" (p. 74). Sanday and Headlam say: "Clearly the *pneuma* here meant is the human *pneuma* which has the properties of life infused into it by the presence of the Divine *pneuma*" (p. 198). Beet comments: "The human spirit, as in ch. 1.9, the highest side of man's nature, in contrast to *the body* in which it dwells" (p. 218). Hodge agrees.

Life   In the previous clause Paul declares that the body is dead (*nekron*, an adjective). But here he says that the spirit is "life" (*zōē*, a noun). Why the change? Godet suggests: "The life of God does not become merely an *attribute* of the spirit in man through the Holy Spirit; it becomes his *nature*, so that it can pass from the spirit to his whole person" (2:74).

Righteousness   The term *dikaiosynē* has various meanings in the NT and even in Paul's Epistles. Perhaps Sanday and Headlam are correct when they say of its use here: "It includes all the senses in which righteousness is brought home to man, first imputed, then imparted, then practised" (p. 198).

The teaching of this clause, then, is that when Christ dwells in us our spirits not only become alive but also become centers and sources of life for the whole personality.

11 Quicken   The thought of verse 10 is carried further in verse 11. There we are told that if the Holy Spirit dwells in us—*oikei*, "makes his home" in us—God will by that same Spirit "quicken" our mortal bodies. And that quickening is related to the resurrection of Jesus Christ.

The verb "quicken" is *zōopoiēsei*. It literally means "make alive" (from *zōē*, "life," and *poieō*, "make"). What is the meaning of the statement here?

Obviously the most natural way is to take it of the believer's final glorification, the redemption of his body (cf. v. 23). Denney writes: "The indwelling spirit is that of Him who raised Jesus from the dead, and as such it is the guarantee that our mortal bodies also (as well as our spirits) shall share in immortality" (EGT, 2:647). Beet says: "Even the mortal clay which has been the organ of the Spirit will live for ever" (p. 219). However, he goes on to say that Paul's language in 1 Cor. 15:43–44, 50 indicates that our present and future bodies will not "consist of the same particles" (*ibid.*).

Godet underscores the difference in "raised" as applied to Jesus and "quicken" in referring to the believer's body. He writes: "The death of Jesus was a sleep, unaccompanied with any dissolution of the body . . . it was therefore enough to *awake* (*egeirein*) Him. In our case, the body, being given over to destruction, must be entirely reconstituted; this is well expressed by the word *quicken*" (2:74–75).

Mortal   The Greek word for "mortal" in this passage is *thnēta*. Thayer says that the adjective *thnetos* means "*subject to death*, and so still living" (p. 291). This has led some to suggest that Paul is not speaking here of our bodily resurrection after death, but rather of a quickening of our mortal bodies *in this life* by the indwelling Holy Spirit. In spite of the fact that no leading commentator seems to support this view, it should probably not be ruled out completely.

12 ***Debtors***   Paul says that "we are debtors," but "not to the flesh." In other words, we owe the flesh nothing. The word for "debtors," *opheiletēs*, means "one who owes another." A secondary definition is "one held by some obligation, bound to some duty" (Thayer). Perhaps that is the sense here. Sanday and Headlam paraphrase the verse thus: "Such a destiny has its obligations. To the flesh you owe nothing" (p. 201). Godet has: "We are under obligation" (p. 307).

13 ***Die***   The first part of the verse reads: "For if ye live after the flesh, ye shall die." The literal Greek is: "ye are about to die." Godet paraphrases the meaning thus: "There is nothing for you but to die; such is the only future which awaits you" (p. 308).

Mortify   The last part of the verse says: "But if ye through the Spirit do mortify the deeds of the body, ye shall live." That the real meaning of *mortify* is not commonly understood is shown by the popular expression "I was mortified to death." Translated into correct English

that simply means, "I was greatly embarrassed."

In contrast is an account written by a missionary. One day, after a tiresome journey in the jungle, he was resting on a camp cot, relaxing by reading his Greek New Testament! He happened to lower the book for a moment and found himself confronted by a very deadly snake, whose head was less than two feet from his face. (Please don't draw the conclusion that it is dangerous to concentrate on *your* Greek Testament.) He said he performed the gymnastic miracle of leaping from that cot without raising himself, found an iron poker by the fire, and "mortified" the snake.

That missionary knew his Greek, for the verb *thanatoō* does not mean "embarrass" but "put to death, destroy, render extinct." That is what we are to do with "the deeds of the body."

Paul is not here pleading for a rigorous asceticism. He is not advocating the suppression of all physical desires and the denial of any enjoyment of physical pleasure. What he is saying is that all the bodily activities carried on independently of the Spirit and in defiance of His dominion should be put to death. The previous clause clearly indicates this.

14 ***Sons of God***   Literally this verse reads: "For as many as are led by God's Spirit, these are God's sons." In the Greek there is no definite article with "sons." This makes it more emphatic. The anarthrous construction (without the article) indicates *character* or *kind*. The statement means that those who are led by God's Spirit have (perhaps also display) the character or nature of God's sons. They not only belong to the family but act like it!

15 ***Bondage***   Here the word *douleia* occurs for the first of five times in the NT. It is found again in verse 21; in Gal. 4:24; 5:1; and Heb. 2:15. Its simple meaning is "slavery." So the phrase here, "the spirit of bondage . . . to fear," means a slavish spirit of being afraid. That is what the Jews under the law had—a constant fear of breaking one of the multitudinous rules and regulations of the Mosaic law or the tradition of the elders. But Christianity brings a spirit of freedom, the Holy Spirit in our hearts guiding and enabling us in doing God's will.

Adoption   The word *huiothesia* likewise occurs here for the first of five times in the NT. It is used only by Paul (Rom. 8:15, 23; 9:4; Gal. 4:5; Eph. 1:5). It means literally "a placing as son" (from *huios*, "son," and *tithēmi*, "set, put, place"). Though rare in the NT, it is common in the Greek inscriptions of the Hellenistic period (ca. 300 B.C.–A.D. 300). The Jews did not practice adoption. So Paul evidently derived the idea and this technical, legal term from Greek sources.

Abba, Father The Greek has *abba patēr*. The first word is Aramaic, the second Greek. Both mean "father."

This same combination is found elsewhere in the NT only twice. In Mark 14:36, Jesus prays in Gethsemane: "Abba, Father, all things are possible unto thee." In Gal. 4:6 we have almost exactly the same statement as here. Sanday and Headlam comment: "It gives greater intensity of expression, but would only be natural where the speaker was using in both cases his familiar tongue" (p. 203).

16 Itself The KJV reads: "The Spirit itself beareth witness with our spirit, that we are the children of God." The RSV changes "itself" to "himself."

Orthodox Christianity has always held to the deity of Jesus Christ and the personality of the Holy Spirit. Modern liberalism has frequently denied both. The KJV rendering here would seem to deny the personality of the Holy Spirit, calling Him an "it." Even if one is reading the KJV in the pulpit he should always change "itself" to "himself." By doing so we affirm our faith in the Holy Spirit, not as an impersonal influence, but as a living Person who dwells in our hearts.

The question may well be raised: Why does the KJV use "it" in referring to the Spirit? The simple answer is that the Greek word for "spirit," *pneuma*, is neuter. Hence it is necessary for grammatical reasons that the pronoun referring back to a neuter noun as its antecedent should also be neuter in form. But not in meaning! This is just one of many examples of an accidental disharmony in the grammatical usages of two different languages. As every student of foreign languages knows, the precise distinction between masculine, feminine, and neuter to which we are accustomed in English is little known outside our language. We have to translate the thought, not just the mechanical form of the word. Paul believed in the personality of the Holy Spirit! This very verse is the declaration of a personal function: The Spirit witnesses.

17 Joint-heirs The word *synklēronomos* occurs here for the first of four times in the NT (cf. Eph. 3:6; Heb. 11:9; 1 Pet. 3:7). As children of God, we are His heirs. But since Jesus is the Son of God, we are fellow heirs with Him. How cheaply some people forfeit this priceless privilege!

18 Reckon For the meaning of this word see the note on Rom. 6:11. Sanday and Headlam comment that the term *logizomai* is used "here in its strict sense, 'I calculate,' 'weigh mentally,' 'count up on the one side and on the other' " (p. 206). Denney declares: "It does not suggest a more or less dubious result of calculation; rather by litotes [understatement to increase the effect] does it express the strongest assurance" (EGT, 2:648). Of the outcome of life for the Christian, Paul had not the slightest doubt. He knew that all the sufferings of this life would be far outweighed by the future glory. "In fact it is nothing short of an universal law that suffering marks the road to glory" (SH, p. 206).

19 Earnest Expectation This expression is the translation of one Greek word, *apokaradokia*, found only here and in Phil. 1:20. It is composed of three parts: *apo*, "from"; *kara*, "head"; *dokeō*, "watch" (in Ionic Greek). So it means "to watch with outstretched head, watch anxiously." Denney says that it "denotes absorbed, persistent expectation—waiting, as it were, with uplifted head" (EGT, 2:649). Sanday and Headlam comment: "A highly expressive word 'to strain forward,' lit. 'await with outstretched head' " (p. 206). Arndt and Gingrich would translate the whole phrase: "the eagerly awaiting creation." Cremer says it means "to expect on and on, to the end."

Manifestation The word for "manifestation" here and the one for "revealed" in the previous verse both come from the same root. In verse 18 it is the verb *apocalyptō*, "uncover, reveal." In verse 19 it is the noun *apocalypsis*, which has been taken over into English as "apocalypse." The RSV correctly renders it "the revealing."

The word occurs some 18 times in the NT. In the KJV it is translated "revelation" 12 times and "revealed" twice. It should be rendered this way here, not only to keep the connection with the previous verse, but also to show its relation to 2 Thess. 1:7, where the same word occurs.

19–22 Creature The word "creature" occurs in the KJV in verses 19, 20, and 21, but "creation" in verse 22. In Greek the word is the same in all four places. Most modern versions correctly translate it "creation" in each case.

The word is *ktisis*, found 18 times in the NT. In the KJV it is translated 4 different ways, "creation" only 6 times. Most scholars would agree that "creation" is the best translation in almost every instance. It literally means "that which is created."

20 Vanity The word *mataiotēs* occurs several times in the Psalms (LXX) and nearly 40 times in Ecclesiastes. In fact, it is the keynote of the latter book. But it is found only 3 times in the NT (cf. Eph. 4:17; 2 Pet. 2:18). It means "vanity, emptiness, frailty, folly" (A-S). Arndt and Gingrich give "emptiness, futility, purposelessness, transitoriness" and suggest the very meaningful translation here: "The creation was subjected to frustration" (p. 496). Sanday and Headlam write: "That is *mataion* which is 'without result' (*matēn*), 'ineffective,' 'which does not reach its end'—the opposite of *teleios*: the word is therefore appropriately used of the *disappointing* character of present existence, which nowhere reaches the perfection of which it is capable" (p. 208). Denney agrees, when he says: "The idea is that of looking for what one does not find—hence of futility, frustration, disappointment" (EGT, 2:649).

21 Liberty "Delivered" and "liberty" are from the same root in the Greek. Literally the verse reads: "Because the creation also itself shall be freed from the slavery of corruption into the freedom of the glory of the children of God"—or "liberated . . . into the liberty." It is a glorious prospect. Sanday and Headlam comment wisely: " 'Glorious liberty' is a poor translation and does not express the idea: *doxa*, 'the glorified state,' is the leading fact, not a subordinate fact, and *eleutheria* (liberty) is its characteristic, 'the liberty of the glory of the children of God' " (p. 208).

22 Groaneth and Travaileth There are two compound verbs both found only here in the NT. The first, *synstenazō*, means "groan together." The second, *synōdinō*, means "travail together." It is here translated "travaileth in pain together." In this word "there is the suggestion of the travail out of which the new world is to be born" (EGT, 2:650). With regard to both terms Godet writes: "The preposition *syn*, with, which enters into the composition of the two verbs, can only refer to the *concurrence* of all the beings of nature in this common groaning" (p. 316). It is a cosmic concept.

23 Firstfruits Paul goes on to say that it is not only "dumb" creation which groans, but we

Christians also. We have received the firstfruits, but this makes us groan all the more for the perfection that is yet to come.

The word *aparchē* was a "sacrificial technical term for first-fruits of any kind (including animals), which were holy to the divinity and were consecrated before the rest could be put to secular use" (AG, p. 80). The phrase "of the Spirit" is the genitive of apposition; the Holy Spirit is Himself the Firstfruits of our future glory (cf. "earnest," Eph. 1:13–14). He is, says Denney, "the foretaste of heaven, the heaven begun in the Christian, which intensifies his yearning, and makes him more vehemently than nature long for complete redemption" (EGT, 2:650). In a similar vein Godet writes that the apostle means: "We ourselves, who, by the possession of the Spirit have already entered inwardly into the new world, still groan, because there is a part of our being, the outer man, which does not yet enjoy this privilege" (p. 318). Full and final redemption, the culmination of our "adoption," will include the transformation of our bodies into a glorified state. Paul speaks elsewhere of this groaning with deep desire for the exchange of our mortal body for an immortal one (cf. 2 Cor. 5:2). It is the Christians' hope (vv. 24–25).

26 Helpeth Paul asserts: "Likewise the Spirit also helpeth our infirmities." The word for *help* is an interesting double compound, found only here and in Luke 10:40. It is the verb *synantilambanomai*. Abbott-Smith suggests the meaning: "*take hold with at the side* for assistance." Robertson writes: "The Holy Spirit lays hold of our weakness along with (*syn*) us and carries his part of the burden facing us (*anti*) as if two men were carrying a log, one at each end" (Rob. Gram., p. 573). Bloomfield says that the verb means "lay hold of any weight to be carried, on the opposite side, and so helping a person to shoulder it." He adds: "It of course implies our *concurrence* with this heavenly aid" (2:52). Godet writes: "The verb *synantilambanesthai* (*to support, come to the help of*) is one of those admirable words easily formed by the Greek language; *lambanesthai* (the middle) *to take a burden on oneself; syn, with* some one; *anti, in his place;* so: to share a burden with one with the view of easing him" (p. 320). Sanday and Headlam give the meaning as simply: " 'to take hold of at the side (*anti*), so as to support'; and this sense is further strengthened by the idea of association contained in *syn*" (p. 213). The Berkeley Version reads: "In a similar way the Spirit joins in to help us in our weakness." The ANT has: "So too the (Holy) Spirit comes to our aid *and* bears us up in our weakness."

All this means that the Holy Spirit takes hold of our burdens with us, helping us day by day to carry our load. To offset our weakness He supplies divine power. As long as we have Him assisting us we need not fall under the sometimes crushing weight of life. But we must also do our part, furnishing faith, obedience, and willingness to work.

Intercession The verb "maketh intercession" is also a double compound—*hyperentyngchanō*, found only here in the NT. Moulton and Milligan say that it "does not seem to occur outside early Christian literature" (VGT, p. 653). They give its meaning as "supplicate on behalf of." Robertson writes: "It is a picturesque word of rescue by one who 'happens on' (*entyngchanei*) one who is in trouble and 'in his behalf' (*hyper*) pleads 'with unuttered groanings' (instrumental case) or with 'sighs that baffle words' " (4:377).

As this quotation suggests, there are two possible translations of *alalētois*—"unuttered" or "unutterable." The latter is adopted in almost all English translations and is strongly defended by some commentators. Both the Berkeley Version and RSV have "sighs too deep for words." The ANT brings out the double meanings of verb, adjective, and noun in its rendering: "The Spirit Himself goes to meet our supplication *and* pleads in our behalf with unspeakable yearnings *and* groanings too deep for utterance."

Alford describes beautifully the meaning of this verse. He writes: "The Holy Spirit of God dwelling in us, knowing our wants better than we, Himself pleads in our prayers, raising us to higher and holier desires than we can express in words, which can only find utterance in sighings and aspirations" (2:397).

That "inexpressible" is the proper meaning here of *alalētois*, Meyer says, "is decided by the fact that only the latter sense can be proved by linguistic usage, and it characterizes the depth and fervour of the sighing most directly and forcibly" (p. 332).

Intercessory prayer reaches its deepest depths when it passes beyond the realm of words and becomes a series of groans. Spirit-filled Christians are familiar with this agony of soul which is the Holy Spirit praying in them. This intercession is "according to the will of God" (v. 27). One of the important ministries of the Spirit is that of aiding us in prayer.

28 *All Things* This is one of the favorite promises of all Bible-loving Christians. It has been a comfort to thousands in time of perplexity and test, when everything seemed to be going wrong. Most mature believers could recount numerous instances when this promise has proved to be true.

Probably every reader can quote the first half of the verse from memory: "And we know that all things work together for good to them that love God." But the RSV reads: "We know that in everything God works for good with those who love him." Why the difference?

The answer is that in some ancient manuscripts "God" appears twice in this verse—not only as the object of "love" but also as the subject of "works."

Is this the correct Greek text? No one can give a dogmatic answer to that question. But the validity of this added reading has been given further support by recent discovery.

When the KJV was made in 1611 only about a half dozen Greek manuscripts formed the basis of the text to be translated, as against some 5,000 available today. In 1628, too late to be used by the King James translators, the great Alexandrian manuscript (from the fifth century) was brought to England. About 100 years ago the Vatican manuscript (fourth century) was made available to scholars. Both of these have the added reading, *ho theos*. So does the Sahidic (Egyptian). Origen (third century), the greatest Bible scholar of the Early Church, quoted the verse this way.

Because of these facts, Westcott and Hort placed the added *ho theos* in their text, but in brackets. This famous Greek text was published in 1881, the same year as the ERV. Though the revision committee had the use of prepublication copies of this new text, the added reading was not adopted. Nor did it appear in the ASV (1901). The RSV (1946) has it.

Meanwhile some private modern-speech translations had adopted it. Moffatt (1922) has: "We know also that those who love God, those who have been called in terms of his purpose, have his aid and interest in everything." Goodspeed (1923) makes it still more explicit: "We know that in everything God works with those who love him, whom he has called in accordance with his purpose, to bring about what is good."

Scholars today have stronger support for adopting this reading than did the two just cited. For in the 1930s the so-called Chester Beatty Papyri were discovered and edited. The most significant find was almost an entire papyrus manuscript of Paul's Epistles from the third century—100 years older than Vaticanus and Sinaiticus, hitherto our oldest Greek manuscripts. And this, called Papyrus 46, has the added *ho theos*.

It is not surprising, then, to find this reading in some recent translations. The Berkeley Version (NT, 1945) has: "But we know that for those who love God, for those called in agreement with His purpose, He cooperates in all things for what is good." The ANT (1958) reads: "We are assured *and* know that [God being a partner in their labor], all things work together *and* are [fitting into a plan] for good to those who love God and are called according to [His] design *and* purpose." The reason the additional reading is in brackets is that this new version is based on the Westcott and Hort Greek text, as clearly stated in the Preface.

What should be our position? In 1914 (before the discovery of Papyrus 46) A. T. Robertson said the reading was "more than doubtful" (Rob. Gram., p. 477). But in 1931 he commented about *ho theos* as the subject of *synergei*: "That is the idea anyhow. It is God who makes 'all things work together' in our lives 'for good' " (WP, 4:377). That is certainly what the passage teaches. Whether or not the original Greek text specifically stated it, we know that God is the acting Subject who controls all things for our good.

29 Foreknow Verses 29–30 speak of five great phases of divine redemption: foreknowledge, predestination, calling, justification, glorification. These will be discussed in turn. Each occurs in verb form in the aorist tense. These are facts both crucial and completed in the purpose of God.

The word is *proegnō*, from *proginoskō*. The simple verb *ginoskō* means "know" and *pro* means "before." So "foreknow" is the clear connotation. The noun is *prognōsis*, taken over bodily into English with the meaning: "Act or art of foretelling the course and termination of a disease." (Almost all medical terms today come from the Greek.)

The latest and best one-volume Greek-English lexicon of the NT is that by Arndt and Gingrich (1957). For this passage they suggest the translation "choose beforehand" (p. 710). Wuest agrees with this. He argues that in Acts 2:23 "counsel" and "foreknowledge" (*prognōsis*) mean the same thing. Also in 1 Pet. 1:20, KJV translates *proginoskō* as "foreordain." Wuest adds: "The word should also be so translated in Rom. 8:29" (p. 144). However, in 1 Pet. 1:20 the ERV and the ASV have "foreknew," although the RSV has "destined." Calvin, as might be ex-

pected, makes *proginoskō* here in Rom. 8:29 refer to our adoption (p. 227).

But this theological connotation is unsupported by the majority of the best authorities. Liddell and Scott in their monumental (2, 111 pp.) *Greek-English Lexicon* (rev. ed., 1940) give no such meaning for the term. Abbott-Smith has simply "know beforehand, foreknow." Thayer agrees and interprets 1 Pet. 1:20 as: "foreknown by God, although not yet 'made manifest' to men" (p. 538). Cremer seems to fall somewhere between. He writes: "*Proginoskō*, however, essentially includes a self-determining on God's part to this fellowship (Rom. vii. 29, *whom God had beforehand entered into fellowship with*)" (p. 161).

Alford, pioneer of the modern grammatico-historical method of interpretation, notes Calvin's rendering here ("elected, adopted as His sons"). Then he adds: "But I prefer taking the word in the ordinary sense of *foreknew*" (2:399).

Meyer points out that the Early Church fathers (e.g., Origen, Chrysostom, Augustine, Jerome) interpreted the term as signifying foreknowledge rather than foreordination. He declares that the meaning is not "to be decided by dogmatic presuppositions, but simply by the usage of the language, in accordance with which *proginoskō* never in the NT (not even in xi.2, I Pet. i.20) means anything else than *to know beforehand* . . . That in classic usage it ever means anything else, cannot be at all proved" (p. 335).

It is being increasingly recognized that one of the most important backgrounds for the use of words in the NT is the LXX (Greek OT). This was the Bible of the earliest Christians.

It is in this vein that Sanday and Headlam write: "The meaning of this phrase must be determined by the Biblical use of the word 'know,' which is very marked and clear. . . . In all these places the word means 'to take note of,' 'to fix the regard upon,' as a preliminary to selection for some especial purpose" (p. 217).

Denney takes a similar view. He says: "Yet we may be sure that *proegnō* has the pregnant sense that *ginoskō* often has in Scripture . . . hence we may render, 'those of whom God took knowledge from eternity' (Eph. i.4)" (EGT, 2:652). The ANT reads: "For those whom He foreknew—of whom He was aware (in the divine plan)." Charles Williams makes it a little stronger in his translation: "on whom He set His heart beforehand." In a footnote he asserts that this usage is found in the LXX.

Vincent speaks vigorously on the subject. He declares of *proginoskō*: "It does not mean *fore-*

ordain. It signifies prescience, not preelection." In a footnote he adds:

> This is the simple, common-sense meaning. The attempt to attach to it the sense of preelection, to make it include the divine decree, has grown out of dogmatic considerations in the interest of a rigid predestinarianism. The scope of this work does not admit a discussion of the infinitesimal hair-splitting which has been applied to this passage, and which is as profitless as it is unsatisfactory (3:95).

The relation of this term to its context is correctly stated by Vine when he writes: "The foreknowledge of God is the basis of his foreordaining counsels" (2:119).

One of the best treatments of this passage is in Godet's *Commentary on the Epistle to the Romans,* where he devotes over a page of rather fine print to this one word alone. He writes:

> Some have given to the word *foreknow* the meaning of *elect, choose, destine beforehand.* . . . Not only is this meaning arbitrary, as being without example in the NT . . . but what is still more decidedly opposed to this meaning is what follows: *He also did predestinate* (p. 324).

After discussing several views held regarding this word, Godet goes on to say (p. 325): "In what respect did God thus *foreknow* them? . . . There is but one answer: foreknown as sure to fulfil the condition of salvation, viz. faith; so: foreknown as His *by faith.*"

Predestinate   The Greek verb is *proorizō.* As in the previous word, *pro* means "before." The simple verb *horizō* comes from *horos,* "boundary." So its primary meaning is "mark off by boundaries." That is the basis of Williams' translation for *proōrisen,* "He marked off as His own."

But to what are we "foreordained" (ASV) or "predestined" (RSV)? Not to eternal individual salvation, as often claimed. The text says, "to be conformed to the image of his Son."

The word *conformed* is *symmorphous,* an adjective found only here and in Phil. 3:21. It comes from *syn,* "with," and *morphē,* "form." While one meaning of this is "outward appearance," Trench says: "The *morphē,* then, it may be assumed, is of the essence of a thing" (p. 265).

Lightfoot, in his great commentary on Philippians, discusses the term at length. He writes: "It comprises all those sensible quali-ties, which striking the eye lead to the conviction that we see such and such a thing" (p. 127). Yet he concludes his discussion of Phil. 2:6–8 by saying: "Thus in the passage under consideration the *morphē* is contrasted with the *schēma,* as that which is intrinsic and essential with that which is accidental and outward" (p. 133). So Sanday and Headlam are probably justified in their statement that *symmorphous* "denotes inward and thorough and not merely superficial likeness" (p. 218).

"Image" is *eikon.* Abbott-Smith says: "*Eikon* is a *derived* likeness and like the head on a coin or the parental likeness in a child, implies an archetype" (p. 131). Arndt and Gingrich would translate it here as "appearance."

30 *Called*   The verb is the very common *kaleō.* Godet says that this call "embraces the outward invitation by preaching, and the inward drawing by the Spirit of grace" (p. 327).

Justified   The word is *edikaiōsen.* Since we have discussed the verb *dikaioō* at length (cc. 3–5), the term need not detain us here.

Glorified   With regard to these three verbs in verse 30, Sanday and Headlam write: "These are not quite exhaustive: *hēgiasen* [*hagiazō,* 'sanctify'] might have been inserted after *edikaiōsen:* but it is sufficiently implied as a consequence of *edikaiōsen* and a necessary condition of *edoxase* (glorified)" (p. 218). With regard to this term Denney declares: "The tense in the last word is amazing. It is the most daring anticipation of faith that even the N.T. contains" (EGT, 2:652). In the divine foreknowledge our glorification is already seen as an event accomplished.

In connection with the last clause of verse 28, Sanday and Headlam have some general remarks on the five words we have noted in verses 29–30. They write: "With this clause St. Paul introduces a string of what may be called the technical terms of his theology, marking the succession of stages into which he divides the normal course of a Christian life." Then they make this very sane observation:

> There can be no question that St. Paul fully recognized the freedom of the human will. The large part which exhortation plays in his letters is conclusive proof of this. But whatever the extent of human freedom there must be behind it the Divine Sovereignty. It is the practice of St. Paul to state alternately the one and the other without attempting an exact delineation between them. And what he has not done

we are not likely to succeed in doing (pp. 215–16).

32 *Spared Not* The greatest human sacrifice on record is that of Abraham offering his son Isaac. When God saw that Abraham was willing to do what He commanded, even to the sacrificing of his beloved son, He said: "Because thou hast done this thing, and hast not withheld thy son, thine only son . . ." (Gen. 22:16). In the LXX the Greek word for "withheld" is *epheisō*. In Rom. 8:32, "spared" is *epheisato*, the same verb. Perhaps Paul had this OT passage in mind. At any rate it serves to underscore the sacrifice on God's part when He spared not His own Son, but gave Him (John 3:16) as the Sacrifice for our sins. This was no impersonal business transaction or legal case. God's love flowed freely at Calvary.

Freely Give This verse asks a question to which there is only one answer—He will! Will do what? "Freely give us all things."

"Freely give" is *charisetai*, from *charis*, "grace." The verb *charizomai* means "give freely or graciously as a favor." It is used this way again in 1 Cor. 2:12—"that we might know the things that are freely given us of God."

But a dozen times in the NT *charizomai* means "forgive" (e.g., Luke 7:42–43; 2 Cor. 2:7, 10; Eph. 4:32; Col. 3:13). Bengel, in his *Gnomon*, translates it that way in this passage—"Forgive us all things" (3:111). But a check of a dozen translations of the NT failed to discover one that adopted this.

Since *charis* means "grace," one is tempted to favor the rendering given by Ballantine in the *Riverside New Testament*—"graciously give." The ANT has "freely and graciously give."

33–34 Affirmation or Question? The latter part of verses 33 and 34 is treated as declarative in the KJV and the ASV. But in the RSV the second one is translated as a question.

Which is correct? The answer is that we do not know. In the early Greek manuscripts there are no punctuation marks such as are constantly used today. Hence the same Greek sentence may be rendered as declarative or interrogative.

Sanday and Headlam prefer to take both of these as affirmations. In this they agree with Origen and Chrysostom in the early church and with the commentators Ellicott and Denney.

But Alford prefers to treat these clauses as questions, partly because this is rather clearly the correct form in verse 35. Olshausen writes:

"I prefer, with Augustine, the interrogative form throughout; the vividness of the language is greatly enhanced by it" (4:68).

Meyer thinks that the last sentence of verse 33 should be linked with the first sentence of verse 34. The two verses would then read: "Who shall raise accusation against the elect of God? God is the justifier, who the condemner? Christ is He that has died . . ." (p. 339).

There is a difference of opinion among translators. Weymouth prefers all as questions: "Who shall impeach those whom God has chosen? Will God, who acquits them? Will Christ, who died . . . ?" Moffatt has a similar rendering: "Who is to accuse the elect of God? When God *acquits, who shall condemn?* Will Christ?—the Christ who died, yes and rose from the dead! the Christ who is at God's right hand, who actually pleads for us!"

Goodspeed follows Meyer's interpretation, which is that of Origen, Chrysostom, and later of Erasmus. He translates the passage: "Who can bring any accusation against those whom God has chosen? God pronouncing them upright; who can condemn them? Christ who died, or rather who was raised from the dead, is at God's right hand, and actually pleads for us." *The Twentieth Century New Testament* also adopts this handling of these verses. It reads: "Who will bring a charge against any of God's Chosen People? God acquits them; so who is there to condemn them? Christ Jesus died for us—or rather, he was raised from the dead, and he is now at God's right hand and is also pleading on our behalf."

It should be noted that this is the punctuation in Westcott and Hort's NT, as also in Nestle's text. As already stated, the earliest Greek manuscripts have no signs of punctuation at the ends of the sentences. In fact, there is no separation between sentences, or even between words. But the editors of the Greek text have concluded that this is the best way to punctuate here. Westcott and Hort, as well as Nestle, have at the close of verse 33 a raised period, which is equivalent to the modern semicolon.

The RSV follows the ASV in the first instance, putting a semicolon at the end of verse 33. But it changes the last part of verse 34—after "who is to condemn?"—making it a question.

As indicated at the beginning of this discussion, there is no way of being sure which is the best punctuation to adopt. But the meaning of the passage is clear, whatever way it is punctuated.

One word in these two verses calls for special notice. It is *engkalesei*, translated in the

KJV "shall lay to the charge of." The verb means literally "call in" (*en, kaleō*); so it signifies "bring a charge against," "accuse." In some of the translations quoted above it is vividly rendered "impeach." Fortunately we have Christ as our Lawyer to plead our case. And the Judge is our Heavenly Father. So as long as our hearts are right with God we know we are safe.

35 Separate The last paragraph of the eighth chapter (vv. 35–39) forms the climax of the great doctrinal division of this Epistle (cc. 1–8). It all hinges on the question, "Who shall separate us from the love of Christ?"

The more common word for "separate" in the NT is *aphorizō*, which means "mark off by boundaries," and so "set apart" (e.g., Rom. 1:1). A good example of this latter use occurs in Acts 13:2, where the Holy Spirit says: "Separate me Barnabas and Saul for the work whereunto I have called them."

Rather different is the word here. The verb *chōrizō* comes from the noun *chōra*, which in classical Greek meant "space" or "place." In the NT it is variously translated as "country," "region," "land," "field," and so forth.

The verb, which occurs in Romans only here and in verse 39, is found 13 times in the NT. Eight times it is rendered "depart," twice "put asunder" (Matt. 19:6; Mark 10:9), and 3 times "separate" (Rom. 8:35, 39; Heb. 7:26).

Because the basic meaning of *chōra* is "space," A. T. Robertson suggests that the question means: "Can any one put a distance between Christ's love and us . . . ? Can any one lead Christ to cease loving us?" (WP, 4:379). To ask the question is to answer it.

Distress The noun *stenochōria* is one of three that are translated "distress" in the NT. It comes from *stenos*, "narrow," and *chōra*, "space." It thus has just the opposite connotation from *chōrizō*. In the latter the emphasis is on distance, in the former on the lack of it.

The word *stenochōria* is found only four times in the NT. In Rom. 2:9—where it also follows "tribulation"—it is translated "anguish." Here and in 2 Cor. 6:4; 12:10 it is rendered "distress."

Abbott-Smith gives the literal meaning as "narrowness of space, want of room." It is thus very close in meaning to *thlipsis*, "tribulation," with which it is associated in both passages in Romans. The idea is equivalent to our modern expression "a tight squeeze," or the slang phrase "a bind." It describes a condition of being hemmed in by hard circumstances until one is in a dreadfully difficult place.

Persecution The Greek word is *diōgmos*, from the verb *dōkō*. The latter means "pursue"—though it is never rendered thus in the KJV—or "persecute" (28 times in the NT). It is rather weakly translated "follow" in Heb. 12:14, where the Greek says: "Keep on pursuing peace with all men and that sanctification apart from which no one shall see the Lord." It is interesting in this connection to note that the four Hebrew words translated "persecute" in the OT all mean "pursue." In fact one means "pursue hotly after." That is the basic idea of persecution.

In two parallel passages in the Gospels (Matt. 13:21; Mark 4:17) persecution is likewise associated with tribulation. This is somewhat obscured by the fact that *thlipsis* is rendered "tribulation" in the former but "affliction" in the latter. Both passages read alike in the Greek, except for the introductory conjunction.

Famine For millions of people in the world, even today, *famine* is a term to strike terror to the heart. The prevalence of famine in ancient times is shown by the occurrence of 3 Hebrew words for it a total of nearly 100 times in the OT.

The Greek word *limos* is found only a dozen times in the NT. It means very literally an absence of food.

Nakedness This term today suggests indecency on parade. Then it meant a lack of clothes simply because one had no ways or means of getting any.

The word *gymnotēs* occurs only 3 times in the NT. In 2 Cor. 11:27, Paul speaks of being "in fastings often, in cold and nakedness." Here one gets the connection. It is suffering due to insufficient clothing for the cold weather.

The third passage (Rev. 3:18) speaks of "the shame of thy nakedness." This reflects the frequent OT usage, found especially in Leviticus (22 times in chapter 18 and 8 times in chapter 20). But the thought here is a physical suffering from inadequate protection against the cold.

Peril The Greek word *kindynos* means "danger, risk." Outside of this passage it is found in the NT in only one verse (2 Cor. 11:26), where it occurs 8 times! It bulked large in Paul's vivid memory of his many exciting experiences as a missionary.

Today we who live at home may be strangers to most of the perils mentioned by the apostle. But it is important for us to realize that always we are surrounded by countless spiritual perils, which threaten our safety if we do not watch and pray.

37 More than Conquerors The entire clause "we are more than conquerors" is all one word in the Greek—*hypernikōmen*. It is compounded of *hyper* (Latin *super*), meaning "above," and *nikaō*, from *nikē*, "victory." So it means literally "we are super victors." Paul did not believe in barely getting by, in hardly holding his head above water. He experienced the more abundant life which Jesus said He came to bring (John 10:10).

The word is found only here in the NT. It was formerly thought that it was not used by anyone prior to Paul, that the great apostle coined it himself. But Arndt and Gingrich (1957) cite the use of it by the Greek physician Hippocrates—source of the Hippocratic oath administered to young doctors today—who lived about 400 B.C., as well as Menander of about 300 B.C. But at least we can say that the term was rare. Arndt and Gingrich translate it here: "We are winning a most glorious victory."

38 Persuaded Paul writes, "I am persuaded." The verb *peithō* means "convince." So the perfect passive here, *pepeismai*, may be rendered, "I stand convinced." Arndt and Gingrich would translate it, "I am certain." Paul had no uncertainty in the matter.

39 In Christ Everyone who believes the Bible believes in eternal security. But we need to see what kind of eternal security the Bible teaches. It is eternal security "in Christ." That phrase, as all good scholars recognize, is the heart of Paul's theology.

As long as we are "in Christ" we are secure. But just as we become "in Christ" by the choice of our own wills, so by the same method we can cease to be in Christ. Then we are no longer secure.

What Paul is saying in this great, climactic peroration is that nothing in all of God's great universe outside of ourselves can possibly separate us from the love of God. There is only one thing that can separate us from that love—our own wills!

9:1 Lie Not Paul was about to make a startling statement. So he fortified it with the assertion, "I lie not." The verb is *pseudomai*. Since the prefix *pseudō*, in both Greek and English, means "false," we might render the clause: "I do not speak falsely."

In Christ The significance of this phrase as used in the first verse is beautifully expressed by Denney. He writes: "*En Christō* means that he speaks in fellowship with Christ, so that falsehood is impossible" (EGT, 2:656). Could you lie if you were fully conscious that Christ was standing by your side?

Witness To further strengthen his assertion of truthfulness Paul adds: "my conscience also bearing me witness in the Holy Ghost." The verb *symmartyreō* occurs here for the third and last time in this Epistle. In 2:15 we find almost the same expression as here. In 8:16 it is the Holy Spirit bearing witness with our human spirits. Do our consciences bear witness with us or against us? Paul asserted that his inner conscience concurred with his outer testimony.

The apostle not only claimed the witness of his conscience, which he alone could bear, but also the witness of the Spirit. James Morison writes that the concurrent testimony of his declaration and of conscience was "the echo of the voice of God's Holy Spirit" (quoted in Vincent, 3:99).

Ghost The expression "Holy Ghost" occurs over 80 times in the KJV of the NT. "Holy Spirit" is found 4 times (Luke 11:13; Eph. 1:13, 4:30; 1 Thess. 4:8). Both are translations of exactly the same Greek expression, *hagion pneuma*.

The RV (1881) shows an even greater inconsistency. Vincent sums up the situation thus:

> Throughout Matthew, Mark, and Luke they use *Ghost*, with *Spirit* in margin, as also throughout Acts and Romans. In John, *Spirit* throughout, except in xx.22, for no apparent reason. In 1 Corinthians, both; in 2 Corinthians, *Ghost* throughout; in Ephesians, *spirit*. In 1 Thessalonians, both. In Timothy, Titus, 1st and 2nd Peter, *Ghost*, in Jude, *Spirit*.

The ASV has "Holy Spirit" always.

Today the word *ghost* is used for the spirit of a *dead* person. It should not be applied to the Spirit of the living God.

2 Heaviness, Sorrow The apostle declares that he has "heaviness" and "sorrow" in his heart. The Greek words are *lypē* and *odynē*. The first is the most common word for "sorrow" in the NT, being translated that way 11 out of its 16 occurrences. The second word occurs only here and in 1 Tim. 6:10. Both words are used for pain of body or mind. Perhaps the first carries slightly more the idea of "grief," and the second of "distress." Moffatt translates them "pain" and "anguish." Weymouth has "grief" and "anguish," as does Williams. Verkuyl (Berkeley) seems best with "intense grief and unceasing distress." ("Unceasing" is the literal meaning of *adialeiptos*.) Sanday and Headlam comment: "*lypē* . . . appears to mean grief as a state of mind; it is rational or emotional: *odynē* on the other hand never quite loses its physical associations; it implies the anguish or smart of the heart . . . which is the result of *lypē*" (p. 227).

3 Could Wish Paul writes: "I could wish that myself were accursed from Christ for my brethren, my kinsmen according to the flesh." A better translation is: "I could have wished." The form *ēuchomēn* is the imperfect of *euchomai*, "pray." Alford says: "The imperfect is not *historical*, alluding to his days of Pharisaism, as Pelagius and others, but *quasi-optative* . . . 'I was wishing,' had it been possible. . . . The sense of the imperfect in such expressions is the proper and strict one. . . . the act is unfinished, an obstacle intervening" (2:403). Sanday and Headlam translate it: "The wish was in my mind," or, "The prayer was in my heart." A. T. Robertson calls it the idiomatic imperfect, "I was on the point of wishing" (WP, 4:380). In his *Grammar* he labels it the potential imperfect and comments on this passage: "Paul almost expresses a moral wrong. He holds himself back from the abyss by the tense" (p. 886). Vincent writes: "The imperfect here has a tentative force, implying the wish *begun*, but stopped at the outset by some antecedent consideration which renders it impossible" (3:99).

Godet agrees with this interpretation. He says: "The imperfect indicative *ēuchomēn*, literally, *I was wishing*, has in Greek the force of throwing this wish into the past, and into a past which remains always unfinished, so that this expression takes away from the wish all possibility of realization" (p. 339).

Denney shows the basis of the apostle's statement, when he writes: "Paul could wish this if it were a wish that could be realized for the good of Israel" (EGT, 2:657).

I . . . Myself The Greek is emphatic—*autos egō*. Sanday and Headlam write: "The emphasis and position of these words emphasize the willingness for personal sacrifice; and they have still more force when we remember that St. Paul has just declared that nothing in heaven or earth can separate him from the love of Christ" (p. 228).

Accursed The Greek word for "accursed" is found half a dozen times in the NT, but only here in Romans. The term has a long and interesting history. It was first used for a votive offering set up (*anatithēmi*) in the Temple. In the LXX it ordinarily means "devoted to destruction."

Commenting on this passage, Cremer writes: "Some have supposed that *anathema* . . . simply denotes an act of church discipline, just as the Hebrew *herem* sometimes signifies the second stage of excommunication from the synagogue. . . . But the words *apo tou Christou* show that the reference is not to mere excommunication from the church, but to estrangement from Christ and His salvation. . . . The word denotes not punishment intended as discipline, but *a being given over*, or *devotion to divine condemnation*" (pp. 547–48).

Sanday and Headlam agree with this conclusion. They say: "The attempt to explain the word to mean 'excommunication' from the society—a later use of the Hebrew in Rabbinical writers and the Greek in ecclesiastical—arose from a desire to take away the apparent profanity of the wish" (p. 228).

Paul's prayer reminds us of that of Moses: "Yet now, if thou wilt forgive their sin—; and if not, blot me, I pray thee, out of the book which thou hast written" (Exod. 32:32). Bengel well says: "It is not easy to estimate the measure of love, in a Moses and a Paul. For the narrow boundary of our reasoning powers does not comprehend it; as the little child is unable to comprehend the courage of warlike heroes" (3:120).

Alford points out the fact that this does not mean that Paul loved his nation more than his Lord. Rather, "It is the expression of an affectionate and self-denying heart, willing to surrender all things, even, if it might be so, eternal glory itself, if thereby he could obtain for his beloved people those blessings of the Gospel which he now enjoyed, but from which they were excluded" (2:404).

Dorner has best caught the significance of Paul's prayer. He calls it "a spark from the fire of Christ's substitutionary love" (quoted in EGT, 2:657).

4 Service In verses 4 and 5 eight special privileges of the Israelites are enumerated: the adoption, the glory, the covenants, the giving of the law, the service, the promises, the fathers, the human birth of Jesus. What a heritage!

The word for "service" is *latreia*, which occurs only five times in the NT (John 16:2; Rom.

9:4; 12:1; Heb. 9:1, 6). In the LXX it always refers to "divine service." That is the way it is translated in Heb. 9:1. It first meant "the state of hired labourer" (LSJ, p. 1032). But even in classical Greek it was used for the service of the gods. In modern Greek it means "adoration, worship." In the NT it is used only for service to God.

5 Christ, God Is Christ God? The only answer to that in orthodox theology is an unequivocal "Yes." But the question that concerns us now is whether Christ is here equated with God. The KJV, ASV, and NASB make that connection. The RSV, NAB, and NEB, by putting a period after *Christ*, do not.

Again the problem is that in the earliest Greek manuscripts there are no punctuation marks. The placing of commas, periods, and question marks is therefore a matter of editorial opinion—hence a rather subjective matter.

The Westcott-Hort text places a comma before "who," thus affirming the ascription of deity to Christ. This reading is supported by most of the church fathers. But Nestle and the Bible Societies' text place a raised period there (equivalent to the modern semicolon). That would make the closing part simply a benediction to God.

As would be expected, Moffatt adopts the latter interpretation. So do Goodspeed and Ballantine. But Weymouth and Williams, along with the majority of translators, do not. What decision are we to make?

Alford argues at length for the traditional punctuation and consequent interpretation: Christ is here called God. He concludes (2:406):

> The rendering given above is then not only that most agreeable to the usage of the Apostle, *but the only one admissible by the rules of grammar and arrangement.* It also admirably suits the context: for, having enumerated the historic advantages of the Jewish people, he concludes by stating one which ranks far higher than all—that from them sprung, according to the flesh, He who is God over all, blessed for ever.

Bengel also connects the closing clause with Christ. He would paraphrase the passage: "Christ is of the fathers, according to the flesh; and at the same time was, is, and shall be over all, inasmuch as He is God blessed for ever. Amen!" (3:124).

James Denney presents clearly the three main arguments in favor of the traditional punctuation. Then he rather surprises us by setting them aside. His conclusion is as follows: "I agree with those who would put a colon (semicolon in U.S.) or a period at *sarka*, and make the words that follow refer not to Christ but to the Father" (EGT, 2:659).

Godet spends four pages defending the use of the comma rather than the period. He writes: "The entire primitive church seems to have had no hesitation as to the meaning to be given to our passage" (p. 343). After surveying the opposing arguments he concludes: "It seems to us, therefore, beyond doubt that Paul here points, as the crown of all the prerogatives granted to Israel, to their having produced for the world the Christ, who now, exalted above all things, is God blessed forever" (p. 345).

Meyer agrees that none of the fathers of the church makes the closing part a doxology to God. He adds: "Now the decision, which of the two leading interpretations fits *the meaning of the apostle*, cannot be arrived at from the language used, since, so far as the words go, both may be equally correct . . . nor yet from the immediate connection, since with equal reason Paul might . . . feel himself induced to set over-against the human side of the being of Jesus its divine side . . . or might be determined by the recital of the distinctions of his nation to devote a doxology to God, the Author of these privileges, who therefore was not responsible for the deeply-lamented unbelief of the Jews" (p. 361).

One of the main arguments which Meyer emphasizes is this: "Besides the insuperable difficulty would be introduced, that here Christ would be called not merely and simply *theos*, but even *God over all* . . . which is absolutely incompatible with the entire view of the NT as to the dependence of the Son on the Father." Hence he concludes: "Accordingly, the doxology of our passage cannot be referred to Christ, but must be referred *to God*" (p. 362).

But Meyer seems to miss the point. Of course Paul would not assert that Christ was over the Father. The word "all" means "all things," as elsewhere. That Christ is over all things is based on His creatorship of all things (Col. 1:16).

The reader is perhaps wondering why we have devoted so much space to this one problem. Sufficient vindication may be found in the following statement by Sanday and Headlam: "The interpretation of Rom. ix.5 has probably been discussed at greater length than that of any other verse of the NT" (p. 233). They themselves devote over five pages of fine print to a special note, "The Punctuation of Rom. ix.5."

First of all they note that there are four main interpretations, as follows:

(a) Placing a comma after *sarka* and referring the whole passage to Christ . . .

(b) Placing a full stop after *sarka* and translating "He who is God over all be blessed for ever," or "is blessed for ever" . . .

(c) With the same punctuation translating "He who is over all is God blessed for ever" . . .

(d) Placing a comma after *sarka* and a full stop at *panton*, "who is over all. God be (or is) blessed for ever" (*ibid.*).

They add: "The question is one of interpretation and not of criticism. The original MSS of the Epistles were almost certainly destitute of any sort of punctuation" (*ibid.*).

As far as the grammar is concerned, Sanday and Headlam think that "concerning the flesh" would most naturally have an expressed antithesis, as in Rom. 1:3–4. In connection with the Jews, especially, Paul would be careful to assert the deity, as well as the humanity, of Christ. They also note that the words *ho ōn* ("who is") imply very strongly that the words following relate to what precedes. This seems to us a significant point. Then, too, the position of "blessed" (*eulogētos*) favors the ascription to Christ. These three grammatical points add up to considerable weight.

A second main argument is that of the connection of thought. Sanday and Headlam write: "Probably not many will doubt that the interpretation which refers the passage to Christ admirably suits the context" (p. 236). It forms a natural climax to the list of special privileges enjoyed by the Jews. Also, the doxology seems unnatural in this passage filled with sadness.

The third main argument treated by Sanday and Headlam relates to Pauline usage. It has been affirmed that the apostle would not apply the name "God" to Christ. But he clearly and repeatedly calls Jesus "Lord," and this for the Jews meant Deity (p. 237). And while the term *blessed* was reserved by the Jews primarily for God Himself, yet later NT books have doxologies addressed to Christ (e.g., Rev. 5:13; 2 Pet. 3:18).

The final conclusion of Sanday and Headlam is expressed in the following words: "In these circumstances with some slight, but only slight, hesitation we adopt the first alternative and translate 'Of whom is the Christ as concerning the flesh, who is over all, God blessed for ever. Amen' " (p. 238). The judgment of these careful, thorough scholars may well be accepted.

In the appendix to volume 2 of Westcott and Hort's *The New Testament in the Original Greek* we discover a rare phenomenon—these two great collaborators expressing differing opinions. In connection with their joint statement, Hort adds in brackets concerning the punctuation in the margin: "which alone seems adequate to account for the whole of the language employed, more especially when it is considered in relation to the context." Thus he favors applying the doxology to God alone. But Westcott, also in brackets, expresses the opposite opinion. He feels that the close connection of the clauses "seems to make a change of subject improbable" (p. 110).

What is to be our conclusion concerning this much controverted question? First of all, we should recognize that the problem is linguistic rather than theological. The fact that such a conservative scholar as James Denney, author of the famous classic *The Death of Christ*, should favor ascribing the doxology only to God should warn us against labeling or libeling those who may prefer that interpretation. Nevertheless, with all the evidence in hand, we feel that the KJV is here preferable to the reading of the RSV.

6 *Hath Taken None Effect* A good example, among many, of the fact that a Greek word may be translated a variety of ways in English is found in the first part of the sixth verse. The KJV reads: "Not as though the word of God hath taken none effect." The ERV and the ASV say: "hath come to nought." Berkeley reads, "fell short." Weymouth, Williams, Goodspeed, and Phillips all translate it, "has failed." Moffatt and the RSV read, "had failed."

The Greek word is *ekpeptōken*, the perfect tense of *ekpiptō*. The verb *piptō* means "fall." The preposition *ek* means "out." So the compound verb has the meaning "fall out, fall from, fall off." For this passage alone Abbott-Smith suggests "fall from its place, fail, perish"; Thayer, "fall powerless, fall to the ground, be without effect"; Arndt and Gingrich, "fail, weaken." It appears that the best translation, as found in most modern versions, is "failed."

This verse, then, strikes a note often sounded in both Testaments. One is reminded of Isa. 55:11—"So shall my word be that goeth forth out of my mouth: it shall not return unto me void, but it shall accomplish that which I please, and it shall prosper in the thing whereto I sent it." Many of the psalms emphasize the unfailing character of the Word of God. Men may fail, but God's Word will never fail.

7 *Seed* There are no fewer than 21 passages in the NT that speak of Abraham's "seed." That fact highlights two great truths: the importance of God's covenant with Abraham, and the futility of trying to understand the NT without the OT. We also find 3 references to "the seed of David," which reminds us of another great covenant. In 7 NT passages *seed* is used in a botanical sense, as we most commonly employ it today. In 1 John 3:9 there is a unique use of *seed*, which is a study in itself.

The Greek word is *sperma* in every case. Liddell and Scott say that this term is found in Homer (oldest Greek writer) only once, in a metaphorical sense. They give as its first meaning: "mostly, *seed* of plants" (p. 1626). But it is also used of the seed of animals. The Greek poets often use *sperma* in the sense of "offspring." That is its most common meaning in the NT.

But this use of *seed* in English for "offspring" is "now *rare* except in Biblical phraseology" (OED, 9:383). So in spite of the fact that this rendering is retained in RV and ASV it would seem that for modern readers it should be changed. Berkeley uses "offspring." The RSV has "descendants." The latter is probably the most understandable translation.

8 Flesh We have already noted that in Paul's Epistles, and outstandingly in Romans, the term *flesh* is used in two senses: physical and spiritual. In verse 8 it is clearly the physical meaning which is employed. Paul is exploding the idea held by too many Jews of his day that being a physical descendant of Abraham automatically made one a child of God. Today children of so-called Christian parents are apt to think that this fact guarantees them membership in the kingdom of God.

11 Election Here we come to one of the crucial ideas in biblical theology. What is meant by God's "election"?

The Greek word is *eklogē*. It is found only seven times in the NT (translated "chosen" in Acts 9:15). Not surprisingly, four of these occurrences are in this section of Romans (cf. 11:5, 7, 28).

The noun comes from the verb *eklegō*. This is composed of *ek*, "out of," and *legō*, which is translated in the KJV most commonly as "say."

But this meaning of *legō* is rare in Homer and Hesiod (ca. 7th cent. B.C.). Thayer gives as its first definition: "1. to collect, gather; to pick out. 2. to lay with; count with; to enumerate, recount, narrate, describe" (p. 373). Abbott-Smith says that in Homer the word means: "to pick out, gather, reckon, recount" (p. 265).

That prepares us for the specialized meaning of the compound *eklegomai* (it is always middle in the NT). It means "choose," "pick

out," "select," both in the LXX and the NT. Thayer writes on this word: "Especially is God said to *eklexasthai* those whom he has judged fit to receive his favors and separated from the rest of mankind to be peculiarly his own and to be attended continually by his gracious oversight" (p. 197).

When we turn to the noun *eklogē* we find that it means "choice," "selection," or, as a technical term, "election." In the NT it is used only of the divine election, although the verb is employed also in a general sense.

Sanday and Headlam have a good discussion of the expression "the purpose of God according to election." They define it as meaning "the Divine purpose which has worked on the principle of selection." They add: "These words are the key to chaps. ix–xi and suggest the solution of the problem before Paul." Regarding the word *purpose* they state: "From Aristotle onwards *prothesis* has been used to express purpose; with St. Paul it is 'the Divine purpose of God for the salvation of mankind,' the 'purpose of the ages' determined in the Divine mind before the creation of the world" (p. 244).

On the term *election* they write:

> *Eklogē* expresses an essentially O.T. idea . . . but was itself a new word, the only instances quoted in Jewish literature earlier than this Epistle being from the *Psalms of Solomon*, which often show an approach to Christian theological language. It means (1) "the process of choice," "election" (pp. 244–45).

They quote Gore as saying:

> The absolute election of Jacob—the "loving" of Jacob and the "hating" of Esau,—has reference simply to the election of one to higher privileges as head of the chosen race, than the other. It has nothing to do with their eternal salvation.

Barrett comments thus on the latter part of the eleventh verse: "Not works but faith leads to justification; not works but God's call admits to the promise. These are different ways of expressing the same truth" (pp. 182–83).

12 Elder The Greek says literally "greater" (*meizon*) and "lesser" (*elasson*). There are examples in Greek literature and in the LXX (Gen. 29:16) of the use of *meizon* clearly for "older." But Meyer favors the literal meaning, "greater" and "smaller" (p. 372). Vincent agrees. He says: "The reference is not to age, but to their relative position in the theocratic plan" (3:103). In the 44 passages in the NT where *meizon* occurs, it seems never to mean "elder," though it is translated that way here by most scholars.

13 Hated Rather obviously the term *hated* carries with it no idea of malice, but rather of moral antipathy. Sanday and Headlam think the meaning should not be softened to "love less" (cf. Matt. 6:24; Luke 14:26). They wisely suggest: "But it is really better to take the whole passage as corroborating the previous verse by an appeal to history" (p. 247). It is true that the nation of Israel was blessed and Edom (Esau) cursed. But we believe God's election was based on His foreknowledge.

15 Mercy, Compassion The first verb is *eleeō*, from *eleos*, "mercy, pity, compassion." So it means to "have pity" or "show mercy." The second verb is *oiktirō* (only here in the NT). It means "to pity, have compassion on." Cremer notes that the former verb "when applied to God, means to have mercy upon any one, to make him a partaker of saving grace, Rom. ix.15, 16" (p. 249).

It is obvious that the two words are practically synonymous. However, Thayer does point out a slight difference, as follows:

> *Eleeō*—to feel sympathy with the misery of another, especially such sympathy as manifests itself in act, less frequently in word; whereas *oikteirō* denotes the inward feeling of compassion which abides in the heart. A criminal begs *eleos* of his judge; but hopeless suffering is often the object of *oiktirmos* (p. 203).

He also indicates that the second verb is from *oiktos*, "pity," which in turn comes from the interjection *oi*, "Oh!" (p. 442). It refers, therefore, to the pity or compassion that is aroused by the sight of suffering.

In connection with the long quotation above, it might be well to note that etymologically *compassion* and *sympathy* mean exactly the same thing. The former is from the Latin, the latter from the Greek. The literal meaning of both is "suffering with."

16 Runneth On first thought, the combination in this verse may seem a bit odd. Paul writes: "So then it is not of him that willeth, nor of him that runneth, but of God that sheweth mercy." What connection does running have with willing?

The point that Paul is making is that neither determination nor effort on our part can save us. Salvation is only by the mercy of God. Sanday and Headlam explain it this way:

"God's mercy is in the power not of human desire or human effort, but of the Divine compassion itself" (p. 254).

With regard to the meaning of *trechō* ("runneth") in this passage, Abbott-Smith says: "Metaphorically, from runners in a race, of swiftness or of effort to attain an end" (p. 450). In a similar vein Arndt and Gingrich write: "Using the foot-races in the stadium as a basis ... *exert oneself to the limit of one's powers in an attempt to go forward, strive to advance,* Ro. 9:16 (the emphasis is entirely upon the effort which the person makes ...)" (p. 833).

Paul is not discounting the importance of faith and repentance. What he is saying is that no amount of self-effort can save anyone.

17 Raised ... Up Here is another quotation (cf. v. 15) from Exodus (9:16) in which God declares that He "raised up" Pharaoh in order that He might display His power in him. What is meant by "raised up"?

Arndt and Gingrich hold that here *exegeirō* means "cause to appear, bring into being." But Sanday and Headlam object to this idea. They write: "The interpretation which makes *exegeirein* mean 'call into being,' 'create,' has no support in the usage of the word" (p. 256).

They call attention to the fact that some have favored the meaning: "I have preserved thee and not taken thy life as I might have done." But they add:

> The correct interpretation ... is therefore one which makes St. Paul generalize the idea of the previous passage, and this is in accordance with the almost technical meaning of the verb *exegeirein* in the LXX. It is used of God calling up the actors on the stage of history (*ibid.*).

Denney is in complete agreement with this. He says that Paul means: "For this reason I brought thee on the stage of history" (EGT, 2:662). Knowing that Pharaoh would stubbornly rebel, God made a public example of him.

18 Whom He Will Here is one of the strongest NT statements about the sovereign will of God: "Therefore hath he mercy on whom he will ... and whom he will he hardeneth." How should we interpret this?

The first thing that should be said is that we must balance this with the many invitations in the NT to believe and accept Christ. All of these imply freedom of the human will, or the language is a farce.

Sanday and Headlam have noted this well. After pointing out that Paul has already said practically the same thing in Rom. 1:20–28, they write: "In both passages he is isolating one side of the Divine action; and in making theological deductions from his language these passages must be balanced by others which imply the Divine love and human freedom" (p. 257). They also go on to make a very important point: "The Apostle says nothing about eternal life or death. . . . He never says or implies that God has created man for the purpose of his damnation" (p. 258).

One of the finest statements on divine election that we have ever seen comes from the pen of Dr. A. B. Simpson, the sainted founder of the Christian and Missionary Alliance. We jotted it down years ago and are not able to document it now. It reads: "Redemption is a sacred temple, on whose front we read, 'Whosoever will may come'; but when we enter in, we find inscribed on the walls, 'Chosen in Him before the foundation of the world.' "

While on the subject of divine election it might be worthwhile to note a few items in Sanday and Headlam's summary of this topic.

After pointing out the prominent place this holds in the OT, in both the Pentateuch and the Prophets, they say: "But between the conception as held by St. Paul's contemporaries and the O.T. there were striking differences. In the O.T. it is always looked upon as an act of condescension and love of God for Israel" (pp. 248–49). They continue (p. 249):

> But among the Rabbis the idea of Election has lost all its higher side. It is looked on as a covenant by which God is bound and over which He seems to have no control. Israel and God are bound in an indissoluble marriage . . . the holiness of Israel can never be done away with, even although Israel sin, it still remains Israel . . . the worst Israelite is not profane like the heathen . . . no Israelite can go into Gehenna . . . all Israelites have their portion in the world to come . . . and much more to same effect.

These beliefs—all of which are documented—were held by the Jewish rabbis of Paul's day. Israel was to enjoy God's favor and mercy, but the Gentiles were to be destroyed. As Sanday and Headlam say, "The Jew believed that his race was joined to God by a covenant which nothing could dissolve. . . . This idea St. Paul combats" (p. 249).

The emphasis on the absolute, divine predestination of each human soul for either heaven or hell has its roots in rabbinical Judaism, not

in the NT. We must read Paul's Epistles in the light of the controversies of his day. The great apostle was correcting some extreme views of his contemporaries. He was seeking to give the Christian view of divine election in the light of the OT.

19 *Find Fault*   The apostle's imaginary opponent raises the objection: "Why doth he yet find fault?" The verb *memphomai* is found (in the best text) only here and in Heb. 8:8. It means "blame." The question implies, "Why does God blame us for a condition for which we are not responsible?"

Resisted   Paul asks the question, "For who hath resisted his will?" The word for "resist" is *anthistēmi*. Literally it means "stand against." Vincent prefers "withstand" rather than "resist." He writes: "The idea is the *result* rather than the *process* of resistance. A man may *resist* God's will, but cannot *maintain* his resistance. The question means, who *can* resist him?" (3:105).

Though Sanday and Headlam object, a number of the modern versions reflect this interpretation. Williams has: "For who can resist His will?" Knox has, "since there is no resisting his will?" Moffatt reads: "Who can oppose his will?" The ANT seeks to give the full force in its rendering: "For who can resist *and* withstand His will?" Probably the best translation is that found in the TCNT. It reads: "For who can withstand his purpose?"

Will   The last word of this verse is not the common one for *will* in the NT (*thelēma*, rendered "will" 62 out of 64 times). Rather it is *boulēma*, found only once elsewhere in the Textus Receptus. In Acts 27:43 it clearly means "purpose" and is so translated in the KJV. In the earliest Greek manuscripts *boulēma* is also found in 1 Pet. 4:3 (the late MSS have *thelēma*). On this passage in 1 Peter, Lenski comments: "*Boulēma* is what one intends, hence 'counsel'; in v. 2 *thelēma* is what one wills or has decided" (p. 181). On its use here in Romans, Sanday and Headlam say that *boulēma* "seems to be substituted for the ordinary word *thelēma* as implying more definitely the deliberate purpose of God" (p. 259). It seems that "purpose" is the best translation here.

20 *Repliest Against*   The opening words of verse 20 are unusually full and emphatic in the Greek. Robertson translates them: "O man, but surely thou who art thou?" (WP, 4:383).

The verb "repliest against" is a double compound, found only here and in Luke 14:6. It means "answer to one's face." The language is startling. Berkeley reads: "O man, who are you anyway, to talk back to God?" That puts it well. *The Twentieth Century New Testament* says: "Who are you, frail mortal, who are arguing with God?" Vincent notes that the verb means "answer by contradicting" (3:106).

Formed The giving of blood plasma and the manufacture of plastics are rather recent functions. But the words are old. The apostle asks, "Shall the thing formed [*plasma*] say to him that formed it [*plasanti*] . . .?"

The verb *plasso* means "form" or "mold." It is found only here and in 1 Tim. 2:13—"Adam was first formed, then Eve." The noun *plasma*, "that which is molded or formed," occurs only here. The same is true of the adjective *plastos*, from which comes *plastic*. First used as a substitute for glass, and now also for steel, plastics are so called because they are molded materials. In ancient Greek days the molding was done with wax or clay.

21 Potter This modern term also comes from the Greek. The word for *potter* is *cerameus*. The adjective *ceramicos* is found only once in the NT (Rev. 2:27). It is from this the word *ceramics* is taken directly.

22 Willing Perhaps the greatest single defect in the Greek language is its abundant use of the participle. This very often makes for ambiguity of interpretation. In English we use clauses instead. But the problem that faces us frequently in the NT exegesis is this: How shall we translate the Greek participle? Often there are half a dozen possibilities: as *since, because, although, while, in order that*. Which is the one to choose? Robertson writes: "Does a given circumstantial participle bear the notion of 'because' or 'although'? Only the context can tell, and men do not always interpret the context correctly" (Rob. Gram., p. 1125).

The participle "willing" is a case in point. Sanday and Headlam say that "most commentators" prefer "because God wishes to show his wrath" (p. 261). Perhaps through the influence of their monumental work on Romans, the situation is different today. Most recent commentators are agreed that "although" is preferable. Sanday and Headlam interpret the verse thus: "God, although His righteous anger might naturally lead to His making His power known, has through His kindness delayed and borne with those who had become objects that deserved His wrath" (p. 261). Robertson agrees that the

participle should be taken as concessive rather than causal (WP, 4:384). The last clause would seem to demand this.

Fitted The verb *katartizō* occurs 13 times in the NT (only here in Romans) and is translated 8 different ways in the KJV. This is the only place where it is rendered "fitted."

Abbott-Smith lists this passage under the meanings "to furnish completely, complete, equip, prepare" (p. 238). The form is the perfect middle or passive participle. Most commentators and translators treat it as passive. But Arndt and Gingrich suggest it might be taken as middle, with the meaning: "having prepared themselves for destruction" (p. 419). This rendering would have obvious advantages theologically.

In any case, the sense seems to be "ripe and ready" (Moffatt). Goodspeed has "already ripe." Weymouth reads, "who stand ready," bringing out the full force of the perfect tense (existing state resulting from completed action). The idea is that these disobedient ones are ready and ripe for the destruction they deserve. It definitely is not said that God has made them thus.

23 Afore Paul says that the vessels of mercy were "afore prepared." The correct form now, of course, would be "prepared beforehand."

Attention should be called to the change of verb, as compared with verse 22. This one is *proetoimazō*. The only other place in the NT where it occurs is Eph. 2:10. There it is translated "before ordained." But that seems to be an unjustifiably strong rendering. The simple verb *hetoimazō* is found 40 times in the NT. It is rendered "prepare" 29 times, "make ready" 10 times, and "provide" once. The compound does not seem to carry the connotation "foreordain," for which another verb is used. Denney comments: "How much is covered by *proētoimasen* is not clear, but the text presents no ground whatever for importing into it the idea of an unconditional eternal decree" (EGT, 2:665).

25, 27, 29 Osee, Esaias There are a few hints for the public reading of the Scriptures which everyone should heed. One of them is highlighted by these two strange names. It is this: Always use the familiar OT form of OT characters' names. If you read, "Osee," some of your hearers will not catch the connection at all. So by all means say, "Hosea," and, "Isaiah." And that goes for *Elijah* instead of *Elias, Elisha* instead of *Eliseus, Jeremiah* instead of *Jeremias*, and so for many others. The pattern is set for us in Neh. 8:8—"So they read in the book in the law of God distinctly, and gave the sense, and caused them to understand the reading." Following the above hint will help.

27 Remnant The doctrine of the remnant bulks large in Isaiah and Jeremiah. Paul quotes twice from the former (vv. 27, 29).

Some Greek manuscripts have *hupoleimma*, some *kataleimma* (both only here in the NT). The former means that which is left over, the latter that which is left behind. A remnant, but only a remnant, of Israel will be saved.

28 Finish, Cut Short Two interesting verbs occur here, *synteleō* and *syntemnō*. The first means "bring to an end"; the second, "cut off." Robertson takes the prefix *syn* as intensive, meaning "completely" finish and cut off. Vincent takes it in its literal sense, "together," and says it means "summarily." Both could be true. These two words suggest that God's judgment will be conclusive and concise.

30–31 Attained Two different Greek words are here translated "attained." The former is *katelaben*, the latter *ephthasen*. The first means "grasped, seized, overtook." The second signifies "arrived at." Vincent comments: "The meaning is substantially the same, only the imagery in the two words differs; the former being that of *laying hold of a prize*, and the latter *arriving at a goal*" (3:110).

32 Stumbled The verb "stumbled" is *proskoptō*, which means "strike [one's hand or foot] against." It almost suggests the idea of stubbing one's toe and falling as the result. The tragedy was that the Jews stumbled over Jesus, their Messiah.

10:1 Desire The Greek word here translated "desire" is not the one which most naturally means that. Rather, it is *eudokia*, found almost exclusively in Jewish and Christian writings. Out of nine occurrences in the NT, this is the one place it is rendered "desire."

Abbott-Smith gives only these meanings: "good pleasure, good-will, satisfaction, approval." But Thayer allows "*desire* (for delight in any absent thing easily begets a longing for it)" as the sense in this passage (p. 258). Arndt and Gingrich do the same, "inasmuch as a desire is usually directed toward something that causes satisfaction or favor" (p. 298). Vine defines the word thus: "Lit., good pleasure . . . implies a gracious purpose, a good object being in view, with the idea of a resolve, shewing the

willingness with which the resolve is made" (1:298). Moulton and Milligan feel that the meaning "good pleasure" or "goodwill" is found "in all its NT occurrences, even in Rom. 10:1" (VGT, p. 260).

Robertson is uncertain about the matter. He comments: "No example for 'desire' unless this is one." Denney writes: "His heart's *eudokia* is that in which his heart could rest with complacency; that which would be a perfect satisfaction to it." He adds: "This is virtually the same as 'desire' " (EGT, 2:668). But Sanday and Headlam disagree. They affirm: " 'good will,' 'good pleasure,' not 'desire,' which the word never means" (p. 282).

What is to be our conclusion? Goodspeed has: "My heart is full of good will toward them." Similarly Williams renders it: "My heart's good will goes out for them." That seems to represent the sense.

Prayer There are 7 different words for prayer in the Greek NT. The one found here, *deēsis*, occurs 19 times (only here in Romans). Twelve times it is translated "prayer," 6 times "supplication," and once "request."

Each of the 7 words has its own distinctive emphasis. The one used here means "prayer for particular benefits," or "petition" (Trench, 189). Probably it is best rendered "supplication," as it is regularly in the RV and in the ASV.

4 The End "For Christ is the end of the law for righteousness to every one that believeth." What is meant by "end"?

The word *telos* regularly signifies "end." But does Paul here mean that Christ is the *fulfillment* of the law or its *termination?*

Arndt and Gingrich would allow both. They say, "Christ is the goal and the termination of the law at the same time" (p. 819). Thayer prefers only the latter interpretation: "Christ has brought the law to an end" (p. 620).

The commentators are ranged on both sides. Calvin says: "The word fulfilling seemeth unto me not to serve amiss in this place" (p. 284). Wesley defines it this way: "The scope and aim of it" (p. 561). But Meyer objects to this. He prefers "end" or "conclusion," which he says is the meaning "adopted after Augustine by most of the modern expositors" (p. 405). That seems to be true. Sanday and Headlam say: "Law as a method or principle of righteousness had been done away with in Christ" (p. 284). Denney writes: "With Christ in the field law as a means of attaining righteousness has ceased" (EGT, 2:669). The context suggests that this is the correct interpretation, though both may be allowed.

The Law The KJV says "the law." But there is no article in the Greek. Denney comments: "*Nomon* without the article is 'law' in the widest sense; the Mosaic law is only one of the most important instances which come under this description" (*ibid.*).

7 The Deep The Greek word *abussos* is translated "deep." Here it means the place of departed spirits. In all its other occurrences in the NT (Luke 8:31 and seven times in Revelation) it refers to the abode of demons. It is rendered "deep" in Luke, but Revelation has "bottomless pit" or simply "bottomless." The best way to treat the word is to transliterate ("the Abyss") rather than translate it.

9 Believeth, Confession The first clause should probably be ended with "Jesus as Lord" rather than "the Lord Jesus." That is the way most modern versions give it.

Verse 10 is often quoted in connection with evangelism. There is sometimes a difference of opinion as to exactly what is meant. Are "righteousness" and "salvation" two different things? Do we gain the one by faith and the other by confession?

Denney's comment is helpful: "To separate the two clauses, and look for an independent meaning in each, is a mistake; a heart believing unto righteousness, and a mouth making confession unto salvation, are not really two things, but two sides of the same thing" (EGT, 2:671).

11 Ashamed This verse contains a quotation from Isa. 28:16—"Whosoever believeth on him shall not be ashamed" (already quoted in 9:33). The idea seems to be that no one who believes on Jesus will fail to have his hopes realized. The LXX uses the term to express shame because of unfulfilled hopes (A-S). Weymouth, Moffat, and Goodspeed all have "disappointed" instead of "ashamed."

17 By Hearing . . . by the Word of God The earlier Bible translations frequently fail to distinguish between Greek prepositions with different meanings. Here we read: "So then faith cometh by hearing, and hearing by the word of God." But the first preposition is *ek*, "out of," and the second *dia*, "through." Furthermore, "of God" (*theou*) is "of Christ" (*Christou*) in the oldest Greek manuscripts. Williams gives the correct translation: "So faith comes

from hearing what is told, and hearing through the message about Christ."

18 Sound "Their sound went into all the earth." The word for "sound" is *phthongos*, which occurs elsewhere in the NT only in 1 Cor. 14:7. It was used first for the sound of musical instruments. But here it seems to mean "voice." That is the way it is translated in many modern versions. The OT passage (Ps. 19:5) refers to the voice of God in nature. Paul here applies the passage to the preaching of the gospel which had by then reached to all parts of the Roman world.

19 Foolish The Greek word is *asynetos*. It occurs five times in the NT and is three times translated "without understanding." That is its literal meaning. Therefore most recent translations render it by "senseless." It is used of those who fail to understand the clear, simple things of God, who do not have sense enough to know the truth.

21 Gainsaying This is a participial form of *antilegō*. Literally it means "speak against," and that is the way it is translated (KJV) 5 out of the 10 times it occurs in the NT. It is used in the sense of "contradict," "oppose," or "resist." Goodspeed and Williams render the last two participles "disobedient and obstinate" (so also Arndt and Gingrich). Weymouth has "self-willed and fault-finding." Moffatt and the RSV have "disobedient and contrary." All of these bring out the thought much more clearly than "gainsaying."

11:1 Cast Away The verb is *apotheō*. It occurs 6 times in the NT and is translated 5 different ways in KJV—"cast away" (Rom. 11:1–2), "thrust away" (Acts 7:27), "thrust from" (Acts 7:39), "put from" (Acts 13:46), "put away" (1 Tim. 1:19). It may also be translated "push aside" (Arndt and Gingrich's first choice). Williams says "disowned." Moffatt, Goodspeed, Berkeley, and Phillips all have "repudiated." The RSV has "rejects."

It should be noted that *mē* in the Greek indicates that a negative answer is expected. Also the verb is in the aorist tense. Literally the question reads: "God did not reject His people, did He?" Paul's answer is an emphatic "God forbid"—*mē genoito:* "By no means!", "Not at all," "No, indeed!"

2 Wot This is a quaint old word in English which occurs 10 times in the KJV. But what does it mean?

Actually "wot" here is a translation of the very common verb *oida*, which occurs 317 times in the NT and is almost always (281 times) rendered "know." Why the KJV translators should have chosen a few times to represent it in English by "wot" is a question that will probably never be answered.

Of Elijah   The standard English versions say "of Elijah." But the Greek preposition is *en*, "in." Denney writes: "The sections of the Bible were designated, not as now by chapter and verse, but by some descriptive phrase. . . . Many references are made in this form by Hebrew writers" (EGT, 2:676). So here it means "in the section of Scripture which narrates the story of Elijah" (SH, p. 310). Moffatt puts it well: "in the passage called 'Elijah.' "

Intercession   The verb "maketh intercession" is *entyngchanō*. Its primary meaning is "fall in with"; then, "meet with in order to converse." Finally it came to mean "appeal" (Goodspeed), or "plead" (Moffatt, RSV).

The essential idea of the verb is that of having an interview with someone. That suggests the basic function of intercession. It means to have an interview with God concerning someone else. We do not engage in intercession until we have consciously come into the presence of God.

3 *Digged Down*   Elijah complains that his contemporaries have "digged down" God's altars. The verb *kataskoptō* is found only here in the best Greek text. It means "tear down, raze to the ground." So it is well translated "demolished" (Moffatt, Goodspeed, RSV).

The LXX (1 Kings 19:10) has *katheilan*, "pulled down." That seems more appropriate for destroying an altar than "digged down."

Altars   The Greek word is *thysiastēria*, which means altars of sacrifice (not incense altars). The plural suggests that in Elijah's day there was more than one altar of sacrifice, though the Law (Deut. 12:13–14) commanded that there should be only one.

Left Alone   Elijah feels that he is "left alone" as a follower of God. The verb is *hypoleipō*, found only here in the NT. It means "leave behind." Goodspeed captures Elijah's mood: "I am the only one left."

Life   *Psyche* is a good English word. The dictionary defines it as "the human soul." But here the Greek word *psychē* is translated "life."

Psychē has about the same spread of meaning in Greek that *soul* has in English. We say that a ship went down with so many souls lost. Yet of those who were drowned we say that some souls were saved and some lost. And the same goes for the survivors.

Actually the Greek word is very difficult to define. *Psychē* occurs 105 times in the NT. It is translated "soul," "life," "mind," and "heart." Arndt and Gingrich remark: "It is often impossible to draw hard and fast lines between the meanings of this many-sided word" (p. 901).

The most common word for *life* in the NT is *zōē*, from which comes zoology. Another word is *bios*, basis of *biology*. But *psychē* occurs more often, even translated as "life," than *bios*. Once (Rev. 13:15) *pneuma* is rendered "life."

What does *psychē* mean? It comes from *psychō*, "breathe" or "blow." So it was first used for "breath, breath of life, life." In Aristotle it signifies the vital life principle. It was thought of as the seat of the will, as well as the emotions. At the same time it may seem occasionally to suggest the intellect.

It is almost impossible to distinguish between *pneuma* (spirit) and *psychē* (soul). Sometimes they seem practically synonymous. The identification of *psychē* as the principle of animal life, often made by earlier writers, seems untenable.

While God is declared to be *pneuma* (John 5:24), the word *psychē* is never used of Him. When used of Christ, it applies to His humanity.

Vincent sums up the meanings of *psychē* thus: "(1) The individual life, the seat of personality; (2) The subject of the life, the person in which it dwells; (3) The mind as the sentient principle, the seat of sensation and desire" (3:122).

Answer of God   This is all one word in Greek, *chrēmatismos*, found only here in the NT. Originally it meant a business transaction or political negotiation. Then it was used for a decree or ordinance having public authority. In the LXX and NT it means an "oracular response, divine injunction or warning" (LSJ, p. 2005).

Baal   In the OT we find that with the Israelites Baal was Jehovah's main rival. Jehu destroyed the worshipers of Baal in Israel (2 Kings 10).

At first *Baal* was a word in good standing. It was incorporated in such names as Jerubbaal (Judg. 6:32), Eshbaal (1 Chron. 9:39), and Meribbaal (1 Chron. 9:40). But when the word came to be associated with the worship of the Phoenician god Baal, its use in Israel was forbidden (Hos. 2:16–17). In line with this, an effort was made to eliminate the term *Baal* from the Scriptures, substituting for it *Bosheth*, "abomination" or "shame." The Greek word for "shame" is *aischynē*, a feminine noun. So the feminine article came to be used with *Baal*. That is what we find here.

5 Remnant The word *leimma* (or *limma*) is found only here in the NT. It comes from *leipō*, "leave." So it means "what is left."

8 Slumber The phrase "spirit of slumber" is quoted from Isa. 29:10. There the Hebrew has "spirit of a deep sleep."

But the Greek word *katanyxis* (only here in the NT) has a somewhat different connotation. It comes from the verb *katanyssō*, "strike violently" or "stun." So the noun means properly "the stupefaction following *a wound* or *blow*" (Vincent, 3:124). Denney makes the wise comment: "It is God Who sends this spirit of stupor, but He does not send it arbitrarily nor at random: it is always a judgment" (EGT, 2:677). That is, the people's disobedience is the cause of their condition.

Sanday and Headlam describe the condition thus: " 'a spirit of torpor,' a state of dull insensibility to everything spiritual, such as would be produced by drunkenness, or stupor" (p. 314). A drunkard may claim that he is not responsible for what he does. But he is accountable for getting into that state. So with those whose hearts are dulled by disobedience. Robertson suggests the seriousness of this guilt when he writes: "The torpor seems the result of too much sensation, dulled by incitement into apathy" (WP, 4:393). Goodspeed uses the phrase "a state of spiritual insensibility." Probably the best translation is "stupor" (Phillips, RSV, Weymouth).

9 Snare, Trap, Stumblingblock The original Greek words could all be translated "trap." The first is *pagis*, used of a snare for birds or beasts. The second is *thēra* (only here in the NT). It first meant "a hunting, chase," then "prey, game," and finally a "net" in which game was caught. The third is *scandalon*. Its original use was for the bait stick or trigger of a trap. Then it came to be used for the snare or trap as a whole.

The word *table* suggests feasting. So the thought of the verse is this: "Their presumptuous security will become to them *a snare, a hunting, a stumbling-block*" (Vincent, 3:124). While lounging at the table they are suddenly

caught and destroyed. Sanday and Headlam express it thus: "The image is that of men feasting in careless security, and overtaken by their enemies, owing to the very prosperity which ought to be their strength" (p. 315). This is certainly a timely lesson for us as nations and as individuals. Daniel 5 is a good example.

Recompense The term *antapodoma* is a strong double compound, found only here (in bad sense) and in Luke 14:12 (in good sense). It comes from the verb *antapodidōmi* (*didōmi*, "give"; *apo*, "back"; *anti*, "in exchange for"), "to give back as an equivalent." Vincent comments: "It carries the idea of a *just retribution*" (3:124).

10 Bow The word for "bow down" is the compound *synkamptō*, found only here in the NT. It means "bend completely" or "bend together." Since we usually speak now of bowing ourselves and bending others, the better translation here is "bend."

12 Diminishing "Diminishing" is *hēttēma*, found here and in 1 Cor. 6:7 ("fault"). It means "defeat" (AG). It is variously translated "defection" (Moffatt), "overthrow" (Williams), "failure" (Phillips, RSV), and "defeat" (Weymouth, Goodspeed). The last meaning is clearly what the word has in Isa. 31:8. That is probably best here. The Jews had failed to find the Messianic kingdom because they rejected Jesus as Messiah. This was for them a fatal defeat.

13 Office The word *diaconia* occurs 34 times in the NT. Sixteen times it is translated "ministry," 6 times "ministration," and 3 times "ministering." Only here is it rendered "office." It is related to *diaconos*, which finally became the technical term for *deacon*. Most modern versions correctly use "ministry" here—"I glorify my ministry." That is a constant challenge to every preacher.

14 Emulation "Provoke to emulation" translates the same Greek verb *parazēloō* rendered "provoke to jealousy" in verse 11. The latter is the correct translation, which is used in the other two places where this verb occurs (Rom. 10:19; 1 Cor. 10:22). "Emulation" is not exactly synonymous with "jealousy."

16 Firstfruit, Lump What is the connection between these two terms? The word for "lump" (*phyrama*) has already occurred in 9:21. It literally means "that which is mixed or kneaded" (A-S). It is used of clay in 9:21, but here of dough. The term *firstfruit* (*aparchē*) we generally connect with fruit, grain, or vegetables. The connection between the two is thus explained by Vincent:

> The apparent confusion of metaphor, *firstfruit, lump,* is resolved by the fact that *firstfruit* does not apply exclusively to harvest, but is the general term for the first portion of every thing which was offered to God. The reference here is to Num. xv. 18–21; according to which the Israelites were to set apart a portion of the dough of each baking of bread for a cake for the priests. This was called *aparche, first-fruits* (3:126).

17 Branches . . . Broken Off There is a play on words here. *Klados,* "branch," and *ekklaō,* "break off," are from the same root.

17, 19, 23–24 Graffed In The verb *enkentrizō,* "graft in," is found only in this paragraph. The correct spelling today is "grafted." The word is derived from *kentron,* "a sting." So the emphasis is on the incision made in grafting.

In horticulture it is normally the cultivated branch which is grafted on the wild tree or vine. Paul realized that this natural process was being reversed in the church, a wild olive being grafted on the original tree, Israel (cf. "contrary to nature," v. 24).

17 Fatness In the best Greek text "and" (*kai*) between "root" and "fatness" is omitted. The latter word is *piotes* (only here in the NT). Weymouth has "a sharer in the rich sap of the olive root." Moffatt reads: "share the rich growth of the olive-stem." Goodspeed puts it: "share the richness of the olive's root." The RSV has "share the richness of the olive tree." This is based on the fact that the oldest Greek manuscript (Papyrus 46), with a few others, omits "root and."

22 Goodness The word is *chrēstotēs*. Its earliest meaning was "goodness" or "uprightness." But it is used by Aristotle and later writers in the sense of "kindness" or "generosity." That is apparently its meaning here. "Kindness" is adopted by Weymouth, Moffatt, and the RSV.

Severity The term *apotomia* is found only here in the NT. It comes from the verb *apotemnō,* "cut off." It suggests the idea of abrupt judgment from God on those who persevere in their disobedience.

12:1 Beseech The verb is *parakaleō*. It comes from *para,* "beside," and *kaleō,* "call." So

it literally means "call alongside." It was first used in the sense of "call to one's side, summon." It probably has this meaning in Acts 28:20 ("called for"). It may simply mean "invite" (e.g., Matt. 20:28). Sometimes it carries the stronger connotation, "summon to one's aid, call upon for help." But its main three meanings in the NT as reflected in the KJV are as follows: "beseech" (43), "comfort" (23), "exhort" (21). It occurs altogether 108 times.

A check of several translations shows a variety of renderings: "appeal to" (Moffatt, Goodspeed, Knox, RSV, ANT), "beg" (Ballantine, Berkeley, Phillips, Williams, Wuest), "entreat" (TCNT, Montgomery, Spencer), "pray" (Wand), "plead with" (Weymouth). All of these seem to be synonymous with "beseech." However, Godet prefers "exhort." But he stands nearly alone in this.

Present "That ye present" is the aorist infinitive, *parastēsai,* "to present." Arndt and Gingrich cite the verb as here "a technical term in the language of sacrifice: *offer, bring, present*" (p. 633). They suggest the meaning "offer" in this passage.

The force of the aorist tense is brought out vividly in Williams' translation: "to make a decisive dedication." A footnote explains: "Aor. infin., *once for all.*" Similarly Wuest has: "by a once-for-all presentation to place your bodies at the disposal of God." The language here clearly refers to the crisis of complete consecration.

Bodies The call to present our "bodies" may seem strange at first thought. Many commentators (e.g., Godet, Sanday and Headlam) take this literally as referring to the physical body. Denney makes that only the starting point. He writes: "The body is in view here as the instrument by which *all* human service is rendered to God" (EGT, 2:687). Weymouth translates it: "all your faculties." It would seem that this is the correct interpretation of what Paul meant, namely, "your whole being."

Reasonable Service The Greek is *logikēn latreian*. The first word is an adjective meaning "rational" (cf. "logical") or "spiritual." It occurs only one other place in the NT (1 Pet. 2:2). There it is translated "of the word" (cf. *logos*).

The second term is a noun. It is a technical religious word meaning "service" or "worship." In the LXX it means "the service of worship of God according to the requirements of the levitical law" (Thayer, p. 372). Occurring five times in the NT, it is translated "service" four

times and "divine service" once. The point is
that this word as used in the Bible refers to religious service, not secular.

Sanday and Headlam define the two words
together thus: "A service to God such as befits
the reason (*logos*), i.e. a spiritual sacrifice and
not the offering of an irrational animal" (p.
353). Godet explains it as follows: "the service
which rationally corresponds to the moral
premises contained in the faith which you profess" (p. 426). Denney translates the phrase
"spiritual worship." Phillips has: "intelligent
worship." Weymouth has: "a spiritual mode of
worship." The Berkeley Version reads: "your
worship with understanding."

2 Conformed This is *syschēmatizesthe*,
which occurs only here and in 1 Pet. 1:14. It
comes from *syn*, "with" or "together," and
schēma, which means "form." So the English
word *conform* (*con*, "with") exactly expresses
the idea. The present imperative means "stop
being conformed."

World The term *aiōn* is translated "world"
38 times in the KJV and "age" only twice. But
the latter is the more usual meaning of the
term. Basically it means a segment of time,
"age." It is used of the present age, the age to
come, and also of eternity. But a distinction
should be made between *cosmos* (world) and
aiōn (age).

Transformed The verb is *metamorphoō*. It
occurs only four times in the NT. Two occurrences are actually one usage—parallel accounts of the Transfiguration (Matt. 17:2; Mark
9:2). There it is rendered "transfigured." In the
fourth place it is translated "changed" (2 Cor.
3:18).

The word comes from *meta*, "across," and
morphē, "form." So it means to change across
from one form to another. The biological expression "metamorphosis" comes from it.

The three uses of the word in the NT give
some insight as to how we may live the transfigured life. On the Mount of Transfiguration, the
glory of Jesus burst through the veil of flesh
and the disciples caught a glimpse of His eternal glory. Just so, when we are filled with the
Holy Spirit, something of the divine glory
within will shine out through our lives.

The present passage indicates that transfiguration comes through the renewing of one's
mind. The verb is in the present imperative. It
therefore means: "Go on being continually
transfigured (more and more, day by day)."

This comes by the constant renewing of our
minds. Phil. 4:8 gives some idea of this process.

The third passage (2 Cor. 3:18) suggests that
transfiguration takes place as we reflect the
glory of God, just as the moon reflects the light
of the sun.

Sanday and Headlam bring out the difference between the Greek words for "conform"
and "transform" with this paraphrase: "Do not
adopt the external and fleeting fashion of this
world, but be ye transformed in your inmost nature" (p. 353).

Prove The verb is *dokimazō*. See discussion
at Rom. 2:18. It means "test," "prove" by testing, or "approve" as the result of testing. But it
may also mean "discover" or "discern." Moffatt
translates it "make out." Goodspeed has "find
out." Weymouth says "learn by experience."
The Twentieth Century New Testament reads
"discern." That seems to be the clearest translation. Williams has "find and follow," with the
footnote: "Vb. means *test and approve*, so *find
and follow*." The Berkeley Version reads: "sense
for yourselves." These would all seem to indicate, in agreement with some of the best commentators, that "discern" may be preferable to
"prove."

3 Think This verse has an interesting play
on words: *hyperphronein . . . phronein . . . phronein . . . sophronein*—"not *to be high-minded*
above what he ought *to be minded*, but *to be
minded* unto the *being sober-minded*." The verb
phroneō means "think" or "be minded," "have
an opinion of oneself" or "think of oneself." Occurring 29 times in the NT, it is translated a
dozen different ways in the KJV. The most common, "think," (5 times) fits well here, as does
also "regard" (4 times).

The first compound, *hyperphroneō*, is found
only here in the NT. It means "think too highly
of oneself, be haughty" (AG). It suggests "assuming an air of superiority over others." The idea
is that of being "overproud, high-minded."

The other compound, *sophroneō*, occurs 6
times in the NT. Twice it is translated "be in
right mind" and twice "be sober." One can see
the logic of A. T. Robertson's remark: "Self-
conceit is here treated as a species of insanity"
(WP, 4:403).

4 Office The last word is *praxis*. It comes
from the verb *prassō*, which means "do, accomplish." Hence it signifies "acting, activity, function." The last is the translation chosen for it in
this passage by Arndt and Gingrich. It was also
adopted by Moffatt, Weymouth, Goodspeed,

Williams, and other modern translators. Unquestionably it is preferable to "office."

6 Prophecy The main emphasis of NT prophecy is not on *prediction* but on *preaching* God's message. Apparently the prophets spoke with a strong sense of divine inspiration. They were to prophesy "according to the proportion [*anologia*] of faith"; that is, "according to the strength, clearness, fervour, and other qualities of that faith . . . so that the character and mode of their speaking is conformed to the rules and limits, which are implied in the proportion of their individual degree of faith" (Meyer, p. 473).

7 Ministry The word is *diaconia*. It occurs three times in Romans and is translated three different ways (cf. 11:13, "office"; 15:31, "service"). It is used in Luke 10:40 of preparing a meal. But almost always in the NT it refers to service in the Christian church, whether of a common sort in the local congregation or of the apostolic office and its administration. It is not clear just what type of service is intended here. Vincent comments: "As it is distinguished here from prophecy, exhortation, and teaching, it may refer to some more practical, and, possibly, minor form of ministry" (3:157). In the same vein Godet writes: "In our passage this term *ministry*, placed as it is between prophecy and the function of teaching, can only designate an activity of a practical nature, exerted in action, not in word" (p. 431). Sanday and Headlam think it has to do with "the administration of alms and attendance to bodily wants" (p. 357). It is rendered "practical service" by Moffatt, Goodspeed, and Williams, and in the Berkeley Version. That seems to be its meaning here, rather than the preaching or teaching ministry, which are mentioned separately.

8 Exhorteth, Exhortation The verb "exhorteth" is *parakaleō*. It occurs three other times in Romans (12:1; 15:30; 16:17). In all three of those places it is rendered "beseech." But that does not seem to fit here. It also means "comfort" or "encourage." Thayer writes, "It combines the ideas *exhorting* and *comforting* and *encouraging* in Romans XII:8" (p. 483). Interestingly, however, he defines the noun here, *paraklēsis*, as indicating "powerful hortatory discourse." It would appear that "exhortation" is the best translation.

Simplicity The word is *haplotēs*. Its basic meaning is "simplicity, sincerity, uprightness,

frankness," but it may also mean "generosity, liberality." Arndt and Gingrich prefer the latter here. Godet writes: "According to the etymological meaning, the word signifies: the disposition not to turn back on oneself; and it is obvious that from this first meaning there may follow either that of *generosity*, when a man gives without letting himself be arrested by any selfish calculation, or that of simplicity, when he gives without his left hand knowing what his right does. . . . This second meaning seems to us preferable here" (p. 433).

Moffatt and Goodspeed both prefer "liberality," as do Weymouth, Williams, the Berkeley Version, and the RSV. It seems that this is somewhat more acceptable.

Ruleth "He that ruleth" might appear to suggest political or civil office. But the context here clearly has to do with the relations of church members. So something in this frame of reference must be found to render the word here.

The term *proistamenos* literally means "the one standing in front"; in other words, what we today would call the "leader." Weymouth has: "One who presides should be zealous." Williams renders it: "one who leads others." The Berkeley Version calls him simply "the leader." That appears to be the best translation.

Cheerfulness The Greek word for "cheerfulness" is *hilarotēs*, found only here in NT. It gives us our word *hilarity*. It means "cheerfulness, gladness, graciousness" (AG). That is the true kind of Christian hilarity.

There are some who would say that hilarity has no place in the life of the consecrated Christian. But such have a sadly distorted concept of Christ. It is true that He was "a man of sorrows, and acquainted with grief." But He also said that when one fasts he should not "look gloomy" like the Pharisees. That Jesus had a keen sense of humor is shown by His remark about straining out a gnat and swallowing a camel and also about a camel going through the eye of a needle.

Halford Luccock, writing as "Quintus Quiz" in the *Christian Century* (Aug. 27, 1947), made this very wise observation: "Hilarity goes well with true and undefiled religion." But frivolity is something else. Here is his statement worth pondering: "Frivolity in the Christian Church is a denial of religion; hilarity is its sure evidence. Humor in its true use of it springs out of the peace of God."

9 Dissimulation Can there be such a thing? Paul seems to imply the possibility when he writes, "Let your love be unhypocritical" (lit. Gk.). The word means "without hypocrisy," and so "genuine" or "sincere." Of course, love that is insincere is not really love at all. In this, as in other attitudes of life, sincerity is the most essential thing. We must be sure that we are genuine. Sanday and Headlam call attention to an interesting fact: "It is significant that the word is not used in profane writers except once in adverbial form, and that by Marcus Aurelius" (p. 360). Sincerity did not receive its full credit in the ancient world.

Abhor The Greek word for "abhor" is the present participle *apostygountes*, found only here in the NT. It is a very strong term meaning "hate" or "abhor." Expressing extreme dislike, it may be translated "loathing," as it is in Moffatt and the NEB. Weymouth has: "Regard evil with horror." Williams emphasizes, as usual, the force of the tenses (both present). He renders the latter part of the verse thus: "You must always turn in horror from what is wrong, but keep on holding to what is right." Sanday and Headlam say of the term: "The word expresses a strong feeling of horror" (p. 360). The RSV renders it "hate."

Cleave The Greek word for "cleave" is the verb *kollaō*, which means "glue." It may be represented in English by either *cleave* or *cling*. It suggests that we are to be cemented securely to what is right.

On first sight this verse seems to contain an odd combination of ideas. But there is warning here that is very relevant to modern life. Paul urges his readers to be sure that their love is genuine, that it is not just hypocritically parading as love. Be sure, he says, that you hate evil and hold tightly to the good. Only thus can you escape the temptations that cause many to fall.

10 Kindly Affectioned "Be kindly affectioned" is an adjective, *philostorgos*, found only here in NT. The first part, *philos*, means "beloved." The second is from the noun *storgē*, meaning "family affection." Vincent points out the implication of this when he writes: "The word here represents Christians as bound by a family tie" (3:159). "Brotherly love" is one word in the Greek, *philadelphia*.

These two verses (9–10) emphasize two important corollary truths. Our love for our fellow Christians (brothers) must be affectionate, but at the same time it must be pure. This cannot be emphasized too strongly.

The exact meaning of the second clause of verse 10 has been a matter of dispute. The verb "preferring" (*proegeomai*) literally means "go before as a leader," to show the way. The ancient versions (Old Latin, Vulgate, Syriac, Armenian) take this passage as meaning "try to outdo one another in showing respect." That is the sense adopted by RSV: "Outdo one another in showing honor." Vincent would render it: "leading the way in showing the honor that is due" (3:159). The sense of the KJV is preferred by Denney and also by Sanday and Headlam.

11 Business The word translated "business" is *spoudē*. It means "speed, haste," and so "eagerness, earnestness." For some reason, the KJV elsewhere renders it "diligence," "haste," "care," "forwardness," but only here "business." Probably the best translation is "earnestness" (Williams) or "zeal" (Weymouth, Moffatt, RSV). Denney writes: "It denotes the moral earnestness with which one should give himself to his vocation" (EGT, 2:692).

Slothful The Greek word is *oknēros*, which means "shrinking, hesitating, timid" (A-S) or "idle, lazy, indolent" (AG). It is used by Jesus for the slothful servant (Matt. 25:26).

The phrase is best rendered, "Let not your zeal slacken" (Weymouth); or, "Never let your zeal flag" (Moffatt); or still more simply, "Never flag in zeal" (RSV). Luther put it: "In regard to zeal be not lazy."

Fervent The word *fervent* is the present (continuous action or state) participle of the verb *zeō*, which means "boil." In the NT the word is found only here and Acts 18:25. Goodspeed seeks to bring out the original force of the word in his translation, "on fire with the Spirit." Very similar is "Be aglow with the Spirit" (RSV). Moffatt has, "Maintain the spiritual glow." Weymouth says, "Have your spirits aglow." Williams agrees closely with Goodspeed. He renders it, "always on fire with the Spirit."

It is obvious that one problem is that of translating *to pneumati*. Does it mean "in your spirit" or "with the Spirit"? Sanday and Headlam wisely suggest the combination: "the human spirit instinct with and inspired by the Divine Spirit" (p. 361).

12 Patient The Greek word is *hypomenontes*, present participle. The verb *hypomenō* means literally "remain under." It has the metaphorical meaning "stand one's ground, hold out, endure" (AG). Sanday and Headlam suggest that the idea here is "endurance in persecution" (p. 362).

It seems surprising that so many have retained "patient" here (e.g., Weymouth, Williams, RSV). The Berkeley Version has "endure," which more correctly conveys the basic meaning of the verb. "Patient" tends to be too passive a term in modern English to represent adequately the Greek. Moffatt has, "Be stedfast in trouble." Goodspeed agrees: "steadfast in time of trouble." That seems better.

Instant The KJV reads: "Continuing instant in prayer." The true idea here, however, is "insistent" rather than "instant." But the word "insist" was a new term in 1611.

The verb is a very strong one, *proskartereō*. It means "attend constantly, continue stedfastly." The thought is brought out correctly by most modern versions: Goodspeed and Berkeley both have "persistent in prayer." Williams brings out more fully the continuous force of the present participle. He renders it, "ever persistent in prayer." Denney writes: "The strong word suggests not only the constancy with which they are to pray, but the effort that is needed to maintain a habit so much above nature" (EGT, 2:692).

13 Distributing The Berkeley Version has the latter. The simple Greek is "sharing in the needs of the saints." The verb *koinoneō*, here in the present participle, means "have in common," and so "share." In the case of giving to those who are in need it could well be rendered "contributing." But why not adopt the simplest term, *sharing*? The only objection would be that we share with people in need rather than with their needs. But neither do we contribute or distribute to their needs!

Hospitality The Greek word *philoxenia* means literally "love of strangers." That is what real hospitality is. The word is used only here and in Heb. 13:2. There, and elsewhere in the NT, it is clear that "hospitality was recognized as one of the most important of Christian duties" (SH, p. 363).

"Given to" is literally "pursuing" (*diōkontes*). Some of the recent versions say: "Practice hospitality." That is the right idea.

16 The Same Mind The first clause reads: "Be of the same mind one toward another." The literal Greek is: "thinking the same thing toward one another." Arndt and Gingrich say it means "be in agreement, live in harmony." The latter rendering is adopted in RSV. Williams

has: "Keep on thinking in harmony with one another." Compare, "In your relations with one another, cultivate a spirit of harmony" (TCNT).

Men of Low Estate The middle sentence poses a problem frequently encountered in translating and interpreting the NT. "High things" is undisputed, for it is clearly the neuter plural accusative. But does the second clause of the sentence refer to lowly things or lowly men? No final answer to that question can ever be given. As Denney says, "Certainty on such points must always be personal rather than scientific" (EGT, 3:693).

The problem arises from the fact that in the genitive and dative cases the forms are exactly alike for the masculine and neuter. Only the context can decide which of the two is preferable. Unfortunately the context in this case does not help us much.

Denney prefers to take the adjective as masculine (as it always is elsewhere in the NT) "lowly men." So did Luther, but Calvin favored the neuter. Among the early English translations of the Bible, Wyclif's has the neuter sense, Tyndale's and the Geneva Bible the masculine. Sanday and Headlam say: "The neuter seems best to suit the contrast with *ta hypsēla* (the high things) and the meaning of the verb" (p. 364). On the other hand, Brown says the masculine sense agrees best with the verb (JFB, 4:267). Lange agrees. So does Alford. Meyer, however, says emphatically that the adjective is neuter. The passage means: "Instead of following the impulse to high things, rather yield to that which is humble, to the claims and tasks which are presented to you by the humbler relations of life" (p. 479). Godet interprets "high things" as denoting "distinctions, high relations, ecclesiastical honors," and declares that the reference of "lowly" is to "the most indigent and ignorant, and least influential in the church" (p. 437). He therefore adopts the masculine sense. So does Olshausen, who draws this parallel: "The Son of God teaches the faithful to consort with publicans and sinners, in order to win them for his kingdom" (4:147). Bengel favors the neuter. So does Vincent.

A glance at a few translations discovers similar disagreement: "Associate with humble folk" (Moffatt); "Accommodate yourselves to humble ways" (TCNT); "Be content with humble things" (Ballantine); "Keep on associating with lowly people" (Williams); "Accept humble tasks" (Goodspeed); "Willingly adjust yourselves to humble situations" (Berkeley); "Falling in with the opinions of common folk" (Knox); "Condescend to the lowly" (Confraternity); "Don't become snobbish but take a real interest in ordinary people" (Phillips); "Condescend to things that are lowly" (ASV); "Associate with the lowly" (RSV); "Go about with humble folk" (NEB). It is of interest to note that while the English and American Revised versions took the adjective as neuter, RSV and NEB returned to the masculine sense adopted by KJV. This was the meaning favored in the early church, as especially expressed by Chrysostom: "That is, bring thyself down to their humble condition, ride or walk with them; do not be humbled in mind only, but help them also, and stretch forth thy hand to them."

Is it possible for us to come to any kind of conclusion in the matter? One of the best answers to this question is that offered by C. K. Barrett in his volume on Romans in the "Harper's New Testament Commentaries" ("Black's" in the British Isles). He writes thus: "It is impossible to feel confident that either translation is correct to the exclusion of the other. It is well to remember that Greek occasionally allows an ambiguity impossible in English; Paul may have been aware, and may have approved, of both ways of taking his words" (pp. 241–42).

Condescend to   Part of the problem that has perplexed us is due to difficulty in ascertaining the exact meaning of the verb involved (*synapagō*). It is rare in the NT, being found elsewhere only in Gal. 2:13 and 2 Pet. 3:17. In the former Paul speaks of Barnabas being "carried away with their dissimulation." In the latter Peter warns against "being led away with the error of the wicked." The meaning in these two passages is clear.

The verb is a double compound. *Syn* means "with"; *apo*, "away from"; and *agō*, "lead." Always passive in the NT, it has the meaning "be led or carried away with." So Sanday and Headlam would translate this passage: "Allow yourself to be carried along with, give yourself over to, humble tasks" (p. 364). This agrees with Thayer's understanding of it: "To suffer one's self to be carried away together with . . . i.e. to yield or submit one's self to lowly things, conditions, employments,—not to evade their power" (p. 601). Vine prefers "be led along with"—its literal meaning. Vincent seeks to bring out the full force of the prepositions. He says the idea is this: "Set not your mind on lofty things, but be borne *away* (*apo*) from these by the current of your Christian sympathy *along with* (*syn*) things which are humble" (3:161).

But it seems that the natural meaning of the verb fits better with the masculine sense than the neuter. Having come to this conclusion, we would definitely prefer "associate with" rather than "condescend to." An attitude of condescension toward others is something less than Christian. In fact it is the very thing that Paul is speaking strongly against here, as Phillips' translation very well brings out.

Of course it should be recognized that when the KJV was made the modern connotations of *condescend* were absent. Then it meant "to stoop voluntarily and graciously . . . 'to depart from the privileges of superiority by a voluntary submission; to sink willingly to equal terms with inferiors' . . . to make concessions; to comply, consent, concur, agree" (OED, 2:783). But now it usually means "to bestow courtesies with some air of superiority; to assume a patronizing air; to stoop as a favor or benevolence" (WNID, p. 556). Such an attitude is obviously unchristian.

18 *As Much as Lieth in You*   This phrase has been much misunderstood and abused. It has been offered as an alibi for failing to live at peace with others. "The Bible says, 'as much as lieth in you,' and it doesn't lie in me to live peaceably with that person!"

Most modern versions render the Greek here more accurately. They agree rather closely on this translation: "so far as it depends on you" (Weymouth). That is the correct idea. If there is to be any quarreling, do not let it come from you (*ex hymōn*). If one will maintain this attitude in a consistent and kindly way, much of the trouble between people can be eliminated.

19 *Wrath*   Paul warns: "Avenge not yourselves, but rather give place unto wrath." The ASV reads: "the wrath *of God*." But this loses some of its significance in the light of the fact that the Greek usually places the definite article before abstract nouns, an idiom which is not followed in English. So it is not always possible to tell whether the article should be translated into English or left untranslated (as it usually is). Only the context can decide the matter.

Here the latter part of the verse would seem to suggest that, instead of taking personal vengeance on those who wrong us, we should "leave it to the wrath of God" (RSV). The NEB agrees in its rendering: "Leave a place for divine retribution." That seems to be the correct meaning. After all, what does "give place unto wrath" mean? Does it mean we "let go" with our wrath? Clearly not that! Shelve it aside? It seems better to say, "Let God take care of the situation."

13:1 *Be Subject*

It is important to note in connection with vv. 1–2 that "be subject," "ordained," "resist" (first time), and "ordinance" are all from the same root. Also, the first "resisteth" in verse 2 is, in the original, an entirely different word from the second "resisteth" and "resist."

The verb *hypotassō* is a compound of *tassō*. The latter was primarily a military term meaning "draw up in order, arrange." The former was also used in a military sense as "place under" (*hypo*). In the middle, as here, it means "subject oneself, obey." Both translations are equally correct. The NEB has "submit." Goodspeed, Moffatt, Williams, and Phillips have "obey." Weymouth has "be obedient" and Berkeley "render obedience." There is no problem with the dative case following the verb, since *obey* takes the dative in Greek.

Power

There are two different Greek words translated as "power" in the KJV. The first is "*dynamis*," from which come *dynamo, dynamic, dynamite*. This is correctly rendered "power." But the term here is *exousia*. In the KJV it is translated "power" 69 times, "authority" 29 times (out of a total of 103 times). It comes from the verb *exesti*, which means "it is permitted, it is lawful." So it properly signifies liberty or power to act. Later it came to be used for "right" or "authority."

Practically all recent translations have "authorities" in this passage. Unquestionably that is the more correct rendering. It means "governing authorities" (Berkeley, Moffatt, RSV), "ruling authorities" (Weymouth), or "civil authorities" (Williams, Phillips). The NEB has "supreme authorities." The phrase includes the participial modifier *hyperechousais*, which means "holding over or above," and so "being superior."

It is true that we do speak of the "Western powers," or "great powers." But these expressions refer to nations. Here the primary emphasis is on the *authority* of governments to rule. It should not be inferred from this passage that all *rulers* are chosen by God, but rather that all *rule* is divinely ordained. Governments are set to enforce law. Since most people will not be ruled by love, they must be ruled by law. That is inevitable in an imperfect world. So God has ordained that there should be ruling authorities to keep law and order. It is probably true, in the last analysis, that any government is better than no government. Anarchy is the worst state into which human society can come. When and where there is no governmental authority, human life and property are unsafe.

Where there is no strong central authority, the resulting anarchy is chaotic confusion and devastating destruction.

Ordained

The KJV states that the existing authorities have been "ordained" by God. Moffatt, Weymouth, and Berkeley have "constituted." Goodspeed and Williams have "established." The RSV and NEB have "instituted." Phillips has "appointed under God."

The form is the perfect passive participle of *tassō*. As noted above, it was originally a military term meaning "draw up in order, arrange." It also signified "assign, appoint." Perhaps Phillips' rendering here is the simplest and best. Again it should be noted that it is not the party or person in power that is appointed under God, but the fact of government.

2 Resisteth

As already noted, two different Greek words have both been translated "resist" in the KJV. The ERV and the ASV indicate the distinction, rendering the first "resist" and the second "withstand." It is true that both verbs may be translated "resist." But it would seem that the difference in the Greek should be indicated in English.

The first verb is *antitassō*, another compound of *tassō*. *Anti* means "against." So the verb signifies "set in array against." In the middle (as always in the NT) it means "oppose, resist, set oneself against." The other verb is *anthistēmi*. It is composed of *anti* (against) and *histēmi* (stand). So it means "withstand, resist, oppose."

In an attempt to use different words in English the various translators have gone in different directions. Weymouth, Berkeley, and the NEB have "rebel" for the first, "resist" for the second. Moffatt and Goodspeed have "resist" for the first, and "oppose" for the second, which may be best.

Ordinance

The word is *diatagē*. It comes from *diatassō* (still another compound of *tassō*), which means "charge, give orders to, appoint, arrange, ordain" (A-S). The noun carries the strong verbal force. So the phrase has been translated "what God has ordained" (Goodspeed), "a divine institution" (NEB). Perhaps the simplest translation is "God's appointment" (Weymouth, Berkeley).

Damnation

The translators of the KJV were fond of the word *damnation*. They used "damnable" once (2 Pet. 2:1), "damned" three times, and "damnation" 11 times. This sort of language is common in Shakespeare, who wrote in the same period. But it is doubtful whether it is wise today for Christians to use such a term as "damned," in view of its prevalence in profanity.

Actually, the Greek word here does not mean "damnation." It is *krima*, from *krinō*, "I judge." So it simply means "judgment"—no more, no less.

Does this mean civil punishment or divine judgment? Denney writes: "The judgment or condemnation which those who offer such resistance shall receive, is of course a Divine one" (EGT, 2:696). But most commentators prefer to think of it as the judicial punishment bestowed by civil government on those who oppose its authority. It would seem that the context favors this interpretation. The word does, of course, frequently carry the idea of condemnation by God. But it is not clear that that is the main emphasis here.

3 Terror? Paul says that rulers are not a "terror" to good works. The word is *phobos*. In 41 out of its 47 occurrences in the NT it is translated "fear" in KJV. Three times it is rendered "terror." That seems to be its proper meaning here.

The earliest connotation of the term (in Homer) is "panic flight"; then that which caused the flight, "panic fear"; and finally the "object or cause of terror" (LSJ, 1947).

Wilt "Wilt thou then not be afraid of the power?" The translation is not completely clear. Literally the Greek says: "Do you wish not to fear the authority?" The Berkeley Version reads: "You do not want to fear the authority, do you?" It is not simple futurity that is expressed, but the question of a wish.

4 Minister The ruler is called a "minister" of God. The word is *diaconos*. In NT it is translated "minister" 20 times, "servant" 7 times, and "deacon" 3 times. It seems to have the technical sense of "deacon" in the 3 passages where it is thus rendered (Phil. 1:1; 1 Tim. 3:8, 12).

But the commonest meaning is simply "servant." There are no less than 6 Greek words translated "servant" in the KJV. This one suggests a servant in relation to his work. Goodspeed and the NEB have "God's agents."

The objection to using "minister" here is that the term has a connotation today in church circles which is foreign to its general use in the NT. Except for the three passages noted above, it simply means "servant" and should be so translated. The original meaning of "minister" as being a servant is very significant for those of us who are ministers of the gospel. It is our responsibility to *serve* the people as well as "minister" in the pulpit.

Revenger The word is *ekdikos*. In its only other occurrence in the NT (1 Thess. 4:6) it is translated "avenger." That would be better here. "Revenge" has a connotation that does not fit the character of God or His servants. *Webster's New International Dictionary* (2nd ed.) says: "In present usage to AVENGE is to inflict punishment, either in behalf of oneself or of others, for the sake of vindication or just retribution; as to *avenge* an insult, to *avenge* the injuries of the helpless and innocent. . . . To REVENGE is to inflict pain or injury in resentful or malicious retaliation" (p. 190). Obviously the former word applies to God, not the latter.

6 Pay Ye The first clause reads: "For for this cause pay ye tribute also." That sounds like a command. The ASV has: "For for this cause ye pay tribute also." Most, if not all, of the recent translations treat this as a statement rather than a command. The problem arises from the simple fact that in the second person plural of the present tense the indicative and imperative forms are exactly the same. Only the context can suggest which it may be in any given passage. Here the indicative seems to be preferable.

Tribute In place of "tribute" all the recent translations have "taxes," which is the term we would use today. We employ "tribute" more frequently in the sense of a compliment.

The Greek word is *phoros*. It comes from *pherō*, which means "bear" or "carry." So literally it would mean "something carried." But in both classical Greek and that of the NT it regularly signifies taxes. The word occurs three times in verses 6 and 7 and only twice elsewhere in the NT (Luke 20:22; 23:2). It is used primarily of taxes paid by the people of a subject nation.

Ministers The word for "ministers" in verse 6 is a different one from that in verse 4. This one is *leitourgos*, from which comes *liturgy*. Contrary to the case in the fourth verse, most of the recent translations use "minister" here.

The reason for this is that *leitourgos* in classical Greek first meant one who served a public office at his own expense. Then it was used more generally for a public servant, one who served the state. A specialized meaning was "one who performed religious service." From this comes our modern idea of a minister.

Of course, it is not religious service that is performed by the government for its citizens. But it acts for God in serving the public in various ways, just as a minister of state serves his own government.

7 Render The verb is *apodidōmi*. It means "give up or back, restore, return"; and so "to render what is due, to pay" (A-S). Deissmann shows that this word was used regularly in the papyri for a promise to pay back borrowed money. The emphasis is on the payment of a debt (LAE, p. 331). The NT consistently teaches that taxes are a debt which one owes the government, and that paying them is therefore a legal and moral obligation.

Custom The word for "tribute" is the same as in verse 6. We noted there that a better translation would be "taxes."

But how about "custom"? The Greek word is *telos*. The common meaning for this is "end" (so 36 out of 42 times in the NT). But it was also used in classical Greek, as well as in NT (only here and Matt. 17:25) for "custom." Thayer says it refers to "an indirect tax on goods" (p. 620). Arndt and Gingrich agree. For this special meaning Abbott-Smith offers "toll, custom, revenue."

The connection of all this with the root meaning "end" seems obscure. Vine makes this suggestion: "what is paid for public ends, a toll, tax, custom" (1:263).

Deissmann gives a photo of an ostracon of A.D. 32–33 which is a tax receipt (LAE, p. 111). It contains the word *telos* for *taxes*. Sanday and Headlam distinguish the two words for *taxes* thus: "*Phoros* is the tribute paid by a subject nation, while *telos* represents the customs and dues which would in any case be paid for the support of the civil government" (p. 368).

Fear The word is *phobos*, the most common meaning of which is "fear." But what kind of fear is meant here? Arndt and Gingrich suggest that the word may mean "reverence" toward God, or "respect" toward officials, as here. "Respect" is the translation found here in many recent versions. There can be little doubt that it is best.

An excellent discussion of *phobos* is given by William Barclay in *A New Testament Wordbook* (pp. 92–97). He shows that every time it is used in the Synoptic Gospels and Acts it indicates awe or reverence in the face of divine power. Toward one's fellowman the attitude is respect. Sanday and Headlam say that it is "the respectful awe" felt for one in power (p. 368).

8 Love Paul declares that the only thing we should owe our fellowman is love. He thereby implies that this debt will never be discharged.

Sanday and Headlam have an excellent note on "the history of the word *agapē*" (pp. 374–77). We can only summarize the main points.

There are three Greek verbs for *love*. The first, *eraō*, means "strong passionate affection." Because of its frequent connection with sensual passions this word is not used at all in the NT.

The second word is *phileō*. It signifies "warm domestic affection." The third verb is *agapaō*.

The difference between these last two is that *phileo* expresses "greater affection," *agapaō* "greater esteem." The latter was much preferred by biblical writers. In the LXX *agapaō* occurs 268 times, *phileō* only 12 times. The NT uses *agapaō* 138 times, *phileō* (for *love*) 22 times. The noun *agapē*, not found in classical writers, appears only occasionally in the LXX but is frequent in the NT (116 times).

9 Comprehended Paul says that all the obligations of man to man are "comprehended" in the one great commandment to love one's neighbor as oneself. The Greek verb is *anakephalaioō*. It comes from *ana*, "up," and *kephalē*, "head." It means "to sum up, gather up." Elsewhere in the NT it is found only in Eph. 1:10, where it is rendered "gather together" (KJV). But here almost all recent translations have "summed up."

11 The Time In the NT there are two words for *time*. The first is *chronos*, from which comes *chronology*. It means "time in the sense of duration" (A-S, p. 226). The second is *kairos* (used here). It first meant "due measure, fitness, proportion," and so, "time in the sense of a fixed and definite period" (*ibid.*). Thayer says that when *ho kairos* is used alone (as here) it signifies "the time when things are brought to a crisis, the decisive epoch waited for" (p. 318). As compared with *chronos*, *kairos* means "a definitely limited portion of time, with the added notion of suitableness" (p. 319).

It is interesting to note that in modern Greek, *kairos* means "weather," while *chronos* means "year." Cremer says that here *kairos* suggests "a time in some way limited or defined" (p. 324). Lightfoot suggests that it means "the right moment" (*Notes*, p. 70). Vine defines it as "a fixed or definite period, a season" (4:138). Arndt and Gingrich say that here it means "the present (time)." Denney writes: "*Ho kairos* is not 'the time' abstractly, but the time they lived in with its moral import, its critical place in the working out of God's designs" (EGT, 2:699).

It is in keeping with this emphasis that the NEB translates this passage: "Remember how critical the moment is." The RSV has: "You know what hour it is." Williams says: "You know the present crisis." We do not feel that James Barr has successfully refuted this distinction between *chronos* and *kairos*.

In this passage Paul is emphasizing the need for keeping alert and awake in view of the significance of passing time. Cullmann comments: "Every passing minute brings us nearer to the end point, and from the viewpoint of redemptive history every passing minute, when seen from the center (the Christ-event), is important in the Church" (*Christ and Time*, p. 148).

The KJV fails to bring out the difference between *chronos* and *kairos*. The former it renders "time" 33 times and "season" 4 times; the latter, "time" 63 times and "season" 13 times. It is significant of the NT emphasis that *kairos* occurs more frequently (86 times) than *chronos* (53 times). In the Scriptures time is thought of in its redemptive and often eschatological significance.

All the recent translations seek to bring out the biblical emphasis of the term *kairos*. The RV changed "time" to "season" in some 20 places. More recent versions go even further.

Salvation What is meant here by "salvation"? Were we not saved "when we believed"? Denney gives the meaning as follows: "*Hē sotēria* has here the transcendent eschatological sense" (EGT, 2:699). That is, it refers to our final salvation in heaven.

13 Walk The Greek word is *peripateō*, which means "walk," or literally "walk around." But in the NT it is used very frequently in the metaphorical sense of "live." This usage is especially prominent in Paul's Epistles (33 times). Elsewhere in the NT it occurs 16 times.

Honestly The Greek adverb is *euschēmonōs*. It comes from *eu*, "well," and *schēma*, "fashion." So it means "decorously" or "becomingly." The latter is a common rendering in the recent translations (so Weymouth, Williams, RSV).

One might wonder about the reason for "honestly" in the KJV. The answer is that *honest* originally meant "honorable." The first meaning given in the *Oxford English Dictionary* is "held in honour; holding an honourable position; respectable" (5:361).

Rioting The term *rioting* is apt to have political overtones today. A riot is a disturbance of the public peace by an unlawful assembly of people. The Greek word *kōmos* does not suggest that. Originally it was used for "a festal procession in honor of Dionysius, then a joyous meal or banquet" (AG, p. 462). In the NT it always has the bad sense of "carousing" or "revelry."

Chambering "Debauchery" is the translation of Moffatt, RSV, and NEB. Weymouth has "lust," Williams "sexual immorality," Goodspeed "immorality," and Berkeley "prostitution." These strong renderings are justified by the Greek word *koitē*. First it meant "bed," then the marriage bed, then illicit relations. It is debauchery at its worst.

Wantonness The Greek word here is *aselgeia*. It is translated "sensuality" (Moffatt), "lust" (Weymouth), "indecency" (Goodspeed), "vice" (NEB), and "licentiousness" (Williams, RSV). The last seems best today.

Envying In the NT, *zēlos* has both the good meaning "zeal" and the bad connotation "jealousy." Here it is obviously the latter. Almost all recent translations have "jealousy."

14:1 Weak in the Faith "Him that is weak" and "who is weak" (v. 2) are both present participles. We might assume that by "weak" is meant worldly or indifferent. But verse 2 indicates clearly that Paul has in mind the type of person who makes a major issue out of minor matters, one whose religion consists of being a vegetarian and observing meticulously manmade rules and regulations. This is not the freedom available to us in Christ. We are to be strong, robust Christians, enjoying doing what is proper and wholesome. Christianity is a life dominated by love, not law. Goodspeed translates "weak" as "overscrupulous."

Doubtful Disputations The meaning of the last clause is not altogether clear. That is shown by the variety of ways it has been translated. The ASV has "yet not for decision of scruples." Similarly, the RSV reads "but not for disputes over opinions."

On the other hand, Goodspeed says, "Do not criticize their views." Moffatt has "but not for the purpose of passing judgment on his scruples." Phillips says, "but not with the idea of arguing over his scruples."

The Greek is *mē eis diakriseis dialogismōn*. The first two words mean "not to" or "not for." The noun *diakrisis* is "the act of *judgment, dis-*

cernment." Thayer suggests that the clause means "not for the purpose of passing judgment on opinions, as to which one is to be preferred as the more correct" (p. 139). Arndt and Gingrich define the noun as "distinguishing, differentiation." They also note that in Polybius it seems to have the idea "quarrel." So they would translate this clause as "but not for the purpose of getting into quarrels about opinions" (p. 184).

The last word of the clause is the noun *dialogismos,* "a thought, reasoning, inward questioning" (A-S, p. 109). Thayer says that in Greek writers from Plato down it means "the thinking of a man deliberating with himself" (p. 139). In the KJV it is translated "thought" nine times and once each "reasoning," "imagination," "doubtful" (here), "disputing," "doubting." Vincent writes: "The primary meaning of *dialogismos* is a *thinking-through* or *over.* Hence of those speculations or reasonings in one's mind which take the form of *scruples*" (3:167). A. T. Robertson thinks the meaning of the clause is this: "The 'strong' brother is not called upon to settle all the scruples of the 'weak' brother" (WP, 4:412).

Alford identifies the weak Christian as an overscrupulous Jew who had been converted, but whose "over-tender conscience" caused him to continue abstinence from meat and observance of days. Alford explains the two nouns thus: "disputes in order to settle the points on which he has scruples" (2:451). Denney writes: "The weak man is one who does not fully appreciate what his Christianity means" (EGT, 2:700). That is, he does not realize that salvation is by faith, not by scrupulous observance of legal regulations. In a similar vein Sanday and Headlam say: " 'Weakness in faith' means an inadequate grasp of the great principle of salvation by faith in Christ" (p. 384). They paraphrase this verse thus: "Receive a scrupulous Christian cordially. Do not be continually condemning him" (p. 383).

2 Herbs This verse describes the "weak" person as one who eats "herbs." Recent translations agree in having "vegetables." That is the correct meaning of the Greek word *lachanon,* which occurs here and once in each of the Synoptic Gospels. A check of a dictionary will show that the two English words are not synonymous. The Greek word comes from a verb meaning "to dig"—so something that comes out of the ground.

4 Servant Six different Greek words are translated by "servant" in the KJV. *Diaconos,*

which is rendered "deacon," means an "attendant." *Doulos* is a "slave." *Therapon* refers to a voluntary "servant." *Oiketēs,* used here, means a "house servant" (from *oikos,* "house"). *Pais* may refer to either "child" or "servant." *Hypēretēs* (literally, "under-rower") emphasizes the idea of subordination.

The KJV reads: "Who art thou that judgest another man's servant? to his own master he standeth or falleth. Yea, he shall be holden up: for God is able to make him stand."

The first thing that should be noted is that in the last clause the oldest Greek manuscripts have *kyrios* (lord) instead of *theos* (God). But *kyrios* is the same word which is translated "master" in the middle of the verse. Furthermore, "another man's" is probably an overtranslation. The Greek simply says "another's." Berkeley wisely capitalizes this: "Another's." The RSV has in the last clause: "for the Master is able to make him stand." With admirable consistency the NEB goes a step further. It reads: "Who are you to pass judgement on someone else's servant? Whether he stands or falls is his own Master's business; and stand he will, because his Master has power to enable him to stand."

Paul is not talking about "another man's servant." He is referring to the weak, overscrupulous brother, who is yet the Master's servant, not ours. So we have no right to condemn him.

5 Fully Persuaded The verb is *plērophoreō,* which occurs only five times in the NT (elsewhere in Romans only at 4:21). It comes from the adjective *pleres* (full) and the verb *phero* (bear, carry). So its first meaning is "*to bring in full measure,* hence, *to fulfil, accomplish*" (A-S). Then it came to mean "*to persuade, assure* or *satisfy fully*" (*ibid.*). Arndt and Gingrich prefer here "fully convinced."

6 Regardeth The verb is *phroneō.* It comes from *phrēn* (mind). So it means "*to think,* to be *minded* in a certain way" (A-S). Occurring some 29 times in the NT, it is translated a dozen different ways. Here probably the best rendering is "observes."

10 Set at Nought The verb *exoutheneō* is the same one which is translated "despise" in verse 3. It means "to set at nought, despise utterly, treat with contempt" (A-S). Here it may be translated "look down upon" (Weymouth, Moffatt, Goodspeed) or "despise" (RSV). The last is perhaps the clearest.

Judgment Seat Paul declares that we must all stand before "the judgment seat of God" (so the best Greek text). He is the Judge, not we. Therefore we should stop judging.

The word for "judgment seat" is *bēma*. One can see the term today carved on the wall where Gallio once sat on the judgment seat at Corinth (Acts 18:12, 16–17). It is used of the place where Pilate sat to judge (Matt. 27:19; John 19:13), and also Festus (Acts 25:6, 17). All these were Roman governors. So it refers to the official tribunal, where the governor could pass judgment on offenders or exonerate the innocent.

Paul uses the similar expression "the judgment seat of Christ," in one other place (2 Cor. 5:10). It is clear that he had a keen consciousness that one day he, and all of us, must stand before the great Judge of all. No wonder he sought always to have "a conscience void of offense toward God, and toward men" (Acts 24:16).

13 ***Stumbling Block*** In this verse we find two synonyms, both of which are sometimes translated "stumblingblock" in the KJV. Here one is rendered "stumblingblock" and the other "occasion to fall."

The first is *proskomma*. It comes from *proskoptō*, "strike against." Its main meaning in the NT is "stumble" (strike one's foot against). The second word is *scandalon*. We have already noted that this word originally meant the bait stick on a trap or snare and then the trap or snare itself. Hogg and Vine comment: "In the New Testament *scandalon* is always used metaphorically, and ordinarily of anything that arouses prejudice or becomes a hindrance to others, or causes them to fall by the way" (Vine, p. 262).

Translators differ in their treatment of these words. We find "obstacle or stumbling-block" (Weymouth, NEB), "stumbling block or hindrance" (Moffatt, RSV), "hindrance or obstacle" (Goodspeed), "hindrance or a stumbling block" (Berkeley).

In spite of this variety of translations, Paul's meaning is clear. He is warning the meat-eaters not to do anything that would be a spiritual hindrance to the vegetarians. In other words, we should not selfishly glory in our religious freedom in such a way as to cause a weaker, overscrupulous brother to stumble and fall. True love will put the interests of others before our own. It is the same principle that Paul set forth in answering the question of the Corinthian Christians about eating meat offered to idols. To them he wrote: "But take heed lest by any means this liberty of yours become a stumblingblock to them that are weak" (1 Cor. 8:9). His own magnanimous spirit is shown in the declaration: "Wherefore, if meat make my brother to offend, I will eat no flesh while the world standeth, lest I make my brother to offend" (1 Cor. 8:13). Nothing is worth enjoying if it causes someone to lose his soul.

14 ***Unclean*** This exact expression is found in Acts 10:14, where Peter declares that he has never eaten anything "common or unclean." The first Greek word is *koinos*, which simply means "common." The second is *akatharton* (*a*-negative, and *katharos*—"pure, clean"). The reference is to animals considered unclean in the Jewish law.

Here *koinos* is translated "unclean" three times. This usage reflects the difference between the sacred and the secular. Avoidance of "unclean" meats, eaten commonly by the Gentiles, was one of the main manifestations of the fact that Israel was a separate nation, God's holy people.

The principle which Paul is enunciating here is that in and of themselves *things* are non-moral. It is the use we make of them which constitutes them pure or impure. That is true, for instance, of the human body. Morality does not attach to matter, but to spirit. Sin is something inside a man, though it may manifest itself outwardly. Paul recognized the fact that there can be no such thing as "unclean" animals. It is only a matter of one's attitude toward them. Our choice of foods should not be based on religious scruples but on scientific knowledge. Since our bodies belong to God, we should care for them properly as His possessions, eating what will be conducive to good health.

The question might be raised at this point as to why pork, for instance, was forbidden to the Jews in the Mosaic law. The answer is simple. Of all meats, pork is one of the quickest to spoil and the most apt to communicate disease. Cooks know that while rare beef may be safe as well as palatable, pork should always be cooked thoroughly. In a hot climate with no means of refrigeration, the Israelites needed to be protected against the ever constant danger of food poisoning. So religious sanctions were attached to the regulations about food, in order that God's people would be afraid to eat what was forbidden. Common sense lies behind the dietary laws of ancient Israel. But against the Judaizers Paul contended that true religion is a matter of the spirit, not of outward rules and regulations.

Esteemeth It should be recognized that the Greek word for "esteem" in this verse has no relation to the one translated that way in verse 5. There it was *krinō*, "judge." Here it is *logizomai*, which properly refers to a numerical calculation, and so means "count" or "reckon." The best translation here is "considers" (Moffatt, Berkeley, NEB).

15 Grieved The Greek word is *lypeō*. It means "*to distress, grieve, cause pain* or *grief*" (A-S). Arndt and Gingrich give the basic meaning as "grieve, pain." They would translate the passage here, "if your brother's feelings are hurt because of food." But they note that the verb can also mean "injure, damage." It would seem that the best rendering might be "is being injured" (Moffatt, RSV).

Destroy No less than 10 Greek verbs are translated "destroy" in the KJV. The one used here, *apollymi*, means "destroy utterly."

But the thing that concerns us is that this word is used frequently in the NT of sinners *perishing* without salvation. So here the idea is not of the weak brother having his reputation ruined or his life wasted in this world. The peril is that in causing him to stumble by our own selfish liberties we may be responsible for his soul perishing forever. That danger should always act as a deterrent to any thoughtlessness toward others on our part. We may say that it is nobody's business what we do. But no one can hide behind that deceptive alibi. How we live *does* affect others, whether we want it to or not. In a very real sense every one of us is his brother's keeper.

16 Evil Spoken Of The Greek word is *blasphēmeō*, from which comes *blaspheme*. Its earliest meaning was "speak profanely of sacred things." Then it came to mean "*speak ill, or to the prejudice of* one, *slander*." In the KJV it is rendered "blaspheme" 17 times and "speak evil of" 10 times. Clearly the latter is the meaning here. While we have limited the use of *blaspheme* to speaking irreverently of God, in the Greek the word refers also to slandering men.

It is not enough to do what we feel is right. We must guard against doing anything that could cause criticism from others. Of course this is not always possible. But the principle holds good, nevertheless. We should be concerned about the impression we make on others, as well as the relation of our own consciences to God.

17 Meat and Drink The discussion of whether or not to eat certain foods becomes the occasion for Paul making a profound statement of truth: "For the kingdom of God is not meat and drink; but righteousness, and peace, and joy in the Holy Ghost."

The Greek word for "meat" is *brōsis*. It is from the same root as *brōma* in verse 15. But the latter means "food" (not "meat"), while the one here means "eating." Likewise the Greek word for "drink," *posis*, means "drinking." So the correct translation here is "eating and drinking."

The principle is clearly stated, though too often forgotten. The kingdom of God, or true religion, is not a matter of externals—how we dress or eat. It is rather "righteousness, and peace, and joy in the Holy Ghost." Those who major on externals are prone not to show a right spirit, nor to maintain peace. And too often their lives do not radiate the joy of the risen Christ.

19 Follow After The verb "follow after" is *diōkō*, which means "pursue." It is used in Heb. 12:14, where the literal rendering is, "Keep on pursuing peace with all men." This passage has a similar emphasis: "Let us keep on pursuing the things of peace."

Edify The last clause literally reads, "and the things of upbuilding to each other." The noun is *oikodomē*, which comes from *oikos*, "house," and *demō*, "build." Literally it would mean the building of a house. But it came to refer to any building process. It is used of the beautiful "buildings" of the Temple (Matt. 24:1; Mark 13:1–2). Elsewhere it is found only in Paul's Epistles (15 times). There it always has a metaphorical sense and is usually translated "edifying" or "edification." It may be that this word is thoroughly understood by many Bible readers. But it is doubtful whether the idea of "building up" is conveyed today by this term. The clear sense is this: "Let us then pursue what makes for peace and for mutual upbuilding" (RSV).

20 Destroy The Greek word for "Destroy" is different from that in verse 15. This one is *katalyō*. It is translated "break down" by Moffatt. Arndt and Gingrich prefer "tear down." Abbott-Smith suggests "overthrow," which fits very well here.

Offense The Greek word for "offense" is the same one which is translated "stumblingblock" in verse 13—*proskomma*. Occurring 6 times in the NT (only in Paul), it is rendered "stumbling" or "stumblingblock" in every other case.

That idea should probably be retained here. The Berkeley Version reads, "It is wrong for a man to eat what means a stumbling block."

22 Alloweth "Alloweth" translates the Greek verb *dokimazō*, which means "test," then "prove" by testing, and finally "approve" as the result of testing. It comes from the same root as *dokimos*, which is translated "approved" in verse 18. Probably the best rendering here is "approves."

22–23 Damned "Condemneth" is the verb *krinō*. "Doubteth" is the verb *diakrinō;* and "damned," *katakrinō*. The simple word *krinō* meant first of all "to separate, select, choose"; then "to be of opinion, judge, think"; then "to decide, determine, decree"; and finally "to judge, adjudge, pronounce judgment" (A-S).

The compound *diakrinō* means "to distinguish, discriminate, discern"; then "to settle, decide, judge, arbitrate." In the NT and ecclesiastical writers it often means "to be divided in one's mind, to hesitate, doubt" (A-S). It is the last sense which fits best here.

But what about *katakrinō?* Literally it means to "judge down" or "give judgment against." Occurring 19 times in the NT, it is translated 17 times as "condemn" and twice as "damn" (here and Mark 16:16). The point hardly needs to be labored that the latter is an over-translation amounting to a mistranslation. Eternal damnation, if one uses that expression, is not suggested here. Rather, one is "condemned" if he does not act in faith.

15:1 Strong "Strong" is the plural of the adjective *dynatos*, which means "strong, mighty, powerful." (See note on 13:1.) "Weak" is the plural of the adjective *adynatos* (the alpha-privative *a-* plus *dynatos*). Hence it means "powerless." The Berkeley Version gives a very accurate translation: "We who are strong ought to put on ourselves the weaknesses of those who lack strength." Perhaps better: "We powerful ones should bear the weaknesses of the powerless."

1–3 Please Once each in the first three verses of this chapter we find the word *please*. That is the most common meaning of *areskō*. But Abbott-Smith thinks that in verses 1 and 3 it means "render service to."

The basis for this is pointed out by Moulton and Milligan as follows: "For the idea of *service* in the interests of others which underlies several of the NT occurrences of this verb (I Thess. 2:4; Rom. 15:1, 3; I Cor. 10:33), we may compare its use in monumental inscriptions to describe those who have proved themselves of use to the commonwealth" (VGT, p. 75). This was a usage of the word in that period.

One can see the advantage of translating the first clause of verse 3, "For even Christ served not himself." That fits with His own statement: "For the Son of man also came not to be served but to serve, and to give his life as a ransom for many" (Mark 10:45, RSV).

3 Reproaches Almost all translations have "reproaches." But it may be that this is not forceful enough today. The verb here, *oneidizō*, means "reproach, revile, heap insults upon" (AG). The noun *oneidismos* means "reproach, reviling, disgrace, insult" (*ibid.*). With us "insults" seems stronger than "reproaches," and so may be preferable.

4 Learning The word rendered "learning" is *didaskalia*. Its usual meaning is "teaching, instruction." The term *learning* today has two meanings. It is used not only for the process of learning, but also in such statements as, "He is a man of great learning." This would not fit here. So unquestionably the best translation is "instruction."

Patience The rendering "patience" for *hypomonē* is too weak and passive, as we have noted earlier. The word has the stronger, active sense of "steadfastness." Perhaps even better it might be rendered "fortitude" (NEB). That is what a Christian needs more than "patience." Fortitude keeps us in the race until the goal is reached.

8–31 Minister Three different Greek nouns are translated as "minister" in the KJV. One of them, *hypēretēs*, does not occur in Romans. It is used most frequently in the Gospels (15 times), where it is usually translated "officer," but also "servant" and "minister" (twice). It occurs 4 times in Acts (twice "officer," twice "minister"), and only once elsewhere in the NT (1 Cor. 4:1). There it is used for "ministers" of Christ.

The literal meaning of *hypēretēs* is "under rower." It signifies a subordinate who takes orders from his superior. That, of course, is one important aspect of the Christian ministry.

The two Greek words for "minister" found in chapter 15 of Romans are *diaconos* (v. 8) and *leitourgos* (v. 16). The former is found 30 times in the NT. Twenty times it is translated "minister," 7 times "servant," and 3 times "deacon"—the English word which is derived from it. This technical meaning is found only in Philippians (1:1) and 1 Tim. (3:8, 12).

The use of *diaconos* for "servant" in such passages as Matt. 22:13; 23:11; and John 2:5, 9 indicates clearly that the main emphasis of this term is on the minister as a servant—of God and of his people. The ministry is a service to others. One who is not willing to be a servant has no place in the Christian ministry.

The other word for "minister" in Romans 15 is *leitourgos* (v. 16). It occurs only 5 times in the NT. Twice in Romans and twice in Hebrews it is rendered "minister." In the other passage (Phil. 2:25) it is translated "he that ministers."

This word has already been discussed at its other occurrence in Romans (13:6). It was used for a public servant of the state, and then in a specialized way for one who performed religious service (cf. *liturgy*). That seems to be its meaning here.

A check of Young's or Strong's concordance will show that there are 9 different Greek verbs that are rendered "minister" in KJV. It is generally agreed that in the case of 5 of these there was an error in translation. Three of the others correspond to the 3 nouns we have just noticed. The fourth is a unique term, found only once in the NT (Rom. 15:16).

This last mentioned verb, *hierourgeō*, is based on *hieros*, which means "holy, sacred, consecrated." The neuter of this adjective is used for the Temple at Jerusalem, signifying the whole Temple area. The noun *hiereus* means "priest." So the verb signifies "to perform sacred rites, to minister in priestly service" (A-S). Arndt and Gingrich would translate the phrase here: "serve the gospel as a priest." So the emphasis of this word is on the priestly function of the ministry, an aspect too often neglected in nonliturgical churches.

Of the other 3 verbs, the first is *diaconeō* (v. 25). As our study of *diaconos* has already indicated, the main emphasis here is on serving.

The next verb is *leitourgeō* (v. 27). Again, our study of the cognate noun will show that it signifies usually the performance of religious service. But here it seems to be used in the general sense of "serve."

It remains for us to note the Greek word for "service" in verse 31. It is *diaconia*, which occurs 34 times in the NT. Sixteen times it is translated "ministry," 6 times "ministration," and 3 times "ministering." Only here and in Rev. 2:19 is it rendered "service." The emphasis of this word is on service as the main aspect of the ministry.

19 By Power The first part of the verse reads: "Through mighty signs and wonders, by the power of the Spirit of God." What the KJV obscures is the fact that the expressions "through mighty" and "by the power" both translate exactly the same Greek phrase—*en dynamei;* literally, "in power." The ASV correctly renders this passage as follows: "in the power of signs and wonders, in the power of the Holy Spirit." Paul's ministry to the Gentiles had been characterized by the power of the Holy Spirit (cf. 1 Thess. 1:5), which sometimes manifested itself in signs and wonders; that is, miraculous interventions of divine power. One is reminded of the apostle's recovery after being stoned at Lystra (Acts 14:19–20) and of the earthquake at Philippi (Acts 16:25–26).

27 Carnal Paul declares that the Gentiles who had shared in the spiritual blessings of the Jewish Christians should minister to them in "carnal" things. The adjective is *sarkikos*, which we have already met in 7:14—"But I am carnal, sold under sin." It occurs 11 times in the NT and is rendered "carnal" in 9 places ("fleshly" in 2 Cor. 1:12 and 1 Pet. 2:11).

While the translation "carnal" does seem most suitable in Rom. 7:14 and in 1 Cor. 3:1, 3, 4, it certainly does not fit well here nor in a very similar passage (1 Cor. 9:11). In these two places the correct meaning is clearly "material." The term "carnal," while derived from the Latin *carnis*, "flesh," is used today in a theological sense which is entirely foreign to this passage. Webster indicates that the use of *carnal* for *material* is archaic. Unfortunately this outdated rendering is still found in the ASV. But most twentieth-century translations give the correct meaning. The thought of this passage is very clearly and beautifully expressed in the NEB: "For if the Jewish Christians shared their spiritual treasures with the Gentiles, the Gentiles have a clear duty to contribute to their material needs."

16:1 Commend The 16th chapter of Romans consists of a letter of recommendation for Phoebe as she transferred from one church to another. Such formal communications are still employed today. It is interesting to note this custom beginning as early as the apostolic age.

The opening word here is *synistēmi*. It literally means "place together," and so "introduce" one person to another. It is used commonly in the sense of "commend" or "recommend." Denney says that it is "the technical word for this kind of recommendation, which was equivalent to a certificate of church membership" (EGT, 2:717). Sanday and Headlam comment: "These letters played a very large part in the organization of the church, for the tie of hospitality (cf. xii.13), implying also the reception to communion, was the great bond which united the separate local churches together, and some protection became necessary against imposture" (p. 416).

Servant Phoebe (correct spelling) is called a "servant" of the church at Cenchreae (eastern harbor for Corinth). The Greek word is *diaconos*. It is translated "deaconess" in many recent versions.

The difficulty of translating *diaconos* is well expressed by Denney. He says: "It is not easy to translate *diaconos*, for 'servant' is too vague, and 'deaconess' is more technical than the original" (EGT, 2:717). After discussing some of the general functions of hospitable Christians, he adds: "On the other hand it must be remembered that the growth of the Church, under the conditions of ancient society, soon produced 'deaconesses' in the official sense, and Phoebe may have had some recognized function of *diaconia* assigned to her" (p. 718). By "conditions of ancient society" Denney probably has reference to the rigid separation between the sexes in the East, which would necessitate female deaconesses. Even today there are some countries where missions must include women doctors on the staff and even have separate hospital wings for men and women.

In the *Apostolic Constitutions* (ca. 3rd cent.) the female workers in the church are referred to under the term *diaconos* in the earlier part (2:26; 3:15), but *diakonissa* (feminine) in the latter part (8:19–20, 28). It is clearly indicated that widows were considered inferior to the deaconesses, though the latter may well have been chosen from the former. Sanday and Headlam conclude: "*Diakonos* is technical, but need hardly be more so than *prostatis* in ver. 2" (p. 417).

Pliny (ca. A.D. 112) refers to two *ministrae* whom he had tortured. These female ministers were probably deaconesses.

Vincent elaborates a little more on the work of these deaconesses. He says: "Their duties were to take care of the sick and poor, minister to martyrs and confessors in prison, to instruct catechumens, to assist at the baptism of women, and to exercise a general supervision over the female church-members" (3:177).

2 Assist Paul urged the church to receive Phoebe as a fellow Christian and to "assist" her

in any need she had. The NEB says "stand by her." That is exactly what *parastēte* means. Abbott-Smith indicates that from Homer to Xenophon the verb *paristēmi* carried the sense: "*to stand by* for help or defence."

Succorer The Greek for "succorer" is *prostatis*. Abbott-Smith gives its meaning as "a patroness, protectress." It occurs only here in the NT. The masculine form *prostatēs*—found in early Christian literature, but not in NT—means "defender" or "guardian." Sanday and Headlam write of the word here:

> It is the feminine form of *prostatēs*, used like the Latin *patronus* for the legal representative of the foreigner. In Jewish communities it meant the legal representative or wealthy patron.... Here the expression suggests that Phoebe was a person of some wealth and position who was thus able to act as patroness of a small and struggling community (pp. 417–18).

3–16 Greet No less than 16 times in these 14 verses we find the word *aspasasthe*. It is the aorist imperative of *aspazomai*, which means "greet" or "salute." In the KJV of this passage it is translated "greet" 4 times and "salute" 12 times. This is evidently to avoid repetition in the English, though it is there in the Greek. The ASV uses "salute" altogether, for consistency. The RSV employs "greet" throughout, as being the more correct rendering today.

Moulton and Milligan say of *aspazomai*: "The papyri have shown conclusively that this common NT word was the regular technical term for conveying the greetings at the end of a letter" (VGT, p. 85). They cite examples to support this. Paul was following the accepted custom of his day.

Deissmann asserts the same thing on the basis of his pioneering work with the papyri. He says: "It is easy to produce parallels from the papyrus letters, especially for the one most striking peculiarity of this letter, viz. the apparently monotonous cumulation of greetings" (LAE, p. 234). After calling attention to a couple of examples, he adds: "Their resemblance to Romans xvi is most striking; Paul, however, enlivens the monotony of the long list of greetings by finely discriminating personal touches" (LAE, pp. 234–35).

3 Priscilla In this verse, the KJV has *Priscilla;* but the ASV and the RSV, following the best Greek text, have *Prisca*. The latter means "old woman"; the former, "little old woman." The name occurs 6 times in the NT. At the three places in Acts (18:2, 18, 26), the correct form is *Priscilla*. But according to the oldest Greek manuscripts it should be *Prisca* each time in Paul's Epistles (Rom. 16:8; 1 Cor. 16:19; 2 Tim. 14:19). But we think of her more commonly as Priscilla.

In the best Greek text, Priscilla's name occurs before that of her husband in 4 out of the 6 places where they are mentioned. (The two exceptions are Acts 18:2 and 1 Cor. 16:19.) This seems to imply that Priscilla was perhaps the stronger character of the two, or at least the one with the greater leadership ability.

7, 11, 21 *Kinsmen* The word *syngenēs* is an adjective meaning "congenital" or "akin to." But in the NT it is used as a substantive with the meaning "kinsman." However, Abbott-Smith suggests that the idea in this chapter is that of "tribal kinship," as it clearly is in Rom. 9:3. Arndt and Gingrich note that in Josephus it has the broader sense of "fellow country-man," which obviously is the way it must be taken in Rom. 9:3 and perhaps also in this chapter. Moulton and Milligan indicate that the meaning of the word is extended "to denote all of the same *nationality* (as in Rom. 9:3) or of the same *tribe* (as in Rom. 16:7, 11, 21)" (VGT, p. 595).

Sir William Ramsay has an interesting discussion of this point. After noting that in Rom. 16:7–21 six persons are called "kinsmen" by Paul, he says:

> The word can hardly mean here kinsmen by right of birth and blood in the ordinary sense . . . for there is reason to think that the family to which the Apostle belonged had not come over to the Christian Church in such numbers, but rather had condemned his action and rejected him. Nor can it mean simply members of the Jewish nation, for many of the others mentioned in this passage without this epithet were undoubtedly Jews. . . . The word "kinsman" here means fellow-citizen and fellow-tribesman, for all the six were doubtless Jews and therefore members of the same Tribe in Tarsus (*Cities of St. Paul*, p. 177).

It should be noted that by "Tribe" Ramsay does not mean one of the 12 tribes of Israel. Rather, the term refers to a grouping of citizens in a Greek city. All the Jewish community in Tarsus would constitute such a "tribe" in that city. Ramsay thinks that is Paul's reference here.

Meyer says that *"kinsmen* is to be preferred" (p. 567). But many of the best recent commentators do not agree with him. "Fellow-country-men" or "Jews" is the choice of Sanday and Headlam—"St. Paul almost certainly means by 'kinsmen,' fellow-countrymen, and not relations" (p. 423). Denney, Godet, Olshausen, and C. K. Barrett would seem to concur.

Among the translators "fellow-country-men," or its equivalent, was adopted by Moffatt, Weymouth, Goodspeed, and Williams. In view of the fact that this is clearly the sense in Rom. 9:3—the only other occurrence of the term outside the Gospels and Acts—as also the unlikelihood of Paul having so many Christian "kinsmen," it seems best to use "fellow country-men" here.

1 Corinthians

1:2 *Sanctified ... Saints* In the light of 3:1, where Paul says the Corinthian "brethren" are not spiritual but carnal, it is obvious that "sanctified" here is used in a restricted sense. It expresses a relationship of having been set apart to God. Findlay puts it well: "This initial sanctification is synchronous with justification" (EGT, 2:758).

These born-again believers were "called to be saints" (cf. Rom. 1:7). The term "saints" is the plural of *hagios*, "holy," which is the root of the verb "sanctified" (*hagiazō*). So saints are literally "holy ones." Again, the term is used in its limited, sacramental sense of "belonging to God." This is the main meaning of "holy" in the Old Testament, though the personal and ethical meaning comes to the front in Isaiah and some other prophets and becomes dominant in the New Testament. However, it is clear that Paul here uses the term "saints" for all Christians, as those who are called to belong to God.

7 *Coming* The Greek word is *apocalypsis*, which literally means an "uncovering," and so "revelation." That is the way it is usually translated in the KJV (12 out of 18 times). Only in this passage is it rendered "coming."

The Second Coming will be a revealing of Christ, who for over 1,900 years has been veiled from sight. We are told that when He comes again, "every eye shall see him," even "they also which pierced him" (Rev. 1:7; cf. John 19:37).

10 *Divisions* This is a strong word in the Greek, *schisma*, from which we get our word "schism." The noun comes from the verb *schizō*, which means "split, divide, separate, tear apart, tear off" (AG, p. 805). It is used literally for a "rent" in a garment (Matt. 9:16; Mark 2:21). Elsewhere in the NT it is used figuratively, where it is translated "division" five times and "schism" once (1 Cor. 12:25).

Division was the main problem in the church at Corinth. There were four parties or cliques in the congregation (v. 12), and Paul devotes the first four chapters of this epistle to dealing with that crucial situation.

Perfectly Joined Together Instead of being divided into quarreling cliques, Christians should be "perfectly joined together"—all one word in the Greek, *katērtismenoi*, the perfect passive participle of *katartizō*. This verb literally means "put in order, restore ... restore to its former condition" (AG, p. 418). It is used of fishermen "mending" their nets (Matt. 4:21; Mark 1:19). Here in Corinthians it means "make one what he ought to be" (Thayer). Lias (CGT) says the idea is that of being "*fitted together*, as the fragments in a piece of mosaic, in which each minute portion exactly fills its proper place" (p. 34).

Perhaps Alford is a little closer to the true picture when he comments: "*katartizō* is the exact word for the healing or repairing of the breaches made by the *schismata*" (2:476).

In the ICC volume on 1 Corinthians, Robertson and Plummer write: "The word is suggestive of fitting together what is broken or rent (Matt. iv. 21). It is used in surgery for setting a joint (Galen), and in Greek politics for composing factions (Hdt. v. 28)" (p. 10). All three of these uses apply well to this passage.

Judgment Of the Greek word used here, Lias says: "*gnōmē* is usually employed in the sense of *opinion*. But it has also the sense of *purpose* or *consent*." After citing a passage in Polybius, he affirms: "There, as here, the decision of the

215

mind is meant, rather than the opinion on which it was formed" (p. 34). For this passage Arndt and Gingrich suggest "purpose" or "intention."

11 Contentions The word *eris* means "strife, wrangling, contention" (A-S, p. 180). Arndt and Gingrich suggest that in the plural, as here, it means "quarrels." Robertson and Plummer say, "The divisions became noisy" (p. 11). Findlay writes: "*erides* signifies the personal *contentions*, due to whatever cause, which lead to *schismata*" (EGT, 2:763). And so it is today that church quarrels lead to church splits.

17 Preach the Gospel This is one word in the Greek, *euangelizō*. Paul declares: "Christ sent me not to baptize, but to evangelize." That is the main mission of the church.

18 Preaching Paul says that "the preaching of the cross" is foolishness to those that perish. But the Greek word for "preaching" is simply *logos*, which is translated "word" 218 out of the 330 times it occurs in the NT. It is "the word of the Cross" (that is, the word about the Cross) that perishing sinners despise. What the world still ridicules is the message of the Cross, the Good News of salvation through Christ's death for us at Calvary. Too many people would rather try to save themselves than to let Christ save them.

21 Preaching *Kērygma* is still another word that is translated "preaching" in the KJV. It has become established in theological circles as an English term in good standing.

The word comes from the verb *kēryssō*, which means "herald" or "proclaim." In classical Greek the noun meant "that which is cried by a herald, a proclamation" (A-S, p. 246). In the NT it is used in the sense of "proclamation" or "message," "that is, the substance as distinct from the act" (*ibid.*). Lightfoot declares: "It refers . . . to the subject, not to the manner of preaching" (*Notes*, p. 161). Lias comments: "The word translated *preaching* should rather be rendered *what is preached*" (p. 38). In agreement with all this, Findlay writes that *kerygma* "signifies not the act of proclamation, but *the message proclaimed* by God's herald" (EGT, 2:769).

On the basis of the KJV rendering many have thought that it is the *method* of preaching that is considered foolish. Rather, it is the *message*.

In Kittel's *Theological Dictionary of the New Testament*, Friedrich spells out what this message is. He writes:

> At the heart of the New Testament *kērygma* stands the lordship of God. Preaching is not a lecture on the nature of God's kingdom. It is proclamation, the declaration of an event (3:710).

Friedrich goes on to point out that the central emphasis of apostolic preaching was not the words of Jesus, but the historical fact of His life, death, and resurrection. He says:

> The reality of the resurrection constitutes the fulness of the early Christian *kērygma*. This is a fact which cannot be apprehended like other historical events. It has to be continually proclaimed afresh (3:711).

Commenting on 1 Cor. 1:21, he affirms: "The foolish message of Jesus crucified saves those who believe" (3:716). That is what the gospel is. And that is the Good News which every preacher is commissioned to proclaim.

22 Require The verb is *aiteō*. Basically it means "ask for something." Thayer lists this as one of the passages in which it probably carries the stronger sense of "demand," a meaning which Arndt and Gingrich support.

Sign The first thing we would note is that in the oldest and best Greek manuscripts, the word *semeia* is plural, not singular. This term literally means "signs." It first refers to a distinguishing "mark" by which something is known. But it also means "*a sign, prodigy, portent*, i.e., an unusual occurrence, transcending the common course of nature" (Thayer, p. 573). It is used "of miracles and wonders by which God authenticates the men sent by him, or by which men prove that the cause they are pleading is of God" (*ibid.*). When it is used in this way, Arndt and Gingrich would simply translate it as "miracle" (cf. NEB: "Jews call for miracles"). Perhaps a more adequate translation would be "miraculous signs" (NIV).

This tendency of the Jews to demand a miraculous sign is vividly illustrated by an incident related to us some years ago by the superintendent of a Hebrew Mission. He told of a young lady who had almost come to the place of accepting Jesus as her Savior, but she wanted to be certain that this Jesus was really the promised Messiah.

Right in the midst of her crucial struggle the superintendent and his wife were out for a drive one day with the young lady in the back seat. Suddenly, out of the clear sky, a ball of fire hit the highway in front of the car, causing the startled superintendent to jam on his brakes. But from the rear seat came the joyous exclamation: "Thank You, Lord, for giving me this proof; now I know that Jesus is Your Messiah." She then told how that very morning she had prayed: "O God, if Jesus is the true Messiah, give me a sign today to prove it." Evidently the Lord accommodated himself to her "demand." From that time on she was a devoted, faithful Christian, even though disowned and persecuted by her family.

In contrast to the Jews, said Paul, the Greeks "seek" or "look for" wisdom. They wanted intellectual evidence; for them logic was stronger proof than miracle. Actually, neither one is absolute evidence. The greatest proof of the truth of Christianity is the conscious presence of the living Christ in our hearts.

23 Preach This verse has an important message for all preachers. Paul said: (1) "we *preach*," not just talk, explain, teach; (2) "we preach *Christ*," not our own opinions, or even just principles and propositions; (3) "we preach Christ *crucified*," not just Christ as our example, but as our crucified Redeemer.

26 Noble One of the besetting sins of the church members at Corinth was pride. This was a leading cause of their divisions. So Paul reminds them that not many of them were "wise according to worldly standards" (RSV), not many were "mighty"—*dynatoi*, "powerful," perhaps meaning "of the ruling class" (Phillips)—not many were "noble." The Greek word is *eugenēs*, which literally means "well-born," that is, "high-born" or from families of the nobility. "Noble" might mistakenly be taken as meaning "of noble character." The idea here is rather "of noble birth."

27 Confound The Greek word is *kataischynō*. It means "to disgrace, dishonour, put to shame" (A-S, p. 233)—which is hardly what we mean now by "confound." Most modern translations correctly have "shame."

28 Base The word is *agenēs*, which is the opposite of *eugenēs* (v. 26). The latter is compounded of *eu*, "well," and *genēs*, "born." The former is composed of *a*, "not," and *genēs*, "born." Thayer defines *agenēs* thus: "*of no family*, a man of base birth, a man of no name or reputation; often used by profane writers, also in the secondary sense *ignoble, cowardly, mean,*

base. In the New Testament only in I Cor. i. 28, *ta agenē tou cosmou*, i.e., those who among men are held of no account" (p. 6). Arndt and Gingrich say that its original meaning, as used by Xenophon and Plato of the fourth century B.C., was "not of noble birth," but that it was used "more commonly" in the secondary sense of "base, low, insignificant" (p. 8).

The adjective *agenēs* is in the neuter here. So most translations take it as referring to things, as in the KJV. But some translators follow Thayer in giving it a personal application. For instance, the *Berkeley Version* has: "God also has chosen the world's low-born and contemptibles and nobodies."

29, 31 Glory Once in verse 29 and twice in verse 31 we find the verb "glory." The Greek *kauchaomai* comes from the noun *kauchēma*, which means "boast." So the simplest translation of the verb is "boast," which is probably clearer today than "glory."

30 Wisdom We read that God has made Christ Jesus to be to us "wisdom, and righteousness, and sanctification, and redemption." However, the Greek reads literally: "But of him you are in Christ Jesus, who has been made wisdom to us from God, both righteousness and sanctification and redemption." That is, the last three terms are additional explanations of "wisdom." God's wisdom in Christ is shown in our righteousness, sanctification, and redemption. Godet suggests that "wisdom" here means "the *understanding* of the Divine plan communicated to man by Jesus Christ" (p. 118). This divine plan is our salvation in Christ Jesus as He becomes our "righteousness" (*dikaiosyne*), "sanctification" (*hagiasmos*), and "redemption" (*apolytrōsis*).

Godet defines "redemption" as "our complete and final deliverance" (cf. Rom. 8:18–30). One could almost suggest that we find here the "three works of grace" in salvation: justification, sanctification, and glorification. The first two are available to us in this life; the third will come in the next.

2:4 Enticing The adjective *peithos* occurs only here in the NT. Not only that, but it has not been found anywhere else in Greek literature. It is formed from the verb *peithō*, which means "persuade." So it clearly means "persuasive," with none of the negative overtones that "enticing" suggests. The apostle was not using mere human persuasiveness nor superstitious manipulation.

The word *Peithō* was also the name of a

Greek goddess, "Persuasion." Some of the Early Church fathers (Origen, Eusebius) thought that Paul here intended a reference to this goddess.

Demonstration The Greek word *apodeixis* is found only here in the NT. It first meant a "display" or "showing off." Then it came to be used for "demonstration," in the sense of conclusive proof. All scholars agree that this is its meaning here.

Findlay says that *apodeixis* was "the technical term for a proof drawn from facts or documents, as opposed to theoretical reasoning; in common use with the Stoics in this sense" (EGT, 2:776). Godet writes: "The word *apodeixis* indicates a clearness which is produced in the hearer's mind, as by the sudden lifting of a veil; a conviction mastering him with the sovereign force of moral evidence" (1:129). Such conviction comes only from "the Spirit" who works on our hearts in "power." Lias comments: "The 'power' of which he speaks was not so much that of working miracles in the ordinary sense of the word, as of touching the heart. He is referring to that conviction of sin, righteousness and judgment (John xvi. 8), which the Spirit of God produces in the spirit of man, and of the power to produce a change of heart and life which is the leading characteristic of the Gospel" (p. 43).

Robertson and Plummer make this helpful observation: "St. Paul is not dealing with scientific certainty; but he claims that the certitude of religious truth to the believer in the Gospel is as complete and as 'objective'—equal in degree, though different in kind—as the certitude of scientific truth to the scientific mind" (p. 33). Those who experience the reality of Christ's presence within and the illumination of His Spirit can surely say a hearty "Amen" to this.

In relation to the preaching of Paul in the context here, the words "demonstration of Spirit and power" mean "a proof by the Spirit and power of God, operating in me, and stirring in the minds of my hearers the most holy emotions and thus persuading them" (Thayer, p. 60).

In view of the current use of the word "demonstration" in our country, it would seem that "proof" would be a better translation here. It is also clearer and simpler. Then too, "demonstration" in religious circles means something outward, whereas the "proof" of the Spirit's power here is an inward conviction of one's sin and of the truth of the gospel.

6 Perfect The adjective *teleios* is translated "perfect" (KJV) 17 out of the 19 times it occurs

in the NT. In 1 Cor. 14:20 it is rendered "man," and Heb. 5:14 "of full age."

It comes from *telos*, "end." So it really means "having reached its end, finished, mature, complete, perfect" (A-S, p. 442). In Heb. 5:14 it refers to persons who are physically full grown. In our passage here, and in 14:20, it is used for those who are "spiritually mature." That is probably the best translation here (cf. Phillips).

The objection to the word "perfect" is that it is often misunderstood. Some people say we should use it because "it's in the Bible." But that is begging the question. It is in the KJV, to be sure, but whether or not it is a precise translation of *teleios* is a matter of question. The term "perfect" has been much misunderstood as meaning that everything one does is beyond criticism. We are all human still and subject to faulty judgment and action. What is called "Christian Perfection" takes this into account. It is the inner, heart relationship to God which is to be perfect.

It is often said that we can receive purity in a moment, but that it takes time to reach maturity. There is much truth in this, of course. But it might also be affirmed that every Spirit-filled Christian is in a real sense "spiritually mature" because he is under the guidance of the Holy Spirit. In any case, the idea of maturity fits the present passage very well.

13 Spiritual Things with Spiritual The Greek says: *pneumaticois pneumatica*. The word for "spirit" is *pneuma* and so the adjective *pneumaticos* simply means "spiritual."

The second form here, *pneumatica*, is clearly neuter (both are plural). But the first word is in the dative case, which has the same form for both the masculine and neuter. This makes for ambiguity because *pneumaticois* may be translated "with" (or, "to") "spiritual things" or "spiritual people."

The KJV takes it as neuter and says "spiritual things." Weymouth also assumes the neuter but gives a more specific rendering: "adapting spiritual words to spiritual truths." The TDNT similarly has: "and so we explain spiritual things in spiritual language." Goodspeed is basically the same: "giving spiritual truth a spiritual form."

But many recent versions take *pneumaticois* as masculine. The RSV has: "interpreting spiritual truths to those who possess the Spirit" (cf. NEB). More simply, Phillips puts it this way: "explaining spiritual things to those who are spiritual." This was the way it was handled in the earliest English Bible by Wyclif (1382).

218

14 *Natural* The Greek word is *psychicos*, from which we get "psychical." It is here, as in Jude 19, placed in contrast to *pneumaticos*, "spiritual." In James 3:15 it is equivalent to *epigeios*, "earthly." In both these places the KJV translates it "sensual." These are the only two places in the NT where *psychicos* is used outside 1 Corinthians. Besides our present passage, it occurs three times in chapter 15 (vv. 44, 46). There it refers to the "natural body" which is buried in the grave, in contrast to the "spiritual body" we shall receive in the resurrection.

How should *psychicos* be translated here? Lias thinks that "natural" is "fairly satisfactory," and then adds: "But the term 'worldly,' as used by the divines, seems most nearly to approach to the precise meaning of the Apostle" (p. 47). Findlay says that the term "describes to the Corinthians the unregenerate nature *at its best*" (EGT, 2:783). Robertson and Plummer say: "The *psychicos* is the 'unrenewed' man, the 'natural' man (AV., RV.), as distinct from the man who is actuated by the Spirit" (p. 49). Perhaps the best translation is "the unspiritual man" (AG, RSV, Phillips, NEB).

3:1–4 *Carnal* The term "carnal" occurs four times (KJV) in these four verses. The difficulty of understanding the Greek word here is evidenced by the variety of renderings found in modern translations.

The confusion begins in the Greek text. The Textus Receptus (basis of KJV) has *sarkikos* in all four places. But the Textus Criticus, derived from the oldest and best Greek manuscripts, has *sarkinos* in verse 3 (twice) and *anthrōpos* (man) in verse 4.

What is the relation of *sarkikos* to *psychicos* (2:14)? Trench calls attention to the difference between classical and NT usage at this point. He writes: "*Psychicos*, continually used as the highest in later classical Greek literature—the word appears first in Aristotle—being there opposed to *sarkikos* . . . and constantly employed in praise, must come down from its high estate, another *pneumaticos* so much greater than it being installed in the highest place of all" (p. 268). He goes on to say: "According to Scripture the *psychē* (soul), no less than the *sarks* (flesh), belongs to the lower region of man's being . . . and it is at any rate plain that *psychicos* is not a word of honour any more than *sarkikos*, being an epithet quite as freely applied to this lower" (pp. 268–69). He concludes: "The *psychicos* of Scripture is one for whom the *psychē* is the highest motive power of life and action; in whom the *pneuma*, as the organ of the divine *Pneuma*, is suppressed, dormant . . .

whom the operations of this divine Spirit have never lifted into the region of spiritual things" (p. 269).

What is the difference between *sarkikos* and *sarkinos*? Trench notes that words ending in *-inos* designate "the stuff of which anything is made," and so *sarkinos* properly means "fleshy," "that is, having flesh for the substance and material of which it is composed" (p. 272). *Sarkikos* is a more ethical term, meaning "fleshly." Trench says: " 'Fleshly' lusts . . . are lusts which move and stir in the ethical domain of the flesh, which have in that rebellious region of man's corrupt and fallen nature their source and spring" (p. 273).

Findlay makes this same distinction. He comments: "*-inos* implying nature, *-icos* tendency or character" (EGT, 2:785). Arndt and Gingrich agree with this. They say: "*sarkikos* means 'belonging to the sarks', having the nature and characteristics of *sarks* . . . 'fleshly'; on the other hand, *sarkinos* is 'consisting' or 'composed of flesh', 'fleshy' " (p. 750).

Thayer suggests that *sarkikos* means "governed by mere human nature." Of the use of *sarkinos* in the best text of 3:1 he says that "unless we decide that Paul used *sarkikos* and *sarkinos* indiscriminately, we must suppose that *sarkinos* expresses the idea of *sarkikos* with an emphasis: *wholly given up to the flesh, rooted in the flesh as it were*" (p. 569).

Vincent translates *sarkinos* in verse 1 as "made of flesh" and *sarkikos* in verse 3 as "having the nature of flesh." He comments on verse 3: "Here the milder word is used. . . . In verse 1, Paul would say that he was compelled to address the Christians as unspiritual, *made of flesh*. Here he says that though they have received the Spirit in some measure, they are yet under the influence of the flesh" (3:200). But as we shall note in a moment, it may well be that *sarkinos* (v. 1) was intended as the milder term—"merely human"—while *sarkikos* (v. 3) was a stronger word of condemnation: "You are still somewhat under the domination of your lower nature; instead of letting Christ be Lord of all in your lives." This is what we mean by a "carnal" Christian.

Schweizer thinks that Paul uses the two terms interchangeably in this passage (TDNT, 7:144). Grosheide thinks the difference between the two "is not great, but suggests that Paul may have used *sarkinos* in verse 1 in an attempt to avoid a stronger term at this point" (p. 78, n. 1). That is, he softened his approach to the Corinthians in denouncing them for their carnal attitudes.

What is the meaning of *anthrōpoi* (men) in

verse 4, in comparison with *sarkikoi* (v. 3)? Robertson and Plummer comment: "The Corinthians were *anthrōpoi* in failing to rise to the higher range of motives; they were *sarkikoi* in allowing themselves to be swayed by the lower range" (pp. 54–55). They would translate the clause: "Are ye not mere human creatures?"

9 Husbandry The term *geōrgion* is found only here in the NT. It means "cultivated land" or "field." Bengel says it is "a word of wide and comprehensive meaning, comprising the field, the garden, and the vineyard" (3:218). The Christian congregation at Corinth is pictured in this verse as "God's farm, God's building" (Goodspeed). The first of these two metaphors looks back to verses 6–9: Paul planted, Apollos watered, God made the seed grow. The second metaphor looks forward to verses 10–17: Paul laid the foundation, Jesus Christ; let everyone be careful how he builds on that foundation.

Both the pastor and the people of every church need to face the implications of these two figures used by Paul. The pastor is to plant the seed of God's Word, see that it is watered with the showers from heaven (God's blessing on the services) and cultivate carefully the tender plants that grow. The verb *potizō*, "watered" (v. 6), was used in ancient Greek for irrigating a field. So we may think of preaching as also watering the hearts of the listeners. By faithful attendance and a spirit of cooperation and response, the people will benefit by his ministry.

But the congregation is also a building erected as a "temple of God" (v. 16). It should be a fit temple for Him to dwell in.

10 Masterbuilder The Greek word (only here in NT) is *architectōn*, from which we get "architect." Of this term Plato writes: "The architect does not work himself, but is the ruler of workmen" (*Statesman*, p. 259).

But probably our concept of an architect today does not fit this passage. Findlay writes: "The Gr. *architectōn* was not a designer of plans on paper; he was like the old cathedral builders, the *master-mason*, developing his ideas in the material" (EGT, 2:790). Godet says: "The *master builder* is not only he who draws the plan of the building—in this sense the title would revert to God—but also the man who directs its execution" (1:179–80).

In the NT, God has furnished us the plan for the building. We are to carry out that plan in working with Christ in building His church—including the local congregation, as here.

Because the modern term "architect" could

be misleading, almost all English versions have "master builder." That is what Paul was. J. I. Packer says that this word means "a head builder, masterbuilder, contractor, or director of works" (*The New International Dictionary of New Testament Theology*, 1:279).

13 Try Paul declares that "the fire shall try every man's work." The verb is *dokimazō*. The first definition given by Thayer is: "to *test, examine, prove, scrutinize* (to see whether a thing be genuine or not), as metals" (p. 154). Trench comments: "As employed in the New Testament *dokimazein* almost always implies that the proof is victoriously surmounted, the *proved* is also *approved*" (p. 278). For this latter emphasis he cites 2 Cor. 8:8; 1 Thess. 2:4; 1 Tim. 3:10.

But this does not seem necessarily to attach to this passage. For the apostle presents two possible results of the testing. If any man's work stands the test, he will receive a reward (v. 14), but "if any man's work shall be burned, he shall suffer loss" (v. 15). Both alternatives are possible.

To understand what he is talking about, we have to go back to verse 11. There is only one foundation, Jesus Christ. But on this foundation people build with different materials. Some build solidly with "gold, silver, precious stones." These are the works that will "abide" (remain) through the testing by fire (v. 14). But other people build foolishly with "wood, hay, stubble." These inflammable materials will be burned up—"but he himself shall be saved; yet so as by fire" (v. 15). This suggests that some Christians whose experience is actually founded on Christ will waste their lives in useless endeavor, so that all their flimsy works will be in vain. It is a sad thing to contemplate a person working all his life without producing some permanent results. Winning souls is the kind of work that will survive the test by fire.

16 Temple Paul writes that the Corinthian congregation is "the temple of God," because the Spirit of God dwells in them. It was His presence that made them sacred.

Two different Greek words are translated "temple" in the NT. (A third word, meaning "house," is incorrectly translated "temple" in Luke 11:51.) The first is *hieron*, which means a sacred place. It occurs 70 times in the Gospels and Acts—where it refers to the Temple area—and once elsewhere (1 Cor. 9:13). The second, *naos*, refers to the sanctuary itself, containing the holy place and the holy of holies. It is found 46 times scattered throughout the NT, most frequently in Revelation (16 times). *Naos* is the word used here. In a sense it could be said that the Christians together constituted God's dwelling place in Corinth. What a high view of the local church!

17 Defile The first part of verse 17 reads: "If any man defile the temple of God, him shall God destroy." But in the Greek both verbs are the same. The correct translation is: "If anyone destroys the sanctuary of God, God will destroy him."

It must be remembered that this passage is a part of Paul's discussion of the problem of division in the church at Corinth. He devotes the first four chapters of the Epistle to this subject. What he means here, then, is that those who are dividing the church are destroying it.

This is because the church of Jesus Christ is a living organism, not just an organization. You can divide a pie into 6 pieces without destroying it; you are just preparing to serve it. This is because a pie is an organization. But if you divide a dog in two, you have destroyed him, because he is an organism. The Corinthian church was being divided into four cliques or parties (1:12). Thus it was in danger of being destroyed.

This passage sounds a solemn warning against those who would do anything to bring about a church quarrel, leading to a church split. In God's sight they have murdered a living organism.

The time to take care of problems is in the earliest stage, when they are small. At first in a personal quarrel only two people are involved, and that is all the pastor has to deal with. But if he ignores the problem and lets the quarrel continue, others get involved, and a church fuss is in the making. The problem is much more difficult to handle, because relatives and close friends have formed strong feelings about the situation. The pastor will have to straighten out two groups of people.

We could illustrate it this way. When a lion is a little cub, a man might play around with it freely. But when the lion is a year or two old, it isn't as safe to handle! Problems are like that; they get out of hand. And the pastor who tries to handle a church split is likely to get hurt in the process.

19 Taketh The verb *drassomai* is found only here in the NT, quoted from the Septuagint. It means "catch" or "seize" (AG, p. 205). Some recent versions have "trap."

Craftiness The noun *panourgia* originally meant "cleverness," almost always in a bad sense in classical Greek. It is sometimes translated "cunning." No matter how clever the "wise" men are, God traps them in their cleverness.

21 Glory We have already met this verb *kauchaomai* in 1:29. There we noted that "boast" is probably clearer—and, we might add, more contemporary—than "glory" (cf. 4:7).

Here we should like only to call attention to the fact that aside from twice in James (1:9; 4:16) this verb is used only by Paul (36 times). He uses it most frequently in 2 Corinthians (21 times). It is found 5 times each in Romans and 1 Corinthians. These three epistles were written at the same period in Paul's life (A.D. 54–56), when he was greatly plagued in spirit by the boastful attitude of the quarreling Corinthian church members.

4:1 **Ministers**

The noun is *hyperetēs*, used by Paul only here. Literally it means "under-rower." So the basic emphasis is on one who is subordinate. Thayer defines it thus: "Any one who serves with his hands; a servant," and adds that it is used "in the N.T. of the officers and attendants of magistrates" (p. 641). Arndt and Gingrich say it means "*servant, helper, assistant*, who serves a master or a superior" (p. 850).

Occurring 20 times in the NT, this word is translated "officer" 11 times, "minister" 5 times, and "servant" 4 times. Probably "servant" is the best translation in most instances, though the sense of police "officers" fits well in many cases—for instance, of the "officers" (policemen) employed by the Sanhedrin. The term is used twice each in the three Synoptic Gospels, 9 times in John, and 4 times in Acts. The only places where it can possibly be translated "minister," meaning pastor or preacher, are Luke 1:2 and Acts 26:16.

Stewards The word *oikonomos* occurs only 10 times in the NT and is correctly translated "steward" in all places except Rom. 16:23 ("chamberlain") and Gal. 4:2 ("governors"). It should be "steward" always.

The word comes from *oikos*, "house," and *nemō*, "manage." So it literally means "a house manager." Wealthy men employed slaves or freedmen to manage their households for them. It is used in this literal sense 4 times in Luke (3 times in the Parable of the Unjust Steward, 16:1–8). In the present passage (1 Cor. 4:1–2) it is used metaphorically for those who are stewards of God's grace, responsible for giving it out to people. The same usage is found in Titus 1:7 and 1 Pet. 4:10.

3 Judgment Paul said that it was a very little thing for him to be judged by the Corinthians, or by "man's judgment." The Greek literally says "by human day" (*hypo anthrōpines hēmeras*). This is clearly in contrast to the statement in 3:13, "Every man's work shall be made manifest; for the day shall declare it"; that is, the day of divine judgment. All of us face that Judgment Day. But Paul says he is not concerned about man's judgment day. He is not answerable to that, but only to God.

In the light of the whole picture here Abbott-Smith suggests the rendering "human judgment." But Lightfoot writes: "The word is put here because it is in opposition to *hē hēmere* of iii. 13 'The Lord's day.' The meaning is 'by any day fixed by man.' The idea of a day as implying judgment is common in Hebrew, and would be directly assisted by such expressions as 'diem dicere,' 'to fix a day for judgment.' Compare the English 'daysman' [Job 9:33, judge], which contains the same idea" (*Notes*, p. 198).

4 By Lightfoot correctly observes that " 'I know nothing by myself' is simply an archaism" (*ibid.*). The context clearly demands the translation, "I know nothing against myself." In the Greek "myself" (*emautō*) is in the dative case without any preposition. But the meaning is obvious. In the time of King James (1611) "by" was used in the sense of "against," but such a usage now is misleading.

6 Transferred "I have in a figure transferred" is all one word in the Greek, *meteschēmatisa*. Its usual meaning is "*to change in fashion or appearance*" (A-S). But here (alone in NT) it has a specialized sense. Thayer spells it out very well; "to shape one's discourse so as to transfer to one's self what holds true of the whole class to which one belongs, i.e., so as to illustrate by what one says of himself what holds true of all: 1 Co. iv. 6, where the meaning is, 'by what I have said of myself and Apollos, I have shown what holds true of all Christian teachers' " (p. 406). Arndt and Gingrich translate the passage, "I have applied this to Apollos and myself." They say that it means, "I have given this teaching of mine the form of an exposition concerning Apollos and myself" (p. 515).

7 Differ In the Greek "maketh . . . to differ" is *diacrinei*. The essential idea of this verb is "to separate," and so "to distinguish, discriminate" (A-S). Thayer thinks that here the verb means "to prefer," that is, "yield to him the preference or honor." Arndt and Gingrich translate it in this passage, "Who concedes you any superiority?"

In similar fashion Robertson and Plummer suggest: "For who sees anything special in you?" They go on to say: "The verb has a variety of meanings . . . and these meanings are linked by the idea of 'separate' in one sense or another; here it means to distinguish favorably from others." The next question, "What hast thou that thou didst not receive?" they paraphrase: "Let us grant that you have some superiority. Is it inherent? You know that you have nothing but what you have received. Your good things were all of them *given* to you" (p. 82).

There are three questions in verse 7. Concerning the first, Findlay writes: "This question stigmatises the partisan conceit of the Corinthians as *presumptuous;* those that follow . . . mark it as *ungrateful;* both ways it is egotistic" (EGT, 2:800).

8 Full The first half of this verse consists of three ironical statements: "Now ye are full, now ye are rich, ye have reigned as kings without us." The verb "full" is *corennumi*. It is found only here (in a metaphorical sense) and in Acts 27:38 (in a literal sense). It comes from *coros*, "surfeit," and so in the passive means "be satisfied." The tragic thing about these Corinthians was that they were too well satisfied with themselves.

Robertson and Plummer reveal the attitude of the Corinthians. They write: "The Apostle now directly attacks the self-esteem of his readers in a tone of grave irony. 'You may well sit in judgment upon us, from your position of advanced perfection, whence you can watch us struggling painfully to the heights which you have already scaled' " (p. 83).

I Would to God The Greek text has nothing in it about God. All this expression in English is one word in Greek, *ophelon*, which simply means "would that."

9 Set Forth The verb *apodeiknymi* was used for exhibiting gladiators in the arena of the amphitheater. Paul says it seems as though God has exhibited us apostles "last," that is, "to make the best sport for the spectators." Lightfoot adds: "The Apostles were brought out to make the grand finale, as it were" (*Notes*, p.

200). Godet writes: "Down to the end of the verse the apostle is alluding to the gladiators who were presented as a spectacle in the games of the amphitheatre, and whose blood and last agonies formed the joy of a whole population of spectators" (1:224).

Another possible picture is suggested in Goodspeed's translation: "God has exhibited us apostles at the very end of the procession." This might refer to the triumphal procession at Rome, when the emperor or a general would have his captives of war led in a long parade to humiliate them and exalt his own prowess. The ones at the end of the procession would be the most despised ones, left until the last.

Findlay combines the two ideas in his explanation. He writes: "One imagines a grand procession, on some day of public festival; in its rear march the criminals on their way to the arena, where the populace will be regaled with their sufferings" (EGT, 2:801). In a similar vein Robertson and Plummer say: "There is a great pageant in which the Apostles form the ignominious finale, consisting of doomed men, who will have to fight in the arena until they are killed" (p. 85).

Appointed to Death This is one word in Greek, the adjective *epithanatios* (only here in NT). In the apocryphal additions to the Book of Daniel it is used in the story of Bel and the Dragon to describe "condemned conspirators who were thrown to the lions, two at a time, daily . . . Dionysius of Halicarnasus, about B.C. 8, uses it of those who were thrown from the Tarpeian rock" (*ibid.*). Lightfoot suggests that the adjective should be translated "condemned criminals." Moffatt renders the clause: "Like doomed gladiators in the arena." That seems to catch the picture here.

11 *Naked* The verb *gymniteuo* occurs only here in the NT. It means to be scantily clad. Arndt and Gingrich give only the definition: "be poorly clothed."

Buffeted The verb *kolaphizō* comes from the noun *kolaphos*, meaning "a fist." So it literally means "to strike with the fist." Moffatt translates it: "knocked about." It would seem that "buffeted" is a little weak (cf. "brutally treated," NIV).

Have No Certain Dwellingplace Again this is one word in Greek, the verb *astateō*. It comes from the adjective *astatos*, which means "unstable." So it signifies: "to be unsettled, be homeless, lead a vagabond life" (A-S, p. 65). It could be translated "are vagabonds," or "are homeless" (NIV).

12 *Suffer* The verb *anechō* literally means "hold up." In the NT it is always in the middle voice and carries the idea of "bear with" or "endure." The rendering "suffer" gives a somewhat different connotation to the modern reader.

13 *Defamed* The verb *dysphēmeō* is found only here in the NT. It means to speak ill of somebody. In 1 Macc. 7:41 it is used of the insults hurled at the Jews by Rabshakeh, the representative of King Sennacherib. Probably "slandered" (NIV) gives the best meaning today.

Filth, Offscouring Both Greek words, *perikatharmata* and *peripsēma*, are found only here in the NT. Arndt and Gingrich define the first term as meaning "*that which is removed as a result of a thorough cleansing, i.e. dirt, refuse, off-scouring*, also as a designation of the 'off-scouring' of mankind (Epict. 3, 22, 78)" (p. 653).

The second term comes from the verb meaning "to wipe off all around." So it means "that which is wiped off, off-scouring" (A-S, pp. 358–59).

Of these two words Godet writes: "The term *perikatharma, filth,* denotes literally what is collected by sweeping all around the chamber (*peri*); and *peripsēma* the dirt which is detached from an object by sweeping or scraping it all around" (1:228).

Lightfoot says that the first term means "sweeping, offscourings." He then comments:

> This is the primary meaning of the word. But the Apostle is carrying on the metaphor of *epithanatios* above. Both *perikatharmata* and *peripsēma* were used especially of those condemned criminals of the lowest classes who were sacrificed as expiatory offerings, as scapegoats in effect, because of their degraded life. It was the custom at Athens to reserve certain worthless persons who in case of plague, famine or other visitations from heaven might be thrown into the sea, in the belief that they would cleanse away, or wipe away, the guilt of the nation (*Notes*, pp. 200–201).

Arndt and Gingrich feel that the first of these two terms may have the meaning of "propitiatory offering." They say that "it is probably better to translate *scapegoats for the world*" (p. 653), in this passage (for "filth of the world"). Phillips' rendering is colorful: "We are the world's rubbish, the scum of the earth."

15 *Instructors* The word *paidagōgos* occurs only here and in Gal. 3:24–25 (see notes there). It comes from *pais*, "child," and *agōgos*, "a leader," and so literally means "a child leader"; that is, a guide and guardian of boys. Both Thayer and Abbott-Smith give just one definition, "tutor."

Thayer has a rather full treatment of this term, which is worth quoting. He writes:

> Among the Greeks and Romans the name was applied to trustworthy slaves who were charged with the duty of supervising the life and morals of boys belonging to the better class. The boys were not allowed so much as to step out of the house without them before arriving at the age of manhood . . . The name carries with it an idea of severity (as a stern censor and enforcer of morals) in 1 Cor. iv. 15, where the father is distinguished from the tutor as one whose discipline is usually milder, and in Gal. iii. 24f. where the Mosaic law is likened to a tutor because it arouses the consciousness of sin, and is called *paidagōgos eis Christon*, i.e., preparing the soul for Christ, because those who have learned by experience with the law that they are not and cannot be commended to God by their works, welcome the more eagerly the hope of salvation offered them through the death and resurrection of Christ, the Son of God (p. 472).

16 *Followers* Our words "mimic" and "mimeograph" both come from the Greek word here, *mimetai*, which occurs seven times in the NT (cf. 11:1; Eph. 5:1; 1 Tim. 1:6; 2:14; Heb. 6:12; 1 Pet. 3:13). It always means "imitators," which is a stronger term than "followers." Paul wanted the Corinthian Christians to imitate him, as he was imitating Christ (11:1).

18 *Puffed Up* The verb *physioō* is used 6 times in this epistle—3 times in this chapter (4:6, 18, 19; 5:2; 8:1; 13:4)—and only once elsewhere in the NT (Col. 2:18). This reflects the spiritual pride of the Corinthians, which was their main problem.

The word comes from *physa*, which means "bellows." So it means "*to puff up* or *blow up*, inflate" (A-S). In the New Testament the verb is always used metaphorically in the sense of being puffed up with pride.

The context suggests that "arrogant" (Weymouth, RSV) may be the best translation here. Some members of the Corinthian congregation were carrying on arrogantly, assuming that Paul would not come and straighten things out.

19, 20 *Speech, Word* "Speech" (v. 19) and "word" (v. 20) are both translations of *logos*.

The RSV is consistent in having "talk" in both places. This is perhaps the best rendering. Paul's opponents in Corinth were doing a lot of talking, but they lacked real power. The apostle asserts that the kingdom of God is not mere talk; it is the power of the Holy Spirit, which these self-inflated Corinthians sadly lacked.

5:1–5 *To Deliver . . . unto Satan* Chapter 5 deals with a case of flagrant immorality in the church at Corinth. One of its members was living with his stepmother. This is what is called "incest," and it was particularly abhorrent even to the pagans of that day. So this sin in the church was bringing serious reproach on the name of Christ. Yet the proud, stubborn Corinthians were arrogant when they should have been repentant.

In verse 2 Paul says that they should have put the guilty person out of church, should have excluded him from their fellowship. He concludes his discussion of this problem by saying that the "wicked person" should be "put away from among you" (v. 13). This rather clearly means excommunication.

But what is the apostle talking about in verses 3–5? He says that he has already rendered a judgment in the case. With apostolic authority he has moved "to deliver such an one unto Satan for the destruction of the flesh, that the spirit may be saved in the day of the Lord Jesus" (v. 5). Paul uses similar language in 1 Tim. 1:20.

H. A. W. Meyer writes helpfully on this passage. He suggests that while the church could excommunicate an erring member, it was the prerogative of only the apostles to consign a man to Satan. He calls the latter "the *intensified* penalty of excommunication" (p. 112).

Meyer also calls attention to the fact that what is to be destroyed is the *sarx*, "the flesh," not the body. The object of Paul's judgment of the man was that "his *sinful fleshly nature*, which is turned to account by the indwelling power of sin as the workplace of his desires and lusts, might be emptied of its energy of sinful life by the pains of bodily sickness, and might in so far perish and come to nought. It is not his *soma* (body) that is to *die*, but his *sarx* (flesh)" (p. 113). He goes on to say: "Observe that it is with an *anti-Christian purpose* that Satan smites the man delivered over to him with bodily misery, but that against his own will this purpose of his is made to *serve God's* aim of *salvation*" (pp. 113–14). The delivering to Satan was penal, but it had a remedial purpose.

6 Leaven Paul quotes an old proverb: "A little leaven leavens all the dough." To regular readers of the KJV the term "leaven" is familiar. But many readers of the Bible today might not be aware of the fact that "leaven" means "yeast." Of course, in this day when very little baking is done at home, probably most young people would not even know what yeast is! It is true that "leaven" has become deeply ingrained in our language as a symbol of evil, although it is sometimes used for a good influence. Basically it means what affects the whole group or society.

10 Fornicators In verses 10 and 11 the apostle mentions various types of sinful people. He says that we cannot avoid associating with such people in this world, but we are not to tolerate them in the church.

We have already noted that the Greek word translated "fornication" can refer to many kinds of immorality, including adultery and probably homosexuality. So "fornicators" (*pornois*) here should be rendered as "the immoral."

10, 11 Covetous The noun *pleonektēs* occurs in both these verses and in 6:11. Elsewhere in the NT it is found only in Eph. 5:5. It refers to a "greedy" person, as we would say today.

10 Extortioners The adjective *harpax*, used here as a substantive, comes from the verb *harpazō*, which means "to seize, catch up, snatch away, carry off by force" (A-S, p. 60). So the reference here is to what we would call "robbers" (RSV) or "swindlers" (NEB, NIV).

11 Railer The noun *loidoros* is found only here and in 6:10, where it is translated "reviler" in KJV. It comes from the verb *loidoreō*, which means "to abuse, revile" (A-S). Perhaps the best contemporary translation would be "an abusive person."

6:2, 4 To Judge . . . Judgments For the one who tries to translate the Greek of these verses there are obvious difficulties. Both the above expressions render *criterion*, which basically has the same meaning in Greek as we have given it in English. Thayer defines it thus: "1. properly *the instrument* or *means of trying* or *judging anything; the rule by which one judges* (Plat., Plut., al). 2. *the place where judgment is given; the tribunal of a judge; a bench of judges:* plur. I Co. vi.2; Jas. ii.6.3. in an exceptional usage, *the matter judged, thing to be decided, suit, case:* plur. I Co. vi.4" (p. 362).

This definition helps out in translating verse 4. But "tribunals" hardly seems to fit verse 2, unless we render it: "Are you unworthy of being tribunals for smallest matters?"

This is the way Meyer takes it. He writes: "*Criterion* does not mean *matter of dispute, case at law*, as most expositors . . . wish to take it, with no evidence at all from the usage of the language in their favour, but *place of judgment* (*tribunal, seat of justice*, Jas. ii. 6) . . . or *judicial trial* which is held . . . The latter sense, *judicial trial* . . . is the true one here, as is evident from ver. 4. We render therefore: *Are ye unworthy to hold very trivial trials?* i.e. trials in which judgment is to be given upon very insignificant matters" (p. 129).

There is no question that "tribunal" or "judgment seat" fits very well in Jas. 2:6, the only other passage in the NT where this word occurs. There Arndt and Gingrich would translate the passage, "drag you into court." But they continue: "It is not easy to fit this meaning into the two other passages in our literature where *criterion* is found." They hold that the clause in verse 2 "could perhaps mean: *are you unfit to form even the most insignificant courts* (i.e. those that have jurisdiction over the petty details of every-day life)?" For verse 4 they suggest: "*if you have* (need for) *courts for the matters of everyday life, do you appoint insignificant men* (as judges)?" Then they add: "However, in both cases the tendency is now to prefer for *criterion* the sense . . . *lawsuit, legal action*" (p. 454). The idea then would be: "Are you unworthy (*anaxios*, only here in NT) to take care of the least important legal actions?" (v. 2).

The problem still remains: Is verse 4 to be taken as a command (KJV) or as a question (most Greek texts)? If the former, Paul must be speaking ironically. For instance, Findlay suggests: "Paul says in sarcasm, 'If you have lawsuits in secular affairs, set up the lowest amongst you (for judges of these low matters)!' " Actually, Findlay agrees with Meyer in insisting that *criterion* "signifies *place* rather than *matter* of judgment" (EGT, 2:814), and so prefers the translation: "Well then, for secular tribunals—if you have men that are made of no account in the Church, set these on the bench!" (EGT, 2:815).

Robertson and Plummer (ICC) have a full treatment of the matter. They write:

> If *cathizete* (set) is imperative, then these words mean "those in the Church who are held of no account," i.e. the least esteemed of the Christians. The apostle sarcastically tells them that, so far from there being any excuse for re-

sorting to heathen tribunals, any selection of the simplest among themselves would be competent to settle their disputes about trifles. Let the insignificant decide what is insignificant.

If *cathizete* is indicative [the same Greek form is used for both in second person plural of the present tense] and the sentence interrogative, then these words mean, "those who, in the Church, are held of no account," viz. the *adikoi* (unjust) of v. 1.

They add: "Both constructions are possible, and both make good sense."

After listing many authorities on both sides, they conclude: "We must be content to leave the question open. The general sense is clear. The Corinthians were doing a shameful thing in going to heathen civil courts to settle disputes between Christians" (pp. 113–14).

7 Fault The word *hēttēma* occurs only here and in Rom. 11:12. The translation "fault" (KJV) is inaccurate in terms of what that means today. The Greek word means "loss" or "defeat." The latter is its use in the OT (LXX). Arndt and Gingrich translate this passage: "it is an utter defeat for you" (p. 350).

Lightfoot seems to capture the real significance. He translates: "it is a loss to you, a defeat." That is, "You trust to overreach, to gain a victory: it is really a loss, a defeat, before the trial even comes on" (*Notes*, p. 212). Even if a Christian won money in a damage suit against a fellow Christian, he had already sustained a great spiritual loss, perhaps even the loss of his own soul. This has happened many times. Paul goes on to suggest, "Better sustain a material loss than lose your salvation."

7, 8 Defraud The verb *apostereō* means "*to defraud, deprive of, despoil* (in classical Greek, chiefly of the misappropriation of trust funds)" (A-S, p. 54). Thayer even gives the meaning "rob," and Arndt and Gingrich give, "steal, rob." Goodspeed translates verse 8: "But it is you who wrong and rob others, and your own brothers at that!"

What Paul is saying to the Corinthian Christians is: "Better to be robbed than to rob. But you are actually robbing each other by unjust lawsuits against each other." The church at Corinth was a constant heartache and heartbreak to the apostle who had founded it.

9 Effeminate Two Greek words at the end of verse 9 seem to refer to much the same thing. The first is *malakos*, translated "effeminate." This adjective, in the plural here, literally means "soft" and was properly used of what is

soft to touch. It occurs elsewhere in the NT in only two parallel passages (Matt. 11:8; Luke 7:25) where it describes "soft clothing."

But, as Arndt and Gingrich note, it was also used "of persons *soft, effeminate*, especially of *catamites*, men and boys who allow themselves to be misused homosexually" (p. 489). This was a common thing in that day. Deissmann gives a photographic facsimile of a third-century papyrus letter from a wealthy Egyptian to a police official, asking that "Zenobius the effeminate," a musician, be sent to him (LAE, p. 164).

"Abusers of themselves with mankind" is all one word in Greek, *arsenokoitai* (only here and 1 Tim. 1:10). It is compounded of *arsēn*, "male," and *koitē*, "bed," and so means "one who lies with a male as with a female, a sodomite" (Thayer, p. 75). The same sin is described graphically in Rom. 1:27.

Because these two words evidently refer to the same type of person, they are combined in many modern translations. In the Berkeley Version we find simply "partakers in homosexuality." The RSV followed suit with only one word, "homosexuals," but a footnote explains: "Two Greek words are rendered by this expression." The NEB ties these two words in with the previous term and reads: "none who are guilty either of adultery or of homosexual perversion."

In keeping with its policy of representing every Greek word in the English translation, NASB has both "effeminate" and "homosexuals." But today "effeminate" is popularly used to describe a fellow who acts like a "sissy." So it is hardly a correct translation here. The Jerusalem Bible has "catamites, sodomites," but it is doubtful if either of those terms would convey much to the average reader today. The New American Bible represents both terms together by "sodomites." The NIV has: "nor male prostitutes nor homosexual offenders."

In much of modern society in America and Europe homosexuality is no longer even frowned upon. Several church denominations have officially stated that homosexual relations between consenting adults should no longer be considered a crime. Congregations of homosexuals have sprung up in this country and have even formed themselves into an association like a denomination. Marriages of two men or two women are not uncommon. These homosexual "Christians" claim that they should be recognized as God's children just as readily as those who prefer the traditional way of life.

In the face of all this permissiveness we need to realize afresh what God's Word says about this practice. In both the Old Testament and the New it is categorically condemned. Certainly we need to be sympathetic with those who have a psychological problem at this point. But the Scriptures label homosexuality as a sin. Paul states very clearly here that no homosexual will inherit the kingdom of God. The same thing is implied in Rom. 1:27. Sodomy was the sin for which God destroyed ancient Sodom.

11 Sanctified Paul writes: "And such were some of you: but ye are washed, but ye are sanctified, but ye are justified in the name of the Lord Jesus, and by the Spirit of our God."

The first thing that should be noted is that in all three cases the verb is in the aorist tense, not the present, in the original. The Greek says: "You were washed . . . sanctified . . . justified." One of the main weaknesses of the translators working 350 years ago was their failure to accurately translate the Greek tenses.

In the second place, it will be observed that "sanctified" occurs between "washed" and "justified." The order of the terms would suggest that the verb *hagiazō* has here its lesser meaning of "set apart to God." All three terms seem to refer to the initial experience of conversion. At that time those to whom Paul is writing had their sins washed away—the compound verb *apolouō* (only here and Acts 22:16) means "wash off" or "wash away"—they were set apart to God, and they were "justified" (made and declared righteous in God's sight).

12–18 Corinthian Antinomianism Paul twice writes: "All things are lawful for me." But it seems clear that he is quoting his critics. So the statement should be put in quotation marks both times (cf. RSV, NIV). In each case the apostle gives his answer to the proud claim of those who wanted to do as they pleased. The same goes for the first part of verse 13: "Food for the stomach, and the stomach for food" (literal translation).

It appears that there were those in the church at Corinth who gloried so much in their freedom from the Mosaic law and their liberty in Christ that they had become almost libertines. This is evidently the reason for the apostle's strong castigation of immorality in the preceding verses. He goes on to warn against participation in the pagan worship that involved relations with sacred prostitutes in the temple (vv. 15–16). He warns them to "flee immorality" (v. 18). Corinth was perhaps the most wicked city of that day, and the Christians needed to be particularly careful.

20 Body . . . Spirit? Paul concludes his discussion by reminding his readers that they have been "bought with a price," the precious blood of Christ, and so they are to "glorify God in your body." The added words, "and in your spirit, which are God's," are not in any of the oldest and best Greek manuscripts—from the third, fourth, and fifth centuries. They must have been inserted in the text by a later scribe.

Gnosticism taught that all matter is evil; only spirit is good. Therefore the human body is essentially evil. Unfortunately, Gnostic ideas crept into the Early Church, causing an unwholesome emphasis on asceticism. To tone down the strong admonition here to glorify God in our bodies, a copyist added "and in your spirit." (All modern translations correctly end the chapter with "body.")

The teaching of both the Old Testament and the New is that our physical bodies were made by God and so are good. It is how we use them that matters. They can be used for sinful purposes. But they can also be used for holy purposes, and so glorify God.

7:2 Fornication "Nevertheless, to avoid fornication, let every man have his own wife, and let every woman have her own husband." This seems to suggest a low motive for marriage. But instead of "to avoid fornication," the Greek reads: "on account of the fornications." The NASB renders it correctly, "because of immoralities;" *porneia* is used in the NT for all kinds of immorality, including adultery and homosexuality. The NIV reads: "But since there is so much immorality."

The reason for Paul's admonition was that Corinth was at that time perhaps the most immoral city in the world. Cases of immorality were to be seen on every side. The Christians at Corinth were safer to be married, since they had to live in such immoral surroundings.

See also discussion at Matt. 5:32.

3 Due Benevolence The Greek is simply *tēn opheilēn*. This comes from the verb *opheilō*, which means "I owe." So it means "one's due." The correct translation is "what is due her" (NEB). The context suggests that the reference is to her conjugal rights, that is, normal marriage relationships. Both husband and wife owe this to each other. People who are not prepared to do this should not be married.

5 Defraud The verb is *apostereō*. Its earliest meaning was "steal, rob." Then it came to signify "defraud," as we use that term today. But the context (cf. v. 3) suggests that Paul is saying, "Do not deprive each other" (NIV). Phillips, with his paraphrase, spells it all out: "Do not cheat each other of normal sexual intercourse." This is the correct meaning.

Consent It is the adjective *symphōnos*, which is compounded of *syn*, "together," and *phōnē*, "sound." So the literal meaning is "agreeing in sound." Metaphorically it is used in the sense of "harmonious, agreeing." So the phrase here means "by agreement."

This adjective occurs only here in the NT. The same is true of the noun *symphōnia* (Luke 15:25), which meant a musical symphony. The language suggests that our married life should be a true symphony, with no jarring, discordant sounds. It's the "sour notes" in marriage that ruin the symphony. We keep in tune with each other when we both follow the maestro, Christ.

Give We do not find here the common word for "give"—*didōmi*. Rather the verb is *scholasēte*, from which we get "scholastic." What's the connection?

The verb *scholazō* comes from the noun *scholē*. Originally this meant "freedom from labor, leisure." In later Greek it was used for "a place where there is leisure for anything, a school" (Thayer, p. 610). This is its meaning in the only place where it is found in the NT (Acts 19:9). Learning takes time. Someone has said, "Without leisure there is no true education." Probably that is the reason there are so few really educated people today! Most of us don't take time to think.

The verb used here originally meant "to cease from labor," then "to be free from labor, to be at leisure . . . to have leisure for a thing, i.e., to give one's self to a thing" (Thayer, p. 610). Abbott-Smith spells it out even more clearly: "*to be at leisure*, hence, to have time or opportunity for, *to devote oneself to*," (p. 436). The best translation here is "devote" (NIV).

Fasting Paul says that the husband and wife should not deprive each other of normal married relationship except by mutual agreement for a short time, "that ye may give yourselves to fasting and prayer." But the oldest and best Greek manuscripts—the third-century Papyrus 46, together with all the fourth- and fifth-century manuscripts and the earliest versions—do not have "fasting" here. They simply mention "prayer." The strong emphasis on fasting was a part of the development of asceticism in the Early Church, under the evil influence of Gnosticism. This heresy taught that all spirit is

good and all matter is evil: so the physical body must be suppressed as an evil thing.

The first chapter of Genesis teaches that God created matter and called it "good." When He crowned it all with the creation of man He surveyed the results and pronounced them "very good" (Gen. 1:31). Asceticism is a denial of biblical theology.

Incontinency This is an archaic translation of *akrasia* (only here and Matt. 23:25). The proper rendering today is "lack of self-control" (Weymouth, RSV, NEB, NASB, NIV).

6 Permission The apostle states that in the advice given in verse 5 he speaks "by permission and not of commandment." The noun *syngnōmē* means "concession." Robertson and Plummer write: "The word occurs nowhere else in N.T. and is very rare in LXX." In a footnote they comment: " 'By permission' (A.V.) is ambiguous: it might mean, 'I am permitted by God to say as much as this' . . . It means 'By way of concession': he is telling people that they may marry, not that they must do so" (p. 135).

9 Contain The verb *engkrateuō* occurs only here and in 9:25. It means "to exercise self-control," and that is the way to translate it here.

Burn On the surface this verse could be taken as meaning: "It is better to marry than to burn forever in hell." It is true that the verb *pyroō* (from *pyr*, "fire") means "to be set on fire, to burn" (A-S, p. 394); it is always passive in the NT. But almost all the modern translations agree that the correct meaning is "to be aflame with passion" (RSV). Weymouth has: "For marriage is better than the fever of passion." As usual, the NASB gives a literal rendering, "to burn," but it adds in the margin: "i.e., *burn with passion*" (cf. NIV).

Robertson and Plummer call attention to the fact that the verbs "contain" and "burn" are in the present tense of continuous action. They comment: "A prolonged and painful struggle seems to be intended, a condition quite fatal to spiritual peace and growth" (p. 139).

It is true that in our day, as in ancient Corinth—when the Christian is surrounded by flagrant, blatant immorality—the safest condition for most people is a normal married life. That was what God ordained in Eden, and it is still His pattern for human beings.

11, 12, 13 Put Away . . . Leave This is the translation found at the end of these verses.

But in the Greek the verb is the same in all three places. It is *aphiēmi*, which means "send away," and is so translated in all three places in NASB. Since in the context here this would mean "divorce," the word is rendered that way in RSV and NIV. Among the Jews a woman could not divorce her husband. This fact probably accounts for the change in translation in KJV for verse 13. But 1 Corinthians was written to a Gentile church, and we know that Greek and Roman women could divorce their husbands. Many modern translators use "divorce" here.

17 Distributed Paul says that each man should keep the place in life which the Lord has "distributed" to him. It is true that the verb *merizō* means "to divide" or "distribute." But the meaning that fits this passage is "assigned" (NIV).

21 Servant The noun *doulos* comes from the verb *deō*, which means "bind." So the noun means a bond-servant, or slave. This is clearly the connotation here, for it speaks of being "made free," not fired.

The last clause of this verse is somewhat ambiguous in the Greek. What does "use it rather" mean? By equally competent scholars it has been taken with opposite meanings.

Weymouth (1902) rendered the last two clauses: "And yet if you can get your freedom, you had better take it." Moffatt (1913) similarly has: "If you do find it possible to get free, you had better avail yourself of the opportunity." But Goodspeed (1923) goes in the other direction: "Even if you can gain your freedom, make the most of your present condition instead."

The majority of recent translations have followed Weymouth and Moffatt, rather than Goodspeed. But both RSV and NEB give the alternative rendering in the margin, since there is no way of being certain which was intended in the original. The NIV follows the majority: "although if you can gain your freedom, do so."

Among the commentators there is likewise a division of opinion, with equally good authorities lined up on each side. But Robertson and Plummer make a strong case for the view adopted above. The aorist tense of "use" suggests a new condition. They conclude: "The advice, thus interpreted, is thoroughly in keeping with the Apostle's tenderness of heart and robustness of judgment" (p. 148).

31 Abusing "And they that use this world, as not abusing it." This is a good attempt to bring over into English the play on words in

Greek. "Use" is the verb *chraomai*, "abuse" is *katachraomai*. The prepositional prefix *kata* has the intensive force. So the compound verb means "to make full use of, use to the uttermost, use up" (A-S, p. 240). This is expressed well in NEB: "Nor those who use the world's wealth on using it to the full." We are to use the material resources of this world for the good of the Kingdom, but we must not use them selfishly upon ourselves. To do so is to abuse our privileges, rather than use them.

32 Carefulness The adjective *amerimnos* occurs only here and in Matt. 2:14. It means "free from anxiety." Paul is not telling us to be "without carefulness." One of the most important of the ABCs of life is: "Always Be Careful!" But he does express the wish that his readers should be "without anxiety," or "free from anxious care."

35 Snare The word *brochos* is found only here in the NT. Thayer defines it as "*a noose, slip-knot, by which any person or thing is caught, or fastened, or suspended.*" Used with the verb *epiballō*, as here, the phrase means "*to throw a noose upon one*, a figurative expression borrowed from war (or the chase) . . . i.e., by craft or by force to bind one to some necessity, to constrain him to obey some command" (p. 106).

Metaphorically it means "restraint," as here. Robertson and Plummer comment: " 'Cast a snare upon you' (AV., RV.) gives a wrong idea: *brochos* is a halter or lasso, not a trap . . . He has no wish to curtail their freedom, as one throws a rope over an animal that is loose, or a person that is to be arrested" (p. 158).

Comely The adjective *euschēmon* literally means "elegant, graceful, comely." But here it is used in its moral sense of "seemly, becoming." The simplest translation is "proper."

Attend . . . Without Distraction This verse has three words used only once in the NT. We have already noted *brochos*. Two more occur near the end of the verse. The first is *euparedros*, "constantly attendant or waiting on." The second, *aperispastōs*, is an adverb meaning "without distraction." It comes from the alpha-privative *a-* and the verb *perispaō*, "distract," found only in Luke 10:40. There we read that Martha was "cumbered" (distracted) with much serving. Paul wished that workers in the church might sit at the Master's feet, as did Mary, not be distracted as Martha.

The great apostle was so wrapped up in the

business of the Kingdom that he had no time for anything else. He would liked to have applied this ideal to everybody. But in reading this paragraph (vv. 25–40) we should always keep in mind the opening verse: "Now concerning virgins I have no commandment of the Lord: yet I give my judgment, as one that hath obtained mercy of the Lord to be faithful" (v. 25). He also closes the discussion by saying that he is giving his own judgment (v. 40). So the guidelines he suggests here are not binding on the Christian—they state Paul's own preferences, as he is careful to tell us. It should also be noted that he was dealing with a special, abnormal type of situation in Corinth. That the apostle had a high view of marriage is clearly seen in Eph. 5:25–27.

36, 37 *Virgin* The English Revised Version (NT, 1881), the ASV (1901) and the NASB (NT, 1963) all have "virgin *daughter*." The older commentaries (e.g., CGT, ICC, EGT) support this rendering, mainly because of the expression "giveth her in marriage" in verse 38. Thayer's *Lexicon* takes it that way.

The Greek simply has *parthenos*. Under *gamizō*, "give in marriage," Arndt and Gingrich note that the verb may here be used for *gameō*, "marry." They go on to say: "In the context of vv. 36–8 *parthenos* would then mean either a Christian's fiancee . . . or perhaps even his 'spiritual bride,' who lived with him as a virgin" (p. 150). The RSV takes it in the former way—"If anyone thinks he is not behaving properly toward his betrothed" (v. 36). The NEB adopts the other view: "But if a man has a partner in celibacy" (v. 36) . . . "and if he has decided in his own mind to preserve his partner in her virginity" (v. 37). Probably the NIV rendering is best: "the virgin he is engaged to" (v. 36), "the virgin" (vv. 37, 38).

8:1 *Things Offered unto Idols* This is all one word in Greek, *eidolothyta*. It is compounded of *eidolon*, "idol," and *thyō*, "sacrifice." So it literally means "things sacrificed to idols." The term is used four times in this chapter (vv. 1, 4, 7, 10), twice in chapter 10 (vv. 19, 28), twice in Acts (15:29; 21:25) and twice in Revelation (2:14, 20). Thayer says that it denotes "the flesh left over from the heathen sacrifices; it was either eaten at feasts, or sold (by the poor and the miserly) in the market" (p. 174). Arndt and Gingrich (p. 220) note: "From the Jewish viewpoint it was unclean and therefore forbidden" (cf. Num. 25:2; Ps. 106:28). Dean Stanley observes: "This identification of a sacrifice and a feast was carried to the high-

est pitch among the Greeks. Sacrifices are enumerated by Aristotle and Thucydides amongst the chief means of social enjoyment" (Quoted by Lias, *Romans*, p. 94).

Edifieth The Greek word is *oikodomeō*, which literally means "build a house," and so more generally "build." One could translate the last part of this verse: "Knowledge blows up, but love builds up." The first verb is *physioō*, which comes from *physa*, "bellows." So it means "blow up" or "inflate."

The picture here is a striking contrast. Intellectualism often inflates a person with pride. We can blow up a balloon in a minute or two, and collapse it in a second with a pin prick. So it is with self-important intellectuals. They can be deflated with a single remark.

But building up with love is something else. Just as one has to lay stone on stone or brick on brick in order to construct a solid building, so we must lay one loving deed on another if we would build a solid life that will last.

9:3 *Answer* The word is *apologia*, from which we get "apology." But the Greek term means "a speech in defense." Actually the original meaning of "apology" in English was "defense."

4 *Power* The term used here (vv. 4, 5, 6, 12, 18) is not *dynamis*, "power," but *exousia*, "right, privilege, authority." Paul first asks "Have we not power to eat and to drink?"—that is at the church's expense. Some evidently insisted that because Paul was not one of the original 12 apostles, he had no right to be maintained by the church.

In the second place, Paul asks if he does not have just as much right to be accompanied by a wife as had other apostles and the Lord's brothers and Peter. The third question the apostle asked is: "Or I only and Barnabas, have we not power to forbear working?" (v. 6). The last two words are literally "not to work." What Paul is asking is this: "Are Barnabas and I the only ones who do not have the right to refrain from working?"

Lias comments: "The reason why Paul and Barnabas refused to accept payment for their services is not hard to discover. They went on a mission to the Gentiles, the other Apostles to the Jews. The latter fully understood that the ministers should be maintained by the offerings of the worshippers. The Gentiles, on the contrary, had so long known what it was to be plundered by greedy sophists who lived by their wits, that it was above all things necessary for the Apostles of Christ to avoid being confounded with such persons" (pp. 102–3).

7 Goeth a Warfare This is one word in the Greek, *strateuetai*. The verb simply means "serve as a soldier." It is used literally here and in Luke 3:14 and 2 Tim. 2:4. In the other four occurrences in the New Testament (2 Cor. 10:3; 1 Tim. 1:18; James 4:1; 1 Pet. 2:11) it is used metaphorically of making war in a spiritual conflict.

Charges The word *opsōnion* meant "provisions, provision-money, soldier's pay" (A-S, p. 332). That is how it is used here and in Luke 3:14. In 2 Cor. 11:8 it is used in a more general sense for wages, and in Rom. 6:23 for the "wages" of sin. The general sense of "wages" is found in the papyri (BS, p. 148). The correct translation of the first question in verse 7 is: "Who at any time serves as a soldier at his own expense?" (NASB).

11 Carnal Paul writes: "If we have sown unto you spiritual things (*pneumatika*), is it a great thing if we shall reap your carnal things (*sarkika*)."

The *Oxford English Dictionary* (2:123) indicates that the earliest meaning of "carnal" was "of or pertaining to the flesh or body; bodily, corporeal." But it labels this "obsolete." It then came to mean "pertaining to the body as the seat of passions or appetites; fleshly, sensual." This is the usual way that the word "carnal" is taken today, but obviously this is not what Paul is talking about here. Another definition, labeled "archaic," is "material, temporal, secular." That is the sense in which it is used here. The correct translation is "material things," or, "money." What the apostle is saying in this passage (vv. 11–14) is that the one who dispenses food for the soul should be paid for this just as is the grocer who furnishes food for the body.

13 Live Paul says that those who work at holy tasks in the temple "live of the things of the temple." Instead of "live" the Greek has "eat" (*esthiousin*). This refers to the fact that the priests were entitled to get their meat from the sacrifices offered in the temple, as ordered in the law of Moses (Num. 18:8–20). They shared ("partakers with") the food that was placed on the altar.

17 Willingly... Against My Will In the Greek there is a play on words: *hekōn... akōn*. The latter is found only here in the New Testament; the former occurs only here and in Rom.

8:20. Obviously the translation should be: "willingly"... "unwillingly."

Dispensation The word *oikonomian* means "dispensation" in its original meaning of "a dispensing." Paul was dispensing the gospel to others. But today the term "dispensation" usually refers to a period of time, and so its use here is misleading. The proper translation is "stewardship."

19 Servant Paul declared that although he was free from domination by any man, yet he had made himself "servant" to all men, "to win as many as possible" (NIV). The verb *douloō* means "make (myself) a slave to" (see discussion at Rom. 6:18–22). So probably the better translation here is "slave" (NASB, NIV).

Gain The verb *kerdainō* regularly means to "gain," in the sense of gaining *things*. "That I might gain the more" (KJV) would most naturally be thought of as gaining more possessions. But with *persons* the correct word is "win"—"that I might win the more" (RSV, NASB). This applies to vv. 19–22.

23 This "This" (KJV) is *panta*, "all things." Whatever Paul did was for a definite purpose— "I do all this for the sake of the gospel" (NIV).

24 Race The Greek word for "race" in this passage is *stadion*, which was taken over into English in its Latin form "stadium." It means "a stadium, i.e. (1) a measure of length equal to 600 Greek feet or one-eighth of a Roman mile ... this being the length of the Olympic course, (2) a racecourse: 1 Cor. 9:24" (A-S, p. 415). Later it came to mean the "arena ... on or in which the foot races and other public athletic contests were held" (AG, p. 771)—which is what "stadium" means now.

25 Striveth for the Mastery This is all one word in the Greek, *agōnizomenos*. The verb *agōnizō* is used here in its literal meaning of "contend for a prize" (A-S, p. 8). (It is used metaphorically in Col. 1:29; 4:12; 1 Tim. 4:10; 6:12; 2 Tim. 4:7). Here "competes in the games" (NASB, NIV) translates the verb well.

"Is temperate" is better rendered "exercises self-control." That is what athletes have to do in order to win. And that is what Christians must do to win in the race of life. The verb *engkrateuō* is found (in NT) only here and 7:9.

Crown The Greek word is *stephanos*. It does not usually mean a royal crown (Greek, *diadēma*) but the victor's crown. This was a laurel wreath (NIV) given to the one who won in an athletic contest, particularly the Marathon race. Grundmann writes: "Like Philo . . . Paul draws on the perishable crown which is given to the victor as an award in the games . . . and he compares the Christian life to a sporting contest. The point of comparison is the self-controlled abstinence . . . which is practised for the sake of the goal" (TDNT, 7:629).

26 *Uncertainly* The adverb *adēlōs* (only here in NT) is compounded of *alpha*-negative and *dēlos*—"visible, clear." While it does have the general meaning "uncertainly," yet "aimlessly" fits better in connection with a race. Paul is saying that he is running "not aimlessly, i.e., not as one who has no fixed goal" (AG, p. 16). Changing the figure, he says, "I do not box (*pykteuō*, only here in NT) as a man beating the air"—or, shadowboxing.

27 *Keep Under* The verb *hypōpiazō* is found only here and in Luke 18:5, where KJV has the very weak translation "weary." It literally means "to strike under the eye, give a black eye" (A-S, p. 463). Thayer defines it: "properly, to beat black and blue, to smite so as to cause bruises and livid spots." Here Paul is saying, "Like a boxer I buffet my body, handle it roughly, discipline it by hardships" (p. 646). Weiss says of Paul: "He has in view the physical mistreatment he has received, the scars this has left on his body, the hardships to which his body is constantly exposed, and the results of these" (TDNT, 8:591).

Bring It into Subjection This is all one word in Greek, *doulagōgō* (only here in NT). Thayer defines this: "to lead away into slavery, claim as one's slave . . . to make a slave . . . to treat as a slave, i.e., with severity, to subject to stern and rigid discipline" (p. 157). The simplest translation is "make it my slave" (NASB, NIV). Paul believed that his spirit should dominate his body, not vice versa.

A *Castaway* The Greek word *adokimos* means "rejected after testing." Robertson and Plummer comment: "Manifestly exclusion from the contest, as not being qualified, is not the meaning; he represents himself as running and fighting: It is exclusion from the prize that is meant. He might prove to be disqualified" (p. 197). For that reason "disqualified for the prize" (NIV) may be a more adequate translation than simply "disqualified" (RSV, NASB).

Seneca, the pagan philosopher, has a passage that is amazingly appropriate to these verses of Paul's. He wrote: "What blows do athletes receive in their faces, what blows all over their bodies. Yet they bear all the torture from thirst of glory. Let us also overcome all things, for our reward is not a crown or a palm branch or the trumpeter proclaiming silence for the announcement of our name, but virtue and strength of mind and peace acquired ever after" (*Moral Epistles*, 78:16). How much greater the Christian's reward in heaven!

10:7 *Play* The verb *paizō* (from *pais*, child) originally meant to "play like a child." Then it came to mean "*to play, sport, jest; to give way to hilarity*, especially by joking, singing, dancing" (Thayer, p. 473).

This is the only place where *paizō* occurs in the NT, and it is found here in a quotation from the Septuagint of Exod. 32:6. Bertram says, "There can be no doubt that Exod. 32:19 refers to cultic dances" (TDNT, 5:629). Similarly Robertson and Plummer write: "The quotation, therefore, indicates an idolatrous banquet followed by idolatrous sport" (p. 204). So "play" may be "indulge in pagan revelry" (NIV).

10 *Murmur* The verb *gongyzō* is an onomatopoetic word; that is, its sound suggests its sense. The only trouble with "murmur" is that we use it now of speaking softly, and probably the Israelites were not that quiet! For this reason "grumble" is better. Both words are onomatopoetic.

11 *Ensamples* It is odd that earlier translators adopted "ensamples" here in place of the more familiar "examples" of v. 6. The noun in v. 6 is *typos*, from which we get "types." In v. 11 it is the adverb *typicōs*, "typically." For this passage Arndt and Gingrich suggest, "*typologically, as an example* or *warning*, in connection with the typological interpretation of Scripture" (p. 837). For v. 6 they say for *typoi*; "of the *types* given by God as an indication of the future, in the form of persons or things" (p. 838). Lias thinks that both "examples" and "types" fit well (p. 113).

13 *A Way to Escape* The Greek says *tēn ekbasin*, "the way out." Robertson and Plummer say this means "the necessary way of escape, the one suitable for such a difficulty" (p. 209).

Bear The verb *hypopherō* means "to bear up under, to endure patiently." Robertson and Plummer say: "Temptation is probation, and

God orders the probation in such a way 'that ye may be able to endure it' " (*ibid*.).

14 Idolatry Our English word comes directly from the Greek *eidōlatria* which is compounded of *eidōlon*, "image," and *latreia*, "worship." So idolatry is the worship of images.

16 Communion The Greek word is *koinōnia*. It comes from the adjective *koinōnos*, which means "common," but when used as a substantive means "a partaker, sharer" (see "partakers," v. 18). So the noun *koinōnia* may here be translated "a sharing" (NASB) or "a participation" (RSV, NIV). These terms make Paul's point a little clearer. However, since the reference is probably to the Lord's Supper, "communion" is also meaningful here. Arndt and Gingrich suggest "participation." But they offer as an alternative: "a means for attaining a close relationship with the blood (body) of Christ" (p. 440). that is what the Communion service is supposed to be. Hauck says that *koinōnia* "denotes 'participation, fellowship,' especially with a close bond" (TDNT, 3:798).

25 Shambles The word *makellon* is found only here in the NT. "Shambles" (KJV) does not convey the correct meaning today. A more accurate rendering is "meat market" (RSV, NASB, NIV). But Schneider writes: "The word means not only a meat market but a food market in general. The meat market is part of the *makellon*" (TDNT, 4:371). When Pompeii was excavated, the Macellum (Latin form) was found to be a rectangular court of pillars, covered by a dome-shaped roof, with booths on the sides.

28 Offered in Sacrifice This is all one word in Greek, *hierothyton*, which is compounded of the word *hieros* ("consecrated to the deity, sacred") and the verb *thyō* ("sacrifice"). So it meant "offered in sacrifice." Arndt and Gingrich say that here, as a substantive, it denotes "meat sacrificed to idols" (p. 373). Schrenk points out that it was regularly used to indicate "the flesh of sacrificial animals" (TDNT, 3:252).

The KJV rendering, "offered in sacrifice unto idols," is based on the reading *eidōlothyton*, which is found in the late manuscripts. G. G. Findlay observes: "The genuine reading, *hierothyton* (slain as sacred, i.e., in sacrifice), takes the statement as from the mouth of unbelievers; a Jew or a Christian would presumably say *eidōlothyton*" (EGT, 2:868)—which is genuine in v. 19, but not here. So the

translation "offered in sacrifice" (RSV, NIV) is more accurate than "meat sacrificed to idols" (NASB).

Incidentally, the repetition of "for the earth is the Lord's and the fulness thereof" (from v. 26) occurs only in a few, very late manuscripts. It is obviously a scribal addition, not a part of the original text.

32 Give None Offence The translation "give no offense" (RSV, NASB) is practically the same as "Give none offence" (KJV). The Greek says, "Become *aproskopoi*." This Greek word is compounded of the alpha-privative *a*- and the verb *proskoptō*, which in the transitive means "strike against" and in the intransitive "stumble." Abbott-Smith defines the adjective *aproskopos* as meaning "not causing to stumble." Probably the best translation is "Do not cause anyone to stumble" (NIV).

11:2 Ordinances The Greek word *paradosis* comes from the verb *paradidōmi*, which in this verse is translated "delivered." The verb means "to hand down, hand on, or deliver verbally" (A-S, p. 339). So the noun refers to what has been handed down. Today we call these "traditions" (RSV, NASB). Probably Paul is referring primarily to the doctrines of the Christian faith, but also to apostolic injunctions for Christian conduct. The KJV renders *paradosis* as "traditions" in all the other 12 places where it occurs in the NT. Why an exception here?

6 Shorn Today we speak of shearing sheep. That is the way the verb *keirō* is used in Acts 9:32, in a quotation from Isaiah. But here it is used for cutting off a woman's hair ("be shorn"). So the better translation now is "have her hair cut off" (NASB, NIV). Paul was alluding to customs that were current in Corinth at that time.

10 Power The word is not *dynamis*, "power," but *exousia*, "authority." But what does it mean when it says that a woman should have authority on her head? The bare statement seems to require something additional in order to make sense. That is why we find "*symbol* of authority" (NASB)—the italics indicate there is no word in the Greek—or "sign of authority" (NIV). The RSV goes a step farther by saying, "That is why a woman ought to have a veil on her head," with the footnote: "Greek *authority* (the veil being a symbol of this)." That is probably the correct meaning, in keeping with the custom that Paul reflects here.

11 Without The Greek preposition *chōris* means "separate from, apart from." The translation "without" seems a bit weak. Probably "independent of" (RSV, NASB, NIV) is more adequate, and so, more accurate. God originally created mankind "male and female" (Gen. 1:27). Husband and wife are to be "one flesh," not independent of each other. It should be noted that the words for "man" and "woman" mean "husband" and "wife," and they are often translated that way in the NT. That is the meaning here.

15 Covering Abbott-Smith thinks that the word *peribolaion*, "that which is thrown around," means "a veil." But Robertson and Plummer translate the second half of this verse: "Long hair is a permanent endowment (*dedotai*) of woman, to serve as an enveloping mantle" (p. 235). They also make this comment on v. 14: "At this period, civilized men, whether Jews, Greeks, or Romans, wore their hair short" (*ibid.*). We would agree with their observation: "While fanaticism defies nature, Christianity respects and refines it; and whatever shocks the common feelings of mankind is not likely to be right" (*ibid.*).

16 Contentious *Philoneikos* (only here in NT) is an adjective compounded of *philos*, "loving," and *neikos*, "strife." So it means "fond of strife" or "contentious." Unfortunately, most churches have some who are fond of strife, who, as we say, would rather argue than eat.

25 Testament The Greek word is *diathēkē*. In the NT (KJV) it is translated "testament" 13 times and "covenant" 20 times. Most scholars agree that it means "covenant" in almost every case. It is claimed that the Hebrews did not make wills or testaments as the Greeks and Romans did. But they did make covenants, as we find in many places in the OT.

Robertson and Plummer translate here: "This cup is the new covenant, and it is so in virtue of My Blood." They go on to say: "The Atonement is implied, without which doctrine the Lord's Supper is scarcely intelligible. . . . The choice of *diathēkē*, rather than *synthēke*, which is the common word for covenant, is no doubt deliberate, for *synthēke* might imply that the parties to the covenant contracted on equal terms. Between God and man that is impossible. When He enters into a contract He disposes everything, as a man disposes of his property by will" (p. 247).

12:1 Spiritual Gifts Here and in 14:1 the Greek says simply *tōn pneumaticōn*, "the spiritual (things)." But the use of gifts in vv. 4, 9, 28, 30, and 31 seems to show conclusively that "spiritual gifts" is a correct interpretation—as almost all versions have. The opening words of chapter 12, "Now concerning," clearly introduce a new problem, and unquestionably the problem of chapters 12–14 is that of spiritual gifts, or gifts of the Spirit.

3 Accursed Paul declares that no one speaking "by" (or "in") the Spirit of God "calleth Jesus accursed"—literally, "says, '*Anathema Iēsous*.' " Furthermore, only by the Holy Spirit can one "say that Jesus is Lord"—literally, "say 'Lord Jesus.' " The Holy Spirit alone can enable us to submit to the Lordship of Christ.

The basic meaning of the Greek word *anathema* is "something dedicated or consecrated to the deity." It was used first "of the consecrated offerings laid up in the temple," and second, for "something delivered up to divine wrath, dedicated to destruction and brought under a curse" (Behm, TDNT, 1:354). Paul always uses it in the latter sense—"the object of a curse" (*ibid.*).

Robertson and Plummer write: "The blasphemous *Anathema Iēsous* would be more likely to be uttered by a Jew than a Gentile. . . . It is not improbable that Saul himself used it in his persecuting days, and strove to make others do so (Acts 26:11). . . . Unbelievers, whether Jews or Gentiles were admitted to Christian gatherings (16:24), and therefore one of these might suddenly exclaim in the middle of public worship '*Anathema Iēsous*.' To the inexperienced Corinthians a mad shout of this kind . . . might seem to be inspired. . . . St. Paul assures them that this anti-Christian utterance is absolutely derisive. It cannot come from the Spirit" (261). *Anathema* "is one of the 103 words which in NT are found only in Paul and Luke" (*ibid.*).

4, 5, 6 Diversities, Differences? In these three verses we find (KJV): "diversities . . . differences . . . diversities." In the Greek it is exactly the same word all three times—*diaireseis* (used only here in NT).

Thayer defines it as first, "division, distribution," and second, "distinction, difference," and then adds that in particular it means "a distinction arising from a different distribution to different persons" (p. 137).

Schlier, after noting the different meanings of *diairesis* (sing.), says: "So far as concerns 1C. 12:4ff., this can be decided only from the context. The plural *diaireseis*, the opposition *to de auto pneuma* [but the same spirit], and the parallelism with the basic concept of *hē phanerōsis tou pneumatos* (v. 7) all favour 'distribution' rather than 'distinction.' The one Spirit is manifested in apportionments of gifts of the Spirit" (TDNT, 1:185).

The corresponding verb *diaireō* is used in v. 11, where "dividing" (KJV) should be "distributing." In His sovereign will—"as he will"—the Holy Spirit distributes His gifts to different individuals. It is not God's intention that everyone should have the same gift (see vv. 28–30). The failure to recognize this clearly stated truth has led to a great deal of confusion in our day. The strong emphasis of vv. 4–11 is on one Spirit distributing many gifts to many people.

5 *Administrations* Here we find the common Greek word *diaconia*, which means "service." It is translated "administration" only here and in 2 Cor. 9:12. The most frequent translation is "ministry" (15 times). It is being increasingly recognized that in the church there are many types of ministries in which different members of the church should be involved.

6 *Operations* In this verse "operations" is *energēmatōn* and "worketh" is *energōn*. Obviously these have the same basic root. Why not show in English this close connection in Greek? This is easily done: "There are different kinds of working, but the same God works all of them in all men" (NIV). It is interesting to note that the same noun is translated "working" in v. 10 (KJV). That fits best here too.

10 *Discerning* One of the gifts is labeled "discerning of spirits." The first word is *diacrisis*. It comes from the verb meaning to "judge." Buechsel says that in the NT it usually means "differentiation" (TDNT, 3:949). Thayer defines it as "a distinguishing, discerning, judging" (p. 139). Robertson and Plummer make this comment: "The gift of discerning, in various cases (hence the plural) whether extraordinary spiritual manifestations were from above or not; they might be purely natural, though strange, or they might be diabolical" (p. 267).

11 *Will* Paul declared that the Holy Spirit distributes the gifts "as he will." The Greek has *bouletai*, which is a strong verb meaning "to wish, desire, purpose" implying "the deliberate exercise of volition" (A-S, p. 84). So "just as he determines" (NIV) is a more adequate translation.

12 *Members* The Greek word here is *melos*, which means a member, or part, of the body. In classical Greek it is used regularly in the plural for the parts of the body, and this usage is reflected in the Septuagint and the papyri.

The metaphor of Christians as members of the Body of Christ is introduced very effectively by Paul in Rom. 12:4–5, with its application to differing functions in the church (vv. 6–8). In 1 Corinthians the apostle elaborates this figure, devoting 16 verses to it (12:12–27).

He declares that the body is not one member, but many (v. 14). No individual Christian should try to dominate the whole church. Paul illustrates this by the relation of the two most active parts outwardly, the hand and the foot (v. 15). Then he speaks of the ear and the eye (v. 16). There are "many members, yet but one body" (v. 20). All are needed (vv. 21–25).

Finally he makes the spiritual application: "Now you are the body of Christ, and each one of you is a part of it" (v. 27, NIV).

There are two arguments for using "part" rather than "member" as the translation. The first is that today we speak of "parts of the body" rather than "members of the body." The second is that when we use the expression "members of the body" we mean a person who is a member of a duly constituted body, such as the Congress. But the Body of Christ, the true Christian Church, is not an *organization;* it is an *organism.* It is not a social institution but a spiritual union. As Horst remarks, "Membership does not consist in belonging to a social body" (TDNT, 4:564). One of the great tragedies of history is that many people have thought that salvation comes by being a "member" of some church. We need to recapture Paul's emphasis on the nature of the church as a spiritual organism, with each true Christian functioning as a vital organ of Christ's Body. That is the main thrust of 1 Corinthians 12.

23, 24 *Uncomely, Comely* The first word is *aschēmona* (plural adjective), the second *euschēmona*. The first prefix is *alpha*-negative. The second, *eu*, means "good" or "noble."

Aschēmon (singular) occurs only here in the NT. *Schēma*, from which we get "scheme," means "figure" or "fashion." Schneider notes that it "always refers to what may be known from without" (TDNT, 1:954). *Aschēmon* is defined by Thayer as meaning "indecent, unseemly"—what is usually covered up, so that it cannot be seen.

Euschēmona is used here for "the comely parts of the body that need no covering" (Thayer, p. 263). Greeven says that the adjective literally means "of good external appearance" (TDNT, 2:771).

The application that Paul seems to be making is that the members of Christ's Body who do not receive much public honor are still necessary. Each Christian is an essential part of the Body of Christ.

28 Apostles In this verse Paul mentions 8 types of ministry in the church. The first is that of apostles.

Who were the apostles in the Early Church? Are there still apostles in the church of today? Neither of these questions is easy to answer.

The Greek noun *apostolos* comes from the verb *apostellō*, which means "send with a commission, or on service." So *apostolos* is "a messenger, one sent on a mission." Abbott-Smith continues his definition by saying: "In NT, an *apostle* of Christ (*a*) with special reference to the Twelve . . . , equality with whom is claimed by St. Paul . . . (*b*) in a wider sense of prominent Christian teachers, as Barnabas, Acts 14:14, apparently also Silvanus and Timothy, 1 Thess. 2:6, and perhaps Andronicus and Junias (Junia?), Rom. 16:7 . . . ; of false teachers, claiming apostleship" (p. 55). It is evident that the word has a variety of applications in the NT.

In his long article on *apostolos* in Kittel's *Theological Dictionary of the New Testament*, Rengstorf shows that in classical and early Hellenistic Greek there is no parallel to the NT use of this word. This is true even of the Septuagint, Josephus, and Philo (1:408).

The word is found 79 times in the NT. Paul and Luke (his close companion) each use it 34 times (68 out of the 79). It occurs 3 times in Revelation, twice in 2 Peter, and once each in Matthew, Mark, John, Hebrews, 1 Peter, and Jude. Paul has it at the beginning of 9 of his 13 Epistles.

Apostolos is used for messenger, "one sent" in John 13:16. In 2 Cor. 8:23 Paul applies this term to the commissioned representatives of local church congregations. "Finally, *apostoloi* is a comprehensive term for 'bearers of the NT message' " (TDNT, 1:422). It is used primarily for the 12 apostles chosen and commissioned by Christ. This is the dominant usage in Luke's Gospel and Acts.

Then we also find the wider spread suggested by Abbott-Smith. Paul and Barnabas were first of all apostles of the church at Antioch. But Paul calls himself, at the beginning of his epistles, "an apostle of Jesus Christ." Luke does not hesitate to speak of Paul and Barnabas as apostles (Acts 14:4, 14).

The first apostle was Jesus himself (Heb. 3:1), sent from God. Rengstorf comments: "Here the only possible meaning of *apostolos* is that in Jesus there has taken place the definitive revelation of God by God himself (1:2)" (TDNT, 1:423). All other apostles are direct representatives of Jesus.

Are there apostles today in the Church? In a general, unofficial, nontechnical sense, yes. But it may well be questioned whether apostolic authority as found in the first-century Church has carried over to subsequent centuries. Acts 1:21–22 indicates that an apostle was to be one who had been in close contact with Christ during His earthly ministry and who could be a witness of His resurrection. Paul fulfilled the latter requirement (1 Cor. 15:8), but not the former one. However, he was careful to state that he had "received" the necessary information (1 Cor. 15:3).

Charles H. Spurgeon was perhaps a bit severe when he characterized apostolic succession as laying empty hands on empty heads. But many of those who claim apostolic succession today hardly show themselves to be true representatives of the Christ of the NT.

Prophets The Greek *prophētēs* comes from the verb *prophēmi*, which means "speak forth." So it signifies "one who acts as an interpreter or forth-teller of the Divine will" (A-S, p. 390). Contrary to popular usage today, the biblical meaning of "prophecy" is not foretelling, but forth-telling. Put in simplest terms, the prophet is one who speaks for God.

In Kittel's *Theological Dictionary of the New Testament*, Friedrich has a lengthy article on *prophētēs* and its cognate terms in the New Testament. He notes some differences between OT and NT prophets. He says that "prophecy is not restricted to a few men and women in primitive Christianity. According to Acts 2:4, 4:31, all are filled with the prophetic Spirit and, according to Acts 2:16ff., it is a specific mark of the age of fulfilment that the Spirit does not only lay hold of individuals but that all members of the eschatological community without distinction are called to prophesy" (6:849).

But our present passage, as well as Eph. 4:11, shows that there was a special gift of prophecy in the Early Church. It is ranked first, as the best gift after "apostles," in our present passage as well as 14:1.

Has the gift of prophecy continued? In the second century the Montanists went to unfortunate extremes in their claims for this gift. Friedrich writes: "With the repudiation of Montanism prophecy came to an end in the

Church" (TDNT, 6:860). On the other hand, many Bible scholars believe that the NT prophets were essentially preachers, and so this gift of the Spirit is present today.

Helps   The Greek word *antilēmpsis* (only here in NT) is used in the Septuagint and papyri in the sense of "help." Abbott-Smith thinks that here it is used for the "ministrations of deacons" (p. 41). Cremer says that the word is "taken by the Greek expositors uniformly as answering to *deacons* (implying the duties towards the poor and sick)" (p. 386).

Governments   *Kybernēsis* is likewise found only here in the NT. It comes from the verb meaning to guide or steer. In classical Greek it referred to the piloting of a boat. Then it was used metaphorically for "government." Beyer writes that, in view of its literal meaning and attested usage, "The reference can only be to the specific gifts which qualify a Christian to be a helmsman to his congregation, i.e., a true director to its order and therewith of its life" (TDNT, 3:1036). The word may be translated "gifts of administration" (NIV).

13:1 *Tongues of Men*   The form *lalō*, "I speak," can be either indicative or subjunctive. But the *ean* at the beginning of the sentence shows that it is subjunctive. Charles B. Williams, in his translation *The New Testament* (1937), always makes a careful distinction between the Greek moods and tenses. He renders this: "If I could speak." F. F. Bruce, in his *The Letters of Paul: An Expanded Paraphrase* (1965), has: "I may speak."

The Corinthians prided themselves on their elegance and eloquence in public speaking. Paul, the Jew, was not their ideal. His opponents in the church at Corinth sneered: "His bodily presence is weak, and his speech contemptible" (2 Cor. 10:10). So Paul says, "If I could speak with the tongues of men."

Tongues of Angels   He did not stop with "men," but added: "even of angels." (The Greek *kai* can be translated by either "and" or "even.") It was a remote possibility—"but if."

Chapters 12, 13, and 14—all three—deal with the problem of speaking in tongues at Corinth. The abuse of this gift was causing confusion and division in the church. The Corinthian Christians were far more concerned about the gifts of the Spirit than the Giver of those gifts. They were forgetting the great Gift, the Holy Spirit (Acts 2:38). And so they were divided.

The place that chapter 13 occupies is clearly indicated by the last verse of chapter 12 and the first verse of 14. In 12:31 he says: "But covet earnestly the best gifts"—not tongues which is at the bottom of the list (vv. 28–30), but prophecy (cf. 14:1)—"and yet shew I unto you a more excellent way"—the way of love (c. 13). Then in 14:1, after describing love, he commands: "Follow the way of love" (NIV).

But the reference to speaking in the tongues of angels shows the connection also. Evidently some of those who spoke in tongues at Corinth claimed to be speaking the language of angels. A few years ago the official organ of a certain denomination made this claim for those who now speak in tongues. Such an attitude fosters spiritual pride—the worst pride of all—and causes schisms in the Church of Jesus Christ today, as it did in ancient Corinth.

Charity   Paul declared that even if he could speak in the tongues of men or angels, it would all be hollow and meaningless if he did not have "love." The word is *agapē*, the highest word for "love" in the NT.

The verb *agapaō* occurs 142 times in the NT. In the KJV it is translated "love" 135 times ("beloved" 7 times). The noun *agapē* is found 116 times. It is translated "love" 86 times and "charity" 27 times.

One of the most pronounced blunders of KJV translators was the use of "charity" for "love." Nearly 100 years ago Lias wrote: "The AV has unfortunately departed here from the earlier rendering *love* of Tyndale and Cranmer (which the Revised Version has restored) and has followed the Vulgate *caritas*. Thus the force of this eloquent panegyric on love is impaired, and the agreement between the various writers of the New Testament much obscured. . . . The English word *charity* has never risen to the height of the Apostle's argument. At best it does but signify a kindly interest in and forbearance towards others. It is far from suggesting the ardent, active, energetic principle which the Apostle had in view" (p. 146).

The KJV (1611) was largely a revision of the Bishop's Bible (1568) and since the bishops of the Church of England at that time were barely out of the Roman Catholic church, their love for the Latin Vulgate was still strong. So they used "charity," and 43 years later it was retained in the KJV.

The Greeks had three verbs for *love: eran, philein,* and *agapan* (to cite the infinitive forms). Stauffer writes: "*eran* is passionate love which desires the other for itself" (TDNT, 1:35). From the Greek noun *eros* we get *erotic,* with all its sensual connotations. That is why *eros* and *eran* are not found in the NT.

The second verb, *philein* (*phileō*) occurs 25 times. It is translated "love" 22 times and "kiss" 3 times. This shows that it refers to the love of the affections. The noun *philia* is found only once (James 4:4) and is translated "friendship." So *philia* is affectionate friendship.

We have already noted how frequently *agapē* and *agapaō* occur in the NT. Of the relationship between this concept and that of *eros*, Stauffer says: "*Eros* is a general love of the world seeking satisfaction wherever it can. *Agapan* is a love which makes distinctions, choosing and keeping to its object.... *Agapan* relates for the most part to the love of God, to the love of the higher lifting up the lower, elevating the lower above others. *Eros* seeks in others the fulfilment of its own life's hunger. *Agapan* must often be translated 'to show love'; it is a giving, active love on the other's behalf" (TDNT, 1:37). He adds: "It is indeed striking that the substantive *agapē* is almost completely lacking in pre-biblical Greek" (*ibid.*). The Greek *agapaō* occurs about 275 times in the Septuagint, most often in the Psalms. *Agapē* is found only 20 times. In the NT it is the dominant word for "love." God is *agapē* (1 John 4:8, 16). His love for the world of sinners is expressed by the verb *agapaō* (John 3:16). We are commanded to love (*agapan*) God with all our being (Matt. 22:37) and to love our neighbor as ourselves (Matt. 22:39). Christian love is *agapē* love.

Tinkling *Alalazon* is a participle of the verb *alalazō* (only here in NT). It comes from a battle cry of that day, "*Alala!*" So it literally means "raise a war cry." Obviously "tinkling" is too tame a translation. Robertson and Plummer write, "*Alalazon* imitates loud and prolonged noise" (p. 289). They go on to say:

> Cymbals are often mentioned in the OT, but nowhere else in the NT: and in St Paul's day they were much used in the worship of Dionysus, Cybele, and the Corybantes. Seeing that he insists so strongly on the unedifying character of the Tongues (XIV), as being of no service to the congregation without a special interpreter, it is quite possible that he is here comparing unintelligible tongues in Christian worship with the din of gongs and cymbals in pagan worship. Or he may be pointing out the worthlessness of extravagant manifestations of emotion, which proceed not from the heart, but from hollowness. Cymbals were hollow, to increase the noise. Or he may be saying that tongues without Christian love are as senseless

as the unmusical and distracting noise of a soulless instrument (*ibid.*).

3 Feed the Poor "Bestow ... to feed the poor" is all one word in Greek, *psōmisō* (only here and Rom. 12:20). The verb comes from the noun *psōmos*, "a morsel." So it means "*to feed with morsels* (as children, or the sick), hence, generally in late writers, *to feed, nourish*" (A-S, p. 489). Lias suggests: "If I feed people one by one with all my goods" (CGT, in *loco*). C. B. Williams translates it: "If I should dole out everything I have for charity."

Burned C. B. Williams reads: "And give my body up to torture in mere boasting pride." Goodspeed has: "And give myself up, but do it in pride." What is the basis for this?

The answer is that the three oldest manuscripts of 1 Corinthians—Papyrus 46 (3rd century), Vaticanus and Sinaiticus (4th century)—have *kauchēsōmai* (to boast) rather than *kauthēsōmai* (to burn). (In the Greek the difference is only one letter.) But many feel there is stronger internal evidence for *kauthēsōmai* and so most versions have "burned."

4 Suffereth Long, Kind Having shown the absolute necessity of love (vv. 1–3), the apostle now goes on to describe the characteristics of love (vv. 4–7). He first says that it "suffereth long, and is kind" (KJV). In the Greek this is: *makrothymei, chrēsteuetai*. The first verb is from the adjective *makrothymos*, "long-tempered," and so means "is patient or long-suffering." The second (only here in the NT) means to be kind. The first is passive—not retaliating. The second is active—bestowing benefits. The best translation is: "Love is patient, love is kind." The twofold statement stands as a daily challenge to every Christian.

Vaunteth Not Itself The verb *perpereuomai* is found only here in the NT—or LXX. Robertson and Plummer translate: "Does not play the braggart." They add: "Ostentation is the chief idea." Today we would say, "it does not boast" (NIV).

5 Unseemly "Behave itself unseemly" is *aschēmonei* (only here and 7:36, where it is translated "behaveth himself uncomely"). It means "act unbecomingly, behave dishonourably" (A-S). F. F. Bruce reads: "Never acts dishonourably." G. G. Findlay writes: "Love imparts a delicacy of feeling beyond the rules of politeness" (EGT, 2:899).

Not Easily Provoked   There is no basis in the Greek for the modifier "easily." It has been suggested that it was added because King James had such a violent temper! The verb is *paroxynetai* (only here and Acts 17:16).

Robertson and Plummer comment: "Not merely 'does not fly into a rage' but 'does not yield to provocation'; it is not embittered by injuries, whether real or supposed" (ICC, *in loco*).

Thinketh No Evil   The verb is *logizomai*, which literally means "count" or "reckon." Then it has the metaphorical sense of "take into account." Thayer notes that it is "a favorite word with the Apostle Paul, being used (exclusive of quotations) some 27 times in his epistles, and only 4 times in the rest of the NT" (p. 379). For this passage he suggests the translation "to pass to one's account, to impute." So the Greek literally says, "does not impute the evil"; that is, "it keeps no records of wrong" (NIV).

7 Beareth   The verb *stegō* is related to the noun *stegē*, which means "a roof." Its literal meaning is "to cover closely, to protect by covering" (A-S). In 1 Thess. 3:1, 5, and 1 Cor. 9:12 (its only other NT occurrences), it seems to mean "endure." But Kasch says, "The most difficult passage is 1 Cor. 13:7" (TDNT, 7:586). He favors the translation "covers all things" (*ibid.*, p. 587). Another rendering is "it always protects" (NIV).

8 Fail . . . Vanish Away   After pointing out the Primacy of Love (vv. 1–3) and the Perfection of Love (vv. 4–7), Paul now asserts the Permanence of Love (vv. 8–13). He declares that love never "fails." The Greek is *piptei*, which literally means "falls." But here, as in some other places, it carries the idea of falling into ruin.

This verse affords an illustration of a frequent translator's fault—translating two different Greek words by the same English word, and translating the same Greek word by two English words. "Faileth," as we have just noted, is the verb *piptō*. But "fail" is *katargeō*, which at the end of the verse is rendered "vanish away." The verb *katargeō* means "put out of action." Prophecies will disappear when the reality comes.

Tongues   In view of the discussion of the gift of tongues in chapters 12 and 14, the most natural way to take *glossai* would be as meaning speaking in tongues, which will finally cease. But the word also means "languages." So the reference could be to the fact that the various

languages which began at Babel will come to an end in the beautiful unity of eternity. There will be no language barrier in heaven.

11 Childish Things   The Greek could equally well be translated "things" or "ways." But the latter is much more meaningful. Many "adults" (chronologically, not psychologically) have put away their *things* of childhood—dolls and toys—but they have never given up their childish *ways* of reacting to life. They still throw a fit when they can't have their own way.

12 Glass   The Greek word *esoptron* is found (in NT) only here and in Jas. 1:23. It simply means "mirror." Findlay writes: "Ancient mirrors made of burnished metal—a specialty of Corinth—were poor reflectors; the art of silvering glass was discovered in the 13th century" (EGT, 2:901). So "mirror" is the better translation.

Darkly   This is two words in Greek, *en ainigmati*, "in an enigma, or riddle" (only here in NT). The Greek says: "For we see at present by means of a mirror in a riddle." When we can see only enigmatically we should be careful how we speak dogmatically!

14:1 *Follow After Charity*   The Greek literally says, "Keep on pursuing love." A good paraphrase would be: "Make love your lifelong pursuit." The verb *diōkō* means "zealously to follow" (Oepke, "*diōkō*," TDNT, 2:230).

This may suggest that love is a rather elusive thing. And this is true. We do not find love by wishful thinking or by halfhearted effort. We have to pursue it eagerly every day, if we are going to find it operating in our lives as it should. We must ask the Holy Spirit, who makes us perfect in love, to help us express that love to others constantly in a Christlike way. When one makes love his lifelong pursuit, he discovers that his capacity for loving those around him grows with the years.

2 Unknown   We hear a great deal these days about speaking in unknown tongues. The supposed scriptural support for this is the fact that five times in this chapter (vv. 2, 4, 14, 19, 27) Paul talks about speaking "in an unknown tongue."

However, the word "unknown" is in italics in every case, indicating thereby that it is not in the Greek. So we have no right to quote it as support for argument. The Greek simply says, "in a tongue." This could mean a foreign language, as it clearly does in Acts 2:4–11. "No man understandeth him" would then mean that no one present understood this particular foreign language.

3 *Edification* The Greek word is *oikodomē*. It comes from *oikos*, "house," and *demō*, "build." So it literally means "the act of building." In the NT it is used only in the metaphorical sense of "building up."

Does the word "edification" suggest to us the idea of "building up," as one would build a house? Perhaps not. Arndt and Gingrich (p. 561) say that *oikodomē* has the figurative sense of "spiritual strengthening" (cf. NIV). Michel writes: "In the N.T. *oikodomē* is a familiar figure of speech which is primarily used for the community" (TDNT, 5:145). This is clearly its context in verse 5, and probably throughout this chapter (vv. 3, 5, 12, 26). Paul had already said in 3:9, "Ye are God's building" (*oikodomē*). So here he is pleading for the building up of the Corinthian congregation as a "temple of God" (3:16), where God can dwell and manifest himself. And here in verse 4 he declares that it is prophesying—that is, preaching the Word of God—which builds up the church, not speaking in tongues.

That is the main test of tongues in this chapter. In public worship we should have only what "builds up" the church.

Exhortation The Greek word is *paraclēsis*. In the New Testament (KJV) this noun is translated "consolation" 14 times, "exhortation" 8 times, and "comfort" 6 times—plus "entreaty" once. Since the last word in this verse (*paramythia*, only here in NT) clearly means "comfort," some other translation is used for *paraclēsis*.

The meaning of this word oscillates between "exhortation" and "comfort." It would seem that "encouragement" (NIV) best spans the gap between these two senses, which are rather different in English.

This is a good example of the frequently illustrated fact that no two words in different languages have exactly the same meaning. Dr. Nida of the American Bible Society says, "Words in different languages do not have formal equivalence; they have only dynamic equivalence." Anyone who works at the job of translating soon discovers how true this is.

7 *Pipe* The word *aulos* (only here in NT) comes from *aō*, a verb meaning "to blow." So it refers to a "wind instrument," probably a flute. It is joined here with *kithara*, "harp." The two

terms together, then, could be thought of as representing all the wind and stringed instruments of music.

9 *Easy to Be Understood* This is one word in Greek, the adjective *eusēmon* (only here in NT). It literally means "good sign" (*eu*, "good," plus *sēma*, "sign"). So it indicates here a word that signifies something. It may be translated "intelligible" (NIV). G. Abbott-Smith says that it means "clear to the understanding, distinct" (p. 189). Arndt and Gingrich translate the whole phrase "utter intelligible speech" (p. 326).

10 *Without Signification* The Greek word is *aphōnon*. It is composed of *alpha*-negative and *phōnē*, "sound." So it literally means "soundless" or "voiceless." But here it carries the connotation of "unintelligible" (A-S, p. 72).

11 *Barbarian* The Greek word (twice here) is *barbaros*. Windisch says, "The basic meaning of this word . . . is 'stammering,' 'stuttering,' 'uttering unintelligible sounds.'" Then we have "the transition to the most important usage, i.e., 'of a strange speech,' or 'the one who speaks a strange language' (i.e., other than Greek)" (TDNT, 1:546).

It is in the first sense that the word is used here. The one who utters "unintelligible sounds" in a church service does not help anybody. Paul says, "Try to excel in gifts that build up the church" (v. 12, NIV).

14–15 *Understanding* The term *understanding* is found three times in these two verses. The Greek word is *nous*, "mind." Paul says that he will pray and sing not only with his spirit but also with his mind. God made us intelligent creatures, and He expects us to use that intelligence, not scuttle it. True worship involves the intellect, the emotions, and the will. It is the whole person worshiping God.

16, 23, 24 *Unlearned* The Greek word in all three of these verses is *idiōtēs*. Aside from here, it is found (in NT) only in Acts 4:13 ("ignorant") and 2 Cor. 11:6 ("rude").

The term comes from the adjective *idios*, which means "one's own," or "private." So it first meant a private individual as distinct from a public person or official. Schlier shows that in Greek usage it finally signified "the 'outsider' or 'alien' as distinct from a member" (TDNT, 3:216). He also notes that there is no fixed translation for this word; it takes its exact sense from the context.

What does it mean here in 1 Corinthians 14? Schlier says that it is "the one who does not have the gift of tongues or the interpretation of tongues. He is expressly described as one who 'does not know what thou sayest,' and who consequently cannot say Amen to the charismatic thanksgiving of the man who speaks with tongues" (TDNT, 3:217).

In vv. 23 and 24 the *idiōtēs* is linked with "unbeliever." On this basis Schlier writes: "The *idiōtai* are those who do not belong to the community though they join in its gatherings. They are first characterized as such by the fact that they do not understand speaking with tongues, and then by the fact that they are not members (v. 24)" (*ibid.*).

20 *Understanding* This is not the same word that is translated "understanding" in vv. 14–15 (see above). Rather, it is *phrēn* (only here in NT), which Thayer defines as "the faculty of perceiving and judging" (p. 648).

The literal meaning of the word was the physical diaphram which controls the breath. Bertram notes that the term "was early regarded as the seat of the intellectual and spiritual activity" (TDNT, 9:220). With regard to its use here, he says: "To give preference to speaking with tongues as an immediate utterance of the Spirit is childish, 1 Cor. 14:20. The Corinthians should use their reason, which includes emotion and will, and achieve perfection therein" (TDNT, 9:230). Probably the best translation is "thinking" (NASB, RSV, NIV).

Malice Today "malice" means "the desire to harm others, or to see others suffer" (*American Heritage Dictionary*, p. 790). But here the Greek word is simply *kakia*, which means "evil" (so in most modern versions).

Be Ye Children This is one word in Greek, *nēpiazete* (only here in NT). It comes from *nēpios*, "infant," and so means literally "be an infant." Paul is urging the Corinthian Christians to stop being (pres. tense) childish in their thinking, but at the same time to be always (pres. tense) childlike in regard to evil: that is, be innocent.

Men The word translated "men" (KJV) is the adjective *teleios*, "complete," "perfect," or "mature." A good rendering of this verse is: "Brothers, stop thinking like children. In regard to evil be infants, but in your thinking be adults" (NIV).

26 *Doctrine* The Greek word *didachē* occurs 30 times in the NT. In the KJV it is rendered "has been taught" once, and "doctrine" all the other times. But the noun comes from the verb *didaskō*, which is always correctly translated "teach" (97 times). So the noun should be "teaching." "Doctrine" is too theological a term.

29 *Judge* Paul says that only two or three prophets should speak in a service, and let the listeners "judge." The verb is *diakrinō*. Properly it means "distinguish, discriminate, discern," but Abbott-Smith goes on to suggest that here it means "settle, decide, judge" (p. 108). Arndt and Gingrich (p. 184) give for this place: "Pass judgment" (NASB). But "weigh" (RSV) or "weigh carefully" (NIV) seems to fit well. However, Buechsel suggests the meaning "assess," and comments: "The reference is not so much to what the prophets say as to the spirits of the prophets, 12:10" (TDNT, 3:947).

40 *Decently* Besides this place, the adverb *euschēmonōs* is found (in NT) only in Rom. 13:13 and 1 Thess. 4:12. In both places it is translated "honestly"—"walk honestly" (KJV). Arndt and Gingrich suggest for our passage "properly" (cf. NASB). The NIV translates this verse: "But everything should be done in a fitting and orderly way." This is the way we should conduct our church services.

15:2 *Keep in Memory* The Greek has one word, *katechete*. The verb *katechō* means "hold fast" (NASB) or "hold firmly" (NIV). Paul clearly asserts here that our finally being saved depends on our holding firmly to the Word of the gospel.

4 *Rose* The verb is *egeirō*. Arndt and Gingrich say that it means "figuratively *raise, help to rise,*" as of a fallen or sick or dead person, and specifically "of the raising of Jesus" (p. 213).

Here and in v. 12 the form is the perfect passive, *egēgertai*, which literally means "has been raised" (see v. 12, NASB, NIV). The English Revised Version (1881) reads "hath been raised." Vincent approves this and notes: "*Died* and *was buried* are in the aorist tense. The change to the perfect marks the abiding state which began with the resurrection. He hath been raised and still lives" (3:273). The perfect tense in Greek indicates completed action and a continuing state with primary emphasis on the continuation.

Paul's theology stresses the fact that God

raised Christ from the dead (6:14; 15:15; 2 Cor. 4:14). That is the reason for the translation "was raised" in the NASB and NIV.

5–8 *Was Seen* Four times in these four verses we have the expression "he was seen" (KJV). This is the literal translation of *ōphthe* (aorist passive of *horaō*, "see"). The aorist tense suggests a single event in each case—the risen Christ was seen by different ones at different times.

This word may also be translated "appeared" (NASB, NIV). And so we find in 1 Corinthians (A.D. 55) the earliest list of the post-resurrection appearances of Jesus. (The four Gospels were written later.)

Paul begins with Christ's appearance to Peter (v. 5), although we know from the Gospels that He appeared first to the women who came early on Easter Sunday morning (John 20:11–18; Matt. 28:9). But Peter was the first prominent leader in the Early Church. It was he who assumed charge of the 120 in the Upper Room (Acts 1:15) and who delivered the sermon on the Day of Pentecost (Acts 2:14) that resulted in 3,000 being saved (Acts 2:41). The Lord used him in the healing of the cripple at the Beautiful Gate of the Temple (Acts 3:4–7) and in preaching the subsequent sermon (Acts 3:12–26). The same Peter who had denied his Lord, now filled with the Holy Spirit, stood boldly before the Sanhedrin and accused the Jewish leaders of murdering their Messiah (Acts 4:8–12).

The last appearance was to Paul ("me also," v. 8). The significant thing is that Paul uses the same verb that he used for the previous appearances. He thereby claims that he actually saw Jesus in visible form. It was no hallucination. That is why Paul emphasizes the Resurrection so strongly in his Epistles.

5 *Cephas* This is a Greek transliteration of the Aramaic word for "stone." See discussion at John 1:42; Matt. 16:18.

8 *One Born out of Due Time* In the Greek this is simply the definite article with the noun *ektrōma* (only here in the NT). It may be translated "one untimely born" (NASB) or "one abnormally born" (NIV).

Arndt and Gingrich define *ektrōma* as meaning "untimely birth, miscarriage." They go on to say: "So Paul calls himself, perhaps taking up an insult hurled at him by his opponents" (p. 246).

Wyclif translated the word as "a dead-born child." Marvin Vincent writes: "Paul means

that when Christ appeared to him and called him, he was—as compared to the disciples who had known and followed Him from the first, and whom he had been persecuting—no better than an unperfected foetus among living men. The comparison emphasizes his condition at the time of his call" (3:274).

9 *Meet* More than 800 words in the KJV have changed their meaning in the last 350 years. "Meet" is one of them. The Greek adjective is *hikanos*, one of whose meanings is "fit, appropriate, competent, qualified . . . worthy" (AG, p. 375). The simplest translation is "fit." In the light of his previous persecution of the "church of God," Paul felt that he was not fit to be called an apostle. However, he adds the significant assertion: "But by the grace of God I am what I am" (v. 10).

10 *Labored More Abundantly* This translation is accurate, but hardly contemporary. The verb is *kopiaō*, which means "work hard, toil" (AG, p. 444). "More abundantly" is the word *perissoteron*, which Arndt and Gingrich translate as "even more." Today we would say, "I worked harder" (Phillips, NIV).

12–17 *Rose* The verb *egeirō* occurs 9 times in these 6 consecutive verses. In the NT it is found 141 times. Of these, 73, or slightly more than half, refer to the resurrection of the dead. Of these 73, again, some 48, or about two-thirds, refer to the resurrection of Jesus. There are other references in the NT to the resurrection of Jesus, but about 50 places use this word.

The verb occurs many times in each of the four Gospels. But there are less references to the resurrection from the dead and comparatively few to the resurrection of Jesus. That is easily understood, because most of the material of the Gospels relates to Jesus' ministry before His death and resurrection.

When we come to Acts, the picture changes abruptly. Seven of the 14 occurrences of this word refer to resurrection, and all but one to the resurrection of Jesus. In Romans we find the word 10 times, 9 of which refer to the resurrection of Jesus.

But it is in the great Resurrection Chapter (1 Corinthians 15) that we find it most frequently (19 times). In every instance it refers to resurrection from the dead, 9 times to the resurrection of Jesus.

We have already noted (on v. 4) that the best translation here is not "rose," but "has been raised" (NASB, NIV). God raised Christ from the dead (v. 15): that is Pauline theology.

12 *Resurrection* After the introductory section on the resurrection of Christ (vv. 1–11), Paul deals in this chapter with two basic matters: (1) The fact of the resurrection (vv. 12–34), and (2) The nature of the resurrection (vv. 35–58). These are the two main divisions of this chapter. The first topic is introduced with the question: "How say some among you that there is no resurrection of the dead?" (v. 12). The second is triggered by the twofold question: "How are the dead raised? With what kind of body will they come?" (v. 35, NIV).

The word for "resurrection" here is *anastasis*, which occurs 38 times in the NT. Nine of these times it refers to the resurrection of Jesus. Literally it means "a standing up." Over half of its occurrences are in the Gospels (16 times) and Acts (11 times).

In the Greek inscriptions around the time of Christ *anastasis* is used for the "erection" of a monument or the "setting up" of a statue. But the idea of a resurrection from the dead was foreign to Greek thinking, as Paul's experience at Athens shows. Oepke says that for the Greeks "Resurrection is impossible" (TDNT, 1:369).

The noun *anastasis* comes from the verb *anistēmi*, which means "raise up." It is used some 23 times for the resurrection of Jesus. The noun *egersis* (from the verb *egeiro*) is found only once in the NT (Matt. 27:53). The same is true of *exanastasis*, literally "a standing up out of," found only in Phil. 3:11. Putting all these words together, we find that there are over 80 definite references in the NT to the resurrection of Jesus. It is a striking fact that the word "resurrection" does not occur in the OT.

How may we be certain that we shall share in the "resurrection of life" (John 5:29)? The answer is plain. If we have experienced an inner, spiritual resurrection, we have abundant assurance of our final resurrection.

15 *Of* Paul says, "We have testified of God that he raised up Christ" (KJV). The NASB reads "against God" and the NIV "about God." Which is right?

The Greek preposition is *kata*, the root meaning of which is "down." It sometimes does have the meaning "down upon" and so "against." Arndt and Gingrich devote 6 columns to defining this small word. They give as one meaning "with respect to" (p. 408). In their volume in the ICC series, Robertson and Plummer say: "The meaning 'respecting' or 'about' is fairly common in classical Greek, although not in the NT, and is perhaps to be preferred here" (pp. 348–49). We agree.

19 *Miserable* The word is *eleeinoteroi*, the comparative of the adjective *eleeinos* (only here and in Rev. 3:17). The comparative in Greek often signifies the superlative. It comes from the noun *eleos*, "mercy" or "pity," and the verb *eleeō*, "have pity or mercy on." So it means "most pitiable" or "most to be pitied" (NASB, NIV).

33 *Communications* The noun *homilia* (only here in NT) means "company, association" (A-S, p. 316). Later on it came to be used for a sermon given in a church, and so we have "homily" and "homiletics." But here Arndt and Gingrich (p. 568) say that the adjective and noun mean "bad company" (NASB, NIV).

Manners The Greek word *ethos* (only here in NT) is used in the sense of "custom" or "manner." But Robertson and Plummer translate this old Greek proverb: "Evil companionships mar good morals" or "Bad company spoils noble characters" (p. 363). The NASB has "morals," the NIV "character."

36 *Fool* Four different Greek words in the NT are translated "fool" in the KJV. *Anoētos* (6 times) and *asophos* (only in Eph. 5:15) are mild terms. The first means "thoughtless," the second "unwise." A third word, *mōros* (accusative, *mōron*) sometimes has moral connotations. It occurs 13 times in the NT.

But the word here is *aphrōn* (11 times in the NT). It literally means "mindless" or "senseless." Arndt and Gingrich define it as "foolish, ignorant" (p. 127). Bertram writes: "In 1 Cor. 15:36, Paul is not pronouncing a definitive judgement with his *aphrōn*. It is a rhetorical appeal for true understanding. To cling to the negative view is to adopt the position of the *aphrōn* which is close to that of ungodliness" (TDNT, 9:231).

In view of all this, "Thou fool" (KJV) or "You fool!" (NASB) seems a bit too harsh. A better rendering would seem to be "you foolish man!" (RSV) or "How foolish!" (NIV).

Quickened The verb is *zōopoieō*, from *poieō*, "make," and *zōos* "alive." So it means "come to life" (RSV, NASB, NIV). Of the 12 times this verb occurs in the NT, it is translated "quicken" 9 times (see v. 45). But that is obsolete terminology.

42, 50 *Corruption* The Greek word *phthora* does mean "corruption" or "destruction." But Arndt and Gingrich note that in the world of nature (including the human body, as here), it signifies "perishable." Here it means the "state of being perishable" and in verse 50 "that which is perishable" (p. 865). Today the word "perishable" (RSV, NASB, NIV) conveys the sense better than "corruption."

44 Natural This verse is the crucial one in answering the second question of verse 35: "With what kind of body will they come?" (NIV). Here Paul says: "It is sown a natural body; it is raised a spiritual body."

What is meant by "natural"? The Greek word is *psychicos*, "psychical."

Abbott-Smith says that *psychicos* means "of the psyche (as the lower part of the immaterial in man), EV, *natural*" (p. 489). Arndt and Gingrich write: "*pertaining to the soul* or *life*, in our literature always denoting the life of the natural world and whatever belongs to it, in contrast to the supernatural world, which is characterized by *pneuma*" (p. 902). They translate here "a physical body" (cf. RSV). They also suggest "physical" in verse 46.

Schweizer writes: "The psychical is neither sinful as such nor does it incline to the *pneuma*. But it is corruptible and finds no access into God's kingdom, v. 50" (TDNT, 9:662).

Commenting on verses 42–44, Robertson and Plummer say (p. 372):

> Hitherto the answer to the second question (of v. 35) has been indirect: it now becomes direct. The risen body is incorruptible, glorious, powerful, spiritual. It is quite obvious that the corpse which is "sown" is none of these things. It is in corruption before it reaches the grave. . . . It is absolutely powerless, unable to move a limb. The last epithet, *psychicon*, is less appropriate to a corpse, but it comes in naturally enough to distinguish the body which is being dissolved from the body which will be raised. The former was by nature subject to the laws and conditions of physical life (*psyche*), the latter will be controlled only by the spirit (*pneuma*), and this spirit will be in harmony with the spirit of God. In the material body the spirit has been limited and hampered in its action; in the future body it will have perfect freedom of action and consequently complete control, and man will at last be, what God created him to be, a being in which the higher self is supreme.

F. Godet, in his two-volume *Commentary on the First Epistle of St. Paul to the Corinthians*, has the best discussion of verse 44 that we have found. He translates the first half of the verse, "It is sown a psychical body, it is raised a spiritual body," and then comments (2:413):

The terms *animated* or *animal-body* are the only ones in our language by which we can render the term reproduced in our translation by the Anglicized Greek term. The meaning of the epithet is clear; it denotes a body, not of the same substance as the soul itself—otherwise it would not be a body—but formed by and for a soul destined to serve as an organ to that breath of life called *psyche*, which presided over its development. Neither, consequently, is the *spiritual* body a body of a spiritual nature—it would still be less than a body in that case—but a body formed by and for a principle of life, which is a spirit, and fully appropriated to its service.

Then comes a very beautiful description of the change that will take place in the resurrection (2:413–14):

> The law of the beings belonging to nature is to revolve uniformly in the same circle; the privilege of spiritual being is to surmount this iron circle and to rise from the natural phase, which for it is only the means, to a higher sphere which is its end. This contrast arises from the wholly different mode of being possessed by the soul and the spirit. The soul is only a breath of life endowed with a certain measure of power, capable of taking hold of a material substance, subjecting it to itself, converting it into its agent, and using this organ for a fixed time up to the moment when it will no longer lend itself to such use. The characteristic of the spirit is that it possesses a life which is constantly being renewed. . . . In a new order of things, after extracting from the body an organ adapted to its nature, it will perpetually renew its strength and glory. Such a body will never be to the principle of its life what the earthly body so often is to the inhabiting soul, a burden and a hindrance: it will be the docile instrument of the spirit, fulfilling its wishes and thoughts with inexhaustible power of action, as we even now see the artist using his hand or his voice with marvelous freedom, and thus foreshadowing the perfect spiritualization of the body. If any one should deny the capacity of matter thus to yield to the action of the spirit, I should ask him to tell me what matter is: then, by way of showing what spiritualized matter may be, I should invite him to consider the human eye, that living mirror in which all the emotions of the soul are expressed in a way so living and powerful. These are simple foreshadowings of the glory of a resurrection body.

53–54 Immortality The Greek word is *athanasia* (only here and in 1 Tim. 6:16, where it is applied to God). It comes from *alpha*-negative and *thanatos*, "death." So it literally means "deathlessness." Bultmann writes: "The OT has no equivalent for *athanasia*," and adds: "In 1 Cor. 15:53 ff. the incorruptible mode of existence of the resurrected is called *athanasia* as in Hellenistic Judaism, the thought being not merely that of eternal duration but of a mode of existence different from that of *sarx* (flesh) and *haima* (blood)" (TDNT, 3:24).

16:1–2 *Collection*

The first thing we note is that "collection" (v. 1) and "gathering" (v. 2) is the same word in the Greek and obviously should be translated the same way in both places.

The Greek word is *logeia* (only here in NT). Deissmann says: "It comes from *logeuō*, 'I collect,' a verb which, like the derivate, was found for the first time comparatively recently in papyri, ostraca, and inscriptions from Egypt and elsewhere. We find it used chiefly of religious collections for a god, a temple, etc., just as St. Paul uses it of his collection of money for the 'saints' at Jerusalem" (LAE, p. 105).

In verse 2 we have a hint of Christian tithing. On the first day of the week each one was to "set aside a sum of money in keeping with his income" (NIV).

3 *Liberality*

In only one other place in the KJV is the word "liberality" found (2 Cor. 8:2). There the Greek is *haplotēs*, which literally means "simplicity" or "sincerity."

But here it is a very different Greek word, *charis*. Occurring 156 times in the NT, it is translated "grace" 130 times. Here most recent versions have "gift," which is obviously the meaning in this context. But since there are other Greek words that mean "gift" in the sense of something given, the most adequate translation here would be "gracious gift."

These three verses suggest three principles governing our giving. First, it is to be *systematic*—"upon the first day of the week" (v. 2). Second, it is to be *proportionate*—as one is prospered (v. 2). Third, it is to be *voluntary*—a gracious gift, given freely (v. 3). God does not want what is given grudgingly, but what is given gladly. Paul did not want to put on the pressure when he arrived.

11 *Conduct*

"Conduct him forth" suggests something formal and public. The verb *propempō* has this meaning in Acts 20:38 and 21:5. But for this passage Arndt and Gingrich give: "*help on one's journey* with food, money, by arranging for companions, means of travel, etc., *send on one's way*" (p. 716). "Send him on his way" (NASB, NIV) is the simplest translation.

13 *Quit You Like Men*

This is all one word in Greek, *andrizesthe* (only here in NT). Arndt and Gingrich define this verb as "conduct oneself in a manly or courageous way" (p. 63). Abbott-Smith has simply "play the man" (p. 35). This verb occurs in the Septuagint three times (2 Sam. 10:12; Ps. 27:14; 31:25) in combination with "be strong" (*krataiousthe*), as here. Robertson and Plummer render the two, "Be not only manly but mighty" (p. 394).

14 *Charity*

The correct translation is: "Do everything in love" (NIV). That is a most significant command for all of us!

15 *Addicted*

In these days of addiction to drugs, alcohol, and tobacco, it is refreshing to read of a family that "addicted themselves to the ministry of the saints." These first converts of Paul in Achaia (specifically Corinth) were now ministering to others.

The verb is *etaxan*, "arranged, ordered, appointed." Robertson and Plummer comment: "They had spontaneously taken this service upon themselves. Just as the brethren appointed (*etaxan*) that Paul and Barnabas and others should go to Jerusalem about the question of circumcision (Acts 15:2), so Stephanas and his household appointed themselves (*etaxan heautous*) to the service of their fellow-Christians. It was a self-imposed duty" (p. 395).

Such spontaneous consecration to a ministry to others is an expression of true love. Probably the best translation today is "devoted themselves" (NASB, NIV).

22 *Anathema*

In most other places in the NT this word is translated "accursed" (see comments on Rom. 9:3 and Gal. 1:8). But here it is transliterated from the Greek. The one who does not love the Lord Jesus Christ is under a divine curse. (Paul is addressing professing Christians.) Behm says that the word means "something delivered up to divine wrath, dedicated to destruction and brought under a curse" (TDNT, 1:354).

Maran-atha

In the KJV there is no punctuation between Anathema and Maran-atha, though it seems there should be a period. A. T. Robertson says, "It was a curious blunder in the King James Version that connected *Maranatha* with *Anathema*" (WP, 4:204)—a blessing or prayer, and a curse.

Also, the Bible Society Greek Text has "Maranatha" undivided. According to Edgar J. Goodspeed, the first edition of the KJV (1611) also read, "Let him be Anathema Maranatha," with no separation in the last word (*Problems of NT Translation*, p. 166).

Arndt and Gingrich say that *Maran-atha* means "(our) Lord has come." But they immediately add "better separated *marana-tha* . . . (our) *Lord, come!* an Aramaic formula which, according to *Didache* 10:6, was used in the early Christian liturgy of the Lord's Supper" (p. 492).

The *Didache* comes from the second century. The passage cited is a part of the Thanksgiving that was to be repeated aloud at the close of the Communion service. The people were to say: "Hosannah to the God of David. If any man be holy, let him come! If man be not, let him repent: Maranatha, Amen" (*The Apostolic Fathers* [Loeb Classical Library], 1:325). A footnote in this Loeb edition reads: "A transliteration of Aramaic words meaning 'Our Lord! Come!' "

This Didache passage reminds us of the closing promise and prayer of the NT (Rev. 22:20): " 'Yes, I am coming quickly.' Amen. Come, Lord Jesus" (NASB).

Robertson and Plummer call attention to a slight problem. They write: "Why St. Paul gives this warning in Aramaic rather than Greek writing to Corinth is unknown. The most probable conjecture is that in this language it had become a sort of motto or password among Christians, and familiar in that shape, like 'Alleluia' with ourselves" (p. 401). The Didache seems to give some support to this view.

It is our privilege and responsibility to live in constant expectation of our Lord's return. This attitude is one of the strongest safeguards against carelessness in conduct, and it also is a powerful incentive to devoted service for our Master.

2 Corinthians

1:3–7 *Consolation, Comfort* In the KJV we find the noun "comfort" twice in verses 3 and 4, and "consolation" 4 times in verses 5–7. The Greek has the same word, *paraklēsis*, throughout. Helpfully and consistently the NASB and NIV have "comfort" in all 6 places.

We note also that the verb "comfort" (*parakaleō*) occurs 3 times in verse 4 and once in verse 6. "The God of all comfort" comforts us in all our affliction. By retaining "comfort" for both the noun and the verb we get the full force of the original.

Paul is fond of these words. *Parakaleō* occurs 103 times in the NT, 54 of these in Paul's Epistles. *Paraklēsis* is found 29 times, almost always in Paul (20 times). John and James do not use them at all.

Schmitz calls 2 Corinthians 1 "the great chapter of comfort in the NT" (TDNT, 5:797–98). He goes on to say, "Thus the fellowship of suffering between the apostle and the church becomes a fellowship of comfort, and both in rich measure, 2 C. 1:5–7" (p. 798). Schmitz concludes his discussion of these words by saying:

> The meaning "to comfort," "comfort," "consolation," which is rare in both the Greek world and Hellenistic Judaism, but the more common in the translation Greek of the LXX, is influenced by the OT, and especially by Is. (and the Ps.) when the reference is to salvation history (cf. the "consolation of Israel" in later Judaism). It expresses the divine aid which is already lavishly granted to the members of the suffering community of Jesus by present exhortation and encouraging events, and which will reach its goal when the NT people of God is delivered out of all its tribulations (TDNT, 5:799).

Verse 4 shows why Christians, and especially ministers, must suffer. It is that they may comfort others by the comfort they have themselves received.

4 *Tribulation* The basic meaning of *thlipsis* is "pressure" (see notes on Rom. 2:9). It is the pressures of life that tend to crush us, so that we need the sustaining grace of God.

Both "tribulation" and "trouble" in this verse are *thlipsis* in the Greek. So the translation should be the same in both cases—either "affliction" (NASB) or "trouble" (NIV).

8 *Pressed* The verb *bareō* comes from the noun *baros*, which means "weight" or "burden." This passage suggests the words, "with burdens too heavy to bear." The NASB translates the verb, "we were burdened."

Out of Measure In the Greek this is *kath' hyperbolēn*, which is more accurately translated "beyond measure" (Gal. 1:13). In Rom. 7:13 the KJV has "exceeding," and in 1 Cor. 12:31 it reads "more excellent." Aside from these three passages, *hyperbolē* is found only in 2 Corinthians (four times).

The word is compounded of *hyper*, "above" or "beyond," and *ballō*, "throw." So it literally means "a throwing beyond." In the NT it is used metaphorically in the sense of "excellence" or "excess" (as here). So the NASB translates the phrase, "excessively."

Despaired The verb *exaporeō* (only here and in 4:8) is a strong compound, meaning "to be utterly at a loss, be in despair" (A-S, p. 159). Paul felt as if he was at the end of his rope, as far as this life was concerned.

9 Sentence Most modern versions follow the KJV in using "sentence" here. The literal meaning of *apokrima* (only here in NT) is "answer." But Buechsel notes: "It is a technical term of official and legal speech and denotes an official resolution (on an enquiry or petition) which decides the matter" (TDNT, 3:945). He goes on to say: "By human judgment Paul could only reckon that his position was like that of a man condemned to death who had made a petition for mercy and received the answer that he must die" (p. 946).

Arndt and Gingrich agree with this and give the definition: "official report, decision." But probably "sentence of death" communicates the idea best.

11 Helping Together Paul is fond of compounds beginning with *syn;* he had a strong sense of "togetherness." Here we have another one, *synypourgeō* (only here in NT). It means "join in helping us" (AG; cf. NASB).

Gift The word is *charisma*, which (in KJV) is translated "gift" 15 times and "free gift" twice. Found 6 times in Romans and 7 times in 1 Corinthians, it occurs only this one time in 2 Corinthians (plus 1 Tim. 4:14; 2 Tim. 1:6; 1 Pet. 4:10). It comes from *charis*, "grace," and so means "a gift (freely and graciously given), a favor bestowed" (AG, p. 887). It is obvious that "favor" (NASB) or "gracious favor" (NIV) is the preferable translation. The context indicates that it is the favor of being granted deliverance from death.

12 Rejoicing The noun is *kauchēsis*. In the KJV it is translated "boasting" 6 times and "rejoicing" 4 times (plus "glorying" or "glory" twice). The correct meaning is "boast" (NIV) or "proud confidence" (NASB). The same is true of the related noun *kauchēma*, translated "rejoicing" in verse 14.

Simplicity The KJV uses this term, but the NASB and NIV have *holiness*. It is a matter of textual criticism. "Simplicity" translates *haplotēti*, which is found in the fifth century manuscript D and most of the Old Latin manuscripts. But Papyrus 46 (third century), our only two fourth-century manuscripts (Vaticanus and Sinaiticus), and two fifth-century manuscripts (A, C), plus many others, have *hagiotēti*, "holiness." This seems clearly to be the original word.

13–14 Acknowledge The verb is *epiginoskō*. Occurring 42 times in the NT, it is trans-

lated "know" 30 times. Only here (3 times) and twice in 1 Corinthians (14:37; 16:18) do we find "acknowledge." The best translation is "understand" (NASB, NIV).

15 Benefit Paul says that he had wanted to visit the Corinthian Christians, in order that they might have a second "benefit." The noun is *charis*, "grace." The NASB notes correctly in the margin that the literal meaning is "have a second grace," but translates in the text: "That you might twice receive a blessing." Similarly the NIV has, "That you might benefit twice." Arndt and Gingrich render it: "That you might have a second proof of my goodwill" (p. 886). Most recent versions follow these general lines. The *Modern Language Bible* (*New Berkeley Version*) has: "So that you might enjoy a double blessing."

22 Sealed, Earnest The two very significant Greek words here are discussed in the comments on Eph. 1:13–14. We like the NIV of this verse: "Set his seal of ownership on us, and put his Spirit in our hearts as a deposit, guaranteeing what is to come."

2:1 Determined It is the aorist of the verb *krinō*, which most frequently in the NT is used in the sense of "to judge" (so translated 88 out of 114 times in NT). But its original meaning was to "divide" or "select." Buechsel writes: "The most common meaning is 'to decide' ... 'to judge,' 'to assess' ... Hence, though the word is most commonly found in legal terminology, it does not belong here either exclusively or by derivation" (TDNT, 3:922). The definition that fits here is the third one given by Arndt and Gingrich: "reach a decision, decide" (p. 452).

1–5 Heaviness, Sorrow, Grief In these five verses we find the noun *lypē* twice and the verb *lypeō* five times. The noun also occurs near the end of verse 7. It is translated "heaviness" in the first verse, but "sorrow" in verses 3 and 7. The verb is rendered "make sorry" in verse 2, "grieved" or "caused grief" in verse 5. The NASB consistently translates it "cause sorrow" (vv. 2, 5) or "made sorrowful" (vv. 2, 4). This is probably best—to catch the repeated emphasis.

4 Anguish The word *synochē* (only here and Luke 21:25) comes from the verb *synechō*, "hold together" or "press on every side," and so "oppress." Koester says of this passage: "Paul is referring to the tribulation and affliction which he suffered through hostility at Corinth. He uses the same terms as those used by the OT Psalmist when speaking of the distress which God's enemies caused him" (TDNT, 7:887).

5 Overcharge Today "overcharge" means to charge too much. This is not the idea here at all. The verb is *epibareō* (only here and in 1 Thess. 2:9; 2 Thess. 3:8). It literally means "to put a burden on, be burdensome" (A-S, p. 168).

Arndt and Gingrich say that *hina mē epibarō* in this passage "seems to have the meaning 'in order not to heap up too great a burden of words' = *in order not to say too much* (cf. NASB) . . . although there are no examples of it in this meaning. Other possibilities are *exaggerate, be too severe with*" (p. 290). The NIV probably catches the correct sense: "If anyone has caused grief, he has not so much grieved me as he has grieved all of you, to some extent—not to put it too severely."

6 Punishment The noun *epitimia* (only here in NT) comes from the verb *epitimaō*, which first meant to honor someone. Then the verb came to have the sense: "to mete out due measure," and so "to censure, rebuke" (A-S, p. 176).

Similarly, the noun first had a good meaning. But in Greek inscriptions it means "punishment." Stauffer says that here it is a "a technical term in congregational discipline for the censure of the church" (TDNT, 2:627). The guilty member had been sufficiently punished by public censure.

11 Satan This is a Hebrew word taken over into Greek (and other modern languages). It means "adversary."

Alfred Plummer, in the ICC volume on 2 Corinthians, writes: "Of the Scriptural designations of the evil one, four are found in this Epistle: 'Satan' (here, xi. 14, xii. 7), 'the serpent' (xi. 3), 'Belial' (vi. 15), 'the god of this age' (iv. 4). Elsewhere St. Paul calls Satan 'the tempter' (1 Thess. iii. 5), 'the devil' (Eph. iv. 6, etc.), 'the evil one' (Eph. vi. 16), 'the prince of the power of the air' (Eph. ii. 2)" (p. 63).

He goes on to say:

> It is not necessary to dwell on the obvious fact that here and elsewhere he regards the evil power which opposes God and the well-being of man as a personal agent. Excepting xii. 7, *Satanas* [Greek form] always has the article in the Pauline Epistles. So also most frequently in the rest of the N.T. But, whether with or without the article, *Satanas* in N.T. is

always a proper name which designates the great Adversary of God and man (pp. 63–64).

Devices The word *noēma* is found five times in 2 Corinthians (2:11; 3:14; 4:4; 10:5; 11:3) and only once elsewhere in the NT (Phil. 4:7). It is translated three ways in the KJV: "mind," "device," "thought."

This noun comes from the verb *noeō*, which in turn comes from *nous*, "mind." So it basically means "thought." But Arndt and Gingrich note that in classical and Hellenistic Greek it also meant: "*purpose*, in a bad sense *design, plot*" (p. 542). The NASB and NIV both have "schemes."

13 Rest The Greek word is *anesin*, which has been taken bodily over taken into English as a trade name for a relaxant. "Rest in my spirit" is translated "peace of mind" in the NIV.

14 Causeth Us to Triumph In the Greek this is *thriambeuonti hēmas*. The verb *thriambeuō* had a technical meaning. In the Liddell-Scott-Jones *Greek-English Lexicon*, two interesting definitions are given. The first—"*lead in triumph*, of conquered enemies"—applies to Col. 2:15. The second—"*lead in triumph*, as a general does his army"—fits here (LS-J, p. 806).

Plummer thinks that the first of these definitions fits both passages. He says of the present one: "The victorious commander is God, and the Apostles are—not His subordinate generals, but His captives, whom He takes with Him and displays to all the world. St. Paul thanks God, not for 'always *causing* him to triumph (AV), but for at all times *leading* him in triumph.' The Apostles were among the first to be captured and made instruments of God's glory" (p. 67).

But why not both? Delling majors on the first point, but seems to approach the second. After speaking of the prisoners of the Roman emperor being led in the triumphal procession, he says: "In 2 C. 2:14 Paul describes himself as one of these prisoners. But he regards it as a grace that in his fetters he can accompany God always and everywhere in the divine triumphant march through the world" (TDNT, 3:160).

14, 16 Savor The Greek word is *osmē*. ("Savor" in verse 15 is another word, *euodia*, which we might differentiate by translating as "aroma.") The best rendering for *osmē* is "fragrance."

Plummer expresses beautifully the meaning of this in the light of the context. He writes:

When a Roman *imperator* triumphed, clouds of incense arose along the route; and in the triumphtrain [procession] of the Gospel the incense of increased knowledge of God is ever ascending. The Apostles cause this increase of knowledge, and therefore they themselves are a fragrance to the glory of God, a fragrance that is life-giving to those that are on the road to salvation, but will prove deadly to those who are on the other road (p. 67).

In this last sentence Plummer is including the context of verses 15–16.

17 Corrupt The verb *kapeleuō* (only here in NT) comes from *kapelos*, "a huckster" or "peddler." Thayer says that the verb means—with the accusative of the thing (here "the word of God")—"to make money by selling anything; to get sordid gain by dealing in anything, to do a thing for base gain" (p. 324). He goes on to say: "But as peddlers were in the habit of adulterating their commodities for the sake of gain . . . *kapeleuein ti* was also used as synonymous with *to corrupt, to adulterate*" (pp. 324–25). He favors this sense here. But "peddle" (NASB, NIV) is certainly a viable translation, and perhaps the best. Paul was not peddling the gospel to make money.

3:1 Commend "Commend" is the verb *synistanein*, which is a variant of *synistēmi*. Arndt and Gingrich define it as "(re)commend someone to someone" (p. 798). See discussion at Rom. 16:1.

From this comes the adjective *systatikos* (only here in NT), meaning "introducing, commendatory" (AG, p. 802). In the last part of the verse the KJV is more full than the Greek, which simply says (NASB): "letters of commendation to you or from you." But the technical term today for this is what the NIV has: "letters of recommendation to you or from you."

3 Of Christ Is the genitive case here subjective (written by Christ), objective (telling about Christ), or possessive (belonging to Christ)? As in other cases in the New Testament, we cannot be certain. Plummer (ICC) and Bernard (EGT) prefer the first. This is well represented in the NIV, "a letter from Christ."

Ministered by Us The Greek is *diaconētheisa hyph' hēmon*, literally "have been served (ministered) by us." The connection with the preceding expression is well brought out by Bernard: "the Apostle conceiving of himself as his Master's amanuensis" (EGT, 3:53). This idea is caught by Weymouth—"penned by

us." Paul says that the Corinthian Christians were "the result of our ministry" (NIV). The most important result of his ministry was what was written on the hearts of his converts.

Tables "Tables of stone" is evidently a reference to the two pieces of stone on which the Ten Commandments were written (Exod. 31:18). The Greek *plax* occurs only here (twice) and in Heb. 9:4—"the stone tablets of the covenant" (NIV). The word literally means something flat, and so here a flat stone. But the correct term today is "tablets."

Contrasted with "tablets of stone" are "tablets of human hearts" (NASB, NIV). Incidentally, "in" should be "on."

5 Sufficient Paul's statement here, "But our sufficiency is of God" is an answer to his very pertinent question in 2:16—"And who is sufficient for these things?" The connection is also brought out in the NASB: "And who is adequate for these things? . . . but our adequacy is from God." The adjective is *hikanos* (frequent in NT). The noun is *hikanotēs* (only here). But the KJV of verse 6, "made us able," fails to indicate that there the verb is *hikanoō* (only here and Col. 1:12), which is derived from *hikanos*. The NASB correctly represents this: "made us adequate." Our adequacy comes from Christ.

6 Testament The word *diathēkē* occurs 33 times in the NT. In the KJV it is translated "covenant" 20 times and "testament" 13 times. Most commentators agree that it should probably be rendered "covenant" except in Heb. 9:16–17, and possibly Gal. 3:15 (see comments at the latter place).

The Letter *Gramma* (from which we get "grammar") first meant a letter of the alphabet. Then it came to mean what is written, and so a document (usually in the plural), an epistle, and even a book. Arndt and Gingrich feel that it is used here "of the literally correct form of the law" (p. 164).

Paul says that the letter kills, but the spirit (*pneuma*) makes alive. Plummer comments:

But we must not be misled by the common contrast in English between "letter" and "spirit," which means the contrast between the literal sense and the spiritual or inward sense of one and the same document or authority. By *gramma* and *pneuma* St. Paul means two different authorities; *gramma* is the written code of the Law, *pneuma* is the operation of the Spirit in producing and promulgating the Gospel (p. 87).

Schrenk agrees with this when he writes: "Any suggestion is to be rejected which would have it that the spirit of Scripture is here opposed to its letter, or its true or richer sense to the somatic body" (TDNT, 1:767). The contrast is between the written Law and the life-giving Spirit.

7–9 Ministration The Greek word *diaconia* (4 times here) occurs 34 times in the NT and is translated "ministry" 16 times in the KJV. That is clearly the correct translation here (cf. NASB, NIV).

Incidentally, it should be noted that "engraven in stones" (v. 7) should be "engraved in letters on stone" (NIV). That is what the Greek text says. The reference, of course, is to the Ten Commandments.

12 Plainness *Parrēsia* occurs 31 times in the NT and is translated "boldness" 8 times, "confidence" 6 times, "openly" 4 times, and "plainly" 4 times. Only here is it rendered "plainness of speech."

The word comes from *pas*, "all" and *hrēsis*, "speech." So it basically means "freedom of speech." Abbott-Smith says: "In LXX, Josephus, and NT, also (from the absence of fear which accompanies freedom of speech), *confidence*, boldness" (p. 347).

Schlier writes: "Above all, the discussion in 2 C. 3:12ff. shows that for Paul *parrēsia* to God—the uncovered face of Paul looking towards Him, 3:18—implies an uncovered face which men can see as Israel could not see the covered face of Moses, 3:13. He who lifts up his face uncovered to God also turns uncovered to men" (TDNT, 5:883).

So we have here the ideas of openness and boldness. The latter is perhaps not only "in *our* speech" (NASB), but in general (NIV).

13–16 Veil The noun *kalymma* is found once each in these four verses, and nowhere else in the NT. It comes from the verb *kalyptō*, "cover," and so means "a covering."

13 Abolished While the verb *katargeō* does have "abolish" as one of its meanings, "fading away" (NASB, NIV) fits much better here. It was the glory on Moses' face that faded away after a while.

The reference is to Exod. 34:33, where the KJV reads: "Till Moses had done speaking with them he put a veil on his face." Plummer says:

This is erroneous. The correct translation is, "*When* Moses had done speaking with them

he put a veil on his face" (cf. NASB). He knew that the brightness was caused by converse with Jehovah, and would fade away when he was absent from the divine presence. He did not wish the people to see the disappearance of the brightness, and therefore, when he had delivered his message, he covered his face, until he returned to the presence of the Lord (pp. 96–97).

18 Open The Greek for "open" is *anakekalymmenō*, the perfect passive participle of *anakalyptō*. This verb is found only here and in verse 14, where it is translated "taken away." It literally means "to unveil" (A-S, p. 30), and so the correct translation here is "unveiled" (NASB, NIV).

Glass "Beholding as in a glass" is all one word in Greek—*katoptrizomenoi*, the present middle participle of *katoptrizō* (only here in NT). In the middle it means "to reflect as a mirror" (A-S, p. 242). Since they did not have glass mirrors (only bronze) in Paul's day, "glass" is incorrect.

Changed The verb is *metamorphoō*, which is rendered "transformed" in Rom. 12:2 (see comments there). This is the literal meaning of the verb and the correct translation here.

4:1 Faint Today the verb "faint" is used as a synonym for "swoon"—becoming dizzy and falling down. But the verb *enkakeō* means "become weary" or "lose heart" (AG, p. 214). Achilles comments: "Weariness here is not physical but spiritual" (DNTT, 1:563). The correct translation is "lose heart" (RSV, NASB, NIV).

2 Dishonesty It is difficult to see where the translators got the word "dishonesty" here. The Greek simply says, "the hidden things of shame."

But what does this mean? Arndt and Gingrich suggest, "What one conceals from a feeling of shame" (p. 24). This idea is taken over in the NASB: "The things hidden because of shame." The NIV puts it a little more generally: "Secret and shameful ways."

Craftiness In the Septuagint *panourgia* means "cleverness," in a good or neutral sense. But in classical Greek and the NT it is used in a bad sense—"craftiness" or "deception" (NIV).

Handling ... Deceitfully In the Greek this is the present participle of the verb *doloō*, which comes from the noun *dolos*, a "bait" or "snare." So the verb literally means "ensnare." But both noun and verb are used metaphorically in the sense of "deceit" or "treachery." Arndt and Gingrich say that the verb means "falsify, adulterate" (p. 202)—it was used in secular Greek for adulterating wine. One could deduce the idea here: "Don't water down the Word of God!"

3 Hid The Greek word here is not related to the one translated "hidden things" in verse 2. There it was the adjective *cryptos*, from which we get "cryptic." Here it is the verb *calyptō*, "to cover or veil." So the best translation here is "veiled" (RSV, NASB, NIV).

Lost Evangelical Christians are familiar with the thought that the unsaved are "lost." But does this word communicate the truth accurately and adequately to an outsider?

The verb *apollymi* in the active voice means "destroy" (cf. 1 Cor. 1:19). In the middle voice, as here, it means "perish." So it seems that the best translation is "those who are perishing" (NASB, NIV). It is the same verb that is translated "perish" in John 3:16. The main argument for using "lost" here would be a connection with the three parables of the lost in Luke 15, where this verb is rendered "lose" or "lost" (7 times). But we also find the prodigal son saying, "I perish (*apollymai*) with hunger" (v. 17).

We should not discontinue using the term "lost" to describe the condition referred to here. But the other concept is also important. Oepke says that *apollymi* indicates "definitive destruction, not merely in the sense of the extinction of physical existence, but rather of an eternal plunge into Hades and a hopeless destiny of death" (TDNT, 1:396).

5 The Lord Paul declared, "We preach not ourselves, but Christ Jesus the Lord" (KJV). In the Greek there is no article before "Lord." So the correct translation is "as Lord." Alfred Plummer comments: "To 'preach Christ as Lord' is to preach Him as crucified, risen, and glorified, the Lord to whom 'all authority in heaven and earth has been given' " (p. 118).

The alert reader may have noted that NASB has "Christ Jesus as Lord," whereas NIV has "Jesus Christ as Lord." Which is right? The answer is, "We cannot be sure." Our two oldest Greek manuscripts of the NT (as a whole) come from the fourth century. Of these two, Vaticanus has *Christon Iesoun* and Sinaiticus has *Iesoun Christon*. All three fifth-century manuscripts have the latter. That is probably why this reading was adopted in the United Bi-

ble Society Greek Testament, now considered the best in print. It may be noted that the correct reading at the end of v. 6 is "Christ" (NASB, NIV), not "Jesus Christ." In this case the Greek is very clear.

·7 Earthen The adjective *ostracinos* is found only here and in 2 Tim. 2:20. Arndt and Gingrich say that here it is used "as a symbol, denoting breakableness" (p. 591).

This adjective is the basis of the archaeological term "ostraca," used for broken pieces of pottery that often have ancient writing inscribed on them.

Vessels The word *skeuos* is rendered "vessel" in the KJV 19 out of the 23 times it occurs in the NT. Most of the time it refers to what we today would call "jars" or "containers." "Vessel" is now used more for a ship. Here "jars of clay" (NIV) is more contemporary than "earthen vessels" (RSV, NASB).

What is meant? Gen. 2:7 suggests that God made man's body from clay. So some have thought that the reference here is to the physical body. But Plummer writes: "It was in the man as a whole, and not in his body in particular, that the Divine treasure which was to enrich the world was placed to be dispensed to others" (p. 127). He notes that this metaphor is common in the OT (Isa. 29:16; 30:14; 45:9; 64:8; Jer. 18:6).

The figure used here emphasizes the frailty of our humanity. This is in contrast to the greatness of God's power and glory.

8 Troubled The Greek word is the present passive participle of *thlibō*, the verb meaning "to press." Occurring 10 times in the NT, it is translated "troubled" 4 times and "afflicted" 3 times. But since the basic meaning is "press," it seems that "hard pressed" (NIV) is best here. Plummer declares: "Here the radical signification of 'pressure' (Mk. iii. 9) must be retained, because of *stenochōroumenoi*" (p. 128).

Distressed The verb *stenochōreomai* is found in the NT only here and in 6:12 (twice), where the KJV has "straitened." This catches better the distinctive meaning of the word. It comes from *stenos*, "narrow," and *chōros*, "space." So it means "to compress." This idea is caught by "crushed" (NASB, NIV).

Perplexed But Not in Despair The Greek has "*aporoumenoi* [but not] *exaporoumenoi*." *Ex* (*ek*) is a prepositional prefix meaning "out of." It acts here, as often, in the sense of a strong intensive of the simple verb. Plummer suggests: "in despondency, yet not in despair" (p. 129).

The first verb, *aporeō*, occurs four times in the NT. It means "be at a loss, in doubt, uncertain" (AG, p. 97). *Exaporeō* is found only here and in 1:8. It has the force of being "utterly at a loss," and so "in despair."

9 Cast Down   "Struck down" is preferred for *kataballomenoi* by the NASB and NIV, as being more contemporary. Phillips puts it very vividly: "We may be knocked down, but we are never knocked out!"

14 By   The KJV says "by Jesus" and "with you." The Greek has the same preposition in both places—*syn*, which means "(together) with."

15 Redound   "Redound" is an archaic word. The verb is *perisseuō*, which occurs 39 times in the NT. In the KJV it is translated "abound" 17 times and "redound" only here. The former gives the correct sense.

17 Far More Exceeding   This represents another play on words in the Greek: *kath' hyperbolēn eis hyperbolēn*. Arndt and Gingrich define the first part of this as "beyond measure." To get the full force of the double expression they suggest "beyond all measure and proportion" (p. 848). The NASB has "far beyond all comparison," the NIV "that far outweighs them all."

5:1, 4 Tabernacle   The feminine noun *skēnē* occurs 20 times in the NT and is translated "tabernacle" all but once ("habitation," Luke 16:9) in the KJV. It often refers to the Tabernacle in the Wilderness. But here alone we have *skēnos* (neuter).

Today "tabernacle" suggests a large plain building, seating big crowds. So "tent" is a better translation in this place. Paul thinks of the human body as a tent pitched here in this world. It is only our temporary home. In heaven our glorified bodies will be our eternal "house."

1 Dissolved   The verb *katalyō* means "destroy, cast down" (A-S, p. 236). "Dissolved" carries a somewhat different connotation today. The best translation is "torn down" (NASB) or "destroyed" (NIV).

2 House   The most common word for "house" in the NT is *oikos* (114 times). *Oikia* (95 times) is the term used twice in the first verse here. Abbott-Smith distinguishes these two words thus:

> *oikos*, which in Attic law denoted the whole *estate*, *oikia*, the *dwelling* only. In classical poets *oikos* has also the latter sense, but not in prose, except in metaphorical usage, where it signifies both *property* and *household*. The foregoing distinction is not, however, consistently maintained in late Greek (p. 312).

Michel agrees. He says: "Originally Greek distinguished between *oikos* and *oikia*.... *Oikos* had then a broader range than *oikia*, being the whole of a deceased person's possessions . . . whereas *oikia* is simply his residence" (TDNT, 5:131). But in the NT the two are used interchangeably.

In verse 2, however, we have *oikētērion* (only here and Jude 6). It comes from *oikētēr*, "an inhabitant," and so means "habitation." Today we would say "dwelling" (NASB, NIV).

4 Mortality   The Greek is *to thnēton*. An adjective, *thnētos* means "mortal" (see 4:11), that is, "subject to death." With the definite article *to* (neuter) it means "what is mortal" (RSV, NASB, NIV), not the abstract idea of "mortality."

5 Earnest   See discussion at Eph. 1:14.

6, 8, 9 At Home . . . Absent   There is an interesting play on words in the Greek: *Endēmountes . . . ekdēmoumen*. The first verb means "to be at home," the second "to be away from home." They both occur only here (three times each).

11 Terror   Out of its 47 occurrences in the NT, the noun *phobos* is translated as "fear" 41 times. Only 3 times is it rendered "terror" (Rom. 13:3; here; and in 1 Pet. 3:14). "Terror" seems too strong a translation.

14 Constraineth   The verb is *synechō*, literally "hold together," which occurs only twice in Paul's Epistles (here and Phil. 1:23). Koester says that in these two passages it means "to be claimed, totally controlled." Commenting on verses 14–15 he says: "It is the love of Christ which 'completely dominates' Paul . . . so that on the basis of Christ's death the only natural decision for him, as for all other believers, is no longer to live for self but to live for Christ" (TDNT, 7:883).

In the David Livingstone Memorial in

Blantyre, Scotland (just outside Glasgow), one can see on the wall of the last room a cross. To the left are the words: "The love of Christ constraineth us—St. Paul." To the right: "The love of Christ compels me—David Livingstone." The NIV has "compels" here (v. 14).

Is the genitive "of love" subjective, objective, or possessive? Since we cannot be sure which, we can use all three for a sermon outline:

1. Christ's love for me compels me to crucial commitment.
2. My love for Christ compels me to complete consecration.
3. Christ's love in me compels me to compassionate service.

16 *After the Flesh*   The phrase (twice here) is *kata sarka*—literally, "according to flesh." Plummer says that it means "according to external distinctions," "by what he is in the flesh" (p. 176).

What did Paul mean when he said that he knew Christ *kata sarka?* Plummer writes: "Almost certainly he is alluding to some time *previous* to his conversion. . . . At that time he knew Christ as an heretical and turbulent teacher, who was justly condemned by the Sanhedrin and crucified by the Romans" (p. 177). But now he knows Him in a new way.

Know Him   The KJV says, "Yet now henceforth know we *him* no more." Taken in its absolute sense, that statement of course is not true.

The Greek simply says, "But now no longer we know" (*alla nun ouketi ginōskomen*). The KJV added "him" in italics, to try to make the meaning clearer. Most translators have felt it necessary to add something for better sense in English, such as "thus" (NASB) or "so" (NIV).

17 *Creature*   The NASB (as KJV) has "creature," whereas the NIV has "creation."

The noun *ktisis* first means "the act of creating." Then it came to mean "what has been created." Arndt and Gingrich write: "The Christian is described by Paul as *kainē ktisis a new creature* 2 Cor. 5:17, and the state of being in the new faith by the same words as *a new creation* Gal. 6:15" (p. 457). Some prefer to translate this second clause of the verse: "there is a new creation" (NASB margin).

Passed Away . . . Become New   The KJV reads: "Old things are passed away; behold, all things are become new." But this fails to represent the difference in tenses. "Are passed away"

is the aorist tense (*parēlthen*), which indicates a crisis experience. "Are become new" is the perfect tense (*gegonen*), indicating a continuing state. "The old things passed away; behold, new things have come" (NASB).

18–20 *Reconciled, Reconciliation*   The two greatest passages on reconciliation in the NT are this one and Rom. 5:10–11 (see comments there). The noun *katallagē* occurs twice here (vv. 18, 19) and twice in Romans (5:11; 11:15), and nowhere else in the NT. The verb *katallassō* is found three times here (vv. 18, 19, 20) and once in Rom. 5:10. In the only other place where it occurs in the NT (1 Cor. 7:11) it is used of an estranged wife being reconciled to her husband.

Buechsel says of Paul's ministry of reconciliation (*katallagē*): "It brings before men the action by which God takes them up again into fellowship with Himself" (TDNT, 1:258). Of the verb he writes: "*katallassein* denotes a transformation or renewal of the state between God and man, and therewith of man's own state. . . . By reconciliation our sinful self-seeking is overcome and the fellowship with God is created in which it is replaced by living for Christ" (TDNT, 1:255).

6:1 *Workers Together*   "As workers together with him" is all one word in Greek, *synergountes*. Literally it means "working together (with)"—from *syn*, "together," and *ergon*, "work." The NIV has "as God's fellow workers."

We have already noted that Paul's strong sense of "togetherness" is shown by his fondness for compound words with a *syn* prefix. A quick check discovered over 50 of these.

2 *Succored*   The verb is *boētheō*. It comes from *boē*, "a cry," and *theō*, "run." So it literally means to "run at a cry for help"—that is, "hurry to help someone who is in need." That is what God does for us. The noun *boē* occurs only in James 5:4, where it represents "the cry of the oppressed" (TDNT, 1:411).

3 *Offence*   The noun *proskopē* is found only here in the NT. It comes from the verb *proskoptō*, which is used for striking one's foot against a stone or other obstacle in the path, and so means "to stumble." Thayer suggests that the entire phrase here means "to do something which causes others to stumble, i.e. leads them into error or sin" (p. 547).

The NASB, "giving no cause for offense in anything," is accurate. But the NIV, "We put no stumbling block in anyone's path," communicates the idea more clearly.

Not Blamed The verb *mōmaomai* is found only here and in 8:20. The minister is to conduct himself in such a blameless way that his ministry will not be "discredited" (NASB, NIV).

4 Patience Again the word is *hypomonē* (see comments on Rom. 2:7; 5:3). The correct translation is "endurance" (NASB, NIV).

Plummer notes that following "endurance" (KJV, "patience") in verse 4 we have three triplets that, taken together, illustrate the full meaning of endurance. Of the first of these (v. 4) he says: "This triplet consists of troubles which may be independent of human agency, and it is probably intended to form a climax: 'afflictions' . . . which might be avoided; 'necessities' . . . which cannot be avoided; 'straits' . . . out of which there is no way of escape" (p. 194).

He suggests that the second triplet (v. 5) "consists of troubles inflicted by men." Then he observes: "It is doubtful whether there is any climax; but St. Paul might think 'stripes' . . . less serious than 'imprisonments' . . . which stopped his work for a time, and imprisonments less serious than 'tumults,' which might force him to abandon work altogether in the place in which the tumult occurred" (p. 194).

Plummer says that the third triplet (v. 5) "consists of those troubles which he took upon himself in the prosecution of his mission." He goes on to say: "There is order in this triplet also, and perhaps one may call it a climax: *kopoi* disturb the day, *agrypniai* the night, and *nēsteiai* both" (p. 195).

Necessities The KJV represents the original, literal meaning of *anangkē*—"necessity." But for this passage (and 12:10; Luke 21:23; 1 Cor. 7:26; 1 Thess. 3:7) Thayer says: "In a sense rare in the classics (Diod. 4, 43), but very common in Hellenistic writers . . . *calamity, distress*" (p. 36). Moulton and Milligan cite evidence of this usage as early as the third century B.C. (VGT, p. 31). Grundmann says that here the word indicates "such afflictions as those experienced by the apostle Paul, or afflictions which derive from the tension between the new creation in Christ and the old cosmos" (TDNT, 1:346). It is thus related closely to the preceding word "afflictions" and the following word "distresses." It may be rendered "hardships" (NASB, NIV).

5 Stripes In the KJV *plēgē* is translated "plague" 12 times in Revelation and "wound" 4

times (plus once in Luke 10:30). Elsewhere in the NT (5 times) it is rendered "stripe" (Luke 12:48; Acts 16:23, 33; 2 Cor. 6:5; 11:23). The correct translation here is "beatings" (NASB, NIV). That is what Paul had suffered often (11:23).

Tumults *Akatastasia* (5 times in NT) basically means "disturbance" (AG). Oepke says that in this passage it signifies "personal unrest" (TDNT, 3:446). But Plummer feels that here it means "tumults," as in Luke 21:9. He comments: "Popular tumults against St. Paul are frequent in Acts" (p. 194). The contemporary term for this is "riots" (NIV).

Labors *Kopos* means "labor." But today we would probably say "hard work" (NIV).

Watchings The noun *agrypnia* is found only here and in 11:27. Basically it means "sleeplessness." But Plummer writes:

> The word covers more than sleeplessness; it includes all that prevents one from sleeping. At Troas Paul preached until midnight and yet longer (Acts xx. 7, 9). In LXX the word is almost confined to Ecclesiasticus, where it is frequent and commonly means forgoing sleep in order to work. The Apostle no doubt often taught, and travelled, and worked with his hands to maintain himself by night (p. 195).

The word should be translated here either as "sleeplessness" (NASB) or, perhaps better, as "sleepless nights" (NIV).

Fastings The word *nēsteia* is used in the same way here and in 11:27. Aside from these two places, the best Greek text has it only in Luke 2:37 and Acts 14:23; 27:9. In the first two of these three it is connected with prayer and so has a religious connotation. Acts 27:9 borders on this. But what does it mean here? Plummer says: "Not 'fasts' in the religious sense; but, just as *agrypnia* is voluntary forgoing of sleep in order to get more work done, so *nēsteia* is voluntary forgoing of food for the same reason." He adds: "We infer from xi. 27 that *nēsteiai* are *voluntary* abstentions from food, for there they are distinguished from involuntary hunger and thirst" (p. 195).

6 Pureness Following a dramatic list of nine hardships endured by Paul (vv. 4–5), we find a striking contrast in the nine virtues named in verses 6–7. The first virtue is *hagnotēs* (only here and 11:3). It comes from the adjective *hagnos*, "pure" (9 times in NT). The noun is rare, not occurring at all in classical Greek or in the Septuagint. Hauck defines it as "moral purity and blamelessness" (TDNT, 1:124). Rather than "pureness," today we would say "purity" (NASB, NIV).

Unfeigned "Unfeigned" precisely represents the Greek adjective *anypocritos*, "unhypocritical" (found once each in Romans, 2 Corinthians, 1 & 2 Timothy, James, 1 Peter). But the term is outdated; "sincere" (NIV) says it today.

7 Armor The Greek has the plural of *hoplon*, which originally meant a "tool" or "instrument." It is used that way in Rom. 6:13. Always plural in the NT, it often means "weapons"—literally in John 18:3, figuratively in Rom. 13:12; 2 Cor. 6:7; 10:4).

"On" (KJV) should be "in" (NIV) or "for" (NASB), indicating where the weapons are held.

8 Honor In the KJV *doxa* is translated "glory" 145 times and "glorious" 10 times in its 168 occurrences in the NT. It should be "glory" here.

Evil Report and Good Report In the Greek this is *dysphēmia* and *euphēmia* (both only here in NT). The first means "slander."

12 Bowels Verse 12 is difficult to understand in the KJV. It means, "We are not withholding our affection from you, but you are withholding yours from us" (NIV).

13 Recompence *Antimisthian* is found only in Rom. 1:27, in a bad sense, and here, in a good sense—and nowhere in secular Greek literature. Arndt and Gingrich translate the clause here: "Widen your hearts in the same way in exchange" (p. 74).

14 Unequally Yoked Together The Greek verb *heterozygeō* (only here in NT) literally means "to come under an unequal or different yoke." Here it is used metaphorically in the sense "to have fellowship with one who is not an equal" (Thayer, p. 254).

15 Infidel This is the same word, *apistos*, which is translated "unbeliever" in verse 14. "Infidel" now has a technical connotation that does not fit here.

16 Agreement The word is *synkatathesis* (only here in NT). It is compounded of the verb

meaning "place" or "put" (stem *the*), *kata*, meaning "down," and *syn*, "together." It was used for a joint deposit of votes (Thayer, p. 592), and so means "assent" or "agreement."

7:1 Filthiness The noun *molysmos* (only here in NT) comes from the verb *molynō*, which means "to stain, soil, defile" (A-S, p. 296). So it means "defilement." Arndt and Gingrich translate and interpret the passage this way: "*from all defilement of body and spirit*, i.e. outwardly and inwardly" (p. 528). J. I. Packer says that it signifies "the moral and spiritual defilement that comes from embracing the pagan lifestyle" (DNTT, 1:449).

Perfecting The verb *epiteleō* comes from *telos*, "end." The prefix *epi* is a preposition meaning "upon," but here probably has the intensive function—"bring fully to completion." In 8:6 it means "complete" (NASB) or "bring to completion" (NIV). Delling notes that one meaning of *telos* is " 'completion' as a state, 'perfection' " (TDNT, 8:49). "Perfecting" seems to be the best translation here.

Holiness The word *hagiōsyne* occurs only three times in the NT (Rom. 1:4; here; and 1 Thess. 3:13) and its cognate *hagiotēs* only once (Heb. 12:10).

But the adjective *hagios*, "holy," from which these are derived, is found 229 times. The verb *hagiazō*, "sanctify," occurs 29 times, and the noun *hagiasmos*, "sanctification" 10 times. So there is a great deal of emphasis on holiness in the NT.

In Kittel's *Theological Dictionary of the New Testament* 27 pages are devoted to *hagios* and its derivatives. Procksch says that *hagiōsyne* "means 'sanctification' or 'holiness' rather than sanctifying, but as a quality rather than a state" (TDNT, 1:114). It is the quality of being holy. The sanctified Christian needs to have his whole inner being and outward life so permeated by the Holy Spirit that it all becomes holy.

2 Receive At least 18 Greek verbs in the NT are translated as "receive" in the KJV. In most cases it is either *lambanō* (133 times), *dechomai* (52 times), or one of the numerous compounds of these verbs (e.g., *paralambanō* 15 times).

In contrast to these, the verb here is *chōreō* (9 times in NT), which is translated "receive" only here and in Matt. 19:11. It comes from the noun *chōros*, which means "place" or "space." Thayer says that here the verb means "make room for one in one's heart" (p. 674). So both

NASB and NIV have: "Make room for us in your hearts"—a very meaningful translation.

Defrauded The verb *pleonekteō* is found mainly in 2 Corinthians (2:11; 7:2; 12:17, 18)—elsewhere only in 1 Thess. 4:6. Its basic meaning is that of taking advantage of someone (cf. NASB). The proper word for that today is "exploit" (NIV), which the *American Heritage Dictionary* defines as "1. To employ to the greatest possible advantage. . . . 2. To make use of selfishly or unethically" (p. 463). "Defraud" (KJV) means "to take by fraud," which is not the exact point here.

4 Boldness of Speech This is one word in Greek, *parrēsia* (see comments on 3:12). Paul is not here talking about "boldness of speech" but "confidence" (NASB, NIV).

Glorying "Boasting" (NASB) is the better translation of *kauchēsis* (see on 1:12). It may be rendered "take pride" (NIV).

5 Troubled "Troubled" seems too weak a translation for *thlibō* (see comments at 4:8). "Afflicted" (NASB) is used today mostly for physical ailments. So probably "harassed" (NIV) is better.

Fightings The noun *machē* (related to *machaira*, "sword") literally means "a fight." But in the NT (2 Cor. 7:5; 2 Tim. 2:23; Titus 3:9; Jas. 4:1) it is "only in plural and only of battles fought without actual weapons" (AG, p. 497). So it means "a strife, contention, quarrel" (A-S, p. 280). "Conflicts" (NASB, NIV) expresses it well.

Bauernfeind notes that as early as Homer's *Iliad* the word was used "in the general sense of conflict, for battles of words." But he adds the observation: "It is not clear whether the *machai* to which Paul was exposed in 2 C. 7:5 embraced physical threats" (TDNT, 4:527–28).

7 Earnest Desire For *epipothēsis* all the standard lexicons give "longing." In the NT it occurs only here and in verse 11, where it is rendered "vehement desire."

Schoenweiss observes: "When Paul speaks of desire and longing in a good sense, he uses *epipotheō . . . epipothesis . . .* and *epipothia*"—the last found only in Rom. 15:23. He adds: "This word-group is used 13 times in the NT, 11 of them being in the Pauline writings and always in a good sense" (DNTT, 1:458). Paul was a man of strong feelings and he uses strong terms.

Fervent Mind The Greek word here, *zēlos*, is used more frequently (5 times) in 2 Corinthians than in any other book of the NT. In this Epistle the apostle is expressing strong emotions, more than in any other of his letters.

Our word "zeal" comes from this word, and it is translated that way most often (6 times) in the KJV. But it is also translated "envying" five times and "envy" once. Only here it is rendered "fervent mind." In 2 Corinthians it carries a good sense always except in 12:20 ("envyings"). In 11:2 it is translated "jealousy," but in a good sense.

8 Repent The more common Greek verb for "repent" in the NT (34 times) is *metanoeō*, which is always translated "repent" in the KJV. The word here (twice) is *metamelomai* (6 times), also rendered "repent" always. Each of these two words, interestingly, occurs in only one passage in Paul's Epistles (*metanoeō* in 12:21). Aside from that *metanoeō* is found exclusively in the Synoptic Gospels, Acts, and Revelation. However, the noun *metanoia*, "repentance," occurs 4 times in Paul (see comments on Rom. 2:4). It is found here in verses 9 and 10.

After emphasizing the fact that the two verbs seem to be used somewhat interchangeably in Greek literature, Thayer concludes: "But that *metanoeō* is the fuller and nobler term, expressive of moral actions and issues, is indicated not only by its derivation, but by the greater frequency of its use, by the fact that it is often employed in the imperative (*metamelomai* never), and by its construction with *apo*, *ek*" (p. 405). He also notes that *metamelomai* properly means, "it is a care to one afterwards," whereas *metanoeō* means "change one's mind."

Trench, in his *Synonyms*, says that in both sacred and secular writers there is "a very distinct preference for *metanoia* as the expression of the nobler repentance." He adds: "He who has *changed his mind* about the past is in the way to change everything; he who has an *after care* may have little or nothing more than a selfish dread of the consequences of what he had done" (pp. 260–61).

Michel has an excellent treatment of the words in their context in this passage. He writes:

In 2 C. 7:8–10 there is again a plain distinction between *metamelesthai* and *metanoein*. Paul is not sorry that he sent a severe letter (*ou metamelomai*, 7:8). Even if it caused pain, this was according to God's will. . . . It is now clear to him that the pain was necessary to bring the Corinthians to a change of heart (*. . . eis metanoian,* 7:9). Suffering which corresponds to God's will brings about a change of heart which is to salvation and which will not be rued (*. . . metanoia ametameletos,* 7:10) (TDNT, 4:628–29).

The adjective *ametameletos* (only v. 10 and Rom. 11:29) is properly translated "without regret" (NASB). And of course the verb *metamelomai* in verse 8 should be rendered "regret" (NASB, NIV).

11 Carefulness *Spoude* literally means "haste" (as in Mark 6:25; Luke 1:39). Then it came to mean "eagerness, earnestness" (AG, p. 771). "Earnestness" is the best translation here (NASB, NIV).

Clearing The adjective *hagnos* literally means "pure," as in 11:2. But for this passage Arndt and Gingrich suggest "innocent" (p. 11), as does Hauck (TDNT, 1:122). That fits very well (NASB, NIV).

16 Have Confidence The verb *tharreo* is almost confined to 2 Corinthians in the NT (5:6, 8; 7:16; 10:1, 2). Elsewhere it is found only in Heb. 13:6. Its heavy use in 2 Corinthians reflects the fact that Paul was overjoyed that his confidence in the Corinthian Christians had been restored.

8:1 We Do You to Wit Obviously this communicates little to the modern reader. The Greek simply says, *gnorizomen hymin,* "we make known to you."

The verb *gnorizo* occurs 24 times in the NT and in the KJV is translated "make known" 16 times. Only here is it rendered "do to wit," and in Phil. 1:22 "wot." Both terms are obsolete.

2 Liberality The word *haplotes* occurs eight times in the NT. Three times it is translated "simplicity"—1:12; 11:3; Rom. 12:8 (see comments there). Here it is "liberality," in 9:11 "bountifulness," and in 9:13 "liberal." In Eph. 6:5 and Col. 3:22 it is "singleness." (These two passages are closely parallel to each other.)

"Liberality" fits very well here. Perhaps "generosity" (NIV) is slightly more contemporary.

4 Gift In the KJV the noun *charis* is translated "grace" 130 out of the 156 times it occurs in the NT. The next most frequent translation is "favor" (6 times), which fits best here

(NASB). Only in this one passage is it translated "gift."

6–7 Grace In these two verses "grace" (KJV) is *charis* in the Greek. Since Paul here is talking about taking up an offering for "the poor saints in Jerusalem" (Rom. 15:26), "gracious work" (NASB) is a little more specific.

This passage emphasizes the important fact that giving is a grace. This is brought out beautifully in the NIV of verse 7: "See that you also excel in this grace of giving."

"The Grace of Giving" would make an excellent sermon subject. The thought is elaborated further in verses 9 and 19.

10 Forward The Greek is *thelein,* which means "to be willing" or "desire" (NASB, NIV). It is correctly translated "to will" in verse 11. The second half of verse 10 is rendered very helpfully in the NIV: "Last year you were the first not only to give but also to have the desire to do so."

11 Perform "Perform" and "performance" (KJV) are more accurately rendered "finish" and "completion" (NASB, NIV). The verb is *epiteleo,* which is correctly translated "finish" in verse 6. "Performance" is the articular aorist infinitive of the same verb (*to epitelesai,* "to have completed").

11, 12, 19 Readiness, Willing Mind, Ready Mind The Greek word *prothymia* occurs five times in the NT and is translated five different ways in the KJV. It is found four times in the immediate context: in this chapter "readiness" (v. 11), "willing mind" (v. 12), "ready mind" (v. 19), and in 9:2 "forwardness of mind." In Acts 17:11 it is "readiness of mind."

The noun means "eagerness, willingness, readiness" (A-S, p. 381). The NIV uses "eagerness" in Acts and in 11:19; 9:2, but "willingness" in 8:11, 12. The NASB has "eagerness" in Acts and "readiness" in 2 Corinthians. Rengstorf suggests "cheerful resolution" for the passages in 2 Corinthians (TDNT, 6:700).

12 First Instead of "there be first," the NASB has "is present" (cf. NIV). The verb *prokeimai* means "lie before, be present" (AG, p. 714).

17 Exhortation Arndt and Gingrich give three basic meanings for *paraclesis:* (1) "exhortation," (2) "appeal," (3) "comfort." They comment: "2 Cor. 8:17 could stand under 1, but probably may better be classed with 2" (p.

623). In keeping with this we favor "appeal" (RSV, NASB, NIV). It seems to fit better here.

Of His Own Accord The Greek adjective *authairetos* is found (in NT) only here and in verse 3 ("of themselves"). It is compounded of *autos*, "self," and the verb *haireomai*, "choose." So it basically means "self-chosen." The NIV has here, "on his own initiative."

19 Chosen The verb *cheirotoneō* is found only here and in Acts 14:23 "ordained"; better "appointed" (RSV, NASB, NIV). It comes from *cheir*, "hand," and *teinō*, "stretch." It originally meant "to vote by stretching out the hand" in the Athenian assembly. Then it came to mean simply "appoint." Lohse says that the sense here is "to select" (TDNT, 9:437).

21 Providing The verb *pronoeō* (only here, Rom. 12:17; 1 Tim. 5:8) literally means "think of beforehand," and so "take care, care for, provide" (AG, p. 715). Behm says that here and in Rom. 12:17 (closely parallel passages) "the meaning is 'to have regard for' what is noble and praiseworthy" (TDNT, 4:1011). "Honest things" (KJV) as the object of this verb is too narrow for *kala*, which means "good, noble" or "honorable" (RSV, NASB).

23 Fellow Helper The Greek word *synergos* is compounded of *syn*, "together," and *ergon*, "work." So it clearly means "fellow worker" (NASB, NIV).

Messengers *Apostolos* occurs 81 times in the NT and is translated "apostle" 78 times in the KJV. Only here and in Phil. 2:25 is it rendered "messenger." In John 13:16 it is "he that is sent." The word literally means "one sent on an errand or with a commission." Here it refers to the appointed "representatives" (NIV) from the various churches, who traveled with the offering to Jerusalem.

24 Show ... Proof There is a play on words here in the Greek (*endeiknymi ... endeixis*) that doesn't show up in English translations. The verb "show" is *endeiknymi*, which in the middle (as here) means "to show forth, prove" (A-S, p. 152). "Proof" is the noun *endeixis*, which comes from this verb. It means a proof in the sense of something that is clearly shown to be.

9:2 Provoked The verb *erethizō* is found only twice in the NT. In Col. 3:21 it has the bad sense, "provoke" or "irritate." But here it is used in the good sense of "stir" or "stimulate." Since "provoke" usually carries a bad connotation today, "stir" is more satisfactory here.

3 In Vain The verb is *kenoō*, which comes from the adjective *kenos*, "empty." So it means "made empty" (NASB).

5 Make Up Beforehand This is one word in Greek, the verb *prokatartizō* (only here in NT). The idea is: "finish the arrangements" (NIV).

Bounty The noun *eulogia* occurs twice in this verse and twice in verse 6 ("bountifully"). Its regular meaning is "blessing," and that is the way it is translated 11 out of its 16 occurrences in the NT. (In Rom. 16:18 it is rendered "fair speech," its etymological sense.)

Arndt and Gingrich point out the transition to its meaning in these two verses. They write: "Since the concept of blessing carries with it the idea of bounty, *eulogia* gains the meaning *bountiful gift, bounty*" (p. 323).

Beyer finds a connection with the verb "bless" (*eulogeō*) in Matt. 5:44—"Bless them which curse you." He writes: "Because it springs from such unconditional love, *eulogia* can also be used ... for the gift which Paul seeks as a collection for Jerusalem" (TDNT, 2:763). "Generous gift" (NIV) is perhaps slightly more contemporary than "bountiful gift" (NASB).

Whereof Ye Had Notice Before This is all one word in Greek, *proepēngelmenēn*. The verb *propangellō* is found only here and in Rom. 1:2, where it is translated "promised afore." That is probably the correct meaning here. In the active the verb means "to announce before." But in the middle, as in both these references, it means "to promise before" (A-S, p. 380). Arndt and Gingrich give only the second meaning and translate the passage "the bountiful gift which was (previously) promised" (p. 712).

Surprisingly, Plummer writes: "It is not quite clear that the participle means 'promised long before' by the Corinthians. It might mean 'announced long before' by St. Paul" (p. 255). But almost all recent versions and commentaries adopt the first meaning.

7 Cheerful Giver The Greek word for "cheerful" is *hilaros* (only here in NT), from which comes "hilarious." God loves a hilarious giver! It is a simple fact that when people give "generously" (v. 6, NIV), the Lord's blessing descends.

259

8 *Always . . . All* This is one of the most
striking verses in the NT—"all . . . always . . .
all . . . all . . . every." And it is just as forceful in
the Greek: *"pasan . . . panti pantote pasan . . .
pan."* Only Paul could have written such a passage; it exactly reflects his enthusiastic personality.

10 *Minister* The verb is *chorēgeō* (only here
and 1 Pet. 4:11), which comes from *choros*, "chorus," and *hegēomai*, "lead." So it meant: "1. to
lead a *choros*. 2. to defray the cost of a *choros*,"
and then in later writers metaphorically, "to
supply, furnish abundantly" (A-S, p. 482). So
the proper translation here is "supply." The
verb "ministereth" ("supplies") is the intensive
compound *epichorēgeō* (five times in NT).
"Minister" (KJV) should be "will supply."
The verb is future and expresses not a wish but
a promise.

Fruits "Seed" and "bread" indicate that
grain is meant, not "fruits." The Greek word is
genēma (only here in Paul). It comes from the
verb *ginomai*, which means "come into being."
The correct translation here is "harvest"
(NASB, NIV).

12 *Service* For a discussion of *leitourgia* see
the comments on Phil. 2:17.

13 *Experiment* The correct meaning of
dokimē is not "experiment" but "proof" (NASB).
This noun comes from the verb *dokimazō*,
which meant (1) "test," (2) "prove by testing,"
(3) "approve as the result of testing." Plummer
(ICC) comments here: "Affliction tested the reality of the Macedonians' Christianity (viii. 2), benevolence will be a proof in the case of the Corinthians" (p. 266). *Dokimē* is translated "trial"
in 8:2, but "proof" in 2:9; 13:3, and Phil. 2:22.
That is what it should be here.

15 *Unspeakable* *Anekdiēgētos* (only here in
NT) contains four elements: the alpha-
privative *a-*; *ek*, "out"; *dia*, "through"; and
hēgeomai, "lead." The verb *diēgeomai* means "to
set out in detail, describe" (A-S, p. 35), or "inde-
scribable" (NASB, NIV).

10:1 *Base* The adjective *tapeinos* originally meant "low." Then it came to mean
"poor, lowly, undistinguished," and in a bad
sense "subservient, abject". (AG, p. 811). It is in
the last sense that it was used here by Paul's opponents in Corinth. This is brought out in the
NIV by putting "timid" and "bold" in quotation
marks, to indicate that these were terms applied to Paul by his critics. By using "meek"
here, the NASB confuses it with "meekness"
(first clause), which is an entirely different
term in Greek.

1–2 *Bold* In the last part of verse 1 and the
first part of verse 2 "bold" is the verb *tharreō*,
which means "be bold or courageous." But in
the middle of verse 2 "bold" is the verb *tolmaō*,
which has much the same meaning. Thayer differentiates them in this way: *"Tharreō* denotes
confidence in one's own strength or capacity,
tolmaō boldness or daring in undertaking" (p.
628). To distinguish the two words, the NASB
helpfully uses "courageous" for *tolmaō*.

4 *Strongholds* The word *ochyrōma* (only
here in NT) means a "stronghold" or "fortress,"
and then metaphorically "anything on which
one relies." Thayer goes on to say that here the
word is used metaphorically for "the arguments and reasonings by which a disputant endeavors to fortify his opinion and defend it
against his opponent" (p. 471).

5 *Imaginations* In and of itself *logismos*
simply means "a reasoning, thought" (A-S, p.
270), and it is usually translated in Rom. 2:15
(the only other place it occurs in the NT) as
"thoughts." But here it is used in a bad sense
for "the thoughts of a reason which in its self-
vaunting shuts itself off from God" (Heidland,
TDNT, 4:287).

7 *Outward Appearance* The Greek has
one word, *prosōpon*, which means "face." Both
the Hebrew and Greek words for "face" are
used in a variety of ways.
"After the outward appearance" is *kata
prosōpon*. In verse 1 the same expression is
translated "in presence" (NASB and NIV have
"face to face with"). But here it means "on the
surface of things" (NIV).
In the KJV the first sentence of this verse is
a question. But most versions today treat it as
an affirmation, which is better. In the early
Greek manuscripts there are no punctuation
marks, and the Greek uses the same order of
words for a question as for a statement—instead of reversing the order as we do in English. Since in the second person plural of the
present tense the same form is used for the imperative as for the indicative, this sentence
can be taken as a command: "Look at what is
before your eyes" (RSV). All three possible
ways of taking it are meaningful.

8 Destruction The noun *kathairesis* comes from the verb *kathaireō*, which means "to put down by force, pull down, destroy" (A-S, p. 222). So it literally means "a pulling down."

The verb is found in verse 5, where it is translated in the KJV "casting down." The noun is rendered "pulling down" in verse 4, but "destruction" here and in 13:10 (the only three places where it occurs in NT). Since the Greek word for "edification" (*oikodomē*) means "building up," the NIV is especially good here: "the authority the Lord gave us for building you up rather than pulling you down."

9 Terrify The verb *ekphobeō* (only here in NT) means "frighten, terrify" (AG, p. 246)—from *phobos*, "fear." But "frighten" (NIV) seems to fit better here. Letters are more likely to frighten people than to terrify them.

11 Absent . . . Present These two contrasting words in English come from the Latin. But they are also somewhat parallel to the Greek words here: *apontes*, "being away," and *parontes*, "being beside."

12 Make . . . of the Number This is one word in the Greek, the infinitive of the verb *engkrinō* (only here in NT). *Krinō* means "judge" and *en* "among" (with the plural). So this compound verb means "*to reckon among, judge among . . . to judge one worthy of being admitted* to a certain class" (Thayer, p. 167). This is well expressed by "class" (NASB) or "classify" (NIV).

"Classify or compare" (NIV) is in the Greek *engkrinai . . . synkrinai.* Paul is fond of such play on words.

13 Rule The word *canōn* is found three times in this chapter. In verses 13 and 15 it is translated "rule" and in verse 16 "line." It is also translated "rule" in the only other place (in NT) where it occurs (Gal. 6:16).

Thayer defines *canōn* as follows: "Properly a rod or straight piece of rounded wood to which anything is fastened to keep it straight . . . a measuring rod, rule; a carpenter's line or measuring tape," and so in 2 Cor. 10: "a definitely bounded or fixed space within the limits of which one's power or influence is confined; the province assigned to one; one's sphere of activity" (p. 324). But in Gal. 6:16 it is used in the sense of a rule or standard (*ibid.*).

Beyer takes exception to this. He would apply the second sense to 2 Cor. 10:13–16, which he calls "a linguistically difficult passage." He says of Paul: "He thus has a canon or standard

for his work and for the associated claim to apostolic authority which he has not conferred on himself but received from God." He concludes: "The measure given to Paul is not, then, a sphere marked out in space in which he alone is to work. It is the orientation laid upon him, the *charis* granted to him . . . and the blessing which God has caused to rest on his missionary activity" (TDNT, 3:599).

After discussing the idea of "sphere" (cf. NASB), Plummer comments: "But *kanōn* is generally used of *length*, and *to metron* [measure] *tou canonos* would mean 'the length of one's tether,' the length of the radius from one's centre. In this case it would mean the distance which God told the Apostle to go in his missionary work" (p. 287).

This seems to fit the passage well. But perhaps we should accept both concepts: "sphere" and "rule" or "standard."

17 Glory As in other places where we have met the verb *kauchaomai*, we would note that the more accurate translation today is "boast." The word occurs 5 times each in Romans and 1 Corinthians, and 21 times in 2 Corinthians. Outside of Paul's Epistles the term is used only by James (1:19; 4:16).

11:1 Would to God This phrase translates one word in the Greek, *ophelon*—"2 aor. of *opheilō*, without the augment . . . used to express a fruitless wish . . . *would that*" (A-S, p. 330). This is an example of the fondness of the KJV translators for the expression, "Would to God" even though it is not in the Greek (cf. also "God forbid," 15 times). The correct translation is simply "I wish" (RSV, NASB), or "I hope" (NIV).

Folly? Aside from Mark 7:22, the Greek word *aphrosynē* is found only in this chapter (vv. 1, 17, 21). It comes from *aphrōn*, which means "senseless, foolish." Probably "foolishness" is more contemporary than "folly." In Mark the NIV uses "folly" because a bad moral connotation is clearly suggested by the context.

Ye The last clause of this verse is in the form of an imperative in the KJV and RSV, but of an indicative in the NASB and NIV. Once more we have a second person plural (*anechesthe*), which can be taken either way. It is difficult here to decide between the two.

2 Espoused The verb is *harmozō* (only here in NT). It comes from *harmos*, "a joining," the origin of our word "harmony." Today we espouse a cause, not a wife. So "betroth" (NASB) is better. The idea here is that of joining one person to another in marriage.

3 Simplicity The KJV has only "simplicity," but the NASB adds "and purity" (cf. RSV, NIV). Why?

The answer is that the added words are found in the oldest Greek manuscripts—Papyrus 46 (third century), Vaticanus and Sinaiticus (fourth century), and Bezae (fifth century)—as well as in the best minuscule manuscripts of the Middle Ages (33, 81, 88).

4 Might The KJV has: "Ye might . . . bear with." But the Greek is *anechesthe* again, probably better translated as a statement, "you bear" (NASB, cf. RSV, NIV).

5 Very Chiefest Paul takes his stand as not being a whit behind the "very chiefest" apostles. The Greek adverb *hyperlian* is found only here and in 12:11, in a parallel context. It is compounded of *hyper*, "above," and *lian*, "very, exceedingly." So it means "over much; pre-eminently" (Thayer, p. 641). Arndt and Gingrich suggest the translation, "super-apostles" for the combination expression here, and this was adopted in the NIV.

To whom is Paul referring? Arndt and Gingrich write: "These are either the original apostles . . . or, perhaps with more probability, the opponents of Paul in Corinth" (p. 849).

Plummer agrees with this. He says: "It is improbable that St. Paul would use such an expression as *hoi hyperlian apostoloi* of any of the Twelve." He adds that "there is little doubt that the phrase . . . is a sarcastic description of the Judaizing leaders, who claimed to be acting with the authority of the Twelve against one who had no such authority" (p. 298).

6 Rude The noun *idiōtēs* (only here and in Acts 4:13; 1 Cor. 14:16, 23, 24) comes from the adjective *idios*, "one's own"—that is, what is private and personal. So the noun means first "a private person" and then "one without professional knowledge, unskilled" (A-S, p. 213). The last definition fits well (cf. NASB). The NIV has here: "I may not be a trained speaker, but I do have knowledge." The current use of "rude" does not fit.

7 Offence The Greek word here is *hamartia*, which simply means "sin" and is translated that way 173 out of the 174 times it occurs in the NT. Why the translators chose to render it "offence" in just this one place is a mystery.

Freely *Dōrean* is the accusative of *dōrea*, "a gift," used as an adverb. So it means "as a gift, without payment, gratis" (AG, p. 209). "Free of charge" (NIV) communicates this more accurately than "freely." Today preaching "freely" means speaking "with freedom."

9 Chargeable *Katanarkaō* is a rare verb in Greek literature, but is found here and in 12:13, 14, where it is translated "be burdensome." That is probably the meaning here. Literally it means "to grow numb," and so metaphorically "to be inactive, be burdensome" (A-S, p. 236). Etymologically it is unrelated to the adjective *abarēs* (only here in NT), which in the last part of this verse is translated "kept from being burdensome." The NASB and NIV have in the first instance, "I was not a burden to anyone," and in the second place, "I (have) kept myself from being a burden to you."

13 False Apostles This is one word in Greek, *pseudapostolos* (only here in NT). Paul first calls his opponents in Corinth "super-apostles" (v. 5). Then he becomes more specific and calls them "false apostles," because they were not sent by Christ, as they claimed to be.

13, 14, 15 Transform Elsewhere in the KJV "transform" is found only once—Rom. 12:2, where it is the translation of the verb *metamorphoō*, which means "change form." But the verb here is *metaschēmatizō*, which means "change appearance." This is conveyed better by "disguise" (NASB) or "masquerade" (NIV).

16, 19 Fool(s) Besides half a dozen other places, the adjective *aphrōn* is found twice in verse 16 and once in 19, plus 12:6, 11. It is usually treated as a substantive, "fool." Hart says that the term expresses "want of mental sanity and sobriety, a reckless and inconsiderate habit of mind" (quoted in A-S, p. 72).

Bertram writes (TDNT, 9:231):

> In 2 C. 11 and 12 *aphrōn* and *aphrosynē* are used in self-criticism. The apostle's *aphrosynē* is that in the difficult conflicts with the church or congregation he apparently or provisionally sets himself on the carnal plane of self-boasting rather than on the spiritual plane. This is what Paul has in view when he speaks of his *aphrosynē* in 2 C. 11:1. In the situation at Corinth foolish boasting . . . before God and men has become necessary for him, 11:16f.

19, 20 Suffer This is again the verb *anechō* (see vv. 1 and 4, where it is three times correctly translated "bear with," as in NASB). In verse 20, "suffer" can be very misleading, suggesting that the readers are undergoing pain. This is not the idea. The NIV helpfully has "put up with" in all four verses. That is the way we would say it today.

23 Fool In parentheses we have the statement: "I speak as a fool." This is not *aphrōn*, but *paraphronōn*, participial form of the compound verb *paraphroneō* (only here in NT), which means "to be beside oneself, be deranged" (A-S, p. 343). The sentence may be translated "I speak as if insane" (NASB), or "I am out of my mind to talk like this" (NIV).

26 Perils The word *kindynos* occurs only in Rom. 8:35 (once) and 8 times in this verse. It means "danger" or "risk" (AG, p. 433).

27 Painfulness *Mochthos* (found also in 1 Thess. 2:9; 2 Thess. 3:8) means "toil, labour, hardship, distress" (A-S, p. 297). Comparing *kopos* ("weariness") with this, Thayer says that *kopos* gives prominence to the fatigue and *mochthos* to the hardship (p. 355).

Watchings *Agrypnia* occurs only here and in 6:5 (see discussion there). Its primary meaning is sleeplessness (cf. NASB, NIV).

Fastings *Nēsteia*, usually indicating fasting, probably means lack of available food here and in 6:5 (see comments there). It is properly translated "without food" (NASB, NIV).

33 Basket *Sagarnē* literally means "a plaited rope," and so a basket made of ropes. The word is found only here in the NT.

12:1 Expedient *Sympheron* means "profitable" or "advantageous." The word "expedient" hardly communicates that today. The first part of the verse may rather literally be rendered: "Boasting is necessary, though it is not profitable" (NASB). The whole verse is well expressed: "I must go on boasting. Although there is nothing to be gained, I will go on to visions and revelations from the Lord" (NIV).

4 Paradise This comes directly from the Greek *paradeisos* (here, Luke 23:43; Rev. 2:7), which is thought to be of Persian origin. Among the Greeks it was first used by the historian Xenophon in reference to the parks of Persian kings and nobles (A-S, p. 338). He describes it

as shady and well watered. And so it came to mean "a garden, pleasureground; grove, park." Here it is used for "an upper region in the heavens" (Thayer, p. 480).

Joachim Jeremias devotes eight pages to a discussion of this word. He asserts that it is "a loan word from old Persian" (TDNT, 5:765), and adds: "Already by the 3rd. cent. B.C. it can then be used generally for a 'park'" (p. 766). The Persian term was adopted into Hebrew and Aramaic, but only in a secular sense. It was used for the Garden of Eden in Genesis 2.

Jeremias agrees with other writers (e.g., Plummer) in saying that we cannot be sure whether Paul equates "the third heaven" (v. 2) with Paradise (v. 4). It seems to us that he does.

7 Thorn The word *skolops* (only here in NT) means "something pointed." In classical Greek it meant "a stake." But in the Septuagint it clearly is used, for the first time, in the sense of "splinter" or "thorn"—never for stake (TDNT, 7:410–11). And this is unquestionably its meaning in the papyri (VGT, pp. 578–79). "In the flesh" suggests it was a physical affliction, probably chronic malaria or poor eyesight. The idea of pain seems suggested by the context.

Buffet The verb *kolaphizō* comes from the noun *kolaphos*, "the knuckles, the closed fist." So it literally meant "to strike with the fist" (A-S, p. 252). Since thorns do not buffet a person, it seems that "torment" (NIV) is justified here.

10 Reproaches The word *hybris* occurs here and in Acts 27:10 (of physical disaster). Thayer says that it means "insolence, impudence, pride," and then "a wrong springing from insolence, an injury, affront, insult." He adds this comment: "in Greek usage the mental injury and wantonness of its infliction being prominent" (p. 633). It seems that "insult" conveys this better than "reproach."

12 Patience, Signs, Wonders, Deeds The KJV of this verse sounds as if the signs of an apostle were wrought by Paul in four ways: patience, signs, wonders, and mighty deeds. But the Greek clearly names only three. The correct translation is found in the NASB: "The signs of a true apostle were performed among you with all perseverance, by signs and wonders and miracles." *Hypomonē*, usually translated "patience" in the KJV, actually means "perseverance."

Three words are here used for miracles, as in the Synoptic Gospels. The first is *semeiois*, "signs." The second is *terasin*, "wonders." The third is *dynamesin*—literally, "powers," or "powerful works." *Dynamesin* is the term usually translated "miracles" in the Synoptic Gospels and Acts, as here in the NASB and NIV.

The miracles of Christ and His apostles were "powerful works." But they were also "signs," signifying a spiritual truth. And they were called "wonders" because they excited wonder in those who saw them.

16 Crafty The adjective *panourgos* (only here in NT) literally means "ready to do anything." In classical Greek it was used mainly in a bad sense. But in the Septuagint it is used frequently in the Book of Proverbs in a good sense—"clever" or "prudent."

What does Paul mean by his use of it here? Arndt and Gingrich (p. 613) suggest a logical explanation: "Paul says, taking up an expression used by his opponents . . . crafty fellow that I am" (see NASB, NIV).

20 Debates, Envyings, Wraths, Strifes, Backbiting, Whisperings, Swellings, Tumults Most of these terms do not convey correct meanings today. The first is *eris*, which basically means "strife" (NASB) or "quarreling" (NIV). The second, *zelos*, means "jealousy." The third, *thymoi*, suggests a boiling over. It is better rendered as "angry tempers" (NASB) or "outbursts of anger" (NIV). The fourth, *eritheiai*, suggests "factions" or "disputes." The fifth, *katalaliai*, literally means acts of speaking against. It may be translated "slanders" (NASB). The sixth, *psithyrismoi* (only here in NT) does literally mean "whisperings," but today we would call this "gossip" (NASB, NIV). The seventh, *physiōseis* (only here in NT), in the singular means "a puffing up," and so, "*swelling* with pride" (A-S, p. 476). Perhaps "arrogance" (NASB, NIV) best expresses it today. The last, *akatastasiai*, literally means "disorders" (cf. NIV) or "disturbances" (NASB).

Paul feared that he would meet these things when he returned to Corinth. No wonder he dreaded to go.

13:1 Mouth The second sentence of this verse is a free quotation from Deut. 19:15. Probably the meaning is clear enough. Today, however, we would say "by the testimony" (NASB, NIV).

Word Abbott-Smith notes that *hrēma* is used "properly, of that which is said or spoken," and so "a word." Then it was extended to mean "a saying, statement." Parallel to the Hebrew *davar*, it finally came to be used, as here, for "a

thing, matter," as "that which is the subject of speech" (p. 397). In the KJV "matter" is used in Deut. 19:15, where the Septuagint has *hrēma*. What is stated or reported has to be confirmed by two or three witnesses.

2 Heretofore Have Sinned The verb *proamartanō* is found only here and in 12:21 (the immediate context). Properly it means "to sin before" (A-S, p. 378)—from *pro*, "before," and *hamartanō*, "sin." In 12:21 it is translated "have sinned already," and in 13:2 "heretofore have sinned."

In both cases, however, it is the perfect active participle, which not only indicates completed action but also emphasizes a continuing state. So these incorrigible opponents of Paul at Corinth were still sinning.

The first part of the verse in the KJV is a literal translation of the Greek; but it makes rather awkward English and can be misunderstood. It is given more clearly in the NIV: "I already gave you a warning when I was with you the second time. I now repeat it while absent. . . ."

3 Mighty At the end of verse 3 we find the verb *dynamai* translated "is mighty," whereas in verse 4 the noun *dynamis* is twice rendered "power." By using "is powerful" in verse 3 the NIV points up the connection.

5 Examine . . . Prove The two verbs are *peirazō* and *dokimazō*. Thayer defines the first as "*to try, make trial of, test:* (someone), for the purpose of ascertaining his quality" (p. 498). The second, he says, means "*to test, examine, prove, scrutinize* (to see whether a thing be genuine or not), as metals" (p. 154).

While these two terms seem to be used rather interchangeably in the NT, Trench warns us that "they are not perfectly synonymous." He goes on to say: "As employed in the N.T. *dokimazein* almost always implies that the proof is victoriously surmounted, the *proved* is also *approved* . . . just as in English we speak of *tried* men . . . meaning not merely those who have been tested, but who have stood the test" (p. 278).

On the other hand, *peirazō* "means properly no more than to make experience of . . . to pierce or search into." Trench continues: "It came next to signify the trying intentionally, and with the purpose of discovering what of good or evil, of power or weakness, was in a person or thing . . . or . . . revealing the same to the tried themselves; as when St. Paul addresses the Corinthians . . . 'examine yourselves' " (p. 280).

The two verbs may be translated "exam ine . . . prove" (KJV), "test . . . examine" (NASB), or "examine . . . test" (RSV, NIV). They have much the same meaning here.

5, 6, 7 *Reprobates*   The word is *adokimoi*. It means "rejected after testing." See discussion at Rom. 1:28. The term "reprobates" does not convey that meaning today. We would now probably say "fail the test" (NASB, NIV). Paul affirms that he has not failed the test, and he hopes that his readers will not.

In the middle of verse 7 we have "approved" and at the end "reprobates." The Greek had "*dokimoi . . . adokimoi*." The NASB expresses this play on words by using "approved . . . un-approved." On the other hand, the NIV pre-serves the continuity of the three occurrences of *adokimoi* by having in verse 7: "stood the test . . . may seem to have failed."

9 *Wish*   The verb is *euchomai*, which is cor-rectly translated "pray" in verse 7. That is the only meaning that Abbott-Smith's *Lexicon* gives for this word, though others allow "wish." But we would agree with Greeven when he writes: "In 2 C. 13:7 Paul expressly mentions God, to whom he prays that the Corinthians may do no evil. We should understand v. 9 also of intercessory prayer rather than as a mere wish" (TDNT, 2:776).

The verb *euchomai* occurs only 7 times in the NT. Already the compound *proseuchomai* had begun to supplant the simple verb in the Septuagint, and in the NT it became dominant (87 times).

9, 11 *Perfection*   In verse 11 it is the verb *katartizō*, discussed at Rom. 9:22. In verse 9 it is the derivative noun *katartisis* (only here in NT). On the latter Delling writes: "Similarly *katartisis* denotes inner strength, whether of the community (*oikodomē*) in its organic rela-tionship, or of the character of its members, i.e., their maturity as Christians (2 C. 13:9)" (TDNT, 1:476). Both "perfection" (KJV, NIV) and "completion" (NASB) fit well here. But the verb in verse 11 must be translated consis-tently with this.

10 *Sharpness*   It is the adverb *apotomōs* (only here and Titus 1:13). Abbott-Smith says it means: "abruptly, curtly," and so "sharply, se-verely" (p. 55). Plummer says of Paul: "He writes sharply, that he may not have to act sharply" (p. 378).

Edification . . .   Destruction   The first noun is *oikodomē*, which literally means "build-ing up." The second is *kathairesis* (see com-ments on 10:4, 8), which means "pulling down." So the correct translation here is: "for building up and not for tearing down" (NASB; cf. NIV).

Galatians

Paul's Epistle to the Galatians ranks second only to Romans in its theological importance. But it served a unique and invaluable purpose in pointing Martin Luther to the truth which he embodied in the Protestant Reformation. He himself said of it: "The Epistle to the Galatians is my epistle. To it I am as it were in wedlock."

The case of John Bunyan is also striking. Seeking desperately for deliverance from his awful sense of sin, he found an old copy of Martin Luther's *Commentary on Galatians*. Here is what he says about that experience:

> When I had but a little way perused, I found my condition in his experience so largely and profoundly handled, as if his book had been written out of my heart. I prefer this book of Martin Luther on the Galatians (excepting the Holy Bible) before all the books that ever I have seen, as most fit for a wounded conscience.

Paul wrote to free the Galatian Christians from the bonds of Judaistic legalism in his day. Martin Luther wrote to free the people of his generation from the yoke of Roman Catholicism, with its religion of works-righteousness. The message of the epistle is still very pertinent. The purpose of these studies is to open some word windows for glimpsing that message more clearly.

1:1 *Apostle* Our English word is a transliteration of the Greek *apostolos*, which comes from the verb *apostellō*, "send away, send on an errand, send with a commission." The earliest use of *apostolos* was for a fleet, an expedition. Herodotus used it for a messenger, or one sent on a mission. That was its common meaning in New Testament times.

Though used rarely in classical Greek, it occurs some 80 times in the NT. Eight of these occurrences are in the Synoptic Gospels. Cremer comments: "Perhaps it was just the rare occurrence of the word in profane Greek that made it all the more appropriate as the distinctive appellation of 'the Twelve' whom Christ chose to be His witnesses" (p. 530). In the Synoptic Gospels (mostly Luke) it regularly carries the technical sense of one of the Twelve. (In John's Gospel it is found only in 13:16, where it is translated "he that is sent.")

In the first part of the Book of Acts this usage continues. But in connection with the Gentile mission we find a broadening of the term. In Acts 14:14 we read of "the apostles Barnabas, and Paul." Since these were the two great missionaries sent out by the church at Antioch, we find here a suggestion of the modern application of the term. Today an apostle is a missionary, commissioned and sent forth. In a very real sense every preacher is an apostle. In a still more definite sense every true missionary of Christ is an apostle.

But that does not exhaust the meaning of the term. It has been suggested that the best translation for *apostolos* is "envoy." In the volume on Galatians in the *New International Commentary on the New Testament*, Ridderbos has this to say: "An *apostle* is a minister plenipotentiary" (p. 40). In connection with Gal. 1:1 he comments: "Paul is God's own and special ambassador" (p. 41).

No wonder Paul asserts his apostolic authority in opposing the heretical teachers in the churches of Galatia. He did not wear a badge pinned on him by some earthly potentate or pope. He carried in his heart the consciousness of a divine call and commission to be Christ's ambassador to men. What greater authority could one ask?

2 Church The Greek word for church is *ekklēsia*. This comes from the verb *ekkaleō* (*ek*, "out"; *kaleō*, "call"), "call out." It has therefore often been emphasized that the Church is a body of "called out ones."

But the first question that should be asked is: What was the common meaning of the term in Paul's day? Because usage, rather than etymology, is the main factor in determining the meaning of a word at any given period or in any particular place.

Ekklēsia was the name applied to the assembly of free citizens in a Greek city. We find the term used in exactly that way in Acts 19:32, 39, 41 (particularly as in v. 39 of a "lawful assembly"; that is, one regularly convened). This would be the usage most familiar to the Gentile readers of Paul's epistles.

But there is another important background. The Septuagint (Greek translation of the OT, made 200 years before Christ) uses *ekklēsia* for the "congregation" or "assembly" of Israel. This usage is reflected in the NT, in Acts 7:38.

In the time of Christ the Jewish gathering for worship was called the synagogue. Perhaps it was partly because of the severe persecutions from the Jews that the Christians chose *ekklēsia* rather than *synagogē* as the designation for their place of worship and for the congregation gathered there.

In the NT we find a distinct, twofold use of *ekklēsia:* "(I) The entire congregation of all who are called by and to Christ, who are in the fellowship of His salvation—the Church. (II) The N.T. churches as confined to particular places" (Cremer, pp. 334–35). The latter sense is obviously the one in which the word is used in this passage.

3 Grace The Greek *charis* is one of the most beautiful and meaningful words in the NT. Abbott-Smith's *Manual Greek Lexicon of the New Testament* gives an excellent summary of its varied meanings, which we quote in part:

> 1. Objectively, that which causes favourable regard, *gracefulness, grace, loveliness* of form, *graciousness* of speech. 2. Subjectively, (a) on the part of the giver, *grace, graciousness, kindness, goodwill, favour*; esp. in N.T. of the divine *favour, grace*, with emphasis on its freeness and universality; (b) on the part of the receiver, a sense of favour received, *thanks, gratitude* (p. 479).

A rapid check of Moulton and Geden's *Concordance to the Greek Testament* shows that *charis* occurs in all the NT books except Matthew, Mark, and 1 John. Paul uses it dozens of times in his Epistles.

The first emphasis of this word was on physical gracefulness. But as usual, the NT gives largest place to the highest meaning. Cremer writes: "*Charis* has been distinctively appropriated in the N.T. to designate the relation and conduct of God towards sinful man as revealed in and through Christ, especially as an act of *spontaneous favour*" (p. 574).

It would be impossible to compass the tremendous scope of this term or even to delineate its particular theological signification. Here we must content ourselves with two brief observations.

First, we fear that too many conservatives glory in the orthodoxy of their emphasis on the wonderful grace of God shown in the forgiveness of our sins—the unmerited favor of God in pardoning our guilt and accepting us as His children—without facing all the implications of this beautiful term. It is not enough to thank God for His grace. We must ask, Does that grace make us more gracious? We read in the OT that God is "gracious." When Jesus spoke, the people wondered at the "gracious words" that proceeded from His mouth (Luke 4:22). Has our preaching ever produced that reaction? But, more importantly, do we rightly represent God by being gracious in all our relations with our fellowmen? To be boorish in our personal relations in life shows a tragic lack of the "grace" of God, however orthodox we may be and whatever experience we may profess.

The other observation is that this term is used for "the grace of giving." In 2 Cor. 8:7 Paul urges his readers to "abound in this grace also." In 1 Cor. 16:3 the word "liberality"—meaning an offering—is *charis* in the original. Since God has so freely given to us, we should be liberal in giving to the work of His kingdom. The greatest incentive to giving perhaps lies in this word "grace."

Peace The word "peace" (*eirēnē*) means more than freedom from outward strife. It means essentially an inner harmony, something that can be brought about only by the grace of God.

Someone has defined grace as meaning "the divine adequacy." We would like to suggest that peace means "the consciousness of the divine adequacy." As Christians we have adequate resources at our disposal, in the grace of an infinite God, to meet all the emergencies of life. But we only feel peaceful as we are conscious of that adequacy.

Paul, of course, had in mind the Hebrew word for peace, *shalom*, which meant "total well-being for time and eternity" (IB, 10:447). That was the kind of "peace" that he wished for his readers. And he knew full well that that kind of peace could come to them only from "God our father and the Lord Jesus Christ." The "God of peace" is the only source of true peace.

4 Sins The Greek word here for sin (*hamartia*) means "missing the mark." It is derived from the verb *hamartanō*, which is used in Homer some hundred times of a warrior hurling his spear but missing his foe. In classical Greek the verb came to be used for missing the right, going wrong, sinning. The noun was used in the sense of "guilt, sin," though more frequently for "fault, failure." In the NT it always has the theological connotation. Stahlin says that the NT "uses *hamartia* to denote the determination of human nature in hostility to God" (TDNT, 1:295).

Cremer has some pertinent comments. He says that *hamartia* "would seem to denote primarily, *not sin considered as an action, but sin considered as the quality of action*, that is, *sin generically* . . . Sin is not merely the quality of an action, but a principle manifesting itself in the conduct of the subject" (pp. 100–101). Paul prefers to use other words for sinful acts, reserving *hamartia* largely for the generic idea of sin as a principle, what we call the carnal nature. However, in the plural, as here, it may denote sinful acts as such.

World The word translated "world" in the KJV is *aiōn*, which properly means "age" and is so rendered in most recent translations.

Originally *aiōn* meant "lifetime," the duration of a human life. Then it came to be used for a "generation," which is a life span. Finally it was expanded to mean unlimited duration, eternity.

In verse 4 it is used for "the present evil age," which is under the domination of "the prince of this world" (John 12:31; 14:30; 16:11). In John it is *cosmos*, this world-system. But here it is the time element which is indicated. It is the period of evil rule.

In verse 5 the expression "for ever and ever" is literally "to the ages of the ages." This is the fullest phrase in the NT to indicate eternity. What a glorious thought that for the saints eternity will be a never ending succession of age after age of bliss and blessing. Certainly we ought to put up with this "light affliction which

is but for a moment" (2 Cor. 4:17), while living in this present evil age, with our hopes set steadfastly on that blessed life that shall never end.

6–7 Another Gospel The language of these verses seems strange. Paul writes: "I marvel that ye are so soon removed (lit., removing) from him that called you into the grace of Christ unto another gospel: which is not another." What does he mean by saying that it is "another" and "not another"?

Two different Greek words are used in verses 6 and 7. The KJV translates them both by "another." Recent versions more correctly read "different" in verse 6 and "another" in verse 7. The first is *heteros*, the second *allos*. The distinction between these two words is well pointed out by Trench in his *Synonyms of the New Testament*. He writes: "*Allos*, identical with the Latin 'alius,' is the numerically distinct. . . . But *heteros*, equivalent to the Latin 'alter' . . . superadds the notion of qualitative difference. One is 'divers,' the other 'diverse' " (p. 357).

When Jesus promised another Comforter (John 14:16) the word *allos* is used. The Holy Spirit would be a distinct Personality; but He would not be a different (*heteros*) kind of Paraclete. Rather, He would be another of the same kind (*allos*).

Now the language of Paul is clear. He bemoans the fact that the Galatian Christians are turning to a "different" gospel, which is really "not another" gospel. What they were now following was not the glad, good news that men can be saved through faith in Christ but the very depressing idea that one must work for his salvation. Legalistic Judaism did not present another way of salvation. It was heterodoxy, "different opinion"; not orthodoxy, "straight opinion." There is only one true gospel, Paul would say, only one way of salvation. That is not to be found in the law, but in Christ.

6 Gospel Our English word comes from the old Anglo-Saxon *godspell*, "good tidings." The Greek word is *euangelion*. A cognate noun is *euangelistēs*, which we have taken over into English as "evangelist."

The word *euangelion* was first used in classical Greek for "a reward for good tidings," or "sacrifice for good tidings." Later Greek writers use it for the good news itself. In the NT it carries the specialized sense of "the good tidings of the kingdom of God and of salvation through Christ."

In his excellent article on *euangelion* in the

Theological Dictionary of the New Testament Gerhard Friedrich writes: "For Paul the heart of the good news is the story of Jesus and His suffering, death and resurrection" (2:730). He also declares: "The Gospel does not merely bear witness to salvation history; it is itself salvation history. It breaks into the life of man, refashions it and creates communities" (2:731).

The verb *euangelizō*, which gives us "evangelize," occurs many times in the NT. Usually it is translated "preach" or "preach the gospel," whichever fits more smoothly into the context.

But there are two passages that illustrate the original meaning of the word: "bring glad tidings." One is Luke 1:19. The angel Gabriel said to Zacharias: "I . . . am sent . . . to *shew* thee these *glad tidings*." The other is 1 Thess. 3:6. Here Paul says that Timothy came from Thessalonica "and *brought* us *good tidings* of your faith and charity." Aside from these two passages the word usually has the technical meaning of publishing the good tidings of the gospel.

6-7 Removed, Pervert   There are two interesting Greek words in verses 6 and 7. The first is *metatithesthe;* the second, *metastrepsai.* In the RSV the former is translated "you are deserting"; the second, "to pervert." The KJV also has "pervert" for the second, but "ye are removed" for the first. The RSV translation suggests that the Galatians were deserters, and their teachers perverters.

The first word, *metatithēmi*, means "transfer to another place, change." Vincent notes that in classical Greek it is used "of altering a treaty, changing an opinion, deserting an army" (WS, 4:85). It is this last usage which has suggested the striking translation of the RSV.

The other word, *metastrephō*, means "turn about, change, reverse"; and in an evil sense, "pervert, corrupt." Vine (3:180) says the word means "to transform into something of an opposite character." As an illustration of its meaning here we might cite Acts 2:20, "the sun shall be turned into darkness." That is what the false teachers in Galatia were doing: turning the glorious sunlight of God's truth into the darkness of error. They were transforming the gospel of Christ into something that was not a gospel at all. That is the keynote of verses 6–10. These Galatian Christians were being duped and deceived by this erroneous teaching and were deserting Christ and His free gospel of salvation.

8 Angel   Paul goes so far as to say that even if "an angel from heaven" should preach to them a gospel contrary to what he had preached, "let

him be accursed." It is difficult to imagine what stronger language he could have used to assert the utter uniqueness of the gospel he preached.

The word "angel" is taken directly from the Greek *angelos,* which means "messenger." It occurs about 200 times in the NT. More than one-third of these instances (some 76) are found in the Book of Revelation. Luke also refers frequently to angels in his Gospel and Acts.

In practically all instances the word is transliterated as "angel." But the literal translation "messenger" occurs in 7 places in the NT. Three of them are in the quotation of Mal. 3:1 in Matthew, Mark, and Luke. A fourth case is found in 2 Cor. 12:7, where Paul refers to his thorn in the flesh as "the messenger of Satan."

The other 3 occurrences are clear examples of the simple meaning "messenger." In Luke 7:24 we read of the messengers (*angeloi*) whom John the Baptist sent to interrogate Jesus. In Luke 9:52 we are told that Jesus sent messengers on ahead to make arrangements for the night's lodging. And in James 2:25 mention is made of the messengers sent by Joshua.

What then is an angel? The answer is found in Heb. 1:14—"Are they not all ministering spirits, sent forth to minister for them who shall be heirs of salvation?" The angels are God's messengers, running errands and carrying messages for Him.

Yet Paul declares that even if one of these heavenly messengers should preach a different gospel from what he preached, he should be accursed. Either Paul was a bigoted egotist, a fanatical fool, or else he had a valid and overwhelming consciousness of a divine inspiration that certified the infallible source of his message. Nineteen centuries of Christian history have proved that the latter was the case. The authority of Paul's gospel is authenticated by the transformation it has wrought in millions of men and women who have heard and obeyed it.

Accursed   The Greek noun *anathema* occurs only 7 times in the NT, and the verb *anathematizō* 4 times.

The noun is found in the Septuagint as the translation of the Hebrew *cherem.* This word had two distinct meanings. It is translated "accursed," "accursed thing," etc. But it is also translated "devoted," "devoted thing." The cognate verb *charam* is rendered in the KJV at least 12 ways: "consecrate, destroy, devote, make accursed, utterly destroy (40 times), utterly slay, be devoted, be forfeited, be utterly destroyed," etc. The essential idea of the noun is "*devoted to destruction*, something given up to death on account of God" (Cremer, p. 547).

That is the regular meaning of *anathema* in the NT. Some have tried to weaken its force in one or two places to the sense of excommunication. But Cremer objects to this. He holds that the word "denotes not punishment intended as discipline, but *a being given over*, or *devotion to divine condemnation*" (p. 548). In other words, it always in the NT has the idea of a curse attached to it, as it did in the secular Greek of that time.

Paul says here, If we as ministers of the Word preach any other gospel than that clearly revealed in the NT we place ourselves under the awful curse of God. Better never to have entered the ministry than to stand in the pulpit and preach some substitute for the gospel. Those who reject the atonement of Christ are teaching basically the same heterodox human opinions that were being circulated in Galatia in the first century, namely, that one is saved through his own work-righteousness rather than through the divine righteousness provided in Christ. A Christless gospel is no gospel at all. Salvation by works either presents man with a ladder he can never climb or else it lulls him to sleep in the false security of self-righteousness.

12 Revelation Paul declares that his gospel is not human, for neither did he receive it from man nor was he taught it, but it came to him by direct divine revelation. Oepke says that the mystery hidden from the ages became known to Paul "through the self-revelation of Jesus Christ. . . . This is how Paul received his Gospel (Gal. 1:12, 16). . . . God used revelation to convince him of the resurrection of the Crucified. This altered at a stroke his whole attitude to what he already knew of Jesus. The lying message became the message of salvation, and Paul's task was now to pass it on" (TDNT, 3:584).

The Greek word for "revelation" is *apocalypsis*, which we have taken over into English as "apocalypse," the name often given to the Book of Revelation in the NT.

The noun comes from the verb *apocalyptō*, which means "uncover, disclose." It "refers primarily to the removal of what conceals, an uncovering, and in some cases the choice of the word seems to be due to the thought of a previous concealment" (Burton, p. 433). Consequently *apocalypsis* means "an uncovering, disclosing, laying bare."

Burton gives a good outline of the NT usage of *apocalypsis*:

1. An appearance or manifestation of a person, a coming, or coming to view; used of the coming of Christ.
2. A disclosure of a person or thing such that its true character can be perceived.
3. A divine revelation or disclosure of a person in his true character, of truth, or of the divine will, made to a particular individual, and as such necessarily involving the perception of that which is revealed (p. 434).

Cremer says of *apocalyptō:* "The word serves especially in the N.T. to denote the act of divine revelation" (p. 342). He notes that *apocalypsis* is rare in secular Greek. Then he adds: "In the N.T. it is applied exclusively to disclosures and communications proceeding from God or Christ, of objects of Christian faith, knowledge, and hope, that are in and by themselves hidden, unknown, and unrecognized" (p. 343).

It has long been a conviction of the writer that we do not have a firm faith in the deity of Jesus unless and until there is a revelation of the divine Christ to our own hearts. No amount of instruction can produce that sense of certainty that takes the crook out of question marks and thereby turns them into exclamation points. We may be logically persuaded as to the reasonableness and scripturalness of the doctrine of the deity of Jesus. But we need more than that if we are going to preach with the conviction that produces convictions.

Preaching opinions learned from others will never carry authority. The people were astonished because Jesus taught them with authority, and not as the scribes (Matt. 7:29). What was the difference? The scribes discussed and debated the traditions of the elders. Jesus spoke with a sense of inner certainty that gripped His hearers. We today can have a revelation of Jesus Christ to our own hearts by the Holy Spirit that will carry complete conviction of the truth of His deity. No man has the right to stand in the pulpit to preach unless he is dead sure of the deity of Jesus Christ. That is the *sine qua non* of the ministry.

13 Conversation There are three different Greek words which are translated "conversation" in the KJV of the NT. But none of them has to do with "conversation" as we use that term today.

The first is *politeuma*, found only in Phil. 3:20. It comes from *politeuō*, "be a citizen, live as a citizen." That verb comes from *politēs*, "citizen," which, in turn, comes from *polis*, "city" (cf. Indianapolis, Minneapolis, etc.). So the meaning of *politeuma* is "citizenship," as correctly rendered in the ASV (1901).

The second word translated "conversation" in the KJV is *tropos*, which means "way or manner." The third, found here, is *anastrophē*, which literally means "a turning down or back, a wheeling about." But in later writers, as in the NT, it is used in the sense of "manner of life, behavior, conduct." One could well cross out "conversation" wherever it occurs in the KJV of the NT (Gal. 1:13; Eph. 4:22; 1 Tim. 4:12; Heb. 13:5, 7; Jas. 3:13; 1 Pet. 1:15, 18; 2:12; 3:1, 2, 16; 2 Pet. 2:7; 3:11) and write "conduct" above it as a more correct rendering. The trouble is that our English word "conversation" has greatly narrowed its meaning in the last 300 years, so that it no longer refers to all of one's conduct, but only to "talk." But the Greek words mean much more than that. The one exception is Phil. 3:20, where it should be translated "citizenship" or "commonwealth."

The two occurrences of "conversation" in the OT (Ps. 37:14; 50:23) should be changed to "way."

Wasted In verses 13 and 23 of this chapter we find the verb *portheō*. In the KJV it is rendered "wasted" in verse 13 and "destroyed" in verse 23 (as also in Acts 9:21, its only other occurrence in the NT). In the earliest Greek writers, such as Homer, *portheō* is a military term. It was used of destroying or ravaging cities. It regularly conveyed the idea of violent destruction. In the NT it is used only to describe Paul's activities. The imperfect tense would suggest that Paul "was ravaging" the Church and trying to destroy it, but that he did not completely succeed.

14 Profited We read that Paul "profited" in the Jews' religion (Gk., Judaism). The word is *prokoptō*, literally meaning "cut before," and so "advance." The figure is that of a runner in a race cutting ahead of others. Paul was way out in front, already a leader as a young man.

Equals Paul says that he advanced beyond "many my equals." What does he mean? The word in the original is *sunēlikiōtēs*, which occurs only here. Its meaning is "one of the same age, an equal in age." Even as a young man in Judaism Paul was forging away ahead of his "contemporaries." The glorious thing is that as a Christian he did exactly the same thing again.

18 See After his conversion Paul went into Arabia—probably the quiet countryside near Damascus—to meditate and think through the implications of his newfound faith in Jesus, the Messiah. After some few weeks or months he returned to Damascus. "Then after three years" he went up to Jerusalem (vv. 17–18).

What was the purpose of Paul's journey to Jerusalem? The KJV says that he went up to "see" Peter. But the term thus translated is not one of the five common Greek words for "see," which together occur hundreds of times in the NT. This is a more rare term, found only here in the NT. It is *historeō*, from which we get our word "history." Originally it meant "inquire into, learn by inquiry," and then "narrate, record"—suggesting "history." However, in late writers it came to mean "visit, become acquainted with." This is its meaning here.

Paul is emphasizing the fact that he did not go up to Jerusalem to take a course of theological instruction under the apostles. Rather he went to get acquainted with Peter, and he paid him a brief visit of only two weeks. That would not have given him time to be "taught" (v. 12) the gospel, which instead he received by divine revelation.

2:2 Reputation Paul states that he went up to Jerusalem and "communicated unto them that gospel which I preach among the Gentiles, but privately *to them which were of reputation.*" These last 6 words are only 2 in the Greek, *tois dokousin*. This is the definite article with the present participle of *dokeō*. The same combination occurs twice again in verse 6 and once in verse 9. In verse 6 it is translated "who seemed" and "who seemed to be somewhat." In verse 9 it is translated "who seemed." The RSV translates: "those who were of repute" (v. 2), "those who were reputed," and "those who were of repute" (v. 6), "who were reputed" (v. 9). It could be rendered "those in esteem."

The verb *dokeō* means "be of opinion, think, suppose." It also means "seem, be reputed." It occurs 63 times in the NT. In the KJV it is translated "think" 33 times, "seem" 13 times, "suppose" 7 times, "seem good" 3 times, "please" and "account" twice each, and once each it is rendered "trow," "be of reputation," "pleasure."

What does Paul mean by these men who were "of reputation"? Some have thought he was ironical. But the majority of the best scholars are agreed that he was not. For instance, Trench says of *dokeō*: "There is ever a predominant reference to the public opinion and estimate, rather than to the actual being; however the former may be a faithful echo of the latter. Thus, while there is no touch of irony, no shadow of depreciation, in St. Paul's use of *hoi dokountes* at Gal. 2:2 (and 6) and while manifestly there could be no slight intended, seeing that he so characterizes the chief of his fellow Apostles, the words for all this express rather the reputation in which these were held in the Church than the worth which in themselves they had, however that reputation of theirs was itself the true measure of this worth" (pp. 305–06).

The other side of the picture, however, is found in Galatians 6:3—"For if a man think himself to be something, when he is nothing, he deceiveth himself." Here *dokeō* ("think") obviously refers to an opinion of oneself which is sadly distorted. But in Galatians 2, it is the opinion of others which is indicated; that is, one's reputation. One's opinion of himself may be much farther from the truth than the reputation which he has.

We should be concerned as to what men think of us, more concerned as to what we think of ourselves, but most concerned as to what God thinks of us. And always we should strive to make sure that what we *seem* to be is what we actually are.

4 Privily Paul speaks of "false brethren unawares brought in, who came in privily to spy out our liberty which we have in Christ Jesus." The expression "unawares brought in" is all one word in Greek, the adjective *pareisaktous*. "Came in privily" is likewise one word, the verb *pareisēlthon*. Both are double compounds, with the two prepositional prefixes *para* (beside) and *eis* (in). The rest of the adjective is from *agō*, "lead, bring," and the simple verb is the second aorist of *erchomai*, "go, come." The adjective is correctly translated "brought in secretly." The verb means "came in secretly."

"Privily" is the obsolete term for "privately." But the real meaning here is "secretly." These false brethren sneaked in underhandedly "to spy out" the liberty which the Gentile Christians were enjoying. Lightfoot comments: "The metaphor is that of spies or traitors introducing themselves by stealth into the enemy's camp" (p. 106).

6 Person "God accepteth no man's person." The Greek here is *prosōpon*, which means "face." This literal translation is usually found in the KJV. Other renderings, however, are: "presence," "countenance," "appearance," "before," and "fashion."

Here the Greek literally says, "God does not receive a man's face." One is reminded of the words of the Pharisees and Herodians—quoted in all three Synoptic Gospels (Matt. 22:16;

Mark 12:14; Luke 20:21)—"Thou regardest not the person of men" (lit., "look not on men's faces"). The idea goes back to the OT, where "face" often means "presence." The meaning here is clearly indicated by the RSV, "God shows no partiality," or by the NIV, "God does not judge by external appearance."

8 Wrought Here we find the same Greek word translated by two rather different expressions. "Wrought effectually" and "was mighty" are both translations of *energeō*, from which we get "energy" and "energize." It means, "be at work, be in action, operate." Moulton and Milligan state that the verb "seems always to have the idea of effective working" (VGT, p. 214). They prefer the translation "by (4:201). Peter" rather than "in Peter" (KJV) or "for Peter" (ASV). The RSV renders v. 8 "for he who worked through Peter for the mission to the circumcised worked through me also for the Gentiles."

One can hardly refrain from commenting that if ever there was an "energetic" individual that one was the apostle Paul. His counterpart in modern times was John Wesley. No one can visit John Wesley's home in London, kneel in his prayer room, and stand in his pulpit in City Road Chapel, without being tremendously impressed with the almost measureless "energy" of this small but mighty man whose incomparable life spanned the eighteenth century. One comes away with the cry in his heart: "O Lord, make me more like John Wesley, and the apostle Paul, but especially like the Christ who inspired them both."

9 Fellowship The word is *koinonia*, from *koinos*, "common." Thayer defines it as "fellowship, association, community, communion, joint participation . . . the share which one has in anything" (p. 352). The word is translated "fellowship" in almost all English versions. In KJV it is rendered "fellowship" 12 times, "communion" 4 times, "contribution," "communication," "to communicate," and "distribution" once each.

Moulton and Milligan show that in the papyri (contemporary with NT times) the word was clearly used in the sense of "partnership." Hauck calls attention to "partners" in Luke 5:10, where the same root (*koinonoi*) is used (TDNT, 3:804).

This adds a beautiful thought here. Not only were James, Peter, and John displaying a good spirit of Christian fellowship towards Paul and Barnabas, but they were shaking hands as partners in a business enterprise. Wisely they decided on a distribution of labor. The first three were to minister to Jews; the latter two were to go to the Gentiles.

11 Blamed The verb *kataginōskō* means "blame, condemn." But in the only other two occurrences of the word in the NT (1 John 3:20, 21) the KJV uses "condemn"—"If our heart condemn us," "if our heart condemn us not." Clearly that is the right translation there. Should it be translated the same way here?

The answer of practically all good scholars and commentators is, "Yes." Lightfoot says: "Not 'reprehensible', but 'condemned'. His conduct carried its own condemnation with it" (p. 111). Burton affirms that this is "evidently much more appropriate in a clause in which Paul gives the reason for resisting Peter" (p. 103). Huxtable, in the *Pulpit Commentary*, says: "The rendering *to be blamed*, correct so far as it reaches, is inadequate in expressing the sense which St. Paul had of the *gravity* of St. Peter's offense" (p. 80).

13 Dissimulation The verb translated "dissemble with" is *synypokrinomai*, which occurs only here in the NT. The noun "dissimulation" is *hypokrisis*, which gives us our English word "hypocrisy." ("Hypocrite" is also from the Greek *hypokritēs*.)

The verb *hypokrinomai*—to which *syn* ("with") is added here—means literally "answer from under"; that is, from under a mask as an actor would do when playing his part. Vine (1:242) writes: "It was a custom for Greek and Roman actors to speak in large masks with mechanical devices for augmenting the force of the voice." So the verb here, *synypokrinomai*, means "join in acting the hypocrite, in pretending to act from one motive, whereas another motive really inspires the act" (Vine, 1:324). Probably the best translation of this verb is "play the hypocrite." And "dissimulation" should be changed to "hypocrisy," as in most of the recent versions.

How could their conduct be thus labeled? Vincent says: "Their act was *hypocrisy*, because it was a concealment of their own more liberal conviction, and an open profession of still adhering to the narrow Pharisaic view." (4:102). Peter and Barnabas had both associated freely with Gentile Christians. In his present attitude Peter was repudiating the light he had received at Joppa on the housetop (Acts 10). Paul saw clearly the serious consequences for the Church in dividing it into Jewish and Gentile branches. That is why he dealt so firmly with the situation.

Wilckens points out the fact that in distinction from classical Greek, the Septuagint uses these words in a bad sense (TDNT, 8:563). This negative sense is also found in Philo and Josephus, as well as in the literature of Dispersion Judaism in general (p. 565). Of our present passage Wilckens writes: "Paul's charge is not that they deceived the envoys from Jerusalem by their sudden change of practice. Their *hypocrisis* was not culpable tactical hypocrisy.... The real point was that by breaking off table fellowship between Jews and Gentiles in the one Church they were not walking straight according to the truth of the gospel, Gal. 2:14" (p. 569). Cremer writes: "The hypocrite seeks to appear before men as he ought to be but is not before God" (p. 380).

14 Walked Not Uprightly The verb is *orthopodeō*, found here for the first time in Greek literature. It comes from *orthos* ("straight") and *pous* ("foot"). The expression means "make a straight path, pursue a straight course." Vine says that it is "used metaphorically in Gal. 2:14, signifying a course of conduct by which one leaves a straight track for others to follow" (4:195). The implication is that Peter and Barnabas had swerved aside from the path of truly Christian conduct. Burton writes: "The present word is apparently not simply a general ethical term for doing right, but, as the context implies, denotes straightforward, unwavering, and sincere conduct in contrast with the pursuing of a crooked, wavering, and more or less insincere course, such as Paul had just attributed to Peter and those who followed him" (p. 110). Williams (CGT) agrees with Vine in holding that the word "suggests not only a crooked walk but the crooked track thereby made, likely to lead others astray." Perhaps the best translation is, "They were not walking straight."

16–17 Justified The verb *dikaioō* occurs three times in v. 16 and once in v. 17. It is uniformly translated "justify" in most English versions. However, Goodspeed has "made upright" and Young has "declare righteous." Verkuyl inconsistently has "made righteous" the first two times and "justify" the last two times. Williams employs the rather lengthy circumlocution "Come into right standing with God."

What does *dikaioō* really mean? The difficulty is shown somewhat by the fact that Cremer devotes 16 pages in his *Lexicon* to *dikaios* and its cognate terms.

He defines the adjective *dikaios* as meaning

"what is right, conformable to right, pertaining to right—just." He then goes on to say (p. 184): "Righteousness in the biblical sense is a condition of rightness the standard of which is God, which is estimated according to the divine standard, which shows itself in behaviour conformable to God, and has to do above all things with its relation to God, and with the walk before him." He further notes that it designates "the normal relation of men and their acts, etc., to God."

Under *dikaiosyne* (righteousness) Cremer comes closer to our problem, when he writes: "The Pauline conception of righteousness denotes the state of the believing man called forth by the divine acquittal" (p. 193).

The verb *dikaioō* occurs rarely in classical Greek. But in the NT it is found 39 times (27 in Paul), while its cognate terms occur about 200 times. Unquestionably it is one of the central ideas of the NT.

Cremer gives as its fundamental meaning in the NT, "to recognize, to set forth, as righteous, to justify" (p. 195). He also says that with Paul it "denotes nothing else than the *judicial act* of God, whereby man is pronounced free from guilt and punishment" (p. 197).

Abbott-Smith defines righteousness as "conformity to the Divine will in purpose, thought and action." He gives the meaning of the verb in the NT as "show to be righteous." Thayer agrees with this. He says that negatively it means to "declare guiltless," positively to "declare acceptable."

Burton (ICC) has 15 pages on *dikaios* and its cognate terms. He notes that *dikaios* in classical Greek was "fundamentally a forensic or court term" (p. 460). But in Hebrew usage the corresponding words are "prevailingly moral as well as forensic" (p. 466). In the NT "righteousness" means "conduct and character which satisfy the ethical requirements of God, and so render one acceptable to him." It also means, in a more forensic sense, "acceptance with God" (p. 469). It includes forgiveness. "Since, according to Paul, 'all have sinned and are destitute of the divine approval,' forgiveness is included in righteousness, either distinctly and explicitly, or by implication" (*ibid.*).

But is this all that the term implies? Vincent objects strongly to that conclusion. He says: "The meaning *to declare* or *pronounce righteous* cannot be consistently carried through Paul's writings in the interest of a theological fiction of imputed righteousness." He calls attention to passages that speak of justification by works of law, and then observes: "If one is justified by the works of the law, his righteousness is a real

righteousness, founded upon his conformity to the law. Why is the righteousness of faith any less a real righteousness?" (4:104).

In connection with Rom. 3:20, Vincent gives an extended discussion of *dikaioō*. After recognizing the fact that the main emphasis in classical Greek is judicial, he defines its NT meaning as indicating "the act or process by which a man is brought into a right state as related to God." He further emphasizes the idea of a right state by saying: "Justification aims directly at *character*. It contemplates making *the man himself* right" (3:39). He concludes with this significant statement: "Justification which does not *actually remove* the wrong condition in man which is at the root of his enmity to God, is no justification. In the absence of this, a legal *declaration* that a man is right is a fiction" (3:40).

So although, as many commentators note, the philological background of *dikaioō* suggests primarily the judicial sense, yet the strong moral emphasis of the NT demands that God shall *make* righteous those whom He *declares* righteous.

3:1 *Foolish* Paul's strong emotions while writing this letter are revealed in the opening words of chapter 3: "O foolish Galatians." The word is *anoētos*, which Young, Ballantine, and Verkuyl render "thoughtless." Moffatt, Goodspeed, and Williams translate it "senseless." It is a combination of *nous* (mind) and *alpha-privative*, which negates the meaning of a word to which it is attached (e.g., amoral means nonmoral). So the fundamental meaning of this adjective is "not thinking."

But the translation "thoughtless" seems too weak to convey the force of the expression here. Vincent notes that "*nous* is used by Paul mainly with an ethical reference, as *the faculty of moral judgment*." Hence his deduction: "*Anoētos* therefore indicates a folly which is the outgrowth of a moral defect" (4:110). If we take "foolish," not as a half-playful expression, but as a serious, earnest accusation of moral and mental failure, then perhaps it is a better rendering than either "thoughtless" or "senseless," both of which may seem to stress the mental aspect more than the moral.

Bewitched *Baskainō* (only here in NT) originally meant "slander, speak ill of one." Then it came to have the meaning "blight by the evil eye, fascinate, bewitch." Vincent says: "Paul's metaphor here is: *who hath cast an evil spell upon you?*" (4:111). Concerning the use of this word in the papyri, Moulton and Milligan write: "The popular belief in the power of the evil eye, underlying the Pauline metaphor in Gal. 3:1, is well illustrated by the common formulas in closing greetings" (VGT, p. 106). As an example they cite these words from a papyrus letter of about A.D. 25: "But above all I pray that you may be in health unharmed by the evil eye and faring prosperously." The entire phrase "unharmed by the evil eye" is one word in Greek, *abaskantos*.

This does not mean, of course, that Paul believed in magic, although the masses of his contemporaries apparently did. Paul is simply saying: "You folk are acting as though someone has bewitched you. You seem charmed by these false teachers who are leading you astray."

How often we feel that way today about vacillating Christians or prospects who suddenly turn away! The only adequate explanation seems to be the influence of some satanic power that diverts them from God.

Evidently Set Forth Paul declares that, before the very eyes of the Galatians, Jesus Christ "hath been evidently set forth." The phrase is one word in the Greek, *proegraphē*. The ASV translates it "openly set forth." Moffatt renders it "placarded" and the bulk of the best commentators favor this translation. Weymouth has "portrayed" and the RSV "publicly portrayed."

The verb *prographō* literally means "write beforehand," and that is its use in Rom. 15:4. But it very early took on the meaning, "write up in public, placard." Lightfoot says: "It is the common word to describe all public notices or proclamations." And he makes the pertinent observation: "This placard ought to have kept their eyes from wandering, and so to have acted as a charm against all Judaic sorceries" (p. 134). Vincent puts it well: "Who could have succeeded in bringing you under the spell of an evil eye, when directly before your own eyes stood revealed the crucified Christ?" (4:112).

The homiletical hint here is obvious. We need to warn people to keep their eyes on Jesus in order that they may not become "fascinated" (Latin for casting a spell) by the worldly allurements around. When our eyes are filled with the bright shining of the Light of the World, we shall not be captivated by the dazzling neon signs of the world's pleasures. When we are following *the* Light, other little flashes may annoy us, but they will not divert us from the narrow way that leads to life and light eternal.

3 Spirit The perplexing question confronts the translator: Should "spirit" be spelled with a capital or a small *s*? He must ask, "Is the reference here to the human spirit or the Holy Spirit?" Almost all English translators have taken it in the latter sense and so have written "Spirit." One exception is Ballantine (*Riverside New Testament*), who uses a small *s*. Weymouth paraphrases the question: "Having begun by the spiritual, are you now going to reach perfection by the external?" That wording is true to the Greek, and gives clear meaning to the passage.

Of course the Greek manuscripts give us no help here, since the oldest copies have large, square "uncial" letters and the later copies have a running ("cursive") script. In each case the letters are all the same.

The Greek word is *pneuma*, from which we get "pneumonia," "pneumatic," etc. It originally meant "a movement of air, wind, breath." But when a person's breath leaves his body, he is dead; that is, his spirit is gone. So the word for "breath" was also used for "spirit."

Vine writes:

> In Gal. 3:3, in the phrase "having begun in the Spirit," it is difficult to say whether the reference is to the Holy Spirit or to the quickened spirit of the believer; that it possibly refers to the latter is not to be determined by the absence of the article, but by the contrast with "the flesh"; on the other hand, the contrast may be between the Holy Spirit who in the believer sets His seal on the perfect work of Christ, and the flesh which seeks to better itself by works of its own (4:63–64).

Obviously, this is an open question, where dogmatism is out of place. But the meaning is much the same whichever way we take it. It is the Holy Spirit who gives us spiritual life. The main emphasis is on keeping the spiritual, rather than the material, supreme. Probably we should follow the majority of translators in capitalizing "Spirit" here.

5 Ministereth The Greek word *epichorēgōn* is translated "ministereth" in KJV and "supplies" in RSV. The verb *chorēgeō* comes from *choros* (chorus, choir) and *hēgeomai* (lead). So the word originally meant "lead a chorus"; then, "supply a chorus"; that is, defray the expense of providing a chorus at a public feast. In later Greek it means simply "furnish, supply." But it also carries the added idea of supplying lavishly or abundantly. Probably the prepositional prefix *epi* in the compound verb here emphasizes still further the idea of abundance (so Lightfoot, Burton).

The form here is the present participle, which would suggest continuous action—"the

275

one supplying to you the Spirit." While there is a crisis moment in which the Holy Spirit comes into the believer's heart, yet there is also a sense in which the Spirit is being supplied richly to us as we walk in the light.

6 Accounted Abraham's believing "was accounted to him for righteousness." The RSV has "was reckoned to him as righteousness" and the NIV "credited." As is frequently the case, all these translations are entirely correct.

The verb is *logizomai*. It is a favorite word with Paul, "being used (exclusive of quotations) some 27 times in his Epp., and only 4 times in the rest of the N.T." (Thayer, p. 379). Its original usage was mathematical: "reckon, count, compute, calculate." There is probably an example of this in Luke 22:37, in a quotation from the Septuagint: "He was reckoned among the transgressors." Then the word came to be used metaphorically in the sense "reckon, take into account." That is the meaning here, where the statement is quoted from the Septuagint of Gen. 15:6.

Cremer exhibits a strange and strong Calvinistic bias in his treatment of *logizomai* in relation to this verse and similar passages in Romans. He stresses the ideas of imputation and substitution. For instance, we find this statement, all in italics: "That is transferred to the subject in question, and imputed to him, which in and for itself does not belong to him" (p. 399). Again he says: "But faith is now put in the place of righteousness" (*ibid.*). He seems to imply that though a man is not actually righteous he is reckoned so in God's sight. We hold that God could not "reckon" a man as righteous unless and until He had made him righteous. Faith is put to one's account as the grounds of making righteous, not as a substitute for righteousness.

9 Faithful Those who come to God by the faith route are blessed with "faithful" Abraham. The Greek word has two distinct meanings: (1) "faithful, trustworthy"; (2) "believing, trusting." That the second is the proper meaning here is clear from the context. It does not mean here "faithful to God" but "full of faith." The KJV translates it correctly in John 20:27— "Be not faithless, but *believing*." It should be so translated here—"believing Abraham."

Heidland writes: "Faith is reckoned for righteousness because this is pleasing to the will of Yahweh, not because faith has this value intrinsically" (TDNT, 4:289).

13 Tree At the end of this verse we find a quotation from the Septuagint of Deut. 21:23, which reads: "Cursed is every one who hangs upon a tree."

The last word is *xylon*, which is found 20 times in the NT (including Rev. 22:19, which reads "book of life" instead of "tree of life" in the KJV). Exactly half of these times it is translated "tree." In its first 5 occurrences—all connected with the arrest of Jesus in Gethsemane—it is rendered "staves," in the dual phrase "with swords and staves." We would say "clubs" today.

Three times *xylon* is translated "wood" and once "the stocks" (Acts 16:24). In the latter case the meaning is that they were wooden stocks which held the feet of Paul and Silas in the Philippian jail. One of the references where it is translated "wood" is 1 Cor. 3:12, where we find the combination "wood, hay, stubble."

The basic meaning of *xylon* is "wood." Liddell and Scott give "wood, cut and ready for use; firewood, timber" as the earliest usage. Then comes "piece of wood, log, beam, peg or lever." A further development is represented in "cudgel, club, gallows, stake, stocks," which we have found illustrated in the NT. Finally the word came to be used for "live wood, a tree," as 10 times in the NT. It is used 4 times in the last chapter of the Bible (Revelation 22) for the tree of life.

The typical Greek word for "tree" is *dendron*, which is also our biological term for tree. It is so translated in all 26 of its occurrences in the NT.

While in later Greek *xylon* was used for a live tree, yet modern Greek has gone back to its original meaning, "wood." In the papyri, which come from the Hellenistic period in which the NT was written, the word has both meanings. Moulton and Milligan cite passages for "tree" and also those which use it in the sense of "beam, staves, log." Always the idea of "wood" is dominant.

Three times in Acts we find *xylon* used for the cross of Christ (Acts 5:30; 10:39; 13:29). It is translated "tree," as in our passage in Galatians, for lack of a better word to express the exact idea.

The only trouble with this translation is that when we read of a person "hanging on a tree" we form a mental picture of a person strangled with a rope around his neck, dangling from the limb of a tree, as was done with horse thieves in the frontier days. But that, of course, is not the correct picture when applied to Christ.

Actually crucifixion was not a Jewish, but a Roman, method of punishment. The typical

Jewish method of capital punishment was stoning, as illustrated in the case of Stephen. That was what was ordained in the Law of Moses for Sabbath-breakers, blasphemers, etc. After the person had been stoned, sometimes his body was hung from a tree until sundown, as a warning example to others (Deut. 21:22). This was considered to be a particularly disgraceful fate. That apparently is the background of the statement quoted from Deuteronomy: "Cursed is every one who hangs upon a tree." So "tree" is best here.

15 *Covenant* In both vv. 15 and 17 we find the word "covenant." The first is in a general statement of principle. The second relates to the covenant made with Abraham. There is practically no question about the meaning of the word in v. 17, although Moffatt uses "will" there. But there is considerable debate as to whether the word should be "covenant" or "will" (testament) in v. 15. Several translations (including the RSV) give the latter rendering.

The Greek word is *diathēkē*, which occurs some 33 times in the NT. In the KJV it is rendered "covenant" 20 times and "testament" 13 times. It is obvious that the word carries both meanings. But which should we adopt in Gal. 3:15?

Burton gives a full treatment of the subject in his commentary on Galatians (pp. 496–505). He notes first of all that in classical Greek *diathēkē* normally meant a will or testament. However, it sometimes was used for "an arrangement or agreement between two parties in which one accepts what the other proposes or stipulates" (p. 496). This, of course, is close to the idea of a covenant. It also has been shown that such an agreement could be revoked only by mutual consent of both parties.

The word *diathēkē* occurs over 300 times in the Septuagint. There it is normally the translation of the Hebrew word *berith*, which uniformly means "covenant" or "compact." It is most commonly used for "a covenant between God and men in which case the initiative being thought of as wholly with God, the compact assumes in general the form of a gracious promise on God's part to do certain things, accompanied by the imposition of certain conditions and obligations upon men" (Burton, p. 497).

The ordinary Greek word for a compact was *synthēkē*. But this term was avoided by the Septuagint translators because it suggested the equal rank of the two parties, whereas the OT *berith* is used for "a relationship between God and man graciously created by God, and only accepted by man" (p. 498).

In the Greek papyri *diathēkē* always means "a will." Since many of these are dated in the first century it is clear that such a will would be the main sense of the term among the Greeks when the NT was written. On the other hand, the Jewish usage at this time was still "covenant." Burton states clearly the difference in the two ideas: "The essential distinction between the two meanings is that in a testament the testator expresses his will as to what shall be done after his death, esp. in respect to his property; the covenant is an agreement between living persons as to what shall be done by them while living" (p. 500).

The question then remains: Is Paul using *diathēkē* in the Greek sense or the Hebrew sense? Behm says, "The many legal terms in the passage make it clear that he is here using the word *diathēkē* in the sense of Hellenistic law" (TDNT, 2:129). Sir William Ramsay also argues for this in Gal. 3:15. He feels that the context clearly indicates it, especially the mention of "inheritance" in verse 18 and the discussion of "heir" in chapter 4 (pp. 349–70). But Burton presents convincing answers to these arguments.

In his commentary on Hebrews, B. F. Westcott has a lengthy note likewise on *diathēkē* (pp. 298–302). He feels that its meaning in the New Testament should be determined first of all by its use in the Septuagint. We have already noted that that is definitely "covenant." Westcott says: "There is not the least trace of the meaning 'testament' in the Greek Old Scriptures, and the idea of a 'testament' was indeed foreign to the Jews till the time of the Herods" (p. 299).

But what about its use in the NT? Westcott is positive on this point: "In the N.T. the sense of 'covenant' is unquestionable, except in two passages: Gal. 3:15; Heb. 9:15f."

How are we to translate *diathēkē*, then, in Gal. 3:15? We incline toward Meyer, Alford, Ellicott, Lightfoot, and Burton—the most scholarly commentators on Galatians—that the best translation here is "covenant." That accords best with the regular usage of the NT, and specifically of Paul, and seems to fit the context better here. It would seem best to make Heb. 9:15ff. the only exception to this translation in the NT.

17 *Of None Effect* The expression "make of none effect" is all a translation of *katargēsai*, the aorist infinitive of *katargeō*. Exactly what does this word mean?

It occurs 27 times in the NT. In the first of these (Luke 13:7) it has its weakest meaning, "make idle." The KJV translates it "cumbereth."

Katargeō is a peculiarly Pauline term in the NT. Aside from Luke 13:7, it occurs outside of Paul's Epistles in only one passage, Heb. 2:14, where it is translated correctly in the KJV as "destroyed."

The meaning of this word is a bit flexible. (It is translated 15 different ways in the KJV in its 27 occurrences in the NT.) Frankly, it must be admitted that in the papyri it usually has the weaker sense of "hinder." But does this define its Pauline usage? Cremer says that with Paul "it clearly signifies more than hindering, or cessation from outward activity" (p. 260). Then he goes on to make this very significant assertion: "With him it always denotes a complete, not a temporary or partial ceasing. Elsewhere it signifies a putting out of activity, out of power or effect; but with St. Paul it is—to *annihilate, to put an end to, to bring to nought*" (p. 261, italics his).

We need make no apology, then, for retaining the word "destroy" in Rom. 6:6—"that the body of sin might be destroyed." Godet, the outstanding conservative French commentator, supports that rendering. Cremer says it means "annihilate."

Even in Gal. 3:17 "destroy" makes good sense. The promise would be destroyed if the law superseded it.

18–21 Law . . . Promise In this section of the Epistle, Paul asks a very pertinent question, one which might well occur to the reader: "Why then the law?" It would seem from his previous discussion that there was no need for the law at all.

The apostle answers the question by saying that the law was added (to promise) on account of transgressions. It was a temporary arrangement in God's dealing with man, to produce a consciousness of sin and compel men to seek salvation.

22–23 Concluded, Shut Up "Concluded" in v. 22 and "shut up" in v. 23 are translations of the same verb, *synkleiō*. It means "shut in on all sides, shut up completely."

The prepositional prefix *syn* normally means "with" or "together." Hence some give the meaning of *synkleiō* as "shut together, enclose." It is clearly used in that sense in Luke 5:6—"they inclosed a great multitude of fishes." In Rom. 11:32 (the only other place where it occurs in NT) it is translated "hath concluded," as in Gal. 3:22.

While "shut together" fits the passage in Luke, the majority of scholars would rule it out in Romans and Galatians. In the papyri it is used of being "shut up" in prison. And it is used of only *one* person being confined. So it seems better to take the *syn* as intensive, and render it "shut up." This is obviously its meaning in the Septuagint of Josh. 6:1—"Jericho was *straitly shut up.*"

The figure in Galatians and Romans is that of being confined in prison. In Romans it says that God has shut them all up in unbelief. In Galatians it says that "the scripture" has shut up all under sin.

In Gal. 3:22 sin is the jailer that holds people in prison. In v. 23 it is the law that acts as jailer.

24–25 Schoolmaster The Greek term in question occurs in only one other passage in the NT (1 Cor. 4:15). There it is translated "instructor."

The word is *paidagōgos*. Alford says of it: "The *paidagōgos* was a faithful slave, entrusted with the care of the boy from his tender years till puberty, to keep him from evil physical and moral, and accompany him to his amusements and studies" (3:36). Lenski translates the word "slave-guardian." Literally it means "child-leader," from *pais* ("child") and *agō* ("lead"). Young renders it "child-conductor." Weymouth gives it as "tutor." The RSV has "custodian." Actually there is no word in English which exactly represents the meaning of this Greek word. Goodspeed and Williams use "attendant" which seems best.

But does it mean "schoolmaster"? Scholars answer with almost one voice, "No!" Vine writes: "In this and allied words the idea is that of training, discipline, and not impartation of knowledge. The *paidagōgos* was not the instructor of the child; he exercised a general supervision over him and was responsible for his moral and physical well-being" (2:265).

Lightfoot agrees. He says: "Thus his office was quite distinct from that of the *didaskalos* (teacher), so that the English rendering, 'schoolmaster,' conveys a wrong idea" (p. 148).

What we need is an English word to represent the masculine counterpart to "governess." The *Pulpit Commentary* ("Galatians," p. 142) gives a very interesting passage from Plato, showing that the attendant took the child to the teacher's house. Socrates is questioning a young man. " 'But as to this, who has the ruling of you?' 'This man here,' he said, 'a *tutor.*' 'Being a slave, eh?' 'But what of that?' said he. 'Yes, only a slave of our own.' 'An awfully strange thing this,' I said, 'that you, freeman that you are, should be under the ruling of a slave. But further, what does this tutor of yours, as your ruler, do with you?' 'He takes me,' said he, 'to a teacher's house, of course.' "

Because of this clear meaning of the word, some have held that the law is pictured as a slave taking the Jews to Christ, the Schoolmaster. But the context does not support this latter idea. Lightfoot says: "The tempting explanation of *paidagōgos eis Christon*, 'one to conduct us to the school of Christ,' ought probably to be abandoned. . . . There is no reference here to our Lord as a *teacher*" (p. 149). The best commentators are in agreement on this point.

27 Put On The Greek verb is *endyo*. It is used most naturally of putting on clothing. This meaning occurs in the papyri. In modern Greek a similar verb form means "dress." Paul says that the believers "have put on Christ." Probably a better translation would be, "You clothed yourselves with Christ" (aorist middle indicative).

Rendall gives the background for understanding Paul's statement. He writes:

> At a certain age the Roman youth exchanged the *toga praetexta* for the *toga virilis* and passed into the rank of citizens. . . . Here the author evidently has in mind the change of dress which marked the transition from boyhood to manhood. Greeks and Romans made much of this occasion and celebrated the investment of a youth with man's dress by family gatherings and religious rites. The youth hitherto subject to domestic rule, was then admitted to the rights and responsibilities of a citizen, and took his place beside his father in the councils of the family (EGT, 3:174).

This interpretation fits well with the context. In v. 26 Paul writes: "You are all sons of God through faith in Christ Jesus" (Weymouth). Under the law they were minors, as he notes in the next chapter. But now they have come into the glorious liberty of being sons of God. No longer are they under a *paidagōgos*.

4:1 Child Paul reminds his readers that as long as the heir is a *nēpios* ("child") he has no more authority than a servant, though he will finally be lord of all his father's estate.

Etymologically, *nēpios* is equivalent to the Latin *infans*. Both literally mean not-speaking (*nē*, "not"; *epos*, "word"). That is, *nēpios* refers most strictly to an infant without the power of speech, not yet able to talk. That is its sense in Matt. 21:16—"Out of the mouths of babes and sucklings thou hast perfected praise."

But then it came to be used in a more general sense. Six times in the KJV it is translated "babe." Seven times it is translated "child" and once "childish." It occurs four times in 1 Cor. 3:11. Always it has as its dominant emphasis the idea of immaturity. This is especially evident in 1 Cor. 3:1 and Heb. 5:13.

But what is its meaning here? Vine says it is used "of the Jews, who, while the law was in force, were in a state corresponding to that of childhood, or minority, just as the word 'infant' is used of a minor, in English law" (1:93).

Nēpios does not appear to have been used in a technical, legal sense in Greek circles of Paul's day. Lightfoot says: "*Nēpios* seems to be here 'a minor' in any state of minority." Rendall (EGT) agrees with this when he writes: "*Nēpios* is not a legal term, but an appropriate description for a child of tender years, naturally subject to the control of guardians."

2 Tutors and Governors Paul says that this "minor" is under "tutors and governors" (KJV) until he becomes of age. The Greek words are *epitropos* and *oikonomos*. The former has the general meaning of "administrator, steward," and is so used in the only two other places where it occurs in the NT (Matt. 20:8; Luke 8:3). In both of those passages it is translated "stewards." It comes from the verb *epitrepō*, "commit, entrust." In the papyri it is used frequently for the guardian of a minor, as here.

The second word is from *oikos*, "house," and *nemō*, "manage." Hence it properly means the manager of a household or estate, a house steward. It is the more common word for "steward" in the NT (eight times). In Rom. 16:23 it is used for the city treasurer ("chamberlain," KJV). But it is also used four times in the Epistles for Christians as stewards "of God," "of the mysteries of God," "of the manifold grace of God."

Apparently, then, *epitropos* refers primarily to a personal "guardian," *oikonomos* to a "steward" of property. Lightfoot renders the whole expression, "controllers of his person and property" (p. 166).

Rendall gives the background for Paul's language here:

> The illustration is obviously borrowed from testamentary systems prevailing among Greeks and Romans (not among Hebrews) which enabled a father to appoint guardians for his orphan children during their minority. These testamentary powers differed considerably in different parts of the Roman world according to the municipal laws of various cities.

Whereas Roman citizens became wards of the state at fourteen, so that the powers of testamentary guardians were strictly limited, the discretion of the father was allowed a wider range in Greek cities. At Athens, for instance, the guardians of Demosthenes retained control over his property till he became a full citizen after eighteen; and in Asiatic Greece the custody of property was sometimes prolonged to twenty-five, though the personal authority ceased at fourteen (EGT, 3:175).

What Paul is contending is that the rule of law was not a permanent regime. It was just a preparatory period before the coming of Christ.

3 *Elements*   In this verse we find the phrase "elements of the world," and in v. 9 "weak and beggarly elements." In the ASV "elements" is changed to "rudiments."

The Greek word is *stoixeion*, which properly means one of a row (*stoixos*) or series. It was used for an elementary sound or letter of the alphabet. Then it was used for the elements or rudiments of knowledge. That seems to be its meaning here and in Heb. 5:12. In 2 Pet. 3:10, 12 it apparently refers to the material elements of the universe. The word was also used for the heavenly bodies. Recently scholars have held that it sometimes means demons or "tutelary spirits of nature." Deissmann holds that in this Galatian passage it means "cosmic spiritual beings" (VGT, p. 591).

This is apparently the background for the translation of the RSV, "elemental spirits." We question, however, whether this is the best rendering. It seems to us more likely that Paul is using the word *stoixeia* in the simpler sense of "elements" or "rudiments." The latter avoids the suggestion of physical "elements." The KJV uses "elements" in Gal. 4:3, 9, but "rudiments" in Col. 2:8, 20 and "principles" in Heb. 5:12. In 2 Pet. 3:10, 12 it is translated "elements" again.

The Early Church fathers usually interpreted this word as referring to the observance of days and seasons, which are regulated by the heavenly bodies. One man, Victorinus, even interpreted it as meaning the influence of the stars on the heathen before the time of Christ. Augustine held that Paul was referring to "the Gentile worship of the physical elements." (See Lightfoot, p. 167.)

Alford argues for the simpler meaning as being more natural. He would agree with Conybeare in rendering "elements of the world" as "elementary lessons of outward things." Lightfoot says that "elementary teaching" is "probably the correct interpretation." He concludes: "St. Paul seems to be dwelling

still on the rudimentary character of the law, as fitted for an earlier stage in the world's history" (p. 167). Delling (TDNT, 7:684–85) supports this idea.

5 *Redeem*   Paul introduces one of his rather frequent statements on the Atonement. He says that God sent forth His Son "to redeem them that were under the law."

The word "redeem" is *exagorazō*. It is a Pauline term and is translated "redeem" in all four places where it occurs in the NT (Gal. 3:13; 4:5; Eph. 5:16; Col. 4:5).

The word literally means "buy out of." The Greek word *agora* means "marketplace." So *agorazō* means "buy" in the marketplace. *Exagorazō* has the added idea of buying "out" or "up." It may also mean "buy back."

The word was used frequently of ransoming slaves. Lightfoot says categorically that this meaning "is required here." In spite of the objection of some scholars we feel that he is correct. Christ came to ransom the Jews from their slavery under law and give them freedom as sons of God.

Adoption   This verse contains another interesting word, *huiothesia*, "adoption." It is a compound of *huios*, son, and *thesis*, a placing (from *tithēmi*, "place" or "put"). So the word clearly means a placing as son.

Paul uses it in Rom. 8:15, 23; 9:4; and Eph. 1:5, besides this passage in Galatians. Older commentators state that it occurs nowhere else in Greek literature. But in recent years it has been found in a number of inscriptions. Martitz says, "The word is attested only from the 2nd cent. B.C. and means 'adoption as a child'" (TDNT, 8:397).The usage there suggests that adoptions were frequent in the Greek world of Paul's day, and so his readers would be familiar with the term (BS, p. 239). Moulton and Milligan also show that it was common in the papyri, though it is not in the LXX.

Probably "adoption as sons" (RSV) is a little clearer and more accurate than "adoption of sons" (KJV). It is our adoption by God as His sons that the apostle is talking about. What a glorious privilege is ours! Though born as aliens to God, we can by acceptance of Jesus Christ be adopted into the family of God.

13 *Infirmity of the Flesh*   In verse 13 the apostle states that "through infirmity of the flesh" he had preached the gospel in Galatia, during his former visit there. What was this weakness of the flesh?

"Flesh" here does not mean the carnal nature. Paul is clearly talking about some bodily affliction. This passage is usually connected by Bible students with 2 Cor. 12:7, where Paul mentions his "thorn in the flesh." It seems likely that the reference in both passages is to the same physical infirmity. What was its nature?

The most common answer is that it was poor eyesight. This idea is derived from several allusions in Paul's Epistles. In 4:15 the apostle declares that the Galatian Christians would have plucked out their eyes and given them to him. This has been taken as a suggestion that these new converts felt sorry for Paul's difficulty with his poor eyesight. But this is far from being positive proof of such a condition. The apostle may simply mention the eyes as being the most precious part of the body. The Psalmist prays: "Keep me as the apple of the eye" (Ps. 17:8). The prophet Zechariah (2:8) comforts the people with this assurance from the Lord: "He that toucheth you toucheth the apple of his eye."

In Gal. 6:11 Paul says: "You see with how large letters I wrote (epistolary aorist—'I write') to you with my own hand." It is generally assumed that this suggests poor eyesight on the part of the apostle.

Then again, in Acts 23:5 Paul declares that he did not recognize the high priest when he stood trial before the Sanhedrin in Jerusalem. Perhaps the most natural explanation is that Paul could not see very well.

A second identification of the "thorn in the flesh" has been epilepsy. Sholem Asch has popularized this in his novel *The Apostle*. It has been pointed out that many great geniuses, such as Napoleon Bonaparte, were epileptics. But there is no clear indication of this in the case of Paul, and there seems no reason for accepting it.

Perhaps the best suggestion is that made by Sir William Ramsay in *St. Paul the Traveler* and in his commentary on Galatians. He holds that the apostle's particular affliction was chronic malaria.

Through The KJV reads "through infirmity of the flesh I preached the gospel." Now *dia* with the genitive means "through"; but with the accusative it means "because of, on account of." Here "infirmity" (literally, "weakness") is in the accusative. So what Paul is saying here is that it was "because of weakness of the flesh" that he preached the gospel to the Galatians.

Ramsay suggests that Paul had a severe attack of malaria in the low, swampy seacoast of Pamphylia. Hence, he informed Barnabas that

he would have to move immediately to the mountains. So instead of evangelizing the province of Pamphylia, Paul and Barnabas climbed the hills to the high, interior province of Galatia.

We cannot be sure what Paul's ailment was. But we can agree with Burton's summary statement: "The language can refer only to some physical ailment hard to bear, and calculated to keep him humble and, in some measure, to repel those to whom he preached" (p. 239).

14 *My Temptation* Speaking further of his affliction, Paul writes: "My temptation which was in my flesh ye despised not, nor rejected." But a majority of the oldest Greek manuscripts have, "Your temptation in my flesh." This suggests the idea that the apostle's repulsive appearance was a trial to his hearers. It may have been to them a "temptation" to reject both him and his message.

We cannot be sure that "your" is the correct reading, since the third-century Chester Beatty papyrus (our oldest manuscript) has "my." The general reference to the effect of Paul's affliction on his hearers is the same, whichever reading we adopt.

The Greek word translated "rejected" is a very strong one and occurs only here in the NT. Literally it means "spit out" (*ekptuō*). The word is onomatopoeic; that is, the sound of it suggests the sense. Paul's hearers might have been tempted to express their disgust of him as one might spit out some objectionable thing. But instead they received him as an angel of God.

16 Question or Exclamation? One of the problems connected with translating the NT is that the early Greek manuscripts have no punctuation marks. Furthermore, the indicative mood is used for both questions and assertions. So the only way one can decide whether a sentence is interrogative or declarative is by the context—and this is not always decisive.

Verse 16 is one such instance in the NT. In many English versions it is translated as a question. But Burton prefers to treat it as an exclamation: "So that I have become your enemy by telling you the truth!"

17–18 *Affect* The word "affect" in these verses does not fit very well. It leaves both verses, especially 17, rather obscure in meaning.

The Greek verb, which occurs three times, is *zēloō*. It first meant "be jealous," and is so used a number of times in the NT. But then it swung over nearer to our meaning "be zealous." In several passages it means "seek or desire eagerly." That is clearly its meaning here. Burton renders it: "They zealously seek you, not honestly, but wish to shut you out that ye may seek them. But it is good to be zealously sought after in a good thing, always, and not only when I am present with you."

What was it from which the Judaizers were trying to exclude the Galatian Christians? The most obvious answer is that it was Christ, or the privileges of the gospel. The Judaizers wished these new converts to submit to the law of Moses. It was necessary to separate them from Christ in order to get them to follow the Judaizers.

Another interpretation is possible. One of the best ways to cause people to want to join an organization is to make its membership exclusive. It is human nature to be indifferent to accessible territory until a fence is put up around it. Then we become eager to get in.

It may be that the Judaizers held the Galatian believers at arm's length, thus causing them to "zealously seek" admittance to the Judaistic group. Thus the latter would seek to win them away from loyalty to Paul and his gospel.

The apostle reminds them (v. 18) that he had sought after them for a good purpose when present with them. Now, far away from them, he travails over them that they may be renewed once more in Christ.

22 Bondmaid Five times (vv. 22, 23, 30, 31) we find the Greek word *paidiskē*. In the KJV it is translated "bondmaid" in v. 22, but "bondwoman" in the other four instances. It is the same Greek word throughout.

The original and proper meaning of *paidiskē* was "young girl, maiden." But it came to be used colloquially for a young female slave or a maidservant. Vincent says that the word in classical Greek "means also a free maiden; but in N.T. always a slave." In the Septuagint it has both meanings, though more frequently the latter. In the NT it may be translated "bondwoman," "slave woman," "bondmaid," or a number of other ways.

This illustrates the unreasonableness of insisting that a certain word has only one meaning and cannot be translated in other ways with equal accuracy and propriety. No one can devote much time to the arduous and exacting work of translating the Scriptures without feeling keenly the many distressing difficulties of the task.

Free Woman In contrast to the bondwoman, Hagar, Paul places the free woman, Sarah. The word for "free woman," is *eleuthera*, the feminine form of the adjective used as a substantive. Cremer says of this adjective that in its absolute sense it means "free, unconstrained, unfettered, independent, or one who is not dependent upon another." Of this passage he says: "The social relationship serves, in Gal. IV. 22–31, to illustrate the difference between the Old and New Test. economy" (p. 250).

How thankful we ought to be for this glorious freedom which we enjoy in Christ, "unconstrained" and "unfettered" by the minute rules and regulations of the Mosaic law! How careful it ought to make us to use our freedom for God's glory and man's good!

24 Allegory The word "allegory" is *allegoroumena*, the present participle of *allegoreō*, which is found only here in the NT. It refers to speaking or interpreting allegorically; that is, "not according to the primary sense of the word, but so that the facts stated are applied to illustrate principles" (Vine, 1:47). Allegorizing does not deny the literal, historical sense of statements in the OT, but it gives them an added spiritual application.

The present participle of the verb is used here, rather than the noun *allegoria*. It would therefore seem most natural to translate it, "Which things are being spoken allegorically." Indeed, Young in his *Literal Translation of the Holy Bible*, uses "allegorized." But Burton argues at length that the best translation is, "Which things are allegorical utterances," the participle being taken as "an adjective participle used substantively" (p. 253).

The allegorical interpretation of the Old Testament was greatly overworked by Philo, an Alexandrian Jew contemporary with Christ. It was also carried to unfortunate extremes by such Early Church fathers as Origen and Augustine. But that does not justify us in ruling it out altogether; Paul clearly uses it here. However, it should be used with restraint, because men's imaginations can contrive all sorts of foolish speculations.

25 Answereth to The verb is *systoicheō*. It is from *syn* (with) and *stoicheō* (be in a row or line). Hence it means "be in the same row with." The modern equivalent is "corresponds to."

In military connections the word meant "stand or march in the same file with." In a metaphorical sense, as used here, it carries the idea of being in the same category.

What Paul is saying is that Hagar and Ishmael correspond to the old covenant and the earthly Jerusalem, whereas Sarah and Isaac correspond to the new covenant and the heavenly Jerusalem.

This is in line with Paul's emphasis throughout this Epistle on the bondage of the law. Those who are under the law are confined in prison, or under the rule of stewards, or in the care of pedagogues. But the gospel has brought freedom from all this. Grace is the gift of God and makes us free.

27 Rejoice ... Break Forth ... Cry Paul uses strong words to express the joy of the barren woman who becomes the mother of children. He says, "Rejoice!" The word means "make joyful, be delighted with." Here it is in the aorist passive and is best rendered, as in most English versions, by "rejoice." It is used in Greek literature of making merry at a feast.

The next exclamation begins with a word that means to break forth into speech. Its original meaning was "rend, break asunder." All three Synoptic Gospels use this verb in Jesus' saying about new wine bursting old wineskins (Matt. 9:17; Mark 2:22; Luke 5:37). Just as fermenting wine will burst old, already stretched wineskins, so a newfound joy must find means of expression. Thayer gives "break forth into joy" as the proper translation in v. 27.

The third verb in this quotation is *boaō*, translated in the KJV "cry." A better rendering would be "cry out." The RSV has "shout." Thayer gives as its meaning "to cry aloud, shout."

Three different Greek words in the NT may properly be translated "cry out"—*kaleō, boaō, krazō*. The first signifies crying out for a purpose, involving intelligence particularly. The third suggests a harsh cry, perhaps inarticulate. But *boao* refers to crying out as a manifestation of feeling, and so relates primarily to the sensibilities.

5:1 Free According to the best Greek text, this verse reads: "For freedom Christ set us free; keep on standing, therefore, and do not be entangled again with a yoke of bondage."

The phrase "for freedom" has an interesting usage in the papyri. Deissmann explains this in *Light from the Ancient East* (1927 English edition, p. 322). A slave who wanted to become free could pay the price of his freedom to the temple of his god. Then the owner would bring him there, receive the money from the temple treasury, and turn his slave loose. Thereupon the slave would become the property of the god. "Against all the world, especially his former master, he is a completely free man."

Deissmann gives (p. 323) a Greek inscription from Delphi, of about 200 B.C. It states that the god Apollo "bought from Sosibius of Amphissa, *for freedom*, a female slave ... *with a price*." (The last expression is found in 1 Cor. 6:20 and 7:23.) The inscription ends with the repeated words *ep eleutheriai*, "for freedom," the exact phrase found in Gal. 5:13, where the KJV has "unto liberty."

There is one marked difference between this ancient pagan custom of freeing a slave and our release from the bondage of sin and the law. In preparation for the pagan rites the slave had to pay to the temple treasury the price of his freedom. Only by a threadbare fiction did the god buy him out of slavery. But in our case we could never by any means have paid the purchase price for our freedom. It was Christ himself who paid the price of His own blood to set us free. Ours should be an undying gratitude for this precious token of His love.

7 Who Did Hinder You The verb here is *enkoptō* which literally means "cut in or into." Paul says to the Galatians: "You were running well; who cut in on you?" The figure is that of a runner in a race who is making good progress until someone cuts into his path.

The person who has the inside lane on a circular track is at an advantage. But if another runner chooses to block him by cutting in on him he may more than lose his advantage. The Galatians had made an excellent start in the Christian race. But the Judaizers were blocking their path and hindering them from running. We find the same danger suggested in Heb. 12:1–2.

12 Cut Off The verb "cut off" is *apokoptō* (*apo*, "from"; *koptō*, "cut"). This literal meaning of the word seems clear enough in the active voice, as in John 18:10 and other passages. But here the middle voice is used, hence Abbott-Smith's *Lexicon* gives "to mutilate oneself, have oneself mutilated." Thayer's *Lexicon* agrees. He says it is incorrect to interpret this as "cut themselves off from the society of Christians."

Alford says that the verb cannot be passive, as the KJV takes it. He continues: "It can hardly mean 'would cut themselves off from your communion.'" He agrees with the Early Church fathers and "the great consensus of ancient and modern commentators" that the word here refers to physical mutilation. He concludes: "It seems to me that this sense *must be adopted*, in spite of the protests raised against it" (3:55–56).

One of those who protests against it is Ellicott. In his excellent commentary he decides in favor of the other meaning. So does Barnes. But they stand almost alone among leading commentators in this position.

Lightfoot paraphrases the thought: "Why do they stop at circumcision? Why do they not mutilate themselves, like your priests of Agbele?" He then explains what seems to be a very extreme position taken by Paul. "Circumcision under the law and to the Jews was a token of a covenant. To the Galatians under the gospel dispensation it had no such significance. It was merely a bodily mutilation, as such differing rather in degree than in kind from the terrible practices of the heathen priests" (p. 207).

Rendall (EGT) supports this interpretation. Findlay (EB) holds to the literal interpretation, but thinks that Paul was speaking sarcastically rather than seriously.

Not only did the word have this clear usage in the then pagan world, but this is also its meaning in the Septuagint. It occurs in Deut. 23:1 (v. 2 in LXX), where it is translated "whose male member is cut off" (RSV). Such a person was to be excluded from the congregation of the Lord.

Vincent calls this word "perhaps the severest expression in Paul's Epistles." He gives what seems to be a good explanatory paraphrase: "These people are disturbing you by insisting on circumcision. I would that they would make thorough work of it in their own case, and, instead of merely amputating the foreskin, would castrate themselves, as heathen priests do. Perhaps this would be even a more powerful help to salvation" (4:162).

Paul has been accused of stooping to the use of vulgar language here. But one must remember that such terms were common on the lips of even the best people of his day.

13 Liberty The Greek word for "liberty" is *eleutheria*. It was used especially in NT times of the freeing of slaves. Paul says that the Christian is not to use his new freedom "for an occasion to the flesh"—or, "as an opportunity for the flesh"—"but by love serve one another."

True liberty is governed by love. But too often license is dominated by lust instead of taking our freedom as an opportunity for loving service to others. It is *freedom to do right* which

the Christian enjoys and which the one who is shackled by sin does not have.

Flesh The term "flesh" (*sarx*) has been used in a physical sense thus far in this Epistle. But here in chapter 5 it is employed with an ethical meaning, indicating that it is the part of man's nature which seduces to sin—what is often called the carnal nature. Paul uses the term in both senses frequently. One of the important problems in the exegesis of his Epistles is deciding which meaning the word *sarx* has in any particular passage. In this chapter it appears to have primary reference to the carnal self, or the sinful nature within.

In the "works of the flesh" enumerated in verses 19–21 we find not only sins related to the physical body but also wrong attitudes of the spirit. In fact, all 9 mentioned in verse 20 are of the latter type. It is obvious that here "flesh" is not synonymous with "physical body," as many have contended.

16–18 Spirit The problem in this passage relates to the word "spirit." In vv. 16 and 18 the Greek word *pneuma* occurs twice without the article. In v. 17 it is found twice with the article. The question is: Are we going to spell it with a capital *S* and thus refer it to the Holy Spirit, or are we going to spell it with a small *s* and refer it to the human spirit? Such distinctions are not indicated in Greek. So the problem becomes one of interpretation. We have to decide how we are going to interpret *pneuma* before we can write our translation in English.

Since the article occurs in v. 17, it is rather clear that the translation here is "the Spirit." But in vv. 16 and 18, where *pneuma* is found without the definite article, the matter is more difficult.

The division of opinion is not along theological lines. One of the most conservative commentators of our generation, Lenski, argues strongly that *pneuma* here refers to the human spirit. On the other hand, Burton, who is rather liberal, is equally emphatic in insisting that the reference is to the Holy Spirit. How are we to decide? Perhaps the answer lies partly in the fact that the human spirit is in a sense dead apart from the Holy Spirit. Hence, a spiritual life and a Spirit-led life mean the same thing. So, although the difficulty of translation here is an insoluble problem, the essential interpretation of the passage is the same whichever way we translate it. The only way to avoid fulfilling fleshly desire is to keep walking in the Spirit, or in the realm of spirit rather than in that of flesh.

The Holy Spirit comes in His fullness to cleanse our hearts from all sin. But the only way we can keep clean is to keep filled with the Spirit. The only way we can keep sanctified is to let the Holy Spirit dwell in our hearts unhindered.

16–17 *Lust* The word "lust" is found many times in the KJV. In most of the recent translations this is changed to "desire." Why?

"Lust" is usually too strong a rendering for the noun *epithumia* and the verb *epithumeō*. These words properly refer to desire of any kind, whether good or bad. That is the usage of classical Greek writers and even of the Septuagint. Not only so, but we find the same spread of meaning in the NT, where only the context can indicate whether the desire is good or evil.

Of its use in these verses Burton says: "It is clearly without moral colour in the present passage" (p. 300). It is clear that the term "lust" is not a correct translation for us today, however satisfactory it may have been 300 years ago. A better translation for our day would be "desire."

6:1 *Overtaken* The verb *prolambanō* means "take beforehand, be beforehand, anticipate." But it also means "overtake, surprise."

Some scholars have held that the reference here speaks of a Christian being surprised in his sin by some fellow Christian who caught him in the act. But it seems much more natural to hold that it refers to the believer being himself overtaken by sin, perhaps to his own surprise. That is, it suggests the deceitfulness of sin in causing us to stumble before we realize fully the danger we are in. Burton says that it means being taken by surprise or seized unawares. The element of surprise should be emphasized.

ible *Fault* The word *paraptōma* means "a false step, a blunder, a misdeed, trespass" (A-S). Moulton and Milligan (VGT) say that in the papyri the word is used for "a 'slip' or 'lapse' rather than a wilful 'sin.' " Though it is one of the many Greek words for sin in the NT, it suggests the less serious type of sin, that which is not deliberate or premeditated.

This word is translated in the KJV in a variety of ways. It is rendered 9 times by "trespass," 7 times by "offence," 3 times by "sin," and twice each by "fault" and "fall."

There is a very real sense in which all of us are guilty of "trespasses" against others' rights. The proper attitude is to ask forgiveness or

apologize as soon as we become aware of the offense.

But the word in this context seems to carry a somewhat stronger connotation. It refers to a lapse in Christian experience which requires a restoration. The unfortunate one, however, has been overtaken or seized suddenly and unexpectedly. That often happens, especially to the new convert.

"*Spiritual*" We have put this word in quotation marks because the question may well be raised as to whether the term is to be taken literally or ironically. A comparison with 1 Corinthians suggests that there were in the Early Church what might be called "supersaints." They prided themselves on being more spiritual and looked down on all other church members as being less spiritual. In Corinth they were the ones who said they were "of Christ" (1 Cor. 1:12). Probably they were the most contentious ones in the whole church, speaking in tongues and putting a high premium on spiritual gifts and ecstatic experiences. In the earlier part of this Epistle, Paul has also been dealing with professed Christians whose spirit was entirely foreign to the spirit of Christ.

It may be, however, that the word here should be taken literally, rather than ironically. In that case the verse is an exhortation to the more spiritual members of the church to watch over the weaker ones with loving care and solicitous prayer.

In any case it is definitely an admonition that we should not criticize those who may lose out spiritually, but that we should seek to restore them. It is always easier to condemn than to assist, to push a person down than to lift him up. Too often Christians take the easier, selfish way in such cases.

Restore The verb *katartizō* means "mend, repair." It is used in Matt. 4:21 and Mark 1:9 of the fishermen on the Lake of Galilee mending their nets. It speaks here, then, of a broken relationship that needs to be repaired.

2, 5 *Burden(s)* On the surface it would seem that these verses contradict each other. The first commands: "Bear ye one another's burdens." The second declares: "For every man shall bear his own burden." But when we examine the Greek we find two different words for "burden." The distinction in their meanings will eliminate the seeming contradiction.

The word in v. 2 is *baros*. It comes from *bareō*, which means "depress, weigh down." The verb is used in 2 Cor. 1:8 ("we were pressed out of measure") and 5:4 ("do groan, being burdened").

It obviously refers to being pressed down by a crushing weight. The adjective *barus* is translated in the KJV "heavy," "weighty," and "grievous."

The word in v. 5 is *phortion*. It comes from the verb *pherō*, which means "bear, carry." So *phortion* means "something carried."

Putting these two verses together we get the thought clearly. When any Christian has an extra heavy, crushing burden—such as unexpected illness, sudden death of a loved one, loss of home, financial pressure, or the like—other Christians should help to lift the pressing burden, lest it crush him to the ground. But that does not mean that we are to shirk our regular responsibilities in life. Verse 2 is no excuse for laziness or expecting others to do our work. We like to translate v. 5: "For every man must carry his own load." We are to shoulder our own responsibilities and not push them off on others.

6 Communicate The word "communicate" in this passage does not mean what it does to us today. It is one of over 200 words in the KJV that have radically changed their meaning since 1611.

The Greek word is *koinōneō*. It means "to share in (something) with (someone)." Now the passage becomes clear. Those who are taught spiritual truth should share their material goods with the teacher. It is in line with Paul's regular teaching that ministers of the gospel should receive financial remuneration in order that they may devote their full time to spiritual duties.

11 Letter The word Paul uses is *grammasin* (dative-instrumental plural). The Greek word *gramma*—from which we get our word gram-

mar—was used first for "that which is traced or drawn, a picture." Then it meant "that which is written." It is used primarily of letters of the alphabet. Only once in the NT is it used for an epistle (Acts 28:31).

The usual Greek word for "letter" in the sense of a document is *epistolē*, from which our word *epistle* comes. But that is not the word used here. The Greek does not say, "You see what a lengthy letter I have written." It very clearly says: "You see with how large letters I wrote to you with my own hand."

Why did Paul write with large letters? Three answers might be given. The first is that he was writing under the pressure of strong feeling. He was excited and distressed over the situation in the churches of Galatia. So he "scrawled" with large letters. Another suggestion is that he may have had poor eyesight—as hinted elsewhere—and so had to make his letters large. A third possible reason is that Paul wanted to emphasize the importance of what he was saying. The large letters would then have the force of underlining or of boldface type.

17 Marks The Greek term is *stigma*, which has been taken over into English. It occurs only here in the NT.

Betz writes: "*Stigma*, from *stizō* 'to prick,' 'tatoo,' 'mark' with a sharp instrument . . . means basically 'prick,' 'point,' then the mark burned on the body with hot iron, then generally 'distinguishing mark'" (TDNT, 7:657). He goes on to say, "Branded marks were carried especially by domestic animals, slaves, criminals, and later soldiers" (p. 658).

Paul often speaks of himself as a slave of Christ. So we may translate here: "I bear in my body the brandmarks of the Lord Jesus."

What were these marks? Betz suggests: "The most convincing explanation is that the reference is to his wounds and scars" (p. 663).

Ephesians

1:1 *Saints* The word "saints" occurs more frequently (9 times) in Ephesians than in any other book of the NT, with the exception of Revelation. It is found once in Matthew (27:52) but nowhere else in the Gospels. In Acts it occurs 4 times. It is used twice in Hebrews, twice in Jude, and 13 times in the Book of Revelation. But it is in Paul's Epistles that it is most frequently used (40 times) making a total of 62 times in the NT. It is always plural except in Phil. 4:21.

The Greek word is the adjective *hagios*, which means "holy" and is so translated 162 times in the NT. Thus its literal meaning is "holy ones," and this is the translation in Spencer's *The New Testament* (1937).

The earliest meaning of *hagios* was "devoted to the gods," and so "sacred, holy" (LS-J, p. 9). Thayer notes that it comes from the noun *hagos*, "religious awe, reverence." Hence its meanings are: "1. properly *revered, worthy of veneration* . . . 2. *Set apart for God, to be, as it were, exclusively his* . . . 3. of sacrifices and offerings; *prepared for God with solemn rite, pure, clean* . . . 4. in a moral sense, *pure, sinless, upright, holy*" (pp. 6–7).

Cremer notes, as most writers do, that it was used very rarely in classical Greek (p. 36). After tracing the use of *qadosh* in the OT he concludes: "God's holiness, accordingly, must manifest itself in and upon Israel, Israel must participate in it. 'Ye shall be holy, for I am holy,' is henceforward the keynote and the norm of the union subsisting between God and His people; so that the 'I am holy' is explained, 'I am holy, Jehovah, who sanctifieth you,' Lev. 21:8; Ex. 31:13" (p. 43).

Pursuing further the OT presentation, Cremer writes: "It thus appears how fully *righteousness* . . . is the necessary correlative of holiness" (*ibid.*). He continues: "Man's true relationship to God's holiness accordingly is that *blending of fear and trust* which we find in Holy Scripture throughout" (p. 46). Again he says: "Opposition to sin is the first impression which man receives of God's holiness. . . . God's holiness signifies *His opposition to sin, manifesting itself in atonement and redemption or in judgment*" (pp. 46–47).

Shifting to the NT picture, Cremer notes: "As God's holiness becomes sanctification, and believers are received into the fellowship of the redeeming God . . . the predicate *hagios* is suitable of them also, seeing that it expresses the special grace which they experience who are in the fellowship and possession of the New Testament salvation" (p. 51).

It seems clear that in the NT the term "saints" is used for all Christians. Vine is correct when he says: "In the plural, as used of believers, it designates all such and is not applied merely to persons of exceptional holiness" (3:315). It designates Christians as those who are set apart to God in a saving relationship to Him through Jesus Christ. As such they partake of His nature and so are in a very real sense "holy ones."

3 *Blessings* The word "blessing" (singular in the Greek) is *eulogia*, from which we get "eulogy." The verb—"who hath blessed"—is *eulogeō* ("eulogize"), which means "to speak well of, praise . . . bless, prosper, bestow blessings on" (A-S, p. 187). The first "blessed" of this verse is the adjective *eulogētos*. The *New English Bible* translates it "praise be to." Perhaps that conveys about as accurately as can be done what it means to "bless" God. It suggests offering praise to Him who deserves it preeminently.

287

In Heavenly Places "In the heavenlies" is the literal Greek for "in heavenly places." Arndt and Gingrich say that it means simply "in heaven" (p. 306). This agrees with Thayer: "*the heavenly regions,* i.e., heaven itself, the abode of God and angels" (p. 247). Traub is in accord with this, asserting that the expression is equivalent to "in the heavens" (TDNT, 5:539). Vine says it means "heavenly, what pertains to, or is in, heaven (*epi,* in the sense of 'pertaining to,')," and so describes "the present position of believers in relationship to Christ" (2:209).

Salmond says of "spiritual": "It is best . . . to take *pneumatikē* to define the blessings in question as *spiritual* in the sense that they are blessings of grace, blessings of a Divine order, belonging to the sphere of immediate relations between God and man" (EGT, 3:246).

The phrase "in the heavenlies" occurs five times in this Epistle and nowhere else in the NT. It is the key phrase of Ephesians.

Lightfoot has a beautiful comment on the significance of this expression. He writes: "The heaven, of which the Apostle here speaks, is not some *remote locality,* some *future abode.* It is the heaven which lies within and about the true Christian" (p. 312).

This passage states a tremendous truth. God blesses us "with every spiritual blessing" (ASV) in the heavenlies in Christ. He has not promised everything *material* that we might wish. But He does offer every *spiritual* blessing. These spiritual blessings come to us in heavenly fellowship with Christ. We cannot have the blessings without Him. The greatest blessing any man can enjoy is the conscious presence of Christ in his heart.

In Christ This is the key phrase of Paul's Epistles—*en Christō.* It is the heart of his theology. Of its use here Salmond says: "The phrase expresses the supreme idea that pervades the Epistle" (EGT, 3:247). The great apostle saw clearly that all the blessings we receive from God come to us "in Christ." Paul's theology is definitely Christocentric. We cannot bypass Christ and find God. Neither can we find any spiritual blessings except as we seek them in Christ. He is in every sense the Mediator between God and men (1 Tim. 2:5).

The Greek preposition *en* (in) occurs three times in the latter half of this verse. God has blessed us *in* every spiritual blessing *in* the heavenlies *in* Christ. Lightfoot notes the force of this: "We are united to God *in* Christ; so united we dwell *in* heavenly places; so dwelling we are blessed *in* all spiritual blessings" (p. 312).

The challenge that confronts every Christian is to make sure that he remains "in Christ." Here alone are safety and salvation, peace and protection. Blessing comes through abiding in Him. As long as we are in Him we are His.

4 *Chosen . . . in Him* The doctrine of election bulks rather large in Ephesians. Paul here places a great deal of emphasis on the inevitable carrying out of God's eternal, sovereign purpose.

The word for "chosen" is *eklegō.* It means "*to pick out, choose.* In NT always middle . . . *to pick out for oneself, choose*" (A-S, p. 139). Occuring 21 times in the NT, it is regularly translated in the KJV as "choose" (choose out, make a choice). But the adjective derived from it, *eklektos,* is translated "elect" 16 times and "chosen" 7 times. Thus the idea of election is definitely involved.

On this passage Cremer makes the pertinent comment: "Ephesians 1:4 . . . cannot be taken to imply a division of mankind into two classes according to a divine plan before history began; it simply traces back the state of grace and Christian piety to the eternal and independent electing-love of God." He also points out that this verb is always used in Scripture for "God's dealings towards men in the scheme of redemption" (p. 404).

Schrenk writes: "This is the one place in the NT where we find *eklegesthai* with an accent on eternity." He goes on to say: "The purpose of election is described as responsible calling to a consecrated walk in the presence of God, in love" (TDNT, 4:175).

Alford prefers the idea of selection rather than election. He writes: "I render *selected,* in preference to *elected,* as better giving the middle sense,—'Chose for himself'—and the *eks,* that it is a choosing *out* of the world" (3:70).

On the general import of this doctrine Salmond says: "The idea of the divine election in the NT is not a philosophical idea expressing the ultimate explanation of the system of things or giving the *rationale* of the story of the human race as such, but a religious idea, a note of grace, expressing the fact that salvation is originally and wholly of God" (EGT, 3:249).

Without Blame The adjective *amōmos* is used in the Septuagint in connection with animals to be sacrificed on the altar. There it means "without blemish." But it also carries the ethical connotation, "blameless." Arndt and Gingrich note that it is used in this moral and religious sense in a number of secular Greek writers (p. 47).

This is the first occurrence of the adjective in the NT. It occurs again in 5:27. In the 7 places where it is found in the NT it is translated 6 different ways in the KJV.

Trench objects to the translation "without blame." He thinks that in later Hellenistic Greek it always means "without blemish" (p. 379). That is the way it is uniformly rendered in the English Revised Version. Vine approves this, but notes that it is used in the sense of "blamelessness in character and conduct" in the Psalms and Ezekiel (1:132).

Salmond emphasizes the fact that "blameless" is the meaning in classical Greek and the inscriptions. He concludes: "Little indeed depends on the decision between the two senses; for both terms, 'without blemish' and 'without blame,' may have *ethical* applications" (EGT, 3:249).

Concerning the two terms in this verse, "holy" and "without blame," Eadie writes: "The first is inner consecration to God, or holy principle—the positive aspect; the latter refers to its result, the life governed by such a power must be blameless and without reprehension—the negative aspect" (p. 21). He further adds: "The eternal purpose not only pardons, but also sanctifies, absolves in order to renew, and purifies in order to bestow perfection. It is the uniform teaching of Paul, that holiness is the end of our election, our calling, our pardon and acceptance" (pp. 21–22). The election here described is not that of the sinner to salvation but of the saint to sanctification.

In somewhat the same strain Alford says: "This holiness and unblamableness must not be understood of that justification by faith by which the sinner stands accepted before God: it is distinctly put forth here (see also ch. 5:27) as an ultimate *result* as regards us, and refers to that sanctification which follows on justification by faith, and which is the will of God respecting us. 1 Thess. 4:7" (3:71).

The expression "before him" is both a warning and a consolation. It is a warning because His all-seeing eye will miss nothing. One cannot harbor insincerity in his soul and get by with God. But it is also a comforting thought. One can never hope to be blameless in the eyes of men; Jesus was not. But God's eyes of love will overlook our faults and see our worthy motives. Alford expresses it beautifully thus: "*Before Him* (i.e. in the deepest verity of our being—thoroughly penetrated by the Spirit of holiness, bearing His searching eye, ch. 5:27: but at the same time implying an especial nearness to His presence and dearness to Him—and bearing a foretaste of the time

when the elect shall be 'before the throne of God,' Rev. 7:15)" (3:71).

5 *Predestinated* The verb "predestinate" is *proorizō*. In Acts 4:28 it is rendered "determined before." Its other five occurrences are all in Paul's Epistles. It is translated "predestinate" twice in Romans (8:29, 30) and twice in Ephesians (1:5, 11). In 1 Cor. 2:7 it is rendered "ordained," which is an inadequate translation, since the *pro-* is equivalent to *fore-* or *pre-*. The verb means "foreordain" or "predestinate"; that is, "to determine or decree beforehand" (Cremer, p. 462). Cremer also insists that the main emphasis of this verb lies on the purpose of the decree. He writes: "The matter to be considered when the word is used is not who are the subjects of this predestination, but what they are predestined to" (*ibid.*).

Eadie has a good comment here:

> Foreknowledge, which is only another phase of electing love, no more changes the nature of a future incident, than afterknowledge can affect a historical fact. God's grace fits men for heaven, but men by unbelief prepare themselves for hell. It is not man's nonelection, but his continued sin, that leads to his eternal ruin (p. 24).

Adoption What is that to which God has foreordained us? The answer is: adoption. The Greek word is *huiothesia*, which occurs three times in Romans (8:15, 23; 9:4), once in Galatians (4:5), and here. It is a typically Pauline expression. Literally the term means "a placing as son."

"Adoption of children" should be "adoption as sons." We become children of God by the new birth; we become sons of God by adoption. The latter is a legal term.

Adoption was not a Jewish custom, but a Roman one (Latin, *adoptio*). After noting the informal adoption of Esther by Mordecai (Esther 2:7), Salmond states: "Adoption in the sense of the legal transference of a child to a family to which it did not belong by birth had no place in the Jewish law." He continues: "Thus among the Romans a citizen might receive a child who was not his own by birth into his family and give him his name, but he could do so only by a formal act, attested by witnesses, and the son thus adopted had in all its entirety the position of a child by birth, with all the rights and privileges pertaining to that" (EGT, 3:251–52).

This custom is reflected in the inscriptions of that period, though very rare in the literature. Deissmann writes: "The frequency with which these formulae occur permits of an inference as to the frequency of adoption, and lets us understand that Paul was availing himself of a generally intelligible figure when he utilized the term *huiothesia* in the language of religion" (BS, p. 239).

Moulton and Milligan cite an interesting example of a legal form of adoption, found on a fourth-century papyrus at Oxyrhynchus, Egypt. It reads: "We agree, Heracles and his wife Isarion on the one part, that we have given away to you, Horion, for adoption (*eis huiothesian*, same phrase as here) our son Patermouthis, aged about two years, and I, Horion, on the other part, that I have him as my own son so that the rights proceeding from succession to my inheritance shall be maintained for him" (VGT, pp. 648–49). We, as adopted sons, are heirs of God and joint heirs with Christ (Rom. 8:17).

6 Accepted "Accepted in the beloved" is a beautiful phrase. The expression "he hath made ... accepted" is all one word in the Greek, *echaritōsen*. Its only other occurrence in the NT is in Luke 1:28—"thou that art highly favoured." The verb *charitoō* comes from the noun *charis*, "grace." It means "to endow with *charis*," or "to cause to find favour" (A-S, p. 480). The idea here is that God has extended His favor or grace to us in Christ.

7 Redemption This word occurs more frequently in Ephesians (1:7, 14; 4:30) than in any other book of the NT (twice in Romans and twice in Hebrews; once each in Luke, 1 Corinthians, and Colossians). The Greek term *apolytrōsis* was formed from *lytron*, "a ransom." It was used originally for "*buying back* a slave or captive, *making* him *free* by payment of a ransom" (AG, p. 95). Buechsel says: "It means 'setting free for a ransom,' and is used of prisoners of war, slaves, and criminals condemned to death" (TDNT, 4:352). The ransom price paid is indicated by the phrase that follows: "through his blood." The NEB has "release" instead of "redemption," but the KJV translation is somewhat fuller in meaning.

Forgiveness The word *aphesis* occurs 8 times in the Gospels and 5 times in Acts, but only twice in Paul's Epistles (here and Col. 1:14) and twice in Hebrews. In the KJV it is translated "remission" 9 times, "forgiveness" 6 times, and once each "deliverance" and "liberty." The last two are in a quotation from the OT in Luke 4:18.

Thayer defines the word thus: "1. *release*, as

from bondage, imprisonment, etc. . . . 2. *aphesis hamartion*, *forgiveness*, *pardon*, of sins (properly *the letting them go*, as if they had not been committed), *remission of their penalty*" (p. 88). Abbott-Smith gives first "*dismissal, release*" and then "*pardon, remission* of penalty" (p. 70). Arndt and Gingrich have: "1. *release* from captivity. . . . 2. *pardon, cancellation* of an obligation, a punishment, or guilt . . . with *hamartion forgiveness of sins*, i.e., cancellation of the guilt of sin" (p. 124). Cremer gives its meaning in the NT as "setting free, remission" (p. 297).

Deissmann has made an interesting study of the use of *aphesis* in the Septuagint (BS, pp. 98–101). There it is translated "brooks" (Joel 1:20) and "rivers" (Lam. 3:47). He shows that this is probably due to the use of the term in Egypt—the Septuagint was made in that country—for the "releasing" of water by opening the sluices. Then there is the common use in the Septuagint of *aphesis* for the Year of Jubilee. It was a time of release of land. In Egypt the word was used for the "release" of land from the payment of taxes. This usage is found both on the famous Rosetta Stone (196 B.C.) and the papyri. The Septuagint also uses it for the sabbatical year (Exod. 23:11).

Moulton and Milligan carry the matter a step farther. They write: "A nearer approach to the Pauline use for 'forgiveness' is afforded by the occurrence of the word in inscriptions for remission from debt or punishment" (VGT, p. 96). Vine points out that it is never used in the Septuagint for the remission of sins (2:123).

On the other hand, says Trench, "*aphesis* is the standing word by which forgiveness, or remission of sins, is expressed in the New Testament" (p. 114). He explains its meaning thus: "He, then, that is partaker of the *aphesis*, has his sins forgiven, so that, unless he bring them back upon himself by new and further disobedience (Matt. 18:32, 34; 2 Pet. 1:9; 2:20), they shall not be imputed to him, or mentioned against him any more" (p. 119).

Is "remission" or "forgiveness" the better translation? That is hard to answer. The former is more technically correct, but "forgiveness" is more understandable today.

Sins The word here is *paraptōma*. It is translated "trespass" 9 times, "offence" 7 times (all in Romans), "sin" 3 times (Ephesians and Colossians), "fall" twice (Romans) and "fault" twice. The first is accurate and probably should have been used throughout the NT, as it is, indeed, in Eph. 2:1.

The earliest meaning of the term is "a false

step, blunder," and so "a misdeed, trespass" (A-S, p. 342). Literally it means "a falling beside." Trench defines it as: "an error, a mistake in judgment, a blunder" (p. 246). Eadie writes: "The word, therefore, signifies here that series and succession of individual acts with which every man is chargeable, or the actual and numerous results and manifestations of our sinful condition" (pp. 41–42).

8 Prudence The word *phrēnesis* occurs only once elsewhere in the NT (Luke 1:17). There it is rendered "wisdom." Coming from *phrēn*, "mind," it literally signifies "way of thinking." Trench says that it means "a right use and application of the *phrēn*" (p. 284). Arndt and Gingrich give: "understanding, insight, intelligence" (p. 874).

Comparing *phrēnesis* with *sophia* ("wisdom"), Eadie writes: "*Sophia* is the attribute of wisdom, and *phrēnesis* is its special aspect, or the sphere of operation in which it develops itself." He goes on to say: "Intellectual action under the guidance of *sophia* is *phrēnesis*—intelligence" (p. 47).

The concensus today is that "insight" is the best translation (so Moffatt, Goodspeed, Berkeley, RSV, NEB). *The Twentieth Century New Testament* and Knox have "discernment." The question as to whether "in all wisdom and prudence" modifies "abounded" or "having made known" is much debated and cannot be settled.

9 Good Pleasure The word is *eudokia*. It is translated "good pleasure" here and in v. 5, as well as Phil. 2:13 and 2 Thess. 1:11. But in Luke 2:14 and Phil. 1:15 it is rendered "good will." Which is better?

Cremer says that *eudokia* denotes: "a *free will* (willingness, pleasure), *whose intent is something good*" (p. 214). Moulton and Milligan note that the term "is apparently confined to Jewish and Christian literature." After citing several instances of the word in the papyri, they say: "All these passages confirm the meaning 'good pleasure,' 'goodwill,' which *eudokia* seems to have in all its New Testament occurrences" (VGT, p. 260).

Abbott-Smith defines the meaning as: "good pleasure, good-will, satisfaction, approval" (p. 185). Arndt and Gingrich prefer "favor, good pleasure" here (p. 319). Vine says that the word "implies a gracious purpose, a good object being in view, with the idea of a resolve, shewing the willingness with which the resolve is made" (1:298). Westcott defines *eudokia* as meaning "gracious purpose" (p. 13). The *Modern Language Bible* (Berkeley) reads "kind in-

tent." It is difficult to decide between "good pleasure" and "good will." The term seems to denote both ideas.

10 Dispensation The Greek word is *oikonomia*. It comes from *oikos*, "house," and *nemō*, "manage." An *oikonomos* is a house-manager or "steward," as the word is correctly translated in the NT. So *oikonomia* rightly means "the office of a steward" and is properly translated "stewardship" in Luke 16:2–4. But that does not seem to fit well here. Some modern attempts are "arrangement" (Berkeley), "plan" (RSV) and "arranging" (Goodspeed).

The difficulty here is highlighted by Alford: "After long and careful search, I am unable to find a word which will express the full meaning of *oikonomia*" (3:76). He finally settles for "economy." Salmond says the meaning here is "an *arrangement* or *administration* of things" (EGT, 3:259). Though the term "dispensation" has been abused in recent times, it is difficult to find a satisfactory substitute. The necessary thing is to hold to its original meaning of "a dispensing," which is what "stewardship" really is. Westcott writes: "The exact meaning which it conveys appears to be in each case that of a distribution of Divine treasures, which have been committed by God to chosen representatives, that they may be faithfully administered by them" (p. 13).

Fulness of Times There are two Greek words for "time." Westcott differentiates them thus: " 'Time' (*chronos*) expresses simply duration; 'season' (*kairos*) a space of time defined with regard to its extent and character" (*ibid.*). *Kairos* is the term used here. The whole phrase, "the fulness of times" refers, not to the end of this age, but to "the whole duration of the Gospel times" (Alford, 3:76). It means "the filling up, completing, fulfillment, of the appointed seasons, carrying on during the Gospel dispensation . . . the giving forth of the Gospel under God's providential arrangement" (*ibid.*).

Gather Together in One The whole phrase "that . . . he might gather together in one" is a single word in Greek (*anakephalaiōsasthai*). The term was used in classical Greek for "*repeating summarily* the points of speech." Salmond continues: "In late Greek the verb means also to present in *compendious form* or to *reproduce*" (EGT, 3:261).

The meaning is well expressed by Westcott: "The word here expresses the typical union of all things in the Messiah, a final harmony answering to the idea of creation" (p. 14).

11 _Inheritance_ The verb *klēroō* (only here in NT) is from *klēros*, "lot." It therefore signifies properly: "(1) to cast lots. (2) to choose by lot. (3) to assign by lot, assign a portion" (A-S, p. 249). Arndt and Gingrich would translate here: "in whom our lot is cast" (p. 436). Eadie defines the verb as, "I assign an inheritance to someone"; in the passive, "I have an inheritance assigned to me"; and would render it here: "We have been brought into possession" (p. 59).

Salmond notes the connection with the assignment of territories by lot to the various tribes of Israel, and adds: "Thus the idea of *lot* or *portion* passed over into that of *inheritance*." He prefers here to translate either "we were made a heritage" or "we were taken for God's inheritance" (EGT, 3:263). Ellicott, in his commentary on the Greek text of Ephesians, adopts: "In whom we were also chosen as His inheritance" (p. 26). Recent translations support this; e.g., "made a heritage" (Berkeley), "have been given our share in the heritage" (NEB).

Counsel, Will The first word is *boulē*, the second *thelēma*. The former occurs 12 times in the NT and is rendered "counsel" 10 of these times (once "will"; once "advise"). The cognate *boulēma* is found twice and is translated "purpose" and "will." The verb *boulomai* occurs 34 times and is rendered "will" 15 times and "would" 11 times.

Abbott-Smith defines *boulē* as: "*Counsel, purpose* (in classics, especially of the gods.)" (p. 84). The meaning of *boulomai* is: "*to will, wish, desire, purpose, be minded,* implying more strongly than *thelō* the deliberate exercise of volition" (*ibid.*). Arndt and Gingrich define the noun as "resolution, decision," although they say that *boulomai* is "no longer different in meaning from *thelō*" (p. 145). Thayer thinks the former indicates deliberation, the latter inclination (p. 286).

The second word, *thelēma*, occurs 64 times in the NT. It is translated "will" all but two of these times (once "desire"; once "pleasure"). It comes from *thelō*, which is found over 200 times and is almost always rendered "will." In later Greek (including NT) it seems to be used interchangeably with *boulomai*, taking over the functions of the latter. Salmond says: "The distinction between *boulē* and *thelēma* is still much debated, scholars continuing to take precisely opposite views of it." Nevertheless he concludes:

> In a connection like the present it is natural to look for a distinction, and in such cases the

idea of *intelligence* and *deliberation* seems to attach to the *boulē*. This appears to be supported by the usage which prevails in point of fact in the majority of NT passages, and particularly by such occurrences as Matt. 1:19. Here, therefore, the will of God which acts in His foreordaining purpose or decree, in being declared to have its *boulē* or "counsel," is set forth not *arbitrarily*, but *intelligently* and by deliberation, not without reason, but for reasons, hidden it may be from us; yet proper to the Highest Mind and Most Perfect Moral Nature (EGT, 3:264).

Ellicott says that the entire phrase ("counsel of his own will") "solemnly represents the Almighty Will as displaying itself in action; *thelēma* designating the *will* generally, *boulē* the more special expression of it" (p. 27).

12 _Trusted_ The verb is *proelpizō*, found only here in the NT. Since the KJV correctly translates *elpis* as "hope" 53 out of the 54 times it occurs (once "faith"), it is difficult to understand why it uses "trusted" in this passage. All modern versions have the correct rendering, "hoped." Literally the verb means "hoped before," though "first hoped" is used in recent versions (RSV, NEB; cf. NIV).

13 _Sealed_ By the Holy Spirit the sanctified Christian is "sealed." The verb *sphragizō* is from the noun *sphragis*, a "seal" or "signet," or the impression made by this seal. Arndt and Gingrich give as one meaning of the verb: "*mark* (with a seal) as a means of identification . . . so that the mark which denotes ownership also carries with it the protection of the owner" (p. 804).

The *Harper's Bible Dictionary* has an excellent article on the "seal." Thousands of tiny seals, many of them like small spools in shape and size, have been found in excavations in the Middle East. They were "used to affix the ancient equivalent of written signatures to documents" and also "widely used whenever security from molestation was important," as in sealing jars of wine and oil, or bales of goods (p. 657).

The dominant idea of a seal is that it was a mark of ownership. When a person surrenders himself completely to Christ, to belong wholly to Him and no longer to be his own property, then he is "sealed" with the Holy Spirit as a sign that he belongs no more to himself, but to God.

Eadie comments as follows: "The sealing followed the believing, and is not coincident with it" (p. 66). The aorist participle, "having believed," normally signifies action antecedent to that of the main verb. He also writes: "The Divine image in the possession of the Spirit is impressed on the heart, and the conscious enjoyment of it assures the believer of perfection and glory. . . . That seal unbroken remains a token of safety" (*ibid.*).

14 *Earnest* The word *arrabōn* was a "legal and commercial technical term" meaning "*first instalment, deposit, down payment, pledge,* that pays a part of the purchase price in advance, and so secures a legal claim to the article in question, or makes a contract valid. . . . In any case, *arrabōn* is a payment which obligates the contracting party to make further payments" (AG, p. 109). Behm writes: "The Spirit whom God has given them is for Christians the guarantee of their full future possession of salvation" (TDNT, 1:475). So the Holy Spirit is the Christian's down payment on his heavenly inheritance, the guarantee that he will receive the rest, as well as being a foretaste of what heaven will be like. Moulton and Milligan say: "The above vernacular usage (found in the papyri of that period) confirms the NT sense of an 'earnest,' or a part given in advance of what will be bestowed fully afterwards" (VGT, p. 79).

But they also note that in Modern Greek *arrabona* is used for "the engagement-ring" (*ibid.*). This suggests that after the Christian has fallen in love with Christ he will someday be confronted with the challenge: "Will you be wholly mine, be my bride and belong to no other?" When a full, final Yes is given to that question, the Holy Spirit is given as an engagement ring, sealing our betrothal to Christ. Keeping this engagement ring—the Holy Spirit dwelling ungrieved in our hearts—assures us of final union with our Lord at the Marriage Supper of the Lamb (Rev. 19:7–9).

Possession The word *peripoēsis* is here translated "purchased possession." Occurring five times in the NT, it is rendered five different ways in the KJV—"to obtain" (1 Thess. 5:9); "the obtaining" (2 Thess. 2:14); "the saving" (Heb. 10:39); and "peculiar" (1 Pet. 2:9). The true sense of the term is described by Vincent: "The word originally means *a making to remain over and above;* hence *preservation; preservation for one's self; acquisition; the thing acquired,* or *a possession*" (3:369).

The rendering "purchased possession" is an overtranslation, found first in Tyndale (1535). The word denotes no more than "possession." It is possible that "purchased" was introduced from Wyclif, who had "purchasynge." The

Genevan version had "that we might be fully restored to liberty." The Rhemish (Catholic) version correctly says, "the redemption of acquisition."

The question is whether this is our possession in Christ or God's possession in us. Salmond favors the latter, as being more in line with the Old Testament concept of Israel as the people God acquired for himself (EGT, 3:270).

15 *Faith* One of the more difficult problems of textual criticism occurs in this verse. The words *tēn agapēn* ("love") are omitted in the earliest Greek manuscripts we have. They are missing not only in the two great fourth-century manuscripts, Vaticanus and Sinaiticus, but also in the third-century Papyrus 46. These are the three oldest manuscripts of Ephesians extant. Add to this Alexandrinus of the fifth century and it makes a formidable array of evidence against the genuineness of the words.

But without "love" the passage reads awkwardly. What is meant by faith toward the saints? Salmond rightly observes: "The documentary evidence is on the side of the omission. But the difficulty is to find in that case a suitable sense." He goes on to say: "The *pistis*, in short, if it belong to both clauses, must be introduced in two different aspects, as *belief* in the first clause and as *faithfulness* in the second" (EGT, 3:271). He doubts the reasonableness of doing this.

Westcott and Hort considered the words to be an interpolation from Col. 1:4 and omitted them from their Greek Testament. For that reason, apparently, they were omitted in the English Revised Version of 1881, which Westcott and Hort helped to produce. Though their Greek text was published that same year, advance copies of it were made available to the translation committee.

On the other hand, "love" is included in the ASV (1901), the RSV (1946), and the NEB (1961). It appears in the Nestle text. The translators of RSV and NEB were instructed to make their own decisions about variant readings as they went along, rather than following any printed text.

It is impossible to solve the problem with the data now at hand. Perhaps the best course is to leave "love" in the passage, without placing undue weight on it.

17 *Spirit* This is one of many passages in the NT where it is difficult to decide whether the reference is to the human spirit or the Holy Spirit. The older English versions have the former. But Salmond argues for the latter. He writes: "It is necessary, therefore, to take *pneuma* as = the *Holy Spirit*" (EGT, 3:274). Ellicott follows this interpretation, as do Eadie and Meyer. This seems to be preferable (cf. NIV).

Revelation   One of the strong reasons for interpreting *pneuma* in this passage as "Spirit" rather than "spirit" is this word *revelation*. The human spirit may possess "wisdom," but not "revelation." As Salmond rightly points out, *apocalypsis* (literally, "an uncovering") "has the stated meaning not of *understanding* mysteries but of *disclosing* them . . . not a *susceptibility* for knowledge, nor a *mind open* to revelation" (*ibid.*). Rather, *apocalypsis* is always used in the NT (18 times) for a divine disclosure. The verb *apokalyptō* is translated "reveal" in every one of its 26 occurrences. "Wisdom" may in a limited way be postulated of the human, but never "revelation." And the most important revelation is "the knowledge of him," which is beyond all merely human understanding.

Knowledge   The regular Greek word for "knowledge" is *gnōsis*. Paul uses it 23 times (out of 29 in NT). But the word here is *epignōsis*, which the apostle employs 15 out of the 20 times it occurs in the NT. Is there any difference?

Trench writes: "Of *epignōsis*, as compared with *gnōsis*, it will be sufficient to say that *epi* must be regarded as intensive, giving to the compound word a greater strength than the simple word possessed" (p. 285). Lightfoot says: "The compound *epignōsis* is an advance upon *gnōsis*, denoting a larger and more thorough knowledge" (*Colossians*, p. 138). And Salmond agrees: "It means a knowledge that is true, accurate, thorough, and so might be rendered 'full knowledge' " (EGT, 3:274).

Paul is fond of compound words. This fact seems to be a reflection of his powerful personality. He felt deeply and expressed himself strongly. His use of compounds with the intensive *epi* was but a projection of his very intense nature, which manifested itself also in a life of unsurpassed devotion to his Lord.

18 Understanding   For "eyes of your understanding" the Greek has "eyes of your heart" (*kardia*). The RSV is to be complimented for bringing this out in English. It is true that the Greek *kardia* (cf. cardiac), like the Hebrew *leb*, has a broader connection than is usually included in the English "heart." It is related to the intellect and will, as well as to the emo-

tions. In the OT it is used for the physical organ, but never so used in the NT. Matthew 12:40 has the expression "the heart of the earth." But the regular use of the term in the NT is thus defined by Abbott-Smith: "In a psychological sense, the seat of man's collective energies, the focus of personal life, the seat of the rational as well as the emotional and volitional elements in human life, hence that wherein lies the moral and religious condition of the man" (p. 230).

This spread of meaning is emphasized by Thayer. He gives these definitions: "The soul or mind, as it is the fountain and seat of the thoughts, passions, desires, appetites, affections, purposes, endeavors" (p. 325). Arndt and Gingrich make the main definition, "The seat of physical, spiritual, and mental life" and especially emphasize it "as center and source of the whole inner life, with its thinking, feeling, and volition" (p. 404).

Salmond points out the reason for the phrase here: "The knowledge is a *spiritual* knowledge; hence 'the eyes of the heart,' *kardia* being the 'inner man,' the seat and centre of the mental and spiritual life" (p. 275).

Inheritance   The word *klēronomia* (already in v. 14) is related to the verb *klēroō* (v. 11). As noted there, the root *klēros* means "lot." But all the cognate terms gradually lost sight of the method of casting lots and came to be related only to the idea of an inheritance or an inheritor ("heir").

What is meant by "his inheritance"? Salmond sounds a word of caution: "The *klēronomia* is not the inheritance which God has in us (a sense which the word seems never to have in the NT), but the inheritance which God gives to us and which is the object of our hope" (*ibid.*). The inheritance is "his" in that it comes from Him as its source of origin. Of the nature of this heritage Meyer comments: "*Doxa*, glory, is the essential character of the Messianic salvation to be received from God as an inheritance at the Parousia" (*Ephesians*, p. 340).

It should be noted that some very good exegetes explain "his inheritance in the saints" as meaning "the inheritance which *God* has in *His* people," as well as "that which they have in Him" (Alford, 3:84). Perhaps a combination of these meanings is best.

19 Exceeding   The verb *hyperballō* (twice in 2 Corinthians, three times in Ephesians, nowhere else in NT) literally means "throw over or beyond" or "run beyond." In the NT it is always used metaphorically with the idea of "to exceed, surpass, transcend" (A-S, p. 458).

Vincent makes the apt observation: "Compounds with *hyper, over, beyond,* are characteristic of Paul's intensity of style, and mark the struggle of language with the immensity of the divine mystery, and the opulence of divine grace" (3:371). A glance at the *Englishman's Greek Concordance* or Moulton and Geden's *Concordance to the Greek Testament* will show that of 25 compounds with *hyper* in the NT, 16 are found only in the Pauline Epistles and others are used mainly by Paul. They reflect the apostle's strong personality and his almost frustrated desire to seek to express in words the inexpressible greatness of God's grace.

This sense of the inadequacy of language to convey spiritual truths is even more prominent in the Greek text than in English translation. Paul is struggling to say what cannot be said. It is utterly impossible to put the fullness of divine reality in human language, to compress the infinite into what is finite. That is why one cannot receive the full impact of the meaning of the Word of God except as the Holy Spirit illuminates his mind to understand it. Just so, Paul struggled to express the great thoughts with the words which so weakly convey them. It is with words that we have to deal. But our goal is always to get behind those words to the meaning. Biblical interpretation is the most challenging, demanding task that anyone can undertake.

The sincere student, and especially preacher, of the Word of God will seek to use all the human tools he can get hold of—study of the original Greek and Hebrew, the best reference works available, the studies made by careful scholars. The minister who fills his shelves only with canned sermons and popular "how-to" books is not true to his calling. What he needs is spades with which to dig out eternal truths. Above and beyond all this he needs the Holy Spirit's help and guidance.

Greatness The word *megethos* is found only here in the NT. Such Pauline *hapax legomena* (words used only once) again reflect the outreach of the great apostle's mind in seeking to describe the wonders of divine redemption. One can almost see words stretching at their seams as Paul tries to pour more meaning into them.

Power The word *dynamis* occurs here for the first of five times in Ephesians. It is twice translated "might," but "power" is the best English equivalent. The terms derived from it—dy-namic, dynamite, dynamo—suggest something of the thrust of this word, which is found 120 times in the NT.

Who Believe "Who believe" is, in the Greek, "who are believing" (present participle of continuous action). This underscores the fact that this power is operating not in those who only once upon a time believed in Jesus Christ, but in those who are right now constantly believing in Him.

The Working "Working" is *energeia*. Abbott-Smith defines it: "*Operative power* (as distinct from *dynamics, potential power*)" (p. 153). Salmond agrees with this when he writes that it denotes: "power as *efficiency, operative, energising* power" (EGT, 3:276). The term is used only by Paul—6 times in the three Christological Epistles (Ephesians, Philippians, Colossians), and twice in 2 Thessalonians of Satan. In every case it is superhuman power.

Mighty Power The Greek has *kratos* of His *ischus.* Vincent comments:

> The A.V. frequently impairs the force of a passage by combining into a single conception two words which represent distinct ideas; translating two nouns by an adjective and a noun. . . . The idea is thus diluted, and the peculiar force and distinction of the separate words is measurably lost (3:371–72).

Eadie agrees with this when he writes: "To suppose that the apostle uses these terms including *energeia* without distinction, and for no other purpose than to give intensity of idea by the mere accumulation of synonymns, would indeed be a slovenly exegesis" (p. 94).

He distinguishes the meaning thus:

> *Ischus* . . . is—power in possession, ability or latent power, strength which one has, but which he may or may not put forth. . . . *Kratos* . . . is that power excited into action—might. *Energeia,* as its composition implies, is power in actual operation. *Ischus,* to take a familiar illustration, is the power lodged in the arm, *kratos* is that arm stretched out or uplifted with conscious aim, while *energeia* is the same arm at actual work, accomplishing the designed result (pp. 94–95).

Salmond supports these distinctions. He writes: "*Kratos* is power as *force, mastery,* power as shown in *action: ischus* is power as *inherent,* power as possessed, but passive. The phrase, therefore, means 'the efficiency of the active power which expresses inherent might' " (EGT, 3:276).

Vincent expresses the same general ideas in somewhat different language, as follows:

> *Strength* (*kratous*) is used only of God, and denotes *relative* and *manifested* power. *Might* (*ischuos*) is *indwelling* strength. *Working* (*energeian*) is the active, efficient *manifestation* of these. Hence we have here God's *indwelling* power, which inheres in the divine nature (*strength*); *the relative quality* or *measure* of this power (*might*); and the *efficient exertion* of the divine quality (*working*) (3:372).

The best translation of the entire phrase would probably be: "that working of the strength of his might" (ASV). The next verse gives an illustration of this in the case of the resurrection of Christ.

On the reason for the striking combination of those forceful words Eadie has this good comment:

> The use of so many terms arises from a desire to survey the power of God in all its phases; for the spectacle is so magnificent, that the apostle lingers to admire and contemplate it.... The mental emotion of the writer is anxious to embody itself in words, and, after all its efforts, it laments the poverty of exhausted language (p. 95).

21 *Principality* Four parallel terms are used in this verse. The first, *archē*, literally means "beginning." That is the way it is translated in the first verse of Mark's and John's Gospels. It is so rendered in 40 out of the 58 times it occurs in the NT. Eight times it is "principality," as here.

For its meaning in this passage Thayer suggests: "the first place, principality, rule." He adds: "Hence the term is transferred by Paul to angels and demons holding dominions entrusted to them in the order of things" (p. 77). Arndt and Gingrich's explanation is similar: "Also of angelic and demonic powers, since they were thought of as having a political organization" (p. 112).

Cremer carries the discussion a point farther. He notes that *archē* used in conjunction with the other terms in this verse signifies "supramundane powers," and then writes:

> The several synonymous designations by no means indicate a relationship of the angels one to another, nor a difference of rank ... for the synonymousness of the designations forbids such a distinguishing. They rather bear upon the relation and conduct of angels to-

ward mankind.... We have therefore no indication of, or connection whatever with, the Rabbinical or Neo-Platonic angelology, which in itself, upon closer comparison, is found to be altogether inappropriate (p. 115).

J. Massie thinks differently. He says that the four terms used here, "or their linguistic equivalents, are found among the orders of angels in Jewish-Christian books ranging over the New Testament period or its immediate neighbourhood" (HDB, 1:616). So perhaps this idea should not be ruled out altogether.

Meyer feels that the picture given here is of ranks of angels. He says that the group of terms here

> is neither to be understood ... of the *Jewish hierarchs*, nor ... of the various grades of *Gentile rulers*, nor ... of *human powers in general*, nor of ... 'any kind of glory and dignity'; but, as is shown by the immediate context ... and the analogous passages, iii. 10, Col. i. 16, Rom. viii. 38 (comp. also I Pet. iii. 22), of the *angels* who are designated according to their *classes of rank* ... and, in fact, of the *good* angels, since the apostle is not here speaking (as in I Cor. xv. 24) of the victory of Christ over *opposing* powers, but of His exaltation above the *existing* powers in heaven.

Meyer adds, however, that "the Rabbinical theory of classes of angels, elaborated under the influence of Platonism, yet dissimilar, is not in keeping with the designations of the apostle, and has evidently been elaborated at a later date" (pp. 342–43).

Power The word is *exousia*, which is more correctly translated "authority." Abbott-Smith defines the word thus: "1. properly, *liberty* or *power* to act, freedom to exercise the inward force or faculty expressed by *dynamis*. ... 2. Later ... of the power of *right, authority*" (pp. 161–62). Cremer maintains this distinction between *exousia* and *dynamis* when he writes: "If the latter imply the possession of ability to make power felt, the former affirms that free movement is ensured to the ability" (pp. 236–37).

Might This is *dynamis*, which is properly translated "power." Arndt and Gingrich note that while the first meaning of the word is "power, might, strength, force," it may also signify "*power* as a personal supernatural spirit or angel" (p. 207).

Dominion The word *kyriotēs* is from *kyrios,* "lord." So it properly means "lordship." The King James rendering comes from the Latin word for "lord," which is *dominus.* Arndt and Gingrich indicate that while the term is used especially for "the majestic power that the *kyrios* wields," it is employed in this passage (and Col. 1:16) for "a special class of angelic powers" (p. 461).

What do these four terms taken together signify? We have already noted several opinions, but might add two or three more. Eadie connects them thus: "Whoever possesses the *archē* enjoys and displays *exousia;* and whoever is invested with the *dynamis,* wields it in his appointed *kyriotēs.*"

Alford gives a rather careful discussion of distinctions. He writes:

> The most reasonable account of the four words seems to be this: *hyp. pas. archēs* gives the highest and fullest expression of exaltation: *k. exousias* is added as filling out *archēs* in *detail: exousia* being not only government, but every kind of official power, primary and delegated.... Then in the second pair, *dynamis* is mere *might,* the raw material, so to speak, of power: *kyriotēs* is that preeminence or lordship, which *dynamis* establishes for itself. So that in the first pair we descend from the higher and concentrated, to the lower and diffused: in the second we ascend from the lower and diffused, to the higher and concentrated. The following shows that in this enumeration not only earthly, nor only heavenly authorities are to be included, but both together,—so as to make it perfectly general (3:85).

Finally we note Salmond's conclusions. He opposes all idea of a graduated scale of angelic or demonic powers. Says he: "It is true that in the non-canonical writings of the Jews . . . the idea of variety of ranks among the angels appears, and that in the later Rabbinical literature it took strange and elaborate forms." Then he adds: "But between these and the simple statements of the New Testament there is no real likeness, and there is nothing here to point either to an ascending *scale* or to a *descending*" (EGT, 3:278).

Salmond summarizes his attitude toward this passage as follows:

> We must take the terms, therefore, not as dogmatic terms either teaching or implying any doctrine or graduated ranks, differentiated functions, or organized order in the world of angels, but as rhetorical terms brought together in order to express the unique suprem-

acy and absolute sovereignty proper to Christ, and meaning simply that whatever powers or dignities existed and by whatever names they might be designated, Christ's dominion was above them all (*ibid.*).

That seems to be a wise interpretation. Actually it does not differ radically from that of Alford. Verkuyl expresses it similarly in his *New Berkeley Version.* He translates the words: "All government and authority, power and lordship." Then he adds this in a footnote: "No classifying of spiritual orders, but a mention of the whole seen and unseen realm."

22 *Put All Things Under* The word "put" is *hypotassō.* It was originally used as a military term, meaning "to place" or "rank under"; then, "to subject, put in subjection" (A-S, p. 463). "All things" (*panta*) will not only be placed under Christ's feet, but put there in a state of complete subjection to Him. Only then will there be peace among men.

The verb is in the aorist tense, indicating that this has now been done. But this might almost be called a prophetic aorist. In the mind and purpose of God everything is already in subjection under His Son. But the actual completing of this will, in action, waits for the end of this age (Heb. 2:8–10).

Gave The verb is *didōmi,* which means "*to give*—in various senses, according to context—*bestow, grant, supply, deliver, commit, yield*" (A-S, p. 114). Arndt and Gingrich prefer the translation "made" (so RSV). The NEB has "appointed." But Alford objects to this rendering. He says: " '*Presented;*' keep the literal sense: not 'appointed' " (3:86). Eadie agrees when he writes, "There is no reason for changing the ordinary meaning of *edōke,* and rendering it 'appointed' " (pp. 104–5). Salmond also takes this position, against Calvin and some other earlier exegetes. He says: "The *edōken* is not to be taken in the technical sense of *appointed, installed* . . . but, as is indicated by the simple dative *tē ekklesia,* in its ordinary sense of gave" (EGT, 3:280).

In the Greek "him" precedes the verb, which is the emphatic position. More than that, the pronoun—which in Greek is included in the verb—is expressed separately as well. This is done only in cases where the writer desires to give added prominence to it. So the position and separate expression of the pronoun give double emphasis to Christ. The thought is this: *Him*—the One whom God raised from the dead and exalted to His right hand (v. 20), far above every power and name (v. 21)—God has given to the Church as its Head. What a glorious thought!

Head The word *kephalē* occurs 76 times in the NT and is always translated "head." But the term is used both literally (of the physical head) and figuratively. In general one can say that the word is used literally in the four Gospels, Acts, and Revelation, as well as a few times in the Epistles. The metaphorical use is confined largely to Paul—1 Cor. 11:3 (3 times), Ephesians (4 times), and Colossians (3 times). In addition we have the expression "head of the corner" used of Christ several times (Matt. 21:42; Mark 12:10; Luke 20:17; Acts 4:11; 1 Pet. 2:7). One might also say that the figurative sense is found in Rom. 12:20 and Acts 18:6.

Church The Greek word *ekklēsia* occurs 62 times in Paul's Epistles. Salmond gives a good summary of its meaning:

> Used by the Greeks to designate an *assembly of the people called for deliberation* (cf. Acts xix. 39), and by the Septuagint as the equivalent of the Hebrew *qahal, the congregation* of Israel, especially when called in religious convention (Deut. xxxi. 30, 35c.) it expresses in the New Testament the idea of the fellowship or assembly of believers meeting for worship or for administration. And it expresses this in various degrees of extension, ranging from the small company gathering for worship in one's house (. . . Rom. xvi. 5; I Cor. xvi. 19, etc.), or the single congregation of village or city (Acts v. 11; viii. 3; I Cor. iv. 17, etc.), to the larger Christian communities of provinces and countries (I Cor. xvi. 1, 19; II Cor. viii. 1; Gal. i. 2, 22) and finally to the Church universal, the Church collectively, the whole fellowship of believers throughout the world (Matt. xvi. 18; I Cor. xii. 28; Phil. iii. 6; Col. i. 18, 24, 35c.). Here and in the other occurrences in this Epistle the word has this largest extension of meaning, with the further mystical idea of a unity vitally related to Christ, incorporated in Him, and having His life in it (EGT, 3:280).

23 Body The word *sōma* was used by Homer (about ninth century B.C.) for a *dead* body. But beginning with Hesiod (eighth century B.C.) it came to be employed for *living* bodies, whether of animals or men. Metaphorically it is "used of a (large or small) *number of men united into one society,* or *family as it were; a social, ethical, mystical body;* so in the *New Testament of the church*" (Thayer, p. 611).

This figure of the Church as the "body" of Christ is found 10 times in the NT. As would be

expected, it occurs most frequently in the Christological Epistles—5 times in Ephesians (1:23; 4:12, 16; 5:23, 30) and 3 times in Colossians (1:18, 24; 2:19). It is also found once each in Romans (12:5) and 1 Corinthians (12:27). Besides this, the Church is referred to as a "body" in several other passages without specifically stating "the body of Christ" (1 Cor. 10:17; 12:13; Eph. 2:16; 4:4; Col. 3:15). The meaning of the latter phrase in 1 Cor. 10:16 may be open to debate.

Concerning the significance of the Church as the Body of Christ, Alford writes: "He is its Head; from Him comes its life; in Him, it is exalted; in it, He is lived forth and witnessed to; He possesses nothing for Himself,—neither His communion nor His glorified humanity,—but all for His Church" (3:86).

Salmond points out the implication of "body" in this way: "The relation between Christ and the Church, therefore, is not an external relation, or simply one of Superior and inferior, Sovereign and subject, but one of life and incorporation" (EGT, 3:281). The Church is "the instrument also by which He works" (*ibid.*). The last sentence is a very solemnizing thought.

Eadie points out a bit more specifically some further implications. He says:

> There is first a connection of life: if the head be dissevered, the body dies. The life of the church springs from its union to Christ by the Spirit, and if any member or community be separated from Christ, it dies. There is also a connection of mind: the purposes of the head are wrought out by the corporeal organs—the tongue that speaks, or the foot that moves. The church should have no purpose but Christ's glory, and no work but the performance of His commands. There is at the same time a connection of power: the organs have no faculty of self-motion, but move as they are directed by the governing principle within . . . Energy to do good, to move forward in spiritual contest and victory, and to exhibit aggressive influence against evil, is all derived from union with Christ. There is, in fine, a connection of sympathy. The pain or disorder of the smallest nerve or fibre vibrates to the Head, and there it is felt. Jesus has not only cognizance of us, but He has a fellow-feeling with us in all our infirmities and trials (pp. 107–8).

The above has been quoted at length because it presents a splendid, usable outline for a sermon on this subject. Aside from a contemplation of the members of the Trinity, there are few topics more rich in blessing and helpfulness for the Christian than the relation of

Christ to His Church. A sermon on this subject should serve to inspire and uplift, to challenge and comfort. The trouble with most Christians is that they live—in their conscious thoughts and feelings—too much in isolation from Christ, the Head.

Fulness The word is *plērōma*. Thayer says of it: "1. etymologically it has a passive sense, *that which is* (or *has been*) *filled;* very rarely so in classical Greek." He further suggests: "In the New Testament the body of believers, as that which is filled with the presence, agency, riches of God and of Christ" (p. 158). Somewhat similarly Cremer writes that in this passage the fullness of Christ "is a name given to the church, because the church embodies and shows for all that Christ . . . is" (p. 501).

The word comes from the verb *plēroō*, which means "fill, make full, fill to the full." Abbott-Smith goes on to define *plēroma* thus: "the result of the action involved in *plēroō* . . . , hence, 1. in passive sense, *that which has been completed,* complement, plenitude, fullness" (pp. 365–66).

Arndt and Gingrich indicate the difference of opinion as to the exact meaning of *plērōma*. Under the definition "that which makes something full or complete, supplement, complement," they say: "Figuratively, perhaps of the church which, as the body, is *to plērōma*, the complement of Christ, who is the head Eph. 1:23"; then they add: "Much more probably the Ephesian passage belongs under 2. *that which is full of something*" (p. 678).

Alford agrees with this, as he says: "Here, the simple and primary meaning is by far the best,—'*the thing filled,*'—'*the filled up receptacle*' . . . the meaning being, that the church being the Body of Christ, is dwelt in and filled by God: it is His *plērōma* in an especial manner—His fulness abides in it, and is exemplified by it" (3:87).

Eadie has a long discussion of *plērōma*. He first asserts, against Erasmus and others, that it is in apposition with *sōma* (body). That seems clearly correct. He further rejects the idea that *plērōma* means either multitude or the divine glory. Finally he sets aside the active connotation of *plērōma*—the thought that the Church complements Christ—held by Chrysostom, Calvin, and others. He comments: "The idea is a striking, but a fallacious one. It is not in accordance with the prevailing usage of *plērōma* in the New Testament, and it stretches the figure to an undue extent" (p. 112). He writes: "The word, we apprehend, is rightly taken in a passive sense—that which is filled up." And then he concludes: "So the church is named *plērōma,* or fulness, because it holds or contains the fulness of Christ" (p. 113). It is obvious that this is in agreement with Alford's interpretation.

With this consensus Salmond agrees. He says: "Hence *plērōma* is to be taken in the passive sense here, as is done by most commentators, and the idea is that the Church is not only Christ's body but that which is *filled by Him.*" After comparing this usage with the similar one in Colossians, he concludes: "Here the conception is that this plenitude of the divine powers and qualities which is in Christ is imparted by Him to His Church, so that the latter is pervaded by His presence, animated by His life, filled with His gifts and energies and graces" (EGT, 3:282).

In his commentary on Colossians and Philemon, Lightfoot has an extensive special note, "On the meaning of *plērōma*" (pp. 257–73). He points out, as do all lexicons, that the verb *plēroun* has two distinct meanings—(1) "To fill," or (2) "To fulfil, complete, perfect, accomplish"—and adds: "The word occurs about a hundred times in the New Testament, and for every one instance of the former sense there are at least four of the latter" (p. 257). He differs from the majority of commentators in insisting that it is this second meaning which should be applied to the noun. He writes: "As *plēroun* is 'to complete,' so *plērōma* is 'that which is completed,' i.e. the complement, the full tale, the entire number or quantity, the plenitude, the perfection" (p. 258). He believes this agrees with "its commonest usages in classical Greek" (*ibid.*).

After noting the use of *plērōma* in the Gospels, Lightfoot finally comes to a comparison of its meaning in Colossians and Ephesians. This is governed by the differences in aim in the two Epistles. He continues:

> While in the former the Apostle's main object is to assert the supremacy of the Person of Christ, in the latter [Ephesians] his principal theme is the life and energy of the Church, as dependent on Christ. So the *plērōma* residing in Christ is viewed from a different aspect, no longer in relation to God, so much as in relation to the Church. It is that plenitude of Divine graces and virtues which is communicated through Christ to the Church as His body. The Church, as *ideally* regarded . . . becomes in a manner identified with Him. All the Divine graces which reside in Him are imparted to her; His "fulness" is communicated to her: and thus she may be said to be His *plērōma* (p. 263).

Westcott is in essential agreement with Lightfoot. He says: "For while, on the one side, Christ gives their true being to all things by His presence . . . and Christians in a special sense reach their 'fulness,' their complete development, in Him . . . on the other side, all things are contributary to Him, and He himself finds His fulness in the sum of all that He brings into a living union with Himself" (p. 28).

It would appear that we should allow both meanings: the Church as the receptacle of divine fullness, and the Church as the completion of Christ. The second interpretation is dismissed by many commentators as being too daring. But F. W. Beare helpfully suggests that this completion of Christ is not to be referred to His divine nature, which obviously was eternally complete, but rather to "the contingent manifestation of him in his function as Messiah. . . . In this contingent sense the church is necessary to his completion" (IB, 10:637). Beare quotes Westcott (above) approvingly and adopts his interpretation of *plērōma*.

2:1 *Quickened*

This verse serves as a good example of the apparent necessity for supplying words in an English translation which have no direct support in the Greek. For this purpose the King James translators used italics, to indicate that such words were not represented in the original.

Often the added words in italics dilute the effectiveness and force of the Greek text (e.g., 1 Thess. 4:3). At other times they actually distort the true sense of the passage. For instance, "somewhat" in Rev. 2:4 is positively misleading. The Greek says clearly: "But I have against you that you neglected (or left) your first love."

But in the case of the passage before us, some addition seems necessary. Literally it reads: "You [plural] being dead in your trespasses and sins." The Greek has no main verb in the first three verses of this chapter, which seem to constitute a sentence. A Greek sentence can be complete without any verb; but that is not the case in English. Usually, though, it is only the copulative verb ("to be") which must be supplied. Here something more is needed—or so it seems.

The first printed English New Testament was by Tyndale (1525). His translation became the main basis for the KJV. He has: "And hath quickened you also that were deed in trespasse and synne." The Great Bible (1539) comes a little closer to the KJV. It reads: "And you hath he quyckened, where as ye were deed in trespasses, and synnes." The Geneva Bible (1560) introduced the use of italics for words not in

the original. It has: "And you *hath he quyckened also*, that were dead in trespasses and synnes."

Weymouth (1902) varies strikingly in placing the verb at the end of verse 3—"to you God has given Life." But other private translators have usually supplied the copulative verb. *The Twentieth Century New Testament* (1901) has: "To take your own case again. Once you were, so to speak, dead because of your offences and sins." Moffatt (1913; rev. ed., 1922) reads rather similarly: "As with us, so with you. You were dead in the trespasses and sins" (continuing the sentence to the end of verse 3). Goodspeed (1923) also carries on the sentence. He has: "You also were dead because of the offences and sins in the midst of which you once lived." Charles B. Williams (1937) follows this same line: "You too were dead because of the shortcomings and sins in which you once lived." Verkuyl's *New Berkeley Version* (1945, 1959, 1969) reads very similarly: "You, too, were dead in your trespasses and sins" (cf. NIV). It is obvious that modern translators prefer to supply the copulative verb so as to make a complete sentence.

The English Revised Version (1881) followed the general lead of the KJV, only modifying it to read: "You *did he quicken*, when ye were dead through your trespasses and sins." The ASV (1901) simply changed *did he quicken* to *did he make alive*. The RSV followed rather closely, with this wording: "You he made alive, when you were dead through the trespasses and sins." But the NEB (NT, 1961) conforms more nearly to the pattern set by private translations in this century. It reads: "Time was when you were dead in your sins and wickedness."

The question is: Does the context justify the insertion found in similar terms in the three standard versions? The verb "quicken" does not occur until verse 5. It would seem that the copulative verb, as in the above recent translations, is adequate and less open to criticism.

Trespasses and Sins

The Greek noun *paraptōma* (trespass) has already been noted (1:7). What is the difference between "trespasses" and "sins"? Vincent makes this distinction: "*Trespasses*, special acts. *Sins*, all forms and phases of sin: more general" (3:374). Salmond says: "Etymologically, *paraptōma* points to sin as a *fall*, and *hamartia* to sin as *failure*." But he adds: "It is impossible to establish a clear distinction between the two nouns in the plural forms, as if the one expressed *acts* and the other *states* of sin, or as if the former meant single trespasses and the latter all kinds of sins" (EGT, 3:283). He takes the whole as a general declaration that it is by sin we are made dead.

But most commentators find some distinction. Eadie writes: "Perhaps while the first term refers to violations of God's law as separate and repeated acts, the last . . . may represent all kinds of sins, all forms and developments of sinful nature" (p. 118). He says more specifically: "Thus *paraptōmata*, under the image of 'falling,' may carry an allusion to the desires of the flesh, open, gross, and palpable, while *hamartiai*, under the image of 'missing the mark,' may designate more the desires of the mind, sins of thought and idea, of purpose and inclination" (p. 119). This seems to be a helpful, as well as valid, distinction. It is in agreement with what Olshausen had already declared: "The plural *hamartiai* of course denotes also workings of sins, not, however, sinful *acts*, so definitely as *paraptōmata*, but rather inward sinful movements of the soul in desires and words" (5:54).

The thought seems to be that what makes the natural man spiritually dead is not only his violation of God's laws. This would constitute him condemned to die. But it is something deeper. He is not only subject to death or even under the sentence of death; he is actually dead, because under the control of a sinful nature.

In Is it "in trespasses and sins" or "through trespasses and sins"? In the Greek no preposition occurs; it is simply the dative case, which can be rendered several ways. The "in trespasses" form would be called the locative dative; "through trespasses" would be the instrumental dative.

The older translators took it the first way. "In" is used by Wycliffe, Tyndale, the Great Bible, the Geneva Bible, and the KJV. But the RV (English and American) has "through," which is equivalent to "by means of." Weymouth agrees. *The Twentieth Century New Testament* is even more specific. It reads: "because of," as do Goodspeed and Williams. The RSV has "through," but the NBV and the NEB have "in."

What do the commentators say? Olshausen writes: "Men are of course here called *dead* through transgressions" (5:54.). Salmond says emphatically: "The dative is the instrumental dative, 'by trespasses,' not *in* them" (3:283). Alford makes it "causal dative," which would be much the same. Similarly, Meyer writes: "The dative denotes the 'efficient cause' of the death" (p. 356). Ellicott prefers "by," not "in," holding that the dative here indicates the instrumental cause. Westcott adopts "through." A. T. Robertson, however, says that it is the locative here.

It is evident that the matter is not fully settled. Probably the best solution is to allow both meanings to the dative. It is certainly true that sin is the cause of our spiritual death. But it is just as correct to say that we are dead "in" our sins.

When two possible interpretations of a grammatical construction in the Greek seem equally well supported, it may be the part of wisdom to adopt both, rather than committing oneself irrevocably to either one alone. Often both applications may be made in preaching, even in the same sermon.

2 *Walked* The verb *peripateō* is used 39 times in the Gospels, always for physical walking. Seven out of the 8 times it occurs in Acts it is also in the literal sense (exception—21:21). But Paul uses the term only in the metaphorical sense (32 times in his Epistles). It occurs most frequently in Ephesians (8 times).

Thayer notes that by Paul it is used "Hebraistically, *to live*"; specifically, "to regulate one's life, to conduct one's self" (p. 504). Arndt and Gingrich write: "In the New Testament this use of the word is decidedly Pauline. . . . Elsewhere it is reasonably common only in the two small Johannine letters, *live, conduct oneself, walk*, always more exactly defined" (p. 655).

Literally the verb means "walk *about*, implying *habitual* conduct" (Vincent, 3:67). Weymouth's translation brings this out: "Which were once habitual to you while you walked."

Though most English versions give the literal translation "walk," the metaphorical term "live" is used by Goodspeed, Williams, and NIV. Both renderings are equally acceptable.

Course How did they formerly live? Literally the answer is: "According to the age (*aiōn*) of this world (*cosmos*)." But that does not seem to make good sense in English.

Of the 128 times *aiōn* occurs in the NT, it is translated "ever" 71 times, "world" 38 times, and "age" only twice in KJV. The basic meaning of the term is "*a space of time, as,* a lifetime, generation, period of history, an indefinitely long period; in New Testament of an indefinitely long period, *an age, eternity*" (A-S, p. 122).

But what is its meaning in this passage? Eadie and Salmond agree that "course" is the most suitable translation here. The former says: "*Aiōn* sometimes signifies in the New Testament—'this or the present time'—certain aspects underlying it . . . It is its 'course,' viewed not so much as composed of a series of superficial manifestations, but in the moving principles which give it shape and distinction" (p. 122). Salmond writes: "In such a connection as the present *aiōn* comes near what we understand by 'the spirit of the age,' but is perhaps most happily rendered *course*, as that word conveys the three ideas of *tenor, development*, and limited continuance" (EGT, 3:283).

World   What is the distinction between *aion* and *kosmos*, two words often translated the same way in KJV? A. T. Robertson speaks of the "curious combination" of the two terms here and differentiates them thus: "*aiōn* (a period of time), *kosmos* (the world in that period.)" (4:524). Similarly Salmond observes: "The *kosmos* is the world as the objective system of things, and that as evil. The *aiōn* is the world as a world-period, the world as transitory" (EGT, 3:283). Goodspeed renders the whole clause clearly: "In the midst of which you once lived under the control of the present age of the world."

Prince of the Power of the Air   The RSV retains this translation, perhaps because it has become a fixed biblical phrase in the minds of Christians. Other versions vary considerably. Verkuyl (NBV) has "The prince of the aerial powers." Williams reads, "The mighty prince of the air." Goodspeed has "The master-spirit of the air." *The Twentieth Century New Testament* reads, "The Ruler of the Powers of the air." The NEB has "The commander of the spiritual powers of the air."

The first term, *archōn*, means "ruler," from *archō*, "I rule." The second, *exousia*, means "authority." The third, *aēr*, is obviously the origin of English "air" (cf. "aerial"). It was used by Homer and other early writers for the lower and denser atmosphere in distinction from *aither* (cf. "ether"), which referred to the higher, rarer realms. Arndt and Gingrich translate the phrase: "The ruler of the kingdom of the air" (p. 20).

Meyer agrees with most commentators in identifying this as the devil, ruling over demons, who were supposed by the Jews to have their main base of operations in the air. He writes: "The *devil* Paul here represents as *the ruler of the might of the air*, in which *exousia* is *collective*, denoting the totality of the mighty ones (the demons, Matt. xii. 24) concerned.

This *exousia* has its seat in the air, which exists between heaven and earth" (p. 358).

Children of Disobedience   "Sons of disobedience" is a more accurate translation. The phrase is a typical Hebraism. "Sons of disobedience" (RV) suggests "belonging to disobedience as sons to a parent" (Vincent, 3:375). It is the same construction as "sons of light" (1 Thess. 5:5). Salmond comments: "The term *huios* (son) in its topical sense and followed by the genitive of a *thing*, expresses what is in intimate relation to the thing, what belongs to it and has its innate quality. 'Sons of disobedience' are those to whom disobedience is their very nature and essential character, who belong wholly to it" (EGT, 3:284). Thayer notes that in the NT *apeitheia* (disobedience) carries the connotation of "obstinate opposition to the divine will" (p. 55).

Prince, Spirit   These two words seem to be in apposition in this verse, both referring to the devil. But the former is in the accusative case and the latter in the genitive. So grammatically they cannot be appositives. "Spirit" has to modify "prince," as does *exousia* in the previous clause.

The correct explanation seems to be that, just as we have the Spirit of God or Christ, so we have the spirit of Satan—"that particular Spirit whose domain and work are in evil men" (EGT, 3:284). God influences men through His Holy Spirit. Satan influences them through His evil spirit. This can also be thought of as his hosts of demons who carry out his will in seeking to defeat God's will. C. S. Lewis, in his *Screwtape Letters*, has indicated something of the manner in which these demonic forces operate to tempt men and lead them astray.

3 Conversation   There are three different Greek words which are translated "conversation" in the KJV, and none of them means "conversation" as we use the term today.

"Had our conversation" is all one word in the Greek, *anestraphēmen*. The verb *anastrephō* occurs 11 times in the NT and is translated 8 different ways in KJV: "return" (Acts 5:22; 15:16); "have . . . conversation" (here and 2 Cor. 1:12); "live" (Heb. 13:18; 2 Pet. 2:18); "abide" (Matt. 17:22); "overthrow" (John 2:15); "behave" (1 Tim. 3:15); "be used" (Heb. 10:33); "pass" (1 Pet. 1:17).

A look at the lexicons shows that the word does suggest a variety of meanings. Thayer has "1. to turn upside down, overthrow . . . 2. to turn back . . . to return . . . 3. to turn hither and thither ... to turn one's self about, sojourn, dwell ... to conduct one's self, behave one's self, live" (p. 42).

The verb is compounded of *ana*, "again," and *strephō*, "turn." Hence it literally means "turn again." Arndt and Gingrich note that transitively it can mean "upset, overturn," as in John 2:15. In the passive it is used reflexively in the sense "turn back and forth." Figuratively it is used of human conduct, with the meaning "act, behave, conduct oneself, live"; that is, practice certain principles (p. 60).

Deissman, in his *Light from the Ancient East*, insists that this ethical use of *anastrephō* is not necessarily Semitic—as Thayer held—since it is found commonly in non-Semitic Greek situations. He cites an example from an inscription at Pergamum (p. 312), and several more from the same place in his *Bible Studies* (p. 194). Moulton and Milligan furnish quotations from the papyri in which the verb is used with the connotation "conduct oneself, behave" (VGT, p. 38).

For this passage Arndt and Gingrich suggest: "live in the passions of the flesh," which means "be a slave to physical passion" (p. 61). It is quite clear that the best translation of the verb here is "lived" (ASV, RSV, NEB, NASB, NIV).

Desires The word *thelēma* occurs 64 times in the NT and is translated "will" 62 times, including 6 times in Ephesians. Here alone it is rendered "desire"; and in Rev. 4:1, "pleasure."

It comes from the verb *thelō*, which basically means "wish" or "will." It may refer primarily to desire (wish, wish to have, desire, want) or to purpose (wish, will, wish to do) (AG, p. 355).

The word "fulfilling" is literally "doing" (*poiountes*). So Arndt and Gingrich would translate this clause "doing what the flesh desires" (*ibid.*).

Mind The Greek word translated "mind" is not *nous*, but *dianoia* (in the plural). It means "understanding, intelligence, mind" (as the organ of thinking), but also "*mind* as a kind of thinking, disposition, thought." Here it suggests "*senses, impulses* in a bad sense" (AG, p. 186). Moffatt has "impulses."

In spite of the fact that the translation "mind" is retained in ASV and RSV, it would seem that the better rendering is "thoughts" (so Weymouth, Williams, Goodspeed, NIV).

5 Sins "Sin" in the KJV New Testament is usually the translation of *hamartia* (172 times)

or the related term *hamartēma* (4 times). But here the Greek word is *paraptōma*, the most common rendering of which is "trespass" (so 9 times in KJV, 7 times "offence," and 3 times "sin"). Almost all the modern versions correctly have "trespasses" here.

Quickened In the time when the KJV was made, the verb "quicken" meant "to live or restore life to, to make alive" (OED, 8:54). It was only a little later (1626) that Bacon used it in its modern sense, "to hasten, accelerate" (*ibid.*, p. 55).

The Greek word is *synzōopoieō*, found only here and in Col. 2:13. It is compounded of *syn*, "together," *zōē*, "life," and *poieō*, "make." Hence the ASV gives the correct rendering for today: "Made us alive together." This brings out the proper connection and contrast with "dead."

Paul was especially fond of compounds with *syn*. He believed in a spiritual "togetherness"! That much-used term today would have been very meaningful for him. In verses 5 and 6 he has 3 of these compounds: make alive together, raise up together, and make to sit together. There are over 175 Greek compound words in the New Testament with the prefix *syn*, and many of these are found only in Paul's Epistles.

7 Exceeding The great apostle was also fond of compounds with *hyper*, the equivalent of the Latin *super*. He believed ardently and enthusiastically in a super religion—not just barely getting by, but an abundant life in Christ Jesus.

The word "exceeding" is a participle, *hyperballon*. The verb *ballō* means "throw" or "cast." So *hyperballō* is literally "throw beyond." But in the NT it is used only figuratively (five times) in the sense "exceed, surpass, transcend" (A-S, p. 458). The participle would therefore mean "exceeding" or "surpassing." Arndt and Gingrich translate the participle as "surpassing, extraordinary, outstanding" (p. 848). The NBV and RSV both have "immeasurable."

10 Workmanship The Greek word is *poiēma*, from *poieō*, "I make." It occurs elsewhere in the NT only in Rom. 1:20, where it is translated very literally "the things that are made." Abbott-Smith defines the word as meaning "that which is made or done, a work" (p. 369). *The Twentieth Century New Testament* (1900), Weymouth (1902), and the NEB (1961) have "handiwork." This and "workmanship" (KJV, ASV, RSV, NASB, NIV) are equally good.

12 Without Paul writes that his Gentile readers were once "without Christ" (KJV), "separated from Christ" (RSV), "outside Christ" (Moffatt), "apart from Christ" (Weymouth).

The word *chōris* is properly an adverb, meaning "separately, apart." But in the NT (with the exception of John 20:7) it is used as a preposition—"separate from, apart from, without" (A-S, p. 486). The King James translators adopted the weakest rendering, "without" (35 out of 39 times). "Apart from" fits better in most passages. Probably here the strongest meaning should be chosen—"separate from" (NEB, NASB, NIV).

Aliens The Greek has the perfect passive participle of *apallatrioō*, "being in a state of alienation from." Arndt and Gingrich would translate it: "excluded from" (p. 79). Because it is a verb form, "alienated from" (RSV) is preferable to "aliens" (KJV).

Commonwealth Most English translations follow the KJV in adopting "commonwealth." The NBV has "the right of Israel's citizenship."

The Greek word *politeia* has both meanings. In the NT it occurs only one other time, in Acts 22:28, where it clearly means "citizenship." But does it have that sense here?

The word comes from *politeuō*, "to be a citizen," which is from *politēs*, "a citizen," and in turn from *polis*, "a city." This is due to the fact that "politics" was first related to the Greek city-state. One was not a citizen of a country, but of a city, such as Athens or Sparta. These were independent and autonomous.

While *politeia* can mean both "commonwealth" and "citizenship" (or the rights of a citizen), Salmond correctly observes: "The first of these is most in harmony with the theocratic term *tou Israel*, and so is understood by most" (EGT, 3:292). Eadie comments: " 'The commonwealth of Israel' is that government framed by God, in which religion and polity were so conjoined, that piety and loyalty were synonymous, and that to fear God and honor the king were the same obligation" (p. 164).

Without God The Greek word is *atheoi* (only here in NT), and one is tempted to translate, or rather transliterate, it, "atheists." But this temptation must be resisted. While it does mean "atheists in the original sense of being without God and also in the sense of hostility to God from failure to worship him" (WP, 4:526), yet Eadie is probably correct in objecting: "Not 'atheists' in the modern sense of the term, for

they held some belief in a superior power" (p. 167).

In classical Greek the word meant "slighting or denying the gods" (Plato), "godless, ungodly" (Pindar), or "abandoned by the gods" (Sophocles). But in the NT it means "without God, not knowing God" (A-S, p. 11).

Cremer says there are two main meanings of the term. First it was used actively in the sense "godless, forgetful of God." In the second place it was used passively—"without divine help, forsaken by God, excluded from communion with God." The latter is its meaning here (p. 281).

Salmond writes: "The adjective *atheos*, which is never found in the Septuagint or in the Apocrypha, and only this once in the NT, in classical Greek means *impious* in the sense of denying or neglecting the gods of the State; but it is also used occasionally in the sense of knowing or worshipping no god, or in that of abandoned by God." He goes on to say: "Three renderings are possible here—*ignorant* of God, *denying* God, *forsaken* of God" (EGT, 3:292). While Ellicott and Meyer prefer the third, probably the first fits best here. Arndt and Gingrich note that the term is used in this place "without censure" (p. 20).

14 The Middle Wall of Partition The Greek is *to mesotoichon tou phragmou;* literally, "the middle wall of the fence"—"the *fact* of separation being emphasized in *wall*, and the *instrument* of separation in *fence*" (WS, 3:378).

The first noun is a rare one, occurring only here in the NT. Moulton and Milligan cite only one example from the papyri and one from an inscription (VGT, p. 400). It is a compound of *mesos*, "middle," and *toichos*, "a wall." So it is translated literally here.

The second noun is from the verb *phrassō*, "fence in, stop, close." So it properly means "a fencing in." But in the NT it means a "fence" or hedge." The latter is the KJV translation in the other three places where the word occurs (Matt. 21:33; Mark 12:1; Luke 14:23). Eadie says: "*Phragmos* does not, however, signify 'partition;' it rather denotes inclosure" (p. 172). He concludes: "Any social usage, national peculiarity, or religious exclusiveness, which hedges round one race and shuts out all others from its fellowship may be called a 'middle wall of partition'; and such was the Mosaic law" (p. 173).

15 Law, Commandments, Ordinances These three words occur together only here. The first is the most general and occurs about 200 times in NT. The second is more specific, suggesting particulars, and found some 70 times. The third, Greek *dogma*, occurs only 5 times. Three of these occurrences are in Luke's writings (Luke 2:1; Acts 16:4; 17:7), where the word is translated "decree." Paul uses it here and in Col. 2:14, in both of which places it is rendered "ordinances" (KJV, RSV). It may be translated "regulations" (NBV, NEB, NIV).

Probably Weymouth shows best the relationship of these three words: He has: "The Law with its commandments, expressed, as they were, in definite decrees."

18 *Access* The word *prosagōgē*, literally "a bringing to," is found three times in the NT (Rom. 5:2; here; and in 3:12). Most translations have "access" (KJV, RSV, NEB, NASB, NIV). But Williams has "introduction." Eadie writes: "*Prosagōgē* . . . is 'introduction,' entrance into the Divine presence—an allusion, according to some, to approach into the presence of a king by the medium of a *prosagōgeus* (introducer); according to others, to the entrance of the priest into the presence of God . . . —not access secured but introduction enjoyed" (pp. 186–87).

19 *Strangers and Foreigners* Paul indicates that his Gentile readers were formerly "strangers and foreigners," or "strangers and sojourners" (RSV). Weymouth has "mere foreigners or persons excluded from civil rights."

It is obvious that the two Greek words here mean much the same thing. The first, *xenos*, is properly an adjective. It means "foreign, alien." With the genitive case following, as in the twelfth verse of this chapter, it denotes "strange to, estranged from, ignorant of"; as a substantive it means "a foreigner, stranger" (A-S, p. 307). In the KJV it is always translated "strange" (3 times) or "stranger" (10 times), except Rom. 16:23, where it is rendered "host"; that is, one who entertains strangers. The term indicates one who is not a citizen.

The second word is also an adjective—*paroikos*. It is compounded of *para*, "beside," and *oikos*, "house." So its original connotation in classical Attic was "dwelling near, neighbouring"; and as a substantive, "a neighbour" (A-S, p. 346). But in late writers, as in the Septuagint and in Philo, it is used in the sense of "foreign, alien"; and so as a substantive, "an alien, a sojourner" (*ibid.*). Arndt and Gingrich note that it is used "figuratively, of the Christians, whose real home is heaven" (p. 634).

As in the case of the former term, the *paroikoi* are contrasted with citizens. In inscrip-

tions of the second century B.C. the *politai* (citizens) and the *paroikoi* are noted as two segments of the population.

Moulton and Milligan say: "Hicks . . . has shown that *paroikos*, while never losing the idea of 'a sojourner,' 'a stranger' . . . is often found in the inscriptions in the sense of the classical *metoikos* to denote 'a licensed sojourner' in a town, 'whose protection and status were secured by the payment of a small tax,' as contrasted with *xenos*, a mere passing stranger (cf. Eph. 2:19)" (VGT, p. 496).

Whether Paul intended this distinction or simply used the two terms synonymously, we cannot be sure. But since he was himself a Roman citizen and had traveled widely, he was doubtless aware of this fine point, and may have had it in mind here. In that case, Bishop Wand's translation brings out the exact thrust of the passage: "You are no longer foreigners, or even licensed immigrants." Instead they were *sympolitai*, "fellow citizens" (so almost all the versions and translations). More than that, they were *oikeioi*, members of the "household" or "family" of God.

20 *Foundation?* It is often assumed that Paul here declares the "apostles and prophets" (probably NT prophets) to be the foundation on which the Church is built. But Meyer strongly objects. He says: "The apostles and prophets are *not* the foundation, but have *laid* it (I Cor. 3:10). *The foundation laid by the apostles and prophets* is the gospel of Christ, which they have proclaimed, and by which they have established the churches" (p. 393). Alford takes it as simply genitive of possession, not apposition.

Chief Corner Stone This is all one word in the Greek, *akrogōniaios*. It comes from *akros*, "highest," and *gōnia*, "an angle." Found only here and in 1 Pet. 2:6, it means "the corner foundation stone" (A-S, p. 18). Arndt and Gingrich note that the term is "purely biblical." Thayer comments: "For as the cornerstone holds together two walls, so Christ joins together as Christians, into one body dedicated to God, those who were formerly Jews and Gentiles" (p. 24).

21 *Fitly Framed Together* This again is one word in the Greek—*synarmologoumenē*. It is used "only in Christian writers" (AG, p. 792). In the NT it occurs only here and in Eph. 4:16.

22 *Builded Together* "Ye are builded together" is one word—*synoikodomeisthe*. It is a double compound, formed of *syn*, "together," *oikos,* "house," and *demō,* "build." The word occurs only here in the NT.

Habitation The word *katoikētērion,* "habitation," is likewise a rare one. It is found (in NT) only here and in Rev. 18:2.

One of the remarkable features of these four verses (19–22) is that they contain 6 compounds of *oikos,* "house." In verse 19 are *paroikoi*—those who are "beside" (*para*) the "house," not in it—and *oikeioi,* signifying those who "belong to the house" or family. In verse 20 occurs *epoikodomeō,* "build upon" (*epi*). In verse 21 is *oikodomē,* from *oikos,* "house," and *demō,* "build"; originally the act of building, and then the building itself, as here. Verse 22 has *synoikodomeō,* already noticed, and *katoikētērion.*

Paul thinks of the individual Christian, of the local church congregation, and of the Church of Jesus Christ as a "habitation" where God, through His Spirit, dwells. He also calls the Church a "holy temple" (v. 21). The word for "temple" is not *hieron,* which is used for the whole Temple area, but *naos,* which means "sanctuary." The latter is the better translation, because it was in the sanctuary itself that God's presence dwelt. The Holy Spirit is the Shekinah, the glorious presence of the Lord, in our hearts and in the Church.

3:1 Prisoner The word is *desmois,* from the verb *deō,* "bind." So it literally means "one who is bound." It is used regularly in the NT (16 times) in the sense of "prisoner."

Here Paul refers to himself as "the prisoner of Jesus Christ." The same expression occurs in Philemon, verses one and nine. In Eph. 4:1 and 2 Tim. 1:8 he calls himself a prisoner of the Lord.

This reflects an amazing faith. Actually Paul was a prisoner of the Roman Empire. But instead of bemoaning his fate—the lack of opportunity for preaching and traveling about in missionary work—he saw himself as the personal prisoner of Jesus Christ. He was bound in body, but free in spirit.

A very busy and widely traveled Christian worker once found himself flat on his back in bed. Tempted to feel sorry for himself and frustrated at his enforced inactivity, he turned for comfort to the twenty-third psalm. As he read the familiar words, "He maketh me to lie down," the Spirit suddenly put a period right at that point. The man went no farther. Here was the truth he needed. It was not ultimately the sickness that made him lie down, but the Lord—who wanted to talk quietly with His servant who had been too busy to listen attentively.

The great apostle was one of the busiest men of his day. Preaching, traveling, writing, organizing new churches—he had little time for meditation. Now he was "the prisoner of Jesus Christ," bound physically that he might be freed mentally and spiritually to meditate and pray. His thinking had time to settle, and in these Prison Epistles he has skimmed off the cream and given it to us.

2 Dispensation The word *oikonomia* is translated "stewardship" in the Gospel of Luke and "dispensation" in the Epistles of Paul (KJV)—the only places where it occurs in the NT. We have met it already in 1:10, where neither meaning seemed to fit very well in that place.

However, here the correct sense, "stewardship," fits exactly. To Paul was committed the "stewardship of God's grace" (RSV), that he might administer this grace to the Gentiles.

5 Ages The word is not *aiōn,* "age," but *genea,* "generation." Most recent English translations have "generations" (RSV, NEB, NASB, NIV). Out of 42 occurrences in the NT, *genea* is translated "generation" 37 times in the KJV, "time" twice, "age" twice (here and v. 21), and "nation" once.

The meaning of the term is "1. literally, those descended from a common ancestor . . . 2. basically, the sum total of those born at the same time, expanded to include all those living at a given time," and so "generation." It can, however, mean "3. *age,* the time of a generation" (AG, p. 153). For this passage Arndt and Gingrich suggest "other times."

6 Fellow Heirs In this verse three related terms occur. They all begin with the same prefix, but this is obscured in most English translations.

The words are *synklēronoma, synsōma,* and *synmetocha* (as spelled in Westcott and Hort). The prefix *syn* is a preposition "expressing association, fellowship and inclusion" and means "with, together with" (A-S, p. 424).

The first of these three terms is translated "fellow-heirs." Deissmann gives examples of this use in inscriptions of this period at Ephesus and Thessalonica (LAE, p. 92). The second word is rendered "of the same body" ("members of the same body," RSV). *Sōma,* "body," is used for the Church 8 times in this Epistle (not counting the compound, which is found only here in NT). The third term, found only here and in 5:7, means "joint partaker." The simple form, *metochos*, means "partaker" or "partner."

The ASV (1901) helpfully represents the common prefix of these three Greek compounds by translating them "fellowheirs, fellow-members of the body, and fellow-partakers."

7 Minister *I Was Made a Minister* is the title of the fascinating autobiography of the late Methodist bishop, Edwin Holt Hughes. The book vividly documents the fact that God makes His own ministers.

The phrase is translated by both Moffatt and Williams, "I was called to serve." Ballantine has, "I became a servant"; and Goodspeed, "I became a worker."

The noun is *diakonos*. Occurring 30 times in the NT, it is rendered (in KJV) "minister" 20 times, "servant" 7 times, and "deacon" 3 times. It is the word from which comes the English term "deacon," and is probably correctly translated this way in Phil. 1:1 and 1 Tim. 3:8, 12.

But in the other instances is "minister" or "servant" more accurate? Thayer defines the term thus: "One who executes the commands of another, especially of a master; a servant, attendant, minister" (p. 138). Abbott-Smith lists these last three meanings.

To us today "minister" does not primarily connote "servant." But that is its earliest meaning. The *Oxford English Dictionary* indicates "servant, attendant" as the first meaning, but labels this usage "obsolete" (4:473). Next it gives "one who waits upon, or ministers to the wants of another." This also it calls "archaic." The use of the term "minister" in an absolute sense for a clergyman began in Protestant circles in the 16th century, partly as a protest against the designation "priest" (4:474).

In the light of all this it is clear that in the NT "servant" is a more accurate translation of *diakonos* than "minister." The primary meaning of the Greek word is "one who serves." That is not what the English word "minister" connotes today.

There is a strange inconsistency in the translation of *diakonos* in Matt. 20:26 and 23:11 in the KJV. In both passages Jesus says that whoever would be great among the disciples should be their *diakonos*. But this is translated "minister" in the first instance, and "servant" in the second. The latter is, of course, correct. The same inconsistency occurs in Mark 9:35 ("servant") and 10:43 ("minister")—*diakonos* in both places.

The true meaning of the word is shown by its use in Matt. 22:13 for "servants" of a king and in John 2:5, 9 for the "servants" at the marriage in Cana. Commenting on these passages, Stott says: "In none of these instances is the *diakonos* working in his private capacity; he is the representative of a higher authority whose commission and command he is fulfilling" (John R. Stott, *The Preacher's Portrait*, p. 104).

8 Less than the Least This is an interesting phrase. How can one be "less than the least"? What is less than zero?

The adjective *elachistos* means "smallest, least." It is already a superlative form. But here we have *elachistoteros*—a comparative formed from a superlative! Thayer writes: "It is well known that this kind of double comparison is common in the poets; but in prose, it is regarded as faulty." He defines it: "less than the least, lower than the lowest" (p. 202).

What the apostle is seeking to say is that he felt himself the least worthy of God's grace and mercy. This passage is parallel to 1 Cor. 15:9—"For I am the least of the apostles, that am not meet to be called an apostle, because I persecuted the church of God."

Unsearchable The adjective *anexichniastos* is found only here and in Rom. 11:33. It means "that cannot be traced out" (A-S, p. 36). It is used in the Septuagint in Job 5:9; 9:10; 34:24. Moulton and Milligan think that Paul borrowed the word from Job, "and it is re-echoed in early Fathers" (VGT, p. 41). It simply emphasizes the fact that no one can plumb the depths or fathom the greatness of God's grace. The riches of Christ cannot be comprehended. Yet we are "joint-heirs with Christ" (Rom. 8:17)! Salmond notes that the term is used here "not in the sense of *inexhaustible*, but rather in that of *unfathomable*" (EGT, 3:306).

9 Fellowship The expression "fellowship of the mystery" seems a bit odd. As Salmond notes, the reading *koinōnia* (fellowship) "has the slenderest possible authority" (EGT, 3:307). All the oldest and best Greek manuscripts have *oikonomia*. We have already noted the meaning of this word in connection with its use in 1:10 and 3:2; in both places the KJV translates it "dispensation." Here it means: "the *dispensation* or *arrangement* of the mystery, to wit the admission of the Gentiles on equal terms with the Jews; the *mysterion* here having the same application as in iii.6" (*ibid.*).

Beginning of the World "Beginning of the World" is all one word in the Greek, *aiōnōn*, "ages." Salmond writes: "The formula *apo tōn* *aiōnōn* occurs in the NT only here and in Col. 1:26. . . . It means literally 'from the ages,' 'from the world-periods,' that is, *from the beginning,* or *since the world began*" (*ibid.*). Ellicott defines the expression here as meaning: "From the commencement of the ages when intelligent beings, from whom it could be concealed, were called into existence" (p. 71).

10 *By* One of the weaknesses of the KJV is its translation of Greek prepositions. "Of" is used constantly in the sense of "by," which it does not mean today. Here it is not "by the church," but "through the church." God will manifest His manifold wisdom *through* the Church of Jesus Christ. It is His placard display.

Manifold The Greek term is *polypoikilos,* an old, rare word (only here in NT). It literally means "much-variegated," or "having a great variety of forms." Salmond says: "The adjective is used of the rich variety of colours in cloths, flowers, paintings, etc." (EGT, 3:309).

It is difficult to represent this striking Greek term by any single word in English. Moffatt has, "the full sweep of the divine wisdom." *The New English Bible* says, "in all its varied forms"—a phrase which very correctly defines the meaning of the adjective. Perhaps the best single-word rendering is that adopted by Goodspeed and Verkuyl (NBV): "many-sided."

11 *Purposed* One might suppose that "purpose" and "purposed" are related terms in the Greek. But such is not the case. The first is *prothesin,* the second *epoiesen.*

The expression "eternal purpose" is literally "purpose of the ages"; that is, "the purpose which pertained to, existed in, was determined on in the ages" (Ellicott, p. 72).

The Greek word for "purpose" is *prothesis;* literally, a "placing before," or a "setting forth." It is used this way in the Synoptic Gospels, as also in Heb. 9:2 for the shewbread—literally, "the presentation of the loaves." But in Acts and Paul's Epistles it means "plan, purpose, resolve, will"—a sense found commonly in the classical Greek writers (AG, p. 713).

"Purposed" is something else. It is the exceedingly common (576 times in NT) verb *poieō,* which is translated "do" 357 times, "make" 114 times, and dozens of other ways in the KJV. It has two main meanings: first, "to make, produce, create, cause"; second, "to do, perform, carry out, execute" (A-S, p. 369).

Which is the dominant idea here? "Constituted" is preferred by Calvin, while others adopt "carried out, executed." After noting the latter, Alford writes: "I can hardly think that so indefinite a word as *poieō* would have been used to express so very definite an idea, now introduced for the first time. . . . The aorist seems to refer the act spoken of to the origination of the design." Then he adds: "Both senses of *poieō* are abundantly justified" (3:107).

Ellicott perhaps has a little broader perspective. He says: "The mention of the eternal purpose would seem to imply rather '*constituit*' . . . than '*exsecutus est*' . . . as the general reference seems more to the appointment of the decree than to its historical realization . . . ; still the words *en Christō Iēsou to kyrio hēmōn* seem so clearly to point to the realization, the carrying out of the purpose in Jesus Christ—the Word made flesh . . .—that the latter . . . must be considered preferable" (pp. 72–73).

With this judgment the majority of recent translators agree. Goodspeed, NBV, and NASB all have "carried out." Williams has "executed." Moffatt and the RSV have "realized." That seems to be the thought of the passage. God's purpose of the ages was finally "realized" in Christ Jesus, our Lord.

12 *Boldness* The Greek word is *parrēsia.* It comes from *pas,* "all," and *rhēsis,* "speech." Its earliest usage in classical Greek is for "*freedom of speech, plainness, openness, freedom* in speaking" (A-S, p. 347). In the Septuagint, Josephus, and also the NT, "from the absence of fear which accompanies freedom of speech" it means "confidence, boldness" (*ibid.*).

In the NT the word occurs a number of times in the dative case and is translated adverbially as "openly" or "plainly." In the noun sense it is rendered "boldness" 8 times and "confidence" 6 times. Its basic idea is that of "freedom" (NIV).

Confidence The term "confidence" here is quite another word—*pepoithēsis.* It comes from the perfect tense of *peithō,* "persuade," and so literally means "full persuasion." It is a late and rare word in Greek writers, but is found half a dozen times in the NT. In 2 Cor. 3:4 it is translated "trust," though the usage seems to be exactly the same as "confidence" in 2 Cor. 1:15 and elsewhere in the NT.

Access We have already noted the Greek word *prosagōgē* in Rom. 5:2 and Eph. 2:18, the only other places in the NT where it occurs. Some prefer the rendering "introduction" rather than "access."

The reason for mentioning this word again is that we wish to note the significance of the combination of the three terms here. Many translators paraphrase the passage. Moffatt has: "through whom, as we have faith in him, we enjoy our confidence of free access." Goodspeed reads: "Through union with him and through faith in him, we have courage to approach God with confidence."

15 Whole Family The Greek is *pasa patria*, translated in the KJV "the whole family." But since there is no article in the Greek, most modern translations have "every family." This is in keeping with strict grammatical usage.

Family The word *patria* is from *patēr*, "father." It was used by Herodotus in the sense of "lineage, ancestry" (A-S, p. 349). But more commonly in classical Greek it signified "a family or tribe." It is used only three times in the NT and is translated three different ways in the KJV—"family" (here); "lineage" (Luke 2:4); "kindreds" (Acts 3:25).

Thayer defines it as follows: "1. lineage running back to some progenitor, ancestry. . . . 2. a race or tribe, i.e. a group of families, all those who in a given people lay claim to a common origin . . . 3. family . . . nation, people" (p. 495). He thinks that *pasa patria en ouranois* means "every order of angels" (p. 496).

Cremer gives the various usage of the term in classical Greek and in the Septuagint and then concludes:

> The explanation of Eph. 3:14, 15 . . . is difficult, *from whom all that is called after a father, that bears his name, i.e.* the name of a *patria*. For, . . . *pasa patria*, since *pater* . . . is named, can only mean those *patriai* who are to be traced to *this pater*, the *patriai of the children of God*. . . . Thus Luther's translation, *over all who bear the name of children*, recommends itself as best (pp. 473–74).

The following translations are at least worthy of consideration: "from whom all fatherhood in heaven and on earth is named" (Spencer); "from whom all fatherhood, earthly or heavenly, derives its name" (Phillips). It should be noted however, that A. T. Robertson rejects "fatherhood" here (WP, 4:532) as does Salmond (EGT, 3:312).

16 Might The KJV (also RSV) has "strengthened with might." The Greek word for "might" is *dynamis*, which is correctly translated "power" in Acts 1:8—"But ye shall receive power, after that the Holy Ghost is come upon you." So the ASV is much superior here—

"strengthened with power." It is the dynamic power of the Holy Spirit that strengthens us in the inner man.

The King James translators correctly rendered *dynamis* as "power" in verse 20—"according to the power that worketh in us"; that is, the inward operation of the Holy Spirit. It would have been much better if they had been consistent and done so in verse 16.

17 Rooted and Grounded This combination is a favorite one with Paul—agriculture and architecture (cf. 1 Cor. 3:9). The first suggests roots going down deep into the soil. The second indicates the laying of a solid foundation.

The former participle is from the verb *rhizoō*, which means "to cause to take root," but is used metaphorically in the sense "to plant, fix firmly, establish" (A-S, p. 397). In the NT it occurs only here and in Col. 2:7. The latter is the verb *themelioō*, which means "to lay the foundation of, to found" (A-S, p. 205). Both are perfect passive participles, indicating a fixed state.

Most commentators feel that the two terms are intended to convey the same general thought, that of being firmly fixed or established. For instance, Salmond writes: "So here the two words probably express the one simple idea of being *securely settled* and *deeply founded*" (EGT, 3:314).

18 Able The word is *exischuō*. It is a compound of *ischuō*, which means "be strong, powerful . . . have power, be competent, be able" (AG, p. 384). The compound means "have full strength" or "be fully able." Salmond says: "The strong compound *exischuein* = to be *eminently able*, to *have full capacity*, occurs only this once in the New Testament and is rare in ordinary Greek" (EGT, 3:315). It should be translated "be fully able."

19 Passeth The RSV brings out much better than the KJV the full force of the strong Greek term used here. Instead of "passeth" it has "surpasses." The Greek is the compound participle *hyperballousan*. The whole phrase means literally "the knowledge-surpassing love of Christ" (*ibid.*).

20 Exceeding Abundantly Above This is all one word in the Greek—*hyperekperissou*. *Hyper* is the equivalent of the Latin *super*, "above." *Ek* means "out of." *Perissos* means "more than sufficient, over and above, abundant" (A-S, p. 357). So this double compound signifies "superabundantly, exceeding abundantly" (A-S, p. 458). Elsewhere in the NT it occurs only in 1 Thess. 3:10; 5:13. Arndt and Gingrich note that it is found nowhere else but in two Greek editions of Dan. 3:22 and in the *Testament of the Twelve* (Joseph 17:5). They give its meaning as "quite beyond all measure (highest form of comparison imaginable)" and would translate it here "infinitely more than" (p. 848). Ellicott renders it "superabundantly beyond" (p. 81).

21 *World Without End* The closing words of this chapter are literally: "to all the generations of the age of the ages; amen." The suggestion is that of the age being composed of generations and at the same time of succeeding ages. It is the strongest possible way of saying "for ever and ever."

4:1 *Walk* Five times in chapters four and five Paul instructs his readers as to how they should walk. In 4:1 he says, "Walk worthy of the vocation wherewith ye are called"; in 4:17, "Walk not as other Gentiles walk"; in 5:2, "Walk in love"; in 5:8, "Walk as children of light"; in 5:15, "Walk circumspectly." These passages make splendid texts for a series of sermons on "The Christian's Walk in a World Like This."

The verb *peripateō* occurs 96 times in the NT. In the KJV it is translated "walk" in all but three places. In these it is rendered "go" (Mark 12:38), "walk about" (1 Pet. 5:8), and "be occupied" (Heb. 13:9).

The word has its literal meaning "walk" in the four Gospels, where it is found 39 times. It is the same for the first 7 occurrences in Acts. But in the 8th (Acts 21:21) it is used metaphorically, as in Ephesians. As would be expected, this is the dominant usage in the Epistles. The 5 occurrences in Revelation all carry the literal sense.

Abbott-Smith says that the word is used "metaphorically, of living, passing one's life, conducting oneself" (p. 356). This is clearly occ meaning here.

Vocation Since "vocation" (KJV) is the same root as "called," it is better to translate the former as "calling" (ASV). This brings out the close connection between the two in Greek.

2 *Lowliness* The word *tapeinophrosynē* (seven times in NT) is defined as "lowliness of mind, humility" (A-S, p. 439). Thayer gives the following explanation of its meaning: "having a humble opinion of one's self; a deep sense of one's (moral) littleness; modesty, humility, lowliness of mind" (p. 614).

The compound is derived from the adjective *tapeinos*. Cremer traces the development of the latter. Figuratively it meant:

> (a.) low, unimportant, trifling, small, paltry . . . (b.) humbled, cast down, oppressed . . . (c.) . . . modest, humble . . . submissive subject. . . . Further, the word is used in profane Greek (d.) very often in a morally contemptible sense cringing, servile, low, common . . . and it is (e.) a notable peculiarity of Scripture usage that the Septuagint, Apocrypha, and New Testament know nothing of this import of the word, but rather, in connection with (c.), deepen the conception, and raise the word to be the designation of the noblest and most necessary of all virtues (pp. 539–40).

Trench agrees fully with this characterization of the use of *tapeinos* in classical Greek. He says: "The instances are few and exceptional in which *tapeinos* signifies anything for them which is not grovelling, slavish, and mean-spirited." As far as *tapeinophrosynē* is concerned, "no Greek writer employed it before the Christian era, nor, apart from the influence of Christian writers, after" (p. 148). The word is used in Josephus, but only in a bad sense.

Christianity took the pagan idea of humility as suggesting a cringing, servile attitude and made it the finest, noblest virtue of all. This is one of the glories of the Christian religion.

Jesus set the example when He said, "I am meek and lowly in heart" (Matt. 11:29). The two adjectives He used correspond exactly to the two nouns in this clause, "with all lowliness and meekness." There is no place in the life of the true follower of Christ for pride and self-assertion.

"Lowliness" is used here by most standard English versions. However the NEB and NIV have "humble." The NBV has "humility," as does also the NASB. Moffatt has "modesty." But that is inadequate. As noted in the quotation from Cremer, Greek writers used the adjective *tapeinos* in the sense of "modest." After describing its higher meaning, Trench says: "Such is the Christian *tapeinophrosynē*, no mere modesty or absence of pretension, which is all that the heathen would at the very best have found in it" (p. 150). Cremer agrees with this when he writes: "Humility with the Greeks was in fact nothing higher than *modesty, unassuming diffidence*" (p. 540).

Meekness The word *prautēs* is defined by Abbott-Smith as "gentleness, meekness" (p. 377).

Occurring 11 times in the NT, it is always translated "meekness" in the KJV.

But the NEB and NIV have "gentle"; and "gentleness" is the rendering in Moffatt, Goodspeed, Williams, and the NASB. Certainly there is no meekness which does not manifest itself in gentleness. The Christian must make sure that his inward grace of meekness, implanted by the Holy Spirit, manifests itself in the outward graciousness of "gentleness."

Trench seems to have caught the true meaning of this term. He notes that it is not "mere natural disposition. Rather is it an inwrought grace of the soul; and the exercises of it are first chiefly towards God." He continues: "It is that temper of spirit in which we accept his dealings with us as good, and therefore without disputing or resisting; and it is closely linked with the *tapeinophrosynē*, and follows directly upon it (Ephes. iv. 2; Col. iii. 12), because it is only the humble heart which is also the meek" (p. 152). Put in simplest terms, meekness is submissiveness to the will of God.

3 *Endeavoring* The verb is *spoudazō*, which literally means "to make haste," and so "to be zealous or eager, to give diligence" (A-S, p. 414). In the KJV it is translated "endeavor" in two other places, but be "diligent," do or give "diligence" five times, and once each "was forward," "labor," and "study" (2 Tim. 2:15). "Eager" (RSV) expresses the idea of the Greek more accurately and adequately than "endeavoring."

Unity? The Greek word is *henotēs*, which occurs only here and in v. 13. It comes from *hen*, "one," and so very literally means "oneness."

True ecumenicity is not a union of denominations, but "the unity of the Spirit." In other words, the thing the NT teaches and that Christ desires is not organizational union but spiritual unity.

4–6 *One Body, One Spirit* This "unity of the Spirit" (v. 3) is spelled out more specifically in vv. 4–6. The true Church of Jesus Christ is "one body" spiritually because it is maintained by "one Spirit." Here is the ecumenical emphasis of the NT. It is still God's design and desire. When we are working for this we are "workers together with him." The Middle Ages had a far greater organizational unity of the Church than obtains today. But does that mean that the one, monolithic church was more spiritual and doing a greater evangelistic work than the many evangelical denominations today? To ask the question is to answer it.

The 5th verse is of interest to those who know Greek. For it contains all three genders of the word "one"—*heis, mia, hen*—the only place like it in the New Testament. The word "one" occurs 7 times in verses 4–6.

The 4th verse stresses the spiritual unity of the Church; the 5th verse, its oneness in loyalty, doctrine, and fellowship. The 6th verse points to the ultimate source of all authority in the Church—God the Father, who is "above all" (transcendent), "through all" (pervasive), and "in all" (immanent).

8 *Captivity Captive* The rendering of the KJV is a literal translation, but it does not make clear sense in English. Abbott-Smith says that the abstract noun translated "captivity" is used for the concrete, "captives" (p. 15). Thayer agrees, as do Arndt and Gingrich, who render it, "prisoners of war" (p. 26). The NBV conveys this thought with its translation: "He led the captured away in captivity." The simplest and clearest rendering is: "He led a host of captives" (Goodspeed, RSV).

9 *Lower Parts of the Earth* This strange expression has provoked an endless amount of discussion, especially in the older commentaries. There are two main interpretations. The first would refer it to a descent into Hades (cf. the Apostles' Creed). The second would apply it to the Incarnation. Some of the Early Church fathers, such as Irenaeus, Tertullian, Jerome, together with Erasmus, Bengel, Meyer, Alford, and others, took the former view. On the other hand, Calvin proposed the latter, and many modern commentators have followed him.

Salmond says: "Neither grammar nor textual criticism gives a decisive answer" (EGT, 3:326). If "of the earth" is taken as a genitive of apposition, it means "the lower parts which are the earth." The possessive genitive would be "the lower parts belonging to the earth"; that is, Hades. The comparative genitive would mean "the parts lower than the earth." Salmond comments: "The *katotera* may mean the parts lower than the earth itself, i.e., Hades; but it may also mean the parts lower than heaven, i.e., the earth" (EGT, 3:327). A comparison with the great kenosis passage in Phil. 2:5–10 suggests that the latter interpretation is preferable. Salmond adopts this conclusion.

Eadie thinks the same. He says: "We agree with the majority of expositors who understand the words as simply denoting the earth" (p. 283). He further points out the fact that the comparative—"lower parts of the earth"— could very well describe Christ's lowly birth in a manger, His lowly occupation as a carpenter, His humiliating death, and His "extemporized and hasty" funeral (pp. 294–95). All this fits in with Paul's emphasis in the kenosis passage. Christ not only became a man but a servant, and humbled himself to death, "even the death of the cross." It does not seem necessary to look farther for the meaning of this obscure phrase in Ephesians.

11 Apostles The noun *apostolos* comes from the verb *apostellō*, which properly means "*to send away, to dispatch* on service; 1. to send with a commission, or on service" (A-S, p. 54). Jesus was the first "apostle," and He chose 12 disciples to be His apostles to the world. In John 17:18 He prays: "As thou hast sent me into the world, even so have I also sent them into the world" (cf. John 20:21).

Barnabas and Paul are also called apostles (Acts 14:14). Vincent writes: "The distinguishing features of an apostle were, a commission directly from Christ: being a witness of the resurrection: special inspiration: supreme authority: accrediting by miracles; unlimited commission to preach and to found churches" (3:389).

Prophets The word is taken directly from the Greek *prophētēs*. This comes from the verb *prophēmi*, which literally means "say before," but which can also mean "speak forth" or "speak for." Liddell and Scott note that the noun was used in classical Greek for "one who speaks for a god and interprets his will" (p. 1540). In the NT it means "inspired preacher and teacher, organ of special revelations from God" (*ibid.*). Arndt and Gingrich note that it is used "also in other senses, without excluding the actual prophets, of men who proclaim the divine message with special preparation and with a special mission" (p. 731). In the NT it seems to mean "preacher."

Evangelists The word, which is a transliteration of the Greek *euangelistēs*, is found only two other places in the NT. In Acts 21:8 Philip is referred to as "the evangelist." In 2 Tim. 4:5 the young Timothy is admonished to "do the work of an evangelist."

The term comes from the verb *euangelizō* ("evangelize"), which means "proclaim glad tidings." An evangelist, then, is one who preaches the "gospel" (Greek *euangelos*), the good news that Christ has died to save men. The evangelists in the Early Church were probably itinerant preachers.

Pastors and Teachers "Pastor" is the Latin term for "shepherd." The Greek word *poimēn* also means "shepherd." It is used of Christ (John 10:11, 14, 16; Heb. 13:20; 1 Pet. 2:25). Here it is used of Christian pastors. Homer, in his *Iliad*, refers to "pastors of the people" (*poimena laōn*). The pastor is to be the shepherd of his flock.

Apparently the pastors and teachers were the same. Vincent comments: "The omission of the article from *teachers* seems to indicate that pastors and teachers are included under one class" (3:390).

12 Perfecting Instead of "perfecting," some recent translations prefer "equipment" (RSV) or "to equip" (NEB).

The Greek word is *katartismos* (only here in NT). It comes from the verb *katartizō*, which means "to make *artios*"; that is, "fit" or "complete." The verb is used for mending nets (Matt. 4:21; Mark 1:19). Its basic meaning was "put in order, restore—a. restore to its former condition, put to rights . . . b. put into proper condition, complete, make complete" (AG, p. 418).

Salmond calls attention to the fact that in Polybius and Herodotus the verb carries the idea of "preparing, furnishing, equipping." So he would translate the phrase here, "with a view to the full equipment of the saints" (EGT, 3:330–31).

The comma after "saints" should be omitted. The correct meaning apparently is "for the equipping of the saints for the work of service" (NASB) or "to prepare God's people for works of service" (NIV).

Edifying The word is *oikodomē*. It comes from *oikos*, "house," and *demō*, "build." So it refers to the act of building. In the Gospels it is used for the buildings of the Temple (Matt. 24:1; Mark 13:1–2). In the Epistles (Romans, 1 & 2 Corinthians, Ephesians) it is always used metaphorically. It is translated "building" in 1 Cor. 3:9; 2 Cor. 5:1; and Eph. 2:21. In most other passages it is rendered "edifying" or "edification." Since these are rather outdated terms now, it is better to translate the word as "building up."

13 Come The verb *katantaō* properly means "come" or "arrive." But here it is used in the figurative sense of "attain." That seems to be the better translation here (NASB).

Perfect The word "perfect" is a bone of contention in ecclesiastical and theological circles. At the one extreme are those who bristle at the very mention of the term in a religious connection. At the other extreme are those who when they see the word "perfect" or "perfection" immediately assume that it refers to the crisis experience of entire sanctification. Both attitudes are mistaken.

The Greek adjective *teleios* comes from *telos*, "end." So it means "having reached its end, finished, mature, complete, perfect" (A-S, p. 442). In Heb. 5:14 it is used literally of a fully grown or mature person in contrast to a "babe," and is translated in the KJV "of full age." Here in Ephesians and in other passages in Paul's Epistles, it is employed in an ethical sense. It is translated "man" in 1 Cor. 14:20, but elsewhere in the KJV as "perfect" (17 times). The RSV renders it "mature" seven times.

The contrast with "children" (v. 14) suggests that "full-grown" is the basic connotation here, and that is the way it is given in the ASV. Salmond comments: "The state in which *unity* is lacking is the stage of immaturity; the state in which oneness in faith and knowledge is reached is the state of mature manhood in Christ." In relation to the use of "man" here in the singular, he says: "The goal to be reached is that of a new Humanity, regenerated and spiritually mature in all its members" (EGT, 3:332).

It seems evident that "mature" (RSV, NEB, NASB, NIV) is a more accurate translation here than "perfect." It should be noted that "perfecting" (v. 12) and "perfect" (v. 13) are from two entirely different Greek roots; and "perfect" is not the basic idea of either.

Fulness of Christ

What is meant by the *plērōma* of Christ? Salmond says: "The *Christou* is the *possessive genitive,* and the phrase means the fulness that belongs to Christ, the sum of the qualities which make Him what He is" (EGT, 3:333). Vincent carries it one point farther: "Which belongs to Christ and is imparted by Him" (3:391).

14 Children "Children" is the translation in all the standard English versions. But "babes" occurs in the NBV and Weymouth, while "babies" is used by Goodspeed and Williams.

The noun *nēpios* literally means an "infant." But it is used of children, and of legal minors not yet eligible to inherit the family estate. It may very well be that the idea of babyishness is intended here (cf. Heb. 5:13–14). The NIV has "infants." At any rate, the admonition is to "grow up"!

Tossed To and Fro

The expression "tossed to and fro" is all one word in the Greek, *klydōnizomenoi* (only here in NT). It comes from *klydōn*, which means "billow" or "wave." Hence the verb literally means "to be tossed by waves." Metaphorically it signifies "to be tossed like waves" (A-S, p. 250). Williams renders it "like sailors tossed about."

The second word, *peripheromenoi*, is literally "carried about," and is so translated in most versions. The combination of the two terms is expressed in different ways. Moffatt has "blown from our course and swayed by every passing wind of doctrine." The NEB has perhaps the most "breezy" translation: "tossed by the waves and whirled about by every fresh gust of teaching."

Sleight The word *cubeia* (only here in NT) comes from *cubos*, "cube" or "dice." So it literally means "dice-playing." It may be rendered "cunning" (RSV, NBV) or "trickery" (Goodspeed, Williams, NASB). While the word "sleight" is still used in the phrase "sleight of hand performance," the basic idea is that of "trickery," which is probably the best translation.

Cunning Craftiness

This is one word in the Greek, the noun *panourgia*. It comes from the adjective *panourgos*, which literally means "ready to do anything." In the classics it means "cleverness," nearly always in the bad sense of "craftiness" (A-S, p. 336). The one word "craftiness" is perhaps an adequate rendering (RSV, NASB, NIV).

Lie in Wait to Deceive

The last part of v. 14, is rendered in ASV "after the wiles of error." The Greek is literally "to the method of deceit."

The word *methodeia* comes from the verb *methodeuō*, which first meant "to treat by rule," and then "to employ craft." So the noun means "craft, deceit." It is found here and in 6:11, but nowhere in earlier Greek literature. It occurs in later papyri (fifth century and following) in the sense of "method," which has been taken over into English. Arndt and Gingrich would translate the whole phrase here, "in deceitful scheming" (p. 500; adopted in NASB, NIV). Vincent says that literally it should be rendered, "tending to the system of errors," since *methodeia* means "a deliberate planning or system." He adds that "error" includes the idea of "deceit or delusion" (3:392).

15 Speaking the Truth This is one word in the Greek—*alētheuontes.* The verb *alētheuō* occurs only here and in Gal. 4:16. Thayer and Abbott-Smith give only one meaning, "to speak the truth." Arndt and Gingrich have "be truthful, tell the truth."

16 *Joined Together* Paul's favorite prefix for compound verbs is *syn*, "with" or "together." Two of these occur in this verse. They are translated "fitly joined together" and "compacted" (KJV). The first, *synarmologeō*, has already been encountered in Eph. 2:21. There it is used of a building "framed together," that building being the Church, a "holy temple in the Lord." Here it is employed for the Church as the Body of Christ. The two figures are closely related.

The second verb, *synbibazō*, means "to join or knit together, unite" (A-S, p. 426). It is used of the physical body, which is held together by joints and ligaments. It speaks eloquently of the unity of the spiritual Body of Christ, His Church. It is framed together as a building and joined together as a body. The first figure suggests the ancient Tabernacle in the wilderness, and also Solomon's Temple. They were both built as "the house of the Lord." In like manner the Church is "builded together for an habitation of God through the Spirit" (Col. 2:22).

The second figure is more complicated. It has to do with a vital, pulsating, moving union of parts by joints and ligaments that hold them together. Both are meaningful representations of the Church of Jesus Christ. Eadie writes: "The two participles express the idea that the body is of many parts, which have such mutual adaptation in position and function, that it is a firm and solid structure" (p. 322). The simplest translation is "joined and held together" (NIV).

That Which Every Joint Supplieth
"Through every joint of the supply" is the literal Greek for the KJV phrase, "by that which every joint supplieth."

The word for "joint" is *haphē* (only here and Col. 2:19), which Arndt and Gingrich define as "ligament" (p. 124). "Supply" is *epichorēgia*, which occurs only here and in Phil. 1:19.

Salmond gives a good summary of the meaning of this verse: "The idea, therefore, appears to be that the body is fitly framed and knit together by means of the joints, every one of them in its own place and function, as the points of connection between member and member and the points of communication between the different parts and the supply which comes from the head" (EGT, 3:337). The NIV has "by every supporting ligament."

17–18 *Mind, Understanding* Paul exhorts the Ephesian Christians not to walk (i.e., "live")

as the Gentiles (heathen) walk, in the vanity of their "mind." The Greek word is *nous*. Arndt and Gingrich say that it "denotes the faculty of physical and intellectual perception, then also the power to arrive at moral judgments" (p. 546). Thayer defines it thus: "The mind, comprising alike the faculties of perceiving and understanding and those of feeling, judging, determining" (p. 429). For this passage he adopts the meaning: "Reason in the narrower sense, as the capacity for spiritual truth, the higher powers of the soul, the faculty of perceiving divine things, of recognizing goodness and hating evil" (*ibid.*).

This, among the Gentiles, had become vain; that is, empty. Thayer defines the Greek word for "vanity" as meaning "what is devoid of truth and appropriateness," and for this passage he gives "perverseness, depravation" (p. 393). The key word of Ecclesiastes is "vanity." The Greek word is used there (in LXX) 40 times. The context in Ecclesiastes will suggest something of the meaning of the term. Those who adopted the heathen worship and way of life found it all to be "vanity"—sheer emptiness. When one rejects the truth, the mind is filled with unreality, and so empty of all that is eternal.

"Understanding" is the compound *dianoia*. Of this word Cremer writes: "*Dianoia*, strictly *a thinking over, meditation, reflecting*, is used in the same range, and with the same signification as the original *nous*, . . . save that the preposition '*dia*' gives emphasis to the act of reflection; and in keeping with the structure of the word, the meaning *activity of thinking* precedes the borrowed meaning *faculty of thought*" (p. 438). That is, the latter is more properly *nous*, the former *dianoia*. Cremer further notes that in the NT "*dianoia* is specially the *faculty of moral reflection, of moral understanding*" (p. 439). In this passage the two words are translated correctly in the KJV.

18 *Ignorance* The word *agnoia* comes from the same root. It means "*want of knowledge, ignorance*, which leads to mistaken conduct, and forbids unconditional imputation of the guilt of the acts performed" (Cremer, p. 163). This concept seems to fit Acts 3:17; 17:30; 1 Pet. 1:14—the only other places in the NT where the word occurs.

But here it seems to be used "with sense of wilful blindness" (A-S, p. 6). Moulton and Milligan write: "The connotation of wilful blindness, as in Ephesians 4:18, is found in *The Tebtunis Papyri* I, 24.33 (B.C. 117), where an official reports the misconduct of certain persons whose plans he had frustrated, so that *legontes tēs agnoias* they left the district" (VGT, p. 5). Cremer, who wrote before the great era of papyrus discoveries, discerned this distinction in usage. He says: "This *agnoias* is with St. Paul the characteristic of heathendom, Acts xvii. 30, Ephesians iv. 18, compare verse 17, and is a state which renders repentance necessary, Acts xvii. 30, . . . and therefore eventually furnishes ground for blame, Ephesians iv. 18, as otherwise for forbearance" (p. 163).

Blindness   The KJV has "blindness;" the NIV, "hardening." The Greek word is *pōrōsis*. It means "a covering with a callus, hardening" (A-S, p. 395). Arndt and Gingrich define it as: "hardening, dulling, . . . dullness, insensibility, obstinacy" (p. 739). Thayer thinks that in this passage it indicates "stubbornness, obduracy" (p. 559). It is obvious that "hardness" or "hardening" is a more accurate rendering than "blindness."

19 Past Feeling   The Greek verb is *apalgeō* (only here in NT). Its basic meaning is "to cease to feel pain for," while in late Greek it signifies "to become callous, reckless" (A-S, p. 44). The RSV, following Goodspeed, reads, "They have become callous." The essential idea is that of callousness, so that it fits closely with "hardening" above.

Lasciviousness   *Aselgeia* is the Greek word. It means "licentiousness, wantonness, excess" (A-S, p. 63). Arndt and Gingrich define it as "licentiousness, debauchery, sensuality" and suggest for this passage, "give oneself over to debauchery" (p. 114). Thayer has a long list: "unbridled lust, excess, licentiousness, lasciviousness, wantonness, outrageousness, shamelessness, insolence" (p. 79). Moffatt, Goodspeed, and NIV have "sensuality." This seems to be the most meaningful translation for today.

22 Conversation   The word "conversation" has changed its meaning considerably since the KJV appeared in 1611. The *Oxford English Dictionary* gives as a definition of this term: "The action of living or having one's being *in* a place or *among* persons. Also figuratively of one's spiritual being" (2:940). But this meaning is labeled "obsolete."

As early as 1580 the word had come to mean, as now: "Interchange of thoughts and words; familiar discourse or talk" (3:941). This meaning finally prevailed. The correct translation here is "manner of life" (NASB) or "way of life" (NIV).

The Old Man   Most translations today use for this "old nature" or "old self." Weymouth, however, has a stronger rendering: "your original evil nature." This was "displayed in your former mode of life."

"The old man" (KJV) is the literal meaning of the Greek *ton palaion anthrōpon*. So the recent translations are to a certain extent interpretive. The word *palaios* means "old, ancient." It is used "of things not merely old, but worn by use" (A-S, p. 334). Thayer suggests: "We, as we were before our mode of thought, feeling, action, had been changed" (p. 494). Arndt and Gingrich say that *palaios* means "in existence for a long time, often with the connotation of being antiquated or outworn," and give the whole phrase: "*the old* (i.e., earlier, unregenerate) *man*" (p. 610).

Archbishop Trench's *Synonyms of the New Testament* is still the standard work in the field, though it very much needs to be brought up to date. It was written before the great era of the papyrus discoveries, which have shed much light on the meanings of New Testament terms. Furthermore, Trench builds largely on classical Greek, and it is universally recognized that the Koine Greek of the New Testament age was definitely different in many details from the classical language of an earlier day.

Trench indicates that *archaios* and *palaios* often appear to be used in the same sense. But when the emphasis is on "old in the sense of more or less worn out, . . . this is always *palaios*" (p. 252).

In regard to the meaning of "the old man," Eadie writes: "The words are, therefore, a bold and vivid personification of the old nature we inherit from Adam, the source and seat of original and actual transgression" (p. 339). Salmond defines it as: "the former unregenerate self in its entirety" (EGT, 3:342).

24 The New Man   The Greek is *kainon anthrōpon*. The other word for "new" is *neos*, from which the English word comes. Trench points out well the distinction between these two terms. He says: "Contemplate the new under aspects of *time*, as that which has recently come into existence, and this is *neos*." He then adds: "But contemplate the new, not now under aspects of *time*, but of *quality*, the new, as set over against that which has seen service, the outworn, . . . and this is *kainos*" (p. 220). So "the new man" refers to the new quality of life that comes with Christ's entrance into the human heart.

Of the contrast between "the old man" and "the new man" Olshausen writes: "As in *the old* lies at the same time the idea of the obsolete, so in *the new* is that of the original, of that which corresponds with its ideal." He comments further: "But while the laying aside the old, and the putting on the new, is here referred to man, of course it is not Paul's meaning that sanctification is accomplished by our own power: Christ is our sanctification, as he is our righteousness (see on 1 Cor. 1:30); but all, that Christ through the Holy Spirit works in man, can in the form of Law be put to him as a demand, because man by his unfaithfulness can hinder the operation of the Spirit" (5:117). We do not "put off" and "put on" in our own strength, but by faith in Christ and in the power of the Holy Spirit.

As to the identity of "the new man," Ellicott writes: "It is scarcely necessary to observe that *kainon anthrōpon* is not Christ, but is in direct contrast to *ton palaion anthrōpon*, and denotes 'the holy form of human life which results from redemption' " (p. 109).

Righteousness and True Holiness Paul states that the "new man" is created "in righteousness and holiness of truth" (literally). What is meant by "righteousness" (*dikaiosynē*) and "holiness" (*hosiotēs*)? Salmond notes that Plato "defines *dikaios* as the *generic* term and *hosios* as the *specific;* and he describes the former as having regard to our relations to *men,* the latter to our relations to God" (EGT, 3:344).

Olshausen writes: "*Dikaiosynē* denotes the right relation inwardly between the powers of the soul, outwardly to men and circumstances." He further states: "On the other hand, *hosiotēs* denotes . . . integrity of the spiritual life, and the piety towards God which it supposes" (5:118–19).

The word *hosiotēs* occurs in only one other passage in the NT, Luke 1:75. There it is also connected with *dikaiosynē,* only in the opposite order. The basic meaning of the word is "piety." Thayer defines it thus: "Piety towards God, fidelity in observing the obligations of piety, holiness" (p. 456). Cremer describes it as "holiness manifesting itself in the discharge of pious duties," and adds that "it denotes the spirit and conduct of one who is joined in fellowship with God" (p. 464).

26 Be Ye Angry and Sin Not This verse furnishes an interesting example of what one of-ten finds in NT quotations from the OT. Paul is quoting Ps. 4:4. But in the KJV, Ps. 4:4 reads: "Stand in awe, and sin not."

The explanation of the apparent misquotation is that Paul quotes the Septuagint, which has exactly the same Greek words as here in Ephesians—*orgizesthe kai mē hamartanete.* Why, then, the common English translation of Ps. 4:4? The answer is that the Hebrew word literally means "tremble" (cf. NASB)—which may be with either awe or anger. English versions have usually chosen "awe," whereas the Septuagint translators chose "anger." *The Amplified Old Testament* (1962) has combined the ideas, with an added "but"—"Be angry, *but* stand in awe and sin not."

At first sight this seems like a strange command. Understandably there have been many attempts by interpreters to blunt its shock. Olshausen, following Chrysostom and other early writers, takes the first imperative hypothetically: "If ye are angry, as it is to be foreseen will happen, at least sin not in anger" (5:120). Beza, Grotius, and others took the first verb as interrogative: "Are ye angry?" It is doubtful if either of these explanations is valid—that is, supported by good Greek grammar.

Winer takes the first imperative as permissive. He says: "In the passage from Ephesians Paul's meaning is unquestionably this: we should not let anger lead us into sin" (p. 312). Meyer objects to Winer's position. He says: "The mere *kai* is only logically correct when both imperatives are thought of in the *same* sense, not the former as permitting and the latter as enjoining" (p. 479). His interpretation is: "In anger do not fall into transgression" (p. 478). In the seventh edition of Winer (by Lunemann) Meyer's objection is answered (it seems effectively) as follows: "For, the assertion (Mey.) that of two closely connected Imperatives the one cannot denote a permission and the other a command, is incorrect; we may say with perfect propriety: Well, then, go (I give you leave), but do not stay above an hour" (p. 312).

Eadie seems to prefer a fourth view: "The phrase is idiomatic—'Be angry'—(when occasion requires), 'but sin not;' the main force being on the second imperative with *mē*" (p. 348).

Salmond suggests a fifth interpretation: "The *kai* has here the rhetorical sense which is found also in *atque,* adding something that seems not quite consistent with the preceding or that qualifies it, 'and yet' " (EGT, 3:345).

Alford seems to strike a mediating position. He says: "The first imperative, although jussive (expressing a command), is so in a weaker degree than the other: it is rather assumptive, than permissive" (3:125). Somewhat in line with this is the comment of Bengel: "Anger is neither commanded, nor quite prohibited; but this is commanded, not to permit sin to enter into anger: it is like poison, which is sometimes used as medicine, but must be managed with utmost caution" (4:98). He further notes that often the force of the imperative mood "falls only upon a part of what is said, Jer. x. 24" (*ibid.*).

Blass and Debrunner state that for the most part the imperative in the New Testament stays within the same limits as in classical usage. They continue: "As in the latter it is by no means confined to commands, but also expresses a request or a concession." For an illustration of this they cite Eph. 4:26 and offer the following paraphrase: "You may be angry as far as I am concerned (if you can't help it), but do not sin thereby" (p. 195).

Arndt and Gingrich approach the problem from another direction—the meaning of *kai* ("and"). They note that it can mean "but" (p. 393). The translation they offer for this passage is: "Be angry, but do not sin" (p. 583) (so also RSV). Trench says it means: "Be ye angry, yet in this anger of yours suffer no sinful element to mingle" (p. 134).

Many commentators call attention to the fact that Jesus was angry (cf. Mark 3:5). So there is an anger that is holy and just.

Moule has given a good explanation of the difference between righteous and unrighteous anger. He writes:

> Anger, as the mere expression of wounded personality, is sinful; for it means that self is in command. Anger, as the pure expression of repugnance to wrong in loyalty to God, is sinless where there is true occasion for it. The Apostle practically says, let anger, when you feel it, be *never* from the former motive, always from the latter (p. 122).

Wrath The last part of the verse reads: "Let not the sun go down upon your wrath." The last word is *parorgismos*, found only here in the NT, though occasionally in the Septuagint. Moulton and Milligan say that it "does not seem to occur outside biblical Greek" (VGT, p. 496). Salmond writes: "It differs from *orgē* in denoting not the *disposition* of anger or anger as a lasting mood, but *provocation, exasperation,* sudden, violent anger" (EGT, 3:346). Eadie explains it thus: "*Parorgismos,* a term peculiar to biblical Greek, is a fit of indignation or exasperation: *para*—referring to the cause or occa-

sion; while the *orgē,* to be put away from Christians, is the habitual indulgence of anger" (p. 349). J. Armitage Robinson writes: "Here *parorgismos* is the state of feeling provocation, 'wrath' " (p. 192). But most commentators prefer "indignation" or "provocation" as the translation here. In any case, anger is not to be retained in us.

27 Neither Give Place The KJV gives a good literal translation: "Neither give place to the devil." The word for "place" is *topos.* It means "a portion of space viewed in reference to its occupancy or as appropriated to a thing" (Thayer, p. 628). This is evidently the basis of Phillips' translation (tying it in with what precedes): "Don't give the devil that sort of foothold." That is, don't give him any place of occupancy by harboring anger in your heart. Arndt and Gingrich suggest for this passage: "*Do not give the devil a chance* to exert his influence" (p. 831). Beck follows this closely in his rendering: "Don't give the devil a chance to work." The RSV also builds on this: "And give no opportunity to the devil." Moffatt and Goodspeed use "chance." Weymouth has: "And do not leave room for the devil." Perhaps the most striking translation is that of the NEB: "Leave no loophole for the devil."

29 Corrupt Communication The noun here is the common term *logos,* which means "word," and is so translated 218 out of the 330 times it occurs in the NT. But in the other places (including here), it is rendered in different ways.

The adjective is *sapros.* Thayer gives among others the following definitions: "rotten, putrid, of poor quality, bad, unfit for use, worthless" (p. 568). Arndt and Gingrich give: "decayed, rotten." They note that it is used of spoiled fish, of rotten grapes on the ground, of crumbling stones. In general it means "unusable, unfit, bad." For this passage they suggest "evil word" or "evil speech."

In the NT it is used of trees and fruit (Matt. 7:17–18; 12:33; Luke 6:43), and of fish (Matt. 13:48). Only in this place is it used metaphorically. Salmond says: "Here it does not seem to mean *filthy,* but, as the following clause suggests, bad, *profitless, of no good to any one*" (EGT, 3:347).

However, some scholars prefer the stronger meaning. Eadie renders the clause, "Let no filthy word come out of your mouth." Phillips has "foul language," and the NBV "foul speech." The standard versions read "corrupt speech" (ASV), "evil talk" (RSV), and "bad language" (NEB). Moffatt and Goodspeed have "bad word." But Weymouth has "unwholesome words" (cf. NASB). This agrees with Salmond's conclusion, noted above. The best way to interpret the passage is to say that no bad words or even worthless words should come out of the Christian's mouth. Rather it should always be "something good" (literal Greek).

The Greek reverses the order of the words "to the use of edifying." It has "edifying of the use." The word translated "edifying" means literally "building up," from the idea of building a house. "Use" is *chreia*, "necessity" or "need." But how does this make sense in English?

Salmond suggests that *chreias* (genitive case) is either the objective genitive, "edification applied to the need," or the genitive of remote reference, "edification in reference to the need (the present need)" (EGT, 3:347). The thought seems to be that our talk should be suitable for building people up in the faith, so as to meet any needs that may be present. Eadie puts it this way:

> The precious hour should never be polluted with corrupt speech, nor should it be wasted in idle and frivolous dialogue.... Conversation should always exercise a salutary influence, regulated by special need. Words so spoken may fall like winged seeds upon a neglected soil, and there may be future germination and fruit (p. 353).

It should be noted that the admonition, "Grieve not the Holy Spirit of God," follows right after this. Evidently one way that we may grieve the Holy Spirit is by frivolous, worthless conversation. Actually, time is too short and valuable to be wasted. It needs to be spent in edifying words and works.

31 Bitterness Arndt and Gingrich define *pikria* as meaning figuratively: "bitterness, animosity, anger, harshness" (p. 663). Elsewhere in the NT it is found only in Acts 8:23; Rom. 3:14; and Heb. 12:15.

Eadie says that *pikria* is "a figurative term denoting that fretted and irritable state of mind that keeps a man in perpetual animosity—that inclines him to harsh and uncharitable opinions of men and things—that makes him sour, crabbed, and repulsive in his general demeanour—that brings a scowl over his face, and infuses venom into the words of his tongue" (p. 357).

Wrath, Anger The two Greek words are *thymos* and *orgē*. The first occurs only this one

place in Ephesians. The second is found in 2:3 and 5:6, but is translated "wrath" in both places. This fact points up the confusion between the exact meanings of the two terms. *Thymos* occurs 18 times in the NT. It is translated (KJV) "wrath" 15 times, "fierceness" twice, and "indignation" once. *Orgē* is found 36 times. It is rendered "wrath" 31 times, "anger" 3 times (including here), "vengeance" and "indignation" once each. So the dominant translation for both words is "wrath." What is the difference between them?

Trench is the most helpful authority on such distinctions. He says: "*Thymos* ... is more of the turbulent commotion, the boiling agitation of the feelings," whereas *orgē* suggests "more of an abiding and settled habit of mind" (p. 131).

Clamor The Greek word is *kraugē*. The cognate verb means "cry out, shout." So the noun means "outcry" (cf. Acts 23:9), or "shouting." The reference seems to be to noisy arguing and quarreling. Eadie suggests that it signifies the "expression of this anger—hoarse reproach, the high language of scorn and scolding, the yelling tones, the loud and boisterous recrimination, and the fierce and impetuous invective that mark a man in a towering rage" (p. 358).

Evil Speaking In the Greek this is *blasphēmia*, from which we get "blasphemy." The word literally means "railing" or "slander." When used of slandering God it is technically called "blasphemy." But here it means "slander" or "abusive speech," what is hurtful to the reputation of others.

Malice The Greek word is *kakia*, from the adjective *kakos*, "bad." It is defined by Abbott-Smith as meaning "wickedness, depravity, malignity" (p. 227). Eadie says: "Kakia is a generic term, and seems to signify what we sometimes call in common speech bad-heartedness, the root of all those vices" (p. 358).

32 Forgiving One Another In contrast to the carnal characteristics of v. 31, Paul suggests the proper spiritual attitude toward those who have wronged us. We are to be kind and tenderhearted, "forgiving" others as God has "forgiven" us.

The verb is *charizomai*. It comes from *charis*, "grace." So it means "forgive freely"—graciously, not grudgingly. That is the way God has forgiven us; so that is the way we should forgive others.

"For Christ's sake" is simply *en Christō* "in

Christ." It is only in Christ that we have this gracious forgiveness from God.

5:1 *Followers* "Be ye therefore followers of God." The Greek is *mimētai*, from *mimos*, "a mimic, actor." So it means "imitators." That is the rendering found in many modern translations and is grammatically correct. It is more precise than "followers."

Dear The adjective is *agapēta*, from *agapaō*, "I love." It occurs 62 times in the NT. Forty-seven times it is rendered "beloved," 9 times "dearly beloved," 3 times "well beloved," and 3 times "dear." "Beloved" or "dearly loved" (NIV) is the correct translation. Be imitators of God because you are His children, beloved by Him. As Christians we should demonstrate daily the fact that we are children of God by acting like Him.

2 *Walk in Love* As beloved children we should "keep on walking (present imperative) in love, just as Christ also loved you." The best way that we can imitate God, and thus prove that we are His beloved children, is to walk continually in love, for "God is love" (1 John 4:8, 16). Imitators of God, then, will love as He loves.

One of the worst travesties of Christianity is people who profess not only that they are children of God, but also that they are sanctified wholly, made perfect in love, and yet they are "cranky," sour, critical, unkind. We have no right to claim to be God's children unless we are seeking by the help of the Holy Spirit to be like Him in our daily lives. We disgrace the family when we fail to walk in love.

Offering, Sacrifice These words may carelessly be thought of as synonymous. But they are not. The first, *prosphora*, literally means "something brought to." It aptly describes an "offering," which was "brought to" the altar. It might be composed of meal or oil, or even be a drink offering.

On the other hand, "sacrifice" is *thysia*. It comes from *thyō*, one of the meanings of which is "slay" or "kill." So it refers to animal sacrifices which were slain and offered on the altar.

Christ was both. It takes all the offerings of the OT—described in detail in the early chapters of Leviticus—to typify the many-sided work of Christ in His redemption of humanity.

Sweetsmelling Savor Christ's offering for us is described as "a sweetsmelling savor." But "savor" is now used mostly for taste rather

than smell. So this rendering is not the best. But worse is the awkward "an odor of a sweet smell" (ASV).

The Greek phrase means "a smell of fragrance," and so "a fragrant smell." Recent translations tend to combine this into a single adjective, giving the rendering "a fragrant offering and sacrifice to God" (Moffatt, Goodspeed, RSV, NIV).

4 *Filthiness, Foolish Talking* The Greek word for "filthiness" is found only here in the NT. Arndt and Gingrich define its meaning as "ugliness, wickedness" (p. 24). Thayer gives "baseness, dishonor" (p. 17). The word is *aischrotēs*, from *aischos*, "shame, disgrace." Vine says that it refers to "obscenity, all that is contrary to purity" (2:98). Salmond writes: "It denotes shameless, immoral conduct in general" (EGT, 3:352).

"Foolish talking" is *mōrologia*. Trench calls attention to the fact that "fool," "foolish," and "folly" have ethical significance in the Scriptures, and gives this definition: "It is that 'talk of fools,' which is foolishness and sin together" (p. 121).

"Jesting" is *eutrapelia*. Originally this word had a good connotation—"versatility," or "keen wit," what we sometimes call "quick repartee" in conversation. But gradually it took on bad meanings, indicating "coarse jesting" or "ribaldry." The context indicates that this is the sense here.

All three of these words are *hapax legomena* (literally, "said once for all"), and are found only here in the NT. They seem to indicate Paul's acquaintance with Greek literature. The apostle says that, instead of filthiness or even foolishness in talk, the Christian should indulge in "giving of thanks." This is always in order.

5 *For This Ye Know* The ASV has here "For this ye know of a surety." The RSV reads, "Be sure of this." Why add "of a surety" or change to "Be sure of this"?

The Greek literally says: "For this you know, knowing." That is an expression for "You surely know." But the Greek word for "you know" may be either indicative or imperative. In the second person plural of the present tense the form is exactly the same for both. That will explain the RSV reading here. It will also account for the change in John 5:39 from "Search the scriptures" (KJV) to "Ye search the scriptures" (ASV) and "You search the scriptures" (RSV). There are many passages in the NT where we can never be certain whether the writer intended the word to be taken as indicative or imperative.

This is one of the ambiguities of language, some of which still exist even in the rigid demands of our day for scientific exactness. Linguistic ambiguity in the Greek, often attaching also to the English, is one of the inescapable problems of NT exegesis. One can only do his best to interpret such ambiguous terms in the light of the context—which is not always definitely determinative. The NIV has: "For of this you can be sure."

Whoremonger, Unclean In v. 3 there are three abstract nouns: "fornication," "uncleanness," and "covetousness." They are balanced in the fifth verse with three concrete nouns: "whoremonger," "unclean person" (one word in the Greek), and "covetous man" (one word). "Whoremonger" should be translated "fornicator," to show its connection with "fornication" (same root in the Greek). Such connections in the Greek should be preserved in English translation, if possible.

It is a black picture of heathen immorality which is suggested here, with overtones reminiscent of Rom. 1:21–32. *Pornos* ("whoremonger, fornicator") originally meant a "male prostitute." Then it came to be used in the universal meaning of "fornicator."

The modern technical distinction between adultery and fornication is not maintained in the Greek NT. While *porneia* is always translated "fornication" in the KJV (26 times), it clearly means adultery in Matt. 5:32; 19:9. There is a distinct word for "adultery," however, which occurs only 4 times in the NT (Matt. 15:19; Mark 7:21; John 8:3; Gal. 5:19)—as also "adulterer" 4 times.

Covetousness The word for "covetous man," *pleonektēs*, occurs (in NT) only here and in 1 Cor. 5:10, 11; 6:10. The abstract noun *pleonexia* (v. 3), is found 10 times in the NT. It is translated "covetousness" in every place but one (Eph. 4:19—"greediness"). The word is a compound from *pleon*, "more," and *echō*, "have." So it means "greedy desire to have more" (Thayer, p. 516).

As in this passage, "covetousness" is usually found in the NT in very bad company. Arndt and Gingrich cite numerous instances of this same association in the secular Greek writers (p. 573). Trench writes: "Not merely is *pleonexia*, as signifying covetousness, joined to sins of impurity, but the word is sometimes used, as at Ephes. v. 3[5:3] . . . to designate these sins themselves" (p. 83).

Salmond thinks that in some passages in the NT (e.g., Luke 12:15; 2 Cor. 9:5; 1 Thess. 2:5) the word means simply "covetousness," but that here in v. 3 it may have "the acquired sense of *sensual* greed" (EGT, 3:352).

Eadie objects to interpreting *pleonexia* as signifying lustful desire. His explanation of the association here is: "And it is joined to these preceding words, as it springs from the same selfishness, and is but a different form of development from the same unholy root." He defines the word thus: "It is greed, avarice, unconquerable love of appropriation, morbid lust of acquisition, carrying in itself a violation of almost every precept of the decalogue" (p. 370).

Lightfoot agrees. He writes on Col. 3:5: "The attempt to give pleonexia here and in other passages the sense of 'impurity' . . . is founded on a misconception." He also observes: "Impurity and covetousness may be said to divide between them nearly the whole domain of human selfishness and vice" (p. 212).

But why is the "covetous man" called an "idolator" (and in Col. 3:5 "covetousness" called "idolatry")? Eadie suggests: "The covetous man makes a god of his possessions, and offers to them the entire homage of his heart" (p. 375). Ellicott comments: "Covetousness is truly a definite form of idolatry, it is the worship of Mammon (Matt. vi. 24) instead of God" (p. 120). Grayston writes: "Since ruthless self-assertion is the very essence of idolatry (Eph. 5:5; Col. 3:5), the word forms a bridge between sexual vice and idolatry, and may in some quarters have been a euphemism for ritual fornication" (TWBB, p. 64).

6 Vain The apostle warns his readers: "Let no man deceive you with vain words"—or, "empty words" (NASB, NIV). The Greek for "vain" is *kenos*, translated literally as "empty" in Mark 12:3; Luke 20:10–11. Arndt and Gingrich note that it is used figuratively as meaning "without content, without any basis, without truth, without power" (p. 429).

That is what it means here. "Vain" is not a bad translation, but "empty" brings out more forcefully the exact sense of the term.

9 Spirit In this verse the KJV reads "the fruit of the Spirit," whereas the Revised Versions have "the fruit of the light." Why the change?

The answer is that the majority of the oldest Greek manuscripts have "light." The matter is complicated by the fact that of the two third-century papyri that contain this passage, one (P 46) has "spirit" (*pneumatos*), while the other

(P 49) has "light" (*phōtos*). But the latter is supported by the two fourth-century manuscripts, Vaticanus and Sinaiticus.

It seems altogether likely that the phrase "the fruit of the Spirit" was borrowed from Gal. 5:22. So the internal evidence of probability combines with the external evidence of the manuscripts to suggest that "the fruit of the light" is the correct reading. This ties the ninth verse more closely to its context in the eighth verse, where "light" is the dominant word. "The fruit of the light" means what the light produces. This is "found in all that is good and right and true" (RSV); or, as Weymouth puts it, "the effect of the Light is seen in every kind of goodness, uprightness, and truth."

10 *Proving* What is meant by "proving what is acceptable unto the Lord"? The verb *dokimazō* is fairly common in the NT (23 times). It means "test, try, prove, approve." Which does it mean here? Probably "test."

The NASB has "trying to learn what is pleasing to the Lord." The NIV reads: "Find out what pleases the Lord."

The contrast between "the unfruitful works of darkness" (v. 11) and "the fruit of the light" (v. 9)—further evidence in favor of this reading—is strikingly parallel to that between "the works of the flesh" and "the fruit of the Spirit" (Gal. 5:19, 22). The plural ("works") suggests the divisiveness of sin. The singular ("fruit") symbolizes the unity and unifying quality of the good.

11, 13 *Reprove(d)* The verb *elegchō* means "convict," or "reprove," or "rebuke." But Abbott-Smith gives for this passage "expose." He says that the verb "implies rebuke which brings conviction" (p. 144). Thayer defines the word thus: "to *convict, refute, confute*, generally with a suggestion of the shame of the person convicted" (p. 202). He also gives for this passage: "by conviction bring to light, expose" (p. 203). The first meaning given by Arndt and Gingrich is: "bring to light, expose" (p. 248). Our present passage is listed under this particular definition. So it seems that the best translation here is "expose" (RSV, NASB, NIV).

This also fits best in v. 13—"But everything exposed by the light becomes visible" (NIV). It is the light that makes a thing visible and so exposes it. The best way to combat sin is to expose it. Turn on it the light of truth, so that people can see its horrible hideousness. A. T. Robertson says that the verb *elegchō* means "convict by turning the light on the darkness" (4:543).

14 *He Saith* The quotation in this verse has caused considerable discussion, because these exact words are found nowhere in the OT. Robertson says that they are "apparently a free adaptation of Isa. 26:19 and 60:1" (*ibid.*). The NBV changes "he saith" to "it says," and adds this footnote: "Apparently from an early Christian hymn, based on Isa. 60:1." The NEB incorporates this idea right in its translation: "And so the hymn says."

This, however, is a good example of overtranslation, involving a high degree of interpretation. Considerable restraint needs to be exercised at such points in translation work. Since the idioms of Greek and English are so different, a certain amount of interpretation is necessary to make sense. Fundamentally the demand is that we translate the words. But the ultimate obligation is always that of correctly translating the thought; for it is the spirit, not the letter, that makes alive.

The Greek verb in this introductory formula (*legei*) can with equal accuracy be rendered "he says" or "it says." The majority of recent translations treat it as neuter, "it says" or, more freely, "it is said" (NIV).

15 *Circumspectly* Five times in the fourth and fifth chapters of Ephesians, Paul says, "Walk." First, it was, "Walk worthy of the vocation wherewith ye are called" (4:1); second, "Walk not as other Gentiles walk" (4:17); third, "Walk in love" (5:1); fourth, "Walk as children of light" (5:8). Now comes the fifth, "Walk circumspectly."

The Greek word is *akribōs*. It means "with exactness, carefully." Thayer says, "exactly, accurately, diligently" (p. 24). Vine suggests: "The word expresses that accuracy which is the outcome of carefulness" (1:25). The adverb occurs only five times in the NT. Twice it is translated "diligently" in the KJV (Matt. 2:8; Acts 18:25). The best rendering here is "carefully" (RSV, NEB, NASB).

Fools Paul goes on to say that we are to walk "not as fools, but as wise." In the Greek there is a play on words: it says: "not as *asophoi*, but as *sophoi*." This can be brought out in English by rendering it: "not as unwise, but as wise" (RSV, NASB, NIV).

16 *Redeeming the Time* The verb is *exagorazō*. The noun *agora* meant the marketplace (or forum). So the verb *agorazō* literally means "buy in the market." It came to be used in the general sense of "purchase." The prepositional prefix ex (*ek*) means "out." So *exagorazō*

321

literally meant "buy out of the market." It was used for "redeeming" or "ransoming" slaves (cf. Gal. 3:13; 4:5). But in the middle voice, as here, it means "buy up for oneself." It is used the same way in the parallel passage in Col. 4:5. These are the only four times it occurs in the NT.

Arndt and Gingrich say that the middle form in Eph. 5:16 and Col. 4:5 "cannot be interpreted with certainty." They go on to suggest: "The best meaning is probably *make the most of the time* (which is severely limited because of the proximity of the Parousia as well as for other reasons)" (p. 271). A good translation here is "making the most of the time" (RSV), or "making the most of your time" (NASB). Since the Greek word for "time" (*kairos*) does not signify merely chronological time (*chronos*) but an opportune or appointed time, this passage may be rendered: "making the most of every opportunity" (NIV).

17 Unwise The adjective translated "unwise" is a different one from that in v. 15. Here it is *aphrones*. The "a" is what is called "*alpha*-negative"; as a prefix it negates the rest of the word. English equivalents are "un" or "in," or even the same "a," as in "amoral" and "amillennial."

The *phrones* is from *phrēn*, "mind." So *aphrones* literally means "mindless." Abbott-Smith defines it as "*without reason, senseless, foolish*, expressing 'want of mental sanity and sobriety, a reckless and inconsiderate habit of mind'" (p. 72). Thayer's definition is: "Without reason, senseless, foolish, stupid; without reflection or intelligence, acting rashly" (p. 90). It is a stronger term than the one in v. 15. The best translation here is "foolish" (RSV, NASB, NIV). The only way one can avoid being foolish is by "understanding"—literally, putting together—"what the will of the Lord is."

18 Excess Paul admonishes his readers not to be "drunk with wine, wherein is excess." The last word is in the Greek *asōtia*. Here again we find the *alpha*-negative, this time with *sōtia*, which comes from the verb *sōzō*, "save." So it is the opposite of salvation. Abbott-Smith defines the word as "prodigality, wastefulness, profligacy" (p. 66). Thayer says: "an abandoned, dissolute life; profligacy, prodigality" (p. 82). Arndt and Gingrich suggest: "debauchery, dissipation, profligacy" (p. 119). The best translation is "debauchery" (RSV, NIV) or "dissipation" (NEB, NASB).

Be Filled Instead of being "drunk with wine," Paul says that Christians should be "filled with the Spirit." Evidently he is suggesting that what people seek in drinking—relaxation, escape from the unendurable—one may find in being filled with the Holy Spirit. The verb is in the present imperative, which means "be continually filled with the Spirit." This is not to be a transitory experience, but an abiding one. Jesus said: "I will pray the Father, and he shall give you another Comforter, that he may abide with you for ever" (John 14:16).

19 Psalms, Hymns, Songs This verse is closely related to v. 18. The Spirit-filled person will find a song in his soul. The Holy Spirit will be singing within, and some of this symphony of the soul ought to come out through the lips. Paul uses three terms to describe this heavenly music coming out of the human heart.

The first word is *psalmos*. It means: "1. *a striking, twitching* with the fingers (Euripides, others), hence, *a striking* of musical strings (Aeschylus, others), and hence in later writers, 2. *a sacred song* sung to musical accompaniment, *a psalm* (Septuagint)" (A-S, p. 487).

Psalmos occurs 70 times in the Septuagint. Most of these occurrences are in the titles of the psalms. It is obvious that the current usage of the term was for sacred songs that were to be sung to the accompaniment of musical instruments. The etymological derivation of the term suggests that these were primarily stringed instruments—which are mentioned a number of times in the psalms.

This word is used for the Book of Psalms in Luke 20:42 and Acts 1:20; for an individual psalm in Acts 13:33; for the third division of the Hebrew canon (the Writings) in Luke 24:44; and for Christian psalms in 1 Cor. 14:26, here in Ephesians, and in Col. 3:16. These are all the occurrences in the NT.

The second word is *hymnos*. Abbott-Smith describes its usage thus: "(a) in classics a festal song in praise of gods or heroes; (b) in LXX and NT a song of praise addressed to God" (p. 455). It is found elsewhere in the NT only in the parallel passage, Col. 3:16.

The third word is *ōdē*, which means "*a song, ode*, whether sad or joyful; in LXX and NT always in praise to God or Christ" (A-S, p. 490). It is found three times in Revelation (5:9; 14:3; 15:3) as well as in Col. 3:16. Since it is a general word for "songs," it is accompanied by the adjective "spiritual" (*pneumatikais*).

These three terms are also found together in the parallel passage in Col. 3:16. So they call for a comparison. Some commentators find no difference between them, insisting that Paul was not trying to classify the various forms of Christian poetry. While admitting the truth of the latter claim, Trench asserts: "But neither, on the other hand, would he have used, where there is evidently no temptation to rhetorical amplification, three words, if one would have equally served his turn" (p. 295).

Concerning the "psalms," Trench observes: "In all probability the *psalmoi* of Ephes. v. 19, Col. iii. 16, are the inspired psalms of the Hebrew Canon" (p. 296). That is its meaning elsewhere in the NT, as we have noted, except in 1 Cor. 14:26—where it could also mean this.

The distinguishing feature of a "hymn" is that it is always addressed to God. Trench says: "Augustine in more places than one states the notes of what in his mind are the essentials of a hymn—which are three: 1. It must be sung; 2. It must be praise; 3. It must be to God" (p. 298). This is still a correct description of a hymn.

It may not be out of the way to observe here that hymns should regularly be used in the Sunday morning worship service. The minds and hearts of the people should be directed away from themselves and their own feelings, toward God in adoration and worship. Trench says: "A 'hymn' must always be more or less of a *Magnificat*, a direct address of praise and glory to God" (*ibid.*). Hymns like "Holy, Holy, Holy," "All Hail the Power of Jesus' Name," "Majestic Sweetness," or "Come, Thou Almighty King" point people toward God. That is what is needed at least one hour a week.

Lightfoot summarizes the distinction between the three words as follows: "While the leading idea of *psalmos* is a musical accompaniment and that of *hymnos* praise to God, *ōdē* is the general word for a song, whether accompanied or unaccompanied, whether of praise or on any other subject" (p. 225). Eadie comments: "The hymn was more elaborate and solemn in its structure than the ode" (p. 400).

"Speaking to yourselves" is probably better rendered "speaking to one another." This spiritual music is to be for mutual blessing and edification.

"Singing" is the Greek verb *adō*. It is used three times in Revelation (5:9; 14:3, 15:3) with the object *ōdē*. Aside from that it is found in the NT only here and in the parallel passage, Col. 3:16. It comes from the same root as *ōdē* and means "to celebrate something or someone in song" (TDNT, 1:163).

"Making melody" is one word in the Greek, *psallontes*. The verb *psallō* meant first to strike the strings of a harp or lyre. Then it meant to "strike up a tune." Finally it was used in the sense "to sing." The phrase here could be translated "singing and psalming."

This is to be "in your heart." The relation of this to "speaking to one another" is thus explained by Lightfoot: "This external manifestation must be accompanied by the inward emotion. There must be the thanksgiving of the heart, as well as of the lips" (p. 226). That is, while one is singing these songs aloud, he should be hymning them in his heart. Also, after singing together on Sunday we should carry a melody of song in our souls all the week.

The primary emphasis of all our religious singing should be "giving thanks always for all things unto God and the Father in the name of our Lord Jesus Christ" (v. 20). Probably it would be correct to say that all of us are behind in expressing our gratitude to God. The heart that is filled with praise to Him is a happy heart. One of the surest secrets of success and victory in the Christian life is forming the habit of thanking the Lord frequently throughout each day. Praise is a great dispeller of doubt and darkness.

21 Submitting "Submitting yourselves" is the present middle participle of *hypotassō*, which is thus defined by Abbott-Smith: "1. as a military term, *to place* or *rank under* (Polybius). 2. *to subject, put in subjection.* . . . Middle, "to subject oneself, obey" (p. 463). Most of the recent versions (e.g., RSV, NEB, NASB) use "subject" rather than "submit." The KJV does this in verse 24, where the verb is the same as here. The NIV has "submit" in both places.

25 Husbands, Love Your Wives After telling the wives to be in subjection to their own husbands, Paul confronts the men with a much more difficult demand. To them he says: "Husbands, love your wives, even as Christ also loved the church."

Aside from Mark 12:38, where a word meaning "wish" is rendered by "love" (in KJV), there are two verbs that are translated "love" in the NT—*agapaō* and *phileō*. *Agapaō* is found 142 times. It is rendered "love" 135 times and "beloved" 7 times. On the other hand, *phileō* occurs only 25 times. It is translated "love" 22 times and "kiss" 3 times.

In classical Greek there is a third verb for love, *eraō*. Concerning this term Cremer writes: "*Eran* denotes the love of passion, of vehement, sensual desire; but so unsuitable was this word, by usage so saturated with lustful ideas, to express the moral and holy character of that love with which Scripture in particular has to do, that it does not occur in a good sense even in the O.T., save in Prov. iv. 6; . . . and . . . not at all in the N.T." (p. 10).

Trench is in essential agreement with this. Regarding the nonuse of *eros* and *erao* in the Greek OT (LXX) he says: "It is in part no doubt to be explained from the fact that, by the corrupt use of the word, they had become so steeped in sensual passion, carried such an atmosphere of unholiness about them . . . , that the truth of God abstained from defiling contact with them; yea, devised a new word rather than betake itself to one of these" (p. 43).

The "new word" is the noun *agapē*, of which Trench says: "There is no trace of it in any heathen writer whatever" (*ibid.*). Similar is the statement of Cremer: "Not found in profane writers" (p. 13).

Today these statements may need revising. Trench wrote 100 years ago (1855, 1863), and Cremer also (Eng. trans. of 2nd ed., 1878). Arndt and Gingrich say: "Now we have an inscription that is surely pagan"—from the third century A.D. (p. 5).

But *agapē* can still be spoken of as practically unknown in pagan sources. It is used 16 times in the Septuagint, all but 5 of these in the Song of Solomon. The verb *agapaō* is used nearly 300 times in the Septuagint.

What is the difference between *agapaō* and *phileō*, the two verbs for love in the NT? It is noted above that *phileō* is 3 times translated "kiss"—all in connection with Judas Iscariot's betrayal of Jesus (Matt. 26:48; Mark 14:44; Luke 22:47). This gives a clue as to the distinctive meaning of the term. It describes the love of the affections. On the other hand, *agapaō* expresses the love of the will. Cremer sums it up well: "*Philein* denotes the love of natural inclination, affection,—love, so to say, originally spontaneous, involuntary (*amare*); *agapan*, on the other hand, love as a direction of the will (*diligere*)" (p. 11).

The most thorough recent treatment of *agapaō* is to be found in the first volume (1964) of the new English translation of a monumental work—Kittel's *Theologisches Woerterbuch zum Neuen Testament* (English: *Theological Dictionary of the New Testament*).

The greater part of this article on *agapaō* is written by the famous German scholar, Ethelbert Stauffer. He says: "*Eran* is passionate love which desires the other for itself" (TDNT, 1:35). He also writes: "*Eros* seeks in others the fulfillment of its own life's hunger. *Agapan* must often be translated 'to show love'; it is a giving, active love on the other's behalf" (TDNT, 1:37). Christ "loved the church, and gave himself for it."

The verb which is used twice in Eph. 5:25 is *agapaō*. From the above discussion it will be seen that this means something more than affectionate love, though this is included. The emphasis is rather on an intelligent, voluntary love. This is the kind of love that will last. Feelings fluctuate. Emotions ebb and flow. Affections are often affected by changing circumstances. But the love of commitment can remain firm and loyal through every vicissitude of life. This is the kind of love that a husband is commanded to have for his wife. It is an unselfish love that seeks the best good of its object. This kind of love will hold a marriage together "as long as ye both shall live."

After discussing the difference between *agapaō* and *phileō*, Abbott-Smith writes: "If this distinction holds, *agapaō* is fitly used in NT of Christian love to God and man, the spiritual affection which follows the direction of the will, and which, therefore, unlike that feeling which is instinctive and unreasoned, can be commanded as a duty" (p. 3).

One further thought might be suggested here. While we cannot directly control our feelings, we can control our thoughts. The man who thinks loving thoughts about his wife will experience loving feelings toward her.

26 Sanctify and Cleanse In vv. 25–26 Paul moves from the love of husbands for their wives to the love of Christ for His Church. The Greek says: "In order that He might sanctify it (or *her*), having cleansed (her) by the washing of water in (by, with) word"—"with the word" (RSV, NASB).

We speak of pardon and purity, of conversion and cleansing, as related to distinct experiences in grace. This is accurate. But there is also a purity that comes with pardon, and a cleansing that comes with conversion. When we confess our sins to God and believe in Jesus Christ, not only are our sins forgiven, but the stain of committed sins is washed away. However, there is still needed a deeper cleansing from all sin, from the carnal nature with which every human being is born.

Word The meaning of this term is not entirely clear. The Greek word is *rhēma*. The most common term for "word" is *logos*, which occurs some 330 times in the NT. It is translated "word" 225 times, with dozens of other renderings for the remaining occurrences. On the other hand, *rhēma*, found 70 times, is translated "word" 56 of those times and "saying" 9 times.

The distinctive idea of *rhēma* is that it properly refers to what is said or spoken, whereas *logos* can be used for a written word. Thayer defines the term as basically meaning: "that which is or has been uttered by the living voice, thing spoken, word" (p. 562). He interprets the phrase here, *en rhēmati*, thus: "according to promise (properly *on* the ground of his *word* of promise, namely the promise of the pardon of sins)" (*ibid.*). Arndt and Gingrich say with regard to *rhēma* in this and similar passages: "Generally the singular brings together all the divine teachings as a unified whole, with some such meaning as *gospel*, or *confession*" (p. 743).

This Greek term *rhēma* is found again in 6:17—"the sword of the Spirit, which is the *word* of God." The same phrase, "word of God" (using *rhēma* rather than *logos*) occurs in Heb. 6:5 and 11:3. In 1 Pet. 1:25 reference is made to "the word of the Lord" which is preached.

It seems clear that the cleansing is to be accomplished by the power of God's word, however it may be expressed.

27 *Spot, Wrinkle?*

The word for "spot" (*spilon*) first meant a rock or cliff. Later it came to mean a "spot" or "stain" (NIV). Here it is used metaphorically for "a moral blemish." The Greek word for "wrinkle" is found only here in the NT. The phrase "not having spot, or wrinkle" suggests the idea of "washed and ironed." Christ wants His bride, the Church, to be neat as well as clean. When we are concerned only with being a "clean people," but do not give attention to making our personal appearance and personality attractive, so that we may attract others to Christ, we fail to be what He wants us to be.

Without Blemish

This is one word in the Greek—*amōmos*. It was used of sacrificial animals, which the law required should be without blemish (Num. 6:14; 19:2). So it is applied to Christ, the Lamb of God sacrificed for the sins of men (1 Pet. 1:19; Heb. 9:14). By classical Greek writers it was employed in the sense of "blameless," morally and religiously. In Jude 24 the word is translated "faultless"—"present you faltless before the presence of his glory." This forms a striking parallel to Eph. 5:27.

Verses 25–27 may be taken together as the basis for a textual sermon. Verse 25 shows us "The Provision for Sanctification" in the death of Christ. Verse 26 gives "The Prerequisite for Sanctification" in the washing of regeneration. Verse 27 shows "The Purpose of Sanctification" in our presentation to Christ as His bride.

28 *So Ought Men*

"So ought men to love their wives as their own bodies." The verb translated "ought" is *opheilō*. It means "to owe, be a debtor" (A-S, p. 330). Of a similar use of the term in 1 John 2:6, Westcott says: "The obligation is represented as a debt" (*Epistles of John*, p. 50).

That is the meaning here. The husband *owes* it to his wife to love her as he loves (cares for) his own body. The one who fails to do so is not paying his honest debts.

29 *Nourisheth and Cherisheth*

To express the loving care that a man should have for his wife, Paul used two terms. The first, *ektrephō*, is found only here and in 6:4. There it is used for bringing up children. Thayer defines it thus: "1. *to nourish up to maturity;* then universally *to nourish* . . . Eph. v. 29. 2. to nurture, bring up . . . Eph. vi. 4" (p. 200). It suggests the idea of a husband caring tenderly for his wife, as a mother might care for her child.

"Cherisheth" is the verb *thalpō*. It literally means "keep warm," and so figuratively "cherish, comfort" (AG, p. 351). Thayer writes: "Like the Latin *foveo, to cherish* with tender love, *to foster* with tender care" (p. 282). The word is found only here and in 1 Thess. 2:7.

31 *Two Shall Be One Flesh*

This verse consists of a quotation of Gen. 2:24, an important OT passage quoted earlier by Jesus (Matt. 19:5; Mark 10:7). The verb "be joined" is literally "be glued." What many marriages need today is more of the glue of genuine, unselfish love, so that they will "stick together."

Paul is incurably and inexorably practical. He starts out by commanding husbands to love their wives (v. 25). This leads to a contemplation of Christ's love for His Church (vv. 25–27). Then he comes down to earth with a "thump" again: "So ought men to love their own wives as their own bodies" (v. 28). Once more he takes off into orbit in the heavenlies, as he speaks of Christ and the Church (vv. 29–30). In v. 31 it is human marriage again, but in v. 32 Christ and the Church. His final note, however, is on practical Christian living in the social relationship between husband and wife (v. 33).

6:1 *Obey*

The Greek word for "obey" here is *hypakouō*. It is a compound of *akouō*, which means "hear, listen." So it literally means "to listen." Thayer defines it thus: "1. properly: of one who on a knock at the door comes to listen who it is . . . Acts xii. 13. . . . 2. *to hearken to a command*, i.e. *to obey, be obedient unto, submit to* (so in Greek writers from Herodotus down)"

(p. 638). Children are admonished by Paul to "listen to" their parents, which means doing what they ask.

3 *Live Long* This reads literally: "In order that it may become well with thee, and thou shalt be [future tense] of long duration upon the earth." "Of long duration" is one word in the Greek, the compound adjective *makrochronois. Makros* means "long," *chronos* "time." So the adjective literally means "long-timed." Found only here in the NT, and rare in secular Greek, it may be translated "long-lived."

Earth This is a quotation from Deut. 5:16 (cf. Exod. 20:12). In the OT passages it is a promise that if the children will honor their parents the nation will continue long in the land of promise. But Paul is now writing to Gentile Christians living in Asia Minor. So the correct rendering here is "on the earth" (KJV, RSV, NASB, NIV), not "in the land" (NEB).

4 *Provoke Not Your Children* "Provoke . . . to wrath" is one word in Greek, *parorgizō*. It occurs only here and in a quotation from the Septuagint in Rom. 10:19. A good free translation of this clause is: "You fathers, again, must not goad your children to resentment" (NEB). This is the other side of the coin of parent-child relationship—"Children obey your parents."

Nurture and Admonition The first of these two terms is *paideia* in the Greek. It comes from *pais*, "child." Abbott-Smith gives the following comprehensive definition of it: "1. *the rearing of a child* (Aeschylus). 2. *training, learning, instruction* (Plato, others): Eph. 6:4; II Tim. 3:16. 3. As in the Septuagint (Prov. 3:11; 15:6, others), *chastening, discipline:* Heb. 12:5, 7, 8, 11" (p. 333). These are all the occurrences in the NT.

The second word is *nouthesia*. Literally it means a "putting in mind." It is found elsewhere in the NT only in 1 Cor. 10:11 and Titus 3:10. In each instance it is rendered "admonition." Arndt and Gingrich translate the phrase here: "discipline and instruction" (p. 608). That is about as close to the Greek as one can come.

6 *Eyeservice* This term closely represents the Greek compound *ophthalmodoulia*. Arndt and Gingrich say it means "service that is performed only to attract attention . . . , not for its own sake nor to please God or one's own con-

science" (p. 604). The word occurs in the parallel passage in Col. 3:22, but nowhere else in Greek literature.

Menpleasers This compound, *anthrōpareskos*, is likewise found in the NT only here and in Col. 3:22. Moulton and Milligan say that the word, "which starts in the Septuagint and *Psalms of Solomon*, was presumably as much a coinage as our own 'men-pleasers,' but made in a language where compounds are more at home than in ours. If this is a 'Biblical' word, it is only an instance of the fact that every Greek writer made a new compound when his meaning required one" (VGT, p. 43).

7 *Good Will* The Greek word is *eunoia* (only here in NT). Arndt and Gingrich give its meaning for this passage as "zeal, enthusiasm."

9 *Forbearing Threatening* The verb is *aniemi*. Originally used in the sense of "loosen, unfasten," it came to mean "give up, cease from" (AG, p. 69). That is its meaning here. Bultmann writes: "The basic meaning of the word *aniemi* is the relaxation of tension" (TDNT, 1:367). This is the sort of thing that is needed in human relationships.

Eph. 5:21–6:9 deals with the social application of the gospel to three areas of life: the relationship of husbands and wives, parents and children, masters and slaves. The same 6 classes are instructed in a similar fashion in Col. 3:18–4:1. This is one of several close parallels between these two Epistles of Paul. The apostle was interested not only in theology but also in practical Christian living.

10 *Finally* In Greek it is *tou loipou*. The Textus Receptus (late MSS) has *to loipon* (accusative case), which means "for the rest." The meaning of *tou loipou* (genitive case) is given in Blass and Debrunner as "from now on, henceforth"; that is, genitive of time (p. 100). But Arndt and Gingrich say: "In Eph. 6:10 the meaning is probably rather finally, bringing the matter to a conclusion" (p. 481). Phillips translates it, "In conclusion."

Be Strong The verb is *endynamoo*. It comes from *dynamis* (dynamo, dynamic). One is tempted to translate it, "Be dynamic!" The whole clause is paraphrased in NEB: "Find your strength in the Lord."

The Power of His Might The first noun is *kratos*, which is used in Homer for bodily strength. The second is *ischys*, which means "strength, power, might" (AG, p. 384). But neither noun is *dynamis*, which is most properly translated "power." So the best rendering here is "the strength of his might" (RSV, NASB).

11 The Whole Armor Paul exhorted his readers: "Put on the whole armor of God." The verb is used regularly of putting on clothes. It may be translated "be clothed with." "Whole armor" is one word in Greek, *panoplia*. It comes from *pan*, which means "all," and *hopla*, "arms, weapons." The word is used metaphorically here and in v. 13. Elsewhere in the NT it occurs only in Luke 11:22, where it has the literal sense, "*full armor* of a heavily-armed soldier" (AG, p. 612). Vine writes: "Among the Greeks the *panoplia* was the complete equipment used by heavily armed infantry" (1:75). The different parts of this armor are mentioned in the verses that follow v. 13.

Wiles of the Devil In the Greek, "wiles" is *methodeias*, from which comes the English word "methods" (cf. Phillips).

The cognate verb, *methodeuō* is found in the Septuagint, but not in the NT. On the other hand, the noun *methodeia* has not been discovered in any earlier writings. In the NT it occurs only in 4:14 (see comments there), here, and in verse 12 in Papyrus 46 (third century).

The treatment of this word in modern reference works furnishes a striking example of recent progress in this field. Among older scholars, Thayer declares that *methodeia* "is not found in profane authors" (p. 395); that is, secular writers. Abbott-Smith says, "not found elsewhere" (p. 282). But Moulton and Milligan give several examples of the use of this word in the papyri of the 5th and 6th centuries (VGT, p. 394), always in the sense of "method." Arndt and Gingrich include this information in their lexicon and suggest the translation, "stratagems" (military context).

The context indicates that here the word carries an evil connotation. Perhaps the best translation is "the devices of the devil" (NEB).

12 We Wrestle Not Literally the first part of this verse reads: "Because there is not to us the wrestling against blood and flesh." The word for wrestling is *palē*. Thayer notes that beginning with Homer this word was used to describe "a contest between two in which each endeavors to throw the other, and which is decided when the victor is able *thlibein kai katechein* (to press and to hold down) his prostrate antagonist, i.e., to hold him down with his hand upon his neck" (p. 474). Paul taught

that Christians should be "more than conquerors" through Christ (Rom. 8:37).

Principalities, Powers, Rulers, Wickedness In this verse the apostle names four things against which we wrestle (cf. 1:21). The first is "principalities." The Greek word is *archē*, which literally means "beginning" (cf. John 1:1). But here it means "sovereignty, principality, rule" (see rather full discussion on 1:21).

Delling writes: "*Archē* always signifies 'primacy,' whether in time: '*beginning*' ... or in rank: 'power,' 'dominion,' 'office'" (TDNT, 1:479). It is used both ways in the Septuagint and the New Testament. With regard to the use here, Delling says: "They are spiritual beings (Eph. 6:12), related to angels according to Rom. 8:38" (p. 483).

The second term, "powers," is literally "authorities" (*exousias*). This is also found in 1:21, where its sense is explained in the comments there.

The other two terms, however, differ from those in 1:21. Both are expressed in phrases. The first is "the rulers of the darkness of this world"; literally, "the world-rulers [one word] of this darkness." Arndt and Gingrich define this as meaning: "the rulers of this sinful world" (p. 446).

The last expression is "spiritual wickedness in high places"; literally, "the spirits of wickedness in the heavenlies." This underscores the truth that there are wicked spirits which may tempt men in their highest moments of spiritual fellowship.

13 Stand Again Paul urges his readers to take up "the whole armour (panoply) of God." With this they can "withstand in the evil day"—the day when the devil makes his heaviest assaults. He adds: "and having done all, to stand." The ASV and RSV translate this exactly the same way. The NASB improves this somewhat by strengthening the second verb: "and having done everything, to stand firm."

The expression "having done" hardly seems adequate for the Greek *katergasamenoi*. This emphatic compound verb (from *ergazomai*, "work") means "to effect by labour, achieve, work out, bring about" (A-S, p. 240). Thayer defines it as "to perform, accomplish, achieve," and says that here it means: "having gone through every struggle of the fight" (p. 339).

Arndt and Gingrich suggest two interpretations. The first is that of doing everything prescribed, putting on every piece of the armor. But they also find support in Herodotus and

Thucydides (Greek historians) for the meaning "overpower, subdue, conquer," and give for this passage: "after proving victorious over everything, stand your ground" (p. 423).

Many of the best commentators object to the meaning "overpower" in this passage. While admitting that *katergazō* has that sense in classical Greek, they insist that it does not in the NT. Alford writes: "To finish, or accomplish, is the invariable Pauline usage of the word when taken in a good sense" (3:146). Meyer says that the verb "retains its ordinary signification, 'to achieve, accomplish, complete,' and is not . . . to be taken in the sense of . . . *overpower*, in which sense it is . . . usual enough, but is never so employed by Paul . . . or elsewhere in the N.T." (p. 542). Eadie agrees with this. Salmond writes: "There is no reason to depart from the ordinary sense of the verb . . . *doing thoroughly, working out*, especially (the *kata* being intensive) accomplishing a difficult task" (EGT, 3:385). He adds: "The ability to withstand when the fight is on is to be sought with a view to holding one's position when the conflict is at an end,—neither dislodged nor felled, but *standing* victorious at one's post" (*ibid.*). Lenski thinks that the neuter "all" rules out "overpower," which would require the masculine. But he holds that *stēnai* means: " 'to stand' as victors" (p. 663). It would seem that, while we cannot stress the idea of "having overcome all things," yet this is implied in the closing word, *stēnai*—"stand as victors."

14 *Girt About with Truth*

Paul writes: "Stand therefore, having your loins girt about with truth." But the latter verb is middle, not passive, and so is correctly translated: "having girded your loins with truth" (RSV, NASB). The NEB renders this clause: "Buckle on the belt of truth."

Vincent notes that the loins constituted "the point of junction for the main pieces of the body-armor, so that the girdle formed the common bond of the whole," and adds: "Truth gives unity to the different virtues, and determinateness and consistency to character." Helpfully he defines "truth" as meaning "the agree-

ment of our convictions with God's revelation" (3:408).

Concerning the different items mentioned here, Vincent remarks: "The principal terms in this description of the Christian armor are taken from the Septuagint of Isaiah" (p. 407). The girdle of truth is mentioned in 11:5; the breastplate of righteousness and helmet of salvation, in 59:17; the sandals of peace, in 52:7. In addition, one might find an allusion to the Sword of the Spirit in 49:2.

Breastplate of Righteousness

The Greek word for breastplate is *thōrax*, first meaning "breast" and then "breastplate." "Of righteousness" is the genitive of apposition. It means the breastplate which is righteousness. This refers to the righteousness of Christ, made available to us through faith. Lenski says of this: "It is the central part of all saving truth. The heart of the Word makes our heart invulnerable against Satan" (p. 667). (The function of the breastplate was to cover the vital organs of the body, particularly the heart.)

Vincent describes the breastplate in the Roman armor as being a "corselet of metal scales fastened upon leather or linen, or of flexible bands of steel folding over each other" (p. 408). The "cuirasses" were heavy breastplates of chain mail worn by the Roman spearmen.

15 *Shod with . . . Peace*

The literal wording is: "And have shod yourselves as to the feet in readiness of the gospel of peace." Lenski writes: "The general sense is: 'ready, eager courage that is due to the gospel which fills us with the peace of God' " (p. 667).

The Greek word for "preparation" is found only here in the NT. Vincent says of it: "*Hētoimasia* means *readiness;* but in Hellenistic Greek it was sometimes used in the sense of *establishment* or *firm foundation*, which would suit this passage: *firm-footing*" (3:409). The Roman soldiers wore sandals, "bound by thongs over the instep and round the ankle, and having the soles thickly studded with nails" (*ibid.*). God's peace gives us firm footing in fighting the enemy.

Philippians

1:1 Bishops The Greek word for "bishop" is *episcopos* (cf. *episcopal*). It occurs five times in the NT. In Acts 20:28 it is translated "overseers." In 1 Pet. 2:25 it refers to Christ, "the Shepherd and Bishop of your souls." It is found twice in the Pastorals (1 Tim. 3:2; Titus 1:7) and is correctly translated "bishop." ("Office of a bishop" in 1 Tim. 3:1 is another word, *episcopē*.) Critics have sometimes insisted that the technical use of *episcopos* for "bishop" in the Pastoral Epistles reflects a later development in church organization and so demands a second-century date for these letters. But the same usage here in Philippians (written about A.D. 61) undercuts that argument.

The word *episcopos* comes from *scopos*, "a watcher." So it means "a superintendent, guardian, overseer" (A-S). Thayer notes that it has this same comprehensive sense in Homer's *Iliad* and *Odyssey* and in classical Greek writers from that time on (p. 243). The large *Lexicon* of Liddell-Scott-Jones (1940) gives as the first meaning of *episcopos* "one who watches over," and lists numerous examples of this use (p. 657). "This was the name given in Athens to the men sent into subdued states to conduct their affairs" (Cremer, p. 527). The word was used 14 times in the Septuagint in the sense of "overseer," or "inspector." Deissmann notes that in Rhodes, *episcopos* was "a technical term for the holder of a *religious* office" (in the temple of Apollo), as well as being used in the plural for "communal officials" (BS, pp. 230–31).

Lightfoot mentions its use at Athens, and adds: "The title however is not confined to Attic usage; it is the designation for instance of the inspectors whose business it was to report to the Indian kings . . . ; of the commissioner appointed by Mithridates to settle affairs in Ephesus . . . ; of magistrates who regulated the sale of provisions under the Romans . . . ; and of certain officers in Rhodes whose functions are unknown" (p. 95).

Beyer writes: "In Greek *episcopos* is first used . . . with a free understanding of the 'onlooker' as 'watcher,' 'protector,' 'patron.' " Then it came to be used "as a title to denote various offices" (TDNT, 2:609). He notes that protective care is "the heart of the activity which men pursue as episcopoi" (TDNT, 2:610). This is its classical usage.

By the end of the second century we read of diocesan bishops. Early in the second century Ignatius indicates that in each church was one bishop, a group of presbyters, and a group of deacons. But in Paul's Epistles (here and in the Pastorals) "bishop" and "presbyter" seem to be used synonymously. Lightfoot observes: "It is a fact now generally recognized by the theologians of all shade of opinion, that in the language of the New Testament the same officer in the Church is called indifferently 'bishop' (*episcopos*) and 'elder' or 'presbyter' (*presbyteros*)" (p. 95). In TDNT, Coenen thinks it "probable that the terms *presbyteros* and *episcopos* (bishop) are interchangeable" (1:199).

Deacons The word *diaconos* occurs no less than 30 times in the NT. But it has the technical meaning of "deacon" only 3 times—here and in 1 Tim. 3:8, 12. Elsewhere in the KJV it is translated "minister" 20 times and "servant" 7 times. But since "minister" usually carries an ecclesiastical connotation today, it would be better rendered simply as "servant" (except in the 3 passages noted above).

Thayer defines the word thus: "one who executes the commands of another, especially of a master; a servant, attendant, minister"; it was also used for "a waiter, one who serves food and drink" (p. 138).

In pre-Christian inscriptions the term was already employed for an "*attendant* or *official* in a temple or religious guild" (LSJ, p. 398). From this it was an easy transition to the church "deacon."

Moulton and Milligan cite approvingly Hort's rendering of this passage: "with them that have oversight, and them that do service" (VGT, p. 245). But it seems better to take "bishops and deacons" as referring to the titles of officers in the church.

4 Prayer, Request "Always in every prayer of mine for you all making request with joy." But "prayer" and "request" are the same word in Greek, *deēsis*. The word literally means "a wanting, need," and so "an asking, entreaty, supplication" (A-S, p. 99). Probably the two occurrences of the term should be rendered consistently: "always in every prayer of mine for you all making my prayer with joy" (RSV)—an excellent literal translation of the Greek (cf. NASB, NIV).

5 Fellowship Paul thanks God for the "fellowship" of the Philippians in proclaiming the gospel. The word is *koinōnia*. It is translated "fellowship" in Gal. 2:9; Eph. 3:9; and 3 times in this Epistle (1:5; 2:1; 3:10), as well as 4 times in 1 John (1:3 [twice], 6, 7). Altogether it occurs 20 times in the NT.

H. A. A. Kennedy notes that the reference here is to "their common participation with Paul in spreading the Gospel" (EGT, 3:418). So it would seem better to translate the term as "partnership" (RSV, NIV).

6 Perform Paul expresses his confidence that the One who had begun a good work in his readers would "perform" it until the day of Jesus Christ. The Greek verb is *epiteleō* from *epi*, "upon," and *telos*, "end." So it clearly means "to complete, accomplish, execute" (A-S, p. 175). Occurring 11 times in the NT, it is translated 7 different ways in KJV. The best rendering here is "bring it to completion" (RSV, NEB, Berk.).

7 I, You A good example of the perplexing ambiguity sometimes found in the Greek NT is furnished by this verse. The second clause reads, "because I have you in my heart" (KJV, ASV). But the margin of the ASV has "ye have me in your heart." Which is correct?

The problem arises because of the difference in Greek and English idiom and the presence of two accusatives with the infinitive *echein*. Very

literally the Greek reads: "On account of the to have me in the heart you." A. T. Robertson writes: "One accusative is the object of the infinitive *echein*, the other is the accusative of general reference. There is no way to decide which is the idea meant except to say that love begets love" (WP, 4:436). That is, the pastor's love for his people will beget in their hearts a love for him. This seems to be the most natural way to take Paul's statement: He holds the Philippian Christians in his heart (cf. RSV). The majority of the translators have taken it this way. Exceptions are: "you have me in your hearts" (Ballantine) and "you hold me in such affection" (NEB). We prefer "I have you in my heart" (NIV).

8 Bowels This verse provides one of the best examples of the fact that a literal translation may actually be an incorrect translation. Paul says that he longs after the Philippians in the "bowels" of Jesus Christ.

The Greek word is *splanchnon*, which means "bowels" or "inward parts." It is used literally of these physical organs in Acts 1:18. But elsewhere in the NT (10 times) it is employed metaphorically. The Greeks thought of the bowels as the center of affection. But we use the term "heart" for that. So the translation "bowels" here is actually misleading. Not only does it convey entirely the wrong idea, but it is apt to start the mind off on a sidetrack of unpleasant thought that will divert the attention away from the true meaning of the passage. Therefore any well-informed person reading the Bible in public will change the word "bowels" to something else like "tender mercies" (ERV, ASV) or "affection" (RSV, NASB, NIV). In Acts 1:18, where the word is used literally, "bowels" could be changed to "inward parts."

It is interesting to note that in Luke 1:78 the King James translators rendered what is literally "bowels of mercy of our God" as "tender mercy of our God." Evidently they balked at speaking of the bowels of God! But is "bowels of Jesus Christ" in our present passage any better? In 2 Cor. 7:15 they rightly used "inward affection" for *splanchnon*.

9 Judgment The last word translates a Greek term found only here in the NT— *aisthēsis*. Thayer defines it as: "perception . . . cognition, discernment" (p. 17). The last of these terms is perhaps the best rendering here (so ASV, RSV, NASB), or "insight" (NIV). Arndt and Gingrich suggest, "*become rich in every* (moral) *experience*" (p. 24).

10 *Approve ... Excellent* This phrase is translated much the same way in KJV, ERV, ASV, RSV, and NASB. Phillips suggests: "recognize the highest and best." *The Berkeley Version* has "distinguish differences." Weymouth comes perhaps closest to the Greek when he renders it "testing things that differ." One of the most striking translations is that of Moffatt: "enabling you to have a sense of what is vital" (cf. Goodspeed). This is one of the many passages in the NT where a comparison of different translations and versions can add much richness to one's study and preaching. "Discern what is best" (NIV) puts it very simply.

Sincere The Greek word is *heilikrines*, found only here and 2 Pet. 3:1, where it is translated "pure." Its basic meaning is "unmixed." Buechsel writes: "*Heilikrines* derives from *heile* (*halea, helios*), meaning 'warmth or light of the sun," and *krino*, so that the full sense is 'tested by the light of the sun,' 'completely pure' " (TDNT, 2:397). He goes on to say that the word always denotes "moral purity" (p. 398). C. B. Williams translates the whole phrase: "Be men of transparent character and blameless life"—a very meaningful wording. After considering this possibility, however, Trench writes: "It is not so much the clear, the transparent, as the purged, the winnowed, the unmingled" (p. 319).

In either case, the idea of purity or sincerity is dominant. Barclay favors combining the two figures of suggested etymologies. He writes: "The Christian purity is a purity which is sifted until the last admixture of evil is gone, a purity which has nothing to conceal and whose inmost thoughts and desires will stand the full glare of the light of day" (NTW, p. 33).

12 *Furtherance* The word is *prokope*. It literally means "a striking forward." First indicating progress on a journey, it came to be used metaphorically for progress in any realm. The best translation is "progress" (ASV, NASB)—here and in the other two places where the word occurs (v. 25; 1 Tim. 4:15)—or "advance" (NIV).

13 *Palace* Paul tells the Philippians that his "bonds in Christ"—that is, his imprisonment in the cause of Christ—have become well known in the whole "palace." The Greek word is *praitorion*. Elsewhere in the NT it is found once each in Matthew, Mark, and Acts, and four times in John. It is translated "common hall" in Matt. 27:27, and "Praetorium" in Mark 15:16.

In John and in Acts 23:35 it is rendered "judgment hall" (once "hall of judgment"). In each of these cases it refers to the governor's palace. But what does it mean in Philippians?

The first use of *praitorion* (which comes from the Latin) was for the headquarters in a Roman camp, the tent of the commander in chief. Then it was used (as in the Gospels and Acts) for the palace in which the governor of a province resided. In the third place it referred to the camp of Praetorian soldiers (Thayer, p. 534).

The most thorough treatment of this term is in the commentary by Lightfoot. He calls attention to the fact that the Greek fathers interpreted the word here as referring to the imperial palace at Rome. But he affirms: "Not a single instance of this usage has been produced. ... the imperial residence on the Palatine is not once so called" (p. 100).

Lightfoot declares that a second interpretation—the Praetorian barracks attached to the palace—"is equally destitute of authority" (p. 101). The same can be said for a third suggestion, that it refers to the great camp of the Praetorian soldiers. He concludes: "All attempts to give a local sense to 'praetorium' thus fail for want of evidence" (*ibid.*).

What, then, does it mean? "Praetorium signifies not a place, but a body of men"; it most frequently "denotes the praetorian regiments, the imperial guards" (pp. 101–2).

This fits best with the phrase which follows. In KJV this reads: "and in all other *places*." It will be noted that "places" is in italics, indicating that it is not in the original. The Greek simply says "to [or 'in'] all the remaining." This can mean remaining people or places. Probably the best translation is still that of the ASV (1901): "throughout the whole praetorian guard, and to all the rest," or "throughout the whole palace guard and to everyone else" (NIV). Arndt and Gingrich say: "If the letter was written from Rome, the words *en holo to praitorio* are best taken to mean *in the whole praetorian* (or *imperial*) *guard*" (p. 704).

Vincent calls attention to the fact that Paul was probably chained at all times to a member of the imperial guard, since he was an imperial prisoner. He adds: "His contact with the different members of the corps in succession, explains the statement that his bonds had become manifest throughout the praetorian guard" (3:420).

In Acts 23:35 the word clearly refers to the palace of Herod at Caesarea. In the Gospels it means the governor's official residence at Jerusalem. But there is still a dispute as to whether that was the palace of Herod the Great or the Tower of Antonia.

14 Many Paul rejoices that "many" of the brethren have been emboldened by his imprisonment to speak the word of God fearlessly. The Greek for "many" is *pleionas*. This is the comparative degree of the adjective for "many." So it would literally mean "more." But since in the NT the comparative is usually used for the superlative, the proper rendering is "most." That is what is found in "most" recent translations.

16–17 Contention The careful reader will note that these verses are in reverse order in the revised versions, as compared with KJV. As in all such cases, the more recent translations follow the better Greek text of the earliest manuscripts, while KJV is based on later manuscripts.

In verse 16 (17 in the better text) Paul declares that some of his contemporaries were preaching Christ "of contention." The Greek word is *eritheias* (genitive case). It means "ambition, self-seeking, rivalry" (A-S, p. 179). Cremer notes that the general meaning of the term is "selfishness, self-willedness" (p. 263). Thayer gives: "a courting distinction, a desire to put one's self forward, a partisan and factious spirit . . . partisanship, factiousness" (p. 249).

Arndt and Gingrich state that before NT times the word is found only in Aristotle, "where it denotes a self-seeking pursuit of political office by unfair means" (p. 309). The KJV rendering "contention" is based on the older theory that *eritheia* comes from *eris*, which is correctly translated "strife" in verse 15. But this view is rejected by scholars today. The true meaning is "selfishness, selfish ambition" (*ibid.*).

The term is now commonly held to be derived from a verb meaning to work for hire. H. A. A. Kennedy says: "Now that which degraded the hired worker, in the estimation of antiquity, was his labouring wholly for his own interests, while it was a sign of the noble to devote himself to the common weal" (EGT, 3:425). Moulton and Milligan write: "The meaning of 'selfish' rather than 'factious' ambition perhaps suits best all the New Testament occurrences of *eritheia*" (VGT, p. 254). A good translation, then, would be, "out of selfish ambition" (NASB, NIV).

16 Sincerely The Greek word is *hagnos*, which means "purely." A. T. Robertson points

out the true meaning: " 'Not purely,' that is with mixed and impure motives" (WP, 4:439).

18 Pretence The Greek word is *prophasis*. According to Abbott-Smith it comes from *prophēmi*, "speak forth"—"the ostensible presentation often untrue" (WP, 4:439). It "is the 'ostensible reason' for which a thing is done, and generally points to a false reason as opposed to the true" (VGT, p. 555). Occurring 7 times in the NT, it is translated four different ways in the KJV.

19 Salvation Paul asserts his faith that whatever happens will turn out for his "salvation." But was he not already "saved"?

The Greek word is *sotēria*. Its classical meaning was "deliverance, preservation" (LSJ, p. 1751). Moulton and Milligan state that this word "is common in the papyri in the general sense of 'bodily health,' 'well-being,' 'safety' " (VGT, p. 622).

Foerster says that the verb *sōzō* and the noun *sotēria* "mean first 'to save' and 'salvation' in the sense of an acutely dynamic act in which gods or men snatch others by force from serious peril" (TDNT, 7:966). He also notes that these words sometimes have more the idea of preservation from danger.

Arndt and Gingrich note that in Philo and Josephus (both first century) the term is used "generally of preservation in danger, deliverance from impending death" (p. 808). The latter meaning fits Paul's case perfectly. He was hoping to be freed safely from his imprisonment, instead of being executed (cf. 2:24). Rather obviously, then, the correct rendering here is "deliverance" (RSV, NEB, NASB, NIV). Phillips seems to miss the point entirely when he translates it: "for the good of my own soul."

Supply The Greek word for "supply" is *epichorēgia*. It comes from *chorēgos*, "chorus-leader." The verb *epichorēgeō* first meant to furnish a chorus at one's own expense, then simply to supply. So the noun is normally translated "provision" (NASB), "supply," or "support" (AG). It is a late and rare word, found in only one inscription (from A.D. 79). Vincent says: "The word implies *bountiful* supply" (3:423). This seems to be the best translation (so Weymouth, C. B. Williams). Regarding the following phrase, "of the Spirit of Jesus Christ," Vincent comments: "Either the supply furnished by the Spirit, or the supply which is the Spirit. It is better to take it as including both" (*ibid.*).

20 *Earnest Expectation* This is one word in the Greek, *apokaradokian*, found only here and in Rom. 8:19. Vincent defines it thus: "From *apo* away, *kara* the head, *dokein* to watch. A watching with the head erect or outstretched" (3:22). Lightfoot comments: "The idea of eagerness conveyed by the simple word *karadokein* is further intensified by the preposition which implies abstraction, absorption" (p. 91). The term may be translated either "earnest expectation" (KJV, ASV, NASB) or "eager expectation" (Weymouth, C. B. Williams, RSV).

Boldness Paul hopes that with "all boldness" he may magnify Christ. The Greek for "boldness" is *parrēsia* (see comments on Eph. 3:12). Arndt and Gingrich give as its meaning: "1. *outspokenness, frankness, plainness* of speech, that conceals nothing and passes over nothing. . . . 2. 'Openness' sometimes develops into *openness to the public*, before whom speaking and actions take place. . . . 3. *courage, confidence, boldness, fearlessness*, especially in the presence of persons of high rank" (pp. 635–36). Weymouth adopts the first of these definitions. He renders the phrase "by my perfect freedom of speech." Arndt and Gingrich prefer the second. But most recent translators adopt the third—"unfailing courage" (TCNT, Goodspeed), "fearless courage" (Moffatt), "full courage" (RSV). The context seems to favor "sufficient courage" (NIV).

Magnified The Greek verb is *megalynō*, from *megas*, "great." It means "to make great" or "to declare great." "Magnified" is a good translation. So also is "honored" (TCNT, C. B. Williams, RSV). The same idea is expressed in "do honour" (Moffatt) and "honor" (Phillips). Weymouth has "glorified" ("exalted," NIV). A good paraphrase is: "The greatness of Christ will shine out clearly in my person" (NEB).

22 *Fruit of My Labor* This verse seems a bit ambiguous. Perhaps the meaning is best expressed by C. B. Williams: "But if to keep on living here means fruit from my labor, I cannot tell which to choose" (cf. NIV).

Wot This archaic word occurs no less than 10 times in the KJV. In every case it renders a Hebrew or Greek term meaning "know." This history of the word goes back to around A.D. 1300. It had definitely become obsolete by the beginning of the 20th century. Retained in ERV (1881), it was changed to "know" in ASV (1901). In fact, "wot" does not occur in the latter version. Many recent translations use "tell" here—

"I cannot tell." Closely related to "wot" is "wit," used 3 times in KJV in the sense of "know." The past tense of "wot" is "wist." This occurs 14 times in KJV.

23 *In a Strait* Paul says that he is "in a strait betwixt two." The Greek literally says, "I am held together (*synechomai*) out of the two" (*ek tōn duo*). The verb means "to hem in, press on every side" (A-S, p. 428). Thayer says that the thought here is: "I am hard pressed on both sides, my mind is impelled or disturbed from each side" (p. 604). Lightfoot suggests: "*I am hemmed in on both sides*, I am prevented from inclining one way or the other." He adds: "The *duo* are the two horns of the dilemma, stated in verses 21, 22" (p. 93). The best translation is, "I am hard pressed between the two" (RSV), or "I am hard pressed from both directions" (NASB).

25 *Abide and Continue* Paul is convinced that for him to "abide in the flesh" is more necessary for the Philippian Christians (v. 24). So he declares: "I shall abide and continue with you."

These two verbs in the Greek are from the same root—*menō* and *paramenō*. The prefix of the second is a preposition meaning "beside." In order to bring out the connection of the two words in the original, the TCNT has, "I shall stay, and stay near you all." C. B. Williams renders it, "stay on and stay by." Lightfoot offers, "bide and abide" (p. 94). The second verb may be translated "stand by" (Phillips, NEB). H. A. A. Kennedy writes: "*Paramenō* (which is best attested) has in later Greek the special sense of 'remaining alive'" (EGT, 3:429). So Moffatt has, "remain alive and serve."

26 *Coming* *Parousia* occurs 24 times in the NT. In all but 6 of these instances it is used for the second coming of Christ. Literally it means "presence" (see Phil. 2:12). But it was also employed in the sense of "arrival." Here "coming . . . again" means "return" (Moffatt). The literal meaning is reflected by "my being with you again" (Weymouth, NIV).

27 *Conversation* Paul admonishes his readers: "Only let your conversation be as it becometh the gospel of Christ." "Let your conversation be" is all one word in the Greek, *politeuesthe*. This verb occurs (in NT) only here and Acts 23:1, where it is correctly translated, "I have lived."

The word comes from *politēs*, "citizen" (Luke 15:15; 19:14; Acts 21:39). This, in turn, is from *polis*, "city," just as our English word "citizen" comes from "city." The reason for this derivation goes back to the Greek city-states. One was not a citizen of a country, as today, but a citizen of a city.

The verb *politeuō*, used here, literally means "to be a citizen, live as a citizen" (A-S, p. 371). Thayer develops the usage of the word further, as follows: "*to behave as a citizen; to avail one's self of or recognize the laws;* so from Thucydides down; in Hellenistic writings *to conduct oneself as pledged to some law of life*" (p. 528). Here it may mean "Discharge your obligations."

Vincent says, "The exhortation contemplates the Philippians as members of the Christian *commonwealth*," and adds: "The figure would be naturally suggested to Paul by his residence in Rome, and would appeal to the Philippians as a Roman colony, which was a reproduction of the parent commonwealth on a smaller scale" (3:426). A. T. Robertson comments: "The Authorized Version missed the figure completely by the word 'conversation' which did refer to conduct and not mere talk as now, but did not preserve the figure of citizenship" (WP, 4:441). The correct translation is, "Conduct yourselves in a manner worthy of the gospel of the Christ" (NASB, NIV). Lightfoot paraphrases the first part of verse 27 as follows: "But under all circumstances do your duty as good citizens of a heavenly kingdom; act worthily of the Gospel of Christ" (p. 105).

Striving　Paul hopes he may hear that the Philippian believers are "with one mind [literally, 'one soul'] striving together for the faith of the Gospel." The verb is *synathleō*, found only in this Epistle (cf. 4:3). It is a compound of *syn* ("with" or "together") and *athleō* ("to be an athlete, contend in games"). The simple verb is found only in 2 Tim. 2:5.

Thayer defines the compound as meaning "*to strive at the same time with* another" (p. 600). The whole phrase may be translated, "joined in conflict for the faith of the Gospel" (Berkeley). A good rendering is, "contending as one man for the faith of the gospel" (NIV).

28 Terrified　Paul also hopes to hear of his readers that they are "in nothing terrified by your adversaries." The strong word "terrified" has been changed to "affrighted" (ASV) or "frightened" (RSV, C. B. Williams, NIV).

The verb is *ptyromai* (only here in NT). It means "to be startled, frightened" (A-S, p. 392). Arndt and Gingrich translate the phrase here, "in no way intimidated by your opponents" (p. 735). *The Berkeley Version* adopted this meaning—"not for a moment intimidated by the an-

tagonists." Typical paraphrases are "not caring two straws for your enemies" (Phillips) and "meeting your opponents without so much as a tremor" (NEB).

Perdition　The Greek word is *apōleia*. It means "destruction, waste, loss, perishing" (A-S, p. 56). In the NT it has the particular sense of "the destruction which consists in the loss of eternal life" (Thayer, p. 71). Of its use in Rev. 17:8, Oepke says: "What is meant here is not a simple extinction of existence, but an everlasting state of torment and death" (TDNT, 1:397). The best translation here is "destruction" (Goodspeed, Weymouth, C. B. Williams, RSV, NASB).

30 Conflict　The Greek word for "conflict" is *agōn*. This comes from the verb *agō*, which means "lead" or "bring." So the noun means: "1. *a place of assembly* (in Homer); specifically the place in which the Greeks assembled to celebrate solemn games (as the Pythian, the Olympian); hence 2. *a contest*, of athletes, runners, charioteers. In a figurative sense . . . any struggle with dangers, annoyances, obstacles, standing in the way of faith, holiness, and a desire to spread the gospel" (Thayer, p. 10). The rendering "contest" (NEB) points best to the athletic background of the term.

Ethelbert Stauffer has a good summary of the main emphasis of this paragraph (vv. 27–30) on the Christian's contest. We must "stand firm in one spirit, contending as one man" (v. 27). The victory over our adversaries is assured (v. 28). Faith in Christ costs suffering (v. 29). Stauffer concludes of Paul: "He thinks of the conflicts and sufferings of the Christian life itself as a life which in its totality stands under the sign of the cross and in this sign carries the cause of Christ to victory" (TDNT, 1:139).

2:1 Consolation　The Greek word is *paraklēsis*. It comes from *parakaleō*, "call to one's side." So the noun literally means "a calling to one's aid," then "exhortation" or "encouragement," and finally "consolation" or "comfort." Abbott-Smith lists this passage under the second of these three sets of meanings, as do also Thayer and Arndt and Gingrich.

The word occurs 29 times in the NT. In the KJV it is translated "consolation" 14 times, "exhortation" 8 times, "comfort" 6 times, and "intreaty" once. It appears that the best rendering here may be "encouragement" (RSV, Phillips, NASB, NIV). Arndt and Gingrich and ASV both prefer "exhortation," as does H. A. A. Kennedy (EGT, 3:432).

Comfort   In contrast to the fairly frequent occurrence of *paraklēsis*, the Greek word *paramythion* ("comfort") is found only here. Thayer gives only one meaning, "persuasive address" (cf. Berkeley, "persuasive appeal"), although he notes (p. 485) that in the classics it was used in the sense of "consolation" (NEB, NASB). Abbott-Smith has "an exhortation, persuasion, encouragement." Arndt and Gingrich would translate the phrase here, "if there is any solace afforded by love" (p. 626).

Lightfoot says about this word: " '*incentive*,' encouragement, not 'comfort,' as the word more commonly means" (p. 107). Kennedy comments: "Almost equivalent to *paraklēsis*, but having a suggestion of tenderness involved" (EGT, 3:432). Vine agrees with this. Of the closely related word *paramythia* he writes: "primarily a speaking closely to anyone, (*para*, near, *mythos*, speech), hence denotes consolation, comfort, with a greater degree of tenderness than *paraklēsis*" (1:207).

In his excellent article in the TDNT, Staehlin notes that these similar terms have "the favourable sense of a friendly relation" and that "it is almost impossible to separate the elements of petition, admonition and consolation." He says also that the basic sense "can develop along two main lines: with reference to what ought to be done, 'to admonish to something,' and with reference to what has happened, 'to console about something' " (5:817).

Staehlin affirms that both *paraklēsis* and *paramythion* "are characterized by the twofoldness of admonition and comfort" and adds: "In the NT . . . admonition becomes genuine comfort and *vice versa*, so that it is hard to distinguish between the two. . . . The unity of admonition and consolation is rooted in the Gospel itself, which is both gift and task" (5:821). He also notes: "All thoughts of comfort in the NT are in some way orientated to Christ" (5:823). That is the case here.

There is still something to be said for the rendering "incentive" (Moffatt, Goodspeed, RSV). Weymouth and Charles B. Williams have, "if there is any persuasive power in love." Wand translates: "of the persuasive influence of love." But the NIV returns to the traditional "comfort."

Fellowship   This is the famous word *koinōnia*, which has become well known in church circles today. It is a favorite term with Paul. He uses it 14 out of the 20 times it occurs in the NT. John also has it 4 times in his First Epistle.

The noun comes from the adjective *koinos*, "common." So its basic idea is that of sharing something in common. Thayer notes that its first meaning is "the share which one has in anything, participation" (p. 352). This is brought out by Weymouth's rendering, "any common sharing of the Spirit" (cf. C. B. Williams: "any common share in the Spirit"). The NIV and NASB have "fellowship."

Bowels   The Greek word is *splangchnon*, which literally means "bowels." But this physical sense is found only once in the NT (Acts 1:18). The other 10 times it occurs it is used metaphorically and should be rendered "heart" or "affection" (or some similar expression). Abbott-Smith says: "The characteristic LXX and NT reference of the word to the feelings of kindness, benevolence and pity, is found in papyri" (p. 414). The correct translation here is "affection" (RSV, NEB, NASB) or "tenderness" (NIV).

Mercies   The Greek word *oiktirmos*, like the previous term *splangchnon*, primarily refers to "the viscera, which were thought to be the seat of compassion" (Thayer, p. 442). Both words are usually in the plural in the NT and OT (LXX). For a comparison of the two, Lightfoot says: "By *splangchna* is signified the abode of tender feelings, by *oiktirmoi* the manifestation of these in compassionate yearnings and actions" (p. 108).

Oiktirmos occurs only five times in the NT. In the KJV it is regularly translated "mercies" (once, "mercy"). Probably a preferable rendering is "compassion" (NEB, NASB, NIV), or "sympathy" (RSV, Phillips). Actually "compassion" (from the Latin) and "sympathy" (from the Greek) both have exactly the same literal meaning—a "suffering with." Real sympathy or compassion demands that we become involved.

2 *One Accord, One Mind*   Paul desires that the Philippians shall be "of one accord, of one mind." The first expression is one word in Greek, *sympsychos* (found only here in NT). Literally it means "together-souled," and so "harmonious, united in spirit" (AG, p. 789).

The second expression is an entirely different construction. Literally it reads: "thinking the one thing." Obviously it is a bit difficult to put these two together. Charles B. Williams has: "your hearts beating in unison, your minds set on one purpose." *The Berkeley Version* reads: "your fellowship of feeling and your harmonious thinking." The NASB has: "united in spirit, intent on one purpose." The NIV reads: "being one in spirit and purpose." That is about as well as can be done with the passage.

Strangely, Phillips reverses these: "as though you had only one mind and one spirit between you." The similarity of meaning of these two expressions leads Lightfoot to make this cogent observation: "The redundancy of expression is a measure of the Apostle's earnestness" (p. 108).

3 Strife The Greek word is *eritheia*. It means "ambition, self-seeking, rivalry" (A-S, p. 179). The best translation would seem to be either "rivalry" (Phillips, NEB), "selfishness" (RSV, NASB), or "selfish ambition" (NIV).

Vainglory Paul also warns against being motivated by *kenodoxia* (only here in NT). Arndt and Gingrich say it means "vanity, conceit, excessive ambition" (p. 428). For this passage they suggest "empty conceit," the rendering which was chosen for NASB. The prefix *kenos* means "empty," while *doxa* means "opinion." The idea, then, is of one having an empty, or groundless, opinion of himself.

Lowliness of Mind The phrase "lowliness of mind" is a compound word in Greek, *tapeinophrosynē*. It has already been discussed at length in connection with Eph. 4:2. After noting that in pagan writers it meant "grovelling" or "abject," Lightfoot says: "It was one great result of the life of Christ (on which St. Paul dwells here) to raise 'humility' to its proper level; and if not fresh coined for this purpose, the word *tapeinophrosynē* now first became current through the influence of Christian ethics" (p. 109). Arndt and Gingrich list only two occurrences of the term, one in Epictetus and one in Josephus (both in a bad sense). These are later than Paul.

5 This Mind "Let this mind be in you" has the same Greek verb that is found twice in verse 2, where it reads "be likeminded" and "of one mind." The latter of these is a participial construction.

The verb is *phroneō*, which means "think" or "have in mind." Literally the passage reads: "Think this in you [plural]—or among you— which also in Christ Jesus." Obviously this needs some amplification to make sense in English. Arndt and Gingrich suggest the following translation: "Have the same thought among yourselves as you have in your communion with Christ Jesus" (p. 874). The NEB gives a good paraphrase: "Let your bearing towards one another arise out of your life in Christ Jesus." Phillips puts it a bit more briefly: "Let Christ Jesus be your example as to what your attitude should be" (cf. NIV). Probably the most meaningful rendering is that given by Lightfoot: "Reflect in your own minds the mind of Christ Jesus" (p. 110).

6 Robbery The second clause reads, "Thought it not robbery to be equal with God." The ASV has, "Counted not the being on an equality with God a thing to be grasped." The RSV and NIV read almost exactly the same.

"A thing to be grasped" is all one word in Greek, *hapargmos*. Most modern expositors are agreed that it does not have the active meaning, "the act of seizing" or "robbery," but rather the passive meaning, "a thing seized" or "a prize." For instance, Lightfoot paraphrases the passage: "*Though* He pre-existed in the form of God, *yet* He did not look upon equality with God as a prize which must not slip from His grasp" (p. 111). Ellicott favors this interpretation: "*He did not deem the being on an equality with God a thing to be seized on*, a state to be exclusively (so to speak) clutched at, and retained as a prize" (p. 56). Marvin Vincent (ICC) says that the correct meaning is "thing seized" (p. 58). Thayer gives for this passage the sense: "A thing to be seized upon or to be held fast, retained" (p. 74). Probably a good translation for the whole phrase is that given here by Vincent: "Counted it not a prize to be on an equality with God." Somewhat smoother would be this wording: "He did not consider being equal with God a prize to be retained."

7 Of No Reputation Paul goes on to say that Christ "made himself of no reputation." The verb here is simply *ekenōsen*—literally, "he emptied." That is why this is called the "kenosis" passage. It describes the self-emptying of the Son of God. The correct translation is: "He emptied himself." Of what? All orthodox theologians are agreed that it does not mean that He emptied himself of His divine nature. Rather, it was His heavenly glory—"The glory which I had with thee before the world was" (John 17:5).

Oepke writes: "What is meant is that the heavenly Christ did not selfishly exploit His divine form and mode of being, but by His own decision emptied himself of it or laid it by, taking the form of a servant by becoming man. . . . The essence remains, the mode of being changes" (TDNT, 3:661).

Vincent (ICC) issues a salutary note of warning at this point. He says of the verb employed here: "Not used or intended here in a metaphysical sense to define the limitations of Christ's incarnate state, but as a strong and graphic expression of the completeness of his self-renunciation. It includes all the details of humiliation which follow, and is defined by these" (p. 59).

6–8 *Form, Fashion*

The former word (vv. 6–7) is *morphē* in the Greek, the latter (v. 8) *schēma*. Regarding the first word Trench writes: "The *morphē* then, it may be assumed, is of the essence of a thing" (p. 265). Concerning the latter he comments: "The *schēma* here signifying his whole outward presentation" (p. 263).

Lightfoot emphasizes the idea that *morphē* means "what He *is* in Himself"—truly God become truly servant—but *schēma* indicates "what He *appeared* in the eyes of men" (p. 112). Of the latter Vincent (ICC) writes: "*Schēma* is the outward *fashion* which appeals to the senses" (p. 60). The former word refers to the inner being, the latter to the outer appearance. Christ not only *appeared* to be a servant in His incarnation; He *was* one. There was no playacting here. But manifesting himself to men as a man, He yet humbled himself further to the ignominious death on the Cross.

9 *Highly Exalted*

Because Christ humbled himself to become obedient to a shameful, but sacrificial, death on the Cross, God has "highly exalted him, and given him a name which is above every name." This refers to His ascension and glorification.

The verb translated "highly exalted" is *hyperypsoō*. It is not found in classical Greek and occurs only here in the NT—though it is used in the Septuagint several times. Abbott-Smith defines it thus: "To exalt beyond measure, exalt to the highest place" (p. 459). Similarly Arndt and Gingrich say that it means to "raise to the loftiest height" (p. 849). Vincent (ICC) writes: "Paul is fond of *hyper* in compounds, and the compounds with *hyper* are nearly all in his writings ... Its force here is not 'more than before,' nor 'above his previous state of humiliation,' but 'in superlative measure' " (p. 61).

Given

The Greek verb translated "given" is *charizomai*. It comes from the noun *charis* which means "grace." So the verb signifies. "1. *to show favour or kindness* ... 2. *to give freely*, bestow ... 3. In late Gk. ... *to grant forgiveness*, forgive freely" (A-S, p. 479).

The verb occurs 23 times in the NT. About half the time it means "give," and the other half "forgive." In both cases the emphasis is on the idea of doing it freely or graciously.

The KJV rendering here is correct and proba-

bly adequate, and is followed in most modern translations. But because of the derivation from *charis*, one is tempted to favor the wording of *The Berkeley Version*: "God ... has graced him with a name that surpasses every name."

A Name

The best Greek text has "the name." The definite article is omitted in the late, medieval manuscripts, which formed the basis of the KJV. The ASV (1901) has "the name." Weymouth (1902) reads: "God ... has conferred on Him the Name which is supreme above every other name." That expresses it well. "Name" signifies "title and dignity" (Lightfoot, p. 113).

10 *At*

The tenth verse says, "That at the name of Jesus every knee should bow." The preposition "at" is *en*, which properly means "in." That gives a very different sense here and is obviously more fitting. It is not a matter of bowing at the mention of the name of Jesus.

What does it mean to bow "in the name of Jesus"? Vincent (ICC) writes: "Paul follows the Hebrew usage, in which the name is used for everything which the name covers, so that the name is equivalent to the person himself" (p. 62). To bow in the name of Jesus is to recognize Him as Lord, exalted at the right hand of the Father.

Things

The KJV specifies what knees will bow by saying: "of *things* in heaven, and *things* in earth, and *things* under the earth." It will be noticed that the word *things* in all three instances is italicized, indicating that it is not in the original.

In the Greek there are simply three adjectives. The first is *epouranios*, which means "*in* or *of heaven*, *heavenly*" (A-S, p. 177). In the oldest Greek writer, Homer, it is used of the gods. The second adjective is *epigeios*, "of the earth, earthly." The third is *katachthonios*, "subterranean, under the earth." It is used in classical Greek for the infernal gods.

These three adjectives are in the genitive plural ("of ——s"). Unfortunately, in the Greek of most adjectives the same form is used for the masculine and neuter in genitive and dative cases. (The feminine is a different form usually.) Hence it is impossible to tell whether the masculine or the neuter is meant, except as the context may indicate. In English we put a noun with the adjective to make the matter specific. But the Greek has the habit of using an adjective, usually with the definite article, as a substantive. For instance, the key phrase of Ephesians, "in heavenly *places*," is in the Greek simply "in the heavenlies."

In the case of the Ephesian phrase it seems clear that the adjective must be neuter. But the matter is not so evident in the passage before us; so the commentators differ in their interpretation. For instance, Lightfoot thinks the reference is to "all creation, all things whatsoever and wheresoever they be. The whole universe, whether animate or inanimate, bends the knee in homage and raises its voice in praise." He goes on to say, "It would seem therefore that the adjectives here are neuter" (p. 115).

Vincent (ICC) considers Lightfoot's arguments for the neuter to be a case of "over-subtilising." He interprets the language as indicating: "The whole body of created intelligent beings in all departments of the universe" (p. 62). He and Abbott-Smith agree in interpreting the third adjective as referring to "the departed in Hades." It seems that this is about as definite as we can be.

Looking at the modern translations, we find that Weymouth has: "Of beings in the highest heavens, of those on the earth, and of those in the underworld." Similarly, Charles B. Williams reads: "So that in the name of Jesus everyone should kneel, in heaven, on earth, and in the underworld." Likewise Goodspeed has "everyone." John Wesley (1755) had "of those in heaven, and those on earth, and those under the earth," taking the adjectives as masculine. In spite of the fact that ERV (1881) and the ASV (1901) followed the KJV in using "things," most modern translators have preferred the masculine form. The RSV, NEB, and NIV avoid the issue by simply saying, "every knee should bow, in heaven." That is perhaps the safest way to treat the passage. However, the use of "tongue" in verse 11 seems definitely to favor the reference in verse 10 as being to persons rather than "things."

12 Presence, Absence In the Greek there is a play on words. "Presence" is *parousia*, which literally means "being beside," while "absence" is *apousia*, "being away from." The Philippian Christians were to be as faithful in Paul's absence as when he was with them.

Work Out Paul said: "Work out your own salvation." The verb is *katergazesthe*. It means "work on to the finish," or "carry out to the goal." While Christ purchased our salvation and offers it to us as a free gift, yet there is a part that we must do if the salvation is to be completed in our case.

A. T. Robertson, the great Baptist Greek scholar, makes an excellent observation on the relation between these two ideas. He says of

Paul: "He exhorts as if he were an Arminian in addressing men. He prays as if he were a Calvinist in addressing God and feels no inconsistency in the two attitudes. Paul makes no attempt to reconcile divine sovereignty and human free agency, but boldly proclaims both" (WP, 4:446). We should pray as if all depended on God and "work to the end" as if all depended on us.

Fear It is with fear (*phobos*) that we are to "work out"—or "make sure of"—our salvation. Vincent says of this fear: "Not slavish terror, but wholesome, serious caution" (3:437). He gives this excellent quotation from the old Scottish preacher, Wardlaw: "This fear is self-distrust; it is tenderness of conscience; it is vigilance against temptation; it is the fear which inspiration opposes to high-mindedness in the admonition 'be not high-minded but fear.' It is taking heed lest we fall; it is a constant apprehension of the deceitfulness of the heart, and of the insidiousness and power of inward corruption [in the unsanctified]. It is the caution and circumspection which timidly shrinks from whatever would offend and dishonor God and the Savior" (*ibid.*).

13 Worketh in You As we "work out" our own salvation, we find that God "worketh in" us. The verb is *energeō*, which means "energize." We do not have to depend on our own strength, but let the all-powerful One energize us.

Will, Do "To will and to do" is literally "the willing and the working." As we submit to let Him, God wills and works in us in accordance with "his good pleasure." Augustine expressed it this way: "We will, but God works the will in us. We work, therefore, but God works the working in us" (quoted in Vincent, 3:438). In this verse "do" is the same verb as the "worketh in" of the previous verse. The point is that our energy comes from Him.

Good Pleasure Only as we let God work in us can we fulfill His "good pleasure." This is one word in Greek, *eudokia*. It means "good pleasure, good-will, satisfaction, approval" (A-S, p. 185). Cremer says that *eudokia* denotes "*a free will* (willingness, pleasure), *whose intent is something good*—benevolence, gracious purpose." Here it describes "God's purpose of grace" (p. 214).

Of this beautiful word Schrenk writes: "*Eudokia* is not a classical word. It is almost completely restricted to Jewish and Christian literature and occurs for the first time in the Greek Bible" (TDNT, 2:742). Concerning its use here he says: "The meaning of Phil. 2:13 is that the operation of God, which evokes the will and work of believers, takes place in the interests of the divine counsel, i.e., fulfils the ordination therein foreseen." The term expresses "His gracious resolution to save" (ibid., pp. 746–47).

Arndt and Gingrich suggest the translation here: "in his (God's) good will" (p. 319). This stresses the fact that the divine sovereignty is on the side of man's best good. God's pleasure is man's well-being.

14 Murmurings The Greek word gongysmos sounds like the buzzing of bees. It is what is called an onomatopoetic term: the sound suggests the sense. Robertson comments: "It is the secret grumblings that buzz away till they are heard" (WP, 3:72). In the Septuagint it is used for the murmuring of the children of Israel in the wilderness. The phrase in this passage may be translated "without complaining" (NIV). We are to do our assigned work cheerfully, not grumblingly (cf. RSV—"without grumbling"). Whispering tongues sometimes sound like buzzing bees, about ready to sting!

Disputings This is the word dialogismos, from which we get dialogue. It means "a thought, reasoning, inward questioning" (A-S, p. 109). But it sometimes, as here, signifies "doubt, dispute, argument" (AG, p. 185). Whereas gongysmos occurs only 4 times in the NT (John 7:12; Acts 6:1; Phil. 2:14; 1 Pet. 4:9), dialogismos is found 14 times. It is a favorite term in Luke's Gospel (6 times).

Lightfoot gives an interesting comparison of these two terms. He says: "As gongysmos is the moral, so dialogismos is the intellectual rebellion against God" (p. 117). The latter word may be rendered "arguing" (Phillips, NIV) or "wrangling" (NEB).

15 Blameless The adjective amemptos means "free from fault" (A-S, p. 24), or "deserving no censure" (Thayer, p. 31). It is found commonly in epitaphs on tombs of this period. Trench points out that the precise sense of the word is "unblamed" (p. 380).

Harmless This adjective, akeraios, means "unmixed, pure," and so "guileless, simple" (A-S, p. 17). It occurs only two other places in the NT (Matt. 10:16; Rom. 16:19). Trench says that the rendering "harmless" is based on a misunderstanding of the derivation of the word. The correct translation is "simple" or "sincere," the fundamental idea being that of "the absence of foreign admixture" (p. 206).

Concerning these adjectives in verse 15, Lightfoot writes: "Of the two words here used, the former (amemptoi) relates to the judgment of others, while the latter (akeraioi) describes the intrinsic character" (p. 117). In essential agreement is the observation of Ellicott. He says the desire for the Philippians was "that they might both outwardly evince (amemptoi) and be inwardly characterized by (akeraioi) rectitude and holiness, and so become examples to an evil world around them" (p. 66).

Without Rebuke "Without rebuke" is one word in Greek, the adjective amōmos. In the Septuagint it is used for sacrificial animals, indicating "without blemish." That is the correct translation here (cf. RSV). The adjective is appropriately applied to Christ, who offered himself "without spot" to God (Heb. 9:14). As Christians we should seek to be both "unblamed" (amemptos) and "blameless" (amōmos). Goodspeed translates the latter "faultless," NIV "without fault."

Crooked The Greek word is skolios. Literally it means "curved, bent, winding" (Luke 3:5), metaphorically "crooked, perverse, unjust" (A-S, p. 409)—Acts 2:40; Phil. 2:15; 1 Pet. 2:18—or "unscrupulous, dishonest" (AG, p. 763). It might be translated "warped" (Phillips, NEB).

Perverse This is the perfect passive participle of diastrephō, which means "distort, twist, pervert." So it signifies being in a perverted state—"perverse, corrupt, wicked" (Thayer, p. 142). Arndt and Gingrich say it means "perverted in the moral sense, depraved" (p. 188). Lightfoot renders it "distorted" (p. 117).

Nation The Greek word is genea. It means "race, stock, family," but in the NT always "generation" (A-S, p. 89). That is the translation here in most modern versions. Arndt and Gingrich note that the term means "literally, those descended from a common ancestor," but "basically, the sum total of those born at the same time, expanded to include all those living at a given time, generation, contemporaries" (p. 153).

Jesus denounced His contemporaries as "a wicked and adulterous generation" (Matt. 16:4), as a "faithless and perverse generation" (Matt. 17:17). The passage in Philippians is an echo of this. And how sadly true are these words as applied to our generation!

17 *Offered* The Greek word for "offered" is *spendomai*, which means "*I am poured out or offered as a libation* (in the shedding of my life-blood)" (A-S, p. 413). It occurs only here and in 2 Tim. 4:6—"For I am now ready to be offered" (cf. NEB—"As for me, already my life is being poured out on the altar"). Paul wrote to the Philippians during his first Roman imprisonment, knowing it might end soon in death. He wrote his second letter to Timothy shortly before his second Roman imprisonment terminated in his execution. In the latter instance he knew that martyrdom for the faith was almost inevitable.

The correct translation here is: "But even if I am being poured out like a drink offering on the sacrifice and service coming from your faith" (NIV). It has sometimes been objected that the drink offerings (libations) of the Jews were poured around the altar, not "upon" the sacrifice. But the same Greek preposition as here, *epi*, is used in Lev. 5:11 (LXX) for this. Lightfoot comments: "On the other hand, as St. Paul is writing to converted heathens, a reference to heathen sacrifice is more appropriate (comp. II Cor. ii. 14); while owing to the great prominence of the libation in heathen rites the metaphor would be more expressive" (p. 119).

Service Instead of "service," Phillips, RSV, and NEB all have "offering." Is the change justified?

The Greek word is *leitourgia*, from which comes "liturgy." It occurs only 6 times in the NT. In Luke 1:23 it is used of Zechariah's priestly "ministration" in the Temple. In 2 Cor. 9:12, Paul employs it for the "service" which the Gentile Christians were rendering to their Jewish brethren in the form of a love offering. It is used similarly in Phil. 2:30. Finally, it occurs twice in Hebrews: for Christ's "ministry" (8:6), and for the "ministry" in the Tabernacle.

The word has a long history. In ancient Athens it was used for "the discharge of a public office at one's own expense" (A-S, p. 266). Then it came to be employed for referring to religious service, which is what it always means in the LXX and NT. Moulton and Milligan give instances in the papyri of the term as applied to the Egyptian priesthood (VGT, p. 373). It would appear that "service" is the best translation here.

Nevertheless it is closely related to "sacrifice" (*thusia*). Lightfoot points up the connection of the whole clause in these words: "The Philippians are the priests; their faith (or their good works springing from their faith) is the

sacrifice: St. Paul's life-blood the accompanying libation" (p. 119).

17–18 *Rejoice* It has been said that the Philippian letter might be summed up in four words: "I rejoice; rejoice ye!" That is based on the last part of verse 17 with verse 18. Paul says, "I am rejoicing (*chairō*) and rejoicing together (*synchairō*) with all of you. In the same way do you rejoice (*chairete*) and rejoice together (*synchairete*) with me."

Paul is especially fond of compounds with *syn* (cf. *synthetic*), which means "with" or "together." The average Greek lexicon has some half a dozen pages listing words in the NT that begin with *syn* as a prefix. A large part of these are found only in Paul's Epistles. He had a great appreciation of "togetherness" in the Christian life.

19 *Comfort* The verb *eupsycheō* is translated "be of good comfort." RSV, NIV, and Phillips have "be cheered" (cf. NEB—"it will cheer me"). Abbott-Smith gives as its meaning "to be of good courage" (p. 191). Thayer has "to be of good courage, to be of a cheerful spirit" (p. 264); Arndt and Gingrich, "be glad, have courage" (p. 330). Since the verb comes from the adjective *eupsychos*, "courageous," it would seem that the best translation is: "so that I also may be encouraged when I learn of your condition" (NASB).

20 *Likeminded* Paul says of Timothy: "For I have no man likeminded." The adjective is *isopsychos*, from *isos*, "equal," and *psychē*, "soul," just as the word above was from *eu*, "good," and *psychē* (lit., "good-souled"). Both terms occur only here in the NT.

For the adjective, Thayer gives "equal in soul." Arndt and Gingrich suggest "of like soul or mind." NASB translates it "of kindred spirit."

19, 24 *Trust* One would assume that "I trust" in verses 19 and 24 is the same in the Greek. But such is not the case. In verse 19 it is *elpizō*, "I hope," from the noun *elpis*, "hope." In verse 24 it is *pepoitha*, the perfect tense of *peithō*, "have confidence." So it would mean, "I have a settled confidence." Paul seemed to have a firm conviction that he was going to be released from prison. This is one reason why we date the Epistle to the Philippians near the close of his first Roman imprisonment (probably in A.D. 61).

25 Suppose The verb is *hēgeomai*. It means "think, consider, regard" (AG, p. 344). Phillips translates the phrase, "I have considered it desirable." RSV and NASB both use "thought." Weymouth has "I deem it important." Thayer says that *hēgeomai* denotes "a belief resting not on one's inner feeling or sentiment, but on the due consideration of external grounds, the weighing and comparing of facts . . . deliberate and careful judgment." So "thought" is better than "supposed."

Fellow Soldier As has been noted before, Paul is particularly fond of words beginning with *syn*, the Greek preposition which means "with" or "together with." Two of these occur here.

The first is *synergon*, translated "companion in labour." This is the only place (out of 13 times in NT) where it is rendered this way. Four times it is correctly translated "fellow-laborer." The literal meaning is "fellow worker" (RSV, NIV)—*ergon* means "work."

The other word, *systratiōtēs*, is accurately rendered "fellow soldier." To Paul the Christian life was both work and warfare. Fortunately there were a few faithful souls who were engaged in both with him.

Messenger Paul says that Epaphroditus was the "messenger" of the Philippians, conveying their love offering to him in prison, probably so that he could dwell "in his own hired house" (Acts 28:30)—"in his own rented apartment" (Phillips)—at Rome instead of in a miserable dungeon.

The word for "messenger" is *apostolos*. In 78 out of the 81 times this significant word occurs in the NT it is rendered "apostle." In only one other place (2 Cor. 8:23) is it translated "messenger." In John 13:16 it is rendered "he that is sent."

This noun comes from the verb *apostellō*, which means "send on an errand or mission." The Philippian church had sent Epaphroditus as its "apostle" to Paul, to minister to his needs.

26 Heaviness Epaphroditus was longing for the Philippians and was "full of heaviness" because they had heard he was sick. The word is *adēmonōn*, the present participle of *adēmoneō*, "be troubled or distressed." In recent translations it is usually rendered "distressed" (Weymouth, RSV, NEB, NIV) or even "greatly distressed" (Goodspeed).

28 Sent "I sent" is in the aorist indicative (*epempsa*), which normally signifies past time.

But this is what is called the "epistolary aorist"—writing from the standpoint of the reader. When the Philippians received the letter, the messenger would have already been sent by Paul. But he had not yet gone when the apostle wrote this statement. So the correct translation is, "I am sending him"—that is, with this letter. Epaphroditus was now to be Paul's "apostle," carrying his letter to the Philippian church.

Carefully Paul said that he was sending the bearer of the Epistle "the more carefully." This is all one word in the Greek, *spoudaioterōs*, the comparative degree of the adverb *spoudaiōs*. It comes from *spoudē*, which means "haste." So the adverb means "*with haste or zeal, i.e., earnestly, zealously, diligently . . . hastily, speedily*" (A-S, p. 415). Probably the best translation is "all the more eagerly" (NASB).

29 Receive Though many versions have "receive," the compound verb *prosdechomai* is perhaps better represented by "welcome" (Phillips, NEB, NIV). *Pros* means "to." So the idea is "welcome to oneself."

Reputation "In reputation" is one word in Greek, *entimos*. It is from *timē*, "honor," and so means "esteemed, highly honored." The best translation here is "hold men like him in high regard" (NASB), or simply "honor men like him" (NIV).

3:1 Grievous Paul says that to repeat what he has already written is not "grievous." The Greek word is *oknēros*. Its basic meaning is "shrinking, hesitating, timid." It is translated "slothful" in Matt. 25:26 and Rom. 12:11. Here it means "troublesome" or "irksome" (ASV, RSV).

Safe "Safe" is the literal meaning of *asphalēs*, which inherently means "not in danger of being tripped up," and so "certain, secure, safe" (A-S, p. 66). The thought of the passage is better indicated, however, by rendering the phrase "your safety" (Charles B. Williams) or "a safeguard for you" (NEB, NASB, NIV).

2 Dogs The Greek word is not *kynarion*, which means "little dog" or "pet dog" and might be rendered "doggie" (Matt. 15:26–27; Mark 7:27–28). Rather it is *kyon*, a term used for the scavenger dogs and which Phillips here translates "curs." This was the term of reproach and contempt which the Jews commonly used for the Gentiles. But Paul here turns the tables and applies it to the Judaizers themselves. They were the ones who were actually barking and biting.

Concision The Greek word is *katatomē*. It is found only here in the NT. In the LXX the corresponding verb is used for mutilations of the body practiced in heathen religions but forbidden to the Israelites (Lev. 21:5). What Paul is saying here is that the Jews have lost the sacredness of circumcision as a sign of God's covenant with Abraham (Gen. 17:10). What they are actually doing is just mutilating the body, as the heathen did. So the apostle refers to them as "the mutilation faction" (Berkeley), "those mutilators of the flesh" (NIV).

3 Circumcision The Greek word *peritomē* literally means "a cutting around." That exactly represents the physical operation. The English word "circumcision" comes from the Latin and means the same thing. Paul is emphasizing here that the true circumcision is that of the heart, not the body.

Rejoice It might be assumed that "rejoice" in verse 3 is the same as "rejoice" in verse 1. But such is not the case. In the first verse it is *chairō*, which most versions render as "rejoice." But here it is *kauchaomai*, which means "boast" or "glory." Most modern translations correctly render it "glory."

3–4 Confidence, Trust The word "confidence" occurs in the last part of verse 3 and the first part of verse 4. In the latter part of verse 4, "hath whereof he might trust" is the same verb in the Greek as "have confidence" in the two previous cases. It would seem more consistent to translate it the same way, "have confidence," in all three places, as is done in the ASV (1901) and most translations since.

5 Stock The Greek word is *genos*. Used rather widely in the NT, it is translated 10 different ways in the KJV.

It comes from the verb meaning "become," the root stem of which is *gen*. So it signifies "family . . . offspring . . . race, nation" (A-S, p. 91). Arndt and Gingrich give the following meanings: "1. *descendants* of a common ancestor . . . 2. *family relatives* . . . 3. *nation, people*" (p. 155). The best translation here is "people" (RSV, NIV) or "nation" (NASB).

8 Excellency The Greek word is *hyperechon*. It is a participial form of the verb *hyperechō*, which means "to rise above, overtop," and so

metaphorically "to be superior, excel, surpass." Here it means "the surpassing worth" (A-S, p. 458). Arndt and Gingrich suggest "the surpassing greatness" (p. 848). The best translation is probably "the surpassing worth" (RSV) or "the surpassing value" (NASB).

Knowledge The Greek word *Gnōsis* is translated "knowledge." It literally means "a seeking to know, inquiry, investigation," but in the NT is used especially for "the knowledge of spiritual truth" (A-S, p. 94). Arndt and Gingrich would translate the phrase here "personal acquaintance with Christ Jesus" (p. 163).

Since the Gnostics claimed a special, superior *gnōsis* which others did not possess, it may well be that Paul is here countering their ideas. He asserts that the supreme *gnōsis* is "the knowledge of Christ Jesus."

Dung The Greek term is *skybala*, found only here in the NT. Abbott-Smith gives its meaning as "*refuse*, especially *dung*" (p. 410). Arndt and Gingrich give "refuse, rubbish, leavings, dirt, dung" (p. 765). The choice seems to lie between "refuse" (ASV, RSV, Moffatt) and "rubbish" (Goodspeed, NASB, NIV). "Garbage" (NEB) seems a little far out. Paul is using the strongest term he could get hold of to show how little he valued everything else in life in comparison with possessing Christ.

12 Attained The Greek word is *elabon*, the second aorist of *lambanō*. This verb occurs 263 times in the NT and is translated some 20 different ways in the KJV. Only here is it rendered "attain." In all but 24 instances it is translated either "receive" (133 times) or "take" (106 times).

By way of definition Abbott-Smith gives: "1. to take, lay hold of . . . 2. to receive" (p. 263). For this passage Thayer suggests "to get possession of, obtain, a thing" (p. 370). Arndt and Gingrich take a somewhat different slant: "*make one's own, apprehend* or *comprehend* mentally or spiritually (class.) of the mystical apprehension of Christ . . . *I have made* (*him*) *my own*" (p. 466). That is, Paul has not fully comprehended Christ.

It seems clear that "obtain" (RSV, NASB, NIV) is preferable to "attain." Weymouth has: "already gained this knowledge." Goodspeed reads: "Not that I have secured it yet." Phillips gives a good paraphrase: "I do not consider myself to have 'arrived' spiritually."

Perfect The verb is *teleioō*. It comes from the adjective *teleios* (v. 15). This, in turn, is derived from the noun *telos*, "end." So the adjective means "having reached its end, mature, complete, perfect." For verse 15, Abbott-Smith gives "full-grown, mature." In this chapter Thayer thinks the verb means "to bring one's character to perfection" (p. 618).

Arndt and Gingrich think that *teleios* is used here as "a technical term of the mystery religions, which refers to one initiated into the mystic rites . . . the *initiate*" (p. 817), and that the verb carries the same connotation. Many scholars, however, object to this interpretation. It does not seem justifiable to make that connection.

With regard to the adjective, Lightfoot writes: "The *teleioi* are 'grown men' as opposed to children . . . They are therefore those who have passed out of the rudimentary discipline of ordinances (Gal. iv. 3, 4), who have put away childish things (I Cor. xiii. 10–12)" (p. 153).

On the basis of the same Greek root in verses 12 and 15 it would seem that KJV and NASB were more consistent in using "perfect" in both places. But since Paul denies perfection in verse 12 and seems to claim it in verse 15, it may well be that one is justified in using "perfect" in verse 12 and "mature" in verse 15 (RSV, NEB, NIV). A. T. Robertson comments on verse 15: "Here the term *teleioi* means relative perfection, not the absolute perfection so pointedly denied in verse 12" (WP, 4:455). The context suggests that in verse 12 Paul is denying resurrection perfection. We may say that in verse 15 he claims what John Wesley called Christian perfection.

Follow After The verb is *diōkō*, translated "press" in verse 14. Properly it means "pursue." But here it is used with no object. So Abbott-Smith suggests: "*follow on, drive,* or *speed on*" (p. 119). Thayer gives for this passage: "*to press on*: figuratively, of one who in a race runs swiftly to reach the goal" (p. 153). Arndt and Gingrich have: "hasten, run, press on" (p. 200). It would seem that the best translation here is "press on" (RSV, NEB, NASB, NIV), which makes it consistent with the translation of the same verb in verse 14.

Apprehend The word is *katalambanō*, a compound of the simple verb translated "attain" in this same verse. Thus there is a word play in Greek which does not come out in English.

The verb *katalambanō* means "to lay hold of, seize, appropriate" (A-S, p. 235). Of its use in this passage Thayer writes: "in a good sense, of Christ by his holy power and influence laying

hold of the human mind and will, in order to prompt and govern it" (p. 332).

It would appear that the best translation is "lay hold of that for which also I was laid hold of by Christ Jesus" (NASB), or "take hold of that for which Christ Jesus took hold of me" (NIV).

Reaching Forth The verb (only here in NT) is *epekteinō*. It is a double compound of *teinō*, "stretch" or "strain," with *ek*, "out" and *epi*, "upon." So it means "stretch forward." Here it is in the middle voice, and so means "stretching myself forward to." A. T. Robertson says that it is the "metaphor of a runner leaning forward as he runs" (WP, 4:455). Bengel comments: "The eye goes before (outstrips) and draws on the hand, the hand goes before (outstrips) and draws on the foot" (*Gnomon*, 4:147). The best translation is probably "stretching forward" (Weymouth, ASV).

14 *Mark* *Skopos* means "*a mark* on which to fix the eye" (A-S, p. 410). It is found only here in the NT. Since the figure Paul is using is that of a runner in a race, the correct translation here is "goal," as in most modern versions.

Prize The Greek word is *brabeion*. It comes from *brabeus*, "umpire," and so properly means a prize won in a race or in the games. Phillips translates it "reward." But the entire context favors "prize." Ignatius wrote in his letter to Polycarp (ii): "Be temperate as God's athlete. The prize is incorruption and eternal life."

16 *Attained* The verb *phthanō* originally meant "come before." But in later Greek it simply meant "come" or "arrive." Weymouth gives an excellent translation of this verse: "But whatever be the point that we have already reached, let us persevere in the same course."

17 *Followers Together* This is one word in the Greek, *synmimētai*, found only here in the NT. The prefix *syn* is the preposition meaning "with" or "together with." The simple noun *mimētai*, meaning "imitators," occurs 6 times in the NT, always in Paul's Epistles. Apparently Paul made up the compound here, for it is not found elsewhere in Greek literature. It means "a fellow imitator" or "an imitator with others." Arndt and Gingrich give "fellow-imitator," but suggest for the whole phrase: "*join* (with the others) in following my example" (p. 786). That is, the readers were to join other Christians in following Paul's example in imitating Christ (cf. 1 Cor. 11:1). Lightfoot suggests for here: "Vie with each other in imitating me" or "one and all of you imitate me" (p. 154).

Mark   The verb is *skopeō*. It means "to look at, behold, watch, contemplate"; in the NT it is used only in the metaphorical sense, "to look to, consider" (A-S, p. 140). Arndt and Gingrich offer "notice" here. The TCNT has "fix your eyes on" (cf. *skopos* in v. 14). Weymouth says "carefully observe." Perhaps the simplest translation is "observe" (NASB) or "take note" (NIV).

Ensample   The Greek word is *typos*, from which we get "type." Originally it meant "the *mark* of a blow" (John 20:25), and so "an *impression, impress,* the *stamp* made by a die; hence, a *figure, image*" (Acts 7:43); "form" (Rom. 6:17); "an example, pattern"; once, "*type*" (Rom. 5:14)—the meaning which has been taken over into English (A-S, p. 452).

Obviously, "ensample" is an obsolete form of "example." The choice here lies between "example" (RSV) and "pattern" (NASB, NIV).

20 Conversation   We have noted before that there are three Greek words which are translated "conversation" in the KJV, and not one of them signifies what we mean by conversation today. The one here is *politeuma* (only here in NT). It is derived from the verb *politeuō*, which occurs only in Phil. 1:27 (see notes there) and Acts 23:1.

It comes from *polis*, "city." Properly it means "an act of administration" or "a form of government" (A-S, p. 371). But in the NT it is equivalent to *politeia*, "a commonwealth" or "state." Moulton and Milligan say that most quotations from the papyri and inscriptions favor "community" or "commonwealth" (VGT, pp. 525–26).

Moffatt made a bold departure when he translated the opening part of this verse: "But we are a colony of heaven." This finds added appropriateness in the fact that Philippi, to which this letter was written, was a colony of Rome. But Moulton and Milligan question whether this meaning is supported in Greek literature.

Goodspeed has: "But the commonwealth to which we belong is in heaven." Similarly, Arndt and Gingrich prefer: "Our commonwealth is in heaven" (so RSV). But it seems to us just as accurate and more meaningful to say: "Our citizenship is in heaven" (NASB, NIV)—cf. "We are citizens of heaven" (Phillips, NEB, Beck).

21 Change   The verb is *metaschēmatizō*. It is composed of *meta*, which has the idea of ex-

change or transfer, and *schēma*, which means "appearance" or "form." The compound means "*to change in fashion* or *appearance*" (A-S, p. 288). Thayer gives: "to change the figure of, to transform" (p. 406). It seems to us that the literal meaning of the Greek word is best represented in English by "transform" (NASB).

Vile   The KJV states that Christ will change our "vile body." This is a completely unjustifiable translation. The *Oxford English Dictionary* (13 vols.) does not seem to give any example of exactly this usage.

The Greek has here simply "the body of our humiliation." The word *tapeinōsis* means "abasement, humiliation, low estate" (A-S, p. 440). This is the way it is used by Plato, Aristotle, and later writers. Arndt and Gingrich have: "humility, humble station, humiliation" (p. 812). Cremer gives the essential meaning as "humiliation" or "lowness" (p. 541).

It should be obvious that the correct translation is not "vile body" but "lowly body" (RSV). Phillips seems off-beat when he uses "wretched body." Far more accurate is "the body belonging to our humble state" (NEB). This gives exactly the sense of the Greek. Lightfoot says: "The English translation, 'our vile body,' seems to countenance the Stoic contempt of the body, of which there is no tinge in the original" (pp. 156–57). It is also contrary to the teaching of the NT.

Fashioned Like   For the clause "that it may be fashioned like," the best Greek text has simply one word, the adjective *symmorphos* (only here and in Rom. 8:29). This is compounded of *syn*, "with," and *morphē*, "form." So the English equivalent is "conformed to." The first definition given by Arndt and Gingrich is: "having the same form" (p. 786).

The NEB has here: "give it a form like that of his own resplendent body." The best translation is: "will transform our lowly bodies so that they will be like his glorious body" (NIV).

4:3 Yokefellow   The Greek word for "yokefellow" is *syzygos*, found only here in the NT. It is an adjective (used here as a substantive) meaning "yoked together." Concerning this word Thayer says:

> Used by Greek writers of those united by the bond of marriage, relationship, office, labor, study, business, or the like; hence, *a yokefellow, consort, comrade, colleague, partner.* Accordingly, in Phil. iv. 3 most interpreters hold that by the words *gnesie syzyge* Paul ad-

dresses some particular associate in labor for the gospel. But as the word is found in the midst of (three) proper names, other expositors more correctly take it as a proper name . . . and Paul, alluding (as in Philem. 11) to the meaning of the word as an appellative, speaks of him as "a genuine Synzygus," i.e., a colleague in fact as well as in name (p. 594).

The fact that the Epistle is addressed "to all the saints . . . at Philippi" makes it impossible to identify this "loyal comrade" (NEB) unless it is taken as a proper name.

Fellow Laborers The RSV has "fellow workers," seemingly a distinction without a difference. The KJV rendering would naturally be thought of as parallel to "labored with" in the first part of the verse. However, the Greek roots are entirely different. The verb "labored with" is *synathleō*, found only here and in 1:27 (see notes there). Our word "athletics" comes from it. So it is properly translated "shared my struggles" (NEB).

"Fellow laborers" is one word in the Greek, *synergon*. It is compounded of *syn*, "with," and *ergon*, "work." The correct translation is "fellow workers."

5 Moderation The word *epieikes* has perhaps been more variously translated in modern versions than any other term in the NT. It is difficult to settle on a "best" translation.

Actually *epieikes* is an adjective. In Homer it meant "seemly, suitable" and later "equitable, fair, mild, gentle" (Thayer, p. 238). Arndt and Gingrich give "yielding, gentle, kind," and for this passage "your forbearing spirit" (p. 292).

Lightfoot adopted "your forbearance" (cf. RSV). He says: "Thus we may paraphrase St. Paul's language here: 'To what purpose is this rivalry, this self-assertion? The end is nigh, when you will have to resign all. Bear with others now, that God may bear with you then' " (p. 160).

Preisker makes this helpful observation: "Because the *kyrios* (Lord) is at hand, and the final *doxa* (glory) promised to all Christians will soon be a manifest reality, they can be *epieikeis* towards all men in spite of every persecution" (TDNT, 2:590).

Trench gives careful attention to the meaning of the related noun, *epieikeia*. He says: "It expresses exactly that moderation which recognizes the impossibility cleaving to all formal law, of anticipating and providing for all cases that will emerge, and present themselves to it for decision; which, with this, recognizes the

danger that ever waits upon the assertion of *legal* rights, lest they should be pushed into *moral* wrongs . . . which, therefore, urges not its own rights to the uttermost" (p. 154). That is, one should not insist on his lawful rights, contrary to the law of love.

On the difficulty of translation he makes this interesting comment:

> It is instructive to note how little of one mind our various Translators from Wiclif downward have been as to the words which should best reproduce *epieikeia* and *epieikes* for the English reader. The occasions on which *epieikeia* occur are two, or reckoning to *epieikes* as an equivalent substantive, are three (Acts xxiv. 4; II Cor. x. 1; Phil. iv. 5). It has been rendered in all these ways: "meekness," "courtesy," "clemency," "softness," "modesty," "gentleness," "patience," "patient mind," "moderation." *Epieikes*, not counting the one occasion already named, occurs four times (I Tim. iii. 3; Tit. iii. 2; Jam. iii. 17; I Pet. ii. 18), and appears in the several versions of our Hexapla as "temperate," "soft," "gentle," "modest," "patient," "mild," "courteous." "Gentle" and "gentleness," on the whole commend themselves as the best; but the fact remains . . . that we have no words in English which are full equivalents of the Greek. The sense of equity and fairness which is in them so strong is more or less wanting in all which we offer in exchange (pp. 156–57).

It would seem to us that "gentleness" (NIV) might be the best translation, though inadequate.

6 Careful The verb is *merimnaō*, which primarily means to "be anxious." It comes from *merizō*, "be drawn in different directions." So it suggests the idea of being distracted by many cares.

The KJV rendering is obviously incorrect. Paul is not forbidding us to be careful! He would doubtless agree with the ABC of safety: "Always Be Careful." What he is saying is "Do not be anxious about anything" (NIV). Phillips has caught the idea rightly in his rendering: "Don't worry over anything whatever." Carefulness is a Christian virtue. Worry, as John Wesley declared, is a sin.

7 Passeth The verb is *hyperechō*. It means "rise above, surpass, excell" (AG, p. 848). The correct translation here is "surpasses" (NASB) or "transcends" (NIV).

Keep The word is *phroureō*. It comes from *phrouros*, "a guard." So it means "*to guard, keep*

345

under guard, protect or keep by guarding" (A-S, p. 474). Thayer gives as the literal meaning: "to guard, *protect by a military guard.*" The English word "keep" may mean "hold on to" and so is not satisfactory.

The better translation here is "guard" (NASB, NIV). Phillips expresses it well: "And the peace of God, which transcends human understanding, will keep constant guard over your hearts and minds as they rest in Christ Jesus."

Through   There seems to be no justification for the rendering "through Christ Jesus." The Greek says *en,* "in." Practically all modern translations give it correctly: "in Christ Jesus." What this means is well represented by Phillips, as quoted above. As long as our hearts and minds are resting in Christ, the peace of God stands guard over them.

8 Honest   It is the adjective *semnos,* which means: "1. *reverend, august, venerable,* in classics of the gods and also of human beings. 2. *grave, serious;* of persons: I Tim. 3:8, 11; Tit. 2:2; of things: Phil. 4:8" (A-S, p. 404). For its use with things Arndt and Gingrich give: "honorable, worthy, venerable, holy" (p. 754).

Trench says of *semnos:* "It is used . . . constantly to qualify such things as pertain to, or otherwise stand in any very near relation with, the heavenly world" (p. 346). After noting that in Greek literature it is often associated with such adjectives as "holy," "great," "valuable," he observes: "From all this it is plain that there lies something of majestic and awe-inspiring in *semnos*" (p. 347). He speaks of "honest" as "an unsatisfactory rendering," and suggests "honorable" (*ibid.*). This is the choice of most modern versions (ASV, RSV, NASB), though "noble" (NIV) is also good.

Lovely   The adjective *prosphilēs* occurs only here in the NT. Arndt and Gingrich give its meaning as: "pleasing, agreeable, lovely, amiable" (p. 727). Vincent says it means "adapted to excite love, and to endear him who does such things" (3:459). While the favorite rendering is "lovely," several translators offer "lovable" (TCNT, Weymouth, NEB). It would be difficult to decide between the two.

Of Good Report   The adjective (only here in NT) is *euphēmos.* It comes from *eu,* "well," and *phēmi,* "say." Abbott-Smith gives its meaning as: "primarily, *uttering words* or *sounds of good omen,* hence, 1. *avoiding ill-omened words, religiously silent.* 2. *fair-sounding, auspicious*" (p.

190). Thayer says that here it is used of "things spoken in a kingly spirit, with goodwill to others" (p. 263). Arndt and Gingrich say that in this passage it "can be interpreted in various ways: *auspicious, well-sounding, praiseworthy, attractive, appealing*" (p. 327).

H. A. A. Kennedy affirms that the exact meaning is "high-toned" (EGT, 3:468). Lightfoot says: "Not 'well-spoken of, well-reputed,' for the word seems never to have this passive meaning; but with its usual active sense, '*fair-speaking,*' and so 'winning, attractive' " (pp. 161–62). A good translation is "gracious" (NEB).

Virtue   The Greek noun *aretē* occurs outside this passage only in the Epistles of Peter (1 Pet. 2:9; 2 Pet. 1:3, 5). Abbott-Smith gives its meaning as follows: "properly, whatever procures pre-eminent estimation for a person or thing, in Homer any kind of conspicuous advantage. Later confined by philosophical writers to intrinsic eminence—*moral goodness, virtue*" (p. 58).

Thayer notes that it is "a word of very wide signification in Greek writers; *any excellence of a person* (in body or mind) or *of a thing, an eminent endowment, property,* or *quality*" (p. 73). Here he thinks it means "moral excellence."

Praise   "Praise" is the literal meaning of the noun *epainos.* But "praiseworthy" (NIV) or "worthy of praise" (RSV, NASB) seems to be more appropriate in English.

9 Do   The verb is *prassō.* It sometimes is used as synonymous with *poieō,* "do." But here it would seem that the better translation is "practice" (NASB, NIV). The NEB gives an excellent paraphrase of this passage: "The lessons I taught you, the tradition I have passed on, all that you heard me say or saw me do, put into practice."

10 Flourished   The verb is *anathallō,* found only here in the NT. Since *ana* means "again," and *thallō* means "flourish," the KJV rendering is accurate. Intransitively the word means "*grow up again, bloom again*"; transitively it signifies "*cause to grow or bloom again*" (AG, p. 53). Arndt and Gingrich say that in this passage both meanings are possible: either "You have revived, as far as your care for me is concerned" or "You have revived your care for me" (*ibid.*). The second one is more commonly adopted today.

Care "Care" and "ye were . . . careful" are different forms of the same verb, *phroneō*. The first is the present infinitive, treated as a substantive. The second is the imperfect indicative, signifying continual concern for the apostle.

The verb *phroneō* means: "1. to have understanding . . . 2. to think, to be minded . . . 3. to have in mind, be mindful of, think of" (A-S, p. 474). It is obviously in the third sense that it is used here.

Weymouth gives an excellent translation of this passage: "But I rejoice in the Lord greatly that now at length you have revived your thoughtfulness for my welfare. Indeed you have always been thoughtful for me, although opportunity failed you." The idea is well expressed thus: "You have revived your concern for me; you were indeed concerned for me" (RSV; cf. NASB, NIV).

11 *Content* The Greek word (only here in NT) is *autarkēs*. It is compounded of *autos*, "self," and *arkeō*, "suffice." Abbott-Smith says: "As in classics, in philosophical sense, *self-sufficient, independent*" (p. 69). Vincent writes: "A stoic word, expressing the favorite doctrine of the sect, that man should be sufficient to himself for all things; able by the power of his own will, to resist the shock of circumstance. Paul is *self-sufficient* through the power of the *new self*: not *he*, but *Christ* in him" (3:460–61).

Though most of the English versions have "content," the TCNT reads: "For, however I am placed, I, at least, have learnt to be independent of circumstances" (cf. NEB). Arndt and Gingrich say that here the word means "*content*, perhaps self-sufficient" (p. 122).

12 *Instructed* The verb is *mueō*. In classical Greek, as Abbott-Smith notes, its main meaning was "to initiate into the mysteries" (p. 297). Many of the modern versions have: "I have learned the secret," which is an excellent rendering. The TCNT translates this verse: "I know how to face humble circumstances, and I know how to face prosperity. Into every human experience I have been initiated—into plenty and hunger, into prosperity and want."

14 *Communicate* The verb is *synkoinōneō*. It means "to become a partaker together with others" or "to have fellowship with a thing" (Thayer, p. 593). The best translation here is "share."

18 *Odor* "Odor of a sweet smell" is two words in Greek—*osmēn euōdias*. The first means "smell," the second "fragrance." So it is literally "a smell of fragrance"; that is, "a fragrant smell." Today the word "odor" is offensive. Perhaps the best translation here is simply "a fragrant offering" (RSV, NEB, NASB, NIV), or "the *sweet fragrance* of a sacrifice" (TCNT).

Colossians

1:7 *Fellow Servant* The Greek word is *syndoulos*, which literally means "fellow slave." Only in Colossians (1:7; 4:7) does Paul use this term. It is found five times in Matthew—four times in the parable of the unmerciful servant (18:28, 29, 31, 33), plus 28:49. Elsewhere in the NT it occurs only in Revelation, once of fellow saints (6:11) and twice of angels (19:10; 22:9). Paul had a strong sense of "togetherness" with his fellow laborers in the Kingdom.

9 *Knowledge* Paul desires that his readers might be filled with the "knowledge" of God's will. The Greek word is *epignōsis*.

The prefix *epi* perhaps intensifies the meaning of *gnōsis*, "knowledge." Should an attempt be made to bring out this distinction in English?

Paul uses *epignōsis* 15 out of the 20 times it is found in the NT. But he also uses *gnōsis* 23 out of its 29 occurrences. He has the cognate verb *epiginōskō* 12 out of its 42 appearances. He uses the simple verb *ginōskō* 48 times (out of 223 in NT). So it can hardly be said, as sometimes has been claimed, that Paul prefers the stronger terms and so uses them as synonymous with the simple verb and noun.

Arndt and Gingrich feel that in some cases (e.g., 1 Cor. 13:12) *epiginōskō* means "know completely," but that most of the time it is simply equivalent to *ginōskō*. The same would go for the nouns *epignōsis* and *gnōsis*.

Thayer puts the case more strongly. After noting that "*epi* denotes mental direction towards, application to, that which is known," he gives as the first definition for *epiginōskō*: "to become thoroughly acquainted with, to know thoroughly; to know accurately, know well" (p. 237). For *epignōsis* he gives: "precise and correct knowledge." Trench agrees with this when he writes: "Of *epignōsis*, as compared with *gnōsis*, it will be sufficient to say that *epi* must be regarded as intensive, giving to the compound word a greater strength than the simple possessed" (p. 285). Likewise Cremer says that *epignōsis* signifies "*clear and exact knowledge*, more intensive than *gnōsis*, because it expresses a more thorough participation in the object of knowledge on the part of the knowing subject" (p. 159). Lightfoot concurs. Commenting on this passage, he writes: "The compound *epignōsis* is an advance upon *gnōsis*, denoting a larger and more thorough knowledge" (p. 138).

But J. Armitage Robinson takes exception to all this. In his scholarly commentary on the Greek text of Ephesians he has a long additional note (7 pages) on the meaning of *epignōsis*.

He first notes: "The word *epignōsis* is not found in Greek writers before the time of Alexander the Great" (p. 248). The cognate verb does occur a few times in the classical writers. But after citing a number of passages from the older writers, Robinson affirms: "There is no indication that *epiginōskein* conveys the idea of a fuller, more perfect, more advanced knowledge" (p. 249). He adds: "We find a large number of compounds in *epi*, in which the preposition does not in the least signify *addition*, but rather perhaps *direction*" (*ibid.*). His conclusion is: "Thus *ginōskein* means 'to know' in the fullest sense that can be given to the word 'knowledge': *epiginōskein* directs attention to some particular point in regard to which 'knowledge' is affirmed. So that to perceive a particular thing, or to perceive who a particular person is, may fitly be expressed by *epiginōskein*" (*ibid.*). The difference between the nouns may be stated thus: "*Gnōsis* is the wider word and expresses 'knowledge' in the fullest sense: *epignōsis* is knowledge directed towards a particular object, perceiving, discerning, recognizing: but it is not knowledge in the abstract: that is *gnōsis*" (p. 254).

The latest thorough study of *ginōskō* and its derivatives is by Bultmann. Speaking of early Christian usage, he says: "*Epiginōskein* is often used instead of *ginōskein* with no difference in meaning. . . . In fact the simple and compound forms are used interchangeably in the papyri, where *epiginōskein* really means 'to affirm' or 'to confirm.' " (TDNT, 1:703). He adds: "In the Septuagint the two terms are often used as equivalents," as well as in Philo. He cites several parallel passages in the Gospels where he finds no distinction in meaning between these words (p. 704). So it would seem that any supposed difference should not be overemphasized.

12 Made Us Meet The verb is *hikanoō*. It comes from the adjective *hikanos*, which means "sufficient, competent, fit." So it signifies "make sufficient, render fit" (A-S, p. 215), or "qualify" (AG, p. 375). Probably the best translation in this passage is: "who has qualified us" (RSV, NASB).

It should be noted, in passing, that the Bible Society Greek text has "you" instead of "us." The two oldest uncial manuscripts, Vaticanus and Sinaiticus, have "you." But the bulk of the early as well as late manuscripts have "us." Unfortunately, the still earlier papyri do not help us at this point, because of breaks in the fragile material. The NIV reads "who has qualified you."

15 Image The Greek word is *eikōn*, from which comes the English "icon." It means a "likeness"—not, however, an accidental similarity, but a derived likeness such as that of "the head on a coin or the parental likeness in a child" (A-S, p. 131). Thayer says the term is here applied to Christ "on account of his divine nature and absolute moral excellence" (p. 175).

In the Synoptic Gospels this word is used for the image of the emperor on a silver coin, the denarius (Matt. 22:20; Mark 12:16; Luke 20:24). Josephus uses it repeatedly in the same way. it thus signifies an exact representation. Philo employs this term to describe the Logos. Paul himself speaks of Christ as "the image of God" in an earlier Epistle (2 Cor. 4:4).

Lightfoot writes: "Beyond the very obvious notion of *likeness*, the word *eikōn* involves two other ideas: (1) *Representation* . . . *eikōn* implies an arche-type of which it is a *copy*. . . . (2) *Mani-*

festation . . . The Word, whether preincarnate or incarnate, is the revelation of the unseen Father" (p. 145). Ellicott comments: "Christian antiquity has ever regarded the expression 'image of God' as denoting the eternal Son's perfect equality with the Father in respect of His substance, nature, and eternity" (p. 134).

Eadie has a beautiful approach to the study of this passage. He writes: "The clause dazzles by its brightness, and awes by its mystery. . . . The invisible God—how dark and dreadful the impenetrable veil! Christ His image—how perfect in its resemblance, and overpowering in its brilliance! We must worship whilst we construe; and our exegesis must be penetrated by a profound devotion" (p. 43).

He further comments: "Visibility is implied in the very notion of an image. The spirit of the statement is, that our only vision or knowledge of the Father is in His Son" (p. 45). He goes on to say: "In His incarnate state He brought God so near to us as to place Him under the cognizance of our very senses—men saw, and heard, and handled him—a speaking, acting, weeping, and suffering God" (pp. 45–46). But he adds: "Still, too, at the right hand of the Majesty on high, is He the visible administrator and object of worship" (p. 46).

Kleinknecht writes part of the article on *eikōn* in Kittel's TDNT. He says: "Thus *eikōn* does not imply a weakening or a feeble copy of something. It implies the illumination of its inner core and essence" (2:389). Kittel himself says that in Col. 1:15 "all the emphasis is on the equality of the *eikōn* with the original" (2:395).

Phillips has a happy phrasing of this passage. He translates it: "Now Christ is the visible expression of the invisible God." Jesus himself said: "He that hath seen me hath seen the Father" (John 14:9). Paul is simply affirming the same truth about his Lord.

Firstborn of Every Creature The Greek word *ktisis* may be translated either "creature" or "creation." Unfortunately the Greek does not distinguish between "all" and "every." The same word is used for both. So there is an option between the two renderings given above. But there is a general agreement today that the better translation is "all creation" (NIV).

To say that Christ is "the firstborn of all creation" certainly poses a problem. Ever since the days of Arianism in the Early Church, those who deny the deity of Jesus have seized on this verse as proof that He was a created being—even though the first one created by God.

The Greek word for "firstborn" is *prōtotokos*, from *prōtos*, "first," and *tiktō*, "beget." Abbott-

Smith thinks it was "originally perhaps a Messianic title" (p. 392). Lightfoot quotes a rabbinical interpretation and says: "Hence 'the first-born' *ho prōtotokos* used absolutely, became a recognized title of Messiah" (p. 146). He states that the expression conveys two ideas: priority to all creation and sovereignty over all creation. He then adds: "In its Messianic reference this secondary idea of sovereignty predominated in the word *prōtotokos*, so that from this point of view *prōtotokos pasēs ktiseōs* would mean 'Sovereign Lord over all creation by virtue of primogeniture' " (p. 147). (Cf. "His is the primacy over all created things," NEB.)

Eadie holds that the genitive ("of all creation") "may be taken as that of reference. . . . The meaning therefore is, 'first-born in reference to the whole creation' " (p. 51).

The clauses immediately preceding and following this passage show clearly that it cannot be interpreted as meaning that Christ was a created being. For it is explicitly stated: "By him were all things created" (cf. John 1:3). The NIV has "over all creation."

16 Thrones Verse 16 enumerates four things that were created by Christ (cf. a similar list in Eph. 1:21). To what do these refer? Lightfoot says: "Some commentators have referred the terms used here solely to earthly potentates and dignities. There can be little doubt however that their chief and primary reference is to the orders of the celestial hierarchy, as conceived by these Gnostic Judaizers" (p. 152). He adds: "The names, too, more especially *thronoi*, are especially connected with the speculations of Jewish angelology" (*ibid.*). But he thinks that earthly dignitaries may also be meant.

"Thrones" comes directly from the Greek *thronoi*. Lightfoot writes: "In all systems alike these 'thrones' belong to the highest grade of angelic beings, whose place is in the immediate presence of God" (p. 154). Paul is here declaring that Christ is supreme, far superior to all the celestial powers postulated in the Gnostic schools of thought.

Dominions The Greek word *kyriotēs* (from *kyrios*, "lord") means "power or position as lord" (Foerster, TDNT, 3:1096). Its literal meaning would be "lordships."

17 Consist The last word is *synestēken*, from *synistēmi*. A better translation than "consist" is "cohere" or "hold together." Lightfoot says of Christ: "He is the principle of cohesion in the universe. He impresses upon creation that

unity and solidarity which makes it a cosmos instead of a chaos" (p. 156).

Christ is not only Creator but Coherer. He upholds that which He brought into being (cf. Heb. 1:3).

Some years ago a noted scientist said: "If the creative force residing in the universe should be withdrawn for a moment, the whole universe would collapse." This is what Jeans wrote about in *The Spiritual Nature of the Physical Universe*. The Bible tells us that this creative force is Christ.

18 Preeminence The Greek verb is *prōteuō*, found only here in the NT. It comes from *prōtos*, "first," and so means "be first" or "have first place." The best translation of this clause is: "so that He Himself might come to have first place in everything" (NASB), or "might have the supremacy" (NIV).

19 Fulness A favorite term with the Gnostics was *plērōma*. In Colossians, Paul was concerned to oppose the incipient Gnosticism which was invading the churches of the Lycus valley. His answer to all the Gnostic heresies consisted essentially of one word: Christ. He alone was "fulness." Lightfoot comments that this was "a recognized technical term in theology, denoting the totality of the Divine powers and attributes" (p. 159).

Delling has an excellent statement on this. He writes: "The word *plērōma* emphasizes the fact that the divine fulness of love and power acts and rules in all its perfection through Christ" (TDNT, 6:303).

Dwell This is a strong term, *katoikeō*. It means "dwell permanently."

20–21 Reconcile The strong double compound *apokatallassō* occurs only here and in Eph. 2:16. It means "reconcile completely" (A-S, p. 51). Lightfoot comments: "The false teachers aimed at effecting a partial reconciliation between God and man through the interposition of angelic mediators. The Apostle speaks of an absolute and complete reconciliation of universal nature to God, effected through the mediation of the Incarnate Word" (p. 159). He adds: "Their mediators were ineffective, because they were neither human nor divine. The true mediator must be both human and divine" (*ibid.*). He must have the fullness of the divine nature, and at the same time be born as a man. Jesus Christ was the only One who ever fulfilled these conditions (1 Tim. 2:5).

22 Unreproveable The adjective *anegklētos* is found only in Paul's Epistles. It is composed of *alpha*-negative and the verb *egkaleō*, "call in" or "bring a charge against." So it literally means "not to be called to account" or "that cannot be called to account." The meaning is that before God no charge can be laid to our account. We are accepted before Him, because, and only because, we are in Christ.

23 Continue There is a condition attached to the above promise: "If ye continue in the faith." The word for "continue" is a compound, *epimenō*. The simple verb *menō* means "remain." So *epimenō* means "remain on" or "stay." Figuratively it has the sense of "persist" or "persevere."

Grounded The Greek has the perfect passive participle of *themelioō*, "lay the foundation of." Figuratively it means "firmly established" (NASB). That is perhaps the best translation. But the background sense should be kept in mind. It means to have one's foundations securely laid.

Settled The adjective is *hedraios*. Elsewhere in the NT it occurs only in 1 Corinthians (7:37; 15:58), where it is translated "stedfast." It comes from *hedra*, "seat," and so literally means "sitting" or "seated." The best rendering is probably "steadfast."

Not Moved The verb is *metakineō* (only here in NT). It means to "remove" or "shift." Since it is a present participle, indicating continuous action, it should be rendered "not constantly shifting"—or, perhaps, "not being moved away."

24 Fill Up The word is a double compound *antanaplēroō* (only here in NT). It is composed of *anti*, "over against"; *ana*, "again"; and *plēroō*, "fill." So it means "I fill up in turn" (A-S, p. 40) or "I fill up on my part." Lightfoot suggests that the force of the *anti* here is to signify that "the supply comes *from an opposite corner* to the deficiency" (p. 165).

That Which Is Behind This is an awkward clause in English. The Greek has simply *ta hysterēmata*, "the things lacking" or "that which is lacking." (A neuter plural in Greek may often be translated as a singular in English.)

But what does Paul mean by saying that he is completing what is lacking in the sufferings of Christ for the Church? Roman Catholics have used this passage as a basis for their doctrine of the merit of the saints, and so the system of indulgences.

As usual, Lightfoot gives a helpful explanation. He says that the sufferings of Christ may be considered from two different points of view. "From the former point of view the Passion of Christ was the one full perfect and sufficient sacrifice, oblation, and satisfaction for the sins of the whole world." But—"From the latter point of view it is a simple matter of fact that the afflictions of every saint and martyr do supplement the afflictions of Christ. The Church is built up by repeated acts of self-denial in successive individuals and successive generations." He adds: "But St. Paul would have been the last to say that they bear their part in the atoning sacrifice of Christ" (p. 166). In a very real sense it is still true today that only a suffering ministry can be a saving ministry. The preacher of the gospel must live redemptively if he is going to be used by his Master in redeeming men from sin.

25 Dispensation Again we meet this word *oikonomia*, which clearly means "stewardship." The term "dispensation" has come so generally to be used in a prophetic sense for a period of history that it fails completely to convey the correct idea here. The Christian's task today, as was Paul's in the first century, is a stewardship from God.

28 Preach The verb is *katangellō*, which occurs 17 times in the NT (6 in Paul, 11 in Acts). Ten of these times it is rendered "preach" in KJV. Thayer gives its meaning as: "to announce, declare, promulgate, make known; to proclaim publicly, publish" (p. 330). Schniewind says: "As with all the *angel*-verbs . . . it has the constant sense of 'proclaiming' " (TDNT, 1:70). The preferable translation is "proclaim" (RSV, NEB, NASB, NIV).

Warning The verb *noutheteō* is translated "warning" in most versions. But the only meanings that Abbott-Smith gives are: "to admonish, exhort" (p. 304). Thayer adds "warn" and Arndt and Gingrich "instruct." The verb is compounded of *nous*, "mind," and *tithēmi*, "put." So it literally means "put in mind." It would seem that "admonish" (ASV, NASB, NEB) is a little closer to the original. Actually KJV renders it "warn" four times and "admonish" four times.

29 Labor The verb *kopiaō* occurs in Luke 5:5—"We have toiled all the night" (see also Matt. 6:28; Luke 12:27). In John 4:6 it is translated "being wearied." Elsewhere (19 times) it is rendered "labor" or "bestow labor." Thayer notes that in the contemporary writers Josephus and Plutarch the word means "*to grow weary, tired, exhausted,* (with toil or burdens of grief) . . . in biblical Greek alone, *to labor with wearisome effort, to toil*" (p. 355). Arndt and Gingrich say that the general idea is "work hard." For this passage they suggest: "This is what I am toiling for" (p. 444).

Hauck notes that the word means "to make great exertions" or "to wear oneself out" (TDNT, 3:828). It was used in burial inscriptions for severe, strenuous work. So it would seem that "I toil" (RSV) or "I am toiling" (C. B. Williams) expresses it well.

Striving   Our word "agonize" comes directly from the Greek *agōnizō*, which is used here. Occurring only 7 times in the NT, it is rendered "strive" 3 times (here; Luke 13:24; 1 Cor. 9:25), "fight" 3 times (John 18:36; 1 Tim. 6:12; 2 Tim. 4:7), and "labour fervently" once (Col. 4:12).

The root of this word is the noun *agōn*. Literally this means "a gathering." But since the main gatherings in the Graeco-Roman world were for athletic contests—as in America today—the word came to be applied to the contests themselves. Thus the verb meant "to contend for a prize" or "to compete in an athletic contest." The thought is conveyed correctly by Beck's rendering: "struggling like an athlete." Paul did not go at his work for the Lord in any halfhearted manner. He struggled as strenuously as any athlete would do to win. Weymouth words it beautifully: "To this end, like an eager wrestler, I exert all my strength in reliance upon the power of Him who is mightily at work within me."

Eadie translates the participle *agōnizomenos* "intensely struggling." He writes: "It was no light work, no pastime; it made a demand upon every faculty and every moment" (p. 104). He continues: "It would seem from the following verses, that it is to an agony of spiritual earnestness that the apostle refers—to that profound yearning which occasioned so many wrestlings in prayer, and drew from him so many tears" (pp. 104–5). Eadie concludes:

> When we reflect upon the motive—the presentation of perfect men to God, and upon the instrument—the preaching of the cross, we cease to wonder at the apostle's zeal and toils. For there is no function so momentous—not that which studies the constitution of man, in order to ascertain his diseases and remove them; nor that which labours for social im-

provement, and the promotion of science and civilization; nor that which unfolds the resources of a nation, and secures it a free and patriotic government—far more important than all, is the function of the Christian ministry (p. 105).

This is a truth which every minister of Christ needs to recall frequently to spur him on.

Working   The noun is *energeia*. Abbott-Smith says it signifies "*operative power* (as distinct from *dynamis, potential* power)" (p. 153).

It is a bit difficult to translate this verse satisfactorily. "Working" and "worketh" are cognate noun and verb in the Greek (*energeia, energeō*). This connection is missed in RSV— "For this I toil, striving with all the energy which he mightily inspires within me." Probably the most literal translation is: "according to His energy which is being energized in me in power" (*dynamis*).

It is comforting to know that though we must strive earnestly, yet it is only God's power which enables us to do this successfully, and so we rely on that dynamic energy. Eadie expresses this thought beautifully. He says:

> It was, indeed, no sluggish heart that beat in the apostle's bosom. His was no torpid temperament. There was such a keenness in all its emotions and anxieties, that its resolve and action were simultaneous movements. But though he laboured so industriously, and suffered so bravely in the aim of winning souls to Christ and glory, still he owned that all was owing to Divine power lodged within him—

> *The work to be perform'd is ours,*
> *The strength is all His own;*
> *'Tis He that works to will,*
>   *'Tis He that works to do;*
> *His is the power by which we act,*
>   *His be the glory too* (p. 105).

2:1 Conflict   The Greek word for "conflict" is *agōna*, from the same root as in *agōnizō* in the previous verse. We noted there that the term is primarily an athletic one, referring to engaging in an athletic contest. It would seem that this connection should somehow be brought out. With its "striving" (1:29) and "conflict" (2:1) KJV fails to do this. The RSV does maintain the relationship by using "striving" and "how greatly I strive for you." But in order to do this it changes the noun here into a verb.

The NASB misses the connection by using "striving" and "struggle." Beck has "struggling like an athlete" in 1:29 and "how much I'm struggling for you" in 2:1.

2 Comforted The verb is *parakaleō;* literally, "call to one's side." In usage it has three distinct connotations: (1) beseech, entreat; (2) admonish, exhort; (3) cheer, encourage, comfort (A-S, p. 340). Thayer says that here it means "to encourage, strengthen" (p. 483). Arndt and Gingrich prefer "comforted" (p. 623). But the majority of recent translations use "cheered" (Weymouth, Goodspeed, Berk.) or "encouraged" (TCNT, Moffatt, Phillips, RSV, NASB, NIV). Lightfoot says it means " 'comforted' in the older and wider meaning of the word . . . but not with its modern and restricted sense" (pp. 172–73).

Knit The verb is a compound, *symbibazō.* It means "to join together, put together." So the passive here signifies "united" or "knit together." Weymouth, followed by Berkeley, has "welded together."

A thoughtful reader might ask why Moffatt has: "May they learn the meaning of love!" It is because *symbibazō* in the Septuagint always has the sense of "instruct." So in this passage the Vulgate has *instructi.* This is the correct meaning in 1 Cor. 2:16 and Acts 19:33. But Lightfoot argues well that here it must be taken as "united" (NIV), the connotation it clearly has elsewhere in Colossians and Ephesians.

Full Assurance The Greek word is *plērophoria,* from *plērēs,* "full," and *phoreō,* "bear." So the literal meaning is "fullness"; or "abundance," which Thayer prefers here. Abbott-Smith and Arndt and Gingrich give "full assurance" as the first meaning. It may also denote "certainty" or "confidence." Moffatt uses "conviction" in this passage (cf. TCNT, Beck). Lightfoot feels that the word always means "full assurance" in the NT, though "fullness" might possibly fit most passages (p. 173). Arndt and Gingrich agree. Delling suggests "superabundance" (TDNT, 6:311).

Acknowledgment The word *epignōsis* is translated "knowledge" in KJV in 16 out of its 20 occurrences in the NT. Three times it is rendered "acknowledging" and only here "acknowledgement." Abbott-Smith gives only three meanings: "acquaintance, discernment, recognition"; Thayer, "precise and correct knowledge." Since we have already discussed this word at length in connection with its use in 1:9, we shall simply note that here "knowledge"

(RSV) or "true knowledge" (NASB) is probably preferable to "acknowledgment."

3 Hid The adjective *apocryphos* (only here; Mark 4:22; Luke 8:17) is the basis for the expression "apocryphal books." This was used not only for the noncanonical (more accurately, deutero-canonical) books of the OT, but also for the secret writings of the Gnostics. Against their claims to esoteric knowledge, Paul asserts that all true knowledge is hidden—"stored up, hidden from view" (Weymouth)—in Christ.

Since *apocryphos* is an adjective, it would seem that "hidden" (NASB, NIV) is more accurate than "hid" (KJV, RSV).

4 Beguile The term *paralogizomai* occurs only here and in Jas. 1:22. It first meant "to miscalculate," and then "to reason falsely" and so "mislead" (A-S, p. 341). Thayer gives: "to deceive by false reasoning," and so, as here, "to deceive, delude" (p. 484). For this passage Arndt and Gingrich give "deceive, delude." It would seem that "delude" (RSV, NASB) or "deceive" (NIV) is more exact than "beguile."

Enticing Words This is one word in Greek, the compound *pithanologia* (only here in NT). It comes from the adjective *pithanos,* "persuasive" or "plausible," and *logos,* "speech." So it means "persuasive speech." Arndt and Gingrich say that here it means "*plausible* (but false) arguments" (p. 663). Probably the best translation is "persuasive argument" (NASB) or "fine-sounding arguments" (NIV).

T. K. Abbott makes the following observation on the two significant words of this verse: "*Pithanologia* expresses the subjective means of persuasion, the personal influence; *paralogizomai* the objective, the appearance of logic" (p. 242).

5 Steadfastness The Greek word *stereōma* (only here in NT) first meant "that which has been made firm," and finally "firmness, steadfastness" (Thayer, p. 587). The preference perhaps lies slightly with "firmness" (RSV, cf. NIV).

Lightfoot feels that both "order" (*taxis*) and "steadfastness" are military terms. He suggests for the former "orderly array" and for the latter "solid front" or "close phalanx" (p. 176). Apparently this is the basis for the popular translation "solid front" (TCNT, Weymouth, Moffatt). For the two terms NEB has: "your orderly array and the firm front."

Bertram translates here, "orderly and firm." He also calls attention to the fact that *taxis* is a military term and adds that *stereōma* "might also suggest a military metaphor in the sense of a castle or bulwark." He goes on to say that the righteous, as at Colosse, "are pressed by enemies, but they can stand fast in the stronghold of their faith and trust" (TDNT, 7:614).

To all of this Abbott takes exception. He writes: "But neither word has this military sense of itself, but from the context, and here the context suggests nothing of the kind." He concludes: "Here the idea of a well-ordered state lies much nearer than that of an army. The apostle rejoices in the orderly arrangement of the Colossian Church" (p. 243).

Meyer agrees with this. He says: "Hence, if we would avoid arbitrariness, we can only abide by the view that here *taxis* means the *orderly state of the Christian church*, which has hitherto not been disturbed by sectarian divisions or forsaken by the readers." He adds: "To this *outward* condition Paul then subjoins the *inner* one, by which the former is conditioned: *and the solid hold of your faith in Christ*" (p. 287).

It would be our feeling that the military metaphor might be used homiletically as an illustration of one kind of order and firmness. This could be done without insisting that this is the only, or even primary, application of the words.

6 Walk The verb is *peripateō*, which literally means "walk around." It may be translated "go about," as in Mark 12:38. More often it has the general meaning "walk."

But in the NT it is frequently used in the figurative sense. This is especially true of Paul's Epistles, where it has this metaphorical meaning 32 times. The same usage is found in the three Johannine letters 10 times. It occurs 4 times in the Epistle to the Colossians. Used thus it means "to regulate one's life, to conduct one's self" (Thayer, p. 504).

The majority of recent translations prefer "live." While the NASB follows the ASV in retaining "walk," Goodspeed has: "So just as you once accepted the Christ, Jesus, as your Lord, you must live in vital union with him." Since *peripateō* is in the continuous present tense here, a better rendering is: "continue to live in him" (NIV).

7 Rooted and Built Up Paul here portrays the Christian as being rooted in Christ and built upon Christ as the Foundation. In Eph. 3:17 he speaks of being "rooted and grounded in love." These are the only two passages in the

NT where the Greek verb for "root" occurs. (The noun is found 16 times.)

In this verse "rooted" is a perfect passive participle, whereas "built up" is a present passive participle. The NASB seeks to carry this distinction over into English by saying: "having been firmly rooted and now being built up in him." Charles B. Williams has: "with your roots deeply planted in Him, being continuously built up in Him."

8 Spoil The verb is *sylagōgeō*, found only here in the NT. It comes from *sylē*, "booty," and *agō*, "carry." So it literally means "to carry off as spoil, lead captive." Arndt and Gingrich say that it is used "figuratively of carrying someone away from the truth into the slavery of error" (p. 784). So "capture" is the correct meaning here, and some form of this verb is found in most modern versions. In the KJV here the verb "spoil" is used in its earliest meaning, "to strip or despoil, or to strip (persons) of goods or possessions by violence or force; to plunder, rob, despoil" (OED, 10:650). The *Oxford English Dictionary* gives several examples of this usage at about 1611, when the KJV was translated. But this is not what the term connotes today.

Philosophy This comes directly from the Greek *philosophia* (only here in NT). Literally it means "love of wisdom." Of its usage here, Thayer writes: "Once in the N.T. of the theology, or rather theosophy, of certain Jewish-Christian ascetics, which busied itself with refined and speculative inquiries into the nature and classes of angels, into the ritual of the Mosaic law and the regulations of Jewish tradition respecting practical life" (p. 655).

The term "philosophy," taken in itself, carries no bad connotation. It is said to have come as the result of the humility of Pythagoras, who called himself "a lover of (divine) wisdom." Lightfoot observes: "In such a sense the term would entirely accord with the spirit and teaching of St. Paul; for it bore testimony to the insufficiency of the human intellect and the need of a revelation. But in his age it had come to be associated generally with the idea of subtle dialectics and profitless speculation; while in this particular instance it was combined with a mystic cosmogony and angelology which contributed a fresh element of danger" (p. 179). Phillips translates the word here "intellectualism."

Vain Deceit The literal meaning of *kenos* is "empty." That fits best here. Deceit is always an empty thing. Only what is true is solid. Goodness is positive; evil is negative.

Rudiments The Greek word *stoicheia* occurs only seven times in the NT. Here and in verse 20 it is translated "rudiments." In Hebrews 5:12 it is "principles." But four times it is rendered "elements" (Gal. 4:3, 9; 2 Pet. 3:10, 12). Some recent versions (RSV, NEB) have "elemental spirits." Probably a more acceptable translation would be "elementary principles" (NASB) or "basic principles" (NIV).

The primary meaning of *stoicheia* was "the letters of the alphabet." So it came to mean "rudimentary instruction." Many Early Church fathers interpreted this expression as referring to the heavenly bodies. But this seems a mistake. The application to "elemental spirits" also seems questionable.

9 Godhead The Greek word is *theotēs* (only here in NT). It comes from *theos*, "God." The preferable translation is "deity" (RSV, NASB, NIV). That is a simpler and more commonly used term today than "Godhead." It means the essence of the divine nature.

10 Complete The Greek form here is *peplērōmenoi*. Since it is based on the same root as *plērōma* ("fulness") in the previous verse, it would seem wise to show the connection. The RSV expresses it well: "You have come to fulness of life in him." The NIV reads: "You have this fullness in Christ."

Principality The Greek word is *archē*. Most frequently in the NT it means "beginning." But in a number of passages in Paul's Epistles it has the sense of "dominion" or "rule." It always signifies "primacy," whether in time or in rank (TDNT, 1:479).

Power The word is *exousia*, which properly means "authority"—in distinction from *dynamis*, "power." The correct combination here is "rule and authority" (RSV, NASB).

12 Of the Operation It is obvious that the expression "through the faith of the operation of God" is meaningless. The word for "operation" is *energeia*, from *ergon*, "work." It means "working." A meaningful translation is: "through faith in the working of God" (RSV, NASB).

13 Sins, Trespasses? The word is *paraptōma*, translated here as "sins" and "trespasses." Literally, it means "a falling beside."

The proper Greek word for "sin" is *hamartia*. The preferable translation here is "trespasses" (RSV).

14 Blotting Out The KJV gives the literal meaning. The verb *exaleiphō* is used in the LXX in the sense of "to plaster, wash over," and so came to mean "to wipe off, wipe out" (p. 159). This literal connotation is found in Rev. 7:17; 21:4. It has the idea of "erase" in Rev. 3:5. But here it is used in a metaphorical sense. Most of the recent versions follow TCNT, Moffatt, and Goodspeed in translating it "canceled."

Handwriting The Greek word is found only here in the NT. It is the adjective *cheirographon;* literally, "handwritten." Here it is used as a substantive, meaning "a handwriting." Thayer notes that it meant "specifically a note of hand, or writing in which one acknowledges that money has either been deposited with him or lent to him by another, to be returned at an appointed time ... metaphorically applied in Col. ii. 14 ... to the Mosaic law, which shows men to be chargeable with offences for which they must pay the penalty" (p. 668).

Lohse says the word has the sense of "promissory note." He continues: "The reference is to God's pronouncement that the note which testifies against us is cancelled. The phrase is obviously based on a thought which is common to Judaism, namely that God keeps an account of man's debt ... and that He imposes the penalty" (TDNT, 9:435). Lohse concludes: "God has forgiven sins. He has cancelled the note of indebtedness by taking it and fixing it to the cross of Christ" (p. 436).

Deissmann points out the fact that the idea of canceling a promissory note has been abundantly illustrated by the ancient Egyptian papyri discovered in modern times. He writes: "We have learnt from the new texts that it was generally customary to cancel a bond (or other document) by crossing it out with the Greek cross—letter Chi (X). In the splendid Florentine papyrus, of the year 85 A.D.. . . . the governor of Egypt gives this order in the course of a trial:

'Let the handwriting be crossed out.' . . .

We have moreover recovered the originals of a number of 'crossed-out' I. O. U.'s" (LAE, pp. 333–34).

"Cancelled the bond" is the TCNT wording. This rendering has been followed by many versions (e.g., RSV, NEB). NASB reads: "having cancelled out the certificate of debt." The NIV has "the written code."

Ordinances The Greek word is *dogma*, which has been taken over into English. It meant a public decree. In the NT it is used for the decrees of Roman rulers (Luke 2:1; Acts 17:7), of the Jewish law (Eph. 2:15; Col. 2:14), and of the apostles (Acts 16:4).

Since Paul is here addressing the Gentiles as well as Jews, Lightfoot suggests: "The *dogmata* [plural] therefore, though referring primarily to the Mosaic ordinances, will include all forms of positive decrees in which moral or social principles are embodied or religious duties; and the 'bond' is the moral assent of the conscience, which (as it were) signs and seals the obligation" (p. 187). Josephus uses *dogma* for the Mosaic law.

In the KJV, "decrees" is used in the three passages written by Luke, but "ordinances" here and in the parallel passage in Eph. 2:15. Inconsistently the NASB has *"contained* in ordinances" in Eph. 2:15 but "consisting of decrees" here. Either term will fit in these two Pauline passages. (NIV has "regulations.")

Contrary To The Greek word (only here and in Heb. 10:27) is *hypenantios*, an adjective which literally means "set over against, opposite" (A-S, p. 457), and so "opposed, contrary, hostile" (AG, p. 846). Lightfoot translates the clause: "which was directly opposed to us" (p. 188). Moulton and Milligan assert that this strong sense is illustrated by its use in a second-century papyrus from Oxyrhynchus (VGT, p. 651). Charles B. Williams gives a good brief rendering of this passage: "cancelled the note that stood against us, with its requirements." But the full force of the Greek is best brought out in TCNT: "the bond standing against us, which was in direct hostility to us."

15 Spoiled The strong double compound *apekduō* means *"to strip off* clothes or arms" (A-S, p. 46). Here the form is the aorist middle participle, which literally would mean "having stripped off from himself." Lightfoot argues for that meaning here (cf. NEB). Others feel that the middle is used in this case for the active. This is perhaps the best conclusion, giving the translation "disarmed" (RSV, NIV, NASB) or "stripped" (C. B. Williams, Beck). This seems to fit in more naturally with the last two clauses of the verse.

Show *Deigmatizō* is a "very rare verb" (VGT, p. 137). Thayer speaks of it as "a word unknown

to Greek writers" (p. 126). But it has now been found in a Tebtunis papyrus from about 14 B.C. Lightfoot says that it means " 'displayed,' as a victor displays his captives or trophies in a triumphal procession" (p. 191). He also asserts: "Nowhere does the word convey the idea of 'making an example' (*paradeigmatisai*) but signifies simply 'to display, publish, proclaim' " (*ibid.*).

However, Arndt and Gingrich give as their definition "expose, make an example of" and suggest for this passage: "mock, expose" (p. 171). The last word is adopted by Phillips here, while the RSV has: "made a public example of them." A more neutral rendering, in line with Lightfoot's protest, would be "made a public display of them" (NASB).

In either case, the picture is made clear by the last clause of the verse. This is brought out in the paraphrase: "He made a public spectacle of them and led them as captives in his triumphal procession" (NEB). It was the familiar scene of a conqueror returning to Rome and leading the captured kings and warriors in chains in his triumphal processions. This is what Christ did on the Cross.

16 Meat *Brōsis* is found 11 times in the NT. In the KJV it is most frequently translated "meat." But the use of "meat" for "food" is now obsolete.

Literally the word meant "eating," and this is the sense in Matt. 6:19–20, where it is translated "rust." Lightfoot (p. 193) renders the double phrase here: "in eating and in drinking" (cf. TCNT, C. B. Williams). Arndt and Gingrich support this meaning here. Many translators prefer "by what you eat or drink" (NIV).

Holyday The word *heortē* occurs 27 times in the NT and is translated "feast" in every place but here. The reference is to the annual "feasts" of the Jews, mentioned frequently in both Testaments.

But the term "feast" is not entirely satisfactory. It emphasizes the idea of eating. But one of the annual "feasts" was the Day of Atonement. On that day the people fasted, not feasted. So the word "festival," in the sense of a celebration, is better. This is what is used here by most modern translations.

17 Body The word *sōma* literally means "body." It is used frequently in the NT for the physical body. Paul uses it many times for the Church as the body of Christ.

But here we have something different from either of these senses. The meaning is rather clearly that of "substance" in contrast to shadow. Most recent translations have "substance." The sacred rites of the Hebrew religion "have at most only a symbolical value" (Phillips). The "reality" (NIV) is found in Christ. This is the sense preferred here by Schweizer (TDNT, 7:1066).

18 Beguile The expression "beguile you of your reward" does not adequately communicate to the modern reader the real meaning of *katabrabeuō* (only here in NT). This comes from *brabeus*, "an umpire." So it means "*to decide as an umpire against* one, *to declare* him *unworthy of the prize; to defraud of the prize of victory*" (Thayer, p. 330).

It is in the last sense that Lightfoot takes the word. He writes:

> The Christian's career is the contest of the stadium.... Christ is the umpire, the dispenser of the rewards (2 Tim. iv. 8); life eternal is the bay wreath, the victor's prize (*brabeion*, I Cor. ix. 24, Phil. iii. 14). The Colossians were in a fair way to win this prize; they had entered the lists duly; they were running bravely: but the false teachers, thrusting themselves in the way, attempted to trip them up or otherwise impede them in the race, and thus to rob them of their just reward (p. 195).

For this extremely rare word Arndt and Gingrich give these meanings: "*decide against* (as umpire), *rob of a prize, condemn*" (p. 410). It is certainly a much stronger term than "judge" in verse 16. Perhaps the best rendering is either "disqualify" (RSV, NIV) or "rob you of your prize" (ASV, Lightfoot).

Humility The word *tapeinophrosynē* carried a bad connotation in the pagan world. To heathen moralists humility was a vice. It was Christianity that made it a virtue. But Lightfoot well observes: "Humility, when it becomes self-conscious, ceases to have any value" (p. 196).

And that is the situation described here. "Voluntary" is in Greek the present participle *thelōn*. It means "taking delight in" or "devoting himself to." Goodspeed translates the phrase: "persisting in studied humility." Probably the best rendering is: "delighting in self-abasement" or "delights in false humility" (NIV). These false teachers made a religion out of asceticism.

Intruding into The verb *embateuō* (only here in NT) seems to be related to *embainō*, and

so to mean "enter." But just what it means here has been much debated.

It ought first to be noted that the object following this verb—"those things which he hath not seen"—should be "those things which he has seen." There is no negative in the best Greek text.

Arndt and Gingrich call attention to two possible meanings of *embateuō*. The first is: "*enter into* a subject, to investigate it closely, *go into detail* . . . hence in Col. 2:18 perhaps *entering at length upon the tale of what he has seen* in a vision" (p. 253). With regard to the second they write: "Three inscriptions of Asia Minor (second century A.D.) . . . show that *embateuō* was a technical term of the mystery religions. Then perhaps . . . *taking his stand on what he had seen* in the mysteries" (*ibid.*). This last idea is developed at length by Moulton and Milligan (VGT, p. 206).

The passage is admittedly difficult. About the best that can be done is: "goes into great detail about what he has seen" (NIV).

23 Will Worship The compound *ethelothrēskia* is found only here in the NT. It means "*voluntary, arbitrary worship* . . . i.e. worship which one devises and prescribes for himself, contrary to the contents and nature of the faith which ought to be directed to Christ; said of the misdirected zeal and practices of ascetics: Col. ii. 23" (Thayer, p. 168). Abbott-Smith gives "self-imposed worship" (cf. NEB). Arndt and Gingrich have "self-made religion." Probably as good a translation as any of this verse is: "Such regulations indeed have an appearance of wisdom, with their self-imposed worship, their false humility and their harsh treatment of the body, but they lack any value in restraining sensual indulgence" (NIV).

3:2 Affection "Set your affection" is one word in Greek, the verb *phroneite*. It comes from the noun for "mind" (*phrēn*). Homer and other early writers used it in the sense of "have understanding." Then it meant "to think." Here it means: "to have in mind, be mindful of, think of" (A-S, p. 474). For this passage Arndt and Gingrich suggest "set one's mind on, be intent on" (p. 874). Thayer has: "to direct one's mind to a thing" (p. 658). The best translation is probably, "Set your mind on things above" (NIV).

5 Mortify *Nekrōsate* is from *nekros*, "dead." So it literally means "put to death." Thayer suggests that here it means "to deprive of power, destroy the strength of" (p. 424). But why dilute the full force of the verb? Arndt and Gingrich translate the clause: "Put to death what is earthly in you" (p. 537). "Mortify" is hardly an adequate rendering because it is used too loosely today.

Inordinate Affection The KJV has a long translation for a short word—*pathos*. This comes from the second aorist stem (*path*) of *paschō*, "suffer." Basically it means "that which befalls one, that which one suffers," and so "a passion, passionate desire" (A-S, pp. 332–33). It occurs only here, in Rom. 1:26, and in 1 Thess. 4:5. Thayer notes that, while it was "used by the Greeks in either a good or a bad sense," yet "in the N. T. (only) in a bad sense, *depraved passion*" (p. 472). Doubtless "passion" is a more meaningful rendering today, and so it is found in most modern translations.

Evil Concupiscence The word *concupiscence* is also an antiquated expression, unused today. The Greek *epithymia* means "desire." It is used in the NT for the natural desire of hunger (Luke 15:16; 16:21). But in Paul's Epistles it usually has a bad connotation. Buechsel writes: "The essential point in *epithymia* is that it is desire as impulse, as a motion of the will. . . . *Epithymia* is anxious self-seeking" (TDNT, 3:171). Since the adjective "evil" is affixed to the term here, clearly the best translation is "desire."

8 ***Blasphemy*** The Greek word is *blasphēmia*. But originally this did not have the modern connotation of blasphemy. It meant "slander, detraction, speech injurious to another's good name," and only later "impious and reproachful speech injurious to the divine majesty" (Thayer, p. 102). So the correct translation here, as in numerous other places in the NT, is "slander."

Filthy Communication This is one word in the Greek; *aischrologia* (only here in NT). It means "abusive language" (A-S, p. 14). Thayer says: "Foul speaking . . . low and obscene speech" (p. 17). Arndt and Gingrich have: "*Evil speech* in the sense of *obscene speech* . . . or *abusive speech*" (p. 24).

Lightfoot combines both these ideas in his translation, "foul-mouthed abuse." After noting that the word is defined by Clement of Alexandria as "filthy-talking" and used by Polybius in the sense of "abusive language," he continues: "If the two senses of the word had been quite distinct, we might have some difficulty in choosing between them here. . . . But the sec-

ond sense is derived from the first. The word can only mean 'abuse' when the abuse is 'foul-mouthed.' And thus we may suppose that both ideas, 'filthiness' and 'evil-speaking,' are included here" (p. 214).

Trench insists that the meaning of the word should not be confined to obscene discourse, as the Greek Fathers usually took it, but should also include "*every* license of the ungoverned tongue employing itself in the abuse of others" (p. 121). T. K. Abbott feels that "the connexion here shows that it means 'abusive' rather than 'filthy' language," and adds that "the sins of uncleanness have been dealt with in ver. 5, and the other substantives here regard want of charity" (p. 283).

In the light of all this discussion it would seem that "foul talk" (RSV), "abusive speech" (NASB), and "filthy language" (NIV) are all correct.

11 ***Barbarian*** The Greek word is the adjective *barbaros*. It is probably an onomatopoetic word; that is, its sound suggests its sense. Thayer gives this ample definition: "1. properly, *one whose speech is rude, rough, harsh,* as if repeating the syllables *barbar* . . . hence 2. *one who speaks a foreign* or *strange language which is not understood by another.* . . . 3. The Greeks used *barbaros* of *any foreigner ignorant of the Greek language and the Greek culture* . . . with the added notion, after the Persian war, of rudeness and brutality" (p. 95).

Scythian This word refers to "an inhabitant of Scythia, i.e., Russia and Siberia, a synonym with the Greeks for the wildest of barbarians" (A-S, p. 410). Lightfoot comments: "The savageness of the Scythians was proverbial" (p. 218). But in Christ there are no distinctions of race or color, of culture or education.

Windisch points out that each of the other three pairs in this verse is in the form of an antithesis; so presumably this one (Barbarian/Scythian) is also. He suggests that Paul "contrasted the barbarians generally with a particularly notorious barbarian people" (TDNT, 1:553).

12 ***Bowels*** Again we meet this word *splanchna*, which literally means "bowels," but is used metaphorically for the seat of the affections. Instead of "bowels of mercies" we should read "a heart of compassion" (NASB).

13 ***Forbearing*** In the active the verb *anechō* means "hold up." But in the NT it is always in the middle and means "bear with."

Though most versions retain "forbearing," it would seem that "bearing with" (NASB) is slightly more meaningful (cf. "bear with," NIV).

Forgiving The verb is *charizomai*. It comes from *charis*, which means "grace." So it means "forgive graciously." The more common word for "forgive" in the NT is *aphiēmi*, which literally means "leave off." But the word here carries a deeper sense of wholehearted forgiveness. It should be translated "freely forgiving" (C. B. Williams). Weymouth has "readily forgiving." That is the right idea. Our forgiveness of others must be given, not grudgingly, but gladly.

Quarrel The Greek word *momphē* occurs only here in the NT. It literally means "blame" or "complaint." The correct translation here is "complaint" or "grievances" (NIV). Even if we have a just cause for complaint against someone, we should "forgive as freely as the Lord has forgiven you" (Phillips). We want God's forgiveness of us to be immediate, gracious, and complete. That is the kind of forgiveness we must extend to others.

14 Charity This is one of the most unfortunate renderings found in the King James Version. The Greek word is *agapē*, which means the highest kind of unselfish, holy love. Yet 27 times the KJV renders it "charity," which today suggests handouts and cast-off clothes. The word should always be translated "love."

Bond of Perfectness The Greek phrase is a bit difficult to translate into English. This is shown by the fact that one can hardly find two versions that agree exactly.

"Bond" is *syndesmos*. It comes from the verb *syndeō*, which means "bind together." So it signifies "that which binds together."

"Perfectness" is *teleiotētos* (only here and in Heb. 6:1), which means "completeness." It comes from *telos*, "end."

What this passage states is that love is "the power, which unites and holds together all those graces and virtues, which together make up perfection" (Lightfoot, p. 222). Since the figure that Paul uses here is that of putting on clothing (v. 12), it would seem that love may be thought of here as the belt which holds all the rest in place. This is to be put on "above all these things," to tie them together. Phillips perhaps suggests this when he says that "love is the golden chain of all the virtues." Lightfoot thinks of love rather as the outer garment, to be worn over all the rest. He paraphrases this passage: "And over all these robe yourselves in love; for this is the garment which binds together all the graces of perfection" (p. 220).

15 Rule The Greek word for "rule" is *brabeuō* (only here in NT). It comes from *brabeus*, which means "an umpire." So it properly means "act as an umpire," and thus "arbitrate, decide" (A-S, p. 85). Lightfoot paraphrases this clause: "And let the one supreme umpire in your hearts, the one referee amidst all your difficulties, be the peace of Christ" (p. 220). He comments on this passage: "Wherever there is a conflict of motives or impulses or reasons, the peace of Christ must step in and decide which is to prevail" (p. 223).

It is true that some commentators object to adopting the literal meaning of *brabeuō* here. For instance, Meyer writes:

> It means primarily: *to arrange and conduct the contest* . . . then *to confer the prize of victory,* to be *brabeus, i.e.* umpire; finally: *to govern* generally. Considering its very frequent occurrence in the latter sense, and its appropriateness in that sense to (in your hearts), and seeing that any reference to the Messianic *brabeion* (comp. ii. 18) is foreign to the context, the majority of modern expositors have rightly interpreted it: the peace of Christ must *rule, govern* in your hearts (p. 362).

Moulton and Milligan cite several examples of this more general meaning in papyri of the second century B.C. But they find also definite reference to the athletic games in other cases. They conclude: "We may endorse accordingly . . . Lightfoot's insistence on the element of *award* or *decision* in a conflict between two impulses, in the remarkable phrase of Col. 3:15: whether the figure of the games is present we need not argue" (VGT, p. 116). In connection with this passage Stauffer says: "Paul uses the verb of the peace which settles all strife and preserves the unity of the Christian community" (TDNT, 1:638). So it seems to us that the idea of "arbitrate" fits well here. C. B. Williams has: "Let the peace that Christ can give keep on acting as umpire in your hearts." He also brings out the force of the (continuous) present imperative in the last clause of this verse by rendering it: "And practice being thankful."

18 Submit The verb is *hypotassō*. It was first used as a military term, with the sense "place under" or "arrange under." In the middle, as here, it means "subject oneself, obey"

(A-S, p. 463). Perhaps the better rendering here is "be subject to" (RSV, NEB, NASB).

Fit Paul says that the subordination of the wife to the husband is "fit" in the Lord. The Greek word is the verb *anēkō*. Thayer gives this definition: "In Greek writers *to have come up to, arrived at, to reach to, pertain to* . . . hence in later writers . . . *something appertains to one, is due to him* . . . and then ethically *what is due, duty* . . . impersonal *hōs anēke, as was fitting* . . . Col. III. 18" (p. 45). Charles B. Williams brings out this idea of obligation when he translates this clause: "For this is your Christian duty."

19 *Bitter* The verb is *pikrainō*. It comes from *pikros*, which is found only in Jas. 3:11, 14. This adjective is defined by Abbott-Smith as follows: "1. *sharp, pointed*. 2. *sharp* to the senses; of taste, *bitter* . . . metaphorically, *harsh*, bitter" (p. 360). So the verb in the passive, as here, means "to be embittered, irritated" (Thayer, p. 509). But many of the translations use "harsh" (RSV, NEB, NIV), and this seems to fit well. T. K. Abbott writes: "The word would seem, then, to correspond more nearly with the colloquial 'cross' than with 'bitter' " (p. 293). As usual, Phillips gives a free but meaningful paraphrase: "Husbands, be sure you give your wives much love and sympathy; don't let bitterness or resentment spoil your marriage."

21 *Provoke* The problem here is partly as to which Greek word is original. The Textus Receptus, on which the KJV is based, has *parorgizete* (only here and in Rom. 10:19). This means "provoke to anger." But the reading found in the very earliest manuscripts (Papyrus 46, Vaticanus) is *erethizete*. In the only other place in the NT where it occurs it has a good sense—"stir up, stimulate." But here it has the bad sense—"stir up, provoke" (A-S, p. 179). Arndt and Gingrich say that it means: "*Arouse, provoke* mostly in a bad sense, *irritate, embitter*" (p. 308). It would seem that the best translation here is "irritate" (TCNT, Moffatt, Goodspeed, Beck) or "exasperate" (NEB, NASB). Weymouth gives a rather full paraphrase: "Fathers, do not fret and harass your children, or you may make them sullen and morose." In line with this, Lightfoot comments: " 'Irritation' is the first consequence of being too exacting with children, and irritation leads to moroseness" (p. 227).

Discouraged The verb *athymeō* (only here in NT) is compounded of the alpha-privative *a-* and *thymos*. The latter comes from *thyō*, which means "rush along" (cf. thymus gland). The idea of *athymeō* is "to be disheartened, dispirited, broken in spirit" (Thayer, p. 14). This is a tragic thing to have happen to children. Lightfoot suggests that the idea here is that irritated children will "go about their task in a listless, moody, sullen frame of mind" (p. 227). Probably the best translation is "disheartened" (TCNT, NEB) or "lose heart" (Goodspeed, NASB), though "discouraged" is also accurate and meaningful.

23 *Do* The KJV reads: "Whatsoever ye do, do it heartily." But this ignores the fact that whereas the first *do* is the common verb of that meaning, *poieō*, the second *do* is *ergazō*, which means "work." The correct translation is: "Whatever you do, work at it with all your heart" (NIV).

Heartily The latter is a little nearer the Greek, which has *ek psychēs*—literally, "out of the soul." Like the English word "soul," the Greek *psychē* has many meanings. The one that fits here is apparently "heart." This admonition means: "Let your hearts be in your work" (Weymouth). Phillips' paraphrase is excellent: "Put your whole heart and soul into it."

24 *Reward* The Greek word *antapodosis* is found only here in the NT. It is a double compound, composed of *didōmi*, "give"; *apo*, "from"; and *anti*, "in exchange for." It comes from the verb *antapodidōmi*, which Abbott-Smith defines as: "*To give back as an equivalent, recompense, requital* (the *anti* expressing the idea of full, complete return)" (p. 40). For the noun he gives "recompense." The point is that we shall receive our heavenly inheritance as a full reward or recompense for all that we have relinquished down here. We shall be paid in full.

25 *Receive* The verb is not the same as the one translated "receive" in verse 24. There it was the more general word *apolambanō*, which has the idea mainly of receiving from another. Here it is *komizō*, which Abbott-Smith defines as: "1. *to take care of*. 2. *to carry off safe*. 3. *to bear or carry*: Lk. 7:37. Middle, *to bear for oneself*, hence *(a) to receive* . . . *(b) to receive back, recover* . . . metaphorically, of requital . . . Col. 3:25" (p. 253).

Thayer writes: "Since in the rewards and punishments of deeds, the deeds themselves are as it were requited and so given back to their authors, the meaning is obvious when one is said *komizesthai* (to be requited) *that which he has done*, i.e. either the reward or punishment of the deed" (p. 354).

Perhaps the best translation is "be paid back" (Goodspeed, RSV). Moffatt puts it exactly: "The wrongdoer will be paid back for his wrongdoing."

4:1 *Give* The verb translated "give" is not the common *didōmi* or one of its compounds. It is *parechō*. Lightfoot renders it "exhibit on your part" and comments: "The middle *parechesthai*, 'to afford from oneself,' will take different shades of meaning according to the context. . . . Here the idea is 'reciprocation,' the master's duty as corresponding to the slave's" (p. 230).

Possibly "grant" is a little more nearly exact than "give." All versions, however, present the meaning well.

Equal The Greek word is *isotēs*, which literally signifies "equality." But in this passage it probably means "equity" or "fairness." Lightfoot writes: "It seems a mistake to suppose that *isotēs* here has anything to do with the treatment of slaves as *equals* (comp. Philem. 16). When connected with *to dikaion* ("that which is just"), the word naturally suggests an even-handed, impartial treatment, and is equivalent to the Latin *aequitas*. . . . Thus in Aristotle . . . *to dikaion* and *to ison* are regarded as synonymns, and in Plutarch . . . the relation of *isotēs* to *dikaiotēs* is discussed" (p. 230).

T. K. Abbott is in essential agreement. He says: "*Isotēs* differs from *to dikaion* nearly as our 'fair' from 'just,' denoting what cannot be brought under positive rules, but is in accordance with the judgment of a fair mind" (p. 296). So it would seem that the best translation here is: "Masters, provide your slaves with what is right and fair" (NIV).

2 Continue The Greek has a strong compound, *proskartereō*. It is composed of *pros*, "to," and *karteros*, "strong, steadfast." So it means: "to occupy oneself diligently with something," "to pay persistent attention to," or "to hold fast to something" (TDNT, 3:618). This word is used in connection with praying in Acts 1:14; 2:42; 6:4; and Rom. 12:12.

It is obvious that "continue" is an inadequate rendering. The compound verb demands "continue steadfastly" (RSV) or "persevere" (NEB).

Watch The verb is *grēgoreō*, which means "to be awake" or "to keep awake." Arndt and Gingrich would translate it here: "be wide awake about it" (p. 166). Since the form here is a present participle, a better rendering than "watch" is "being watchful" (NIV).

Lightfoot makes a helpful comment. He observes: "Long continuance in prayer is apt to produce listlessness. Hence the additional charge that the heart must be *awake*, if the prayer is to have any value." He adds that "thanksgiving" is "the crown of all prayer" (p. 231).

3 *Of Utterance* Paul solicits the prayers of the Colossian Christians that God might open for him (apparently at Rome) "a door of utterance." In the Greek the last term is *logos*, which means "word." So the better translation is "a door for the word" (RSV, NASB). What is meant is well expressed thus: "that God may open a door for our message" (NIV). That he received this open door is indicated by Acts 28:31.

5 *Walk* The Greek word *peripateō* properly means "walk." It is used in this literal sense countless times in the Gospels and Acts. But Paul employs it over 30 times in a figurative sense. With him it means "live" or "conduct oneself." In this passage a better translation is, "Conduct yourselves" (RSV, NASB). Weymouth catches the thought of this clause well in his paraphrase: "Behave wisely in relation to the outside world."

Redeeming The verb *exagorazō* literally means to buy something "out of" (*ex*) the marketplace (*agora*). But it came to be used technically in the sense of "ransom" or "redeem" slaves. That is the basis of its metahorical use in Gal. 3:13; 4:5. But here and in Eph. 5:16 (the only other places it occurs in NT) it is found in the present middle participle. Used this way it means "buying up for oneself." Thayer says that in these two passages "the meaning seems to be *to make a wise and sacred use of every opportunity for doing good*, so that zeal and well-doing are as it were the purchase-money by which we make the time our own" (p. 220).

A meaningful translation is: "making the most of the time" (RSV; cf. NASB). Since the word for "time" is *kairos*, which means "opportune time," a good rendering is: "make the most of every opportunity" (NIV). Lightfoot gives this full paraphrase: "Walk wisely and discreetly in all your dealings with unbelievers; allow no opportunity to slip through your hands, but buy up every passing moment" (p. 230).

6 Grace, Salt Paul writes: "Let your speech be alway with grace, seasoned with salt." It would seem that *salt* is closely related to *grace*. Weymouth brings it out this way: "Let your language be always seasoned with the salt of grace."

In the Greek comic writers the verb *artyō*, "season," referred to the seasoning with the salt of wit. But too often this degenerated into off-color jokes. Paul says that the Christian's speech should be "with grace," or "gracious."

Salt gives both flavor and preservation, making food tasty and wholesome. A very helpful translation of this verse is: "Let your conversation be always gracious, and never insipid; study how best to talk with each person you meet" (NEB).

8 Your Estate The KJV says that Paul was sending Tychicus to the Colossian church "that he might know your estate." Why do the NASB and NIV have "that you may know about our circumstances"?

The answer is that the latter translation represents what scholars believe to be the best Greek text, though admittedly the manuscript evidence in this case is rather evenly balanced. But the reading adopted by most modern translators is parallel to that in Eph. 6:22, where Paul is apparently saying the same thing.

In any case, "estate" is an archaic rendering here. Today "estate" means property belonging to someone. Here the Greek literally says: "the things concerning us (*or you*)." The correct idea is: "that you may know how we are" (RSV).

Comfort The verb *parakaleō* literally means "call alongside (to help)." It is variously translated as "beseech," "exhort," "comfort," or "encourage." Only the context can decide the choice. It would seem that "encourage" fits best here, as most translators have agreed. The correct thought is expressed by such a rendering as "put fresh heart into you" (NEB). Lightfoot feels that in this passage, as in Eph. 6:22 and 2 Thess. 2:17, the real meaning is "encourage you to persevere" (p. 235).

10 Sister's Son The KJV presents Mark as the nephew of Barnabas. But the Greek word *anepsios* (only here in NT) really meant "cousin" at the time. Lightfoot writes: "The term *anepsioi* is applied to cousins german, the children whether of two brothers or of two sisters or of a brother and sister, as it is carefully defined in Pollux iii. 28" (p. 236). (Pollux wrote his famous Greek dictionary, entitled *Onom-*

asticon, in the second century after Christ.) Abbott says of *anepsios*: "The use of it for 'nephew' is very late" (p. 300).

Receive Paul says that he had already given instructions that if Mark should come, the Colossians were to "receive" him. The verb is *dechomai* (not the same word as "received" earlier in the verse). It means "accept" or "welcome." Most of the recent translations have adopted "welcome" or "make him welcome." The importance of this idea is underlined by T. K. Abbott. After calling attention to the correct term above, "cousin," he says: "The relationship explains why Barnabas was more ready than Paul to condone Mark's defection, Acts xv. 37–39. At the same time the passage throws light in turn on the rather remarkable form of commendation here, 'if he comes unto you, receive him.' The Pauline Churches, which were aware of the estrangement, might not be very ready to give a very hearty welcome to Mark" (p. 300). So Paul is urging: "Give him a hearty welcome" (Phillips).

11 Comfort The Greek noun here is not from the same root as the verb for "comfort" in verse 8. There it was *parakaleō*. Here it is *parēgoria* (only here in NT). Lightfoot notes that the latter has an even wider range of meaning than the former. He writes: "The verb *parēgorein* denotes either (1) 'to exhort, encourage' . . . (2) 'to dissuade' . . . (3) 'to appease,' 'quiet' . . . or (4) 'to console, comfort.' The word, however, and its derivatives . . . were used especially as medical terms, in the sense of 'assuaging,' 'alleviating' . . . and perhaps owing to this usage, the idea of consolation, comfort, is on the whole predominant in the word" (p. 239). The English word *paregoric* comes from this Greek term. The NASB has "encouragement," but almost all recent translations have adopted "comfort" (so NIV).

12 Laboring Fervently The verb *agōnizō* has given us our English word "agonize." As we have noted in previous studies, this was primarily an athletic term. Properly it meant "to contend for a prize" (A-S, p. 8), or "engage in a contest" (AG, p. 15). Here the thought is of "wrestling in prayer." It would seem that "wrestling" is the best translation here (so Weymouth, NIV).

Complete This is again a matter of variant readings. "Complete" is based on *peplēromenoi*, the perfect passive participle of *plēroō*, which means to fill, complete, or fulfill. "Fully assured" (RSV, NASB, NIV) is the rendering preferred by Lightfoot, Abbott, and the other best commentators. It is based on *peplērophorēmenoi*, the perfect passive participle of *plērophoreō*. This verb means: "1. to bring in full measure . . . fulfill, accomplish . . . 2. to persuade, assure or satisfy fully" (A-S, p. 365). Though Delling prefers the former sense (TDNT, 6:310), the latter is its meaning in the papyri, as Deissmann has demonstrated.

13 *Great Zeal*   The word "zeal" is the translation of *zēlon*. But the oldest Greek manuscripts have *ponon*. The original meaning of this word was "labor" or "toil." Then it came to mean "great trouble, intense desire" (Thayer, p. 531). Aside from this passage the word *ponos* occurs only in Revelation (16:10–11; 21:4), where it means "pain" or "distress." Most recent translations have "is working hard" (NIV) or something similar. But there is much to be said for "deep concern" (NASB; cf. Weymouth).

1 Thessalonians

1:3 *Without Ceasing* This is an adverb in the Greek, *adialeiptōs*. It comes from the alpha-privative -*a* and the verb *dialeipō*, "leave off (for a time)." So it means "not leaving off." Paul prayed for his converts "constantly" (RSV, NASB) or "continually" (NEB, NIV). His unremitting prayer life is a challenge to all of us in our day when busy activity too often takes the place of prayer.

It is interesting to note that this word occurs three times in this Epistle (1:3; 2:13; 5:17), and elsewhere in the NT only in Rom. 1:9. It underscores the faithful, unselfish character of the great apostle.

Patience The Greek word *hypomonē* is translated "patience" (KJV) in 29 out of its 32 occurrences in the NT. In the other three places it is more correctly rendered "enduring" (2 Cor. 1:6), "patient continuance" (Rom. 2:7), and "patient waiting" (2 Thess. 3:5). The word "patience" is too passive a term to represent the Greek original. *Hypomonē* means "endurance" or "patient endurance." It is more adequately translated "steadfastness" (RSV, NASB). Phillips brings out the full force of it in his paraphrase: "The hope that you have in our Lord Jesus Christ means sheer dogged endurance."

Lohmeyer puts it well: "*hypomonē* is an endurance which is grounded in waiting, a waiting which expresses itself in endurance" (TDNT, 4:588).

4 *Election* The word "election" is a powerful and polemical term in theological circles. Those who have heard it used frequently and expounded at great length may be surprised to learn that it occurs only 6 times in the entire Bible (Rom. 9:11; 11:5, 7, 28; 1 Thess. 1:4; 2 Pet.

1:10). The Greek word is found also in Acts 9:15, where it is translated "chosen."

The term is *eklogē*. It signifies a "choice" or "selection" and is used this way in the papyri of the period. Because of the sometimes unfortunate theological overtones of "election," it is better to translate *eklogē* as "choice" (NASB).

6 *Followers* The Greek word *mimētai* is found seven times in the NT and always translated "followers" (KJV). It comes from *mimos*, "a mimic" or "an actor." Both the verb *mimeomai* and the noun *mimētēs* are used always in the NT in a good sense. "Followers" is not an adequate translation. The word *mimētai* should be rendered "imitators" (RSV, NASB, NIV).

7 *Ensamples* The Greek word is *typos*, from which comes "type." It is used in this sense in Rom. 5:14. But in a majority of instances in the NT it carries the connotation of "example" (so most translations here) or "pattern" (Weymouth). "Ensamples" is obviously an archaic form. Goppelt says that here it means "a model for others" (TDNT, 8:249).

8 *Sounded Out* The word *execheō* is found only here in the NT. It comes from *ex*, "out," and *echos* (Eng. "echo"), "noise" or "sound." Abbott-Smith says the verb means "*to sound forth* (as a trumpet, or thunder)" (p. 160). Milligan thinks of it here as "pointing to the clear, ringing nature of the report as of a trumpet" (p. 12). (Cf. "rang out," NEB, NIV.)

Spread Abroad The form here is *exelēlythen*, the perfect tense of *exerchomai*, which means "go out." So rather than "is spread abroad," the correct translation is: "has gone forth" (RSV, NASB).

9 Show The word *apangellō* is used "of a messenger, speaker, or writer, *to report, announce, declare*" (A-S, p. 14). It is obvious that "show" is hardly an exact rendering. More accurate is "report" (RSV, NASB, NIV).

Entering In The Greek word *eisodos* literally means "a way into." Here it signifies the act of entering. Probably the idea of the passage is well conveyed by "welcome" (RSV) or "reception" (NASB, NIV). However the same word is rendered "visit" (RSV, NIV) and "coming" (NASB) in 2:1.

10 Wait The term *anamenō* is found only here in the NT. It is a compound of *menō*, "remain," and *ana*, "up." Milligan comments: "The leading thought here seems to be to wait for one whose coming is expected . . . perhaps with the added idea of patience and confidence" (p. 14). Probably "await" (Weymouth) best conveys the meaning (so Abbott-Smith).

2:2 Suffered Before This is one word in Greek, *propathontes*, found only here in the NT. It is the second aorist participle of the verb *propaschō*, which literally means "suffer before." But "already suffered" (RSV, NASB) is smoother English. The fact that Paul had suffered at Philippi just before coming to Thessalonica (Acts 17) is brought out well by "just suffered" (C. B. Williams).

Shamefully Entreated This is a single term in Greek, the verb *hybrizō*. It is a strong word found five times in the NT (cf. Matt. 22:6; Luke 11:45; 18:32; Acts 14:5). It comes from *hybris*, the basic meaning of which was "insolence" or "insult." Thayer adds: "In Greek usage the mental injury and the wantonness of its infliction being prominent" (p. 633).

So the verb means: "treat in an arrogant or spiteful manner, mistreat, scoff at, insult" (AG, p. 839). Milligan comments: "More than the bodily suffering it was the personal indignity that had been offered to him as a Roman citizen . . . that had awakened a sense of *contumely* (humiliation) in St. Paul's mind" (p. 16). It may be that "insulted" (NIV) is the best rendering here.

With Much Contention The KJV gives an entirely wrong connotation. It suggests that Paul preached with a very contentious spirit. But the correct thought is "in spite of strong op-

position" (NIV) or "amid much opposition" (NASB).

Literally the text says "in much conflict" (*en pollō agōni*). The Greek word *agōn* (cf. "agony") was originally an athletic term, referring to the "contest" or "struggle" of the Olympic Games. The Christian life is compared to an athletic competition in which the participants strive to win. Christians need this same spirit if they are to be winners in the game of life.

3 Exhortation or Appeal? The word *paraklēsis* is difficult to translate into English. Occurring 29 times in the NT, it is rendered "consolation" (14 times), "exhortation" (8), "comfort" (6), and "intreaty" (1). It comes from the verb *parakaleō*, which literally means "call alongside (to help)." In the NT the verb carries three main connotations: beseech, comfort, exhort.

For this passage Thayer suggests that the meaning of the noun is: "persuasive discourse, stirring address—instructive, admonitory, consolatory; powerful hortatory discourse" (p. 483). Milligan says that *paraklēsis* "implies something more in the nature of an appeal . . . having for its object the direct benefit of those addressed, and which may be either hortatory or consolatory according to circumstances" (p. 17). It is interesting to note that the general word "appeal," suggested by Milligan, has been adopted for many translations (e.g., TCNT, Weymouth, Moffatt, Goodspeed, RSV, NEB, NIV).

Deceit The Greek word *planē* means: "*A wandering, a straying about*, whereby one, led astray from the right way, roams hither and thither. . . . In the N.T. metaphorically mental straying, i.e. *error, wrong opinion* relative to morals or religion" (Thayer, p. 514).

Milligan says that *planē* is used "apparently always in the N.T. in the passive sense of 'error' rather than in the active sense of 'deceit' " (pp. 17–18). The word "deceit" is a proper rendering of *dolos* ("guile") at the end of the verse (cf. NASB).

4 Allowed The KJV "allowed of God" is taken from Tyndale (1525), which surprisingly was followed by the Geneva Version (1560). More accurate was the first English Bible, that of Wyclif (1382), which had "preued" (proved). The Catholic Rheims Version (1609) was still better. It had "approved."

The Greek word is *dokimazō* in the perfect passive indicative. Thayer defines the verb as follows: "1. *to test, examine, prove, scrutinize* (to see whether a thing be genuine or not), as metals. . . . 2. *to recognize as genuine* after examination, *to approve, deem worthy.*" For this passage he suggests: "We have been approved by God to be intrusted with the business of pointing out to men the way of salvation" (p. 154). Arndt and Gingrich have: "We have been found worthy" (p. 201).

Milligan translates the clause: "But according as we have been approved by God," and comments: "*Dokimazō* means originally 'put to the test' . . . but in the N.T. generally conveys the added thought that the test has been successfully surmounted, in accordance with the technical use of the word to describe the passing as fit for election to a public office" (p. 18). Most recent translations correctly have "approved by God" in this passage.

It is the same verb, *dokimazō*, which is translated "trieth" at the end of this verse. A better rendering is "tests" (NIV). Because it is the present participle which is used here, a more adequate translation is: "who is continually testing our hearts" (NEB). Charles B. Williams brings out the double meaning of the verb in his rendering: "who proves and finds approved our hearts."

5 *Flattering* Lightfoot says of the Greek term here: "*Kolakeia*, a word which occurs here only in the New Testament, is defined both by Theophrastus . . . and Aristotle . . . to involve the idea of selfish motives. It is flattery not merely for the sake of giving pleasure to others but for the sake of self-interest" (p. 23).

In the same vein Milligan writes that *kolakeia* "carries with it the idea of tortuous methods by which one man seeks to gain influence over another, generally for selfish ends." He adds: "How easily such a charge might be brought against the Apostles is evident from what we know of the conduct of the heathen rhetoricians of the day" (p. 19).

Cloak Thayer defines the Greek word here, *prophasis*, as follows: "A pretext (alleged reason, pretended cause) . . . such as covetousness is wont to use, I Th. ii. 5 (. . . the meaning being, that he had never misused his apostolic office in order to disguise or hide avaricious designs)" (p. 552). Arndt and Gingrich note that originally the word *prophasis* meant "actual motive or reason, valid excuse," but that it soon came to mean "falsely alleged motive, pretext, ostensible reason, excuse"—and so here "pretext" (pp. 729–30). This is probably the best rendering.

6 *Burdensome* The Greek literally says "to be in a burden" (*baros*). Milligan gives a clear explanation of this word. He writes: "*Baros* is here understood (1) in its simple meaning of 'weight,' 'burden' . . . with reference to the Apostle's right of maintenance . . . or (2) in its derived sense of 'authority,' 'dignity' . . . pointing to the honour they might have expected to receive at the Thessalonians' hands" (p. 20). He goes on to say: "The two meanings are however compatible, and it is probable that St. Paul plays here on the double sense of the phrase" (pp. 20–21). Lightfoot agrees (p. 24).

The standard lexicons favor the second meaning here. For instance, Arndt and Gingrich have for this passage: "Wield authority, insist on one's importance" (p. 133). So also do most of the modern translations. Weymouth, for example, has: "We might have stood on our dignity" (cf. NASB—"We might have asserted our authority").

Schrenck says that "the reference can hardly be to financial cost . . . it is rather to conscious self-assertion. Though the apostle maintains his apostolic authority, he does not think it necessary to support it by a particularly imposing appearance" (TDNT, 1:556).

7 *Children* Some translations have "children" (KJV, C. B. Williams, Beck), from *epioi*; others have "gentle" (RSV, NEB, NASB, NIV), from *nepioi*. Undeniably the latter has the stronger support of the earliest manuscripts. But the former seems to fit better in the context. Milligan writes: "The reading here is doubtful. If *nēpioi* . . . be adopted, the whole clause is the avowal on the writers' part of their becoming as children to children, speaking . . . baby-language to those who were still babes in the faith. . . . On the other hand, if the well-attested *ēpioi* . . . be preferred, the Apostolic 'gentleness' is placed in striking contrast with the slanders that had been insinuated against them. . . . This agreement with the context leads most modern editors and commentators to favour *ēpioi*" (p. 21). However, Lightfoot seems to defend *nēpioi* (p. 24).

The extreme difficulty of deciding between these two readings is shown by the fact that of two equally good scholars, Moffatt has, "We behaved gently when we were among you," while Goodspeed has, "We were children when we were with you." Probably we shall prefer to go along with the majority of recent versions in reading "gentle" here. This fits perfectly with the next clause, "even as a nurse cherisheth her children."

Nurse The Greek word is *trophos* (only here in NT). It comes from the verb *trephō*, which means to give food to, and is used of a mother nursing a baby at her breast (Luke 23:29). So some (e.g., Weymouth, Moffatt, Goodspeed, C. B. Williams, NASB) prefer "nursing mother" here. But "nurse" is still widely used (e.g., RSV, Phillips, NEB). NIV has simply "mother."

Cherisheth Of the verb *thalpō* Thayer says: "1. properly *to warm, keep warm* . . . 2 . . . *to cherish* with tender love, *to foster* with tender care" (p. 282). The word is found only here and in Eph. 5:29. Probably the best translation for our day is "tenderly cares for" (NASB).

8 *Affectionately Desirous* The verb is *homeiromai*. It means "to desire earnestly, yearn after" (A-S, p. 316). Charles B. Williams gives the sense well: "We were yearning for you so tenderly."

9 *Labor and Travail* The first noun is *kopos*, the second *mochthos*. Lightfoot points out very well the distinction between the two when he writes: "*Kopos* (from *koptō*) is properly a 'blow' or 'bruise,' and hence signifies 'wear and tear,' the fatigue arising from continued labour, and hence the labor which brings on lassitude. In *mochthos* on the other hand the leading notion is that of struggling to overcome difficulties" (*Notes*, p. 26). Perhaps the best translation is "labor and hardship" (NASB) or "toil and hardship" (NIV).

Chargeable The Greek has the infinitive of the verb *epibareō*. This is from *baros*, the noun which occurs in verse 6 above. So it literally means "be a burden upon" (*epi*). Paul had labored and toiled night and day, so that he might not be a financial burden upon his first converts at Thessalonica. This shows the unselfish love and consecrated devotion of this man of God.

16 *Forbidding* The verb *kolyō* is translated "forbid" 17 times in the NT (KJV) and "hinder" only twice. Once (Rom. 1:13) it is rendered "let," which in modern language is just the opposite of what the Greek word means. It occurs also in Acts 11:17 ("withstand"), Acts 27:43 ("keep from"), and Heb. 7:23 ("not suffer").

The word comes from *kolos*, which means "lopped" or "clipped." So it literally means to "cut off" or "cut short," and so "to hinder, prevent, forbid" (Thayer, p. 367). It would seem that "hindering" is slightly more exact than "forbidding." In view of the fact that it is the present participle here, the most accurate translation may be: "trying to keep us from speaking" (C. B. Williams).

17 *Taken from* The word (only here in NT) is *aporphanizō*. It is compounded of *apo*, "away from," and the adjective "*orphanos*," meaning "orphan" or "fatherless." This adjective is used literally in Mark 12:40 and Jas. 1:27, and metaphorically in John 14:18 ("comfortless")—the only places in the NT where it occurs. So the verb means "to bereave of a parent" (Thayer, p. 67). Arndt and Gingrich say that the passive form here is used "figuratively, of the apostle separated from his church . . . *made orphans by separation from you*" (p. 97). Lightfoot seeks to bring out the full force by a double rendering: "bereft of and separated from" (*Notes*, p. 36).

Presence "In presence" is *prosōpō*, the dative of *prosōpon*, "face." Arndt and Gingrich translate the phrase here: "*orphaned by separation from you in person, not in heart* or *outwardly, not inwardly*" (p. 728). It would seem that "person" (NIV) is somewhat clearer than "presence."

Endeavored The verb *spoudazō* occurs 11 times in the NT and is translated 7 different ways in the KJV: "be forward" (Gal. 2:10); "endeavor" (Eph. 4:3; 1 Thess. 2:17; 2 Pet. 1:15); "study" (2 Tim. 2:15); "do diligence" (2 Tim. 4:9, 21); "be diligent" (Titus 3:12; 2 Pet. 3:14); "labor" (Heb. 4:11); "give diligence" (2 Pet. 1:10).

The literal meaning of *spoudazō* is "hasten" or "hurry," and so "be zealous or eager, take pains, make every effort" (AG, p. 771). Milligan comments on this passage: "a sense of *eagerness* being present in *espoudasamen*, which we do not usually associate with our English 'endeavored' (A.V., R.V.)" (p. 33). A good translation here is: "were all the more eager with great desire to see your face" (NASB).

18 *Would Have* The Greek literally says, "We wished (*ēthelēsamen*) to come to you." So the better rendering is "wanted to come" (Weymouth and most recent translations).

Once and Again The Greek is literally "once and twice" (*hapax kai dis*). It means "repeatedly." The best English rendering is "more than once" (TCNT, Moffatt, NEB, NASB) or "again and again" (Weymouth, Goodspeed, RSV, NIV).

Hindered This is not the same Greek word which we translated "hindering" in verse 16. Here it is *enkoptō*. Thayer gives this definition: "*to cut into, to impede one's course by cutting off his way;* hence universally to *hinder*" (p. 166). Arndt and Gingrich give: "hinder, thwart" (p. 215).

Stahlin notes that this word "took on its main sense of 'obstacle' . . . from the military practice of making slits in the street to hold up a pursuing enemy. Hence the basic meaning is 'to block the way' " (TDNT, 3:855). He also says that "the term is used in the metaphor of running on the racetrack" (p. 856). So it would seem that the best translation is "thwarted" (NEB, NASB).

19 Crown The word is *stephanos*, already noted in Phil. 4:1. Abbott-Smith gives this full definition: "1. *that which surrounds* or *encompasses* (as a wall, a crowd: Homer, others). 2. *a crown*, i.e. the wreath, garland or chaplet given as a prize for victory, as a festal ornament, or as a public honour for distinguished service or personal worth (so to sovereigns, especially on the occasion of a *parousia*)" (p. 417).

Rejoicing The Greek word *kauchēsis* occurs 12 times in the NT. In the KJV it is translated "boasting" 6 times and "rejoicing" 4 times. Thayer defines the term as "the act of glorying" and thinks the meaning of the two Greek words here is "crown of which we can boast" (p. 342). Arndt and Gingrich say: "*crown of pride*, i.e. to be proud of" (p. 427). (Cf. NEB.) Some versions prefer "boasting" (e.g., RSV). But it seems to us that "exultation" (NASB) expresses better the point of view of the apostle (cf. NIV).

3:1, 5 Forbear The verb *stegō* comes from the noun *stegē*, which means "roof." So it signifies: "1. *to protect* or *keep by covering, to preserve* . . . 2. *to cover over with silence: to keep secret; to hide, conceal* . . . 3. *by covering to keep off* something which threatens, *to bear up against, hold out against*, and *so to endure, bear, forbear*" (Thayer, p. 586). This is an excellent example of the way words change their meanings in the course of time.

This verb is found elsewhere in the NT only in 1 Cor. 9:12; 13:7. There, as here, it seems to carry the third sense given above. For the fifth verse of this chapter Arndt and Gingrich have: "since I could not bear it any longer" (p. 773). Kasch writes: "Paul, impelled by his missionary task, can no longer bear not to have an influence on the development of the young church in Thessalonica" (TDNT, 7:586).

1 To Be Left One of the weaknesses of the KJV is its failure, in many cases, to distinguish between simple verbs and their compounds. *Leipō* means "leave." But the verb here is *kataleipō*, which means "leave behind." What it implies in this passage is expressed well by Moffatt: "Paul shrank from loneliness, especially where there was little or no Christian fellowship; but he would not gratify himself at the expense of the Thessalonians. Their need of Timothy must take precedence of his" (EGT, 4:31). So he sent Timothy to them, and stayed behind in Athens alone, with only Silas as a companion. Calvin comments: "It is . . . a sign of unusual affection and anxious desire that he is willing to deprive himself of all consolation for the purpose of succouring the Thessalonians" (p. 352).

2 Establish The verb *stērizō* is thus defined by Thayer: "a. *to make stable, place firmly, set fast, fix* . . . b. *to strengthen, make firm;* tropically [figuratively] (not so in profane authors) *to render constant, confirm, one's mind*" (p. 588). Most recent translations have "strengthen."

Comfort This is again the verb *parakaleō*. While it may be rendered "exhort" (RSV), most translators prefer "encourage." That seems to fit best here. It combines the ideas of "comfort" and "exhort."

3 Moved This might seem like a simple verb, but its meaning is a bit complicated. *Sainō* originally was used, as in Homer and in Aesop's fables, for a dog wagging its tail. Thus it came to mean "fawn," as a dog does when it wags its tail and meekly lowers its head. The term was then employed in a metaphorical sense for persons who "fawn upon, flatter, beguile" (A-S, p. 400). And so Milligan comments: "What the Apostles evidently dreaded regarding the Thessalonians was that they would allow themselves to be 'drawn aside,' 'allured' from the right path in the midst of (*en*) the afflictions . . . which were then . . . falling upon them" (p. 38).

Lightfoot follows the same trail. He says that *sainō* signifies "fondle, caress, flatter, coax, wheedle, allure, fascinate, deceive," and adds: "This seems to be the meaning here; 'that no one, in the midst of these troubles, desert the rough path of the truth, drawn aside and allured by the enticing prospect of an easier life' " (*Notes*, p. 42). Frame agrees with this (p. 128).

Arndt and Gingrich come to a different conclusion. After noting that many prefer "so that no one might be deceived," they say: "However, a more suitable meaning is the one preferred without exception by the ancient versions and the Greek interpreters [Church Fathers]: *move, disturb, agitate . . . so that no one might be shaken or disturbed*" (p. 747). On the other hand, Lightfoot asserts that no passages in Greek literature can be cited which bear this meaning.

This difference of opinion is reflected in modern translations. One finds "shaken" (TCNT, NEB), "disturbed" (Moffatt, NASB), and "moved" (RSV) on the one hand, and "led astray" (Goodspeed) or "deceived" (C. B. Williams) on the other. It is very difficult to decide the matter. But in view of the total scholarship represented on the translation committees of the RSV and the NEB, it would seem the part of wisdom to settle in favor of "moved" or "shaken." It should be noted that "beguiled away" is given as an alternative in the margin of NEB. The NIV has "unsettled."

6 Brought Us Good Tidings This is the verb *euangelizō*. Its most common rendering in the NT (KJV) is "preach" (23 times), or "preach the gospel" (22 times). But here and in Luke 1:19 it is used in the literal sense of "bring good tidings" (or "good news"). Of course, that is what the preaching of the gospel is—good news for the needy sinner.

10 Perfect The verb is *katartizō*. Thayer notes that it means "properly to *render artios* i.e. *fit, sound, complete . . .* hence a. *to mend* (what has been broken or rent), *to repair . . .* to *complete*" (p. 336)—as in this passage. Arndt and Gingrich also give "complete" for this place (p. 418). Milligan notes that the verb "is used in the N.T. especially by St. Paul and in the Epistle to the Hebrews in the general sense of 'prepare' or 'perfect' anything for its full destination or use" (p. 42). Lightfoot comments: "This sense of completion is borne out by the not uncommon application of *katartizein* to military and naval preparation, e.g. in Polybius, where it is used of manning a fleet . . . of supplying an army with provisions" (*Notes*, p. 47). So the NIV has "supply."

4:2 Commandments Thayer says that *parangelia* properly means "announcement, a proclaiming or giving a message to," and so "a charge, command" (p. 479). It was used by Xenophon for a military order and by Aristotle for instruction. Arndt and Gingrich think that here is meant "instructions" (p. 618).

Milligan comments: "*Parangelia . . .* is found elsewhere in the Pauline Epistles only in I Tim. i. 5, 18, where it refers to the whole practical teaching of Christianity. Here the plural points rather to special precepts . . . or rules of living, which the writers had laid down when in Thessalonica, and which they had referred to the Lord Jesus . . . as the medium through whom alone they could be carried into effect" (p. 47).

4 Vessel Paul wants every one of his readers to "know how to possess his vessel in sanctification and honour." But what does "vessel" mean? The most natural answer would seem to be that it refers to the physical body. This is the interpretation of several recent translations— "learn to control his body" (Phillips); "learn to gain mastery over his body" (NEB, cf. NIV).

On the other hand, a large number of modern versions have "take a wife," or its equivalent. This is the rendering of Weymouth, Moffatt, Goodspeed, C. B. Williams, RSV, Beck. Why?

The answer lies partly in the true meaning of "possess." The Greek verb is *ktaomai*. It means "to procure for oneself, get, gain, acquire" (A-S, p. 259). One does not acquire a body, but he does acquire a wife.

The word *skeuos* (vessel) has a variety of uses—for containers, household utensils, etc. But it is clearly used for one's wife in 1 Pet. 3:7. On the other hand, it is rather obviously used for the human body in 2 Cor. 4:7. Which does it mean here?

Frame translates the passage: "That each of you get in marriage his own wife" (p. 150). He calls attention, as do others, to the fact that the verb *ktasthai* is used in both classical Greek and the Septuagint for getting a wife.

Milligan writes of this interpretation:

> The latter view, advocated by Theodore of Mopsuestia . . . and St. Augustine . . . has been adopted by the great majority of modern commentators, principally it would appear on account of the objections that can be urged against the former. But though supported by certain Rabbinic parallels . . . it is not, it will be admitted, at first sight the natural view, and is suggestive of a lower view of the marriage-state than one would expect in a passage specially directed to enforcing its sanctity. . . . On the whole therefore it seems better to revert to the meaning 'his own body' which was favoured by the Greek commentators generally" (pp. 48–49).

The matter must be left open.

Maurer comments: "The most probable interpretation of 1 Th. 4:3f. is as follows: '. . . that every one of you know how to hold his own vessel in sanctification and honour (i.e., live with his wife in sanctification and honour).' . . . Material as well as linguistic considerations favour 'wife' rather than 'body' in interpretation of 1 Th. 4:4" (TDNT, 7:366–67).

5 *Lust* The Greek word is *pathos*, found elsewhere in the NT only in Rom. 1:26 and Col. 3:5. In both of those it is rendered "affection." But the best translation is "passion."

Concupiscence The word *epithymia* is generally translated "lust" in the KJV. While "desire" is preferable in some instances, "lust" seems to fit best here. So the phrase would mean "passion of lust" (RSV). Arndt and Gingrich suggest "lustful passion" (cf. Weymouth, NASB), but the NIV has "passionate lust."

6 *Any Matter* The Greek has simply *en tō pragmati*, "in the matter" (cf. NASB). There is no support for "any matter" (KJV). The context clearly suggests that the meaning is "this matter"; that is, the matter of fornication or adultery. Frame, quoting Lillie, would broaden it to be "a euphemistic generalization for all sorts of uncleanness" (p. 152).

7 *Holiness* The word *hagiasmos* occurs 10 times in the NT and is translated "holiness" 5 times and "sanctification" 5 times. It has already occurred twice in this chapter (vv. 3, 4) where it is rendered "sanctification." But here it is "holiness." Which is preferable?

The word comes from the verb *hagiazō*, which means "sanctify." So it properly means "sanctification." There are other words (*hagiotēs, hagiosynē*) which signify the resultant state of holiness. Even though *hagiasmos* sometimes is used for the latter, it would seem better to translate it "sanctification." Here it is literally "in sanctification."

8 *Despiseth* The verb is *atheteō*. Out of the 16 times it occurs in the NT it is translated "despise" 8 times and "reject" 4 times. But the latter is more accurate. Thayer gives for this passage: "to reject, refuse, slight" (p. 14). It literally means "declare invalid, nullify, set aside," and so "reject, not recognize" (AG, p. 20). Abbott-Smith gives for this passage "reject" (p. 11). The reference is to those who deliberately reject God's prescribed way of holy living.

9 *Brotherly Love* The Greek word *philadelphia* is found six times in the NT (Rom. 12:10; 1 Thess. 4:9; Heb. 13:1; 1 Pet. 1:22; 2 Pet. 1:7, twice). It was adopted by William Penn and his Quaker associates as the name for the new city which they founded as a haven of rest for persecuted people of Europe. Incidentally, Philadelphia was the first capital of the United States (1781–1800). In the NT the word refers to the love of Christian brethren for each other.

_Of_ The most overworked term in the KJV is the little word "of." It is used repeatedly in places where modern English usage would employ other prepositions.

"Taught of God" is one word in Greek—*theodidaktos*, from *theos*, "God," and *didaskō*, "teach." It is found only here in the NT. The correct translation is "taught by God."

11 *Study* The word "study" occurs only here and in 2 Tim. 2:15, where it is a translation of *spoudazō*, "hasten, be eager." Here the Greek word is *philotimeomai*. It is compounded of *philos*, "love," and *timē*, "honor." So it literally means "to love or seek after honour," and hence "to be ambitious" (A-S, p. 471). Lightfoot suggests: "to make the pursuit of a thing one's earnest endeavour" (p. 61).

We would take issue with Phillips' rendering: "Make it your ambition to have no ambition!" This would be all right if revised to read: "no self-ambition." A preacher with no ambition to be and do something for God's cause does not belong in the pulpit or pastorate.

The verb here occurs elsewhere in the NT in Rom. 15:20 ("strived") and 2 Cor. 5:9 ("labour"). This is another example of how frequently the KJV translates the same Greek word differently in various locations. This shows the inadequacy of using an English concordance to trace words through the NT. For the one who knows Greek, the *Englishman's Greek Concordance* is an invaluable tool. For those who do not use Greek, the same task can be accomplished, with somewhat more labor, by using Strong's *Exhaustive Concordance* or Young's *Analytical Concordance*. The latter is a bit easier to use.

12 *Honestly* The adverb *euschemonōs* occurs elsewhere in the NT only in Rom. 13:13 ("honestly") and 1 Cor. 14:40 ("decently"). It comes from the adjective *euschemon*, which means: "of elegant figure, shapely, graceful, comely, bearing one's self becomingly in speech or behavior" (Thayer, p. 263). Arndt and Gingrich think that "walk honestly" is best translated "behave decently" (p. 327). The KJV "honestly" comes from the Latin Vulgate *honeste*. The etymology of the Greek term would suggest that the best translation here is "becomingly" (Weymouth). Greeven says that it "denotes the external aspect of the Christian life" (TDNT, 2:771).

Nothing The KJV translates the Greek word as "nothing," while the RSV has "nobody." Which is correct?

The answer is that both are equally accurate translations. The Greek form *mēdenos* may be either masculine or neuter. Frame properly observes: "Nor does it matter logically, for in either case the reference is to dependence upon the brotherhood for support. . . . Contextually, the masculine is probable" (p. 163). What Paul is saying is that Christians should attend to their own business, earn their own living, and not be dependent on others for support.

13, 14, 15 *Asleep* The verb *koimaomai* occurs 18 times in the NT. In 4 instances (Matt. 28:13; Luke 22:45; John 11:12; Acts 12:16) it is used in the literal sense of "be asleep." But in all the other cases it is used metaphorically and euphemistically for being dead. (In 1 Cor. 7:39 it is translated "be dead.") This use of sleep for death goes as far back as Homer's *Iliad*. But there is one marked difference here: the Christians "sleep in Jesus." In the resurrection they will awaken to live forever with Him.

15, 17 *Remain* Half a dozen different Greek words are translated "remain" in the KJV. The one found here, and only here in the NT, is *perileipō*. It comes from *peri*, "around," and *leipō*, "leave." So it means "left around" or "left behind" (C. B. Williams).

15 *Prevent* The word is *phthanō*. In classical Greek it meant "to come before, precede." Thayer interprets this passage as meaning: "We shall not get the start of those who have fallen asleep, i.e., we shall not attain to the fellowship of Christ sooner than the dead, nor have precedence in blessedness" (p. 652).

Because there is a double negative in the Greek preceding the verb, Arndt and Gingrich have: "We will by no means precede those who have fallen asleep" (p. 864). The Jews held the view that a special blessedness attached to those who were alive at the setting up of the Messianic kingdom. A similar belief was found in the Early Church (e.g., Clementine, *Recognitions*). Paul is here emphatically refuting any such idea.

The word "prevent" comes from the Latin *prevenio*, which means "go before." But today "prevent" means "hinder" or "stop," which is not at all the idea here. It is interesting to note that Lightfoot still used "prevent" as the proper translation in his day (he died in 1889). But the ASV (1901) correctly gave "precede."

16 *Shout* The Greek word (only here in NT) is *keleusma*. It comes from *keleuō*, which means "command (mostly of one in authority)." So the noun signifies: "a call, summons, shout of command" (A-S, p. 244). It is used in Herodotus for the word of command in battle. So it appears that the best translation here is "with a cry of command" (RSV, Arndt and Gingrich).

5:1 *Times, Seasons* The first noun is *chronos*, from which comes "chronology." It means: "*Time*, mostly in the sense *a period of time*" (AG, p. 896). The term occurs 53 times in the NT. It is rendered "time" 33 of these, and "season" four.

The second noun is *kairos*. It is found 86 times and is translated "time" in 63 of these and "season" in 13.

The same combination of words is found in Acts 1:7, where Jesus said to His disciples: "It is not for you to know the times or the seasons, which the Father hath put in his own power." Yet in a general way, Paul declares, Christians are aware of the times and seasons.

Kairos is a more distinctive term than *chronos*, as shown by its rendering in these two passages. Trench points out the difference as follows: "*Chronos* is time, contemplated simply as such; the succession of moments. . . . *Kairos* . . . is time as it brings forth its several births" (p. 210). Commenting on Acts 1:7, he writes: " 'The times' (*chronoi*) are, in Augustine's words 'ipsa spatia temporum,' and these contemplated merely under the aspect of their duration, over which the Church's history should extend: but 'the seasons' (*kairoi*) are the joints or articulations in these times, the critical epoch-making periods foreordained of God" (p. 311).

Abbott-Smith summarizes well the early history of *kairos*: "1. *due measure, fitness, proportion* (Euripides, Xenophon, others). 2. Of Time (classical also) in the sense of a fixed and definite period, *time, season*" (p. 226). Arndt and Gingrich say that *kairos* means "*point of time* as well as period of time" (p. 395). They define it as "the right, proper, favorable time"—and so it may be translated "opportunity" in some passages in the NT—and so as "definite, fixed time can also refer to the last things, hence *kairos* becomes . . . one of the chief eschatological terms, *ho kairos, the time of crisis, the last times*" (pp. 395–96). On Acts 1:7 and this passage they say: "*Times and seasons*, which must be completed before the final consummation" (p. 396).

Delling notes that the sense of the "decisive moment" is found in Greek philosophers from the time of Sophocles. The Pythagoreans placed especially strong emphasis on *kairos*. In the Septuagint the term is used for the "decisive point of time," though not as markedly as in later Christian writings. In the NT it means: "The 'fateful and decisive point,' with strong, though not always explicit, emphasis (except at Acts 24:25) on the fact that it is ordained by God" (TDNT, 3:459).

Lightfoot sums up well the difference between these two terms. He writes: "Here *chronoi* denotes the period which must elapse before and in the consummation of this great event, in other words it points to the date: while *kairoi* refers to the occurrences which will mark the occasion, the signs by which its approach will be ushered in" (p. 71).

It is interesting to note that in modern Greek *chronos* means "year," that is, a measurement of time, whereas *kairos* means "weather." This follows out of the idea of "season."

3 Safety The Greek word is *asphaleia*. It first meant "firmness," then "certainty" (Luke 1:4), and finally "security" (Acts 5:23; 1 Thess. 5:3; not elsewhere in NT). In the papyri it is used as a law term, in the sense of "proof, security" (A-S, p. 66). Moulton and Milligan say: "The noun occurs innumerable times in the commercial sense, 'a security' " (VGT, p. 88).

Many recent translations use "security" here instead of "safety." In this day of constant emphasis on "social security" and "national security" it would seem that this rendering is more meaningful. No vaunted "security" can guarantee against sudden disaster.

Sudden The adjective *aiphnidios* means "unexpected, sudden, unforeseen" (Thayer, p. 18). It is difficult to bring this out in a simple English translation. The word occurs elsewhere in the NT only in Luke 21:34, where it is rendered "unawares." Here it probably means that the destruction will come both suddenly and unexpectedly.

5 Children The Greek word is *huioi*, which means "sons," not *techna*, which is the proper word for "children." "Sons of light" (so most recent translations) is a Hebrew idiom, meaning people who have the character of light. This fea-

ture occurs many times in the NT. We read of "sons of the kingdom" (Matt. 8:12), "son of Gehenna" (Matt. 21:5), a "son of peace" (Luke 10:6), "sons of this age" (Luke 16:8), "sons of truth" (Eph. 2:2). The very expression here, "sons of light," is found in Luke 16:8. They are contrasted with the "sons of this age." As sons of God we are sons of light, for "God is light" (1 John 1:5).

6 Watch The verb *grēgoreō* means "to be awake," as well as "watch." In view of the previous part of the verse—"Therefore let us not sleep, as do others"—it seems evident that the best translation here is "keep awake" (RSV). The same verb is translated "wake" in verse 10, where it means "alive," not sleeping in death.

Be Sober The verb *nephō* was originally used in a literal sense of abstaining from drinking wine. But in the NT it is employed only in the figurative sense, "Be free from every form of mental and spiritual 'drunkenness,' from excess, passion, rashness, confusion, etc., *be well-balanced, self-controlled*" (AG, p. 540).

11 Edify The verb is *oikodomeō*. It comes from *oikos*, "house," and *demo*, "build." So at first it means "build a house." Then it came to be used in the general sense of "build." Probably "build each other up" (NIV) is more meaningful today than "edify one another."

12 Know Here we have the infinitive of *oida*, which ordinarily means "know." But Thayer says that in this passage it is used Hebraistically in the sense of "to have regard for one, cherish, pay attention to" (p. 174). Abbott-Smith also notes that it is found here "in unique sense of *respect, appreciate*" (p. 311). For this verse Arndt and Gingrich give "respect."

Lightfoot holds that the word here means " '*to know*,' with a pregnant meaning, i.e. 'to see in their true character, to recognize the worth of, to appreciate, to value' " (p. 79). Milligan agrees that this is "evidently" the sense here, though he declares that it is "a usage of the word for which no adequate parallel has yet been produced from classical or Biblical Greek" (p. 71).

Apparently the best translation is "respect" (Weymouth, Moffatt, Goodspeed, RSV, NIV) or "appreciate" (NASB, Beck).

14 Warn It is the same verb here that is translated "admonish" in verse 12. Why not here also?

Noutheteō is compounded of *nous*, "mind,"

and *tithēmi*, "place" or "put." So it literally means "put in mind." Abbott-Smith gives: "To admonish, exhort" (p. 305). Arndt and Gingrich have: "admonish, warn, instruct" (p. 546).

Unruly The adjective is *ataktos*, found only here in the NT. It is derived from alpha-negative, and the verb *tassō*, "draw up in order" or "arrange." So it means "disorderly, out of the ranks" (Thayer, p. 83).

From the adjective *ataktos* comes the adverb *ataktōs*, found in 2 Thess. 3:6, 11, and the verb *atakteō*, which occurs only in 2 Thess. 3:7. It is a striking fact that all three of these cognate terms are found only in the Thessalonian letters, the main emphasis of which is on preparation for the Second Coming. So the words must be interpreted in that light.

These three cognate terms are treated at considerable length in an additional note by Milligan. He starts with the adjective, "which means primarily 'out of order,' 'out of place,' and hence . . . is readily employed as a military term to denote a soldier who does not keep the ranks, or an army advancing in disarray." He goes on to say: "From this the transition is easy to disorderly or irregular living of any kind as in Plato's reference to *ataktoi hēdonai* . . . or in Plutarch's rebuke to those who, neglecting a 'sane and well-ordered life' . . . hurl themselves headlong into 'disorderly and brutal pleasures' " (p. 152).

Of the verb Milligan writes: "Like its adjective, it is frequently applied to soldiers marching out of order, or quitting the ranks, and hence is extended to every one who does not perform his proper duty" (p. 153).

Especially interesting and illuminating are two examples of the use of *atakteō* in the papyri. The first is in an Oxyrhynchus papyrus of A.D. 66, about 15 years after Paul wrote to the Thessalonians. It is a contract of apprenticeship. The boy's father agrees not to take away his son during the period specified. There is also the further stipulation that if there are any days on which the boy "plays the truant" (*ataktese*), the father is to return him for an equivalent number of days after the regular period has ended (p. 153).

The second Oxyrhynchus papyrus is dated about 120 years later. In it there is the specification that a weaver's apprentice is permitted to have 20 holidays in the year, "but if he exceeds this number of days from idleness (*ataktese*) or ill-health or any other reason," he must make up his absences without added pay (p. 154).

Milligan concludes: "If then these instances can be taken as typical of the ordinary colloquial sense of the verb, we can understand how readily St. Paul would employ it to describe those members of the Thessalonian Church who, without any intention of actual wrongdoing, were neglecting their daily duties, and falling into idle and careless habits, because of their expectation of the immediate Parousia of the Lord" (*ibid.*).

It is doubtless in the light of this papyrus usage that Arndt and Gingrich, after noting that *ataktos* means "disorderly, subordinate," conclude: "The sense *idle, lazy* is to be preferred here" (p. 119). It is also in line with this that Moffatt translates the clause, "keep a check on loafers"; and Goodspeed, "warn the idlers" (cf. RSV, NIV).

Feebleminded The word is *oligopsychos* (only here in NT). It is composed of *oligos*, "little," and *psychē*, "soul." So it might literally be rendered "little-souled." But all authorities agree that the correct meaning is "fainthearted." The rendering most widely used today is: "Encourage the fainthearted."

23 *Wholly* Sometimes we are asked: "Where do you get the expression, 'entire sanctification'? I don't find it in the New Testament."

The answer is 1 Thess. 5:23—"The very God of peace sanctify [aorist tense] you wholly." The last word is *holoteleis* (only here in NT).

It is compounded of *holos*—"whole, entire, complete"—and *telos*, "end." So it would require some such hyphenated expression as "wholly-completely" or "completely-entirely" to bring out the full force of this compound adjective. Martin Luther translated it *durch und durch*, "through and through" (cf. NIV).

Whole The word is *holoklēros*. This is a compound of *holos* and *klēros*, "lot." Thayer defines it as "complete in all its parts, in no part wanting or unsound, complete, entire, whole," and says that in this passage it should be taken ethically as meaning "free from sin, faultless" (p. 443). Arndt and Gingrich translate it: "May your spirit be preserved complete or sound" (p. 567).

2 Thessalonians

1:3 **Bound** The first part reads literally: "We are obligated to give thanks to God always for you, brothers, even as it is fitting." The thought of this passage is expressed strikingly in the liturgy of the Church of England: "It is very meet, right, and our bounden duty that we should at all times and in all places give thanks."

The verb "be obligated" is *opheilō*, which originally meant to owe someone a financial debt. It is translated "owe" in Rom. 13:8. So here it carries a strong sense of obligation. Thayer says that when it is followed by an infinitive (as here) it means "to be under obligation, bound by duty or necessity, to do something" (p. 469).

Meet The word is *axios*. It is translated "worthy" (KJV) in 35 out of 41 of its occurrences in the NT. But when used impersonally, as here, it means "fitting" or "proper."

Aboundeth Paul uses two strong verbs. He says that the faith of the Thessalonian believers grows abundantly and their love superabounds.

The first word, *hyperauxanō*, is found only here in the NT. The simple verb *auxanō* occurs 22 times. Twelve of these times it is rendered "grow," and 7 times "increase." The compound here means "to increase beyond measure" (A-S), or "grow wonderfully, increase abundantly" (AG). The Greek *hyper* is equivalent to the Latin *super*.

The second term, *pleonazō*, is found 9 times. It may be translated either "abound" or "superabound." Of these two verbs Lightfoot writes: "The words *hyperauxanei* and *pleonaxei* are carefully chosen; the former implying an internal, organic growth as of a tree; the other a

diffusive, or expansive character, as of a flood irrigating the land" (p. 98).

5 Manifest Token The word *endeigma* (only here in NT) comes from *endeiknymi* (11 times), which means "to mark, point out" and in the middle "to show forth, prove" (A-S). The patient endurance and faith of the Thessalonian Christians was a clear evidence of God's righteous judgment which would be poured out on their persecutors. The best translation here is "evidence" or "proof."

6 Tribulation, Trouble The use of these two words fails to bring out the connection in the Greek. The noun is *thlipsis*, the verb *thlibō* (same in v. 7). The literal meaning of the verb is "*to press* (as grapes), *press hard upon*" (Thayer). Metaphorically it means "to trouble, afflict, distress" (*ibid.*). The best way to indicate that the noun and the verb have the same root is to translate the phrase: "Repay with affliction those who afflict you" (RSV, NASB).

7 Rest A superficial reading of KJV might suggest that "rest" is a verb. But it is the noun *anesis*. Literally it means "a loosening, relaxation," but here "relief" from afflictions (A-S). Arndt and Gingrich translate the whole expression: "Grant, in turn, rest to those who are oppressed." Either "rest" or "relief" (NIV) fits well. But the contrast with "afflictions" somewhat favors the latter (cf. NASB).

9 Be Punished "Be punished" is in the Greek a combination of verb and noun. The verb *tinō* (only here in NT) means "pay."

Dikē has an interesting history, as given by Thayer. First it meant "custom" or "usage," then "right" or "justice." Then it came to have the technical meaning of "a suit at law." The next step was "a judicial hearing, judicial decision," especially "a sentence of condemnation." The final step was "execution of the sentence, punishment" (p. 151).

So the noun and verb together mean "pay the penalty" or "suffer punishment." The judicial sentence is "everlasting destruction from the presence [literally, 'face'] of the Lord."

10 *Admired* The verb is *thaumazō*. Occurring 46 times in the NT, it is translated (KJV) "marvel" 30 times and "wonder" 14 times. Only here is it rendered "admire," and once "have in admiration" (Jude 16). It is obvious that this is not its usual meaning.

The word is found most frequently in the Gospels (33 times), where it expresses the wonder and amazement caused by Jesus' miracles. It seems clear that the idea of wonder or astonishment is inherent in the term. The best translation here is "marveled at" (ASV, RSV, NASB, NIV).

2:1 *Beseech* The original meaning of *erōtaō* was "ask" in the sense of "ask a question." This is found not only in Homer but also in the papyri and nearly always in the Septuagint. It carries the same connotation regularly in the Gospels. But in the rest of the NT, except for Acts 1:6, its predominant meaning is "to request." Thus it becomes almost equivalent to *aiteō*. Greeven points out the slight difference thus: "In distinction from *aiteō*, which often suggests a claim or passion, *erōtaō* denotes a genuine request which is humble or courteous" (TDNT, 2:686).

2 *Troubled* The verb *throeō* comes from a noun meaning "tumult." In classical Greek it was used in the active with the sense of "cry aloud, make an outcry." In the NT it is always passive and means "*to be troubled*, as by an alarm" (A-S). Thayer suggests: "to be troubled in mind, to be frightened, alarmed" (p. 292). For this passage Arndt and Gingrich give, "*be disturbed* or frightened" (p. 364).

Attention should be called to the fact that this verb is in the present, whereas the previous one (shaken) is in the aorist tense. Milligan observes: "The present tense should be noted as pointing to a continued state of agitation following upon a shock received" (p. 96).

Is at Hand The Greek has *enestēken*. This verb literally means "to place in." For this passage Thayer suggests "to be upon, impend, threaten." Abbott-Smith prefers "to be pres-

ent." Arndt and Gingrich render the expression here: "The day of the Lord has come." Milligan agrees: "as if the day of the Lord is now present" (p. 97). He comments: "The verb is very common in the papyri and inscriptions with reference to the *current* year." Perhaps the best translation is "has already come" (NIV).

3 *A Falling Away* The KJV says "a falling away." But the Greek has *hē apostasia*, "The Apostasy." The noun occurs only here and in Acts 21:21. In the latter passage it is translated "to forsake." Abbott-Smith defines the term as follows: "defection, apostasy, revolt." Lightfoot writes: "The word implies that the opposition contemplated by St. Paul springs up from within rather than from without. In other words, it must arise either from the Jews or from apostate Christians, either of whom might be said to fall away from God" (p. 111).

This emphasis on an apostasy from within takes on added significance in the light of recent developments in the church world. There was a day when the Bob Ingersolls railed and ranted against Christianity. Now this opposition comes from within the church. When teachers of theology in leading theological seminaries in America tell their ministerial students that God is dead, and when a prominent denominational leader declares that it is a sin to believe in individual salvation, it would seem that "The Apostasy" has come.

Sin Instead of "man of sin" the two oldest Greek manuscripts have "man of lawlessness"—*anomias* rather than *hamartias*. It is the same word (*anomias*) which is translated "iniquity" in verse 7—"mystery of iniquity." Furthermore "that Wicked" in verse 8 is in the Greek "the Lawless One"—*ho anomos*. This striking connection in these three verses is entirely lost to the readers of the KJV. Those who are dependent on the KJV are deprived all too often of both the accuracy and the richness of a correct translation of the best Greek text.

Again we should note the application to the present day. Never before has there been such a spirit of lawlessness in the United States as we are witnessing now. It stalks our streets and ravages our university campuses. Apostasy in the church and lawlessness in the land—these are two dominant features of American life today.

Perdition The Greek word is *apōleias*. It comes from the verb *apollumi*, which means "perish." Frame (p. 254) notes that the phrase *ho huios tēs apōleias* ("the son of perdition") equals *ho apollumenos* (literally, "the perishing one"). The latter expression is found in the plural in verse 10—*tois apollumenois* ("in them that perish"; literally, "in those who are perishing"). So it would seem that the best translation here is "the son of perishing" or "the son of destruction."

What does this mean? Frame says the phrase is "a Hebraism indicating the one who belongs to the class destined to destruction, as opposed to the class destined to salvation" (*ibid.*).

Thayer gives the passive meaning of *apōleia* as "a perishing, ruin, destruction" (p. 70). Arndt and Gingrich note that in the New Testament the term is used "especially of eternal destruction as punishment for the wicked" (p. 103). Oepke writes: "What is meant here is not a simple extinction of existence, but an everlasting state of torment and death" (TDNT, 1:397). It should be noted that exactly the same phrase is used for Judas Iscariot in John 17:12.

6–7 *Letteth* A typical vagary of translation in the KJV is found in verses 6 and 7. Exactly the same verb is translated "withholdeth" in verse 6 and "letteth" in verse 7. Neither rendering is correct today, though "withholdeth" comes closer.

The word is *katechō*. It means "to hold back, detain, restrain" (A-S, p. 241). Here it indicates "to restrain, hinder" (Thayer, p. 339).

The present participle (continuous action) is used in both verses. But in verse 6 the form is neuter, while in verse 7 it is masculine. Arndt and Gingrich correctly give the meaning as "that which restrains" and "he who restrains"; that is, "what prevents the adversary of God from coming out in open opposition to him, for the time being" (p. 423). They note that both the ancient church fathers and present-day interpreters take verse 6 as referring to the Roman Empire and verse 7 to the emperor. This would be the first application. Theodore of Mopsuestia referred verse 6 to the preaching of Christian missionaries and verse 7 to the Apostle Paul. Chrysostom mentions the Holy Spirit as the One who restrains. Does the passage mean that the Holy Spirit in the Church is restraining lawlessness in this age and that when He leaves this world in the rapture of the saints the man of lawlessness (the Antichrist) will be revealed? One cannot be dogmatic in insisting that only one possible interpretation is correct. But this is at least a live option.

8 *Spirit* It is stated that the Lord will consume the lawless one with the "spirit" of His mouth. It is true that *pneuma* is almost always translated "ghost" or "spirit" in the NT. However, in John 3:8 it is rendered "wind"—"The wind blows where it wishes." The word *pneuma* comes from the verb *pneō* ("bloweth" in John 3:8). So the earliest meaning was "wind," then "breath." Then it came to signify "the spirit, i.e. the vital principle by which the body is animated" (Thayer, p. 520). When one breathes his last breath, the spirit leaves the body.

But the meaning which seems to fit best here, as Arndt and Gingrich note, is "the breathing out of air, blowing, breath" (p. 680). Christ, as it were, will blow His consuming breath upon the Antichrist, destroying him.

Incidentally "destroy" here is *katargeō*, which is translated the same way in Rom. 6:6. Some have argued for a weaker rendering there. But probably no one would deny that "destroy" is correct here, and the context of Rom. 6:6 demands it there.

Brightness, Coming Here we find two of the three words used in the NT for Christ's second coming. The most common term for this is *parousia*, translated "coming." The other is *epiphaneia*, rendered "brightness." (The third is *apocalypsis*, "revelation," taken over into English as *apocalypse*.)

In the NT, *epiphaneia* is found elsewhere only in the three Pastoral Epistles, where it is always translated (five times) "appearing." It comes from the verb *epiphainō*, which means "appear, become visible." In the transitive it can be rendered "manifest." So "manifestation" is sometimes used to translate the noun here. But Thayer gives "an appearing, appearance," and adds: "Often used by the Greeks of a glorious manifestation of the gods, and especially of their advent to help; in 2 Maccabees of signal deeds and events betokening the presence and power of God as helper" (p. 245). In a similar vein Arndt and Gingrich write: "As a religious technical term it means a visible manifestation of a hidden divinity, either in the form of a personal appearance, or by some deed of power by which its presence is made known" (p. 304). For this passage they prefer "appearance." That seems to be the most accurate rendering. In his *The Letters of Paul: An Expanded Paraphrase* (Eerdmans, 1965), F. F. Bruce has "the bright shining of His advent."

11 *Strong Delusion* That is the literal Greek of "strong delusion." The first noun, *energeia* (cf. energy), is translated "working" in verse 9. It means "*operative power* (as distinct from *dynamis, potential power*), working" (A-S). In the NT it is used only of superhuman power (God, Satan, demons).

The second noun is *planē*. It literally means "a wandering, a straying about" (Thayer). In the NT it is used of mental straying, and so means "error." Hence we find "a working of error" (ASV). Thayer thinks the phrase means "the power which error works." Arndt and Gingrich take the second noun as a descriptive genitive and translate the whole expression "a deluding influence" (cf. NASB).

J. Armitage Robinson writes: "In all the passages where it occurs in the New Testament *planē* will bear the passive meaning, 'error,' though the active meaning, 'deceit,' would sometimes be equally appropriate. There is no reason therefore for departing from the first meaning of the word, 'wandering from the way'; and so, metaphorically, 'error,' as opposed to truth" (p. 185).

Moulton and Milligan (VGT, p. 516) note that the word sometimes means "deceit" in the papyri, but add: "In the NT *planē* is generally, if not always, used in the passive sense of error" (VGT, p. 516). However, Ellicott renders the phrase: "an (effective) working of delusion" (p. 118).

A Lie The Greek has the definite article. It is not that those who perish should believe "a lie," but "the lie"—"this (great) Lie" (Milligan). The expression is in contrast to "the truth" in verse 12. The truth is the gospel of Jesus Christ, that one must accept Christ as his Savior and live a holy life if he is to be saved. "The lie" is the teaching of the man of lawlessness (v. 3) that one can live in unrighteousness (vv. 10, 12) as long as he submits to the rule of the Antichrist (or to the dominion of Satan).

12 Damned The verb *krinō* occurs no less than 114 times in the NT. In 88 of these instances it is correctly translated "judge." Only in this passage is it rendered by the strong Puritan term "damn." The compound *katakrinō* is twice translated "damned" (Mark 16:16; Rom. 14:23). It should not be necessary to try to convince any thoughtful person today that the use of "damned" 3 times in our common English Bible is unfortunate, to say the least. It certainly creates problems with our children that could easily be avoided by a correct translation.

But what does the verb *krinō* mean? In classical Greek it first meant "to separate, put asunder, to pick out, select, choose" (Thayer). Later it conveyed the sense: "to determine, resolve, decree," and then "to pronounce an opinion concerning right and wrong." In the passive (as here) it meant "to be judged," that is, "summoned to trial that one's case may be examined and judgment passed upon it." Thayer continues: "Where the context requires, used of condemnatory judgment, i.q. *to condemn*" (p. 361). Abbott-Smith notes that sometimes in the NT it is used as the equivalent of *katakrinō*, which properly means "condemn." In fact, the simple verb *krinō* is translated "condemn" five times in the KJV.

Arndt and Gingrich note that *krinō* came to be used as a legal technical term meaning "judge, decide, hale before a court, condemn . . . hand over for judicial punishment" (p. 452). They write: "Often the emphasis is unmistakably laid upon that which follows the Divine Judge's verdict, upon the condemnation or punishment." And so the verb comes to mean "condemn, punish" (p. 453).

The doctrine of divine judgment is not a minor emphasis in the NT. In the article on *krinō* in TDNT, Buechsel says of the preaching of Jesus in the Synoptic Gospels: "Here the thought of judgment is central. Jesus' call to repentance is urgent because God's judgment hangs over every man" (3:936). He repudiates the modern "rationalistic criticism" which rejects the NT concept of judgment as mythical and unethical. Buechsel declares: "In face of this we must stress the fact that in the NT judgment is not capricious or emotional. . . . It is an inwardly necessary consequence of the sin of man" (3:940). He concludes: "The concept of judgment cannot be taken out of the NT Gospel. It cannot even be removed from the centre to the periphery. Proclamation of the love of God always presupposes that all men are moving towards God's judgment and are hopelessly exposed to it" (3:941).

Altogether there are a dozen words which are translated "judge" or "judgment" in the KJV NT. This opens up a whole field of study in preparation for preaching on the Judgment—a topic which is surely relevant today.

3:1 Have Free Course It is one word in Greek, *trechō*, which simply means "run." It is used of those who run in a race. So it has here the metaphorical idea of swiftness—"proceed quickly and without hindrance." So say Arndt and Gingrich, who suggest for this passage: "that the word of the Lord might spread rapidly" (p. 833). This has been adopted by NASB and is probably a more adequate translation than the literal rendering "run" (ASV).

2 *Unreasonable* The Greek word *atopos* is composed of the alpha-privative *a-* and *topos*, "place." So literally it means "out of place." It came to have the sense of "strange, paradoxical" (LSJ) or "unusual, surprising" (AG). In later Greek it took on the ethical connotation, "improper, wicked." That is its meaning here.

In his excellent commentary on the Greek text of the Thessalonian letters (reprinted by Eerdmans, 1952), George Milligan cites an interesting use of *atopos* in a papyrus document of around A.D. 100. The parents of a prodigal son posted a public notice that they would no longer be responsible for his debts or for *atopon ti praxe*—whatever he did "out of the way." Milligan adds: "It is in this sense accordingly implying something morally amiss, that, with the exception of Ac. xxviii. 6, the word is found in the LXX and the N.T. . . . And in the passage before us it is best given some such rendering as 'perverse' or 'froward' rather than the 'unreasonable' of A.V., R.V." (p. 110).

Concerning the second adjective ("wicked," KJV) he observes: "Similarly *poneros* . . . is used not so much of passive badness as of active harmfulness, while the prefixed article shows that the writers have here certain definite persons in view, doubtless the fanatical Jews who at the time were opposing their preaching in Corinth (Ac. xviii. 12ff.), as they had already done in Thessalonica and Beroea (Ac. xvii. 5, 13)" (*ibid.*).

3 *Keep* The verb *phylassō* comes from the noun *phylax*, "guard" or "sentinel." So it means "guard, protect" (AG). Thayer puts it this way: "*To guard* a person (or thing) *that he may remain safe*, i.e. lest he suffer violence, be despoiled, etc., i.q. *to protect*." It is obvious that "protect" (NASB, NIV) is a more adequate translation than "keep" (KJV).

Lightfoot paraphrases the second part of the verse as follows: "He will not only place you in a firm position, but also maintain you there against assaults from without" (p. 125).

Evil Ellicott holds to the rendering "from the Evil One." He writes: "Here as elsewhere in the N.T., it is extremely doubtful whether *tou ponērou* refers to evil in the abstract . . . or to the Evil One. . . . The context alone must decide; and this in the present case . . . seems rather in favour of the masculine,—(1) in consequence of the seeming reference to the Lord's prayer, where the Greek commentators (whose opinion in such points deserves full consideration) adopt the masculine,—and (2) from the

tacit personal antithesis suggested by the preceding *Kyrios* [Lord]" (p. 125).

Milligan agrees with this. He comments:

> The precise sense to be attached to these words is best determined by the meaning assigned them in the petition of the Lord's Prayer (Mt. vi. 13), of which we have apparently a reminiscence here. . . . As the general consensus of modern scholarship is to understand *ponērou* there as masculine rather than as neuter in accordance with the predominant usage of the N.T. . . . and the unanimous opinion of the Greek commentators, we follow the same rendering here, and translate "from the evil one": a rendering, it may be noted further, which forms a fitting antithesis to *ho kyrios* of the preceding clause, and is moreover in thorough harmony with the prominence assigned shortly before to the persons of Satan and his representatives (ii. 1–12), and more especially to the *evil men* (*ponērōn anthrōpōn*) of the preceding clause (p. 111).

5 *Patient Waiting* The word *hypomonē* means "a remaining behind . . . patient enduring, endurance" (A-S). Arndt and Gingrich define it as follows: "Patience, endurance, fortitude, steadfastness, perseverance"; and add: "especially as they are shown in the enduring of toil and suffering." For this passage they give: "*a Christ-like fortitude*, i.e. a fortitude that comes from communion with Christ" (p. 854). But they also allow the meaning "(patient) expectation," which they think is clearly correct in Rev. 1:9 and perhaps here and in Rev. 3:10. Thayer prefers "a patient, steadfast waiting for" in all three of these passages. Abbott-Smith does not even cite this meaning.

Ellicott is rather adamant at this point. He says: "Analogy with what precedes would suggest (a) a genitive *objecti*, 'waiting for Christ' . . . but would introduce a meaning of *hypomonē* that is apparently not lexically defensible, and certainly is contrary to the usage of the N.T." (p. 127).

Again Milligan agrees. He declares that "the subjective interpretation of the second clause is rendered almost necessary by the regular meaning of *hypomonēn* in the N.T., 'constancy,' 'endurance' . . . not 'patient waiting' " (p. 112).

But Hauck takes exception to this. While agreeing that the verb *hypomenō* in the NT is "used comparatively rarely for 'to wait,' 'to wait for,' 'to expect,' " he yet goes on to say: "There is an example of the Godward use, corresponding to that of the LXX, in 2 Th. 3:5. The *hypomonē tou Christou* is here expectation of the Christ who will come again in glory. . . .

Similarly in Rev. 1:9 the *hypomonē Jesou* is to be construed as expectation of Jesus, since the saying of the exalted Christ in 3:10 . . . is plainly intended to praise the loyal preservation of faith in the *parousia* in the community." Then he adds this beautiful comment: "Pious waiting for Jesus is the heart-beat of the faith of the NT community" (TDNT, 4:586).

It is obvious that both "patient waiting for Christ" (KJV) and "steadfastness of Christ" (RSV, NASB) are live options.

6 *Disorderly*   The Greek word is the adverb *ataktōs*, found only here and in verse 11. The cognate adjective occurs only in 1 Thess. 5:14, where KJV renders it "unruly"; that is, not living according to the rules. The verb *atakteō*, derived from this, is also a *hapax legomenon*, being found only in 2 Thess. 3:7 (the next verse here). There it is translated "behave disorderly." It will be seen, then, that these three cognate terms do not occur in the NT outside the Thessalonian letters. It looks as though there was a hippie community at Thessalonica!

This suspicion is given further support when we look at the contemporary usage of these terms. Moulton and Milligan note that the verb *atakteō* has the "original connotation of riot or rebellion." One is reminded of the riots and disorderly demonstrations precipitated by hippies on our university campuses. But the authors go on to say: "Like its parent adjective *ataktos*, and the adverb, this verb is found in the NT only in the Thessalonian Epistles, where their context clearly demands that the words should be understood metaphorically. Some doubt, however, has existed as to whether they are to be taken as referring to actual moral wrong-doing, or to a certain remissness in daily work and conduct. . . . The latter view is now supported by almost contemporary evidence from the *Koine*" (VGT, p. 89).

This evidence is found in a papyrus contract of apprenticeship (A.D. 66). The father agrees that if there should be any days when his son (the apprentice) "plays truant" or "fails to attend," he must later make up for them. Also in a papyrus of A.D. 183 a weaver's apprentice is bound to appear for an equivalent number of days in case he exceeds, from idleness or ill health, the 20 days' vacation he is allowed during the year. These illustrations show that the verb *atakteō* was used in that day for being idle or failing to discharge one's responsibilities. For this passage (2 Thess. 3:6) Arndt and Gingrich suggest the rendering "live in idleness."

7 *Follow*   The verb *mimeomai* occurs (in NT) only four times: here; verse 9; Heb. 13:7; and 3 John 11. In the KJV it is always translated "follow." Likewise the noun *mimētēs* (7 times in NT) is always "follower." But "follow" is *akoloutheō*. The correct meaning of *mimeomai* is "imitate." Perhaps the best rendering here is "follow our example" (NASB, NIV).

8 *For Nought*   The Greek word *dōrean* comes from the verb *didōmi*, "give." So it means "as a gift, without payment, gratis" (AG). TCNT and NIV translate it "without paying for it." That is still the best rendering. It is favored by Arndt and Gingrich.

Chargeable   The verb *epibareō* literally means "to put a burden on, be burdensome" (A-S). In 1 Thess. 2:9 it is translated as here, "be chargeable." The only other place where it occurs in the NT is 2 Cor. 2:5, where it is rendered "overcharge." Again TCNT gives the correct meaning: "so as not to be a burden upon any of you" (cf. NIV).

9 *Power*   The basic meaning of *exousia* was liberty of action or freedom of choice. Paul is saying that he was free to accept financial support. Later the word came to signify "right" or "authority." The correct meaning here is "not because we had not a right to receive support" (TCNT; cf. NASB, NIV).

11 *Busybodies*   There is a play on words in the Greek: "not at all *ergazomenous* but *periergazomenous*." This is brought out in the heading above about as nearly as can be done in English. Literally the Greek means "not at all working, but working around."

The second verb, *periergazomai*, is found only here in the NT. It means "to bustle about uselessly, to busy one's self about trifling, needless, useless matters." Thayer goes on to say that the verb is "used apparently of a person officiously inquisitive about others' affairs" (p. 502). Demosthenes employs it in that sense. This seems also to be the meaning in a papyrus letter written in A.D. 41 by the Emperor Claudius to the Alexandrians. In it he says: "And, on the other side, I bid the Jews not to busy themselves about anything beyond what they have held hitherto" (VGT, p. 505).

14 *Have No Company*   The verb is a strong compound, *synanamignymi*. Literally it means "to mix up together," and so "to associate with" (A-S). Perhaps the best translation is: "Do not associate with him" (NASB, NIV). In the NT it is used only here and in 1 Cor. 5:9. The idea that Christians, and especially pastors, should be "good mixers" is not exactly scriptural.

17 Token The Greek word *sēmeion* means "*the sign* or *distinguishing mark* by which something is known." Arndt and Gingrich translate the passage: "This is the mark of genuineness in every letter." The verse may be translated: "I, Paul, add this farewell in my own handwriting. Every letter of mine is signed in this way. This is the way in which I write" (TCNT; cf. NIV).

1 Timothy

1:1 *God Our Savior*   This unique phrase is used by Paul only in the Pastoral Epistles (1 Tim. 1:1; 2:3; 4:10; Titus 1:3; 2:10; 3:4). Elsewhere in the NT it occurs just twice and then in liturgical passages (Luke 1:47; Jude 25). It is also found in the Septuagint version of Deut. 32:15. It fits in perfectly with Old Testament theology, as well as that of Paul. There is no reasonable justification for using it as an argument against the Pauline authorship of the Pastoral Epistles. God is our Savior just as truly as Jesus Christ is our Savior.

2 *My Own*   The word *gnēsios* properly means "lawfully begotten, born in wedlock" (A-S), and so "true" or "genuine." The KJV "my own" suggests this, but is perhaps not strong enough. Strangely, NEB has "his true-born son" (cf. Moffatt, "his lawful son"). Probably the best translation is "my true son" (NIV).

3 *Teach . . . Other Doctrine*   Paul, unlike John, was particularly fond of compound words. Some of them he evidently coined himself. An example is found at the end of verse 3. "That they teach . . . other doctrine" is all one word in Greek—*heterodidaskalein*. It is composed of *heteros*, "different," and *didaskaleō*, "teach." The term (only here and 6:3 in NT) is used by Ignatius in his letter to Polycarp (ca. A.D. 115). Eusebius, in his *Ecclesiastical History* (A.D. 326) employs the cognate noun *heterodidaskaloi* to designate heretical teachers. In verse 7, Paul has *nomodidaskaloi*, "law-teachers." So the "different" teaching here in verse 3 was evidently that of Judaizers, who asserted that Gentile Christians had to keep the Jewish law (cf. Acts 15).

4 *Fables*   The Greek word is *mythos*, from which we get "myth." In the NT it is found four times in the Pastoral Epistles (1 Tim. 1:4; 4:7; 2 Tim. 4:4; Titus 1:14) and in 2 Pet. 1:16. In all five places it is rendered "fables" in KJV.

The term first meant "a speech, word, saying," then "a narrative, story"—whether true or fictitious—and finally "an invention, falsehood" (Thayer). It is thus distinguished from *logos*, "a historical tale" (Vincent, 4:203).

Kittel's TDNT devotes no less than 34 pages to this word alone. Because of the vague and varied ways in which the term is used today by biblical scholars, it might be well to give it some attention.

The article in TDNT is written by Staehlin. He notes that some use "myth" for that which is unhistorical and yet has religious value. Then he asserts: "But if the concept of myth is brought into antithesis to both historical reality and to truth as such, and if reality and truth are thought to be essential to genuine revelation and the only possible basis of faith, myth can have no religious value" (4:765). Two results follow. Either the NT stories are "dismissed as myths, as errors and deceptions," or a sharp line is drawn between Gospel and myth. He notes that the latter is "the judgment of the NT itself" which contrasts myth with history (2 Pet. 1:16) and with truth (2 Tim. 4:4; Titus 1:14). His conclusion is incisive: "The Christian Church, insofar as it is true to itself, accepts this judgment that myth is untrue and consequently of no religious value" (*ibid.*). This is a welcome antidote to Bultmann!

Plato made much use of myth, but Aristotle argued that *logos* alone has educational value; myth merely pleases (4:775). For the Stoics myth was valid as a symbol (4:777). Staehlin concludes his study of myth in the Greek world by saying: "There is, however, no fundamental repudiation on religious grounds until we come to the NT and the Christian writers of the first centuries" (4:779).

In the Septuagint the word *mythos* is found only in the apocryphal books (twice). Later rabbis made use of Greek myths as parables (4:781).

Coming to "Mythoi in the NT," Staehlin reiterates his earlier statements. He says: "The position of the NT regarding what it calls *mythos* is quite unequivocal. . . . There is obviously a complete repudiation of *mythos*. It is the means and mark of an alien proclamation, especially of the error combatted in the Pastorals" (*ibid.*).

What is the nature of these myths which Paul warns against? Staehlin says, "It is highly probable that the Pastorals are concerned with the early form of a Gnosticism which flourished on the soil of Hellenistic Jewish Christianity" (4:783).

Staehlin concludes that "myth as such has no place on biblical soil" (4:793). Against those who defend it as a form of religious communication he asserts: "In the Bible, however, we have from first to last the account and narration of facts. This may undergo certain changes in form and consciousness from the childlikeness of many of the ancient stories to the maturity of the Johannine view of Christ. But the essential theme is the same throughout, namely, what God says and what God does" (4:793–94).

Pagan myths were sometimes used as parables. But Staehlin insists that "the NT uses genuine parable rather than myths" (4:794). Myths were finally thought of as symbols. Staehlin's answer to this argument is clear and direct. He says: "The central symbol of the Gospel, however, is the cross, and this embodies a hard and unromantic historical reality. No myth can be integrated into or imposed upon this symbol in any form" (*ibid.*). In a footnote he adds: "Hence the use of expressions like the Christ myth, which is common in form criticism, is to be strictly avoided."

This German writer maintains his position without equivocation. He raises the question as to whether there is some other way to make myth at home in the biblical world. He answers: "But no matter how the term is understood, and no matter how it is extended, as e.g., by Bultmann, there is within it an inherent antithesis to truth and reality which is quite intolerable on NT soil" (*ibid.*).

We have quoted at unusual length from this article because it touches on a very relevant problem in current NT studies. It is the most scholarly, constructive treatment we have seen to date.

Minister　The word is *parechō*, which literally means "hold beside." As used here it signifies "cause, bring about" (AG). Vincent suggests "afford, furnish, give occasion for" (4:204).

Questions　The Greek term *ekzētēsis* occurs only here in the NT and is not found in the Septuagint or classical Greek. It carries the idea of "seekings *out*" (*ek*). For these two words together in this verse Arndt and Gingrich suggest the rendering, "give rise to speculations" (cf. RSV). Perhaps the best translation is "cause questionings." N. J. D. White defines the second term as: "*Questionings* to which no answer can be given, which are not worth answering" (EGT, 4:93). Lock suggests "out-of-the-way researches" (p. 9).

Edifying　The best Greek text does not have *oikodomēn*, "edifying," but *oikonomia*. The latter word primarily means "stewardship" (cf. Luke 16:2–4). In later writers it came to have the more general sense of "administration" or "dispensation" (A-S). Aside from the above passage in Luke, the word occurs in the NT only in Paul's Epistles (1 Cor. 9:17; Eph. 1:10; 3:2; Col. 1:25), where it is always translated "dispensation" in KJV. Here Arndt and Gingrich (p. 562) think the meaning is: "They promote useless speculations rather than divine training that is in faith" (cf. RSV). Michel, in TDNT (5:153), agrees. He writes: "In 1 Tim. 1:4 it is said of the false teachers that they proclaim fables in which there is more questioning than godly instruction in faith." Lock (p. 9) gives what seems to us an especially good interpretation: " 'God's stewardship,' *i.e.* they do not help them to carry out the stewardship entrusted to them by God."

5 End　The simple meaning of the word *telos* is "end." But it also has in this passage the specialized sense, "the end to which all things relate, the aim, purpose" (Thayer, p. 620; cf. A-S, p. 443). Arndt and Gingrich give here: "The preaching has love as its aim" (p. 819).

Commandment　The noun here has the same stem as the verb "charge" in verse 3. The connection is retained by translating it similarly. The goal of Timothy's charge to the Ephesian Christians was "love out of a pure heart." And that is the ultimate aim of all true Christian preaching.

Unfeigned The adjective *anypocritos* is from the alpha-privative *a-* and *hypocrites,* "hypocrite." So it literally means "unhypocritical." Perhaps the best modern equivalent is "sincere" (NIV).

6 Swerved The verb *astocheō* (only in the Pastorals) literally means "miss the mark." Arndt and Gingrich say that here it signifies "deviate, depart." Lock (p. 10) thinks the idea is "taking no pains to aim at the right path." A possible translation is "straying" (NASB) or "wandered" (NIV).

Vain Jangling This is one word in the Greek, *mataiologia* (only here in NT). Literally it means "vain talking, empty talk" (Thayer). It could be translated "empty prattle" (TDNT, 4:524) or "meaningless talk" (NIV). Arndt and Gingrich give the sense here as "fruitless discussion" (cf. NASB).

7 Law "Teachers of the law" is all one word in the Greek, *nomodidaskaloi*—literally, "law-teachers." Since it is obviously the Mosaic law which is meant here, it is best to capitalize "Law" (cf. NASB).

Affirm The term is a strong compound, *diabebaiountai* (only here and Titus 3:8). It means "affirm strongly, assert confidently" (Thayer). The NIV renders it well: "They so confidently affirm."

9 Disobedient The adjective is a double compound, *anypotaktos.* It is formed from the alpha-privative *a-, hypo* ("under"), and *tassō.* The last is a verb wieh primarily the military connotation of "draw up in order." So the compound means "that cannot be subjected to control . . . unruly" (Thayer). It may well be translated "disorderly" or "insubordinate." The first two adjectives here signify "the general refusal to obey all law" (Lock, p. 12). The next two, "ungodly and sinners," refer to "the general refusal to obey the law of God"; and the next two, "unholy and profane," to "the more detailed opposition to the law of God" (*ibid.*). The verse finishes with the mention of patricides, matricides, and homicides. It is obvious that in this list of sinners (vv. 9–10) there is indicated a progression in sin.

10 Whoremongers The term "adulterous" is preferable today for *pornois,* though "immoral persons" (RSV) may be better. "For them that defile themselves with mankind" is all one word in Greek, *arsenokoitais.* It is correctly translated "sodomites" (RSV), though the usual term used today for this is "homosexuals" (NASB). "Menstealers" (*andrapodistais,* only here in NT) refers to slave traders or "kidnappers." "Perjured persons" (*epiorkois,* only here in NT) is better translated "perjurers" (NIV).

Sound The term is *hygianousei,* from the verb *hygiainō* (cf. "hygiene"). This verb is found 3 times in the Gospel of Luke (5:31; 7:10; 15:10); 8 times in the Pastoral Epistles, and once in 3 John (v. 2, "be in health"). It means "to be sound, to be well, to be in good health" (Thayer, p. 634). With regard to its use in the Pastorals, Arndt and Gingrich write: "Thus in accord with prevailing usage, Christian teaching is designated as the *correct* doctrine, since it is reasonable and appeals to sound intelligence" (p. 840). Some scholars prefer "healthful" or "wholesome." Lock specifically rejects the latter, choosing "sound" (p. 12). Vincent (4:209) supports both "sound" and "healthful." While the basic idea of the Greek verb may suggest "healthy" rather than "healthful," we know that teaching, like food, is either conducive to moral and spiritual health or a hindrance to it. For that reason, "healthful" seems to be a justifiable translation.

This list of common sins at Ephesus in the first century, for which there is abundant documentation from secular sources, is a shocking one. But every item mentioned here can be duplicated from contemporary society in America and Europe. Some of these sins are perhaps more prevalent now than at any time since Roman days.

13 Injurious The word *hybristēs* is found (in NT) only here and in Rom. 1:30, where it is translated "despiteful" (KJV). It is a noun meaning "a violent, insolent man" (A-S). It suggests "one who, uplifted with pride, either heaps insulting language upon others or does them some shameful act of wrong" (Fritzsche, quoted by Thayer). The great humility of Paul is seen in his describing his pre-Christian life in this way. Vincent writes: "*Hybristēs* is one whose insolence and contempt of others break forth in wanton and outrageous acts. Paul was *hybristēs* when he persecuted the church" (4:211).

15–16 Chief, First The superlative degree form *prōtos* is defined thus by Abbott-Smith: "*first,* 1. of Time or Place. . . . 2. Of Rank or Dignity, *chief, principal.* . . . 3. Neuter, *proton,* as adverb, *first, at the first*" (pp. 389–90).

Prōtos is translated "chief" in verse 15 (second meaning above) and "first" in verse 16 (first meaning). Vincent defends this. He says of *prōtos* in verse 16: "Not the chief sinner, but the representative instance of God's long-suffering applied to a high-handed transgressor" (4:212). Arndt and Gingrich agree. They translate the phrase in verse 16: "in me as the first" (p. 733). A. T. Robertson interprets it this way: "Probably starts with the same sense of *prōtos* as in verse 15 (rank), but turns to order (first in line). Paul becomes the 'specimen' sinner as an encouragement to all who come after him" (WP, 4:564). Alford follows much the same line. He writes on verse 16: "It can hardly be denied that in *prōtō* here the senses of '*chief*' and '*first*' are combined. . . . Though he was not in time 'the first of sinners,' yet he was the first as well as the most notable example of such marked long-suffering, held up for the encouragement of the church" (3:309). Lock agrees with these interpretations (starting with "chief," but also implying "first") (p. 16).

In spite of this array of scholarly opinion we prefer to go along with J. H. Bernard in the *Cambridge Greek Testament*. He says that the Revised rendering "in me as chief," "certainly brings out the connection with . . . the preceding verse better than A.V. 'first' " (p. 33). The NASB preserves this connection by using "foremost" (v. 15) and "in me as foremost" (v. 16).

16 All Longsuffering The KJV has simply: "that in me first Jesus Christ might show forth all longsuffering." This could be interpreted as meaning Paul's patience with others. But the Greek has the definite article, with the possessive force. So the correct meaning is "all his longsuffering" (ASV); that is, the long-suffering of Christ toward Paul. The NASB has: "might demonstrate His perfect patience" (cf. NIV: "might display his unlimited patience").

Pattern Paul normally uses the simple word *typon* (9 times), from which comes "type." But here and in 2 Tim. 1:13 we find the compound *hypotypōsis*. Originally it meant an outline or sketch. Then it came to be used in the metaphorical sense of an example—"to show by the example of my conversion that the same grace which I had obtained would not be wanting also to those who should hereafter believe" (Thayer, p. 645). Arndt and Gingrich feel that here it suggests "prototype," whereas in 2 Tim. 1:13 it means "standard." The majority of recent translations have wisely adopted "example."

17 Only Wise God The best Greek text does not have the adjective "wise." The Eternal King is not just the "only wise God" but the "only God"—period! There is no other real God of any kind, wise or unwise.

18 Went Before The verb *proagō* was used transitively in the sense of "lead on, lead forth," and intransitively as "lead the way" or "go before." The English Revised Version (NT, 1881) followed the KJV in reading, "which went before on thee." But it also placed in the margin an alternative rendering, "led the way to thee." This marginal reading was adopted in the American Standard Edition of the Revised Version (ASV), put out in 1901. It is preferred by Abbott-Smith in his *Lexicon* and by Bernard (CGT).

But Thayer thinks the participle in this passage means "preceding i.e. prior in point of time, previous." Similarly Arndt and Gingrich suggest here: "in accordance with the prophecies that were made long ago" (p. 709).

Lock (p. 18) allows both of these meanings: "*Either* according to the previous . . . prophecies about thee . . . *or* according to the prophecies leading me towards you." But in his paraphrase he adopts the latter: "recalling to mind the words of the Christian prophets which led me to choose you to help me in my work" (p. 17). The reference seems to be to Timothy's ordination (4:14), although the quotation just given would relate it to Acts 16:3. At one time or the other—perhaps both—there were inspired utterances about Timothy's future.

Warfare The KJV has "war a good warfare." Because there is a definite article in the Greek, the ASV has more accurately, "war the good warfare."

The NASB adopts the rendering given in Arndt and Gingrich: "fight the good fight." Perhaps this is too narrow. Of the noun Vincent says: "Not *fight* (*machēn*), but covering all the particulars of a soldier's service" (4:215).

The verb is *strateuō*, which means "to serve as a soldier" (A-S); "do military service, serve in the army" (AG). The noun *strateia* was used for "an expedition, a campaign, warfare" (A-S). The point to emphasize, of course, is that the Christian's fight with evil is not a single battle; it lasts until death. It has been truly said: "There is no discharge in this war." Possibly "war the good warfare" is best, or "wage the good warfare" (RSV). On the other hand, "fight the good fight" (Weymouth, Moffatt, Goodspeed, NIV) may be a better contemporary translation.

19 Put Away The KJV translation is not strong enough. The verb *apōtheō* means "to thrust away" and in the middle (always in NT) it signifies "to thrust away from oneself, refuse, reject" (A-S). Bernard says: "The verb is expressive of a wilful and violent act" (p. 35). Schmidt observes that it is "used in Greek poetry and prose from the time of Homer to the papyri with both the literal and figurative meaning of 'to repel' or 'reject' " (TDNT, 1:448).

Faith The noun has the definite article in the Greek: "concerning the faith." A. T. Robertson writes: "Rather, 'concerning their faith' (the article here used as a possessive pronoun, a common Greek idiom)" (4:566). Lock agrees with this. He feels that the context and the stress on faith throughout the chapter "make the subjective meaning more probable" (p. 19).

2:1 Supplications, Prayers, Intercessions, and, Giving of Thanks In this verse we find four words for prayer. This is the only place in the NT where they all occur together. There are some points of distinction between them.

The first term is *deēsis*, the second *proseuchē*. *Deēsis* simply means "petition," whether made to God or man. But *proseuchē* is used only for prayer to God.

The third noun is *enteuxis*, which occurs only here and in 1 Tim. 4:5. In his classic work, *Synonyms of the New Testament*, R. C. Trench notes that *enteuxis* "does not necessarily mean what intercession at present commonly does mean—namely, prayer in relation to others. . . . [Rather] it is free, familiar prayer, such as boldly draws near to God" (pp. 189–90).

Concerning these three words Thayer comments: "*Deēsis* gives prominence to the expression of personal need, *proseuchē* to the element of devotion, *enteuxis* to that of childlike confidence, by representing prayer as the heart's converse with God" (p. 126).

The fourth expression, "giving of thanks," is one word in the Greek—*eucharistia*. Of this Trench writes: "Regarded as one manner of prayer, it expresses that which ought never to be absent from any of our devotions (Phil. iv. 6; Eph. v. 20; I Thess. v. 18; I Tim. ii. 1); namely, the grateful acknowledgement of past mercies, as distinguished from the earnest seeking of future" (p. 191).

Now to look at each of these terms more closely. *Deēsis*, from the verb *deomai*, first meant "a wanting, need" and then "an asking, entreaty, supplication" (A-S, p. 99). Arndt and Gingrich note that it is used "with *proseuchē*,

the more general term, to denote a more specific supplication" (p. 171). In the NT it is employed only for prayer to God. The word is "frequently used for intercession" (TDNT, 2:41). Occurring 19 times in the NT, *deēsis* is 12 times translated "prayer," 6 times "supplication," and once "request."

In contrast, *proseuchē* is found 37 times in the NT and is regularly translated "prayer" ("pray earnestly" in Jas. 5:17). It is the most general word for prayer in the NT.

The noun *enteuxis* comes from the verb *entynchanō*, which signifies "to fall in with a person; to draw near so as to converse familiarly." Vincent continues: "Hence, *enteuxis* is not properly *intercession* in the accepted sense of that term, but rather approach to God in free and familiar prayer" (4:216). Ellicott says that *enteuxis* refers to "prayer in its most individual and urgent form . . . prayer in which God is, as it were, sought in audience . . . and personally drawn nigh to" (p. 42).

The term *eucharistia* suggests another important aspect of prayer. It occurs 15 times in the NT and is variously rendered "thanksgiving," "giving of thanks," "thankfulness," and simply "thanks."

N. J. D. White thinks that Paul did not have in mind strong distinctions between the first three terms: "His object in the enumeration is simply to cover every possible variety of public prayer" (EGT, 4:102). In line with this J. H. Bernard, in his volume on "The Pastoral Epistles" in the *Cambridge Greek Testament*, writes: "The four words are not to be too sharply distinguished, inasmuch as they point to different moods of the suppliant rather than to the different forms into which public prayer may be cast" (p. 38). But he later goes on to say: "To sum up, then, we may (1) with Origen, regard the four words as arranged in an ascending scale: the needy suppliant (*deēsis*) as he goes on is led to ask for larger blessings (*proseuchē*), and then becoming bold he presents his *enteuxis*, which being granted, his devotion issues in thanksgiving. Or (2) we may more simply take the words in two contrasted pairs, *deēsis* being related to *proseuchē* as the particular to the general, and *enteuxis* to *eucharistia* as petition to thanksgiving" (pp. 38–39).

2 Authority The Greek word is *hyperochē*. It is found only here and in 1 Cor. 2:1, where it is translated "excellency." It was first used for an eminence, such as a mountain peak, and then metaphorically in the sense of "preeminence." The Greek phrase here occurs in an inscription of the second century B.C. at Pergamum.

Deissmann (BS, p. 255) renders it "persons of consequence." Perhaps the best translation is "high office" (NEB).

Quiet and Peaceable   The two Greek words, *ēremos* and *hēsychion*, are defined exactly the same way in Abbott-Smith's *Lexicon:* "quiet, tranquil." The former is found only here in the NT; the latter occurs also in 1 Pet. 3:4. Vincent points out the distinction between the two. "*Ēremos* denotes quiet arising from the absence of outward disturbance: *hēsychios* tranquillity arising from within" (4:217). We are to pray for our rulers, that we may enjoy the former. Meanwhile, God's grace can give us the latter.

Honesty   The Greek word is *semnotēs*. Thayer gives this definition: "That characteristic of a person or a thing which entitles to reverence or respect, *dignity, gravity, majesty, sanctity*" (p. 573). The last two ideas apply especially to God, the other two to man. Abbott-Smith gives only "gravity." But this term is not commonly used today. Arndt and Gingrich say that when used of men *semnotēs* means: "Reverence, dignity, seriousness, respectfulness, holiness, probity."

Vincent opts for "gravity." He comments: "*Honesty*, according to the modern acceptation, is an unfortunate rendering" (4:217). In place of "godliness and honesty," if one likes alliteration he can use "godliness and gravity" (ASV) or "piety and probity" (Goodspeed). Perhaps the best translation for the second word is "dignity" (NASB) or "holiness" (NIV).

4 Will Have   The KJV rendering might be taken as indicating simple futurity. But the Greek word is *thelō*, which signifies "wish" or "will," in the sense of desire or purpose (cf. NIV: "wants"). Both ideas apply here.

5 Mediator   Besides this passage, *mesitēs* occurs twice in Galatians (3:19–20) and three times in Hebrews (8:6; 9:15; 12:24). It is regularly translated "mediator" in most versions.

Thayer explains the term as meaning "one who intervenes between two, either in order to make or restore peace and friendship, or to form a compact, or for ratifying a covenant." Of this passage he writes: "Christ is called *mesitēs theou kai anthrōpōn*, since he interposed by his death and restored the harmony between God and man which human sin had broken" (p. 401). Arndt and Gingrich refer to it as "this many-sided technical term of Hellenistic legal language" (pp. 507–8). It is used many times in

the papyri for an arbitrator in connection with both legal and business transactions.

The word comes from *mesos*, "middle," and so means a middleman; that is, "a man who stands in the middle and who brings two parties together." The Greek term occurs only once in the Septuagint, when Job complains: "Neither is there any daysman betwixt us, that might lay his hand upon us both" (Job 9:33). As indicated in the *Oxford English Dictionary*, "daysman" is an archaic term for "an umpire or arbitrator; a mediator" (3:53).

In his meaty little volume *A New Testament Wordbook*, William Barclay has an excellent discussion of *mesitēs*. He says that it had two main meanings in classical Greek. The first was "arbiter." Both Greek and Roman law gave considerable attention to arbitration. Barclay writes: "An arbiter, a mediator, a *mesitēs*, is therefore fundamentally a person whose duty it is to bring together two people who are estranged and to wipe out the differences between them" (p. 86). He adds that this is what Jesus did between us and God.

The second meaning is "a sponsor, guarantor, or surety." Barclay says: "A man who went bail for another's appearance in court was so called. But the words are especially used of guaranteeing or standing surety for a debt" (*ibid.*). So Jesus stands surety for our debt to God. This usage is found several times in the papyri of the second and third centuries (VGT, p. 399).

In TDNT Oepke devotes to *mesitēs* 27 pages, much of it in fine print. His thorough survey of the history of this term and its theological significance ends with a twofold observation. After noting the almost complete absence of *mesitēs* in early Christian writings, he says: "In Roman Catholicism the Church and its agent largely took over the mediatorial function. In contrast, Reformation theology looked to the one Mediator, Christ." And then he adds this striking statement: "It is no accident that in the 20th century, when, after a period of liberal and rational thought, theology was finding its way back to the biblical and Reformation message, the word 'mediator' became one of the slogans of the new outlook" (4:624). In our estranged generation the message of Christ the Mediator needs to be sounded again and again.

6 Ransom   Christ gave himself as a "ransom" on behalf of all. Only here in the NT do we find the compound *antilytron*.

The simple form *lytron* is found twice, in Matt. 20:28 and Mark 10:45—"For even the Son of man came not to be ministered unto [served], but to minister [serve], and to give his life a ransom for many." The literal meaning of *lytron* was "a price for release." It was used especially for the price paid to free a slave. The noun comes from the verb *lyō*, which means "to loose." Still earlier it was used to designate "the money paid to ransom prisoners of war" (TDNT, 4:340). There does not seem to be any basic difference between *lytron* and *antilytron*. The prefix *anti*, "instead of," follows *lytron* in the saying of Jesus. Here it is incorporated with the simple noun to emphasize the fact that Christ died in our place to ransom us from the slavery of sin. White makes the helpful suggestion: "*Lytron anti* merely implies that the exchange is decidedly a benefit to those on whose behalf it is made" (EGT, 4:105). Bernard says: "Here we have the compound *antilytron* preceding *hyper pantōn*, which suggests that both the elements represented by *anti* 'instead of," and *hyper* 'on behalf of' must enter into any Scriptural theory of the Atonement" (p. 42).

8 Doubting The word *dialogismos* occurs 8 times in the Gospels—6 in Luke, 1 each in Matthew and Mark—where it is rendered "thought(s)" with the exception of Luke 9:46 ("reasoning"). It occurs 5 times in Paul's Epistles and is translated five different ways in the KJV! It is found once elsewhere, in Jas. 2:4 ("thoughts").

The noun comes from the verb *dialogizomai*, "to consider, reason," and so means "a thought, reasoning, inward questioning" (A-S). Thayer notes that from the time of Plato it signified "the thinking of a man deliberating with himself" (p. 139).

Schrenk notes that the most common meaning in ancient Greek was "deliberation" or "reflection." He states: "The sense of 'evil thoughts' is predominant in the NT" (TDNT, 2:97). But it can also be used for "anxious reflection" or "doubt." With regard to our passage he writes that the translation "without wrath or disputing" (cf. ASV) "yields good sense." But after pointing out the fact that the idea of contention is not necessarily inherent in the term, he concludes: "We thus do better to follow the linguistic instinct of the Greek exegetes and interpret *dialogismos* as doubt or questioning" (2:98).

Our own inclination, however, follows that of Lock. He says, "probably 'disputing,' " and adds that "the idea of doubt is alien to the context, which emphasizes man's relation to his fellow men" (p. 31). Huther, in Meyer's commentary series, thinks that here it should be taken in the sense of evil deliberations against one's

neighbor (p. 102). Bernard prefers "disputation." Likewise E. K. Simpson (p. 45) opts for "controversy," though allowing "the primary Platonic meaning of the word, *cogitation, reasoning.*"

9 Modest Apparel In a day of "undress" this famous passage on how women should dress takes on added significance. We need to find out exactly what the Scripture says here.

The word for "apparel" is *katastolē*, which is found only here in the NT. The latter part of this (cf. English "stole" for a scarf) comes from the verb *stellō*, which meant "to set, place, arrange, fit out" (A-S).

The prefix *kata* means "down." So *katastolē* first meant "a lowering, letting down," and then "a garment let down, dress, attire" (Thayer). In classical Greek it also was used in the sense of "modesty, reserve" (LSJ). Arndt and Gingrich furnish this definition: "*Deportment*, outward, as it expresses itself in *clothing* . . . as well as inward . . . and probably both at the same time" (p. 420). Ellicott says: "*Katastolē* is not simply 'dress' . . . a meaning for which there is not satisfactory authority, but 'deportment,' as exhibited externally, whether in look, manner, or *dress*" (p. 50). Simpson writes: "*Katastolē* can signify *dress;* but usage favours the wider sense of demeanour, so that the entire phrase bespeaks a well-ordered carriage" (p. 46).

However, Abbott-Smith says that in the Septuagint and NT the word means "a garment, dress, attire." As in the case of the NT, the word occurs only once in the Septuagint, in Isa. 61:3, where it is translated "garment" (of praise). This would, of course, be metaphorical.

The adjective "modest" is *cosmios*. It is found only here and in 3:2, where it is translated "of good behaviour." It comes from *cosmos*. This is the regular term for "world" (186 times in NT), but in the similar passage in 1 Pet. (3:3) it is rendered "adorning."

The original meaning of *cosmos* was "order" (Homer, Plato, and others). Then it came to be used in the sense of "ornament" or "adornment," especially in relation to women. Only in later writers did it take on the popular usage for "world" or universe, as an ordered system. Finally it came to be used as equivalent to "the earth."

So *cosmios* signifies "well-arranged, seemly, modest" (Thayer). White says: "It means *orderly*, as opposed to disorderliness in appearance" (EGT, 4:108). Perhaps the emphasis here is as much on *neatness* of dress as on *modesty*. The ideal is to combine these two aspects. A good translation here is "becoming attire" (Berkeley). The NIV reads: "I also want women to dress modestly."

Adorn   The verb is *cosmeō*, which also comes from *cosmos*. Originally it meant "to order, arrange, prepare" (A-S). Homer used it for marshalling armies. In Matt. 25:7 it refers to trimming the wicks on lamps. In Matt. 12:44 and Luke 11:25 it is used for a house "put in order" (RSV). In Rev. 21:2 the New Jerusalem is described as like "a bride adorned for her husband." In contrast to this, a passage in an Oxyrhynchus papyrus speaks of women "adorned for adultery" (AG, p. 445).

Shamefacedness   This unfortunate translation leaves the implication that Christian women should go around in public with heads bowed and eyes averted, as if they were ashamed of themselves. Not so. Actually this rendering appears to be an error. *The Oxford English Dictionary* says that the adjective "shamefaced" was "originally an etymological misinterpretation of *shamefast*" (9:620) which carries the idea of discreetness. Wyclif's earliest English version of the Bible (1382) has the correct term here, "shamefastness." This is used in the ASV (1901), but, of course, even this word is obsolete today.

The Greek term is *aidos*, found only here in the NT. Bernard says that it implies "(1) a *moral* repugnance to what is base and unseemly, and (2) *self-respect*, as well as restraint imposed on oneself from a sense of what is due to others." He goes on to say: "Thus *aidos* here signifies that modesty which shrinks from overstepping the limits of womanly reserve" (p. 45). In our opinion, that states the case with accuracy and relevance. In this day when many careless women seem to have no sense of shame (cf. Jer. 8:12—"They were not at all ashamed, neither could they blush"), it is refreshing to see a proper "womanly reserve." Here, as in all else in life, it is "the golden mean" which should be sought, something between shamefacedness and boldfacedness. Instead of "shamefacedness and sobriety," the NIV has: "with decency and propriety." That says it.

Broided   The KJV expression "broided hair" is obviously obsolete. Today we speak of "braided hair" (RSV). The phrase is one word in Greek, *plegmasin*, found only here in the NT (a similar term is found in 1 Pet. 3:3). Literally it means "what is woven or twisted." It is used of baskets and nets.

History goes in strange circles. Women who say that the Bible forbids them to cut their hair wear it long and often braided over their heads. Yet this is apparently condemned here! Long hair at one time was considered the sign of a conservative Christian. Later it became the emblem of the hippies.

But what is the correct meaning of the passage? Combining "braided hair" with "gold," TCNT has, "Not with wreaths or gold ornaments for the hair." The NEB reads: "Not with elaborate hairstyles, not decked out with gold." Probably this is what the admonition means.

Costly   The adjective "costly" is a strong compound, *poluteles*. Thayer says it means "requiring great outlay, very costly." Perhaps "expensive" (Moffatt, NIV) conveys the idea best.

Array   The Greek word is *himatismos*, not the common NT term for clothing—*himatia*. Trench says: "*Himatismos*, a word of comparatively late appearance . . . is seldom, if ever, used except of garments more or less stately and costly. It is the 'vesture' . . . of kings; thus of Solomon in all his glory . . . is associated with gold and silver, as part of a precious spoil" (p. 185).

The 6 occurrences of this word in the NT all bear this out. It is used for Christ's expensive seamless tunic, called "vesture," for which the soldiers cast lots (Matt. 27: 35; John 19:24). Luke 7:25 speaks of those who are "gorgeously apparelled" and live in luxury. The "raiment" of Jesus glistened on the Mount of Transfiguration (Luke 9:29). Paul testified that he had coveted "no man's silver, or gold, or apparel" (Acts 20:33). A good translation here is "expensive clothes" (NIV).

11 ***Subjection***   The Greek word *hypotagē* occurs only four times in the NT (2 Cor. 9:13; Gal. 2:5; 1 Tim. 2:11; 3:4). It is regularly and correctly translated "subjection." But as applied to women it seems that "submission" (NIV) is less harsh and yet adequate.

12 ***Usurp Authority***   This is one word in Greek, the infinitive *authentein*. The verb occurs only here in the NT. It means "have authority, domineer . . . over someone" (AG). "Usurp" is an over-translation. "Have authority" (NIV) is more accurate.

Man   The Greek word *anēr* means both "man" and "husband". So it is an open question as to whether the primary emphasis here is on the wife's submission to her husband or women's subordination to men—some say to ecclesiastical authorities. Perhaps Paul had both in mind.

15 *In* The KJV says that under certain conditions the woman will be saved "in" childbearing. But the Greek preposition is *dia*, which with the genitive case (as here) signifies "through."

But what does this mean? How can a woman be saved "through childbearing"? The simplest suggestion is that, in spite of Eve's sin, godly women will be preserved through childbirth; that is, as a usual thing. Some think the context may imply that a woman's spiritual salvation is helped by her giving herself to motherly duties in the home, rather than seeking to dominate the church. Since the Greek has the definite article, *tēs teknogonias* (the noun is found only here in NT), others have interpreted "*the* childbearing" as referring to "the childbearing of Mary, which has undone the work of Eve" (Lock, p. 33).

3:1 *Bishop* The first 7 verses of chapter 3 are devoted to outlining the qualifications of a bishop. As a leader in the church he must be a man of exemplary character.

"The office of a bishop" is all one word in Greek, *episcopē*. Elsewhere in the NT it is used in this sense only in Acts 1:20, in a quotation from the Septuagint.

In verse 2 "bishop" is *episcopos*, from which comes "episcopal." It occurs only five times in the NT. In Acts 20:28 it is translated "overseers" and applied to the Ephesian elders by Paul. He also refers to the "bishops and deacons" at Philippi (Phil. 1:1). In Titus 1:7 and following, we again find what is required of a "bishop." Finally, in 1 Pet. 2:25, Christ is called "the Shepherd and Bishop of your souls."

The word *episcopos* is made up of *epi*, "upon" or "over," and *scopos*, "watcher." So it literally means "one who watches over." Thayer defines it thus: "*An overseer*, a man charged with the duty of seeing that things to be done by others are done rightly, *any curator, guardian,* or *superintendent* . . . specifically, the *superintendent, head* or *overseer of any Christian church*" (p. 243).

It will be seen that the basic meaning of *episcopos* is "overseer." The ancient Greeks thought of their gods as *episcopoi*. This usage is found in Homer's *Iliad* and many later writings.

Then it came to be used of men in various functions. Beyer says: "Protective care, however, is still the heart of the activity which men pursue as *episcopoi*" (TDNT, 2:610). Homer applies the term to ships' captains and merchants, who must be "overseers" of goods.

In the fourth and fifth centuries before Christ *episcopos* was used at Athens as a title for state officials. The same thing was true at Ephesus and in Egypt. But more common was the use of *episcopoi* (plural) for local officials and officers of societies. This brings us closer to the Christian *episcopos*.

In the Septuagint *episcopos* is used both for God, who oversees all things, and for men as supervisors in various fields of activity. The latter usage is found in the earlier, as well as the later, books of the OT.

Turning to the NT, we discover one fact immediately: there is no mention of any diocesan bishop. In the one church at Philippi there were *episcopoi*, "bishops" (Phil. 1:1). The apostles are never given this title. The bishop was a local official, and there were several of these in each congregation.

Furthermore, the "elders" (*presbyteroi*) and "bishops" (*episcopoi*) were the same. This is shown clearly in Acts 20. In verse 17 it says that Paul called for the "elders" (*presbyteroi*) of the church at Ephesus. In verse 28 he refers to them as *episcopoi*—"overseers" (KJV), "guardians" (RSV). The same people are designated by both titles. We shall find this same phenomenon clearly indicated in the Epistle to Titus. In the NT Church each local congregation was supervised by a group of elders or bishops and a group of deacons. It seems likely that the former had oversight of the spiritual concerns of the congregation and the latter of its material business.

When we come to Ignatius early in the second century (about A.D. 115), we find a very different picture. Now there is one bishop over each local church, together with several elders and several deacons. The bishop is supreme in authority. One of the keynotes of Ignatius' 7 letters is, "Obey your bishop." To the Trallians he wrote: "For when you are in subjection to the bishop as to Jesus Christ it is clear to me that you are living not after men, but after Jesus Christ. . . . Therefore it is necessary (as is your practice) that you should do nothing without the bishop, but be also in subjection to the presbytery, as to the Apostles of Jesus Christ. . . . And they also who are deacons of the mysteries of Jesus Christ must be in every way pleasing to all men" (*The Apostolic Fathers*, "Loeb Classical Library," 1:213–15). Here we see the beginnings of the episcopal hierarchy that flowered during the second century. But "in the beginning it was not so."

2 *Blameless* There are 6 Greek adjectives that are rendered "blameless" in the KJV. At the same time, one of these adjectives, *amōmos*, occurs 6 times in the NT and is translated 6 different ways in the KJV. Two of these are incorrect; the other 4 are acceptable.

The term here is *anepilēmptos* (only here; 5:7; 6:14). It comes from the alpha-privative *a-* and the verb *epilambanō*, which means "take hold of." It literally means "not apprehended, that cannot be laid hold of," and so "that cannot be reprehended, not open to censure, irreproachable" (Thayer, p. 44). Trench prefers "irreprehensible" and says the word indicated "affording nothing which an adversary could take hold of, on which he might ground a charge" (pp. 381–82). Arndt and Gingrich give a single definition: "irreproachable." That is the most accurate translation here. No one—not even a bishop—can hope to live without being blamed. But a Christian's conduct must be above reproach. It is important to remember that "bishop" here may indicate any leader in a local church.

Vigilant The Greek term here is *nēphalios*. It occurs only three times in the NT, all of them in the Pastoral Epistles. It is used of bishops (here), of women (v. 11), and of elders (Titus 2:2).

The word was first used literally to describe drink which was "unmixed with wine." The ancient Greeks used to give to the Muses offerings of water, milk, and honey. It was forbidden to mix wine with these. The prohibitions went a step further: the wood burned with the sacrifices must not include the twigs of grapevines. There must not be the slightest contact with that which caused drunkenness.

Applied first to materials, it later referred to persons. The meaning then was "abstaining from wine." Some commentators take the adjective here in this literal sense. But it probably should be taken metaphorically. Bauernfeind writes: "The reference is to the clarity and self-control necessary for sacred ministry in God's work" (TDNT, 4:941). Bernard says: "Primarily having reference to sobriety in the case of wine, it has here the more extended sense of *temperate*" (p. 53).

Sober This is another pastoral word, *sōphrōn*. It is found here and three times in Titus (1:8; 2:2,5). In the KJV it is translated three different ways in the three passages in Titus—"sober," "temperate," "discreet."

It is the adjective related to the noun *sōphrosynē* (2:9, 15). Basically it means "of sound mind, sane, in one's senses," and then "curbing one's desires and impulses, self-controlled, temperate." The ASV renders it "sober-minded."

There are two objections to "sober." One is that this term is often used as the opposite of "drunk." Much more than that is meant here. The other is that it often suggests a solemn demeanor, such as we find in "Mr. Sobersides." This too often is a denial of that radiant countenance which is the hallmark of the true Christian. "Self-controlled" (NIV) is best here.

Of Good Behavior This is the adjective *cosmios*, already noted in 2:9, where it is translated "modest." But the basic meaning is "orderly," and that fits well in this context. If a church official does not lead a well-ordered life, the work will suffer. Bernard says of *cosmios*: "This expresses the outward manifestation of the spirit of *sōphrosynē*" (p. 53). That is, inward self-control will be reflected in an outward life that is "orderly."

Given to Hospitality This is a single word in Greek, the adjective *philoxenos* (found also in Titus 1:8 and 1 Pet. 4:9). It is compounded of *philos*, "friend" or "lover," and *xenos*, "stranger." So it means "loving strangers, hospitable" (A-S), or "generous to guests" (Thayer). It's obviously best translated "hospitable," which is all that Arndt and Gingrich give for it.

Apt to Teach This is also one word in Greek, the adjective *didacticos* (cf. *didactic*). It is found only here and in 2 Tim. 2:24. The meaning is "skillful in teaching." It may be rendered "able to teach" (NASB, NIV)—a necessary qualification of bishops.

3 *Not Given to Wine* In Greek this is *mē*, which means "not," and the adjective *paroinos*—from *para*, "beside," and *oinos*, "wine," which suggests "one who sits long at his wine." It also has the secondary meaning, "quarrelsome over wine" (Thayer). That is why the ASV has "no brawler." Ellicott translates it "violent over wine" and says that it includes "drunkenness and its manifestations" (p. 58). But since "striker" (*plēktēs*) follows immediately, Bernard feels that the more moderate meaning, "given to wine," fits better. These two Greek words are found in the NT only here and in Titus 1:7.

Patient In the best Greek text the words translated "not greedy of filthy lucre" are omitted. So we pass by that phrase and come to the next word, rendered "patient."

The term is *epieikēs*. Simpson bluntly asserts: "*Epieikēs* defies exact translation." He goes on to say: "*Gracious, kindly, forbearing, considerate, magnanimous, genial,* all approximate to its idea" (p. 51).

The earliest meaning (from Homer down) seems to be "seemly, suitable." Thayer thinks that in the NT it means "equitable, fair, mild, gentle." Arndt and Gingrich give "yielding, gentle, kind." Vincent prefers "forbearing" (4:230), as does Bernard (p. 54). In 3 out of the 5 occurrences of this word in the NT it is translated "gentle" in KJV. That is the best rendering here (cf. NIV).

Brawler The expression "not a brawler" is one word in Greek, *amachos*, found only here and in Titus 3:2. By Xenophon, the historian, it is used in the sense of "abstaining from fighting, noncombatant." Then it took on the metaphorical sense, "not contentious" (A-S). Perhaps the best translation here is "not quarrelsome."

Covetous "Not covetous" is *aphilargyron* (only here and Heb. 13:5). Literally it means "not loving silver (money)." Perhaps the best we can do in English is "not a lover of money" (NIV).

4 Ruleth The Greek verb *proistēmi* literally means "put before" and so "set over." It can mean "rule" or "govern." But perhaps a more fitting translation here is "manage" (RSV, NASB, NIV) or "preside over." The same applies to "rule" in verse 5 (same word).

Gravity This is the same word which is translated "honesty" in 2:2 (see discussion there). The best rendering is probably "respect" (NIV).

6 Novice The word is *neophytos* (only here in NT), taken over into English as "neophyte." Literally it means "newly planted" and is so used in the Septuagint. In Christian literature alone it is used figuratively in the sense of "newly converted." So the most accurate translation is "new convert" (NASB) or "recent convert" (NIV).

Lifted Up with Pride This is all one word in the Greek, *typhoō* (found only in the Pastoral Epistles). It comes from *typhos*, "smoke," and so literally means "wrap in smoke." The first meaning given in Liddell-Scott-Jones is "delude," leading to "filled with insane arrogance"

(p. 1838). It is used only metaphorically, with the sense of "puffed up" or "conceited" (NIV). This was "the condemnation incurred by the devil" (NASB).

8 Grave The Greek adjective is *semnos*, from which comes the noun *semnotēs* (2:2; 3:4; Titus 2:7). The adjective is also found three times in the Pastorals (1 Tim. 3:8, 11; Titus 2:2), and only once elsewhere in the NT (Phil. 4:8; see comments there).

Trench says that "the *semnos* has a grace and dignity not lent him from earth; but which he owes to that higher citizenship which is also his" (p. 346). He adds that there is something "majestic and awe-inspiring in *semnos*" (p. 347).

Probably the best discussion of this term is in William Barclay's *More New Testament Words* (Harper, 1958), an exceedingly valuable little book. He says that *semnos* has in it "the majesty of divinity" (p. 141). It is used to express royalty and kingliness, as well as what is stately and dignified in language. The term is found frequently inscribed on tombs as a term of great respect. Barclay devotes nearly two pages to Aristotle's use of this term. He also mentions an ambassador who described the Roman senate as "an assembly of kings." That, declares Barclay, is what the Christian church should be. And each believer should manifest in his life "the majesty of Christian living."

It should be noted that this adjective is applied not only to the deacons in our present passage, but also to their wives in verse 11 and to elderly men in Titus 2:2. It carries with it the suggestion of the dignity and seriousness which should characterize leaders and older Christians.

Doubletongued The term *dilogos* (only here in NT) literally means "saying the same thing twice." And so it has the sense "*doubletongued, double in speech, saying one thing with one person, another with another* (with intent to deceive)" (Thayer, p. 152). Arndt and Gingrich suggest the translation "insincere," which is probably too general. The idea is conveyed well by "indulging in double talk" (NEB).

Greedy of Filthy Lucre This is all one word in Greek, *aischrokerdēs*, occurring only here and in Titus 1:7—in relation to a bishop there, to a deacon here. It means "eager for base gain" (Thayer) or "fond of dishonest gain" (AG).

10 Proved The verb *dokimazō* is used for three stages. Basically it means "test." But it also can mean "prove" by testing and even "approve" as the result of being tested. Perhaps all three ideas are included here.

The Office of a Deacon Again it is one word, the verb *diaconeō*. It is from *diaconos*, a "servant," especially one who waits on table. So *diaconeō* means "serve." But in the Christian Church *diaconos* finally took on the technical connotation "deacon." So here and in verse 13 (nowhere else in NT) the verb means "serve as deacons" (NIV).

11 Slanderers The Greek is *diabolous* (v. 11), plural of *diabolos*, "devil." In fact, the word is translated "devil" 35 out of the 38 times it occurs in the NT. It is rendered "false accuser" in 2 Tim. 3:3 and Titus 2:3—both times of human beings who engage in slander. Perhaps the modern equivalent would be "gossips" (Goodspeed; cf. "malicious gossips," NASB). This suggests the idea that those who indulge in gossip or slander are doing the devil's business!

13 Degree Today we think of obtaining a "degree" in academic circles. But the Greek word *bathmos* (only here in NT) means something a little different. Originally meaning "step," it is here used for "a grade of dignity and wholesome influence in the church" (Thayer, p. 129). Arndt and Gingrich say that the entire phrase here means "win a good standing (or rank) for oneself" (p. 92).

15 House The Greek word is *oikos*, the common term for "house." But since "the house of God" might be taken as referring to the church building, it is better to use "household" (NIV). *Oikos* here means the family, not the home.

Ground The word *hedraiōma* (only here in NT) is an ecclesiastical term. It means "a support," "bulwark." Either of these is a good translation. The church is to protect and defend the truth.

4:1 Expressly The noun *rhēma* means something said or spoken. So the adverb here, *rhētōs*, is well translated "expressly." But "explicitly" is a more contemporary term.

Latter Times The Greek literally says "later seasons." But Arndt and Gingrich suggest for this passage "in the last times." It would thus be equivalent to "the last days" (2 Tim. 3:1).

2 Seared with a Hot Iron This is all one word in the Greek, the perfect passive partici-

ple *kekaustēriasmenōn*. The verb *kaustēriazō* (only here in NT) means "to mark by branding, brand" (A-S), or "to burn in with a branding iron" (Thayer). Schneider develops this point further. He sees a reference to the custom of branding slaves and criminals. "Among the Greeks branding was mainly a punishment for runaway slaves.... The mark was usually put on the forehead with an iron" (TDNT, 3:644–45). So these false teachers bear the mark of slaves.

Bernard translates the whole phrase "branded in their own conscience." It is more than "seared," that is, made insensitive. He comments: "But the metaphor more probably has reference to the *penal branding* of criminals ... these hypocrites, with their outward show of holiness and of extreme asceticism ... have the brand of sin on their own consciences" (p. 65). Similarly Schneider writes: "The meaning is that they are in bondage to secret sin" (TDNT, p. 644).

5 Sanctified When applied to things, not persons, the verb *hagiazō* usually means "to set apart for sacred use, consecrate." But that idea hardly seems to fit here. Lock comments: "It becomes holy to the eater; not that it was unclean by itself, but that his scruples or thanklessness might make it so" (p. 48). Probably the best translation here is "sanctified."

The Word of God and Prayer The custom of saying grace before meals was practiced by the Jews and taken over by the early Christians. Often phrases of Scripture were used in this prayer of thanksgiving for the food, as is indicated in the *Apostolic Constitutions* (7:49). "The word of God and prayer" could suggest the reading of a brief biblical passage, followed by a prayer of thanks. This custom is observed at the breakfast table in many Christian homes today. White ties the two expressions together. He thinks it means "a scriptural prayer; a prayer in harmony with God's revealed truth" (EGT, 4:122). All of these suggestions may be employed in "asking the blessing" before meals.

6 Put ... in Remembrance In the active, the verb *hypotithēmi* means "place under" or "lay down." This is the way it is used in the only other place where it occurs in the NT (Rom. 16:4). But here it is in the middle voice and means "to suggest" (A-S) or "point out" (AG). It refers to teaching the truth.

Attained The verb is *parakoloutheō*, from *akoloutheō*, which means "follow," and *para*, "beside." So it means "follow closely." Here and in 2 Tim. 3:10 it suggests "follow faithfully" a rule or standard (Thayer). Timothy had faithfully followed the good teaching ("doctrine," KJV) of Paul. Now he was to pass this on to those to whom he ministered.

Paul belonged to the first generation of Christians, Timothy to the second. The continuance of Christianity depended on the faithfulness of the new generations of believers. This puts a heavy responsibility on us today, if the faith is to survive.

7 Profane The adjective *bebēlos* occurs five times in the NT. Twice it is applied to persons (1 Tim. 1:9; Heb. 12:16). Three times it describes things (1 Tim. 4:7; 6:20; 2 Tim. 2:16). In every case it is translated "profane" in KJV. Arndt and Gingrich suggest "worldly" for our passage here, but "profane" for the other two applications to things. With regard to persons, they prefer "godless" for 1 Tim. 1:9 and "irreligious" for Heb. 12:16 (as a description of Esau).

J. C. Lambert points out the origin of the word. He writes:

> *Bebēlos* is the almost exact equivalent of Latin *profanus*, whence English "profane." *Profanus* (from *pro*—"before," and *fanum*—"temple") means "without the temple," and so "unconsecrated," as opposed to *sacer*. *Bebēlos* (from *baino*—"to go," whence *bēlos*—"threshold") denotes that which is "trodden," "open to access," and so again "unconsecrated" in contrast to *hieros* (sacred) (HDCG, 2:422).

Arndt and Gingrich point out the fact that while *bebēlos* is used in the OT in a ritualistic sense, it occurs in the NT always as an ethical and religious term. That is "profane" which is secular, not sacred, which leaves God out of account.

Hauck says this about *bebēlos* in our passage: "As applied to material things in the Pastorals, the word refers to Gnostic teachings which are scornfully described as profane and unholy *mythoi* (1 Tim. 4:7)" (TDNT, 1:604). It would seem that "worldly" (Goodspeed, NASB) fits well here.

8 Exercise The noun (only here in NT) is *gymnasia*, from which obviously comes *gymnasium*. The verb is *gymnazō* (v. 7, "exercise"), which comes from *gymnos*, "naked." This calls attention to the fact that Greek athletes customarily wore no clothes when exercising. Since the idea of athletic training is inherent here, it would seem that "training" (NIV) is a more adequate translation than "exercise."

This gives a bit of added thrust to the verb "exercise" in verse 7. We are to "train" (AG) ourselves daily in spiritual things, if we wish to maintain good health spiritually.

10 Suffer Reproach This is a matter of textual criticism. The bulk of the medieval manuscripts have *oneidizometha*. But the original reading seems to have been *agōnizometha*. The verb *agōnizō* literally means "compete in an athletic contest" (cf. Col. 1:29). The best translation of this passage is either "toil and struggle" (Goodspeed) or "labor and strive" (NASB, NIV).

Trust These two words do not mean exactly the same thing. The Greek clearly has "hope"; literally, "have set our hope."

12 Conversation We have already met the Greek word *anastrophē* and noted that it refers to the whole "manner of life." "In word, in conversation" is obviously redundant. The Greek has two distinct items: "in word, in conduct."

13 Doctrine The Greek word *didaskalia* has no theological overtones, such as attach to our word "doctrine." What this verse says is that Timothy is to perform three essential functions as pastor: (1) the public reading of the Scriptures; (2) exhorting the people to walk in the light of God's Word; (3) teaching them what the Word means.

14 The Presbytery This comes directly from the Greek word *presbyterion*. Elsewhere in the NT the term occurs only in Luke 22:66 and Acts 22:5. In both those places it refers to the Jewish Sanhedrin. Here it means the group of elders who laid their hands on Timothy, evidently at the time of his ordination into the Christian ministry.

15 Meditate The verb is *meletaō*. It comes from *meletē*, "care," and so means "to care for," "to attend to" (A-S). It is from the stem of the verb *melō*, "to care for." In verse 14 "neglect" is the verb *amelō*, *melō* with the the alpha-privative *a-*. There is thus a play on words in the Greek which is lost in English. In verse 14, Paul says to Timothy, "Don't be careless about the gift you received at your ordination"—perhaps the "gift" (Greek, *charisma*) of prophecy, or prophetic preaching. In verse 15 he says, "Be constantly careful about these things."

In Greek the second clause, "Give thyself

wholly to them," literally reads, "Be in these things."

Profiting The word *prokopē* means "a cutting forward," "an advance." Its clear and simple meaning is "progress." Aside from this passage it occurs only in Phil. 1:12, 25, where it is rendered "furtherance." It should be "progress" in all three places (cf. NIV).

The NASB has properly caught the meaning of this verse. It reads: "Take pains with these things; be *absorbed* in them, so that your progress may be evident to all."

5:1 Rebuke The verb *epiplēssō* is a strong compound (cf. NASB, "sharply rebuke"), occurring only here in the NT. Literally it means "strike at" or "beat upon." Paul warns young Timothy not to strike at an older man in the church. (The reference to "elder women" in verse 2 suggests that "elder" here is not used in an official sense.)

Incidentally, we must not think of this "youth" (cf. 4:12) as a teenager or even a young man in his twenties. Probably he was around 20 years old when Paul, at Lystra on his second missionary journey, took on Timothy as an associate. That was at least 15 years before this Epistle was written. By now Timothy would have been in his upper thirties. But in the Roman Empire one was referred to as a "young man" until he was 45.

4 Nephews The word *ekgona* is found only here in the NT. All lexicons are agreed that the proper translation is "grandchildren," which also fits the context better.

Requite The one word in English represents two in Greek. The first is a verb which literally means "return," "render what is due," or simply "pay." The second is the noun *amoibē* (only here in NT), which means a "return" or "recompense." Arndt and Gingrich translate the passage: "Make a return to those who brought them up" (p. 46). The idea is that children and grandchildren should repay the care that was given them when they were growing up.

5 Desolate The Greek has *memonōmenē*, the perfect passive participle of *monoō* (only here in NT). This comes from the adjective *monos*, "alone," and so means "leave alone." The best rendering here is "left alone" or "all alone" (NIV).

6 Pleasure Lock suggests that the word *spatalōsa* is "probably akin to *spaō*, to suck

down, hence to live luxuriously, self-indulgently" (p. 58). Moffatt writes: "The modern term *fast*, in which the notion of prodigality and wastefulness is more prominent than that of sensual indulgence, exactly expresses the significance of this word" (EGT, 4:129). But in his translation of the New Testament he has: "The widow who plunges into dissipation."

8 Infidel The Greek has the adjective *apistos*, which simply means "unbelieving." It is used frequently in the Corinthian letters for "unbelievers," as opposed to Christians. What Paul is saying here is that a professing Christian who does not take care of his family is worse than a non-Christian.

9 Taken into the Number "Let . . . be taken into the number" is all one word in Greek, *katalegesthō*. This verb (only here in NT) is used by ancient writers for enrolling soldiers. The correct translation here is "enrolled."

There has been a great deal of discussion as to whether there was an official "order" of widows in the NT Church. Vincent writes: "The Fathers, from the end of the second century to the fourth, recognized a class known as *presbytidēs*, *aged women* (Titus ii. 3), who had oversight of the female church-members and a separate seat in the congregation. The council of Laodicea abolished this institution, or so modified it that widows no longer held an official relation to the church" (4:257).

Somewhat different is the opinion of Moffatt. He says: "In the references to widows in the earliest Christian literature outside the N.T. (with the exception of Ignatius *Smyrn.* 13) they are mentioned as objects of charity along with orphans, etc. . . . None of these places hints at an order of widows" (EGT, 4:130).

At any rate, we know that widows, especially elderly ones, were cared for by the church (Acts 6:1). But they must be widows in real need.

10 Afflicted "She have brought up children" and "she have lodged strangers" are each one word in Greek—two compound verbs found only here in the NT. The second is more accurately rendered "shown hospitality to strangers."

"Afflicted" is a participle of the verb *thlibō*, which means "to press." It includes all those who are suffering from the various pressures of life. Today "afflicted" generally suggests one who is ill. The term here has a wider application. Probably "distressed" or "oppressed" gives the idea better.

11 Wax Wanton The verb is *katastrēniaō* (only here in NT). It literally means "to feel the impulses of sexual desire" (Thayer, p. 337). Arndt and Gingrich translate the clause, "when they feel sensuous impulses that alienate them from Christ" (p. 420). Lock suggests that the meaning here is "to grow physically restless and so restive against the limitations of Christian widowhood" (p. 60). Bernard says, "The metaphor is that of a young animal trying to free itself from the yoke" (p. 82). Schneider says the meaning is that "they become lascivious against Christ" or that "they burn with sensual desire in opposition to Christ" (TDNT, 3:631).

Hendriksen (pp. 175–76) thinks that evil desire is not necessarily indicated here. It is natural for young widows to wish to remarry. For that very reason they should not be put on the official list of widows, lest they be more concerned with finding a husband than serving the Lord in the church. Hendriksen suggests "grow restless with desire." Unfortunately we have no secular example of this verb—this is the only passage cited in the two-volume *Lexicon* of Liddell-Scott-Jones—so that the meaning is not completely clear. Goodspeed has, "When their youthful vigor comes between them and Christ," which is a minimum rendering. The NEB puts it more strongly: "For when their passions draw them away from Christ" (cf. NIV).

12 Damnation The term "damnation" occurs about a dozen times in the KJV (all in NT). This is considered by most to be an over-translation. The word here literally means "judgment." The strongest rendering it can properly be given is "condemnation."

Faith The Greek word is *pistis*, which in the KJV is translated "faith" 239 of the 244 times it occurs in the NT. But the original classical connotation was "faithfulness, reliability" (AG). Then it means "solemn promise, oath." Thirdly, it signified "proof, pledge." Finally it came to have the religious signification of "trust, confidence," or "faith" in the active sense of believing.

The context indicates that here it clearly means "pledge"; that is, the pledge they made to give full loyalty to Christ (cf. NIV: "they have broken their first pledge").

13 Tattlers The term *phluaros* is found only here in the NT. It comes from the verb *phluō*, which means "to boil up" or "throw up bubbles" of water, and so "to indulge in empty and foolish talk" (Thayer). Actually the word here is an adjective, meaning "gossipy" (AG). The best translation here is "gossips" (NIV) which is used more today than "tattlers."

14 Guide Paul advises younger women to marry, bear children, and "guide the house." This is one word in Greek, compounded of *oikos*, "house" or "household," and *despotēs*, "master" or "lord" (cf. our "despot"). So the verb (only here in NT) literally means "to rule a household" (A-S) and is translated that way in the ASV. But since the NT suggests that the husband should be the head of the house, "manage their homes" (NIV) is the basic idea. The NEB expresses it well: "preside over a home." That is what the wife and mother should do.

16 Charged The Greek verb is *bareō*. It comes from *baros*, which means a "weight" or "burden." So the verb means "weigh down" or "burden." In the passive, as here, it signifies "be burdened." The church was not to be burdened with the care of widows who had relatives that could provide for them. Only those who were widows without support should be on the rolls.

Donald MacKenzie says:

> The Apostle makes it clear that no widows were to be relieved who had children or grandchildren able to support them. This was not simply to save the scanty finances of the Church, but much more in order to enforce a binding moral principle. There is every reason to believe that there were families who tried to evade what was a cardinal obligation of piety by attempting to get their widowed mothers or grandmothers to be supported by the Church. Possibly some widows were themselves eager to do so, so as to gain thus greater personal liberty. Against this St. Paul is emphatic in declaring that descendants ought to support their widowed relatives. He repeats this duty thrice. . . . Church support is not a substitute for filial indifference or neglect (HDAC, 3:676).

The Early Church gave much attention to the care of widows. Polycarp speaks of widows as an "altar of sacrifice," on which Christians should lavish their offerings. Hermas urges believers to buy "oppressed souls" instead of more fields. Ignatius criticizes the heretics for failing to care for their widows and orphans. Aristides in his *Apology* says that Christians "do not turn away their countenance" from widows.

It was the Church of Jesus Christ which set

the pattern for the care of the needy, providing orphanages, hospitals, and schools. Today the state has taken over many of these functions. But we as Christians still need to feel a personal compassion for those who are in need. It is a part of our Christian duty.

17 Honor The Greek word is *timē*. Originally it signified "*a valuing by which the price is fixed;* hence *the price* itself: of the price paid or received for a person or thing bought or sold" (Thayer, p. 624). It is used that way several times in the NT and is translated "price" (Matt. 27:6, 9; Acts 4:34; 5:2–3; 19:19; 1 Cor. 6:20; 7:23). On the other hand, it is translated "honor" (KJV) 33 times. Moulton and Milligan cite clear examples of both meanings in the papyri. The word was used for the "price" of oil, wheat, hay, and medicine. As one of the meanings of *timē*, Arndt and Gingrich give "honorarium, compensation" and suggest that this is "perhaps" the sense here. Under *diplous* ("double") they cite the case of an emperor giving double wages to a prophet for his services.

Most of the versions have "honor" in this passage. However, the NEB reads, "Elders who do well as leaders should be reckoned worthy of a double stipend." And the *Jerusalem Bible* has "double consideration," with the marginal suggestion "doubly paid." Pastors will appreciate the way Charles B. Williams renders it: "should be considered as deserving twice the salary they get." N. J. D. White says: "*Remuneration* is a better rendering of *timē* than pay, as less directly expressive of merely monetary reward." Liddon suggests the rendering "*honorarium*" (EGT, 4:134). That this is the meaning of *timē* here is clearly indicated by the fact that Paul has just been talking about the church's support of needy widows and that he goes on (v. 18) to say, "The worker deserves his wages" (NIV).

Doctrine The word *didaskalia* occurs 21 times in the NT. In the KJV it is rendered "doctrine" 19 times and "teaching" only once. This order should be reversed. Paul is not talking about doctrine in the sense of theology. "The word and doctrine" simply means "preaching and teaching" (NIV).

19 Before The Greek word translated "before" is *epi*, which means "upon." By extension it means "on the basis of," and that is the correct idea here (cf. NASB).

20 Rebuke The word *elenchō* first meant "*to convict* . . . generally with a suggestion of the

shame of the person convicted" and here means "*to reprehend severely, chide, admonish, reprove*" (Thayer, p. 203). For this passage Arndt and Gingrich suggest "reprove, correct." The NEB has "expose publicly." It appears that either "rebuke" or "reprove" fits well here.

21 Preferring, Partiality We find two Greek words that occur only here in the NT. The first, *prokrima*, is rendered in the KJV "preferring one before another." The word literally means "prejudging," and so "prejudice." That is perhaps the best translation here. Arndt and Gingrich suggest "discrimination," which sounds contemporary.

The second word is *prosklisis*, which means "inclination, partiality" (A-S). Cremer writes: "*Prokrima* includes an unfavourable *prejudgment* against one; *prosklesis*, nothing but positive *favour, partiality*" (p. 378).

22 Suddenly The word is *tacheōs*, which means "quickly, hastily." Abbott-Smith goes on to say that here, in Gal. 1:6, and in 2 Thess. 2:2 it carries the "suggestion of rashness." Arndt and Gingrich give for these same passages: "too quickly, too easily, hastily." The thought of the command is expressed well in the NEB: "Do not be over-hasty in laying on hands in ordination."

23 Water, Wine This verse has posed a problem for many Christians, particularly in the United States. Why would the Apostle Paul tell his young associate Timothy no longer to drink water, but to use a little wine because of his stomach (Greek, *stomachon*) and his frequent "infirmities" (lit., "weaknesses," or "illnesses")?

Some have tried to dissolve the difficulty by saying that there are two Greek words for *wine*. *Gleukos* (cf. *glucose*) means "sweet new wine," that is, unfermented grape juice. *Oinos* simply means "wine." True. But the problem is that *oinos* is the word used here and in the story of Jesus turning the water into wine (John 2:9). So this suggestion is of no help at all.

The important thing to note is that *oinos* is used in the Septuagint for both fermented and unfermented grape juice. Since it can mean either one, it is valid to insist that in some cases it may simply mean grape juice and not fermented wine.

It has often been objected that in those days of no refrigeration it would have been impossible to keep grape juice from fermenting. But the Roman writer Cato, in his treatise *On Agriculture*, gave this prescription: "If you wish to keep new wine sweet the whole year round, put new wine in a jar, cover the stopper with pitch, place the jar in a fishpond, take it out after the thirtieth day; you will have sweet wine all the year round."

Probably the question cannot be settled on the basis of Greek words, but rather on moral and scientific principles. Does fermented wine have medicinal value? The present writer once put this question to a noted surgeon, the head of a department in a university medical school. His answer was an emphatic no.

One thing, of course, must be insisted on: Paul was not advocating the general use of wine as a beverage. The most that can be said is that he was suggesting that Timothy, because of frequent stomach illness, should take "a little wine" as medicine. And the possibility is still open that the apostle referred to unfermented grape juice, which of course is good for a weak stomach.

24–25 Open Beforehand, Manifest Beforehand

The expression "open beforehand" (v. 24) and "manifest beforehand" (v. 25) are both translations of the same Greek adjective, *prodēlos* (only here and Heb. 7:14). It means "evident beforehand" or "clearly evident" (A-S). Thayer defines the term as "openly evident, known to all, manifest." White comments: "Not *open beforehand* (AV), but *evident* (RV). . . . The *pro* is not indicative of antecedence in time, but of publicity" (EGT, 4:139). "Going before" (v. 24) is literally "leading the way." Men's evident sins lead them to the judgment.

6:1 Masters

Elsewhere in his Epistles, Paul uses the word *kyrios* for masters of slaves. But in the first two verses of this chapter and in Titus 2:9 we find the term *despotēs*. The only other place in the NT where this usage occurs is in 1 Pet. 2:18. The other 6 times that the word is found in the NT it applies to God as the sovereign Lord of all. Thayer says the term "denoted absolute ownership and uncontrolled power." Similarly Trench says that "the *despotēs* exercises a more unrestricted power and absolute domination" (p. 96). That is why the ancient Greeks applied this word only to their gods. It was when the slave-masters became more autocratic that the term was used for them. Originally the word carried none of the opprobrium attached to the modern English derivative *despot*.

Luke is the only one of the Evangelists to use *despotēs*, once in his Gospel (2:29) and once in Acts (4:24). It has been suggested that Luke may have actually composed the Pastoral Epistles for Paul, under his direction, when the

apostle was elderly and needed the care of his physician and secretary.

From this passage, and many others, it is clear that the NT did not directly attack the institution of slavery. It is claimed that half the population of the Roman Empire in Paul's day consisted of slaves. To have launched a frontal assault on slavery would probably have resulted in the extinction of Christianity. What the NT does do is to lay down the principles of love and justice which finally brought about the abolition of this accursed custom of long standing.

3 Wholesome

The heterodox teacher does not consent to the use of "wholesome" words. The adjective is actually a participial form of the verb *hygiainō*, from which comes *hygienic*. Elsewhere in the Pastoral Epistles it is regularly translated "sound" (cf. 1:10).

Aside from the Gospel of Luke (3 times) and the Pastorals (8 times), the word is found only in 3 John 2, where it conforms to the customary greeting of those days. This fact also suggests that Luke may have had a considerable part in the composition of the Pastoral Epistles. We know that he was the amanuensis for 2 Timothy, for Paul says, "Only Luke is with me" (4:11).

4 Doting

"Doting" is the present participle of *noseō* (only here in NT). Literally the verb means "to be sick." In classical Greek it was used metaphorically for mental illness. Thayer says that here it means "to be taken with such an interest in a thing as amounts to a disease, to have a morbid fondness for" (p. 429). Arndt and Gingrich suggest the translation "have a morbid craving for" (cf. Goodspeed). White says of the person described here: "His disease is intellectual curiosity about trifles" (EGT, 4:141).

Strifes of Words

The literal meaning of the compound *logo-machias* (only here in NT) is "word battles." It is rendered in the KJV "strifes of words." A good translation for this section of the verse is: "He has a morbid interest in controversial questions and disputes about words" (NASB). This is a form of illness that is not only psychological and social; it is also a spiritual sickness. Too many church members are afflicted with it.

Surmisings

The term *hyponoiai* (only here in NT) is best translated "suspicions" (NIV). Moulton and Milligan give several examples of this meaning in the papyri. White defines the phrase here: "*Malicious suspicions* as to the honesty of those who differ from them" (EGT, 4:142). This is a serious judgment for people to make, but it is often done.

5 *Perverse Disputings* The double compound *diaparatribai* (only here in NT) has basically the idea of friction or irritation. Thayer says it means "constant contention, incessant wrangling or strife." Bernard comments that "the first of two prepositions in a composite word governs the meaning, and thus *dia* is emphatic, signifying the persistency and obstinacy of the disputes" (p. 94). White agrees. He says that it "denotes *protracted* quarrelings."

Destitute The form here is the perfect passive participle of *apostereō*. Abbott-Smith gives this definition for the verb: "*To defraud, deprive of, despoil* (in classics chiefly of the misappropriation of trust funds)" (p. 54). For this passage he suggests "bereft of" (cf. RSV). White comments: "*Apostereō* conveys the notion of a person being deprived of a thing to which he has a right. . . . This is expressed in R.V., *bereft of*. The truth was once theirs; they have disinherited themselves. The A.V., *destitute of*, does not assume that they ever had it" (EGT, 4:142). The best translation is "deprived of" (NASB).

Gain is Godliness This is obviously an incorrect rendering. The word for "godliness" is clearly the subject, for it has the article, while "gain" does not. The correct translation is: "supposing godliness to be a means of gain." The word for "means of gain," *porismos* ("a gainful trade"), is found in the NT only in this passage (vv. 5–6).

6 *Contentment* The first meaning of *autarkeia* is "sufficiency" or "competence." Then it came to mean "contentment" or "self-sufficiency" (AG). This was a favorite virtue of the Stoics. Bernard comments: "That riches are not essential to true well-being was a commonplace of pre-Christian philosophy, which laid great emphasis on *autarkeia* or the 'self-sufficiency' of the wise man. . . . St. Paul's words go deeper, inasmuch as they lay stress on *eusebeia* (godliness) as a chief condition of happiness, and recognize the proper place of *autarkeia*, as *contentment*, not *self-sufficiency*" (p. 95). The word occurs elsewhere in the NT only in 2 Cor. 9:8, where it carries the original meaning, "sufficiency."

White feels that "contentment" is not strong enough here. He writes: "*Autarkeia* is more profound, and denotes independence of, and indif-

ference to, any lot; as man's finding not only his resources in himself, but being indifferent to everything else besides. This was St. Paul's condition when he had learnt to be *autarkes*, Phil. iv. 11" (EGT, 4:142).

8 *Food and Raiment* Both of these terms in Greek are found only here in the NT. The first, *diatrophas*, signifies "means of subsistence," and so may have a broader connotation than simply food, though the primary reference is to that which nourishes or sustains. In a papyrus contract of apprenticeship from Oxyrhynchus, Egypt, and dated A.D. 66—perhaps the very year that 1 Timothy was written—this word occurs in the sense of board and room. Five drachmas was to be paid for the boy's "keep" (VGT, p. 156).

The second term is *skepasma*. Literally it means a "covering." Though used mainly for clothing, it sometimes referred to a house (as in Aristotle's *Metaphysics*). In the broadest sense it means "protection." So these two terms taken together would cover the necessities of life, which we refer to today as "food, clothing, and shelter."

9 *Hurtful* This is another word found only here in the NT. *Blaberos* comes from the verb *blaptō*, which means hurt, harm, injure, or damage. Probably "harmful" (NIV) is a more contemporary translation than "hurtful."

10 *All Evil* The Greek says "all evils." Most modern versions have either "all kinds of evil" (ASV, NIV) or "all sorts of evil" (NASB). As Patrick Fairbairn says, "There is no kind of evil to which the love of money may not lead men, when it once fairly takes hold of them" (*Pastoral Epistles*, p. 239).

Sorrows The word *odynē* occurs scores of times in the Septuagint, translating no less than 26 different Hebrew words. But in the NT it is found only twice. In Rom. 9:2, Paul uses it to express his mental distress over the unbelief of his fellow Jews. Here it is used for the remorse of conscience. Moffatt has "many a pang of remorse."

The verb *peripeirō*, "pierced . . . through," occurs only here in the NT. "Erred from the faith" is literally "have been led astray from the faith." That is, they have forsaken the straight path of truth. Bernard comments: "Struggling out of this they get entrapped among the briars and thorns of the world, and pierce themselves" (p. 97). This is what always happens to those who go astray.

11 Meekness The word *praupothia* is found only here in the NT. The cognate adjective means "gentle," and "gentleness" (NIV) is the best translation for this noun. Michaelis writes: "The meaning is not so much 'meekness' in the sense of 'tractability' but 'composure' . . . which can take wrongs calmly" (TDNT, 5:939).

12 Fight The verb is *agōnizomai*. The noun is *agōn*. They come from the verb *agō*, which means "lead." So the basic idea of *agōn* was a gathering. But since the largest gatherings of the first century, as usually also of the twentieth century, were for athletic contests, the term came to be used for such events. The verb signified "to compete in an athletic contest." So Goodspeed translates this passage, "Enter the great contest of faith!" Since the leading event in the ancient contests was the long-distance race (e.g., the Marathon race), *The New English Bible* has, "Run the great race of faith." White thinks that "the metaphor has its full force here . . . *Engage in the contest which profession of the faith entails*" (EGT, 4:145).

Bernard agrees with this. He writes: "The metaphor of life as a gymnastic contest was one which naturally suggested itself to those who had witnessed the Olympian or Isthmian games which played, even as late as the Apostolic age, so important a part in Greek national life. Philo uses the illustration again and again" (pp. 97–98). It is reflected in Heb. 12:1. It was a favorite figure with Paul (cf. 1 Cor. 9:24; Phil. 3:12, 14; 2 Tim. 4:7).

Though the original meaning of the noun and verb was that of "contest" in an athletic sense, the words came to be used generally in the sense of "struggle" or "fight." But it should be remembered that the primary reference is athletic rather than military.

12–13 Profession, Confession? "Profession" (v. 12) and "confession" (v. 13) are exactly the same in Greek. Consistency would seem to suggest that we use the same translation in both cases, but which is better?

The word is *homologia*. In the KJV it is translated "profession" everywhere else in the NT (Heb. 3:1; 4:14; 10:23; cf. 2 Cor. 9:13). The cognate verb *homologeō* ("professed," v. 12) occurs 23 times in the NT. In the KJV it is rendered "confess" 17 times, "profess" 3 times, and once each "promise" (Matt. 14:7), "give thanks" (Heb. 13:15), and "confession is made" (Rom. 10:10).

The literal meaning of the verb is "say the same thing" (*legō-homos*), and so means not to

deny but "to declare." In Matt. 14:7 it suggests "not to refuse," and so "to promise."

Thayer points out the basic difference between "confess" and "profess" by calling attention to their roots in Latin. *Profiteor* means "to declare openly and voluntarily," *confiteor* "to declare fully"—"implying the yielding or change of one's conviction" (p. 446). So one professes his faith but confesses his sin. Arndt and Gingrich think that the meaning here is "bear testimony to a conviction." They would translate the combination of verb and noun in verse 12, "make the good profession of faith." They go on to say, "Jesus, the first Christian martyr . . . bore witness to the same *good profession of faith* vs. 13" (p. 571).

Michel notes that the Greek sense of the verb is "to state solemnly," "to affirm," "to attest." He says that it signifies "a solemn declaration of faith in the Christian sense of proclamation" (TDNT, 5:207).

Michel also has some helpful observations about the noun. He writes: "*Homologia* implies consent to some thing felt to be valid, and in such a way that it is followed by definite resolve and action, by ready attachment to a cause. The aim in *homologia* is not a theoretical agreement which does not commit us, but acceptance of a common cause" (TDNT, 5:200). With regard to our passage he comments: "Just because Timothy has made this binding confession he is committed to passing on the proclamation, keeping the commandment and walking without blame until Christ is manifested" (p. 211). He also holds that the reference here is to Timothy's ordination, when the young preacher made a good confession before the congregation (p. 216). Others think it refers to the time of his baptism.

Which shall it be, "confession" or "profession"? The choice is difficult. Weymouth and Moffatt have "confession," but Goodspeed has "profession." However, most of the recent versions agree on "confession" (ASV, RSV, NASB, NEB, NIV). The majority of the best commentators support this.

15 Potentate The Greek word is *dynastēs*, from which we get *dynasty*. Literally it means "the one who can do something" (from *dynamai*, "I am able"). Grundmann writes: "It was used from an early period for 'ruler,' 'the one who is powerful,' 'the one who exercises authority and rule'" (TDNT, 2:286).

The word occurs only three times in the NT, with three different connotations. In Luke 1:52 it is used for "rulers." In Acts 8:27 it describes a court official. But here it clearly refers to God, who is the "Sovereign" of the universe.

16 *Immortality* Two Greek words are translated "immortality" in the NT. In this passage it is *athanasia*, which literally means "deathlessness." It occurs only here and in 1 Cor. 15:53–54.

The other word is *aphtharsia*, "incorruptibility." Only twice is it translated "immortality" (Rom. 2:7; 2 Tim. 1:10). Four times is it rendered "incorruption" and twice "sincerity." The English adjective "immortal" is found only once (1 Tim. 1:17), though the Greek original, *aphthartos*, is given its more literal translation in half a dozen other passages. The two nouns seem to be used interchangeably by Paul in his great treatise on the Resurrection (1 Corinthians 15). There *athanasia* is found in verses 53 and 54, *aphtharsia* in verses 42, 50, 53, and 54.

Approach "Which no man can approach unto" is all one word in Greek, *aprositos*. It simply means "unapproachable" (NIV). Paul probably had in mind the experience of Moses (Exod. 33:20).

17 *Highminded* The compound verb *hypsēlophroneō* is found only here in the NT. E. K. Simpson (*Pastoral Epistles*, p. 90) calls it "a compound probably of Pauline mintage." The more common Greek term of that day was *megalophroneō*. Both mean "haughty, arrogant, proud." Bernard comments: "The pride of purse is not only vulgar, it is sinful" (p. 101).

Trust in Uncertain Riches The Greek says, "Set their hope on the uncertainty of riches." The word for "uncertainty," *adēlotēs*, occurs only here in the NT. There is nothing in this life more uncertain than riches, as many men have found to their sorrow.

18 *Distribute, Communicate* Both the Greek words are found only here in the NT. They are adjectives, introduced by *einai*, "to be." The first, *eumetadotos*, "is best rendered 'ready to impart' " (VGT, p. 263). Thayer adds to this "liberal," whereas Arndt and Gingrich simply give "generous." The second, *koinōnokos*, comes from *koinos*, "common." It is related to *koinōnia*, "fellowship." In classical Greek it first meant "sociable, ready and apt to form and maintain communion and fellowship," and then "inclined to make others sharers in one's possessions, inclined to impart, free in giving, liberal" (Thayer, p. 352).

Bernard suggests that the second adjective

"seems to express a wider idea" than the first, and adds: "As is often the case, the larger word is placed second, by way of explanation; a kind heart as well as a generous hand is demanded of the rich" (p. 102). Lock spells it out a little more fully. He says that the distinction between the adjectives is either "quick to give away to others in charity . . . and ready to share with one's friends that which is one's own," or "*eumetadotos*, of action, 'openhanded' . . . *koinōnikos*, of demeanour and temper, 'gracious,' with true sense of human fellowship, the antithesis of *hypsēlophronein*" (pp. 74–75). Since God is so rich toward us (v. 17), we should be rich toward others.

Probably the best translation of the latter half of verse 18 is "to be generous and willing to share" (NIV).

19 *Laying Up in Store* This is all one word in Greek—the participle *apothēsaurizontas*. It comes from *thēsauros*, which first meant "a treasury" and then "a treasure." The idea here is evidently that by giving generously people will be "storing up for themselves the treasure of a good foundation for the future" (NASB).

Eternal The best Greek text has "that which is life indeed" rather than "eternal life." The correct wording obviously has great homiletical possibilities.

20 *Committed to Thy Trust* The KJV has, "Keep that which is committed to thy trust." A literal translation of the Greek would be, "Guard the deposit." The expression is found again in 2 Tim. 1:12, 14 (the only other places where *parathēkē*, "deposit," occurs in NT). This deposit was the truth of the gospel, to be guarded against heresies.

Science Falsely So Called The use of the word "science" here is obviously incorrect. The Greek has *gnōsis*, "knowledge." Science is only a part of human knowledge. Paul was not antiscientific!

"Falsely so called" is one word in Greek, *pseudonymos* (cf. *pseudonym*), found only here in the NT. It literally means "falsely named." The reference is probably to the false claims of the Gnostics that they had the true *gnōsis*. With them "knowledge" was the key word. They found contradictions between the OT and the NT, as elaborated in Marcion's famous second-century work, *Antitheses*. But this does not mean, as some older critics claimed, that the Pastoral Epistles were written later than Marcion's time. Now we know that Gnosticism had already penetrated Judaism before the time of Christ.

Hort, however, feels that the primary reference here is to "the endless contrast of decisions, founded on endless distinctions, which played so large a part in the casuistry of the scribes as interpreters of the law" (*Judaistic Christianity*, p. 140, quoted approvingly by both Bernard and Lock).

2 Timothy

1:3 *Forefathers* The Greek word *progonos* is an adjective meaning "born before." But in the plural it is used as a substantive. It occurs (in NT) only here and in 1 Tim. 5:4. There it refers to living parents or grandparents. Here it means "ancestors."

6 *Stir Up* Found only here in the NT, the verb is *anazōpyreō*. The prepositional prefix *ana* has two meanings, "up" and "again." The middle item, *zō*, means "life." The last root, *pyr*, is "fire." If we take *ana* as "again," the full translation would be "stir alive again into a flame." Arndt and Gingrich give here the simple rendering "rekindle" (cf. NASB, "kindle afresh").

But probably a majority of the best commentators agree that *ana* here means "up" rather than "again" (re-). Ellicott writes: "The simple form *zōpyrein* is 'to kindle to flame,' the compound *anazōpyrein* is either (a) to 'rekindle' . . . or (b) as here, 'to kindle *up*,' 'to fan into a flame,' without, however, involving any *necessary* reference to a *previous* state of higher ardor or of fuller glow" (p. 124). Lock says that the verb properly means "to stir up smouldering embers into a living flame," or "to keep at white heat" (p. 85). In line with this, Donald Guthrie comments: "There is no necessary suggestion, therefore, that Timothy had lost his early fire, although undoubtedly, like every Christian, he needed an incentive to keep the fire burning at full flame" ("The Pastoral Epistles," *Tyndale New Testament Commentaries*, p. 126). In a similar vein Hendriksen writes: "The flame had not gone out, but it was burning slowly and had to be agitated to white heat" (NTC: *Pastoral Epistles*, 229). The best translation here is "fan into flame" (NIV).

General Booth of the Salvation Army once made this pertinent observation: "The ten-

dency of fire is to go out; watch the fire on the altar of your heart." Anyone who has burned wood in a fireplace knows that periodically it is necessary to add fresh fuel and sometimes to fan the embers into a flame. We need to keep alive the inner flame by adding the fuel of the Word of God and fanning it with prayer.

Gift Charisma is the Greek word here translated "gift." Paul reminds Timothy that he had received this gift "by the putting on of my hands." In 1 Tim. 4:14 it was "the hands of the presbytery," a rather clear reference to ordination. Here it may refer to the time when Paul chose to take Timothy along with him as a helper. Bernard comments: "The *charisma* is not an ordinary gift of God's grace, such as every Christian may seek and obtain according to his need; but is the special grace received by Timothy to fit him for his ministerial functions" (p. 109).

7 *Fear* Three Greek nouns are translated as "fear" in the NT (KJV). *Deilia* is found only here. The most frequent one is *phobos* (47 times). *Eulobeia* occurs twice (Heb. 5:7; 12:28). Trench points out these differences between them: "Of these three words the first, *deilia*, is used always in a bad sense; the second, *phobos*, is a middle term, capable of a good interpretation, capable of an evil, and lying indifferently between the two; the third, *eulobeia*, is quite predominantly used in a good sense" (pp. 34–35). In Heb. 12:28 it is translated "godly fear."

Thayer defines *deilia* as meaning "timidity, fearfulness, cowardice." The last of these is what Arndt and Gingrich suggest for the passage here. Bernard comments: "Of the gifts of the Holy Spirit cowardice is not one; a Christian man, a Christian minister, has no right to be a coward, for God has given him the spirit of *power*" (p. 109).

Sound Mind

The noun *sōphronismos* is found only here in the NT. Lock says it suggests "the power to make *sōphrōn* (sane, sensible, self-controlled); whether to discipline others . . . or to discipline oneself, to keep oneself in hand, free from all excitement or hesitation; it is 'the sanity of saintliness,' cf. Bishop Paget, *Studies in the Christian Character*, pp. 64–67. The context probably limits the reference here to self-discipline. . . . The Christian minister must be strong, efficient, courageous, but never forget personal tenderness for others . . . or control of his own temper" (p. 86).

N. J. D. White discusses the relevance of this exhortation. He writes: "There was an element of *deilia* in Timothy's natural disposition which must have been prejudicial to his efficiency as a Church ruler. For that position is needed (a) force of character, which if not natural may be inspired by consciousness of a divine appointment, (b) love, which is not softness, and (c) self-discipline, which is opposed to all easy self-indulgence which issues in laxity of administration" (EGT, 4:155).

Timothy had been brought up by his mother and grandmother (v. 5), two devout Jewish Christians. His Greek father (Acts 16:1), who was probably a pagan, evidently left the religious training of his son to the two women. These factors may have contributed to the fact that Timothy's personality was more gentle than rugged. Throughout Paul's two letters to Timothy he exhorts his young associate to be firm, and even stern (cf. 2:1; 4:2). From Paul's correspondence with the Corinthians we gather that the apostle sent Timothy to try to straighten out the sad state of affairs among them. But the gentle-hearted young man was no match for Paul's harsh opponents in Corinth. Soon afterward, Titus succeeded where Timothy had failed.

It has been suggested that the "love" and the "self-discipline" must be present to control the "power." One might use the automobile for an analogy. The higher the horsepower of the engine, the more one needs power brakes and power steering. And the man behind the wheel must be in control at all times.

8 Partaker of the Afflictions

"Be thou partaker of the afflictions" is all one word in Greek, *synkakopotheō* (only here and 2:3 in NT). It literally means "suffer evil with," and so "suffer hardship together with." Arndt and Gingrich suggest here: "Join with me in suffer-

ing for the gospel." That is evidently the idea. It is thought that Paul coined this term.

9 Before the World Began

The literal meaning of *pro chronōn aiōniōn*, which in the KJV is translated "before the world began," is "before times eternal" (v. 9). It probably means "long ages ago," or "from eternity."

12 Committed unto Him

"That which I have committed unto him" is *tēn parathēkēn mou*, "my deposit." It may also be translated "what has been entrusted to me" (RSV; cf. NEB). Obviously "my deposit" is somewhat ambiguous. White says that the Greek expression is best taken as "that which I have deposited for safe keeping." He adds: ""Here it means 'my soul' or 'myself'" (EGT, 4:157–58).

E. K. Simpson agrees with this. He writes: "The apostle is looking at home. Philo applies the term to the soul (ii. 37), our costliest treasure, and it is that entrustment the saints, especially in prospect of taking flight, commit into Immanuel's steadfast hands" (p. 127).

Lock also favors this interpretation. He says that the Greek phrase means "that which I have deposited with Him . . . all my precious things which I have put under His care. He does not define or limit; it will include his teaching . . . his apostolic work, his converts . . . his life which has been already in God's keeping and which will remain safe there even through death. . . . The last is perhaps the primary thought" (p. 88).

Bernard takes a different view. He comments: "In I Tim. vi. 20 and 2 Tim. i. 14 *parathēkē* plainly means the doctrine delivered to Timothy to preach; and hence it appears that here *tēn parathēkēn mou* = the doctrine delivered to Paul by God" (p. 111). He notes that this also ties in more closely with the admonition of the next verse: "Hold fast the form of sound words."

In an extended note, Lock observes that "*parathēkē* . . . always implies the situation of one who has to take a long journey and who deposits his money and other valuables with a friend, entrusting him to restore it on his return" (p. 90). He goes on to say: "In the N. T. the substantive is only used in the Pastoral Epistles: it comes naturally from one who is preparing for his last long journey, but the verb occurs elsewhere, and the word was used metaphorically in many applications. (*a*) Of the body of truth which Christ deposits with the Apostle and the Apostle with Timothy, cf. 2 T 1:18 . . . 6:20 . . . 2 T 1:14, and which Timothy has to hand on to others when he takes his journey to Rome, 2 T 2:2 . . . (*b*) Of our true self which the Creator has handed over to us to keep safe . . . (*c*) Of good works deposited with God in heaven: a very common Jewish thought . . . (*d*) Of persons entrusted to the care of others . . . (*e*) Of our life deposited with God at death. . . . The life which at first was God's deposit with us becomes our deposit with God" (pp. 91–92). The NIV has "what I have entrusted to him."

13 *Form* The word *hypotypōsis* occurs only here and in 1 Tim. 1:16. In that place it is best rendered "example"—the example of Paul's life. But here it means "the pattern placed before one to be held fast and copied" (Thayer). Lock suggests that "the signification of a *summary, outline*, which Galen assigns the word, best tallies with this context" (p. 127). Timothy was to hold fast the summary or outline of the gospel as expressed in sound words. This suggests the beginnings of a Christian creed.

Once more Timothy is admonished, "Guard the good deposit" (v. 14). He can do this only "by the Holy Spirit," who is the great Conservator of orthodoxy.

15 *Asia* In view of the current use of "Asia" it is important to note that in the NT the term never refers to a continent. It designates the Roman province of Asia, on the western end of the peninsula which we now call Asia Minor (modern Turkey). It was only one of half a dozen Roman provinces in that area.

The main city in that province was Ephesus, where Timothy was in charge of the Christian work (1 Tim. 1:3). It is a pathetic report that the apostle gives here. Lock suggests: "Possibly all the Asiatic Christians who were in Rome at the time, cf. 4:6, failed to support him at his trial and had now returned to Asia"—they were now "in Asia" and known to Timothy—"or all the Christians in Asia at the time when he was arrested there failed to help him or come with him to Rome" (p. 89).

16 *Refreshed* The verb is *anapsychō*, found only here in the NT. It comes from *psychō*, which meant "to breathe, to blow," and so "to cool, to make cool" (Cremer, p. 588). The compound then means "to make cool, to refresh" (*ibid.*). The Latin Vulgate has *refrigeravit*. When Onesiphorus came to see Paul in the stuffy dungeon, it was as if the air conditioning had been turned on!

2:4 *Chosen . . . to Be a Soldier* "Him who hath chosen him to be a soldier" is in

Greek simply the definite article with the participle *stratologēsanti*. Literally it means "the one who enlisted him."

Today we generally use "enlist" in the intransitive sense. A man enlists in the army or navy; that is, he enters voluntarily, is not drafted. But the first meaning of "enlist" is transitive, "to persuade to enter the armed forces."

Actually, there are three steps involved. First, God invites us to enlist, seeks to persuade us to do so. Second, in response to this we volunteer to join. Third, God then enlists us; that is, records us as soldiers in His army. And enlistment is not for a short term of three or four years; it is for life! Our duty and pleasure are to please our Commander in Chief. We should beware of absenteeism or going AWOL.

5 *Strive* "Strive for masteries" is one word in Greek—*athlei*, from which we get *athlete*. The verb is found only here in the NT (twice in this verse). It means "to compete in an athletic contest." The adverb *nomimōs*, "lawfully," means "according to the rules." The one who does not keep the rules is disqualified from the contest. We need to study the Bible in order that we may be familiar with the rules of the game.

Typically, Paul uses three figures here to illustrate the life of the Christian. The follower of Christ is to be a soldier (vv. 3–4), an athlete (v. 5), and a farmer (v. 6). These could well be used for the three points of a sermon, or, better still, for a series of three sermons on the Christian life.

9 *An Innocent Sufferer* Paul says, "I suffer trouble," as though I were "an evildoer." The compound verb is *kakopatheō*, literally, "suffer evil." The compound noun is *kakourgos*. It is used elsewhere in NT only for the "malefactors" crucified on either side of Jesus (Luke 23:32–33, 39). The righteous Paul was being treated like one of them. In this way, as in many others, the apostle was being identified with his Lord.

10, 12 *Endure* "Endure" has no direct relation to "endure" in verse 3. There it is a double compound, *synkakopatheō*, "suffer evil together," and is found elsewhere only in 1:8— "Be thou partaker of the afflictions."

But here the verb is *hypomenō*, literally, "remain under." Of itself it does not suggest suffering, but "I am patiently enduring."

The same verb, *hypomenō*, is found in verse 12, where it is wrongly translated "suffer." The passage should read: "If we patiently endure [keep steadfast to the end], we shall also reign with him."

14 Subverting Catastrophē is exactly the Greek word translated "subverting." It means "ruin" or "destruction." That is what Paul declares results when people "strive about words." The verb *logomacheō* means to "fight with words." It is found only here in the NT. The corresponding noun, *logomachia*, occurs only in 1 Tim. 6:4. Word battles bring catastrophe wherever they occur.

15 Study In contemporary language the verb *study* is used mostly for reading books. While this occupation is commendable, the word thus translated in verse 15 has no direct reference to reading. It is the verb *spoudazō*. It means "*to make haste; hence, to be zealous* or *eager, to give diligence*" (A-S). Arndt and Gingrich define it as "*be zealous* or *eager, take pains, make every effort.*" It is obvious that it takes in a lot more territory than "study."

Approved This English word is based on the root *prove*. But it is doubtful if the average person is aware of this when he uses the term.

The Greeks were probably more conscious of the connection. They realized that the adjective here, *dokimos*, was related to the verb *dokimazō*, which meant "test, try, prove." So *dokimos* was used primarily of metals, in the sense "tested, accepted, approved" (A-S). In other words, a thing or person must first be "proved" before being "approved." Arndt and Gingrich define *dokimos* as follows: "*approved* (by test), *tried and true, genuine.*" God can approve only those who have proved themselves true in the tests of life.

Rightly Dividing This KJV translation has caused much confusion in biblical interpretation. To many people this phrase is the key to understanding the Bible, and so they have gone down the dead-end street of extreme dispensationalism—which holds, for instance, that the Sermon on the Mount does not apply to us today; it applies to the millennium. So we Christians are robbed of some of the most important teachings of Jesus for daily living.

"Rightly dividing" is one word in Greek, *orthotomounta*. It comes from *orthos*, "straight," and *temnō*, "cut." So the verb *orthotomeō* (only here in NT) means "cut in a straight line." The Liddell-Scott-Jones *Lexicon* gives for this passage: "teach aright" (p. 1250). It was used for cutting a straight furrow in a field, or laying out a straight road. In the

Septuagint it is used in the sense of "direct, make straight, make plain."

N. J. D. White says: "This use of the word suggests that the metaphor passes from the general idea of a workman to the particular notion of the minister as one who 'makes straight paths' for the feet of his people to tread in (Heb. xii. 13)" (EGT, 4:165). In a similar vein Vincent writes: "The thought is that the minister of the gospel is to present the truth rightly, not abridging it, not handling it as a charlatan . . . not making it a matter of wordy strife (ver. 14), but treating it honestly and fully, in a straightforward manner" (4:302). E. K. Simpson prefers the idea of "cut a road," and adds the observation: "It enjoins on every teacher of the Word straightforward exegesis" (p. 137).

The translation we prefer is that found in the margin of the ERV: "holding a straight course in the word of truth." Instead of detouring on devious and crooked ways, or going recklessly down side roads, the preacher should "hold a straight course" in the middle of the road, offering a sane, sensible interpretation of Scripture. This is the kind of preaching that will build up people in the most holy faith.

16 Vain Babblings The noun *kenophōnia* occurs only here and in 1 Tim. 1:16. It is compounded of *kenos*, "empty," and *phōnē*, "sound." So it literally means "empty sounds." Perhaps the best translation is "empty chatter" (NASB).

In both passages where the word is found it is preceded by *bebēlos*, "profane." Arndt and Gingrich would combine this adjective with the compound noun and translate the whole expression as "godless chatter" (NIV). This is what we are told to avoid.

17 Canker The word *gangraina* is found only here in the NT. Thayer defines it as follows: "*A gangrene*, a disease by which any part of the body suffering from inflammation becomes so corrupted that, unless a remedy be seasonably applied, the evil continually spreads, attacks other parts, and at last eats away the bones" (p. 107). Abbott-Smith calls it "a gangrene, an eating sore." Arndt and Gingrich say, "*Gangrene, cancer* of spreading ulcers, etc. (medical term since Hippocrates)." They note that it is used figuratively here, as in Plutarch. The one-volume Hastings *Dictionary of the Bible* (rev. ed., 1963) defines *gangraina* as "a medical term for spreading ulcers." Since it is not a doctrinal term, it is not discussed in TDNT.

The root question is: Can we translate this

term as "cancer"? In spite of Arndt and Gingrich's use of that word, it seems that the safer rendering is "gangrene" (NIV). This appears to be the correct medical term today.

19 Sure The word is *stereos*, which has been taken over into English for stereo records and record players. The original meaning is "firm, solid, compact, hard, rigid," and as used here to describe a foundation it means "strong, firm, immovable" (Thayer). The correct translation here is "firm" (NIV) or "solid."

20 Earth The adjective ("of earth") is *ostrakinos*, found only here and in 2 Cor. 4:7. It means "made of clay." Today we speak of "earthenware" dishes. The plural noun *ostraca* has been taken directly over into English for potsherds, or broken pieces of pottery that are found in archaeological excavations. The last clause of this verse is best translated, "some for great occasions and some for ordinary use" (Goodspeed).

21 Meet for . . . Use The adjective *euchrēstos* occurs only here, in 4:11, and in the eleventh verse of Philemon. It means "useful" (NIV) or "serviceable."

22 Follow Timothy is admonished to flee from youthful lusts but to "follow" good things. The Greek word *diōkō* literally means "pursue" (NIV). Furthermore, it is in the continuous present. So it means "keep on pursuing."

23 Unlearned The adjective *apaideutos* is found only here in the NT. It comes from the alpha-privative *a-*, and the verb *paideuō*, which means "train a child" (*pais*). So the adjective means "without instruction and discipline, uneducated, ignorant, rude" and here indicates "stupid questions" (Thayer, p. 53). Arndt and Gingrich translate this phrase "stupid speculations." Probably "ignorant" (ASV, NASB, NEB) is better than "unlearned."

Gender Strifes The KJV rendering of *gennōsin machas* is certainly correct. But "breed quarrels" would be more contemporary. The KJV is also right in using "strive" in verse 24 for *machesthai*, since the noun and verb have the same root. "Quarrel" (v. 24, NIV) would fit better now.

24 Patient Paul says that the Lord's servant must not be quarrelsome, but "gentle" (or "kind") and "apt to teach" (or "skillful in teaching"; see 1 Tim. 3:2), and "patient."

The last word is the rendering of *anexikakos*, found only here in the NT. It is compounded of *anechō*, "hold up," and *kakos*, "bad" or "evil." So it means "holding up under wrong." That is something more than just being patient. Thayer defines it as "patient of ills and wrongs, forbearing" (cf. RSV). Arndt and Gingrich suggest "bearing evil without resentment" (cf. Goodspeed, "unresentful"). Grundmann (TDNT, 3:487) says it means "tolerant of evil or calamity" (cf. NEB, "tolerant"). The NASB uses a phrase, "patient when wronged." This is needed, perhaps, to convey the full sense of the compound term in Greek (cf. NIV: "not resentful").

25 Instructing The verb *paideuō* literally means to "train children." But it is also used in the Septuagint and in the papyri in the sense of "correct." That is the meaning given for it here by Thayer, as well as Arndt and Gingrich.

Those That Oppose Themselves In the Greek this is simply the definite article with the participle *antidiatithemenous* (only here in NT). The verb is a double compound, composed of *anti*, "against," *dia*, "through," and *tithēmi*, "place." So it means "place oneself in opposition" (Thayer). Arndt and Gingrich would translate the article and participle "his opponents."

Acknowledging The term *epignōsis* is a compound of *gnōsis*, "knowledge." It means "precise and correct knowledge" (Thayer). For this passage Arndt and Gingrich give "knowledge" or "recognition." Actually, the phrase here in the Greek, *epignōsin alētheias*, "the acknowledging of the truth," is exactly the same as in 1 Tim. 2:4 and 2 Tim. 3:7, where it is translated as "the knowledge of the truth." That is the best translation here. It must be admitted that Paul seems to use *gnōsis* and *epignōsis* interchangeably.

26 Recover The verb *ananēphō* occurs only here in the NT. It literally means "return to soberness." Thayer (p. 40) suggests that the meaning of the passage here is: "To be set free from the snare of the devil and to return to a sound mind ('one's sober senses')." Arndt and Gingrich (p. 57) say the compound verb means "come to one's senses again" and offer this translation: "Come to one's senses and escape from the snare of the devil" (cf. NASB). The addition of "escape" seems necessary for smooth English. However, Bernard offers this translation: "And may return to soberness out of the snare of the devil" (p. 127).

Taken Captive The verb *zōgreō* is found only here and in Luke 5:10. It is compounded of *zōos*, "alive," and *agreuō*, which means "*to catch or take* by hunting or fishing" (A-S). So it literally means "to take alive." Then it came to have the more general sense of "catch" or "capture." But Bernard writes: "*Zōgrein* only occurs elsewhere in N.T. at Luke v. 10 where it means 'to catch alive,' as it does here" (p. 128).

Both Bernard and Ellicott (on Greek text) think that "his will" means "God's will." But we prefer the interpretation of Arndt and Gingrich: "*Held captive by him* (the devil) *to perform his* (the devil's) *will*" (p. 340). The fact that the verb *sōgreō* is here in the perfect passive participle suggests that "held captive" is more accurate than "taken captive." The devil holds as captive everyone he can.

3:1 Perilous The basic meaning of *chalepos* is "hard." Abbott-Smith defines it thus: "(a) *hard to do or deal with, difficult;* (b) *hard to bear, painful* . . . 2 Tim. 3:1; (c) of persons, *hard to deal with, harsh, fierce, savage:* Mt. 8:28" (p. 478). These are the only two times that the word occurs in the NT. For this passage Arndt and Gingrich suggest "hard times, times of stress" (p. 882).

2–4 Lovers In verses 2–4 Paul lists 18 characteristics of men in the last days. Five terms here have the prefix *phil*, which means "friend" or "lover." There are no less than 35 words in the NT beginning with *phil*.

The first term here is *philautoi*, "lovers of self" or "selfish." Bernard comments: "In Greek thought of an earlier age *philautia* had a good sense, and was expressive of the self-respect which a good man has for himself. . . . But a deeper philosophy, recognizing the fact of man's Fall, transferred the moral centre of gravity from self to God; once the sense of sin is truly felt, self-respect becomes an inadequate basis for moral theology" (p. 129).

The second term is *philargyroi*, "lovers of money" (KJV, covetous). The phrase, "despisers of those that are good" is one word in Greek, "*aphilagathoi.*" Literally it means "not loving good people." (This word has not been found anywhere else in Greek literature.) The fourth term is *philēdonoi*, "lovers of pleasure." The last is *philotheoi*, "lovers of God." Probably no one would dare deny that the majority of people in modern society are "lovers of pleasure more than lovers of God." Hedonism is one of the main characteristics of our day.

2 Boasters The word *alazōn* is found only here and Rom. 1:30. It likewise occurs twice in the Septuagint. Coming from *alē*, "wandering," it first meant "a vagabond." It was used for those who were "full of empty and boastful professions of cures and other feats which they could accomplish" (Trench, p. 98). Then it was applied to any braggart or boaster. Phillips translates it, "full of big words." (For "proud" see Rom. 1:30.)

Blasphemers This is an adjective *blasphēmos*, used here for persons as in 1 Tim. 1:3. In Acts 6:11 it describes words. In its only other occurrence in the NT it refers to "railing" accusation (2 Pet. 2:11). It sometimes means "speaking evil, slanderous, reproachful, railing, abusive" (Thayer, p. 103). Bernard writes: "*railers*, or evil-speakers, in reference to their fellow men rather than to God. This is the regular force of *blasphemos* and the cognate words in the Pastoral Epistles" (p. 130).

Unthankful The adjective *acharistos* is found only here and in Luke 6:35. It is compounded of the alpha-privative *a-* and *charis* ("grace"). So its earliest meaning was "ungracious." Homer uses it in the sense of "unpleasing." But beginning with Herodotus it took on the meaning "unthankful." Probably the best translation here is "ungrateful" (NIV), the only meaning given by Arndt and Gingrich. Bernard says: "*Without gratitude.* This follows naturally from the last mentioned characteristic (disobedient to parents), for the blackest form of ingratitude is that which repudiates the claim of parents to respect and obedience" (p. 130). Though written in the nineteenth century, this observation is particularly relevant right now.

Unholy Of the term *anosios*, Hauck writes: "In the NT it occurs twice in the Pastorals for 'impious' persons who impiously reject sacred obligations. In 1 Tim. 1:9 . . . it seems to have the sense of 'ungodly,' but in II Tim. 3:2 the sequence . . . suggests the sense of 'impious,' 'devoid of piety' " (TDNT, 5:492).

3 Without Natural Affection This is all one word in Greek, *astorgoi*. It is composed of alpha-negative and *storgē*, "family affection." The word occurs only here and in Rom. 1:31. Arndt and Gingrich suggest "unloving." The NIV has "without love."

Trucebreakers The term *aspondos* is found only here in the NT. Like one-third of the adjectives in this list (vv. 2–4) it begins with the alpha-privative *a-*. The noun *spondē* meant "a libation, which, as a kind of sacrifice, accompanied the making of treaties and compacts" (Thayer, p. 81). So the adjective here means "that cannot be persuaded to enter into a covenant, implacable" (*ibid.*). Perhaps the best translation is "irreconcilable" (AG). (For "false accusers" see 1 Tim. 3:11.)

Incontinent The basic meaning of *akrateis* (only here in NT) is "*without self-control, intemperate*" (Thayer). Arndt and Gingrich add to this: "dissolute." Bernard says that it means "without self-control, in the widest sense, but more particularly in regard to bodily lusts" (p. 130).

Fierce This adjective, *anēmeros*, also occurs only here in the NT. It literally means "untamed," and so "savage" or "brutal." It would seem that "brutal" (NIV) conveys the idea correctly.

4 Traitors The noun is *prodotēs*, which occurs also in Luke 6:16 (of Judas Iscariot) and Acts 7:22. It means "betrayer" or "traitor." It describes those who are "treacherous" in their dealings with their fellows." Perhaps "treacherous" (NIV) is the best rendering.

Heady The adjective *propetēs* occurs only here and in Acts 19:36. It literally means "falling forwards, headlong" and metaphorically "precipitate, rash, reckless" (A-S). Probably "headstrong" is the term we would use today. (For "highminded" see "lifted up with pride," 1 Tim. 3:6.)

6 Creep The verb is *endynō*, elsewhere in the NT spelled *endyō*. The latter is used literally for putting on clothes, or figuratively for clothing oneself with certain virtues or with Christ (Rom. 13:14).

But since *dynō* means to "enter, sink into," so *endynō* can mean "to enter, press into" (A-S). Only here in the NT does it have that meaning. Thayer suggests for this passage: "to creep into, insinuate one's self into; to enter" (p. 214). Arndt and Gingrich have "worm their way into houses" (p. 263). Since *oikia* means "household" as well as "house," Moffatt reads, "worm their way into families" (cf. NIV). The *Jerusalem Bible* has "insinuate themselves into families." The NASB says, "enter into households." A. T. Robertson thinks that "slip into by insin-

uation" is the meaning here. In the light of the context this unfavorable sense is probably justified.

Silly Women This is one word in the Greek, *gynaikaria* (only here in NT), the diminutive of *gynē*, "woman." So it literally means "little women." As Vincent remarks, "*Silly* is expressed by the contemptuous diminutive" (4:312).

Laden The perfect passive participle of *soreuō* (only here and Rom. 12:20) means "heap together," and so "to overwhelm one with a heap of anything"; here, "to load one with the consciousness of many sins" (Thayer, p. 612). "Loaded down with sins" (NIV) gives the correct idea.

Divers The word *poikilos* occurs 10 times in the NT. In 1 Pet. 1:6; 4:10 it is translated "manifold." The rest of the time it is rendered "divers," the Middle English form of "diverse." The Greek word literally means "many-colored, variegated," and so "of various kinds, diversified." Both meanings are found as early as Homer. The correct translation is "various."

8 Corrupt Minds The Greek phrase is a strong one, carrying the sense "utterly corrupted in their minds." The verb *kataphtheirō* (only here in NT) literally means "destroy entirely," and so in a moral sense, "deprave, corrupt" (A-S). The form here is the perfect passive participle, indicating a thoroughly depraved state of mind. The NIV translates this, "men of depraved minds."

9 Folly The term *anoia* occurs only here and in Luke 6:11, where it is translated "madness." It is compounded of the alpha-negative and *nous*, "mind." So it literally means "mindlessness" or "want of sense."

Manifest The compound *ekdēlos* (only here in NT) is a strengthened form of *dēlos*, which means "*clear* to the mind." So this word means "quite clear, evident" (A-S).

10 Fully Known This is the same verb *parakoloutheō* which is found in 1 Tim. 4:6. There it means "follow faithfully." But here the thought seems to be "followed closely"; that is, you are familiar with what happened to me. Elsewhere in the NT it is found in Luke 1:3, where it means "investigate" or "trace carefully."

Manner of Life The noun *agōgē* (only here in NT) comes from the verb *agō*, meaning "lead." Properly it means "a leading." But it was used figuratively in the sense of "education" or "discipline," and then more generally for "the life led" or "the course of life." Since "doctrine" should definitely be "teaching," a helpful translation here is that of Moffatt: "my teaching, my practice."

12 Godly The adverb *eusebōs* is found only here and in Titus 2:12. Since "godly" is properly an adjective, the best translation is "live a godly life" (RSV, NIV).

13 Seducers The noun *goēs* (only here in NT) comes from *goaō*, "wail" or "howl." So it originally meant a wailer or howler. Then it signified a wizard or enchanter, "because incantations used to be uttered in a kind of howl" (Thayer, p. 120). Here the correct meaning is "impostors" (NIV).

14 Been Assured of Whereas the verb *pisteuō*, "believe," occurs 248 times in the NT, the cognate verb *pistoō* is found only here. It meant "to make faithful, render trustworthy," and then "make firm, establish." In the passive, as here, it means "to be firmly persuaded of; to be assured of" (Thayer, p. 514).

16 Given by Inspiration This is one word in Greek, *theopneustos* (only here in NT). It literally means "God-breathed"—*theos*, "God," and *pneō*, "breathe." That is, God breathed His truth into the hearts and minds of the writers of Scripture. The best translation is "God-breathed" (NIV).

Reproof The noun *elegmos* is found only here in the NT. In the Septuagint it is used for the "conviction" of a sinner, for "reproof," and even for "punishment." Thayer says it means "correction, reproof, censure." While "reproof" is the popular translation, the idea of "conviction" should not be ruled out.

Correction The word (only here in NT) is *epanorthōsis* (*orthos* means "straight"). The term suggests "restoration to an upright or a right state; correction, improvement" (Thayer, p. 228). Arndt and Gingrich prefer the last of these, "improvement," for this passage. Trench says it means "rectification" (p. 111).

Instruction The noun *paideia* comes from *pais*, "child," and the verb *paideuō*, which in classical Greek meant "to train children." So

the literal meaning of *paideia* is "child training." Thayer says it refers to "whatever in adults also cultivates the soul, especially by correcting mistakes and curbing the passions" (p. 473). Trench writes: "*Paideia* is one among the many words, into which revealed religion has put a deeper meaning than it knew of, till this took possession of it. . . . For the Greek, *paideia* was simply 'education.' " But biblical writers "felt and understood that all effectual instruction for the sinful children of men, includes and implies chastening" (p. 111). Since "instruction" is thought of as mainly intellectual, "training" is a more adequate translation.

17 Perfect In the Greek there is a play on words that is lost in English translation. The adjective "perfect" is *artios* (only here in NT), and "thoroughly furnished" is the perfect passive participle of the verb *exartizō*, based on the adjective. The verb is found here and in Acts 21:5 ("accomplished"; that is, "finished").

The basic meaning of *artios* is "fitted" or "complete." Trench comments: "If we ask ourselves under what special aspects completeness is contemplated in *artios*, it would be safe to answer that it is not as the presence only of all the parts which are necessary for that completeness, but involves further the adaptation and aptitude of these parts for the ends which they were designed to serve. The man of God, St. Paul would say (2 Tim. iii. 17), should be furnished and accomplished with all which is necessary for the carrying out of the work to which he is appointed" (p. 77).

Delling writes: "At 2 Tim. 3:17 *artios* is used . . . to denote what is right or proper, and more particularly what is becoming to a Christian, obviously with a moral accent, as shown by what follows. At 2 Tim. 3:17 *exartizō* means to bring to a suitable state for Christian moral action" (TDNT, 1:476).

The meaning of the passage is "that the man of God may be complete, equipped for every good work" (RSV).

4:1 Quick The Oxford English Dictionary has no less than 9 long columns on the use of "quick" in our language. Its original meaning was "living," and that is all the Greek word here, *zōntas*, means. It has no relation to our modern concept of "quick." The archaic use of "quick" for "living" in the KJV is found 4 times in the NT (Acts 10:42; 2 Tim. 4:1; Heb. 4:12; 1 Pet. 4:5).

2 Instant The verb *ephistēmi* is translated "be instant" in verse 2 and "is at hand" in verse

6. It literally means "be on hand" and so "be ready." The former sense fits verse 6; the latter, verse 2.

"In season, out of season" is *eukairōs akairōs*. Lock has an excellent comment on this for preachers: "*Both* whether or no the moment seems to fit your hearers, 'welcome or not welcome,' and 'whether or no it is convenient to you,' 'on duty or off duty,' 'in the pulpit or out of it,' 'take or make your opportunity'" (p. 113). That is the way Paul preached.

3 *Itching* The verb *knēthō* (only here in NT) literally means "scratch" or "tickle." In the passive (as here) it means "itch." Arndt and Gingrich remark that the word is here used "figuratively of curiosity, that looks for interesting and spicy bits of information" (p. 438). Weymouth puts it well: "wanting to have their ears tickled."

6 *Offered* The statement "I am now ready to be offered" is much stronger in the Greek: "I am already being poured out as a drink offering." The whole of Paul's life of service was a sacrifice. But as it came to a close, his lifeblood was being poured out on the altar as a final act of dedication. The verb *spendō* is found only here and in Phil. 2:17. Michel writes: "The LXX uses the verb *spendō* . . . in the sense 'to pour out a drink offering'" (TDNT, 7:531).

7 *Fight* For the first clause almost all translations have, "I have fought a [the] good fight." But in the Greek the verb is *agōnizō* and the noun is *agōn*, from which we get *agonize* and *agony*.

These words came from the verb *agō*, which means "lead." An *agōn* was a gathering. But since the largest gatherings, then as now, were for athletic contests, it came to be used for the contest itself. So Paul's meaning here is probably, "I have competed well in the great contest of life."

The climax of all the contests of that day was the marathon race (26 miles). The winner of this was given the highest honors. He was greeted as a great hero. He had "agonized" and won the *agōna*.

This fits in perfectly with the second clause, "I have finished my course." The Greek word for "course" is *dromon*, which comes from the verb meaning "to run" (second aorist, *edramon*). So it definitely refers to a race-course. TDNT has correctly captured the thought: "I have run the great Race, I have completed the Course."

The third clause, "I have kept the faith,"

could possibly suggest: "I have kept the rules; I have not been disqualified." It may well be that Paul, who was especially fond of athletic metaphors, thus intended that all three of these clauses be taken as referring to the Christian life as a long-distance race. This is the figure which is clearly used in Heb. 12:1–2.

Verse 8 also fits into this pattern. The "crown" which Paul knew was awaiting him was not the royal diadem (Greek, *diadēma*) but the victor's wreath (*stephanos*). It would be given him by the Lord, who is the righteous "judge," or Umpire. He stands at the end of each Christian's race, waiting to give him the victor's crown and welcome him into his eternal home. What an encouragement to all of us to keep pressing on to the end! This is the apostle's dying testimony, and it is a glorious one.

9 *Shortly* "Do thy diligence to come shortly unto me" is literally, "Make haste to come to me quickly." Winter was coming on. In his damp, dingy dungeon, the apostle was already beginning to suffer from the cold. And so he urged Timothy to come as quickly as possible, bringing Paul's "cloke" (v. 13), his warm outer robe. The Greek is *phailonēs* (only here in NT).

13 *Books, Parchments* The first word is *biblia*, which probably refers to papyrus rolls or scrolls. These could have been copies of Paul's own Epistles, although the identification is uncertain. Our word *Bible* comes from this.

The second word is *membranas*, "skins" (only here in NT). It refers to scrolls made of the skins of animals. These may have been scrolls containing at least some of the books of the OT.

16 *Answer* The word is *apologia*. Today an *apology* is generally a confession that one is sorry for some wrong he has done. But the original meaning of *apology* in English is "defense"—not saying, "I'm sorry; I was wrong," but, "I am innocent." And that is exactly what *apologia* means: "a speech made in defense." So the reference here is not to some obscure "answer" but to Paul's defense at his trial before the emperor. No person stood by him—except the Lord (v. 17), who "strengthened" (Greek, "empowered") him. At Paul's first trial he was delivered out of the lion's mouth (that is, from death). But the previous verses show that he realized his next trial would result in his execution, for which he was ready.

Titus

1:2 *That Cannot Lie* This is a single word in Greek, *apseudēs*, found only here in the NT. It means "free from all deceit," and so "truthful" or "trustworthy" (AG). As here, it is used as an adjective to describe God in Polycarp's last prayer before his martyrdom. God has promised eternal life, and this promise will not fail even in the face of physical death.

Before the World Began The Greek says "before times eternal" (*pro chronōn aiōniōn*). This evidently means "long ages past, age-long periods ago" (Lock, p. 126). Weymouth translates it "from all eternity."

3 *In Due Times* Literally it reads, "In His own appointed times" (*kairois idiois*). Lock comments: "The thought of the Incarnation taking place at the right moment in the world's history is a favourite one with St. Paul (Gal. 4:4; Rom. 5:6; Eph. 1:10; Acts 17:26), springing from apocalyptic expectations, summed up by the Lord (Mk. 1:15) and expanded by himself in his philosophy of history, Rom. 1–3" (*ibid.*). The exact phrase is found only here and in 1 Tim. 2:6; 6:15; but the singular occurs in Gal. 6:9.

Preaching The word *kērygma* is widely used as a theological term today, signifying the *message* preached by the Early Church.

The term is derived from the noun *kēryx*, "herald," and the verb *kēryssō*, "to herald or proclaim." In classical Greek it signified "that which is promulgated by a herald or public crier, a proclamation by herald." In the NT it means "the message or proclamation by the heralds of God or Christ" (Thayer, p. 346). In the papyri it is used for "a public announcement" (VGT, p. 343). C. H. Dodd writes that the word "signifies not the action of the preacher, but that which he preaches, his message, as we sometimes say" (p. 7).

This is in agreement with the earlier declaration of J. B. Lightfoot. He says that *kērygma* means " 'the thing preached,' 'the proclamation.' . . . It refers therefore to the subject, not to the manner of the preaching. There is only the very slightest approach in classical writers to this [latter] sense of the words *kēryssein*, *kērygma*, etc., as denoting 'instruction,' 'teaching' " (*Notes*, p. 161; commenting on 1 Cor. 1:21). Ellicott equates *kērygma* here with "the Gospel."

This contention of the earlier writers, and popularized by Dodd, that *kērygma* refers to the *content* rather than the *act* of preaching has been challenged of late. Even Thayer says that in 2 Tim. 4:17 (the only other place in the Pastoral Epistles where it occurs) it means "the act of publishing." But in the only 2 places where it is found in the Synoptic Gospels (Matt. 12:41; Luke 11:32) he says it indicates "the proclamation of the necessity of repentance and reformation made by the prophet Jonah." In 1 Cor. 1:21; 2:4; 15:14; and Rom. 16:25—making 8 times the word occurs in the New Testament—Thayer thinks it refers to "the announcement of salvation procured by Christ and to be had through him" (p. 346).

Arndt and Gingrich define *kērygma* in the NT as simply "proclamation, preaching," and they seem by this to mean the *act*. They would translate it here, "The preaching with which I have been entrusted."

Friedrich says that at 1 Cor. 2:4 "*Kērygma* is the act of proclaiming." But of 1 Cor. 1:21 he writes: "The foolish message of Jesus crucified saves those who believe." He continues: "At Rom. 16:25, too, the reference is to the message with a very definite content" (TDNT, 3:716). He thinks, however, that in Titus 1:3 it is the *act* of preaching.

It seems obvious that we are confronted here with a both/and rather than an either/or situation. The noun *kērygma* means *both* the act *and* the content of preaching.

This statement is illustrated in the usage of various versions today. Whereas the KJV translates *kērygma* in all 7 places by "preaching," the ASV (1901) has "message" in the two Pastoral passages. The NASB (1963) has "the message preached" in 1 Cor. 1:21 and "the proclamation" in the Pastoral Epistles. The NEB (1961) also has "proclamation" in these two passages. This can mean the act, but probably its primary emphasis is on what is proclaimed. Certainly too much emphasis should not be put on the idea that preaching is God's only way of getting the gospel to a lost world. The printed page and personal witnessing are both powerful methods of evangelism.

Committed   A comparison with 1 Tim. 1:11 favors definitely the idea that "preaching" in this verse means the message rather than the act. In the earlier passage we read: "According to the glorious gospel of the blessed God, which was committed to my trust." It appears evident that "preaching" in Titus 1:3 is parallel to "gospel" in 1 Tim. 1:11.

The phrase "which was committed to my trust" (1 Tim. 1:11) is exactly the same as "which is committed unto me" (Titus 1:3)—*ho episteuthēn egō*. It is correctly translated in the RSV: "With which I have been entrusted." Commenting on the Timothy passage, E. K. Simpson writes: "*Egō* is emphatic. Paul thrills with joy at the thought of his high commission of proclaiming a gospel so ablaze with the divine perfections" (p. 32). Here the *egō* may point up more especially his heavy sense of responsibility.

4 Mercy   All 13 Epistles of Paul have the twofold greeting, "Grace and peace." In the two letters to Timothy "mercy" is added. It appears here also in the KJV. But the oldest and best Greek manuscripts do not have it in Titus, and so it must be rejected as a later scribal addition.

Perhaps "mercy" was added by Paul in the letters to Timothy because the apostle's younger colleague was overly gentle and timid by nature. Simpson makes this comment about "mercy": "That sounds a tender chord, suggested possibly by Timothy's fragile health" (p.

26). The additional "mercy" is found also in 2 John 3.

5 Set in Order   The verb *epidiorthoō* (only here in NT) is compounded of *orthos*, "straight"; *dia*, "through"; and *epi*, "upon" or "further." (In analyzing a compound verb, we begin with the simple root and work backwards through the prepositional prefixes.) So it means "*set right* or *correct in addition* (to what has already been corrected)" (AG, p. 292).

Paul writes to Titus that he had left him on the island of Crete to complete the organization of the churches there. It is interesting to note that on this very island a second-century inscription has been found that contains this compound verb.

Wanting   Titus was to set in order "the things that are wanting" (*ta leiponta*). The best translation is "what remains" (to be done) or "what was left unfinished" (NIV).

Ordain   Titus was to "ordain elders in every city." This was the simplest form of church government. It was patterned after the Jewish synagogues, each of which was controlled by a group of elders. It was the method Paul and Barnabas used in establishing the Gentile churches on their first missionary journey— "when they had ordained them elders in every church" (Acts 14:23).

Today in ecclesiastical circles "ordain" has a specific technical meaning. It is used for installing a person in the office of elder. How this is done depends on the kind of church government involved. In the Episcopal church it is done only by the bishop. In Presbyterian churches it is the responsibility of the presbytery. In churches with a congregational form of government, as the Baptists, a person is ordained by a group of his fellow ministers.

Was Titus assigned the authority to ordain elders? Because the answer to that question is a bit uncertain, it might be well to use "appoint" (NIV) instead. It does not carry the ecclesiastical overtones inherent in "ordain." Beyer prefers the word "appoint" here (TDNT, 2:617).

5–7 Elders, Bishop   In verses 5 and 6 we find the qualifications of elders in the church; verse 7 says, "For a bishop must be blameless." This seems to indicate rather clearly that the same church officials were called bishops (*episcopoi*) and elders (*presbyteroi*). The name "elders" emphasizes the fact that the leaders of the church were to be older men, as was the case with the elders of Israel. The word *episcopos* (bishop) literally means "overseer." So it refers to the function and office of an overseer of the church.

That "bishop" and "elder" are used for the same person is even asserted by Bishop Lightfoot of the Church of England. In his commentary on the Greek text of the Epistle to the Philippians he writes: "It is a fact now generally recognized by theologians of all shades of opinion, that in the language of the New Testament the same officer in the Church is called indifferently 'bishop' (*episcopos*) and 'elder' or 'presbyter' (*presbyteros*)" (p. 95).

He goes on to show that not only was *episcopos* used in classical Greek for various officials, but it is common in the Septuagint. There it signifies "inspectors, superintendents, taskmasters" (e.g., 2 Kings 11:19; 2 Chron. 34:12, 17; Isa. 60:17). He comments: "Thus beyond the fundamental idea of *inspection*, which lies at the root of the word 'bishop,' its usage suggests two subsidiary notions also: (1) Responsibility to a superior power; (2) The introduction of a new order of things" (p. 96).

Lightfoot gives 6 evidences that bishop and elder are the same: (1) In Phil. 1:1, Paul salutes the bishops and deacons. He could not have omitted mention of the elders unless they were included in the "bishops." (2) In Acts 20:17, Paul summoned to Miletus the elders of the church at Ephesus. But then he calls them "overseers" (*episcopoi*) of the flock. (3) Peter does a similar thing (1 Pet. 5:1–2). (4) In 1 Timothy, Paul describes the qualifications of bishops (3:1–7) and deacons (3:8–13). The fact that he omits elders here would argue that they were the same as bishops. (5) Titus (1:5–7). (6) Clement of Rome's First Epistle (*ca.* A.D. 95) clearly uses "bishops" and "elders" interchangeably.

It is not without significance that Jerome, writing near the end of the fourth century, recognizes this identity of the two. He says: "Among the ancients, bishops and presbyters are the same, for the one is a term of dignity, the other of age." Again he writes: "The Apostle plainly shows that presbyters are the same as bishops." In a third passage he says: "If any one thinks the opinion that the bishops and presbyters are the same, to be not the view of the Scriptures, but my own, let him study the words of the apostle to the Philippians." Other Church Fathers, such as Chrysostom, asserted the same thing. Lightfoot goes so far as to say: "Thus in every one of the extant commentaries on the epistles containing the crucial passages, whether Greek or Latin, before the close of the fifth century, this identity is affirmed" (p. 99).

6 Blameless Five different Greek words are translated "blameless" in the NT. They all begin with the alpha-privative *a-*, but have little else in common. *Amemptos* (five times) is rendered "faultless" in Heb. 8:7. It literally means "free from fault." *Amōmētos* occurs only once in the best Greek text (2 Pet. 3:14). *Anaitios*, "guiltless," is found only in Matt. 12:5, 7. *Anepilēmptos* (1 Tim. 3:2; 5:7; 6:14) means "without reproach." The word here, *anengklētos* (five times in NT), literally means "not called to account," and so "unreproveable" (Col. 1:22). It is obvious that the idea of blamelessness bulks large in Paul's thinking about church officials.

The apostle proceeds to designate some ways in which a bishop or elder must be blameless. He must not be:

7 Selfwilled *Authadēs* (only here and 2 Pet. 2:10) literally means "self-pleasing." It carries the idea of "stubborn" or "arrogant." Bauernfeind says that in the NT "the reference is to human impulse violating obedience to the divine command" (TDNT, 1:509).

Soon Angry *Orgilos* is found only here in the NT. It is based on *orgē*, "anger," and so means "inclined to anger." Probably "quick-tempered" (NIV) is the way we would say it now.

Not Given to Wine The word *paroinos* (only here and 1 Tim. 3:3) is compounded of *para*, "beside," and *oinos*, "wine." It describes one who stays by the wine. This was obviously a common fault in that day. *Plēktēs*, "striker" or "brawler," is also found only here and in 1 Tim. 3:3. *Aischrokerdēs* (greedy of base gain, "given to filthy lucre") occurs only here and in 1 Tim. 3:8. It is a sad commentary on those times that bishops would have to be warned against such conduct!

8 Good Men In verse 8 there are two compounds of *philos*, "lover." The first, *philoxenon*, literally means "a lover of strangers," and so "hospitable." The second is *philagathon* (only here in NT). It means "lover of good"—not "good men," but a lover of what is good. It denotes high moral character, not just an affection for good people (cf. NIV).

Temperate The word *enkratēs* is found only here in the NT. Basically it means, "strong, powerful." Then it came to mean "self-controlled" (NIV). Someone has defined gentleness as "strength under control." That is what real

413

gentleness is. Meekness isn't weakness. It is power in the control of divine love.

10 *Deceivers* In verse 10 there are two *hapax legomena*—words found only once in the NT. The first is *mataiologoi*, "vain talkers," those who talk idly. The second is *phrenapatai*, "deceivers." Literally it means "a deceiver of his own mind" (A-S). Goodspeed translates the whole phrase, "who deceive themselves with their empty talk."

16 *Abominable* The word *bdelyktos* is found only here in the NT. It is a strong term, meaning "abominable" or "detestable" (NIV). Probably the second term is more contemporary.

2:3 *As Becometh Holiness* This phrase is one word in Greek, *hieroprepēs* (only here in NT). It means "suited to a sacred character." Every Christian is set apart to God, and so is sacred. We should suit our daily lives to that exalted and exalting concept.

Given The apostle warns that the "aged women" (*presbytidas*, only here in NT) should not be "given" to much wine. This is the perfect passive participle of *douloō*, which means "to enslave." So the best translation here is "not slaves to much wine."

5 *Keepers at Home* This rendering does not catch the exact emphasis of the original. The term *oikourgos* (only here in NT) means a "worker at home." The young women are urged to take care of the home as their first responsibility.

8 *That Cannot Be Condemned* This phrase is one word in Greek, the adjective *akatagnōstos* (only here in NT). It literally means "not open to just rebuke." We can hardly hope in this life to escape all condemnation from men. But we should seek to live in such a way as to avoid any justifiable criticism.

14 *Peculiar* There is perhaps no word in the KJV that is more misleading today than the term "peculiar." That English term now means "odd" or "eccentric." The Greek word has nothing to do with such a caricature of Christianity.

The word *periousios* simply means "one's own, of one's own possession" (A-S). Cremer notes that the term signifies "more than a mere possession"; it is rather "a treasure." He adds: "Accordingly *periousios* is what constitutes *a costly possession, a specially chosen good, that which is a costly possession*" (p. 242). Arndt and

Gingrich suggest that the real meaning is "chosen." They note that a married man is called *periousios*, "the chosen one."

Preisker writes: "By Jesus' work of redemption God has created for Himself a people which is for Him a costly possession" (TDNT, 6:58). He also quotes Debrunner as saying that *periousios* is "the people which constitutes the crown jewel of God" (p. 57).

The time was when one would occasionally hear somebody testify, "I praise the Lord that I am one of God's *peculiar* people." The person who talked that way had a sad misconception of what this passage means. When we say today that a certain person is "peculiar," we mean that he is queer, that he's an oddball. It doesn't bring any glory to God or the church when we try to be odd in order to prove that we are holy.

The best advertising of holiness of life is not done by those who dress, act, or talk in a "peculiar" way. It is done by those who are Christlike in their attitudes and who are "zealous of good works." One can be so absorbed—if not actually obsessed—with being "peculiar" that he fails to emphasize as he should the last phrase of this verse. If he were as zealous about doing kind deeds to others as he was about trying to prove that he was "different" from them, he might win many more people to the Lord. Fortunately there are those who have caught this truth and by their kind, friendly attitude are winning new converts.

Despise In 1 Tim. 4:12, Paul says to his younger colleague, "Let no man despise thy youth." There the word is *kataphroneō*, "think down on." Here it is *periphroneō*, "think around" (on all sides). That is, don't let anyone think around you. A. T. Robertson says that the term in 1 Tim. 4:12 is a stronger word of scorn, "but this one implies the possibility of one making circles around one and so 'out-thinking' him." Then he adds this pertinent observation: "The best way for the modern minister to command respect for his 'authority' is to do thinking that will deserve it" (WP, 4:605).

3:1 *Put Them in Mind* The verb *hypomimnēskō* occurs seven times in the NT. It means "cause to remember." In three passages (2 Tim. 2:14; 2 Pet. 1:12; Jude 5) it is translated "put in remembrance." In John 14:26 it is "bring to remembrance." The simplest translation in all cases is "remind" (NIV).

Principalities and Powers The Greek simply says that we are to be in subjection "to rulers (*archais*), to authorities (*exousiais*)." Today "principality" refers to a territory ruled by a prince.

To Obey Magistrates The Greek has only one word, *peitharchein*, "to be obedient." Polybius said that the Cretans were notorious for a revolutionary spirit. Paul urges here, as in Rom. 13:1, that Christians must be in subjection to governmental authorities. We should be "ready to every good work," so that we won't get in trouble with the authorities, for "rulers are not a terror to good works, but to evil" (Rom. 13:3).

2 Speak Evil The verb is *blasphēmeō* from which we get "blaspheme." That is what it means when directed toward God. When directed to man, it means "to revile, to rail at, slander" (A-S). There is another verb, *kakologeō*, that means "speak evil of." The one here is better translated "slander" (NIV).

No Brawlers The adjective *amachos* occurs only here and in 1 Tim. 3:3. It literally means "not fighting." Probably the best translation is "not contentious," or simply "peaceable" (NIV). A quarrelsome Christian is a troublemaker in the church and a disgrace to the cause of Christ. One who likes to fight with people should shut himself up alone with God until divine grace has changed his disposition.

3 Serving Again it is the verb *douleuō*, which means to be a slave to someone or something. People are not just serving sin; they are enslaved to it. This has been vividly and horribly illustrated in the last few years by those who are addicted to drugs.

Hateful The adjective *stygētos* is found only here in the NT. It is a strong word. The cognate adjective *stygeros* means "*hatred, abominated, loathed,* or *hated, abominable, loathsome*" (LSJ, p. 1657). So *stygētos* means "hated, abominated, hateful" (*ibid.*).

Speaking of the train of "lusts and pleasures" mentioned earlier in this verse, E. K. Simpson refers to "the malice and jealousy it breeds and the seething cauldron of hatred it foments" (p. 114). This is in startling contrast to the beautiful picture of God's grace in the next verse.

It will be noted in the definitions given above that the first meaning of *stygētos* is "hated." This is adopted in many recent versions. The TCNT has, "Detested ourselves and hating one another." Weymouth reads, "Deserv-

ing hatred ourselves and hating one another." The NEB has, "We were odious ourselves and we hated one another." Similar is Goodspeed: "Men hated us and we hated one another." It may well be that this is the preferable translation, since "hateful, and hating one another" would be repetitious. The NIV has "being hated."

4 Kindness ... Toward Man The kindness of God toward men is put in striking contrast to the unkindness of men to each other (v. 3). The adjective *chrēstotēs* is used only by Paul in the NT (10 times). In the KJV it is translated "goodness" (or "good") 5 times, all in Romans. Elsewhere it is "kindness," except "gentleness" as a fruit of the Spirit (Gal. 5:22).

Its original meaning was "goodness" or "uprightness," and it probably has that sense in Rom. 3:12. Then it came to mean "kindness" or "generosity." Trench speaks of it as "a beautiful word, as it is the expression of a beautiful grace" (p. 232). Jerome (fourth century) speaks of it as a spontaneous disposition to bless. Bernard says that it "signifies the *graciousness* of the Divine love for man" (p. 177). It has also been said that John 3:16 indicates what it really means.

Love ... Toward Man This is one word in Greek, *philanthrōpia*, from which comes *philanthropy*. Compounded of *philia*, "love," and *anthrōpos*, "man," it literally means "love for man." In the NT it is found only here and in Acts 28:2.

In Hastings' *Dictionary of Christ and the Gospels*, W. W. Holdsworth has a helpful article on "Philanthropy." In it he makes this significant observation: "Philanthropy is the immediate product of the Incarnation" (2:357). He shows how Christ took the instinct of human pity for human suffering and transformed it into "love unto the uttermost" (p. 356). The article closes with this beautiful statement: "Philanthropy is love without limit, and love is of God, for God is LOVE" (2:359).

5 Washing Two verbs are translated "wash" in the NT. *Niptō* means to wash a part of the body, as the hands or face. But *louō* means to bathe the whole body. The noun here, *loutron*, is derived from the second. It occurs (in NT) only here and in Eph. 5:26, where we find the expression "washing of water by the word." That apparently means the same as "the washing of regeneration" here—what Weymouth calls "the bath of regeneration." This underscores the fact that in the experience of regeneration all our sins are washed away and the stain of them is gone.

Regeneration

The word *palingenesia* is compounded of *palin*, "again," and *genesis*, "birth." So it literally means a new birth—an expression we use today for conversion. In the NT it occurs only here and in Matt. 19:28, where it is used for the regeneration of the earth. Here, of course, it describes the new birth of the individual.

Renewing

The noun *anakainōsis* (only here and Rom. 12:2) comes from the verb meaning "to make new." Since it is a noun, probably "renewal" (NIV) is a better rendering than "renewing." It refers to the work of the Holy Spirit in the new birth, making us new creatures in Christ Jesus.

10 *Heretic* The Greek word is *haireticos* (only here in NT), from which we get "heretic." An adjective, it comes from the verb meaning "to choose." So it literally means "capable of choosing" and then (as in Plato) "causing division." While Arndt and Gingrich allow that it may "perhaps" mean "heretical," they prefer "factious, causing divisions." That is probably its correct meaning here, rather than doctrinal deviation.

In secular Greek *hairesis* was used for a doctrine and for a school which held this particular teaching. Josephus uses it for the three *haireseis*—Pharisees, Sadducees, and Essenes. We would call them "sects" of Judaism. Finally, in Rabbinic Judaism the term was used for groups that were opposed by the rabbis, and so were stigmatized as "heretical." This usage was taken over by Christianity and applied especially to Gnostic sects. (See article by Schlier in TDNT, 1:180–85.)

Philemon

1 ***A Prisoner of Jesus Christ*** Paul could truthfully have said, "I'm a prisoner of the Roman emperor." Instead he identified himself as "a prisoner of Christ Jesus" (NIV). He was a prisoner not of fate, but in the divine will. That made all the difference.

The word for "prisoner" is *desmios*, which comes from the verb *deō*, "bind." So this adjective means "bound" or "captive," and as a substantive, "a prisoner."

We find the same phrase as here in Eph. 3:1 and similar expressions elsewhere in these Prison Epistles. Kittel writes: "There can be no doubt that the actual imprisonment of Paul everywhere underlies the usage. But this real imprisonment is set in relation to Christ and the Gospel" (TDNT, 2:43).

Perhaps we can go a step further and say that Paul was bound to Christ as His prisoner. That made him actually a free man in the Roman prison.

6 ***Communication*** This is the familiar word *koinōnia*, which means "fellowship" or "communion." But the sense that fits best here is "sharing." Paul wanted his converts to be effective in sharing their faith.

Acknowledging Thayer says that *epignōsis* means "*precise and correct knowledge;* used in the N.T. of the knowledge of things ethical and divine" (p. 237). The better translation is "knowledge" (NASB) or "full understanding" (NIV). Lightfoot calls attention to an interesting fact: "In all the epistles of the Roman captivity St. Paul's prayer for his correspondents culminates in this word *epignōsis*" (p. 336). (See Eph. 1:17; Phil. 1:9; Col. 1:9.)

7, 12, 20 ***Bowels*** We have already discussed the term *splanchnon* in Phil. 1:8 (see comments there). But here it occurs three times in this short Epistle of one chapter. One should avoid reading the KJV of these passages in public worship. The correct translation is "heart," not "bowels."

8 ***Enjoin*** The word *epitassō* is a strong compound verb meaning "order, command" (AG, p. 302). Occurring 10 times in the NT, it is translated (in KJV) "command" 8 times and "charge" once. Only here is the weak rendering "enjoin" found. The best translation is "order" (NASB, NIV).

Convenient The verb *anēkō* is used here in an impersonal way with an ethical sense: "it is fitting (or, proper)." The KJV "convenient" is completely misleading today. In the seventeenth century "convenient" did mean "fitting" (OED, 2:935). But now "what is convenient" may be exactly the opposite of "what is proper." The latter, of course, is the correct meaning here (cf. NASB, NIV). Doing "what is convenient" rather than what is right is bad ethics.

9 ***The Aged*** The Greek word is *presbytēs* (only here and in Luke 1:18; Titus 2:2). In the other two passages it clearly means "an old man," the translation adopted here in the NIV (cf. "the aged," NASB). But in the Septuagint it is just as clearly used as an alternative form for *presbeutes*, "an ambassador." Lightfoot argues strongly for that meaning here (pp. 338–39). But Vincent says, " 'Ambassador' does not seem quite appropriate to a private letter, and does not suit Paul's attitude of entreaty" (ICC, p. 184).

11 *Unprofitable, Profitable* It is well known that the name Onesimus (v. 10) means "profitable." But a different root is used here. In verse 11 the Greek has *achrēston . . . euchrēston.* The first of these two words begins with the alpha-negative *a-*, followed by *chrēston*, "useful"—so "useless" (NASB, NIV). The second has the prefix *eu*, which means "good" or "well."

14 *Mind* The Greek word *gnōmē* did have the meaning "mind" in classical Greek (A-S). But Bultmann shows that it is used in the sense of "consent" in 2 Maccabees and Josephus (TDNT, 1:717). Thayer suggests that translation for this passage (p. 119), as do also Arndt and Gingrich (p. 162). It seems that the best rendering is, "without your consent" (NASB, NIV).

20 *Joy* The verb is *oninēmi* (only here in NT). Arndt and Gingrich translate this passage, "Let me have some benefit from you in the Lord" (p. 573).

21 *Wrote* The KJV uses the past tense in verse 12 ("I have sent"), in verse 19 ("I have written"), and in verse 21 ("I wrote"). The NIV gives the correct (present tense) translation: verse 12, "I am sending"; verse 19, "I am writing"; verse 21, "I write." It is true that the Greek has in each case the aorist indicative, which ordinarily indicates past time. But we have here what is called "the epistolary aorist." From the standpoint of the reader of the letter the action was past. But from the standpoint of the writer it was just taking place. Paul was at that very moment "writing," and he was getting ready to send Onesimus back to his master Philemon with this personal letter. So from the standpoint of our usage today the past tense in English is incorrect.

22 *Lodging* Paul writes to Philemon, "Prepare me also a lodging: for I trust"—the Greek says "hope"—"that through your prayers I shall be given unto you." The Greek word for "lodging" is *xenia* (now sometimes the name for a city). Literally it means "hospitality." Then it came to mean "a guest room" (AG; cf. NIV). The word occurs only here and in Acts 28:23.

Hebrews

1:1 At Sundry Times and in Divers Manners The first three words of this Epistle are *polymerōs kai polytropōs. Kai*, of course, means "and." That leaves us the two adverbs to look at.

"At sundry times" is one word in Greek, *polymerōs* (only here in NT). *Poly* means "many" (cf. English use as a prefix); *merōs* means "part." So the adverb literally means "in many parts," or "in many portions" (NASB). "In divers manners" is *polytropōs. Tropōs* means "way"—so, "in many ways" (NASB).

Marcus Dods gives an excellent treatment of these two adverbs. He writes:

> *Polymerōs* points to the fragmentary character of former revelations. They were given piece-meal, bit by bit, part by part, as the people needed and were able to receive them. The revelation of God was essentially progressive; all was not disclosed at once, because all could not at once be understood (EGT, 4:247).

Dods goes on to say:

> His speaking was also *polytropōs* . . . not in one stereotyped manner but in modes varying with the message, the messenger, and those to whom the word is sent. Sometimes, therefore, God spoke by an institution [for instance, the Tabernacle and its offerings], sometimes by parable, sometimes in a psalm, sometimes in an act of righteous indignation. . . . These features of previous revelations, so prominently set and expressed so grandiloquently, cannot have been meant to disparage them, rather to bring into view their affluence and pliability and many-sided application to the growing receptivity and varying needs of men (4:248).

2 By His Son The Greek reads *en whiō*—literally, "in a son." This emphasizes the character of the new revelation in Christ; it was a *personal* revelation. The previous revelations had been in prophecies, types, and symbols. But an impersonal revelation of a person must always be an imperfect one. So at last God sent His Son. Only a personal revelation of a person can be a perfect revelation. Christ is the perfect Revelation of God.

The Worlds The Greek says *tous aiōnas*—literally, "the ages." B. F. Westcott makes this helpful comment: "The universe may be regarded either in its actual constitution as a whole (*ho cosmos*), or as an order which exists through time developed in successive stages. There are obvious reasons why the latter mode of representation should be adopted here" (p. 8).

3 Brightness The Greek word *apaugasma* (only here in NT) is used passively in the sense of "reflection" (cf. RSV). But the active meaning, "effulgence" or "radiance" (NASB, NIV), is that adopted by the bulk of the Early Church fathers and so is to be preferred here (Kittel, TDNT, 1:508).

Express Image This is one word in Greek, *charactēr* (only here in NT). It first meant "a tool for engraving," and then "a stamp or impress," as on a coin or seal (A-S, 479). It is that by which a person or thing can be recognized (cf. our use of *character*). Probably the best translation, suggested by Arndt and Gingrich, is "exact representation" (NASB, NIV).

Person The Greek word *hypostasis* has been taken over into English as a technical theological term. It literally means "that which stands under," as a support or foundation. Then it came to mean "reality . . . that in virtue of which a thing is what it is, the essence of any being." Westcott goes on to say that Christ "is the expression of the 'essence' of God. He brings the Divine before us at once perfectly and definitely according to the measure of our powers" (p. 13). Marcus Dods suggests: "To the English ear, perhaps, 'nature' or 'essence' better conveys the meaning" (EGT, 4:251). So we can use "nature" (NASB) or "being" (NIV). Koester suggests that in the Septuagint *hypostasis* is the "underlying reality behind something" (TDNT, 8:582).

7 Spirits This is the plural of the noun *pneuma*, which occurs 385 times in the NT. In over 200 of those times it refers to the Holy Spirit. Only once in the KJV is it translated "wind" (John 3:8). Yet that is the rendering here in the RSV, NASB, and NIV. The reason is the parallel with "flames of fire" in the next line of poetry (see NIV). Westcott says, "*winds*, not *spirits*. The context imperatively requires this rendering" (p. 25).

9 Fellows This is the plural of the adjective *metochos*, which literally means "sharing in" or "partaking of." Used as a substantive here, it means "partners" or "associates," and so "companions" (NASB, NIV).

2:1 Let Them Slip The verb (only here in NT) is *pararreō* (in the second aorist pass. subj.), which means "drift away" (NASB, NIV), as all good commentators and versions agree. The KJV rendering is based on the early use of the verb (as in Plutarch) for a ring slipping away from a finger. It was also used in the sense of "be careless, neglect" (Liddell-Scott, 1322). B. F. Westcott comments:

> The idea is not that of simple forgetfulness, but of being swept along past the sure anchorage which is within reach. . . . We are all continuously exposed to the action of currents of opinion, habit, action, which tend to carry us away insensibly from the position which we ought to maintain (p. 37).

2 Recompence of Reward This is one word in the Greek: *misthapodosia*, which is found only in Hebrews (here; 10:35; 11:26). It literally means "payment of wages." In the other two passages it means "reward." But here, as Arndt and Gingrich note, it has the unfavorable sense of "punishment" (NIV).

7 And Didst Set . . . Thy Hands This clause is not in our oldest Greek manuscript, Papyrus 46 (about A.D. 200), or in the great fourth-century manuscript, B (Vaticanus), as well as a number of later manuscripts (cf. NIV).

10 Captain The Greek word is *archēgos*, which comes from *archē*, "beginning." So it properly means "originator," "founder," or "author" (NASB, NIV). By His death, resurrection, and ascension, Jesus Christ originated our salvation. Moulton and Milligan show that the sense of "author" or "source" is strong in the papyri (VGT, 81).

12 Church The Greek word is *ecclēsia*, which is used mostly in the NT for the Christian Church. But it is also used for a Greek "assembly" (Acts 19:32, 39, 41) and is so translated (KJV, NASB, NIV, etc.). Here we find it in a quotation from the Septuagint, which constantly uses it for the congregation of Israel. So the proper translation here is "congregation" (NASB, NIV).

16 Him the Nature Of It will be noted that in the KJV these words are in italics, which means that they are not in the original. The Greek simply has: "For surely it is not angels he helps" (NIV; cf. NASB).

17 Make Reconciliation The verb is *hilaskomai*. It occurs only here and in Luke 18:13, where it is translated "be merciful"—the prayer of the tax collector in the Temple: "God be merciful to me a sinner." In Hebrews it is rendered "make propitiation" (NASB) and "make atonement" (NIV).

The exact form here is *hilaskesthai* (pres. pass. infin.). Cremer says that this means "to be reconciled, to be gracious" (p. 301). He goes on to say, "In Homer always, and in later Greek in the majority of cases, *hilaskesthai* denotes a religious procedure: *to make the gods propitious, to cause them to be reconcilied*" (ibid.). But Cremer insists that "the idea lying at the foundation of heathen expiations is rejected by the Bible. The heathen believed the Deity to be naturally alienated in feeling from man" (pp. 302–3). Then he adds, "In the Bible the relation is a different one. God is not of Himself already alienated from man" (p. 303). But for righteousness' sake, "an expiation of sin is necessary (a substitutionary suffering of the punishment . . .); and, indeed, an expiation which He Himself and His love institute and give" (ibid.). In further pursuit of this thought, Cremer says, "Nothing happens to God, as is the case in the heathen view; therefore we never read in the Bible *hilaskesthai ton theon*. Rather something happens to man, who escapes the wrath to come" (ibid.).

Wescott puts it this way:

> The essential conception is that of altering that in the character of an object which necessarily excludes the action of the grace of God, so that God, being what He is, cannot (as we speak) look on it with favour. The "propitiation" acts on that which alienates God and not on God whose love is unchanged throughout (p. 57).

In Kittel's *Theological Dictionary of the New Testament* Buechsel says of *hilaskomai* and its compound, *exilaskomai:* "The most striking thing about the development of the terms, however, is that words which were originally used to denote man's action in relation to God cease to be used in this way in the NT and are used instead of God's action in relation to man" (3:317).

This is shown clearly by our passage here in Hebrews: It is not man but God—in the person of His Son, the "merciful and faithful high priest"—who makes reconciliation, propitiation, or atonement. This is the glorious gospel message of the NT.

For further discussion see comments at Rom. 3:25.

3:1 *Consider* The verb *katanoeō* is compounded of *nous*, "mind," and *kata*, which literally means "down" but in compounds also has the intensive or perfective force. So the idea is: "Put your mind down on" or "note carefully, thoroughly." Behm says that it is "closely related to *noeō*, whose literal meaning is intensified, 'to direct one's whole mind to an object' " (TDNT, 4:973), or "to consider reflectively" (p. 974). He also writes, "In Hebrews *katanoeō* is one of the verbal concepts which, used imperatively, impress upon the readers the duties involved in being a Christian: 3:1f . . . the duty of looking to the Mediator of salvation, of concentration upon His exemplary moral conduct" (4:975). B. F. Westcott says that the verb "expresses attention and continuous observation and regard" (p. 74). So it may be translated "consider" (KJV, NASB) or, more forcefully, "fix your thoughts on" (NIV).

Profession The noun is *homologia*. It comes from the verb *homologeō*, which means "confess" and is so rendered 17 times in KJV, as against "profess" 3 times. The noun is used in

Hebrews 3 times (cf. 4:14; 10:23) out of the 6 times it occurs in the NT (see 2 Cor. 9:13; 1 Tim. 6:12, 13). Lexicons and commentaries agree that the correct translation is "confession" (NASB; cf. NIV).

6 *Rejoicing* The noun is *kauchēma*. It literally means "a boast," but also "a ground or matter of glorying" (A-S, 243). Westcott comments, "The Christian hope is one of courageous exultation" (p. 78).

8, 15 *Provocation* Arndt and Gingrich say that the noun (not found elsewhere in NT) *parapikrasmos* means: "*embitterment*, then *revolt, rebellion* against God." They translate the phrase as "in the rebellion" (p. 621). This was adopted in the NIV.

11 *Rest* The noun *katapausis* is found 8 times in Hebrews, twice in this chapter (vv. 11, 18), and 6 times in chapter 4 (vv. 1, 3 [twice], 5, 10, 11). Elsewhere it occurs only in Acts 7:49. Likewise the verb *katapauō* is found only in Acts 14:18 and 3 times in Hebrews 4 (vv. 4, 8, 10). It is here in Hebrews that we find the greatest emphasis on "rest" in the New Testament.

The verb is compounded of *pauō*, "cease," and *kata* (intensive or perfective). It suggests an entire cessation of nervous activity or struggle. The same is true of the noun. God has a beautiful, quiet rest for His people to enjoy.

4:8 *Jesus* It is true that the Greek does have *Iēsous*, "Jesus." But this is the Greek form of the Hebrew *Yehoshua*, "Joshua." In this place the obvious reference is to the OT "Joshua"; so that familiar name should be used. The KJV here is misleading to the casual or uninformed reader.

9 *Rest* Here we find a different Greek word, *sabbatismos* (only here in NT). It means "a keeping sabbath," and so "a Sabbath-rest" (NIV; cf. NASB). The term is used for the deeper rest that the Christian should enjoy.

Westcott says that *sabbatismos* indicates "a rest which closes the manifold forms of earthy preparation and work . . . : not an isolated sabbath but a sabbath life." He adds, "The change of term from *katapausis* is significant" (p. 98).

11 *Labor* The KJV says, "Let us labor therefore to enter into that rest." To say the least, this is an odd combination of ideas.

The Greek verb translated "labor" is *spoudazō*, which means literally "to make haste," and so, "to be zealous or *eager, to give*

421

diligence" (A-S, p. 414). It occurs 11 times in the NT and is translated "labor" only here (in KJV). A much better translation is "be diligent" (NASB) or "make every effort" (NIV).

12 Quick ... Powerful The first Greek word is *zōn*, the present participle of the verb *zaō*, "to live, be alive." So it simply means "living" (NASB, NIV). (The KJV uses the obsolete "quick" for "alive" four times in the NT.)

The Greek for the second word is the adjective *energēs* (cf. *energetic*). It comes from *en* and *ergon*, "work," and so literally means "at work," or "active" (NASB, NIV).

13 Naked It is true that the adjective *gymnos* literally means "naked." But Abbott-Smith notes that metaphorically it is used for things "exposed" (p. 96). So a better translation is "open" (NASB) or "uncovered" (NIV).

Opened The Greek has *tetrachēlisemena*, the perfect passive participle of the verb *trachēlizō* (only here in NT). It is evidently used metaphorically here in the sense of "laid open" (A-S, p. 449) or "laid bare" (NASB, NIV).

5:1 Ordained *Kathistēmi* literally means "set down" or "bring down" (to a place). Then it came to be used most generally in the sense of "appoint." Westcott says that it is "the ordinary word for authoritative appointment to an office" (p. 118). Since "ordained" now has a technical usage, probably "appointed" (NASB, NIV) is better.

2 Have Compassion On The verb *metriopatheō* (only here in NT) means "*to hold one's passions or emotions in restraint;* hence, *To bear gently with, feel gently towards*" (A-S, p. 289). "Deal gently with" (NASB, NIV) best communicates the exact thought.

7 In That He Feared The Greek has the noun *eulabeia* (only here and 12:28). In secular Greek usage this word does commonly have the idea of fear or anxiety. But it also was used in the sense of piety, or reverent awe of God. Bultmann argues for both meanings as valid (TDNT, 2:751–54). He does say that in the Septuagint of Prov. 28:14 it means "religious awe." So we find in recent versions: "for his godly fear" (RSV); "because of His piety" (NASB); "because of his reverent submission" (NIV).

Westcott makes these comments:

Eulabeia marks that careful and watchful reverence which pays regard to every circumstance in that with which it has to deal. It may therefore degenerate into a timid and unworthy anxiety (Jos. *Antt.* vi.2, 179); but more commonly it expresses reverent and thoughtful shrinking from over boldness. . . . Here the word in its noblest sense is singularly appropriate. Prayer is heard as it is "according to God's will" (1 John v.14f.), and Christ by His *eulabeia* perfectly realized that submission which is obedience on one side and fellowship on the other (p. 127).

9 Author *Aitios* is an adjective meaning "causative of" or "responsible for" (A-S, pp. 14–15). In the NT it is used only as a substantive (like a noun). It means "cause," or "source" (NASB, NIV).

10 Called The verb is *prosagoreuō* (only here in NT). It means "call, name, designate." The last of these three is used in the RSV, NASB, and NIV. Westcott says that the verb "expresses the formal and solemn ascription of the title [high priest] to Him to whom it belongs" (p. 130).

11 Hard to Be Uttered This is all one word in Greek, the compound adjective *dysermēneutos* (only here in NT). The prefix *dys* has the idea of "difficult." The rest of the word is based on the verb *hermēneuō*, "explain" or "interpret" (cf. *hermeneutics*). So "hard to explain" (RSV, NASB, NIV) is the correct translation here.

12 For the Time This could be taken as meaning "for the time being." But the Greek literally says, "because of the time" (*dia ton chronon*). The true meaning obviously is "by this time" (RSV, NASB, NIV)—that is, after such a long time as Christians.

The First Principles The Greek is *ta stoicheia tēs archēs*. The noun *stoicheion* (sing.) properly means "one of a series" (*stoichos*). Plutarch uses it for "*an elementary sound* or *letter* of the alphabet" and Aristotle for "*the elements* or *rudiments*" of knowledge (A-S, p. 418). That is clearly its meaning here.

Delling writes, "If letters are the basis of speech and their knowledge the basis of instruction, *stoicheion* can soon come to mean 'what is basic or primary' . . . or the 'elementary details' " (TDNT, 7:679). He goes on to say, "The meaning in Hb. 5:12 is clearly 'first principles' with a slightly derogatory nuance: *ta stoicheia*, 'mere rudiments,' 'ABC.' The idea of first principles is strengthened, or brought to expression, by *tēs archēs*" (7:687). The whole expression literally means the "elements of the beginning" (NASB marg.).

12, 14 *Strong Meat* The Greek is *stereas trophēs* (v. 12, gen. case) and *sterea trophē* (v. 14, nom. case). The adjective *stereos* (*-a, -on*) means "hard, firm, solid." *Trophē* comes from the verb *trephō*, "feed." So the correct translation here is "solid food" (RSV, NASB, NIV). The KJV rather constantly uses "meat" for all food, but this is not good American English and misleads the modern reader.

14 *Of Full Age* This is one word in Greek, the genitive plural of the adjective *teleios*, which comes from the noun *telos*, "end." So it means "having reached its end, finished, mature . . ." (A-S, p. 442). All are agreed that here it means "the mature" (RSV, NASB, NIV). Babies drink milk, but mature persons eat solid food.

6:1 *Perfection* The noun *teleiotēs* occurs elsewhere in the NT only in Col. 3:14, where it is translated "perfectness" (KJV). It comes from the noun *telos*, which means "end." So the basic idea is completeness.

The first part of this verse literally reads: "Therefore, having left the word of the beginning [Gk., *archēs*] of Christ." This ties in with 5:12, where the term *archēs* is used and where both NASB and NIV translate it as "elementary." The writer of Hebrews goes on to say: "Anyone who lives on milk, being still an infant . . . But solid food is for the mature" (5:13–14, NIV). Since "therefore" (6:1) ties our verse right into this, it would seem that "mature" is the best translation here. Delling writes, "In distinction from archē (Hb. 5:12; 6:1) *eleiotēs* is in Hb. the 'highest stage' of Christian teaching (6:1)" (TDNT, 8:79). So the primary emphasis of this exhortation is not on Christian character or experience but on advance in learning the higher teachings of the Christian faith.

5 *World* The Greek word *aiōn* should be translated "age," though the KJV renders it "world" 38 times and "age" only twice.

6 *If* In verses 4–6 there are five aorist participles in parallel construction. The fifth one is *parapesontas*, "and have fallen away." The NASB has the correct translation here: "and then have fallen away." The "if" is not justifiable. The Greek clearly indicates that one may become a partaker of the Holy Spirit—obviously a Christian—and yet fall away and be lost.

Seeing They Crucify This is one word in the Greek, *anastaurountas*—a present participle of continuous action. So the best translation is probably "while they are crucifying."

7 *Herbs* The Greek word (only here in NT) is *botanē* from which we get *botany*. It means "fodder, herb, plant" (AG). So it can be translated "vegetation" (NASB).

Dressed The verb *geōrgeō* (only here in NT) is compounded of *gē*, "earth" or "land," and the verb *ergō* (from *ergon*, "work"). So it means "work the land" (or "ground"). Today we would say "tilled" (NASB) or "farmed" (NIV).

18 *Immutable* The adjective is *ametathetos*—alpha-negative plus the verb *metatithēmi*, "place across" or "change." In verse 17 it is in the neuter and used as a substantive. These are the only two occurrences of this adjective in the NT. God is unchanging and unchangeable in His purpose (cf. NASB, NIV).

Consolation The noun *paraclēsis* occurs 29 times in the Greek NT. In the KJV it is translated "consolation" 14 times, "exhortation" 8 times, "comfort" 6 times, and "intreaty" once. The word that today combines these meanings is "encouragement" (NASB; cf. NIV). That fits well with "hope" here. See further discussion at Acts 4:36.

19 *Anchor* We get our English word from the Greek noun *angkyran*. This is found three times in Acts (27:29, 30, 40) for the anchor of a ship. But here—its only other occurrence in the NT—it is used figuratively for the anchor of the soul, which is hope.

Sure and Stedfast The Greek adjectives are *asphalēs* and *bebaios*. They are practically synonymous. Abbott-Smith defines the former as "certain, secure, safe," and the latter as "firm, secure." *Asphalēs* literally means "not tripped up." The two together suggest "firm and secure" (NIV), which fits well with an anchor.

Veil The Greek word is *katapetasma*. Usually in the Septuagint, and always in the Greek NT, it is used for the inner veil or curtain that separated the holy place from the holy of holies in the Tabernacle and Temple. The NIV spells this out for the reader by saying of hope: "It enters the inner sanctuary behind the curtain," God's dwelling place.

7:3 Without Descent This is one word in Greek, *agenealogētos* (only here in NT). It is compounded of alpha-negative and the verb *genealogeō* (found in NT only in v. 6), "to trace ancestry." So it clearly means "without genealogy" (NASB, NIV)—that is, without a recorded pedigree. We should not assume, as some have wrongly done, that Melchizedek was without human ancestry. The same should be said about the added description: "Having neither beginning of days, nor end of life." It means that the dates of his birth and death are unknown.

Made Like The verb *aphōmoioō* (only here in NT) is in the form of a perfect passive participle. The idea seems to be that Melchizedek was like the Son of God in the timelessness of his priesthood: He had no predecessor or successor. J. Schneider says that in the perfect tense, as here, the verb means, "to be like" (TDNT, 5:198).

16 Carnal The Greek adjective *sarkinos* comes from the noun *sarx*, "flesh." The English word *carnal* (KJV) comes from the Latin word for flesh. But it has taken on a largely pejorative sense, so that it does not fit here, where we are dealing with a matter of "physical requirement" (NASB), or "as to his ancestry" (NIV). Jesus came from the tribe of Judah and so did not meet the requirement of being a physical descendant of Levi (v. 14). Rather, He was a priest in the order of Melchizedek.

Endless The Greek adjective *akatalytos* (only here in NT) is compounded of the alpha-privative *a-* and the verb *katalyo*, "destroy." So it means "indestructible" (NASB, NIV).

21 Repent Today we normally use the word *repent* for feeling remorse for sin or some misdeed. The Greek verb here is *metamelomai*, which usually has that sense. But George Wesley Buchanan points out that this "is formed from the preposition 'after' and the verb 'to care,' 'be anxious about,' 'take thought.' This word, then, means to have an 'after thought' or an 'after care,' to give the matter a second thought." Buchanan concludes, "The claim of both Ps. 110 and the author is that God made a firm decision about this and he would never give it a second thought. It could not come up for reconsideration" (*To the Hebrews*, Anchor Bible, 127). Probably the best translation here is "will not change his mind" (NIV; cf. NASB).

22 Testament This is the first of 17 times that the word *diathēkē* occurs in Hebrews. In the KJV it is translated "covenant" 11 times and "testament" 6 times.

But this is unfortunate. In his monumental commentary on the Greek text of Hebrews, B. F. Westcott writes, "There is not the least trace of the meaning 'testament' in the Greek Old Scriptures [the Septuagint], and the idea of a 'testament' was indeed foreign to the Jews till the time of the Herods" (p. 299).

The ordinary Greek word for "covenant" was *synthēkē*, which does not occur in the NT. This term indicates an agreement made between two or more parties. The reason the sacred writers chose *diathēkē* is clear: *synthēkē* was used for a covenant made between equals, but God's covenant with mankind is a unilateral agreement: God dictates the terms.

For a further treatment of *diathēkē*, see the discussion at Heb. 9:16–17 and Gal. 3:15.

Surety The word is *engyos* (only here in NT). Jesus is the divine "Guarantee." Preisker suggests that He is the "Guarantor" of the promises of God. He writes, "With his life, death and ascension Jesus has given us the assurance . . . that the beginning of the saving work of God will necessarily be followed by its completion" (TDNT, 2:239).

25 To the Uttermost The Greek phrase *eis to panteles* occurs (in the NT) only here and in Luke 13:11 ("at all"). Westcott says that it means "completely, wholly, to the uttermost" (p. 191). The NIV has "completely," whereas the NASB has "forever." Delling notes that outside the Bible the word *panteles* means "complete," and the phrase signifies "completely" (TDNT, 8:66–67). But he combines the two ideas of the NIV and NASB in this interesting observation: "The One who saves 'for ever' . . . is also, however, the One who saves 'altogether,' so that the saying about the 'totality' of the saving work can hardly be expounded in only a single direction" (8:67).

28 Consecrated The Greek has *teteleiōmenon*, the perfect passive participle of the verb *teleioō*, "complete" or "perfect." So the correct translation is "made perfect" (NASB, NIV). Jesus is "perfect" in contrast to the Levitical priests who were "weak" (NASB, NIV).

8:1 *Sum* The word *kephalaion* comes from *kephalē*, "head." In the only other place in the NT where it occurs it means "sum" (of money). See discussion at Acts 22:28. But here it has its primary meaning, "main point" (NASB).

Is Set In the KJV the verb *kathizō* is correctly translated "sat down" twice in Hebrews (1:3; 10:12). But here and in 12:2 it is given the awkward, incorrect rendering "is set."

2 *Of the Sanctuary* The Greek literally says "of the holy things" (*tōn hagiōn*). But here and in 9:1 the adjective is used as a substantive (neuter sing. in 9:1) for the "sanctuary" of the Tabernacle.

5 *Example* The term *hypodeigma* was used in secular Greek for an "example." But it also meant "copy." That meaning fits better here and in 9:23 (NASB, NIV). In the latter passage the KJV has "pattern(s)."

6 *Mediator* See discussion at 1 Tim. 2:5.

13 *Made . . . Old . . . Decayeth* Both of these translate the same verb, *palaioō*, which comes from the adjective *palaios*. Arndt and Gingrich say that the adjective means "*old* = in existence for a long time, often with the connotation of being antiquated or outworn" (*Lexicon*, 605). Seesemann writes, "The word has theological significance only in Hb. 8:13, where it occurs twice . . . the author argues . . . that by setting up the new covenant God has declared the old to be outdated. God himself cancels its validity" (TDNT, 5:720).

Since it is the same verb in 13*a* and 13*b*, it is best to translate: "made obsolete" and "is becoming obsolete" (NASB; cf. NIV). The first form is the perfect active indicative, and the second is the present passive participle. With the coming of the new covenant in Christ, the old covenant made at Sinai is now obsolete. We are not under law but under grace.

Waxeth Old This is the present active participle of the verb *gēraskō* (in NT only here and John 21:18), which comes from the noun *gēras*, "old age" (only in Luke 1:36). It means "growing old" (NASB) or "aging" (NIV).

9:2 *Candlestick* The Greek word is *lychnia*, which means "lampstand" (NASB, NIV). They did not use candles in the Tabernacle. See discussion at Matt. 5:15.

Sanctuary It is true that we have here the neuter plural (*Hagia*) of the adjective *hagios*, "holy." But the translation "sanctuary" does not fit here, because verses 2 and 3 describe two sanctuaries. The first (v. 2) was called "the Holy Place" (NIV; cf. NASB). The second (v. 3), behind the inner curtain, was called "the Most Holy Place" (NIV). The Greek is *Hagia Hagiōn*—literally, "the Holy of Holies" (NASB). These two rooms together comprised one building, which could be referred to as "The Sanctuary." The rest of the Mosaic Tabernacle consisted of open courts or courtyards.

The Showbread In the NT this same term occurs (in KJV) in each of the Synoptic Gospels (Matt. 12:4; Mark 2:26; Luke 6:4). There it is a translation of *tous artous tēs prothēseos*—literally, "the loaves of the presentation" (or, "placing before"). Here the order of the words is reversed: *hē prothesis tōn artōn*. This poses a bit of a problem. Maurer suggests, "When Hb. 9:2 lists not only the table but more specifically *hē prothesis ton arton* as an object in the temple sanctuary, the reference is not so much to the act of placing as to something concrete, perhaps the bread laid on the table . . ." (TDNT, 8:165).

5 *Cherubim* This is the only place in the NT where this term occurs, though it is found scores of times in the OT. It comes directly from the Hebrew *kerubim*. *Im* is the masculine plural ending of Hebrew nouns. So to say "cherubims" (some KJV) is simply not correct; it is like saying "I have three childrens." All good modern versions, of course, have correctly "cherubim" or "cherubs."

9 *Figure* It comes as a bit of a surprise to discover that the Greek word here is *parabolē*, which is translated "parable" (KJV) 46 out of the 50 times it occurs in the NT. It is used for the parables of Jesus 17 times in Matthew, 13 times in Mark (though translated "comparison" in 4:30), and 17 times in Luke. Once in the Synoptic Gospels it is rendered as "proverb" (Luke 4:23). Aside from these Gospels it is found only in Hebrews (9:9; 11:19)—where the KJV has "figure."

The noun *parabolē* comes from the verb *paraballō*, which means "place beside," "compare." Here it may well be translated "illustration" (NIV), which is what the parables were.

10 *Reformation* *Diorthōsis* (only here in NT) comes from the verb *diorthoō*, "set on the right path." Here it is used for the "new order"

(NIV), which replaced the old order found in the Mosaic law—as the first part of this verse indicates.

11 To Come This translation (KJV) is also found in the NASB. But the NIV has: "that are already here." Why the difference?

The simple answer is that the manuscript evidence, including the very earliest Greek manuscripts, goes both ways. Vaticanus (supported by third-century Papyrus 46) has *genomenōn*, "have come." But the other fourth-century manuscript, Sinaiticus, has *mellontōn*, "about to be." The fifth-century manuscripts are similarly divided. So we cannot be sure which was the original reading. Actually, both make good sense. We already enjoy the "good things" in Christ, our High Priest. But we shall also enjoy them even more in the time "to come," in heaven. In this case, we can "have our cake and eat it too"!

Building The Greek has *ktiseōs*, which means "creation" (NASB, NIV). The ancient Tabernacle was the place where God manifested His presence among His people. Now the "greater and more perfect tabernacle," not a part of this earthly creation, is where He manifests His presence. This spiritual tabernacle is where Christ ministers as our High Priest.

16–17 Testament For a full discussion of whether *diathēkē* should be translated as "covenant" or "testament," see our treatment at Gal. 3:15. We would agree with most commentators that the only place where this word means "testament" is Heb. 9:16–17.

The reason for this decision is that here we have an emphasis on the death of the one who made the *diathēkē* (v. 16), with an added statement that it is not in force until then (v. 17). This would not be true of a "covenant," but it is true of a "will" (NIV). The latter term is our usual word for what is legally known as "last will and testament."

22 Shedding of Blood This is one word in Greek, *haimatekchysia* (only here in NT). Apart from this passage, the term is found only in the Early Church fathers. Behm says that it refers here to "the shedding of blood in slaying" (TDNT, 1:176). He goes on to say:

> The main point is that the giving of life is the necessary presupposition of the remission of sins. This was prefigured in the animal sacrifices of the OT, but what could not be actualized in the OT (Heb. 10:4) has now been established as an eternal truth by the death of Christ (p. 177).

Remission The noun *aphesis* comes from the verb *aphiēmi*, which meant "let go, send away," and then "cancel, remit, or pardon" a debt or sin. The noun was used in secular Greek and in the Septuagint for "release" from captivity. Then it came to be used for "*pardon*, cancellation of an obligation, a punishment, or guilt" (AG, 125). Occurring 17 times in the NT, it is translated (KJV) 9 times as "remission" and 6 times as "forgiveness." The latter is more contemporary (NASB, NIV).

24 Figures The word *antitypos* occurs (in NT) only here and in 1 Pet. 3:21. Interestingly, it is used there in the opposite sense from the way it is employed here.

Strictly speaking, *antitypos* is an adjective meaning "corresponding to." But here it is used as a substantive. Goppelt writes: "In Neo-Platonism, though not in Plato himself, *antitypos* denotes the sensual world of appearance in contrast to the heavenly world of ideas, the *authenticon*" (TDNT, 8:248). He would translate *antitypa* (pl.) here as "counterpart" (p. 258).

Though we get our word *antitype* directly from this Greek term, that English word would not fit here. For us, *antitype* means the original. Here *antitypos* means "copy" (NASB, NIV).

25 The Holy Place It is true that the Greek simply has *ta hagia* (literally, "the holy things"). But we know from the OT that the high priest once a year, on the Day of Atonement, entered "the Most Holy Place" (NIV).

27 Appointed Ten different Greek verbs are translated "appoint" in the NT (KJV). Only here is *apokeimai* rendered that way. In Luke 19:20 it is used in its literal sense of "laid up" (KJV) or "laid away" (NIV). In the two other places in the NT where it occurs (Col. 1:5 and 2 Tim. 4:8) it is used for spiritual things "laid up" for the Christian. Here in Hebrews the thought is: "Just as man is destined to die once" (NIV).

10:10 Sanctified Is it "sanctified" (KJV, NASB) or "made holy" (NIV)? The answer is that both are correct. The Greek verb is *hagiazō*, which comes from the adjective *hagios*, "holy," and the causative *z*. So the literal meaning of *hagiazō* is "make holy." Our familiar word *sanctify* comes from the Latin *sanctus*, "holy," and *ficare*, "to make." So it means "make holy."

17 *Iniquities* The Greek word is *anomia*. It is compounded of the alpha-privative *a-* and *nomos*, "law." So it means "lawless deeds" (NASB) or "lawless acts" (NIV).

23 *Faith* The Greek word is not *pistis*, "faith," but *elpis*, "hope" (RSV, NASB, NIV).

24 *Provoke* The first meaning of this word today, as given in the *American Heritage Dictionary* (p. 1054), is "To incite to anger or resentment." Obviously that doesn't fit here. The correct translation is "to stimulate" (NASB) or "spur one another on" (NIV).

26 *If We Sin Wilfully* This might be taken to mean that if a person committed one willful sin after being converted, there would be no more atoning sacrifice for his sins. But the verb "sin" is here in the present participle of continuous action. So the correct translation is "If we go on sinning willfully" (NASB) or "If we deliberately keep on sinning" (NIV).

29 *Done Despite* This is one word, *enybrisas*, which means "has insulted" (NASB, NIV). The verb *enybrizō* occurs only here in the NT.

32 *Fight* The Greek word is *athlēsis* (only here in NT), from which we get our word *athletics*. It comes from the verb *athleō*, which meant to contend in games or athletic contests. So the noun properly means "contest" (NIV).

Afflictions The Greek word here is not at all the one that is usually (and correctly) translated "affliction" in the KJV. Rather, it is the plural of *pathēma*, which means "suffering" (NIV; cf. NASB). The usual word for "affliction" is *thlipsis*, which occurs in the plural in verse 33.

33 *Whilst Ye Were Made a Gazing-stock* This is all one word in Greek, the present participle of the verb *theatrizō* (only here in NT), which means "expose publicly" (AG; cf. NIV). We get our word *theater* from it.

34 *Spoiling* Today this word suggests the spoiling of food. The Greek noun is *harpagē*, which comes from the verb *harpazō*—"steal, carry off, drag away" (AG). Arndt and Gingrich say that the noun is used here for "forcible confiscation of property in a persecution" (p. 108).

So the correct translation is "seizure" (NASB) or "confiscation" (NIV).

36 *Patience* As we have noted in other places (see on Luke 8:15; 21:19), *hypomonē* does not mean "patience" but "endurance" (NASB) or "perseverance" (cf. NIV).

11:5 *Translated*
The Greek verb is *metatithēmi* (twice here), which literally means "convey to another place" (AG). The Greek noun for "translation" is *metathesis*, which has been taken over into English as a chemical term. In the NT it occurs only here and in Heb. 7:12; 12:27.

Today "translate" is used mainly for changing from one language to another. The *American Heritage Dictionary* gives as its 6th definition: "*Theology.* To convey to heaven without natural death" (p. 1364). That is the way it is used here in the KJV. Today we would say "was taken up" (RSV, NASB) or "was taken from this life" (NIV).

7 *Moved with Fear* This is one word in the Greek, the aorist passive participle of *eulabeomai*. In secular Greek this verb was commonly used in the sense of "fear," but it also often has in the Septuagint the idea of "fear of God" (TDNT, 2:752). Bultmann thinks that here it has the sense of "to fear" or have "reverent awe" (2:753). So we find "in reverence" (NASB) and "in holy fear" (NIV).

10 *Builder and Maker* The first noun is *technitēs*, from which we get *technician*. It means "craftsman, artisan, designer" (AG, 814). Arndt and Gingrich suggest for this passage the translation "architect" (NASB, NIV).

The second noun is *dēmiourgos*, which is compounded of *dēmos*, "people," and *ergon*, "work." So it literally means "one who works for the people." Then it came to be used universally in the sense of "builder." The best translation here for the two is "architect and builder" (NASB, NIV).

11 *Abraham (NIV)* In most translations "Sarah," not "Abraham," is the subject of the entire sentence of this verse. Why does the NIV have "Abraham"?

The main problem with the traditional rendering is the expression "to conceive seed" (KJV). The Greek says "for the laying down of seed" (*eis katabolēn spermatos*). This is the act of a male, not a female, in the reproductive process (see on v. 18).

For this reason, F. F. Bruce suggests that

autē Sarra be taken as the dative of accompaniment. (The unpointed text of the Greek manuscripts could be taken as either dative or nominative.) Then the verse would read this way: "By faith he [Abraham] also, together with Sarah, received power to beget a child when he was past age, since he counted him faithful who had promised" (*The Epistle to the Hebrews*, in *New International Commentary on the New Testament*, p. 302). Leon Morris of Australia, in his commentary on Hebrews in the *Expositor's Bible Commentary* (12:119), agrees with this conclusion. These are two leading evangelical NT scholars today. In his *Textual Commentary on the Greek New Testament*, Bruce Metzger concludes on the same note (p. 672).

17 *Offered Up* This expression occurs twice in the KJV of this verse, but the Greek has different tenses. In the first instance it is the perfect active indicative of *prospherō*. The perfect tense indicates completed action. But Abraham did not complete his offering up of Isaac (Gen. 22:1–18). A. T. Robertson gives this helpful explanation: "The act was already consummated so far as Abraham was concerned when it was interrupted" (WP, 5:424).

The second occurrence has the same verb, but this time it is in the imperfect tense of action going on. Robertson suggests that here we have "the imperfect of an interrupted action" (ibid). Abraham was in the process of sacrificing his son, but God intervened in time to save the boy.

The distinction between the two tenses is brought out well by changing the second occurrence to "was ready to offer up" (RSV), "was offering up" (NASB), or "was about to sacrifice" (NIV). Incidentally, the verb *prospherō* literally means "bring to." But it is used many times in the NT (more than a dozen times in Hebrews) for offering up sacrifices. That is the meaning here (see NIV).

18 *Seed* The Greek word *sperma* has a different meaning here from what it has in verse 11. There it apparently means "semen" (a Latin word that we have taken over into English). Here it has the more common use in NT as "offspring" (NIV) or "descendants." (Cf. A-S, p. 413, for the distinction in the two verses.)

19 *Figure* Strangely, the Greek word is *parabolē*. Occurring 50 times in the NT, it is translated (KJV) 46 times as "parable." But in both occurrences in Hebrews (9:9; 11:19) it is rendered "figure." The phrase *en parabolē*, "in a parable," may be translated "figuratively speaking" (NIV, NASB marg.).

21 *Both* The Greek has *hekaston*, which means "each" (NASB, NIV).

22 *When He Died* In verse 21 "when he was a dying" ("when he was dying," NIV) is the present participle of the common Greek word for dying, *apothnēskō*. But in verse 22 it is the present participle of *teleutaō*. This verb comes from the noun *telos*, "end," and therefore means "coming to an end." It is used in the NT frequently for dying. But "when he died" (KJV) does not correctly translate the present participle. It should be "when he was dying" (NASB).

Departing The Greek word is *exodos*, which we have taken over into English as "exodus." It literally means "a going out." Since we refer to the escape of the Israelites from Egypt as the Exodus (recorded in the Book of Exodus), it is better to use here "the exodus" (RSV, NASB, NIV).

23 *Proper* In the NT the adjective *asteios* is used only twice: here and in Acts 7:20 (see comment there). Both times it is applied to the Baby Moses, as it also is in the Septuagint on Exod. 2:2. In Liddell-Scott (p. 260) it is stated that in Exod. 2:2 it meant "pretty, graceful." So in the NASB it is translated "beautiful." The NIV says "no ordinary."

26 *Had Respect* The verb is *apoblepō* (only here in NT). It is compounded of *blepō*, "see" or "look," and *apo*, "away from." Abbott-Smith says it means "to look away from all else at one object" (p. 48). It is the imperfect tense of continuous action. So it is rightly translated "was looking" (NASB) or "was looking ahead" (NIV).

Recompence of the Reward This is all one word in Greek, *misthapodosia*, found only in Hebrews (2:2; 10:35; 11:26). In all three places it is translated as above in the KJV. It is compounded of *misthos*, "wages," and the verb *apodidōmi*, "give back." So it was used primarily for the payment of wages, and then for "reward." Here it is used for the "reward" that comes to those who obey God's will. In 2:2 it refers to the "punishment" (NIV) that people receive for disobedience. But here and in 10:35 it is the reward that God's people get for their faithfulness.

31 *Believed Not* The Greek verb is *apeitheō*, which definitely means "disobey" or "be disobedient." If the writer had meant "believed not," he would have used *apisteō* (from *pistis*, "faith"). Appropriately, Marvin Vincent says *apeitheō* indicates "disbelief as it manifests itself in disobedience" (WS, 4:531). The correct translation is "disobedient" (RSV, NASB, NIV).

33 Subdued The verb is *katagōnizomai* (only here in NT), a perfective compound meaning to "struggle against," and then "conquer" (cf. RSV, NASB, NIV).

37 Were Tempted It is impossible to know today whether this (one word in Greek, *epeirasthēsan*) was, or was not, in the original Greek text. In our oldest manuscript of Hebrews (Papyrus 46, from about A.D. 200) it does not occur. The expression is retained in the NASB, but not in the NIV.

40 Provided The verb is *problepō* (only here in NT). It literally means "see beforehand" (*pro*), and so here "foreseen" (RSV, NASB marg.). Arndt and Gingrich suggest "provided" for this passage. God not only foresaw but "planned" (NIV).

12:1 Weight The noun *ogkos* (only here in NT) literally means a "weight" or "burden," and so metaphorically an "encumbrance" (NASB). The NIV spells it out as "everything that hinders."

Which Doth So Easily Beset This is all one word in Greek, *euperistatos* (only here in NT). Westcott adopts the sense "readily encircling, besetting, entangling" (p. 394). Probably the best rendering is "so easily entangles" (NASB, NIV). Marcus Dods suggests that the reference is to "that which characterises all sin, the tenacity with which it clings to a man" (EGT, 4:365). So we would suggest also the rendering: "the sin which clings so closely to us."

Patience Once more (see comment on 10:36) we note that *hypomonē* does not mean "patience" (KJV). No one ever won a race by patience. It takes "endurance" (NASB) or "perserverance" (NIV). This is a lifelong, long-distance race.

2 Looking The verb *aphoraō* (only here and Phil. 2:23) means "to look away from all else at, fix one's gaze upon" (A-S, 71–72). So we find "fixing our eyes" (NASB) and "Let us fix our eyes" (NIV). Keeping our eyes fixed on Jesus is the only safe way to live in a sinful world. This involves looking "away from all else" that would turn us aside.

Finisher The noun *teleiōtēn*—found only in later Christian writers, after this occurrence (TDNT, 8:86)—comes from the verb *teleioō*, which literally means "bring to an end" (*telos*), and so "make complete or perfect." Probably the best translation here is "perfecter" (NASB, NIV).

3 Contradiction The word *antilogia* literally means "a speaking against." But in Jude 11 it clearly indicates a "rebellion" (NASB, NIV). So here it may mean "hostility" (NASB), a meaning found in the secular papyri of the NT period, or simply "opposition" (NIV).

5–11 Chastening, Chasteneth, Chastisement "Chastening" (vv. 5, 7, 11) and "chastisement" (v. 8) translate the Greek noun *paideia*. "Chasteneth" (vv. 6, 7) and "chastened" represent the verb *paideuō*. All of these are based on the word *pais*, "child." So they all refer to child training. Today we call this "discipline," which conveniently acts as both verb and noun. So the NASB and NIV correctly use "discipline." This includes verse 9, where the KJV has "corrected." The Greek has *paideutas*, "one who disciplines" (here in the pl.).

While we are looking at this section on child discipline, we should like to make one observation: It is difficult to see how any reasonable-minded person could defend the reading aloud of the KJV of verse 8. The fact that the offensive term there was an acceptable word in that period (1611) does not make it so now. Even to give an innocent child or young person a copy of "The Holy Bible" with that "dirty word" in it can create unnecessary problems. The Greek simply says *nothoi*, "illegitimate children" (RSV, NASB, NIV).

14 Follow The Greek word that actually means "follow" is *akoloutheō*. But we have here a much stronger term, *diōkō*, which means "pursue." It is used in classical Greek for an animal pursuing its prey, as a hound dog on the trail of a fox—pursuing all day! So we must "pursue" peace with all people, and holiness—literally, "the sanctification" (NASB)—as long as we live.

16 Morsel of Meat The KJV constantly uses "meat" for all kinds of food, whereas today the term is used only for "edible flesh" (*American Heritage Dictionary*, 812). In the Greek, "morsel of meat" is just one word, *brōsis*, which literally means "eating." So the correct translation is "a single meal" (NASB, NIV).

Birthright　The Greek word is *prōtotokia* (only here in NT), which is compounded of *prōtos*, "first," and *tiktō*, "give birth." So a more adequate translation is "inheritance rights as the oldest [firstborn] son" (NIV). The firstborn son was entitled to a double portion of the family estate.

17 Repentance　The Greek word *metanoia*, as we have noted before, literally means a "change of mind" (NIV). A. T. Robertson says that "it" (which Esau sought with tears) was "the blessing" (see NIV)—not repentance. Robertson adds: "There was no change of mind in Isaac" (WP, 5:438). Esau was not seeking repentance, but to change his father's mind.

22 An Innumerable Company　This is all one word in Greek, the plural of *myrias*, "myriad" (cf. NASB). We get our word *myriad* from the genitive case, *myriados*. It literally means "ten thousand," and so "thousands upon thousands" (NIV). Here it is used hyperbolically for "vast numbers" (A-S, 298; cf. KJV).

23 To the General Assembly　This is one word in Greek, *panēgyrei*, the dative case of *panēgyris* (only here in NT), which meant a "festal assembly" (A-S, 335). In the Greek text this is the final word of verse 22—see NIV, "in joyful assembly"—not the beginning of verse 23.

Written　We have here the perfect passive participle of *apographō*. In the only other places in the NT where it occurs (Luke 2:1, 3, 5), this verb means "enroll" for a census. So here it may be translated "enrolled" (NASB) or "names are written" (NIV).

24 Mediator　See discussion at 1 Tim. 2:5.

28 Let Us Have Grace　The Greek is *echōmen charin*. The noun *charis* does usually mean "grace" in the NT. But in Luke 17:9 the combination, as here, with the verb *echō*, "have," is translated "thank" (KJV, NASB, NIV). "Thanks" and "gratitude" are listed in Greek lexicons as one meaning of *charis*. So here we have "let us show gratitude" (NASB) or "let us be thankful" (NIV).

13:1 Brotherly Love　The Greek word is *philadelphia*. See discussion at 1 Thess. 4:9.

3 In Bonds　The Greek noun *desmios* comes from the verb *deō*, "bind." So it does mean one who is bound. But it is the regular word for "prisoner" (cf. NASB, NIV). Many Christians were Roman prisoners at this time.

4 Is　This word is in italics (KJV), indicating that there is no verb in the Greek text. The rather obvious meaning of the passage is brought out much better in the NASB—"Let marriage be held in honor among all, and let the marriage bed be undefiled"—or the NIV—"Marriage should be honored by all, and the marriage bed kept pure." In numerous places we have to add a verb to make any sense in English.

Whoremongers　This is not acceptable contemporary English. The Greek word *pornos* may be translated "fornicator" (cf. NASB), a term not commonly used today. Actually it means "the sexually immoral" (NIV).

　　The second noun, *moichos*, does mean "adulterer." For the sake of English style the NIV has reversed the order of these terms.

5, 7 Conversation　See discussion at Gal. 1:13.

5 Without Covetousness　The Greek adjective *aphilargyros* (only here and in 1 Tim. 3:3) literally means "without love of money." So it is best translated "free from the love of money" (NASB, NIV).

7 Which Have the Rule　This is the present participle of *hēgeomai*, which primarily means "lead" (cf. NASB), and so "rule" (KJV). Abbott-Smith gives for the present participle: "a ruler, leader." The NIV has adopted the latter as more appropriate for "leaders" in the church (also in vv. 17, 24).

9 Divers　This is Old English for "diverse." The Greek adjective *poikilos* means "variegated," and so "varied" (NASB) or "all kinds of" (NIV).

Meats　The Greek word *brōma* means "food." Here the idea clearly is "ceremonial foods" (NIV) in the Mosaic ritual.

16 Communicate　We use "communicate" now mostly for speaking or writing some message. The Greek word here is *koinōnia*, which means "fellowship" or "sharing." The latter fits the context here.

21 *Make You Perfect* The verb *katartizō* means "furnish completely" or "equip." Probably the latter (NASB, NIV) fits best in this sentence.

23 *Set at Liberty* As this was from prison, we would say "released" (NASB, NIV).

James

1:1 James The Greek form is *Iakōbos*, "Jacob." This James, the brother of Jesus (as most scholars hold), was named after Jacob (Israel), the father of the 12 tribes of Israel.

Scattered Abroad The Greek has *en tē diaspora*, "in the Diaspora"—technical name for the Dispersion of Jews in the Assyrian and Babylonian captivities and from then till the time of Christ. The Jews became "dispersed abroad" (NASB) or "scattered among the nations" (NIV). This Epistle was written primarily to Jews.

2 Temptations The Greek noun is *peirasmos*. It can be, and is, translated "temptation" in some other places. But the context here suggests "trials" (NASB, NIV).

3–4 Patience As we have noted before, *hypomenē* means "endurance" (NASB) or "perseverance" (NIV).

6 Wavereth This is the present passive participle *diakrinomenos*, as also in the previous clause—"nothing" (literally "not at all," *mēden*) "wavering." The verb *diakrinō* literally means "judge between." But in Hellenistic Greek (NT) it came to mean "To be divided in one's mind, to hesitate, doubt" (A-S, 108). So the best translation in this verse is: "without any doubting" and "the one who doubts" (NASB; cf. NIV). Buechsel writes: "Jm. 1:6 gives a vivid description of the man of prayer who is a *diakrinomenos*. He does not stand firm on the promise of God but moves restlessly like a wave of the sea" (TDNT, 3:947).

12 That Endureth Temptation The Greek is *hypomenei peirasmon*. The verb *hypomenō* is, of course, related to the noun *hypomonē* (v. 3). So the best translation is "who perseveres under trial" (NASB, NIV).

When He Is Tried The Greek *dokimos genomenos* is literally "having become approved"—as a result of having been tested. So it may be translated "once he has been approved" (NASB) or "when he has stood the test" (NIV).

13 Cannot Be Tempted The Greek says that God is *apeirastos*. This adjective (only here in NT) is compounded of the alpha-privative *a-* and the verb *peirazō*, "tempt" (which occurs three times in v. 13 and once in v. 14). Literally the statement is that God is "untemptable" by evil.

14 Enticed This is the present passive participle of *deleazō* (in NT only here and 2 Pet. 2:14, 18). It comes from the noun *delear*, "a bait." So it meant to catch fish by bait. Evil desires act as a bait to "hook" us and get us in trouble.

21 Superfluity of Naughtiness The first word is *perisseia*, which means "abundance"; the second noun is the very common term *kakia*, "badness." But in the moral sense, as here, it means "wickedness, depravity." Arndt and Gingrich translate the combination here: "excess of wickedness."

Engrafted The word is *emphyton* (only here in NT). It means "rooted, implanted" (A-S, 150), rather than "engrafted." God's Word is to be rooted in our hearts.

23 Natural The Greek says "the face of his *genesis*"—literally "beginning," and so "birth." That would be his "natural face."

Glass The Greek noun *esoptron* occurs only here and in 1 Cor. 13:12. In those days mirrors were not made of glass but of metal (usually copper or tin). So the correct translation is "mirror."

26 Religious In the Greek this is a noun, *thrēskos* (only here in NT), used as a predicate adjective. A. T. Robertson notes that "it refers to the external observances of public worship, such as church attending, almsgiving, prayer, fasting" (WP, 6:24). He adds: "It is the Pharisaic element in Christian worship."

26, 27 Religion The noun is *thrēskeia* in both places. In verse 26 it carries its primary sense of outward observances, but in verse 27 it seems to include more. It consists not only of righteous acts but also of pure character.

2:1 Of Our Lord This is clearly not a subjective genitive (Jesus' believing) but objective genitive—people believing in Jesus. So the correct translation is not "of" (KJV) but "in" (NASB, NIV).

Respect of Persons This is one word in Greek, *prosōpolēmpsiais*. See discussion at Rom. 2:11. It means "favoritism" (NIV) or "personal favoritism" (NASB).

2 Assembly The Greek word is *synagōgē*, which is compounded of *syn*, "together," and *agō*, "gather." So it literally means a "gathering together," and so "assembly" (KJV, NASB) or "meeting" (NIV). James is the only NT writer who uses this for a Christian gathering. That was because he was writing to Jews (see discussion at 1:1). Elsewhere in the NT *ecclēsia*, "church," is used.

Vile The Greek word *hrypara* means "filthy, dirty" (A-S, 399). And in the *Oxford English Dictionary* (12:201) the first definition given is "despicable on moral grounds." But Tyndale, in the first printed English NT, used "vyle" here and so it got into KJV, which retained most of Tyndale. Today we would say "dirty" (NASB) or "shabby" (NIV).

4 Of "Judges of evil thoughts" (KJV) would suggest judging the evil thoughts of others. But the clear meaning of this passage is "judges with evil thoughts" (NIV). "Thoughts" (*dialogismōn*) is literally "reasonings" (NASB marg.).

6 Despised The verb *atimazō* is compounded of the alpha-privative *a-* and the noun *timē*, "honor." So it literally means "dishonor" (cf. NASB). Abbott-Smith also gives "insult" (cf. NIV).

9 Ye Have Respect to Persons This is one word in Greek, the verb form *prosōpolēmpteite* (cf. noun in v. 1). The NIV helpfully uses "show favoritism" in both places.

Convinced The verb *elengchō* was a technical legal term in the first century, used for being convicted in court. So the proper translation here is "convicted by the law" (NASB, NIV).

14 Can Faith In the first question of the verse *pistis*, "faith," stands alone. But in the second question it has the definite article (*hē*). This is brought out by "that faith" (NASB) or "such faith" (NIV). We are saved through faith, but not by a faith that has no good works or deeds.

15 Naked The adjective *gymnos* does mean "naked." But in classical Greek it is used frequently in the sense of "scantily or poorly clad" (A-S, p. 96). Oepke says that here it means "badly clothed" (TDNT, 1:773–74).

19 Devils The Greek word is *daimonia*, from which we get "demons." There is only one "devil" (*diabolos*), but there are many demons.

Out of the 60 times that *daimonion* (sing.; pl. *daimonia*) occurs in the NT, it is translated "devil(s)" in the KJV 59 times (once, "god," Acts 17:18). This is unfortunate. The distinction should always be made.

3:1 Masters The Greek has *didaskaloi*, "teachers" (from *didaskō*, "teach"). Though the KJV always translates the verb as "teach" (97 times), it renders the noun *didaskalos* (sing.) as "master" 7 times when it does not refer to Jesus. (The NIV uses "Master" for Jesus.) But aside from "Master" for Jesus (40 times), the term "master" in the NT usually refers to a slave master, which is the usage we are accustomed to today. So here the better translation is "teachers" (NASB, NIV).

2 We Offend All This is not a true statement, and the Greek does not have it. "All" is not in the accusative (objective) case but in the nominative (*hapantes*). So it is the subject of the verb, not the object. We do not offend all people, but we do all offend.

The verb "offend" here is *ptaiō* (found also in 2:10). Its regular meaning is "stumble." In this chapter James is speaking particularly about the tongue (vv. 1–12). Honesty compels us to say that in our speech "we all stumble in many ways" (NASB, NIV). Connecting this verse with the admonition of the previous verse, J. H. Ropes makes this interesting observation: "All men stumble, and of all faults those of the tongue are the hardest to avoid. Hence the profession of teacher is the most difficult mode of life conceivable" (ICC, *James*, 228).

Bridle The verb is *chalinagōgeō* (only here and 1:26 in NT). It literally means to "lead with a bridle" (*agō*, "lead," plus *chalinos*, "bridle," as in v. 3). Here it is used metaphorically in the sense of "bridle" or "restrain." It means "keep . . . in check" (NIV).

4 Governor Today we do not speak of the "governor" of a ship. The Greek has the present participle of the verb *euthynō* (only here and John 1:23). Literally it is "the one directing or steering." This would be "the pilot" (NASB, NIV).

Listeth The Greek is *bouletai*, which means "wishes" or "desires" (NASB).

5 Matter The Greek word here, *hylē* (only here in NT), literally meant a "forest." It is true that Greek philosophers, such as Aristotle, used it in the sense of "matter," and the KJV translators were influenced by this fact. But "forest" (RSV, NASB, NIV) fits perfectly.

How Great . . . a Little We have here a very interesting phenomenon: Both of these expressions translate the same Greek adjective! *Hēlikos* properly means "how great." But as used here doubly in the interrogative it means "how great . . . how small" (A-S, p. 199). The NIV expresses it well: "what a great forest is set on fire by a small spark"—such as a smoldering cigarette stub!

6 Body For this word the NIV has "person." See discussion at Rom. 12:1.

Course The Greek noun *trochos* (only here in NT) comes from the verb *trechō*, "run." It was the Greek word for "wheel" (KJV marg.). This may suggest the whole "round" of life.

Nature The Greek word is *genesis*, which literally means "beginning." But here it seems to mean "existence" or "life" (NASB, NIV). That makes the best sense in this passage: "course of life." Incidentally, all commentators recognize this as a difficult verse to interpret.

8 Unruly The Greek *akatastaton* (only here and 1:8) is compounded of the alpha-privative *a*- and the verb *kathistēmi*, "set down" or "set in order." In 1:8 it is translated "unstable" (KJV, NASB, NIV). But here it is perhaps best rendered as "restless" (NASB, NIV). That's what our tongues are!

Deadly The adjective *thanatēphoros* (only here in NT) is compounded of *thanatos*, "death," and the verb *pherō*, "bear." So it means "death-bearing."

11 Place The Greek word is more definite than this. *Opē* (only here and Heb. 11:38) literally means "hole" and is so translated (pl.) in the Hebrews passage (NASB, NIV). Here it means "opening" (NASB).

13 Endued with Knowledge This is one word in Greek, *epistēmōn* (only here in NT). It comes from the verb *epistamai*, "know, understand." So the simplest meaning is "understanding" (NASB, NIV).

Conversation This translation (KJV) is entirely incorrect today. The Greek word is *anastrophē*. See discussion at Gal. 1:13. Here it means "behavior" (NASB) or "life" (NIV).

14, 16 Strife *Eritheia* is found before NT times only in Aristotle, the famous Greek philosopher. He uses it for those who were selfishly seeking political office. Buechsel thinks it is best to understand the word as meaning "base self-seeking" (TDNT, 2:661). This is well indicated by "selfish ambition" (NASB, NIV).

15 Sensual The Greek adjective is *psychikos*. It can be translated "natural" (NASB), as opposed to the spiritual (A-S, p. 489). Probably this is best expressed by "unspiritual" (NIV, NASB marg.).

Devilish The Greek adjective is *daimoniōdēs* (only here in NT). The best translation is "demonic" (NASB).

17 Gentle This is not the usual word for "gentle." It is *epieikēs*. J. B. Mayor says that Thucydides used it of men "who would listen to reason" (p. 131). So it may be translated "reasonable," or "considerate" (NIV).

Easy to Be Entreated *Eupeithēs* (only here in NT) is compounded of *eu*, "well," and the verb *peithomai*, "be persuaded." So the KJV is a literal translation. It may be rendered "reasonable" (NASB) or "submissive" (NIV).

4:1 *Wars and Fightings* The Greek has *polemoi kai . . . machai*. The primary meaning of the first term is "wars," and it is so rendered by NASB and NIV in "wars and rumors of wars" (Matt. 24:6; Mark 13:7). In the singular it is used sometimes for a "battle." A second meaning is figurative, as here, a "conflict" or "quarrel."

The primary meaning of the second noun, *machai*, is "contentions" or "quarrels." Abbott-Smith suggests that here the two terms are equivalent, both indicating "private quarrels" (p. 370). The whole expression may be rendered "quarrels and conflicts" (NASB) or "fights and quarrels" (NIV). The verb forms of these, in reverse order, occur in the middle of verse 2— "quarrel and fight" (NIV).

1, 3 *Lusts* The Greek word is *hēdonē*, from which we get *hedonism*. It means, in the plural, "pleasures" (NASB). The verb "lust" (v. 2) is an entirely different term, *epithymeō*, which basically means "desire" or "want" (NIV) but sometimes has the bad connotation "lust" (NASB).

3 *Amiss* The Greek adverb is *kakōs*, which literally means "badly." In a moral sense, as here, it means "wickedly" or "with wrong motives" (NASB, NIV).

4 *Adulterers and Adulteresses* The oldest Greek manuscripts have only *moichalides*, "adulteresses." The additional masculine form does not appear until the ninth century. The term "adulteress" is here used in the spiritual sense, "friendship with the world" (NASB, NIV), just as Israel in the OT is described as the adulterous wife of the Lord (Jer. 3:20; Hos. 9:1). A later scribe took it in the physical sense and added *moichoi*, "adulterers."

Friendship The Greek word is *philia* (only here in NT). It is related to *philos*, "friend" (also in v. 4), and the verb *phileō*, "love" (with emotion and affection). The Christian must love God with all the heart, and not love the world system with its godlessness.

9 *Be Afflicted* The verb is *talaipōreō* (only here in NT). It means "be miserable" (NASB). The cognate noun *talaipōria*, in the plural, is translated "miseries" in 5:1. Elsewhere in the NT the noun occurs only in Rom. 3:16 (sing.), where it is rendered "misery" (KJV, NASB, NIV). The "sinners" and "double minded" (v. 8) should be miserable in their condition and humble themselves before the Lord (v. 10).

11 *Speak Evil Of* This expression occurs three times in this verse. The Greek verb is *katalaleō*. It is compounded of *laleō*, "speak," and *kata*, "against." So the meaning is "speak against" (NASB; cf. NIV).

12 *Lawgiver* Instead of the usual case of a word being added in the late manuscripts, we have here just the opposite. The early manuscripts (before the ninth century) have "Lawgiver and Judge" (NASB, NIV).

The Greek word for "Lawgiver," *nomothetēs*, is found only here in the NT. It is compounded of *nomos*, "law," and the verb *tithēmi*, "place" or "set"; it means one who gives or sets the law. God is the supreme Lawgiver. So we should not speak against the law (v. 11).

14 *It Is* The NASB and NIV both have "You are." Why the difference? This is a textual problem. Our oldest and best manuscript of the Epistle of James, Vaticanus (fourth century), has *este*, "you are," and so do a number of later manuscripts. The evidence for *estin*, "it is," is much weaker. Since the latter seems more natural as an answer to the question, "What is your life?" it is easier to see how a later scribe would change "You are" to "It is" rather than follow the reverse procedure. In any case, the meaning is essentially the same.

5:1 *Howl* The Greek has the present participle of the verb *ololyzō* (only here in NT). This is what is called an onomatopoetic word—the sound suggests the sense (like "buzz")—and is claimed by one Greek writer (Theander) to be synonymous with *alalazō*. Heidland says that the verb means " 'to make a loud and inarticulate cry' in expression of very great stress of soul." He also notes that it "is found in the LXX in prophecies of judgment" (TDNT, 5:173). The rich will weep and howl at the return of Christ (5:174) because they have lived for self rather than for Him.

2 *Corrupted* The verb is *sepō* (only here in NT). Today we would say "rotted" (NASB, NIV). It is in the perfect tense of completed action. There is nothing permanent or eternal about material "wealth" (NIV).

3 Cankered The verb is *katioō* (only here in NT). It means "have rusted" (NASB) or "are corroded" (NIV). Gold and silver are worth fabulous sums now, but they will be worth nothing then.

4 Reaped Down The verb is *amaō* (only here in NT). It means to "mow" fields (cf. NASB, NIV).

Kept Back by Fraud The verb *aphystereō* (only here in NT) simple means "keep back" or "withhold." Withholding wages that were due was labeled a serious sin in the OT. "By fraud" is not in the Greek.

Sabaoth This word occurs in the NT only here and in Rom. 9:29 (in a quotation from the Septuagint). It is generally taken as meaning "hosts" or "armies." J. B. Mayor writes, "Its immediate reference is to the hosts of heaven, whether angels or the stars over which they preside: then it is used more generally to express the Divine Omnipotence" (cf. NIV, "Lord Almighty"). He goes on to say, "The use of this name is one among many indications serving to show that the Epistle is addressed to Jews" (p. 158).

5 Lived in Pleasure The verb *tryphaō* (only here in NT) comes from the noun *tryphē*, which means "softness, daintiness, luxuriousness." So it may be translated "lived luxuriously" (NASB) or "lived . . . in luxury" (NIV).

Been Wanton *Spatalaō* (only here and 1 Tim. 5:6) has much the same meaning. It is best translated "led a life of wanton pleasure" (NASB) or simply "lived . . . in . . . self-indulgence" (NIV).

7 Husbandman See discussion at Luke 20:9, 10, 14, 16 (WM, 1:260). The word *geōrgos* occurs 19 times in the NT and is always translated "husbandman" in KJV. The correct contemporary translation is "farmer" (NASB, NIV).

9 Grudge The verb *stenazō* literally means to "sigh" or "groan." Mayor writes, "The word denotes feeling which is internal and unexpressed" (p. 162). J. Schneider agrees with this when he says, "The reference is to inner sighing, not to open complaints" (TDNT, 7:603).

This seems evident in Mark 7:34—Jesus "sighed."

10 Suffering Affliction This is one word in Greek, the noun *kakopatheia* (only here in NT). It is related to the compound verb *kakopatheō*, "suffer misfortune," which is found in verse 13. Michaelis says that the sense of the noun (v. 10) is "enduring affliction." The verb (v. 13) "suggests, not so much the distressing situation as such, but the spiritual burden which it brings with it, and which drives us to prayer" (TDNT, 5:937). The OT prophets were examples of the patient suffering of affliction. And we should follow their example.

11 Count . . . Happy The verb is *makarizō* (only here and Luke 1:48). It means "consider blessed" (NIV; cf. NASB). It comes from the adjective *makarios*, which occurs (in the pl.) as the first word of each of the beatitudes (Matt. 5:3–10). This adjective was used by classical Greek authors for divinely bestowed blessedness, not human happiness. We can be "blessed" when we don't feel "happy."

Patience We have noted several times that *hypomonē* does not mean "patience" (KJV) but "perseverance" (NIV). Job often showed some lack of patience with his "comforters," but he did display a wonderful perseverance in his faith in God.

Very Pitiful This is a "pitiful" translation, considering the contemporary meaning of that term. It now means "pathetic."

The Greek has the compound word *polysplangchnos* (only here in NT). It is composed of *poly*, "much," and *splangchnon*—literally, "inward parts," but figuratively, "compassion." So the correct translation here is "full of compassion" (NASB, NIV).

13 Let Him Sing Psalms This is all one word in Greek, *psalletō*. The verb *psallō* originally meant to "pull or twitch" (as a bowstring), then "to play" a stringed instrument with the fingers, and finally "to sing to a harp, sing psalms." In the NT it means "to sing a hymn, sing praise" (A-S, p. 487).

16 Faults The late Greek manuscripts have *paraptōmata*. This literally means (in the sing.) "a falling beside" and could be translated as "faults." But all the early manuscripts have *hamartias*, "sins" (NASB, NIV).

17 Subject to Like Passions as We Are This is two words in the Greek, *homoiopathēs hēmin*. The second word simply means "with us." The first word (only here and Acts 14:15) means "of like feelings or affections" (A-S, p. 317), or "with the same nature." Michaelis says it denotes "one who finds himself in the same or similar relations, whose attitude or feeling is the same or similar" (TDNT, 5:938). The simplest translations are "with a nature like ours" (NASB) or "just like us" (NIV). The point, of course, is that Elijah was not a super-human being when he prayed so effectively, but was just like us, a human being.

1 Peter

1:1 Strangers The adjective *parepidēmos* (only here; 2:11; and Heb. 11:13) is composed of *para*, "beside," *epi*, "upon," and *dēmos*, "people." It is consistently translated "strangers" in the NIV in the three places where it occurs.

Scattered This is the noun *diaspora*, "dispersion," which we have already seen in James 1:1. It occurs one other place in the NT (John 7:35). While used of Jews in James 1:1, it refers also to Gentiles here and in John.

2 Foreknowledge The Greek word (only here and Acts 2:23) is *prognōsis* which we have taken over into English. *Pro* means "before," and *gnōsis* "knowledge."

3 Hath Begotten... Again The verb *anagennaō* (only here and v. 23) is compounded of *gennaō*, "beget," and *ana*, "again." It stresses the "new birth" (NIV)—"has caused us to be born again" (NASB).

Lively The correct translation of *zōsan* is "living." A. T. Robertson notes, "Peter is fond of the word 'living' (present active participle of *zaō*) as in 1:23; 2:4, 5, 24; 4:5, 6" (WP, 6:81).

14,23 Incorruptible The adjective *aphthartos* is compounded of the alpha-privative *a*- and the verb *phtheirō*, "destroy." So it means "imperishable" (NASB, NIV).

5 Kept The verb *phroureō* comes from the noun *phrouros*, "guard." So it may be translated as "protected" (NASB) or "shielded" (NIV).

6 Temptations See discussion at James 1:2.

7 Trial This is *dokimion*, the neuter singular of the adjective *dokimios* (only here and James 1:3). For a long time this word was not given in any Greek lexicon. One scholar (Winer) declared, "There is no adjective *dokimios*." But Adolf Deissmann found it in the papyri of that period. He writes, "Hence, then, the adjective *dokimios*, *proved*, *genuine*, must be recognized, and may be adopted without misgiving in both New Testament passages" (BS, p. 260). He suggests here in Peter: "what is genuine in your faith."

Appearing The Greek word is *apocalypsis*, which Peter uses three times in this Epistle (1:7, 13, 4:13). It means "revelation." The reference here is to the Second Coming. At the end of verse 13 exactly the same Greek phrase as here is translated in KJV: "at the revelation of Jesus Christ." The NASB and NIV wisely have it the same in both places.

13 Gird Up the Loins of Your Mind This is a literal translation of the Greek and represents the way they talked back then. It is almost equivalent to the present expression "tighten your belt."

"Gird up" (literally, "girding up") is the aorist middle participle of the rare verb *anazōnnymi* (only here in NT). A. T. Robertson says that this is a "vivid metaphor for habit of the Orientals, who quickly gathered up their loose robes with a girdle when in a hurry or starting on a journey" (WP, 6:87). What the whole expression means is "Prepare your minds for action" (NIV).

15 Conversation As we have noted before—see discussion at Gal. 1:13—there are three Greek nouns that are translated "conversation" in the KJV, and not one of them means that, as we use the term today. Peter is especially fond of the noun used here, *anastrophē*. He uses it 8 times (1 Pet. 1:15, 18; 2:12; 3:1, 2, 16; 2 Pet. 2:7; 3:11) out of the 13 times it occurs in the NT (see Gal. 1:13; Eph. 4:22; 1 Tim. 4:12; Heb. 13:7; James 3:13). The Greek word literally means the "turnings about" of life. The correct translation is "conduct" (RSV), "behavior" (NASB), or "all you do" (NIV).

17 Without Respect of Persons This is all one word in the Greek, the adverb *aprosōpolēmptōs*—found nowhere else except in the Epistle of Clement of Rome and the so-called Epistle of Barnabas. It is composed of the alpha-privative *a-*, *prosōpon*, "face," and the verb *lambanō*, "receive." It means that God judges "impartially" (NASB, NIV).

20 Foreordained The Greek has the perfect passive participle of *proginōskō*, "know before." It is correctly translated this way (KJV) in 2 Pet. 3:17. Also in Rom. 8:29 the KJV has "did foreknow" and in 11:2 "foreknew." The only other place in the NT where the verb occurs (Acts 26:5) it is used of human beings knowing beforehand.

Bultmann writes, "In the NT *proginōskein* is referred to God. His foreknowledge, however, is an election or foreordination of His people (R. 8:29; 11:2) or Christ (1 Pt. 1:20)" (TDNT, 1:715). We feel, however, that God's foreordination is based on His foreknowledge, and the two should not be confused. The NASB correctly has "foreknown" here.

22 Unfeigned The Greek adjective is *anypocritos*. It comes from *alpha*-negative and the verb *hypokrinomai*, "play a part" or "pretend." So the adjective means "sincere" (NASB, NIV)—literally, "unhypocritical."

2:1 Evil Speakings The noun is *katalalia* (only here and 2 Cor. 12:20). It is compounded of the verb *laleō*, "talk," and *kata*, "against." It may well be translated "slander" (NASB, NIV).

2 Newborn The adjective *artigennētos* (only here in NT) is composed of *arti*, "just now," and the verb *gennaō* (pass., "born").

Desire *Epipotheō* is a strong verb, meaning "long for" (NASB) or "crave" (NIV).

Sincere The adjective *adolos* (only here in NT) is compounded of the alpha privative *a-* and *dolos*, "deceit." So it means "sincere." As ap-

plied to liquids it meant "genuine" or "pure" (NASB, NIV). It can also be translated "unadulterated" milk.

Of the Word This is one word in the Greek, the adjective *logikos* (only here and Rom. 12:1). In both places it probably means "spiritual" (NASB marg., NIV).

4, 7 Disallowed *Apodedokimasmenon* is the perfect passive participle of *apodokimazō*, which means "reject after testing." Christ's contemporaries tested Him, the "living Stone," and then most deliberately rejected Him. So the proper translation here is "rejected" (NASB, NIV).

5 Lively It is the same adjective as "living" in verse 4 and should, of course, be translated that way.

6 Chief Corner Stone This is one word in Greek, the adjective *akrogōniaios* used as a substantive. It is also used in Eph. 2:20. See discussion there.

Be Confounded This is the passive of *kataischynō* and means "be ashamed," or "be put to shame" (NIV).

8 Stumbling . . . Offense The first word is *proskomma*, the second *skandalon*, from which we get "scandal." A. T. Robertson says of these: "*Proskomma* (from *proskoptō*, to cut against) is an obstacle against which one strikes by accident, while *skandalon* is a trap set to trip one, but both make one fall" (WP, 6:98). (See NIV.)

9 Peculiar Today "peculiar" is a pejorative term, meaning "odd" or "queer." Unfortunately, this translation has been misused by Christians who gloried in being "peculiar."

The Greek has *laos*, "a people," followed by *eis peripoiēsin*—literally "a people for possession," that is, "God's own possession" (NASB). The meaning is "precious," rather than "peculiar"!

12 Conversation See discussion at 1:15.

13 Ordinance of Man "Of man" is the adjective *anthrōpinos*, which means "human." For us "ordinance" means a law or regulation. But the Greek word here is *ktisis*. In the Septuagint and the NT it means "creation"; that is, "that which has been created."

The NASB translates the expression as "human institution," the NIV as "authority instituted among men." Foerster notes that this verse has "special difficulties"; the exact meaning is not perfectly clear. He suggests that this verse might well be "the title of the whole section 2:13–3:9" (TDNT, 3:1035). In that light, the reference may be to our fellowmen, as God's creation. The main emphasis seems to be on maintaining the proper relationship with all human beings.

16 Cloke The Greek word *epikalymma* (only here in NT) means "a cover." The idea is that of a "covering" (NASB) or "coverup" (NIV) "for evil." We are not to misuse our Christian freedom.

18 Servants The Greek has *oiketai*, from *oikos*, "house." So it means household servants. The reference to "masters" shows that they were "slaves" (NIV).

19 For Conscience Toward God The Greek word for "conscience" is *syneidēsis*. This comes from the verb *syneidon*, "see together." So the first meaning of *syneidēsis* was "consciousness." Finally, with the Stoics, it developed into the idea of self-judging consciousness, and so "conscience" (A-S, p. 427).

One problem we have here is that in our text *syneidēsis* is followed immediately by *theou*, "of God." (It is also preceded by *dia*, "on account of" or "because of.") So the NIV, perhaps wisely, translates the whole expression: "because he is conscious of God." This makes good sense.

20 Glory The Greek word *kleos* (only here in NT) did mean "fame" or "glory." But perhaps the best translation here is "credit" (NASB, NIV).

Buffeted This is a strong Greek verb, *kolaphizō*. It literally means "strike with the fist." So it may be translated "receive a beating" (NIV).

24 Stripes The word *mōlōps* (only here in NT) means a "wound" received by being beaten. So a better translation here is "wounds" (NASB, NIV). He was horribly wounded that we might be healed!

25 Bishop The word is *episcopos*, from which we get *episcopal*. The term comes from *scopos*, "a watcher," and *epi*, "upon" or "over." So it meant a "superintendent" or "guardian" or "overseer." It finally, in the church, took over the technical form, "bishop." As our "Shep-

herd," Jesus is our "Guardian" (NASB) or "Overseer" (NIV).

3:1, 5 Be(ing) in Subjection For the verb *hypotassō*, see discussion at Eph. 5:21 and Eph. 5:25 (for both sides of the marriage relationship). A better translation here is "be submissive" (NASB, NIV).

1, 2, 16 Conversation See discussion at 1 Pet. 1:15.

3 Adorning The Greek has *cosmos*, which occurs 187 times in the NT. In every other place it is translated "world"! But that usual meaning obviously would not fit here. Both NASB and NIV have "adornment."

The earliest meaning of *cosmos* (in Homer and Plato) was "order." The second usage was "adornment," as here alone in the NT. Then it came to be used universally for the "world," or the orderly "universe."

The noun is related to the verb *cosmeō*, which means to "put in order" or "arrange." That's what the ladies do with the help of *cosmetics*. The verb may also be translated "adorn" (Matt. 12:44; Luke 11:25). That is the way it is used here in verse 5.

Plaiting The Greek word *emplokē* (only here in NT) means "braiding" (NASB; cf. NIV).

4 Meek *Praus* (in NT only here and Matt. 5:5; 11:29; 21:5) may also be translated "gentle" (NASB, NIV). In Matt. 5:5 the NIV retains "meek" because of the familiarity of this beatitude (contra NASB).

Quiet The adjective *hesychiōs* occurs in the NT only here and in 1 Tim. 2:2. See discussion there.

6 Lord The Greek word *kyrios* occurs about 750 times in the NT. In the KJV it is translated "Lord" 667 times, "lord" 55 times, "master" ("Master") 13 times, "sir" ("Sir") a dozen times, and once each "owner" (Luke 19:33) and "God" (Acts 19:20). As one can see, *kyrios* is used not only for Christ or God, but also for slave masters, husbands (as here), or fathers (Matt. 21:30), and even as just a polite form of address (John 12:21, etc.). In our passage here the NIV has "master."

Amazement The noun *ptoēsis* (only here in NT) comes from the verb *ptoeō* (Luke 21:9; 24:37), which means (in the pass.) "be terrified." So the noun means "terror" or "fear" (NASB, NIV).

7 Dwell With The Greek has the present participle (used as imperative) of the verb *synoikeō* (only here in NT). It is composed of *syn*, "together," and *oikeō*, "dwell" (from *oikos*, "house"—so, living together in the same house). Today we would say "live with" (NASB, NIV).

8 Be Pitiful See discussion at James 5:11, third item.

11 Eschew The verb *ekklinō* means "turn away" (NASB).

Ensue The verb is *diōkō*, which means "pursue." In Heb. 12:14 we are likewise told to "pursue peace."

13 Followers The Greek has the plural of the noun *zēlōtēs* and so means "zealous ones" ("zealots"). Here it may be translated "zealous" (NASB) or "eager" (NIV).

14 Happy The Greek adjective is *makarios*. See discussion at James 5:11, first item.

15 Sanctify The verb is *hagiazō*, most commonly translated "sanctify" (literally, "make holy"). It is also used in the sense of "set apart." Since we cannot make God holy, perhaps the best rendering here is "set apart" (NIV; cf. NASB marg.).

The Lord God Instead of *theon*, "God," all the Greek manuscripts earlier than the eighth century have *Christon*, "Christ." So the correct reading here is "Christ as Lord" (NASB, NIV).

18 Suffered The NASB and NIV both have "died" instead of "suffered." Why?

This is a textual problem. *Apethanen*, "died," is found in Papyrus 72 (third century), Aleph (fourth century), A and C (fifth century), and other manuscripts of the eight and ninth centuries, as well as many later manuscripts. On the other hand, *epathen*, "suffered," is the reading in B (fourth century) and two manuscripts of the ninth century, as well as a limited number of later ones. The early versions almost all have "died." Actually, of course, Jesus both "suffered" and "died" on the Cross. So the meaning is much the same.

Quickened The verb is *zōopoieō*, which means "made alive" (NASB, NIV). Incidentally,

since the Greek makes no distinction with capital letters, we cannot be certain whether to have in this verse "Spirit" (KJV, NIV) or "spirit" (NASB). The latter choice was evidently based on the comparison with "in the flesh" (though the margin has "Spirit").

20 By Water The Greek has the preposition *dia* with the genitive, which means "through." Noah and his family were not saved "by water." Rather, they were saved "through water" (NIV; cf. NASB)—that is, saved through the Flood, not destroyed in it.

21 Figure The Greek noun is *antitypon*, which we have taken over as *antitype*. It is an adjective, literally meaning "striking back," but metaphorically (as here) "corresponding to" (NASB). Noah's being saved through the Flood "symbolizes" (NIV) Christian water baptism.

Answer The Greek noun is *eperōtēma* (only here in NT). It comes from the verb *eperōtaō*, "to question," but which later came to mean "to demand of." So the noun took the meaning "a demand." A. T. Robertson comments, "In ancient Greek it never means answer, but only inquiry. The inscriptions of the age of the Antonines use it of the Senate's approval after inquiry" (WP, 6:120). So it may refer here to the "pledge" made by the candidate at his baptism. Since *eis theon* immediately follows *eperōtēma* in the Greek, the NASB has "an appeal to God for a good conscience." We cannot be dogmatic about the exact meaning of the passage but can get help from different versions and even different interpretations.

4:1 Arm The verb *hoplizō* (only here in NT) comes from the noun *hoplon*, which is used several times in the NT in the plural for "arms" (weapons). So it is appropriate to translate the verb as "arm yourselves" (aorist middle imperative—right now!).

Mind The regular Greek word for "mind" is *nous*. But here we have *ennoia*. It occurs elsewhere (in NT) only in Heb. 4:12, where it is translated "intents" (KJV). Abbott-Smith defines it as "thought, purpose, design" (p. 155). It is compounded of *en*, "in," and *nous*, "mind." Behm says that the word means: "What takes place in the *nous*, 'deliberation,' 'consideration' " (TDNT, 4:968). So it may be translated "purpose" (NASB) or "attitude" (NIV).

3 Lasciviousness *Aselgeia* occurs 10 times in the NT and is translated "lasciviousness" 6 times (KJV). Today we would probably say, "licentiousness." It is well rendered "sensuality" (NASB) or "debauchery" (NIV).

Excess of Wine This is one word in Greek, *oinophlygia* (only here in NT). It is compounded of *oinos*, "wine," and *phlyō*, "bubble up, overflow." We call this "drunkenness" (NASB, NIV).

4 Excess *Anachysis* (only here in NT) comes from the verb *anacheō*, "pour out." So it means "a pouring out, overflowing, excess" (A-S, p. 35). This may be represented by "flood" (NIV).

Riot Today "riot" means "a wild or turbulent disturbance created by a large number of people" (*American Heritage Dictionary*, 1120). The Greek word here is *asōtia*, from *a*-negative and the verb *sōzō*, "save." Probably the best translation is "dissipation" (NASB, NIV).

5 Quick See discussion at 2 Tim. 4:1.

7 Be Sober The verb is *sōphroneō*. See discussion at Rom. 12:3.

Watch The verb is *nēphō*. See discussion at 1 Thess. 5:6. Probably the best translation here is "self-controlled" (NIV).

8 Fervent This English adjective is defined as: "Having or showing great emotion or warmth" (*American Heritage Dictionary*, 485). But the Greek word here, *ektenēs* (only here in NT) has a somewhat different connotation. It comes from the verb *ekteinō*, "stretch out"; so it literally means "stretched out." C. E. B. Cranfield says that it "suggests rather the taut muscle of strenuous and sustained effort, as of an athlete" (*First Epistle of Peter*, p. 95). A good translation is "unfailing" (RSV).

9 Use Hospitality There is no verb here in the Greek, just the adjective *philoxenoi* (pl.). See discussion at 1 Tim. 3:2. We obviously have to put a verb here. So we may read: "Be hospitable" (NASB) or "Offer hospitality" (NIV).

10–11 Minister The verb *diakoneō* was used basically for waiting on tables. So it means "serve." It is probably better to use that translation here (NASB, NIV), since the admonition applies to all Christians, not simply to those who "minister" in the pulpit.

12 Strange . . . Strange The second occurrence of "strange" is a correct translation of the adjective *xenos*, "strange, unusual." But "think it . . . strange" is the present passive imperative of *xenizō*, which means "be surprised" (NASB, NIV)—a regular sense found in late Greek writers.

13 Are Partakers Of The verb here, *koinōneō*, means "share" (NASB).

14 Reproached It is interesting that Arndt and Gingrich define the verb *oneidizō* as "reproach, revile, heap insults upon" (p. 570) and that these three meanings are represented in chronological sequence by KJV, NASB, and NIV.

Happy See discussion at 1 Pet. 3:14.

Resteth upon You The rest of the verse is not found in any Greek manuscript earlier than the ninth century and so is properly omitted from scholarly versions today.

15 A Busybody in Other Men's Matters This is all one word in the Greek, *allotriepiscopos* (only here in NT). It is compounded of *allotrios*, "belonging to another," and *episcopos*, "overseer." Charles Bigg writes: "*Allotrioepiscopos* [received Text spelling] is a word not found elsewhere, and probably coined by St. Peter" (*Epistles of St. Peter and St. Jude*, ICC, p. 177). It seems to mean "meddler" (NIV; cf. NASB).

17 House The Greek word *oikos* properly means a "house." But by metonymy it signifies, as here, a "household" (NASB) or "family" (NIV), as Abbott-Smith notes (p. 313).

18 Scarcely *Molis* comes from *molos*, "toil." So it means "with difficulty, hardly, scarcely" (A-S, p. 296). (See NASB, NIV.)

19 In Well Doing In the Greek this is *en agathopoiia* (only here in NT) and is found at the very end of the verse (see NASB, NIV). The noun comes from the verb *agathopoieō—poieō*, "do," and *agathos*, "good."

5:2 Feed The Greek does not have the verb *boskō*, "feed," but *poimainō*. This comes from *poimen*, "a shepherd." So the correct translation is "Shepherd the flock" (NASB; cf. NIV). This involves more than feeding; it means taking care of the sheep.

2–3 Flock It is interesting that the Greek word here, *poimnion*, is used in the NT only in a metaphorical sense, for Christians (also Luke 12:32; Acts 20:28–29).

2 Taking the Oversight This is all one word in Greek, *episcopountes*, the present active participle of *episcopoeō* (only here and Heb. 12:15). It literally means "look upon," and then "visit, care for." The participle may be translated "serving as overseers" (NIV).

By Constraint This is one word in Greek, the adverb *anagkastōs* (only here in NT). It has the force of "because you must" (NIV).

Willingly This is another adverb, *hekousiōs* (only here and Heb. 10:26 in NT). It means "voluntarily" (NASB).

The alert reader may have already discovered that after this word there is an added item in NASB ("according to the will of God") and NIV ("as God wants you to be"). This is because after *hekousiōs* there is an added phrase, *kata theou* ("according to God") in Papyrus 72 (third century), Sinaiticus (fourth century), A (fifth century), a considerable number of later manuscripts, and some early versions. We cannot, at this stage, be absolutely certain as to whether this addition was a part of the original text.

Of a Ready Mind This translates the adverb *prothymōs* (only here in NT), which means "eagerly."

3 Being Lords This is the present participle of the verb *katakyrieuō*. See discussion at Matt. 20:25.

Heritage The Greek has the plural of the noun *klēros*, which means "a lot"—as in "casting lots" or "drawing lots." But here we have the second stage of its use: "that which is obtained by casting" (A-S, p. 249). So the correct translation here is "those allotted to your charge" (NASB) or "those entrusted to you" (NIV). It must be remembered that this is addressed to the "elders" in the church (v. 1).

Incidentally, it should be noted that *"Gods"* (KJV) is in italics, indicating that it is not in the Greek. So we omit it.

4 Chief Shepherd This is one word, *archipoimēn*—only here in NT, though found by Adolf Deissmann in two places elsewhere (LAE, p. 99–101). It is compounded of *archi*, a prefix "denoting high office and dignity" (A-S, p. 62), and *poimēn*, "shepherd."

For pastors we would like to suggest a series of three sermons. The first would be on Psalm 22, depicting the Good Shepherd (John 10) who gives His life for the sheep. The second would be based on Psalm 23, where we see the Great Shepherd (Heb. 13:20) caring for His sheep. The third would be on Psalm 24, the Chief Shepherd in glory.

Crown The Greek word here is not *diadēma* (diadem), the royal crown, but *stephanos*, the victor's crown. See discussion at 1 Cor. 9:25.

Fadeth Not Away This is one word, the adjective *amarantinos* (only here in NT). A. T. Robertson notes that this word gave name to the flower "amaranth"—"so called because it never withers and revives if moistened with water and so used as a symbol of immortality" (WP, 6:132).

5 Be Clothed *Egkomobōsasthe* is the aorist middle imperative of *egkomboomai* (only here in NT)—"clothe yourselves" (NASB, NIV). The verb comes from the noun *kombos*, "a knot." So *egkombōma* meant "a garment tied on others, especially a frock or apron worn by slaves" (A-S, p. 128). Robertson suggests that Peter may be thinking of what Jesus did when He tied a towel around His waist and washed the disciples' feet (John 13).

7 Care The noun is *merimna*, which means "anxiety" (NASB, NIV). "Careth" is the verb *melō*, a different root.

8 Devour The Greek has the second aorist infinitive of *katapinō*, "to drink down." Satan would like to grab us and gulp us down!

9 Afflictions The Greek has the plural of the noun *pathēma*, which means "suffering" (cf. NASB, NIV).

10 Make This (KJV) appears to be in the form of a request. But the Greek has four verbs, all in the future tense—"will Himself perfect, confirm, strengthen and establish you" (NASB). It is a promise, not a prayer.

The first verb is *katartizō*, which means "render *artios*" (fit or complete). It sometimes means "repair" or "restore" (NIV). Then it took on the ethical sense, "to complete," or "perfect" (NASB).

The second verb is *stērizō*, which metaphorically (as here) means "to confirm, establish." The third is *sthenoō* (only here in NT), "to strengthen." The fourth is *themelioō*. It comes

443

from *themelios*, "foundation." So it means "establish."

12 *I Suppose* The Greek has *logizomai*, which was first used for numerical calculation, in the sense of "reckon." Then it came to mean "consider." The best translation here is "regard" (RSV, NASB, NIV).

13 *The Church That Is at Babylon* "Church" is not in the Greek. All it has is: "She who is in Babylon" (NASB, NIV). Some take this as meaning Peter's wife. But most scholars think the reference is to the local church. (*Ecclēsia*, the regular word in the NT for "church," is feminine.)

The identification of "Babylon" is also a matter of dispute. Most take it—rightly, we think—as referring to Rome, where Peter was at this time. It was probably safer for him not to mention Rome as the place where he was.

2 Peter

1:3, 4 *Divine* This is the adjective *theois* (only here [twice] and in Acts 17:29). It comes from the noun *theos*, "God."

3, 5 *Virtue* See discussion of *aretē* at Phil. 4:8, third item.

5 *Diligence* See discussion of *spoudē* at Rom. 12:11. Here the NIV translates the whole phrase: "make every effort" (see also 3:14).

6 *Temperance* *Egkrateia* (only here; Acts 24:25; and Gal. 5:23) should be translated "self-control" (NASB, NIV).

8 *Barren* The adjective *argos* comes from *alpha*-negative and the noun *ergon*, "work." So it means "idle." It may be translated "useless" (NASB) or "ineffective" (NIV).

Unfruitful The adjective *akarpos* comes from the alpha-privative *a-* and *karpos*, "fruit." So it means "unfruitful" (KJV, NASB) or "unproductive" (NIV)—since "fruit" is used in KJV for "crops."

9 *And Cannot See Afar Off* This is all one word in Greek, *myōpazōn*, the present participle of *myōpazō* (only here in NT). It comes from *myōps*, "shortsighted" (NASB), and so means "nearsighted" (NIV). We get our word *myopia* from this.

10, 19 *Sure* The adjective *bebaios* means "firm, secure." Deissmann says that it is used "in the sense of legally guaranteed security" (BS, 109). Peter admonishes Christians ("my brothers"): "Be all the more eager to make your calling and election sure" (NIV)—by abiding in Christ. If we do this, we will "never fall." This implies that if we don't do this, we may fall.

12 *Put . . . in Remembrance* This is one word in Greek, the verb *hypomimnēskō*, the intensive compound of *mimnēskō*, "remind." It is also best translated "remind" (NASB, NIV).

13 *Meet* This is the adjective *dikaios*, which means "just" or "right" (NASB, NIV).

13, 14 *Tabernacle* *Skēnōman* is from the verb *skēnoō*, "dwell"—used in the papyri for living in a temporary dwelling (A-S, 409). Both the noun and verb come from *skēnē*, "tent." The reference here is obviously to Peter's body (cf. NIV). In the only other place in the NT where *skēnōma* occurs (Acts 7:46), it refers to the Temple as God's dwelling.

14 *Showed* The verb *dēloō* comes from the adjective *dēlos*, "clear." So it here means "made clear" (NASB, NIV).

15 *Endeavor* The verb is *spoudazō*, which literally means "make haste." It is interesting to note that of the 11 times it is used in the NT it occurs 3 times in Paul's last letter (2 Timothy) and 3 times in Peter's last letter (2 Peter). Both these men had eager, earnest personalities, and this is reflected in their writings, especially as they approached the end.

Decease The Greek word is *exodos* ("exodus"), which means "departure" (NASB, NIV).

16 *Cunningly Devised Fables* The Greek has *sesophismenois mythois*. The verb *sophizō* (in the perf. pass. part. here) comes from the adjective *sophos*, "clever" or "wise." In the only other place where it occurs in the NT (2 Tim. 3:15) it has the good meaning of "make wise." But here it has the bad sense of being a sophist, cleverly inventing false myths.

For the noun *mythos*, see our long discussion at 1 Tim. 1:4.

The whole phrase here is best translated "cleverly devised tales" (NASB) or "cleverly invented stories" (NIV).

Majesty The noun *megaleiotēs* (only here; Luke 9:43; and Acts 19:27) means "splendor" or "magnificence." Here, as applied to Christ, it means "majesty."

17 Excellent Here we have the adjective *megaloprepēs* (only here in NT). Obviously related to the above word, it means "befitting a great person, magnificent, majestic." The combination with "glory" is best represented here as "the Majestic Glory" (NASB, NIV)—a title for Christ.

19 Dawn The verb *diaugazō* (only here in NT) literally means "shine through."

Day Star This is one word in Greek, *phōsphoros* (only here in NT). It comes from *phōs*, "light," and the verb *pherō*, "bear," and so literally means "light-bringing." This word was applied to Venus as the "morning star" (NASB, NIV). The reference seems to be to the second coming of Christ as the Morning Star of the eternal day to come.

20 Is of Any Private Interpretation The verb here is *ginetai*, which means "becomes" or "comes about." The word "private" translates *idias*, literally "one's own." The noun for "interpretation" is *epilysis*, from the verb *epilyō*, "loose, solve, explain," and so means "interpretation." Probably the correct meaning here is that "no prophecy of Scripture came about by the prophet's own interpretation" (NIV). Verse 20 seems clearly to demand this. Holy Scripture is of divine origin.

21 Came The form here, *ēnechthē*, is the aorist passive participle of *pherō*, "bear" or "carry." Charles Bigg translates this "was borne" and explains: "came from heaven to man" (ICC, *Epistles of St. Peter and Jude*, 270).

The Greek of the last part of verse 21 literally reads: "But being borne along (*pheromenoi*) by the Holy Spirit, men spoke from God" (cf. NASB, NIV). This is perhaps the strongest statement in the New Testament regarding the divine origin and authority of the

Old Testament Scripture. It stands right alongside 2 Tim. 3:16 in asserting this great truth.

2:1 Privily Shall Bring In This is one word in Greek, the verb *pareisagō* (only here in NT). It is a double compound: *agō*, "lead" or "bring"; *eis*, "into" or "in"; *para*, "beside." So it came to mean "bring in secretly," or "secretly introduce" (NASB, NIV).

Damnable This is the genitive case of *apōleia*, "of destruction." This same noun is correctly translated "destruction" in the KJV at the end of this verse and of 3:16. But in the third verse it is rendered "damnation" and in 3:7 "perdition." It should be "destruction" in all those passages. And here the correct translation is "destructive" (NASB, NIV).

Heresies The Greek noun *hairesis* gives us our word *heresy*. It comes from the verb *haireō*, which meant "choose." So the noun first meant "choice." Then it came to mean "what is chosen," and finally "a peculiar opinion" or "heresy." It is used that way here, in 1 Cor. 11:19, and Gal. 5:20.

Lord Here we do not have the common Greek word for "Lord," *kyrios*. Rather we find *despotēs*, which we have taken over as "despot." This Greek noun is applied to Christ (in NT) only here and in Jude 4. The NIV has "sovereign Lord" here and "Sovereign" in Jude 4 (because it is accompanied there by *kyrios*). *Despotēs* indicates complete sovereignty.

2 Pernicious Ways The Greek noun *aselgeia* (here in pl.) means "licentiousness." A good translation here is "sensuality" (NASB).

3 Feigned The Greek adjective *plastos* (only here in NT) first meant "formed, molded" (cf. our "plastic"). Then it came to mean "fabricated, feigned," or "made up" (NIV).

Make Merchandise of The verb *emporeuomai* (only here and James 4:13) first meant to "travel," especially for business, and so "trade." Here it means "make a gain of," or "exploit" (NASB, NIV).

4 Hell There are three Greek words that are translated "hell" in the NT of KJV. The first is *geenna* (Gehenna), which really means "hell" and is so rendered in almost all versions. It occurs 12 times in the NT (7 times in Matthew, 3 times in Mark, and once each in Luke and James).

The origin of this name for hell is very interesting. Gehenna was the Valley of the Son of Hinnom, south of Jerusalem. Ahaz and Manasseh, two wicked kings of Judah, sacrificed their sons there to the heathen god Molech (2 Chron. 28:3; 33:6; Jer. 32:35). Good King Josiah defiled the place (2 Kings 23:10), and it became the city dump, with fires burning on it. Then the Jews made "Gehenna" the name for the final judgment and the place of eternal punishment. Jesus used it that way (11 times).

The second word translated "hell" in the NT (KJV) is *hadēs*. It occurs 11 times in the NT and is translated "hell" 10 of those times (KJV). Once (1 Cor. 15:55) it is "grave." *Hadēs* was the name of the god of the underworld and does not mean the place of everlasting punishment; so it should not be translated "hell." It is used in the NT for the abode of departed spirits. Probably the best procedure is to transliterate the word as "Hades."

Here in 2 Pet. 2:4 we find the third word, *tartarōsas* (only here in NT). It is really the aorist participle of *tartaroō* and so is translated "cast *them* down to hell" (KJV). The verb comes from the noun *tartaros*, used for the dark abode of the wicked dead. In the apocryphal Book of Enoch (20:2) it is used as the place of punishment of the fallen angels (as here in 2 Peter). In English we use the Latin form "Tartarus."

Chains We have another textual problem here. "Chains" (KJV) translates the Greek form *sirais*, found in Papyrus 72 (3rd century) and two 9th-century manuscripts (K, P), as well as the majority of later manuscripts. "Pits" (NASB) is the translation of *sirois*, found in our two 4th-century manuscripts (Aleph, B) and two of the 5th century (A, C). We cannot be certain which was the original form, but the meaning is essentially the same.

5 Flood The Greek word is *cataclysmos*, hich has been taken over into English as "cataclysm." This noun comes from the verb *cataclyzō*, "inundate, deluge" (found only in 2 Pet. 3:6). In the NT the noun is used only for Noah's "flood" (here; Matt. 24:38, 39; and Luke 17:27).

6 Turning . . . into Ashes This is one word in Greek, *tephrōsas*, the aorist participle of *tephroō* (only here in NT). It comes from the noun *tephra* ("ashes"), which one Greek writer used in describing an eruption of Mount Vesuvius.

7 Vexed *Kataponoumenon* is the present passive participle of *kataponeō* (only here and Acts 7:24). The verb means to "wear down" (*kata*), and in the passive to be "oppressed" (NASB) or "distressed" (NIV).

Conversation See discussion of *anastrophē* at 1 Pet. 1:15.

The Wicked The adjective *athesmos* (only these two places in NT) is compounded of the alpha-privative *a-* and *thesmos*, "law" or "custom." So it means "lawless men." Abbott-Smith says that it is used "especially of those who violate the law of nature and conscience" (p. 11).

8 Vexed This is a different verb from the one translated "vex" (KJV) in verse 7. Here it is *basanizō*, which first meant to "examine by torture" and then "torture" or "torment" (cf. NASB, NIV).

10 Uncleanness Here we have the noun *miasmos* (only here in NT). It comes from the verb *miainō* (four times in NT), which meant to "stain" or "defile."

Government The Greek word is *kyriotēs*, "lordship." Here it probably means "authority" (NASB, NIV).

Presumptuous This is the plural of *tolmētēs* (only here in NT). It comes from the verb *tolmaō*, which means "dare" or "be bold." So it may be translated "daring" (NASB) or "bold" (NIV).

Self-willed For *authadēs* see the discussion at Titus 1:7, first item. It has the force of "arrogant" (NIV). Derived from *autos*, "self," and the verb *hēdomai*, "have pleasure," it may well be translated "self-pleasing."

Dignities The Greek has the plural of *doxa*, "glory." This is translated "the glorious ones" (RSV), "angelic majesties" (NASB), and "celestial beings" (NIV). Some commentators refer it to bad angels, some to good angels, and others to angels in general. We simply cannot be certain about the interpretation of this verse.

12 Natural The adjective *physicos* (only here and Rom. 1:26, 27) is from *physis*, "nature." Mayor (p. 130) translates the phrase here: "born creatures of instinct" (cf. NASB).

Brute The adjective *alogos* (in NT only here; Acts 25:27; and Jude 10) is composed of the alpha-privative *a-* and *logos*, "reason." So it means "without reason," or "unreasoning" (NASB). The NIV has returned to "brute," which puts it bluntly.

Perish in Their Own Corruption The verb *phtheirō* (fut. pass. here) and the noun *phthora* (based on it) are from the same root and should be translated alike. This is well done in the NASB: "will in the destruction of those creatures also be destroyed."

13 Feast This is the verb *syneuōcheō* (only here and Jude 12). In the passive, as in both places, it means "feast together with."

14 That Cannot Cease The adjective *akatapaustos* (only here in NT) is composed of alpha-negative and the compound (intensive) verb *katapauō*. Probably the best translation is "that never cease" (NASB).

Beguiling The verb *deleazō* is found (in NT) only here, in verse 18—where it is translated "allure"—and James 1:14 (see discussion there). It may be translated here "enticing" (NASB) or "seduce" (NIV).

Unstable The adjective *astēriktos* (only here and 3:16) is compounded of the alpha-privative *a-* and the verb *stērizō*, "fix firmly" or "establish." So it means "unstable" or "unsettled."

Exercised This translation catches the literal meaning here. We find the perfect passive participle of the verb *gymnazō*, for which see the discussion at 1 Tim. 4:8.

18 That Were Clean Escaped This sounds as if they had completely escaped. The NASB has "who barely escape" and the NIV reads "who are just escaping." Why the difference?

The KJV translation is based on *ontōs*, "being" escaped, found in Aleph (fourth century), C (fifth century), and many late manuscripts. But Papyrus 72 (third century), B (fourth century), A (fifth century), and the early versions have the adverb *oligōs* (only here in NT), which comes from the adjective *oligos*, "little." So the adverb means "scarcely, barely." This seems to be the better reading.

20 Pollutions Here we have the plural of the noun *miasma* (only here in NT), which is equivalent to *miasmos* (see discussion of "uncleanness" at verse 10). *Miasma* has been taken over into English with the meaning "poisonous atmosphere"—which we call air "pollution."

3:1, 6 Epistle The Greek word *epistolē* occurs 24 times in the NT. In the KJV it is translated "epistle" 15 times and "letter" 9 times (regularly "letter" in NIV). It comes from the verb *epistellō*, "send a message" (especially by writing). So the noun *epistolē* meant what was transmitted, and so a "letter."

1 Pure The two main Greek adjectives for "pure" are *hagnos* (8 times) and *katharos* (28 times). Here we have *eilikrinēs* (only here and Phil. 1:10). Thayer notes that this word is "commonly supposed to be from *heile* . . . sunlight, and *krinō* ["judge"], properly found pure when unfolded and examined by the sun's light" (p. 175). But Trench (p. 319) favors a different etymology and writes: "It is not so much the clear, the transparent, as the purged, the winnowed, the unmingled." He thinks that the best English rendering is "sincere" (cf. NASB).

Minds The Greek word here is not *nous*, but the compound *dianoia*, which basically means "thought" or "understanding." So the NIV has the combination: "wholesome thinking."

Remembrance *Hypomnēsis* (only here and 2 Tim. 1:5) is best translated "reminder" (NASB; cf. NIV). It is related to the verb "be mindful" (*mimneskō*) in verse 2.

3 Scoffers This one word (KJV) represents three words in Greek: *en empaigmonē empaiktai*—literally, "in mocking, mockers." Both nouns come from the verb *empaizō*, "mock" (common in the Gospels for the religious leaders mocking Jesus). The first noun is found only here in the NT; the second occurs also in Jude 18. The combination is well represented by "mockers . . . with their mocking" (NASB) or "scoffers . . . scoffing" (NIV).

5, 8 Willingly Are Ignorant Of The verb *lanthanō* means "escape notice" (cf. NASB) or "be hidden from." "Deliberately forget" (v. 5) and "forget" (v. 8) in NIV probably catches the thought correctly.

6 Overflowed This is the aorist passive participle of *kataclyzō* (only here in NT). See discussion at 2 Peter 2:5.

9 Is . . . Slack . . . Slackness The verb is *bradynō*, "be slow" (only here and 1 Tim. 3:15). The noun is *bradytēs* (only here in NT). Both come from *bradys*, "slow." So the best translation is "be slow" and "slowness" (NASB, NIV).

10 *With a Great Noise* This is one word in Greek, *hroizēdon* (only here in NT). It is onomatopoetic. A. T. Robertson says that it means a "whizzing sound of rapid motion through the air like the flight of a bird, thunder, fierce flame" (WP, 6:176).

Shall Be Burned Up The NIV has "will be laid bare." This, again, is a textual problem. Our oldest Greek manuscripts give three different readings here, and we cannot be absolutely certain as to which is original. But, again, the meaning is much the same.

11 *Conversation* See discussion at 1 Pet. 1:15.

The Wicked See discussion at 1 Pet. 2:7.

Stedfastness The noun is *stērigmos* (only here in NT). It comes from the verb *stērizō*, which, as we have noted before, means "make firm or secure" (cf. "secure position," NIV).

1 John

1:1 *Looked Upon* "Seen" is the common verb *horaō*, which means "catch sight of." But "looked upon" is the Greek verb *theaomai*. Abbott-Smith gives this definition: *"to behold, look upon, contemplate, view* (in early writers with a sense of *wondering*), in NT of 'careful and deliberate vision which interprets . . . its object' " (p. 203). John the beloved apostle, the author of this Epistle, not only caught sight of Christ but also, over a period of three years, carefully watched Jesus and came to understand who and what He was, the Eternal Logos. And he had actually "touched" Jesus with his own hands. Christ was no phantom; He was real!

Word For the significance of the term *logos*, see discussion at John 1:1.

2 Show The verb *apangellō* means "to report, announce, declare," which is something stronger than "show." Arndt and Gingrich give for this passage "proclaim" (NASB, NIV). In verse 3 the KJV gives the more adequate translation "declare" for this same verb.

3 Fellowship The Greek word *koinōnia* occurs four times in this chapter (twice in v. 3 and once each in vv. 6 and 7). It is one of the key words of this Epistle.

It comes from the adjective "common" and so means having something in common. That is what fellowship is. It is a sharing. As Hauck observes, "It expresses a two-sided relationship" (TDNT, 3:798). See further discussion at Gal. 2:9.

5 Message . . . Declare The noun is *angelia* (in NT only here and 3:11). The verb is the compound *anangellō*, which originally meant

"bring back word, report," but then was used as equivalent to *apangellō* (see above), "announce" (NASB) or "declare" (NIV).

7 All This was originally translated "every" in the NIV. It is true that the adjective *pasēs* means both "all" and "every." But to be consistent with verse 9 (same word in Greek), "every" was officially changed to "all" in verse 7, as appears in later printings of the NIV. This is definitely preferable.

2:1 *Advocate* The Greek word is *paraclētos*, for which see discussion at John 14:16. In the Gospel the term is used for the Holy Spirit. But here it refers to Christ, and the meaning is clearly that He is our "Advocate" (NASB) or defense lawyer in the court of heaven. The NIV spells it out: "one who speaks to the Father in our defense." All this translates the one word *paraclēton* (accus.).

2 Propitiation The Greek term *hilasmos* (only here and 4:10) comes from the verb *hilaskomai*, which means "propitiate" or "conciliate"—see discussion at Heb. 2:17 and also of *hilastērion* at Rom. 3:25. Since "propitiation" is a technical theological term, not understood by all, the NIV has "atoning sacrifice."

5 Perfected The Greek verb *teleioō* comes from the adjective *teleios*, "having reached its end" (*telos*), and so "complete" or "perfect." Here we may use "perfected" (KJV, NASB) or "made complete" (NIV).

16 Pride *Alazoneia* (only here and James 4:16) basically means "boastfulness." It may well be translated "boastful pride" (NASB; cf. NIV).

18, 22 *Antichrist*   The English term is practically a transliteration of the Greek *antichristos* (only here, four times; and 2 John 7). John uses it to describe anyone who denies the deity (v. 22) or the humanity (4:3; 2 John 7) of Jesus Christ. The latter was denied by the Docetic Gnostics of John's day. They said that Jesus only *seemed* to have a physical body. Following the lead of some Early Church fathers, we have applied the term *antichrist* to the beast of Revelation.

20, 27 *Unction*   The Greek word is *chrisma* (only here in NT). It comes from *chriō*, "anoint" (with oil), and so means "anointing" (NASB, NIV). The reference is to the Christian being anointed with the Holy Spirit, symbolized by olive oil.

20 *Ye Know All Things*   This translation is based on the reading *panta* (neut. pl. accus.), found in many manuscripts. But our two fourth-century manuscripts have *pantes* (nom. pl. masc.). This would make the passage read: "you all know" (NASB; cf. NIV)—that is, the truth (v. 21). It is not true that any Christian knows all things. If the reading of the bulk of later manuscripts is correct, "all things" would have to be taken as meaning all things necessary to salvation (v. 27). But it is probably better to accept *pantes* as original—"you all know."

23 *(italics)*   The second half of this verse is in italics in the KJV, which normally indicates that it is not in the Greek. But here the part in italics *is* found in the bulk of the manuscripts and early versions. So it is represented in modern versions with no marginal note.

24 *Abide . . . Remain . . . Continue*   The translators of the KJV sought for "elegant variation." Here is a good example. The Greek has the same verb, *menō*, in all three places. It is consistently translated "abide(s)" all three times in the NASB. The NIV uses "remain(s).

26 *Seduce*   *Planaō* means "lead astray" or "deceive." We have here the present participle of continuing action. The next verse seems to indicate that these seducers were not succeeding. So the correct meaning is "trying to deceive you" (NASB) or "trying to lead you astray" (NIV).

3:1–2 *The Sons of God*   Two things need to be said about this translation (KJV). The first is that the Greek word is not *whioi*, "sons," but *tekna*, "children." The second is that there

is no article in the Greek text; it is simply "children of God" (NASB, NIV). When the article is missing in the Greek, it emphasizes kind or quality. We will be called "children of God" because we live godly lives.

A quick comparison will show that recent versions have an added statement in the middle of verse 1—"and such we are" (NASB); "And that is what we are!" (NIV). This is because all the early manuscripts and versions (before the ninth century) have *kai esmen*, "and we are." This is a beautiful touch, and it is undoubtedly genuine.

4 *The Transgression of the Law*   The Greek simply has *hē anomia*. *Hē* is the definite article (fem.), but while the Greek usually puts the definite article with an abstract noun—it is here used also with "sin"—we normally leave it out in English. Furthermore, *anomia* is from alpha-negative and *nomos*, "law." So the correct translation here is "sin is lawlessness" (NASB, NIV). This is one of the biblical definitions of sin.

6 *Sinneth . . . Sinneth*   The verb *hamartanō* in both cases is in the present tense of continuing action. This is brought out helpfully by "keeps on sinning . . . continues to sin" (NIV). The one who lives in Christ does not keep on sinning.

This same use of the present tense is found in verse 9. Here again it should be brought out: "No one who is born of God will continue to sin . . . he cannot go on sinning" (NIV).

17 *Good*   The Greek word is *bios*. Here it indicates "means of subsistence." We do not call that "good" but "goods." So the correct translation here is "the world's goods" (NASB) or "material possessions" (NIV). Trench says that here *bios* indicates "the means of life" or "living" (*Synonyms of the NT*, p. 91).

This is the last of 10 times that *bios* occurs in the NT (in 1 John only here and 2:16). There it means "life" as lived on earth, "the course of life." Here it means "livelihood."

Bowels   See discussion at Phil. 1:8.

4:1 *Try*   The verb *dokimazō* occurs 23 times in the NT. In the KJV it is translated "prove" most often (10 times) and "try" (4 times). For various meanings of this verb, see the discussion of "prove" at Rom. 12:2. Here the best translation is "test" (RSV, NASB, NIV).

3 *Antichrist*   See discussion at 1 John 2:18.

9 *Only Begotten* The Greek word is *monogenēs*. It is compounded of *monos*, "only," and *genos*, "offspring." So it literally means "only begotten."

It is interesting to note in the first three of nine times that *monogenēs* occurs in the NT it is translated in the KJV as "only" (Luke 7:12; 8:42; 9:38). Moreover, in Heb. 11:17 Isaac is said to be the *monogenēs* of Abraham. But Ishmael was also begotten by Abraham! So it is obvious that the main thrust of *monogenēs* is not "only begotten" but "only," perhaps in the sense of "unique." Isaac was unique as the "only" son of promise. In the same way Jesus is *the* "only" Son of God in the sense of full deity. Christians are also called "sons of God," as begotten by the Spirit in the new birth.

10 *Propitiation* See discussion at 1 John 2:2.

12 *Perfected* See discussion at 1 John 2:5.

18 *Torment* The noun *kolasis* (only here and Matt. 25:46) comes from the verb *kolazō*, "punish." So the literal meaning is "punishment" (NASB, NIV).

5:3 ***Grievous*** The adjective *barys* is connected with the verb *bareō*, which means "weigh down." So the adjective means "burdensome" (NASB, NIV). We do not use "grievous" that way today.

4 *Overcometh (second time)* The Greek participle is in the aorist tense: "has overcome" (NASB, NIV).

7 *Father ... Word ... Holy Ghost* Anyone who uses a recent scholarly version of the NT will see that these words on the Trinity are not in verse 7. This is because they have no basis in the Greek text. Under Roman Catholic pressure, Erasmus inserted them from the Latin Vulgate. They are not a part of the inspired Bible.

11–12 *Life* The noun *zōē* occurs 134 times in the NT. It is translated "life" every time but one (Luke 16:25), where the KJV has "lifetime." The latter idea is usually expressed by *bios* (see discussion at 3:17).

Bultmann begins his treatment of *zōē* by saying: "Zōē denotes in Greek the physical vitality of organic beings, animals, men, and also plants. Life is understood, not as a thing, but as vitality, as the nature or manner which characterizes all living creatures as such" (TDNT, 2:832).

In classical Greek *bios* had ethical connotations and *zōē* did not. But when we come to the NT we find the case exactly the reverse. Here we find *bios* used in a material and chronological sense. But *zōē* is the word used, especially by John (36 times in his Gospel and 13 times in his First Epistle), mostly for spiritual life that we have from God in Christ. It is not mere existence, but a new "life." R. C. Trench puts it very well when he writes:

> In revealed religion, which thus makes death to have come into the world through sin, and only through sin, life is the correlative of holiness. Whatever truly lives, does so because sin has never found place in it, or, having found place for a time, has since been overcome and expelled. So soon as ever this is felt and understood, *zōē* at once assumes the profoundest moral significance; it becomes the fittest expression for the very highest blessedness (p. 95).

13 *Have I Written* In view of what we wrote at 5:4, someone might ask why we have "I write" in the NIV. It is true that the verb here is in the aorist tense (*egrapsa*). But this is what we call the "epistolary aorist." From the point of view of the reader, it would be past time when he got the letter. But for John it was present: "I am writing." In his large *Grammar of the Greek New Testament* (845–46), A. T. Robertson gives a full discussion of this phenomenon, listing 1 John 5:13 as a possible example. However, in his *Word Pictures* (6:25), he says of our passage: "Not epistolary aorist, but refers to verses 1 to 12 of this Epistle." So we can accept either the NASB or NIV on this verse.

19 *Wickedness* We do not have here the abstract noun, *ponēria*, but the dative masculine of the adjective *ponēros*. So the correct translation is "the evil one" (NASB, NIV). See a similar situation in Matt. 6:13.

2 John

1 Elder The Greek word is *presbyteros*. A. T. Robertson comments: "The word referred originally to age (Luke 15:25), then to rank or office as in the Sanhedrin (Matt. 16:21; Acts 6:12) and in the Christian churches (Acts 11:30; 20:17; 1 Tim. 5:17, 19) as here also" (WP, 6:249).

Elect Lady The Greek has *eclectē kyria*. We cannot be certain whether this means a church or an individual.

8 We . . . We . . . We The first and third verbs are in the second person plural in all manuscripts earlier than the 9th century. So it is "you" instead of "we."

In the case of the second verb ("wrought"), the first person plural ("we") is found in the 4th-century Vaticanus. For this reason we cannot be certain whether it is "we" (NASB) or "you" (NIV).

9 Transgresseth Here we have the present participle of *proagō*—*agō*, "lead," and *pro*, "before." So the verb means "go before, precede, go on ahead." It may be translated here: "goes too far" (NASB) or "runs ahead" (NIV). We are to stay "in step with the Spirit" (Gal. 5:25, NIV).

9–10 Doctrine As we have noted before, the proper translation of *didachē* is "teaching." It comes from the verb *didaskō*, "teach."

10 Bid Him God Speed The Greek has *chairein autō . . . legete*—literally "say a greeting to him" (cf. NASB).

11 Is Partaker Of This is one word in Greek, *koinōnei*—"shares in" (NIV) or "participates in" (NASB).

12 Paper The Greek *chartēs* (only here in NT) was a sheet of "paper," made of papyrus strips.

Ink *Melan* (only here; 3 John 13; and 2 Cor. 3:3) literally means "black." It is used in these three places for "ink."

3 John

2 Wish   The Greek verb is *euchomai*, which means "pray" (NASB, NIV).

Prosper   The verb *euodoō* (in NT only here [twice]; Rom. 1:10; and 1 Cor. 16:2) is compounded of *eu*, "well," and *hodos*, "way." So it originally meant to "have a prosperous journey." Then it was used metaphorically for "prosper."

Be in Health   The Greek has one word, *hygiainein*, from which we get *hygiene*. It means "be sound, healthy, in good health."

6 After a Godly Sort   The Greek has *axiōs tou theou*, "worthily of God." The NASB and NIV both say: "You will do well to send them on their way in a manner worthy of God." That puts it well.

8 Receive   The verb is *hypolambanō*. It first meant "*to take* or *bear up*" (by supporting from beneath), and then "*to receive, welcome, entertain*" (A-S, 461). So we could say "support" (NASB) or "show hospitality" (NIV).

9 Loveth to Have the Preeminence   This is all one word in Greek, the present participle of *philoprōteuō* (only here in NT). The verb is compounded of *phil* (a stem for "love") and *prōtos*, "first." It means "who loves to be first" (NASB, NIV).

10 Prating Against Us   The verb *phlyareō* is found only here in the NT. A. T. Robertson says it means "to accuse idly and so falsely" (WP, 6:264).

Content   The verb *arkeō* in the passive (as here) means to be "satisfied" (NASB, NIV).

11 Follow   The verb is *mimeomai*, from which we get *mimic* (found only here; 2 Thess. 3:7, 9; and Heb. 13:7). It means "imitate" (NASB, NIV).

12 Hath Good Report   This is the perfect passive indicative of the verb *martyreō*, "witness." In late Greek it came to have the meaning in the passive: "to have a good report, to be approved." It means that "Demetrius is well spoken of by everyone" (NIV).

Record   "Bear record" is the same verb, *martyreō*, "witness" or "testify." The second "record" is the noun *martyria*, "witness" (NASB) or "testimony" (NIV).

13 Pen   The Greek noun is *kalamos*. It basically meant "a reed." In the NT the word is used for a "stalk" or "staff" and for a "measuring rod" in Revelation (11:21; 21:15f.). Here alone (in NT) it is used for a "pen."

For "ink" see note at 2 John 12.

Jude

1 Sanctified Again we have a textual problem. Is it "sanctified" (KJV) or "loved" (NIV; cf. NASB). The facts are that *hēgiasmenois*, "sanctified," is not found in any Greek manuscript before the ninth century. Papyrus 72 (3rd century), Aleph and B (4th century), A (5th century), Psi (8th century), many minuscules, and the oldest versions all have here *ēgapēmenois*, perfect passive participle of the well-known verb *agapaō*, "love."

3 Earnestly Contend This is one word in Greek, the present infinitive of the strong compound verb (hence, "earnestly") *epagōnizomai* (only here in NT). The simple verb *agonizomai* first meant to compete in an athletic contest, and then, more generally, to "fight, struggle, strive." We are to be earnest in our defense of the faith.

4 Crept In Unawares This is one word in Greek, the second aorist passive indicative of *pareisdyō* (only here in NT). It is compounded of *para*, "beside," *eis*, "in," and *dyō*, "plunge." So it means to slip in secretly (cf. NIV), as if by a side door.

5 Put You in Remembrance We would say, "remind you" (NASB, NIV). See discussion at 2 Pet. 1:12.

6 First Estate The Greek single word is *archē*. The term literally means "beginning" or "rule." Here it probably means "domain" (NASB) or "positions of authority" (NIV). Jude is discussing the fallen angels.

7 Giving Themselves Over to Fornication This is all one word in Greek, the aorist participle of *ekporneuō* (only here in NT).

As we have noted before, the noun *porneia*, which is always translated "fornication" (26 times) in the KJV, takes in more than that term indicates today. It includes all "sexual immorality" (NIV) or "gross immorality" (NASB). This is further enlarged here by the additional "going after strange flesh," which rather obviously suggests homosexuality.

8 Dignities See discussion at 2 Pet. 2:10.

9 A Railing Accusation The Greek has *krisin . . . blasphēmias*. The noun *blasphēmia* (here in the genitive) first meant "slander," and then, as applied to speaking against God, "blasphemy." *Krisis* (accus. here) means "judgment" (cf. NASB). But the context here suggests for the whole expression: "a slanderous accusation" (NIV).

10 Brute See discussion at 2 Pet. 2:12.

11 Gainsaying *Antilogia* (in NT only here and Heb. 6:16; 7:7; 12:3) literally means "a speaking against" (*anti*). In the papyri it has the meaning "strife." Here it has its strongest meaning, "rebellion" (NASB, NIV).

12 Spots The word is the plural of *spilas*. In the classics it was used for "a *rock* or reef over which the sea dashes" (A-S, 414). This meaning was adopted in the NASB. But Abbott-Smith goes on to note that in later writers it was equated with *spilos*, "spot" or "stain." Both meanings make good sense in this passage, taking the term, in either case, as metaphorical.

15 Convince As we have noted before, the verb *elengchō* should be translated "convict" (NASB, NIV).

16 Murmurers The noun *gongystēs* (only here in NT) is onomatopoetic. It is best translated "grumblers" (NASB, NIV).

Complainers *Mempsimoiros* (only here in NT) is an adjective (pl. here), meaning "complaining of one's fate." It may also be translated "finding fault" (NASB) or "faultfinders" (NIV).

Great Swelling Words This is all one word in Greek, the neuter plural of the adjective *hyperonkos* (only here and 2 Pet. 2:18). The adjective means "excessive, immoderate" and was used in later writers for arrogant speech (cf. NASB).

Having Men's Persons in Admiration This is two words in Greek: *thaumazontes prosōpa*—literally, "admiring faces." It means "flattering people" (NASB; cf. NIV).

Because of Advantage The Greek is: *epheleias charin. Epheleia* (only here and Rom. 3:1) means "profit" or "advantage." *Charin* means "for the sake of" (cf. NASB, NIV).

19 They Who Separate Themselves The Greek has the plural definite article *hoi* and the present participle of the double compound verb *apodiorizō* (only here in NT). It is based on *horos*, "boundary," *dia*, "through," and *apo*, "away from"—to mark off boundaries. Here it is used metaphorically in the sense of "make separations." The reference is to people "who cause divisions" (NASB).

22 Making a Difference The Greek has the plural of the present middle participle of *diakrinō* in the accusative case, which means "doubting." It seems that the true meaning here is "who are doubting" (NASB) or "those who doubt" (NIV).

Revelation

1:1 *Revelation* The very first word of this last book of the Bible is *apocalypsis*. That is why we often refer to this book as "the Apocalypse."

The Greek term literally means "an uncovering." See discussion at Gal. 1:12. That is what we have in the Book of Revelation: an uncovering of the unknown future, what could not at all be known except by a divine revelation.

Signified The Greek verb is *sēmainō* (in the aorist), which comes from *sēma*, "a sign." So it means "to give a sign, signify, indicate" (A-S, p. 405), or "make known, report, communicate" (AG, p. 755). Lange says of it here: "*Esēmanen* is a modification of *deixai* [show], indicative of the signs employed, the symbolical representation" (Revelation, p. 89).

Rengstorf thinks that the verb, as used here, only means "to indicate or declare something" (TDNT, 7:264). But he does note that Philo (first century) used it with the connotation: "this means (in the deeper sense)" (p. 265).

In spite of objections, we do feel that there may be some "significance"—pardon the play on words!—in John's use of *sēmainō* here. He uses the verb three times in his Gospel (12:33; 18:32; 21:19) with what might be called prophetic significance.

In support of our position on its use in Rev. 1:1 we note that Bengel says that "the LXX use *sēmainein* to express a great sign of a great thing: Ezek. xxxiii.3" (*Gnomon of the NT*, 5:185). Vincent observes, "The word is appropriate to the symbolical character of the revelation, and so in John xii.33, where Christ predicts the mode of his death in a figure" (WS, 2:408). The first meaning given for *sēmainō* in the famous Liddell-Scott *Lexicon* is: "show by a sign, indicate, point out" (p. 1592). And Edward McDowell writes, "The author implies that the message he has received is being given to his readers under signs or symbols. Attention to this fact should save us from crass literalism in interpreting the message of the book" (p. 24).

Someone has suggested that if we pronounce "signified" as "*sign*-ified" we would get the right idea. Perhaps so.

4 *Asia* In the NT the term "Asia" never means the continent, as it does for us today. Rather it is "the province of Asia" (NIV), the western part of Asia Minor (modern Turkey).

The Seven Spirits The reference is to the Holy Spirit in all His perfection (the number "seven"). It is the one Holy Spirit manifesting himself and ministering to the 7 churches (v. 4).

5 *Prince* *Archōn* is better translated "ruler" (NASB, NIV).

Washed This translates *lousanti*, from the verb *louo*, "bathe." But all the manuscripts earlier than the 9th century have *lusanti*, from *luo*, "loose." So the correct translation is "released" (NASB) or "freed" (NIV).

6 *Kings* The Greek has *basileian*, which means "a kingdom" (NASB, NIV). Of course, the sense is much the same.

8 *Alpha . . . Omega* These are the first and last letters of the Greek alphabet. So it means "the beginning and the ending" (KJV). But these explanatory words are not in A and C (fifth century), though they are in Sinaiticus (fourth century)—Vaticanus (fourth century) ends at Heb. 9:14. Since the external evidence (manuscripts) is rather evenly balanced, this case has to be settled by internal evidence. Bruce Metzger puts it well: "If the longer text were original no good reason can be found to account for the shorter text, whereas the presence of the longer expression in 21:6 obviously prompted some copyists to expand the text here" (*Textual Commentary on the Greek NT*, p. 732). Again we would note that the meaning of the passage is not affected by this.

9 *Companion* *Sygkoinōnos* (sometimes spelled *synkoinōnos*) is compounded of *syn*, "together," and the adjective *koinos*, "common." So it means a "sharer, partaker, participant."

Patience of Jesus Christ This translation obviously does not make sense in this passage. The Greek says: *hypomonē en Iēsou. En* means "in." We have noted a number of times that *hypomonē* does not mean "patience" but "endurance" or "perseverance." We have this "in Jesus" (NASB, NIV).

For This (KJV) would suggest that John was on Patmos to preach the gospel. But the Greek has *dia* with the accusative, which means "because of" (NASB, NIV). John was there as a political prisoner of the Roman Empire because of his preaching.

10 *The Lord's Day* Some have assumed that this means "the day of the Lord," found often in Scripture. But here "Lord's" is an adjective, *kyriakē*, found only here and in 1 Cor. 11:20—"the Lord's supper." In modern Greek, Sunday is called *Kyriakē*. R. H. Charles says of this passage in Revelation: "Here 'Lord's Day' has become a technical designation of Sunday" (ICC, Revelation, 1:23). Why Sunday? Foerster writes, "The Lord's Day takes its significance from the resurrection of Christ" (TDNT, 3:1096). Jesus was in the grave on Saturday, the Jewish Sabbath. On Sunday we worship the risen Lord!

11 *I Am . . . the Last* All of this is absent in the early manuscripts (before the 9th century). It was added by a later copyist. The same is true of "which are in Asia."

Book The Greek word is *biblion*, from which we get our word "Bible." The reference is to a papyrus "scroll" (NIV), which would be less expensive than parchment (animal skins). The scroll of Revelation would be about 15 feet long.

13 *Candlesticks* The Greek *lychnias* means "lampstands" (NASB, NIV). See discussion at Matt. 5:15.

Girt About the Paps . . . Girdle How much more beautiful is the NIV: "with a golden sash around his chest."

15 *Brass* *Chalkolibanon* (in NT only here and 2:18) is a word not found elsewhere in literature, except in reference to these passages. So we are not sure of the exact meaning. But "bronze" or "burnished bronze" (RSV, NASB) seems the nearest we can get to it.

18 *Hell* The Greek should be transliterated "Hades" (NASB, NIV), the place of departed spirits. "Hell" is the Greek *Gehenna* (not used here).

20 *Angels* The Greek word *angelos* means "messenger" and is used for human messengers in Luke 7:24; 9:52; and James 2:25. It is true that in the 60 or more times that *angelos* occurs in the Book of Revelation it refers to "angels." But we feel that here it may *possibly* mean the pastors of the 7 churches. However, George E. Ladd concludes his study of the term here by saying: "It is best to understand this as a rather unusual symbol to represent the heavenly or supernatural character of the church" (p. 35).

2:2 *Patience* Should be "perseverance" (NASB, NIV). See my commentary on Revelation (BBC, 10:492).

Tried Should be "tested" (NIV; cf. NASB).

3 *Fainted* The Greek verb is *kopiaō*, which means "grow weary." Instead of "hast laboured, and hast not fainted" (KJV), the Greek simply has *kai ou kekopiakas*—"and have not grown weary" (NASB, NIV).

4 *Somewhat* This added word in italics (KJV) gives entirely the wrong meaning to this verse. It is not "somewhat"—some *little* thing that has gone wrong. The Greek very clearly says: "But I have against you that you have left your first love." This was not a trifling matter, as verse 5 points out emphatically. They had to "repent" and start all over again!

6 *Nicolaitans* In spite of speculation by Irenaeus and some other ancient church fathers, we have no knowledge as to who these heretics were. The term *Nicolaitōn* (pl.) occurs only here and in verse 15.

7, 11, 17, 26 Overcometh The verb *nikaō* comes from the noun *nikē*, "victory." So it literally means to "be a victor." In 1 John 5:4 we find the verb twice and the noun once. (*Nikē* occurs only there in the NT.)

7 Paradise See discussion at 2 Cor. 12:4.

9, 13 Works *Erga* is not found in the better Greek manuscripts (with the exception of Aleph in verse 9 but not in verse 13) and so is not included in good versions. It seems like a scribal echo of verse 2.

10 Crown See discussion at 1 Cor. 9:25.

13 Seat The Greek word is *thronos*, from which we get "throne"—the correct translation here (NASB, NIV).

14, 20 Commit Fornication The verb *porneuō* takes in more than fornication. It includes all "sexual immorality" (NIV). See discussion at Matt. 5:32.

17 In The Greek does not have *en*, "in," but *epi*, "upon." The new name was not written "in the stone" (KJV) but "on" it (NASB, NIV).

20 A Few Things This addition (KJV) has practically no support in the Greek manuscripts.

21 Space The Greek word *chronos*, from which we get *chronology*, means "time," not "space."

22 Their The Greek manuscripts give somewhat stronger support to *autēs*, "her" (NASB, NIV), than to *autōn*, "their." Again we would note that a copyist would be more apt to change "her" to "their" than to do the reverse. And once more we would say that the difference in meaning is very slight.

23 Reins *Nephros* (only here in NT) literally meant (in pl.) "the kidneys." It is used in the Septuagint for the kidneys of sacrificed animals (Exod. 29:13, etc.). Then it came to be used figuratively for the inward part of man, as in Job 16:13 (TDNT, 4:911).

We have here a loose quotation from Jer. 11:20. *Nephrous* may be translated "minds" (NASB).

26 Power The Greek word is not *dynamis*, "power," but *exousia*, "authority" (NASB, NIV).

3:2 Be Watchful The Greek has the present imperative of the verb *ginomai*, "become," followed by the present participle of *grēgoreō*, "to be awake." So a good translation is "Wake up" (NASB, NIV).

Perfect This is not the adjective *teleios*, which is usually translated "perfect" (KJV). Rather, it is the perfect passive participle of *plēroō*, "fill." So it means "filled up," or "complete" (NIV; cf. NASB).

4 Defiled The verb *molynō* means to "stain" or "soil" (cf. NASB, NIV). Arndt and Gingrich comment here: "Unsoiled garments as symbol of a spotless life" (pp. 526–27).

3, 12, 21 Overcometh See the discussion at Rev. 2:7.

16 Spue The verb *emeō* (only here in NT) literally means to "vomit," and so "to reject with extreme disgust" (WP, 6:321).

17 I Am . . . Increased with Goods This is all one word in Greek, *peploutēka*, the perfect active indicative of *plouteō*, which means "be rich" and is translated that way in verse 18 (KJV). "I am rich" (v. 17, all versions) is *eimi*, "I am," with the adjective *plousios*, "rich." For variation (as in KJV) the verb here could be translated "have become wealthy" (NASB) or "I have acquired wealth" (NIV).

18 Tried in the Fire This is a striking expression in the Greek: *pepyrōmenon ek pyros*. *Pyr* is the Greek word for "fire" (used throughout NT). It is preceded here by the perfect passive participle of *pyroō*, "set on fire, burn." Clearly the idea here is "refined by fire" (NASB).

19 Chasten *Paideuō* is better translated "discipline" (NASB, NIV). See discussion at Heb. 12:5.

4:1 Was Opened This suggests that John saw a door just being opened in heaven. But the Greek is *ēneōgmenē*, the perfect passive participle of *anoigō*, "to open." The perfect tense indicates a continuing state resulting from a completed act. So the correct translation is "standing open" (NASB, NIV).

2 Spirit The uncial Greek manuscripts (4th to 9th century) have all large letters, while the minuscule (cursive) manuscripts (9th to 15th century) have all small letters. So the Greek does not indicate whether we should have "in the spirit" (KJV)—in a trance—or "in the Spirit"—in the control of the Holy Spirit. The latter (NASB, NIV) seems preferable. The Holy Spirit was giving John a divine revelation of the future.

3 Jasper . . . Sardine The Greek word *iaspis* occurs only here and three times in chapter 21 (vv. 11, 18, 19). Abbott-Smith says of it: "apparently not the modern stone of that name, but a translucent stone" (p. 212). *Sardion* (only here and 21:20) is defined by Abbott-Smith as "the *sardian* stone, *sard* (of which *carnelian* is one variety)" (p. 402). The KJV has "sardine" because the late manuscripts have *sardinos*. Pliny says that the stone was named after the city of Sardis (3:1).

A third item is mentioned here, a "rainbow." The Greek word is *iris* (only here and 10:1), given as a name to the iris plant.

This rainbow is often connected with the "rainbow" of promise after the Flood. But the Greek word there in the Septuagint (Gen. 9:13, 14, 16) is *toxon*. H. B. Swete sounds this note of warning: "Since *iris* is substituted for *toxon*, it is precarious to press a reference to the rainbow of the covenant" (p. 68).

5 Thunderings The Greek word is the plural of *phōnē*, which means "sound, tone, noise," and then "voice" (AG, 870). Here it probably means "sounds" (NASB) or "rumblings" (NIV).

Voices The Greek word is *brontē* (in Revelation 10 out of 12 times in NT), which means "thunder." Since it is in the plural here, it may be translated "peals of thunder" (NASB, NIV).

6 Beasts Here we have the plural of *zōon*, which occurs in Heb. 13:11; 2 Pet. 2:12; Jude 10; and 20 times in Revelation. It is always translated "beast" in the KJV. This is unfortunate, for today "beast" is used mostly for a wild animal or a brutal person. These here were heavenly beings, literally "living creatures" (NASB, NIV)—from *zōē*, "life." The real "beast" of Revelation is indicated by the Greek word *thērion*, "wild beast," which occurs 38 times in this book and is correctly translated "beast."

7 Calf The word is *moschos*. A. T. Robertson says of it: "*Moschos* is first a sprout, then the young of animals, then a calf (bullock or heifer) as in Luke 15:23, 27, 30, or a full-grown ox (Ezek. 1:10)" (WP, 6:329).

11 O Lord The Greek text has *ho kyrios kai ho theos hēmōn*, "our Lord and God" (NIV; cf. NASB).

For Thy Pleasure The Greek says *dia to thelēma sou*—literally, "because of Thy will" (NASB), and so, "by your will" (NIV). In a 10-page discussion of *thelēma* (TDNT, 3:52–62), Schrenk shows clearly that *thelēma* means "will."

They Are and Were Created The Greek has *ēsan kai ektisthēsan*—literally, "they were and were created." This is a bit difficult to translate into meaningful English. Swete gives this helpful interpretation: "The Divine Will had made the universe a fact in the scheme of things before the Divine Power gave material expression to the fact" (p. 75).

5:1 **Book** When we say "book" today we mean a bound volume. But that is not what we have here. Schrenk writes: "The *biblion* with seven seals (5:1–5, 7f) is again in the form of a roll . . . not a codex" (TDNT, 1:618). "Codex" is the technical name for a bound book, such as we find from the fourth century on, but not in the first century. So it is better to say "scroll" (NIV).

2 Loose That is the basic meaning of *luō*. But with "seals" it means "break" (NASB, NIV). When the seals were broken, then it would be possible to "open the scroll" (vv. 2, 3, 4, 5, NIV).

5 Prevailed The verb is *nikaō*, which comes from the noun *nikē*, "victory." So a better translation is "overcome" (NASB) or "triumphed" (NIV). Swete comments:

> The Lion of Judah, the Son of David, conquered the world (Jo. xvi.33 . . .), and one fruit of His victory is that it belongs to Him to open the seals of God's Book of Destiny, i.e. to carry history onward through successive stages to the final revelation (p. 77).

Root The basic meaning of the noun *hriza* is "root." But scholars are agreed that here it means the "shoot" that comes out of the root. For instance, Maurer contends that here *hriza* must be translated "shoot (out) of David"—genitive of origin (TDNT, 6:989). So "Root of David" is basically equivalent to the familiar "Son of David."

6, 8, 12, 13 Lamb Outside the Book of Revelation the Greek noun *arnion* occurs only in

John 21:15, where it is used (pl.) for young believers. It is a diminutive form of *arnē*.

In Isa. 53:7 the word for "lamb" in the Septuagint is *amnos*. Swete writes:

> *Amnos* has passed from the LXX into the other passages in the N.T. where Christ is described as the Lamb (Jo. i.29, 36, Acts viii.32, 1 Pet. i. 19), but it does not occur in the Apocalypse, which uses *to arnion* as a title of our Lord 29 times in 12 chapters (*p. 78*). Swete goes on to say:
>
> The diminutive must not be pressed, . . . but the contrast of the Lamb with the Lion is sufficiently striking in any case, directing attention to the unique combination of majesty and meekness which characterized the life of Jesus Christ (*ibid.*).

8 Odors The word *odor* is generally used today for a bad smell. Unfortunately, the KJV uses it here and in 18:13 for the noun *thymiama* (in the pl.), which means "incense" (NASB, NIV). For some unknown reason, in 8:3 and 4 it is correctly translated "incense" in the KJV.

9 Redeemed The verb is *agorazō*, which comes from *agora*, "marketplace." So it meant "to buy in the market, purchase" (A-S, p. 7). In fact, in the KJV it is translated "buy" in 28 of the 31 times it occurs in the NT. Only here and in 14:3 and 4 is it "redeemed." Christ actually "purchased" (NIV) us with His own blood.

Kindred The Greek word *phylē* means "tribe" (NASB, NIV). It refers over a dozen times to the tribes of Israel. But in Matt. 24:30 and half a dozen times in Revelation it is used for the tribes of the earth. "Tongue," of course, means "language" (NIV). With Christ there is no distinction of race, language, or nationality.

6:1, 3, 5, 7 Come and See Why do all scholarly versions today omit "and see"? The simple fact is that, with the exception of Aleph (4th century), no Greek manuscript earlier than the 10th century has these words. It seems clear that they were not a part of the original text.

"Come and see" (KJV) would be a call to John to come and see what was about to happen. But "Come" was probably a summons to each of the four horsemen to ride out into view. The modern parallel would be a trumpet blast that called a rider on horseback to burst out into the arena in front of the spectators. (For interpretation of the four riders see BBC, 10:540–43.)

5 A Pair of Balances This is one word in Greek, *zygon*, which literally means "a yoke" and is so translated the other five times it occurs in the NT (Matt. 11:29, 30; Acts 15:10; Gal. 5:1; 1 Tim. 6:1). It is used there metaphorically in the sense of submission to authority. But here it is used, as in the Septuagint of Isaiah 40:12, for "a pair of scales" (NASB, NIV). Here it suggests a great shortage of food (v. 6). Rengstorf notes: "Models for the use of scales as a symbol of dearth are perhaps to be found in Lv. 26:26; Ez. 4:16, though the word *zygos* is not used in these passages" (TDNT, 2:898).

6 Measure This term is very indefinite. The Greek word *choinix* (only here in NT) indicated a dry measure equivalent to about a "quart" (NASB, NIV).

Penny The Greek word is *dēnarion*. Occurring 16 times in the NT, it is translated (KJV) 9 times as "penny," 5 times as "pence," and twice as "pennyworth." But this is misleading. The Roman "denarius" (Latin form) was a silver coin worth about 18 cents. Furthermore, it represented a day's wages (Matt. 20:2). In the famine predicted here, a person would have to spend a day's wages just to buy a quart of wheat or three quarts of barley (the food of the poor people). The correct rendering is "denarius" (RSV, NASB) or "day's wages" (NIV)—to represent the enormity of the price.

8 Pale The Greek adjective is *chlōros*. It literally means "green" (Mark 6:39; Rev. 8:7). But it was used by Hippocrates and others for "*pale* as the color of a person in sickness as contrasted with his appearance in health" (AG, p. 882). That is its meaning here.

Death The Greek has *thanatos*, the common word for death (117 times in NT). Why, then, is it here translated "pestilence" (RSV, NASB) and "plague" (NIV)?

The answer is that *thanatos* often means "pestilence" in the Septuagint. Also, there is a close parallel here with Ezek. 14:21, which reads: "How much more when I send my four sore judgments upon Jerusalem, the sword, and the famine, and the noisome beast, and the pestilence." The same four things are mentioned, with the last two in reverse order.

13 Untimely Figs This is one word in Greek, *olynthous* (only here in NT). *Olynthos* (sing.) is defined by Abbott-Smith as meaning "*an unripe fig*, which grows in winter and usually falls off in the spring" (p. 316). So it may be

461

translated "unripe figs" (NASB) or "late figs" (NIV).

14 Departed The verb *apochōrizō* (in NT only here and Acts 15:39) is compound of *apo*, "away from," and *chōrizō*, "divide, separate." So it means "was split apart" (NASB) or "receded" (NIV).

15 Chief Captains The Greek word is *chiliarchos*, a chiliarch or "commander of a thousand men" (used many times in Acts). The plural can well be translated "commanders" (NASB) or "generals" (NIV). "Captain" is a lower rank today.

7:9 Palms Since all human hands have "palms," the KJV "palms in their hands" could be a bit awkward. The Greek word for "palm" is *phoinix*, which means the date-palm tree. This word occurs once elsewhere in the NT (John 12:13). There it is preceded by *baia* (only here in NT), the word for a "palm branch." So the whole expression is translated "branches of palm trees" (KJV). To avoid awkwardness here in Revelation it would be best to say "palm branches" (NASB, NIV).

14 Great Tribulation The Greek has *tēs thlipseōs tēs megalēs*—literally, "the tribulation, the great"; that is, "the Great Tribulation." The article should be retained in English translation.

15 Shall Dwell Among Them The Greek says *skēnōsei ep' autous*. The verb *skēnoō* comes from *skēnē*, "tent" or "tabernacle." And the primary meaning of *epi (ep')* is "upon." So the whole expression here may be translated "shall spread His tabernacle over them" (NASB) or "will spread his tent over them" (NIV). It is a beautiful picture of God's protecting care.

16 Heat The Greek noun *kauma* (only here and 16:9) comes from the verb *kaiō*, which has the strong meaning of "burn, destroy by fire" in some passages. So the noun may be translated "burning heat" (AG, 425) or "scorching heat" (NIV; also AG in 16:9).

17 Feed Once more (see discussion at John 21:16) the KJV falls short. The verb here is not *boskō*, "feed," but *poimainō*. The latter comes from the noun *poimēn*, "shepherd." So it means to "shepherd." Hence, the correct translation is "will be their shepherd" (NIV; cf. NASB).

8:5 Voices See discussion at Rev. 4:5.

7 Sounded The verb is *salpizō*, which comes from the noun *salpix*, "trumpet." So it means to "sound a trumpet" (used mostly in Revelation). It is not necessary to repeat "trumpets" at the end of verse 6, but perhaps it is well in verse 7 to say "sounded his trumpet" (NIV).

Burnt Up This is the compound verb *katakaiō*, intensive form of *kaiō*, "burn." So it means "burn up" or "burn completely."

This occurs twice in the KJV. But in all scholarly versions there is in front of those two clauses another clause: "A third of the earth was burned up" (cf. RSV, NASB). This clause is found in practically all the early Greek manuscripts of the NT. It almost certainly is genuine. With three consecutive clauses ending the same, and the first two beginning the same, it would be very easy for a copyist to omit one. This is a fairly common mistake made by typists today.

10 Lamp This is the Greek word *lampas*, which clearly means "lamp" in the parable of the 10 virgins (five times in Matt. 25:1, 3, 4, 7, 8), because fed with oil. They were tiny clay lamps, such as have been excavated from those days. But here the *lampas* was probably a "torch" (NASB, NIV), which is the first meaning for *lampas* given in Greek lexicons.

13 An Angel The Greek literally says "one eagle," *henos aetou*. So it is properly translated "an eagle" (RSV, NASB, NIV). *Angelos* is found in some late manuscripts and so got into the Textus Receptus. It is easy to see why a later copyist would change *aetos* to *angelos*, as being more natural, but not why anyone would do the reverse. It seems probable, however, that it was an angel who appeared in the form of an eagle for striking effect.

9:1, 2 The Bottomless Pit The Greek says "the shaft of the Abyss" (NIV): *to phrear tēs abyssou*. *Phrear* means "well" (Luke 14:5; John 4:11, 12), and then "shaft." This noun occurs once in verse 1 and three times in verse 2 and is translated "pit" (KJV, NASB). It had this meaning in later Greek.

We get our word *abyss* from *abyssos*. This term occurs in Rom. 10:7 for the abode of the dead—the common Greek usage. In Luke 8:31 it evidently refers to the abode of demons. Then it occurs 7 times in Revelation (9:1, 2, 11, 11:7; 17:8; 20:1, 3).

In classical Greek *abyssos* was an adjective meaning "bottomless." Then it came to be used as a substantive, and is best transliterated simply as "Abyss" (NIV). Cremer says that in this sense "it is only used in biblical and ecclesiastical Greek" (p. 2). Joachim Jeremias writes:

> In the NT *abyssos* is thought of as a "prison for spirits" (Rev. 9:1; 20:1, 3). . . . Its inmates until their release in the tribulation before the end are Antichrist (Rev. 11:7; 17:8 . . .), the prince of the underworld (Rev. 9:11), demons (Lk. 8:13) and scorpion centaurs (Rev. 9:3ff.). After the *parousia* Satan will be shut up in it during the millennial kingdom (20:1, 3) (TDNT, 1:10).

5 Torment This occurs three times in this verse, first as a verb and then twice as a noun. The verb *basanizō* is in the future passive and so is correctly translated in the KJV. The noun is *basanismos.*

The verb properly meant "to rub on a touchstone, put to the test," and then "to examine by torture," and so "to torture, torment" (A-S, 76). The noun, which occurs only in Revelation (9:5; 14:11; 18:7, 10, 15), means "torture" or "torment."

6 Shall Flee *Pheugei* is the present indicative of *pheugō,* "flee," and so literally means "flees" (NASB).

11 Abaddon . . . Apollyon The Hebrew *abaddōn* means "destruction." The Greek noun *apollyōn* comes from the verb *apollymi,* "destroy," and so means "destruction."

14 In The Greek preposition is *epi,* "upon." When referring to a vicinity it means "at" or "by." These four angels were not bound "in" the great river but "at" that place (NASB, NIV). "In" would be the Greek *en.*

Loose The verb *luō* does mean "loose." But "release" (NASB, NIV) is the more contemporary term.

16 Two Hundred Thousand Thousand We would say, "Two hundred million" (NASB, NIV).

17 Of Fire The Greek has the adjective *pyrinos* (only here in NT), which means "fiery." This obviously refers to color, not content. So it is best rendered "the color of fire" (NASB) or "fiery red."

Of Jacinth The Greek has the adjective *hyakinthinos* (only here in NT), "of hyacinth" (NASB). Swete writes, "Here *hyakinthinos* is

doubtless meant to describe the blue smoke of a sulphurous flame" (p. 123). So the NIV simply has "dark blue."

Brimstone The adjective *theiōdēs* (only here in NT) meant "sulphurous." The NIV keeps the color pattern by saying: "yellow as sulphur."

21 Sorceries The Greek noun *pharmakon,* from which we get *pharmacy,* occurs only here in the NT. It literally meant "a drug," and then "an incantation, enchantment" (A-S, 466). Many manuscripts have the plural of *pharmakeia,* which means "magic arts" (NIV). That is probably what is meant, in either case.

Fornication See discussion at Matt. 5:32.

10:6 Time No Longer It is true that the noun is *chronos,* from which we get *chronology,* and that its basic meaning is "time" (in the sense of a period of time). But many Greek writers used it for a "delay," and that seems to be the real meaning here (NASB, NIV). Delling suggests "the 'delay' that is granted to allow time for conversion, Rev. 2:21, or 'postponement' in Rev. 10:6" (TDNT, 9:591). He goes on to say, "Rev. 10:6 does not mean that time itself comes to an end. All that is meant is that the judgment of God will be delayed no longer" (p. 592). That seems clearly to be the meaning here.

7 Declared The Greek verb is *euangelizō,* which basically means "announce good news." It is almost always in the middle or passive in the NT, as in classical Greek. Only in later writers was it used in the active, as we find it here and in 14:6.

In most of the NT it is people who do the announcing. But here it is God. Friedrich writes, "In Rev. 10:7 God has revealed His plan of salvation to His servants the prophets of the OT and the NT. It is good news because it proclaims the coming of the Messiah, of the *basileia tou theou,* after the overthrow of the dominion of Antichrist" (TDNT, 2:721). This is "the mystery of God," mentioned in this verse.

9, 10 Belly In the KJV *koilia* is translated "womb" 12 times and "belly" 11 times. The obvious meaning here is "stomach" (NASB, NIV).

11:1 Reed . . . Rod The first word is *kalamos.* It is most naturally translated "reed" in Matt. 11:7; 12:20; but in Matt. 27:29 and 30 as "staff." In 3 John 13 we found it used a third way, for a reed "pen" with which John was writing. Here it is a reed used for a measuring rod (NIV).

The second word is *hrabdos*, which was often used for a "staff" (NASB) on a journey (e.g., Matt. 10:10). But it was also used for a ruler's staff, or "scepter" (Rev. 2:27; 12:5; 19:15).

The various meanings of these two words account for the variety of translations in the different versions. This is true of many Greek words in the NT. Frustrated readers often ask, "Which is correct?" The answer is: "All."

Them That Worship The NIV says, "Count the worshipers." In the Greek there is no word here for "count." But it seems obvious that John was not told to measure the physical height of the worshipers. A. T. Robertson wisely observes: "Perhaps measuring as applied to 'them that worship therein' implies a word like numbering" (WP, 6:376–77).

Temple The Greek word is not *hieron*, the "Temple area" (Mark 11:15), but *naos*, which refers particularly to the sanctuary itself. John was specifically instructed not to measure the "outer court" (v. 2, NIV), which in Jesus' day was called the Court of the Gentiles.

3 Power As indicated by italics (KJV; "authority," NASB), this is not in the Greek. But it appears to be the proper sense (NIV).

4 Candlesticks The correct translation of *lychniai* is "lampstands." See discussion at Matt. 5:15.

5 Will Hurt This sounds like a simple future. But the Greek says *thelei adikēsai*, "desires to harm" (NASB) or "tries to harm" (NIV). The verb *thelō* precedes *adikēsai* both times in this verse. It also occurs at the end of verse 6 (in the future tense).

7 The Bottomless Pit See discussion at Rev. 9:1.

8 Spiritually The Greek does have the adverb *pneumatikōs* (only here and 1 Cor. 2:14), which comes from *pneuma*, "spirit," and so literally means "spiritually." But, as A. T. Robertson notes, it here indicates "in a hidden or mystical (allegorical) sense" (WP, 6:381). This is represented well by "mystically" (NASB) or "figuratively" (NIV).

11 Spirit *Pneuma* first meant "wind," then "breath," and finally "spirit." It is obvious that

the correct translation here is "breath" (NASB, NIV).

13 Remnant The Greek *loipoi* is from the verb *leipō*, "leave behind." So it means those who were left. We call these "survivors" (NIV).

15 Kingdoms The Greek is singular, *basileia*, "kingdom" (NASB, NIV).

16 Seats The Greek has *thronous*, "thrones" (NASB, NIV).

17 And Art to Come This clause is not in the ancient Greek text (cf. NASB, NIV).

19 Testament *Diathēkē* should be translated "covenant" (NASB, NIV). See discussion at Matt. 26:28.

12:1, 3 Wonder

The Greek word is *sēmeion*, which means "sign" (NASB, NIV). This is the first vision in Revelation that is called a sign, but we find it again in 13:13. In 15:1 the term is correctly translated "sign" in the KJV. It will be remembered that miracles in the Gospels are called both "wonders" and "signs," but the Greek words are distinct in meaning.

3 Dragon The Greek word *drakōn* is found (in NT) only in Revelation (13 times; 8 times in this chap.). Foerster notes that *drakōn* had three meanings: "serpent, dragon, and seamonster" (TDNT, 2:281). It should be remembered that it was "the serpent" who tempted Eve (Gen. 3:14). In Revelation "the dragon" is always Satan. Foerster notes this is "the key image for Satan in the whole book" (p. 282).

In verse 9 the dragon is identified as "that old serpent," called the Devil, and Satan." *Diabolos* ("devil") occurs 38 times in the NT—6 times each in Matthew and Luke, but never in Mark. It is found 5 times in Revelation, and 4 times in 1 John. It means "the slanderer." *Satanas* ("Satan") occurs 36 times in the NT—6 times each in Mark and Luke, and 8 times in Revelation. It means "the adversary." Satan functioned in both capacities, slandering God's people (e.g., Job and v. 10) and opposing God and all His work.

10 Strength The Greek word is *dynamis*, from which we get *dynamite*, and *dynamo*, and *dynamic*. Rather than "strength" (KJV), it means "power" (NASB, NIV).

12 The Inhabiters Of These words are not in the Greek (cf. NASB, NIV), though they may be implied.

13 Persecuted The verb *diōkō* basically means "pursue" and is often used of pursuing good things (Phil. 3:12, 14; Heb. 12:14). But it is used most frequently in a hostile sense, "persecute." Here the dragon (Satan) both "pursued" and "persecuted" the woman.

15, 16 Flood The Greek word is *potamos*, the regular term for "river" in the NT. In the KJV it is translated "flood" only here and in Matt. 7:25, 27 (where the NIV has "streams").

15 Cause . . . to Be Carried Away of the Flood All of this is two words in Greek: *potamophorēton poiēsē*. The verb *poieō* means "make." The long word is an adjective (only here in NT), compounded of *potamos*, "river," and the verb *pherō*, "carry." So it means "swept away by a river"—that is, drowned. The dragon was determined to destroy the woman. For the identification of the "woman" here one must consult commentaries.

13:1 I Stood Instead of *estathēn*, "I stood" (KJV), which is not found in any Greek manuscript before the ninth century, all the early manuscripts have *estathē*, "he stood." This would be a reference to the dragon, and not to John. It is properly a conclusion to the 12th chapter rather than an introduction to the 13th chapter.

Beast The Greek word is *thērion*, which, as we have seen, means "a wild beast." This beast is what we commonly call "the Antichrist."

2 Seat The Greek has *thronos*, "throne" (NASB, NIV).

4, 5 Power The Greek has *exousia*, "authority" (NASB, NIV), not *dynamis*, "power" (KJV).

5 Forty and Two Months It is obvious that the 42 months, the 1,260 days (12:6), and the "time, and times, and half a time" (12:14) all refer to the same period of three and one-half years. This is the length of "the Great Tribulation"—not 7 years, as commonly (and mistakenly) held. This is clear in Revelation and agrees perfectly with Dan. 9:27. It is the second *half* of the 70th "week" (of 7 years).

7 Kindreds . . . Tongues . . . Nations Interestingly, it is here the best Greek text that has the longer reading. It says *pasan phylēn kai laon kai glōssan kai ethnos*—"every tribe, people, language and nation" (NIV; cf. NASB). Incidentally, these are all singular, not plural, in the Greek.

10 Captivity The word *aichmalōsia* occurs twice in this verse and nowhere else in the NT except Eph. 4:8. It comes from *aichmalōtos* (in NT only in Luke 4:18), "captive," and so means "captivity."

The difference in the wording of this verse in different versions is due largely to the uncertainty as to the exact original text. A dozen variant readings are found in the Greek manuscripts. So we cannot be certain. A. T. Robertson suggests this interpretation for the first part of the verse: "Apparently John means this as a warning to the Christians not to resist force with force, but to accept captivity as he had done as a means of grace" (WP, 6:402).

14 Miracles The Greek has *sēmeia*, "signs" (NASB, NIV).

15 Life The Greek has *pneuma*, "breath" (NASB, NIV).

16, 17 Mark The noun *charagma* comes from the verb *charassō*, "to engrave." So it means a stamp or impress made on an object. Aside from Acts 17:29, the word is found only in Revelation (7 times). It was evidently some kind of an official seal impressed firmly on the right hand or forehead. Imperial seals of that period have been found. It is indicated in verse 17 that the "mark" consisted of the Beast's name or number.

14:3 Beasts This should be "living creatures." See discussion at Rev. 4:6.

5 Guile *Pseudos* means a "falsehood" or a "lie" (NASB, NIV). It is stronger than "guile."

Before the Throne of God These words are not in the best Greek text, which simply has *amōmoi eisin*—"they are blameless."

8 That Great City The first part of this verse reads in the Greek: *epesen, epesen Babylōn hē megalē*—literally, "It fell, it fell, Babylon the Great" (cf. NASB, NIV).

Wrath *Thymos* means "passion, hot anger, wrath" (A-S, 210). The NASB has "passion." Rather clearly it means "wrath" in verse 10—"the wrath of God." But that perhaps does not fit here. It may well be that "the maddening wine of her adulteries" (NIV) catches the right thought.

12 *Patience* As we have noted several times, *hypomonē* does not mean "patience" (KJV) but "perseverance" (NASB) or "patient endurance" (NIV).

14 *The Son of Man* Both the NASB and the NIV have "a son of man." This is because there is no article here in the Greek, as we regularly find with the expression "the Son of Man" in the Gospels. In the Septuagint of Dan. 7:13 we find the same anarthrous construction as here. We also have "like a son of man" (NIV) in Rev. 1:13. And yet everyone agrees that the reference there is to Christ standing in the midst of His Church. So it would seem to be wisest to go along with Swete and with such recent commentators on Revelation as George Ladd and Robert Mounce in saying that in 14:14 we have the Messiah, not an angel.

15:1 *Marvelous* The verbal adjective *thaumastos* (from *thaumazō*, to "marvel" or "wonder at") is found in a quotation from the Septuagint (Matt. 21:42; Mark 12:11), in John 9:30, and 1 Pet. 2:9. It is a strong expression.

Filled Up Here we have the aorist passive indicative of *teleō*, which comes from *telos*, "end." So it means "bring to an end, complete, finish"—hence here "finished" (NASB) or "completed" (NIV). "Filled up" (KJV) would be the verb *pleroō*.

3 *Saints* A KJV marginal note says: "or, *nations*, or, *ages*." Actually "saints" (*hagiōn*) has the least support of all three. It is found only in two Greek manuscripts of the 16th century! So it is obviously a late copyist's mistake.

"Nations" (*ethnōn*) is found in A (5th century) and P (9th century), together with the bulk of the minuscule manuscripts (9th to 15th century). "Ages" (*aiōnōn*) is in P⁴⁷ (3rd century) and Aleph (4th century), as well as most of the earliest versions. Personally, we would opt for "King of the ages" (RSV, NIV).

4 *Not* In Greek this is the emphatic double negative, *ou mē*—"not by all means." A holy God is to be feared and worshiped.

5 *The Temple of the Tabernacle of the Testimony* This is a very fulsome title for the sacred place. "Temple" is *naos*, "sanctuary." As we have noted before, "tabernacle" is

skēnē, "tent." And "testimony" is *martyrion*. The reference is rather obviously to "the Tent of the Testimony" (Num. 9:15; 17:7)—that is, the Tabernacle in the Sinai Desert. The sanctuary was the place of God's presence. The word *naos* is also used in verse 6 ("temple").

6 *White* The Greek has the adjective *lampros*, which means "bright" (NASB) or "shining" (NIV).

Girded . . . Girdles How much better the NIV: "wore golden sashes around their chests" (cf. 1:13).

7 *Beasts* This should be "living creatures." See discussion at Rev. 4:6.

Vials The Greek word is *phialē* (sing.), which means a shallow "bowl." It occurs (in NT) only in Revelation (12 times). Today "bowls" is better than "vials."

16:2 *Noisome and Grievous* We would not now use these words to describe something painful. The first adjective is *kakos*, which means "bad, evil, harmful, injurious." It may be translated here as "loathsome" (NASB) or "ugly" (NIV).

The second adjective is a stronger one, *ponēros*. It is used in the NT mainly in an ethical sense—"evil" or "wicked." But here it means "painful, serious." It may be translated "malignant" (NASB) or "painful" (NIV).

2, 11 *Sore* The noun *helkos* (only here and Luke 16:21) means a "sore" or "ulcer." The corresponding verb *helkoō* is found in Luke 16:20—"covered with sores."

3 *Souls* The Greek does have *psychē*. And it is true that it is most commonly translated "soul." But "every living soul" would suggest to most readers "every living human being."

In Kittel's *Theological Dictionary of the New Testament*, vol. 9 (edited by Gerhard Friedrich), Eduard Schweizer treats the term *psychē* with typical German thoroughness (pp. 608–56). He begins by saying:

> At the earliest accessible level, namely, Homer, Greek has no words for our concepts of body and soul. *Sōma . . .* is simply the corpse. . . . *Psychē*, etymologically related to *psychō*, "to blow (to cool)" . . . is . . . the vital force which resides in the members and which comes to expression especially in the breath. . . . This *psychē* leaves man at the mo-

ment of death. . . . The soul goes to the under-world. . . . Neither in life nor death does the *psyche* have anything at all to do with the intellectual or spiritual functions of man (pp. 608–09).

After lengthy discussions of the use of *psyche* in classical Greek, Plato and post-Platonists, the OT, and Judaism, Schweizer finally comes to the NT. Here he treats the word as used in the various NT books, finally arriving at Revelation. Then he writes:

> Very much along OT lines is the use of *pasa psyche* . . . in 16:3 except that the added *zoes* ["living"] emphasizes the fact that the reference is to living creatures. . . . Only here and in 8:9 is *psyche* used for animal life in the NT; in both cases marine creatures are in view (9:653).

The Greek literally says: "and every living *psyche* died, the things [neuter article] in the sea." So it seems that the best translation is "every living thing in the sea died" (NASB, NIV). It was a complete destruction.

5 Lord Instead of "Lord," which would be *kyrios*, the Greek text has *hosios*, "Holy One" (NASB, NIV). The KJV "Lord" comes from the Latin Vulgate but has no support in the Greek manuscripts.

And Shalt Be This clause in the KJV is a late addition made by some copyist (cf. 11:17). It is not in any good Greek text.

6 They Are Worthy This sounds like a commendation, which it obviously is not—quite the opposite! The adjective translated "worthy" is *axios*, which means "befitting." In the NT it is used mostly in a good sense. But in a number of passages (in Luke, Acts, and Romans) it has a bad sense, as here. For this we would say today: "They deserve it" (NASB; cf. NIV).

7 Another out of the Altar Say The Greek simply has: "And I heard the altar saying" (NASB; cf. NIV). The verb *akouo*, "hear," takes the genitive case (as here) for that from whom or from which the message comes. Here it was "the altar saying," or responding "yes" (cf. NIV).

Altar The Greek word *thysiasterion* occurs 23 times in the NT (6 in Matthew and 8 in Revelation). It comes from the verb *thysiazo*, to "sacrifice," and so would normally indicate the altar

on which sacrifices were offered, outside the sanctuary. This is the usage of the term most of the time (outside of Revelation) in the NT. But in Luke 1:11 it is used for the altar of incense (indicated by the addition of the word for "incense").

Which is it here in Revelation? Abbott-Smith lists it under "the altar of incense in the sanctuary," adding "symbolically in Heaven" for all the passages in Revelation except 11:1, where it is clearly the altar of burnt offering. On the other hand, Westcott writes regarding its first use in Revelation: "The altar of sacrifice: vi.9, which proclaims the justice of God's judgments: xvi.7" (p. 454). Robert Mounce observes: "It is significant that throughout Revelation (except in 11:1) the altar is connected with judgment (6:9; 8:3–5; 9:13; 14:18; 16:7)" (*The Book of Revelation*, p. 296). As to which altar it is, probably George Ladd gives the best conclusion: "The context does not determine whether the altar is that of incense or of burnt offering; but in either case, the meaning is the same" (p. 211).

Almighty Aside from 2 Cor. 6:18, *pantokrator* occurs (in NT) only in Revelation (9 times). In the KJV it is translated "Almighty" except in 19:6 ("omnipotent"). The NASB and NIV are consistent in retaining "Almighty" there. The noun comes from *pas*, "all," and the verb *krateo*, "be strong, mighty." Michaelis says that *pantokrator* means "the almighty," "the ruler of all things" (TDNT, 3:914). He goes on to say: "The reference is not so much to God's activity in creation as to His supremacy over all things" (p. 915).

14 Devils *Daimonion* means "demons," not "devils." There is only one devil, but there are many demons. See notes on James 2:19.

Miracles The Greek has *semeia*—"signs" (NASB) or "miraculous signs" (NIV).

Of the Earth And These words are not in any good Greek text, but were added later. The Greek simply says "kings of the whole world." The term for "world" here is not *cosmos* but *oikoumene*, which means "inhabited earth."

16 Armageddon The Greek word is *Harmagedon* (only here in NT). This is generally connected with Megiddo, on the border between Samaria and Galilee. *Har* is Hebrew for "mountain."

21 Talent This would be "about a hundred pounds" (NIV; cf. NASB)—the heaviest hailstones ever to fall from the sky. The Great Tribulation will be a time of the greatest catastrophes ever to befall this earth.

17:1 Whore

The Greek word is *porne* (fem.), from which we get pornography. Occurring 12 times in the NT, it is translated (KJV) "harlot" 8 times and "whore" 4 times. The masculine term *pornos* occurs 10 times—"fornicator" and "whoremonger" each 5 times. The abstract noun *porneia* is found 26 times and is regularly translated "fornication." As we have noted previously, this is too narrow a meaning; it should be "sexual immorality" (NIV), including fornication and adultery. The same is true of the verb *porneuo* (8 times), rendered "commit fornication."

The proper translation today for *porne* is "harlot" (NASB) or "prostitute" (NIV). The reference is to "Babylon the great" (14:8; 16:19), a symbolical name for Rome—as almost all commentators agree. The last verse of this chapter seems to prove it.

2 Committed Fornication . . . Fornication The verb is *porneuo*, the noun *porneia* (see above). The first should be translated "committed acts of immorality" (NASB) or "committed adultery" (NIV). The second means "immorality" (NASB) or "adulteries" (NIV). Swete comments, "The *porneia* of which these kings were guilty consisted in purchasing the favour of Rome by accepting her suzerainty and with it her vices and idolatries" (p. 213).

3 In the Spirit The Greek is simply *en pneumati* (no article). We find the same phrase in 1:10; 4:2; and 21:10. For the first the KJV has "in the Spirit." But for the other three it has "in the spirit." Both the NASB and NIV have "in the Spirit" in all four places.

Some commentators have interpreted the phrase as meaning "in a trance." Others insist that it is John's "spirit"—"in spirit"—not the Holy Spirit. As we have noted before, the Greek does not have our practice of capital letters at the beginning of some words; so it offers no help at this point. But it does seem best to hold that John was under the influence of the Holy Spirit.

Scarlet Colored This is one word in Greek, *kokkinos*. The adjective occurs in Matt. 27:28 and Heb. 9:19, but elsewhere only in Revelation (17:3, 4; 18:12, 16). It comes from *kokkos*,

which outside the NT was used for the scarlet berry (TDNT, 3:811).

Concerning *kokkinos*, Michel notes, "In the prophets scarlet is often linked with ungodly and sinful conduct" (TDNT, 3:812). He further comments, "Purple and scarlet indicate the worldly pomp of the demonic power *Babylon* in Revelation. The woman sits on a scarlet beast . . . , and she is herself arrayed in purple and scarlet." He then goes on to say:

> Only purple and scarlet fit the deeds of this woman, namely licentiousness, seduction by the wine of unchastity, blasphemies, abominations, and murder of the witnesses of Jesus, 17:1–6. Here red epitomizes demonic abomination, ungodly lasciviousness and the power which is hostile to God (p. 813).

6 Martyrs The NASB has "witnesses" and the NIV "those who bore testimony." Why the change?

The answer is that the Greek word here, *martyron* (gen. pl.), is connected with the verb *martyreo*, which means "to be a witness, bear witness, testify" (A-S, p. 278). The noun *martys* (nom. sing.) meant "a witness" and was used mainly for a witness in court, though also for any witness. Occurring 34 times in the NT, it is translated "witness" (KJV) 29 times. Only three times is it translated "martyr" (Acts 22:20; Rev. 2:13; 17:6). In Acts 22:20 it is applied to Stephen, the first Christian martyr. This is the only passage in the NT where the NIV uses "martyr." The NASB does not use it at all. Why?

Swete gives the answer. Referring to Acts 22:20 and Rev. 17:6, he writes:

> It is tempting to translate *martys* by 'martyr' in the last two passages, and even R.V. yields to the temptation in Apo.l.c., though it is content to call Stephen and Antipas 'witnesses.' But it may be doubted whether the word had acquired a technical sense ["martyr"] at the end of the first century (p. 36).

Commenting on Rev. 17:6, Strathmann says, "The term *martyres* cannot be taken here in the later martyrological sense" (TDNT, 4:495). So it is perhaps best to avoid using "martyr" in the NT translation. Apparently, this use of *martyr* did not begin until the second century.

Wondered . . . Admiration The Greek has *ethaumasa . . . thauma*. The verb *thaumazo* means to "marvel" or "wonder." The noun *thauma* (only here and 2 Cor. 11:14 in NT) means "wonder." Literally the Greek says, "I wondered a great wonder." So it may be translated "I wondered greatly" (NASB) or "I was greatly astonished" (NIV). There was certainly no "admiration" (KJV) involved!

7 Marvel This is the same verb, *thaumazo*, as in verse 6.

8, 11 Perdition The literal meaning of *apōleia* is "destruction" (NASB, NIV).

12 Power The Greek word is not *dynamis*, "power," but *exousia*, "authority" (NASB, NIV).

13 Mind The word is *gnōmē*. It occurs again in verse 17, where the KJV translates it "will." The best translation is "purpose" in both places (NASB, NIV).

Power and Strength The Greek has *dynamin kai exousian*, "power and authority" (NASB, NIV).

18:1 Lightened Today a person's heavy load may be "lightened." But the verb here, *phōtizō*, means to "light." The earth was "illuminated" (NASB, NIV) by the angel's glory, or splendor.

2 Mightily with a Strong Voice This is double translation. The Greek simply says: "with a mighty voice" (NASB, NIV)—*en ischyra phōnē*.

Habitation The Greek word is *katoikētērion* (only here and Eph. 2:22 in NT). *Oikos* means "house," and the intensive prefix *kata* suggests really living in the house—so "dwelling place" (NASB) or "home" (NIV). "Babylon the Great" (Rome) had become "a home for demons" (NIV)—not "devils" (KJV).

Hold . . . Cage In both cases it is the same Greek word, *phylakē*. This first meant "a guard," and then the place where people are kept under guard, "a prison" (NASB). In Rev. 20:7 Satan, after a thousand years, is released from "prison" (KJV, RSV, NASB, NIV). It is the same Greek word as here, *phylakē*. Bertram writes, "Similarly in Rev. 18:2 the shattered city of Babylon becomes the kingdom, the final refuge, and also the place of banishment and the 'prison' of unclean spirits and the unclean, hated and sinister birds that are outlawed with them" (TDNT, 9:244).

Hateful Here we have the perfect passive participle (*memisēmenou*) of the verb *miseō*, which means "hate, detest, abhor" (AG, p. 522). So it would normally mean "hated, detested, abhorred." But Arndt and Gingrich prefer for this passage "loathsome" (p. 523). In line with this the NIV has "detestable."

3 Abundance Strangely, the Greek word is *dynamis*, "power." But Arndt and Gingrich give, as one meaning, "resource" (p. 208). They note that in Xenophon's *Anabasis* it is used for "wealth" (NASB).

Delicacies *Strēnos* (only here in NT) is defined by Abbott-Smith as "insolent luxury, wantonness" (p. 420). Arndt and Gingrich (p. 771) give "sensuality" (NASB) and "luxury" (cf. NIV).

Why does the KJV have "delicacies"? In the *Oxford English Dictionary* the first definition of "delicacy" is: "The quality of being addicted to pleasure or sensuous delights; voluptuousness, luxuriousness" (3:159). But this is labeled "obsolete."

7, 9 Lived Deliciously This is the verb *strēniazō* (only here in NT). It means "lived luxuriously or sensually" (see previous discussion at v. 3).

9 Judgment The Greek word is *crisis*, which is especially appropriate. This was the crisis of final judgment on "Babylon."

10, 16, 19 Alas The word *ouai*, doubled here for emphasis, means "alas" (grief) or "woe" (denunciation) in NASB, NIV.

11, 12 Merchandise The Greek word is *gomos* (in NT only here and Acts 21:3, where the KJV has "burden"). The noun comes from the verb *gemō*, "to be full," which was first used (by Xenophon) for a ship being filled (A-S, 80). So the appropriate translation of *gomos* here is "cargoes" (NASB, NIV).

12 Thyine This is practically a transliteration of the Greek word here, *thyinos* (only here in NT). It comes from *thyia*, "an African aromatic tree, with ornamentally veined wood of varying colour" (A-S, p. 209). The Latin name was *citrinus*. So the NASB and NIV have "citron."

Vessels Today "vessel" means a ship. The Greek word here is *skeuos*, which has a great variety of uses. The first meaning given in Arndt and Gingrich is "thing, *object* used for any purpose at all" (p. 754). The most fitting translation here is "articles" (RSV, NIV). The Greek literally says "every article" (NASB).

Ivory   The Greek word is the adjective *elephantinos* (only here in NT). This, of course, is because ivory comes from elephant tusks.

Most Precious   The Greek has the superlative degree (*timiōtatos*) of the adjective *timios*, which means "costly, highly valued." It is used "primarily of money value" (A-S, p. 446). So the correct translation is "costly" (NIV) or "very costly" (NASB).

13 Cinnamon   This is almost an exact transliteration of the Greek word *cinnamōmon* (only here in NT).

Odors   The Greek word is *thymiama* (in the pl.). It means "incense" (NASB, NIV).

13 Spice (NIV)   The Greek word is *amōmon* (only here in NT). The *amomum* (Latin) was "a fragrant plant of India" (A-S, p. 26). The correct translation is "spice" (RSV, NASB, NIV). This Greek word is missing in the Textus Receptus, and so in the KJV.

Ointments   This is *myron*, which occurs 14 times in the NT and is always translated "ointment" in the KJV. A better translation is "perfume" (NASB).

Oil   The Greek word *elaion* comes from *elaia*, "an olive tree." Since we use the word *oil* today mostly for petroleum, it is best here to say "olive oil" (NASB, NIV).

Beasts   As noted before, we use this term today mainly for wild animals. The Greek word *ktēnos* means a "domesticated animal" (AG, p. 455). Arndt and Gingrich go on to say: "*Cattle* alone seem to be meant in the combination *ktēnē kai probata* Rv. 18:13." (*Probata* is "sheep.")

Chariots   The usual word for "chariot" in the NT is *harma* (Acts 8:28, 29, 38; Rev. 9:9). It was a two-wheeled war chariot.

But the Greek word here is *rheda* (only here in NT). It was a four-wheeled vehicle. So perhaps a better translation is "carriage" (NIV).

Slaves   The Greek has *sōmatōn* (gen. pl.), "bodies." In his 70-page article on *sōma* in TDNT, Schweizer notes that the word first appears in Homer for a dead "human or animal body" (7:1025). He holds that here in Rev. 18:13 it refers to a "slave" (p. 1058). Adolf Deissmann says categorically: "In Rev. 18:13 *sōmata* stands for slaves" (BS, p. 160). He notes that the word has this usage in the Septuagint, based on Egyptian custom. Swete calls attention to the fact that "the slave merchant was known as *sōmatemporos*" (p. 234). So "slaves" (KJV, NASB) has considerable support. As for "bodies and souls of men" (NIV), A. T. Robertson makes this suggestion: "Perhaps *kai* ["and"] here should be rendered 'even,' not 'and': 'bodies even souls of men' " (WP, 6:442). It is significant that these come at the very bottom of this list, as least valuable!

14 Fruits   The noun *opōra* (only here in NT) literally meant "late summer, early autumn" (late July through early September). Since that was fruit time, it came to mean "ripe fruits."

Dainty and Goodly   The first adjective is *liparos* (only here in NT). It comes from the noun *lipos*, "fat"—that is, rich food. The second adjective is *lampros*, "bright, splendid"—referring here to expensive clothes. So the idea is "luxurious and splendid" (NASB). The NIV ties this in with "all things" (Greek, *panta*) and translates it: "All your riches and splendor."

15, 19 Wailing   The verb *pentheō* means "mourn" and is translated that way (KJV) in 7 out of the 10 times it occurs in the NT. In 2 Cor. 12:21 it is rendered "bewail" and only here (twice) as "wail." So the participle is correctly translated "mourning" (NASB; cf. NIV).

16 Decked   We have here the perfect passive participle of the verb *chrysoō* (only here and 17:4). It comes from *chrysos*, "gold," and so means "gilded" or "covered with gold." In both these passages it is followed by the noun for gold (*chrysion*, diminutive of *chrysos*, and so meaning gold ornament). The combination may be translated "adorned with gold" (NASB) or "glittering with gold" (NIV).

17 Shipmaster   *Kybernētēs* is found (in NT) only here and Acts 27:11 (see discussion there). It primarily means "pilot" but may also be translated "sea captain" (NIV).

19 Costliness   The noun is *timiotēs* (only here in NT). It obviously comes from *timē*, "honor." But all lexicons agree that it means "costliness" or "wealth" (NASB, NIV).

20 Holy Apostles and Prophets The Greek reads: *hoi hagioi kai hoi apostoloi kai hoi prophētai. Hoi* is the definite article (nom. pl. masc.). *Kai* is "and." *Hagioi* is the nominative plural masculine of the adjective *hagios,* "holy." In the NT this adjective is often used as a substantive: "holy ones" or "saints." The structure here clearly shows that the correct translation is "saints and apostles and prophets" (RSV, NASB, NIV).

22 Harpers *Kitharōdon* (only here and 14:2 in NT) comes from *kithara,* "harp" (1 Cor. 14:7; Rev. 5:8; 14:2; 15:2). Today we would call these players "harpists" (NASB, NIV).

Pipers *Aulētēs* (sing.) is found only here and Matt. 9:23 in NT. It comes from the verb *auleō,* "play on a flute." In the genitive plural here (*aulētōn*) it means "flute players" (NIV).

Craftsman . . . Craft The former is *technitēs* (only here and Acts 19:24, 38; Heb. 11:10). The latter is *technē* (only here and Acts 17:29; 18:3). We get *technician* from *technitēs*.

23 Candle This, of course, is "lamp." They had no candles in those days.

Sorceries The Greek word is *pharmakeia,* from which we get *pharmacy.* See discussion at Rev. 9:21.

19:1 Honor This is not found in the early Greek manuscripts. It is obviously a later addition, not a part of the inspired text.

4 Beasts This should be "living creatures." See discussion at 4:6.

6 Omnipotent This is *pantokratōr.* The better translation is "Almighty" (NASB, NIV). See discussion at Rev. 16:7.

7 Honor The Greek word is *doxa,* "glory" (NASB, NIV).

7, 9 Marriage *Gamos* is better translated "wedding" (NIV). In John 2:1–3 it obviously refers to the wedding festivities more than to the marriage itself. Abbott-Smith defines the word as meaning "*a wedding,* esp. *a wedding-feast*" (p. 88).

11 Opened This is the perfect passive participle of *anoigō,* "open." So it means "standing open" (NIV). See discussion at Rev. 4:1.

12 Crowns Eight times in the Book of Revelation (2:10; 3:11; 4:4, 10; 6:2; 9:7; 12:1; 14:14) we have had the word *stephanos,* which means "a victor's crown." It occurs 10 times in the rest of the NT.

But here we have a different term, *diadēma,* which means "a royal crown." In the NT it is found only 3 times, all in Revelation (12:3; 13:1; 19:12). That is why the NASB has here "diadems" (which we get from *diadēma*). Christ is pictured in Revelation as wearing both kinds of crowns.

17, 21 Fowls Today we use the term "fowls" mainly for chickens. The *American Heritage Dictionary* (p. 520) says that the use of "fowl" for "any bird" is "archaic." The Greek term here, *orneios* (pl.) means "birds" (NASB, NIV). The word is found (in NT) only here and Rev. 18:2.

17 The Supper of the Great God The RSV, NASB, and NIV all have "the great supper of God." Why the difference? The answer is that the Greek says: *to deipnon to mega tou theou.* Obviously *mega,* "great," goes with *deipnon,* "supper," and not with *theou,* which is in the genitive case ("of God").

18 Captains The Greek word is *chiliarchos,* an officer in charge of a thousand men—which is something more than a captain. The correct translation is "commanders" (NASB) or "generals" (NIV). See discussion at Rev. 6:15.

20:1, 2 Bottomless Pit See discussion at Rev. 9:1.

4 Lived The Greek has the aorist tense, *ezēsan.* This may well be the ingressive aorist: "came to life" (NASB, NIV). The same form is found in verse 5: "did not come to life" (NASB, NIV).

9 From God This phrase is not in the text of any manuscript earlier than the ninth century, and so is omitted in all scholarly versions today.

12 Before God The early Greek manuscripts all have "before the throne" (*thronos*), not "God" (*theos*). See the RSV, NASB, and NIV.

13, 14 Hell The Greek word is *hadēs,* which should be transliterated "Hades" (all good versions). As we have noted before, *hadēs* was the place of departed spirits. "Hell," the place of eternal punishment, is clearly designated here

471

as "the lake of fire" (vv. 14–15). The fact that it says that *hadēs* was "cast into the lake of fire" (v. 14) clearly shows that *hadēs* does not mean hell. It should always be called Hades.

21:2 *John*

Lest anyone wonder why this word (KJV) is not in the recent versions, we would simply note that it is not in the Greek.

Adorned This is the verb *cosmeō*, in the perfect passive participle, *kecosmēmenēn*. As we have noted before, *cosmeō* (from which we get *cosmetics*) means to "order, arrange, adorn." The NIV has here: "beautifully dressed."

3 *Heaven* The Greek says *tou thronou*, "the throne" (RSV, NASB, NIV). Some late copyist substituted *ouranou*, "heaven," probably from verse 2, and this got in the Textus Receptus.

6 *Freely* This might be interpreted as meaning abundantly. But the Greek word *dōrea* comes from the verb *didōmi*, "give," and so means "a gift." Here the accusative case, *dōrean*, is used adverbially in the sense of "gratis, without payment," or "without cost" (NASB, NIV).

8 *Fearful* The adjective *deilos* means "fearful," or "cowardly" (NASB, NIV).

Abominable This is the perfect passive participle of *bdelyssō* (only here and Rom. 2:22), which comes from *bdeō*, "stink." So it means "abominable," or "vile" (NIV).

Whoremongers As we have noted before, *pornē* (fem., found in 17:1, 5, 15, 16, 19:2) and the word here (and 22:15), *pornos* (masc.), in the plural meant "immoral persons" (NASB) or "the sexually immoral" (NIV). Immorality was very common in the Roman Empire of the 1st century, and it is rampant in the 20th century!

The Second Death The first death is physical and temporary. The second death is spiritual and eternal. It has well been said: "Born twice, die once; born once, die twice."

10 *In the Spirit* See discussion at Rev. 4:2.

That Great City, the Holy Jerusalem The Greek has : *tēn polin tēn hagian Ierousalēm*. This clearly says: "the holy city, Jerusalem" (NASB; cf. NIV).

11 *Light* *Phōstēr* (only here and Phil. 2:15) means "light-giving body," and so here "splendor, radiance" (AG, 872). A good translation is "brilliance" (NASB, NIV).

16 *Furlongs* The Greek says "12,000 *stadia*" (NIV). A *stadion* was the basic measurement for running in the Greek races, about 600 feet. We have taken over into English the Latin form, *stadium*, for a place where races and other athletic events take place. Here the NASB gives the English equivalent of 12,000 stadia: "fifteen hundred miles." (The NIV often gives the English equivalent for weights and measures, but does not do so here.)

17 *An Hundred and Forty and Four Cubits* The Greek word *pēchys* (Matt. 6:27; Luke 12:25; John 21:8; Rev. 21:17) is used by Homer for "the forearm." Then it came to be used for "a cubit," the principal unit of measurement of length in the Bible. The Egyptians started using the length of the forearm for a standard of measure (about 18 inches), and it was naturally taken over by the Jews for the measurements of the ancient Tabernacle. Here, again, the NASB has the modern English equivalent, "seventy-two yards," while the NIV has "144 cubits" (a literal translation).

18 *Building* The Greek word is *endōmēsis* (only here in NT). It comes from the verb *dōmaō*, "build," and so means "a building in." Abbott-Smith would translate the passage here: "its wall had jasper built into it" (p. 153). Swete suggests the meaning as: "the wall had *iaspis* built into it, it was cased with precious stone, so that it sparkled with crystalline radiance" (p. 290).

19 *Garnished* This again is the perfect passive participle of the verb *cosmeō* (see discussion at v. 2). Here it is translated "adorned" (NASB) and "decorated" (NIV).

20 *Sardius* The Greek word is *sardion* (only here and Rev. 4:3; see discussion there). The NIV translates it "carnelian."

Chrysoprasus The Greek term *chrysoprasos* (only here in NT) comes from *chrysos*, "gold." Swete says that it "was akin to the beryl, but of a paler green" (p. 293). The King James translators were greatly influenced by the Vulgate, and so they give the Latin form here. The RSV, NASB, and NIV have the modern English form, "chrysoprase."

23 *Lighten* See discussion at Rev. 18:1.

Light The Greek word is *lychnos*, "lamp" (RSV, NASB, NIV).

24 Of Them Which Are Saved These words are not in the Greek text and so are omitted in most versions.

And Honor This is not found in the early Greek manuscripts and so should be omitted. It was imported here from verse 26 by some late copyist.

27 That Defileth This is the Greek adjective *koinos*, which literally means "common" (Acts 2:44; 4:32; Titus 1:4; Jude 3). But in the Septuagint and the NT it is normally used in the sense of "unhallowed" or "unclean" (Matt. 7:2, 5; Acts 10:14, 28; 11:8; Rom. 14:14; Heb. 10:29; and here). So the proper translation is "unclean" (NASB) or "impure" (NIV).

22:2 *In the Midst of the Street of It* Should this start a new sentence for verse 2 (KJV), or should it be attached to verse 1, completing the sentence there (RSV, NASB, NIV)? Probably this question is not important enough for us to be "hung up" on it. The essential thing is to get the spiritual truth so vividly portrayed here: "the river of the water of life" and "the tree of life" forming the central focus of the city, guaranteeing eternal life to all who live there. We should perhaps remind ourselves again that the Greek manuscripts have no verse divisions and no punctuation marks. So they do not help us answer our question here.

5 Candle The correct translation is "lamp."

6 The Lord God of the Holy Prophets The Greek reads: *ho kyrios ho theos tōn pneumatōn tōn prophētōn*—"the Lord, the God of the spirits of the prophets" (RSV, NASB, NIV).

8 Saw ... Heard The Greek has: *Kagō Iōannēs ho akouōn kai blepōn tauta*—literally, "and I John, the one hearing and seeing these things." (*Kagō* is for *kai egō*). The best translation is: "and I, John, am the one who heard and saw these things" (NASB; cf. NIV)—an emphatic statement.

11 He That Is Unjust ... The Greek literally reads: "The one doing wrong, let him still do wrong; and the filthy one, let him still be filthy [verb only here in NT]; and the righteous one, let him still do righteousness; and the holy one, let him still be holy."

13 The Beginning ... the First ... These clauses are the reverse of the Greek text (cf. NASB, NIV).

14 They That Do His Commandments This represents the Greek: *poiountes tas entolas autou*. But that is not found in any manuscript earlier than the 10th century. The 4th- and 5th-century manuscripts, with several later ones, have: *plynontes tas stolas autōn*—"who wash their robes" (NASB, NIV).

16 The Bright and Morning Star There is no *kai* in the Greek between the two adjectives. They go together: "the bright Morning Star" (NIV; cf. NASB). The adjective "Morning" is *prōinos* (only here and 2:28). It means "at early morn."

17 Come ... Come ... Come ... All too often we hear this verse read in public as if all three occurrences of "come" were parallel. The readers have given them equal emphasis. But the first two are quotations ("Come!") while the third is indirect and should be sounded differently. This is helped by the wording in the NIV.

21 You All The NASB has just "all," while the NIV has "God's people." Why these differences?

Again we have a textual problem. Manuscript A (5th cent.) has *pantōn*, "all." Aleph (4th cent.) has *tōn hagiōn*, "the saints" or "God's people." Only one extremely late manuscript (16th cent.) has "you all." We cannot be certain what the original text was. But, as we have said before, the essential meaning of the passage is not affected adversely by these variant readings.

Index

Index

Index

Index

Index